Holt Social Studies Curriculum

GENERAL EDITOR EDWIN FENTON

A New History of the United States

An Inquiry Approach

IRVING BARTLETT
Carnegie-Mellon University

EDWIN FENTON
Carnegie-Mellon University

DAVID FOWLER
Carnegie-Mellon University

SEYMOUR MANDELBAUM
University of Pennsylvania

Holt, Rinehart and Winston, Inc.

New York Toronto London Sydney

COVER
The cover shows the Statue of Liberty, Declaration of Independence, and the "Don't Tread on Me" flag used during the American Revolution.

Printed in the United States of America

SBN: 03-054135-2 12345 071 987654

CONTENTS

CHAPTER 22 *National Politics* 539-566

CHAPTER 23 *The United States Becomes A World Power, 1898-1920* 567-592

CHAPTER 24 *The 1920's: A Normal America?* 593-618

CHAPTER 25 *The Depression and the New Deal* 619-644

MAPS, CHARTS, AND GRAPHS

To the Student

This is a new kind of textbook. Most social studies texts you have read in the past probably contained information about a particular subject, like civics or geography. The texts were written by one or two authors who organized their material into chapters, each with an important theme. There were numerous illustrations in the form of pictures, graphs, tables, and charts. You read or examined this material to learn the facts and generalizations it contained.

Instead of twenty or thirty chapters written by one or two authors, this text has one hundred and twenty-two readings. After an introductory chapter entitled "An Introduction to the Study of History," there are twenty-nine chapters most of which have three readings and a historical essay. Each of the readings contains at least one piece of source material, taken from a newspaper, magazine, book, government document, or other publication. An introduction, to connect one reading with others in the course, and study questions, to alert you to important points and issues, open each of the readings. The essays link the historical periods and summarize information contained in the readings. Chapter 30 contains only a historical essay.

Although maps and time lines accompany most chapters, you will not find other illustrations in the text. However, filmstrips, recordings, transparencies for the overhead projector, handouts, and picture cards have been provided for use with the chapters.

Both the text and the audio-visual materials have been chosen with great care. They have been designed so that you will not merely memorize facts and generalizations; you will identify problems, develop hypotheses, or tentative answers to questions, and draw your own conclusions from factual evidence. Throughout this course in American history you will be challenged to think for yourself and to make up your own mind.

Most students are able to study one reading in this text for each night's homework assignment. Because most classes meet about one hundred and eighty times a year and there are only one hundred and twenty-two readings, there will be days when your teacher will not assign readings from this book. He will find a variety of activities for those days. He may give tests, assign supplementary readings, study current events, or hold individual conferences with students. He may also suggest that many students should spend two days on a reading, particularly on the historical essays.

Today the United States ranks as the most influential nation in the world. For many years, the ideals of the American Revolution inspired imitators in lands far removed from North America. The spirit of American enterprise and the ingenious nature of her technology have been imitated everywhere. But admiration and envy are mixed with hatred and scorn. Many people in developing nations believe that the United States has turned its back on the great revolutionary tradition in which it was born. Unless he knows the long history of his nation, no one can hope to understand its place in the modern world. Nor can he understand himself if he is cut off from the past which shaped him.

Instead of trying to pack this volume with factual information, the authors have chosen to select vital elements of the American tradition and to explore them in depth. The historical essays and time lines link the readings together and provide coherence for the American story. We welcome you to an exciting exploration of the American past, confident that it is worth studying, both for its own sake and for the insights it will provide for life in the second half of the twentieth century.

Edwin Fenton
General Editor
Holt Social Studies Curriculum

How to Use This Book

The text of A New History of the United States consists of 122 readings that have been edited from published works or written especially for this course. Except for the historical essays, each reading follows a common pattern:

1. *The introduction.* Each introduction relates a reading to other readings in the course and supplies the essential background information.
2. *Study questions.* A few study questions call your attention to the most important points of the reading so that you can think about them in preparation for class discussion.
3. *The article or source material.* A few articles have been written especially for this volume. Each piece of source material consists of a document, newspaper account, excerpt from a book, article from a magazine, or some other material.

You are expected to read each day's lesson and to take notes on it before you come to class. Since your teacher will distribute dittoed material from time to time, you ought to get a three-ring looseleaf notebook to hold both the material that will be distributed and your homework and classroom notes.

Note-taking is an essential skill. We suggest that you read and take notes (in ink, so that the notes will be legible at final exam time) on the readings in the following manner:

1. *Write the reading number and title at the top of a piece of notebook paper.*
2. *Skim the entire reading.* Read the first sentence in each paragraph of the introduction. Next, read the study questions and fix them in your mind. Finally, read the first sentence in each paragraph of the article or source material. When you have finished, try to state in your own words what the lesson is about. Skimming such as this should take only a few minutes.
3. *Read the introduction and take running notes.* Do *not* read first and then read again for notes. Do *not* underline or mark the text in any way. Write the major ideas from the introduction and any supporting evidence that seems particularly important. You need not use complete sentences; but remember that you may wish to study from the notes some months later, so take down enough information to make the notes meaningful.
4. *Read the article or source material carefully and take running notes.* Do *not* read first and then read again for notes. Do *not* underline or mark the text in any way. Take the same sort of notes you took for the introduction. Put your own ideas and conclusions in parentheses, to show that they are yours.
5. *Go over your notes, underlining key ideas or words.* This procedure is the best way to begin learning the information in the lesson.
6. *Try to answer the study questions.* When you have finished studying your notes, try to answer the study questions for yourself. Do not write out the answers to the study questions. You would only be repeating the information in your notes if you do this. Use this step to see whether or not you found the important points in the reading to prepare for class discussion.

A similar note-taking technique can be used for the historical essays, although they do not contain introductions or study questions. Follow steps 1, 2, 4, and 5 outlined above. After you have finished this work, you should think about the major issues raised by the essays just as if study questions had been provided.

Two additional study techniques will be useful. First, keep a vocabulary list to which you add all new words and their definitions. In many cases, vocabulary words have been defined in the text in brackets or in marginal notes. Second, keep your class notes and your reading notes on a lesson together in your notebook so that you can review for tests without flipping through a mass of paper to find materials that go together.

Your teacher will help you if you have trouble with note-taking. He may occasionally spend time in class to demonstrate good note-taking techniques, and he will criticize your notes in an individual conference if you request one. Do not hesitate to ask for help.

Supplementary Reading Material

At the end of each chapter, you will find at least three paperback books suggested for supplementary reading. In some cases, teachers may add volumes to the lists of Suggested Readings in order to guide you toward books in your school library on topics that may be of special interest to you. Your teacher may have placed these books in the library or in your classroom. He may require you to read some of them or assign some for extra credit.

Following the author and name of each book, you will find a brief description of the volume. The descriptions will help you decide which volumes you want to read. You may also want to leaf through a number of the books first to get a better idea of what they are like. Some of the volumes are easier to read than others. You should choose something appropriate to your own interests and reading skill.

Your teacher may wish to make special rules and regulations about the supplementary reading material. Some teachers may choose not to use it at all. Others may ask you to submit book reviews based on the volume you select. Instructions for writing book reviews have been included as a handout in the audio-visual kit.

An Introduction to the Study of History

STATING THE ISSUE

Today you begin a formal study of American history. The first task is to find out what history is. Is it merely, as one dictionary says, "a narrative of events" or "a systematic written account of events, particularly of those affecting a nation, institution, science, or art, usually connected with a philosophical explanation of their causes"? Is it instead only "one man's interpretation of the past," or as the French philosopher Voltaire said, "a pack of tricks we play on the dead"? Or is it primarily a way of thinking, a set of rules and procedures for making interpretations?

This chapter is designed to encourage you to work out your own definition of history. Not everyone will arrive at exactly the same understanding of the term. Historians disagree with each other about the nature of their discipline. Hundreds of volumes have been written in an attempt to find a definition of history that everyone in the profession will accept. So far no author has achieved this.

You are not expected to understand the nature of history in one week's work. These five assignments merely introduce the topic and present opportunities to help you develop some ideas about the nature of historical investigation. As you continue your study of history, you will have frequent opportunities to increase your knowledge about historical procedures and to apply historical techniques to a great variety of situations. Only by successfully applying the tools of analysis can anyone be certain he has mastered them.

This study of the nature of history concentrates on a few key issues. What does a historian accept as fact? What determines how he classifies facts into groups of related events? How does he develop and validate hypotheses? These are the questions you will try to answer in this chapter.

I. How the Historian Classifies Information

A historian who collects information from newspapers or other sources must arrange the data in his notes for his readers. Usually a historian tries to answer a particular question, for example: "What caused the Civil War?" In a book or article, he gives the evidence on which his answer is based. If he does not arrange evidence to answer a question, he can only list facts helter-skelter. No one would waste his time reading such an account. But what determines the evidence the historian takes down in his notes in the first place? Will all historians doing research on the same subject take the same notes?

Historians often select and arrange facts on the basis of categories. Suppose a historian had uncovered two facts: first, that King John signed the Magna Carta in 1215 and second, that Eli Whitney invented the cotton gin in 1793. He might classify each fact according to historical periods, placing King John in the Middle Ages and Eli Whitney in the modern period. Or, he might categorize them according to aspects of human life, classifying the Magna Carta as a political event, and the cotton gin as a contribution to economic development.

Your study of history begins with the problems of selecting and arranging data. In order to concentrate on these problems without becoming involved in a true historical subject, data have been chosen that would not usually be considered historical at all. In class, however, you will be able to examine the implications of your conclusions for the study of history.

Below you will find a list of eighteen words. You are to arrange in groups those words that seem to belong together for some reason. For example, if you had been given the words *tiger, pine tree,* and *iron ore,* you might classify them as animal, vegetable, and mineral. You can probably think of a number of additional ways to classify these three terms. Think of as many classifications of the following eighteen terms as you can. Come to class prepared to discuss your classifications.

shark	tuna	pike
turkey	condor	eagle
rabbit	ostrich	sheep
cat	lion	pheasant
grouse	black bass	collie dog
rainbow trout	elephant	barracuda

II. How the Historian Inquires into the Past

Many high school students believe that history is a dull story about dead men. Historians would not agree. According to Paul L. Ward, the executive secretary of the American Historical Association, history is "... inquiry, examining a piece of the past systematically in hopes of getting an answer to questions which honestly matter to us." But how do historians determine what questions "honestly matter"? And how do historians examine "a piece of the past systematically"? You will consider one problem at a time.

The questions that matter to historians come from their *frame of reference.* Their personal experiences, their concern for society's problems, their position in society, and their accumulated knowledge all help to shape the questions they ask. A historian who worked his way through college might ask questions about how poor boys obtained an education in colonial times. One who worries about racial discrimination might investigate slavery in colonial times.

Thus, a historian begins his investigation with questions or problems that concern or interest him. He proceeds in a systematic way until he feels he has obtained satisfactory answers to his questions. What is this systematic procedure? Briefly it consists of two steps: developing hypotheses and validating or revising them.

A hypothesis is a tentative answer to a question. Again, a good question is: What caused the Civil War? Once a historian chooses a question to investigate, he accumulates data that will provide him with factual evidence. His interpretations of the facts will suggest hypotheses. But how does he know what data to look for? Many complex factors contributed to the Civil War. How will he know that he has not overlooked something vital? How will he determine which facts are significant and which are unimportant? And how will he relate one fact to other facts? These are the issues involved in forming hypotheses. They are the problems you will consider in this reading. As you read, ask yourself the following questions:

1. What are concepts? What are analytical questions? How are concepts and analytical questions related?
2. Why do investigators ask analytical questions?
3. Restate in your own words the concepts listed in this selection. What other questions do these concepts suggest?
4. If you were to study the laws of an ancient kingdom, how would you apply the analytical questions listed in this reading?

Social Science Concepts and Analytical Questions

How would you go about answering the question: "Why did the Roman Empire decline?" The problem is so complex that it is difficult to know where to begin. Some obvious questions will occur to you. Did the government weaken? Did the economy collapse? Did something disrupt the social structure? Most of us can think in terms of major divisions of a society—government, the economy, and social structure. In the case of Rome, the government had indeed become weak. It could no longer enforce its own laws. The economy had collapsed. Food production had fallen to alarmingly low levels. The social structure had been disrupted. Small farmers, unable to compete with the large landowners, had flocked to Rome seeking relief and reform.

But such simple answers would not satisfy most historians. Why had the government weakened? What brought about the collapse of the economy? What caused the social disorder within the Roman Empire? To investigate these questions, historians often use concepts from social science disciplines as tools for analysis. These social science concepts help historians to isolate the facts they need to develop hypotheses.

Although all societies have unique features, certain activities and forces exist in every society. Investigators classify these common activities and develop concepts around them. Then they use these concepts to analyze events or social conditions. Take the concept "leadership" from political science, for example. A political scientist knows that all societies have people who make decisions for the entire community. What these people are like, how they become leaders, and how they maintain their support are important considerations in the study of a political system.

You could develop some interesting hypotheses by asking questions about leadership in Rome during its declining years. You would discover that many of Rome's leaders had been generals interested primarily in selfish gains. By focusing on the concept of leadership in Rome, it is possible to discover some of the reasons why the government had weakened.

Concepts suggest a number of analytical questions the investigator can ask of data to make facts come to life. The fact that Wilt Chamberlain earns about $200,000 per year playing basketball is only a passing, if awe-inspiring, curiosity. However, when the investigator asks how values influence the distribution of income in American society, Wilt Chamberlain's salary becomes important evidence.

The following list of concepts and analytical questions contains only a few of the categories investigators use to analyze a society. These concepts and questions should help you formulate hypotheses about western society. During the remainder of this course, you will learn additional concepts, and as you proceed through school, even more concepts will become part of your intellectual equipment. As you study this list, think how you would apply the concepts and analytical questions to articles in today's newspapers.

A. Decision-Making—the process by which a political system makes, interprets, and enforces its rulings
Questions: What are the rules for making decisions? In what institutions are decisions made? Who determines which decisions will be made? How does information reach the decision-makers? How do they see that their decisions are enforced?

Institutions are established organizations or practices, like Congress or the principle of the separation of powers.

B. Citizenship—the role an individual plays in the political system
Questions: How does a citizen influence the use of public power? To what degree can a citizen influence the government? How does he gain access to decision-makers? What are a citizen's obligations? How does government regulate a citizen's life?

Role refers to the functions a member of society is expected to fulfill.

C. Resources—the supply of raw materials, capital goods, and human skills available to a society
Questions: What natural resources are available? What capital resources are available? What human resources are available? How are the resources used to produce goods and services?

Natural resources are raw materials, such as land and minerals. Capital resources are tools and equipment used to produce goods and services. Human resources are workers and their skills.

D. Distribution—the process by which consumers in a community receive goods and services
Questions: Who are the consumers in a society? How do they obtain goods? What institutions distribute goods? Who in the society obtains the most goods? Who obtains the least?

E. Norms—the standards of behavior expected of people in their social relationships with other members of the society
Questions: What norms are assigned to given roles? (How are fathers expected to behave toward their children? toward their wives?) How are people with lower status expected to treat people with higher status, and vice versa? (What behavior is expected of employees toward their supervisors? of supervisors toward their employees?)

Status refers to the ranking of some roles as superior to others.

F. Social Class—a broad group of people who share the same general status and social position and who are classified by others in the society as belonging to the same group
Questions: What are the various social classes in a community? What criteria are used to place people in different social classes? What privileges are given to each social class? Can membership in a social class be earned or must one be born into a class?

III. How the Historian Uses Hypotheses

You have seen that a historian begins his investigation of a subject by asking a question: "What caused World War I?" "What was the most important contribution of the Romans to the Western heritage?" He then starts his research—reading and collecting notes about his topic. He selects the data he wants to record in his notes and then selects again from his notes those pieces of evidence (facts) that he will use to prove his point. Every step in the process of writing a book or an article involves selection.

Before long he starts to develop a hypothesis. As he gathers more data, he revises his hypothesis; he may abandon it entirely if he finds enough evidence against it. In this case, he will develop a new hypothesis to guide his research. Eventually, he will form a hypothesis that answers his question and is supported by facts.

This procedure sounds far simpler than it really is. Where does a historian get the idea for a hypothesis in the first place? How does he decide when a hypothesis has been proved? How should he arrange his evidence to support his explanation?

Today you will investigate the way in which two historians developed hypotheses and tried to prove them. The article you will read concerns the controversy about the Kensington Stone, discovered in Minnesota in 1898. Further evidence about this stone will then be introduced. As you read, think about these questions:

1. How does the author begin his article? Do most historians start research in a similar way?
2. What was the original hypothesis about the authenticity of the stone? What evidence made scholars accept this hypothesis?
3. What was the next hypothesis about the stone? What evidence prompted a new investigation? Why have many historians decided that the stone is an authentic relic?
4. Are you convinced that the stone is genuine? Why?

The Kensington Stone Riddle

Did a group of Scandinavians reach this country—and perish under Indian tomahawks—130 years before Columbus came? Recent research on the Kensington Stone, once denounced as a fraud, has reopened the question of its authenticity.

Thomas R. Henry, "The Riddle of the Kensington Stone," **Saturday Evening Post,** vol. 221 (August 21, 1948), p. 25. Reprinted by permission of Mrs. Thomas R. Henry.

A challenging enigma [mystery] confronts American historians. Did a Norwegian knight named Paul Knutson lead an ill-fated band of forty armored soldier-missionaries to the headwaters of the Red River in west central Minnesota 130 years before the first voyage of Columbus? Evidence of such an expedition, accumulating through half a century, is now so substantial that some of this country's foremost archaeologists consider the case nearly proved. A few hard facts jut like mountain crags out from the clouds of New World antiquity.

Archaeologists are scientists who study fossils, relics, monuments, and other cultural remains of early civilizations.

The first of these facts: Late in the autumn of 1354 King Magnus Erikson, first ruler of the combined realms of Norway and Sweden, commissioned Knutson, a "law speaker"—or judge—and one of the most prominent men of his court, to recruit an expedition to rescue the souls of a vanished Norwegian colony on the west coast of Greenland. Presumably the party sailed early the next spring. It was never heard of again.

The second fact: Fifty years ago a stone slab was found clutched in the roots of a tree by a Swedish homesteader near Kensington, Minnesota. It bore what purported to be a message to posterity, carved in runic letters. It recorded an Indian massacre of a group of explorers. Assuming the relic is genuine, these explorers must have been members of Knutson's expedition. The inscription's date was 1362.

The third fact: A few weeks ago [1948] the slab was placed in the great hall of the Smithsonian Institution, in Washington. Dr. Matthew W. Stirling, chief of the Government's Bureau of American Ethnology, called it "probably the most important archaeological object yet found in North America." . . .

Ethnology is the science that deals with the origins, distribution, characteristics, and interrelationships of the different races.

It was back in the summer of 1898 that Olof Ohman, a young Swedish immigrant and homesteader near the village of Kensington, in Douglas County, Minnesota, grubbed up the stump of an aspen tree at the edge of a marsh. Clutched in its roots was a flat, gravestone-shaped piece of graywacke, one of the hard glacial sandstone rocks of the region. It was about the size of a headstone in a Swedish country cemetery. Carved on one face and one edge of this slab were strange letters. . . .

Prof. O. J. Breda [from the University of Minnesota], one of the foremost Scandinavian scholars in America, found little difficulty in deciphering most of the inscription. The letters were Norse runes, the curious first alphabet of the Germanic peoples derived in some roundabout way from the letters of the Greeks and Romans. Some of these symbols meant nothing to Breda. In his translation, he left blank spaces where they occurred. It now is known that they represented numbers.

This is the translation as now accepted: [We are] 8 Goths [Swedes] and 22 Norwegians on (an) exploration journey from Vinland through (or across) the West. We had camp by (a lake with) two skerries [rocky islands] one day's journey north from this stone. We were [out] and fished one day. After we came home [we] found 10 [of our] men red with blood and dead. AV[e] M[aria], Save [us] from evil. [We] have 10 of (our party) by the sea to look after our ships (or ship) 14 days' journey from this island. Year 1362.

Professor Breda was not at all impressed. It was such an obvious hoax, he said, that it was not worthy of further attention from anybody. The language itself was a dead giveaway. It was a mixture of Norwegian, Swedish, and what looked like old English. In the days of runic writings Swedes and Norwegians had been bitter enemies, and it was incredible that they could have been partners on an expedition. The three letters AVM were Latin, not runic. The Roman alphabet had not been introduced into Scandinavia until early in the Middle Ages.

The learned runologist missed the date—1362. The figures representing it were not in the early runic alphabet. Breda quite naturally assumed that any Norsemen who could have reached central Minnesota must have come from the Greenland colonies of Eric the Red sometime in the twelfth century. There was no room here for any argument. The Kensington Stone could not have been carved by any such Greenlander. It was all a crude and silly fraud perpetrated by somebody with a superficial knowledge of runes together with a gross ignorance of Scandinavian history. The hoaxer, whoever he was, hardly could have expected to be taken seriously. He had said that the stone was carved on an island in a lake. There was no lake within twenty miles of Ohman's homestead. . . .

What is "probably the most important archaeological object yet found in North America" very likely still would be in that barnyard had it not been for the interest of an outstanding Norse-American historian, Hjalmar R. Holand of Ephraim, Wisconsin. For thirty years he has given most of his spare time to its study in every aspect—geological, archaeological, geographic, linguistic, and historical. He has taken it to twenty-three European universities for consultation with experts. One after another, the most serious objections to its authenticity have proved the strongest points in its favor. First was the discovery of the meanings of the runic number symbols and the determination of the date. These particular runes were of late origin and local usage in Norway. In the fourteenth century the Latin alphabet had been introduced, and its letters were intermingled quite often with the ancient Germanic symbols. That disposed of the apparent incongruity [inconsistency] of the Roman letters AVM for AV(e) M(aria). This was a well-understood symbol, easy to write. It would have required a lot of space to have produced it in runes.

The biggest break, however, came about twenty years ago with the publication in a Danish archaeological journal of a copy, found by chance in the royal library at Copenhagen, of King Magnus' order to Knutson. It was translated as follows:

"Magnus, by the grace of God king of Norway, Sweden and Skaane, sends to all men who see or hear this letter good health and happiness.

"We desire to make known that you [Paul Knutson] are to take the men who are to go in the Knorr [the royal trading vessel], whether they be named or not named, from my bodyguard and also from among the retainers of other men whom you may wish to take on the voyage, and that Paul Knutson, who shall be the commandant upon the Knorr, shall have full authority to select the men who are best suited either as officers or men. We ask you to accept this, our command, with a right good will for the cause, inasmuch as we do it for the honor of God and for the sake of our soul, and for the sake of our predecessors, who in Greenland established Christianity and have maintained it to this time, and we will not let it perish in our days. Know this for truth, that whoever defies this, our command, shall meet with our serious displeasure and thereupon receive full punishment.

"Executed at Bergen, Monday after Simon and Judah's day in the six and XXX year of our reign (1354). By Orm Ostenson, our regent, sealed."

Thus it was established that a few years before the date found on the Kensington Stone a certain Paul Knutson, one of the most prominent citizens of Magnus' kingdom, had been ordered to recruit and lead an expedition across the Atlantic. Certainly no hoaxer of the nineteenth century could have known this. The date on the stone, eight years after the issuance of the order, would have been a remarkable coincidence with history. Eight years was a reasonable time to have allowed Knutson to have come from Bergen to the headwaters of the Red River. . . .

If the Kensington Stone is genuine, Paul Knutson and his crusading knights were in Central Minnesota in 1362. Evidence increases for the authenticity of the relic. If Farmer Ohman told the truth about the circumstances of the stone's discovery—and this stolid, hard working, unlettered immigrant must have been leading an extraordinary sort of double life if he concocted the story—the tablet had been in the spot where he found it for at least as long as the aspen tree had been growing. Archaeologists have a reasonably accurate means of dating trees and timbers from the rings in the wood; examination of similar trees in the neighborhood has led to the conservative assumption that the tree in whose roots the rune stone was found, was at least forty years old in 1898. This means that, if the relic had been "planted," the attempted deception must have taken place in the 1850's. There were then few white men in that part of Minnesota. It was inhabited by savage and hostile Sioux.

The conglomeration of languages alone was enough to convince Professor Breda that the stone was a fake. But he was thinking in terms of the language of the sagas in which had been related the exploits of Eric the Red and Leif the Lucky. This stone had been inscribed more than three centuries later. Norway then was in contact with all Europe. Some English words had been introduced into the vulgar [common] speech. Both Swedes and Norwegians participated in the expedition. Magnus was king of both countries. It was natural enough that the "crusaders" should have spoken a slight mixture of tongues. . . .

The message stated that some of the party had been left behind to look after the boats by the sea, "14 days' journey from this island." It has been found that the expression "day's journey" was a conventional term of the time, meaning approximately seventy-five miles, or the distance which a vessel could sail in a day with a fair wind. This would be just about the correct distance to the mouth of the Nelson River. The journey probably had taken Knutson's men at least a year.

The inscription indicates that the party was encamped on an island in a lake, seventy-five miles away from another lake containing two rocky islands on the shore of which their comrades had been massacred. It is to be assumed that they had come here for temporary security from the Indians. Ohman found the stone at the edge of a marsh. This now is dry land. Geological surveys show that the slightly elevated, rocky land from which the farmer grubbed the aspen stump was almost certainly an island in 1362. The countryside has been getting progressively drier for the past century [since about 1850].

Just about seventy-five miles away is the only lake with two "skerries," or rocky islands. It is Cormorant Lake, in Becker County. On its shore are large glacial boulders with triangular holes drilled in three of them. This was a common device for mooring boats along the fiords of fourteenth-century Norway. Beside one of these rocks a fourteenth-century Norwegian fire steel was recently picked up. Several other such mooring rocks have been found in this section of Minnesota. The implication is that the explorers continued their journey eastward for a time, probably seeking a waterway back to Vinland. Along the course of the Nelson during the past half century various Norwegian implements have been picked up—three battle-axes, a fire steel, and a spearhead. This may indicate the route followed by Knutson's men. . . .

A fire steel is an implement that is used with flint to start a fire.

IV. How the Historian Decides What Is Fact

In the last reading you discovered that historians use facts to validate hypotheses. You also learned that scholars often disagree about what is fact and what is not. Because of differences in their frames of reference, some historians accept a statement as fact while others reject it.

Sometimes historians have only one source for a statement of fact. In most cases, however, they have two or more sources. But often the sources disagree, because even an eyewitness author has his own frame of reference from which he views events. He will record some things and fail to record others. Another eyewitness will note different events or interpret the same events differently.

This reading gives you an opportunity to decide which facts can be accepted when two authors disagree on many details. Suppose that civilization on earth has long since been destroyed by hydrogen bombs. You have just landed from Mars. (We won't speculate about what you look like or how you got here.) You are able to read both English and Russian because your midget computer makes instant translations into Martian. In a time capsule buried on the site of ancient New York, you discover a yellowed magazine containing an account of a revolution in a place called Hungary. In another time capsule on the site of ancient Moscow, you discover a fading script of a radio broadcast describing the same event. The two accounts are all the information you have. As a historian, Martian variety, it is your task to decide what the facts are.

As you read these two articles think about these questions:

1. Which of these accounts, if either, do you accept? Why? Do you think each might be right in parts and wrong in other parts?
2. Do the two accounts agree about something? If so, are you willing to accept it as fact? Why or why not?
3. What are some of the issues on which the accounts differ?
4. What further information would you have to find in order to decide which, if either, is correct?

Hungary: Five Days of Freedom

"Hungary: The Five Days of Freedom," **Time** (November 12, 1956), p. 40, copyright © 1956 by Time, Inc. Reprinted by permission.

For five frantic days Hungary was free.

From beleaguered Budapest on Tuesday [October 30, 1956] the news flashed that the Soviet tanks were pulling out. Shouted the jubilant announcer: "For long years past this radio had been an instrument of lies. It lied day and night. It lied on all wavelengths . . . From this moment those who mouthed the lies are no longer . . . We who are now facing the microphone are new men." It was the voice of the people of Hungary in that hour: a great burden had been cast off.

The first to see the unfamiliar face of freedom were the young rebels. Their weapons at the ready, their faces filthy with the grime of battle, their clothes often blood-caked, they stood along the arteries of battle leading out of the battered city, happily jeering the departing Soviet tanks as they rumbled sullenly by.

Tank smashing

Only a few hours before, desperate battles had been fought at the Maria Theresa barracks, at the Communist Party headquarters, and at the steel mills at Csepel Island. With their heavy 76-mm. guns, the Soviet tanks had attempted to blast the rebels out of their hiding places, but the "incredible youngsters" had evolved their own technique for dealing with the mighty 26-ton tanks. First they would fire on the tanks from upper-story windows, then as the big T-34s rumbled up, their great guns elevated, a small boy would leap out of a doorway, fling a pail of gasoline over the tank's engine compartment, and leap back to shelter. As the tank took fire and its crew scrambled out of the turret, the young Tommy-gunner firing from the windows above would mow them down. An alternate system was to slosh a bucket of gasoline across a street and throw a match in it just as a Soviet tank plunged past.

Freedom fighters

Now, as they began to realize what had happened and what they had done, the faces of the rebels were lit with a kind of ecstasy. There were vigorous blond students and tough-looking workers among them, but many seemed pitifully young. A correspondent noted a boy who could not have been more than ten years old holding himself at the ready with a rifle as tall as himself. Beside him was a 15-year-old girl with a submachine gun and a forage cap on her head. Gray with the fatigue of four days' ceaseless fighting, almost falling from exhaustion, they solemnly welcomed the foreigners: "We greet you in the name of the Hungarian Freedom Fighters!" Some carried machine-gun ammunition belts slung around their shoulders, and out of almost every pocket and above every inch of belt protruded hand grenades.

Premier Nagy had disowned the city's 10,000-man Communist security-police force, and the Russians had pulled out leaving the hated AVH men to their fate. Most of them had found temporary

In 1949, the Hungarian government created a large Communist state-security police force (AVH). In 1956, when demonstrations broke out against Soviet dictatorship, the AVH fired into the crowds, turning many protesters into revolutionaries. Fighting broke out and quickly spread throughout the country with the civilian police and the army joining the popular front.

ratholes. In a huge concrete bunker below Communist Party headquarters, some 200 were said to be hiding out with political prisoners as hostages. Scores hung from trees and lampposts.

The revolution uncovered terrible evidence of AVH cruelty. On a wooded hill in Buda, in a bright new housing development reserved exclusively for ex-Premier Rakosi and his comrades, rebels found a villa with a built-in torture chamber and prison cells, one padded and soundproofed, another equipped with a powerful lamp beamed on a chair. The rebels remembered having seen closed automobiles driving up to this house at night. At Györ, in the provinces, Western newsmen were shown an AVH headquarters with tiny 2 ft.-wide standup torture cells, and a secret crematory for victims who did not survive AVH treatment. In the same modern building were technical facilities for monitoring all telephone conversations in western Hungary, including a score of tape recorders working simultaneously.

A crematory is a huge furnace for burning bodies.

There was also fun to be had pulling down Soviet war memorials. High on Gellert Hill, antlike figures swarmed around Sculptor Szigmund Strobl's 150-ft. statue of Freedom, a graceful woman guarded by the bronze statue of a Russian soldier. Slowly the crowd, pulling on lines attached to the soldier, rocked the statue back and forth, until he tipped forward on his face. There had been no looting in the city thus far, but to walk abroad at night was to hazard being shot at . . . or stopped by some tough young rebel and made to show identity papers.

Democracy's return

Small newspapers representing political parties long believed defunct suddenly appeared. The old National Peasant Party, the Smallholders Party, and the Social Democratic Party each found its voice. Out of the disorganized Communist Party a new Hungarian Socialist Workers Party with national Communism as its aim was formed by Party Leader Janor Kadar.

What had come over Hungary, without anyone quite realizing it, was democracy.

To continue holding down the premiership, new Premier Nagy was forced to yield to the pressures of the new parties, to promise free elections, to acclaim neutrality, and, above all, to insist that the Russian troops be withdrawn, not only from Budapest, but from Hungary.

From the moment that U.S. correspondents had begun coming into free Budapest the rebels had never ceased to ask, "When are the Americans coming?" During the middle of the fighting a Hungarian had lifted up his son so that a child might touch a U.S. flag on a correspondent's car. Again and again, innocent of world affairs, they had asked if arms would come soon from America. Said one: "If the Russians come back, we can't hold out forever."

The Russians were coming back, and many Americans were leaving Budapest. Sadly the Hungarians watched them go. They had no stake in the revolution; they were at peace with the mighty Soviet Union and hoped to remain so—Hungary's bloodshed was only a drop of what the world would suffer in a total war.

A Soviet Tourist in Budapest

E. M. Bazarina, as quoted in Richard Lettis and William F. Morris, "The Hungarian Revolt," in **The Hungarian Revolt,** Melvin J. Lasky, ed. New York: Frederick A. Praeger, Inc., 1957, pp. 126–27,

Moscow We arrived in Hungary on 19 October with other Soviet tourists. We spent four days touring this beautiful country and were everywhere given a most cordial and hearty welcome. On Tuesday, 23 October, on our way to a theatre we saw crowds of people in the streets of Budapest. They were lined up in ranks and carried placards, many of which bore the inscription "Long live Hungary!" . . . The students together with members of the intelligentsia and workers were demanding the redress of errors and omissions committed by the Hungarian Government. They were legitimate demands. . . .

On that first evening I saw from the hotel in which we were staying a man with a rifle appear in the deserted street. He took up a position in one of the drives and, taking careful aim, began shooting out the street lamps. The lamps went out one by one and darkness enveloped the street. What prompted the marksman to do this? Just hooliganism? Hardly. I think he was one of the bright sparks of the reactionary underground who wanted to create confusion and chaos in the city. Quite soon afterwards there were flashes of gunfire and sounds of battle and we saw wrecked and burning buildings in the streets of Budapest, overturned tram-cars and other vehicles. Firing would die down and then flare up again. Hostile elements were aiming at paralyzing the city's life but the workers of Budapest were repelling the rebels. Detachments of armed workers tried to restore order in the streets and prevent looting. In many places, including the area around our hotel, workers' patrols were posted. . . .

One member of our hotel staff, a middle-aged man with grey hair, told us: "Our workers cannot have had a hand in this looting and rioting. It is fascism raising its head." And that is what it was. The counterrevolutionary underground was in action in Budapest. Fascist reactionary elements had arrived there from abroad. The hostile venture was gathering momentum and the Hungarian Government asked the USSR Government for aid. In response to this request Soviet military units stationed in Hungary under the Warsaw Treaty entered Budapest to help to restore order. The overwhelming majority of Hungarians welcomed this move in the hope that life in the city would quickly return to normal. I myself saw in one street how the people were welcoming the Soviet tanks.

The Warsaw Treaty, signed in 1955, was a twenty-year pact that set up a unified military command for the Soviet satellite nations and provided for the maintenance of Soviet troops in those territories.

One Hungarian, a member of the hotel staff, described the following incident to us. Firemen-volunteers, absolutely unarmed, were putting out a fire in one of the public buildings. Suddenly, from a small house opposite, shots were fired by fascist louts who opened fire on the unarmed firemen. Several of them fell. Our tank was stationed in the street. The tankmen immediately aimed their gun at the house where the bandits were entrenched. This was sufficient to make them run into a side street. Several firemen ran up to the tank and shook hands with the tankmen. This episode gives a good testimony of the attitude of the Hungarians towards the Soviet troops. However, reaction did not cease its activities. When we walked along some of the streets, we saw that the walls of houses were thickly covered with counterrevolutionary posters. . . .

When Soviet troops began withdrawing from Budapest, an unbridled White Terror started in the Hungarian capital. We Soviet tourists recall this time with horror. It is difficult to describe the chaos which reigned in the city where public buildings were destroyed, shops looted, and where crowds of armed bandits, obviously fascists, walked along the streets committing bestial [brutal] murders in broad daylight. I shall never forget what I saw with my own eyes. I think it was on 30 or 31 October. A man in a sports suit walked along the Lenin Boulevard. He might have been one of those who tried to restore order in the city. Several armed ruffians wearing counterrevolutionary tricolours ran up to him. A horrible inhuman cry was heard. A whole crowd of bandits appeared from somewhere. I was unable to see what they were doing with their victim, but in a few minutes he was hanging on a nearby tree with an eye gouged out and his face slashed with knives.

White Terror was a counterrevolutionary movement that occurred during the French Revolution.

Some time ago I read how the fascists in Germany burnt progressive literature on bonfires. We saw similar things . . . A group of some hooligans looted and set fire to the House of Books. Thousands and thousands of books were smouldering in the muddy street. We were there, witnesses of this barbarity. The works of Chekhov, Shakespeare, Tolstoi, Pushkin, and other famous authors were lying in the mud, black smoke rising. We saw an old man who lifted a few books, then carefully wiped the mud with his sleeve, pressed them to his breast and walked slowly away. Many people did the same.

In the Hotel "Peace" the atmosphere in those days was extremely tense. The counterrevolutionaries tore the red star from the front of the hotel and trod it underfoot on the pavement. We were told that the Hotel "Peace" from now on would be called Hotel "Britannia." The person who told us about it looked around and added quietly: "It doesn't matter. It will only be temporary."

More than once we were witnesses to acts which manifested the friendly attitude of the Hungarians towards the Soviet people. This friendly attitude was felt by us Soviet people, when we were leaving Budapest . . . In small groups of two or three people we made our way along the devastated streets toward the Danube in order to board a Red Cross steamer. We were accompanied by a worker . . . a young girl. She led us from one crossroad to another, fearlessly seeking the safest way. At the pier we heartily embraced her. She said: "Someone in the West wants us to pull their chestnuts out of the fire. Don't believe them, dear friends. We Hungarians are for socialism and we are with you." When we were in Czechoslovakia on our way home, we learned that the counterrevolution in Hungary was routed and that life was becoming normal in the country. Now we are at home in Moscow. We shall not forget that Hungarian girl who said that the Hungarians were for socialism and that they were with us. . . .

V. What Is History

In this chapter, you have been studying the way in which historians investigate the past. As you read and as you discussed the readings in class, you should have begun to develop your own interpretation of the nature of historical investigations and your own preliminary definition of history.

For the next class, you are to write a paper of no more than three hundred words, in which you analyze the way you would approach a historical problem. Suppose you wanted to determine the causes of the American Revolution. Describe how you would investigate this problem, using the method of inquiry you just studied.

SUGGESTED READINGS

GUSTAVSON, CARL G., *A Preface to History.* Gustavson introduces his readers to the historian's craft by examining the various forces historical investigators must take into account when conducting their studies.

NEVINS, ALLEN, *The Gateway to History.* One of this country's best-known historians explains his methods. Nevins examines the kind of evidence historians use and the ways they develop conclusions.

WOOLLEY, SIR LEONARD, *Digging Up the Past.* Sir Leonard reveals how archaeologists organize "digs," analyze remains of ancient civilizations, and reconstruct the lives of the people of long ago.

Our Colonial Ancestors

CHAPTER 1

STATING THE ISSUE

We are a nation of immigrants. The Indians whom the first white settlers found here had originally emigrated from Asia across the Bering Straits. In the nineteenth and twentieth centuries, 35 million Europeans crossed the Atlantic to our shores while thousands of Chinese, Japanese, and other Asians entered our western ports. We sometimes forget, however, that two additional groups of Americans were also immigrants: Negro slaves from Africa and our pioneer ancestors who settled the colonies in the seventeenth and eighteenth centuries.

With the exception of the American Indians who brought their own culture into an empty land, all these immigrants shared a common experience: They were uprooted from one way of life and forced to adopt another. The seventeenth-century farmer left the settled English countryside for the danger and opportunity of free land on the edge of a raw wilderness. The nineteenth-century peasant from Ireland or Italy left his familiar village for the strange streets of a vast new city. Today Americans migrate within our country. Thousands of people move each year from farms in the South to take factory jobs in Chicago, New York, Detroit, Los Angeles, or other large cities. The experience of growing up in one culture and moving to another ties us and millions of our ancestors together.

Many of us have shared a similar uprooting experience. Few Americans are born and live and die beneath the same roof. We move from house to house, from city to city, and from state to state. Moving forces us to leave friends, churches, schools, and homes behind to make new lives somewhere else. In a way, we move from one culture to another, from one way of life to a second which is always somewhat different.

Chapter 1 examines the role of migration in our own lives and in the lives of seventeenth-century colonists. Why do modern Americans move? What problems do they encounter when they migrate from place to place? Why did Europeans emigrate to the American colonies in the seventeenth century? What problems did they encounter? How did the environment of the New World help to shape the cultures which Europeans brought with them? These are the major issues raised in Chapter 1.

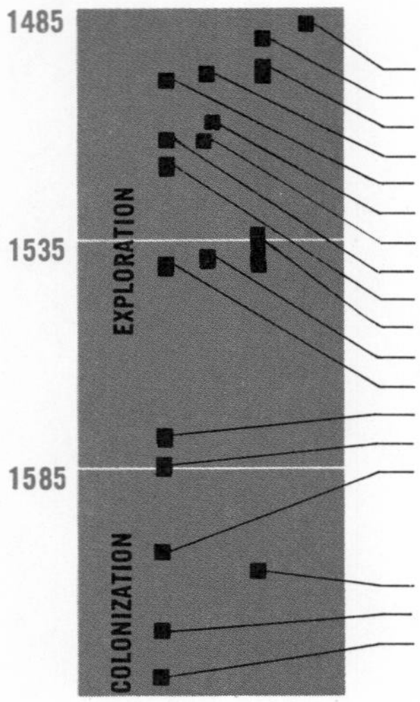

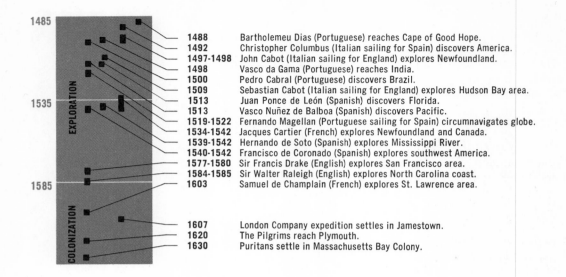

1488	Bartholemeu Dias (Portuguese) reaches Cape of Good Hope.
1492	Christopher Columbus (Italian sailing for Spain) discovers America.
1497-1498	John Cabot (Italian sailing for England) explores Newfoundland.
1498	Vasco da Gama (Portuguese) reaches India.
1500	Pedro Cabral (Portuguese) discovers Brazil.
1509	Sebastian Cabot (Italian sailing for England) explores Hudson Bay area.
1513	Juan Ponce de León (Spanish) discovers Florida.
1513	Vasco Nuñez de Balboa (Spanish) discovers Pacific.
1519-1522	Fernando Magellan (Portuguese sailing for Spain) circumnavigates globe.
1534-1542	Jacques Cartier (French) explores Newfoundland and Canada.
1539-1542	Hernando de Soto (Spanish) explores Mississippi River.
1540-1542	Francisco de Coronado (Spanish) explores southwest America.
1577-1580	Sir Francis Drake (English) explores San Francisco area.
1584-1585	Sir Walter Raleigh (English) explores North Carolina coast.
1603	Samuel de Champlain (French) explores St. Lawrence area.
1607	London Company expedition settles in Jamestown.
1620	The Pilgrims reach Plymouth.
1630	Puritans settle in Massachusetts Bay Colony.

1 Migration: A Class Survey

We cannot clearly understand our ancestors unless we have shared their experience either in our own lives or through reading. Many of us have moved from one place to another. By examining that experience, we can learn something about how our ancestors must have felt when they faced the prospect of leaving their homes in Europe, Africa, or Asia and coming to the New World or leaving homes in one part of the New World for another.

Many American students have never traced the history of their own families. They are often surprised to discover some of their own ancestors represented by statistics in their history books. Somewhere in the past of each of us is an immigrant from another land. Many of us are descended from people who moved from the farm to the city, from south to north or from east to west. Our past becomes more meaningful when we can place our own ancestors within it.

This exercise is designed to help each of us locate our place in American history. It will also introduce us to some of the problems that the early settlers faced as they stood on the brink of the New World. Each student should talk to his parents as he fills out the questionnaire and thinks about the study questions that follow. Even your parents may not know the answers to many of these questions, but do the best you can with them. Write the answers on the copy of the questionnaire supplied by your teacher so that they can be collected and tabulated in class. Do not be concerned if you cannot answer all of the questions accurately. Many of us cannot.

1. If your family has ever moved, what reasons did you have for leaving one home for another? What did you sacrifice by migrating?
2. What problems come up when people move from one home to another, even in the same city?
3. Which would be more difficult, to move from south to north or from Europe to the United States? Why?

Your Family in American History

1.	Were you born in this city?	Yes No
2.	How many houses have you lived in since you were born?	1 2-4 5 or more
3.	Were one, both, or neither of your parents born in this city?	0 1 2
4.	How many of your grandparents were born in this city?	0 1 2 3 4
5.	How many of your great-grandparents were born in this city?	0 1 2 3 4 5 6 7 8
6.	Were you born in the United States?	Yes No
7.	Were one, both, or neither of your parents born in the United States?	0 1 2
8.	How many of your grandparents were born in the United States?	0 1 2 3 4
9.	How many of your great-grandparents were born in the United States?	0 1 2 3 4 5 6 7 8
10.	Estimate as closely as possible the total number of towns, cities, and rural areas in which your family has lived over four generations (you, your parents, your grandparents, and your great-grandparents).	1 2-5 6-10 11-15 16 or more
11.	About what year was your oldest great-grandfather born?	________________
12.	List the countries from which your ancestors came to America.	________________ ________________ ________________

2 The Pilgrims

Moving from one part of a city or one section of our nation to another is a common American experience. In our past, many Americans have faced even more difficult moves. They have uprooted themselves from their accustomed ways and from homes which may have sheltered their families for generations, and they have taken ships to a strange new land. The whole process was filled with danger and was never begun with a light heart. Just as your parents may have spent days discussing the advantages of a new job in a strange city with each other and with you, your ancestors no doubt drew their chairs to the family table to talk about going to America. Some of them were probably poor; a number were actually driven out by starvation; some were even hauled to the banks of the rivers in chains by slavers who had purchased them from their captors. No matter what the reason for migration, it was never easy.

In 1607, after searching their hearts for many years, a band of Englishmen left the small town of Scrooby to settle in the Netherlands. They objected to the Anglican Church, the official church in England, in which they were supposed to worship. Like many other Englishmen, they were *Dissenters,* a term applied to those who disagreed with one or more of the principles or practices of the Anglican Church. Because they wanted to separate from the Anglican Church and establish their own congregation, they were also sometimes called *Separatists.* Hoping to establish a new life in keeping with their religious principles, they settled in Leyden, Holland. In 1620, some of these same people and their descendants took to ships again, heading for Virginia on a small vessel called the *Mayflower.* Eventually, after a harrowing passage, they landed just south of present-day Boston in a place which they called Plymouth. We call these early immigrants *Pilgrims* from the name which their great leader, William Bradford, gave them in his journal.

Instead of being told what the Pilgrims thought of the experience of migration, you will read their own version. As you do so, think about the following questions:

1. What problems did the Pilgrims foresee when they went to Holland? What changes did they have to make in their way of life in a different country?
2. Why did the Pilgrims leave Holland for America? Did they leave for a single reason or for a mixture of reasons? Do you think most emigrants leave one place to go to another for one reason or for several reasons?
3. What problems did the Pilgrims foresee in settling in the New World?

4. Which would be more difficult, to leave England for Holland or Holland for the New World? Would either of these moves be more difficult than changing your home from one American city to another? Why?

Why the Pilgrims Emigrated

In his later life William Bradford, governor of Plymouth Colony, wrote a history of that colony which he called Of Plimouth Plantation. *The text which follows is taken from a modern version of the original book, but it preserves the flavor of Bradford's seventeenth-century prose style.*

E. Brooks Smith and Robert Meredith, eds., **Pilgrim Courage.** Boston: Little, Brown and Company, 1962, pp. 3–4, 14–16.

Of Their Troubles, Persecutions, and Plans To Escape

With the work of some godly preachers many people became enlightened by the Word of God and began to reform their lives. When they began to live in the light of God's Word they were scoffed and scorned by the multitude. The ministers were told to follow the laws of the church or else be silent. And the poor people were sorely vexed by spying of church officers and actions of the courts. They were truly persecuted, yet they bore it with patience for many years.

But they could not long continue in this way. They were hunted and harried [constantly attacked] on every side, so that their former troubles were but as fleabitings in comparison with those which were to come upon them.

Some were taken and clapped up in prison. Others had their houses beset and watched night and day. Most of them decided to flee, leaving their houses and means of livelihood. Seeing themselves thus molested and that there was no hope of staying, they decided by joint consent to go into Holland, where they heard there was freedom of religion for all men. They also heard that some people from other parts of England who had been persecuted for the same cause had gone to Amsterdam and other places in that country.

So they continued together about a year and kept their meetings every Sunday in one place or another, worshiping God among themselves. They decided to get over into Holland as best they could. This was in the year 1607.

To leave their native soil and country, their lands and livings, and all their friends was much. But to go into a country they knew not, where they must learn the language and find a new way of making a living, seemed a most desperate adventure and a misery worse than death. Also Holland was an expensive place to live and a country suffering the miseries of war. They had been used to plain country life and were not acquainted with the trades of the city. These things did not dismay them though they were sometimes troubled by them. Their desires were set on the ways of God and they believed in His providence.

The Netherlands had been at war with Spain since 1568, when Philip II, a Catholic, inherited the Spanish throne and, with it, rule of the Netherlands. Philip attempted to impose religious restrictions on the primarily Protestant Dutch, who rebelled and declared themselves independent in 1581. Peace did not come until 1648, when the Netherlands was officially recognized as an independent republic.

Of the Reasons and Causes for Their Leaving Holland

They lived in this city [Leyden, Holland] for eleven or twelve years, during the time when there was a truce between the Dutch and the Spaniards. Near the end of that time the elders and the wisest members of the congregation began to think about the coming dangers and look into the future for a remedy. They had grown older, some had been taken away by death, and all found living to be hard and the work not of their kind. They began to think about moving to some other place, not because of a giddy desire or newfangledness but for several weighty and solid reasons.

They Show Reasons for Leaving Holland

First, they saw and found by experience that after a few years others who desired to be with them could not endure the hardness of the place. They preferred and chose the prisons in England to the liberty of Holland. Therefore it was thought best to find an easier place of living where they could practice their own trades. Then others would join them where they might have liberty and live comfortably.

Secondly, their leaders saw that although they bore these difficulties cheerfully and courageously, many were becoming old before their time and would sink under their burden. They had better move while they were still able.

Thirdly, because necessity was their taskmaster, they had to oppress their children with heavy labors. Although their children were willing, their bodies bowed under the weight and many became worn out in their early youth. But even worse, some of the children were drawn away from their parents, being tempted by evil examples set by the youth in the city. Some became soldiers, others ran away to sea. Others took even worse courses, further from the ways of their fathers.

Last and most important of all was their hope to lay some good foundation for the kingdom of Christ in remote parts of the world. They had a great desire to be the steppingstones for others to carry out so great a work.

They Argue about Going to America

They discussed the advantages and disadvantages of going to one of those vast and unpeopled countries of America. Although these countries were fit and fruitful to live in, they had no civilized people, only savage brutish men who ranged up and down like wild beasts.

Those who argued against moving to America complained that the long voyage would wear out the weak bodies of the women. They said that the miseries of the land would be too hard to be borne and that they would starve and become naked. The change of air, diet, and drinking, they said, would infect their bodies with sore sicknesses and fatal diseases.

And if they should overcome these difficulties, then there was the continual danger of the savage people, who were cruel, barbarous, and most treacherous in their rage and merciless when they captured. The savages were not only content to kill and take away life, but they delighted in tormenting men in the most bloody manner. They would skin alive some with the shells of fishes and cut off the arms and legs of others by piecemeal. Then they would broil these limbs on the hot coals and eat pieces of their flesh in their sight while they still lived. The very hearing of these things would move the very bowels of men to grate within them and make them weak and to quake and tremble. Those who argued against traveling to America further objected because of the great sums of money it would take to furnish such a voyage. They said that it was hard enough to live in a strange place like Holland, yet it was a neighbor country which was rich and civilized.

Those who desired to move to America argued that all great and honorable actions are always accompanied with great difficulties which must be overcome with courage. They said that many of the things which they feared might not even happen to them, and others by care might be prevented. All of these difficulties, they argued, might through the help of God with courage and patience be borne and overcome. If they remained in Holland with the truce over, the drum would beat again and the Spaniard might be as cruel as the savages of America. The starvation and pestilence might be as bad in Holland as across the seas.

After the arguments on both sides were heard, the majority decided to make plans and preparations for a voyage to America.

3 Other New England Settlers

Society in seventeenth-century England was changing rapidly. Swept along by the wave of religious reform which began in Germany with Martin Luther early in the sixteenth century, England was divided among supporters of the Anglican Church, a number of groups of Dissenters, and some Catholics. These three groups all competed for control of the government and tended to persecute each other when they were in power.

Moreover, the economy was undergoing fundamental changes. In the past, most Englishmen had lived on manors, large agricultural holdings controlled by a lord and worked by a number of peasants, each of whom farmed small plots of land scattered about the estate. Late in the Middle Ages lords began to enclose all the lands of a manor with fences in order to establish large farms or to graze sheep for the increasingly profitable wool industry. Hence large numbers of peasants were forced off the land to find jobs in trade or handicrafts or to join the ranks of the unemployed.

The Tudor family ruled England from 1485 to 1603, when the last Tudor monarch, Elizabeth I, died. James I, the first Stuart king, ruled England after Elizabeth's death.

Finally, intense political rivalry broke out. The Tudor monarchs, like Queen Elizabeth, had learned to get along with the elected members of Parliament. However, their successors, the Stuart kings, who came to the throne in 1603, were determined to rule as they saw fit. They began to do things without the consent of Parliament and eventually to do as they wished even in the face of Parliamentary opposition. In the midst of this turmoil—religious, economic, and political—the New England colonies were born.

Many Americans have been taught that our New England ancestors came to the New World only to seek religious freedom. The documents which follow provide evidence with which you can test this conclusion. One of the issues involved is whether all of the New England settlers were members of religious groups like the ones which settled Plymouth and Boston. Another is whether the *Puritans*—Dissenters who wished to "purify" the Anglican Church of some practices which resembled Catholicism—came to Massachusetts Bay for religious reasons alone.

The two following documents raise a vital historical question: Are most major developments in history the result of one single event (single causation) or the product of a number of forces working together (multiple causation)? Readings 1 and 2 have already raised this issue. As you read, keep the following questions in mind:

1. What evidence can you find in the writings of Peckham and Winthrop that indicate hostile attitudes toward other countries? toward other religions?
2. What reasons does each writer give for going to America? Classify them as political, social, religious, economic, patriotic, etc.
3. In Reading 1 you examined the circumstances under which your family moved, and in Reading 2 you examined a firsthand report of why the Pilgrims moved. After considering the evidence from these two readings and the evidence you find in the readings which follow, are you tentatively a supporter of the idea of single causation or of multiple causation?

An English Pamphleteer Discusses Reasons To Colonize

In 1583, Sir George Peckham wrote a pamphlet entitled Discourse of the Necessitie and Commoditie of Planting English Colonies upon the North Partes of America. *A merchant adventurer interested primarily in profit, he hoped to attract support for colonizing ventures by noting the possible advantages to England.*

Richard Hakluyt, **The Voyages, Navigations, Traffiques and Discoveries of the English Nation.** London: 1600, vol. 3, pp. 173–77. Language simplified and modernized.

It is well worth observing what making voyages of discovery and planting colonies in the East and West Indies have brought to the kingdoms of Portugal and Spain. Because of these new discoveries, there are so many jobs that unemployment has been wiped out. But in spite of all the laws that we have passed, our commonwealth is filled with loiterers and idle vagabonds. We have long been at peace and have had no plagues (two singular blessings of Almighty God), and have grown more populous than ever before. Now there are so many people that they can hardly live together, so many that they often fall to thieving and other evil ways. If we planted colonies, petty thieves might be condemned for a number of years in the new lands, especially in Newfoundland, to work in the forests. They could saw and fell trees, make pitch, tar, resin, and soap ashes, beat and work hemp for cordage, and in the more southern parts, go to work in mines, in planting sugarcane and in planting vineyards.

In short, this enterprise will provide something for all sorts of men to work upon. An English gentleman told me that while he was a prisoner in Spain not long since, he heard the treasurer of the West Indies say that there was no way to hinder his master [King Philip II of Spain] more than to plant a colony upon a coast near Florida. Now thinking about the way King Philip might be injured, I would begin with the West Indies, to lay there the chief foundation to overthrow him. Once we undermine the foundation of his power in the West Indies, his whole empire will collapse around him. If we can cut off for a while the treasure he gets from the Indies, all his territories in Europe outside of Spain will slide away from him and the Moors might even invade Spain itself. The people will revolt in all his foreign territories and cut the throats of the proud, hateful Spaniards, their governors. If you touch him in the Indies, you touch the apple of his eye and take away his treasure. When his treasure is cut off, his armies will soon be disbanded, his purposes defeated, his power and strength diminished, his pride reduced, and his tyranny utterly suppressed.

The Moors came from Morocco and the surrounding area in North Africa. Many of the Muslims who had lived in Spain were Moors.

Let me now give a brief collection of other reasons to induce Her Majesty and the State to take the western voyage in hand and plant colonies there.

The passage there and home is neither too long nor too short, but easy enough to make twice a year.

The passage does not come near the trade routes of any other ruler, nor near any of their countries or territories and is a safe passage and not easily to be interrupted.

The passage can be made at all times of the year.

This enterprise may stop the Spanish king from flowing over the whole face of America. How easy a matter it might yet be to this country, swarming today with valiant youths, to be lord of all those seas, and despoil Philip's Indian navy, and deprive him of his treasure.

King Philip of Spain supported the Pope (whom Peckham, a Protestant, calls "the great anti-Christ of Rome") and Catholicism after England and several other nations had turned to Protestantism and rejected the Pope's authority.

This deed would undermine Spanish pride, and the supporter of the great anti-Christ of Rome, and help to pull down his allies and consequently stop the mischiefs that come to all Europe from the abundance of his Indian treasure, and this without difficulty.

We shall be planting there the glory of the gospel and from England plant sincere religion and provide a safe and sure refuge to receive people from all parts of the world that are forced to flee for the truth of God's Word.

Many men of excellent wit and great talent, overcome by some folly of youth, who are not able to live in England, may there be raised up again and do their country good service.

Many soldiers and sailors who have retired from the army and navy may be sent there to the common profit and quiet of England.

The wandering beggars of England who grow up idly and hurtful and burdensome to this realm, may be sent there and better bred up and may people this waste country to the benefit of England and the country itself and to their own happiness.

John Winthrop Gives His Arguments for Emigration

Born into a wealthy, pious family, John Winthrop attended Cambridge and became a successful lawyer as well as a country gentleman. A staunch Puritan, his religious convictions led him to play a major role in the affairs of the Massachusetts Bay Company, which settled the Boston area in the decade after 1629. As the Company's first governor, he led the migration and played a major role in the colony until his death. The excerpt from his writings which follows contains Winthrop's own analysis of reasons for emigrating.

R.C. Winthrop, **Life and Letters of John Winthrop.** Boston: 1864, pp. 309–11. Language simplified and modernized.

1. It will be an important service to the Church to carry the Gospel into these parts of the world and to raise a barrier against the

kingdom of anti-Christ, which the Jesuits are trying to establish there.

Jesuits are members of the Society of Jesus, a Roman Catholic order founded in 1534. At the time Winthrop wrote this passage, they were the most active missionary group trying to spread Catholicism.

2. All the churches of Europe except ours have begun to embrace sinful ways. Hence, evil times may come upon us. Perhaps God has provided this place as a refuge for those He wants to save. The Church has no better place to fly than into the wilderness. What better work can there be than to go there and provide tabernacles and food for the day when the Church comes there.

3. This land grows weary of her inhabitants so that a man, who is the most precious of all creatures, is here more vile and base than the earth and of less value than a horse or sheep. The government forces masters to take care of servants, parents to maintain their children, and all towns complain of the burden of the poor. Thus it has come to pass that children, servants, and neighbors, especially if they are poor, have become the greatest burdens, while if times were right, they would be our greatest earthly blessings.

4. The whole earth is the Lord's garden and He has given it to the sons of men with a general commission: Genesis: I:28: Increase and multiply and replenish the earth and subdue it. This is so that man might enjoy the fruits of the earth and God might have His due glory. Why then should we stand here, striving for places to live and in the meantime suffer a whole continent to lie waste without any improvement?

5. We have grown so intemperate that no man's income is big enough to let him keep up with his neighbors. And he who fails to keep up lives in scorn and contempt. For this reason it is almost impossible for a good and upright man to pay his bills and live comfortably.

6. The schools and churches are so corrupted that most children are led astray by the many evil examples about them.

7. What can be a better work and more honorable and worthy for a Christian than to help to raise and support a particular church while it is in its infancy and to join forces with a company of faithful people who may grow strong and prosper?

8. If any people who are known to be godly and rich here shall give it all up to join with this church and risk living in poverty and danger, it will be an excellent example to encourage others so that they will join more willingly.

9. It appears to be a work of God for the good of His church, that He has disposed the hearts of so many of His wise and faithful servants, both ministers and others, not only to approve of the enterprise but to interest themselves in it, some by going, some by contributing money, others by giving advice and help and all by their prayers for its welfare. Amos III: The Lord revealeth His secret to His servants and prophets. It is likely that He has some great work

in hand which He has revealed to His prophets among us and has stirred them up to encourage His servants to go to this plantation. He would not permit His own prophets to lead His chosen people astray.

4 Colonizing the New World

HISTORICAL ESSAY

The discovery, exploration, and settlement of America grew out of centuries of European history. No one event and no single trend can explain these dramatic developments. Instead of growing from a single cause, the discovery and settlement of America resulted from four closely related movements which together triggered the expansion of Europe and filled the oceans of the world with European ships.

The first of these developments, an economic revival, began during the tenth century. In the centuries following the collapse of the Roman Empire, the people of Europe had come to live on isolated, self-sufficient manors. Then the Italian cities began to increase their trade with the Far East. As merchants pushed to India and China and Europeans began to demand their goods, a vigorous international trade developed. Cities grew up as trading and manufacturing centers. Stories of new lands, often circulated by Crusaders who had fought to free the Holy Land from the Turks, stirred interest in travel and trade.

Serfs were peasants who, under the feudal system, were bound to the land they worked on and were usually sold with the land.

The economic revival led to voyages of discovery and colonization in a number of ways. It stirred men's desires for new products from the Far East and hence encouraged them to look for new routes around Africa or across the Atlantic. It displaced many men from their traditional role in the economy. Former serfs or free peasants, driven from the countryside when owners of manors turned their estates into more efficient large farms or sheep runs, moved to the cities, where they flooded the labor market. These extra workers could be turned into colonists. Industry began to develop and with it came an increased demand for raw material which colonies could satisfy. Moreover, the companies formed to carry on trade with the Far East, or later with the American colonies, developed ways to raise large sums of money to finance colonies and worked out methods of governing new colonies while they were being established. All these developments growing out of economic revival contributed to the discovery and settlement of America.

The Renaissance also played an important role. Beginning in the fourteenth century, men turned their attention increasingly from thoughts of religion, which had dominated the lives of medieval men, to secular concerns of the world around them. Some men of the Renaissance gained distinction as non-religious painters, architects, sculptors, or writers. Others developed new maps and charts and invented the navigational instruments essential to later voyages of discovery. They also perfected fast new ships capable of sailing in the direction from which the wind was blowing. Renaissance scholars and explorers also spurred interest in new lands, leading to the discovery of a new route around Africa to the East Indies and eventually to the discovery of America.

During and immediately after the Renaissance, a further development helped to prepare Europe for its American adventures. This development was the growth of the five nation-states which did most of the exploring and settling: Portugal, Spain, England, France, and the Netherlands. Stretched along the coast of the Atlantic, these states sought new routes to the Indies, partly so that they might compete for trade with the Italians based in the Mediterranean. These unified nations sometimes provided government funds to finance voyages. A spirit of national rivalry which grew up among them spurred some explorers and colonists to greater efforts.

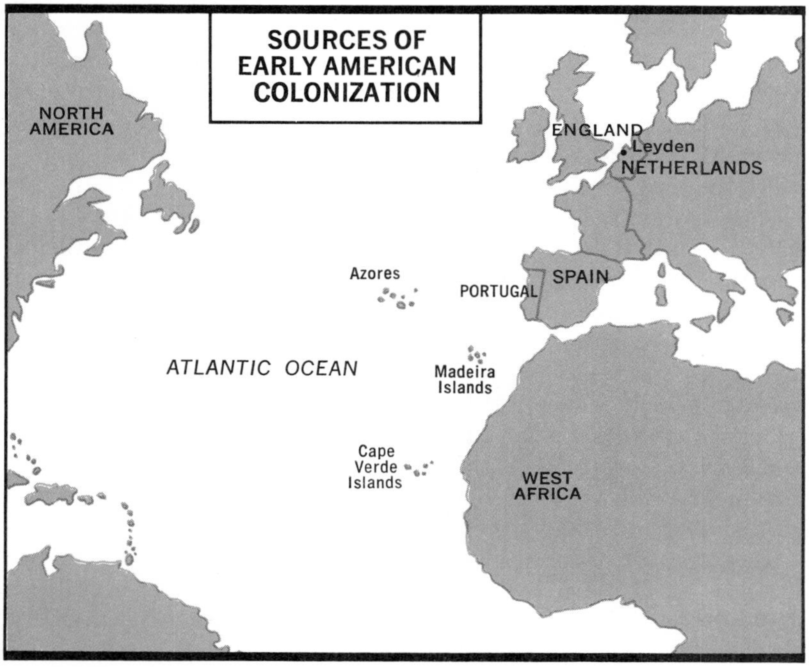

In part, the rush to find a Northwest Passage through the Americas developed because England, France, and the Netherlands wanted routes to the Far East which were under their own control. Practically every promoter of colonies mentioned national rivalry as one of the motives which he thought should drive his country's citizens to colonize.

Finally, the development of the Protestant Reformation, and of the Catholic Reformation which accompanied it, helped to contribute to the settlement of the Americas. Early in the sixteenth century, a movement to reform the Catholic Church, led by such men as Martin Luther and John Calvin, resulted in the establishment of many Protestant churches. Religious wars and religious persecution followed. To escape these ills, a large number of Europeans left their homes, seeking religious freedom elsewhere. Many of these people came to the Americas, where they settled largely in New England and the Middle Colonies. In the meantime, Catholic explorers and missionaries also came to the New World. They played key roles in the exploration and settlement of both Canada and Latin America.

Settlers Come to the Americas

Portugal Although the five exploring and colonizing nations —Portugal, Spain, England, France, and the Netherlands—were influenced by these four developments, they entered the race for colonies at different times and for somewhat different reasons. Portugal was first. The most westerly of the five nations, its long coastline beckoned its people to the sea. For centuries foreign sailors had crowded its ports. A wealthy king ruled Portugal, a nation united since the thirteenth century.

During the fifteenth century, Prince Henry the Navigator (1394–1460) rallied the resources of the Portuguese Crown to push exploration. Prince Henry was anxious to find the legendary Christian kingdom of Prester John, a kingdom supposedly located somewhere in the middle of the African continent. Also, as an ardent student of science, he wanted to develop new navigational instruments and to extend the boundaries of knowledge of geography. Finally, Prince Henry was a practical businessman interested in trade. All these interests and motives helped to whet his appetite for voyages of exploration down the coast of Africa.

Year after year, his sailors pushed back the boundary of the unknown seas. They rediscovered the Madeira Islands and the Azores Islands, sailed down the coast, and found the Cape Verde Islands before Henry's death. In 1488, Bartholomeu Dias rounded the Cape of Good Hope in search of the kingdom of Prester John, only to be turned back by his rebellious crew. Ten years later, Vasco da Gama rounded the Cape and sailed all the way to Calicut, in India, returning to Portugal with a rich cargo of spice and precious stones.

At this time, Portugal was a tiny nation with a small population made up largely of farmers, fishermen, and sailors. Since the Protestant Reformation never reached it, no religious dissension drove some of its peoples abroad. Nor did fundamental economic changes reach its farms and villages until well after the period of colonization. Moreover, its energies were devoted to exploiting the ready wealth of the East Indies. Although one of its captains, Pedro Cabral, stumbled upon Brazil in 1500 when his fleet was driven westward before a storm, Portugal lacked the resources to enter the contest for American colonies. Its influence in the New World never extended beyond Brazil, whose people still speak the language of the Portuguese captains who landed on her shores.

Spain The Spanish had a larger role in colonizing the Americas. Before 1450, five distinct kingdoms, including Portugal, existed on the Iberian peninsula. The population was divided among Christians, Jews, and Muslims. Each king found his authority challenged by great nobles and by independent military organizations designed originally to fight the Muslims. By 1450, some of these organizations had become more powerful than the kings. In the next sixty years, however, four of the five kingdoms were united under the joint monarchy of Ferdinand of Aragon and his wife, Isabella of Castile. Together these two monarchs broke the strength of the nobles, organized a powerful central government, established Catholicism as the state religion, set up the Inquisition to see that all Jews and Muslims had either become genuine converts to Catholicism or had left the country, took over the military organizations, and filled the royal coffers with money. For a century thereafter, Spain was the most powerful state in Europe.

It also dominated the Americas. Starting with the four voyages of Columbus, its soldiers and sailors opened up all the Americas from Florida to Cape Horn. Bent everywhere on the pursuit of gold and the extension of Christianity, the Spanish conquerors subjugated the Indians and sent vast fortunes back to the homeland. But the Spanish colonies turned out to be very different from the English settlements that appeared later to the north. The motives of their settlers and the resources of the home country account for some of these differences.

Like Portugal, Spain was thinly populated. Moreover, many of its best merchants and artisans were driven out of the country after 1492 because they were Jews or Muslims. But the countryside was filled with thousands of restless men, sons of petty nobles, without estates and with slim hopes for the future. Spain obtained its soldiers and settlers from among these men. Captains recruited them, formed them into armies, and conquered not only much of Europe but also most of the Americas. Hence, the Spanish could spread only a thin population over the lands they conquered. They were never able to export their society wholesale since they emigrated as conquerors in small numbers and left their women at home. The population in Spain remained stationary. Spain's natural resources were limited, its commerce fell into the hands of foreigners—particularly after the Jews and Muslims were expelled—and its kings wasted their money in a long series of costly wars. Spain's American colonies became sources of gold and silver for the king and of free land which allowed displaced aristocrats to recover their fortunes.

Along with the soldiers went a host of priests who intended to Christianize the natives and bring them within the fold of the Catholic Church. More than any other country in Europe, Spain succeeded in reforming the Catholic Church. Beginning in the late fifteenth century, the Spaniards proceeded to put an end to one abuse after another. Missionary zeal matched the efforts to reform. All over the Americas, Catholic priests from Spain explored the country, ministered to settlers, and converted the natives. But since the priests came primarily as missionaries and as members of religious orders who could not marry, they did not build settlements of people of European origin like those which Protestant ministers and their congregations established in English-speaking colonies farther to the north.

France France entered the race for colonies in the seventeenth century. United by mid-century under a powerful monarch [Louis XIV] and having a growing economy, France was developing into the most powerful nation in Europe. The voyages to North America sponsored by the king and by trading companies were undertaken to find a Northwest Passage through the Americas to the Far East. When the French discovered the wealth of the fur trade, a few restless souls settled in Canada, in particular along the banks of the St. Lawrence River, where they established trading posts.

But no hosts of dispossessed peoples, ready to settle, populated France. French farmers remained secure on their lands and artisans could find plenty of work in growing crafts and industries. The one group which might have formed the basis for settlements, French Protestants called *Huguenots,* were forbidden by Catholic monarchs to live in France's colonies abroad. Hence, the French colonies, like the Spanish, were lightly settled—largely by single men who took Indian girls for wives and made their living in the fur trade.

The Netherlands The Dutch, who became Protestants in the sixteenth century, fought long and costly wars against the Spanish Catholics who ruled them. Eventually, they drove out the Spanish and established a republic. Their economy was based on trade with Europe and the Far East. Since Holland's small population was occupied with far-flung trading and manufacturing enterprises, few Dutchmen wanted to emigrate with their families to the New World. After Henry Hudson sailed up the Hudson River early in the seventeenth century, a few Dutch traders established posts from Manhattan Island to Albany, but only a few thousand settlers followed. Religious toleration at home, combined with an industry which was developing and which absorbed the labor supply, limited the number of potential settlers. In the 1660's, when England and the Netherlands were at war, the Dutch colonies were conquered by the English, and Dutch colonizing ended in North America.

England Seventeenth-century England was in the midst of economic and social changes which had a marked effect upon the American colonies. The manorial system began to break down as lords enclosed their lands. Uprooted from the soil of their ancestors, farmers flocked to the cities. By 1680, London alone counted 500,000 souls, out of a total English population of 5,000,000. These footloose men flooded the labor market. Cast adrift in society, thousands of them looked across the wide Atlantic for opportunity.

So did many of the wealthy. Some wanted grants of land to establish themselves in the New World as gentry. Others wanted to trade. They had learned to form joint-stock companies in which a number of investors bought shares of stock and, as a result, obtained a vote in company decisions. The New World seemed to offer a fertile ground for profit for these companies. Both the Pilgrims and the Puritans were sent out by joint-stock companies. The charter under which the companies governed themselves provided for control by a governor and a group of assistants elected by the stockholders. Eventually, several charters were turned into governments.

The gentry was a class of people who had wealth but no titles of nobility.

Seventeenth-century England was racked with religious dissension. The Tudor king, Henry VIII, had swept his country into the Protestant camp in 1539 when he established the Anglican Church. But not all Englishmen followed Henry in his beliefs. A small cluster of faithful Catholics continued to worship in their own way. Several Protestant groups urged the Anglican Church to rid itself of the remnants of Catholic practice and belief. As persecution of one group by another mounted, Protestant groups like the Puritans and Separatists decided to settle in New England, while Catholics and Quakers moved to the Middle Colonies.

The Quakers, or the Society of Friends, founded a religious group in England in the seventeenth century. Quakers believed that ministers and ritual were unnecessary in religious services. They were pacifists who would not bear arms. Although Quakers tolerated other persons' beliefs, they were persecuted in seventeenth-century England.

All these changes buffeted the men of seventeenth-century England simultaneously. No one lived in such isolation that only religious dissent or economic change touched his life. The documents which the New England settlers have left behind indicate the complexity of their motives for emigrating to the New World. For the

Puritans, the desire to form a Bible Commonwealth provided a clearly dominant motive. As you have seen, even John Winthrop mentioned, as secondary motives for emigration, the economic, political, and social changes which were sweeping his homeland. The entire movement leading to the discovery, exploration, and settlement of America illustrates the general rule that major developments in history arise from a number of complex causes rather than from a single cause or from the influence of a single man.

The Magna Carta limited the king's absolute power and later became the cornerstone of Britain's unwritten constitution.

In greater degree than any other country in Europe, England had developed a representative government which could check the power of the king. Since the thirteenth century, when English noblemen had forced King John to accept the Magna Carta, Englishmen had believed that their king, like anyone else, was subject to the law. Although the kings had remained powerful, English monarchs had learned to share authority with Parliament. Hereditary nobles sat in the upper chamber of Parliament, the House of Lords, while commoners from counties and towns elected their representatives to the House of Commons. The king could not tax without the consent of Parliament; he could not imprison men at his own whim; nor could he violate legal codes established in the Common Law, that collection of legislative acts and judges' decisions which stood as the legal code for Englishmen. Local government rested firmly in the hands of influential men who were chosen by their neighbors, although the number of men who could vote for them, and for members of Parliament, was most restricted, generally to men who owned property. Englishmen who emigrated to America took with them their belief in the supremacy of law, their devotion to political institutions in which they were represented, their adherence to the Common Law, and their unstated assumption that the rich and powerful should influence political affairs the most.

Social mobility means the ease with which people can move to a higher or lower position in society.

As English colonists traveled across the Atlantic, they took with them many additional beliefs and practices from their homeland, among them the belief that men are born to a certain station, or position in society, and must be content to remain in that station. This belief, however, was not so firmly embedded in the minds of Englishmen that it could not be changed with changing circumstances. As a new economy had developed in England, some men had risen in society while others had fallen. The new life in America encouraged this sort of social mobility. Englishmen believed too in hard work, and even the aristocrats were unashamed to enter business, an ethic which helped to shape the American economic system. The English Protestants who made up the majority of seventeenth-century colonists believed firmly in education, both to train ministers and to insure that every man could read his own Bible. And finally, their strong community spirit led them to expect to settle in congregations which could govern themselves and regulate the lives of the settlers.

Africa As the Portuguese sailed down the coast of Africa in mid-fifteenth century, they began to purchase slaves and to send them back to the homeland. Soon all the major colonizing countries entered the slave trade. It focused in West Africa, particularly on the southern coast of the great bulge of the subcontinent where the Negro population was concentrated in the tropical rain forests and in the grasslands further inland toward the Sahara. These people fell easy prey to the advanced technology of the Europeans.

In previous eras, great kingdoms had grown up in this area of Africa. Slowly, under the attacks of Arabs from the north, they decayed. By the fifteenth century, the kingdoms along the coast had broken up into small tribes unable to offer much resistance to European invaders. The Portuguese, along with other Europeans who followed, began to offer to trade goods unobtainable there in exchange for slaves needed to work in the New World. The men and women who were bought and shipped to America became the ancestors of our present Negro population here.

Negroes from this part of Africa had for centuries lived in villages. Most of them made their livings as farmers. They were also excellent artisans accustomed to the idea of division of labor and to buying and selling goods in a market. Many of them owned slaves of their own; all knew about the institution of slavery and thought that the possibility of their being taken as slaves lay in the hands of the gods. Even their religion—a belief in a supreme God and his messenger who could change the fate of mortals—resembled the idea of the Christian God and his son, Jesus Christ. This cultural heritage—the Africans' patterns of living and their beliefs—was an important factor in the Negroes' adaptation to the culture of the plantation system in America.

The American Environment Challenges the Newcomers

Three features of the New World assumed important roles in the development of the colonies. The first was the natural environment. To the far north, Canada stood cold and inhospitable except to the fur traders and trappers who exploited its animals. In southern Canada and throughout the New England and Middle Colonies, winters were harsh and the land rocky; but soil, rainfall, and temperature were suited to agriculture. Here, any industrious farmer could make a good living. Most of the land was covered with trees which could provide masts, lumber, pitch, and tar for sale in England. The forest-product industries encouraged shipbuilding and trade. The rich fishing and whaling waters off the coast furnished

A staple crop is the principal commodity of a region grown on a regular basis and in large amounts because it is in constant demand.

the basis for another industry. These resources provided the foundation for a diversified economy in which farming, manufacturing, and trade all played their parts. Such an economy demanded skilled workers who could turn their hands to many tasks.

The southern part of what is now the United States, the islands of the Caribbean, and much of the northern half of South America were warm throughout the year. In many of these areas, rich soil and plentiful rainfall encouraged the production of staple crops like sugar, tobacco, indigo, or cotton. All these crops required large numbers of laborers, and their cultivation did not demand the variety of skills essential to success in the North. Hence, the natural environment of the southern areas encouraged the use of slaves who did not have to be trained in a variety of skills new to them.

The presence of Indians represented a second feature of the American environment which played an important role in the development of the colonies. All the American Indians emigrated across the Bering Straits from Siberia perhaps 25,000 years ago and then dispersed over the entire continent over a period of many centuries. Despite their common origins, those Indians north of the Rio Grande differed radically from Indians in Central and South America.

Since their emigration across the Bering Straits, the stone-age cultures of the Indians of North America had shown little change. Neither their primitive tribal organization, which permitted the whites to play one tribe off against another, nor their crude bows and arrows could match disciplined Europeans armed with muskets. If Indians of the north got in the way of colonists, the Europeans could either push them further west or kill them.

Most of the Indian men were hunters and warriors, accustomed to moving from place to place. They looked upon farming as squaws' work, and they preferred death to slavery. When taken as slaves, they soon ran away or died. Nevertheless, despite their primitive culture, they taught the whites many skills, including methods of raising new crops such as corn and tobacco, and of trapping fur-bearing animals from the lakes and streams.

South and Central America, on the other hand, were homes of several advanced Indian civilizations. Unlike their relatives of North America, these Indians had become farmers who built large cities and complex cultures. However, since they had not learned to smelt iron, had never invented the wheel, and had no horses, they were helpless in the face of European soldiers mounted on horses, covered with armor, and carrying guns and swords. The Spanish captured them easily, carried off their gold and silver, and forced many to labor in the mines and on plantations. But these Indians were too numerous to exterminate and too settled to be pushed out of the way. Spanish soldiers took Indian women as wives, and soon Spaniard, Indian, and Negro intermarried to form the basis for the racially mixed nations of Latin America. Traces of pre-Columbian Indian civilizations dot the face of Latin America; they have disappeared almost completely from the area north of the Rio Grande.

Pre-Columbian means before the arrival of Columbus in the New World.

Thus, the physical terrain and the type of Indians encountered north of the Rio Grande differed markedly from the terrain and Indians to the south. These differences combined with the differences in the types of settlers who came to the north and to the south to create vastly dissimilar kinds of settlements in the two areas.

A third feature of the American environment is more difficult to define. In one sense, that feature was space: land free for the taking, a vast wilderness waiting for the plow. In another sense, it was distance: the thousands of miles separating the colonists from the source of authority and from the hand of custom in Europe. Extensive lands meant that a son need not, from fear of disinheritance, obey his father, for he could obtain land of his own. It meant too that a king might reward his servants with generous grants of land, even though eventually such gifts might, by making men rich, tend to encourage independence from European control. Both long distances and slow communications forced colonial rulers to make decisions without consulting the home government, and colonists who grew up in the sight of the forest and never saw the mother country became more and more inclined to make their own decisions. In addition, the harsh conditions of the new land required new types of decisions about different issues than those which occupied the days of European legislators. Taken together, the rich natural resources, the presence of the Indians, and the stretch of free land an ocean removed from Europe played key roles in the process of americanizing the Europeans.

SUGGESTED READINGS

BERGER, JOSEF, & LAWRENCE C. WROTH, *Discoverers of the New World.* This well-illustrated volume traces the history of the men who discovered and explored the American continent.

MORISON, SAMUEL ELIOT, *Christopher Columbus, Mariner.* This beautifully written volume by one of our nation's most distinguished historians summarizes a lifetime of research about Columbus.

WILLIAMSON, JAMES A., *Sir Francis Drake.* This spirited biography traces the life and adventures of the great English sea captain who attacked the Spanish colonies for Queen Elizabeth.

The Growth of English America, 1607–1700

CHAPTER 2

STATING THE ISSUE

In 1600, more than a century after the first voyage of Columbus, the Indians of eastern North America still knew little of Europeans. They lived undisturbed by the Spaniards in Florida, the scattered French traders in Canada, and the occasional European fishermen who visited the North Atlantic coast during the warmer seasons. A century later, the Indians had retreated from most of the Atlantic coastal area.

At first the Spanish and the French seemed to pose the greatest threats to these Indian tribes. The Spanish controlled large parts of the Caribbean, the Gulf of Mexico, and the West Indies. The French explored the area around the Great Lakes and established trading posts deep within the interior. The English had no foothold in America. John Cabot's voyage of discovery in 1497 gave them a claim to part of the New World, but their few feeble attempts at colonization after that failed.

By about 1600, however, the English were ready to expand. Victory over the Spanish Armada in 1588, followed by a peace treaty with Spain in 1604, freed aggressive English merchants to undertake new commercial ventures. A few trading companies decided to establish colonies as a way of making money. Unemployment and religious persecution provided incentives for potential settlers to uproot themselves from accustomed ways. As a result, emigrants by tens of thousands sailed from England, Scotland, and Ireland. By 1700, more than 200,000 persons dwelt in twenty English colonies in the New World. Two of these colonies, Massachusetts and Virginia, had more than 50,000 inhabitants each.

Chapter 2 analyzes the history of the English colonies during the seventeenth century. How did the colonists survive in a strange new environment? How did they attempt to come to terms with the Indians? How did they establish governments in this new land? What sort of economic and social systems evolved during this century in which the roots of a new American life took hold? These are the major issues with which we will be concerned in Chapter 2.

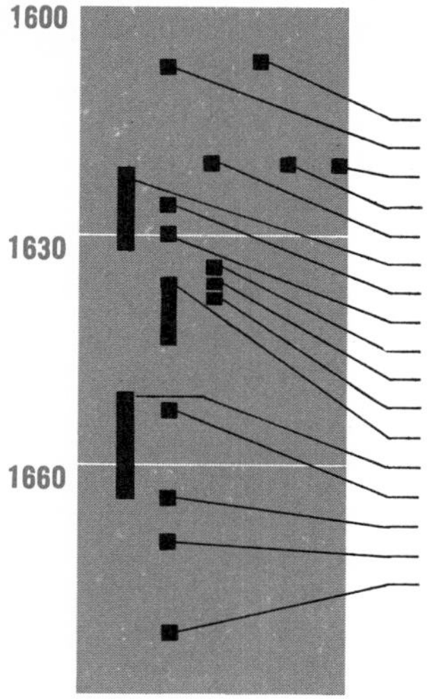

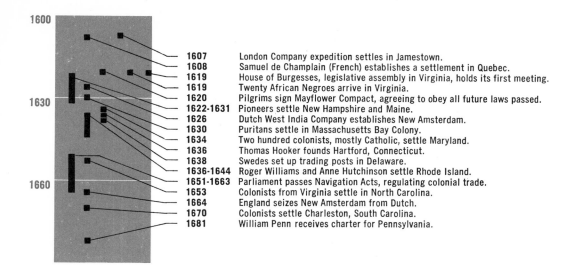

1607	London Company expedition settles in Jamestown.
1608	Samuel de Champlain (French) establishes a settlement in Quebec.
1619	House of Burgesses, legislative assembly in Virginia, holds its first meeting.
1619	Twenty African Negroes arrive in Virginia.
1620	Pilgrims sign Mayflower Compact, agreeing to obey all future laws passed.
1622-1631	Pioneers settle New Hampshire and Maine.
1626	Dutch West India Company establishes New Amsterdam.
1630	Puritans settle in Massachusetts Bay Colony.
1634	Two hundred colonists, mostly Catholic, settle Maryland.
1636	Thomas Hooker founds Hartford, Connecticut.
1638	Swedes set up trading posts in Delaware.
1636-1644	Roger Williams and Anne Hutchinson settle Rhode Island.
1651-1663	Parliament passes Navigation Acts, regulating colonial trade.
1653	Colonists from Virginia settle in North Carolina.
1664	England seizes New Amsterdam from Dutch.
1670	Colonists settle Charleston, South Carolina.
1681	William Penn receives charter for Pennsylvania.

5 The Problem of Survival

English colonists in the New World faced two immediate problems. First, they had to feed and house themselves until they could grow crops and build permanent dwellings. Second, they had to get along peacefully with the Indians while persuading them to sell or give away their claims to land. If persuasion failed, war usually followed. Neither problem was easy to solve.

Most of the promoters who organized expeditions knew very little about the American environment, and what they thought they knew often proved to be inaccurate. Their ships were small and sailed slowly. Into these vessels promoters crowded food and water for the voyage, the ship's crew, the settlers, all the equipment for the new colony, including any animals the colonists wanted to bring along, and supplies to sustain the colonists until crops ripened. Epidemics swept through ships, and colonists sometimes starved once ashore.

Then there were the Indians. When the settlers and the Indians came in contact, it was not altogether certain what social processes would result. The two groups might begin to *amalgamate* by intermarrying. Or they might *assimilate:* one group might adopt the culture of the other, or each group might take on some of the other's ways of life. They might also *accommodate* to each other's presence, by living separate lives in separate cultures. Or one group might expel or *exterminate* the other. When the settlers landed, no one knew which one or combination of these four possibilities was most likely to occur.

In December 1606, the London Company, a group of wealthy merchants and other influential men, sent off an expedition in three small ships to establish a settlement on or near Chesapeake Bay. On board were about a hundred men and four boys destined to remain in America. They had agreed to work for seven years for the company to try to locate valuable minerals, to seek a route to the South Seas [Pacific Ocean] which were thought to be near Virginia, and to find the best places to settle. The company gave command of the expedition to a council which elected one of its members, Edward Wingfield, president. As you read an account of the adventures of this group of men, keep the following questions in mind:

1. How well prepared were the adventurers for what they encountered in Virginia? Were the leaders and men well prepared for their roles?
2. Would you have chosen May as a good month to land? Why?
3. How well did the men take advantage of their new environment?
4. With what attitude did the settlers approach the Indians? How did the Indians approach the settlers? Of the four social processes described, which would be most likely to develop after further contact? Why?

The Founding of Jamestown

One of the best descriptions of the arrival and settlement of the Jamestown colonists comes from one of the settlers, George Percy. The version which follows has been taken from parts of his Observations, *printed in England in 1625. The passage below begins after the expedition had reached the West Indies.*

Lyon G. Tyler, ed., **Narratives of Early Virginia, 1606–1625.** New York: Charles Scribner's Sons, 1907, pp. 9–10, 13–14, 15–16, 19–22. Language simplified and modernized.

The 10th day of April 1607, we set sail out of the West Indies, taking a northerly course. The 14th day, we passed the Tropic of Cancer. On the 21st, about 5:00 at night there began a vehement storm, which lasted all night, with winds, rain, and thunder in a terrible manner. The 26th of April, about 4:00 in the morning, we caught sight of the land of Virginia. The same day we entered into Chesapeake Bay without any obstruction or hindrance. There we landed and explored a little way, but we could find nothing worth speaking of, except fair meadows and fine, tall trees and such fresh waters running through the woods that I was very moved by them.

The leaders were all called "Captain," a military title.

At night, when we were continuing our travels, there came Indians from the hills, creeping upon all fours like bears, with their bows in their mouths. They charged us desperately, hurting Captain Gabrill Archer in both hands and seriously wounding a sailor in two places in his body. After they had used their arrows and had felt the sharpness of our shot, they went into the woods with great noise, and so left us.

On the 4th of May, we came to the territory of the Paspihes, where they entertained us with much welcome. An old Indian made a long speech, making foul noise and uttering his speech with vehement action, but we knew little of what he was saying. While we were with the Paspihes, the chief of the Rapahanna came from the other side of the river in his canoe. He seemed to be displeased at our being with the Paspihes. He would have preferred us to come to his territory. But our captain was unwilling, and seeing that the day was so far spent, he returned to his ships for the night.

The Paspihes had just moved from a site about a mile from Jamestown Island to Sandy Point, a fertile area ten miles above the future settlement.

The Rapahanna Indians lived on the south side of the James River across from the Paspihes.

The next day, the 5th of May, the chief of the Rapahanna sent a messenger to have us come to him. We entertained the messenger and gave him trifles which pleased him. We manned out a shallop [small boat] with muskets and marksmen, and the messenger guided us to where we were to go. When we landed, the chief of the Rapahanna came down to the water with all of his followers, as good men as I have seen among Indians or Christians. The chief led them, playing a flute made of a reed, with a crown of deer's hair colored red and worn in the fashion of a rose fastened about his knot of hair, and a great plate of copper on the other side of his head, with long feathers like a pair of horns placed in the midst of his crown. His body was painted all with crimson, with a chain of beads about his neck, his face painted blue, besprinkled with what we thought was silver ore, his ears all hung with bracelets of pearl, and in either ear a bird's claw through which fine copper or gold was set.

He entertained us in so modest a proud fashion, as though he were a prince of civil government, behaving very seriously and well. He caused his mat to be spread on the ground, where he sat down with great majesty, taking a pipe of tobacco, the rest of his company standing about him. After he had rested a while, he rose and made signs to us to come to his town. He went first, and all the rest of his people and ourselves followed him up a steep hill where his palace was located. We passed through the woods in fine paths, having most pleasant springs which issued from the mountains. We also went through the goodliest cornfields that ever were seen in any country. When we came to Rapahannas Town, he entertained us in good humanity.

The 14th of May we landed all our men, some of whom were set to work on the fortifications while others were made to stand guard as it was convenient. The first night of our landing, about midnight, there came some Indians. Presently an alarm was sounded; upon that, the Indians ran away and we were not troubled anymore by them that night. Not long after, there came two Indians who seemed to be commanders, bravely dressed with crowns of colored hair upon their heads. They came as messengers from the chief of the

Paspihes and told us that their chief was coming and would celebrate with us with a fat deer.

On the 18th, the chief of the Paspihes came himself with one hundred armed Indians who guarded him in a very warlike manner with bows and arrows. The chief signaled us to lay our arms away. But we would not trust him so far. Seeing that it was not the convenient time to work his will, he at length made signs that he would give us as much land as we desired to take.

While the Indians were in a throng in the fort, one of them stole a hatchet from one of our company, who spied him doing the deed and took it from him by force and struck him over the arm. Presently another Indian, seeing that, came fiercely at our man with a wooden sword, thinking to beat out his brains. The chief of the Paspihes saw us take to our arms, and went away in anger.

Bulwarks are solid walls or structures built for defense.

By the 15th of June, we had built and finished our fort, which was triangle-shaped, having three bulwarks at every corner like a half moon and four or five pieces of artillery mounted in them. We had made ourselves sufficiently strong for these Indians. We had also sown most of our corn. It sprang a man's height from the ground. This country has a fruitful soil, bearing many goodly and fruitful trees—mulberries, cherries, walnuts, cedars, cypresses, sassafras, and vines in great abundance.

Corn meant any kind of grain, such as wheat, barley, rye, rice, etc.

Captain Newport commanded the ships which had brought the colonists to Jamestown.

Monday, the 22nd of June, in the morning Captain Newport departed from James Port for England in the flagship. He left behind 104 persons who were very low on food and in danger from the Indians. We hoped for supplies within twenty weeks, as Captain Newport has promised.

On the 6th of August, John Asbie died of dysentery. On the 9th, George Flowre died of the swelling. On the 10th, William Bruster, Gentleman, died of a wound given by the Indians and was buried on the 11th.

On the 14th, Jerome Alikock, Ancient [ensign, an officer], died of a wound; the same day, Francis Midwinter and Edward Moris, Corporal [a soldier], died suddenly.

On the 15th, Edward Browne and Stephen Galthorpe died. The 16th, Thomas Gower, Gentleman, died. On the 17th, Thomas Mounslic died. On the 18th, Robert Pennington and John Martine, Gentleman, died. On the 19th, Dru Pickhouse, Gentleman, died. On the 22nd of August, Captain Bartholomew Gosnold, one of our Council, died; he was honorably buried, having all the ordnance [cannon or artillery] in the fort shot off with many volleys of small shot.

After Captain Gosnold's death, the Council could hardly agree because of the dissension of Captain Kendall.

Captain Kendall was ousted from the council and later was shot and killed in a mutinous outbreak.

On the 24th, Edward Harington and George Walker died and were buried on the same day. On the 26th, Kellam Throgmorton died. On the 27th, William Roods died. On the 28th, Thomas Studley, Cape Merchant [keeper of supplies], died.

On the 4th of September, Thomas Jacob, Sergeant [a soldier], died. On the 5th, Benjamin Beast died. Our men were destroyed by cruel diseases—swellings, dysentery, burning fevers—and by wars, and some departed suddenly, but most died of mere famine.

There were never Englishmen left in a foreign country in such misery as we were in this newly discovered Virginia. We watched every three nights, lying on the bare, cold ground whatever the weather was, and we stood guard all the next day, which brought our men to be most feeble wretches. Our food was but a small can of barley boiled in water for five men for a day; our drink was cold water taken out of the river, which was very salty at high tide and full of slime and filth at low tide, which was the destruction of many of our men. Thus we lived for the space of five months in this miserable distress, not having five able men to man our bulwarks upon any occasion.

If it had not pleased God to have put a terror in the savages' hearts, we would all have perished by those wild and cruel pagans, being in that weak state as we were, our men groaning in every corner of the fort most pitiful to hear. If there were any conscience in men, it would make their hearts bleed to hear the pitiful murmurings and outcries of our sick men without relief, every night and day, for the space of six weeks, some departing the world, many times three or four a night; in the morning their bodies were dragged out of their cabins like dogs to be buried. In this manner did I witness the death of many of our people.

It pleased God, after a while, to send those people who had been our mortal enemies [Indians] to relieve us with food—bread, corn, fish, and meat—in great plenty, which was the salvation of our feeble men. Otherwise we all would have perished.

On the 11th of September, there were certain accusations made against Master Wingfield, who was then president; thereupon he was not only displaced from his presidency, but also from being in the Council. Afterward Captain John Ratcliffe was chosen president.

On the 18th, Ellis Kinistone starved to death. That night Richard Simmons died, and on the 19th, Thomas Mouton died.

[Malaria and other diseases, starvation, and Indian attacks continued to kill the Virginia settlers, who were badly located in a swampy area, ill-organized, and poorly supplied by the Virginia Company. The company continued to send settlers, but failed to send much food with them. By 1616, only 350 persons survived of the 1600 who had gone as settlers to Virginia; by 1624, only 1200 out of 4000 still lived. For several years there appeared to be little economic reason for the colony's survival. The settlers found neither

The Crown created two Virginia companies to settle the New World: the London (or South Virginia) Company and the Plymouth (or North Virginia) Company.

gold nor a route to the Pacific, and the first products they sent back to England were of little value.

The London Company had appointed Captain John Smith to the council. Other leaders distrusted him and kept him under arrest toward the end of the voyage and for the first months in America. After he assumed leadership, he forced the men to work.

Why did the colony survive? Good leadership at crucial times, such as John Smith provided in 1608 and 1609, kept the settlers from dying out altogether. In 1612, the London Company changed its policies. It appointed a single governor and gave him the authority to control the settlers. Also the company permitted settlers to own their own land. Perhaps most important to the survival of Virginia, however, was tobacco, which provided a sound economic base.]

6 Governing a New Colony

In the early summer of 1630, twenty-three years after the founding of Jamestown, an expedition of nearly a thousand men, women, and children landed in Massachusetts. The Massachusetts Bay Colony soon became the largest English settlement on the American mainland. Within ten years, it contained fourteen thousand persons, nearly twice as many as Virginia. What accounted for the early success of the colony?

Unlike the founders of Jamestown, the founders of Massachusetts Bay planned carefully to settle and supply their colony. Competent and experienced leaders such as John Winthrop, who had been a lawyer, a landowner, and a justice of the peace in England, helped direct the colony. The Indians threatened the Massachusetts settlers less than they had the Virginia colonists because the Indian population in eastern Massachusetts had been diminished by an outbreak of smallpox. A strong sense of purpose, lacking among the original settlers at Jamestown, inspired the Puritans, who organized and led the Massachusetts colony. They left England in large numbers in order to establish the kinds of churches they wanted and to make new homes for themselves. Their vision of building a "Holy Commonwealth" in America helped them overcome great difficulties in the early years.

When the Puritans arrived in Massachusetts in 1630, the charter of the Massachusetts Bay Company, the trading company that planned the expedition, provided the only formal government for the colony. A dozen or so men, who had invested much of the money needed to finance the venture, held all power to make decisions for the company. A small group could run a commercial company very well, but could it direct effectively the affairs of hundreds and thousands of people who quickly scattered over a wide area as they cleared land for farms and built towns? Reading 6 explains the government set up by the charter and shows how the settlers modified the government. As you read, consider these questions:

1. According to the charter, who ran the Company? Who elected the officers? How were new freemen (stockholders) chosen?
2. How did a General Court change the charter in October 1630? Why might it have done so? Why should one of the changes have been repealed in 1632?
3. What seems to have been the intention of the restriction on the admission of freemen adopted in May 1631?
4. Why did the freemen demand to see the charter in 1634? Why did they insist that all laws be made by a General Court rather than a Court of Assistants?

The Massachusetts Bay Charter

A group of Puritan gentlemen and businessmen obtained a charter in 1629 from King Charles I granting part of present-day Massachusetts to their company. This charter named the original members and officers of the company. The chart below explains the crucial provisions of how officers and members were to be chosen thereafter, and what their powers were.

Nathaniel B. Shurtleff, ed., **The Records of the Governor and Company of Massachusetts Bay in New England.** Boston: William White, 1853, vol. I, pp. 10–12.

In colonial Massachusetts, court meant a legislative, not a judicial, body.

	How Chosen	**Powers**
Freemen (stockholders in the company)	to be admitted by a vote of the General Court (a general meeting of stockholders and officers held four times a year)	to choose officers together with assistants and officers, at the General Courts, to admit other freemen, to make laws for the good of the company, for the government of the colony, and for the people who inhabit it
Assistants (board of directors)	by vote of the freemen at the General Court held each year at Easter	with officers, to take care of the general business of the company at Courts of Assistants (special meetings held as often as needed)
Governor and Deputy Governor (executive)	by vote of the freemen at the General Court held each year at Easter	the Governor (or the Deputy Governor in his absence) must preside at all company meetings and act as the chief executive in conducting business between meetings

Changes in the Government of Massachusetts Bay, 1630–1634

These excerpts show four stages in the creation of an effective civil government for Massachusetts Bay Colony. They are taken from the records of the Massachusetts Bay Company, as written by its secretary, Simon Bradstreet, and from John Winthrop's Journal. *The editor's explanations appear in brackets.*

Shurtleff, ed., **The Records of the Governor and Company of Massachusetts Bay,** vol. I, pp. 79, 87, 95, 117.
James Kendall Hosmer, ed., **Winthrop's Journal "History of New England," 1630–1649.** New York: Charles Scribner's Sons, 1908, vol. I, pp. 122–23. Language simplified and modernized.

Gentlemen and commoners were terms indicating social rank. Gentlemen had higher rank than common people.

[After two months on shore, Governor John Winthrop, Deputy Governor Thomas Dudley, and six of the assistants held a Court of Assistants to handle public business. All those present were gentlemen rather than commoners. The Court provided that two ministers should be supported at public expense, and it put a limit on the daily wages of certain kinds of skilled workmen. The Court acted on a variety of other matters, including making provisions for law enforcement.

This handful of gentlemen with legal power then had to come to grips with the problem of how to use the company's charter to provide a civil government for the colony. Although only the king could legally make changes in the charter, they promptly set about altering it for their own purposes. It was they, not the king, who had the perplexing job of governing a new colony, and since they kept the charter closely guarded in John Winthrop's possession, perhaps nobody would notice what they were doing.

At the first meeting of the General Court, held a few months later, the members came to some decisions about the location of power in the government. Their decisions may have been influenced by the possibility of the company's opening membership to adult males who were not stockholders. The company's records at this point list the names of 108 men who "desire to be made freemen." More than half of them seem to have been commoners rather than gentlemen. Nobody knows exactly why the decision was later made to broaden the franchise. One reason may be that Winthrop and the other leaders knew that the English government would disapprove of their establishing churches independent of the Church of England, and thus felt it necessary to get the colonists solidly behind the Company's government. The reader can infer from the following excerpt the form of government the leaders of the colony hoped to create.]

October 19, 1630 For the establishment of the government, it was proposed that the freemen should have the power to choose assistants. In turn, the assistants should choose from among themselves a governor and a deputy governor, who, with the assistants, should have the power to make laws and to choose officers to enforce the laws. This was fully assented to by the general vote of the people. (*Company Records*)

[The second stage in the modification of the charter took place seven months later. At a meeting of the General Court, 116 men were admitted as freemen of the Company and thus gained the right to vote. The Court then issued the following explanation of the procedure for electing assistants. It was necessary because many new freemen were unfamiliar with the rules of trading companies. The Court also added a further qualification for becoming a freeman.]

May 18, 1631 For explanation of an order made during the last General Court, it is ordered now, with full consent of all the commons [freemen] then present, that at least once a year a General Court shall be held, at which it shall be lawful for the commons to nominate any person or persons whom they desire to be chosen assistants. If it be doubtful whether the majority of the commons agree to the nomination, a vote shall be taken. A vote shall also be taken when the commons shall wish to remove one or more of the assistants for any reason. So that the body of the commons may be made up of honest and good men, it is likewise ordered and agreed that in the future no men shall be admitted as freemen except those who are members of the churches within the colony. (*Company Records*)

Commons is used here to mean a law-making body similar to the House of Commons, the lower house of Parliament. The House of Commons included both gentlemen and common people at this time.

[One year later, a third stage in the modification of the charter appeared, as the General Court (officers, assistants, and freemen together) repealed one part of the election procedure adopted in 1630.]

May 9, 1632 It was generally agreed upon, by a show of hands, that the governor, deputy governor, and assistants should be chosen by the whole Court made up of governor, deputy governor, assistants, and freemen. It was also agreed that the Governor shall always be chosen out of the assistants. (*Company Records*)

[A fourth, and vitally important, stage in the development of civil government took place in 1634. It had to do with the law-making powers of the General Court, and especially its power to tax. In 1630, the General Court had decided that a Court of Assistants (the Governor and assistants only) could make laws. In the next two years, Courts of Assistants made many laws, including tax laws. Usually the Court ordered each town to pay a sum, the size of which depended mainly on the number of inhabitants. In 1632, several residents of Watertown protested against paying a tax imposed by the Court to provide fortifications for another town. But the Governor and assistants persuaded them that the Court, as a legitimate legislature, had the power of taxation.

Furthermore, Governor Winthrop told them that all freemen could express their grievances at the General Court held each May, when they could remove the assistants and elect others if they chose. Yet dissatisfaction persisted. In England at the time prominent men, including leading Puritans, were imprisoned for refusing to pay taxes that the king had imposed without the consent of Parliament. The men of Massachusetts were naturally sensitive on the subject. They realized that they were being governed on the authority of a charter that few of them had seen. They decided to act, ignoring the advice Winthrop had given them. The results of their actions, and the further modification of the Charter of the Massachusetts Bay Company to meet new conditions, appear in the following excerpt from John Winthrop's own journal of events.]

April 1, 1634 Notice was sent out of the General Court to be held the 14th day of May. The freemen appointed two from each town to meet and consider such matters as they were to act on at the General Court. They met and asked to examine the patent [charter of the Massachusetts Bay Company]. After seeing it, they concluded that all their laws should be made at the General Court [with freemen present and voting]. They also visited the governor to consult with him about it. He told them that when the patent had been granted, the number of freemen was supposed to be (as in similar trading companies) so few that they might easily meet to make laws. Now that they had grown so great in number, it was not possible for them to make or execute laws. They must choose others for that purpose. But at this time they did not have enough qualified men to represent them. They might, however, at the General Court, make an order that once a year a certain number of men would be called by the governor to revise the laws. They would not make any new laws. Instead, they would make their complaints to the Court of Assistants. No tax should be imposed, or lands disposed of, without the consent of such a committee. (John Winthrop's *Journal*)

[The freemen who attended the meeting of the General Court on May 14, 1634, now knew what the charter had said about making laws. They brushed off Winthrop's proposal and offered their own solution. A number of the assistants, led by Deputy Governor Thomas Dudley, who often disagreed with Winthrop, voted with them to adopt the following laws.]

May 14, 1634 It is agreed that none but the General Court has power to choose and admit freemen. None but the General Court has power to make laws; to elect and appoint officers, such as the governor, deputy governor, assistants, treasurer, secretary, captains, lieutenants, ensigns, or any of such importance; to remove officers upon misbehavior, or to determine the duties and powers of the said officers. None but the General Court has power to raise money and taxes and to dispose of lands. (*Company Records*)

[Feeling grew within the colony against Winthrop and some of the assistants. To try to forestall their removal from office, John Cotton, the colony's leading minister, preached a sermon at the church service which traditionally preceded the meeting of the General Court in May. Cotton argued that it was just as unfair to deprive a public official of his office, unless he had been convicted of misbehavior, as it was to deprive a private citizen of his property. Nevertheless, the General Court elected Dudley governor and demoted Winthrop to the rank of assistant. Winthrop took his defeat in good spirit, and three years later the General Court again elected him governor. He served the colony in that office for many more years.]

7 The New Societies

By the end of the seventeenth century, the English colonies in the New World flourished. The settlers now far outnumbered the combined French and Spanish population of the continent. They had developed agriculture, fishing, and trade of great value to themselves and to the mother country.

Successful growth brought perplexing problems. In New England, the expansion of commerce encouraged merchants to amass wealth. Some of the sailors, dock workers, and drifters attracted by the busy waterfront disrupted the orderly life of the growing towns. Religious leaders warned that material success threatened the simplicity and religious dedication of the Puritan colonies. The fact that fewer and fewer of the children and grandchildren of the original settlers joined churches showed that the Puritans were losing their spiritual unity. As merchants grew rich and began to imitate the ways of English gentlemen, they began to compete with the clergy for the top rung of the status ladder.

In Maryland, Virginia, and the Carolinas, tobacco cultivation on a large scale began to make a few men rich and many quite prosperous. The demand for workers to toil for long hours in the hot tobacco fields brought thousands of men and women into the South as indentured servants. An indentured servant had to work for a master for several years in exchange for passage to the colonies. Some signed their indentures, or contracts, voluntarily; others were sent to the colonies as punishment for crimes or debt. In either case, when the indenture was up, they joined the ranks of free farmers and often took servants of their own.

When the supply of these servants ran short, however, plantation owners turned to a new source of labor: West Africa. There Spanish, Portuguese, Dutch, and English traders bought prisoners taken in tribal wars or raids and shipped them to the New World as laborers. In the early seventeenth century, the English colonists treated some

THE THIRTEEN COLONIES (After 1660)

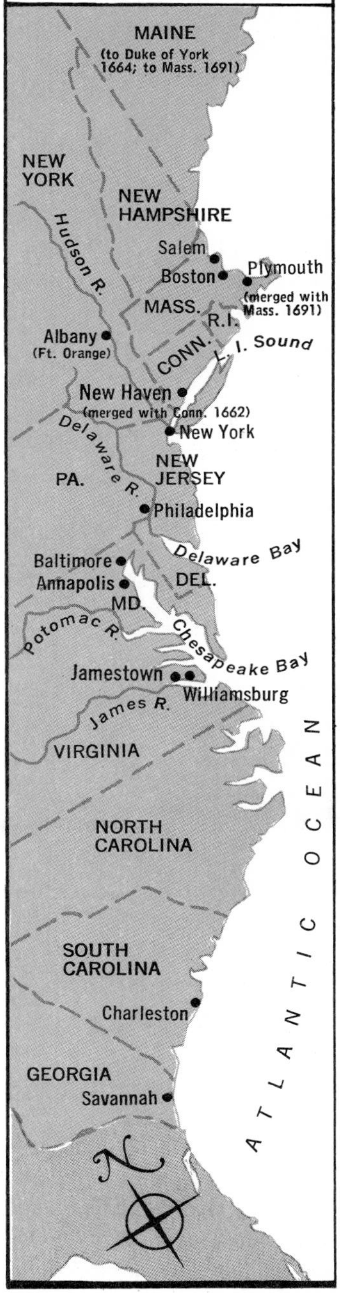

of these African workers as indentured servants, freeing them after a number of years. But eventually the desire for a permanent, stable labor supply—more profitable than the use of indentured servants—together with prejudice against black newcomers worked to place all the arriving Africans and their descendants in permanent slavery.

Out of all these groups—new immigrants, Americans born on this continent, indentured servants, and slaves—a new social structure emerged. Because North and South were different in so many ways, the societies that developed in the two areas took different shapes. Neither duplicated the social structure of the mother country exactly.

The excerpts which follow give insights into the nature of colonial social structure in the seventeenth century. As you read, keep the following questions in mind:

1. Could you easily identify a member of the upper class in one of the colonies? Would you be able to distinguish the difference between a Negro slave and a free Negro if you saw them on the street?
2. Why did the institution of slavery emerge? How much can you tell—or infer—about the treatment of slaves from the Virginia laws or Beverley's account?
3. How were social classes related to economic status in colonial society? What evidence of social mobility can you find in the readings?
4. Judged by today's standards, how democratic was colonial society? How do you account for your conclusion?

Jamestown in 1619

In 1619, John Pory came to Virginia as secretary of state. On September 30, 1619, he wrote a letter to the English ambassador to the Netherlands giving his impressions of the colony. Portions of that letter follow.

Tyler, ed., **Narratives of Early Virginia, 1606–1625,** pp. 284–85. Language simplified and modernized.

All our riches at present consist of tobacco. One man by his own labor in one year raised tobacco valued at two hundred pounds; another with the help of six servants cleared a thousand pounds from one crop. These to be sure are rare examples, yet it is possible for others to do as well. Our principal wealth, I should have said, consists of servants. But they must be furnished with arms, clothing, and bedding, as well as their transportation and other expenses paid while at sea and for their first year in the colony. But if they escape serious illness or death, they prove very hardy and able men.

Now that your lordship may know that we are not the greatest beggars in the world, our cowkeeper here at Jamestown on Sundays dresses all in fresh flaming silk. A wife of a man who in England had been a coal miner, here wears a rough beaver hat with a fair pearl hatband and a silken suit. But to leave the populace and to come to the higher levels of society, when the Governor first came to the colony, he brought only his sword with him. Recently he and his lady returned to London. From the profits he had made in the colony, he was able to spend nearly three thousand pounds for the voyage. Within seven years, I believe that the Governor's position here may be as profitable as the Lord Deputy's of Ireland.

Virginia Laws on Slavery

During the seventeenth century, the southern colonies adopted codes of law to deal with their thousands of slaves. Some of the Virginia laws which helped to define the Negroes' position in society follow.

W.W. Hening, comp., **The Statutes at Large, Being a Collection of all the Laws of Virginia.** Philadelphia: Thomas DeSilver, 1823, vol. III, pp. 26, 170, 260, 267, 270. Language simplified and modernized.

If any English servant runs away with any Negroes, who are already servants for life, the English servant shall serve additional time not only for his absence, but for the Negroes' absence as well. (*1661*)

Some doubts have arisen whether a child is slave or free who has an Englishman for a father and a Negro slave woman for a mother. Be it therefore enacted that all children born in this country shall be slave or free according to the condition of the mother. (*1662*)

Some doubts have arisen whether children that are slaves by birth should by virtue of their baptism be made free. It is enacted that baptism does not alter the person's condition. (*1667*)

Some doubts have arisen whether Negro women who have been set free are still subject to a personal tax [previously paid by their owners because slaves were considered property]. It is declared that Negro women though free ought not to share fully the rights of the English, and they are still required to pay the tax themselves. (*1668*)

The only law in force [requiring service of extra time] for the punishment of unruly servants does not apply to Negroes for they already serve for life. The obstinacy of many Negroes cannot be suppressed except by violent means. Be it enacted that if any slave resisting his master or overseer should die from punishment, the master or overseer will be acquitted. (*1669*)

In order to prevent the abominable mixing of the races by Negroes, mulattoes, and Indians intermarrying with English or other white women, be it enacted for the time to come that any white man or woman who marries a Negro, mulatto, or Indian shall within three months after such marriage be banished forever. (*1691*)

A mulatto in the 1600's was a person who had one black and one white parent.

Slavery and Servitude in Virginia

Robert Beverley, a prominent Virginian and a plantation owner, published in London in 1705 a long and favorable description of the colony and its people. Here he talks about systems of servitude in the colony.

Robert Beverley, **The History of Virginia,** in Four Parts. London: 1722, Book IV, pp. 235–236.

In Virginia, the slaves are Negroes and they remain slaves for life. A Negro child whose mother is a slave becomes a slave at birth. Servants (mainly white Europeans), on the other hand, serve only for a few years according to the time of their indenture or the custom of the country.

Male servants and slaves of both sexes work together tilling the soil and sowing and planting the crops. Some distinction is made between them in their clothes and food, but the work of servants and slaves is the same as what the overseers, freemen, and the planters themselves do.

An overseer directed the work of the servants and slaves. The overseer had usually served as an indentured servant during which time he had acquired skill in managing a plantation. The term freeman, in Virginia, meant a slave or servant who had been freed. This differs from the term as used in Massachusetts, where it meant stockholder or voter.

A distinction is made between female servants and slaves. A white woman is rarely or never put to work in the fields. To discourage all planters from using any white women as field hands, the law imposes the heaviest taxes upon the masters of female servants who are made to work the soil. The masters of all other white women do not have to pay the tax. On the other hand, it is a common thing to work a woman slave out of doors; nor does the law make any distinction in her taxes, whether she works in the fields or at home.

Because I have heard how strangely cruel and severe some people in England believe the labor system of this country is, I can't resist saying that the work of the servants and slaves is no different from what every common freeman does. Neither is any servant required to do more in a day than his overseer does. And I can assure you that generally the slaves are not worked nearly so hard nor so many hours a day as the farmers and day-laborers in England.

The Growth of Towns

Boston, founded in 1630, soon became the largest town in North America. By 1700, it contained about 6700 persons and did a bustling trade with the West Indies and England. Philadelphia, first settled by Swedes, became the center of the colony of Pennsylvania when Quakers led by William Penn arrived in 1682. In this reading, a modern historian, Carl Bridenbaugh, considers the effects of urban growth and prosperity on the manner of living in early colonial society.

The colonists who came to settle in the villages brought with them the social order then existing in England or Holland, and sought with considerable success to set up a similar system in America. While the English nobility did not migrate, many "gentlemen" of wealth and standing came over prepared to assume the functions of an aristocracy in the New World. With these substantial leaders came artisans, tradesmen, and servants, thoroughly indoctrinated with prevailing ideas of social inequality. In this they were all, better, middling, and inferior sorts alike, entirely the children of their age:

Carl Bridenbaugh, **Cities in the Wilderness.** New York: Capricorn Books Edition, 1964; originally published by The Ronald Press Company, 1938, pp. 96–97, 99.

> The people were not democrats then,
> They did not talk of the rights of men,
> And all that sort of thing,

and they certainly had never heard of a classless society. The subsequent addition of Negro and a few Indian slaves provided all the elements for the development of a caste system. . . .

A caste system divides members of society into rigid groups on the basis of birth, wealth, or religion. No social mobility takes place within a caste system.

The leaders of early Boston were gentlemen of considerable wealth who, in association with the clergy, eagerly sought to preserve in America the social arrangements of the Mother Country. By means of their control of trade and commerce, by their political domination of the inhabitants through church and Town Meeting, and by careful marriage alliances among themselves, members of this little oligarchy laid the foundations for an aristocratic class in seventeenth century Boston. As the trade of the little port increased, prosperous merchants accumulated wealth and successfully achieved social prominence. By 1663 the town had become "rich and very populous." . . . Rich Boston merchants erected fine mansions of stone and brick, luxuriously appointed as many in London or Bristol. "Ministers and other persons of Qualitie" began to travel abroad in coaches, calashes or Sedan chairs, to have their portraits painted, to wear periwigs, to adorn their sideboards with . . . silver, and to line their bellies with rich food and good Madeira [wine].

An oligarchy is a small group of people who hold political, economic, and social power in society.

Calashes were light, low-wheeled carriages. Sedan chairs were enclosed chairs, usually holding one person, which two men carried on poles. Periwigs were the kind of wigs men wore during the seventeenth and eighteenth centuries.

Realization of the economic superiority of their class led Boston aristocrats early to disregard the . . . laws prohibiting the wearing of fancy clothes, lace, gold braid, slashed sleeves, etc., enacted in 1634. The Elders seemed powerless to suppress this evil, because "divers [various] of the elders' wives, &c, were in some measure partners in this general disorder." The truth was, however, that the gentledame who inquired "what dress the queen is in this week," and her husband, bedecked in "silver laced coate and gold wrought cap," were birds of a feather. After 1639 the Court neatly solved the problem by denying such brilliant plumage to those of the "Middling" and "Inferiour sort" whose yearly incomes were less than £200. . . . Class lines may have broken down in rural regions or on the frontier, but at

Elders are lay officers who help govern certain Protestant churches.

Boston they seem rather to have tightened as the century progressed. . . .

More wealth was available for the founding of Philadelphia than at any of the other villages. The riches of [some] Quakers . . . enabled them immediately to erect "brave brick houses" with balconies that overlooked the Delaware [River] from Front Street. These favored few began life at Philadelphia in the grand manner. Robert Turner, his daughter and seventeen indentured servants arrived in 1683 to live in the first brick house built in the town. By 1687 Samuel Carpenter's "Slate Roof House" was the show place of the village, though Joseph Growden's country seat, with its orchards near the town, challenged its supremacy. Well might Judge Thomas Holme exclaim:

> Strangers do wonder, and some may say,—
> What mean these Quakers thus to raise
> These stately fabrics to their praise?
> Since we well know and understand
> When they were in their native land
> They were in prison trodden down,
> And can they now build such a town?

The answer is easily found,—profits from commercial ventures as high as one hundred per cent. The Quakers had not yet assumed their garb of "homespun drab and gray," but dressed as did their neighbors in the other villages. Long hair, wigs, side swords and other frippery [bright clothing or ornaments] were as frequently seen in Philadelphia as elsewhere. Elaborately appointed houses, rich and varied foods and choice wines were the daily portion of the heavy drinking aristocrats of Front Street.

8 Growth and Change in England's Colonies

HISTORICAL ESSAY

During the seventeenth century, English settlers spread out over a widening strip of the Atlantic coast of North America. By 1700, the English-controlled area held the fastest-growing and strongest European colonies in the New World. The preceding pages have shown how the settlers struggled to survive, created new governments, and dealt with social changes. These efforts, together with military and commercial achievements, contributed to the growth and strength of English America.

European Competitors in North America

In the early seventeenth century, England, France, and the Netherlands challenged Spain's leadership in the race to dominate the New World. The accompanying map shows each nation's claims in mid-century.

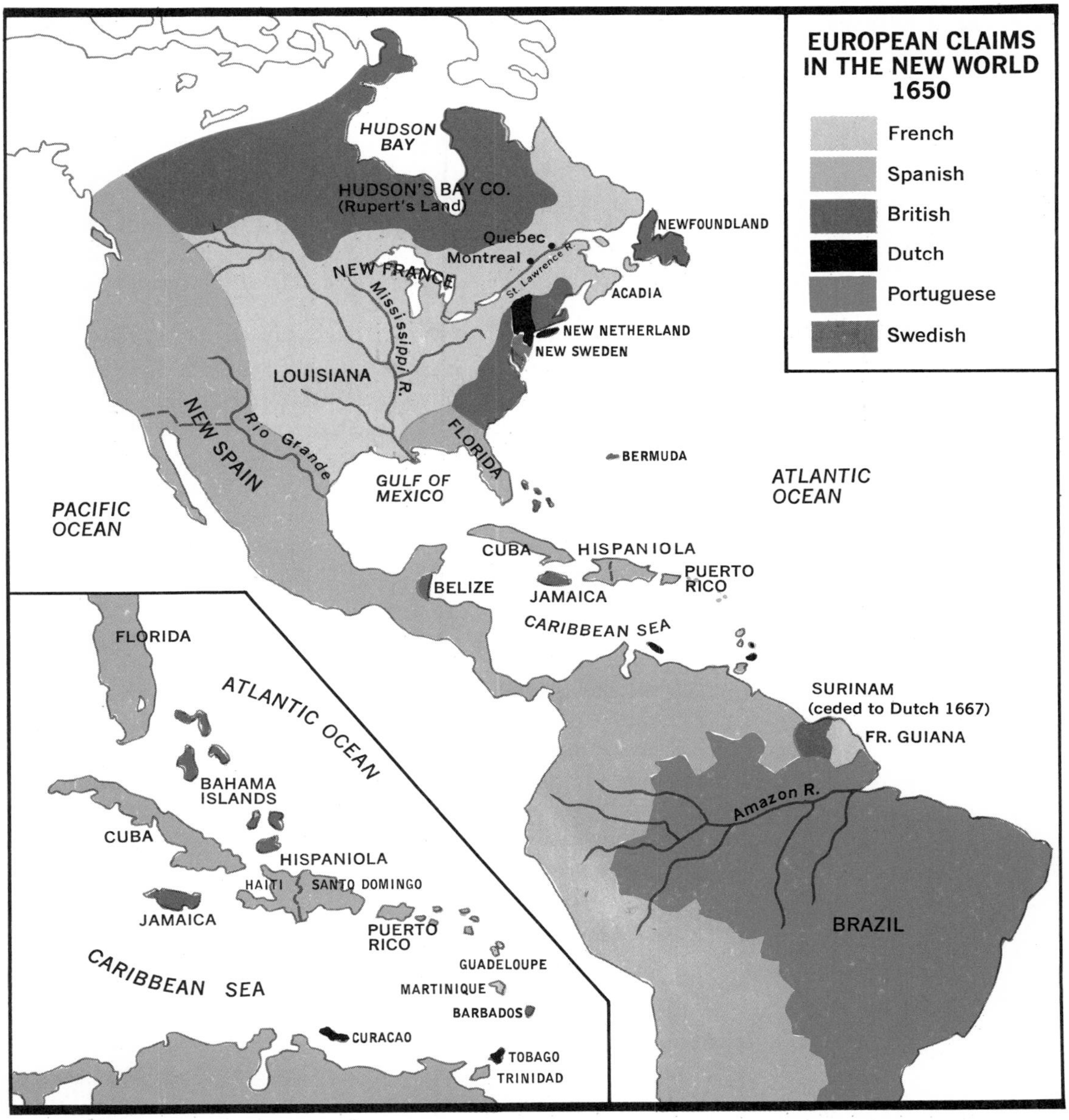

In 1608, the year after Jamestown was settled, Samuel de Champlain established a French trading post at Quebec. Between 1610 and 1613, French traders and missionaries founded outposts in the region they called Acadia (the coasts of present-day Nova Scotia, New Brunswick, and Maine). A party of Englishmen from Virginia raided and burned the Acadian villages in 1613—a grim beginning to a century and a half of French-English conflict over the northern coasts of North America. The French had little difficulty in gaining control over the St. Lawrence Valley and the area north of the Great Lakes.

The Dutch operated further south. Their West India Company sent out parties in 1622 which established trading posts on the site of Albany, New York, and on the Delaware River south of Philadelphia. In 1626, the company founded New Amsterdam, later to become New York City. When the Swedes, in 1638, opened rival trading posts on the Delaware River, the Dutch protested and eventually captured the Swedish settlements. Yet New Netherland remained small, solitary, and weak, and fell into English hands as the result of English-Dutch wars in the 1660's.

England and Holland fought several times for commercial superiority in the 1650's and 1660's. The war fought from 1664 to 1667 ended with the Treaty of Breda, which gave New Netherland to England and Surinam, located on the northeast coast of South America, to Holland.

International conflicts broke out in the islands of the West Indies. The English occupied some of the islands, including Bermuda, and ousted the Spanish from Jamaica in 1655. The French, Dutch, and Danes took over other islands. Spain retained the rich islands of Hispaniola [Haiti and Santo Domingo] and Cuba. She expanded her settlements in Florida and what is now the American Southwest.

The English success in obtaining so much of North America depended partly on seapower. In the seventeenth century, England's navy and merchant marine (including colonial men and ships) became the world's most powerful. English ships usually dominated the Atlantic, protected settlements, and made expansion possible.

Manpower and geographical position also helped to make the English colonies strong and secure. Their inhabitants—thousands of English, and a scattering of Irish, Scots, Dutch, Germans, Africans, Spanish and Portuguese Jews, and French Protestants, made up the largest source of military manpower in the New World. Once these settlers took control of the country inland from the coast, they could not be dislodged unless an enemy could muster greater strength. Only the Indians could occasionally do this.

Self-Government in the Colonies

Settlers in the English colonies lived under governments that were remarkable for the amount of power and participation which the inhabitants enjoyed. This near-independence from the mother country came partly from the failure of the English government to exercise much control over colonization.

Trading companies founded three of the early English colonies in North America—Virginia, Plymouth, and Massachusetts Bay. The Virginia Company of London suffered heavy losses, as seen in George Percy's account of the Jamestown settlement. In 1619, the company gave the colony more political responsibility, when it ordered that a representative assembly be created. The assembly, known as the House of Burgesses, was the first of many legislative bodies in the colonies.

In 1624, Virginia became a royal colony and something of a model for later royal colonies. The king appointed the governor who named a council to advise him. Governors almost always picked the wealthiest and most influential planters to serve on the council, which became, in effect, an upper house of the legislature. But money to run the government came from taxes voted by the Burgesses, who could influence the governor's actions either by threatening to withhold his salary and expenses or by voting him a bonus for his personal use. A pattern of uneasy cooperation and frequent conflict resulted. Often squabbles between the governor and legislators ended with the governor dismissing the legislators (as he had the right to do) and maintaining his position out of his own pocket and such other funds as he could scrape up. This pattern became common in all the royal colonies.

Governments with even greater independence grew in New England. The Pilgrims had been attracted to the New World by an offer from the Virginia Company to give them local self-government. In turn, the merchants who owned the company hoped to profit from their labor. However, because of stormy weather, the Pilgrims landed, not in Virginia, but in New England, where they had been given neither the right to settle nor the right to establish a government. So they took matters into their own hands. Before they landed, the adult males signed the Mayflower Compact, an agreement which set up a "civil body politic" and pledged the signers to frame and obey "just and equal laws." The simple government the Pilgrims soon set up consisted of no more than a governor and an assistant. Later, as Plymouth grew to include several towns, the colonists created a representative assembly. They remained virtually independent of English control in local matters until 1691, when England ordered Plymouth combined with the colony of Massachusetts Bay.

The people who came to Massachusetts Bay in 1630 also came under the authority of a private company, controlled by the Puritans. They had a royal charter which gave them authority over most of Massachusetts. But instead of leaving the charter and the company headquarters in England, as had the Virginia and Plymouth colonists, the Puritans took the charter to Massachusetts and used it as a constitution for local government there.

The Puritans fought against King Charles I and his supporters. The king was captured and executed in 1649. Parliament declared the monarchy abolished and established the Commonwealth under the rule of Oliver Cromwell, a Puritan. In 1660, Parliament invited Charles II to occupy the throne, thereby ending the Commonwealth.

In 1688, Parliament deposed King James II because of his despotic rule and his Catholic sympathies. Parliament invited his Protestant daughter and son-in-law, Mary Stuart and William of Orange, to occupy the throne according to the terms of a Bill of Rights.

Under a feudal system, farmers do not own the land, but work it for the lord who owns it.

These Puritans still considered themselves Englishmen, loyal to the king, but they were well content that England was far away and exercised little control over them. When they suspected in 1634 that the king intended to take away their charter and install his own governor, they fortified Boston harbor against a possible royal invasion. During the English civil wars (1642–1646, 1648) and under the Commonwealth (1649–1660), Massachusetts Bay and the other American colonies became even more independent.

When Charles II recovered the throne in 1660, however, royal officials set about recovering their authority over the colonies. The English government revoked the Massachusetts charter in 1684 and created a Dominion of New England to govern all the colonies north of Pennsylvania. The English Revolution of 1688 touched off successful uprisings in the colonies against the royal governors, and brought an end to the unwieldy Dominion of New England. But the new rulers of England, William of Orange and his wife, Mary Stuart, agreed that England should have more power over the colonies. What was more important, so did Parliament, which, from then on, was the main seat of power in England. A new charter, in 1691, made Massachusetts Bay a royal province, and the king named the governor.

To obtain a royal grant of land, however, a man had to be a wealthy or influential person who happened to be in the king's favor. While these "proprietors," as they were called, often wanted to establish semi-feudal governments and systems of landholding, in every case they ended up granting the settlers representative assemblies and giving them more control over the land they occupied. It was easier to attract settlers who knew they could influence the setting of the rate of taxation on their own property. Moreover, by the late seventeenth century, English settlers had begun to take representative government for granted. Eventually, however, many of the proprietary rights returned to the king.

Connecticut and Rhode Island had been established by migrants from Massachusetts Bay. They were the only two English colonies that retained the virtual independence they had gained before 1660. Both elected their own governors throughout the colonial era, with the exception of the three years under the Dominion of New England. One reason for the English government's liberal attitude toward them was its desire to limit the expansion of the Massachusetts Bay Colony.

A man living in one of the English colonies in America in the late 1600's had more chance of taking part in its political life, as a voter or officeholder, than a man anywhere else in the world. This did not mean that the colonies were "democratic" in the sense that every adult could vote; women, servants, slaves, and most men with little or no property could not vote. It did mean, as we have seen in

The Establishment of American Colonies

Colony	Founder/Proprietor	Date	Reasons for Settlement	1775 Status
Virginia (Jamestown)	London Company	1607	Trade, profit, gold. Conversion of Indians.	Royal
Plymouth	Pilgrims	1620	Religious freedom for Separatists. Economic opportunity.	Merged with Mass. 1691
New Hampshire and Maine	John Mason and Ferdinando Gorges	1622–1631	Escape religious persecution in Massachusetts.	Annexed by Mass. 1641–1820
Massachusetts	Puritans (Winthrop)	1630	Religious freedom for Puritans.	Royal
Connecticut (Hartford)	Thomas Hooker Massachusetts colonists	1636	Escape religious persecution. Economic opportunity.	Self-governing
Rhode Island	Roger Williams and Anne Hutchinson	1636–1644	Achieve complete religious freedom.	Self-governing
Maryland	George Calvert, Lord Baltimore	1634	Trade and profits. Refuge for Catholics.	Proprietary
Delaware (Ft. Christina)	Swedish	1638	Trade and profit.	Proprietary (merged with Pa. 1682)
North Carolina (Albemarle)	Virginians	1653	Trade and profit.	Royal (separated from S.C. 1691)
(New Netherland) New York	Dutch Duke of York	1624 1664	Trade and profit.	Royal
New Jersey	George Carteret and John Berkeley	1664	Trade and profit.	Royal
South Carolina	Eight proprietors	1670	Trade and profit.	Royal
Pennsylvania	William Penn	1681	Religious freedom for Quakers. Economic opportunity.	Proprietary
Georgia	James Oglethorpe	1733	Refuge for debtors. Economic opportunity. Buffer state against Spanish.	Royal

the case of Massachusetts, that the wealthier men, who ran the colonial governments, had to keep in mind the interests of the electorate.

In the English colonies political dissent flourished on a moderate scale. Discontent, however, seldom led to actual rebellion. Episodes, such as Bacon's Rebellion in Virginia in 1676, in which planters who wanted to repress the Indians found themselves in revolt against a governor who refused to let them make war, or Leisler's Rebellion in New York, which was linked to the English Revolution of 1688, were infrequent.

The colonies' political contacts beyond their borders were nearly always with London rather than with each other. Since the colonies were independent of each other, they found it hard to cooperate.

In 1689, when news arrived in America that King James had been deposed, Jacob Leisler seized control of New York City. He governed for several months, but after a new colonial governor arrived from England, he was imprisoned and hanged for treason.

In 1643, Massachusetts Bay, Plymouth, Connecticut, and New Haven formed the New England Confederation to coordinate their policies toward the Dutch, the Indians, and the rival parties in revolutionary England. Massachusetts Bay, much the largest of the four, was suspected, with some reason, by its neighbors of wanting to dominate the policy of the Confederation. Consequently, the alliance served as little more than a discussion group until its end in 1673.

The Ties of Commerce

In contrast to the weakness of political ties, the commerce which sprang up during the 1600's linked the colonies strongly with each other as well as with England. Ships laden with the products of farm and forest sailed from the colonies in increasing numbers for Europe, to return with the manufactured goods and the people so needed in America.

Tobacco soon became the most valuable of colonial exports. By the 1620's, the Virginians produced large quantities and sold it at good prices. During the century, tobacco dominated the colony's economy to such an extent that it was used as a kind of money. Tobacco culture, on a large scale, soon spread north into Maryland and later, on a smaller scale, south into the Carolinas.

Europeans eagerly purchased American furs, timber, and fish. The trading posts that dotted the North Atlantic coast from the late 1500's attracted Indians with furs and skins to trade for implements, ornaments, cloth, and more dangerous goods—firearms and alcoholic drinks. As the settlers cleared the forests, fur-bearing animals dwindled in number, and the trading posts moved inland, one jump ahead of the farmers. In England, where timber was becoming scarce because of the growth of population and manufactures, American oak, hickory, pine, and other woods were especially welcome. European and colonial fishermen pulled rich harvests from the shallow Atlantic waters off New England and Newfoundland. They often dried and salted their catches on the rocky shore to preserve them for the long voyage to Europe.

The settlers grew most of their own food and imported most of their manufactured goods from England. Most colonial manufactures, such as linen or wool cloth, or simple wooden or iron tools, were used or sold near the places where they were made. Shipbuilders, however, found it cheaper to build ships near a supply of good timber. American-built ships soon carried much of the transatlantic trade and also carried goods between England and other European countries.

Intercolonial commerce grew more slowly than did trade with England, but it assumed an increasing importance in the late 1600's as the seaport towns of Boston, Newport, New York, Philadelphia, and Charleston demanded more supplies from the "back country" to feed and clothe their growing populations. Where rich agricultural regions began to concentrate on a single staple crop, such as tobacco in Virginia or sugar in the West Indies, other regions, such as New England or Pennsylvania, with more diversified products, found a ready market for grain, lumber, fish, cattle, or horses.

Until 1651, the colonists shipped their produce where they wanted and sold it as they wanted. Most of it went to England or stayed within the colonies themselves. But a growing share of the lucrative tobacco crop found its way to markets in the Netherlands or elsewhere in continental Europe. Beginning with laws of 1651 and 1660, and later extended by other laws, England required the colonies to ship their tobacco to England for sale or resale there. In turn, England prohibited the growing of tobacco in the home country, thus providing a protected market for the colonial planters. These regulations formed part of a general system of regulations called the Acts of Trade and Navigation. These were supposed to increase English (and colonial) commerce and shipping at the expense of other nations. Under the theory of mercantilism, a nation sought wealth, power, and self-sufficiency by having a favorable balance of trade.

THE NAVIGATION ACTS, 1660

1. All goods and commodities imported into or exported from the colonies had to be shipped in British vessels. The captain and at least three quarters of the crew had to be British subjects.

2. Only British citizens could trade with the colonies. Anyone in authority who did not enforce this law could be dismissed immediately.

3. Major commodities produced in the colonies—such as sugar, tobacco, and cotton wool—could be exported only to British ports.

SOME ADDITIONAL PROVISIONS, 1696

1. English officers were authorized to search all colonial shipping and to confiscate goods that were prohibited to colonial import and export.

2. Any colonial laws that conflicted with Navigation Acts were null and void.

3. Any goods or merchandise leaving the colonies for Ireland or Scotland had to pass first through England and have a duty placed on them.

Under the mercantile system, colonies were urgently needed to provide the mother country with raw materials and also a market for finished products. Colonies also contributed to the mother country's military strength by supplying ships, naval bases, and men.

Some colonists grumbled about the restrictions arising out of this system, especially if, as with tobacco, overproduction drove prices down on the English market. But often the restrictions were not rigidly enforced, and the colonists managed to evade them, either openly, by smuggling, or by bribing port officials.

The Bonds of Society

Immigration and the American environment brought, as we have seen, certain changes in the kind of life European people lived in the colonies.

In England and the rest of Europe, wealth and hereditary titles had created vast differences between the upper classes and the common people. The upper classes in Europe did not have to labor with their hands, but in America gentlemen often had to work hard to get a successful start or to survive. The availability of land—free or at low prices—enabled relatively poor families to own farms and improve their positions. At the same time, wealthy men found it harder to keep laborers or tenants working on huge estates than they did in Europe. Independent farming reduced sharply the social distance between the lower and upper classes and promoted social mobility, as John Pory pointed out in his letter.

The shortage of labor, which lasted through the colonial era, and the cheapness of land benefited one group particularly. Because it was so hard to earn a living in England, many servants renewed their agreements which legally obliged them to obey their masters. Now they had an alternative; thousands of them—perhaps a majority of people who came to the southern and middle colonies—came as indentured servants and then chose freedom. Periods of service for adults lasted usually from four to seven years, or for children, until they became twenty-one. But masters competing for servants reduced the length of service. Because ex-servants could acquire land easily, they were reluctant to sign up for another term, even when offered increased privileges and rewards.

Social mobility was, however, largely limited to Europeans. The same condition—shortage of labor—that offered opportunity to European laborers, denied opportunity to Negroes once the lifetime and hereditary slavery laws, such as those passed in Virginia, were enacted. The profits of farming, especially in the South with its longer growing season, were greater with slaves than with servants. White prejudice made the growth of rigid lifetime slavery for

Africans and their children seem like a necessary system for controlling "dangerous" black strangers. By the last years of the seventeenth century, slave traders brought thousands of Africans by force, under terrible conditions in crowded ships, to the plantations of Virginia, Maryland, and the Carolinas, as well as to the West Indies. At the same time, the number of indentured servants declined sharply in those colonies.

Colonial society largely excluded the Indians, who were forced westward. Occasional pacts and agreements between them and the new settlers were usually broken by hostilities—sometimes provoked by one side, sometimes the other.

By the end of the seventeenth century, other changes were also slowing down the democratizing effects of life in America. The growth of commerce in cities like Boston, Philadelphia, or Charleston made the rich richer, as Professor Bridenbaugh pointed out. A new elite group consisting of the wealthy and colonial officials grew up. Many royal officials were able men, but many of them—especially royal governors—thought of England as home, considered themselves members of the English aristocracy (as sometimes they were), and treated the colonies as places to make money out of their positions and to create a high-toned social life for the colonial elite.

SUGGESTED READINGS

Diary of Samuel Sewall (edited and abridged by Harvey Wish). This Boston judge kept a diary from his graduation from college until the end of his long life. Its entries show a multitude of details of daily life—among them Sewall's unsuccessful courtship of a widow—and his involvement in public affairs, including his unhappy part as a judge in the Salem witchcraft trials.

FISHWICK, MARSHALL W., *Jamestown, First American Colony.* The narrator takes the eventful story of colonial life from the first expeditions of Sir Walter Raleigh in the 1580's to about 1700. Many illustrations add to the interest of this account.

MORGAN, EDMUND S., *The Puritan Dilemma: The Story of John Winthrop.* This brief biography tells the successes and failures of the governor of Massachusetts Bay in his most serious problems: how to maintain religious order among religious rebels and how to make a godly community out of sinful men.

STARKEY, MARION, *The Devil in Massachusetts.* In 1692 people in Massachusetts fell victim to witchcraft hysteria, and before it ended twenty-one victims were dead. This is a colorful account of the panic that gripped a colony.

CHAPTER 3

The Maturing Colonies, 1700–1763

STATING THE ISSUE

Life for most inhabitants of the colonies in the 1700's grew gradually more orderly, safe, and pleasant. Forests yielded to farms and plantations. The number of wild animals dwindled, and Europeans forced the Indians into the back country. Growing villages, towns, and a few cities offered townsmen and visiting farmers opportunities to trade and see new sights and faces. The bountiful supply of cheap land and the demand for colonial products kept unemployment lower and pay higher than anywhere in Europe, encouraged the raising of large families, and drew a steady stream of immigrants across the Atlantic. On the whole, Great Britain provided a stable political system with which the colonists seemed well content. Under these conditions, a prospering colonial population began to look increasingly American rather than European.

During the first half of the eighteenth century, the roots of American culture took firm hold in colonial soil. Anyone who wants to understand the behavior of nineteenth- and twentieth-century Americans should study these eighteenth-century ancestors. Few statistics are available for the period, however, and relatively few firsthand records have come down to us, particularly from the lower classes.

We can, however, learn something about eighteenth-century society from the writings of its leaders. In any society, influential leaders are part of a small group holding a large amount of power, but they often represent the values and aspirations of the men and women who follow them. For this reason, knowledge of the lives of the elite may also help us to learn something about the common man.

Chapter 3 concerns the history of the American colonies during the first half of the eighteenth century. What were the characteristics of three important leaders during this era? What do the lives of these men reveal to us about colonial society? Why did the colonists seem relatively satisfied with their lives at this time? These are the major issues raised in Chapter 3.

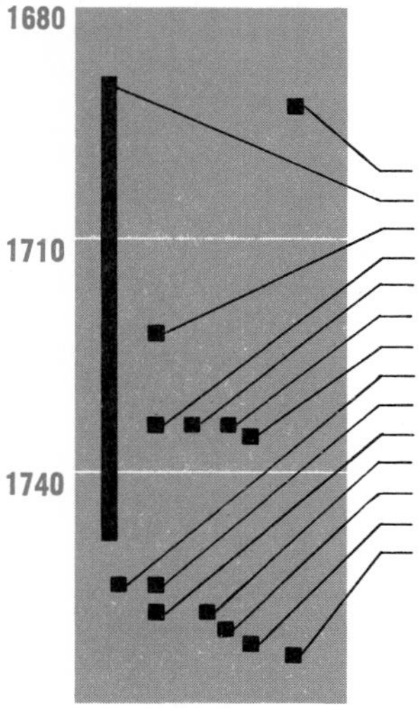

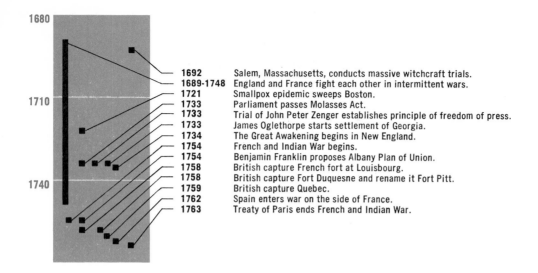

1692	Salem, Massachusetts, conducts massive witchcraft trials.
1689-1748	England and France fight each other in intermittent wars.
1721	Smallpox epidemic sweeps Boston.
1733	Parliament passes Molasses Act.
1733	Trial of John Peter Zenger establishes principle of freedom of press.
1733	James Oglethorpe starts settlement of Georgia.
1734	The Great Awakening begins in New England.
1754	French and Indian War begins.
1754	Benjamin Franklin proposes Albany Plan of Union.
1758	British capture French fort at Louisbourg.
1758	British capture Fort Duquesne and rename it Fort Pitt.
1759	British capture Quebec.
1762	Spain enters war on the side of France.
1763	Treaty of Paris ends French and Indian War.

9 Life Through the Eyes of a Virginia Planter

In the late eighteenth century, large plantations using slave labor dominated the economy of Virginia. Some of these plantations were huge; thousands of acres stretching farther than the eye could see made them truly royal estates. Some of the greatest men in American history owned these lands. George Washington, Thomas Jefferson, and James Madison, three of our first four Presidents, were perhaps the most notable. To be sure, the majority of whites in Virginia in the late seventeenth and early eighteenth centuries owned small farms and had few, if any, slaves. The large plantation owners, however, set the tone of Virginia society and ran its government. Many were educated, public-spirited men as much at home in a London drawing room or at a meeting of a scientific society as they were on horseback riding over their estates. They were the leaders, the decision makers and, therefore, strongly influenced the opinions and style of living of their fellow countrymen. If we wish to learn what shaped Virginia society, we must study their lives.

For more than fifty years, William Byrd II (1674–1744) held a place of power and honor in rural Virginia. He was the son of an Englishman who moved to the New World and established his family securely among the elite of the colony. William Byrd II was educated in England, where his studies included the law. His fellow planters elected him at the age of 22 to the Virginia House of Bur-

The House of Burgesses had become the lower house of the legislature in the colony of Virginia. The Council of State was the upper house. Members were elected to the House of Burgesses, but appointed by the king to the Council of State.

gesses. At 35, he won a seat on the Council of State. Later he was appointed to represent the interests of Virginia in England, so he again crossed the Atlantic to spend several years in London. His estate at Westover on the James River remains today as an example of the setting in which wealthy planters lived.

For much of his life, Byrd kept a diary. As you read the excerpts from it that follow, think about the following questions:

1. What were Byrd's intellectual and economic interests? What were his political responsibilities?
2. What were Byrd's outstanding personal qualities? Why were these qualities particularly useful for a man in his social, economic, and political position?
3. How did Byrd treat his slaves? his wife? visitors? his neighbors? the nearby Indians? What does his behavior reveal about the society?
4. What accounts for Byrd's position of leadership in Virginia society? How could you find out if other Virginia leaders were like him?

The Secret Diary of William Byrd of Westover

In recent years, scholars have deciphered a diary kept by Byrd in an antique shorthand. The frankness of some of his entries indicates clearly that the diaries were written for his eyes alone. He wrote the excerpts which follow in August and September 1709.

Louis B. Wright and Marion Tinling, eds., **The Secret Diary of William Byrd of Westover, 1709–1712.** Richmond, Virginia: The Dietz Press, 1941, pp. 66, 68–71, 78, 79–83. Reprinted by permission of the authors.

Josephus was a Jewish historian of the first century A.D. He wrote some of his works in Greek.

Homer was a Greek poet who lived before 700 B.C. He wrote the **Iliad** and the **Odyssey.**

August 1 I rose at break of day and drank some warm milk and rode to Mr. Harrison's, where I got a permit to load tobacco on board my sloop [a sailing vessel]. . . . I ate some watermelon and stayed till about 9 o'clock, when I returned and read a chapter [probably of the Bible] in Hebrew and some Greek in Josephus. I said my prayers and went to see old Ben [probably a Negro slave] and found him much better. I read some geometry. I ate fish for dinner. In the afternoon the Doctor and my wife played at piquet [a card game]. Joe Wilkinson [a nearby landowner] came and gave me an account of the tobacco that he raised this year and I agreed [to hire him as] my overseer at Burkland [one of Byrd's plantations] the next year. I read some Greek in Homer and took a walk about the plantation. I neglected to say my prayers. I had good health, good thoughts, and good humor, thanks be to God Almighty.

August 2 I rose at 5 o'clock and read two chapters in Hebrew and some Greek in Josephus. I said my prayers and drank whey [the watery liquid left after milk has coagulated] for breakfast. It was terribly hot. I wrote a letter to the Governor of Barbados [in the West Indies], to whom I intend to consign my sloop and cargo. Old Ben was still better and began to complain he was hungry. I ate chicken for my dinner. In the afternoon my wife and the Doctor played at piquet and the Doctor was beat. My neighbor Harrison had the ague but was somewhat better this day. I wrote more letters to Barbados. I walked about the plantation. . . . I said a short prayer. It rained a little. I had good health, good thoughts, and good humor, thanks be to God Almighty.

Ague is a condition of fever and chills; in Byrd's time it often meant a form of malaria.

August 8 I rose at 5 o'clock and read a chapter in Hebrew and some Greek in Josephus. My sloop sailed this morning for Barbados, God send her a good and expeditious voyage. I was angry with B-l-n-m and he ran away. I likewise [punished] Tom [probably a slave]. I said my prayers and ate milk for breakfast. I walked out to see my people at work at the ditch. I read a little geometry. I ate mutton for dinner. In the evening I took a little nap, . . . I walked to the ditch again. In the evening I said my prayers. My man Jack was lame again. I had good health, good thoughts, and good humor, thanks be to God Almighty.

The editors of the diary were unable to determine the full name either because Byrd's shorthand could not be deciphered or because the manuscript was damaged.

August 13 I rose at 5 o'clock and read a chapter in Hebrew and some Greek in Josephus. I said my prayers and ate bread and butter for breakfast. Twelve Pamunkey Indians came over. We gave them some victuals [food] and some rum and put them over the river. I danced my dance. I removed more books into the library. I read some geometry and walked to see the people at work. I ate fish for dinner. I was almost the whole afternoon in putting up my books. In the evening John Blackman came from the Falls [one of Byrd's plantations] and brought me word that some of my people were sick and that my coaler was sick at the coal mine. I scolded with him about the little work he had done this summer. I took a walk about the plantation. I had a little scold with the Doctor about his boy. I said my prayers and had good health, good thoughts, and good humor, thanks be to God Almighty.

The Pamunkey Indians were a small tribe that remained on a reservation in Virginia.

Byrd referred frequently to his dance. It was probably a set of exercises which resembled dance steps.

August 14 I sent away my sloop which came yesterday to Falling Creek. John Blackman returned to the Falls. The old man grew better in his lameness and the [slave] boy who broke his leg was much better, thanks be to God. I ate boiled mutton for dinner. In the afternoon I took a nap. My cousin Betty Harrison came over and stayed till the evening. I took a walk about the plantation with my wife who has not quarreled with me in a great while. . . .

The stock phrases with which Byrd began and ended each day's entry have been eliminated from the remainder of this reading.

August 15 I removed two cases of books into the library. I read some geometry. Old Ben walked a little today which made his leg swell again. Jack was better of his lameness. Mr. Isham Randolph came and dined with us. I ate fish for dinner. In the afternoon I put my books into the cases in the library, notwithstanding Mr. Randolph was here. . . . In the evening I took a walk about the plantation.

September 2 It rained again this day, thanks be to God for his great goodness, who sent us rain almost all day and all the night following. I read some geometry. Notwithstanding the rain Mrs. Ware came to [ask] me to take tobacco for her debt to me, but I refused because tobacco was good for nothing [the price of tobacco was low]. I ate hashed pork for dinner. In the afternoon Mr. Taylor came from Surry [county] about his bill of exchange [a written order to pay a certain amount of money to a specified person]. He told me there was news by way of Barbados that the peace was expected there to be already concluded. The rain kept him here all night but Mrs. Ware went away.

During Queen Anne's War (1702–1713), battles between the English and their opponents, the French and Spanish, took place in the West Indies.

September 3 I said my prayers and ate chocolate with Mr. Taylor for breakfast. Then he went away. I read some geometry. We had no court [the county court which tried local cases] this day. My wife was indisposed [Mrs. Byrd was pregnant] again but not to much purpose. I ate roast chicken for dinner. In the afternoon I beat Jenny [a house servant and probably a Negro slave] for throwing water on the couch. I took a walk to Mr. Harrison's who told me he heard the peace was concluded in the last month. After I had been courteously entertained with wine and cake I returned home, where I found all well, thank God.

September 5 My wife was much out of order and had frequent returns of her pains. I read some geometry. I ate roast mutton for dinner. In the afternoon I wrote a letter to England and I read some Greek in Homer. Then in the evening I took a walk about the plantation and when I returned I found my wife very bad. I sent for Mrs. Hamlin and my cousin Harrison about 9 o'clock and I said my prayers heartily for my wife's happy delivery [of the baby], and had good health, good thoughts, and good humor, thanks be to God Almighty. I went to bed about 10 o'clock and left the women full of expectation with my wife.

September 6 About one o'clock this morning my wife was happily delivered of a son [named Parke, who died July 3, 1710], thanks be to God Almighty. I was awake in a blink and rose and my cousin Harrison met me on the stairs and told me it was a boy. We drank some French wine and went to bed again and rose at 7 o'clock. I read a chapter in Hebrew and then drank chocolate with the women for breakfast. I returned God humble thanks for so great a blessing and recommended my young son to His divine protection. My cousin Harrison and Mrs. Hamlin went away about 9 o'clock and I [rewarded] them for that kindness. I sent Peter [a servant] away who brought me a summons to the Council. I read some geometry. The Doctor brought me two letters from England . . . I ate roast mutton for dinner. In the afternoon I wrote a letter to England and took a walk about the plantation.

September 11 My wife and child were extremely well, thanks to God Almighty, who I hope will please to keep them so. I recommended my family to the divine protection and passed over the creek and then rode to my brother Duke's whom I found just recovered of the ague by means of my physic. Here I ate some roast beef for dinner, and then proceeded to Colonel Duke's, whom I found indisposed.

Physic was medicine. Byrd was an amateur physician who cared for those on his plantation and who also gave medicine and medical advice to his friends.

September 12 I rose at 5 o'clock and said my prayers and then the Colonel and I [talked] about his debt to Mr. Perry in which I promised to be the mediator. . . . Then I met Colonel Bassett and with him rode to Williamsburg [the colonial capital]. . . . Then I went to Mr. President's, where I found several of the Council. The President persuaded me to be sworn, which I agreed to, and accordingly went to Council where I was sworn a member of the Council. God grant I may distinguish myself with honor and good conscience. We dined together and I ate beef for dinner. In the evening we went to the President's where I drank too much French wine and played at cards and I lost 20 shillings. . . .

Mr. President refers to the presiding officer of the Council.

September 13 I rose at 5 o'clock and read some Greek in Lucian and a little Latin in Terence. I neglected to say my prayers and ate rice milk for breakfast. Several people came to see me and Mr. Commissary desired me to frame a letter to the Lord Treasurer which I did and then went to the meeting of the College [of William and Mary, then still a grammar school] where after some debate the majority were for building the new college on the old wall; I was against this and was for a new one for several reasons. . . . I received some protested bills [checks or bills of exchange upon which payment had been refused] and then we went to the President's and played at cards and I lost £4 about 10 o'clock and went home.

Lucian was a Greek satirist and Terence a Roman playwright.

The Commissary was the colonial representative of the Church of England.

10 A Crisis in the Life of a Boston Minister

As the seventeenth century passed, Puritan ministers repeatedly warned their flocks against slackening religious zeal. As noted in Reading 6, many of the children of the Puritans failed to join the churches, and wealthy merchants challenged the ministers for high status and influence.

Although their position was no longer as strong as it had been during the early days of settlement, Puritan ministers were still the most influential men in New England. They were not only its spiritual leaders, but also its most learned men, having been educated in English universities or at Harvard College, which had been founded by the Puritans primarily to assure a steady supply of ministers for the new colony. They held positions in Boston which corresponded in some ways to those of planters in Virginia.

Cotton Mather (1663–1728) was the son of a clergyman, Increase Mather, and the grandson of both John Cotton and Richard Mather, leading ministers of the colony's early days. A leading clergyman in his own right, he was deeply concerned about the lack of piety he saw all around him. In 1692, a shockingly large number of persons were accused of witchcraft in nearby Salem. Mather suspected that the Devil, jealous of the accomplishments of the Massachusetts Bay Colony, had set out to bring about its downfall. Although Mather advised against condemning the accused men and women solely on the testimony of their "victims," he eventually approved of the execution of twenty of them because the evidence in the case seemed overwhelming. Most educated people in the seventeenth century believed in witchcraft.

Three decades later, Mather played an important role in another episode, a role which casts a different light on his character. Like William Byrd, Mather was an avid reader. In a publication of the Royal Society, an English organization devoted to the discovery and dissemination of scientific knowledge, he had learned that the Turks had developed an inoculation against smallpox. When an epidemic swept Boston in 1721, he urged the town's physicians to use this new technique. In a day when few physicians had formal medical training, the opposition of Dr. William Douglass, who had a medical degree from the University of Edinburgh, carried great weight in the community. Only one doctor, Zabdiel Boylston, would agree to inoculate anyone. The results of the inoculation, however, were highly successful.

As you read the excerpts from Mather's diary which describe his feelings during these trying days, think about the following questions:

1. If, as Cotton Mather thought, God sent the smallpox to punish Boston for its wickedness, why did Mather also believe that he was following God's will by using science to fight the disease?
2. What do Mather's experiences during the smallpox epidemic tell us about popular attitudes in the eighteenth century?
3. Why did Mather meet so much opposition from his community? Why was it easier for Byrd to maintain social leadership in Virginia than it was for Mather in Massachusetts?

The Diary of Cotton Mather

Like many other men in the eighteenth century, Mather kept a diary in which he often entered his innermost thoughts. In the excerpts from the year 1721 which are printed below, we find him deeply worried about his duty to his own children and to the community he served.

Worthington C. Ford, ed., **The Diary of Cotton Mather 1709–1724.** Boston: Massachusetts Historical Society, 1911, 7th Series, vol. VIII, pp. 620–58 **passim.** Language simplified and modernized.

May 26 The grievous calamity of the smallpox has now entered Boston. The practice of preventing the smallpox by inoculation has never been used in America. But how many lives might be saved by it, if it were practiced? I will consult our physicians, and lay the matter before them.

May 28 The entrance of the smallpox into the town must awaken in me several thoughts about myself, besides a variety of duties to the people.

First, the glorious Lord employed me a few months ago to lecture the people of the city on approaching trouble and to predict the speedy approach of the Devil. I now must humble myself exceedingly and lie in the dust, for if I am the least vain because my prediction came true, God may do some grievous thing to me.

Secondly, I have two children that are liable to catch the disease. Should I keep them out of town? I must cry to Heaven for direction about it; I am on this occasion called to make sacrifices. If these dear children must lose their lives, the will of my Father must be submitted to.

Thirdly, my own life is likely to be in extreme danger for I must visit the sick.

June 6 My African servant is a candidate for baptism for he is afraid what may happen to him if the smallpox spreads. I must on this occasion try to make him a thorough Christian.

June 13 What shall I do? What shall I do, with regard to my son Sammy? He is home from Harvard College. The smallpox is spreading in our neighborhood and he is reluctant to return to Cambridge [probably for fear of spreading the disease]. I must earnestly look up to Heaven for direction.

My daughter Lizy is in greater fear than her brother. I must improve their states of mind to make their fears less important than their piety.

June 22 I am preparing a little treatise on the smallpox. First I awaken sentiments of piety, which are called for, and then explain the best medicines and methods which the world yet has for managing the disease. Finally, I add the discovery of inoculation, as the way to prevent smallpox. It is possible that this essay may save the lives and the souls of many people. Shall I give it unto the booksellers? I am awaiting direction [from God].

June 23 I am writing a letter to the physicians urging them to take into consideration the important matter of preventing smallpox by the use of inoculations.

June 24 Miserable neglected people are perishing from sickness. I must concern myself to have them looked after.

July 10 I must consider the various distresses of my flock as the grievous disease begins to distress the town. My prayers and sermons must be adapted to their conditions.

July 11 For Sammy, and Lizy, Oh! what shall I do?

July 13 The prayers to be made this day: for it is a day of humiliation throughout the province on the occasion of the calamity now upon miserable Boston.

July 16 At this time, I enjoy an unspeakable comfort. I have instructed our physicians in the method of inoculation to prevent and to lessen the dangers of the smallpox and to save the lives of those that are properly inoculated. The Destroyer [the Devil], being enraged at the proposal of anything that may keep the lives of our poor people from him, has taken a strange possession of the people on this occasion. They rave, they rebuke, they curse; they talk like frantic idiots. And not only the physician who began the inoculations, but I also am an object of their fury, of their furious abuse and insults.

My conformity to my Saviour in this thing, fills me with joy unspeakable and with glory.

July 17 What shall I do for those that have fled into other towns in order to escape the dangers of the smallpox? Give them books of piety. And unto a number of them in the neighboring town, I will go and preach a sermon.

July 18 The cursed clamor of people strangely and fiercely possessed by the Devil, will probably prevent my saving the lives of my two children from the smallpox by means of inoculation. So that I have no way left, but that of my continual and urgent cries to Heaven for their preservation. I urge them to pray for their own preservation.

August 15 My dear Sammy is now receiving a smallpox inoculation. The success of the inoculation among my neighbors, as well as abroad in the world, and the urgent call of his Grandfather for it, have made me think that I could not answer to God if I neglected it. At this time, much piety must be urged upon the child.

This day Sammy's dearest companion and chamber-fellow at college died of the smallpox. He was not inoculated.

August 22 My dear Sammy, having received the smallpox from the inoculation, now has the fever necessary to produce the eruption [the reaction to the inoculation]. But I have reason to fear that he had already caught smallpox when he was inoculated. If he should die, besides the loss of so hopeful a son, I should also suffer a monstrous hatred from an infuriated mob, whom the Devil has inspired with a most hellish rage. My continual prayers and cries, and offerings to Heaven, must be accompanied with suitable religious instructions to the child while our distresses are upon us.

August 25 It is a very critical time with me, a time of unspeakable trouble and anguish. My dear Sammy, has this week had a dangerous and threatening fever, which is beyond what the inoculation for the smallpox had hitherto brought upon others. In this distress, I have cried unto the Lord and he has answered with a measure of restraint upon the fever. The eruption and some degree of his fever still continue. His condition is very hazardous.

August 29 The condition of my son Samuel is very unusual. The inoculation was very imperfectly performed and scarcely any more than attempted upon him. And yet for all I know, it might prove a benefit to him. He is, however, endangered by the ungoverned fever that attends him. And in this distress, I know not what to do; but, O Lord, my eyes are upon thee!

September 4 The flock must hear me take a very solemn and bitter notice, that although the arrows of death are flying around us, and our young people are afraid for their lives, yet we are not aware that any notable effects of piety have been produced among them. Instead thereof, there is a rage of wickedness among us, beyond what was ever known from the beginning [the Creation] to this day.

September 5 Sammy recovering strength, I must now earnestly have him consider what he shall render to the Lord!

November 2 In the sermon this day, I may enlighten a few people of this miserable and detestable town with a talk on the loathsome disease.

November 3 This abominable town treats me in a most malicious and murderous manner, for my doing as Christ would have me do in saving the lives of the people from a horrible death. But I will go on in the imitation of my admirable Saviour and overcome evil with good. I will address a letter to the Lieutenant Governor and other gentlemen of New Hampshire to obtain from their charity a considerable quantity of wood for the poor of this loathsome town under the necessity of the hard winter coming on.

November 14 What an occasion, what an incentive for piety I have this morning. My kinsman, the minister of Roxbury [Massachusetts], being entertained at my house, said that he might undergo the smallpox inoculation and so return to his flock, which have the disease spreading among them.

Toward three o'clock in the night, as it grew toward morning of this day, some unknown hands threw a fired granado [a hand grenade] into the chamber where my kinsman lay and which used to be my bedroom. The weight of the iron ball alone, had it fallen upon his head, would have been enough to have done part of the deadly business for which it was designed. Also the granado was so charged, the upper part with dried powder, the lower part with a mixture of oil of turpentine and powder and what else I know not, that upon its going off, it would have split, and probably killed the persons in the room, and certainly burned the chamber and speedily laid the house in ashes. But this night there stood by me the Angel of the God, whose I am and whom I serve. The merciful providence of God my Saviour, so ordered it that the granado struck the iron in the middle of the casement window which turned it in such a way that in falling to the floor, the fuse was shaken out so the granado did not fire. When the granado was inspected, a paper was found tied to the fuse with a string, which had these words on it: "Cotton Mather, You Dog, Damn you. I'll inoculate you with this, with a pox to you."

November 16 Ought not the ministers of the town be called together so that we may consider what may be our duty and what could most properly be done upon the occasion of the Devil possessing the town.

November 22 I have some relatives and others as dear to me whom I will encourage to save their lives by having the smallpox inoculation.

November 23 I join with my aged father in publishing some *Sentiments on the Small-Pox Inoculated.* Christ crowns the cause for which I have suffered so much, with daily victories. And many lives may be saved by our testimony. Truth also will be rescued and maintained.

November 24 I am writing up the method of giving the inoculation of the smallpox and will send copies of it so that physicians around the country may know how to manage it.

December 14 The smallpox is causing terrible destruction in several parts of Europe. I will send to Holland an account of the astonishing success which we have had here with the inoculation. Who can tell, hundreds of thousands of lives may be saved by this communication.

11 The Public Conscience of a Philadelphia Printer

Modern American society abounds with voluntary organizations. The Community Chest, the Red Cross, the Boy and Girl Scouts, and dozens of similar activities fill the leisure time of millions of Americans. Each year, private citizens give billions of dollars to the public activities of their choice: the United Fund, college endowment drives, churches, and so forth. This great variety of voluntary activities helps to make American culture unique. Voluntary organizations in the United States originated in the thirteen colonies.

Benjamin Franklin (1706–1790) is an early example of this volunteer spirit. Son of a Boston maker of candles and soap, he ran away from his job as a printer's apprentice in 1723 at the age of seventeen. By 1763, he had achieved fame as a wealthy Philadelphia businessman, civic and educational leader, director of the postal system in the colonies, Pennsylvania political leader, colonial agent in London, author, publisher, inventor, and scientist. He gained further renown as a diplomat in France during the American Revolution and as a member of the convention that drew up the United States Constitution in 1787. During his lifetime, his contemporaries hailed him as a universal genius. It is hard to think of a more extraordinary colonial American. Yet Franklin's life reveals the main trends of his times, and his personality shows traits that are widely shared by Americans.

Throughout his life Franklin displayed remarkable qualities of leadership. Self-educated, he worked his way through the ranks of Philadelphia's mobile society to emerge as one of the outstanding leaders of his city, his colony, and the new nation. As you read the excerpts from his *Autobiography* which follow, think about the following questions:

1. What were Franklin's outstanding personal qualities? Why were these particular qualities useful to him in the role he chose to play in Philadelphia society?
2. What interested Franklin? What do these interests reveal about the society in which he lived?
3. Why was Franklin so successful in his attempts to get things done? What techniques did he use to enlist support for his enterprises?
4. How much time, if any, do you think private citizens should devote to volunteer work of the sort Franklin was involved in? What would a person have to give up in order to do volunteer work?

Benjamin Franklin's Autobiography

Epes Sargent, ed., **The Select Works of Benjamin Franklin, Including His Autobiography.** Boston: Philips, Samson and Company, 1854, pp. 200–02, 206–08, 212–16. Language simplified and modernized.

Franklin wrote his Autobiography, *an account of his life until 1757, during the years from 1771 to 1788. In the first part of this famous work, he gave an account of many of the public activities with which he was associated.*

I began now [about 1737] to turn my thoughts a little to public affairs, beginning, however, with small matters. The city watch was

The watch was the guard kept for the protection of the inhabitants of the city and their property.

one of the first things that I thought needed regulation. It was managed by the constables of the wards; each constable had a number of housekeepers attend him on the watch for the night. Those who chose never to attend paid him six shillings a year to be excused, which was supposed to be for hiring substitutes, but in reality was kept chiefly by the constable himself. Walking the rounds, too, was often neglected. I thereupon wrote a paper to be read in Junto representing these irregularities but insisting more particularly on the inequality of this six-shilling tax. A poor widow housekeeper, whose property to be guarded by the watch did not, perhaps, exceed the value of fifty pounds, paid as much as the wealthiest merchant who had thousands of pounds worth of goods in his stores.

I proposed to make the watch more effective by hiring men to do that job, and to make its support more equitable, I proposed a tax that would be proportioned according to the value of the property being protected. This idea was approved by the Junto and communicated to other clubs. The plan was not immediately carried out. Yet by preparing the minds of people for the change, it paved the way for the law obtained a few years after, when the members of our clubs had more influence.

Benjamin Franklin and some of his friends founded the secret Junto Club in 1727 for their mutual improvement. They wrote papers and conducted discussions on philosophical, scientific, and political topics. Other groups organized clubs patterned on the Junto.

About this time I wrote a paper (first read in Junto, but afterwards published) on the different accidents and carelessness by which houses were set on fire. I also included proposals for avoiding fires. This gave rise to forming a company for extinguishing fires and for mutual assistance in removing goods from burning buildings or from buildings threatened by fire. Thirty supporters of this scheme were found. According to our agreement, every member was to keep in good order and fit for use, a certain number of leather buckets with strong bags and baskets [for packing and transporting goods]. These were to be brought to every fire. We agreed to meet once a month and spend a social evening together discussing such ideas as occurred to us upon the subject of fires.

The usefulness of this institution soon appeared, and many more volunteers wanted to be admitted than we thought convenient for one company. They were advised to form another company, which was done. And this went on, one new company being formed after another, until they included most of the inhabitants who owned property. The small fines paid by members for absence from the monthly meetings have been applied to the purchase of fire engines [pumps on wheels], ladders, firehooks, and other useful implements for each company, so that I question whether there is a city in the world better provided with the means of putting a stop to fires.

My business was now continually growing and my circumstances growing daily easier. My newspaper had become very profitable, as for a time it was almost the only one in this and the neighboring provinces [colonies].

I had on the whole good reason to be satisfied with my life in Pennsylvania. There were, however, two things that I regretted: there was no militia nor any college.

With respect to defense, Spain had been at war against Britain for several years. Finally France joined Spain which brought us into greater danger. Because Governor Thomas had failed to get our Quaker Assembly to pass a militia law and to make other provisions for the security of the province, I determined to try what might be done by a voluntary association of the people. To promote this, I first wrote and published a pamphlet, entitled *Plain Truth,* in which I stated our defenseless situation in strong terms, with the need for union and discipline for our defense. The pamphlet had a sudden and surprising effect. I was called upon to draft a plan for a militia. Having settled the draft of it with a few friends, I called a meeting of the citizens. The house was pretty full. I harangued [lectured] them a little on the subject, read the paper, and explained it, and then distributed copies I had printed which the citizens eagerly signed.

Great Britain had declared war on Spain in 1739 (War of Jenkins' Ear) and on France in 1744 (War of the Austrian Succession; King George's War, in America). Franklin was concerned because French and Spanish privateers operated in Delaware Bay.

When the company separated and the papers were collected, we found about twelve hundred had signed. Other copies were distributed in the country, and at length upward of ten thousand signed. These all furnished themselves as soon as they could, with arms, formed themselves into companies and regiments, chose their own officers, and met every week to be instructed in manual exercise and other parts of military discipline.

The officers of the companies composing the Philadelphia regiment met and chose me for their colonel. Believing myself unfit, I declined that position and recommended another man of influence, who was accordingly appointed. I then proposed a lottery to cover the expense of building a battery [an emplacement for artillery] below the town and furnishing it with cannon. We bought some old cannon from Boston, and we wrote to England for more. Meanwhile we borrowed some cannon from Governor Clinton of New York. The volunteers kept a nightly guard while the war lasted. And among the rest I regularly took my turn of duty there as a common soldier.

My activity in these operations was agreeable to the Governor and Council. They took me into their confidence, and I was consulted by them in every measure wherein their agreement was thought useful to the militia. Calling in the aid of religion, I proposed a fast to them to promote reformation and to seek the blessing of Heaven on our undertaking. They agreed, but as it was the first fast ever thought of in the province [Pennsylvania], the Secretary had no precedent from which to draw up the proclamation. My education in New England, where a fast is proclaimed every year, was here of some advantage. I drew up the proclamation in the accustomed style; it was translated into German and circulated through the province. This gave the clergy of the different sects an opportunity to influence their congregations to join the militia.

In order of time, I should have mentioned before that in 1742 I invented an open stove that would warm rooms better and at the same time save fuel. To promote the growing demand for the stove, I wrote and published a pamphlet entitled, *An Account of the New-Invented Pennsylvania Fireplaces.*

When peace was concluded [1748] and the militia business therefore at an end, I turned my thoughts again to establishing an academy. The first step I took was to tell my plans to a number of my active friends, of whom the [members of the] Junto furnished a good part. The next was to write and publish a pamphlet entitled *Proposals Relating to the Education of Youth in Pennsylvania.* This I distributed free among the principal inhabitants. As soon as I could suppose their minds were a little prepared by reading it, I solicited funds for opening and supporting an academy. If I remember right, we got no less than five thousand pounds.

In the proposals for the academy, I stated their publication was not an act of mine, but of some "public-spirited gentleman"; avoiding as much as I could, according to my usual rule, presenting myself to the public as the author of any scheme for their benefit.

Those who contributed funds to carry out the project chose twenty-four trustees and appointed Mr. Francis, then Attorney General, and myself to draw up constitutions for the government of the academy. When that was signed, a house was hired, masters engaged, and the school opened, I think, in the same year, 1749.

It is to be noted that the contributions to this building were made by people of different religious sects. Care was taken in nominating trustees, in whom the building and ground were to be entrusted, that control should not be given to any one sect. It was for this reason that one from each sect was appointed—one Church of England man, one Presbyterian, one Baptist, one Moravian, etc. A vacancy caused by death was to be filled by an election of those who had contributed funds. The Moravian happened not to please his colleagues, and on his death they resolved to have no other of that sect. The difficulty then was, how to avoid having two of some other sect. Several persons were named and for that reason not agreed to. At length one mentioned me, with the observation that I was merely an honest man, and of no sect at all—which caused them to choose me.

The Moravians were a religious group from central Europe who traced their origin to the religious reformer John Huss (1369?–1415).

The trustees of the academy after a while were incorporated by a charter from the Governor; their funds were increased by contributions in Britain and grants of land from the proprietaries [men to whom the King had granted land], to which the Assembly has since made considerable addition. Thus was established the University of Philadelphia [now the University of Pennsylvania].

When I disengaged myself from private business, I flattered myself that, by the sufficient though moderate fortune I had acquired, I had secured leisure for the rest of my life for philosophical studies and amusements. I purchased all of Dr. Spence[r]'s apparatus [for experiments with electricity] who had come from England to lecture here and I proceeded in my electrical experiments with great haste. But the public now considered me a man of leisure. They laid hold of me for their purposes—every part of our civil government imposing some duty upon me. The Governor put me into the commission of the peace; the corporation of the city chose me for the common council and soon after as an alderman. The citizens at large elected me a Burgess to represent them in the Assembly.

I was re-elected to the Assembly every year for ten years without my ever asking any citizen for his vote or indicating either directly or indirectly any desire of being chosen.

12 The Success of British America

HISTORICAL ESSAY

By eighteenth-century standards British America was a flourishing place. Its relatively free religious atmosphere and its abundant economic opportunities continued to attract thousands of immigrants. Its growing commerce created fortunes for merchants in both America and Britain and helped to raise the standard of living of hundreds of thousands of other persons. Its governments, which had a great deal of local control, generally had the warm support of the inhabitants. Its physical security became assured in 1763 when France lost virtually all its possessions in America. Thus, except for Indians and Negro slaves, the British colonies deserved the reputation of a land of opportunity. A French immigrant, Michel-Guillaume Jean de Crèvecoeur, described the society in his classic *Letters from an American Farmer* in 1782:

> The rich and the poor are not so far removed from each other as they are in Europe. Some few towns excepted, we are all tillers of the earth, from Nova Scotia to West Florida. We are a people of cultivators, scattered over an immense territory, communicating with each other by means of good roads and navigable

rivers, united by the silken bands of mild government, all respecting the laws, without dreading their power, because they are equitable. We are all animated with the spirit of an industry which is unfettered and unrestrained, because each person works for himself.

The Colonists Multiply

A good measure of the favorable conditions of life in British America in the 1700's can be found in its rate of population growth, the fastest in the world. The colonists doubled in number every twenty-five years. A man born in 1700 who lived until 1763 saw the population of the mainland colonies grow from about 250,000 to more than 1,600,000, as the graph on this page indicates. Much of this increase resulted from longer lives and more births (Benjamin Franklin estimated, probably with some exaggeration, that the birth rate was double that of Europe), but much also came from the stream of immigrants.

The newcomers came from several areas. Hundreds of thousands of Scottish Presbyterians who had settled in northern Ireland now abandoned the depressed economy of that region. Many thousands of Irish Catholics joined them. Since these settlers were usually impoverished, many came as indentured servants; others moved quickly to the back country where land was cheap. By the 1760's, the Scotch-Irish made up a high proportion of the frontiersmen and small farmers of the Appalachian region, from Pennsylvania south into western Maryland, Virginia, and the Carolinas.

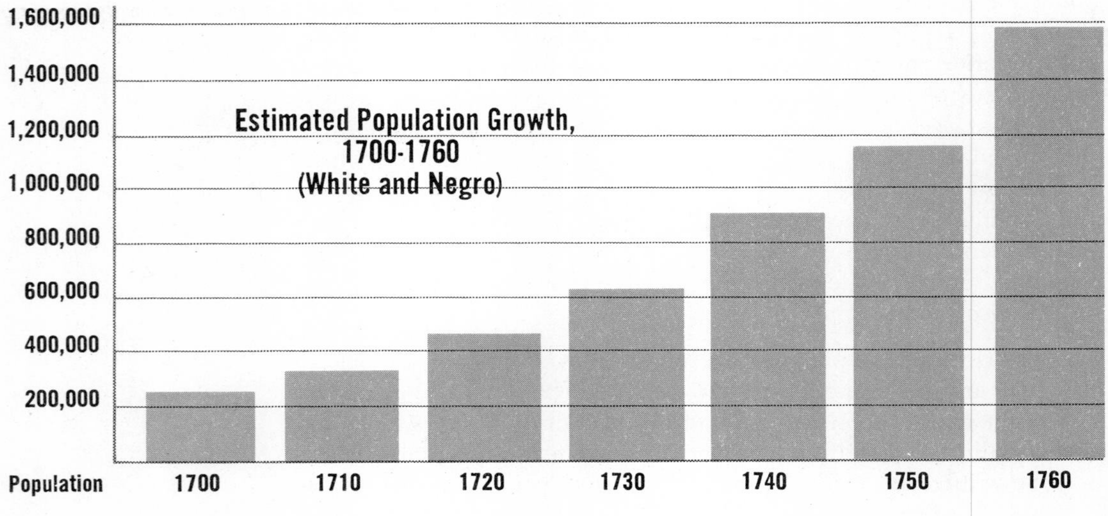

Persecutions of religious minorities and hard economic conditions contributed to the unrest that sent between one and two hundred thousand Germans to the British colonies. Many came as indentured servants, but some came in organized communities. They settled in large numbers in Pennsylvania, with its vast reserves of land suited to farming and its tolerant religious policies.

The Africans who came to America grew to constitute the largest non-English group in the colonies. Here economic opportunity played a cruel role; the booming economy and shortage of labor in the colonies made it profitable to import slaves. Until the late 1600's, there were many slaves in the West Indies, but few in the mainland colonies. When England gave the Royal African Company a monopoly of the slave trade to the colonies, the company brought more than 50,000 slaves to America between 1680 and 1688. During the 1700's, the slave trade, now open to all English or colonial merchants, reached such heights that by 1776 Negroes in the mainland colonies numbered half a million, one fifth of the population. More than nine tenths of the Africans and their descendants lived in the plantation colonies south of Pennsylvania. They outnumbered the whites in South Carolina and Virginia.

While most colonists came from the British Isles, with those of English ancestry still in the majority, the immigration of the 1700's produced a population of which a large minority—perhaps a third—was non-British. Some effects of this new diversity were striking; many German groups remained apart, speaking their own language, and Negroes, even when freed, were kept in an inferior position, either by law or by custom. But English remained the language of law, politics, higher education, and trade. The newer immigrants soon began the slow process of blending with the older.

Town, Farm, Plantation, and City

"We are a people of cultivators," wrote Crèvecoeur in 1782. In 1750, this was even truer; more than ninety percent of the colonists made their living directly from the land by raising crops and animals, or by taking timber and other products from the still abundant forests of the coastal plains and hills. Yet their patterns of life—the ways they spent their hours at work, at worship, in politics, and at leisure—differed considerably from region to region.

Many of the differences that set a Connecticut man apart from a Carolinian, or a New Yorker from a Virginian, had to do with their different economies. New England's hilly, rocky, and sandy lands discouraged the creation of large plantations. Small farms were the rule. At first the landholders of a New England town—the unit of local government—settled close together in villages, surrounded by their fields, pastures, and woodland. Community life centered around a tavern or inn and the meetinghouse, where both religious services and civic affairs took place. As time went on, men who received grants of land in outlying towns often sold it to newcomers or divided it among their children. Farmhouses began to be scattered farther away from the villages.

Elsewhere in the colonies, with few exceptions, social life was more dispersed. On large plantations, such as those in the tobacco, indigo, and rice-growing regions, or on the great estates of the fertile Hudson Valley, landowners lived on their property, often at great distances from their neighbors. This dispersion of population made the county the effective unit of local government. Where the Anglican church was strong, as in Virginia, the church parish assumed responsibility for taxing the inhabitants to provide certain civic services, such as the care of the poor. Both the county justices of the peace and the parish vestrymen were made up mainly of large landowners, like William Byrd.

Each of these kinds of communities—town, village, isolated farm, plantation—concerned itself with the land and its products. Hence all of them had more in common than any of them had with the colonial city. There the merchant, concerned with buying and selling, importing and exporting, dominated the life of the community, to the regret of conservative ministers like Cotton Mather. Of these cities there were but a handful in 1750. Boston, Newport, New York, Philadelphia, Baltimore, and Charleston were the largest, and no other deserved the name of city. The problems of the countryside were still the old ones of weather, crops, and perhaps Indians. The problems of the city, such as Benjamin Franklin found in Philadelphia, were such relatively new ones as fire and police protection, sanitation, pavements, and vice. These urban centers grew rapidly. All were larger than most English cities, and Philadelphia, which reached a population of 40,000 by 1776, was probably the second largest city in the British empire.

The rural and urban worlds of the British colonists thus differed considerably from each other in occupation and social life. Other than their general use of English as a language and their allegiance to Britain, did these worlds have much in common?

Relations among the Colonies

The eighteenth century witnessed rapid growth in kinds of communication that gave colonists more knowledge of each other. All the colonies had printing presses, and colonial newspapers circulated widely. As time passed, the newspapers gradually included more news of America, rather than of Britain or other countries, and showed a greater sense of the identity of the colonists as British Americans rather than as just British. The postal system, which Benjamin Franklin did so much to improve, conveyed private letters as well as newspapers with speed and regularity, although much mail was still carried by private persons. The fact that literacy and education were widespread, especially in New England, made such improvements in communication all the more important.

Colonial religious life, on the other hand, showed less unity. In terms of organization, the colonies had few religious connections. The Anglican Church, which might have been able to unify its parishes in the southern colonies, where it was established as the official Christian church, did not even send a bishop to the colonies. The planters ran their parishes more or less as they pleased. Other Protestant denominations tended to be even more individualistic. Their churches were always splitting over problems of doctrine and the personalities of ministers and lay leaders. The Great Awakening, a religious revival that swept Protestant churches from one end of the colonies to the other during the 1740's and 1750's, divided many Congregational, Presbyterian, and Baptist congregations and ministers between those who welcomed the emotional revivals and those who opposed them. Yet it also increased the flow of communication from North to South and from backwoods to seacoast, and strengthened the deep loyalties of the colonists to individualistic forms of Protestantism.

The Market Economy Grows

Of the several currents that moved in the 1700's to bring colonists closer to one another in knowledge and self-interest, commerce was perhaps the most important.

Crèvecoeur, in his picture of an American paradise, stressed that "each person works for himself." But more and more Americans in the eighteenth century were voluntarily giving up one part of their independence: subsistence agriculture with which they supplied all their own needs and sold none of their products. Instead, wherever landholdings were large, soil was fertile, management was enterprising, or farming was specialized, the farmer produced substantial surpluses for market and quickly became a larger consumer of goods produced elsewhere. He became an important part of a market economy that was often intercolonial or international.

In this way different kinds of farmers, such as the Virginia tobacco planter, the South Carolina rice grower, the Pennsylvania wheat raiser, and the Rhode Island horse breeder, helped to develop colonial commerce. So did the lumberman from New Hampshire, the fisherman from Massachusetts, and the operators of small iron mines and forges scattered through the colonies. In the cities, craftsmen and professional men found themselves bound tightly to the commercial world. Because all these persons now bought and sold in an intercolonial and international market, they became more and more sensitive to prices, the dangers of war to commerce, and governmental regulation of trade. William Byrd's complaints in 1709 about the low price of tobacco and his eager anticipation of the end of the long war with France and Spain illustrate some of their concerns.

Except for the southern planters, whose trade went directly to British markets, most colonists who produced goods for sale put their produce into the hands of a colonial merchant. It was he who usually commissioned the building of ships, arranged to have them manned, and sent them out of harbors laden with produce. Since international business agreements were often hard to enforce, the merchant tried to do business with men he knew he could trust. Thus, often the ship's captain was a relative of the merchant. The merchants to whom goods were consigned in the British West Indies, in other colonial ports, or in London or Bristol in England, were often relatives too.

Since the country which received colonial goods sometimes produced little that the colony wanted in return, merchants and captains often planned triangular voyages to make the greatest profits, as the map on this page indicates. For instance, a Newport, Rhode Island merchant might import a cargo of West Indian molasses and have it turned into rum in one of the colony's many distilleries. He could make great profits with this rum—more than enough to pay the West Indian sugar planters and to cover shipping costs—by sending it to

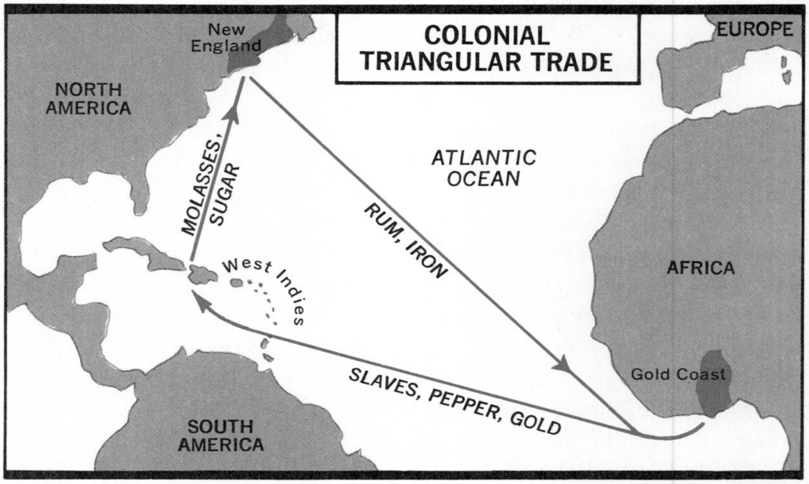

Africa. There the cargo of rum received a warm welcome by traders on the west coast of that continent. With rum they could buy slaves captured in wars or raids by native chiefs, many of whom made a business of supplying the traders. With a cargo of slaves, the Newport captain sailed again for the West Indies. There the harsh life of the sugar plantations, which gave slaves a life expectancy of only six or seven years, demanded a steady supply of this human commodity.

Perhaps, however, the trader dropped anchor at one of the French or Spanish islands in the West Indies, where slaves were also in demand but where molasses was cheaper. With another cargo of molasses aboard, as well as some pieces of gold (if it had been a profitable voyage), the captain appeared again a few weeks later in his home port. To avoid paying the tax of sixpence a gallon on foreign molasses, imposed by Parliament in 1733, the captain or the merchant who financed him had little difficulty in bribing a customs officer. For a penny or so a gallon, the latter might accept false papers from the captain, showing a different port of origin, a different cargo, or a much smaller number of casks of molasses.

A profitable but illegal commerce grew up between colonial shippers and those in France, Spain, the Netherlands, and their colonies. For nearly two thirds of the eighteenth century, the British did little to enforce their customs duties. One reason for this was that they often found themselves at war with France and Spain and needed the cooperation of their American colonies.

Conflicts among Expanding Empires

Bitter international rivalries drew Britain, France, and Spain into war repeatedly. Each war they fought involved their colonists and the Indian tribes in America. The chart on page 86 indicates the major eighteenth-century wars.

In three wars fought between 1689 and 1748 by the British and their colonists against the French and their Indian allies, the French gave up Acadia (Nova Scotia), Newfoundland, and Hudson Bay. Other significant gains were made against the Spanish, who yielded to the British in 1713 the "asiento." This act contributed greatly to British and colonial participation in the slave trade. Then Spain gave way without war in a dispute over the land south of South Carolina, where the British established the colony of Georgia in 1733.

The "asiento" was a contract in which Spain granted the South Sea Company, an English company, the right to carry 4800 Negro slaves a year into Spanish colonies for thirty years.

A fourth war, commonly called the French and Indian War [1754–1763], decided the fate of France in America. This time the colonists were more deeply involved than ever. In 1754, George Washington, a Virginia militia colonel, tried in vain to oust the French from Fort Duquesne, a key position at the fork of the Ohio River. He returned

Dates	War in America	War in Europe	Treaty ending war
1689–1697	**King William's War** English and Iroquois fought French.	**War of the League of Augsburg** England joined the Grand Alliance (League of Augsburg and Holland) to fight France.	**Treaty of Ryswick, 1697** Restored the status in the colonies that existed before the war.
1702–1713	**Queen Anne's War** English colonists fought the French, Spanish, and several Indian tribes.	**War of the Spanish Succession** England, Holland, and the Holy Roman Empire united against France and Spain.	**Treaty of Utrecht, 1713** England received Newfoundland, Acadia (Nova Scotia), and Hudson Bay from France. France kept some small islands in Canada. Spain granted England asiento.
1739–1742	**War of Jenkins' Ear** Southern colonists fought Spanish colonists.	**War of Jenkins' Ear** England declared war on Spain because of abuses of English seamen (provoked by English abuses of asiento).	
1740–1748	**King George's War** English colonists in Northeast fought French and many Indian tribes.	**War of the Austrian Succession** France joined Spain in fight against England. France had been allied with Prussia.	**Treaty of Aix-la-Chappelle, 1748** Restored the status in the colonies that existed before the war.
1754–1763	**The French and Indian War** English colonists and Iroquois fought French and most other Indians.	**Seven Years' War (began 1756)** Britain and Prussia fought France and Austria. Spain joined France in 1762.	**Treaty of Paris, 1763** France ceded to England most of the land east of the Mississippi. England gained Florida and restored Cuba to Spain.

there a year later as a subordinate to General Edward Braddock, commander of a large force of British regulars and colonial militia, only to retreat again as the French and their Indian allies trapped and smashed the expedition, killing Braddock. The French were determined to hold the Ohio Valley and keep the restless British colonists east of the Appalachian Mountains.

The struggle became European in scope in 1756 (Seven Years' War) when Britain formally declared war on France, and Austria and Prussia entered the conflict. For two more years Britain and the colonists suffered nothing but defeats and losses. The tide turned in

1758 under William Pitt, Britain's inspired Prime Minister. Two young, fresh leaders, Generals James Wolfe and Jeffrey Amherst, combined forces to recapture Louisbourg while General John Forbes, aided by George Washington, led an army over the mountains to capture Fort Duquesne. It was renamed Fort Pitt. The following year, Wolfe invaded the St. Lawrence Valley, besieged and then took Quebec at the cost of his own life. Further British victories led to a peace treaty in 1763 that ended France's rule in Canada. France was also obliged to cede Louisiana to Spain as compensation for the loss of Florida to the British.

If the results of this world war constituted a nearly total victory for Britain, she paid a high price for that success. She had financed Prussia to fight the European continental battles against France and Austria and had borne the staggering costs of maintaining supremacy at sea and mounting dozens of campaigns in the New World and in

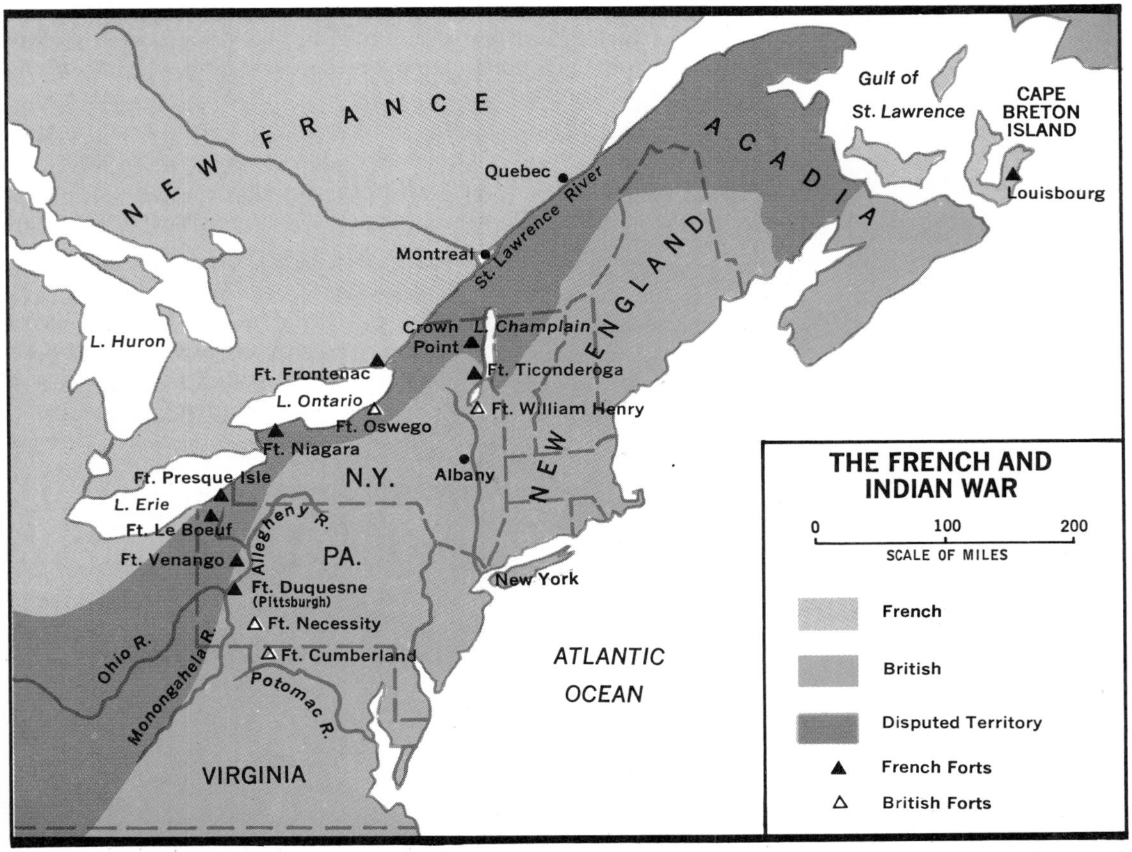

India. The colonies contributed men to campaigns but were repaid for their expenses; it was the only way, Pitt found, to get them to take an effective part in the war. Now several new questions arose. How would Britain and the colonies organize and use their rich new territories and trade? How would the ousting of France from North America affect the relationships of Britain and her colonies, now that they no longer needed each other for defense against the French? How could Britain pay off the heavy costs of the war?

SUGGESTED READINGS

DAVIDSON, BASIL, *The African Slave Trade.* The author recounts the story of the traffic that formed a tragic chapter in the history of the American people.

DONOVAN, FRANK R., *The Many Worlds of Benjamin Franklin.* This fully illustrated book tells the story of the man who was hailed in his own time as both universal genius and typical American.

GALLMAN, ROBERT E., *Developing the American Colonies, 1607–1783.* This slim volume traces the major events in the economic development of the American colonies during the colonial period.

MILLER, JOHN C., *The First Frontier: Life in Colonial America.* The author has compiled a wealth of illuminating and often humorous details about colonial courtship, marriage, children, education, food and drink, sports and recreations, dress, religion, crime and punishment, slavery, and various other topics.

PARKMAN, FRANCIS, *The Seven Years War,* (edited by John H. McCallum). Parkman, one of America's greatest historians, told dramatically the story of the encounters of French, English, and Indians in the wildernesses and settlements of America. Here the editor has chosen selections from three of Parkman's books which dealt with the climactic struggle for control of the continent.

The American Revolution

STATING THE ISSUE

CHAPTER 4

The future of Great Britain and its American colonies looked bright in 1763. The Treaty of Paris signed in that year ended the French and Indian War. Britain now governed all of North America east of the Mississippi River, as well as large parts of India and some previously disputed islands in the West Indies.

The war had created some tensions between the colonists and the mother country, however. To the indignation of English patriots, many colonial merchants had continued to trade with the French West Indies. Moreover, the colonists had paid only a small part of the cost of the far-flung war. Finally, British commanders had frequently belittled colonial soldiers for their lack of discipline and military competence. But the colonists' loyalty to the mother country had stood the test of war. Throughout America, colonists celebrated the British victory and praised both king and mother country.

The colonists now hoped to expand their thriving trade. With the French gone from the interior of the continent and hostilities with the Indians diminished, settlers began to move across the Appalachian Mountains into the Ohio River Valley and the Kentucky wilderness. In increasing numbers, immigrants arrived to swell the growing population of the colonies.

Both the costs of war and the responsibilities of victory brought new problems to Great Britain. Between 1754 and 1763, Britain's national debt had doubled and the expenses of administering the empire had steadily increased. With additional possessions in North America, the West Indies, and India, Britain faced the task of reorganizing her increasingly complex colonial system. It wanted better control of territories but it also wanted the colonists to pay for the costs of administration.

Less than twenty years after the American colonies celebrated the British victory over France, they celebrated their own victory over Great Britain in the American Revolution. Chapter 4 traces the history of the colonies and the new nation between 1763 and 1783. Why did the Revolution break out? How did the colonists justify revolt? How were the Americans able to win their freedom from the mother country? These are the major issues of Chapter 4.

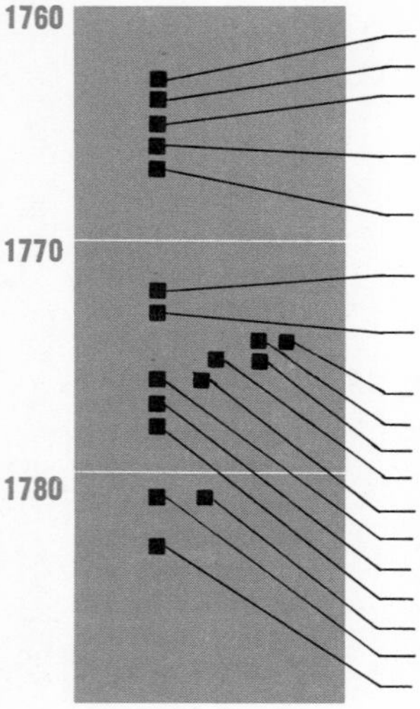

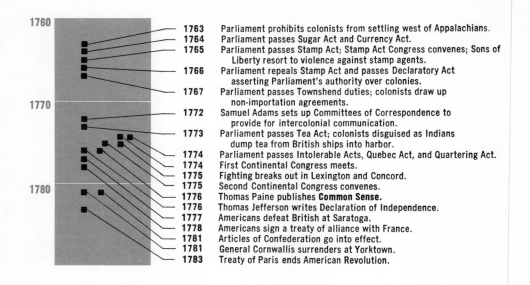

1763 Parliament prohibits colonists from settling west of Appalachians.
1764 Parliament passes Sugar Act and Currency Act.
1765 Parliament passes Stamp Act; Stamp Act Congress convenes; Sons of Liberty resort to violence against stamp agents.
1766 Parliament repeals Stamp Act and passes Declaratory Act asserting Parliament's authority over colonies.
1767 Parliament passes Townshend duties; colonists draw up non-importation agreements.
1772 Samuel Adams sets up Committees of Correspondence to provide for intercolonial communication.
1773 Parliament passes Tea Act; colonists disguised as Indians dump tea from British ships into harbor.
1774 Parliament passes Intolerable Acts, Quebec Act, and Quartering Act.
1774 First Continental Congress meets.
1775 Fighting breaks out in Lexington and Concord.
1775 Second Continental Congress convenes.
1776 Thomas Paine publishes **Common Sense.**
1776 Thomas Jefferson writes Declaration of Independence.
1777 Americans defeat British at Saratoga.
1778 Americans sign a treaty of alliance with France.
1781 Articles of Confederation go into effect.
1781 General Cornwallis surrenders at Yorktown.
1783 Treaty of Paris ends American Revolution.

13 The Colonists Respond to New Regulations

Until 1763, the American colonies had enjoyed a large measure of autonomy under British rule. Great Britain, occupied with its own problems, had controlled the colonies only loosely for a century and a half. Customs officers failed to enforce laws intended to regulate trade, and colonial merchants smuggled goods into the country without paying duties. Colonial legislatures paid the salaries of the governors and, therefore, exercised considerable influence over the king's official representatives. The American colonists had become accustomed to controlling their own affairs.

When the French and Indian War ended, however, Great Britain decided to tighten its control over its large and prosperous empire in North America. The British government announced a number of measures in rapid succession. The new program began with a thorough reform of the customs service. Britain appointed additional customs officers and instructed them to pay strict attention to their duties or face dismissal. In order to enforce the trade laws, the government directed customs officials to keep accurate accounts of all imports and exports, of revenue collected, and of illegal trade. The governors and army and navy officers were ordered to support and protect customs officials as they carried out their responsibilities.

To help ease its financial burdens, Parliament needed additional revenue. In addition to enforcing old regulations, Parliament decided to pass and enforce new laws. In 1764, the Sugar Act lowered the tariff on molasses, but provided machinery to collect duties. Merchants accused of smuggling were to be tried by judges in Vice-Admiralty courts instead of by juries of their peers in civil courts. Colonial merchants complained that the duties would hurt their businesses; colonial lawyers argued that the system of enforcement violated the citizen's right to a trial by jury.

These changes in taxation and administrative policies touched off a vigorous debate among American colonists about the controls exercised by Great Britain. This debate was carried on in pamphlets and newspapers, and in the colonial legislatures for the next twelve years. The two excerpts which follow, written in 1764, are early definitions of the colonial position. As you read, keep these questions in mind:

1. What was the political ideology upon which James Otis based his argument? What did he mean by the phrase "the law of nature" (or natural law)?
2. What conclusion did Otis reach about the rights of the colonies to make decisions for themselves? What conclusion did he reach about the role of Parliament in making decisions for the colonies?
3. In the next to last paragraph in this excerpt, Otis argued that the colonists ought to obey all laws passed by Parliament even though some might seem to violate natural rights. Was this argument consistent with the position he took in the first part of his pamphlet?
4. How did the New York Petition define the relationship between British and colonial political institutions?

Political ideology is the body of ideas, beliefs, attitudes, values, and goals underlying political decisions.

The Rights of the British Colonies

James Otis won his reputation as Boston's most brilliant lawyer. In 1761, representing a number of merchants, he had argued against writs of assistance. After Parliament passed the Sugar Act, he wrote The Rights of the British Colonies Asserted and Proved, *a pamphlet which became famous in the colonies. This reading summarizes the argument Otis presented in that pamphlet.*

The customs officers used writs of assistance, or blanket search warrants, which permitted them to enter homes or warehouses without showing evidence that illegal goods might be stored there.

Is government founded on an agreement between the people and those who govern? Or is government founded on property? It is not altogether founded on either. Then has government any solid foundation that does not change? I think it has an everlasting foundation in the will of God, the creator of nature, whose laws never vary. The same Creator of the universe who made the planets revolve in beauti-

James Otis, **The Rights of the British Colonies Asserted and Proved.** Boston: Edes and Gill, 1764. Language simplified and modernized.

ful order also caused the sexes to attract each other and form families. In turn, families naturally form larger communities which require governments. Government is therefore founded on human nature. It is no arbitrary thing depending merely on an agreement for its existence.

Otis refers here to the ideas of the English scientist and mathematician, Sir Isaac Newton (1642–1727), whose statement of the laws of gravitation promoted the notion that the affairs of men, like the motions of the planets around the sun, might be governed by "natural laws."

Because government is founded on human nature, a supreme power must exist in every society, from whose final decisions there can be no appeal except directly to Heaven. I say this supreme, absolute power is originally and ultimately in the people, and that they can never give this power away since it comes from God.

Government exists to provide for the good of the whole. "Let the good of the people be the supreme law" is the law of nature and part of that grand charter given the human race by God, the only monarch who has a clear and indisputable right to absolute power. Hence, it is contrary to reason that supreme, unlimited power should be in the hands of one man.

Here Otis reflects the ideas of the English philosopher, John Locke (1632–1704), who argued in **The Second Treatise on Government** that nature entitled man to life, liberty, and property.

Since the purpose of government is to promote the welfare of mankind, above all things it should provide for the happy enjoyment of life, liberty, and property. If each individual living by himself could enjoy life, liberty, and property fully, there would be no need for government. But the experience of ages has proved that by nature men are weak, imperfect beings. They cannot live independently of each other, and yet they cannot live together without conflict. To settle conflict, men need an arbitrator.

By nature and by right, the individuals of each society may have any form of government they please. The same law of nature and reason applies equally to a democracy, an aristocracy, or a monarchy. Whenever the administrators of any government depart from truth, justice, and equity [fairness], they should be opposed. If they prove incorrigible, they should be deposed by the people.

The form of government should be settled by an agreement or compact. In Great Britain that compact was made after the abdication of James II. His successors and Parliament agreed to rule under this compact.

After King James II was deposed, and Mary and her husband William of Orange accepted an invitation to become the king and queen of England, they agreed to obey the Bill of Rights. Thereafter, Parliament was the supreme power in Great Britain.

The American colonists, being men, are equally entitled to all the rights of nature. They are also subject to and dependent upon Great Britain. Therefore, Parliament has the authority to make laws for the general good of the colonists.

Every British subject born in America is by the law of God and nature, and by common law and act of Parliament entitled to all the rights of our fellow subjects in Great Britain. One of these rights is that no man's property can be taken away from him without his consent given either personally or through his representative. Any tax levied on those not represented in Parliament deprives them of their most essential rights as free men.

I believe, however, that all acts of the King and Parliament, even those that closely affect the interests of the colonists, must be obeyed while they remain in force. Only Parliament can repeal its own acts. There would be an end of all government if subjects should take it upon themselves to judge the justice of an act of Parliament and refuse to obey it. Therefore, let Parliament lay what burden they please on us; it is our duty to obey. If Parliament can be convinced that its acts are not constitutional or not for the common good, they should repeal them.

To say that Parliament is absolute and arbitrary contradicts natural law. Parliament can in all cases declare what it thinks is good for the whole; but the declaration of Parliament alone does not make a thing good. There is in every instance a higher authority, namely God. Should an act of Parliament violate any of His natural laws, the act would be contrary to eternal truth, equity, and justice, and consequently would be void. Parliament would repeal such an act when it became convinced of its mistake.

The New York Petition to the House of Commons

In October 1764, the New York General Assembly adopted a petition to send to Britain's House of Commons. In the petition, the Assembly gave its definition of what it believed to be Parliament's authority over the colonies. The following selection is from that petition.

Journal of the Votes and Proceedings of the General Assembly of the Colony of New York. New York: 1766, vol. 2. Language simplified and modernized.

Since 1683, the government of this colony has had three branches: a Governor and a Council appointed by the Crown, and an Assembly. The Representatives to the Assembly have been chosen by the people. Besides the power to make laws for the colony, the Assembly has enjoyed the right to tax people for the support of the government.

The founders and early settlers of the colony hoped that they had a constitution under which the rights and privileges of the people would not change.

It is, therefore, with concern and surprise, that they have recently seen indications that the Parliament of Great Britain plans to impose taxes upon people in New York by laws to be passed in Britain. We believe this action would absolutely ruin the colony. So it is our duty to trouble you with our claim that we should be exempt from all taxes that we have not levied ourselves.

We cannot be justly criticized for not raising adequate taxes. The King and the governors have admitted that in the past our taxes have equaled our ability to pay. Our contribution to the French and Indian war surpassed our ability to pay even in the opinion of Parliament.

Exemption from the burden of taxes we have not passed ourselves must be a principle of every free state. Without this right there can be no liberty, no happiness, no security. It is inseparable from the very idea of property, for who can call that his own, which may be taken away by another?

If our contributions to the support of the government or for the maintenance of an army to subdue the Indians were necessary, why would we refuse to raise taxes? It would be in our own interest to do so.

The House of Commons should not interpret this plea as a desire for independence from the supreme power of Parliament. We cannot be guilty of so extravagant a disregard of our own interests. For from where else except Parliament can we hope for protection? We reject the thought of independence from Parliament with the utmost abhorrence.

The peaceful submission of the colonies to Britain during the past century denies such a motive. Has not the whole trade of North America been from the beginning controlled by Parliament? And whatever some people may pretend, his Majesty's American subjects have no desire to invade the just rights of Great Britain to regulate commerce. We think the Mother Country has the indisputable power to make laws for the advancement of her own trade, as long as she does not violate the rights of the colonies. But the colonies claim the right to which they are entitled: exemption from all duties not related to British trade.

Therefore, the General Assembly of New York, in devotion to its constituents, expresses the most earnest plea that Parliament not levy any duties on our commerce, except those necessary to regulate trade. Instead Parliament should permit the legislature of the colony to impose all other taxes upon its own people which circumstances may require.

Furthermore, when we consider the wisdom of our ancestors in establishing trial by juries, we regret that the Laws of Trade have transferred cases from the civil courts to the Vice-Admiralty courts. These military courts do not abide by the civil laws, nor are they always filled by wise and honest judges. We suggest that trials held in these courts assume an amazing confidence in the integrity of judges and such trials give great grief to his Majesty's American subjects.

This sentence refers to the provision of the Sugar Act of 1764 which stated that merchants arrested for violating the act should be tried in a military court rather than by a jury of their peers in a civil court.

The General Assembly of this colony has no desire to take legitimate power away from the Parliament of Great Britain. It cannot, however, avoid pleading against the loss of such rights as we have enjoyed previously.

14 The Conflict Sharpens

In the debate over the political relationship between the mother country and the colonies, the British took the position that Parliament represented all British subjects whether or not they sent representatives to it. The Americans maintained that Parliament could not tax them because they were not represented in Parliament. Yet the colonists spent little effort seeking direct representation in Parliament. They preferred to argue that their interests were largely separate from those of Britain. From their point of view, the colonists had grown and prospered without an elaborate tax program. The broader problems of the empire did not concern them.

The colonists used the argument against "taxation without representation" in the crises precipitated by the passage of the Stamp Act and the Townshend Acts. In 1765, Parliament passed the Stamp Act which required special stamps to be purchased to show that a tax had been paid on newspapers, playing cards, and legal documents such as deeds to property, liquor licenses, and college diplomas. Merchants and lawyers in colony after colony refused to do business requiring the stamps. English merchants whose trade suffered from the boycott argued against the Stamp Act. Parliament repealed it in 1766. But concerned that its authority had been challenged, Parliament passed a Declaratory Act which asserted that it had the power and the right to legislate for the colonies "in all cases whatsoever."

The following year Parliament acted upon this principle by passing the Townshend Acts. With these acts, Parliament resorted to a tax—import duties on glass, lead, paint, paper, and tea—more familiar to the colonists than stamps. But another wave of protest swept the colonies. The colonists argued that the duties were imposed not for the purpose of regulating trade, but "for the single purpose of levying money upon us." Again colonial merchants agreed not to import goods from Britain. Again Parliament repealed the duties, except those on tea.

Conflict over trade died down until 1773 when Parliament granted the East India Company a monopoly on the sale of tea in the colonies. Colonial merchants viewed this action as discrimination against them, since tea was a profitable item to sell. Soon after a consignment of tea arrived in Boston, a band of colonists, dressed like Indians, boarded the ships and dumped the tea overboard.

By the time of the Boston Tea Party, however, taxation and monopoly were but two of many issues dividing the colonists and the British. In another attempt to eliminate smuggling, Britain established an American Board of Customs Commissioners (previously the colonial customs service was located in London) with headquarters in Boston. Three new Vice-Admiralty courts were also set up in the colonies to try suspected smugglers. To help defray the cost of maintaining troops in the colonies, a Quartering Act required colonists to provide food and shelter for the soldiers. The colonists feared that all their rights as British subjects might be in jeopardy. As the debate broadened, the colonists questioned Parliament's right to pass any laws controlling them. These readings which follow show the ways some Americans interpreted British actions and answered the question of Parliament's authority over them. As you read, keep these questions in mind:

1. How did the author of the "Journal" explain the seizure of the *Liberty* and the presence of British troops in Boston?
2. How did "Americanus" interpret the British response to the *Gaspee* incident?
3. How might Baldwin's interpretation of the Intolerable Acts contribute to unrest in the colonies?
4. How did James Wilson define the political relationship between the colonies and Great Britain? How did his argument differ from that of James Otis?

A Journal of the Times

In 1768, the Customs Commissioners seized the Liberty, *a vessel owned by the wealthy Boston merchant, John Hancock. They charged him with smuggling wine. A riot broke out following the seizure, and General Thomas Gage, the commander of the Boston garrison, moved additional troops into the city. An anonymously written "Journal of the Times" gives a contemporary's explanation for the seizure of the* Liberty. *Newspapers throughout the colonies published the "Journal," portions of which follow.*

Oliver Morton Dickerson, Comp., **Boston Under Military Rule, 1768–1769.** Boston: Chapman and Grimes, 1936, pp. 18, 28–29, 79. Language simplified and modernized.

The Sugar Act (1764) had established a tax on wine.

November 3, 1768 This morning Mr. Arodi Thayer, marshal of the Court of Admiralty, came, with a saber at his side, to John Hancock's house. He served Hancock with a warrant for 9000 pounds sterling and then arrested him, demanding bail of 3000 pounds. The Commissioners of the Customs are not satisfied with seizing and confiscating the sloop *Liberty* for not paying the duty on a part of her cargo of wines, which before the Revenue Acts were duty free. They have gone beyond everything of the kind heard of in America. They are prosecuting the owner and each person who they imagined helped unload the wines for the value of the whole cargo plus triple damages. The public can now judge. Was the *Liberty* seized in order to create a turmoil, which would give an excuse for quartering troops in town, instead of at the barracks at Castle-Island [located in Boston Harbor]?

November 30, 1768 A number of gentlemen passed the Town-House during the night. They were hailed several times by the three guards, but they did not answer. They were then stopped and confined to the guard-house for a considerable time. A merchant of the town passed the guard tonight and was challenged by the soldiers. He told them that as an inhabitant he was not obliged to answer, nor did they have any business challenging him. The soldiers replied that this was a garrison town [a town under military rule]. They put their bayonets to his breast and detained him as a prisoner for over half an hour. He got the names of the soldiers and he is prosecuting them. We may expect soon to have it decided whether or not this is a garrison town. Perhaps this treatment of the most respectable of our citizens is intended to impress us with the formidable idea of a military government, so that we may decide to give up such things as rights and privileges.

May 17, 1769 Instances of the indecent and outrageous behavior of the troops still multiply. The citizens of the town have voted to call upon the residents to arm themselves for their defense. Violence always occurs when troops are quartered in a city, but more especially when they are led to believe that they are necessary to intimidate a people in whom a spirit of rebellion is said to exist. To keep arms for their own defense is a natural right which the people have reserved to themselves, and it is a right confirmed by the English Bill of Rights.

The Gaspee Incident

In 1772, the British revenue schooner Gaspee *ran aground in Narragansett Bay while chasing a suspected smuggler. During the night a group of local citizens boarded the* Gaspee, *wounded the commander, and burned the ship. Realizing that Rhode Island juries would probably sympathize with the culprits, the British appointed a special commission to investigate the affair. But no one would talk, and the commission failed to identify the offenders. The popular reaction to the incident is shown in a letter signed "Americanus" that appeared in the* Providence Gazette *on December 26, 1772.*

John R. Bartlett, ed., **Records of the Colony of Rhode Island and Providence Plantations in New England.** Providence: 1856–1865, vol. 2. Language simplified and modernized.

An evil infinitely worse in its consequences than all of the revenue laws that have been passed now threatens this distressed country, which is being piratically plundered by customs officers.

A court of inquisition, more horrid than that of Spain or Portugal, has been established within this colony to investigate the destruction of the schooner *Gaspee*. The commissioners of this new-fangled court have been granted the most excessive and unconstitutional power. They are directed to summon witnesses and to arrest persons suspected, as well as accused, of destroying the *Gaspee*. The commissioners are to turn them over to Admiral Montague, who is ordered to have a ship ready to carry them to England, where they will be tried.

Three of the commissioners are directed to ask General Gage for troops to protect them and to preserve the colony from riots and disturbances.

Is there an American, in whose breast there glows the smallest spark of public virtue, who is not fired with indignation and resentment against a measure so threatening to our free constitution? To be tried by one's peers is a right guaranteed by our [British] constitution. The tools of despotism and arbitrary power have long wished that this important bulwark of liberty might be destroyed.

Ambition and a thirst for arbitrary rule, have already banished integrity, honesty, and every other virtue from those who govern our mother country. Her colonies loudly complain of the violences and vexations they suffer by having their money taken from them, without their consent, by measures more unjustifiable than highway robbery. No private house is free from the avarice of custom-house officers; no place is so remote that the injustice and extortion of these unscrupulous tools of power have not penetrated.

The customs commissioners received one third of the property they seized; another third went to the governors. Hence the colonists viewed the seizures as a form of piracy.

"A Fixed Plan To Enslave the Colonies"

To punish the citizens of Massachusetts for the Boston Tea Party, Parliament, in 1774, passed four acts. The colonists called them the Intolerable Acts. They closed the port of Boston until the colonists paid for the tea; allowed those accused of committing crimes while enforcing the laws to be tried in other colonies or England; changed the colonial charter so as to strengthen the power of the governor and to weaken the local government; and required the colonists to provide food and shelter for British soldiers. These acts intensified the fears and suspicions of the colonists. Ebenezer Baldwin, pastor of the First Congregational Church in Danbury, Connecticut, wrote a statement in 1774 which summarized these suspicions.

Ebenezer Baldwin, **An Appendix Stating the Heavy Grievances the Colonies Labour from Several Late Acts of the British Parliament and Shewing What We Have Just Reason To Expect the Consequences of These Measures Will Be,** published in Samuel Sherwood, **A Sermon Containing Scriptural Instructions to Civil Rulers. . .** New Haven: T and S Green, 1774. Language simplified and modernized.

We have good reason to fear the consequences of the Intolerable Acts. I do not see how anyone can doubt that they are a fixed plan to enslave the colonies and bring them under arbitrary government. The present Parliament has been, by all accounts, more devoted to the interest of the king's ministers, than perhaps any other Parliament. Notwithstanding the excellence of the British constitution, if the ministry secures a majority in Parliament who will vote as they bid them, the ministers may rule as absolutely as they do in France or Spain. The more positions the ministry have to give, the more easily they can bribe a majority of Parliament by bestowing these offices on the members of Parliament or on their friends. This is why they set up so many new and unnecessary offices in America.

Some may imagine it was destroying the tea that caused Parliament to change the government of Massachusetts. If it was, surely it is very extraordinary to punish a whole colony and their descendants for the conduct of a few individuals. I believe, however, that destroying the tea was not the reason for changing the government of Massachusetts. Rather it was a plan fixed long before, and Parliament only waited for an excuse to put it into effect. It has been reported by gentlemen of unquestionable honesty that they had incontestable evidence that more than two years ago the council ordered the crown lawyers to draw up two bills to change the government of Massachusetts.

Now if the British Parliament and ministry continue the course they have entered upon, it seems we must either submit to a dreadful state of slavery or must by force and arms stand up in defense of our liberties. The thoughts of either is enough to make our blood recoil with horror.

Considerations on the Authority of Parliament

The events from 1764 to 1774 forced the colonists to reconsider their constitutional relationship with the mother country. James Wilson, a Pennsylvania attorney, published a pamphlet in 1774 which offered a redefinition of that relationship. Wilson failed to note, however, that after the Glorious Revolution, Parliament, rather than the King, was really supreme in Great Britain.

James DeWitt Andrews, ed., **The Works of James Wilson.** Chicago: Callaghan and Company, 1896, vol. II, pp. 505–43. Language simplified and modernized.

Allegiance to the king and obedience to the Parliament are founded on very different principles. The former is founded on protection; the latter on representation. Inattention to this difference has resulted in much confusion about the connection which ought to exist between Great Britain and the American colonies.

The American colonies are not bound by the acts of the British Parliament because they are not represented in it. How then can anyone claim that the colonies are dependent on Britain and obliged to follow British laws that apply to them? With permission from the crown, the colonists made expeditions to America, took possession of the land, planted it, and cultivated it. Secure under the protection of the king, they spread British freedom. They never swore loyalty to Parliament; they never suspected that such unheard-of loyalty would be required. They never suspected that their descendants would be considered as a conquered people.

Great Britain's authority over the colonies is not justified by law nor by the right of conquest. Because British authority cannot be justified, it ought to be rejected.

There is, however, a more reasonable meaning of the colonies' dependence on Great Britain. The phrase may be used to suggest the obedience and loyalty, which the colonies owe to the kings of Great Britain. Colonists took possession of America in *his* name; they made treaties of war with the Indians by *his* authority; they held the land under *his* grants; they established governments by virtue of *his* charters. No application for these purposes was made to Parliament. Nor did Parliament ratify the colonial charters.

Now we have explained the dependence of the Americans on Britain. They are subjects of the king of Great Britain. They owe him allegiance.

The inhabitants of Great Britain and those of America are fellow-subjects owing allegiance to the same king. The connection and harmony between Great Britain and us, which it is in our mutual interest to promote and on which our mutual prosperity depends, will be better preserved by the crown, than by an unlimited authority by Parliament.

15 Revolt and Independence

British soldiers walked the streets of Boston in 1775. Some had been sent there in 1768 to help unpopular customs officers enforce the laws; many others had arrived as reinforcements in 1774 when Parliament imposed a military government on Massachusetts to punish its resistance to British laws. On the night of April 18, 1775, General Thomas Gage dispatched seven hundred of these soldiers into the countryside to search for the munitions he knew the men of Massachusetts were assembling. The soldiers won skirmishes with the colonial "minutemen" at Lexington and Concord. Their heavy losses, however—73 dead, 174 wounded, 26 missing—at the hands of farmers, sniping from the walls and trees that bordered the road back to Boston, signaled a challenge that no ministry in London could ignore.

Munitions are ammunition, guns, and other armaments.

War had begun. Military action spread quickly to western New England and Canada. Representatives of the rebellious colonies, meeting in Philadelphia as a Continental Congress, took charge of military operations. They appointed George Washington general of the army besieging Boston and assumed other duties of a central government.

But was the break of the colonies from Britain complete, final, and irrevocable? Many colonial leaders, especially those from the middle colonies of New York, New Jersey, Pennsylvania, Delaware, and Maryland, hoped that colonial belligerence, plus the familiar weapon of the boycott, might still cause Britain to give way. And Congress, between May 1775, and July 1776, quarreled heatedly over the question of independence.

The "Pennsylvania Farmer," John Dickinson, led those who sought reconciliation. From his pen came a petition, approved by Congress on July 5, 1775, which pleaded with King George III to restrain his soldiers and his ships from attacks on the colonies so that negotiations between the two sides could begin. But the course of events and the antagonistic attitudes of both the British government and colonial radicals frustrated any chance of reconciliation. As hostilities spread throughout the colonies in the following months, debate shifted to the issue of independence. The three excerpts which follow give the Americans' reasons for severing all ties with Great Britain.

As you read, consider these questions:

1. Compare the tone of the "Declaration of the Causes and Necessities of Taking Up Arms" with that of the Declaration of Independence. How was the tone of each document related to its purpose?
2. How did Thomas Paine justify independence?
3. What authority did the Declaration of Independence give for separation from Great Britain? How did this position compare with the authority James Otis gave for obeying laws of Parliament? which James Wilson gave? Had the political ideology changed?
4. Do you think that the reasons given for revolution in these documents were sufficient to justify all the death, suffering, and destruction that accompanied the war? Under what circumstances can man justify armed revolt?

The Causes and Necessities of Taking up Arms

On July 6, 1775, a year before the Declaration of Independence, the Continental Congress issued a declaration explaining why colonists had taken up arms against their mother country. The declaration was largely written by John Dickinson.

Journals of the American Congress from 1774 to 1788. Washington, D. C.: Way and Gideon, 1823, vol. I, pp. 100–03. Language simplified and modernized.

A reverence for our great Creator, principles of humanity, and common sense, must convince all those who think about it, that the purpose of government is to promote the welfare of mankind. Government ought to be carried out so as to achieve that purpose. Parliament, however, stimulated by passion for power, has attempted to enslave these colonies by violence, and has thereby made it necessary for us to appeal from Reason to Arms. We feel ourselves bound, by obligations of respect to the rest of the world, to make known the justice of our cause.

[After the French and Indian War] Parliament assumed a new power over the colonies. It has undertaken to give and grant money without our consent; laws have been passed to extend the jurisdiction of courts of Admiralty and Vice-Admiralty; to deprive us of the accustomed and inestimable privilege of trial by jury; to suspend the legislature of one of the colonies [Massachusetts]; to close the port of Boston; to alter fundamentally the form of government established by charter; to exempt the "murderers" [British soldiers] of colonists from legal trial, and in effect, from punishment; to erect in a neighboring province [Canada] a despotism dangerous to our very existence; and to quarter soldiers upon the colonists in time of peace. It has also been resolved in Parliament, that colonists charged with committing certain offenses shall be transported to England for trial.

Dickinson here refers to the Quebec Act passed by Parliament at about the same time that it passed the measures which the colonists called the Intolerable Acts. The Quebec Act granted religious freedom to Catholics, and extended Quebec's border southward. It made no provision for representative government, however.

But why should we enumerate our injuries in detail? By one statute [the Declaratory Act] Parliament asserted the right to "make laws to bind us *in all cases whatsoever*." What is to defend us against so enormous, so unlimited a power? For ten years, we have humbly besieged the Throne; we have reasoned; we have argued with Parliament in the most mild and decent language. We have pursued every temperate, every respectful measure. But subsequent events have shown how vain was this hope of finding moderation in our enemies.

We are reduced to the alternative of surrendering unconditionally to the tyranny of irritated ministers, or resisting by force. The latter is our choice. We have counted the cost of this contest, and find nothing so dreadful as voluntary slavery.

Our cause is just. Our union is perfect. Our internal resources are great, and, if necessary, foreign assistance is undoubtedly attainable. With hearts fortified with these animating reflections, we most solemnly, before God and world, declare that we will employ arms for the preservation of our liberties; being with our [one] mind resolved to die free men rather than live slaves.

Lest this declaration should disquiet the minds of our friends and fellow-subjects in any part of the empire, we assure them that we mean not to dissolve that Union which has so long and so happily existed between us, and which we sincerely wish to see restored. We have not raised armies with ambitious designs of separating from Great Britain and establishing independent states. We fight not for glory or for conquest.

Common Sense

Common Sense, *written and printed by Thomas Paine, was published anonymously in January 1776. It was the most famous, most widely read, and probably the most revolutionary pamphlet of those published during the debate over colonial rights.*

Thomas Paine, **Common Sense.** Philadelphia: John Mycall, 1776. Language simplified and modernized.

I offer nothing more than simple facts, plain arguments, and common sense.

Volumes have been written on the subject of the struggle between England and America. Men of all ranks have engaged in the controversy, but all have been ineffectual. The period of debate is over. Arms, as the last resort, must decide the contest.

The sun never shone on a more worthy cause. It is not the affair of a city, a country, a province, or a kingdom, but of a continent. It is not the concern of a day, a year, or an age; posterity are virtually involved in the contest.

By referring the matter from argument to arms, a new era for politics is begun, a new method of thinking has arisen. All plans and proposals made prior to the nineteenth of April [the battles of Lexington and Concord] are out of date and useless now.

As much has been said about the advantages of reconciliation with Great Britain, we should examine the other side of the argument. We should consider some of the many injuries which these colonies sustain, and always will sustain, by being connected with, and dependent on Great Britain.

I have heard some assert that because America has flourished under her connection with Great Britain, that the same connection is necessary for her future happiness. Nothing can be more false than this kind of argument. America would have flourished as much, and probably more, had no European power had anything to do with her. There will always be a market for America's goods, as long as people in Europe continue to eat.

We have boasted that Great Britain has protected us, without considering that she protected us because of her own interest and not because of attachment to us. She did not protect us from our enemies, but from her enemies. France and Spain never were, nor perhaps ever will be, our enemies as Americans, but as subjects of Great Britain, they are our enemies.

Britain is the parent country, say some. The assertion is only partly true. Europe, and not England, is the parent country of America. This new world has been the asylum for the persecuted lovers of civil and religious liberty from every part of Europe.

Whenever a war breaks out between England and any foreign power, American trade goes to ruin, because of her connection with Britain. Everything that is right or natural pleads for separation. Even the distance which the Almighty placed England from America is a strong and natural proof that the authority of the one over the other was never the design of Heaven.

It is repugnant to reason, to the universal order of things, and to all examples from former ages, to suppose that this continent can longer remain subject to any external power. I am clearly, positively, and conscientiously persuaded that it is in our true interest to be separate and independent. Anything short of independence is mere patchwork and it can afford no lasting happiness.

The Declaration of Independence

Thomas Jefferson wrote the Declaration of Independence. The Continental Congress adopted it on July 4, 1776, and severed formal political ties with England. It gives the best known justification for the American Revolution.

When in the course of human events, it becomes necessary for one people to dissolve the political bands which had connected them with another, and to assume among the powers of the earth the separate and equal station to which the Laws of Nature and of Nature's God entitle them, a decent respect to the opinions of mankind requires that they should declare the causes which impel them to the separation.

Unalienable means "not capable of being taken away."

We hold these truths to be self-evident, that all men are created equal, that they are endowed by their Creator with certain unalienable rights, that among these are life, liberty, and the pursuit of happiness. That to secure these rights, governments are instituted among men, deriving their just powers from the consent of the governed. That whenever any form of government becomes destructive of these ends, it is the right of the people to alter or to abolish it, and to institute new government, laying its foundation on such principles and organizing its powers in such form, as to them shall seem most likely to effect [bring about] their safety and happiness. Prudence, indeed, will dictate that governments long established should not be changed for light and transient [passing] causes; and accordingly all experience hath shown, that mankind are more disposed to suffer, while evils are sufferable, than to right themselves by abolishing the forms to which they are accustomed. But when a long train of abuses and usurpations [seizures of power], pursuing invariably the same object evinces [shows clearly] a design to reduce them under absolute despotism, it is their right, it is their duty, to throw off such government, and to provide new guards for their future security. Such has been the patient sufferance of these colonies; and such is now the necessity which constrains [requires] them to alter their former systems of government. The history of the present King of Great Britain is a history of repeated injuries and usurpations, all having in direct object the establishment of an absolute tyranny over these States. To prove this, let facts be submitted to a candid [impartial] world.

[Here the Continental Congress listed many grievances, of which the most important follow.]

He has dissolved representative houses repeatedly, for opposing with manly firmness his invasions on the rights of the people. . . .

He has made judges dependent on his will alone, for the tenure of their offices, and the amount and payment of their salaries. . . .

He has kept among us, in times of peace, standing armies without the consent of our legislature. . . .

He has combined with others to subject us to a jurisdiction foreign to our constitution, and unacknowledged by our laws; giving his assent to their acts of pretended legislation: . . .

For cutting off our trade with all parts of the world:

For imposing taxes on us without our consent:

For depriving us in many cases of the benefits of trial by jury:

For transporting us beyond seas to be tried for pretended offences:

For taking away our charters, abolishing our most valuable laws, and altering fundamentally the forms of our governments:

For suspending our own legislature, and declaring themselves invested with power to legislate for us in all cases whatsoever.

He has abdicated government here, by declaring us out of his protection and waging war against us.

He has plundered our seas, ravaged our coasts, burnt our towns, and destroyed the lives of our people.

He is at this time transporting large armies of foreign mercenaries [hired soldiers] to complete the works of death, desolation, and tyranny, already begun with circumstances of cruelty and perfidy [treachery] scarcely paralleled in the most barbarous ages, and totally unworthy the head of a civilized nation. . . .

Here Jefferson refers to the use of German mercenary soldiers, called Hessians, who were hired by England for use against the colonial armies.

He has excited domestic insurrections amongst us, and has endeavoured to bring on the inhabitants of our frontiers the merciless Indian savages, whose known rule of warfare is an undistinguished destruction of all ages, sexes, and conditions.

In every stage of these oppressions we have petitioned for redress [relief] in the most humble terms: our repeated petitions have been answered only by repeated injury. A prince whose character is thus marked by every act which may define a tyrant, is unfit to be the ruler of a free people.

Nor have we been wanting in attention to our British brethren. We have warned them from time to time of attempts by their legislature to extend an unwarrantable jurisdiction over us. We have reminded them of the circumstances of our emigration and settlement here. We have appealed to their native justice and magnanimity [generous spirit], and we have conjured [appealed to] them by the ties of our common kindred to disavow these usurpations, which would inevitably interrupt our connections and correspondence. They too have been deaf to the voice of justice and of consanguinity [kinship]. We must, therefore, acquiesce [consent] in the necessity, which denounces our separation, and hold them, as we hold the rest of mankind, enemies in war, in peace friends.

We, therefore, the Representatives of the United States of America, in General Congress assembled, appealing to the Supreme Judge of the world . . . do, in the name, and by authority of the good people of these colonies, solemnly publish and declare, that these united colonies are, and of right ought to be free and independent states; that they are absolved from all allegiance to the British Crown, and that all political connection between them and the state of Great Britain is and ought to be totally dissolved . . . And for the support of this declaration, with a firm reliance on the protection of Divine Providence, we mutually pledge to each other our lives, our fortunes, and our sacred honor.

16 The American Revolution and Its Meaning

HISTORICAL ESSAY

The American Revolution grew largely out of changes in Britain's colonial purposes and methods. The American colonists seemed in 1763 to have been content with their status. If Great Britain had not attempted to tighten the loosely knit empire and to make more money out of it, the break between Britain and the colonies would probably not have come when it did or as it did.

Once the rupture occurred, however, changes came fast in Americans' attitudes toward Great Britain and toward their own society.

The fears, hopes, dreams, and material pressures generated by war produced some significant changes in American life.

Nevertheless, America after the war years looked remarkably like colonial America. The American Revolution stands as one of the few modern revolutions in which the main fabric of social relationships was not savagely torn. The conservative nature of the American Revolution must be attributed largely to two circumstances. The first is that the colonists began fighting in an effort to preserve what they already had, rather than to attain a new order. The second is that the war hardly damaged agriculture, the basis of American economy.

Revamping the Empire

After the French and Indian War, the British decided they could no longer afford to neglect their American colonies. The government issued a series of laws and decrees aimed at establishing more effective control over them.

With French power eliminated in America after 1763, colonists moved west and provoked a new Indian war, the Pontiac Conspiracy. To appease the Indians and to gain time to organize the territory acquired from France, Parliament issued the Proclamation of 1763, which forbade the colonists to settle west of the Appalachian Mountains. Then, in 1764, Parliament passed the Sugar Act, which placed new duties on sugar, coffee, wine, and certain other imported products and reduced the tax on molasses, while it provided ways to collect all duties more effectively.

There were only scattered protests to these first measures. But some colonists, such as James Otis, addressed themselves to the basic question of colonial rights within the British Empire. The New York Assembly, in protesting the Sugar Act, advanced the argument—no taxation without representation—which the colonies followed in future financial crises with Great Britain.

A major crisis over taxation quickly followed. In 1765, Parliament passed the Stamp Act. Colonial resistance to the tax it imposed took a number of forms. Colonial leaders organized a voluntary boycott of business and legal activities requiring the use of stamps to show that the tax had been paid. Trade came to a halt, and courts of justice closed since virtually all legal papers needed stamps. Politicians, such as Samuel Adams of Boston, organized bands of patriots, drawn largely from the ranks of workingmen, who called themselves Sons of Liberty. They pressured reluctant businessmen to support the boycott and forced Stamp Act officials to resign by their use of threats and violence. Even more significant than this sporadic violence was a meeting in New York of delegates from nine colonies. This Stamp Act Congress was the first really effective act of political

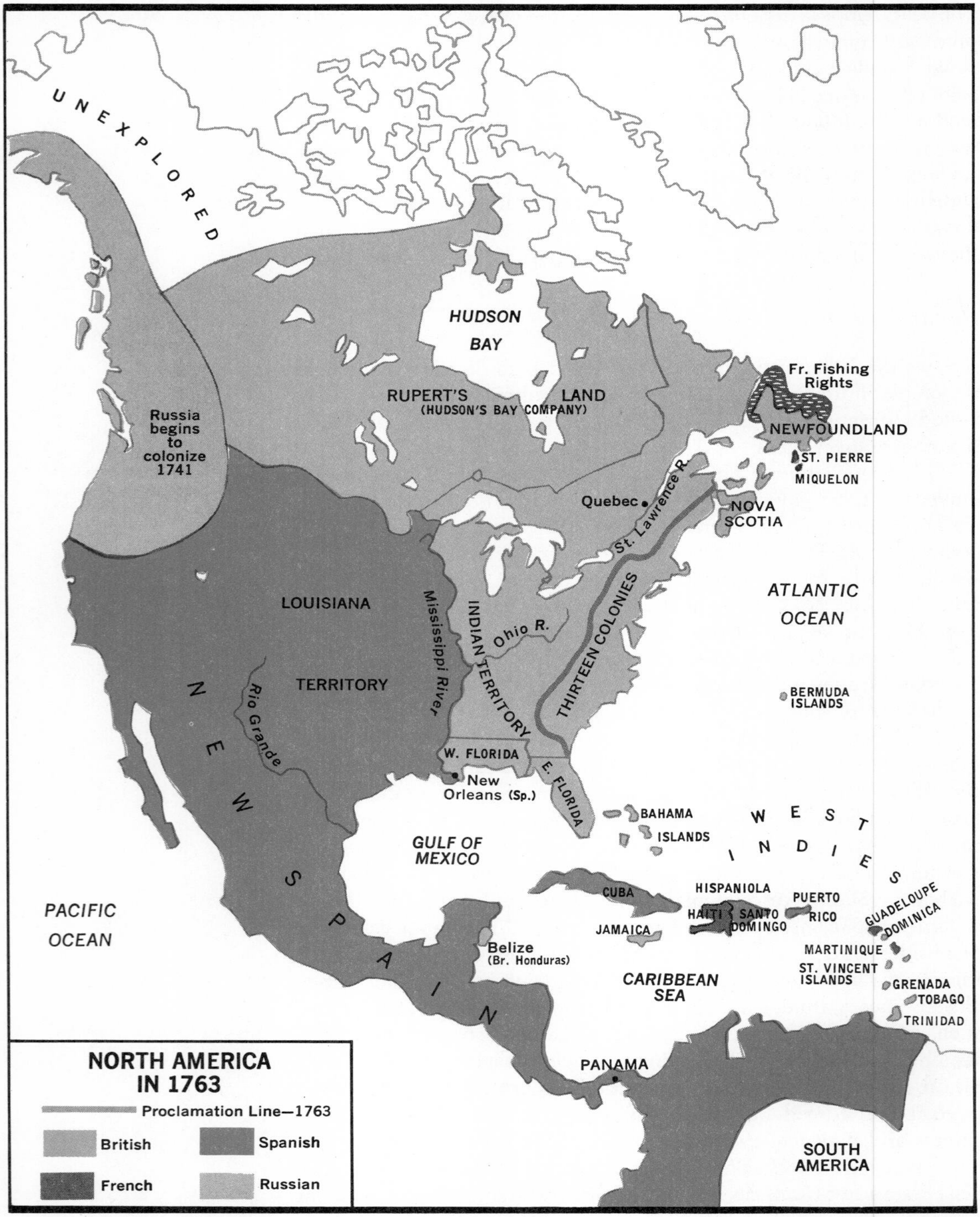
UNEXPLORED
HUDSON BAY
RUPERT'S LAND
(HUDSON'S BAY COMPANY)
Fr. Fishing Rights
NEWFOUNDLAND
ST. PIERRE
MIQUELON
Russia begins to colonize 1741
Quebec
St. Lawrence R.
NOVA SCOTIA
ATLANTIC OCEAN
LOUISIANA
TERRITORY
Mississippi River
INDIAN TERRITORY
Ohio R.
THIRTEEN COLONIES
BERMUDA ISLANDS
Rio Grande
NEW SPAIN
W. FLORIDA
E. FLORIDA
New Orleans (Sp.)
BAHAMA ISLANDS
WEST INDIES
GULF OF MEXICO
CUBA
HISPANIOLA
HAITI
SANTO DOMINGO
PUERTO RICO
GUADELOUPE
DOMINICA
MARTINIQUE
ST. VINCENT ISLANDS
GRENADA
TOBAGO
TRINIDAD
JAMAICA
PACIFIC OCEAN
Belize (Br. Honduras)
CARIBBEAN SEA
PANAMA
SOUTH AMERICA
NORTH AMERICA IN 1763
Proclamation Line—1763
British
Spanish
French
Russian

cooperation among so many colonies. It adopted a series of resolutions protesting the new tax law and other new policies, such as the trials of accused smugglers by Vice-Admiralty courts. British businessmen hurt by the colonial boycott pressured Parliament into repealing the Stamp Act in 1766. At the same time, Parliament reaffirmed its right to pass laws for the colonies.

The following year, Parliament tried again to get the colonies to contribute more money by passing the Townshend Acts. The means of enforcement that accompanied the Acts were as unpopular as the duties they levied. The new American Board of Customs Commissioners often resorted to ruthless tactics. Its members confiscated ships, such as John Hancock's *Liberty,* over minor or technical violations of the law. The customs officers became thoroughly unpopular. In 1768, the soldiers sent to Boston to protect them found a hostile and suspicious atmosphere, as the anonymous author of the "Journal of Our Times" indicated. The colonists felt threatened by the soldiers, and they saw the Quartering Act as another form of taxation. Occasional brawls culminated in the Boston Massacre in 1770 in which the British soldiers shot five members of an unarmed mob. Similar brawls between soldiers and colonists occurred in New York and contributed to the growing antagonism and fear between the colonists and the British.

The first colonist to fall was a Negro, Crispus Attucks.

The Lull and the Storm

In the spring of 1770, British-colonial relations took a marked turn for the better. The redcoats in Boston withdrew to the fort in the harbor to prevent further incidents. A new Parliamentary ministry took office, and its leader, Lord Frederick North, had all of the Townshend duties repealed except that on tea. North allowed the Quartering Act to expire and also promised that no new taxes would be imposed on the colonies. There was rejoicing in the colonies, and for more than two years there seemed to be a real reconciliation.

Then a series of episodes produced serious conflicts that finally led to independence. The first occurred in June 1772, when a group of Rhode Islanders raided and burned the *Gaspee,* a customs vessel. The British decision to try the offenders in England, assuming they could be identified, alarmed the colonists, who saw this as yet another blow to the right of trial by jury. This episode, together with the British decision that the crown, rather than the Massachusetts Assembly, would pay the salaries of the governor and judges in that colony, produced new protest organizations. The colonists organized Committees of Correspondence to keep each other informed about local conflicts between colonial and British authority and to circulate propaganda against British rule.

In 1773, the tea crisis speeded up the final break with Great Britain. The colonists saw the British East India Company's monopoly on the sale of tea as another example of colonial exploitation for British profits. Up and down the Atlantic coast they prevented the sale of tea, and in Boston, the center of colonial protest, a band of citizens destroyed the cargo of tea ships.

Parliament responded angrily in 1774 with the Coercive Acts, labeled the Intolerable Acts by the colonists. At the same time, Parliament passed the Quebec Act, which was not intended as a colonial punishment, but which the colonists interpreted as one.

With the Intolerable Acts, Parliament demonstrated that it intended to enforce British prestige and authority, regardless of the cost to trade and remaining colonial good will. Many colonists interpreted Parliament's actions as part of a conspiracy to deprive them of all their rights. Other spokesmen argued that the colonies owed no allegiance to Parliament. All the colonies united firmly in support of Massachusetts. The Committees of Correspondence organized a Congress, which met in Philadelphia in September 1774 to deal with the mounting crisis. The fifty-five delegates from twelve colonies (Georgia was not represented) voted to support Massachusetts, to denounce Parliament's legislation for the colonies since 1763, and to form a Continental Association to enforce a thorough boycott of trade with Britain.

By the time the delegates to the Second Continental Congress convened in May 1775, the battles of Lexington and Concord had been fought. The Continental Congress explained in the "Causes and Necessities of Taking up Arms" why they had used military force. They tried fruitlessly to get Britain to restore the relationship that had existed prior to 1763. Instead of backing down, Britain began dispatching more troops to the colonies to put down the rebellion.

By the spring of 1776, it became clear to most members of the Congress that reconciliation between the colonies and Great Britain was impossible without a virtual surrender of the colonial position. In all thirteen colonies, the Americans had ousted the royal officials. Disillusionment with the king, who had stoutly supported Parliament, was strengthened by Thomas Paine's bitter attack in *Common Sense* on monarchy in general and on George III in particular. Hundreds of thousands of copies of this pamphlet, which argued for complete independence from Great Britain, circulated among the colonists in 1776. The Continental Congress responded to the events of the year by adopting the Declaration of Independence.

The War and Its Strategy

There is no simple explanation for the Americans' victory in the War for Independence. Their military success owed much to the facts that they fought on home ground, that they received considerable help from France and Spain, and that their commander, George Washington, realized that time was on the American side if he could avoid an early defeat. Washington also received loyal support from the Continental Congress, although it was unable to supply his armies adequately.

The unity of the revolutionaries suffered because many Americans remained loyal to Britain. During the war, however, large numbers of Loyalists fled to Canada or to Great Britain. Those remaining in America could not oppose the war effectively unless they lived in the few places continuously occupied by the British.

The British encountered serious difficulties in bringing their superior strength to bear on the distant rebellion. The war against the colonies was unpopular with many merchants, some members of Parliament, and even some generals. Besides lacking the manpower needed to suppress the revolt—they hired thirty thousand mercenary soldiers from Germany—the British found their navy in bad shape.

With a limited number of troops, the British could not effectively occupy a country that contained vast stretches of farmland and forest. Their strategy for putting down the rebellion was to capture key cities, blockade the coasts, divide the colonies, and beat the Revolutionary armies where they found them.

The British campaign began inauspiciously in June 1775, when the American militiamen besieging Boston dealt the British regulars a savage blow at the Battle of Bunker Hill. The Americans killed and wounded more than a thousand men. In March 1776, the Americans suddenly fortified Dorchester Heights, which overlooked Boston and its harbor, where the British fleet was anchored. Sir William Howe, who had succeeded General Gage, decided to evacuate the city. The British sailed for Halifax and did not return to Boston. Reinforced to 32,000 men, they landed six months later at New York, where Washington had moved his main army. They easily drove Washington's weaker forces into New Jersey and then Pennsylvania.

The Battle of Bunker Hill was actually fought on Breed's Hill.

General Howe and his successor, Sir William Clinton, used New York as a base of operations from then on. They sent British armies out to capture Philadelphia, Savannah, and Charleston, and to try to engage Washington in battle. Washington fought only when he had a good chance to inflict damage on the British forces, and he always kept a way open for retreat. Between 1776 and 1781, the main British and American armies met several times but neither could win.

British control of New York largely cut New England off from the other colonies. But British efforts to isolate New England met a spectacular failure. General John Burgoyne, leading a force of 7700 men south from Canada down the Hudson Valley, found himself blocked by American soldiers. He ran short of supplies and lost nearly 2000

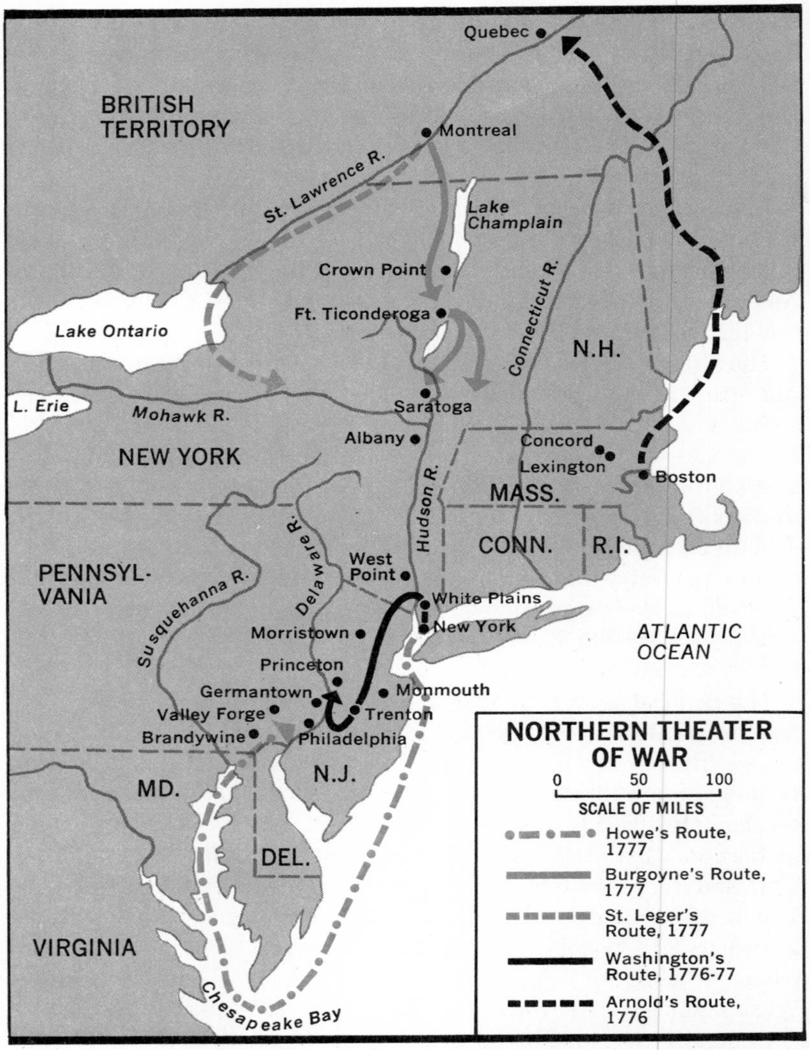

men through casualties and desertions. The American commander, General Horatio Gates, forced Burgoyne to surrender his army at Saratoga, New York, on October 17, 1777. Secret aid from France and Spain contributed to the American victory at Saratoga. When news of the victory reached Paris, France recognized the American government and signed an alliance against Britain.

In the south, Britain's first attempt to capture Charleston failed in 1776. A land force sent north from Florida and a naval expedition from New York captured Augusta and Savannah, Georgia, in late 1778, however. A second expedition against Charleston in early 1780 won that seaport. The British then tried for the next year and a half with a steady loss of men to mop up the opposition in the Carolinas. By late 1781, they controlled little but Charleston and Wilmington.

On the fringes of the main areas of combat, the Americans had some small but important successes. An early thrust into Canada, in the winter of 1775–1776, failed to capture Quebec, and the Americans withdrew. Forces under Benedict Arnold, one of the leaders of that expedition, then blocked a British counterthrust at Lake Champlain the following fall. In the interiors of New York and Pennsylvania, where Loyalists and Indians had been terrorizing frontier settlements, General John Sullivan led a Continental force in 1779 which defeated and scattered the opposition. In the Ohio Valley, George Rogers Clark and a band of Virginia militiamen, aided by the French, conquered British forts at Kaskaskia and Vincennes.

On the sea, the infant American navy played but a small part in determining the outcome of the war. More important were the activities of American privateers. They captured hundreds of British merchant vessels. But Britain's virtual control of the sea kept the Americans from winning a major victory against the British bases on the coast.

Privateers sailed privately owned ships which were given official permission by Congress to attack British ships.

The French fleet sent to aid the Americans finally gave them the opportunity to strike a decisive blow against the British. In 1781, French naval forces gained command of the coast along the middle

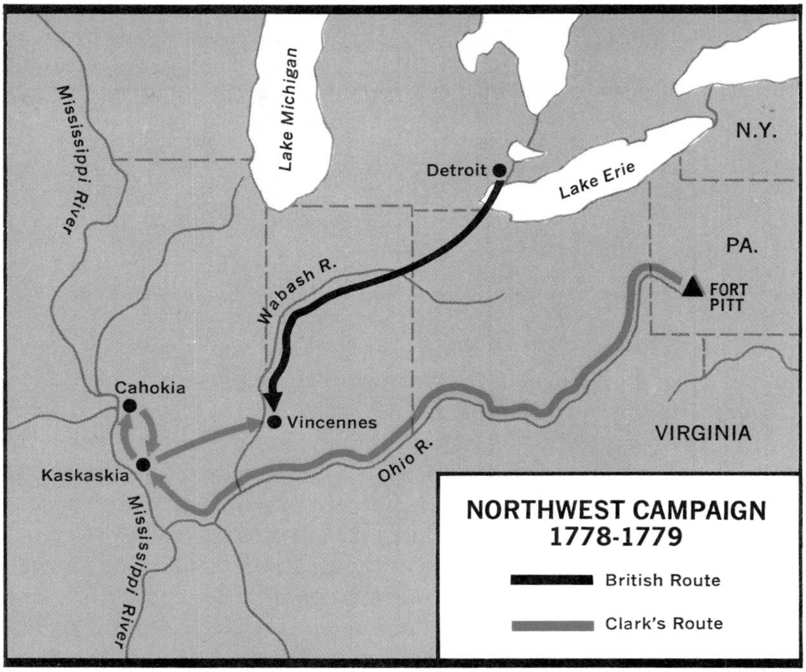

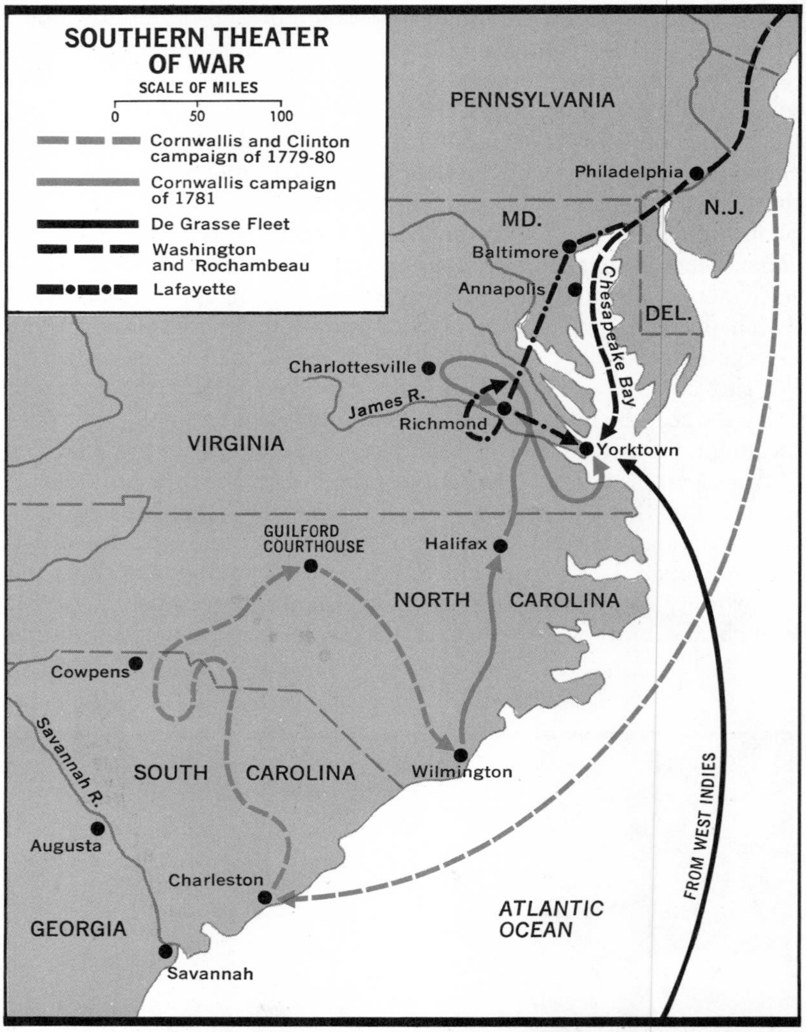

colonies. With masterful timing, Washington and Comte de Rochambeau, commanding the American and French forces outside New York, secretly moved their troops to Virginia to trap a British army under Lord Cornwallis. Cornwallis had marched north from the Carolinas and occupied Yorktown, on a peninsula accessible to British sea power. But the French fleet prevented a British rescue fleet from reaching Cornwallis. He had to surrender.

Parliament, already dismayed at the frustrating course of the war, decided that the victory at Yorktown signaled the end of the war. Peace sentiment swelled in Britain and Lord North's ministry fell. Negotiations with an American peace mission in Paris followed.

At that peace conference, Benjamin Franklin, John Adams, and John Jay won a remarkable diplomatic victory with the signing of the Treaty of Paris in 1783. Great Britain recognized both American independence and American title to the land east of the Mississippi River between the Great Lakes and Florida. Florida went to Spain. The British hoped to lure Americans away from a close attachment to the French by making such a generous settlement.

The Revolution at Home

Revolution against Britain meant the rejection of established authority and implied that the way was open to all kinds of changes within American society. But relatively few changes occurred, revealing the satisfaction of most Americans with their institutions.

State governments were established under new constitutions, beginning in 1776, but they resembled the colonial governments they replaced. Under the new constitutions, the representative assemblies held most political power. Voters in most states elected their gover-

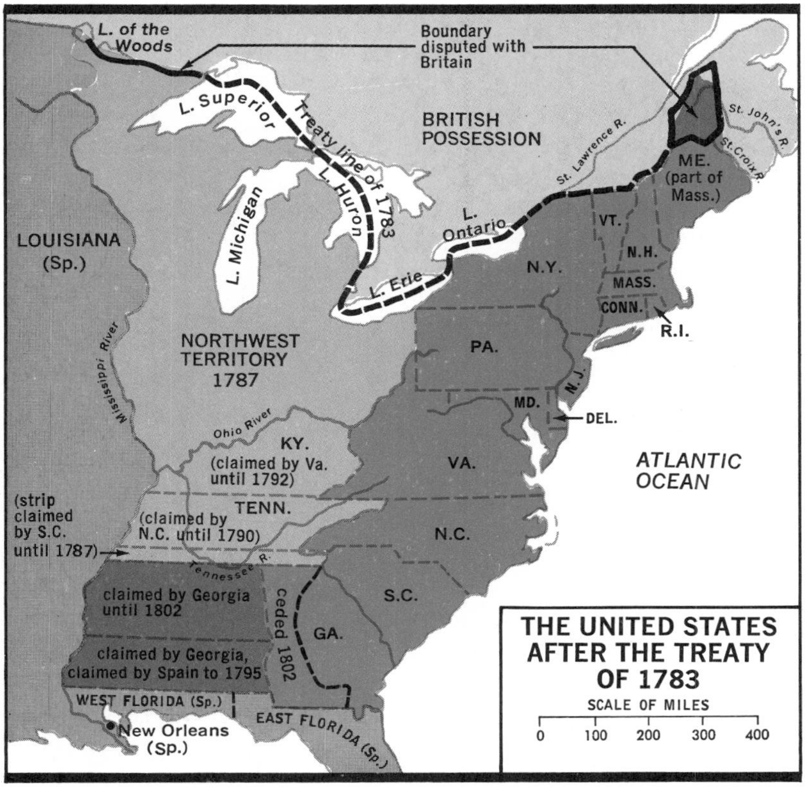

THE UNITED STATES AFTER THE TREATY OF 1783

nors, whose power was reduced. Pennsylvania carried this distrust of executive authority to an extreme by having a committee of its legislature act in the place of a governor.

In most of the colonies, the right to vote had depended on possession of some property. During the war, nearly all property qualifications for voting and officeholding were either lowered or dropped.

The new states guarded their powers jealously. They conceded some authority to the new government of the United States formed under the Articles of Confederation in 1781, but they retained all authority relating to local government. The central government, which itself lacked an effective executive office, directed the army and conducted foreign relations. But it could not regulate commerce, nor did it have the authority to tax citizens directly. It had the right to request money from the states, but could not enforce its requests.

Since many Americans owned farms and businesses, there was little reason for the revolutionaries to overturn existing economic relationships. Merchants and other creditors suffered from the disruption of commerce during the war, while farmers and debtors benefited from the demand for foodstuffs and the creation of a vast supply of paper money by the revolutionary government to pay its debts. Much property owned by Loyalists was confiscated. In most cases, it went to property holders rather than to landless men.

Democratic ideas, stimulated by the war, affected social relationships to some extent. Perhaps the most striking examples were the decisions of several northern states to abolish slavery. Some southern states simplified the process of freeing slaves. The numbers of freed slaves increased, substantially. Most states prohibited the slave trade during the revolution.

Americans emerged from their war of independence, therefore, with a working national political system and a society and economy which were not deeply divided by antagonisms.

SUGGESTED READINGS

CUNLIFFE, MARCUS, *George Washington and the Making of a Nation.* This short biography, richly illustrated, depicts the vital role played by the Virginia soldier-statesman in the creation of the United States.

The Diary of the American Revolution, compiled by Frank Moore and edited and abridged by John A. Scott. This colorful collection of materials about the Revolution is drawn largely from newspapers, pamphlets, broadsides, songs, and letters printed during the war.

LABAREE, BENJAMIN, *The Road to Independence, 1763–1776.* This book contains a brief summary of the sequence of crises that led Americans to throw off their allegiance to Britain in 1776.

The New Government

CHAPTER 5

STATING THE ISSUE

After the Revolutionary War, Americans set up a government that reflected their political ideology. The purpose of a government, they felt, was to protect the rights of individuals. Since a government with unlimited power could threaten a man's life, liberty, or property, its powers had to be carefully established by a constitution.

The Americans also drew upon their experiences in colonial government. Individual colonies treasured their charters, by which king and Parliament had granted them important powers. In all the colonies, executive, legislative, and judicial departments had been established. Those qualifying as voters chose the members of the lower house of the legislature; the king usually appointed the governors, and either the king or the governor appointed the members of the upper house and the principal judges.

The events of the years following 1763 made a profound impression on Americans. They acquired a deep suspicion of a remote, central government that passed laws and issued decrees that seemed to violate natural rights and to disturb customary ways of doing things. Since most colonies had been tied more closely to England than to each other, they were unaccustomed to working together, but the clashes with Britain began to forge the bonds of intercolonial cooperation. The Stamp Act Congress, the non-importation agreements, and the Committees of Correspondence, which arose in response to the imperial crisis, prepared the way for the Continental Congress and the Articles of Confederation, which set up a national government.

During the 1780's, many Americans grew dissatisfied with the government established under the Articles of Confederation. As its weaknesses became apparent, movements to amend the Articles sprang up. Eventually, a new constitution was written, and ratified, and a new government began. Why was the Confederation government changed? What political institutions did the Constitution establish? What formal rules for choosing leaders did the Constitution lay down? What processes were established for making political decisions? What rights did the Constitution guarantee to citizens? What main political ideas guided the men who wrote the Constitution? These are the major issues raised in Chapter 5.

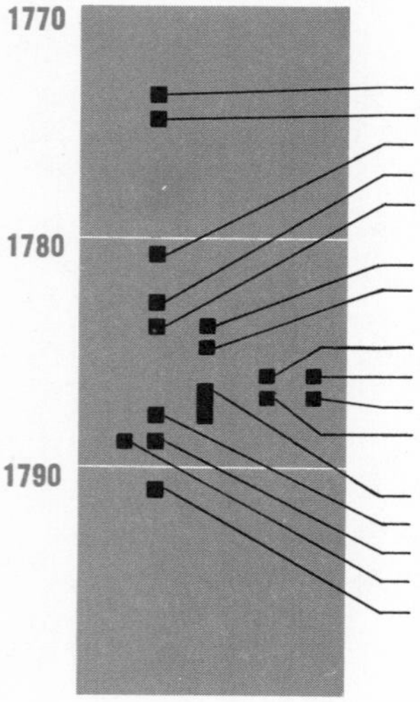

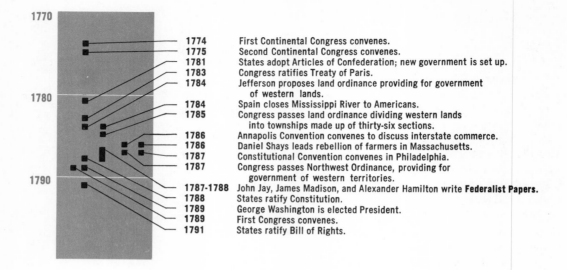

1774	First Continental Congress convenes.
1775	Second Continental Congress convenes.
1781	States adopt Articles of Confederation; new government is set up.
1783	Congress ratifies Treaty of Paris.
1784	Jefferson proposes land ordinance providing for government of western lands.
1784	Spain closes Mississippi River to Americans.
1785	Congress passes land ordinance dividing western lands into townships made up of thirty-six sections.
1786	Annapolis Convention convenes to discuss interstate commerce.
1786	Daniel Shays leads rebellion of farmers in Massachusetts.
1787	Constitutional Convention convenes in Philadelphia.
1787	Congress passes Northwest Ordinance, providing for government of western territories.
1787-1788	John Jay, James Madison, and Alexander Hamilton write **Federalist Papers.**
1788	States ratify Constitution.
1789	George Washington is elected President.
1789	First Congress convenes.
1791	States ratify Bill of Rights.

17 The Challenge of Independence

HISTORICAL ESSAY

Chapters 1–4 have each given three readings followed by a historical essay. In Chapter 5, however, the historical essay precedes the readings. It provides much of the information essential to an understanding of the readings which follow.

Americans, three million strong, settled into peace in 1783. Most people's daily lives as citizens of states did not differ greatly from their lives as subjects of King George III. The state governments had for two years been working together under the Articles of Confederation. Yet some serious problems existed.

The Articles of Confederation had been drawn up in 1776 and approved by the Continental Congress in 1777. They were not ratified by all thirteen states until 1781, at which time the Articles became the official basis for government.

Many difficulties tested the strength of the national unity forged by the Revolution. States found it hard to reconcile the conflicting interests of merchants and farmers, city and country, and seacoast and frontier. A few states had trouble in their direct dealings with other states. Other challenges were national in scope. The United States needed security and respect, and its citizens wanted a fair chance to engage in international trade. Governing and settling the vast western lands won by the United States in the Treaty of Paris, and transferred to the federal government by several states, offered another problem. Above all, the government had to convince its citizens that it was worth supporting.

The Western Country

Perhaps the most appealing opportunity for Americans lay in the west, where millions of acres of fertile land stretched from the Appalachians to the Mississippi River. Even during the war, frontiersmen by the tens of thousands had flooded over the mountains into the Kentucky and Tennessee country, where British influence among the Indian tribes was weak. Although Virginia and North Carolina still held title to these western lands, the frontiersmen had gone beyond the practical limits of eastern control. They began to agitate for new state governments west of the mountains.

With the end of the war, the lands north of the Ohio River lay open to settlement. States with claims to this territory had ceded their claims to the federal government in order to get the "landless" states to accept the Articles of Confederation. Speculators began lobbying to get Congress to sell them large tracts of land cheaply. Meanwhile, frontiersmen began moving into the Ohio country, illegally "squatting" wherever they found good land.

If the process of settlement was to be directed by the government and if the public lands were to provide a source of national income, some kind of land policy had to be worked out. The Continental Congress had promised in 1780 to create new states from the lands ceded to the national government. The new states were to enjoy the same rights as the older ones. Congress now moved to carry out this pledge by adopting the Northwest Ordinance of 1784, an act proposed by Thomas Jefferson, which divided the Northwest into ten parts, each to be governed by the settlers themselves. Each could send a non-voting delegate to Congress as soon as its population reached 20,000 and would be admitted as a state as soon as its population equaled the free population of the smallest existing state. The following year, Congress, in the Ordinance of 1785, adopted a plan to survey the Northwest lands and to lay them out in townships six miles square, with each township having thirty-six sections one mile square. But before much of the Ohio country could be surveyed, Congress yielded to pressure from land speculators and to its own desire to pay off some of the war debts. It sold several million acres of Ohio lands to speculative companies at what amounted to only a few cents an acre.

Many of these mass sales fell through within the next few years. But the land companies pressured Congress into changing the system of government in the Northwest, so that they could exert more influence upon the territorial governments than they could under Jefferson's democratic scheme. Congress passed the Northwest Ordinance of 1787, which served in the future as a model for American territorial organization. It created the Northwest Territory, which

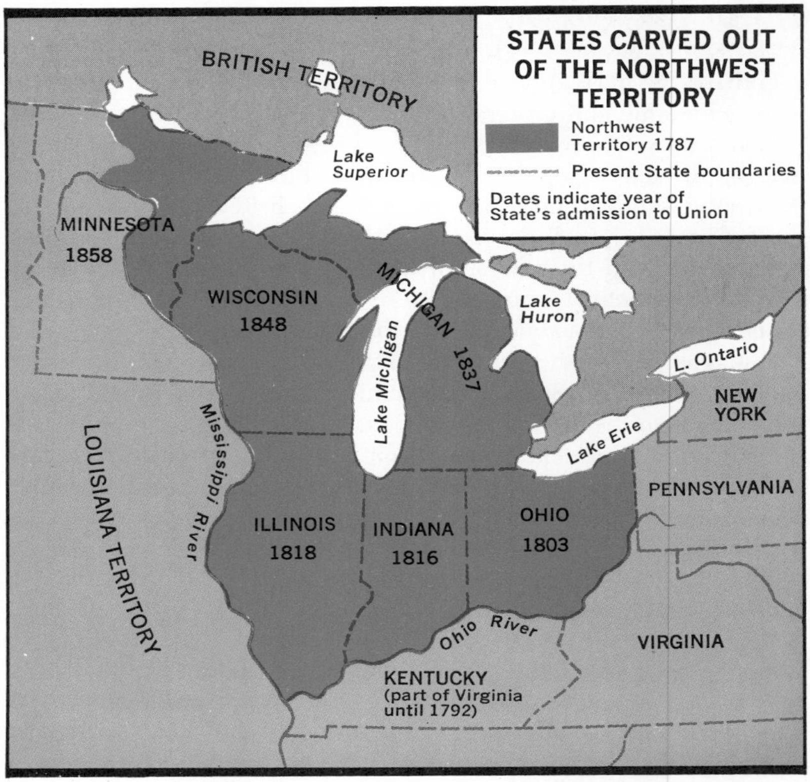

could be divided into three to five new territories. Each was to be ruled by a governor and judges, appointed by Congress, until it gained 5000 adult free males. Then the settlers could elect a bicameral [two-house] legislature, whose laws, however, could still be vetoed by the governor. When the population of a territory reached 60,000, it could adopt a constitution and apply for statehood. This model for territorial government was considerably less democratic than Jefferson's, yet the Northwest Ordinance prohibited slavery and encouraged education. The proceeds from the sale of one square mile in each township went to support public schools.

Indians often lived or hunted on land the government offered for settlement. As the settlers advanced, they killed the Indians or forced them to retreat westward. Sometimes the federal government managed to acquire the land peacefully through treaty or purchase. When the Indians resisted these attempts to dislodge them, small-scale wars often followed. The Indians found that their days on the land were clearly numbered under the pressure of the land-hungry easterners.

Foreign Relations and Foreign Trade

The British gave up the territory south of the Great Lakes in the treaty that followed the Revolutionary War. Yet they violated that treaty by maintaining military posts at Detroit, in northern Michigan, and in northern New York. They kept these posts for several reasons: to retain their trade with the Indians, to put pressure on the United States to fulfill such unpleasant obligations in the treaty as paying Loyalists for confiscated property and allowing British creditors to collect debts from Americans, and to be able to exert influence in case the settlers in areas that were not states decided to break away from the United States. The possibility of settlers breaking away presented a real threat to the new nation. Ethan Allen and his brothers, leaders of the Vermont farmers and frontiersmen during the Revolution, negotiated secretly with the British during the 1780's. Vermont, claimed by both New York and New Hampshire, wanted statehood. The Allens considered organizing an independence movement supported by Britain, or affiliation with Canada.

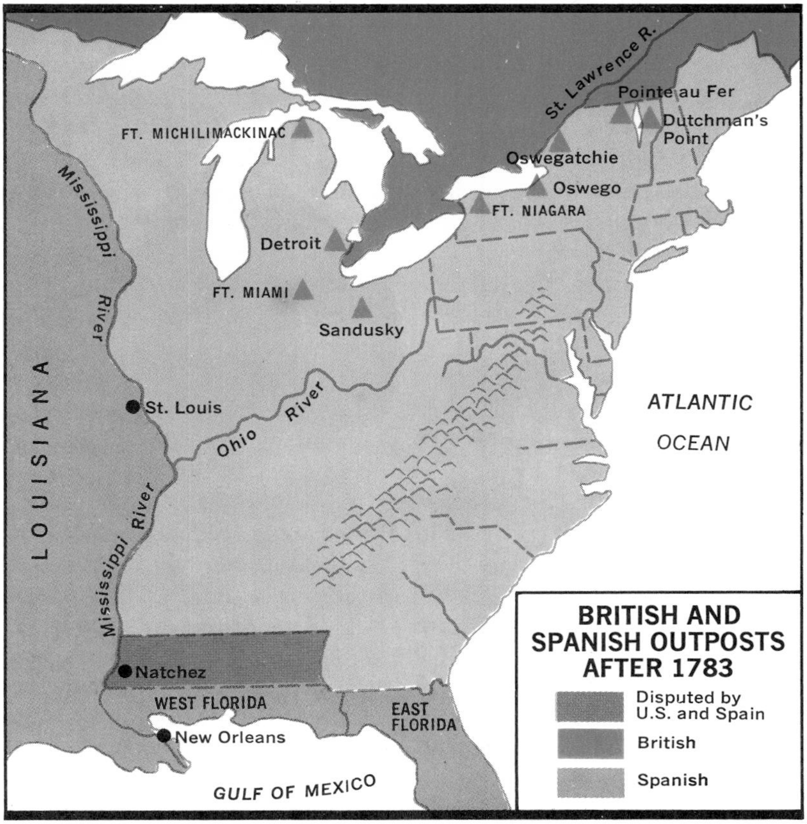

The Spanish threat to the west was even more menacing. From Louisiana and the Floridas, Spain urged the Indian tribes to attack the advancing settlers. In 1784, Spain closed the lower Mississippi River to the settlers, thus blocking their only access to the sea. At the same time, Spain was well aware that many frontiersmen in Kentucky and Tennessee regions felt themselves exploited by land speculators and ignored by the Virginia and North Carolina governments. The Spanish opened secret negotiations with leaders, such as Daniel Boone of Kentucky and John Sevier of Tennessee, hoping they would lead secession movements in return for re-opening the Mississippi to trade and restraining the Indians.

Against the British encroachments in the north and the Spanish plots in the south, American diplomats could do nothing. The British justified their presence by noting that some state governments had interfered with the efforts of British creditors to collect pre-Revolutionary debts. But Congress had no power to restrain the states from such violations of the treaty of peace. John Adams, the American minister to Great Britain, also failed to persuade the British to sign any commercial treaty or to permit American ships to trade with their colonies in the West Indies. The British were so unimpressed with the possibility of the United States becoming unified and powerful that they did not bother to send a diplomatic representative to the country. Spain was willing to talk about a commercial treaty, but only if the United States was willing to give up the use of the Mississippi. John Jay, the American Secretary for Foreign Affairs, who had eastern mercantile interests close to his heart, agreed to such a treaty with Spain. The southern states in Congress refused to approve this sacrifice of western interests.

The United States lacked the military power to make European nations respect it. The states could not cooperate to create a military force.

But despite the weakness of the federal government, American diplomats succeeded in getting commercial treaties with several European nations. After a postwar slump, American merchants and shipowners rapidly increased their trade with Britain, continental Europe, and the Far East. The British West Indian market, too, proved to be as open to illegal American trade as it had been before the Revolution. With Europe at peace, there was little need for an American navy to protect American commerce. Those engaged in international trade in the 1780's complained chiefly about the conflicting commercial regulations of the various states.

The Federal Government

"Each state retains its sovereignty, freedom, and independence, and every power, jurisdiction, and right, which is not . . . expressly delegated to the United States . . ." said the second Article of Confederation. And the powers delegated to the United States were sharply limited. The men who drafted the Articles recognized that the newly independent states were in no mood to replace British rule with a central government which they did not control.

The national government under the Articles of Confederation consisted of a legislature and some permanent employees who transacted government business. Congress had to rely on state courts and state militia to enforce the laws it passed. Its principal sources of income were requisitions on the states, made in proportion to the value of each state's real estate, and loans from abroad. The requisitions were sometimes paid by the states on time, sometimes late or only in part, and sometimes not at all. The foreign loans came mainly from Dutch bankers, who had enough confidence in the future of the United States to keep extending credit throughout the 1780's. But the amount of the foreign debt, and the interest on it, kept increasing. At one point, the failure of Congress to pay interest on its debt to France forced the French government to assume the interest payments for several years.

A more serious problem was the war debt the federal government still owed to Americans, despite the fact that some of the debt had already disappeared. When hundreds of millions of dollars in Continental paper money issued during the war had lost value, Congress had, in effect, declared it worthless. This confiscation of money was a necessary act of war. Congress simply did not have the resources to pay the remaining debt, estimated at about $34 million. Some states assumed the responsibility of paying the portions of the federal debt owed to their own citizens. By 1787, they had paid off large portions of both state and federal war debts. The chart on page 126 reveals some reasons that the state governments, rather than the national government, were the real focus of political action and influence.

Continental paper money lost value in these ways: 1) the government had so little silver and gold that it could not exchange these scarce precious metals for the flood of paper dollars it had printed to pay for war expenses; 2) many people feared the colonies would lose the war and its paper money would become worthless; 3) people who needed supplies had to pay more paper dollars than gold or silver dollars for their purchases. Other forms of debt, such as bonds, lost value temporarily for some of these reasons.

The States and Their Citizens

Although the states often failed to provide Congress with the money and troops it needed, they usually cooperated well with each other in interstate matters, and they usually met the needs of their citizens. The states exercised their right to control their own commerce by placing tariffs on foreign imports, but they rarely taxed each others' products in order to achieve competitive advantages and additional revenue. In some cases, states taxed heavily foreign-produced goods imported from other states. New Jersey and Connecticut, for example, resorted to this tactic to get shippers to bring European goods directly to them instead of to New York. Some noisy squabbles followed, but the actual interference with trade was small.

The states also succeeded, sometimes with the aid of Congress, in settling troublesome disputes between them. Connecticut and Pennsylvania settled a conflicting land claim satisfactorily; Pennsylvania and Virginia agreed on a long-contested boundary; and commissioners from Massachusetts and New York settled their states' common boundary. New Jersey and Pennsylvania signed an agreement to regulate the use of the Delaware River; and Maryland and Virginia agreed in 1785 to regulate the use of Chesapeake Bay and to develop the Potomac River for navigation. The controversy between New York and New Hampshire over control of Vermont continued, but Vermonters wanted statehood.

In the mid 1780's the states, rather than the national government, guaranteed the individual's political and civil rights. While most states required the possession of some property in order for a person to vote and usually a greater amount of property to hold office, the franchise [right to vote] was widely held among adult white males. But the western or frontier areas of most states did not have as many representatives in the state legislatures as their populations justified.

In state after state, farmers found themselves pitted against merchants over the issue of paper money. Farmers were almost always short of hard money, which was usually required for payment of taxes. Throughout the states, they agitated for state-issued paper money, which they could borrow by using their land as security. In turn, they hoped to use the paper money to pay their debts and their taxes. Merchants and professional men feared that the paper money would be issued in such large quantities that it would become worthless. In spite of their objections, seven states issued paper money, and in five of these states the money circulated without great loss in value. In North Carolina and Rhode Island, however, merchants were so bitterly opposed that they refused to accept the paper money at all; their refusal drove its value down sharply. The Rhode Island legislature, controlled by men committed to paper money, ordered fines and loss of citizenship for those who refused to accept the paper money. Creditors sometimes fled the state to avoid being paid. These actions tended to give all paper money an undeserved bad name.

Yet it was, ironically, a conservative rather than a radical financial policy that made many Americans deeply concerned about the ability of the states to survive without a strong central government. Massachusetts, whose government was dominated by east-coast commercial interests, refused to pass a paper money law. At the same time, it agreed to pay its Revolutionary War debt at a rate much nearer the face value of the loans than other states paid. It was trying to pay off this debt rapidly. As a result, taxes were extremely high. The legislature ignored farmers' loud complaints that they were being forced to sell or surrender their property in order to pay taxes and that hundreds of persons were being jailed for non-payment of debts. In 1786, a rebellion of western Massachusetts farmers, led by Daniel Shays, broke out. The uprising was repressed after a few months with little bloodshed, but it caused intense alarm throughout the United States among businessmen and others holding conservative views. Paper money could not cross state lines against a state's wishes, but could a farmers' revolt be so easily limited to a single state?

The Movement for a New Constitution

Shays' Rebellion gave a sharp impetus to a growing sentiment for a stronger central government. This sentiment had been present throughout the war and the postwar period. Such men as Alexander Hamilton of New York pleaded that the security and dignity of the United States demanded a stronger government. Other men looked upon a strong central government as an instrument for aristocracy, corruption, and tyranny.

In 1786, delegates from five states met at Annapolis, Maryland, to discuss mutual commercial problems. The Annapolis Convention set out a call for a convention to meet the following year to revise the Articles of Confederation. Men who advocated stronger government began to crystallize their ideas. Their motives were inevitably mixed, but most of them felt that the government should give more active protection against Indians, British, and Spanish in the west. They believed that it should have the power to collect taxes directly, to control commerce with other nations, and to make prompt arrangements for paying its debts. The government should also, they believed, serve as an effective and imposing arena for men who wanted to serve their country, move quickly and forcefully against rebellions within states, and give the United States a new power and dignity in the world.

There had been many unsuccessful movements to strengthen the federal government. The high quality of the delegates helped greatly in making a success of the Philadelphia Convention. Virginia, a leader among the states seeking the convention, sent a group of men with immense prestige. The group included George Washington; Edmund Randolph, the governor; George Mason, author of the Virginia Declaration of Rights; George Wythe, one of the most eminent legal men of the day; and James Madison. All but three delegates to the Philadelphia convention signed the Constitution they wrote.

In 1776, the Virginia Assembly adopted George Mason's Declaration of Rights, which guaranteed many of the human rights that were included later in the first Ten Amendments to the Constitution.

Other notables in attendance were Benjamin Franklin (Pa.), James Wilson (Pa.), one of the great legal minds of the time, and Alexander Hamilton (N.Y.).

Congress, which had helped to finance the Philadelphia convention and had supplied some of the convention's most active mem-

Flaws in Articles of Confederation	Corrected in Constitution
Two thirds vote (9 states) needed to pass legislation.	Simple majority needed to pass bill.
Unanimous vote needed to amend Articles.	Two thirds of both houses to pass amendment; three fourths of states to ratify it.
Legislators paid by states.	Legislators paid by federal government.
All states, regardless of size, had one vote.	All states have two votes in Senate; vote in proportion to size in House.
No executive to enforce laws.	President is chief executive.
No federal courts existed.	Supreme Court established; Congress could establish lower courts.
Congress could not regulate foreign trade or interstate commerce.	Congress given power to regulate interstate trade and trade with foreign nations; States forbidden to tax imports or exports without Congressional approval.
Congress could levy war, but had to request men from states.	Congress given power to raise and support an army and navy.
Congress could coin money, but had to ask states for gold and silver.	Only Congress could coin money.
Congress could levy taxes, but had no power to collect them.	Congress given power to levy and collect taxes.

bers, now moved to end its own existence by referring the new Constitution to the states. In response to the message by Congress, the states, one by one, arranged for the popular election of delegates to ratifying conventions. In several of these conventions the Federalists [supporters of the Constitution] won easily. In several other states the Constitution was ratified only after long arguments and much pressure. The Antifederalists [opponents of the Constitution], who had a majority in the New York convention, for example, ratified the Constitution in July 1788, by the narrow margin of 30 to 27, partly because they knew that more than the necessary nine states had already ratified, but largely because Alexander Hamilton threatened that New York City might secede from the state if it failed to join the new Union. Only in North Carolina did a convention reject the Constitution. The Rhode Island legislature, which had refused to send delegates to Philadelphia, pursued its dogged independence by refusing to call a ratifying convention. These two states failed to ratify until April 1789. George Washington, chosen unanimously as the first President, and the recently elected First Congress had already set the new government in motion in New York City.

The government began its tasks supported by a burst of nationalist spirit and good will. This support owed much to the fact that the leaders of the new government were still those who had led the country through the Revolutionary period. But the structure of the new system also gave confidence to Americans. The Constitution, while original in some ways, had borrowed heavily for its principles and its details both from the state constitutions and from the Articles of Confederation. While it deliberately provided solutions to the problems that had plagued the government under the Articles, it still remained very much a government of limited powers, responsible to the people and to the states.

18 The Constitution: Institutions

Political institutions are the organizations and established ways in which power is distributed and decisions are made.

Most of the fifty-five men who sat in the Philadelphia Convention in 1787 agreed that the national government needed more power and that a new constitution had to be written to provide it. But they disagreed about the forms of the institutions that would exercise that power. The fiercest controversies centered on two major issues: the distribution of power between the state governments and the national government, and the makeup of the national legislature.

The Articles of Confederation had created a weak national government as a safeguard against oppression. Yet the nation's experience under the Articles had demonstrated that a national government that was too weak lacked the power to deal decisively with foreign countries or to solve such domestic problems as taxation and civil disturbances. The problem before the Convention was to find a way to give the national government greater power than before without destroying the state governments. The solution was to adopt a federal system: the national government had specified powers granted to it, while the individual states retained all powers not delegated to the national government, except those specifically denied by the Constitution. The national government was divided into executive, legislative, and judicial branches, following the pattern of the colonial state governments.

The issue of representation in the legislative branch nearly destroyed the Convention. Governor Edmund Randolph of Virginia had offered a plan that provided for a bicameral national legislature, with the number of representatives from each state in each house to be based on the state's population. One house would have representatives elected "by the people," but the other house would not. The smaller states opposed the "Virginia Plan." They feared that because they would have fewer representatives in the legislature than the larger, more populous states, their interests would be subordinated to those of the larger states. William Paterson, of New Jersey, presented the "New Jersey Plan," which, like the congress under the Articles of Confederation, had a unicameral [one-house] legislature in which each state had one vote.

At the point at which the Convention seemed hopelessly deadlocked over representation, it agreed on the "Great Compromise," in part the work of Benjamin Franklin. The compromise solved the problem of representation by basing membership in the lower house (the House of Representatives) on population, and by giving each state, regardless of size, two seats in the upper house (the Senate).

The clauses in Reading 18, taken from the Constitution, reveal the practical application of the political ideas of eighteenth-century Americans. For purposes of analysis, clauses of the Constitution have been re-organized. To make reading easier, the language has been modernized. The original version of the text of the Constitution can be found in the Appendix.

As you read, think about the following questions:

1. What were the major political institutions established by the Constitution?
2. How did the Constitution distribute power among the three branches of the federal government (legislative, executive, judicial)? How did it distribute power between the federal government and the states?
3. To what degree did the institutions set up in the Constitution reflect the ideology and the political experience of the Founding Fathers?

Separation of Powers: Legislative Branch

Article 1

Section 1. A Congress of the United States, which shall consist of a Senate and a House of Representatives, shall have the power to make all national laws.

Section 2. Clause 3. The number of representatives each state has shall be determined on the basis of the population of the state. The population of a state shall be determined by adding the number of free people, including indentured servants, and three-fifths of the slaves. Each state shall have at least one representative regardless of its population.

One of the compromises reached between Northerners and Southerners at the Convention was to count a slave as three fifths of a person for purposes of both representation and taxation.

In 1868, after the slaves had been freed, the Fourteenth Amendment changed the basis for determining population so that all persons were counted, except Indians who were not subject to taxes.

Section 3. Clause 1. The Senate of the United States shall be made up of two senators from each state, chosen by the state legislatures. A senator's term of office is for six years. Each senator shall have one vote.

The Seventeenth Amendment, adopted in 1913, changed the method of electing senators, so that they are now elected by the qualified voters of each state.

Section 8. Clause 1. Congress has the power to collect taxes of various kinds to pay the debts of the national government, to defend that nation against enemies, and to provide for the welfare of the people. Taxes must be uniform; they must not discriminate against any section of the nation.

Section 8. Clause 2. Congress may borrow money.

Section 8. Clause 3. Congress may control trade with foreign nations, among the states, and with Indian tribes.

Section 8. Clause 4. Congress may make rules concerning how people may become citizens of the United States and laws on bankruptcy.

Bankruptcy is a legal status in which a court has declared that an individual or a corporation cannot fully pay outstanding debts. Once bankruptcy has been declared, the assets, if there are any, are often sold to pay creditors.

Section 8. Clause 5. Congress may coin money and regulate its value. It may also regulate the value of foreign money used in the United States. Congress may set standards of weights and measures.

Section 8. Clause 6. Congress may pass laws specifying how those who counterfeit securities and money should be punished.

Section 8. Clause 7. Congress may establish post offices and roads over which mail is to be carried.

Section 8. Clause 8. Congress may encourage the progress of science and useful arts by securing for authors and inventors exclusive rights to their writings and discoveries for a limited period of time.

Section 8. Clause 9. Congress may set up federal courts under the Supreme Court.

Section 8. Clause 10. Congress may decide on the punishment for crimes committed on the high seas and crimes in which foreign countries are involved.

Section 8. Clause 11. Congress may declare war.

Section 8. Clause 12. Congress may create an army and raise money to pay for its expenses. Only enough money to pay for two years' expenses can be given the army at any one time.

Section 8. Clause 13. Congress may create a navy and provide money to support it.

Section 8. Clause 14. Congress may make rules governing its army and navy.

Section 8. Clause 15. Congress may call out the state militia [similar to the present National Guard] to enforce the laws of the Union, to suppress internal rebellion, and to repel foreign invasions.

Section 8. Clause 16. Congress may organize, arm, and discipline the state militia. The states may appoint the officers of their militia, but must train them in the way Congress directs.

Section 8. Clause 17. Congress may make all rules governing the national capital and all other areas in which national military or naval installations are located.

Clause 18 is known as the "elastic clause." By interpreting it broadly, the powers of the national government could be adjusted to meet new situations.

Section 8. Clause 18. Congress may make all laws necessary and proper to carry out the powers delegated to the national government by this Constitution.

Article 4

Section 3. Clause 1. Congress may admit new states into the Union, but no new states shall be created within the boundaries of another state, nor may any state be formed by combining two or more states or parts of states without the consent both of the legislatures of the states concerned and of Congress.

Section 3. Clause 2. Congress shall have power to make all needful rules and regulations concerning territories or other property belonging to the United States.

Article 5

The Congress, whenever two thirds of both houses shall consider it necessary, shall propose amendments to this Constitution. Or, on the application of the legislatures of two thirds of the states, a convention shall be called for proposing amendments. In either case, amendments shall be valid parts of this Constitution, when ratified by the legislatures of three fourths of the states, or by conventions in three fourths of the states. Either method of ratification may be proposed by the Congress; provided that no state, without its consent, shall be deprived of its equal representation in the Senate.

Executive Branch

Article 2

Section 1. Clause 1. The President of the United States shall have the power to enforce all national laws. He and the Vice-President shall hold office for a four-year term.

Section 1. Clause 7. The President shall receive a salary for his services. It shall not be increased nor reduced during the period for which he has been elected. He shall not receive in that same period any additional payments from the United States nor from any state.

The heads of the executive departments have, since Washington's Administration, constituted the President's Cabinet, a body not specifically established by the Constitution.

Section 2. Clause 1. The President shall be Commander in Chief of the Army and Navy of the United States and of the militias of the several states when they are called into the service of the United States. He may call for written reports from the heads of each of the executive departments upon any subject relating to the work of their departments. He may grant pardons to persons convicted of crimes against the federal government or order their punishment to be delayed, except in the case of impeached government officials.

Section 2. Clause 2. The President shall have the power to make treaties with the advice and consent of the Senate. These treaties must be approved by two thirds of the senators present when the treaties are voted on. The President shall nominate and, with the advice and consent of the Senate, appoint ambassadors, other public ministers and consuls, judges of the Supreme Court, and any other officers of the United States whose appointments have not otherwise been provided for. . . .

Section 3. The President shall from time to time give Congress information concerning the state of the Union. He may suggest for congressional consideration conditions which he feels require legislation. He may call special sessions of Congress and may adjourn Congress if the two houses cannot agree on an adjournment time. He shall receive ambassadors and other public officials. He shall see that all laws are faithfully executed.

Some Presidents have personally delivered the State of the Union Message before Congress; others have sent the message to Congress to be read by a clerk. The Message is now customarily given on the first day that Congress meets.

The power of receiving ambassadors carries with it the power of recognizing or not recognizing the legitimacy of new governments.

Judicial Branch

Article 3

Section 1. The Supreme Court and the lower federal courts established by Congress shall have the power to hear and decide cases. Judges of the Supreme and lower courts shall hold office for life during good behavior, and they shall receive salaries which cannot be reduced during their time in office.

Section 2. Clause 1. Federal courts shall have power to rule on matters affecting this Constitution, federal laws, and treaties. They have the power to rule on disagreements between the federal government and other governments or individuals. They may settle arguments between the states or between citizens of different states or between states or their citizens and foreign countries.

Section 2. Clause 2. The Supreme Court shall have original jurisdiction in cases involving a representative of a foreign government or a state. In all other cases, the Supreme Court shall have appellate jurisdiction.

Original jurisdiction means the authority to try cases for the first time. Appellate jurisdiction means the authority to try cases that have been appealed from a lower court.

States and the Federal Government

Article 1

Section 9. Clause 5. Congress must not tax goods sent out of any state.

Section 9. Clause 6. Congress shall make no laws that would give the ports of one state an advantage over the ports of others.

Section 10. Clause 1. State governments must not do the following: enter into agreements with foreign nations; issue coins or paper money.

Section 10. Clause 2. No state shall, without the consent of Congress, tax goods entering or leaving its territory, except to cover the cost of inspection.

Section 10. Clause 3. No state shall, without consent of Congress, tax ships entering its ports; maintain an army or navy in times of peace; make treaties with other states or with foreign powers; engage in war unless actually invaded or in such immediate danger that delay is impossible.

Article 4

Section 1. Each state shall respect the laws, records, and court decisions of all other states.

Section 2. Clause 1. The citizens of one state shall be entitled to the privileges and immunities of citizens in all states.

Section 2. Clause 2. If a person charged with a crime in one state flees from that state, he shall, on request of the governor, be returned to the state from which he fled.

Section 4. The United States shall guarantee to every state in this Union a republican form of government. It shall protect each state against invasion and, at the request of the state, shall protect each state against domestic violence.

A republican government is one in which the law gives ultimate power to the voters, rather than to the leaders.

Article 5

The Congress, whenever two thirds of both houses shall consider it necessary, shall propose amendments to this Constitution. Or, on the application of the legislatures of two thirds of the states, a convention shall be called for proposing amendments. In either case, amendments shall be valid parts of this Constitution, when ratified by the legislatures of three fourths of the states, or by conventions in three fourths of the states. Either method of ratification may be proposed by the Congress; provided that no state, without its consent, shall be deprived of its equal representation in the Senate.

Article 6

Section 2. The Constitution and the laws of the United States shall be the supreme law of the land. Judges in every state shall be bound by them, even when state laws and state constitutions conflict with the national laws.

19 The Constitution: Decision Making and Leadership

The decision-making process is at the heart of any political system, for a nation's decisions determine such critical issues as war and peace. The leaders who control a democratic government's machinery play a vital role in decision making, even though they must look outside the government itself for support. The Constitution lays down many of the formal rules by which the federal government makes decisions and elects political leaders. Other practices, such as those by which political parties influence decisions, have grown up outside the Constitution. The rules adopted by the delegates to the Philadelphia Convention affected only the formal decisions of government. These rules grew out of the delegates' ideology and their previous experience.

The framers of the Constitution knew that dividing power among the three branches of government and reserving some powers for state governments would not necessarily keep one branch from assuming too much power. The colonial governments had been divided into executive, legislative, and judicial branches, but the governor and king had had the right to veto laws passed by the legislature. No formal machinery existed for overriding an executive veto. The only recourse for a colony was to try to change the executive's mind.

To guard against one branch of government exercising such overwhelming power, the framers of the Constitution worked out a system of checks and balances. Each branch of government was given certain ways to check the power of the others. As a further guard against arbitrary government, the delegates provided that elections to choose congressmen and the President should be held regularly and fairly often. Provision was also made for removing federal officeholders from their positions for misconduct.

The rules the authors of the Constitution adopted for the selection of political leaders are not entirely democratic by twentieth-century standards. Yet they reflect accurately the delegates' colonial experience, in which qualified voters could usually elect only representatives to the lower houses of the assemblies. And by no means all people were qualified voters. Every colony denied women, Indians, and slaves—and usually free Negroes—the right to vote. Some colonies had religious qualifications for voting and all had property requirements. Most white men, however, owned sufficient property to meet those requirements and the religious tests were often overlooked. The delegates to the Philadelphia Convention worked out rules so that some leaders would be elected directly by citizens, but according to voting qualifications established by the states. Other leaders would be elected indirectly by public officials who themselves had been elected to their offices. Others would be appointed by elected officials.

The clauses in Reading 19, taken from the Constitution, give the formal rules for making decisions within the federal government and for recruiting federal leaders. Again, clauses have been reorganized, and language has been modernized. As you read, think about these questions:

1. What formal rules did the Constitution give for decision making?
2. How were powers balanced among the three branches of government? What checks did each branch have on the powers given to other branches? What checks and balances were there between the state governments and the federal government?
3. What were the formal rules governing the election of federal leaders? What was the role of the states in choosing federal leaders? What was the role of individual citizens? How might these Constitutional rules determine the kind of men chosen as potential leaders?
4. To what extent did the process of making decisions and the rules for electing leaders reflect the ideology and the political experience of the Founding Fathers?

Checks and Balances

Article 1

Section 2. Clause 5. The House of Representatives shall have the right to impeach [bring charges against] officials of the United States suspected of serious wrongdoing.

Section 3. Clause 6. The Senate shall have the right to try impeached officials. If the President of the United States has been impeached, the Chief Justice of the Supreme Court shall preside at his trial. No official shall be convicted of the charges brought against him unless two thirds of the senators present at his trial find him guilty.

Article 2

Section 4. The President, Vice-President, and all civil officials of the federal government may be removed from office if Congress impeaches and convicts them of treason, bribery, or other crimes.

The Constitution defines treason, in Article 3, Section 3, as making war against the United States, or supporting its enemies by giving them "aid and comfort."

Article 1

Section 3. Clause 7. Congress can punish impeached officials found guilty only by removing them from office and disqualifying them from ever holding another federal office. After impeachment, however, officials can be tried by a regular court and, if found guilty of crime, punished in accordance with the law.

Section 3. Clause 4. The Vice-President of the United States shall be the President of the Senate, but he may vote only in case of a tie.

Section 3. Clause 5. The Senate shall choose its other officers, and also a temporary president [president *pro tempore*] who shall preside over the Senate when the Vice-President is absent or acting as President.

Section 4. Clause 2. The Congress of the United States shall meet at least once every year.

Some colonial governments had been angered because the governor, who had the power to do so, refused to call colonial legislatures into session.

Section 5. Clause 4. Neither house of Congress shall adjourn for more than three days without the permission of the other house.

Section 7. Clause 1. All bills having to do with the raising of money, or revenue, must be introduced in the House of Representatives. The Senate, however, can offer changes or amendments to revenue bills.

Section 7. Clause 2. Every bill that is passed by the House of Representatives and the Senate shall be presented to the President. If he approves the bill, he shall sign it, thus making it law. If he does not approve, he may veto the bill. If he vetoes the bill, he shall return it, with his objections, to the house where the bill originated. The house shall then reconsider the bill. If, after reconsideration, two thirds of the members of that house still vote to pass the bill, it shall be sent, with the President's objections, to the other house. It shall be reconsidered there, and if approved by two thirds of that house also, the bill shall become law without the President's signature.

If a bill is not signed by the President within ten days (not counting Sundays) of being presented to him, it shall automatically become law unless Congress has adjourned during those ten days, thus preventing the President's returning the bill to it within that time. If Congress adjourns during this ten-day period and the President does not sign the bill, the bill shall not become law.

This procedure of letting a last-minute bill die by simply not signing it after Congress adjourns is called a pocket veto.

Article 2

Section 2. Clause 2. The President shall have the power to make treaties with the advice and consent of the Senate. These treaties must be approved by two thirds of the senators present when the treaties are voted on. The President shall nominate and, with the advice and consent of the Senate, appoint ambassadors, other public ministers and consuls, judges of the Supreme Court, and any other officers of the United States whose appointments have been provided for by law.

How a Bill Becomes Law
(if the bill originates in the House)

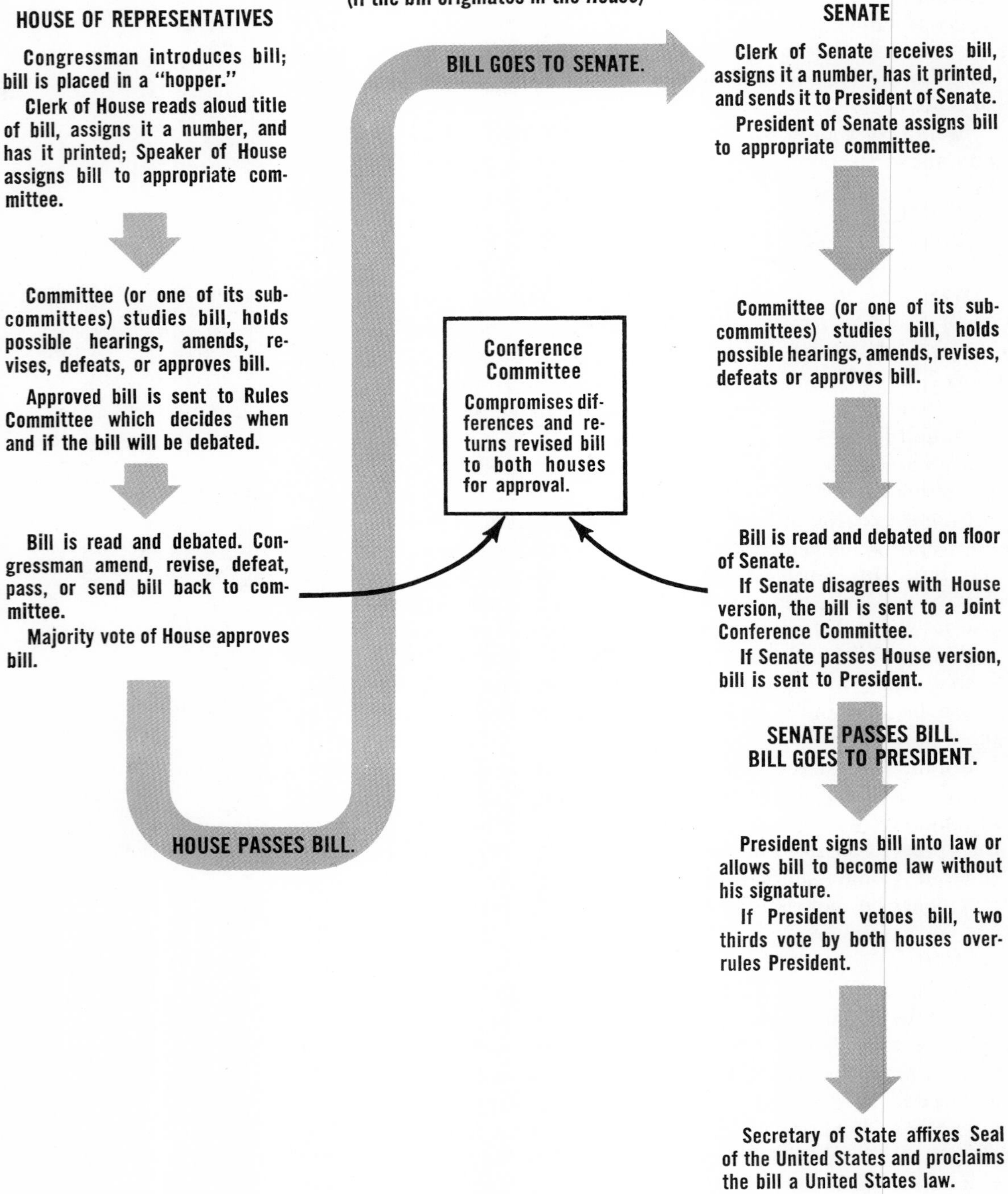
HOUSE OF REPRESENTATIVES
Congressman introduces bill; bill is placed in a "hopper."
Clerk of House reads aloud title of bill, assigns it a number, and has it printed; Speaker of House assigns bill to appropriate committee.
Committee (or one of its subcommittees) studies bill, holds possible hearings, amends, revises, defeats, or approves bill.
Approved bill is sent to Rules Committee which decides when and if the bill will be debated.
Bill is read and debated. Congressman amend, revise, defeat, pass, or send bill back to committee.
Majority vote of House approves bill.
HOUSE PASSES BILL.
BILL GOES TO SENATE.
Conference Committee
Compromises differences and returns revised bill to both houses for approval.
SENATE
Clerk of Senate receives bill, assigns it a number, has it printed, and sends it to President of Senate.
President of Senate assigns bill to appropriate committee.
Committee (or one of its subcommittees) studies bill, holds possible hearings, amends, revises, defeats or approves bill.
Bill is read and debated on floor of Senate.
If Senate disagrees with House version, the bill is sent to a Joint Conference Committee.
If Senate passes House version, bill is sent to President.
SENATE PASSES BILL.
BILL GOES TO PRESIDENT.
President signs bill into law or allows bill to become law without his signature.
If President vetoes bill, two thirds vote by both houses overrules President.
Secretary of State affixes Seal of the United States and proclaims the bill a United States law.

Section 3. The President shall from time to time give Congress information concerning the state of the Union. He may suggest to Congress the matters which he feels require legislation. He may call special sessions of Congress and may adjourn Congress if the two houses cannot agree on an adjournment time. He shall see that all laws are faithfully executed.

Article 3

Section 2. Clause 1. Federal courts shall have power to rule on matters affecting this Constitution, federal laws, and treaties. They have the power to rule on disagreements between the federal government and other governments or individuals. They may settle arguments between the states or between citizens of different states and their citizens and foreign countries.

Leadership

Article 1

Section 2. Clause 1. The members of the House of Representatives shall be elected by the people every two years for a two-year term. The citizens of the states who are qualified to vote for members of the largest branch of the state legislatures may vote for members of the House of Representatives.

Section 2. Clause 2. A representative in Congress shall be at least twenty-five years old and shall have been a United States citizen for seven years. He shall live when elected in the state that elects him.

Section 2. Clause 4. When a representative dies or resigns his office, the governor of his state shall hold an election to fill the vacancy.

Section 3. Clause 1. A senator shall be elected for six years. The state legislatures shall choose the senators.

Section 3. Clause 2. The members of the first senate shall be divided into three groups. The term of office of one group shall expire in two years, of the second group in four years, and of the third group in six years. Therefore, only one third of the senators shall be up for election at the same time.

Section 3. Clause 3. A senator shall be at least thirty years old and shall have been a citizen of the United States for nine years. He shall live when elected in the state that elects him.

Section 4. Clause 1. The times, places, and manner of holding elections to choose senators and representatives shall be decided in each state by its legislature, but the United States Congress may at any time change any of these regulations except regulations concerning where elections shall be held.

Section 5. Clause 1. Each house of Congress may judge whether its members were chosen by a fair election and whether they are properly qualified to be members of Congress. In each house, a majority of members shall constitute a quorum. A representative or a senator may be kept from taking office if a majority of the members of the body to which he was elected vote him ineligible.

A quorum is the number of members of a body required to be present in order to take official actions. A quorum may be more or less than a majority, depending on the rules of the body.

Section 5. Clause 2. Each house of Congress may make rules governing its work. Each may also punish members for behaving improperly and may expel them from the group if two thirds of the members of that house vote to do so.

Section 6. Clause 1. The senators and representatives shall be paid for their services by the United States Treasury. They may not be arrested, except for treason, felony [major crime], or breach of the peace, in Congress or on their way to and from its sessions. They may not be penalized under law for anything they say while in Congress.

Section 6. Clause 2. No senator or representative shall hold any other federal office while serving in Congress, nor, during his term in office, shall he be appointed to a federal office created during that term, or to a federal office for which the pay has been raised during that term.

Article 2

Section 1. Clause 2. Each state shall appoint, in a way established by the legislature, as many electors as it has senators and representatives in Congress. No federal officeholder can become an elector.

Section 1. Clause 3. The electors shall meet in their respective states, and vote by ballot for two persons, of whom one at least shall not be an inhabitant of the same state with themselves. And they shall make a list of all the persons voted for, and of the number of votes for each. They shall sign and certify the list, and send it to the president of the Senate. The president of the Senate shall, in the presence of the Senate and House of Representatives, open all the certificates, and the votes shall then be counted. The person having the greatest number of votes shall be the President, if such number be a majority of the whole number of electors. If more than one candidate has such majority, and has the same number of votes, then the House of Representatives shall immediately choose by ballot one of them for President. If no person has a majority, then from the five highest on the list the House shall in like manner choose the President. But in choosing the President the votes shall

The Twelfth Amendment, adopted in 1804, changed the rules so that electors now vote separately for President and Vice-President. Electors customarily vote for the candidate who receives the majority of the citizens' votes in the elector's state.

be taken by states, with each state having one vote. A quorum for this purpose shall consist of at least one member from two thirds of the states, and a majority of all the states is necessary for a choice. After the choice of the President, the person having the greatest number of votes of the electors shall be the Vice-President. But if there should remain two or more who have equal votes, the Senate shall choose the Vice-President from them by ballot.

Section 1. Clause 4. Congress may determine the time for choosing the electors and the day, to be the same throughout the United States, on which they shall vote for President and Vice-President.

The Presidential elections are held the first Tuesday after the first Monday in November of every fourth year.

Section 1. Clause 5. Only a natural-born citizen or a person who was a citizen of the United States when this Constitution was adopted shall be eligible for the Presidency. To be eligible he must also be at least thirty-five years old and must have lived within the United States for fourteen years.

A natural-born citizen is one who has been born in the United States. The question arises as to whether a child born to American parents abroad is also a natural-born citizen.

Section 2. Clause 2. Judges of the Supreme Court and of lower federal courts shall be appointed by the President of the United States.

Section 4. The President, Vice-President, and all civil officials of the federal government may be removed from office if Congress impeaches and convicts them of treason, bribery, or other crimes.

Article 3

Section 1. The judges of the Supreme Court and of the lower federal courts shall hold office during good behavior and shall be paid for their services and may not have salaries reduced while in office.

20 The Constitution: The Rights of Citizens

In the closing days of the Constitutional Convention, the delegates discussed briefly whether or not they should include a formal statement of individual rights. They decided not to do so, on the grounds that the state constitutions fully protected the rights of individuals. The delegates did, however, write into the Constitution several important guarantees, largely in terms of restrictions placed on the power of Congress and the executive.

In the battles for ratification in the states, it quickly became apparent that the Convention had misjudged the attitudes of many persons. The ideology of the Revolution was important to Americans; they took the natural rights of man seriously. The Constitution strengthened the power of the national government. This in itself reminded many men that a remote and powerful government had violated their rights in the years before the Revolution. They wanted some guarantee that the new American government could not do the same thing. Moreover, the Americans had a long tradition of expecting to find basic rights spelled out in a written document. The colonists had always looked to the charters granted by the king to the trading companies or to the proprietors who had founded the colonies to determine their political rights. They were not likely to accept readily a new government which did not define the rights of citizens as well as the rights of the government. The Antifederalists objected vigorously to the absence of a bill of rights. Five of the first eleven states that ratified the Constitution recommended strongly that a bill of rights be added promptly.

By the time the first Congress met, James Madison, who had been elected to the House of Representatives, recognized that the lack of a bill of rights could become a major focal point for opposition to the new government. Madison took the lead in framing the first ten amendments to the Constitution. They passed Congress quickly, and the necessary three quarters of the states had ratified them by December 1791.

The clauses in Reading 20, taken from the Constitution and its first ten amendments, known as the Bill of Rights, give guarantees of individual rights. Again clauses of the Constitution have been reorganized, and the language has been modernized. As you read, think about these questions:

1. What individual rights did the Constitution guarantee?
2. In what ways did the individual rights reflect the ideology and the colonial experiences of the Founding Fathers?
3. What can a citizen do if he thinks that a governmental action violates a right guaranteed by the Constitution?
4. What are the responsibilities of citizens in protecting individual rights?

Article 1

Section 9. Clause 2. The privilege of the writ of habeas corpus shall not be suspended, except in cases of rebellion or invasion when the public safety requires its suspension.

A writ of habeas corpus is a court order directing an official to show reasons for holding someone prisoner. Unless the official can show sufficient cause for holding him, the prisoner must be released.

Section 9. Clause 3. Congress may pass no bill of attainder. Neither may Congress pass an ex post facto law.

A bill of attainder is a law intended to punish a particular person. An ex post facto law is a law passed to punish someone for an act that was not against the law at the time he did it.

Section 9. Clause 8. No title of nobility shall be granted by the United States.

Section 10. Clause 1. No state shall pass any bill of attainder, ex post facto law, law impairing the obligation of contracts, or grant any title of nobility.

Article 3

Section 2. Clause 3. Except in impeachment cases, any trial for crime shall be decided by a jury. A trial must be held in the state where the crime took place.

Section 3. Clause 1. Treason shall consist only of making war against the United States or of helping enemies of the United States. No one shall be convicted of treason unless two persons testify that they witnessed the act, or unless the accused confesses in court.

Section 3. Clause 2. Congress shall have the power to declare the punishment of treason, but the punishment cannot extend to the families or descendants of a person found guilty of treason.

Article 4

Section 1. Each state shall respect the laws, records, and court decisions of all other states.

Section 2. Clause 1. The citizens of one state shall be entitled to the privileges and immunities of citizens in all states.

Section 2. Clause 2. If a person charged with a crime in one state flees from that state, he shall, on request of the governor, be returned to the state from which he fled.

Section 2. Clause 3. Any indentured servant or slave who escapes from one state to another shall not become free by doing so. If his owner claims him, a runaway must be returned.

This clause has not been applied since 1865, when the Thirteenth Amendment freed all slaves in the United States and its territories.

Article 6

Section 3. No religious test shall ever be required as a qualification for any public office or public trust in the United States.

Amendment 1

Congress shall make no law that has to do with making any religion the official one, or that restricts people from worshiping as they please, or limits freedom of speech or of the press, or keeps them from assembling peaceably, or from petitioning the government if they think they have been treated unfairly.

Amendment 2

Since a well-regulated militia is necessary to the security and freedom of a state, the people shall be allowed to keep and to bear arms.

Amendment 3

People shall not be forced to give room and board in their homes to soldiers in times of peace. Nor shall they be forced to quarter soldiers in time of war unless a law is first passed requiring it.

Amendment 4

A warrant is an order, usually issued by a judge, which authorizes a public official to take action.

Government officials cannot make unreasonable searches or seizures of individuals or their persons, homes, or belongings. No warrant for a search shall be issued unless there is probable cause that a crime has been committed and will be exposed as a result of the search, and unless the places, persons, or things to be searched or seized are specifically described in the warrant.

Amendment 5

Grand juries never try cases; they only determine whether there is sufficient evidence for a trial.

Due process has never been specifically defined by the Supreme Court. Justice Felix Frankfurter defined it as "all those rights which the courts must enforce because they are basic to our free society." There are two types of due process. **Procedural** requires that the government act fairly in its dealings with the people; **substantive** requires that the laws and regulations under which the government acts be fair and just.

No person shall be

(1) tried for a serious crime unless a grand jury has first examined the evidence and decided that a trial is warranted, except in cases arising in the armed forces, or in the militia in times of public danger;
(2) tried for the same crime twice [double jeopardy];
(3) forced, in a criminal case, to be a witness against himself;
(4) executed, imprisoned, or fined without due process of law;
(5) deprived of his property for public use unless he has first been given a fair price for it.

Amendment 6

This is a petit jury usually consisting of twelve persons. The jury weighs the facts of the case to determine whether the accused is guilty or not guilty.

Any person being tried for a criminal offense is entitled to

(1) a speedy and public trial;
(2) an impartial jury chosen from citizens of the state and district in which the crime was committed;
(3) knowledge of why he is being tried;
(4) see and hear the witnesses who testify against him;
(5) force witnesses who can give evidence in his favor to come to court to testify;
(6) assistance by a lawyer in defending himself.

Amendment 7

In law suits involving things valued at more than $20, individuals have the right to a jury trial.

Amendment 8

Bail is a pledge of money or property that the accused will return for trial.

Individuals accused of a crime cannot be required to pay excessive bail. Individuals found guilty of crimes cannot be required to pay excessive fines, nor can cruel or unusual punishments be inflicted.

Amendment 9

The fact that certain individual rights are guaranteed by the Constitution should not be interpreted to mean that rights not specifically mentioned in the Constitution are denied the individual.

Amendment 10

The Constitution delegates certain powers to the national government of the United States. All other powers are retained by the states or by the people, except those powers specifically denied to the states by the Constitution.

SUGGESTED READINGS

BRODERICK, FRANCIS L., *The Origin of the Constitution, 1776–1789.* This brief summary describes the creation of the first federal government, the years under the Articles of Confederation, the Constitutional Convention of 1789, and the ratification of the new Constitution.

MC DONALD, FORREST, *Formation of the American Republic, 1776–1790.* McDonald's book contains a lively political history of the period.

NORTH, DOUGLASS C., *Decisions That Faced the New Nation, 1783–1820.* This tiny pamphlet traces the economic history of the new nation through its trying early years.

VAN DOREN, CARL, *The Great Rehearsal.* This book tells the story of the Constitutional Convention's achievements in Philadelphia during the hot summer months of 1787.

Making Constitutional Government Work

CHAPTER 6

STATING THE ISSUE

The men who created the new American government knew how bold an experiment they were undertaking. Never before in history had men tried to enforce effective government over so wide a geographic area while deliberately limiting its power and making it responsible to popular control. The Founding Fathers placed their faith in federalism, a unique blend of national, state, and local governments. But would the federalism of the new Constitution work?

In 1789, many conditions favored the success of the venture. The United States was at peace, and its economy was prosperous. Although the Continental Congress and the Confederation had been weak, they had given many Americans experience in making political decisions for a nation. Men who had provided leadership to the American states and the Confederation government in the years since 1775 filled the top positions in the new federal government. Many minor federal officeholders, too, had had experience under the Confederation. The first President, George Washington, enjoyed enormous prestige. Most important, American citizens had long ruled themselves and believed firmly in representative government based on a philosophy of natural rights.

Yet serious problems lay ahead. In every state, for example, a minority of men still spoke out in opposition to the Constitution. Even among the men who had signed the Constitution and had stoutly supported its ratification, important differences of opinion remained about the meaning of that document. At Philadelphia, these differences had been compromised or overlooked for the sake of getting a constitution which the delegates could support. But theory now had to be turned into practice. Some men would certainly join the opposition when decisions went against them.

Chapter 6 examines the course of the federal government during its first twelve years. What were the Constitution and the new government going to be like in practice? Could the opponents of the new federal system be reconciled to it, or would they remain its enemies? Could a government wield real power under the Constitution without driving too many men into the opposition? Would men in office accept the results of an election in which they were defeated? These are the major issues raised in Chapter 6.

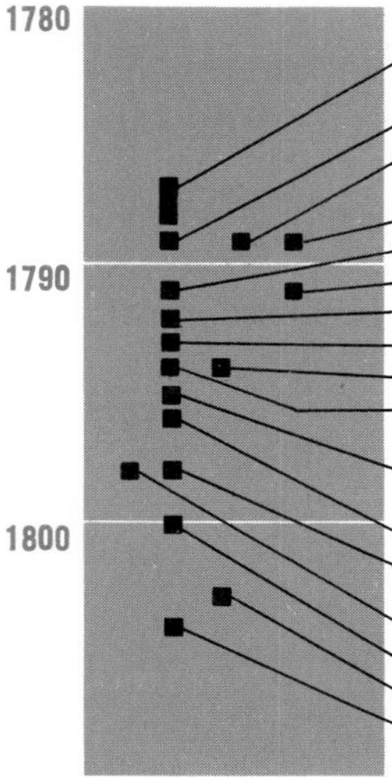

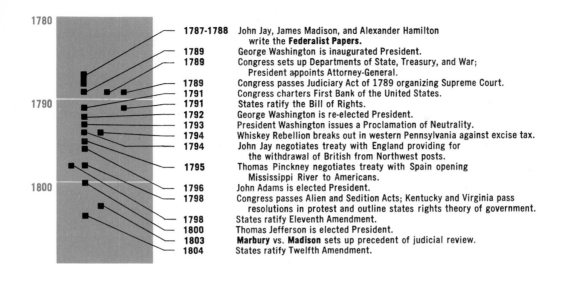

1787-1788	John Jay, James Madison, and Alexander Hamilton write the **Federalist Papers.**
1789	George Washington is inaugurated President.
1789	Congress sets up Departments of State, Treasury, and War; President appoints Attorney-General.
1789	Congress passes Judiciary Act of 1789 organizing Supreme Court.
1791	Congress charters First Bank of the United States.
1791	States ratify the Bill of Rights.
1792	George Washington is re-elected President.
1793	President Washington issues a Proclamation of Neutrality.
1794	Whiskey Rebellion breaks out in western Pennsylvania against excise tax.
1794	John Jay negotiates treaty with England providing for the withdrawal of British from Northwest posts.
1795	Thomas Pinckney negotiates treaty with Spain opening Mississippi River to Americans.
1796	John Adams is elected President.
1798	Congress passes Alien and Sedition Acts; Kentucky and Virginia pass resolutions in protest and outline states rights theory of government.
1798	States ratify Eleventh Amendment.
1800	Thomas Jefferson is elected President.
1803	**Marbury** vs. **Madison** sets up precedent of judicial review.
1804	States ratify Twelfth Amendment.

21 Majority Rule and Minority Rights

Supporters of the Constitution hoped that opposition to it could be reduced by winning decisive votes of approval in each of the ratifying conventions called by the states. The support of New York was particularly important because of its bustling port and its key location between New England and the Middle Atlantic States. Yet Alexander Hamilton of New York, who had joined in the task of drafting the new Constitution, feared that his state might reject it. He called upon two of the nation's most experienced political thinkers, John Jay, author of New York's State Constitution of 1777, and James Madison, the leading figure at the Philadelphia Convention, to help him "sell" the Constitution to the people of New York. These three men wrote a series of letters which were published in New York journals to explain the Constitution's purpose and meaning.

New York might have ratified the Constitution even if the letters had not been written. Nevertheless, their value as a commentary on American government was recognized immediately. They were published together in a volume called *The Federalist,* generally considered the most important discussion of political ideas that has ever been written in America.

Not only did *The Federalist* give explanations of the Constitution which lawmakers, judges, and lawyers still study, but they also contained broad, philosophical discussions of problems that any government must solve. One of the problems examined in *The Federalist* is as real to us today as it was to the Founding Fathers. How can minority rights be protected in a society whose government is based on majority rule?

Two great political thinkers, the Englishman John Locke (1632–1704) and the Frenchman Jean Jacques Rousseau (1712–1778), had each believed in the philosophy of natural rights. Each had also believed that men formed governments by agreement, under a "social contract," in order to protect their natural rights. Yet the two men had different ideas about what should be done with persons whose opinions and interests conflicted with those of the majority. The men who wrote the Constitution were familiar with the ideas of both Locke and Rousseau.

Locke believed that when individual men entered a social contract they reserved for themselves certain basic rights. No just government, even one representing the will of the majority, could violate these rights. Should a government do so, the people could overthrow it and establish a new one. While Locke's argument implied protection of minority rights, it carried with it the potential dangers of disunity and instability.

According to Rousseau, men who entered the social contract agreed to conform to the "general will" of the society, that is, a kind of ideal consensus of what was best. Because Rousseau believed that all men were by nature good, he thought that the "general will" could be trusted to protect the rights of all members of society. But once the "general will" was decided, all had to abide by it. Rousseau did not acknowledge the existence of minorities whose opinions justly differed from the majority, so a government based on his idea could not be expected to tolerate, let alone protect, minority views.

The important question then became whether a government could guarantee a minority the right to political action and still maintain an orderly society. James Madison believed that the Constitution offered an answer to that question. In *The Federalist,* No. 10, he explained how. As you read his explanation, keep these questions in mind:

1. What did Madison mean by a faction? What caused factions?
2. According to Madison, how were factions harmful to society as a whole? to minority groups, in particular? How might a faction be dangerous to you?
3. Does *The Federalist,* No. 10, agree more with the ideas of Locke or those of Rousseau? How might the Constitution have been different if the Founding Fathers had agreed with the philosophy of the other of these two men?
4. What protection for minority rights did Madison think the Constitution offered?

Madison Argues for Minority Rights

James Madison wrote Federalist, No. 10, *portions of which are included in this reading. He explained how the government set up by the Constitution would protect minority rights.*

John C. Hamilton, ed., **The Federalist, also the Continentalist and Other Papers by Hamilton.** Philadelphia: J.B. Lippincott and Company, 1864, pp. 104–12. Language simplified and modernized.

A federation of states can reduce and control factions. By a faction, I mean a group of citizens, either a majority or a minority, who are united by some common interest or strong feeling, which is opposed to the rights of other citizens or to the overall interest of the community. In the past, factions have been one of the greatest dangers to popular governments.

There are two ways to cure the troubles factions cause: either prevent factions from developing or control their effects.

There are, in turn, two ways to keep factions from developing: either by destroying liberty, without which they cannot exist, or by giving all citizens the same opinions, enthusiasms, and interests so that differences will not appear. The first remedy is certainly worse than the disease. Liberty is as essential to factions as air is to fire. But it would be as foolish to destroy liberty, which is essential to political life, because it nourishes faction, as it would be to destroy air, which is essential to animal life, because it feeds fires.

To give all citizens the same opinions is not only impractical, but unwise. As long as men reason erroneously and have the liberty to use their reason, they will form different opinions. And it is man's nature to hold his opinions passionately. The differences in men's abilities, from which property rights originate, also give them different opinions. The first purpose of government is to protect man's unequal abilities for acquiring property. Men possess different amounts and kinds of property. Because of this condition, society divides into different interests and parties.

The basic cause of factions thus exists in man's nature. We see factions all around us. Men zealously hold different opinions about religion and government, and they become attached to different leaders. These differences divide men into parties, inflame them with hatreds and cause them to oppress each other rather than to cooperate for the common good. The tendency of mankind to disagree is so strong that the most frivolous things have kindled unfriendly passions and have stirred up violent conflicts.

But the most common and enduring source of factions has been the unequal distribution of property. Those who have and those who don't have property have always formed distinct interests in society. Creditors and debtors, and landed interests and manufacturing interests divide people into different groups which have different views. The principal purpose of legislation is to regulate these various interests. Thus the operation of government necessarily involves the spirit of party and faction.

It is vain to say that enlightened statesmen will be able to adjust these clashing interests so that the public good will be served. Enlightened statesmen will not always be at the helm.

We must conclude that the causes of faction cannot be removed. The only relief from the harm done by factions is to control their effects.

If a faction consists of a minority, relief is supplied by the republican principle, which enables the majority to defeat the sinister views of the minority by a regular vote. On the other hand, when a majority is included in a faction, popular government gives it power to sacrifice both the public good and rights of other citizens to its own interests. Then the great problem is: How can we protect the public good and the private rights of members of the minority against the danger of a majority faction and keep a popular government?

This task can be done in one of two ways. Either the majority must be prevented from holding the same enthusiasm or interest at the same time or the majority must be prevented from oppressing others. If the majority has both the desire and the opportunity to oppress the minority, then religion and morality cannot be counted on as an adequate control. Religion and morality do not keep individuals from acting unjustly and violently; they are even less effective when a large number of people are joined together.

From this point of view, a pure democracy, that is, a society made up of a number of citizens who personally run the government, cannot cure the dangers of the faction. The majority, in almost every case, will share a common passion or interest. The majority will work together and there is nothing to protect the minority or an obnoxious individual. Hence, pure democracies have been strife-ridden, have failed to provide personal security or protection for property rights, and have, in general, been short-lived. Political thinkers who have supported pure democracies have mistakenly supposed that with equal political rights, mankind would also have equal possessions, opinions, and enthusiasms.

A republic, that is, a representative form of government, promises the cure we are seeking. By comparing a pure democracy and a representative government, we shall understand the benefits of a union of states.

The two points of difference between a democracy and a republic are: First, in a republic, the government is run by a small number of citizens elected by the rest; secondly, a republic may be extended over a greater number of citizens and a larger area.

With a representative government the public view will be refined and broadened because a body of elected citizens may see more clearly the true interests of their country. On the other hand, prejudiced men with sinister designs may get into office and then betray the interests of the people. However, a large republic, rather than a small one, is more favorable for the election of proper public officials. If the proportion of well-qualified representatives is the same in a large as in a small republic, then the large republic will offer a greater choice of candidates. Consequently, there is a greater probability that better qualified officials will be chosen.

Furthermore, each representative will be chosen by a greater number of citizens in a large than in a small republic. It will, therefore, be more difficult for unworthy candidates to use unscrupulous means to get elected. Consequently, wiser and more honest men are more likely to be chosen.

Of course if the electorate is enlarged too much, the representatives will not be well acquainted with local issues. On the other hand, if the electorate is too small, the representative will be too closely attached to local interests and will be unable to see the broader national interest. The Federal Constitution forms a happy combination; national interests will be handled by Congress, while local interests will be served by state legislatures.

Another difference between a democratic and a republican government is that a republic can govern a larger territory. This possibility provides the primary protection that a republic offers against factions. In a small society, there will be fewer distinct interest groups, so a majority will be found more frequently. The smaller the number of individuals making up the majority within a small area, the easier it is for them to carry out oppressive policies. Enlarge the size of the political unit and you take in a greater variety of parties and interest groups. It is then less probable that a majority will have a common motive for invading the rights of other citizens. If such a motive exists, it will be more difficult for those who share it to know their own strength and to act together.

Hence, it clearly appears that a large republic can control factions more effectively than a small republic. A union of states will be more likely to give us representatives whose views will be free of local prejudices and local schemes for injustice. It will increase the variety of parties so that one group will not be able to outnumber and oppress the rest. Finally, it has the advantage of presenting an obstacle to an unjust and self-interested majority.

Leaders of factions may kindle a flame within their particular states, but the fire will be unable to spread through the other states. A religious sect may become a political faction in one state, but the variety of sects found within the United States would protect the nation against such a faction. A rage for paper money, for the abolition of debts, for an equal distribution of property, or for any other improper and wicked scheme will be less likely to spread throughout the Union than throughout a particular state.

In a union of states, therefore, we find a republican remedy for the diseases so commonly found in republics.

22 Interpreting the Powers of Government

Early in Washington's first term, disputes arose over questions which the Constitution had left vague or unanswered. Some involved the form and the style of government. (Should Washington be referred to as "His Highness the President of the United States and Protector of their Liberties"? The answer was "no.") Some involved questions of authority. (Since the President needed the consent of the Senate to appoint department heads, such as the Secretary of State, could he remove them without its consent? The answer was "yes.") As might have been expected, however, the hottest debates about interpreting the Constitution grew out of attempts to define how much power the new government had.

At first the Administration was inclined to take a liberal view of its powers, or as it came to be termed, to adopt a "broad construction" of the Constitution. James Madison, who had had more to do with writing the Constitution and putting it into effect than anybody else, took this view. But Madison and others soon realized that the government could use broad powers to favor some groups at the expense of others.

In 1790, for example, Secretary of the Treasury Alexander Hamilton proposed that the government approve the organization of a national bank by private citizens and advance part of the money to start it. Hamilton saw that a bank could provide credit for business expansion and act as a financial agent for the government. The Constitution, however, said nothing about the government's right to create such a bank. Madison and his close friend Thomas Jefferson, who had become Secretary of State, recognized that a government bank would benefit commercial interests along the northern seaboard more than it would help farmers and planters of the back country and the South. Both these men owned extensive plantations in Virginia. They began moving toward a narrower view of governmental power, a "strict construction" of the Constitution, by denying that the government had the power to charter a bank.

Congress, despite Madison's efforts, passed Hamilton's bank bill. In enacting this bill, Congress and the President obviously interpreted the Constitution; they believed they had the power to create a bank.

But did they have the final voice in such a matter? The members of the Constitutional Convention had not taken a position on this question. Some of them had suggested that the Supreme Court ought to sit with the President as a "Council of Revision" to examine laws passed by Congress. Some had thought that challenges to the constitutionality of laws would naturally come before the Supreme Court for decision. Some also had doubted whether the judges could set themselves above legislators. The issue of the bank raised all these questions.

The first two excerpts which follow are concerned with the question of how much power the Constitution gave to the Congress. The third deals with the power of the Supreme Court. As you read, think about the following questions:

1. On what grounds did Jefferson argue that the Constitution did not give Congress the power to establish a national bank?
2. How did Hamilton justify his argument for a bank?
3. How did Chief Justice John Marshall defend the right of the Supreme Court to pass on the constitutionality of national laws?
4. Suppose that the arguments of the strict constructionists had won out. What difference would this turn of events have made to the effectiveness of the national government, particularly today?

Thomas Jefferson's Views on the Powers of Congress

President Washington asked James Madison, Alexander Hamilton, Thomas Jefferson, and Edmund Randolph, the Attorney General, to send him written comments about whether or not Congress had the power to create a bank. The excerpt below contains a part of Jefferson's reply.

Albert E. Bergh, ed., **The Writings of Thomas Jefferson.** Washington, D.C.: Thomas Jefferson Memorial Association, 1903, vol. III, pp. 146–50. Language simplified and modernized.

I believe that the foundation of the Constitution lies on this principle—that "all powers not delegated to the United States, by the Constitution, nor prohibited by it to the states, are reserved to the states, or to the people." [Tenth Amendment] To take a single step beyond these specific limits to the powers of Congress, is to grasp unlimited power.

The power to incorporate a bank has not, in my opinion, been delegated to Congress by the Constitution. The financial powers granted specifically to Congress are:

1. to lay taxes for the purpose of paying debts of the United States. The Bank Bill, however, does not propose to pay any debt or lay any tax.

2. to "borrow money." The Bank Bill does not propose to borrow money. Nor does it insure that others can borrow from the Bank. The proprietors of the United States Bank will be just as free as any other bank or individual to lend or not to lend money to the public.

3. "to regulate commerce with foreign nations, and among the states, and with the Indian tribes." To establish a bank and to regulate commerce are very different acts. The money from a bank would be used in commerce, but using money in commerce has nothing to do with regulating commerce.

Nor is the power to establish a bank covered by the general powers of Congress, which are:

1. to lay taxes to provide for the general welfare of the United States. Congress is not to lay taxes for any purpose it pleases, but only to pay debts or provide for the welfare of the country. Nor is Congress to do anything it pleases in order to provide for the general welfare; it is only to lay taxes for that purpose. To interpret this clause any other way would make the delegated powers of Congress meaningless. It would reduce the whole Constitution to a single phrase—that of giving Congress the power to do whatever is good for the United States. And it would make Congress the sole judge of good and evil, so it could do whatever evil it wished.

The enumerated powers are those powers the Constitution granted specifically to Congress in Article 1, Sections 1–17.

2. "to make all laws necessary and proper" for carrying out the enumerated powers. But all of the enumerated powers can be carried out without establishing a bank. A bank, therefore, is not necessary, and consequently it is not authorized.

Supporters of the Bank Bill argue that a bank would be a great convenience in collecting taxes. Even if this argument were true, the Constitution allows only for laws which are "necessary," not for those which are merely "convenient" for carrying out delegated powers. If the word "necessary" were interpreted so broadly as to mean convenient, it would swallow up all the delegated powers and allow Congress to pass any laws it wanted to. The Constitution restrained the power of Congress by providing that it pass only necessary laws, that is those laws without which delegated power would be ineffective.

Alexander Hamilton Replies

Hamilton, a New Yorker and a friend of northern commercial interests, sent the following reply to Washington when the President asked him for an opinion on the constitutionality of the Bank Bill.

John C. Hamilton, ed., **The Works of Alexander Hamilton.** New York: John F. Trow, 1850, vol. IV, pp. 107–13. Language simplified and modernized.

Congress has implied as well as express [specifically granted] powers. For the sake of accuracy, it should be mentioned that Congress also has what might be called resulting powers. For example, if the United States conquered a neighboring territory, it would have jurisdiction there. This jurisdiction would come from the whole mass of powers of the government, rather than from any of the specifically enumerated powers.

Thomas Jefferson, the Secretary of State, maintains that no laws passed by Congress are to be considered necessary, except those without which the delegated grant of power would be ineffective. It is vital for the sake of the national government, that so erroneous an idea of the meaning of the term "necessary" should be exploded.

Neither the grammatic meaning nor the popular use of the term supports Jefferson's definition. "Necessary" often means nothing more than needful, requisite, incidental, useful, or conducive to. And this is the way the word is used in the Constitution. The wording of the clause indicates that the Philadelphia Convention intended to give a liberal interpretation to the exercise of delegated powers. The expressions in the clause are comprehensive: "to make all laws necessary and proper for carrying into execution the foregoing powers, and all other powers, vested by the Constitution in the government of the United States, or in any department or officer thereof."

To define "necessary" in the restrictive sense that the Secretary of State does, would be to depart from its obvious meaning. He defines the word as if the clause read "absolutely necessary."

There are many complex ways in which a government can meet national emergencies, prevent national inconveniences, and promote national prosperity. A broad interpretation of the means available to the government to handle these situations is vital. Consequently, the Constitution must be interpreted broadly.

This conclusion does not mean that the government is sovereign in all respects, but it is sovereign to the extent of its specified powers.

Sovereign means having supreme power or authority.

What then is the criterion [standard] for determining what is constitutional and what is not? The criterion is the purpose of legislation; an act of Congress is the means to an end. If the end is clearly within the specified powers of Congress, and if the law has an obvious relationship to that end, and it is not forbidden by any particular provision of the Constitution, then the measure comes within the authority of the national government.

Chief Justice John Marshall Defines the Power of the Supreme Court

The right of Congress to charter a national bank was not challenged until 1819, when the Supreme Court declared that Congress did have that power. But the right of the Supreme Court to de-

cide whether acts of Congress were in conflict with the Constitution went back to 1803. In deciding a case [Marbury *vs.* Madison], *the Court, with Chief Justice John Marshall as its spokesman, simply asserted that it did have this power. Although Jeffersonians disliked the tone and force of this claim of the power of judicial review, they had too much respect for law to try to resist it. Marshall's justification of that power is given here.*

Marbury vs. **Madison,** 1 Cranch, 137 (1803). Language simplified and modernized.

Whether an act contrary to the Constitution can become the law of the land is a question deeply interesting to the United States.

The whole American system is based on the idea that the people have the right to establish such principles for their future government as they think will contribute most to their own happiness. So important a right ought not to be exercised frequently, but when it is exercised, the principles that are established should be considered fundamental and permanent.

Either the Constitution is a supreme law, unchangeable except by amendment, or it is on the same level as ordinary laws passed by Congress and, like other laws, can be changed by Congress.

If the Constitution is the supreme law, then an act of Congress contrary to the Constitution is void. If the Constitution has no more authority than an ordinary law, then constitutions are absurd attempts by people to limit a power that cannot be limited.

Certainly men who have written constitutions think of them as the fundamental and supreme law of the nation. Consequently, the theory behind every government based on a written constitution must be that an act of the legislature which violates the constitution is void. If an act of the legislature which is opposed to the Constitution is void, are not courts obligated to declare such acts invalid?

It is emphatically within the jurisdiction and the duty of the judicial department to say what the law is. Those who apply the rule to particular cases must interpret that rule. If two laws conflict with each other, the courts must decide how each law operates.

So if a law is opposed to the Constitution and if both the law and the Constitution apply to a particular case, the court has two possible courses of action. It must either decide the case in favor of the law and disregard the Constitution, or decide in favor of the Constitution and disregard the law. The court must decide which of these conflicting rules governs the case. This is the essence of judicial duty.

23 The Role of Political Opposition

For a few years, President Washington's Administration met no organized opposition. Jefferson, Madison, and others disliked

Alexander Hamilton's use of federal power to strengthen the commercial interest of the American economy. But to oppose Washington directly seemed a little like treason. He was re-elected unanimously in 1792.

During Washington's second term, however, his fellow Virginians took the lead in organizing a network of political groups. Members of these groups disagreed with many of the policies proposed by Hamilton and adopted by Washington. They called themselves "Republicans," leaving to the Administration's supporters the name of "Federalists."

Many circumstances, besides opposition to the Administration's pro-business policies, contributed to the Republican opposition. Political fights at the state and local level turned some powerful leaders, such as George Clinton of New York, into opponents of the Federalists. The outbreak of war in 1793, between the French revolutionary government and Great Britain, created dissension between sympathizers with Britain, such as Hamilton, and sympathizers with France, such as Jefferson. Federalists also blamed Republican societies, which were influenced by the democratic aims of the French Revolution, for a revolt, in 1794, of western Pennsylvania farmers against a new federal tax on distilled liquor. Then, in 1795, John Jay negotiated a highly unpopular commercial treaty with Great Britain. President Washington used his influence to get the Senate to ratify the treaty over vigorous Republican objections.

While the Republican organization was much too loose and informal to resemble a modern political party, it nearly won the Presidency for Jefferson in 1796. John Adams defeated Jefferson by the narrow electoral margin of seventy-one to sixty-eight. Under the existing rules each elector voted for two men without specifying which one was to be President. Jefferson, with the second highest vote, became Vice-President.

After a brief "honeymoon" between Adams and the Republicans, an even more bitter political fight broke out. Each side had the support of newspapers which vied with one another in denouncing both the leaders and the policies of the opposition. The war between Britain and France entered a more active phase in 1798. American foreign affairs became a violent partisan issue. Both Federalists and Republicans hurled charges of disloyalty to American interests at each other. It became uncertain whether the antagonists could continue to work with each other within a Constitutional framework. Reading 23 examines some aspects of this issue. As you read, keep these questions in mind:

1. What Constitutional issues were involved in the Sedition Act? Why did the Republicans fear its enforcement?

2. What were the implications of the Virginia Resolution for the federal system? for freedom of speech in a democracy?
3. What does Hamilton's estimate of Jefferson suggest about the political position of each man?
4. Does Jefferson's inaugural address sound like the speech of a victorious candidate? What was the significance for the American political system of Jefferson's attitude in 1801?

Sedition means the promotion of discontent with or rebellion against the government.

The Sedition Act

A Federalist Congress passed and President Adams signed a Sedition Act in 1798. Parts of that Act follow.

United States Statutes at Large, vol. I, pp. 596–97. Language simplified and modernized.

If anyone writes, prints, speaks, or publishes, or knowingly assists in writing, printing, speaking, or publishing anything false, scandalous, and malicious against the United States government, either house of Congress, or the President, with the attempt to attack their reputations or to bring them into contempt or disrepute, or to stir up the hatred of the American people against them, such a person, if convicted, shall be punished by a fine not exceeding two thousand dollars and by not more than two years imprisonment. If any person stirs up hatred against a member of Congress or the President, or promotes sedition within the United States, or organizes any unlawful groups to oppose or resist any law of the United States, or any act of the President, or to resist, oppose, or defeat any such law or act, or to aid, encourage or abet [help] any hostile designs of any foreign nations against the United States, their people or their government, such a person, if convicted, shall be punished by a fine not exceeding two thousand dollars and by not more than two years imprisonment.

Congress passed an Alien Enemies Act (1798) giving the President power to expel from the country or arrest alien enemies during wartime. A Naturalization Act (1798) increased from five to fourteen years the time an alien had to live in the United States before qualifying for citizenship.

The Virginia Resolution

The state legislatures of Kentucky and Virginia passed resolutions protesting the Sedition Act and other restrictive laws. Portions of the Virginia Resolution, written by James Madison, are given here.

The Debates in the Several State Conventions on Adoption of the Federal Constitution, collected and revised by Jonathan Elliot. Philadelphia: J.B. Lippincott and Company, 1876, pp. 528–29. Language simplified and modernized.

The Virginia General Assembly deeply regrets that the Federal Government has made clear its intention to enlarge the powers given to it by the Constitution. Certain general phrases of the Constitution are being interpreted in such a way as to destroy the meaning of the enumerated powers which limit general grants of power. This tendency of the Federal Government to assume greater power will gradually consolidate the states into one political unit. This growing federal authority will change the present republican system of the United States government into an absolute, or at best, a mixed monarchy.

The General Assembly particularly protests against the obvious and alarming way in which the Alien and Sedition Acts violate the Constitution. The Sedition Act exercises a power positively forbidden by the First Amendment. This act ought to produce universal alarm, because it is leveled against the right to examine public officials and public acts freely and to communicate freely among the people—a right which is the only effective guardian of all other rights.

The First Amendment forbids Congress to pass any law that restricts people from worshiping freely, speaking freely, assembling peacefully, or from complaining about the government. It also forbids Congress from restricting the freedom of the press.

When Virginia ratified the Federal Constitution, the ratifying Convention expressly declared that among other essential rights "the liberty of conscience and of the press cannot be canceled, abridged, restrained, or modified by any authority of the United States." From its extreme anxiety to guard these rights from every possible attack, Virginia, with other states, recommended an amendment to the Constitution which was passed as the First Amendment.

It would be inconsistent and criminal of us, if we now were indifferent to the violation of one of these rights. Furthermore, it would establish a precedent which might be fatal to other rights.

The General Assembly does solemnly appeal to other states to declare the Alien and Sedition Acts unconstitutional and to cooperate with this state in maintaining the authority, rights, and liberties reserved to the states or to the people [by the Tenth Amendment].

Hamilton's Estimate of Jefferson

In the election of 1800, Thomas Jefferson and Aaron Burr, both Republicans, received exactly the same number of electoral votes. According to the Constitution, the House of Representatives would elect the President in case of a tie. In the House, the Federalists could shift their votes to either Jefferson or Burr. During this crisis, Alexander Hamilton, a bitter enemy of Burr in New York politics, wrote a private letter on January 16, 1801, to James A. Bayard in which he assessed the character of his old opponent, Jefferson.

Hamilton, ed., **The Works of Alexander Hamilton,** vol. VI, pp. 419–20. Language simplified and modernized.

I intend, at some cost to my popularity, to reveal the true character of Thomas Jefferson.

His policies are tinged with fanaticism. He is too enthusiastic about democracy. He has been a mischievous enemy to the principal measures of President Washington's Administration. He is crafty in gaining his objectives, and he is unscrupulous about the means he uses to achieve success. Nor is he mindful of the truth. In short, he is a contemptible hypocrite.

Jefferson had opposed most of Hamilton's financial program and what he considered Washington's pro-British foreign policy.

But it is not true, as some claim, that he is an enemy of executive power or that he is for putting all powers of government into the House of Representatives. In fact, while we served in President Washington's Cabinet, he generally favored an expansion of executive authority. I have more than once reflected that, since he thought about himself as a future President, he was taking care to inherit a strong office.

Nor is it true that Jefferson, while pursuing his principles, would threaten his popularity or his own interests. He is as likely as any man I know to temporize [to suit his actions to the times or circumstances]; to calculate what will be likely to promote his own reputation and advantage. The probable result of such a temperament is to preserve systems, which he once opposed, for systems once established could not be overturned without danger to the person who did it. To my mind, a true estimate of Mr. Jefferson's character leads me to believe that he would temporize rather than change the existing system of government.

It is certainly true that Jefferson has displayed a culpable [blameworthy] partiality for France. But I think his fondness for France is quite as much a result of her popularity among Americans as it is from his own opinions. As French popularity in America diminishes, so will Jefferson's zeal for France. Add to this, the fact that there is no reason to suppose that Jefferson can be corrupted. This is a security that he will not go beyond certain limits.

Jefferson's First Inaugural Address

Because of the tie between Jefferson and Burr in the election of 1800, the House of Representatives had to choose the President. The House voted thirty-six times before Jefferson received the necessary majority. Hamilton disliked Burr, and he finally influenced Federalists to throw the election to Jefferson. The new President later devoted part of his inaugural address to the bitter rivalry which threatened national unity.

Bergh, ed., **The Writings of Thomas Jefferson,** vol. III, pp. 318–20. Language simplified and modernized.

During the election campaign through which we have just passed, heated debates might have confused strangers who are not accustomed to thinking freely and to speaking and writing what they think. But the differences of opinion which divided us have been decided by the voice of the nation and have been announced according to the rules of the Constitution. Now of course, all will abide by the will of the law and unite in common efforts for the common good. All, too, will bear in mind this sacred principle, that though the will of the majority is in all cases to prevail, that will, to be rightful, must be reasonable. The minority have equal rights, which equal law must protect. To violate the rights of the minority would be oppressive.

Let us, then, fellow-citizens, unite with one heart and one mind. Let us restore to social relationships that harmony and affection without which liberty and even life itself are but dreary things. And let us reflect that, having banished from our land that religious intolerance under which mankind so long bled and suffered, we have yet gained little if we approve a political intolerance as despotic, as wicked, and as capable of bitter and bloody persecutions.

During the throes and convulsions of the French Revolution and the accompanying wars, it is not surprising that the agitation should reach even America. Nor is it surprising that this agitation should be felt and feared by some Americans more than by others, and should thus divide opinions over the best ways to preserve the safety of our society. But every difference of opinion is not a difference of principle. We have given people different names who believe in the same principle. We are all republicans, we are all federalists.

If there be any among us who would wish to dissolve this Union or to change its republican form of government, let them stand undisturbed. Errors of opinion may be tolerated where reason is left free to combat it. I know, indeed, that some honest men fear that a republican government cannot be strong, that this government is not strong enough. But would the honest patriot abandon a government, which has so far kept us free, in the fear that this government, the world's best hope, may lack the energy to preserve itself? I trust not. I believe, on the contrary, that this is the strongest government on earth. I believe it is the only one where every man, at the call of the law, would support the law, and would meet invasions of the public order as his own personal concern. Sometimes it is said that man cannot be trusted with governing himself. Can he, then, be trusted with the government of others? Or have we found angels in the forms of kings to govern him? Let history answer this question.

Let us, then, with courage and confidence pursue our own federal and republican principles, our attachment to union and representative government.

24 The Federal Government Survives and Prospers

HISTORICAL ESSAY

In 1789, Americans began a unique experiment in government, the first attempt to establish a government based on the ideology of natural rights. All history offered no evidence that such a system could be made to work. In the twentieth century, scores of failures among new governments have demonstrated how difficult it is to keep them alive and healthy. The fact that the new American system worked and became a model for many other governments is remarkable. The story of the critical years from 1789 to 1803 reveals some of the most important reasons why the new federal government survived and prospered.

The Federalists Absorb Their Opponents

Most of the strong feelings aroused by the battles over ratification of the Constitution died down quickly. Some of the men who had vigorously opposed the Constitution were elected to the First Congress. They may have been attracted to Congress by the prospect of sharing in a new kind of power, or by a desire to guard with sharp eyes the rights of their states against the new central government. In any case they devoted their abilities to the common task of making the federal system succeed. By mid 1790, when all thirteen states had ratified the Constitution, outward opposition to the new system of government had virtually disappeared. The proposal of a Bill of Rights by Congress did much to still the fears of the suspicious. The reputations and talents of the men who took office in George Washington's first Administration quieted those fears further.

Washington's qualities of leadership during the years of the Revolution and the Confederation had influenced his colleagues to make the office of President strong. Washington did not disappoint his supporters as he helped shape the Presidency. His conduct in office won for the new government what it needed most, the confidence of its citizens. While Washington's immense dignity and reserved air kept his subordinates somewhat in awe of him, his rocklike integrity and sound judgment commanded their deep respect. John Adams, who as Vice-President added prestige to the Administration, commented after observing Washington in action for a few months: "No man, I believe, has influence with the President. He seeks information from all quarters, and judges more independently than any man I ever knew." Thomas Jefferson disagreed with many of Washington's policies. Yet, in 1814, he recalled of the first President: "Perhaps the strongest feature in his character was prudence, never acting until every circumstance, every consideration, was maturely weighed; refraining if he saw a doubt, but, when once decided, going through with his purpose, whatever obstacles opposed. His integrity was most pure, his justice the most inflexible I have ever known."

Washington tried hard to get men of high abilities to serve in appointive offices. He also set the precedent of awarding some offices to men from all sections of the nation. This policy was one important way to promote national unity. He selected trusted, former subordinates for two executive positions by appointing Alexander Hamilton of New York as Secretary of the Treasury and Henry Knox of Massachusetts as Secretary of War. He drew upon the largest state, Virginia, for its politically powerful governor, Edmund Randolph, and for its most distinguished political thinker and diplomat, Thomas Jefferson. Randolph became Attorney General and Jefferson became Secretary of State. The six Supreme Court justices were drawn from all parts of the country. John Jay of New York became the first Chief Justice. Of the largest states, only Pennsylvania did not contribute a high-ranking federal officer.

The Constitution provided for a Supreme Court, but did not specify the number of justices. The Judiciary Act of 1789, which established the federal judiciary system, specified that the Supreme Court "shall consist of a chief justice and five associate justices." Congress has varied the number of judges from five to ten. Since 1869, however, the figure has been set at nine.

Programs and Policies

Washington's popularity and his wise appointments, however, did not guarantee that citizens would accept the authority of the new government. The critical test would come when the government had to exert real power where it was needed and still retain the support of a people jealous of their freedom. The political and administrative skill of Alexander Hamilton played an essential part in helping the government meet this test successfully.

Hamilton, as Secretary of the Treasury, was the chief financial officer of the government. He had to obtain an income for the federal government that would free it from dependence upon the states. Hamilton realized that if citizens could be brought to think of the federal government, instead of the states, as the center of financial power and stability, they would identify their own interests with the success of the national government. He set out to develop a sound financial structure.

In 1789, Congress quickly adopted taxes on many imports and established port duties that gave American-owned ships somewhat lower rates. These duties were one source of income for the government. The federal government appointed customs officers to collect the duties and federal marshals to help enforce the laws. A system of federal district courts, parallel in some ways to state courts, was created to hear cases involving the new federal laws. Between the revenue officers and the courts, the government succeeded in getting most importers to obey the laws. Smuggling, a well-established American practice, declined sharply, a fact that testified to the energy and popularity of the new government.

Hamilton arranged a system of "funding," for paying off the national debt. Most of the debt had grown up during the Revolution, and nearly everybody expected the new government to pay that debt. But Hamilton surprised many persons by asking that those holding federal certificates of debt be paid back at face value. Many of the men who held the certificates had bought them at very low prices at times when no one was sure that they ever would be paid off. Some people, such as James Madison, argued that the original holders of the certificates, some of whom had been forced to sell because of hard times, deserved some return for the money they had lost. Hamilton also asked that the federal government be responsible for "assumption," that is, assuming the Revolutionary debts of all the states. This plan was agreeable to states like Massachusetts, with heavy debts still to be paid, but not to states like Virginia, which had already paid most of its debt. Virginians saw this proposal as a scheme for milking their state for the benefit of New Englanders. Madison rallied enough support in Congress to block the passage of bills for funding and assumption.

Yet nearly all national leaders, including Madison, realized the vital necessity of paying the national debt in order to win the confidence of American citizens and of other nations in the stability of the government. Hamilton asked Jefferson to persuade Madison and his followers to back the funding program, in return for Hamilton's support for establishing the new national capital on the Potomac River. The Virginians reluctantly agreed. The federal government then issued new bonds to pay for funding and for the assumption of old debts. Both the old debts and the new bonds were held largely by commercial and professional men in the northern cities, the only group with much available capital.

Hamilton's plan for a national bank drew support from the same group, while many farmers, who often supported Madison and Jefferson, opposed it. According to Hamilton's proposal, the federal government would charter the bank and it would act as the government's financial agent, but the capital and the control of the proposed bank would be largely in private hands. The debate raged partly, as we have seen in Jefferson's and Hamilton's comments to President Washington, over the question of whether Congress could legally create an agency not specifically authorized by the Constitution. But in large part the fight over the Bank represented a clash between rural southern interests and urban northern interests. Washington signed the bill authorizing the bank. It proved to be as successful in ensuring smooth and safe handling of funds and in aiding business transactions as Hamilton and the commercial interests had hoped it would be. But control of the bank fell to northern businessmen, and its profits went largely into northern and foreign hands, just as Jefferson and the agrarian interests had feared.

Agrarian means related to farming interests and agriculture.

The last of Hamilton's imaginative proposals—government subsidies and high tariffs to encourage the development of new industries—failed to pass Congress primarily because of the opposition of the agrarians. Despite the defeat, Hamilton's financial program laid a sound basis, not only for the stability of the new government, but also for the future growth of the American economy. Moreover, in adopting Hamilton's program, the Federalists defined the role of the federal government broadly. Now the government had to demonstrate that it could enforce its authority.

In 1791, Congress adopted an excise tax on liquor distilled within the United States. This act became important not so much for the revenue it produced as for the opportunity it gave to the federal government to meet successfully an open challenge to its authority. Many farmers, who distilled whiskey from their own grain, avoided paying excise taxes. The farther they lived from the heavily settled coastal area, the harder it was to collect taxes from them. In 1794, federal officials decided to collect the whiskey tax in western Pennsylvania. Farmers there resisted by rioting and by terrorizing some of the tax collectors. Washington saw the importance of meeting such challenges. Henry Lee, accompanied by Alexander Hamilton, led an army of about 13,000 hastily recruited militiamen westward over the mountains. Resistance disappeared as word of the approaching army spread among the rebels. Washington had proved his point. He was then wise enough to temper force with leniency. The only persons arrested in the Whiskey Rebellion were eventually released.

An excise tax is a tax levied upon the manufacture, sale, or consumption of goods within a nation or a state. Federal excise taxes have been levied largely upon liquor, tobacco, and other luxury items.

The assertion of federal authority took place with remarkably little conflict between the federal government and the state governments over their respective roles. The new government was actually small in size. The army was tiny and the navy non-existent. Nearly all the public officials that an ordinary citizen met, except for postal employees, worked for state and local governments, rather than for the nation. States did not always approve of federal power, but the first critical years passed without any state challenging federal authority directly.

Many of Washington's decisions established important precedents in defining the role of the President. His prestige helped Congress to accept gracefully his first veto of a bill it had passed. In 1793, during the war between Britain and France, he declared that America would remain neutral. Washington did not assume the responsibility, as modern Presidents have done, of suggesting a legislative program to Congress, but his advisers, especially Hamilton, drafted legislation to be introduced by supporters of the Administration.

The Constitution gave Congress the power to declare war, but it said nothing about the power to declare neutrality.

Federal leaders drew upon colonial and state experiences in ironing out relationships between Congress and the President. Precedents were not clear, however, in determining the role of the Supreme Court. The most important question was whether the Court could declare an act of Congress unconstitutional. Neither the Constitution nor previous experience gave a clear answer. Yet when Chief Justice John Marshall declared in 1803 in the case of *Marbury* vs. *Madison* that part of the Judiciary Act of 1789 was unconstitutional, the decision attracted relatively little opposition.

The Rise of Organized Opposition

The men who designed the Constitution were realists. They expected that those who took part in government would find many reasons to disagree with each other. The delegates to the Philadelphia Convention had built a system of checks and balances into the new government to make it difficult for a distinct interest group to gain control of the whole government. Madison had argued in *The Federalist,* No. 10, that federalism gave protection against the evils of factions. But the authors of the Constitution had not expected that such interest groups would grow into organizations operating openly and peacefully to gain leadership and control in the government. In the 1790's, political parties were not yet a recognized part of the political process, but the beginnings of the American party system date from this period.

DIFFERENCES BETWEEN THE FIRST POLITICAL PARTIES

Federalists	Democratic-Republicans
Party of Alexander Hamilton, John Adams, and John Marshall.	Party of Thomas Jefferson and James Madison.
Led by merchants, bankers, and lawyers living primarily in New England.	Led by planters, farmers, and wage earners living mainly in the South and Southwest.
Favored strong central government.	Favored strong state governments.
Interpreted Constitution loosely.	Interpreted Constitution strictly.
Believed in government by aristocracy; distrusted common man.	Favored rule by the educated masses.
Passed Alien and Sedition Acts.	Supported individual liberties; passed Kentucky and Virginia Resolutions.
Pro-England.	Pro-France.
Favored Hamilton's financial policies: for protective tariff, for National Bank, for manufacturing interests, for assumption of state debts.	Opposed Hamilton's financial policies: against protective tariff, for state banks, for agrarian interests, against assumption of state debts.

The Republicans (later called Democratic-Republicans) informally organized their opposition to the Federalists as early as 1791, when Hamilton pressed his financial program on Congress. The Republicans grew in strength by battling the foreign policies of Washington and Adams, which to the Republicans seemed pro-British and anti-French. But not until 1796, with Washington's retirement from office, did they make a concerted effort to win the Presidency and control of Congress. They failed in both; John Adams became President, and the Federalists maintained their majority in Congress.

The Republicans wanted to gain control of the existing government through regular elections. They promised to administer the government according to the Constitution, but they frightened a good many Federalists who believed that their opponents were really revolutionaries. Federalists had done a good job of representing people with commercial, financial, and urban interests. To many of these men, Jefferson's followers seemed to be enemies of property. Even more frightening to the Federalists was the timing of the Republican challenge. The Republicans became a recognizable group at the very time that the revolutionary government in France, which had executed King Louis XVI and had gone to war with Britain, Austria, and Prussia, reached its most radical and violent stage. Many Republicans, like their leader, Thomas Jefferson, sympathized with the French revolutionaries, who had cast off monarchy in favor of republican government. But conservative men shuddered as they imagined Republicans seizing property and setting up guillotines in the public squares of Philadelphia. Savage criticism of Federalist leaders—even of the revered Washington—in Republican newspapers convinced Federalists that liberty of the press was leading to a breakdown of public order.

Events abroad influenced the tone of the political warfare at home. The American political battle subsided when the French revolutionary government fell into the hands of a more conservative group in 1795, and the European war abated temporarily. Jefferson, in fact, greeted the election of Adams in 1796 cheerfully. His own election as Vice-President suggested that the two discordant groups could be brought together. Hamilton and the most conservative Federalists, however, opposed such a reconciliation. The renewal of the war in Europe aggravated Federalist-Republican differences. Both Britain and France confiscated neutral American ships. Federalists and Republicans accused each other of being in league with a foreign enemy to betray American interests.

The Federalists, with a clear majority in Congress, took steps to repress what to them looked clearly like subversion. In 1798, they passed, and President Adams signed, the so-called Alien and Sedition

Main Provisions of the Twelfth Amendment

The electors meet in their states and vote on separate ballots for President and Vice-President—at least one of whom must be from a different state. They then make lists of all the people who received votes for President and for Vice-President and indicate how many votes each candidate received.

The sealed lists are sent to the President of the Senate. He opens them in the presence of the Senate and the House of Representatives.

The candidate with a majority of the Presidential votes is President; the candidate with a majority of the Vice-Presidential votes is Vice-President.

If nobody receives a majority of Presidential votes, the House of Representatives chooses the President from the three candidates with the largest number of votes. Each state has one vote, and two-thirds of the states must be represented when voting. A majority of the total number of states is necessary for choosing a President. If the House cannot choose a President by March 4, the Vice-President becomes President.

If nobody receives a majority of the votes for Vice-President, the Senate chooses him from the two candidates with the largest number of votes. Two-thirds of all the senators must be present for the vote, and a majority of the total number of senators is necessary for choosing a Vice-President.

Nobody who is ineligible for the Presidency may become Vice-President.

The Twentieth Amendment changed the final date for choosing a President to January 20.

Acts. One of the acts gave the President power to deport any alien he thought was dangerous to the nation. Another provided heavy fines and jail terms for persons who criticized federal officials in "false, scandalous, and malicious" terms. This language was broad enough so that Federalist judges sent several Republican editors and one Republican congressman to jail.

To these challenges the Republicans responded first with protests. In late 1798, the Kentucky and Virginia state legislatures adopted resolutions (written by Jefferson and Madison, respectively) calling the Alien and Sedition laws illegal and declaring that the states had the power to declare federal laws unconstitutional. While these challenges to federal authority set a precedent for later states-rights causes, they drew little support from other states in 1798 and 1799.

A more effective Republican answer to the Federalists came in their vigorous effort to create a party organization at the local level throughout the nation in order to win the election of 1800. This attempt was successful. Jefferson and Aaron Burr of New York received 73 electoral votes each, while Federalists Adams and Charles Pinckney of South Carolina won 65 and 64 respectively. The tie in electoral votes between Jefferson and Burr gave states with Federalist electors a chance to decide the outcome. In the end, Hamilton, who considered Jefferson less dangerous than Burr, as he pointed out in his letter to James A. Bayard, persuaded Federalists to throw the election to Jefferson. The Twelfth Amendment to the Constitution, ratified in 1804, prevented the candidates of the same party from being tied in the vote for President.

Now that the Republicans were in power, what actions would they take against their political enemies? Jefferson gave a conciliatory response in his inaugural address in 1801: "We are all republicans, we are all federalists." Nor did he oust Federalists from appointive offices in large numbers, although he required their loyalty to the new Administration. After the vindictiveness of the 1790's, a calmer spirit prevailed in the nation. A challenge had been met; the leadership of a nation had been changed peacefully. Political opposition within a Constitutional framework would be tolerated and eventually praised rather than driven underground and punished.

SUGGESTED READINGS

ALLIS, FREDERICK S. JR., *Government Through Opposition: Party Politics in the 1790's.* The book presents a brief study of the origins of the Federalist and Republican parties, with some attention to the ways historians have interpreted the growth of the party system.

MILLER, JOHN C., *Crisis in Freedom: The Alien and Sedition Acts.* This book has a full and lively account of the dramatic episode that brought to a head the party struggles of the 1790's.

SCHACHNER, NATHAN, *Alexander Hamilton.* Schachner has written a fine biography of the man whose ideas and actions did most to influence the shape taken by the new national government in its early years.

The Place of the United States in the World, 1778–1823

CHAPTER 7

STATING THE ISSUE

During its first half century as a nation, the United States maintained its independence, increased its political and economic strength, and extended its control over vast new sections of North America. Americans also began to define their country's role in international affairs.

In 1783, the United States had been militarily weak and financially unstable. Its small population, spread so thinly over so wide an area, led many Europeans—and even some Americans—to predict that the republic could never hold together. To the north, the British and the Indians watched and waited for the collapse. To the south and the west, the Spanish and the Indians played the same game. All hoped that the United States' control over its territory would crumble. On the seas, the lack of a protecting navy placed American shipping at the mercy of European fleets and Mediterranean pirates.

Between 1812 and 1815, the United States and Great Britain fought their second war within a generation. Its outcome was neither a victory nor a defeat for the United States, but it stimulated strong nationalistic feelings among Americans. By 1823, the United States had acquired the Louisiana territory and the Floridas, more than doubling its land area. The more rapid communications provided by new highways and canals gave men confidence that the nation could control these new lands effectively. At the same time, a series of national revolutions shattered the Spanish empire in the New World and removed any serious military threat from the south and the west. A new era of security opened for the United States, which was strengthened during the nineteenth century by prolonged peace in Europe and unchallenged British domination of the seas.

Chapter 7 examines some of the ways in which Americans adapted their attitudes and policies to the opportunities and dangers other nations presented between 1778 and 1823. Would an alliance with a more powerful nation best guarantee American safety? Would a policy of discreet neutrality offer the United States the security it needed? What kind of role in world affairs did Americans see for their growing nation? These are the major issues raised in Chapter 7.

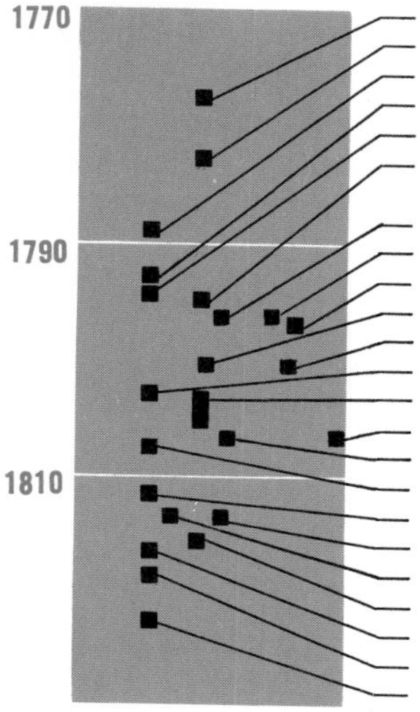

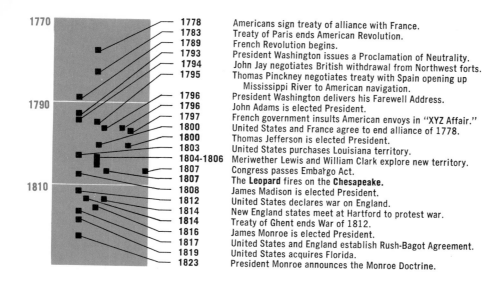

1778	Americans sign treaty of alliance with France.
1783	Treaty of Paris ends American Revolution.
1789	French Revolution begins.
1793	President Washington issues a Proclamation of Neutrality.
1794	John Jay negotiates British withdrawal from Northwest forts.
1795	Thomas Pinckney negotiates treaty with Spain opening up Mississippi River to American navigation.
1796	President Washington delivers his Farewell Address.
1796	John Adams is elected President.
1797	French government insults American envoys in "XYZ Affair."
1800	United States and France agree to end alliance of 1778.
1800	Thomas Jefferson is elected President.
1803	United States purchases Louisiana territory.
1804-1806	Meriwether Lewis and William Clark explore new territory.
1807	Congress passes Embargo Act.
1807	The **Leopard** fires on the **Chesapeake.**
1808	James Madison is elected President.
1812	United States declares war on England.
1814	New England states meet at Hartford to protest war.
1814	Treaty of Ghent ends War of 1812.
1816	James Monroe is elected President.
1817	United States and England establish Rush-Bagot Agreement.
1819	United States acquires Florida.
1823	President Monroe announces the Monroe Doctrine.

25 The United States and the French Alliance

Although the United States emerged as an independent nation from the Revolutionary War, it was not isolated politically. During the war, Americans had eagerly sought the aid of Britain's European enemies; in 1778, France had become a military ally. The United States was grateful for the vital military assistance France had given. Some Americans hoped for even closer ties with France, especially after the French revolutionaries created a republican government in 1792. Should not good republicans stand together against the monarchs of Europe?

In spite of hatreds fanned by the Revolution, common bonds of language and tradition, and often of kinship, still tied many Americans to Britain. Firmly established patterns of trade also linked the two nations; each was the other's best customer. Most important of all, Americans realized that the strong British navy had the power to damage seaborne trade badly in case of war, and Americans depended heavily on international trade for their prosperity. Could the United States afford to antagonize such a powerful nation?

Americans soon had to consider this question seriously. In 1793, Britain and France began another in their seemingly unending series of wars. Americans wanted to trade with both nations, but the British and the French each attacked American ships headed for the ports of the other.

After 1789, a succession of revolutionary governments ruled in France and began foreign wars. In 1799, Napoleon Bonaparte became head of the government. In 1804, he acquired the title of Emperor. By about 1810, Napoleon's armies had conquered most of Europe, including Spain, the German states, Poland, and the Italian peninsula. The allied armies defeated Napoleon in 1814, and after he returned briefly for a last campaign, they exiled him in 1815.

Many Americans sympathized strongly with France, but the wars of the French Revolution and of the Napoleonic Era began to seem increasingly remote from the major interests of settling and developing their nation. Americans came to view the military alliance with France more as a liability than as an asset. In fact, the two nations nearly went to war with each other in the late 1790's.

The excerpts in Reading 25 show the policies that American leaders adopted for their new nation in the troubled years between 1778 and 1801. As you read, keep these questions in mind:

1. What did John Adams assume that the international situation would be after the American Revolution?
2. What did Washington's attitude toward the French alliance seem to be? How do you account for his attitude?
3. What was Jefferson's attitude toward alliances in 1801?
4. Should a nation adopt a policy toward alliances and cling to it consistently, or should it vary its policies toward other countries as circumstances change?

John Adams Assesses the Alliance with France

Francis Wharton, ed., **The Revolutionary Diplomatic Correspondence of the United States.** Washington, D.C.: Government Printing Office, 1889, vol. II, pp. 667–68. Language simplified and modernized.

The Continental Congress sent John Adams and Benjamin Franklin to France to obtain aid for the American revolutionaries. John Adams wrote a letter in 1778 to his cousin, Samuel Adams, assessing the alliance just made with France.

In Adam's time, the term "Canada" referred only to Ontario and Quebec. In 1867, the British North America Act united Ontario, Quebec, New Brunswick, and Nova Scotia into the Dominion of Canada.

I have often heard you make the observation that "France is the natural ally of the United States." This observation is, in my opinion, both just and important for obvious reasons. As long as Great Britain holds Canada, Nova Scotia, or the Floridas, she will be the enemy of the United States.

It is a fact that neighboring nations are never friends. In the times of the most perfect peace between them their hearts and their passions are hostile. This will certainly be the case forever between the thirteen united states and the English colonies.

France and England, as neighbors and rivals, never have been and never will be friends. The hatred and jealousy between these nations are eternal and irremovable. Therefore, we have, on the one hand, good reason to expect the jealousy and hatred of Great Britain. On the other hand, we have the strongest reasons to depend upon the friendship of and the alliance with France. There is no reason in the world to expect her ill will or jealousy, as she has given up every claim to any part of this continent. The United States, therefore, will be for ages the natural bulwark of France against Britain's hostility toward her. France, too, is America's natural defense against the rapacious [greedy] spirit of Great Britain.

France is an extremely important nation that for many centuries has been the dominant European power. She has made a close alliance with our States, and she has enjoyed the benefit of our trade. Together France and America will place a sufficient curb upon British naval power.

The alliance with France will forever gain respect for our States in Spain, Portugal, Holland, and the rest of Europe. European countries will always choose to be upon friendly terms with powers who have numerous cruisers at sea. I presume, therefore, that sound policy, as well as good faith, will persuade us never to renounce our alliance with France, even though that alliance should keep us at war with Britain for some time. The French are as aware of the benefits of this alliance to them as we are, and they are determined as much as we to promote it.

President Washington's Proclamation of April 22, 1793

The alliance signed by the French and American governments in 1778 required that the United States defend the French West Indies "against all other powers." When war broke out between France and Great Britain in 1793, the United States had to decide what it would do should Britain attack one of the French islands. President Washington announced the policy his Administration intended to follow.

James D. Richardson, ed., **A Compilation of the Messages and Papers of the Presidents.** Washington, D.C.: Government Printing Office, 1896, vol. I, p. 156. Language simplified and modernized.

A state of war exists between Austria, Prussia, Sardinia, Great Britain, and the Netherlands, on one side, and France, on the other. The duty and interest of the United States require that it should with sincerity and good faith adopt and pursue friendly and impartial conduct toward the nations at war.

I, therefore, declare that the United States will observe the aforesaid conduct [neutrality] toward the warring nations; and I urge and warn the citizens of the United States to avoid all acts which may in any way violate this policy.

Washington's Farewell Address

In 1796, George Washington decided to retire from public life. At that time, he delivered a farewell statement to his country-

men, in which he advised them about their nation's future relationships with other countries.

Richardson, ed., **Messages and Papers of the Presidents,** vol. I, pp. 221–23. Language simplified and modernized.

It is essential that we not form permanent antipathies [hatreds] against particular nations and passionate attachments for others. Instead we should promote just and friendly feelings toward all nations. The nation that holds a habitual hatred or a habitual fondness for another nation is to some extent a slave to its passions, which may lead it astray from its duty and its interest.

In our conduct toward foreign nations, we should extend our commercial relations, but we should have as few political connections with other countries as possible. We should fulfill with perfect good faith those agreements we have already made. But let us stop there.

Europe has primary interests which are of very little or no importance to us. Hence, she must be engaged in frequent controversies that do not concern us. It would be unwise for us to become involved in European politics, friendships, or wars.

The long distance which separates us from Europe invites and enables us to pursue different policies. If we remain one people, under an efficient government, we may soon be able to protect ourselves from the injury or annoyance of other nations. Should we decide upon a policy of neutrality we may be able to have it scrupulously respected. Warlike nations will not threaten us lightly. We may be free to choose peace or war on the basis of our own interest and sense of justice.

Why should we give up such an advantageous situation? Why should we interweave our destiny with that of any European country? Why should we entangle our peace and prosperity with European ambition, rivalry, or self-interest?

It is our true policy to steer clear of permanent alliances with any foreign nation, insofar as we are now at liberty to do so. Let those agreements [with France] that we have already made be observed honestly. But in my opinion, it is unnecessary and unwise to extend them.

If we always maintain respectable defenses, we may safely trust to temporary alliances whenever extraordinary emergencies arise.

Jefferson's First Inaugural Address

In 1801, in his first inaugural address, Thomas Jefferson included a statement of the foreign policy his Administration intended to pursue. He was able to work with a freer hand because American diplomats had been able to negotiate an end to the French alliance during the last year of John Adams's Administration.

Let us, then, with courage and confidence pursue our own federal and republican principles, our attachment to our union and representative government. Nature has kindly separated this nation by a wide ocean from the havoc of Europe. We are too high-minded to endure the degradations of others. We possess a chosen country, with room enough for our descendants to the hundredth and thousandth generation.

It is proper that you should understand what I consider the essential principles of our government are, and consequently those which ought to shape its administration. Equal and exact justice to all men, whatever their religious or political beliefs; peace, commerce, and honest friendship, with all nations—entangling alliances with none.

Albert E. Bergh, ed., **The Writings of Thomas Jefferson.** Washington, D.C.: Thomas Jefferson Memorial Association, 1904, vol. III, pp. 320–21. Language simplified and modernized.

26 The War of 1812

The United States dramatically reversed its early policies when it declared war on Great Britain on June 18, 1812. Presidents Washington, Adams, Jefferson, and Madison had worked conscientiously to keep the United States out of the wars triggered by the French Revolution and the rise of Napoleon to power in France.

Their task had been difficult, for the desperate struggles between Britain and France created a stormy life for neutral nations. From 1793 to 1812, Britain and other European powers tried to defeat the expanding French. While France won control of most of western Europe and marched into Russia in 1812, Britain swept the French fleet from the seas and tried to enforce a blockade of the continent. In an attempt to keep supplies from reaching the continent, Britain confiscated many American ships and cargoes. The British also forced some sailors serving aboard American ships into the British navy on the grounds, sometimes justified, that they were deserters.

The French badly needed supplies. They raided and confiscated American ships that obeyed the British blockade or that supplied Britain. Americans, however, resented the British seizures more, because many of their raids took place near the American shore, while the French raids occurred near Europe. In 1807, within sight of shore, broadsides from the British ship, the *Leopard,* nearly sank an American naval vessel, the *Chesapeake,* when her commander refused to let the British search his ship for deserters.

In spite of interference from the warring powers, American businessmen and shipowners still reaped large profits from trade with Europe. Wartime prices had risen so high that shipowners could afford to lose ships and cargoes frequently and still make money. Farmers who produced goods which were in great demand, such as timber or wheat, shared in the wartime prosperity. But farmers in the south and west, who had difficulty getting goods to market or who produced crops that were not in great demand, suffered from an agricultural depression in the years before 1812. Settlers in the Ohio country also suffered from an outburst of Indian pillaging, burning, and scalping raids, which they blamed on the British. These considerations influenced the President and the Congress in their decision to go to war against Britain. The excerpts in Reading 26 provide some evidence about the pressures for and against war. As you read, consider these questions:

1. Which Americans might have responded most favorably to Henry Clay's appeal? which ones to John Randolph's? Why?
2. What grounds for war did President Madison offer in his message to Congress? Did the events he described threaten the security of the United States?
3. On the basis of Madison's reasons for war, which Americans would you expect to support the war most enthusiastically? How could you determine the accuracy of your speculations?
4. Do you think the United States should have gone to war in 1812? Why or why not?

Henry Clay's Views of the International Crisis

Henry Clay of Kentucky was the leading spokesman for the West in Congress. On February 22, 1810, in a speech to the Senate, he forcefully presented the course of action he believed the United States should follow.

Annals of the Congress of the United States, 11th Congress, 1st and 2nd Sessions (1809–1810). Washington, D.C.: Gales and Seaton, 1853, vol. I, cols. 579–81.

No man in the nation wants peace more than I. But I prefer war, demanded by the honor and independence of the country, with all its calamities, to the tranquil rottenness of a humiliating peace. Britain stands pre-eminent in her outrage on us. She has violated the sacred personal rights of American freemen, in the arbitrary and lawless imprisonment of our seamen. With the attack on the *Chesapeake,* she has murdered American sailors. I will not dwell on the long catalog of our wrongs and disgraces, which has been repeated until the sensibility of the nation is numbed by the dishonorable detail.

Some say, however, that nothing can be gained by war with Great Britain. In considering war, however, we are to estimate not only the benefit to ourselves, but the injury to be done the enemy. The conquest of Canada is in our power. I trust I shall not be thought overconfident when I state that I believe that the militia of Kentucky alone could place Montreal and Upper Canada at our feet. Is Canada nothing to the British nation? Is it nothing to the pride of her Monarch, to have the last of the immense North American possessions held by him, when his reign began, wrested from his control? Is it nothing to us to extinguish the torch that lights up savage Indian warfare? Is it nothing to acquire the entire fur trade connected with that country?

George III, the British king during the American Revolution, was still on the throne.

A certain amount of military zeal (and that is what I desire) is essential to the protection of the country. The withered arm and wrinkled brow of the illustrious founders of our freedom are sad indications that they will die shortly. Their deeds of glory and renown will then be felt only through the cold pages of history. We shall want the presence and living example of a new race of heroes to supply their places, and to inspire us to preserve what they achieved. Am I counting too much on the valor of my countrymen, when I hope, that if we are forced into war, the American hero now lives, who, upon the walls of Quebec, imitating his glorious example, will avenge the fall of the immortal Montgomery? But we shall, at least, gain the approval of our own hearts. If we surrender without a struggle to maintain our rights, we forfeit the respect of the world and, what is worse, of ourselves.

In 1775, General Richard Montgomery led an American attack on Canada. He took Montreal, but he was killed trying to take Quebec from the British.

John Randolph's Views of the International Crisis

John Randolph of Virginia put the crisis in a different light in speeches he gave in the House of Representatives on December 10 and December 16, 1811.

Annals of the Congress of the United States, 12th Congress, 1st Session (1811–1812). Washington, D.C.: Gales and Seaton, 1853, vol. I, cols. 445–49, 453–54, 529. Language simplified and modernized.

The gentleman from Tennessee, Mr. [Felix] Grundy, has hinted that the recent massacre of our brethren on the Wabash had been plotted by the British Government. Mr. Grundy had no reason to think the Administration believed this. His charge was indeed calculated to excite the feelings of the western people, and it lacked any foundation beyond mere conjecture and suspicion..

In November 1811, American troops fought a battle with the Indians at Tippecanoe, near the Wabash River in Indiana. British weapons found on the battlefield convinced many Americans that the British were backing the Indian resistance to American settlers.

We took advantage of the Indians, whose spirit had been broken by the war that ended in the Treaty of Greenville. Under the authority acquired over them then and by later treaties, they had been confined to restricted areas. We tried to seize the Indians' title to the immense wilderness, which we shall not occupy for half a century. Our own thirst for territory, our own lack of moderation, drove the Indians to desperation.

In 1794, the American general Anthony Wayne defeated the Indians at the Battle of Fallen Timbers on the Maumee River in Ohio. The following year, by the Treaty of Greenville, the Indians surrendered their rights to most of the Ohio region.

The proposed war of conquest against Britain, a war to acquire territory and subjects, is, according to its proponents, to be a holiday campaign. There is to be no loss of blood or money on our part. Canada is to conquer herself; she is to be subdued by the principles of brotherhood.

Go! March to Canada. Leave Chesapeake Bay and her hundred tributary rivers; leave the whole seacoast from Maine to Florida unprotected. But if you take Quebec, have you conquered Britain? Will you seek for the deep foundations of British power in the frozen wastes of Labrador? Will you ask Britain to leave your ports and harbors untouched, until you return from Canada to protect them? The coast will be left defenseless, while men of the interior are reveling in conquest and plunder.

We share common blood, language, religion, and other interests with Britain, not with France and her ruler Napoleon. He holds all the nations he tramples on in contempt, except Britain. Britain he hates because he fears her power.

Suppose France gained possession of the British naval power. What then would be the situation of your seaports and their seafaring inhabitants? What would you expect if the French were the uncontrolled lords of the ocean?

But we are told, and by men of honor too, that we stand pledged to France by the alliance of 1778. Bound to France! If we are, then we have sealed our own destruction.

Will any man argue that we have the right to transfer to a foreign despot [absolute ruler] such as Napoleon, the power to make war for us upon whom he shall please? No, sir, I deny it; such is not our miserable, our hopeless condition. We are not bound to France, and, so help me God, I shall never consent that we should be so bound.

President Madison's Address to Congress

On June 1, 1812, President Madison gave Congress reasons for war against Great Britain.

Richardson, ed., **Messages and Papers of the Presidents,** vol. I, pp. 500–05. Language simplified and modernized.

British cruisers have continually violated the American flag on the high seas. The British have seized and carried off persons sailing under it, not as an act of war against an enemy, but as a right over British subjects. The laws of war forbid captured property to be taken without an investigation before a court. Petty naval commanders of course pay no attention to these laws or to the sacred rights of the persons they seize.

The practice of seizing sailors does not affect British subjects alone. With the excuse of searching for deserters, the British have torn thousands of American citizens from their country and from everything dear to them. They have been dragged on board British ships of war. Under the harshness of British discipline, American sailors have been taken to the most distant and deadly regions to risk their lives in the battles of their oppressors. They have even been forced, while in British service, to fight against and to take the lives of fellow Americans.

British cruisers have also violated the rights and the peace of our coasts. They hover over and harass our ships as they enter and leave port. To the most insulting claims, they have added the most lawless activities in our very harbors. They have even wantonly spilled American blood in areas within our territorial jurisdiction.

By international law, nations generally claim jurisdiction over surrounding waters three miles beyond the shoreline.

Under pretended blockades, our commerce has been plundered in every sea. The great staples of our country have been cut off from their legitimate markets, and a destructive blow has been aimed at our agricultural and commercial interests.

Not content with these occasional attacks on our neutral trade, the Cabinet of Britain ordered a sweeping system of blockades. It has become, indeed, sufficiently certain that the commerce of the United States is to be sacrificed, not because it interferes with the British rights of war, not because it supplies the needs of Britain's enemies (her own merchants trade illegally with Europe), but because our shipping interferes with the monopoly which she wants for her own trade.

The United States tried to get the British Cabinet to repeal its unjust acts. The executive branch of our government told the British that if they lifted the blockade, the United States would go to war with France unless she also lifted her blockade. The British government paid no attention to this communication.

In reviewing the conduct of Great Britain toward the United States, our attention is necessarily drawn to the renewal of Indian warfare on our northwestern frontier. This war spares neither women nor children. It is shocking to humanity. It is difficult to account for the activity which has developed among tribes in constant contact with British traders and garrisons, without connecting the Indian hostility with British influence. In fact, officers and agents of that government have furnished us evidence that the British have encouraged the Indians to attack settlers.

Such are the injuries and indignities which have been heaped on our country. Such is the crisis which our unexampled patience and conciliatory efforts have not been able to avert.

Whether the United States shall continue to bear these accumulating wrongs passively or oppose force with force in defense of its national rights is a solemn question which the Constitution wisely gives to the legislative branch of the government.

27 The Monroe Doctrine

In 1783, Spain controlled the Floridas and the Louisiana territory; in 1820, both belonged to the United States. These were but two areas Spain lost with the collapse of her empire in the New World after 1800. The revolutionary examples of the United States and France influenced the Spanish colonies in Latin America. One by one, they took advantage of the mother country's weakness caused, in part, by Napoleon's occupation of Spain in 1808. Civil disturbances and a British invasion to drive out the French further weakened the Spanish government. Encouraged by Mexico's revolt in 1810, most of the other Latin American colonies ousted the Spanish rulers and set up independent governments. The blow to Spanish power in the Western Hemisphere promised new security to the United States.

This new security, however, as well as the independence of the Latin American republics, soon seemed threatened. Austria, Prussia, Russia, and France cooperated in a "Holy Alliance" to suppress revolutions in Europe. In 1822, they authorized French troops to put down a revolt in Spain. American leaders became concerned that some of the nations in the "Holy Alliance" might help Spain recover its lost colonies. Americans feared the re-establishment of European power in the Caribbean area.

At the same time, another challenge to American security appeared in the Pacific Northwest. Russia began to extend its influence southward from Alaska, which it claimed, along the Pacific Coast. At the time, the United States did not effectively control any of the Northwest nor did any nation recognize its claim to the area. How could Americans possibly resist the Russian thrust so far away from the Atlantic seaboard?

Americans were relieved to learn that Great Britain opposed further European expansion in the Western Hemisphere. British businessmen had been excluded from trade with Latin America while it remained a part of the Spanish empire. With Spain's control broken, British merchants saw promising new opportunities for trade with the Latin American republics. Moreover, Great Britain was not indifferent to Russian expansion in the Pacific Northwest for it too claimed much of that area. The question for Americans no longer was whether European advances could be resisted, but rather what relationship could be worked out with Great Britain to discourage European powers from extending their influence in the Western Hemisphere.

American leaders had to decide what that relationship would be. Reading 27 shows how the leaders made the decision about the policy their young nation would pursue. As you read, consider these questions:

1. What factors influenced the decision about the policy the United States would follow?
2. How did President Monroe get information on which to base a decision?
3. What decision was reached? What was John Quincy Adams's contribution to the policy statement?
4. Which of the documents shows most clearly the way in which foreign policy decisions were made? How would you determine the reliability of those documents?

Notes from the Secretary of State

John Quincy Adams kept a diary from 1794 until 1845. These excerpts are from his entries in 1823 while he was Monroe's Secretary of State. At that time, the government was considering the implications for the United States of the French decision to suppress a revolt in Spain and the Russian expansion in the Pacific Northwest.

Charles Francis Adams, ed., **Memoirs of John Quincy Adams, Comprising Portions of His Diary from 1795–1848.** Philadelphia: J.B. Lippincott and Company, 1875, vol. 6, pp. 137–38, 163. Language simplified and modernized.

March 14, 1823 The President held a Cabinet meeting. John C. Calhoun, Secretary of War, and Smith Thompson, Secretary of the Navy, were present. William H. Crawford, Secretary of Treasury, was ill; William Wirt, Attorney General, was engaged at the Supreme Court. We discussed what is to be done about war between France and Spain. Calhoun is anxious. We need more information. We must act consistently with what we have done in the past. We fear what Britain may do. What are Spain's prospects? There is danger of treachery.

March 15, 1823 Baron de Tuyl, the Russian Envoy, is expected to arrive here next week. A Cabinet meeting was held at two o'clock. Only Calhoun and Thompson were present. Calhoun favors war with Britain if she intends to take Cuba. Thompson favors urging the Cubans to declare their independence if they can maintain it. I take it for granted that they could not maintain their independence and that this nation could not by war prevent Britain from taking Cuba, if they attempt to. The debate was almost warm. There was talk of calling Congress into session, which I thought was absurd. Note—keep cool on this subject.

Cuba was then a Spanish colony that had not overthrown its Spanish rulers.

July 17, 1823 Baron de Tuyl came to the office and asked if he could tell his government that we will forward instructions for negotiating the question of the Northwest Coast. I said he might. He then wanted to know as much as I could tell him about what we intended to propose. I told him as much as I thought prudent. I told him that we dispute Russia's right to any territory on this continent, and that we assume the American continents are no longer open to colonization by any European country.

Background to the Monroe Doctrine

George Canning, the British Foreign Secretary, wrote the letter which follows on August 20, 1823, to Richard Rush, the American Minister to Great Britain. In the letter, he outlined Britain's attitude toward Spain's former colonies in Latin America.

Richard Rush, **Memoranda of a Residence at the Court of London.** Philadelphia: Lea and Blanchard, 1845, pp. 412–13. Language simplified and modernized.

My dear Sir:

Before leaving town, I want to put before you in a clearer, but still in an unofficial and confidential way, the question which we discussed briefly the last time that I had the pleasure of seeing you.

Has not the moment come when our governments might reach an understanding about Spain's American colonies? And if we can arrive at such an understanding, would it not be useful for us and beneficial for all the world, to establish the principles of it clearly and to state them plainly? For we have nothing to hide.

1. We think that Spain's recovery of her colonies is hopeless.
2. We believe that time and circumstances will help decide the question of recognizing them as independent states.
3. We, however, would not in any way oppose an arrangement between them and the mother country [Spain] that is made by amicable [friendly] negotiations.
4. We do not aim at possession of any portion of them ourselves.
5. We could not with indifference see any portion of them transferred to any other power.

If your government and ours share these opinions and feelings, as I firmly believe they do, why should we hesitate to confide them to each other and to declare them to the world?

If any European power has plans to retake the colonies for Spain, or if any power wants to take any part of them for itself, a declaration by your government and ours would be the most effective and the least offensive way of letting them know of our joint disapproval of such projects.

The Cabinet Discusses American Policy

John Quincy Adams kept careful notes in his diary on the discussions American leaders held as they considered Canning's proposals and decided upon the policy their government should follow. These excerpts are taken from his entries in November 1823.

Adams, ed., **Memoirs of John Quincy Adams,** vol. 6, pp. 177–79, 185–86, 199–200. Language simplified and modernized.

Washington, November 7, 1823 The President held a Cabinet meeting from half past one until four. Mr. Calhoun, Secretary of

War, and Mr. Southard, Secretary of the Navy, were present. The subject for consideration was the confidential proposals of the British Secretary of State, George Canning, to Richard Rush and the correspondence between them relating to the intentions of the Holy Alliance upon South America. There was much conversation, without coming to a definite point. Canning appears to have wanted to obtain some public pledge from the United States government against the Holy Alliance helping Spain regain her South American colonies. But we think his real intention was to keep the United States from acquiring any part of the Spanish American possessions for themselves.

In September 1823, President Monroe appointed Samuel Lewis Southard to replace Smith Thompson as Secretary of the Navy.

The 1819 treaty between Spain and the United States drew the western boundary of the United States so that Texas remained in Spanish hands. After Mexico achieved independence from Spain in 1821, Texas belonged to Mexico.

Mr. Calhoun was inclined to let Mr. Rush use his own judgment about joining Great Britain in a declaration against the interference of the Holy Allies, even if we should have to agree not to take Cuba or Texas. Because Great Britain's power to seize them is greater than ours, we should obtain from her the same pledge that we might make ourselves.

I thought the cases were not parallel. We have no intention of seizing either Texas or Cuba. But the inhabitants of either or both may exercise their natural rights and ask to unite with us. They will certainly not unite with Great Britain. By joining with her, in her proposed declaration, we give her an important and, perhaps, inconvenient pledge against ourselves, and we really obtain nothing in return. Without discussing the appropriateness of our annexing Texas or Cuba to our Union, we should at least keep ourselves free to act as emergencies may arise. We should not tie ourselves down to any principle which might immediately afterwards be used against us.

Mr. Southard had much the same opinion.

The President was against any course of action which should give the appearance that we are taking a position unequal to Great Britain's. He suggested sending a special Minister to protest against the interference of the Holy Allies.

I remarked that the communications recently received from the Russian Minister, Baron Tuyl, afforded, I thought, a very suitable and convenient opportunity for us to take our stand against the Holy Alliance, and at the same time, to decline Great Britain's offer. It would be more forthright, as well as more dignified, to state our principles explicitly to Russia and France, than to come in as a cockboat in the wake of the British man-of-war.

November 15, 1823 I received a note saying that the President wished to see me at the office at noon. I went and found him there. He showed me two letters which he had received, one from Mr. Jefferson and one from Mr. Madison giving their opinions on Mr. Canning's proposals. Mr. Jefferson thinks them more important than anything that has happened since our Revolution. He is for agreeing to the proposals, with the idea of pledging Great Britain against the Holy Alliance. He thinks, however, that Cuba would be a valuable and important acquisition for the United States. Mr. Madison's opinions are less clearly pronounced; he thinks, as I do, that Great Britain's offer is motivated more by her own interest than by a principle of general liberty.

November 25, 1823 I made a draft of my observations upon the communications recently received from the Baron de Tuyl, the Russian Minister. I took the President that paper, together with the statement I had prepared of the communication between Baron de Tuyl and me, and all of the papers I had received from him.

The paper itself was written to correspond exactly with a paragraph in the President's message which he had read to me yesterday and which conformed entirely to the policy which I have earnestly recommended for this emergency. It was intended as a firm, spirited, and yet conciliatory answer to all the communications recently received from the Russian government. At the same time, it was a clear answer to the proposals made by Canning to Mr. Rush. It was meant also to be eventually a statement of the principles of this government and a brief statement of the political system which we intend to maintain.

President Monroe's Statement of Policy

On December 2, 1823, in his annual message to Congress, President Monroe announced a United States policy for the Western Hemisphere. That policy statement later became known as the Monroe Doctrine.

Richardson, ed., **Messages and Papers of the Presidents,** vol. II, pp. 209, 218. Language simplified and modernized.

At the proposal of the Russian Government, instructions have been sent to the United States Minister at St. Petersburg, the capital of Russia, to arrange by amicable negotiations the rights and interests of the two nations on the northwest coast of this continent. The government of the United States wishes in this friendly way to show the great value they attach to the friendship of the Russian Emperor and their desire to promote the best understanding with his government. We take this opportunity to assert, as a matter of principle, that the American continents, by the free and independent condition which they have assumed and maintain, are henceforth not to be considered as areas for future colonization by any European powers.

We have always been anxious and interested spectators of events in Europe. We have never taken any part in the wars of the European powers. It is only when our rights are invaded or seriously threatened that we make preparations for our defense. With the affairs of this hemisphere we are necessarily more immediately concerned. The political system of the European nations is essentially different from that of America. We owe it to candor and to the amicable relations existing between the United States and European powers to declare that we should consider any attempt on their part to extend their system of government to any portion of this hemisphere as dangerous to our peace and safety. We have not interfered and shall not interfere with the existing colonies of any European power. But with the Governments who have declared and maintained their independence, we could not view any attempt by any European power to oppress them or in any way control their destiny as other than an unfriendly act toward the United States.

Our policy in regard to Europe, which we adopted at an early stage of the wars there, remains the same: not to interfere in the internal concerns of any European power, to consider the existing government as the legal government for us to deal with, to cultivate friendly relations with it, and to preserve those relations by a frank, firm, and manly policy, meeting in all instances the just claims of every power, submitting to injuries from none.

28 The United States Develops a Foreign Policy

HISTORICAL ESSAY

During the United States' first half-century, its political system grew steadily stronger, and the nation doubled in area, largely without violence. These two impressive developments occurred in spite of a sparse population, military weakness, and the antagonism of the great powers of Europe. What accounts for the political consolidation and geographical growth of the United States?

The answer lies largely in the fact that the United States profited from the quarrels the European nations had with each other. But quarrels in Europe did not guarantee benefits to the United States. Americans had to develop effective policies to guide their relations with the rest of the world.

The World at Peace

The Treaty of Paris of 1783 provided Americans with independence and a vast territory. But in order to repair the damages of war, create a workable government, seek national security, and recover commercial prosperity, they badly needed a period of peace. Fortunately for the United States, nearly ten years of international peace followed the American Revolution. By the time war again swept Europe and the seas around it, the new nation was better prepared to cope with dangers to its security.

In the 1780's, none of the major western European powers especially wanted to disturb the status quo. Britain made no effort to recover the thirteen colonies. Its major goal was to increase its commercial supremacy, for which peace was much more useful than war. The British quickly recovered most of their trade in the New World. Americans were used to doing business with Britain, where they found most manufactured goods cheaper and credit easier to obtain than anywhere else. American shippers, on the other hand, found that trade, without the benefits the British mercantile system had provided, was painfully difficult in some respects. The British discriminated against them in British ports and forbade them to trade with the British West Indies.

France too hoped to gain power through commerce. It had encouraged American trade by a commercial treaty which formed part of the Alliance of 1778 that John Adams had endorsed so warmly. But France was disappointed in its efforts to win the American trade from Britain. It likewise made no effort to recover lost colonies in the New World; its energies were diverted inward by a series of domestic political difficulties. The royal government was falling more deeply into debt each year—part of the deficit had been incurred during the American Revolution—and lacked the strength to obtain new tax revenues.

Spain had more to lose through war than either Britain or France. Its military and naval strength had declined rapidly throughout the eighteenth century. Although it had gained Louisiana from France in 1762 and Florida from Britain in 1783, its widespread colonies were thinly protected and highly vulnerable to attack. Neither Britain nor France saw the United States as an important potential enemy, but Spain knew that if the new nation did expand, Florida and Louisiana would be threatened.

Besides peace, the United States wanted several things from other nations. Its uncertain government and lack of military strength offered little to bargain with. Americans wanted the British to evacuate their military posts in the Northwest Territory and to sign more favorable trade agreements. The French had guaranteed the Treaty of Paris of 1783, but they had little interest in helping to oust the British from their American frontier posts. Although allied to the Americans, the French also limited American trade to their West Indies. Americans tried to increase their trade with Mediterranean ports, only to find that pirates crippled their commerce. Congress lacked funds either to bribe the pirates, as the European powers did, or to build a navy to protect American ships. The United States could neither force Spain to grant free navigation of the Mississippi nor stop the Spanish from intriguing with the Indians and the settlers of the southwest.

The creation of the new Constitution in 1787 and the inauguration of a stronger central government in 1789 brought the United States some minor diplomatic successes. Spain agreed to re-open the Mississippi, France eased some of its restrictions on West Indian trade, and Britain sent a minister to represent it in the United States. But substantial changes in the United States' position had to wait for more dramatic events abroad.

The World at War

The French Revolution of 1789 produced one of the greatest international upheavals of modern times. France attempted to spread the revolution to other countries and to extend French control to other parts of Europe. Most European powers desperately resisted both the revolutionary ideas and the expansion of France. War raged almost uninterruptedly from 1792 to 1815. These struggles, which involved most of the Western world, brought both grave dangers and great opportunities to the Americans.

When Britain went to war against France in 1793, both the dangers and the opportunities were quickly brought into focus. Both nations wanted American supplies, while neither wanted the United States to trade with the other. France threw open its West Indian ports to American commerce; Britain retaliated by seizing hundreds of American ships, which were bound for France or the French colonies, or which were carrying produce from either France or its colonies. The British also stepped up their agitation among the Indians in the Northwest.

Americans, most of whom sympathized with the French Revolution, at least in its early stages, were enraged. The United States moved close to war with Britain. But France, in its turn, captured and confiscated many American ships bound for Britain. Britain also opened its West Indian ports to American trade. This pattern of British and French coercion and competition continued throughout the war.

The pressures on the warring European powers produced some diplomatic benefits for the United States. John Jay, sent as a special envoy to negotiate a treaty with Britain, brought home agreements in which the British finally yielded their frontier posts on American soil, gave American ships the same privileges in British ports as those possessed by any other foreign nation, and allowed a small amount of trade with the West Indies. In the United States, hostility against Great Britain was so strong that many Americans denounced Jay as a traitor because he had been unsuccessful in getting the British to stop seizing American ships. But President Washington wanted to keep relations with Britain from deteriorating further. He realized that Jay's Treaty was the best the new, weak nation could obtain at the time. He threw his influence behind the treaty, and the Senate ratified it. The treaty brought Americans another benefit. The Indians in the Ohio Valley, defeated in battle by the Americans in 1794 and deprived of further British support, signed away a huge tract of land to the United States by the Treaty of Greenville in 1795.

Meanwhile, Spain had withdrawn from the coalition of European nations fighting France. Spain suspected that the improvement of British-American relations, represented by Jay's Treaty, might mean that the two would cooperate to seize its colonies in America. Spain quickly offered the United States a highly favorable treaty, including freedom of navigation on the Mississippi River and the "right of deposit" at the port of New Orleans. The United States thus frustrated Spanish hopes of establishing a strong colony in the Mississippi Valley and of persuading the settlers of Kentucky and Tennessee to secede from the Union. In 1796, the Senate ratified Pinckney's Treaty unanimously.

Thomas Pinckney, minister to Great Britain from the United States, negotiated an agreement whereby Spain recognized the boundaries established by the Treaty of Paris of 1783: the Mississippi River in the west and the 31st parallel in the south. The United States also gained free navigation of the Mississippi and the right to deposit goods at New Orleans to await ocean shipment without paying a duty to Spain.

Further dangers and benefits to the United States followed shortly. The temporary improvement in relations between Great Britain and the United States, represented by Jay's Treaty plus the pressures of war, provoked the French to a new wave of attacks on American ships and cargoes. The insulting treatment the French government gave to three American envoys to France in 1797 increased American sentiment for war. Congress, in 1798, authorized the capture of French armed ships. An unofficial naval war, fought largely in the West Indies against French privateers, continued for more than two years. But John Adams, who succeeded Washington as President, did not wish to fight a war with France. He made the unpopular decision to send new emissaries to France. In 1800, they reached agreements with France which ended both the naval hostilities and the Franco-American treaty of alliance of 1778. There was no longer any danger that the United States would be drawn into a European conflict through the old alliance.

President Adams sent three Americans to Paris to negotiate with the French. Three go-betweens for the French government, known as X, Y, and Z, demanded a bribe from the American Commissioners as the price for any agreement. When Adams told Congress about the "XYZ Affair," a cry went up for war against France.

Reducing tension with France contributed to a far more important development. Louisiana, which included a tract of land ranging from the Gulf of Mexico northward to Canada and westward to the Rocky Mountains, had passed from Spain back to France in a deal arranged in 1800. Control of that vital area by a nation as powerful as France alarmed both President Jefferson and the western farmers. In 1803,

Jefferson sent James Monroe to aid Robert R. Livingston, the American ambassador to France, in an attempt to buy New Orleans and West Florida from Napoleon for $10 million. Such a purchase would guarantee Americans control of the Mississippi.

Napoleon had intended to use Louisiana to further a plan to restore French power in the New World. But a revolt in Haiti, a French island in the West Indies, and an epidemic there of yellow fever frustrated his plan. Napoleon decided instead to sell all of Louisiana. For the bargain price of $15 million, including the assumption of the claims of American citizens against France, the United States doubled its land area and acquired the potential agricultural wealth of the vast western half of the Mississippi Valley. Moreover, the Louisiana Purchase removed the threat that a strong foreign power would occupy territory adjacent to the United States.

Shortly after the purchase, Jefferson launched the first great exploring expedition in American history. Under the leadership of Meriwether Lewis and William Clark the expedition explored the new territory. They pushed up the Missouri River, across the Great Plains and Rocky Mountains, to the Pacific Ocean. The mission proved that an overland route to the Pacific was possible, and it ultimately stimulated new settlement and trade.

The Trial and Failure of Neutrality

During its first twenty years as a nation, the United States had gained favorable treaties with Britain and Spain and had acquired Louisiana without going to war. But staying out of a war, when the rights that Americans claimed as neutrals continued to be violated, became increasingly difficult.

In 1793, Washington had proclaimed that the United States intended to remain "friendly and impartial" toward both Britain and France. The more extreme partisans of France and of England were both disappointed. But Washington's firm stand for neutrality set a pattern that the United States tried to follow for a century and a half. When Washington retired from office in 1796, he cautioned his countrymen, in his famous Farewell Address, against playing favorites with other nations and against making military alliances, except in case of dire need. In 1801, Jefferson seconded these ideas strongly in his First Inaugural Address, in which he gave his well-known advice against "entangling alliances."

But the war between Britain and Napoleonic France resumed in 1803, and both powers again threatened American neutrality. After Great Britain smashed the combined French and Spanish fleets in 1805 off Trafalgar, on the coast of Spain, its navy patrolled the seas unchallenged. Napoleon's armies, however, dominated most of west-

In 1806, Napoleon issued the Berlin Decree, in which he declared that all trade with Great Britain was illegal. Since he lacked naval power, this was only a paper blockade. Great Britain retaliated with the Orders in Council which blockaded most European ports.

ern and central Europe. The British announced a blockade of the thousands of miles of coastline held by Napoleon. To guard all of these shores was obviously impossible. But the British found that they could halt supplies bound for Napoleonic Europe by stopping, searching, and confiscating American ships and cargoes right outside American ports and often within American territorial waters. The British, who suffered from a shortage of seamen for their huge fleet, also took many sailors from American ships and forced them into British naval service. Sometimes the sailors they seized were British subjects who had deserted from the British navy to serve on American ships. But as often as not the sailors who were "impressed," as the practice was called, were American citizens. The United States protested vehemently against impressment, but to no avail. Britain was fighting for its existence as a great power against Napoleon and would risk war with the United States rather than give up impressment. The situation was potentially explosive. On two occasions, in 1807 and 1811, British and American naval vessels fired on each other, killing many sailors.

In 1807, Napoleon issued the Milan Decree which declared that any ship observing the British blockade was subject to seizure by the French.

Napoleon retaliated against the British attempt to strangle the French-controlled economy by declaring a counter-blockade of Britain. He sent privateers to seize any neutral ships which obeyed the British blockade. Americans lost more ships to France than to Britain. Crews of ships seized by the French also suffered harsh treatment. American relations with France deteriorated rapidly.

To preserve both American trade and American neutrality, Presidents Jefferson and Madison (who was elected in 1808) put economic pressure on Britain and France. In December 1807, Jefferson got Congress to place an embargo on foreign trade, which prohibited American merchant ships from sailing to foreign ports. New Englanders, who depended heavily on shipping, opposed the act bitterly and violated it freely. But American trade was reduced sufficiently to hurt Britain badly. British citizens pleaded with their government to relax its pressure on American trade so that the American embargo would be dropped. But pressure from maritime interests in the United States on the American government was even greater. Congress repealed the Embargo Act a few days before Jefferson left office in March 1809. Congress substituted a Non-Intercourse Act which allowed trade with all ports not under French or British control. This act did not achieve the desired purpose of getting the belligerents to cease their attacks on American ships. Congress substituted another Act in 1810, Macon's Bill No. 2, that restored trade with the two belligerents but offered to prohibit imports into America from either belligerent, if the other met American terms.

The President's and Vice-President's terms of office expired on March 4 until the Twentieth Amendment, adopted in 1933, changed that date to "noon on the twentieth day of January."

A belligerent is a party actively engaged in war.

Napoleon took clever advantage of this confusing offer by promising to repeal his restrictions against American commerce. This promise, which Napoleon never fulfilled, convinced an over-optimistic President Madison and Congress that France was ready to cooperate. So the United States adopted the threatened prohibition against British imports in March 1811. The American economic weapon worked so well that Britain ended her restrictions on June 16, 1812. Unfortunately the United States Congress, in response to President Madison's address, declared war on June 18. It did not learn of the British concession until weeks later.

Many Americans, particularly those, such as Henry Clay, who lived in the west, had hoped that Britain was so deeply involved in

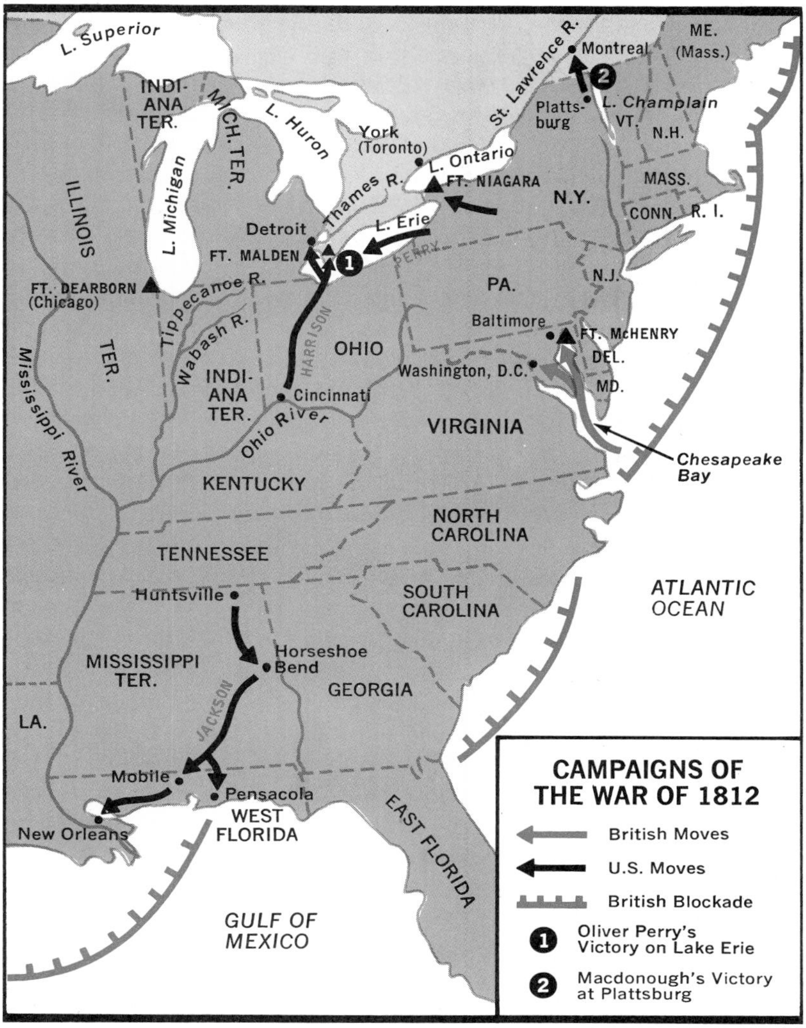

war with France that it would not only concede maritime rights to the United States, but also give up territory in Canada and Florida. Other Americans, such as John Randolph, had opposed the aggressive ambitions of the "War Hawks."

To those who wanted military glory and additional territory, the War of 1812 was a disappointment. Some ships of the small American navy fought brilliant, individual battles with British warships, and American privateers captured hundreds of British merchantmen. But the British navy still ruled the seas, blockaded American ports, and gradually cut down the losses to privateers. Meanwhile, British troops beat back such American attempts to invade Canada as a raid on York, Ontario, where government buildings were burned. The British retaliated with a raid on Washington where they burned the Capitol, the White House, and other buildings.

The United States, unprepared for war, had great difficulty financing any military effort. Moreover, strong anti-war sentiment in New England had actually created a secessionist movement by 1814. Federalist delegates from Connecticut, Rhode Island, Massachusetts, New Hampshire, and Vermont held a secret convention in Hartford, Connecticut. They drew up a resolution calling for several constitutional amendments aimed at making states less vulnerable to federal conscription, taxation, and embargoes. The resolution included a restatement of the philosophy of the Virginia and Kentucky Resolutions. Now it was New England's turn to claim that a state could "interpose its authority" to counteract federal laws it considered unconstitutional. The Convention met too late, however, to have any effect on the outcome of the war.

The British threatened to invade the country from the north, but small, makeshift American fleets defeated similar British fleets on Lake Erie and Lake Champlain, to establish command of these waterways. An equally serious threat came at New Orleans, where a large force of British veterans landed in late 1814 after Napoleon had been defeated. Western militiamen led by General Andrew Jackson crushed the attacking force in early 1815.

In September 1813, Captain Oliver Hazard Perry destroyed the British vessels at Put-in-Bay, near the western end of Lake Erie. The following year Captain Thomas Macdonough destroyed the British ships on Lake Champlain.

Negotiations to end the conflict had actually begun almost as soon as war had been declared. Not until August 1814, however, did British and American representatives meet in Ghent, Belgium. The peace they signed in December recognized that neither party had won; their principal agreement in the Treaty of Ghent was simply to stop fighting. Jackson's victory at New Orleans came two weeks later, before news of the treaty reached the United States.

The five American commissioners were John Quincy Adams, Henry Clay, Albert Gallatin, Jonathan Russell, and James A. Bayard.

The Collapse of the Spanish Empire

With the war ended, the United States continued to reap benefits from the squabbling among European nations. When Napoleon had

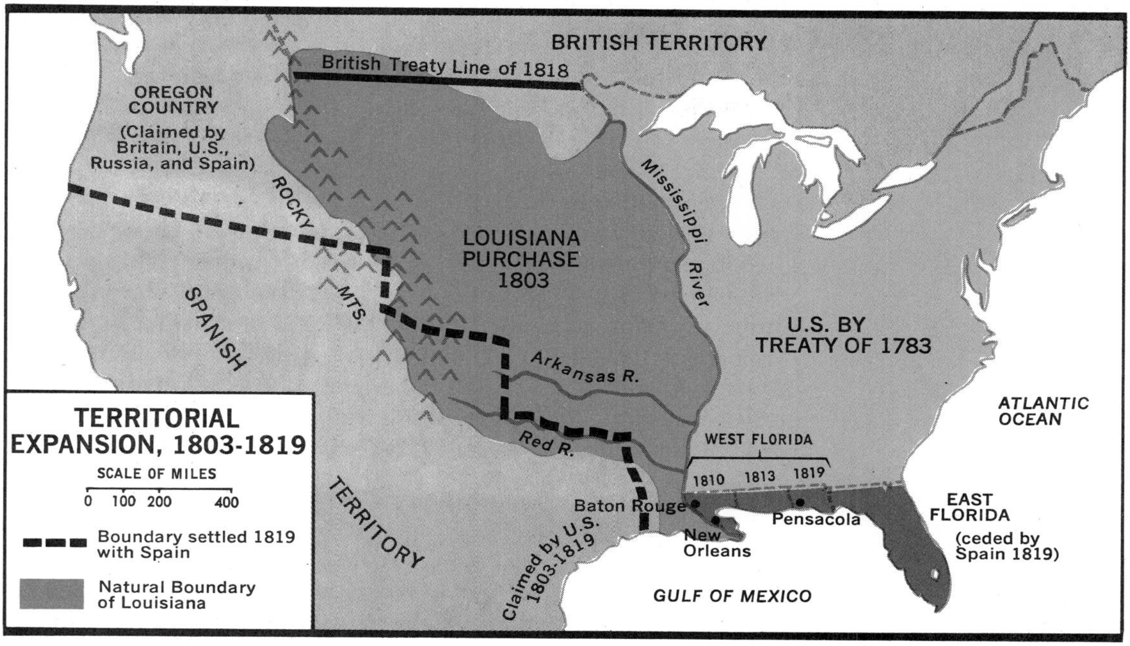

taken over Spain, revolts against the mother country broke out in the Spanish colonies in America. The United States took advantage of this unrest to encourage a revolution in West Florida in 1810 and welcomed the new territory when the rebels asked to have it annexed. Spain ceded East Florida to the United States in 1819 as part of an extensive settlement by which the boundary between the United States and the western Spanish possessions was carefully defined for the first time.

To Americans a great prospect was opening. It was the vision of a Western Hemisphere in which the United States would hold a dominant position. Two possible sources of danger, however, appeared on the horizon. The major European powers, who cooperated through their "Holy Alliance," might try to deprive the new Latin American nations of their independence. And Russia, who owned Alaska, might then extend control down the Pacific coast of North America.

The British navy was the strongest force for resisting any ambitions of European nations. Moreover, Britain opposed the restoration of European control of Latin America and further Russian expansion. Both Britain and the United States issued strong protests against Russian claims. Then, in 1823, the British Foreign Secretary, George Canning, proposed to the United States that the two nations jointly declare their opposition to European intervention in Latin America.

But the shrewd American Secretary of State, John Quincy Adams, recognized that the United States could be sure of British support in keeping Europeans out of the New World. He believed the long-range interests of the United States would be better served by an independent policy statement. This statement came in December 1823, in President James Monroe's annual message to Congress. A few scattered excerpts in the message were later called the Monroe Doctrine. The Doctrine declared that the Americas were no longer open to European colonization, and that the United States had no intention of interfering in the internal affairs or the political disputes of European countries. Since British power was the real deterrent to European action, little attention was paid at the time to Monroe's pronouncement; only later did it become an important and effective part of American foreign policy. But again the United States had profited from disputes among European nations.

SUGGESTED READINGS

COLES, H. L., *The War of 1812.* Coles presents a well-told account of the unpopular and nearly unsuccessful war with Britain, ending, however, with Andrew Jackson's triumph at New Orleans.

Journals of Lewis and Clark (edited by Bernard DeVoto). DeVoto has chosen excerpts from the explorers' own day-by-day report on their epic journey from the Mississippi River to the Pacific Coast from 1804 to 1806.

VAN EVERY, DALE, *Ark of Empire: The American Frontier, 1784–1803.* This volume describes the ways in which Americans won control of the wilderness region between the Appalachian Mountains and the Mississippi River from British, Spanish, and Indian opponents.

The Growth of a National Spirit

CHAPTER 8

STATING THE ISSUE

When Thomas Jefferson came to the White House in 1801, the United States occupied the same land area that it had held in 1783. A quarter of a century later, when John Quincy Adams assumed the Presidency in 1825, the area had more than doubled. A spectacular increase in social and economic growth throughout the country accompanied this increase in size. The population grew from five to eleven million. More people settled in the region west of the Appalachians. An agricultural boom took place in the south, and a manufacturing system began to develop in the north.

The development of conflicts within the country paralleled the growth of the nation as a whole. Some of the conflicts were regional; Americans living in the west, the south, and the north found that they frequently sought different things from the federal government. Other conflicts were economic: factory owners and mechanics, plantation slaveholders and small-farm owners confronted different kinds of economic needs. Although the old rivalry between Federalists and Republicans had largely disappeared, new political rivalries developed.

During this period of growth, change, and conflict another phenomenon developed—the emergence of a strong national spirit. What were the forces which tended to promote the growth of a feeling of national unity during this period? How was the national consciousness expressed? What were the forces that tended to promote division among Americans during the same period? These are the issues we shall be concerned with in Chapter 8.

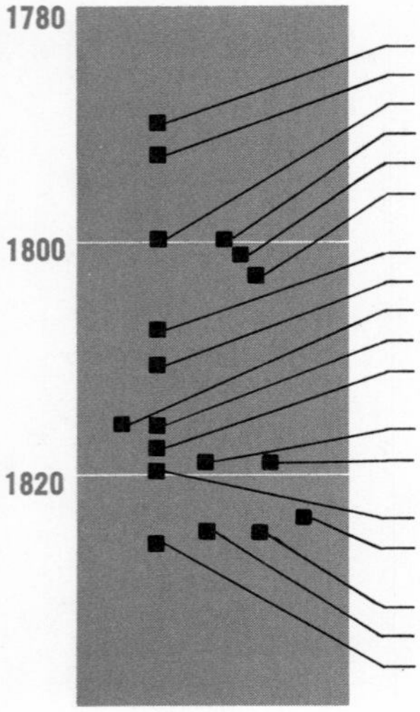

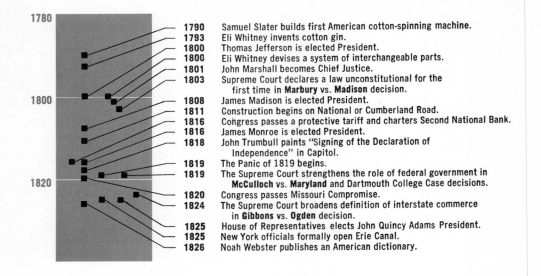

1790 Samuel Slater builds first American cotton-spinning machine.
1793 Eli Whitney invents cotton gin.
1800 Thomas Jefferson is elected President.
1800 Eli Whitney devises a system of interchangeable parts.
1801 John Marshall becomes Chief Justice.
1803 Supreme Court declares a law unconstitutional for the first time in **Marbury** vs. **Madison** decision.
1808 James Madison is elected President.
1811 Construction begins on National or Cumberland Road.
1816 Congress passes a protective tariff and charters Second National Bank.
1816 James Monroe is elected President.
1818 John Trumbull paints "Signing of the Declaration of Independence" in Capitol.
1819 The Panic of 1819 begins.
1819 The Supreme Court strengthens the role of federal government in **McCulloch** vs. **Maryland** and Dartmouth College Case decisions.
1820 Congress passes Missouri Compromise.
1824 The Supreme Court broadens definition of interstate commerce in **Gibbons** vs. **Ogden** decision.
1825 House of Representatives elects John Quincy Adams President.
1825 New York officials formally open Erie Canal.
1826 Noah Webster publishes an American dictionary.

29 The Need for National Communications

By 1820, the American population had grown to nine and a half million, more than twice what it had been when the Constitution was ratified. During the same period, because of the acquisition of Florida and the Louisiana Territory, the land area of the United States had more than doubled. With plenty of room to move around in the new nation, Americans did just that. In 1790, only 100,000 Americans lived west of the Appalachian Mountains. By 1820, more than two million people had moved into the Mississippi River Valley.

To many observers both at home and abroad, the acquisition of new territory and the spread of American settlements over a vast area, seemed to threaten the future of the new nation. Because the American people lived together in bustling river towns and seaports, tiny rural villages, isolated plantations, or far-flung frontier settlements cut off from the coast by vast mountain barriers, their communities frequently seemed to have little to do with each other. This isolation led many American leaders to argue that the government should build and maintain a vast transportation network in order to promote national unity.

Many of us have driven on the great interstate highways that stretch across the United States. We accept the fact that the federal government spends hundreds of millions of dollars each year to construct and maintain these highways. During the early decades of the nineteenth century, however, federal responsibility for building roads was not widely accepted. It was clear enough that better transportation facilities were needed, but whether the construction of roads, bridges, and canals was a public or private responsibility remained an important issue for political debate.

The first selection which follows provides a description of the physical barriers to American unity in 1800. The second selection gives one famous senator's proposal for overcoming the problems caused by these physical barriers. As you read, keep these questions in mind:

1. Suppose you were a farmer on the banks of the Ohio in 1800. Would you be more interested in what was happening in Washington or in New Orleans? Why?
2. What practical problems would America's geographic makeup and the spread of its population have on you in the early 1800's if you were the governor of Pennsylvania? a senator from Tennessee? the President of the United States?
3. How did Calhoun use the experience of the War of 1812 to support his argument?
4. What were the natural "advantages" that Calhoun thought could be exploited to national advantage?

Physical Barriers to National Unity

Henry Adams, the grandson of President John Quincy Adams and author of a famous autobiography, was also a fine historian. The following selection, from his History of the United States of America During the First Administration of Thomas Jefferson, *describes transportation and communication problems in 1800.*

Henry Adams, **History of the United States During the First Administration of Thomas Jefferson.** New York: Charles Scribner's Sons, 1889, vol. 1, pp. 5–8. Language simplified and modernized.

America's physical problems had changed little in fifty years. The old landmarks remained nearly where they stood before. The same bad roads and difficult rivers, connecting the same small towns, stretched into the same forests in 1800, as when the armies of Braddock and Amherst pierced the western and northern wilderness. Only in 1800 these roads extended a few miles farther from the seacoast. Nature was rather man's master than his servant. The five million Americans struggling with the untamed continent seemed hardly more competent to their task than the beavers and buffalo which had for countless generations made bridges and roads of their own.

In 1755, General Braddock (1695–1755) led a force of British and colonial soldiers across the Allegheny Mountains in an unsuccessful attempt to take Fort Duquesne from the French. In 1758, Lord Amherst (1717–1797), a British general, recaptured Louisbourg, Nova Scotia, from the French.

Even by water, along the seaboard, communication was as slow and almost as irregular as in colonial times. The Napoleonic Wars in Europe caused a sudden and great increase in American shipping employed in foreign commerce, without yet leading to general im-

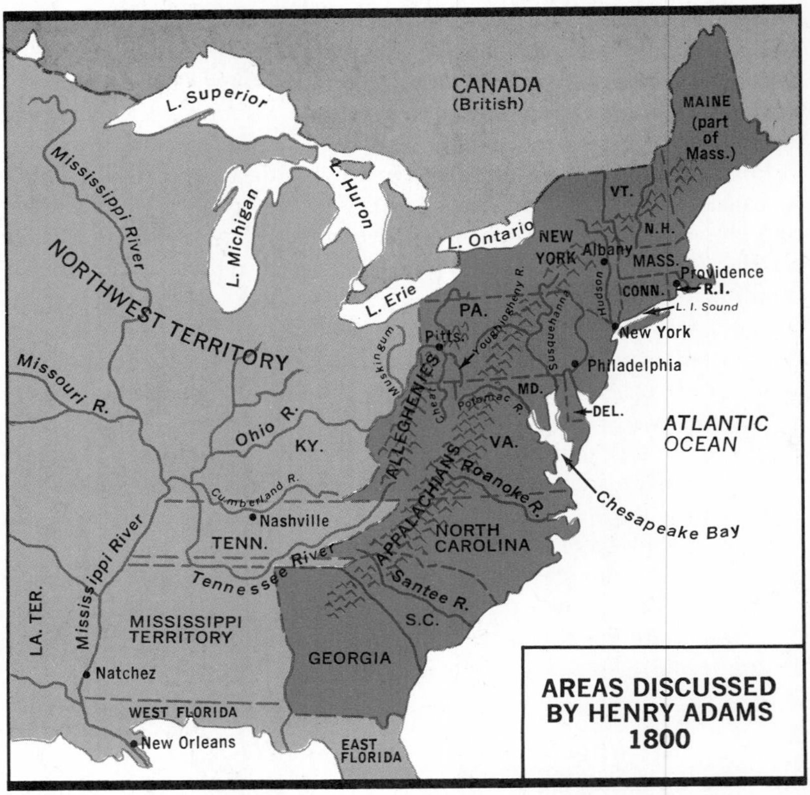

provement in navigation. The ordinary sea-going vessel carried a freight of about two hundred and fifty tons; the largest merchant ships hardly reached four hundred tons; the largest frigate [war ship] in the United States Navy had a capacity of fifteen hundred and seventy-six tons. Elaborately rigged as ships or brigs, the small merchant craft required large crews and were slow sailers, but the voyage to Europe was comparatively more comfortable and more regular than the voyage from New York to Albany or through Long Island Sound to Providence, Rhode Island. No regular packet [boat carrying mail and passengers] plied between New York and Albany. Passengers waited till a sloop was advertised to sail; then they provided their own bedding and supplies. A week on the Hudson River or on the Sound was an experience not at all unknown to travelers.

While little improvement had been made in water-travel, every increase of distance added to the difficulties of the westward journey. The settler, who after buying wagon and horses, hauled his family and goods across the mountains, might buy or build a broad flat-bottomed ark, to float him and his fortunes down the Ohio. The ark was in constant peril of being upset or being sunk. Only light boats with strong oars or boats forced against the current by laboriously poling in shallow water could go upstream. If the settler carried his tobacco and wheat down the Mississippi to the Spanish port of New Orleans, and sold it, he might return to his home in Kentucky or Ohio by a long and dangerous journey on horseback through the Indian country from Natchez to Nashville. Or he might take ship to Philadelphia, if a ship were about to sail, and again cross the Allegheny Mountains. Compared with river travel, the sea was commonly an easy and safe highway. Nearly all the rivers which penetrated the interior were unsafe. Freshets made them dangerous, and drought made them both dangerous and impassable.

Spain held New Orleans until 1800 when the entire Louisiana Territory was turned over to France.

Freshets are a sudden rise in the level of a river due to heavy rain or melting snow or ice.

Yet such as they were, these streams made the main paths of traffic. Through the mountain gorges of the Susquehanna, the produce of western New York first found an outlet. The Cuyahoga and Muskingum were the first highway from the Great Lakes to the Ohio. The Ohio itself, with its great tributaries the Cumberland and the Tennessee, marked the lines of western migration. Every stream which could at high water float a boat became a path for commerce. As General Washington, not twenty years earlier, hoped that the brawling waters of the Cheat and Youghiogheny might become the channel of trade between Chesapeake Bay and Pittsburgh, so the Americans of 1800 risked life and property on any streamlet that fell foaming down either flank of the Alleghenies. The experience of mankind proved trade to be dependent on water communications, and, as yet, Americans did not dream that the experience of mankind was useless to them.

If America were to be developed along the lines of water communication alone, Nature had decided that the experiment of a single republican government must meet extreme difficulties. The valley of the Ohio had nothing to do with that of the Hudson, the Susquehanna, the Potomac, the Roanoke, and the Santee. Close communication by land could alone hold the great geographical divisions together. The union of New England with New York and Pennsylvania was not an easy task, even as a problem of geography, and with an ocean highway. But the union of New England with the Carolinas, and of the seacoast with the interior, promised to be a hopeless undertaking. Physical contact alone could make one country of these isolated empires. To the patriotic American of 1800, struggling for the continued existence of an embryo nation, with machinery so inadequate, the idea of ever bringing the Mississippi River, either by land or water, into close contact with New England, must have seemed wild.

A Program for National Unity

John C. Calhoun (1782–1850) was—along with Daniel Webster and Henry Clay—one of the great "triumvirate" who dominated national politics from the War of 1812 to 1850. Although Calhoun ultimately became a leading spokesman for Southern sectionalism and states' rights, during the early part of his career he was an ardent advocate for the kind of nationalistic legislation suggested in a speech that he delivered in the House of Representatives on February 4, 1817. Portions of that speech follow.

Richard K. Crallé, ed., **Works of John C. Calhoun.** New York: D. Appleton and Company, 1856, vol. II, pp. 188–91. Language simplified and modernized.

Congress ought to take charge of building roads and canals. If we were only to consider the financial advantages of a good transportation system, it might then be left to private enterprise. But when we come to consider how intimately the strength and political prosperity of the republic are connected with transportation, we find the most urgent reasons why we should apply our national resources to it.

In many respects, no country, of equal population and wealth, possesses potential power equal to ours. In muscular power, in hardy and enterprising habits, and in lofty and gallant courage, our people are surpassed by none. In one respect, and, in my opinion, in one only, are we materially weak. We occupy an enormously large land area in proportion to our population. Only with great difficulty can the common strength of our nation be brought to bear on any point that may be menaced by an enemy.

It is our duty, then, in so far as possible, to counteract this weakness. Good roads and canals, carefully laid out, are the proper remedy. In the recent War of 1812, how much did we suffer for the lack of them? Our military movements were slow, while our transportation costs were high. In the event of another war, the savings in the cost of transporting materials and men would go far toward repaying us for the expense of constructing roads and canals.

What can be more important than a perfect unity of feelings and sentiments among the people in every part of the country? And what can help to produce unity more than a transportation system? No free state ever occupied a country as large as this one. Let it not, however, be forgotten—let it be forever kept in mind—that the size of our nation exposes us to the threat of disunity. We are great and growing rapidly. This is our pride and our danger, our weakness and our strength.

We must counteract every tendency to disunion. No doubt the strongest of all cements is the wisdom, justice, and above all, the moderation of this House of Representatives. Yet the great subject on which we are now deliberating deserves the most serious consideration as a means for preventing disunity. Whatever hinders communication between the distant parts of the country and Washington, D. C., the center of the republic, weakens the union. The larger the area within which trade goes on, the greater are the social contacts among people. In turn, the more strongly are we bound together and the more inseparable are our destinies.

Nothing—not even dissimilarity of language—tends more than distance to divide men from each other. Let us, then, bind the republic together with a perfect system of roads and canals. Let us conquer space. The most distant parts of the republic will be brought within a few days' travel of the center; a citizen of the west will read the news of Boston still moist from the press. The mail and the press are the nerves of the nation. They communicate the slightest impression made on a remote part of the country to the whole system; and the more perfect the means of transportation, the more rapid and true the impression.

To aid us in this great work of maintaining the integrity of this republic, our country has most admirable advantages. It is belted around with lakes and oceans and intersected in every direction by bays and rivers. It is blessed with a form of government which combines liberty and strength. We may reasonably raise our eyes to a most splendid future, if we only act in a manner worthy of our advantages. If, however, we neglect them and permit a low, sordid, selfish, and sectional spirit to take possession of the House of Representatives, this happy scene will vanish. We will divide, and misery and despotism will follow.

30 A Common Language and History

What is required to make a nation? Political scientists have identified at least three requirements: independence from outside control, greater communication among citizens than between citizens and outsiders, and the development of a national self-consciousness and pride. The Revolutionary War and the War of 1812 produced and then reasserted the first of these three requirements, independence. The two remaining factors developed rapidly in the early decades of the nineteenth century.

Energetic attempts after the War of 1812 to build an improved transportation and communication system may be interpreted as a step in nation-building. John C. Calhoun's plea to the House of Representatives for support for roads and canals rang with nationalist overtones. But national self-consciousness and pride do not automatically follow new highways. They rest in part on a common cultural heritage and a common language.

National self-consciousness also grows from the pride which a people take in their history and in the leaders who have helped to build the nation. The essential elements of a people's national tradition stay alive in many different ways: through stories, songs, and poems that are handed down orally; through written histories and textbooks; and through the work of painters, architects, and sculptors. The recently established nations in Asia or Africa place murals and statues celebrating the national heroes who led their countries' struggles for independence in almost every public square. Similarly, American artists of the early nineteenth century celebrated the memories of Washington, Franklin, Jefferson, and other great heroes of the American struggle for independence.

The selections below reflect the concern shared by many Americans, during this period, about their language and the heroic events in their history. As you read, keep these questions in mind:

1. What were Webster's objections to the use of conventional English dictionaries by Americans?
2. What observations did Silliman make about the artistic qualities of Trumbull's painting? about the treatment of the subject?
3. If you were an American living in 1819, would you have preferred the earlier or the later version of Trumbull's painting? Why?
4. What other kinds of subjects do you think artists would have been interested in painting during this period? Why might they have been interested in these subjects?

The Reasons for an American Dictionary

Noah Webster (1758–1843) began to work on An American Dictionary of the English Language *in 1800. He completed it in 1828. The following selection is taken from his preface to that dictionary.*

Noah Webster, **An American Dictionary of the English Language.** New York: S. Converse, 1828, vol. 1, Preface. Language simplified and modernized.

It is not only important, but in a degree necessary, that the people of this country should have an *American Dictionary of the English Language*. Although the body of the language is the same as in England, and it is desirable to continue that sameness, yet some differences must exist.

Language is the expression of ideas; and if the people of one country can not preserve an identity of ideas, they cannot retain an identity of language. Now, an identity of ideas depends materially upon a sameness of things or objects with which the people of the two countries are familiar. But in no two portions of the earth, far from each other, can such identity be found. Even physical objects must be different.

The principal differences between the people of this country and of all others, arise from different forms of government, different laws, institutions, and customs. Thus the practice of *hawking* and *hunting*, the institution of *heraldry*, and the *feudal system* of England originated terms which formed, and some of which now form, a necessary part of the language of that country.

But, in the United States, many of these terms are not part of our present language—and they can not be—for the things which they express do not exist in this country. They can be known to us only as out-of-date or foreign words. On the other hand, the institutions in this country which are new and peculiar, give rise to new terms or to new applications of old terms, unknown to the people of England. They cannot be explained by them, and will not be inserted in their dictionaries, unless copied from ours. Thus the terms *land-office, location of land, regent* of a university, *plantation, selectmen, senate, congress, courts,* and *assembly* are either words not belonging to the language of England, or they are applied to things in this country which do not exist in that. No person in this country will be satisfied with the English definitions of the words *congress, senate, assembly, court,* etc. Although these are words used in England, yet they are applied in this country to express ideas which they do not express in that country.

But this is not all. In many cases, the nature of our governments, and of our civil institutions, requires an appropriate language in the definition of words, even when the words express the same thing as in England. Thus the English dictionaries inform us that a *justice* is one appointed by the *king* to make right judgments. He is a *lord* by his office; justices of the peace are appointed by the king's *commission* [authority]—language which is inaccurate in respect to this officer in the United States. So *constitutionally* in England means legally; but in this country the distinction between *constitution* and *law* requires a different definition. In the United States, a *plantation* is a very different thing from what it is in England.

A great number of words in our language require that they be defined in phrases suitable to the condition and institutions of the people in these States. The people of England must look to an *American Dictionary* for a correct understanding of such terms.

The necessity, therefore, of a dictionary suited to the people of the United States is obvious.

The United States commenced their existence under circumstances wholly novel and without example in the history of nations. They commenced with civilization, with learning, with science, with constitutions of free government, and with that best gift of God to man, the Christian religion. Their population is now equal to that of England. In arts and sciences, our citizens are very little behind the most

Hawking is hunting game with a trained falcon, a variety of hawk. **Hunting,** for the English upper classes, is pursuing game for sport. **Heraldry** is the practice of caring for and adorning a knight's armor and of tracing family pedigrees. All of these words designate practices inherited from the Middle Ages, and all are associated with activities of the English aristocracy. The feudal system was the political, economic, and social organization of medieval Europe.

Land-office was a government office which sold public lands to settlers and land speculators. **Location of land** is designated according to townships and sections set up by the Land Ordinance of 1785. A **regent** is a member of the governing board of a university. A **selectman** is a member of a board of town officers in New England chosen to manage certain public affairs.

A constitution is the group of basic principles by which a state or nation is governed. In the United States, it is a written document; in Britain, a group of documents and precedents. A law is any rule that a lawmaking body enacts.

In the United States, a plantation was a large farm on which cotton or tobacco was grown. In Britain, plantation meant a group of planted trees or plants.

enlightened people on earth; in some respects, they have no superiors. Our language, within two centuries, will be spoken by more people in this country than any other language on earth, except the Chinese, in Asia; and even that may not be an exception.

Artistic Expressions of Nationalism

In 1797, the well-known American painter, John Trumbull, painted the signing of the Declaration of Independence on a canvas which measured 21 by 31 inches. In 1818, he painted the same scene for the Capitol rotunda on a canvas which measured 18 by 12 feet. The Capitol painting was widely reviewed in American newspapers and magazines. Benjamin Silliman, a prominent chemist at Yale University, wrote the review from which this selection was taken.

The American Journal of Science and Arts (1818), vol. I, pp. 200–03. Language simplified and modernized.

This is the greatest work which the art of painting has ever produced in the United States. The picture is magnificent both in size and in execution. The dimensions of the canvas are eighteen feet by twelve.

This picture forms one of a series by Mr. Trumbull, in which he intended to represent the most important civil and military events of the American revolution, with portraits of the most distinguished actors in the various scenes. The materials for this purpose were collected many years ago, and two plates have been engraved from paintings of the deaths of General Warren and General Montgomery. But the work was suspended because of the political convulsions, which, for twenty-five years after the war, were so fatal to the arts of peace.

General Richard Montgomery (1738–1775) captured Montreal in 1775 and was killed while trying to take Quebec from the British. General Joseph Warren (1741–1775) was a Massachusetts patriot whom the British shot as he rallied the militia in the Battle of Bunker Hill.

The government of the United States have ordered four of the subjects originally proposed by Mr. Trumbull, to be painted by him, and to be deposited in the national capitol.

No event in human history ever shed a more wholesome influence over the destinies of so great a mass of mankind as the American Revolution did. The wisdom of no political act was ever so soon and so powerfully demonstrated, by such magnificent consequences. And justly may the nation be proud of the Revolution and of those distinguished men, its authors, whose patriotism was calm, dignified, persevering, and always under the guidance of reason and virtue.

The painting represents the Congress at the moment when the committee advanced to the table of the president to make their report. It contains faithful portraits of all those members who were living when the picture was begun, and of all others of whom any authentic representation could be obtained. Of a small number, no

Capitol Building, Washington, D.C.

trace could be discovered. Nothing was included which was not authentic.

This picture is now, by permission of government, exhibited in the Academy of Arts in New York, and will probably be shown in some of our other principal cities, before it receives its final location at Washington.

Yale University

The figures are as large as life; and it may safely be said, that the world has never beheld, on a similar occasion, a more noble group of men. It was the native and untried nobility of great talent, cultivated intelligence, superior manners, high moral aim, and devoted patriotism. The crisis demanded the utmost firmness of which the human mind is capable—a firmness not produced, for the moment, by passion and enthusiasm, but resting on the most able comprehension of both duties and dangers.

This moral effect has been produced in the fullest and finest manner by this great painter. No true American can view this picture without gratitude to the men who, under God, asserted their liberties, and to the artist who had commemorated the event, and transmitted the very features and persons of the actors to future generations. Such artistic efforts tend powerfully also to promote patriotism, and to prompt the rising generation to imitate such glorious examples.

Frenchmen, such as Lafayette, helped the Americans in their fight for independence.

It was a great thing to assert, in principle, the liberties of this country; but it was also a great thing to justify them by arms. We rejoice that Colonel Trumbull is still to proceed, under the authority of government, to paint other scenes, in which Washington and his illustrious American patriots, and the flower of French chivalry, were the actors. Trumbull is in the maturity of his experience, skill, and fame. He has the portraits of most of the great men of the Revolutionary Period and he is himself personally familiar with them and their great deeds. We trust that the government will promptly second what we think the united voice of the nation will demand—that the illustrious artist should dedicate the evening of his life to the country's honor and glory.

31 Emergence of a National Economy

In 1800, more than ninety percent of the American people lived on farms or in tiny villages. These farms and villages formed thousands of separate economies, rather than one "American economy."

Large southern planters and merchants on the Atlantic coast carried on substantial trade with Europe, primarily with Great Britain. The subsistence farm, however, was the characteristic unit of the American economy. In this "family economy," the father and his wife and children spent most of their time producing the basic necessities of life: food, fuel, clothing, and shelter.

By 1820, about 500,000 family economies participated in larger "local economies." Neighboring farmers, for example, bartered crops and shared labor with each other. At village stores or markets, farmers exchanged their excess crops and homemade products. The village usually served as the center for the local market, and small, local industries produced lumber, flour, bricks, wagons, and nails. These products rarely went beyond the local market, which ordinarily did not exceed an area of thirty miles in diameter.

During the first few decades of the nineteenth century, the economy gradually became less local and more national. America had always been involved in the world economy. European countries wanted American agricultural products, such as cotton, tobacco, rice and sugar; in turn, America needed European manufactured goods. Transportation problems, however, had held back trade between distant points within the nation. As more roads, canals, and bridges were built, trade between the various sections increased. More and more local economies began to participate in the same general economy. In turn, economic interdependence between sections of the country increased, as each section specialized in those products it could produce most efficiently and could sell in other areas of the country. Thus economic development in America promoted the growth of nationalism in the first quarter of the nineteenth century.

As you read the following selections, which describe this transformation of the American economy, try to answer these questions:

1. In what ways did the growth of cotton agriculture affect the American economy during this period?
2. How were the Northeast, South, and West economically dependent on each other during this period? What goods flowed between the sections?
3. Why did textile manufacturing develop rapidly in New England after 1815?

The Growth of an Interdependent Economy

This account of economic developments in the United States in the early nineteenth century is taken from the works of the American economic historian, Guy S. Callender.

Guy S. Callender, **Selections from the Economic History of the United States, 1765–1860.** Boston: Ginn and Company, 1909, pp. 272–74.

The influence which rapidly changed [local economies into a national economy] was the introduction of cotton culture into the South and its extension after 1815 over the Southwest. About the same time, also, there was a considerable extension of sugar culture in Louisiana, and tobacco culture in Kentucky and Tennessee. Here was a group of commodities . . . much in demand everywhere . . . and having large value in small bulk so that they were able to bear the expense of land transportation for long distances over the poor roads of new settlements. The soil and climate of a vast region were peculiarly suited to the production of cotton, the demand for which was increasing at a prodigious [extraordinary] rate. This region was covered by a network of navigable streams that could easily and cheaply float this valuable product to tide water. The [steamboat] . . . perfected a natural transportation system entirely adequate for a community devoted to producing a few such commodities and exchanging them with the outside world.

The Southwest, in the early nineteenth century, included the present states of Alabama and Mississippi.

Robert Fulton invented the steamboat in 1807. By 1815, steamboats operated regularly on the Mississippi River.

The effect of these economic advantages was not confined to the South. Very soon they were felt by every other section of the country. The great profit to be secured in the cultivation of cotton and sugar caused the people of South Carolina and the Gulf States to devote themselves chiefly to these industries [crops] and to neglect the other branches of agriculture. . . . [P]lanters with slave labor [took over the production of cotton and sugar]. . . . Mixed farming could not be profitably carried on by slaves in the South; hence the planters were glad to purchase their agricultural supplies, so far as possible, from other producers.

The livestock could be driven overland to the plantations, and the great network of rivers with their flatboats and steamboats provided an easy means of transportation for other supplies. All kinds of produce from such important products as pork, bacon, lard, beef, butter, cheese, corn, flour, and whiskey, to such little ones as apples, cider, vinegar, soap, and candles went down the Ohio and Mississippi in great quantities. This was the first important market which the farmers of Tennessee, Kentucky, and the northwest secured, and it wrought [made] an improvement in their economic situation almost as remarkable as the introduction of cotton culture produced in the southwest.

The prosperity of the South and West now in turn influenced the East. The people of these sections were able for the first time to purchase freely from other communities. The commodities to satisfy their wants were partly imported from abroad, and partly produced in New England and the Middle States. Accordingly, both the commercial and manufacturing interests of this section were greatly stimulated. New York reached out with her Erie Canal to secure a larger share of the growing internal trade, and a keen rivalry sprang up among the commercial cities of the seaboard which has lasted to the present day. Manufactures also began now to feel the influence of that expanding home market which has played so great a part in their development ever since.

The Erie Canal, running from Buffalo, New York, on Lake Erie to Albany, New York, on the Hudson River, was completed in 1825.

This account is sufficient to make clear the general character of internal commerce. Its basis was a territorial division of labor among the three great sections of the country resting upon foreign commerce. The South was able to devote itself chiefly to the production of a few staples, turning out a great surplus of them for export and depending upon the other two sections for much of its agricultural produce, nearly all of its manufactures, and to a large extent for the conduct of its commerce. Both its exports and imports were carried largely by northern shipping, went through northern ports, and were either actually in the hands of northern merchants or financed by northern capital. The northwest devoted itself chiefly to agriculture, depending at first entirely upon the South for its markets, but gradually acquiring after 1840 a home market in the northeast and a foreign one in Europe. New England and the Middle States were devoted principally to commerce and manufactures by which they were enabled to supply the needs of the other two sections, depending at first upon their own farmers for their agricultural supplies and later drawing them partly from the southern seaboard slave states and partly from the northwest, especially from the region about the Great Lakes.

The great streams of commerce which resulted from this territorial division of labor were, first, the trade on the western rivers consisting principally of agricultural produce sent down the river to the planters —little southern produce was brought back except sugar and molasses from Louisiana[.] [S]econd, there was a large coasting trade, consisting of manufactures sent from northern to southern ports with return cargoes of southern staples for the supply of the northeastern states or for export, supplemented by some food supplies for New England[.] [T]hird, there was the trade of the seaboard cities with the West, made up for the most part of manufacture[d goods] . . . sent westward over the canals to the Ohio or the Lakes, and intended to supply the western farmers or to be forwarded down the rivers to the planters of the southwest.

The Growth of Textile Manufacturing

Two important developments spurred the growth of textile manufacturing in the United States. In 1790, a young Englishman named Samuel Slater introduced the English factory system by developing a water-powered machine to spin cotton thread. In 1793, Eli Whitney invented a cotton gin which rapidly separated the cotton seeds from the fibers. This selection, from an American economic historian, Victor S. Clark, describes the growth of textile manufacturing in the early nineteenth century.

Victor S. Clark, **History of Manufacturers in the United States, 1607–1860.** Washington, D.C.: Carnegie Institution of Washington, 1916, Publication No. 215A, pp. 543–51.

While . . . pioneer undertakings [in textile manufacturing] were struggling into life in remoter parts of the country, the cotton manufactures of New England and the Middle States were passing through maturer experiences. Mills that survived the dark years between 1815 and 1820 were generally fitted by location, management, equipment, and resources to continue the industry successfully. So far as the precarious [uncertain] statistics of 1820 are a ground for conclusions, cotton-spinning by this time had nearly recovered the position occupied in 1815. About one-third of the spindles of New England and New York were making yarn for power-looms. The ratio of looms to spindles was higher in Massachusetts than in neighboring states. New Jersey and Delaware mills were engaged chiefly in spinning for Philadelphia manufacturers, but most of the yarn made in Maryland was woven in local factories. Therefore, except for the small but important district tributary [subsidiary] to Philadelphia, the centralized system of manufacture was rapidly extending.

Some cotton manufacturing had been started in Virginia, South Carolina, and Kentucky.

A depression followed the War of 1812. To add to American economic problems, the British dumped their manufactured goods on the American market in an effort to cripple the infant industries.

Spindles are the rods that hold the bobbins on which thread is wound as it is spun.

A loom is a machine for weaving thread or yarn into cloth. Waterpower replaced hand operation of looms.

This concentration affected all aspects of the industry. More processes were performed in one establishment; the capacity of individual mills was enlarged; the plants began to group in narrow areas. Technical and commercial limitations no longer restricted the size of factories so much as formerly; but most mills, and most spindles, even in old manufacturing districts, were still moved by small water-powers . . .

The Merrimac River flows from New Hampshire through Massachusetts to the Atlantic Ocean.

The series of large water-power developments . . . which gave rise to the new manufacturing cities of the Merrimac [River], was anticipated or repeated in a smaller way at several mill villages on rivers tributary to the New England sounds. . . .

Between 1820 and 1832, the number of spindles in Rhode Island increased in round numbers from 70,000 to 240,000. There may have been one mill loom in use for every 160 spindles [at] the former date; there was one for every forty spindles in 1832. Connecticut increased its spindles from 30,000 to 140,000, and its loom capacity in the same ratio as Rhode Island. Massachusetts, with more capital and room for growth, raised its spindles from 52,000 to 340,000, and employed relatively more factory looms than its neighbors. It had now passed Rhode Island as our leading cotton-manufacturing state. . . .

The history of this progress embraces two salient [prominent] features: the appearance of big corporations with plants designed for special goods, and the rise of calico-printing to importance. In 1821 there was a better demand for domestic manufactures than had existed since the war with England, and this condition continued without serious alteration, . . . until towards the end of the decade. . . .

Even the depression following the war did not check the prosperous career of the Boston Manufacturing Company, which produced its first cloth in 1815, built a second larger mill two years later, and added a third factory and a bleachery in 1820. This convinced Boston capitalists that cotton goods could be made profitably in New England and that the Waltham method best suited our conditions of production. Therefore, as soon as the business horizon cleared, measures were taken to start this system of manufacture in other places. Soon after 1820, in addition to smaller enterprises, two groups of large factories were promoted. The first was at Lowell [Massachusetts], and made that city until the Civil War the leading textile center of America; the other was at Dover and Somersworth, in New Hampshire, on the boundary between that state and Maine. The latter mills were built with Boston money, but by different investors from those who supported Waltham and were engaged in founding Lowell. As a consequence of this movement, Boston became the conspicuous financial and commercial supporter of New England's textile development during the years that followed 1820. . . .

A bleachery is a place where cloth is bleached or whitened.

With the Waltham method of manufacturing, introduced in Waltham, Massachusetts, all the processes involved in turning raw cotton into finished cloth were completed in one factory.

The Merrimac Company, which was the original Lowell corporation, was organized in 1822 with $600,000 capital, or the amount then employed by the Boston Company, which was the largest textile concern in New England. . . . And ten years from the time it shipped its first goods to Boston its factories contained over 30,000 spindles and 1000 looms.

Meantime, in 1825, the Hamilton Company was organized, with $600,000 capital, to make drillings—a fabric which it originated—and fancy cloths; in 1828 the Appleton and Lowell companies were chartered, both of which manufactured coarse goods to supply a demand that had outgrown the capacity of Waltham; and in 1830, the Suffolk, Tremont, and Lawrence companies were started. By the end of 1834, these six companies operated 19 cotton mills at Lowell, with 110,000 spindles and 4000 looms. This represented the most remarkable decade of progress, in a single place and industry, as yet achieved in our manufacturing history. . . .

These large corporations, regarded as gigantic in their day, did not monopolize the progress of cotton manufactures during the revival that followed 1820; indeed they did not contribute a major fraction to the spindle increase that then occurred. But these enterprises and others like them were the prominent and, as we see in aftersight, the permanent new feature of the years in question. They expressed the type of industrial organization that eventually was to prevail in America. However, their success at this particular time was aided by the introduction of calico-printing and fancy weaving. . . .

Outside of New England the example of Lowell's big factories had little influence upon manufacturing methods, though in New York and Maryland spinning and weaving were usually combined in one plant. In 1832, the largest mill in New York had less than 10,000 spindles. Hand-loom weaving still prevailed at Philadelphia. . . .

Our principal textile areas continued to be near the New England coast and in the valleys of the Hudson and the Delaware.

32 The Dimensions of Nationhood

HISTORICAL ESSAY

Two contradictory developments took place in the United States during the first quarter of the nineteenth century. On the one hand, spectacular social and economic growth, coming after a second military victory over England, gave a tremendous impetus to national consciousness and pride. The United States had proved its right to be treated as an equal among the great nations of the world, and its people were proud to be called Americans. At the same time, sectional and class feelings grew rapidly. Northerners, southerners, and westerners developed somewhat different societies; farmers, mechanics, slaveholders, and manufacturers began to see different visions of America's future. These contradictory developments created a difficult political problem: how to encourage national growth and at the same time satisfy rapidly differentiating sections and interests within the country.

The "Era of Good Feelings"

Jefferson's friend and Secretary of State, James Madison, succeeded to the Presidency in 1809; he won a second term four years later. In 1817, another political associate of Jefferson, James Monroe, won an easy victory in the electoral college. By this time, the Federalists had so declined in strength that their Presidential candidate, Rufus King, was able to carry only three states: Massachusetts, Connecticut, and Delaware. Because of this overwhelming electoral victory and because Monroe's Administration was generally received with favor, even in New England, the traditional stronghold of Federalism, historians have commonly referred to his two terms of office (1817–1825) as an "Era of Good Feelings." This expression helps us to identify a period in our history when little formal political opposition existed, a period which contrasts sharply with the fierce party wrangling at the end of the eighteenth century. But no amount of surface harmony could make the sectional tensions and contending economic forces disappear. The "Era of Good Feelings" ended with a disputed national election in 1824 and the emergence of new political factions.

After his election, President Monroe toured the country and was received triumphantly everywhere, especially in New England. The prevailing mood of the American people reflected political unity and national pride. Symbols of the American nation became more important than ever before. The stars and stripes of the American flag flew everywhere. The bald eagle, symbol of the soaring strength of the new nation, became a popular decoration and was also stamped on American coins. The figure of "Uncle Sam," clothed in stars and stripes and characterized by shrewdness, industry, tenacity, and strength, emerged to typify the American character. Americans were determined to assert their independence and uniqueness in as many ways as they could. John Trumbull's representation of the signing of the Declaration of Independence and Noah Webster's insistence that the traditional English language could not be made to fit the experience of the new nation are good examples of the nationalistic spirit of the period.

The most important domestic legislation of the period also reflected American nationalism. In 1816, Congress passed the first

American tariff designed primarily to protect new industries rather than to provide income for the federal government. The tariff was a direct response to the rapid growth of cotton mills during the war years when British manufactures were shut out from the American market. When trade with England resumed, Congress believed it was in the national interest to protect new industries, such as the textile industry described by Victor S. Clark. Within a decade, the tariff would become a matter of sharp dispute between Northerners and Southerners. The fact that prominent southern political leaders, such as Calhoun, supported it in 1816 indicates the strength of political unity and national feeling at the time. A similar example can be found in the chartering of the Second Bank of the United States in the same year. Although Jefferson had opposed the establishment of the First Bank of the United States, Jefferson's protégé, Madison, recommended that Congress establish a second bank after the charter to the first had expired.

Internal Improvements

The need for roads and canals to tie the different parts of the country together attracted much public attention during the early part of the century. Although Hamilton had been in favor of federal support for such "internal improvements," it was Jefferson's Secretary of the Treasury, Albert Gallatin, who formally proposed that Congress finance such projects. The Republican administrations were less willing to support this measure than they were the tariff and bank. There were two reasons for this attitude. In the first place, many people doubted the government's constitutional right to build roads and canals. In the second place, despite the fact that a leading New England political leader—John Quincy Adams—and a leading southern leader—Calhoun—advocated these measures, there were many people in New England and the South who could not see the advantages of improved roads and canals. Many New Englanders feared that better transportation facilities would drain off the labor supply in eastern cities. Federal responsibility for internal improvements, therefore, became a lively political issue. It soon became associated with the name of Henry Clay, the dynamic young Speaker of the House of Representatives, and later became one of the most important planks in the platform of the Whig party which Clay helped to organize in the 1830's.

Meanwhile, with the exception of the Cumberland Road which connected the Ohio and Potomac Rivers, state or private money financed most of the roads and canals, which were built or were in the process of being built before 1825. The most famous achievement of this kind was the Erie Canal, opened in 1825.

Although the state governments played a more important role than the federal government in the construction of roads and canals, a national transportation and communication network was coming into existence. Western farmers could sell their crops in eastern markets, and eastern manufacturers could market their goods throughout the country. As a result American dependence on the European economy decreased. Throughout the seventeenth and eighteenth centuries, America combined a subsistence with a staple-producing economy. Most Americans lived on self-sufficient farms. A few produced agricultural products for sale in Europe and bought manufactured goods there. The changes in the economy in the early nineteenth century, such as those Guy S. Callender pointed out, have been described as a "market revolution." Americans were developing a national economy. More and more Americans sold their labor or their farm products in the market to the highest bidder. Instead of determining their own economic welfare, as many subsistence farmers had been able to do, they found their fortunes tied to the general level of prosperity in the country as a whole.

The Strengthening of the Supreme Court

Although the Federalists declined during this period as a political party, many of the "nationalistic" measures which Federalists originally favored, such as the tariff and the bank, were supported by the Republicans. Federalist ideas also continued to have an impact on the government through decisions of the Supreme Court. Probably nothing John Adams did as President had more lasting significance than his appointment in 1801 of John Marshall as Chief Justice of the Supreme Court. For the next thirty-four years, Marshall was the guiding influence on the Court. His own opinions were usually decisive for a majority of the other Justices; he himself wrote about half of the more than 1100 decisions handed down during this period. Because of Marshall's influence, the most important decisions of the Court represented a national rather than a states-rights point of view.

In *Marbury* vs. *Madison* (1803), part of which appeared in Chapter 6, Marshall asserted that the Supreme Court could declare a law of Congress unconstitutional. In 1816, the Marshall court decided two more vital cases. The first related to the right of the New Hampshire legislature to alter the royal charter under which Dartmouth College had been established in 1769. Marshall, speaking for the Court, ruled that the charter constituted a contract and was, therefore, protected from state interference by the Constitution. The Dartmouth College Case was important for two reasons. First, it declared that a state could not pass laws contrary to Constitutional provisions. Second, it placed existing corporations beyond the control of individual states and thus encouraged business growth since corporations felt freer to make plans when they knew that business rules would not be changed arbitrarily by state actions.

In 1819, the Court ruled in the case of *McCulloch* vs. *Maryland.* The issue involved the legal right of Maryland to tax a branch of the Bank of the United States. The decision involved two questions: the constitutionality of the Bank, and the constitutionality of the tax. Marshall started with the assumption that the federal government represented one sovereign nation and not a group of independent states. "The government of the Union," he said, "is emphatically and truly a government of the people. In form and substance it emanates from them, its powers are granted by them, and are to be exercised directly on them, and for their benefit." In deciding that the Bank was constitutional Marshall drew heavily on the reasoning Hamilton had expressed many years before. The Constitution gave the federal government the power to do what was "necessary and proper" for the general welfare. Although the Constitution did not give the federal government the specific power to establish a bank, it could be reasonably assumed that a bank was necessary for the government to carry out its other powers. Marshall spelled this out in language which was enormously important for the rest of American history:

> Let the end be legitimate, let it be within the scope of the Constitution, and all means which are appropriate, which are plainly adopted to that end, which are not prohibited, but consistent with the letter and spirit of the Constitution, are constitutional.

Marshall's insistence that the language of the Constitution should be interpreted broadly set a precedent without which it would have been extremely difficult for the federal government to expand its powers and functions during the nineteenth century. Having determined that the Bank was constitutional, Marshall and the Court decided that the state could not tax it, since the power to tax any institution can be used in such a way as to destroy it.

Another important case, *Gibbons* vs. *Ogden* (1824), involved the question of New York State's right to grant a monopoly to a steamboat company that operated in the waters between New York and New Jersey. Marshall and the Court held that the Constitution reserved to Congress the right to regulate commerce between the states. The immediate effect of this decision was to send steamboats chugging across bays and harbors and up and down rivers without worrying about state restrictions. It thus encouraged national commerce. Years later government regulation of business and labor would be justified on this same principle.

The Growth of Sectionalism

Despite the forces in this period which encouraged national feeling and political unity, Americans in different sections disagreed about the importance of internal improvements. In fact, the three great geographic sections—the Northeast, the South, and the West—were becoming more differentiated than ever. Sectional consciousness was developing along with national consciousness. Forces were building, although still rather muted, that would eventually challenge national unity.

In the Northeast, economic interests were divided. Agriculture remained important in northern New England, upstate New York, and much of Pennsylvania. Traditionally, because of its large cities and seaports, the Northeast had been the commercial center of the nation. By 1820, however, manufacturing had begun to overtake maritime trade in economic importance. While most of the new textile mills grew up in New England where waterpower was abundant, the production of coal and iron had become important in Pennsylvania.

The Northeast was also divided politically. Federalists in New England resented having been shut out of power in the federal government for so long. Manufacturers sought higher tariffs, but were opposed by shipowners and merchants who feared that the tariff would interfere with foreign trade. Northerners distrusted the rising power of the West. They were anxious to hold on to a supply of inexpensive labor. They also looked with distaste on the institution of Negro slavery in the South.

Meanwhile, the South remained almost exclusively devoted to the production of agricultural staples, but the emphasis on particular crops had changed significantly. During the colonial period the principal crop for export had been tobacco grown mostly in the states of the upper South. Hemp and grain were also grown in these states, and rice and sugar were grown in South Carolina, Georgia, and Louisiana. Originally cotton had been a minor crop because of the difficulty involved in separating the fiber from the seeds. In 1793, however, Eli Whitney's cotton gin solved this problem, and the reign of "King Cotton" began in the South. At the time of Jefferson's election in 1800, only about 70,000 bales of cotton were produced in the South. By the time of his death in 1826, cotton production had increased 700 percent. As cotton production increased, so did the number of Negro slaves, although the importation of additional slaves became illegal in 1808. From 1800 to 1820, by which time every northern state had begun to abolish slavery, the number of slaves in the South had almost doubled, growing from about 800,000 to more than one and a half million.

When we speak of the West during this period we must distinguish the Old Northwest (the region beyond the Appalachians from Tennessee and Kentucky northward) from the Old Southwest (the lower Mississippi Valley). During the first quarter of the nineteenth century, the Old Northwest was the most rapidly growing section of the country. By 1820, Ohio, which had not been admitted to the Union until 1803, had a larger population than Massachusetts. The people who settled this section came from both the South and the Northeast. Northern Ohio, Indiana, and Illinois, for example, were largely settled by New Englanders, while the southern parts of these states were settled by immigrants from the South, who tended to support the idea of slavery even if they had no slaves themselves. Generally speaking, the diversified, pioneer farming, typical of the Old Northwest, discouraged the introduction of slavery. Therefore, large slaveholders, who moved westward, usually sought out the rich cotton lands along the lower Mississippi River.

In politics, the Northeast had traditionally supported Federalists and the South, Republicans. The West settled by former residents of the Northeast and South was politically mixed. As demonstrated in Chapter 7, Westerners supported the War of 1812 with great enthusiasm because they wanted the British-backed Indians removed from their frontier. After the war, they tended to support a strong national government because they wanted federal help to solve their most difficult problem, transportation. Whether they would become more closely allied with the Northeast or South would depend largely on the way this problem was solved.

That sectional balance would become a major political problem in the new nation for years to come became obvious in 1819 when the United States suffered its first major depression. Economic uncertainty had characterized the years immediately following the War of 1812. Agricultural production had soared as American farmers sought to take advantage of the newly re-opened European markets. Settlers and speculators had bought up vast amounts of western land on credit, and new untested manufacturing enterprises had rapidly attracted investments. But the economy began to contract as quickly as it had expanded. Farmers found they had produced more than they could sell; banks began to call in loans that borrowers could not repay; land values fell, and the banks ended up owning much of the land. The South and West were most severely hurt. People in these sections tended to blame banks, in general, and the Bank of the United States, in particular, for their plight. Since they associated the Bank with wealthy financial interests in the northeastern states, the panic not only brought economic distress, but sharpened sectional antagonisms as well.

Slavery and Sectionalism

At the same time that the American people were coping with the problems of depression, they were forced to come to grips with another problem—the role of slavery in the American future. By 1819, the Union had grown to 22 states evenly divided between free and slave states. In 1818, Missouri applied for admission as a state, and in 1819, James Tallmadge, a congressman from New York who hated slavery, proposed an amendment to the Missouri statehood law which would have forbidden slavery there. This proposal touched off the most serious sectional debate the nation had yet known. Northern political leaders, already unhappy because of the clause in the Constitution which allowed southern states to count three fifths of their slaves in calculating the number of representatives they could send to Congress, decried the slave system and insisted that Congress had a right to prohibit it in a new state. Southerners warned that they would never support a system of government which refused to let them take their property into new territory. In the end, the Missouri Compromise was reached. It admitted Maine to the Union as a free state and Missouri as a slave state, with the understanding that slavery would be prohibited from the remainder of the Louisiana Purchase north of the parallel 36°30′. Thus an uneasy balance between the slave and free states was preserved. Jefferson wrote to a friend that the Missouri debates were "like a fire bell in the night," tolling the possible end of the Union. "It is hushed indeed, for the moment. But this is a reprieve only, not a final sentence," he said. Thoughtful Americans everywhere feared that Jefferson was right.

The End of Political Unity

By 1824, Monroe's last year in office, the generation of great political leaders which had grown up with the American Revolution was fast passing from the scene. Washington had died in 1799. Hamilton, while still in the prime of life, was killed in a tragic duel growing out of a political quarrel with Aaron Burr in 1804. John Adams and Thomas Jefferson lived on in tranquil retirement, but would soon die on the same day, July 4, 1826.

The political leadership of the new nation was passing into the hands of a younger generation. The election of 1824 symbolized this change. The leading candidates were all Republicans and strong nationalists, and could be distinguished from each other more by their sectional support than by differences in their political platforms. John Quincy Adams, son of the second President, was New England's favorite son. Kentucky nominated Henry Clay, spokesman for the West and the champion of an "American System" of tariffs and internal improvements. Tennessee and other states supported Andrew Jackson, the hero of the Battle of New Orleans. Although Jackson had the broadest national support because of his military reputation, he was particularly strong along the frontier. Calhoun, who was the South's favorite son, originally sought the first office, but dropped from contention to run for Vice-President. When the votes were tallied for President, Jackson received the largest electoral vote, but not the majority required by the Constitution. As a result, the choice of President fell to the House of Representatives, and when Clay advised his supporters to vote for Adams, the latter was elected.

After the election of 1824, the political unity, which on the surface, at least, had characterized the Republican era, disintegrated altogether. When Clay was named Secretary of State, Jackson's followers claimed that he had been robbed of the election because of a "corrupt bargain" between Adams and Clay. The new President was hardly in office before the Jackson men began to plan for 1828.

SUGGESTED READINGS

EATON, CLEMENT, *Henry Clay and the Art of American Politics.* This brief biography describes the man who sought for internal improvements and helped to dominate American politics in the years after 1815.

CUNLIFFE, MARCUS, *The Nation Takes Shape, 1789–1837.* This book by a prominent British historian, provides a good brief analysis of American national growth during the period indicated by the title.

LARKIN, OLIVER W., *Samuel F. B. Morse and American Democratic Art.* This biography shows how the impact of a newly emerging national spirit helped to shape the career of a famous American painter and inventor.

Democratizing American Society

CHAPTER 9

STATING THE ISSUE

We are accustomed to thinking of democracy in political terms. In a political democracy, citizens have an opportunity to influence their government by voting for one party or candidate instead of another and by persuading public officeholders to support particular measures. But democracy has other meanings. Applied to a social system, it means a society in which every man has a chance to change his social status. He can move either up or down the social ladder. In economic terms, democracy means that everyone has an equal opportunity to seek any job and to improve his standard of living. In its broadest meaning, a democratic society offers each person the maximum opportunity to develop himself to the extent of his ability and his willingness to work.

Eighteenth-century America had not been a democracy by our twentieth-century standards. Women, large numbers of men without property, and most Negroes could neither vote nor hold public office. While some social mobility took place, the lines between classes were clearly drawn. Differences in education, dress, and occupation divided aristocrats from ordinary farmers and indentured servants. Laws and customs also limited economic opportunities. The national government owned western lands which it sold only in large parcels. This practice limited opportunities for many men to own their own farms. Moreover, state and national governments had established several monopolies which gave one individual or one company the exclusive right to build a bridge or establish a bank. Such monopolies closed wide areas of economic life to newcomers who sought to compete with the monopolist.

The restrictions on political, social, and economic democracy began to collapse one by one in the early history of the Republic. The movement to democratize American life reached its peak during the Jacksonian Period. Although Andrew Jackson was President only from 1829 to 1837, he so dominated the entire period from 1824 to 1840 that historians frequently refer to it as the "Age of Jackson." How was government made more democratic during this period? How were economic opportunities expanded? Did opportunities for social mobility increase? These are the issues raised in Chapter 9.

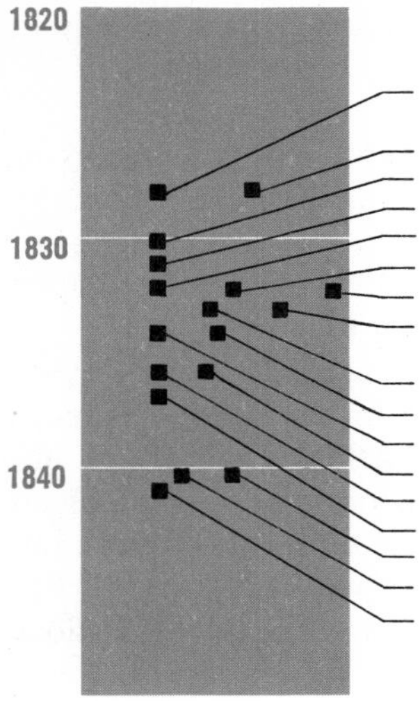

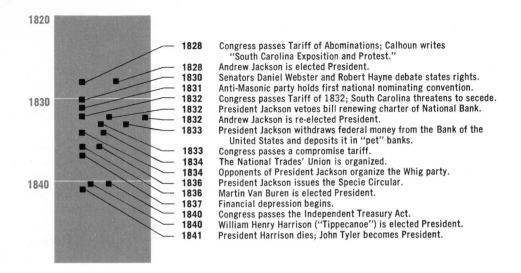

1828 Congress passes Tariff of Abominations; Calhoun writes "South Carolina Exposition and Protest."
1828 Andrew Jackson is elected President.
1830 Senators Daniel Webster and Robert Hayne debate states rights.
1831 Anti-Masonic party holds first national nominating convention.
1832 Congress passes Tariff of 1832; South Carolina threatens to secede.
1832 President Jackson vetoes bill renewing charter of National Bank.
1832 Andrew Jackson is re-elected President.
1833 President Jackson withdraws federal money from the Bank of the United States and deposits it in "pet" banks.
1833 Congress passes a compromise tariff.
1834 The National Trades' Union is organized.
1834 Opponents of President Jackson organize the Whig party.
1836 President Jackson issues the Specie Circular.
1836 Martin Van Buren is elected President.
1837 Financial depression begins.
1840 Congress passes the Independent Treasury Act.
1840 William Henry Harrison ("Tippecanoe") is elected President.
1841 President Harrison dies; John Tyler becomes President.

33 The Democratization of American Life: An Exercise in Hypothesis Formation

Any investigation of the past begins with the identification of a problem. Each of the previous chapters in this book has concentrated on one or two issues. The questions at the end of "Stating the Issue," identify problems considered in each chapter and state them in the form of general questions.

Once a historian identifies a problem, he begins to gather data about it. He reads widely in textbooks, documents written at the time, diaries, letters, and similar source materials and gathers statistics, if any are available. As he accumulates information, he also begins to develop hypotheses—tentative answers to the questions that were the beginning point of his investigation. These hypotheses help to focus his attention on evidence that is important to the question he is trying to answer. The sooner he develops hypotheses, the sooner he can begin to gather meaningful evidence.

Hypotheses often need to be revised. Suppose a historian reads a passage written in 1820 by a man who disagreed with the majority of his fellow citizens. The ideas in the passage might seem to him well worth investigating. Yet, when he gathers evidence from more typical people, he may decide that the original hypothesis he formed is not accurate. In this case, he might revise the hypothesis in the light of new evidence or abandon it completely in favor of a new hypothesis more in keeping with the majority of the evidence.

Reading 33 presents six short excerpts written by Americans or travelers to America during the first half of the nineteenth century. No attempt has been made to select passages which represent—or do not represent—majority views. Hence, any hypotheses developed from these passages must be viewed as highly tentative.

In preparation for class, you are to read each passage carefully. After you have read a passage, write down in one simple sentence in your notebook any hypothesis which you think the passage implies. Then when you have finished all the passages, write—again in one sentence—a hypothesis which pulls together the ideas from the entire set of passages.

Because of the nature of this lesson, there are no study questions provided.

A Discovery Exercise

Unimproved land is land which has not been cleared and prepared for farming.

"Annual Report of the Treasury Department at the Opening of the First Session of 22nd Congress," in **The American Quarterly Review,** vol. XI (June 1832), p. 280. Language simplified and modernized.

1

Land is now sold in tracts of eighty acres, at $1.25 an acre. For $100, an unimproved tract of eighty acres may be purchased. In any of the states west of the Ohio River, a laborer can earn 75¢ per day, and if his living costs 25¢ a day he can, by the labor of two hundred days, or about eight months, purchase a farm. Again, a laborer can get his board and $10 per month, the year round, which would amount to $120 and if $20 be deducted for clothing, he will in this way have earned the purchase money of a farm, in one year.

In 1785, the Massachusetts legislature had incorporated a company called "The Proprietors of the Charles River Bridge."

Charles River Bridge vs. **Warren Bridge,** 11 Peters, 420 [1837]. Language simplified and modernized.

2

The act of incorporation confers upon "The Proprietors of the Charles River Bridge" the ordinary authority of a corporation for the purpose of building the bridge. It also establishes a toll rate to which the company is entitled. This is the whole grant. There is no exclusive privilege given the company over the waters of the Charles River, above or below the bridge. Nor does it have the right to build another bridge. Neither can it prevent other persons from building another bridge, nor can it get a commitment from the State that another bridge shall not be built. No undertaking to limit competition is sanctioned.

In 1834, the city-wide unions of skilled craftsmen from New York, Philadelphia, and four other cities joined together in a National Trades' Union in an effort to gain improved working conditions. Membership had risen to 300,000 by 1837 when a business collapse destroyed the craft-union movement.

3

Resolved, That this Convention of the National Trades' Unions recommend that such of the working classes of these United States as have not already formed themselves into societies for the protection of their industry, do so forthwith.

Resolved, That this committee view with serious alarm the deplorable condition of the male and female children in the cotton and woolen factories of this country and the many deprivations they are subjected to because of the early age they are put to work in factories and the enormous length of time they work each day.

Resolved, That the laws existing in parts of our country, under which Trades' Unions are declared illegal combinations are a clear violation of the Constitution of these United States, and an infringement of the lawful rights of every citizen. This Convention do hereby urge every laboring man to consider seriously the absolute necessity for their repeal.

A number of state courts had ruled that unions were conspiracies which restrained trade. Hence strikers were subject to criminal prosecution. In 1842, in the case of **Commonwealth** vs. **Hunt,** the Massachusetts Supreme Court acknowledged that a union member's refusal to work did not necessarily mean that he was engaged in a conspiracy.

Trades' Union National Convention, **The Man,** vol. II (August 30, 1834), p. 357.

4

Let us suppose you arrived at a New England inn as I did and that you talked with the landlord while he got refreshments for you. He will then sit by your side and carry on the most familiar conversation. He will start asking you about your business and so forth. Then he will raise a political question, for here every individual is a politician. He will force you to answer; then he will contradict and deny what you said. Finally, he will start a quarrel should you not agree with all of his opinions.

Report of an English Traveler in the United States. C. W. Janson, **The Stranger in America.** London: James Cundee, 1807, p. 85. Language simplified and modernized.

5

Should the right to vote, the characteristic and the highest privilege of a freeman, be at the mercy of an accident? I am rich today, but my wealth consists in stock and merchandise; it may be in storehouses; it may be upon the ocean. Suppose I have been unable to get insurance, or there is some concealed legal defect in my policy. Fire or storms devour my wealth in an hour. Am I any the less competent to vote? Have I less of the capacity of a moral and intelligent being? Am I less of a good citizen? Is it not enough that I have been deprived of my fortune—must I also be barred from voting by the community?

George S. Camp, **Democracy.** New York: Harper and Brothers, 1841, pp. 145–46. Language simplified and modernized.

6

It appears, therefore, to the committee that there can be no real liberty without widespread intelligence. The members of a republic should all be alike instructed in the nature and character of their equal right and duties, as human beings and as citizens. Education, instead of being limited as in our public charity schools for the poor, to a simple acquaintance with words and numbers, should tend, as far as possible, to the development of a just disposition, virtuous habits, and a rational self-governing character.

Except for large cities, few communities provided public education on any regular basis. Some communities set up charity schools for poor children. Otherwise, schools in America were private and were usually run by churches.

Workingman's Advocate (March 6, 1830). Language simplified and modernized.

34 Working with Hypotheses, II

A hypothesis is a tentative answer to a question. To find out whether it is right or wrong, a historian must go through several steps. Even after he has been through all of them, he still cannot be entirely sure that the answer to his original question is completely right. Additional evidence, at first unavailable to him, may turn up in documents he was not able to consult. Or he may have made errors in logic as he thought about his problem. Nevertheless, a disciplined way to think about hypotheses helps to reduce the possibility of errors.

Once a historian has a hypothesis, he ought to think through what that hypothesis implies. Suppose he begins with the hypothesis that the colonists won the American Revolution because they had foreign aid. "If this hypothesis is right," he might say, "then foreign aid should have played a key role in each of the decisive battles. If it did not, then something in addition to foreign aid must have been involved."

Given this idea, the historian should then set out to determine the role of foreign aid in key battles: Lexington, Saratoga, Yorktown, and others. To do so, he would have to decide what sources would help him. Then he would have to read those sources, determine whether or not the evidence in them was accurate, take down in his notes the evidence he found, and finally decide whether or not the hypothesis was valid or needed to be modified. Once he has made that decision and has written a statement that the evidence supports, he will have developed a generalization, the end product of his investigation.

In analyzing Reading 33, each student developed his own hypothesis about Jacksonian society. Readings 34 and 35 provide evidence with which these hypotheses can be tested. No study questions are provided because of the nature of the readings. Before you begin to read, you should write out one or two of the logical implications of the hypothesis you developed. Then you should study the material in Reading 34 to gather evidence. As you study, you may get additional ideas, either new hypotheses or new ideas about the implications of the hypothesis you started with. Write out the implications of your hypothesis and include evidence collected from the reading.

Public Land Laws

The United States government acquired title to public lands when the original thirteen states ceded their western land claims to it. Through treaties and agreements, it also acquired territory formerly claimed by Britain, France, and Spain.

Most of the public lands in the United States belonged to the national government. The government sold these lands to settlers and speculators. This chart gives the land laws passed by the confederation and federal governments.

Year	Minimum Purchase	Minimum Price Per Acre	Terms of Sale
		$1.00	Cash
1787	640 acres	$1.00	One third of purchase price in cash; the remainder in three months
1796	640 acres	$2.00	Half of purchase price to be paid within 30 days; half to be paid at end of 12 months
1800	320 acres	$2.00	One quarter of purchase price payable in cash; one quarter payable in 2 years; one quarter payable in 3 years; one quarter payable in 4 years
1804	160 acres (north of the Ohio River)	$2.00 ($1.64, if the entire payment in cash)	Same as in 1800
1820	80 acres	$1.25	Full purchase price in cash
1832	40 acres	$1.25	Full purchase price in cash

Benjamin Horace Hibbard, **A History of the Public Land Policies.** New York: Peter Smith, 1939, pp. 38–39, 41, 82–84, 98. Douglass C. North, **Growth and Welfare in the American Past: A New Economic History.** Englewood Cliffs, N.J.: Prentice-Hall, Inc. 1966, p. 123. George Soule and Vincent P. Carosso, **American Economic History.** New York: Holt, Rinehart and Winston, Inc. 1957, pp. 71–72.

A Frenchman Views American Society

The French government sent Michel Chevalier, a young engineer, to the United States in 1834 to study American transportation and public works. Chevalier was a keen observer of American society. He described his observations and impressions in Society, Manners and Politics in the United States *from which this excerpt is taken.*

Michael [Michel] Chevalier, **Society, Manners and Politics in the United States: Being a Series of Letters on North America.** Boston: Weeks, Jordan and Company, 1839, pp. 398–401. Language simplified and modernized.

In the Northern States, with the exception of the Negro caste, there are only two classes: the middle class and the democracy [the common people]. The middle class consists of manufacturers, merchants, lawyers, physicians, a small number of large landowners, and persons devoted to literature and the fine arts.

The democracy is composed of the farmers and mechanics. In general, the farmers own their own farms; in the West, this is true without exception. Great landholders do not exist, at least as a class, in the North and the Northwest. There is strictly speaking no proletariat. There are day laborers, both in the cities and the country, and many workmen without capital. Yet these men, most of whom are recent immigrants, are apprentices. They, in turn, become proprietors and master-workmen and not infrequently rich manufacturers or wealthy speculators.

The proletariat is the laboring class that works for others, usually in manufacturing.

Capital is wealth either in the form of property or money.

Between these two classes there is, however, no dividing line. The attempts of some groups of people to establish certain fashionable distinctions do not deserve notice for they have no significant influence. The two classes have the same domestic habits, lead the same life, and differ considerably only in terms of the religious sect to which they belong and the pews they occupy in church.

In the Southern States, slavery produces a society quite different from that of the North. Half of the population there, that is the slaves, consists of the proletariat in the strictest sense. Slavery necessarily requires great landed property, whose owners form an aristocracy.

Between these two extremes in the South, an intermediate class of working men and men of leisure has sprung up. Those in commerce, manufactures, and the professions are on the one side; on the other are the landholders, who live on their estates by the sweat of their slaves. They have no taste for work, are not prepared for it by education, and even take little responsibility for the daily business of the plantation.

The equal partition of estates must have increased the numbers of this leisure class, which is numerous in the old Southern States of Virginia, the Carolinas, Georgia, and Louisiana. But we do not find this class in the new states of the South. The new generation there, obsessed with the passion of making money, has become as industrious as the Yankees. The cultivation of cotton offers a wide field of activity. In Alabama and Mississippi, cotton lands are sold at a very low price. The internal slave trade furnishes abundant hands which are easily bought on credit. The sons from the old Southern States sell off their property at home, get a loan, which they are sure of being able to repay promptly, and go to the Southwest to establish a cotton plantation.

In the United States, landowners usually divided property equally among sons instead of following the English practice of primogeniture which left entire estates to the eldest son.

The internal slave trade refers to the practice of raising slaves in the states of the upper South, such as Virginia, and selling them in Alabama and Mississippi.

Thus the part of the middle class which works little, or not at all, is disappearing in the United States. In the Western States, which are the true New World, it no longer exists at all, either in the North or the South. In the West, you meet with no one who is not engaged in agriculture, commerce, manufactures, the professions, or the Church. The United States, then, has no aristocracy, no idle middle class, and no class of mere laborers, at least in the North.

A Historian Analyzes the Social Structure of Western Cities

Richard C. Wade, **The Urban Frontier: The Rise of Western Cities, 1780-1830.** Chicago: The University of Chicago Press, 1964, pp. 105-07, 203-04, 206, 209-10, 212-13, 215-21.

Richard C. Wade, a contemporary American historian, has studied life, between 1790 and 1830, in five western cities—Pittsburgh, Cincinnati, Lexington, Louisville, and St. Louis. His conclusions about social structure, excerpted from his book The Urban Frontier, *are given here.*

. . . Local boosters talked a good deal about egalitarianism in the West [between 1790 and 1815], but urban practice belied the theory. Social lines developed very quickly, and although never drawn as tightly as in Eastern cities, they denoted [indicated] meaningful distinctions. The groupings were basically economic, though professional classes were set apart by their interest and training, and Negroes by their color. No rigid boundaries divided these classes, and movement across them was constant. Yet differences did exist, people felt them, and contemporaries thought them significant. . . .

Egalitarianism is the condition of equality among all men.

The merchants headed this rapidly stratifying [dividing into distinct classes] social structure. Next in influence stood the lawyers, ministers, doctors, teachers, and journalists, who, if they had less income than commercial leaders, often had as much prestige. Beneath them lived most of the people—skilled and unskilled laborers, clerks and shopkeepers—"the respectable workingmen." Lower still in the hierarchy were the transients and rootless—wagoners, rivermen, hangers-on, and ne'er-do-wells—who had no stable connections with the community but whose activities formed an important part of its life. The Negroes, slave and free, occupied the bottom rung of the ladder, performing the most menial tasks and excluded from white society by both custom and law.

The irregular development of the postwar [War of 1812] years put new strains on the social structures of the young Western towns. Larger populations and the expansion of commerce and industry created new groups and interests, thus adding to the complexity and sophistication of city life. Already stratified after a generation of growth, these communities found lines sharpened, class divisions deepened, and the sense of neighborliness and intimacy weakened. . . .

Though the order in the urban hierarchy remained the same in the postwar decades, the distribution of power and influence shifted markedly. The merchants, who had presided over town affairs unchallenged for a quarter of century, saw their supremacy contested by the strengthening of other groups, especially the wage-earning and professional classes. . . .

. . . [B]usinessmen . . . were not only the cities' most prosperous group but also socially the most prominent. Their wives belonged to the same clubs, their children went to the same schools, and they participated in the same amusements and recreations. Nearly all the developments of the twenties—the depression [which began in 1819], the rise of new classes, and mounting urban populations—heightened this sense of separateness. Though new families entered the circle and older ones fell out, the circle itself became tighter and more distinct. . . .

By 1830 the business community represented a well-defined unit. Bound together by economic interest, fortified by constant social contacts, and set apart by wealth and education, the mercantile class presided over urban affairs. Beneath it were several other groups with varying degrees of prestige and esteem, who became increasingly aware of their status. Though the personnel of each level continually changed, the lines between them grew constantly more distinct. To put it another way, there was a double development in urban societies: one was the movement of many individuals up or down the social ladder, the other was the widening of the distance between rungs.

The professional classes were one of the great beneficiaries [receivers of benefits] of postwar urban expansion. As the cities grew, the need for specialized skills multiplied, and in the twenties doctors, lawyers, ministers, teachers, and editors flocked to Western communities. . . .

As the professional classes grew, they became more independent of the business community. To be sure, the old connections were still there. Lawyers continued to seek clients among the wealthy, private-school teachers catered to the children of the well-to-do, and doctors and ministers relied heavily on the elite for support. But the relationship had altered; the dependence of earlier days disappeared. . . . Though not the wealthiest section of Western society, [professional] people enjoyed esteem and influence that greatly exceeded their economic status. In the twenties their numbers and prestige increased as they provided articulate and energetic leadership for almost every division of urban life.

. . . [The numerical growth of the] wage-earning class . . . outstripped that of all other groups. Though the flow of working people into frontier cities slackened during the depression, it never stopped, and in the late twenties it reached flood tide again. Indeed, except during a few years in Pittsburgh and Lexington, the labor supply seldom met the demand. In many instances businessmen issued blanket invitations to migrants, pointing out local openings and promising good wages . . . Opportunities like these drew large numbers of wage-earners to transmontane [beyond the Appalachian Mountains] cities, swelling the ranks of a class which became increasingly aware of its status and strength.

One measure of this growing consciousness was the spread of trade unions. In the first decades of the century, organization had been sporadic and touched only a few crafts. In the twenties, however, the movement developed rapidly, affecting new occupations and influencing political as well as economic affairs. Underneath this upsurge lay not only a desire for better wages and hours, but also new awareness of labor's social position. . . .

Wage-earners could have afforded better housing if it had been available, but their other great requirement, education, was beyond the means of most. The need was twofold: instruction for children and some kind of training for young men and adults. In the twenties progress took place along both these lines. In most cities free public schooling took care of all children for at least a few years, while the establishment of mechanics' institutes and apprentices' libraries extended opportunities to adults. . . . By 1830 Western wage-earners had begun to break down one of the barriers that most clearly separated them from the more fortunate classes.

While the professional and wage-earning classes grew in numbers and influence, another group lost ground. The transients—boatmen, wagoners, migrant laborers, and drifters—suffered a proportional decline, occupying increasingly a peripheral [marginal] position in most cities. As town life became more settled, their importance diminished, even though expanding trade and immigration added somewhat to their ranks. Rough, untutored, unstable, and without meaningful ties to any community, they remained a jangling element. By 1830, however, they were no longer a formidable force. . . .

Contemporaries, confronted with civic problems created by transients, could not see the relative decline of that urban element. There was no doubt, however, about the growth of another class both numerically and proportionally, for Negroes were readily identified. Nor was their increase confined to Southern towns. Pittsburgh and Cincinnati attracted more than their share; indeed in 1828 ten percent of the population of the Ohio city was colored. . . . But whether they lived in North or South, whether free or in bonds, they constituted a menial class. Cut off from the rest of society, denied ordinary opportunities, Negroes still occupied the lowest rung on the social ladder.

35 Working with Hypotheses, III

Like Reading 34, the present reading contains evidence about the nature of American society during the Jacksonian period. You are to continue the exercise begun yesterday adding to the material which you compiled in your notes. In preparation for class, write one paragraph, no longer than a hundred words, in which you state the conclusions you have drawn from your work with Readings 33 through 35.

President Jackson's First Annual Message to Congress

Although Andrew Jackson received more popular and electoral votes than any other candidate in the Presidential election of 1824, the House of Representatives elected John Quincy Adams to the Presidency. Jackson and his supporters believed that he had been "robbed." Jackson won the election of 1828. In his first message to Congress, from which this excerpt is taken, he expressed his ideas on the proper relationship between citizens and public officers.

James D. Richardson, ed., **A Compilation of the Messages and Papers of the Presidents.** Washington, D.C.: Government Printing Office, 1896, vol. II, pp. 447–49. Language simplified and modernized.

The right to elect the President belongs to the people. Their choice should never be defeated, either by the electoral college or by the House of Representatives. Experience proves that as the number of officials to carry out the will of the people increases so does the danger that their wishes will be frustrated. Some officials may be unfaithful; all are liable to make errors. So far, therefore, as the people can speak conveniently, it is safer for them to express their own wills.

In the election of the President, as in all other matters of public concern, as few obstacles as possible should exist to the free expression of the public will. Let us, then, try to amend our system so that no citizen may become President except as a result of a fair expression of the will of the majority.

The duties of all public officers are, or at least could be made, so plain and simple that men of intelligence may readily qualify to perform them. I believe that more is lost by men remaining in office for a long period of time, than is gained through their experience. I submit, therefore, to your consideration whether government efficiency would not be promoted and officeholder's industry and integrity improved by a law which limits officials to a four-year term.

In a country where offices are created solely for the benefit of the people, no one man has any more right to public office than another.

Method of Electing Presidential Electors, 1800–1840

The Constitution provides that state legislatures shall determine the way in which the electors, who elect the President, will be chosen. This chart gives the percentage of states in which the state legislatures, rather than the ordinary voters, chose the Presidential electors between 1800–1840.

U.S. Bureau of the Census, **Historical Statistics of the United States, Colonial Times to 1957.** Washington, D.C.: Government Printing Office, 1960, p. 681.

Percentage of States Choosing Electors by State Legislature

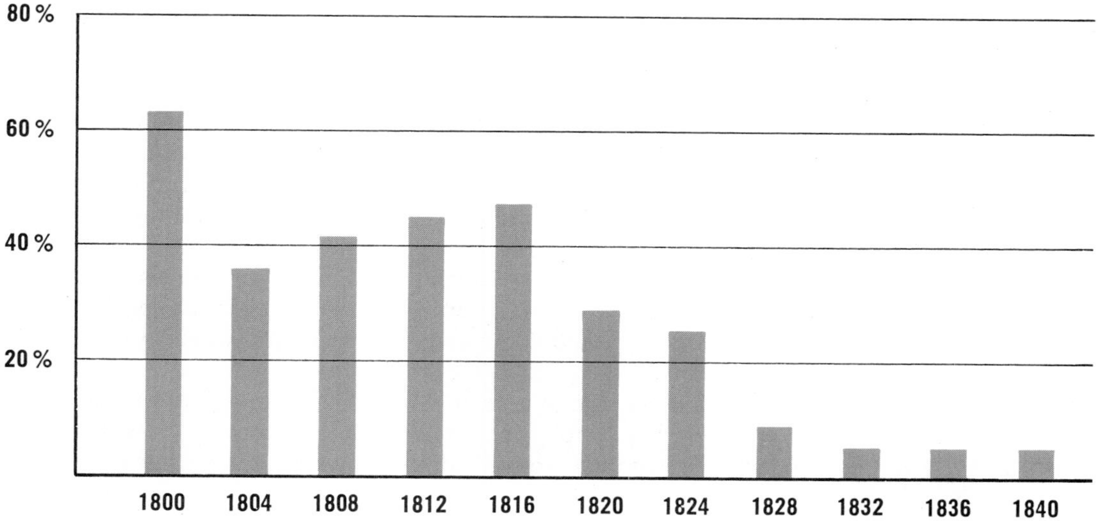

The Nominating Convention

In a political democracy, citizens not only vote for candidates for public office, but they also have some voice in choosing those candidates. Before the Jacksonian Period, a caucus of influential leaders in Congress had selected Presidential candidates. Candidates for local and state offices were either selected by caucuses or they simply announced their candidacy. In the 1820's and 1830's, with the development of well-organized political parties, the caucus

A caucus is a meeting of party members to choose leaders, to decide policies, or to select candidates.

gave way at all levels of government to the nominating convention. Delegates to the convention, elected, at least in theory, by party members, selected the candidates, adopted a party platform, and planned for the election campaign.

Thomas Ford, a Jacksonian Democrat and governor of Illinois from 1842 to 1846, observed these party developments closely in his state. He wrote A History of Illinois, *from which this excerpt is taken, in which he evaluated the nominating conventions as they functioned in his state.*

Thomas Ford, **A History of Illinois.** Chicago: S.C. Griggs, 1854, pp. 201–06. Language simplified and modernized.

Our old way of conducting elections required each person seeking an office to announce himself as a candidate. The more prudent, however, always first consulted a little caucus of select, influential friends. The candidates then traveled around the country or state, making speeches, conversing with the people, soliciting votes, whispering slanders against their opponents, and defending themselves against the attacks of their adversaries.

As party spirit increased more and more, it became necessary to find a way of concentrating party strength. Some settlers from New England and New York introduced into Illinois the convention system of nominating candidates. That system won its way slowly, and now [1847] all the candidates for governor, lieutenant governor, and members of Congress are nominated by conventions. In two thirds of the state, candidates for the state legislature are also nominated by conventions.

The system has some advantages and disadvantages in Illinois. Those in favor of it say it furnishes the only way of concentrating the action of the political party, and of giving voice to the will of the majority.

On the other side, it is argued that the whole convention system is a fraud on the people; that conventions themselves are got up and packed by cunning, active, intriguing politicians, to suit the wishes of a few. Some active men organize conventions by getting a few friends in each precinct of a county to hold primary meetings, where delegates are elected to county conventions. These delegates meet at the county seats, and nominate candidates for the legislature and for county offices and appoint other delegates to district and state conventions to nominate candidates for Congress and for governor.

A precinct is a small electoral district that contains a polling place.

The great difficulty lies in the primary meetings in the precincts. In the Eastern states, where conventions began, they had township governments—little democracies—where the whole people met in person at least once a year, to lay taxes for roads and for the support of schools and the poor. This called the whole people of a township together, enlightened their minds, and accustomed them to take a lively interest in their government. While they were assembled, they elected delegates to conventions. In this way, a convention reflected the will of a party.

But how is it in Illinois? We have no township government, no occasions for a general meeting of the people, except at the elections themselves. The people do not attend the primary meetings. Only a few who live closest to the meeting places attend. These are too often the professional politicians and the loafers about town, who, having but little business of their own, are ever ready to attend to the affairs of the public. This throws the political power out of the hands of the people, merely because they will not exercise it, into the hands of idlers and a few active men, who control them.

A Plea for Expanded Business Opportunities

The state legislatures chartered banks, insurance companies, manufacturing companies, and other corporations. Wealthy men used their influence to obtain special privileges from the legislators. Jacksonian Democrats, such as William Leggett, an editorial writer for the New York Evening Post, *argued for reforms that would expand opportunities for ordinary citizens to set up new businesses. This editorial, written by Leggett, appeared in the* Evening Post *on December 30, 1834.*

Theodore Sedgwick, Jr., ed., **A Collection of the Political Writings of William Leggett.** New York: Taylor and Dodd, 1840, pp. 140–41. Language simplified and modernized.

A week from today the Legislature will meet in Albany. Seldom has a meeting of the Legislature been looked forward to with such interest. The message of Governor Marcy will probably be delivered to both Houses of the Legislature on the first day of the session. By the sentiments of that message the Governor will be judged. That message will either raise him, in our estimation and in the estimation of all truly democratic men, to a most enviable height, or sink him to the level of the gross herd of petty, selfish, short-sighted, and low-minded politicians.

Unequivocal means leaving no doubt as to meaning.

A joint-stock partnership or company is a form of business organization which allows men to combine their capital by purchasing shares of stock. Each share of stock represents ownership and usually entitles its owner to a vote at a shareholders' meeting.

He has the rare opportunity, by one single act, to inscribe his name among those of the greatest benefactors of mankind. We hope he will stand forth as the honest, bold, unequivocal asserter of the great principle of equal rights and strenuously recommend to the Legislature that all acts of special incorporation are incompatible with the fundamental principle of our government. Acts of special incorporation build up a privileged group in society and concentrate all wealth and power in the hands of the few. We urge the Governor to oppose all exclusive privileges. We earnestly recommend instead, the adoption of a general law of joint-stock partnerships which would allow voluntary associations of men, who possess no special privileges. Businessmen would be liable to the same free competition as the merchant, the mechanic, the laborer, and the farmer.

If the Governor should take such a stand, his name will go down to posterity inseparably associated with that of the patriotic and democratic Jackson, who, at the head of the national government, has done so much to restore to the people their violated rights, and check the course of unequal, aristocratic legislation.

Percentage of Adult White Males Voting in Presidential Elections, 1808–1844

One way to measure the vitality of political democracy is to look at the number of citizens who vote for public officials. This chart shows the percentage of qualified voters who actually voted in Presidential elections between 1824 and 1844. Those states for which election data are available are given.

Chart prepared at the Curriculum Development Center, Carnegie-Mellon University. Based on data from Richard P. McCormick, "New Perspectives on Jacksonian Politics," **The American Historical Review,** vol. LXV (January 1960), p. 294.

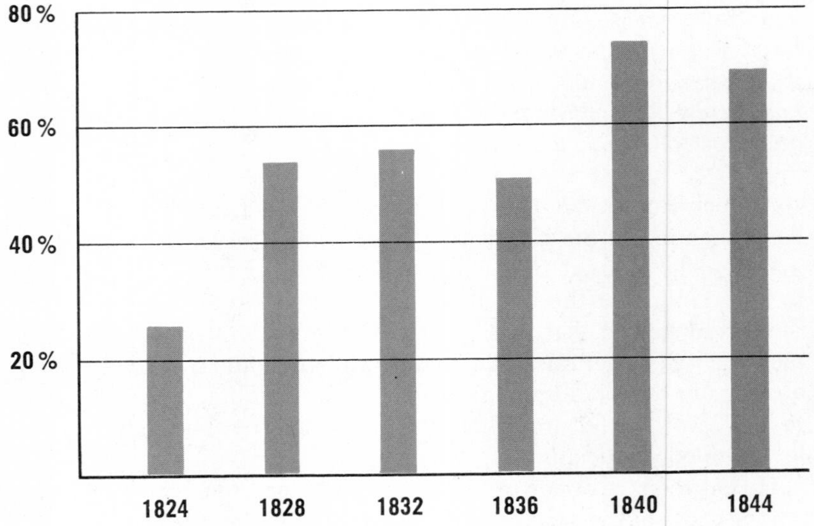

(SELECTED STATES: Maine, New Hampshire, Massachusetts, Rhode Island, New Jersey, Pennsylvania, Maryland, Virgina, Ohio)

Voting Qualifications, 1800–1840

Each state establishes certain requirements that its citizens must meet in order to vote. This chart gives the voting qualifications in all states between 1800 and 1840.

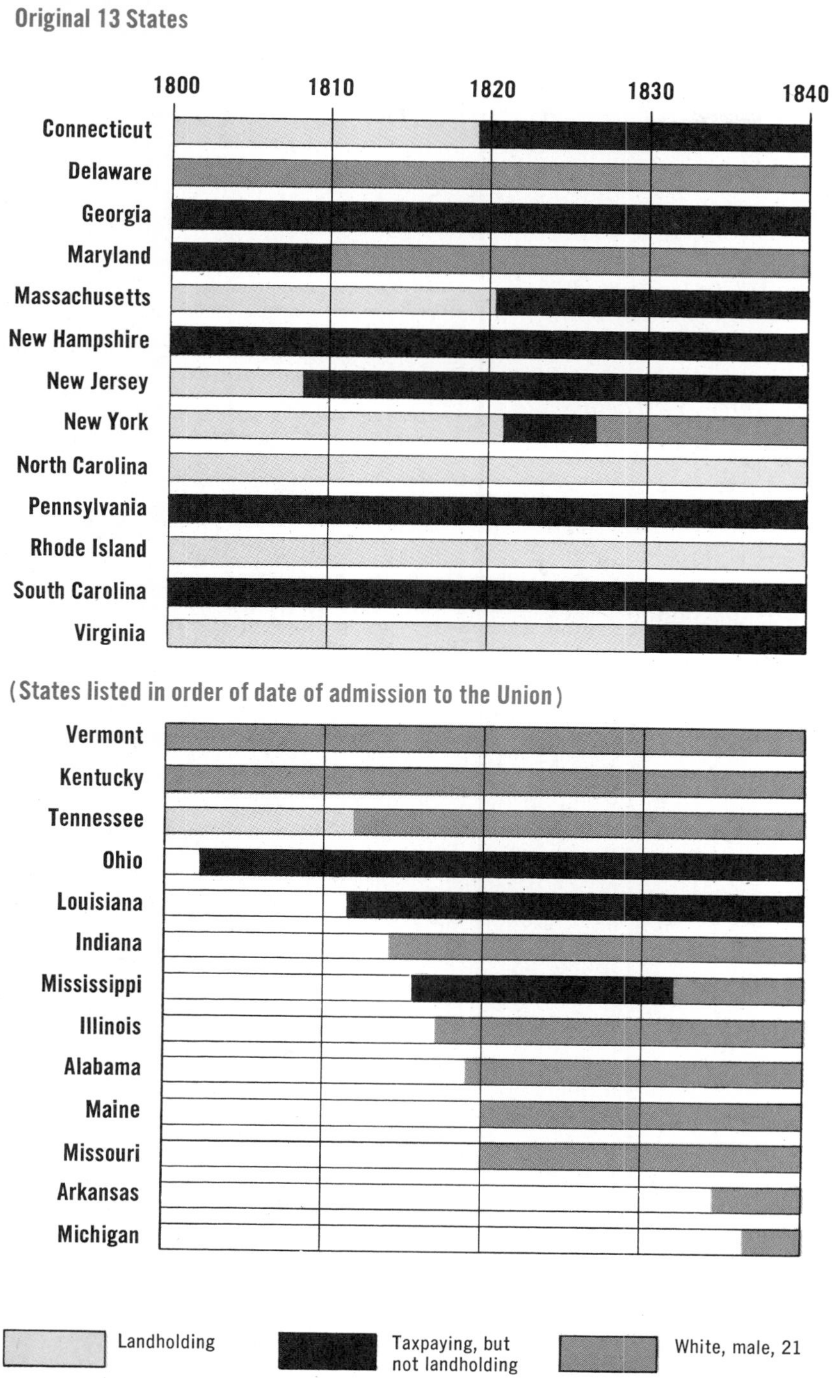

Chart prepared at the Curriculum Development Center, Carnegie-Mellon University. Based on data from Richard P. McCormick, "Suffrage, Classes and Party Alignments: A Study in Voter Behavior," in **Mississippi Valley Historical Review,** vol. XLVI, no. 3 (December 1959), pp. 397–410, and Chilton Williamson, **American Suffrage from Property to Democracy: 1760–1860.** Princeton, N.J.: Princeton University Press, 1960.

Alexis de Tocqueville's Observations on American Political Life

Alexis de Tocqueville, a young Frenchman, came to the United States in 1831 to study prison reforms. He was also deeply interested in America's experiment with democracy. For nine months he traveled throughout the United States, covering seven thousand miles. Upon his return to France he published Democracy in America, *a two-volume work in which he gave his observations and analysis of American ideas, attitudes, and institutions. Scholars still consider De Tocqueville's description, from which this selection is taken, a classic account of American society during the Jacksonian Period.*

Alexis de Tocqueville, **Democracy in America,** ed. and trans. by Henry Reeve. Cambridge, Mass.: Sever and Francis, 1862, vol. 1, pp. 318–19. Language simplified and modernized.

It is possible to imagine the surprising liberty that the Americans enjoy; some idea may also be formed of their extreme equality. But the political activity that pervades the United States must be seen in order to be understood. No sooner do you set foot upon American ground than you are stunned by a kind of tumult. A confused clamor is heard on every side, and a thousand simultaneous voices demand the satisfaction of their social wants. Everything is in motion around you. Here the people of one quarter of a town are meeting to decide upon the building of a church; there the election of a representative is going on; a little farther, the delegates of a district are hastening to the town in order to consult upon some local improvements. In another place, the laborers of a village quit their plows to deliberate upon a project for a road or a public school. People call meetings for the sole purpose of declaring their disapproval of the conduct of the government; while in other assemblies, citizens salute the authorities of the day as the fathers of their country.

It is difficult to say what place is taken up in the life of an inhabitant of the United States by his concern for politics. To take a hand in the regulation of society and to discuss it is his biggest concern and, so to speak, the only pleasure an American knows. This feeling pervades the most trifling habits of life; even the women frequently attend public meetings and listen to political harangues [orations] as a recreation from their household labors. Debating clubs are, to a certain extent, a substitute for theatrical entertainments. An American cannot converse, but he can discuss. His talk falls into a formal discourse. He speaks to you as if he were addressing a meeting.

36 The Impact of Jacksonian Democracy on American Life

HISTORICAL ESSAY

One way to illustrate the new qualities which Jackson brought to the Presidency is to compare him with his predecessor John Quincy Adams. Adams was a man of exceptional intellect, education, and sophistication. He had already served his country ably as a diplomat abroad and as Secretary of State. He believed the federal government should play a positive role in American social and economic life. He tried during his Administration to establish a national university, as well as to promote the more conventional internal improvements, such as roads and canals.

If Adams had been President ten years earlier, he might have been very successful. In the middle of the 1820's, however, he was out of place. Although he yielded to no one in his loyalty to American institutions, Adams came from a family of great prominence. His political opponents easily tagged him an aristocrat. His background, together with his cold temperament, which prevented him from communicating and mingling freely with the masses of the people, proved his undoing as President. In the election of 1828, Jackson received 178 electoral votes to Adams's 83. Jackson drew strong support from every section except Adams's New England.

Jackson was the first American President to come from the ranks of the common people. His parents had been poor Scotch-Irish immigrants. Jackson's rise from a position of total obscurity to a position of prominence as lawyer, planter, soldier, and land speculator in Tennessee was, in many ways, typical of what was happening everywhere in the highly fluid social conditions of early nineteenth-century America. Western farmers, workingmen in the cities, and ambitious businessmen all believed that Jackson would be sympathetic to their aspirations, so they gave him support.

Growth and Limits of Equality

The idea of equality in America had been eloquently expressed in the Declaration of Independence, but it had not been translated completely into political practice. As the chart on page 233 shows, several states, before the War of 1812, restricted the right to vote to property owners. In the years following the war, however, the new western states that entered the Union (Indiana in 1816, Illinois in 1818, Alabama in 1819) gave every white male the right to vote. Several eastern states also took steps to liberalize their voting qualifications. At the same time, the people gained the right to elect more and more of their officials. State legislatures transferred their power to choose Presidential electors to the voters.

Because Jackson believed in the principle of equality, he had great faith in the common people. In all matters of public policy, he told the Congress in his First Annual Message "as few impediments as possible should exist to the free operation of the public will." His respect for the "public will" and the abilities of ordinary citizens led him to rely on what became known as, the "spoils system." He replaced government jobholders with his own supporters. He believed that they represented the public will and that ordinary people were capable of carrying on the business of government.

The term "spoils system" derives from the phrase "to the victor belong the spoils." "Spoils" are the fruits of victory and, in politics, the "spoils system" means the award of government jobs to one's political supporters.

Jackson also sought advice from his "kitchen cabinet," that is, close personal friends who held no official positions in government.

Jackson's attitude toward the public lands in the west also shows his belief in equality. Political leaders disagreed over whether these lands should be sold by the government in order to raise revenue or distributed to prospective settlers at cheap prices. Jackson favored the latter course as a way of making it possible for the largest number of people to own their own land and get a start in the world.

Equality as a condition of life and as an ideal was important during this period. The French traveler Michel Chevalier was impressed with the extent to which the ideal had been achieved. But it is also important to understand that neither the condition nor the ideal included everybody. Professor Wade believes that western urban society became more stratified. Negroes, Indians, and women did not enjoy equality. An abolition movement began to develop during the Jacksonian period. Yet those reformers who believed that the principle of equality should apply to everybody were still a tiny minority. Jackson, himself, supported slavery and owned slaves, and along with almost all of his followers, he believed that the principle of equality should apply only to white males. Many state constitutions, which had originally allowed free Negroes to vote, were amended to deny the vote, while more whites voted.

Meanwhile, something similar happened to the Indian tribes. Jackson favored a land policy that would distribute western lands widely among settlers and thus promote economic opportunities in the west. But he also forced Indian tribes to move to lands west of the Mississippi River. Usually they gave up better land than they received. In the 1830's, the Indian, like the Negro, was still a long way from equal membership in American democracy.

The New Tariff and the Issue of Nullification

Jackson believed that the President should be a strong executive. He believed that the President should use all of his Constitutional powers to execute the public will and that he should not subordinate himself either to the legislature or the judiciary. We can see how

PRE-CIVIL WAR TARIFFS

Name of Tariff	Provisions	Public Reaction
Tariff of 1789	Placed specific duties on 30 items, including molasses, hemp, steel, and nails; average of 8½% *ad valorem* * on listed items; 5% duty on all other goods.	Designed primarily to raise revenue; it met with wide acceptance.
Tariff of 1792	Increased 5% duty to 7½%.	Farmers and New England shippers protested.
Tariff of 1816	A protective tariff, it placed duties of 25% on most woolen, cotton, and iron manufactures.	General support from all sections, small protest from New England commercial interests and the South and Southwest.
Tariff of 1824	Increased duty on cotton and woolen goods to 33⅓%; increased duty on raw wool to 15%.	Favored by Western farmers and manufacturers in New England; opposed by South and Southwest.
Tariff of 1828 (Tariff of Abominations)	Duty of 50% *ad valorem* * plus 4¢ a pound on raw wool, 45% *ad valorem* on woolens, increased duties on iron and hemp.	Supported by Western farmers and middle states; Southwest and New England divided; South opposed.
Tariff of 1832	Increased duty on woolens; placed cheap raw wool and flax on duty-free list; reduced average duties to 35%.	South Carolina adopted Ordinance of Nullification and threatened secession.
Tariff of 1833	Expanded the number of items on duty-free list; provided for gradual reduction of all duties above 20%.	South supported this compromise tariff; New England and middle states opposed it.
Tariff of 1842	Returned tariff to 1832 level; duties averaged 23%–35%.	Democrats opposed it; Whig party passed it.
Walker Tariff of 1846	Reduced average rates to 25%; placed several items on duty-free list.	South supported it; New England and middle states opposed it.
Tariff of 1857	Increased the duty-free list; reduced tariff to average of 20%.	South and Southwest supported it; Northern industrialists opposed it.

**Ad valorem* duties are levied according to value of the goods. Other duties are levied according to weight or quantity.

President Jackson applied these two basic principles—the belief in equality and the belief in a strong executive—by examining two major issues of his Administration: the bank and the tariff.

The most nagging sectional issue during this period centered on the federal government's use of the tariff. Southerners believed that the tariff was contrary to their interests. Opposition to the tariff was particularly strong in South Carolina, where leaders in the state blamed a prolonged economic depression, caused chiefly by soil exhaustion, on the protective tariff. John C. Calhoun, the state's leading political figure, became the spokesman for the anti-tariff position. Calhoun, who served as Vice-President under both Adams and Jackson, had favored the Tariff of 1816. During the 1820's, as opposition to the tariff hardened in his own state, he changed his position. In 1828, Congress passed a tariff bill with particularly high duties. In protest against this "Tariff of Abomination," Calhoun wrote an essay entitled *The South Carolina Exposition and Protest,* in which he proposed a course of action for the South.

Calhoun's arguments were similar to those Madison and Jefferson had used when they wrote the Virginia and Kentucky Resolutions in 1798. Calhoun reasoned that the various sovereign states had organized the federal government and had given it certain delegated powers for the purpose of protecting their interests and rights. If the federal government passed a law that threatened the rights or interests of a state, that state had the right to declare the law unconstitutional and, therefore, null and void within its boundaries. The Congress could then either accept state nullification of a federal law or it could work to get a Constitutional amendment passed which would make the law part of the Constitution. If the law were made part of the Constitution, the state could decide either to remain in the Union accepting the law or become independent.

Calhoun then showed that the southern states made up a great exporting and importing section which the tariff injured. Southern planters sold their cotton at low prices in competitive markets abroad and bought their manufactured goods at high prices in a protected market at home.

Calhoun kept his authorship of the *South Carolina Exposition and Protest* secret in 1828, but a famous debate in the Senate gave the ideas it contained wide public exposure. Daniel Webster from Massachusetts argued for the supremacy of the Union, and Robert Hayne from South Carolina presented Calhoun's point of view.

Jackson's position on the tariff was not very clear. He was sensitive to the charge that the tariff helped manufacturers more than southern farmers, but, at the same time, he wanted tariff revenues to help the government pay its debts. Jackson also sympathized with the position that the rights of the states had to be protected from arbitrary federal power. However, his conviction, that as President he represented all the people in the nation, made it impossible for him to accept the idea that a state could defy federal authority.

The opposing ideas of Webster and Hayne, as well as those of Jackson and Calhoun, were put to the test in 1832. A state convention in South Carolina declared the tariffs of 1828 and 1832 unconstitutional and hence not binding on the people of the state. Calhoun's own views had become public knowledge by now. He resigned his position as Vice-President to represent his state in the Senate and lead the fight for nullification.

In what was probably America's greatest political crisis since the adoption of the Constitution, Jackson stood resolutely by the power of the federal government. He dispatched a warship to Charleston harbor and privately claimed he would like to hang the nullifiers. South Carolina remained defiant, and violence was avoided only when Henry Clay worked out a compromise tariff in 1833. Once again the American people found a practical way to prevent sectional hostility from destroying the Union. The deeper question of sovereign power would not be answered before the Civil War.

The "Bank War"

The second major issue of Jackson's Administration involved his battle with the Bank of the United States. The Second Bank of the United States had been chartered by Congress in 1816 to act as a depository for government funds, to issue paper money, to sell government bonds, and to do a commercial banking business—in general, to serve the financial needs of the rapidly growing nation. Since 1822, the Bank had been run by Nicholas Biddle, a highly able financier who came from an aristocratic Philadelphia family.

Congress had allowed the First United States Bank to die in 1811 at the end of its twenty-year charter.

Jackson based his opposition to the Bank on two assumptions. In the first place, he was highly suspicious of the reckless speculation in land and business activity so characteristic of the time. Numerous state banks, willing to offer generous terms to prospective borrowers and investors, made most of the speculation possible. Too many of these banks rested on shaky foundations. They went through periods of spectacular prosperity, but frequently periods of spectacular failure followed. The result was that the American economy in the decade following the War of 1812 had become highly unstable. Individual speculators made and lost fortunes in rapid succession. Jackson, himself, had tried his hand at land speculation and had suffered disastrous financial losses. He had recovered by resorting to farming. He came to the White House convinced that the agrarian virtues of the early republic were the source of national strength and that banks and speculators threatened American values.

When state banks presented notes and checks to the U.S. Bank, Biddle demanded they be converted into hard money. This caused an extreme shortage of credit.

Jackson also opposed the Bank for the same reason that William Leggett fought against all monopolies. Congress had chartered the Bank, and Jackson and his supporters felt that its great power, derived largely from funds the federal government deposited in it, depended on special privilege, which had no place in a democratic society based on equal opportunity for all.

The Supreme Court had upheld the constitutionality of the Bank in *McCulloch* vs. *Maryland*. This development, however, did not dissuade Jackson. He let it be known that he disagreed with Marshall and would veto any attempt by Congress to recharter the Bank. When Congress passed such a bill in July 1832, Jackson quickly returned it with a veto message attacking the Bank as an example of legislation which favored "the advancement of the few at the expense of the many."

Congress failed to pass the Bank Bill over Jackson's veto. The Bank controversy immediately became the central issue in the Presidential election of 1832. In this campaign the anti-Jackson forces rallied around Jackson's chief opponent, Henry Clay. They claimed that the President was trying to put himself above the Constitution and play the role of a king. Jackson won the election easily, largely because of his attack on the Bank. On the one hand, farmers who shared his agrarian prejudices against banks supported him. The farmers were joined by small businessmen and speculators who felt that the Bank of the United States tended to favor established business interests over newcomers like themselves, who were willing to take big gambles in the struggle for wealth and success. Thus Jackson, like almost all other successful political leaders in American history, attracted support for his policies from different kinds of people for different kinds of reasons. The belief that held these people together, however loosely, was equality of opportunity.

What historians refer to as the "Bank War" did not end with Jackson's veto and re-election in 1832. Jackson transferred government funds from the National Bank to state banks, which his opponents called "pet banks." Nicholas Biddle retaliated by calling in bank loans to such an extent that a depression (the "Bank panic") took place in the winter of 1833–1834. Jackson's support in the Congress remained firm, however, and the Bank finally closed its doors in 1836 with the expiration of its charter.

A New Two-Party System

One of the most important developments during the Jacksonian period was the re-emergence of the two-party system, which contributed to the political interest that De Tocqueville observed in America in 1831. The election of 1828 sounded the death knell for the National-Republicans. The Jacksonians began to call themselves Democrats and to build a strong organization on both the state and national level. In 1836, the Democratic party held its first national nominating convention.

At first, the anti-Jacksonians were a poorly organized coalition centered around National-Republicans like Adams, Clay, Webster, and Calhoun. Opposition to Jackson was about all that held these political leaders together. Under the impact of the bank crisis, however, these men began to draw up a coherent program, which supported internal improvements and sound business enterprise. They made a special appeal to the substantial business interests in the north and those large southern planters with strong commercial ties in the north. These political leaders called themselves Whigs, after the party in England which had stood for liberty before the time of the American Revolution. Calhoun and the advocates of states' rights worked with the Whigs party for a short period but returned to the Democratic party after 1837.

In 1836, Jackson retired from the Presidency. His successor and close political adviser from New York, Martin Van Buren, won a narrow victory over the Whigs, but found himself forced to cope with a long period of economic depression during which the bank issue continued to be debated hotly. Van Buren continued Jackson's economic policies. He refused to expand the supply of paper money and supported legislation which finally took federal deposits out of private banks altogether and deposited them in separate government depositories called subtreasuries.

In the election of 1840, the Whigs found Van Buren vulnerable on two counts. In the first place, his opponents accused him of continuing the depression through disastrous financial policies. In the second place, they accused him of not being a typical representative of American democracy. The Whigs held their first national convention in 1840, and remembering how Jackson had defeated Adams, they nominated William Henry Harrison, an old Indian fighter, as their candidate for President. Harrison had won popularity as a war hero in the Battle of Tippecanoe. The Whigs appealed to the masses of the voters by emphasizing Harrison's rustic background which they contrasted with Van Buren's "aristocratic" manners. They compaigned vigorously with massive rallies and torchlight parades and used log cabin replicas to symbolize the simple beginnings of their candidate. The result was a resounding victory for the Whigs. The American voters went to the polls in greater numbers than ever before to vote for Harrison. In one sense, the Whigs had "out-democratized" the Democrats. In another sense, the election of 1840 revealed the lasting impact of Jacksonian democracy on American politics. From now on every American Presidential candidate, Democratic, Whig, or Republican, would want to be known as "the people's candidate."

SUGGESTED READINGS

ANDRIST, RALPH K., *Andrew Jackson, Soldier and Statesman.* This richly illustrated biography traces Jackson's turbulent career and discusses his impact on American political life.

SMALLEY, DONALD, editor, Frances Trollope, *Domestic Manners of the Americans.* This is a vivid description of many aspects of American life during the Jackson period as seen by a British visitor traveling through the United States in the 1830's.

WARD, JOHN W., *Andrew Jackson—Symbol for an Age.* This interesting book, which reflects the interests of many historians in the use of psychology as a tool for historical research, analyzes the reasons why the American people made Jackson one of their greatest heroes.

The Spirit of Reform

CHAPTER 10

STATING THE ISSUE

During the second half of the twentieth century, Americans, and especially younger Americans, have been protesting in increasing numbers basic issues such as war, poverty, and civil rights. But in South America, Asia, and some parts of Europe, many people seem to accept poverty and injustice as a matter of course. Americans do not. Even though they have enjoyed more freedom and prosperity than any other people in the world, a substantial minority of American citizens have always been dissatisfied with their society and have been determined to make it better.

The spirit of reform in America was very much alive in the northern states during the three decades before the Civil War. A wave of protest against social and moral injustice, covering almost every kind of human activity, accompanied the movement toward greater political, social, and economic democracy, which characterized the Age of Jackson. Every reform cause, whether it was the temperance movement or the movement for more humane treatment of the insane, had its own leaders and organization. Often, however, the members and leaders of different reform groups overlapped. Many people in the American Anti-Slavery Society, for example, also supported the peace movement and the struggle to extend political rights to women.

What were the sources of this outburst of reform activity which swept across the American nation during the three decades before the Civil War? What kinds of people were the reform leaders? What were the motives and tactics of the most important reformers, the American abolitionists? What role have groups of reformers, joined in voluntary association, played in American life? These are the issues we will examine in Chapter 10.

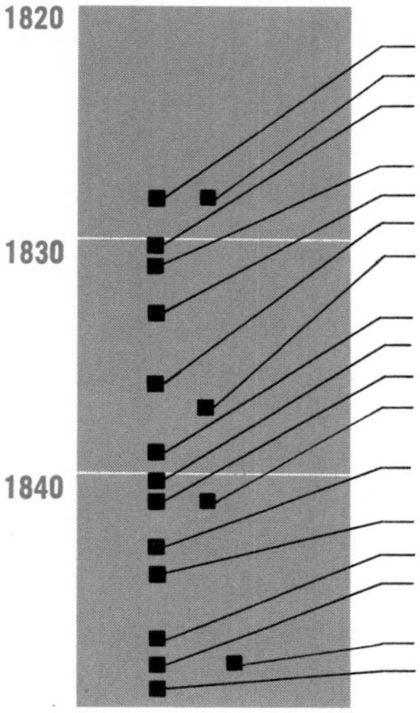

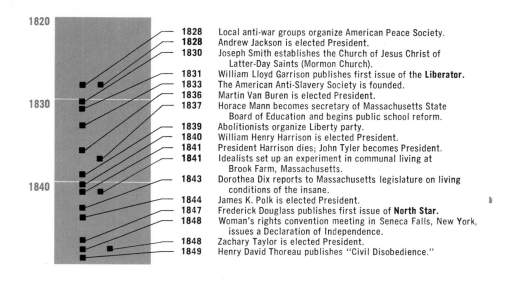

1828	Local anti-war groups organize American Peace Society.
1828	Andrew Jackson is elected President.
1830	Joseph Smith establishes the Church of Jesus Christ of Latter-Day Saints (Mormon Church).
1831	William Lloyd Garrison publishes first issue of the **Liberator.**
1833	The American Anti-Slavery Society is founded.
1836	Martin Van Buren is elected President.
1837	Horace Mann becomes secretary of Massachusetts State Board of Education and begins public school reform.
1839	Abolitionists organize Liberty party.
1840	William Henry Harrison is elected President.
1841	President Harrison dies; John Tyler becomes President.
1841	Idealists set up an experiment in communal living at Brook Farm, Massachusetts.
1843	Dorothea Dix reports to Massachusetts legislature on living conditions of the insane.
1844	James K. Polk is elected President.
1847	Frederick Douglass publishes first issue of **North Star.**
1848	Woman's rights convention meeting in Seneca Falls, New York, issues a Declaration of Independence.
1848	Zachary Taylor is elected President.
1849	Henry David Thoreau publishes "Civil Disobedience."

37 The Philosophic Basis for American Reform

Not everyone who tries to change society is a reformer. A man who stirs up discontent and enflames passions solely to promote his own good is called a demagog. While demagogs threaten a democratic society, reformers frequently play a constructive role. They are concerned more with principles than with personal gain. They are willing to challenge powerful interests and to risk the disapproval of their fellow citizens in order to improve or abolish a given social practice or institution. They are often motivated by religious conviction or a strong sense of social idealism.

Frequently, reformers have been influenced by the words and deeds of people whose personalities and careers may have been quite different from their own. Three Americans who had important influences on the reformers of the 1830's and 1840's were Thomas Jefferson, William Ellery Channing, and Frederick Douglass.

Thomas Jefferson (1743–1826) wrote the Declaration of Independence in 1776 and lived on for more than fifty years to earn almost every public honor the new American republic could bestow. Jefferson would have been great in any country or any age. Living on into the third decade of the nineteenth century in America, he seemed the very embodiment of the new nation's principles.

William Ellery Channing (1780–1842) also had roots in the American revolutionary experience. His grandfather had signed the

Declaration of Independence, and as a boy Channing had met George Washington who stayed at his parents' house when he visited Newport, Rhode Island. As a young minister in Boston, Channing became a leading spokesman for American Unitarianism. Unitarianism was an influential Protestant denomination which broke away from Calvinism in the early nineteenth century and emphasized such doctrines as the love of God and the dignity and rational ability of man. Channing, one of the best known clergymen of his time, urged a whole generation of Americans to apply religious principles to social problems.

Calvinism is the body of religious doctrine and practices derived from the Reformation leader John Calvin (1509–1564). The Puritans were Calvinists.

Frederick Douglass was born a slave in Maryland in 1817. His master's wife began to teach him to read when he became a household servant in Baltimore at the age of seven. When he was twenty-one, he escaped from slavery and quickly became involved in the abolitionist movement where he met William Lloyd Garrison, the editor of the antislavery newspaper, the *Liberator*. Douglass became one of the nation's most effective abolitionist speakers. As editor of *The North Star*, a reform newspaper started in Rochester, New York, he campaigned for abolition, women's rights, free land, free schools, trade unions, and civil liberties.

The following selections from Jefferson, Channing, and Douglass show the intellectual and emotional forces which helped to motivate American reformers before the Civil War. As you read these selections, try to answer the following questions:

1. What did Jefferson mean by "the rights of man"? What people in America at this time were without such rights?
2. Why did Channing think that men are essentially equal and exist on a higher level than other creatures?
3. How might Channing's sermon have influenced the way a member of his congregation looked at American society? Do you think that members of the clergy ought to take stands on public issues?
4. According to Douglass, what must reformers do to achieve their goals? Do you think the rewards are worth the risks?

Jefferson: An Inspiration to Reformers

Thomas Jefferson wrote this letter to Mayor Weightman of Washington, D. C., two weeks before his death in 1826.

Paul L. Ford, ed., **The Writings of Thomas Jefferson.** New York: G.P. Putnam's Sons, 1899, vol. X, pp. 390–92. Language simplified and modernized.

Respected Sir, I am flattered to receive your kind invitation on the part of the citizens of Washington, to attend, as one of the surviving signers of the Declaration of Independence, their celebration of the fiftieth anniversary of American Independence. It adds to my sufferings, that sickness will prevent me from participating personally in the rejoicings of that day.

I should, indeed, have been delighted to meet and exchange congratulations with the small remnant of that host of worthies who joined on that day [July 4, 1776] in the bold and doubtful choice we made for our country—submission to England or the sword. I would have rejoiced with them because our fellow citizens, after half a century of experience and prosperity, continue to approve the choice we made.

May our choice be to the world, what I believe it will be—the signal to arouse men to burst the chains under which ignorance and superstition have bound them, so they may assume the blessings and security of self-government. That form of government which we have developed guarantees the right to the unbounded exercise of reason and freedom of opinion. All eyes are opened, or are opening to the rights of man. The general spread of the light of science has already laid open to every view the obvious truth, that the mass of mankind has not been born with saddles on their backs, so that a favored few could ride them. These are grounds of hope for others. For ourselves, let the annual return of this day forever refresh our recollections of these rights, and increase our devotion to them.

May I express the pleasure with which I should have met my old neighbors of the city of Washington and its vicinity. I passed many years of pleasing social life with them. Their friendship relieved the anxieties of public cares, and left impressions so deeply engraved in my memory that I have never forgotten them. With my regret that ill health prevents me from accepting your invitation, please accept for yourself, and for those for whom you write, the assurance of my highest respect and friendly attachments.

William Ellery Channing's Humanitarianism

William Ellery Channing preached the sermon "Honor Due to All Man" in 1832. Portions of that sermon are given here.

The Works of William E. Channing, D.D. Boston: American Unitarian Association, 1900, pp. 67–73. Language simplified and modernized.

Among the many blessings of Christianity is the new way in which it teaches man to look upon his fellowman. It awakens in us a new interest toward everything human; it gives new importance to the soul; it establishes a new relationship between one man and another. In this respect, Christianity began a mighty revolution, which has been spreading silently through society. I believe this revolution will not stop until new ties take the place of those which have connected the human race previously. Christianity has as yet only begun its work of reformation. Under its influences, a new order of society is advancing, surely though slowly.

I believe that nothing will make men truly love other men, except the discovery of something interesting and great in human nature. We must see and feel that each human being is something of immeasurable importance. We must see and feel the broad distance between the spiritual life within us and the vegetable or animal life around us. I cannot love flowers, however beautiful, enough to make me sacrifice my own welfare for them. You will in vain urge me to love inferior animals wholeheartedly, however useful or attractive they may be. They lack capacity for truth, virtue, and progress. They lack that principle of duty which alone gives permanence to a human being.

A human being deserves a different affection from that which we give to inferior creatures. Man has a rational and moral nature by which he is to endure forever, and by which he may achieve happiness or sink into woe. The only way to love a human being properly is to catch some glimpse of this immortal power within him.

To show why we should honor all men, I might take a survey of the aspects of human nature which are common to all men, and set forth their claims to reverence. I believe that there is one principle of the soul which makes all men essentially equal, which may place the poorest people among the first rank of human beings, and which, therefore, gives the most depressed a right to interest and respect. I refer to the sense of duty, to the power of knowing and doing right, to the moral and religious principle, to the inward voice which speaks in the name of God, to the capacity for virtue or excellence. This is the great gift of God. We can conceive no greater.

This moral power makes all men essentially equal and wipes out all the distinctions of this world. Through this moral power, the ignorant and the poor may become the greatest of the human race; for the greatest is he who is truest to the principle of duty. The noblest human beings are probably to be found in the least favored conditions of society, among those whose names are never uttered beyond the narrow circle in which they toil and suffer. For in this class may be found those who have resisted the severest temptations, who have practiced the most arduous duties, who have been most wronged and have forgiven most. These are the great, the exalted. It does not matter what the particular duties are to which the individual is called or how obscure those duties may be. Greatness in God's sight lies in the power of virtue, in the energy with which God's will is chosen, and with which trial is borne and goodness loved and pursued.

In this sermon, I have spoken of the reasons for and the importance of that honor or respect which we owe to all human beings. I lack time to enlarge on the various ways in which this principle may be shown. I would only say, "Honor all men." Honor man, from the beginning to the end of his earthly life. Honor the child. Welcome the infant with a feeling of its mysterious grandeur, with the feeling that an immortal existence has begun, that a spirit has been kindled which is never to be quenched. Honor the child. On this principle all good education rests.

Again. Honor the poor. This respect is essential to improve the connection between those who are and who are not prosperous. This attitude alone makes goodness truly godlike. We must learn how insignificant are the distinctions between us and the poor. A fraternal union, founded on this deep conviction and intended to lift up and strengthen the poor, will do infinitely more for them than all of our organizations. 'Till Christianity shall have breathed into us this spirit of respect for human nature, we shall do the poor little good.

Perhaps none of us has yet heard or can understand the tone of voice in which a man, thoroughly impressed with this sentiment, would speak to his fellow man. It is a language hardly known on earth. No eloquence, I believe, has achieved such wonders as it is destined to accomplish.

I will close as I began, with saying that the great revelation which man now needs will reveal his true nature to himself. The faith which is most wanted is a faith in what we and our fellow beings may become—a faith in the divine germ or principle in every soul. We need to explore the mystery of our spiritual, accountable, immortal nature. Happy are they who have begun to understand it, and in whom it has awakened feelings of awe toward themselves, and of deep interest and honor toward their fellow creatures.

The Reform Philosophy of Frederick Douglass

Frederick Douglass made this statement in a speech in 1857.

Two Speeches by Frederick Douglass. Rochester: C.P. Dewey, 1857, pp. 21–22.

Let me give you a word of the philosophy of reform. The whole history of the progress of human liberty shows that all concessions yet made to her have been born of earnest struggle. The conflict has been exciting, agitating, all-absorbing. If there is no struggle there is no progress. Those who claim to favor freedom and yet denounce agitation, are men who want crops without plowing up the ground. They want rain without thunder and lightning. They want the ocean without the awful roar of its many waters.

Fugitive slaves—slaves who escaped from their masters in the South and went North—could be hunted down legally and returned to their owners. In 1850, the **Fugitive Slave Act** was passed. It aided slaveholders by rewarding commissioners who returned slaves and fining heavily officers who refused to cooperate.

This struggle may be a moral one, or it may be a physical one, and it may be both moral and physical, but it must be a struggle. Power concedes nothing without a demand. It never did and it never will. Find out what any people will quietly submit to and you have found out the exact measure of injustice and wrong which will be imposed upon them, and these will continue till they are resisted with either words or blows, or with both. The limits of tyrants are set by the endurance of those whom they oppress. In the light of these ideas, Negroes will be hunted in the North, and held and flogged in the South so long as they submit to those devilish outrages, and make no resistance, either moral or physical. Men may not get all they pay for in this world, but they must certainly pay for all they get. If we ever get free from the oppressions and wrongs heaped upon us, we must pay for their removal. We must do this by labor, by suffering, by sacrifice, and, if needs be, by our lives and the lives of others.

The first issue of Douglass's newspaper, The North Star, *carried an editorial, an excerpt from which appears below.*

North Star (December 3, 1847). Language simplified and modernized.

We neither reflect on the good faith nor discount the abilities of our [white] friends and fellow workers when we assert that the man who has suffered wrong should be the man to demand justice—that the man struck is the man to cry out—and that he who has endured the cruel pangs of slavery must advocate liberty. We must be our own advocates and representatives, not alone but independent, not separate from but in connection with our white friends. In the grand struggle for liberty and equality now waging, it is appropriate, necessary, and right that authors, editors, and orators should arise in our [the Negro] ranks, for in these capacities we can contribute the most permanent good to our cause.

38 Three Kinds of Reform

At various times in American history large numbers of people have been reformers. Extension of the suffrage, reform of the federal civil service, control of monopolies, prohibition of the sale of alcoholic beverages—each of these has held the spotlight at a given time in our history when other issues received comparatively little attention.

The reform movement before the Civil War, however, was all-inclusive. So many different kinds of reformers lived in Boston, for example, that some boarding houses advertised rooms "for reformers only." There one could find ardent sectarians who believed that specific religious denominations, such as Baptists, Methodists, or Mormons, were commissioned to save the world. They mingled with people who called themselves "come-outers" because they felt compelled to leave their churches in order to reform society. Other reformers believed that the formula for a better world lay in eating dark bread and taking cold showers. Still others claimed that men and women would find happiness only by giving away their money and property and living together without marriage or government.

A few of these reformers were simple-minded eccentrics. Most of them, however, were strong-minded idealists who, despite their disagreement over precise cures for the ills of society, tended to agree on certain basic principles. They believed, for example, that many social injustices would disappear if all people had an equal chance to improve themselves through education. They believed that women had as much to contribute to reform as men. Consequently, women played leading roles in many reform movements; the crusade to give women greater political rights was itself a leading reform movement of the period. Finally, they believed in the fundamental dignity of every individual person.

An eccentric is an individual who does not conform to the norms of behavior appropriate to his role in society. Society considers such a person peculiar or odd.

The following selections will help you to understand the far-reaching nature of the American reform impulse and the fundamental principles which bound individual reformers together. As you read, think about the following questions:

1. What is the value of universal education according to Mann?
2. To what extent did the Seneca Falls Declaration seem to reflect Jefferson's ideas? What were the rights which women felt they were denied? What is the significance of the last paragraph?
3. What was the fundamental assumption of Dorothea Dix about people with mental diseases? Would Channing have approved of Miss Dix? Why or why not?
4. Do you think that private citizens should devote their lives to causes such as the ones described in these readings?

Horace Mann on Public Education

In 1837, Horace Mann was appointed Secretary of the newly organized Board of Education of Massachusetts. In his Twelfth Annual Report, prepared in 1848, Mann discussed the implications of public education for national welfare.

According to the European theory, men are divided into classes—some to toil and earn, others to seize and enjoy. According to the Massachusetts theory, all are to have an equal chance for earning a living, and equal security in the enjoyment of what they earn. The latter idea tends to make men equal; the former, to promote the

Life and Works of Horace Mann. Boston: Lee and Shepard, 1891, vol. IV, pp. 246–51. Language simplified and modernized.

worst inequalities. Tried by any moral standard, can anyone hesitate, for a moment, to declare which of the two will produce the greater amount of human well-being, and which, therefore, is more in keeping with the divine will? The European theory is blind to what constitutes the highest glory, as well as the highest duty, of a State.

Our state should seek the solution of such problems as these: To what extent can ability to make a living displace pauperism? How nearly can we free ourselves from the low-minded and the vicious, not by driving them from society, but by elevating them within it? To what extent can the resources and powers of nature be converted into human welfare, the peaceful arts of life be advanced, and the vast treasures of human talent and genius be developed? How much suffering, in all its forms, can be relieved or, what is better, prevented? Cannot crime be reduced, and the number of criminals diminished?

Because of its industry and business, Massachusetts has some people who are extremely wealthy and some who are desperately poor. Surely nothing except universal education can counteract this tendency toward the dominance of capital and the servility of labor. If one class possesses all the wealth and the education, while the rest of society is ignorant and poor, it doesn't matter by what name the relation between them may be called. The latter, in fact and in truth, will be the servile dependents and subjects of the former.

But, if education is equally diffused among all members of society, widespread ownership of property will follow. For never have intelligent and practical men been permanently poor. The people of Massachusetts have, in some degree, appreciated the truth that the unexampled prosperity of the state is due to the education which all its people have received. But are they aware of the equally important fact that because of education two thirds of the people are not today the servants of capital?

Education equalizes the conditions of men. I do not mean that it so elevates the moral nature as to make men scorn and hate the oppression of their fellow men. But I mean that it gives each man the independence and the means by which he can resist the selfishness of others. It does better than to disarm the poor of their hostility toward the rich; it prevents poverty.

Seneca Falls Declaration of Sentiments and Resolutions

The Seneca Falls Convention on women's rights, called in 1848 by Lucretia Mott and Elizabeth Cady Stanton, drew up a

Declaration of Independence which marked the beginning of the women's rights movement in America.

E.C. Stanton, S.B. Anthony, and M.J. Gage, eds., **History of Woman Suffrage.** New York: Charles Mann, 1889, vol. I, pp. 70–73. Language simplified and modernized.

When, in the course of human events, it becomes necessary for one portion of the family of man to assume among the people of the earth a position different from that which they have hitherto occupied, but one to which the laws of nature and of nature's God entitle them, a decent respect to the opinions of mankind requires that they should declare the causes that impel them to such a course.

We hold these truths to be self-evident: that all men and women are created equal; that they are endowed by their Creator with certain inalienable rights; that among these are life, liberty, and the pursuit of happiness; that to secure these rights governments are instituted, deriving their just powers from the consent of the governed. Whenever any form of government becomes destructive of these ends, it is the right of those who suffer from it to refuse allegiance to it, and to insist upon the institution of a new government, laying its foundation on such principles, and organizing its powers in such form, as to them shall seem most likely to effect their safety and happiness. Prudence, indeed, will dictate that governments long established should not be changed for light and transient causes; and accordingly all experience hath shown that mankind are more disposed to suffer while evils are sufferable, than to right themselves by abolishing the forms to which they are accustomed. But when a long train of abuses and usurpations pursuing invariably the same object, evinces a design to reduce them under absolute despotism, it is their duty to throw off such government, and to provide new guards for their future security. Such has been the patient sufferance of the women under this government, and such is now the necessity which constrains them to demand the equal station [position] to which they are entitled.

The history of mankind is a history of repeated injuries and usurpations on the part of man toward woman, having in direct object the establishment of an absolute tyranny over her. To prove this, let facts be submitted to a candid world.

He has never permitted her to exercise her inalienable right to vote.

He has compelled her to submit to laws, in which she had no voice in making.

He has taken from her all right in property, even to her wages.

He has monopolized nearly all the profitable employments, and from those she is permitted to follow, she receives but scanty payment. He closes against her all the avenues to wealth and distinction which he considers most honorable to himself. As a teacher of theology, medicine, or law, she is not known.

He has denied her the facilities for obtaining a thorough education for all colleges are closed to her.

Resolved, That woman is man's equal—was intended to be so by the Creator, and the highest good of the race demands that she should be recognized as such.

Resolved, therefore, That, being given by the Creator the same capabilities, and the same sense of responsibility for their exercise as men, it is the right and duty of woman, equally with man, to promote every righteous cause by every righteous means. Especially, it is her right to participate with her brother in teaching the great subjects of morals and religion, both in private and in public, by writing and by speaking, by any proper means and in any proper assemblies. This is a self-evident truth growing out of the divinely implanted principles of human nature. Any custom or authority against it, whether modern or old, is to be regarded as a self-evident falsehood, and at war with mankind.

Dorothea Dix on the Insane

Dorothea Dix (1802–1887), a member of Channing's congregation, was a teacher in a Boston girls' school in 1841, when she accidentally discovered the mistreatment of a group of insane people in a local jail. During the next two years, she investigated conditions in jails and asylums throughout Massachusetts and then composed a report to the Massachusetts Legislature. Massachusetts soon took steps to provide better care for its mental patients, and Miss Dix broadened her efforts throughout the United States and Europe.

Francis Tiffany, **Life of Dorothea Lynde Dix.** Boston: Houghton Mifflin Company, 1891, pp. 76–82. Language simplified and modernized.

I come to present the strong claims of suffering humanity. I come to place before the Legislature of Massachusetts the condition of the miserable, the desolate, the outcast. I come as the advocate of helpless, forgotten, insane, and idiotic men and women; of beings sunk to a condition from which the most unconcerned would start with real horror; of beings wretched in our prisons, and more wretched in our poorhouses. And I cannot suppose it is necessary to use earnest persuasion, or stubborn argument, in order to fix attention upon a subject, only the more strongly pressing in its claims, because it is revolting and disgusting in its details.

I must confine myself to few examples, but am ready to furnish other and more complete details, if required. If my pictures are displeasing, coarse, and severe, my subjects, it must be recalled, have no pleasant features. The condition of human beings, reduced to the extremest states of degradation and misery, cannot be described in pleasant language.

I proceed, gentlemen, briefly to call your attention to the present state of insane persons confined within this Commonwealth in cages, closets, cellars, stalls, pens! Chained, naked, beaten with rods, and lashed into obedience.

To illustrate my subject, I offer the following extracts from my Notebook and Journal:

Lincoln, [Massachusetts. All the other locations were also in Massachusetts.] A woman in a cage. *Medford.* One idiotic subject chained, and one in a close stall for seventeen years. *Pepperell.* One often doubly chained, hand and foot; another violent; several peaceable now. *Brookfield.* One man caged, comfortable. *Granville.* One often closely confined; now losing the use of his limbs from lack of exercise. *Charlemont.* One man caged. *Savoy.* One man caged. *Lenox.* Two in the jail, against whose unfit condition there the jailer protests.

Dedham. The insane disadvantageously placed in the jail. In the almshouse, two females in stalls, situated in the main building; lie in wooden bunks filled with straw; always shut up. One of these subjects is supposed curable. The overseers of the poor have declined to put her in the hospital, as I was informed, on account of expense.

Franklin. One man chained; decent. *Taunton.* One woman caged. *Plymouth.* One man stall-caged; from Worcester Hospital. *Scituate.* One man and one woman stall-caged. *West Bridgewater.* Three idiots. Never removed from one room. *Barnstable.* Four females in pens and stalls. Two chained certainly. I think all. Jail, one idiot. *Wellfleet.* Three insane. One man and one woman chained, the latter in a bad condition. *Brewster.* One woman violently mad, solitary. Could not see her, the master and mistress being absent, and the paupers in charge having strict orders to admit no one. *Rochester.* Seven insane; at present none caged. *Milford.* Two insane, not now caged. *Cohasset.* One idiot, one insane; most miserable condition. *Plympton.* One insane, three idiots; condition wretched.

Gentlemen, I commit to you this sacred cause. Your action upon this subject will affect the present and future condition of hundreds and of thousands.

In this legislation, as in all things, may you exercise that "wisdom which is the breath of the power of God."

39 The Abolitionist Movement

Slavery became increasingly important in the South after Eli Whitney invented the cotton gin in 1793. Whitney's invention made cotton cultivation more profitable than it had been before.

Southern planters quickly opened new plantations on rich lands in Mississippi, Alabama, and Louisiana. As cotton agriculture moved to the Southwest, the demand for slaves increased accordingly. Between 1820 and 1840, cotton production quadrupled and the number of slaves grew from 1,538,000 to 2,487,355.

Since the eighteenth century, slavery had been a controversial part of American life. In the years following the Revolution, it had been abolished gradually throughout the North. Even in the South widespread opposition to slavery grew up during the first three decades of the nineteenth century. By 1840, however, Southerners almost universally defended slavery. This response came in part as a direct reaction to the activities of the American Anti-Slavery Society. Meeting in Philadelphia in 1833, the organizers of the Society admitted that several state constitutions protected slavery. They insisted, however, that immediate emancipation of the slaves was the only morally justifiable course for the nation to take. They also pledged themselves to establish local antislavery organizations and to launch a massive campaign to convince their countrymen that slavery was a monstrous evil.

The abolitionists had strong religious convictions. William Ellery Channing, whose sermon appeared in Reading 37, influenced some of them. The preaching of Charles Grandison Finney, whose views about a Christian's duty with regard to slavery are included in this reading, profoundly affected many others.

The abolitionists were also skillful organizers and effective writers. By 1840, they had recruited about 200,000 members and established over 2000 local antislavery societies. These societies supported the work of antislavery agents such as Theodore Dwight Weld, who lectured and wrote in behalf of their cause. The selections in Reading 39 show some of the ways in which the abolitionists went about trying to destroy slavery. As you read these selections, try to answer the following questions.

1. What did Finney mean by slavery "is a sin of the church"?
2. Why didn't the American Anti-Slavery Society want Theodore Weld to provide people with a detailed plan for emancipation? What connection do you find between Finney's sermon and the goals and strategy of the American Anti-Slavery Society? What did Frederick Douglass contribute to the movement?
3. How did Theodore Weld try to carry out the goals of the American Anti-Slavery Society by writing *American Slavery As It Is*?
4. Do you think that *American Slavery As It Is* was a fair attack on slavery or was it simply propaganda? How do you think it would be received in the North and in the South? Should reform organizations describe such brutality?

The Churches Must Take a Stand on the Subject of Slavery

Charles Grandison Finney (1792–1875) was a great revivalist preacher. He taught that no person could become a Christian unless he renounced his sins and was converted through an individual emotional experience with God. Finney converted tens of thousands of Americans in the North before the Civil War. In 1835, Finney gave a sermon on a Christian's duty with regard to slavery.

American Protestantism went through a Great Revival in the early nineteenth century.

Here the question arises, what is the right stand? FIRST I will state some things that should be avoided.

1. *A bad spirit* should be avoided. Nothing will injure religion, and the slaves themselves more than an angry controversy among Christians on the subject. Those proud professors of religion who think it is a shame to have a black skin may shut their ears because of their prejudices and be disposed to quarrel with those who urge the subject upon them. But I repeat, the subject of slavery is a subject upon which Christians need not and must not differ.

2. Another thing to be avoided is an attempt to be neutral on this subject. Christians can no more take a neutral stand on this subject than they can take a neutral stand on the subject of the sanctification [setting apart as holy] of the Sabbath. It is a great national sin. It is a sin of the church. The churches by their silence, and by permitting slaveholders to belong to their religious group, have been consenting to it. They have virtually declared that it is lawful. Allowing slaveholders quietly to remain in good standing in their churches, is the strongest and most public expression of their views that slavery is not sin. For the church, therefore, to pretend to be neutral on the subject is perfectly absurd. The fact is that she is not on neutral ground at all. While she tolerates slaveholders in her communion, SHE JUSTIFIES THE PRACTICE.

Charles G. Finney, **Lectures on Revivals of Religion.** New York: Fleming H. Revell, 1868, pp. 281–86. Language simplified and modernized.

Church members are God's witnesses. The fact is that slavery is, pre-eminently, the sin of the church. It is the very fact that ministers and professors of religion of different denominations hold slaves, which sanctifies the whole abomination of slavery in the eyes of ungodly men.

It is the church that mainly supports this sin. Her united testimony upon this subject would settle the question. Let Christians of all denominations meekly but firmly come forth, and pronounce their verdict; let them clear their communions, and wash their hands of this thing; let them give forth and write on the head and front of this great abomination, SIN! In three years, a public sentiment would be formed that would carry slavery away. There would not be a shackled slave, nor a bristling, cruel slave driver left in this land.

Instructions to an Abolitionist Agent

Theodore Weld was one of the most successful abolitionist agents. In 1834, the American Anti-Slavery Society, which he had helped to found, appointed him to carry the abolitionists' message into Ohio. At the time of his appointment, the Society sent him a letter containing instructions, portions of which are given here.

Dwight L. Dumond and Gilbert H. Barnes, eds., **Letters of Theodore Dwight Weld, Angelina Grimke Weld and Sarah Grimke.** New York: Appleton-Century-Crofts, 1934, vol. I, pp. 124–28. Language simplified and modernized.

To Mr. T. D. Weld
Dear Sir:

You have been appointed an agent of the American Anti-Slavery Society and will receive the following instructions from the executive committee, as a brief expression of the principles they wish you to teach and the course of conduct they wish you to pursue.

Our object is the overthrow of American slavery. We expect to accomplish this, mainly by showing to the public its true character and legitimate fruits, its denial of the first principles of religion, morals, and humanity, and its special inconsistency with our beliefs as a free, humane, and enlightened people.

You will teach everywhere, the great fundamental principle of IMMEDIATE ABOLITION, as the duty of all masters, on the ground that slavery is both unjust and unprofitable. Insist principally on the SIN OF SLAVERY, because our main hope is in the consciences of men.

We oppose the idea of compensation to slaveholders, because it implies the right of slavery. It is also unnecessary, because the abolition of slavery will be an advantage, as free labor is more profitable than the labor of slaves.

The people of color ought at once to be emancipated and recognized as citizens, and their rights secured, equal in all respects to others, according to the fundamental principle laid down in the American Declaration of Independence.

In covering your territory you will generally find it wise to visit first several prominent places, particularly those where our cause has friends. In going to a place, you will naturally call upon those who are friendly to our objectives and take advice from them. Also call on ministers of the gospel and other leading characters and labor specially to enlighten them and secure their favor and influence. Ministers are the hinges of community, and ought to be moved, if possible.

Form branch societies, both male and female, in every place where it is practicable. Encourage them to raise funds and apply them in purchasing and circulating free antislavery publications.

You are not to take up collections in your public meetings, as the practice often prevents persons from attending, whom it might be desirable to reach.

We shall expect you to write frequently to the Secretary for Domestic Correspondence and give detailed accounts of your proceedings and success. If you receive money for the society, you will send it, by mail, WITHOUT DELAY, to the treasurer.

Frederick Douglass Joins the Cause

Frederick Douglass became a renowned orator in both the United States and Great Britain. In later life, he recalled his unusual contribution to the abolitionist cause.

Frederick Douglass, **Life and Times of Frederick Douglass.** Boston: DeWolfe Fiske and Company, 1895, pp. 268–69.

Among the first duties assigned to me on entering the ranks was to travel in company with Mr. George Foster, to secure subscribers to the *Anti-Slavery Standard* and the *Liberator*. With him I traveled and lectured through the eastern counties of Massachusetts. Much interest was awakened—large meetings assembled. Many came, no doubt, from curiosity to hear what a Negro could say in his own cause. I was generally introduced as a "chattel"—a "thing"—a piece of southern property—the chairman assuring the audience that *it* could speak. *Fugitive slaves,* at that time, were not so plentiful as now [1855]; and as a fugitive slave lecturer, I had the advantage of being a "bran-new fact"—the first one out. Up to that time a colored man was deemed a fool who confessed himself a runaway slave, not only because of the danger to which he exposed himself of being retaken, but because it was a confession of a very low origin.

The only precaution I took, at the beginning, to prevent Master Thomas from knowing where I was, and what I was about, was the withholding of my former name, my master's name, and the name of the state and county from which I came. During the first three or four months, my speeches were almost exclusively made up of narrations of my own personal experience as a slave. "Let us have the facts," said the people. . . . "Tell your story, Frederick," would whisper my revered friend, Mr. [William Lloyd] Garrison, as I stepped upon the platform. I could not always [obey], for I was now reading and thinking. New views of the subject were being presented to my mind. It did not entirely satisfy me to *narrate* wrongs; I felt like *denouncing* them. . . .

Selections from an Abolitionist Best Seller

Theodore Weld, his wife Angelina, and her sister, Sarah Grimke, compiled evidence from thousands of Southern newspapers for a book American Slavery As It Is: Testimony of a Thousand Witnesses. *The book, published in 1839, immediately became a best seller and later served as a source for Harriet Beecher Stowe's* Uncle Tom's Cabin.

American Slavery As It Is: Testimony of a Thousand Witnesses. New York: American Anti-Slavery Society, 1839, pp. 62–63, 77, 125, 127. Language simplified and modernized.

We will in the first place, prove by a number of witnesses, that slaves are whipped with such inhuman severity, as to lacerate and mangle their flesh in the most shocking manner, leaving permanent scars and ridges. After establishing this, we will present a mass of testimony, concerning a great variety of other tortures. The testimony, for the most part, will be that of the slaveholders themselves, and in their own chosen words. A large portion of it will be taken from the advertisements, which they have published in their own newspapers, describing the scars made by the whip on the bodies of their own runaway slaves. We shall insert only so much of each advertisement as will intelligibly set forth the precise point under consideration. In the column under the word "witnesses," will be found the name of the individual, who signs the advertisement, or for whom it is signed, with his or her place of residence, and the name and date of the paper, in which it appeared, and generally the name of the place where it is published. Opposite the name of each witness will be an extract, from the advertisement, containing his or her testimony.

WITNESSES	TESTIMONY
Mr. Robert Nicoll, Dauphin St. between Emanuel and Conception Sts., Mobile, Alabama, in the "Mobile Commercial Advertiser."	"Ten dollars reward for my woman Siby, very much scarred about the neck and ears by whipping."
Maurice Y. Garcia, Sheriff of the County of Jefferson, La., in the "New Orleans Bee," August 14, 1838.	"Lodged in jail, a mulatto boy, having large marks of the whip, on his shoulders and other parts of his body."
James A. Rowland, jailor, Lumberton, North Carolina, in the "Fayetteville (N. C.) Observer," June 20, 1838.	"Committed, a mulatto fellow —his back shows lasting impressions of the whip, and leaves no doubt of his being A SLAVE."
Mr. H. Varillat, No. 23 Girod Street, New Orleans—in the "Commercial Bulletin," August 27, 1838.	"Ranaway, the Negro slave named Jupiter—has a fresh mark of a cowskin on one of his cheeks."

Brandings, Maimings, Gun-Shot Wounds, &c.

We shall adopt under this head, the same course as that pursued under the previous one.

WITNESSES	TESTIMONY
Mr. Micajah Ricks, Nash County, North Carolina, in the Raleigh "Standard," July 18, 1838.	"Ranaway, a Negro woman and two children; a few days before she went off, I burnt her with a hot iron, on the left side of her face, I tried to make the letter M."
Mr. Asa B. Metcalf, Kingston, Adams Co., Miss., in the "Natchez Courier," June 15, 1832.	"Ranaway Mary, a black woman, has a scar on her back and right arm near the shoulder, caused by a rifle ball."
Mr. William Overstreet, Benton, Yazoo Co., Miss., in the "Lexington [Kentucky] Observer," July 22, 1838.	"Ranaway a Negro man named Henry, his left eye out, some scars from a dirk [dagger] on and under his left arm, and much scarred with the whip."
J. A. Brown, jailor, Charleston, South Carolina, in the "Mercury," Jan. 12, 1837.	"Committed to jail a Negro man, has no toes on his left foot."
Mr. J. Scrivener, Herring Bay, Anne Arundel Co., Maryland, in the "Annapolis Republican," April 18, 1837.	"Ranaway Negro man Elijah, has a scar on his left cheek, apparently occasioned by a shot."
Mr. Nicholas Edmunds, in the "Petersburgh (Va.) Intelligencer," May 22, 1838.	"Ranaway my Negro man named Simon, he has been shot badly in his back and right arm."

"Slaveholders are Proverbial for Their Kindness, Hospitality, Benevolence, and Generosity"

Many people claim that the cruelties inflicted upon slaves are fictions because slaveholders are famed for their courtesy and hospitality.

The fact that slaveholders may be full of benevolence and kindness toward their equals and toward whites generally, while they treat with the most inhuman neglect their own slaves, is well illustrated by an incident mentioned by the Rev. Dr. Channing, of

Boston, (who once lived in Virginia) in his work on slavery, p. 162, 1st edition:—

> I cannot, says the doctor, forget my feelings on visiting a hospital belonging to the plantation of a gentleman highly esteemed for his virtues, and whose manners and conversation expressed much benevolence and conscientiousness. When I entered the hospital with him, the first object on which my eye fell was a young woman who was very ill, probably approaching death. She was stretched on the floor. Her head rested on something like a pillow, but her body and limbs were extended on the hard boards. The owner, I doubt not, had, at least, as much kindness as myself; but he was so used to seeing the slaves living without common comforts, that the idea of unkindness in the present instance did not enter his mind.

Mr. George A. Avery, an elder of a Presbyterian church in Rochester, N. Y., who resided some years in Virginia, says:—

> On one occasion I was crossing the plantation and approaching the house of a friend, when I met him, rifle in hand, in pursuit of one of his Negroes, declaring he would shoot him in a moment if he got his eye upon him. It appeared that the slave had refused to be flogged, and ran off to avoid the consequences; and yet the generous hospitality of this man to myself, and white friends generally, scarcely knew any bounds.

40 The Tradition of American Reform

HISTORICAL ESSAY

A high percentage of nineteenth-century American reformers came from the vicinity of Boston, Massachusetts, a city filled with symbolic reminders of the American Revolution. Most of the people who became active in reform causes before the Civil War were born early in the nineteenth century. Their fathers and grandfathers had fought in the Revolution. The ideals of the Declaration of Independence, like the sight of Boston Common, Bunker Hill, and Faneuil Hall, were a part of the living past for these men and women, not merely something to be learned from history books. Wendell Phillips, a well-known abolitionist orator, for example, recalled hearing about Sam Adams and John Hancock

Boston Common is a public area which the Revolutionary patriots used as a meeting place. In the Battle of Bunker Hill, fought in 1775, the Americans inflicted heavy losses on the British. The patriots also used Faneuil Hall, an old market building and public hall, as a meeting place.

throughout his boyhood. Theodore Parker, the Boston minister who played a leading role in helping escaped slaves, kept the musket that his grandfather had used against British troops in the battle of Lexington close by his side to remind him of his own revolutionary heritage.

A second factor helps to explain the importance of Boston as a center of reform. Three hundred years earlier, the Puritans had come to New England to pursue their own religious beliefs and to build a Christian society which would serve as a model for the old world. Many active reformers were descended from the Puritans. Some of them, like Wendell Phillips, took pride in the fact that their ancestors had come to America on the *Arabella* with John Winthrop. Most of them, whatever their own personal background, felt a tie between their mission to reform American society in the nineteenth century and the earlier mission of the Puritans two centuries before.

The Role of the Church

Protestants dominated nineteenth-century reform movements. Only a few Jews lived in America at this time, and the Catholics, although somewhat more numerous, were still very much a minority group. Because the Catholic Church was in a minority position striving to make a place for itself in America, its members shied away from controversial social questions. Consequently, they were less involved in reform causes than members of Protestant denominations.

In the case of some reform causes, most notably abolition, churches played an important role on both sides. Some church people argued that since the Bible treated slavery as a legitimate institution, men should not tamper with it in America; others argued that slavery denied the spirit of Christianity and should be abolished. In addition to the difficulty of deciding what the Bible had to say about slavery, the churches faced a practical problem because they drew their membership from Americans all over the country. By agreeing with the reformers and condemning slavery, the churches might drive out Southern members and thus disrupt their organizations.

Because churches took official positions on slavery slowly, many reformers turned upon the churches themselves as obstacles to reform. These reformers were anti-church but not anti-religious. They believed that if a person expected to find favor from God in the next world, he must struggle against everything unjust and evil in this world. Charles G. Finney preached this message all over the

North and influenced other abolitionists such as Theodore Dwight Weld. Religious zeal played an important role in supporting reform movements before the Civil War.

Perfectionism, Transcendentalism, and Reform

A new school of philosophy in America called transcendentalism also contributed to the ideology of the reformers. The father of the movement was Ralph Waldo Emerson. As a young Unitarian minister, Emerson was very much influenced by William Ellery Channing, but in 1832 he left the ministry because he felt that Unitarians relied too much on the authority of the Bible and not enough on man's own sense of truth and duty. In the philosophy of transcendentalism, which Emerson proclaimed, man became "a God in ruins." By this phrase Emerson meant that all nature, including man, was a part of God and that man could become divine by expressing the spiritual quality within himself and living according to his most profound moral intuitions.

Emerson lived in Concord, Massachusetts, from 1834 until 1882. He finished most of his influential writing before the Civil War. Despite the difficulty of his philosophy, he had a wide following as a writer and lecturer throughout the northern and western states. The heart of his philosophy appealed strongly to Americans. Every man was godlike, he argued, and should stand on his own two feet and pursue his own convictions. One of his most famous essays was called "Self Reliance." This emphasis on individualism gave a kind of philosophical support to the ideals of Jacksonian democracy and also stimulated the reform movement. If all men were a part of God, then it was wrong to treat any man unjustly. Moreover, if a man knew in his heart that an institution such as slavery was wrong, then he was obliged to try to change it.

The case of one of Emerson's most famous followers, Henry David Thoreau, illustrates the implications of transcendentalism. Like Emerson, Thoreau lived in Concord. Not very well known in his own time, he spent most of his life reading, studying nature, and writing in his journal. Thoreau believed that slavery was wrong. In 1846, he refused to pay taxes because he felt that tax money was being used to support a government that protected slavery. The authorities put Thoreau in the Concord jail overnight. On his release he wrote an essay entitled "Civil Disobedience" in which he justified his refusal to obey what he thought were unjust laws. Thoreau believed it was wrong to support slavery in any way, and he preferred to go to jail rather than violate his deepest moral convictions. "Civil Disobedience" is still widely read throughout the world. It influenced Mohandas Gandhi, who attempted to get England to grant independence to India in the 1930's and 1940's, and American civil-rights leaders such as Martin Luther King, Jr.

In addition to the idealism of the American Revolution and the influences of Christianity and transcendentalism, the reform spirit before the Civil War was nourished by the emphasis on equality, which characterized the thinking of many Americans during the time of Andrew Jackson. If the common people were good enough to win political power and to fill responsible positions in government, then, the reformers argued, any institutions which kept them from enjoying equal opportunities should be changed.

Historians often use the word "perfectionism" to stand for all of the influences just mentioned: the idealism of the Declaration of Independence, the moral emphases of Christianity and transcendentalism, and the Jacksonian emphasis on equality. Large numbers of Americans before the Civil War believed that society could and should be made more perfect. This perfectionist faith supported northern reformers and helped to distinguish the North from the South.

Perfectionism led to unusual kinds of reform activity. Many idealistic people, influenced by the ideas of a French reformer named Charles Fourier (1772–1837), wanted to create a society in which each person could enjoy maximum freedom and security. They established small model communities which abolished private property and required everyone to work for the common good. The most famous of these communities, Brook Farm, was located just outside Boston.

Mormonism

Perfectionism and religious zeal went hand in hand and led to the development of new kinds of churches. The most important of these new religious groups, organized in Fayette, New York, in 1830, was the Church of Jesus Christ of the Latter Day Saints. Joseph Smith founded this church after he claimed that he had received a special revelation from God in the form of the Book of the Mormon. Smith accepted the authority of the Bible, but taught that God intended to establish the pure form of Christianity in Mormonism. A centralized form of economic and social life, which clashed sharply with the individualism of the times, characterized the Mormon Church. Mormon group solidarity, together with reports of such unorthodox ideas as their belief in polygyny, aroused the antagonism of their neighbors. Searching for more congenial surroundings, the Mormons moved from New York State to Ohio, Missouri, and Illinois. In 1844, a mob in Nauvoo, Illinois, killed Joseph Smith and drove the Mormons out.

Polygyny is the practice of a husband having two or more wives at the same time.

Brigham Young succeeded Smith as leader of the Mormons. By this time Young and most of his followers had come to feel that they would only find security outside the populated areas of the United States. In 1847, Young led a small group of Mormons west to the Great Salt Lake Valley in what is now the state of Utah. By 1850, more than 11,000 fellow believers had joined him. The Mormon migration makes up one of the great chapters in frontier history. Mormonism, which has since become a powerful world-wide religious order, is one of the most "original" religious organizations ever developed in the United States.

The Variety of Reform Movements

An enormous variety of reform causes concerned Americans before the Civil War. Some of them seem rather frivolous today. A few reformers even campaigned against growing beards, wearing corsets, or eating white bread. Other movements attacked more fundamental problems and have counterparts in active organizations in America. All these diverse groups, however, made one basic assumption: that any pattern of behavior or any social arrangement which degraded the dignity of the individual should be reformed.

Children, forced to work in factories twelve hours a day, could not go to school to prepare themselves for a better life. Rather than press for factory legislation, reformers tried to pass laws requiring all children to go to school. Horace Mann led the fight for free public education; by 1860 many states had passed compulsory school laws. Few children before the Civil War studied beyond the elementary school. Our concern today, however, that every qualified student finish high school and, if possible, continue on to college, grew directly from the pre-Civil War reform spirit expressed in the work of Horace Mann.

Our contemporary concern for world peace also has roots in the early nineteenth century. In 1828, reformers founded the American Peace Society in New York City. This organization denounced the use of force in international disputes and urged the establishment of an organization like the United Nations. Local peace societies sprang up throughout the country, and students in schools and colleges received special prizes from the Society for their essays and orations.

The excerpt from the writings of Dorothea Dix illustrates still another important reform cause during this period: improvement in the ways that society treated the mentally ill and insane. During the pre-Civil War period, reform groups also began to change American prisons from dungeons to correctional institutions designed to rehabilitate their inmates.

Important movements also developed to provide care and educational opportunities for the deaf and the blind. In 1832, Samuel Gridley Howe, a graduate of Harvard Medical School, established Perkins Institute in Boston for the purpose of instructing blind children. In 1857, a Yale graduate and minister, Thomas Hopkins Gallaudet, established a college in Washington, D. C., for the education of the deaf.

The Movement to Abolish Slavery

The antislavery movement, however, occupied the center of the stage. Although the American Anti-Slavery Society was not founded until 1833, slavery had troubled America's conscience long before that. Quakers had organized the first antislavery society in America in 1775. All the northern states took steps to abolish slavery in the years following the Revolution. Even in the South feeling against slavery ran high; a movement providing for gradual emancipation of slaves and for their colonization in Africa remained a powerful influence in the upper South as late as the 1820's. By the 1830's, however, slavery had become accepted in the South as an essential part of the economy, and Southerners resented any criticism of it.

William Lloyd Garrison became the most famous abolitionist. The son of a poor family from Newburyport, Massachusetts, Garrison received little formal education, and after several unhappy apprenticeships, he finally took up journalism. While he was working for a Quaker journalist in Baltimore, Garrison became interested in slavery. In 1831, he founded his own paper, the *Liberator,* in Boston, to crusade against slavery. In the first issue, Garrison indicated how he intended to carry out his crusade:

> I *will be* as harsh as truth, and as uncompromising as justice. On this subject I do not wish to think, or speak or write with moderation . . . I am in earnest—I will not equivocate—I will not excuse—I will not retreat a single inch—AND I WILL BE HEARD.

Garrison was true to his word. In the following years, the *Liberator* became the most famous antislavery newspaper in the country. Although its subscription list was always relatively small, other papers North and South quoted the *Liberator* freely, thus spreading the influence of its crusading editor.

During the 1830's, great troubles vexed the abolitionists despite their growth in numbers. Trouble arose both in the South and in the North. The South took action almost immediately to keep abolitionism from spreading below the Mason-Dixon line. Southern

The southern boundary of Pennsylvania was run in the 1760's by Charles Mason and Jeremiah Dixon at about 39° latitude. This line was extended in 1820 as the boundary between slave and free states under the Missouri Compromise. The term "Mason-Dixon line" thus came to mean the boundary between slave and free states.

states passed laws making it a crime to circulate antislavery literature or to criticize slavery in public. Some states actually posted a reward for the capture of Garrison, dead or alive. Therefore, abolitionists had to find their audiences in the North, and even there, the reception at first was decidedly hostile. Opposition grew in part from the fact that considerable anti-Negro feeling existed in the North before the war. Negroes went to segregated schools; they rode in segregated trains; they even sat in segregated pews in white churches. Abolitionists opposed these practices and thus incurred the wrath of many northern whites. Northern businessmen also opposed abolitionists for fear that agitation would disrupt trade between North and South. As a result, abolitionists often found it hard to get a hearing in the North. Mobs broke up their meetings, and they were sometimes beaten. A mob even killed one of their number, Elijah Lovejoy, in Alton, Illinois, in 1837.

This harassment also had a positive effect, however. By the end of the 1830's, many people in the North had begun to feel that abolitionists were being denied their fundamental right to free speech. On this ground, they began to take new interest in the antislavery movement. Local antislavery societies multiplied rapidly, claiming about 200,000 members throughout the North by 1840.

Most abolitionists limited their activities to paying dues to an antislavery organization, listening to abolitionist orators, such as the famous ex-slave Frederick Douglass, reading antislavery newspapers and pamphlets, and occasionally writing legislators to support antislavery measures. A small number, however, probably not more than 3000, struck directly at slavery by developing a secret organization called the underground railroad. It began in the early 1830's and helped hundreds of slaves to escape from the South every year. The underground railroad was particularly strong in border states. Most of the money to support it came from white people in the North sympathetic to the antislavery cause. Some of its most important agents, however, were escaped Negro slaves, like the courageous Harriet Tubman who, after escaping from a Maryland plantation into Pennsylvania, returned many times to the South and developed a line of underground stations extending from Maryland to Canada.

Four slave states, Missouri, Kentucky, Maryland, and Delaware had one boundary on free territory and were thus called border states.

Dissension divided American abolitionists. People who devote their lives to reform causes are usually strong minded and uncompromising, and frequently find it difficult to get along with each other. In 1840, the American Anti-Slavery Society split into two factions. One faction, under the leadership of men like Theodore Dwight Weld, began to concentrate on political means to destroy slavery. Some of them helped to organize the Liberty party which nominated James G. Birney for President in 1840. Others began to work through the Whig or Democratic parties. These political abolitionists worked to abolish slavery in the District of Columbia and to exclude slavery from federal territories. In the 1850's, the Republican party took over this position.

The other faction, grouped around Garrison and Wendell Phillips, believed that abolitionists could not become involved in politics without compromising their principles and should, therefore, stay aloof from political activity. They advocated extreme measures, such as the secession of the North, so that slavery would no longer stain the entire Union. One of Garrison's slogans carried in the *Liberator* proclaimed, "No union with slaveholders." Because the Constitution of the United States seemed to protect slavery, radical abolitionists refused to honor it. Garrison called the Constitution a "covenant with death and an agreement with Hell." At a public meeting he burned a copy of the Constitution, saying "thus perish all compromises with tyranny."

For thirty years, the radical abolitionists continued to demand immediate emancipation and to denounce those people whose position was more conservative than their own. In one sense they failed. They did not convert the slaveholders, and the majority of people in the North continued to look on them as dangerous fanatics. In another sense, even with all their shortcomings, they succeeded. The abolitionists represented the American conscience. They helped to force the great issue which Abraham Lincoln defined by saying that the American nation could not remain indefinitely half slave and half free. Men who denounce contemporary reformers for their uncompromising stands might well reflect upon the influence of this remarkable band of impassioned people who believed that it was preferable to divide a nation rather than condone injustice.

Voluntary organizations have spearheaded reform in the United States since the earliest days of the republic. Benjamin Franklin helped to organize a number of local reform groups in Philadelphia, as we learned in Chapter 3. During the three decades before the Civil War, reform groups spread their influence across the entire nation, but they gained their most notable successes by promoting legislation on the state level. The next major outbreak of reform activity during the first years of the twentieth century emphasized political and economic reform at the local, state, and national level. During the 1930's, men such as Franklin D. Roosevelt used the national government to reshape the nation's economy and bring new economic and social welfare to millions of citizens. In the 1960's, civil-rights groups, opponents of poverty, and advocates of peace continued to urge reform on government at all levels. They represent a great American tradition—the belief that free men must give their time, money, and energy, indeed their very lives, so that justice and freedom may reign supreme in the land.

SUGGESTED READINGS

BARTLETT, IRVING H., *The American Mind in the Mid-Nineteenth Century.* This volume contains short essays on Emerson, Thoreau, Wendell Phillips, Daniel Webster, and Abraham Lincoln and attempts to distinguish between liberals, radicals, and conservatives in nineteenth-century America.

DOUGLASS, FREDERICK, *Narrative of the Life of Frederick Douglass.* This volume tells the story of America's most celebrated escaped slave in his own words. It is one of the classic autobiographies in American literature.

HAWTHORNE, NATHANIEL, *The Blithedale Romance.* This is a novel about New England reformers before the Civil War by a famous American writer who was critical of them.

NYE, RUSSEL B., *William Lloyd Garrison and the Humanitarian Reformers.* This is the best brief biography of the famous abolitionist editor.

The Slavery Issue

CHAPTER 11

STATING THE ISSUE

By the second quarter of the nineteenth century, the South had developed a civilization which differed in many striking ways from the rest of America. While cities grew rapidly in other parts of the United States, the South remained primarily rural. While the North and Northwest absorbed thousands of immigrants from Europe, the white population, chiefly of British ancestry, in the South remained relatively stable and homogenous. While prosperity in the northern and western states depended primarily on the ability of farmers, manufacturers, and merchants to satisfy the demands of a rapidly expanding domestic market, the economic welfare of the South depended almost exclusively on the ability to sell cotton abroad. While society in the North and West encouraged new ideas in all fields and generally supported reform movements, Southerners remained essentially conservative and discouraged criticism of their social and economic institutions.

But Negro slavery, more than anything else, distinguished the South from the rest of the nation. In the colonial period, slavery had existed throughout America. After the Revolutionary War, the Northern states passed laws providing for its gradual abolition. By 1850, the South was the only area, not only in the United States but in any Western nation, except Cuba and Brazil, where men owned other human beings.

Chapter 11 examines the ways in which slavery shaped the South in the second quarter of the nineteenth century. What was it like to be an American Negro slave? How did Southerners defend slavery? What was the impact of slavery on the economy of the South? How did slavery influence Southern society and attitudes? These are the major issues with which we will be concerned in Chapter 11.

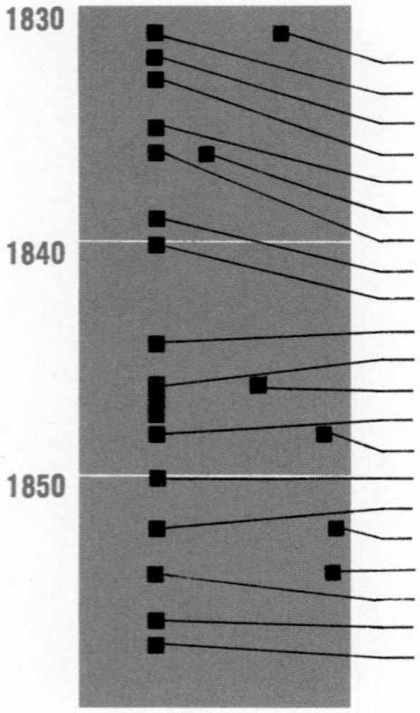

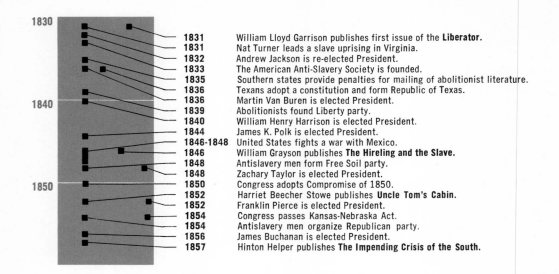

1831	William Lloyd Garrison publishes first issue of the **Liberator.**
1831	Nat Turner leads a slave uprising in Virginia.
1832	Andrew Jackson is re-elected President.
1833	The American Anti-Slavery Society is founded.
1835	Southern states provide penalties for mailing of abolitionist literature.
1836	Texans adopt a constitution and form Republic of Texas.
1836	Martin Van Buren is elected President.
1839	Abolitionists found Liberty party.
1840	William Henry Harrison is elected President.
1844	James K. Polk is elected President.
1846-1848	United States fights a war with Mexico.
1846	William Grayson publishes **The Hireling and the Slave.**
1848	Antislavery men form Free Soil party.
1848	Zachary Taylor is elected President.
1850	Congress adopts Compromise of 1850.
1852	Harriet Beecher Stowe publishes **Uncle Tom's Cabin.**
1852	Franklin Pierce is elected President.
1854	Congress passes Kansas-Nebraska Act.
1854	Antislavery men organize Republican party.
1856	James Buchanan is elected President.
1857	Hinton Helper publishes **The Impending Crisis of the South.**

41 Slavery on the Plantation

Since the Civil War, historians have been trying to determine what it was like to be a Negro slave in the South. They have encountered many difficulties in conducting their investigations. In the first place, slaves led different kinds of lives depending upon where they lived, who their masters were, and what kind of work they did. Some slaves worked as field hands on plantations, while others worked on small farms. Some were house servants on plantations or in cities. Others were skilled craftsmen whom their masters hired out for wages. Slaves who lived and worked under such different circumstances obviously had diverse experiences.

The great plantation, which has been so glamorized in historical fiction and in the movies, was not the typical unit of Southern economic and social life. Although a few plantations had a slave population numbering in the hundreds, only one percent of the slaveowners held more than a hundred slaves each. Two thirds of all slaveholders owned fewer than twenty slaves each; twenty percent owned only one slave. Nevertheless, more than half the four million slaves in the South in 1860 lived in groups of ten or more and worked in the fields planting and harvesting staple crops. Plantation slavery, then, was the experience of the majority of slaves.

What was plantation slavery like before the Civil War? Different sources suggest different answers. Former slaveholders, writing after the Civil War, stressed the harmony of plantation life and the kindness and generosity of the masters. Northern historians, writing in the post-Civil War Period, emphasized the cruelty of the slaveholder and the suffering of the slave. Former slaves, who testified after the Civil War about their experiences as slaves, often gave inconsistent reports.

For a more detached view of slavery, historians frequently consult the accounts of Southern life written by Northern and European travelers who visited the region. Frederick Law Olmsted (1822–1903), a prominent American landscape architect and author, spent most of his life in the North, but he made three trips through the Southern states in the 1850's. The books which he wrote on the basis of these journeys represent one of the most valuable records we have of Southern economic and social life in the decade before the Civil War. Reading 41 gives Olmsted's account of one plantation that he visited. As you read, keep these questions in mind:

1. What is significant about the fact that the owner of the plantation lived "several hundred miles away"?
2. What evidence did Olmsted find that slaves were treated well on this plantation?
3. What evidence was there that the slaves were dissatisfied?
4. How reliable do you consider a traveler's account of slavery?

A Mississippi Plantation

In the late 1850's, Frederick Law Olmsted visited a plantation in lower Mississippi. His observations on the daily life of the slaves are given here.

Frederick Law Olmsted, **A Journey in the Back Country.** New York: Mason Brothers, 1860, pp. 46–51. Language simplified and modernized.

We had a good breakfast in the morning. Immediately afterward we mounted our horses and rode to a very large cottonfield, where the whole field-force of the plantation was working.

It was a first-rate plantation. On the highest ground stood a large and handsome mansion, but it had not been occupied for several years. The owner lived several hundred miles away, and the overseer had not seen him for more than two years.

The whole plantation, including the swamp land, covered several square miles. The nearest neighbor's house was four miles away. There were between thirteen and fourteen hundred acres planted with cotton, corn, and other crops. Two hundred hogs ran at large in the swamp. It was intended that enough corn and pork should be raised to feed the slaves and the cattle. This year, the overseer had to purchase additional provisions, as he probably had to each year. The overseer hinted that the owner had been displeased, and he "did not mean to be caught so bad again."

There were 135 slaves, big and little, of which 67 went to the field regularly—equal, the overseer thought, to 60 able-bodied hands. Besides the field-hands, there were 3 mechanics (blacksmith, carpenter, and wheelwright), 2 seamstresses, a cook, 1 stable servant, 1 cattle-tender, 1 hog-tender, 1 teamster, 1 house servant (the overseer's cook), and 1 midwife and nurse. These were all first-class hands. The overseer said that most of them would be worth more, if they were for sale, than the best field-hands. There was also a driver of the hoe-gang who did not work himself and a foreman of the plow-gang. These two acted alternately as petty officers in the field and in the slave quarters.

A wheelwright made and repaired wheels for wagons and carriages.

A midwife delivers children at childbirth.

The hoe-gang hoed the fields to loosen the soil around the plants and to destroy weeds.

There was a nursery for babies at the quarters. Twenty women, at this time, left their work four times each day for half an hour to nurse the young ones. The overseer counted these women as half-hands, that is, they were expected to do half an ordinary day's work.

The overseer had no runaways out at this time, but he had just sold a bad one to go to Texas. He had been whipping the fellow, when he turned and tried to stab him. The slave then broke from him and ran away. The dogs had caught him almost immediately. After catching him, the overseer kept him in irons until he had a chance to sell him.

Irons were rings and chains made of iron and placed on a slave's wrists or ankles to prevent him from escaping.

His slaves did not very often run away, he said, because they were almost sure to be caught. As soon as he saw that one was gone, he put the dogs on. If rain had not just fallen to remove the scent, the dogs, which were trained especially to run after escapees, soon found him.

Sometimes, however, runaways would outwit the dogs. If they did, they almost always stayed in the neighborhood so they could come back to see their families and get food. As soon as the overseer knew about such visits, he put the dogs on again. Two months was the longest time that any runaway was gone.

In the field, we found thirty plows, moving together, turning the earth from the cotton plants, and from thirty to forty hoers, most of whom were women. A black driver walked about among them with a whip, which he often cracked at them, sometimes allowing the lash to fall lightly upon their shoulders. He also constantly urged them with his voice. All worked very steadily. Though the presence of a stranger on the plantation must have been rare, I saw none raise or turn his head to look at me. A water-toter attended each gang.

A driver's job was to keep the slaves working steadily.

I asked at what time the slaves began to work in the morning. "Well," said the overseer, "I do better by my slaves than most. I keep 'em right smart at their work while they are working, but I generally knock 'em off at 8 o'clock on Saturday mornings and give 'em all the rest of the day to themselves. I always give 'em Sunday off. At pickin' time, and hoein' time, I sometimes keep 'em to it till about sunset on Saturdays, but I never work 'em Sundays."

"How early do you start them out in the morning, usually?"

"Well, I don't never start my slaves 'fore daylight except in pickin' time. Then maybe I get 'em out a quarter of an hour before daylight. But I keep 'em right smart to work through the day." He showed an evident pride in the vigilance of his driver, and called my attention to the large area of ground already hoed over that morning—well hoed, too, as he said.

"At what time do they eat?" I asked. They ate "their snacks" in their cabins, he said, before they came out in the morning, that is before daylight. At this time, the sun rose a little before five, and day dawned about an hour earlier. Then at 12 o'clock their dinner was brought to them in a cart—one cart for the plow-gang and one for the hoe-gang. The hoe-gang ate its dinner in the field, and only stopped work long enough to eat it. The plow-gang drove its teams of mules to the "weather houses," which were open sheds built in different parts of the plantation, under which were cisterns filled with rain water. The water-toters carried water from these cisterns to those at work. The mules were fed as much oats, corn, and fodder as they would eat in two hours. This forage had been brought to the weather houses by another cart. The plowmen had nothing to do but eat their dinner during this time. All worked as late as they could see to work well and had no more food nor rest until they returned to their cabins.

Cisterns are large holes dug in the ground and lined with bricks or stones. They served as reservoirs for water.

At half past nine o'clock, the drivers, each on an alternate night, blew a horn. At ten, the driver visited every cabin to see that its occupants were at rest, rather than spending their strength in fooleries, and to make sure the fires were safe—a very unusual precaution.

The Negroes are generally free, after their day's work is done, till they are called in the morning. When washing and patching were done, wood hauled and cut for the fires, corn ground, etc., I did not learn. Probably all chores that did not have to be done daily, were reserved for Saturday. Custom varies in this respect. In general, the Negroes have to look out for fuel for their cabins themselves. They often have to go to "the swamp" for it, or at least, if it has been hauled, to cut it to a convenient size, after their day's work is done.

The allowance of food was a peck of corn and four pounds of pork for each slave per week. When they could not get "greens," each generally received five pounds of pork. They had gardens, and raised a good deal of food for themselves. They also had chickens and usually plenty of eggs. The overseer added, "The man who owns this plantation does more for his slaves than any other man

A peck is a unit of measurement equivalent to a fourth of a bushel or eight quarts.

Calico is printed cotton cloth.

I know. Every Christmas he sends me up a thousand or fifteen hundred dollars' [about eight to eleven dollars per slave] worth of molasses, coffee, tobacco, calico, and Sunday treats for 'em. Every family on this plantation gets a barrel of molasses at Christmas." (This was not an uncommon practice in Mississippi, though the quantity is rarely so generous. The amount is usually made somewhat proportionate to the value of the last crop sold.)

The overseer also added that the slaves are able, if they choose, to buy certain comforts for themselves—tobacco, for instance—with money earned by Saturday and Sunday work. Some of them went into the swamps on Sunday and made boards. One man sold fifty dollars' worth last year.

42 The Defense of Slavery

Until about 1830, few Americans, either in the North or the South, tried to defend slavery, except to point out that it was so deeply imbedded in the Southern way of life that it could not be eliminated overnight. Several events, however, influenced the positive defense of slavery which began in the South in the early 1830's. In 1831, in Virginia, Nat Turner, a Negro preacher, led a slave revolt in which fifty-seven white people were killed. State and federal troops crushed the revolt, and Turner and his supporters were executed. But the slaves' bid for freedom terrified slaveholders. At about the same time, William Lloyd Garrison began to publish his radical antislavery newspaper, the *Liberator,* which put slave owners on the defensive. Finally, the booming cotton economy in the deep South increased the demand for slave labor.

In 1832, despite the impact which Nat Turner had made and which Garrison was beginning to make on Southern thinking, Southern leaders still argued in public over the merits and evils of slavery. In that year, the members of the Virginia Constitutional Convention debated emancipation proposals which received substantial support. From that time on, however, it became increasingly difficult and dangerous for Southerners to criticize slavery.

During the twenty-five years before the Civil War, Southern leaders, whether they held slaves or not, almost unanimously defended slavery. The "proslavery argument" which they developed took various forms. One argument held that slavery could be justified because the Bible recognized it; another held that it could be justified because Negroes were naturally unequal to white people. The selections in Reading 42 explore the social, political, and economic arguments for slavery. As you read, consider these questions:

1. Why did Calhoun think that the slave was better off than the "free" worker in Europe and the North?
2. How did Calhoun explain the fact that social and political conditions in the South were more stable than in the North? What Northerners do you think he was trying to reach?
3. Why did Brown believe that the non-slaveholder in the South would never be won over by the abolitionists? What do his reasons show about Southern whites' attitudes toward Negroes?
4. Make a list of the reasons Grayson gave for his belief that the slave was better off in America than the free Negro was in Africa? Why, according to Grayson, did the world profit by this change in the Negro's condition?
5. Do you think slavery can ever be justified?

Slavery—"A Positive Good"

Senator John C. Calhoun from South Carolina gave this speech in the United States Senate on February 6, 1837.

Richard K. Crallé, ed., **Works of John C. Calhoun.** New York: D. Appleton and Company, 1856, vol. II, pp. 631–32. Language simplified and modernized.

I believe when two races come together which have different origins, colors, and physical and intellectual characteristics, that slavery is, instead of an evil, a good—a positive good. I must speak freely upon the subject, for the honor and interests of those I represent are involved. I maintain then, that a wealthy and civilized society has never existed in which one part of the community did not, in fact, live on the labor of others. Broad and general as this assertion is, history supports it. It would be easy to trace the various ways by which the wealth of all civilized communities has been divided unequally. It would also be easy to show how a small share has been allotted to those by whose labor it was produced and a large share given to the non-producing classes. Innumerable methods have been used to distribute wealth unequally. In ancient times, brute force was used; in modern times, various financial contrivances [schemes] are used.

I will now compare the position of the African laborer in the South with that of the European worker. I may say with truth that in few countries has so much been left to the laborer's share, and so little expected from him, or where more kind attention is paid to him when he is sick or old. Compare the slaves' condition with that of the tenants of the poorhouses in the more civilized parts of Europe.

I will not dwell on this aspect of the question; rather I will turn to the political issue. Here I fearlessly assert that the existing relationship between the two races in the South, against which these blind fanatics [abolitionists] are waging war, forms the most solid and durable foundation on which to build free and stable political institutions. The fact cannot be disguised that there is and always has been, in an advanced stage of wealth and civilization, a conflict between labor and capital. Slavery exempts Southern society from the disorders and dangers resulting from this conflict. This explains why the political condition of the slaveholding States has been so much more stable and quiet than that of the North.

The Attitude of Non-Slaveholding Southerners Toward Slavery

Senator William H. Seward of New York argued in a Senate speech that the non-slaveholders in the South, who made up a majority of the white population, might be expected to oppose slavery. Senator Albert G. Brown of Mississippi answered Seward on December 22, 1856. Portions of his answer are given here.

Michael W. Cluskey, ed., **Speeches, Messages, and Other Writings of Hon. Albert G. Brown.** Philadelphia: Jas B. Smith and Company, 1859, pp. 484–85. Language simplified and modernized.

This biblical quotation is from **Joshua** 9:21 and means menial workers or servants.

There are, according to the Senator [Seward] three hundred and fifty thousand slaveholding aristocrats in the South. He says that they are men at war with liberty and dangerous to the republic. Only one out of every one hundred of the entire population owns slaves. If you include the children, relatives, and dependents of the slaveholders, he says that the ratio is one in fifteen. Consequently, fourteen out of every fifteen white Southerners have no direct interest in slavery. The non-slaveholders, according to the Senator, are mere "hewers of wood and drawers of water" to the slaveholding aristocrats.

This opens a wide field for speculation. If the Senator expects by such appeals to turn the non-slaveholders against slavery, he will not be successful. They may have no financial interest in slavery, but they have a social interest at stake that is worth more to them than the wealth of all the Indies.

Suppose for the sake of argument that the Senator from New York should succeed in abolishing slavery. What would the social relationship between the two races then be in the South? Could they live together in peace? No one pretends to think that they could. Would the white man be allowed to maintain his superiority if the Negroes were free? Let us examine this question. In my state, there are about three hundred and fifty thousand whites and about an equal number of blacks. Suppose the Negroes were all set free. What would be the immediate and necessary consequence of that? A struggle for supremacy would follow immediately. No more white people would move into the state. The whites already there would have little reason to struggle in the unequal contest between them and the blacks with their millions of sympathizing friends in the free states. The result would be that the wealthy men would gather up their movable property and seek a home in some other country. The poor men, those of little means—the very men the Senator from New York relies on to aid him in carrying out his great scheme of emancipation—would alone be forced to remain behind. Their poverty, not their will, would compel them to stay in Mississippi.

In a few years, with no one going to the state, and thousands upon thousands leaving it in one steady stream, the present balance between the races would be upset. The ratio between the races would be, in a few years, some three, four, or five to one in favor of the blacks. In this state of things, it is not difficult to see what the white man's condition would be. If he were allowed to maintain his equality, he might think himself fortunate; superiority would not be dreamed of. The Negroes, who would be vastly in the majority, would probably claim social ascendency over the whites. If the white man, reduced to such a condition, were allowed to marry his sons to Negro wives, or his daughters to Negro husbands, he might bless his stars. If the Senator from New York expects the aid of non-slaveholders in the South in bringing about this state of social relationships, let me tell him that he is greatly mistaken.

The Hireling and the Slave

William Grayson of South Carolina was a planter, politician, and poet. In 1846, he published a long poem, The Hireling and the Slave, *portions of which are given here. Although the poem has little literary merit, it expresses clearly a point of view widely held in the South.*

William J. Grayson, **The Hireling and the Slave, Chicora, and Other Poems.** Charleston: McCord and Company, 1856, pp. 21–45.

Fallen from primeval innocence and ease,
When thornless fields employed him but to please,
The laborer toils; and from his dripping brow
Moistens the length'ning furrows of the plow;
In vain he scorns or spurns his altered state,
Tries each poor shift, and strives to cheat his fate;
In vain new-shapes his name to shun the ill—
Slave, hireling, help—the curse pursues him still;

primeval: primitive

. . .

Companions of his toil, the axe to wield,
To guide the plow, and reap the teeming field,
A sable multitude unceasing pour
From Niger's banks and Congo's deadly shore;

The Niger River is in West Africa, and the Congo River is in Central Africa. Many slaves came from these regions.

No willing travelers they, that widely roam,
Allured by hope to seek a happier home,
But victims to the trader's thirst for gold,
Kidnapped by brothers, and by fathers sold,
The bondsman born, by native masters reared,
The captive band in recent battle spared;
For English merchants bought; across the main,
In British ships, they go for Britain's gain;
Forced on her subjects in dependent lands,
By cruel hearts and avaricious hands,
New tasks they learn, new masters they obey,
And bow submissive to the white man's sway.
But Providence, by his o'erruling will
Transmutes to lasting good the transient ill,
Makes crime itself the means of mercy prove,
And avarice minister to works of love.
In this new home, whate'er the Negro's fate—
More bless'd his life than in his native state!

. . .

In sloth and error sunk for countless years
His race has lived, but light at last appears—
Celestial light: religion undefiled
Dawns in the heart of Congo's simple child;
Her glorious truths he hears with glad surprise,
And lifts his eye with rapture to the skies;
The noblest thoughts that erring mortals know,
Waked by her influence, in his bosom glow;
His nature owns the renovating sway,
And all the old barbarian melts away.
And now, with sturdy hand and cheerful heart,
He learns to master every useful art,
To forge the axe, to mould the rugged share,
The ship's brave keel for angry waves prepare:
The rising wall obeys his plastic will,
And the loom's fabric owns his ready skill.
Where once the Indian's keen, unerring aim,
With shafts of reed transfixed the forest game,
Where painted warriors late in ambush stood,
And midnight war-whoops shook the trembling wood,
The Negro wins, with well-directed toil,
Its various treasures from the virgin soil.

. . .

These precious products, in successive years,
Trained by a master's skill, the Negro rears;
New life he gives to Europe's busy marts,

Dependent lands refers to the British colonies in North America and the West Indies.

avaricious: greedy

transmutes: changes
transient: temporary

renovating: renewing

The share is the part of a plow that cuts the earth.

The keel is the main timber or, in modern ships, the steel piece, that extends the entire length of the bottom of a ship to support the frame.

marts: markets

To all the world new comforts and new arts;
Loom, spinner, merchant, from his hands drive
Their wealth, and myriads by his labor thrive;
While slothful millions, hopeless of relief,
The slaves of pagan priest and brutal chief,
Harassed by wars upon their native shore,
Still lead the savage life they led before.
Instructed thus, and in the only school
Barbarians ever know—a master's rule,
The Negro learns each civilizing art
That softens and subdues the savage heart,
Assumes the tone of those with whom he lives,
Acquires the habit that refinement gives,
And slowly learns, but surely, while a slave,
The lessons that his country never gave.

. . .

Hence is the Negro come, by God's command,
For wiser teaching to a foreign land;
If they who brought him were by Mammon driven,
Still have they served, blind instruments of Heaven;
And though the way be rough, the agent stern,
No better mode can human wits discern,
No happier system wealth or virtue find,
To tame and elevate the Negro mind:
Thus mortal purposes, whate'er their mood,
Are only means with Heaven for working good;
And wisest they who labor to fulfill,
With zeal and hope, the all-directing will,
And in each change that marks the fleeting year,
Submissive see God's guiding hand appear.

myriads: large numbers of people

Mammon: the false god of material wealth

mode: way

43 The Impact of Slavery on the South

Only a minority of Southern white people owned slaves. Yet because of slavery, the economic, intellectual, and psychological life of the South developed differently from that of the North.

During the thirty years before the Civil War, industry expanded at a tremendous rate in Northern states. Factories multiplied, railroad mileage increased rapidly, and cities grew at a rapid rate. As the North became more urban and more industrial and as its economy became more diversified, the South found itself fastened to a staple agricultural economy based on slave labor. Economic life in the South centered around cotton. Planters sold their cotton crop on the world market for millions of dollars each year. Southerners bragged that because it was America's most profitable export, "cotton was king." But the South was not as prosperous as the North.

The reform movements in the Northern states went hand in hand with industrial expansion and urbanization. During the pre-Civil War decades, free discussion flourished on almost every conceivable subject. Some of the most gifted writers and orators in the North launched intense, prolonged attacks on slavery. Southerners, however, frowned upon reform activity of any kind, and they practically outlawed any criticism of slavery. The economic well-being of many Southerners depended upon slavery. In addition, Southerners feared that criticism would promote unrest among the slaves.

The selections in Reading 43 show the impact of slavery on the economy, the rights of whites and Negroes, and the psychology of the South. As you read, keep these questions in mind:

1. In what ways were Southern planters dependent upon Northern businessmen? What did Southerners mean when they talked about their colonial status?
2. How did Southerners justify their censorship of the mails? Do you think such censorship is ever justified?
3. Why did Clement Eaton make a comparison between the South before the Civil War and South Africa today? Is it valid?
4. How was the emotional climate of the South affected by alleged abolitionist plots and slave revolts? How could such an emotional climate contribute to the coming of the Civil War?

Clement Eaton Describes the South Before the War

Clement Eaton is one of America's leading historians specializing in the South before the Civil War. The excerpts that follow come from two of his books, The Growth of Southern Civilization, 1790–1860, *and* Freedom of Thought Struggle in the Old South.

The Economic Relationship Between North and South

Clement Eaton, **The Growth of Southern Civilization, 1790–1860.** New York: Harper & Row, Publishers, 1961, pp. 196, 216, 218. Abridged.

The most striking characteristic of Southern economy was that although the colonial connection with England had been broken, a new colonialism arose with respect to Northern business. Southern trade in the first half of the nineteenth century came increasingly under the control of Northern men and particularly under the dominance of the port of New York. Credit was a vital need of the

Southern farmers and planters; the North furnished this credit on its own terms. The protective tariff policy, moreover, contributed toward the dependence of the South on the North. The colonial status of the South was underlined by the highly unfavorable balance of trade of the Southern ports. They exported far more than they imported, and European goods destined for Southern consumers were channeled through the port of New York. Northern businessmen were largely the middlemen, the shippers, the bankers, the insurers, that took a lion's share of the profits of Southern agriculture. Every spring and autumn the trek of Southern merchants to Northern mercantile centers dramatized the colonial status of the region below the Potomac. . . .

The dependence of the Southern states on the North for credit, especially for manufactured goods, was the most salient [noticeable] aspect of its colonial status. It was a psychological as well as economic relation. James D. B. De Bow, editor of *De Bow's Review,* pointed out that country merchants in South Carolina who did not have the means to go to New York to buy goods and were forced to buy in Charleston carefully obliterated [blotted out] every mark on a box that indicated the goods were purchased there instead of in New York. "It was quite a plume in the cap of a trader," he reported, "to say he was just from New York, and had purchased his supplies there." Many merchants made the trip to New York not only because of the delusion that they could get cheaper goods there but because of desire to see the life of a big city. Dependence on New York even went so far as to have the Charleston hotel keepers feeding their guests (so rumor said) on turkeys and chickens fattened in abolitionist Ohio and shipped via New York. . . .

The South was . . . exploited by a ruthless industrial power. It became a bitter jest below the Mason-Dixon Line that Southerners began life as babies rocked in Northern cradles and ended it buried in Northern coffins, and that throughout their existence they were dependent on the North for virtually all their manufactured articles. It is ironic that De Bow, the great crusader for Southern economic nationalism, had his industrial review published in the North (after trying several New Orleans printers) and that three fourths of his income from advertisements came from Northern businesses.

The Southern Response to Abolitionist Publications

In the summer of 1835 the Southern people became keenly aware of a new danger that threatened the tranquility of their social system. A powerful, concerted effort of propaganda had been launched against the Southern way of life by the abolition societies of the North. Both the American and the New England antislavery

Clement Eaton, **Freedom of Thought Struggle in the Old South** (New York: Harper Torchbook, 1964, pp. 197–200). Copyright 1940 by Duke University Press, and reprinted with permission.

societies had resolved upon an aggressive campaign to distribute their publications in the South. It was not the object of these societies, so they declared, to distribute such abolitionist literature among slaves or free Negroes in the South. They hoped, rather, to revolutionize public opinion below the Mason and Dixon line by scattering their radical publications "unsparingly" throughout the land of Dixie. Accordingly, tons of antislavery pamphlets, magazines, and newspapers were sent through the mails to prominent Southerners—justices of the peace, ministers, editors, members of Congress, state officials—in other words, leaders of public opinion.

The impact of this deluge of fervid [impassioned] publications on the Southern mind produced a wave of excitement and of anger. In the summer of 1835 a mob of citizens, led by ex-Governor Robert Y. Hayne, entered the post office at Charleston, South Carolina, and destroyed several sacks of mail containing antislavery pamphlets.

One of the most effective measures of safeguarding Southern society from subversive propaganda was the exercise of a censorship over the incoming mails. In 1836 the Virginia legislature passed a law requiring postmasters to notify justices of the peace whenever they received incendiary [inflammatory] publications or publications "denying the right of masters to property in their slaves and inculcating [teaching] the duty of resistance to such right." The justice of the peace should then inquire into the circumstances of the case, and if he were convinced that such writings were dangerous, he should have such books, pamphlets, and other publications burned in his presence and should arrest the addressee, if the latter subscribed for the said book or pamphlet with intent to aid the purposes of the abolitionists or antislavery societies. This law gave a single justice of the peace inquisitorial [arbitrary] power over the mails and, by extension, a dictatorship over the kind of mental food his neighbors were permitted to enjoy. A Maryland act of 1841 commanded the grand juries to summon before them at every term of court all the postmasters in their respective counties and examine them as to whether they had received publications of an inflammatory character, "having a tendency to create discontent among and stir up to insurrection the people of color of this State."

The Southern Response to Attacks on Slavery

Eaton, **The Growth of Southern Civilization, 1790–1860**, pp. 313, 323. Abridged.

William M. Pratt, the Baptist minister at Lexington, Kentucky, wrote in his diary, January 11, 1856, "James Brady, principal of Morton School no. 1, was mobbed, taken out of his house, head shaved and varnished on the face with varnish—he had written a letter to Ohio reflecting severely on the institution of slavery and on Mr. Berkeley, Episcopal preacher. The committee discharged him and he was advised to leave immediately." Pratt condemned the mob spirit, but he commented that the principal had acted foolishly in writing such a severe letter on the Kentuckians and their institutions, thus depriving himself of a good position that paid him a salary of $900. . . .

The "sovereign people" showed little regard for minority opinion within the section. The Charleston merchant, Jacob Schirmer, recorded in his diary in 1848 an instance of it: "a man selling Birds in Broad St. made use of some expression in regard to our domestic institution—was knocked down by Mr. Geo. Walter & was then taken to the Police Office and he left here this afternoon in the Wilmington Boat." Nor did the sovereign people or their leaders have that decent respect for the opinion of mankind to which Jefferson had appealed in the Declaration of Independence. Like South Africa today, the aroused South of 1860 was prepared to defy world opinion and go it alone. When Johnston J. Pettigrew made the minority report to the South Carolina legislature in 1858 against reopening the African slave trade, he said: "The opinion, then, of the outside world on slavery is entitled to less weight than upon almost any other subject, being destitute of every foundation which renders opinion respectable."

The Republic of South Africa has cut itself off from the western world in order to defend its racial policies, called apartheid, which subordinate blacks within the society.

The Psychological Impact of Slavery

Eaton, **Freedom of Thought in the Old South,** pp. 99–100, 116–17.

Although the South was untroubled by any actual insurrections of the slaves after [the revolt led by Nat Turner in] 1831, it was racked at intervals by dark rumors and imagined plots. In the autumn of 1856 it suffered one of the worst panics of fear concerning slave insurrection that it had experienced. In that year the Southern people were disturbed by the prospect of a Republican victory electing Frémont as President. The discovery of most of the actual or supposed plots, however, came after the election. The height of the alarm was reached in December, for it was believed that the rising of the slaves was set for the Christmas holidays. The striking characteristic of this panic was that it spread . . . all over the Southern States, plots being detected in Mississippi, Louisiana, Missouri, Arkansas, South Carolina, Tennessee, Kentucky, and Virginia. The British consul at Richmond reported to his government that the wide diffusion of the plot of servile insurrection and the implication of whites in it indicated that the movement had been planned in the North. This stampede of fear led to the arrest of a number of Negroes, who were severely whipped to secure confessions. The Memphis *Eagle and Enquirer* estimated that during

The Republican party was founded in 1854. In 1856, John C. Frémont, a soldier-explorer, was the first Republican candidate for President. The Republicans favored an end to the extension of slavery.

the excitement not less than forty Negroes were hung for plotting insurrection.

The factor which made the insurrectionary scare of 1856 so intense was the belief that abolition agents had instigated [stirred up] the slaves to revolt. The Savannah *Daily Republican* explained the reports of slave plots all over the South as due to the widespread activities of white instigators. Johnson J. Hooper, editor of the *Daily Montgomery Mail,* believed that the numerous reports of insurrection extending over such a wide area in the South indicated that these plots had been instigated by an organized band of white cutthroats. The same suspicion of abolitionists disaffecting the slaves was expressed by Barksdale, editor of the Jackson *Daily Mississippian.* In an editorial on "Servile Insurrections," he declared: "The conspiracies detected among slaves in Tennessee, Kentucky, South Carolina, and Texas show that the vile emissaries of abolition, working like moles under the ground, have been secretly breathing the poison of insubordination into their minds." These newspapers advocated summary punishment of such meddling white men. . . .

This fear of servile insurrection was not constant but grew so intense at certain times as to amount to a panic or hallucination and then subsided until another stimulus was provided. The period from 1793 to 1801 was one of these storm centers of fear; the years from 1829 to 1832 mark another; in 1845 the Lower South was affected by a hysteria with respect to servile insurrection; while the swift half-decade before the Civil War was in general a time of disquiet and apprehension. Moreover, the Southern press was alarmist in tone, especially during the campaign years of 1856 and 1860. After the discovery of the incendiary pamphlet of David Walker there was always the suspicion that some abolitionist might disaffect the normally contented slaves, or that inflammatory literature might fall into the hands of some brooding Nat Turner. This fear of servile insurrection cannot be dismissed in assessing the causes for [denial of civil liberties in the South].

David Walker was a Negro abolitionist from Boston. In 1829, he published a pamphlet which he distributed to slaves in the South. It urged them to use violence in order to gain their freedom.

44 A Cotton Kingdom Built on Slavery

HISTORICAL ESSAY

Slavery dominated the social, economic, and political life of the South before the Civil War. To understand what slavery was really like, we must distinguish between theory and practice.

Slavery in Theory and Practice

In theory, American slavery was extremely harsh. Some South American countries, such as Brazil, guaranteed slaves certain fundamental rights by law. But slaves in the United States had no rights, for the law defined them as property rather than as persons. Americans considered the freedom of a person to control his property in his own way as a fundamental right. So slaveholders could buy and sell slaves just as they could any other property. The slave had no right to marry, to govern his own children, to learn to read or write, to worship as he pleased, or to sell his own labor.

In practice, slavery was probably not as severe as its legal definition suggests. Slaves were valuable property and common sense led most people to protect and care for their property. Moreover, both slaves and slave owners were human beings, who frequently lived and worked together on close terms and developed strong ties of affection for each other.

On the other hand, the use of violence and brutality helped the slave owners and overseers to wield absolute power over their slaves. Many masters controlled unruly slaves with the whip, as Olmsted saw on the plantation he visited. The scars, brandings, and mutilations mentioned in Southern advertisements for escaped slaves were real enough. No matter how barbarously an owner treated a slave, the slave had no legal recourse. His testimony against a white man could not be heard in court. When Mark Twain was a boy in Hannibal, Missouri, he saw a clumsy Negro slave clubbed to death by an angry overseer. "Nobody in the village approved of the murder," Twain later recalled, "but, of course, no one said much about it. Considerable sympathy was felt for the slave's owner, who had been bereft of valuable property by a worthless person who was not able to pay for it."

The Social Structure of the Pre-War South

We cannot understand life in the South before the Civil War unless we distinguish sharply between romantic descriptions of the South given in the Hollywood movies and the historical novels of the first half of the twentieth century, and the South as it actually was. The stately mansion house, attended by hundreds of faithful Negroes, shielded by graceful magnolias, and surrounded by vast well-tended cotton fields was not entirely a myth. Such places actually did exist in the South, but they were even less common than millionaires' mansions are in our society today.

At the risk of some oversimplification, we can divide the free population of the South into five large social classes. The first group, representing the top of the Southern economic and social order, consisted of planters. A man needed to have twenty slaves devoted to agriculture and to own a minimum of 500 to 1000 acres of land to belong in this elite class. The census of 1860 counted only about 46,000 planters. Of this number only about 2000 were large planters who owned 100 or more slaves. In the entire South in 1860, only thirteen planters owned more than 500 slaves.

It is clear, therefore, that vast plantations are far more common in the romantic legends, which Americans have spun about the South, than they ever were in historical fact. The great majority of planters lived rather simply on small plantations. But statistics cannot tell the whole story, because the planters possessed an influence far greater than their numbers indicate. The large planters, who represented the social ideal for almost all white Southerners, came as close to being aristocrats as any people have in American history. They patterned their lives after the style of English country gentlemen, and their distaste for commerce and industry helped to keep the South agricultural. In politics, they were the most important group in the South. Their political power rested on a sound economic base because the planters, large and small, produced most of the crops which the South sold to the North and in Europe.

By far the largest group in the South, comparable to the middle class in the North, consisted of farmers. In states such as North Carolina and Louisiana, two thirds of all farms contained less than 100 acres. Some farmers owned a few slaves and worked alongside them in the fields, but most farmers did not have enough capital to buy slaves. The average farmer owned his own land, lived in a two-room log house, grew enough cotton or tobacco to get money for taxes and store-bought goods which he could not produce himself, and spent most of his energy raising food crops and livestock. These farmers were the backbone of the South. They were not as well educated as their counterparts in the North, but they were hard working and ambitious. Some farmers were successful enough to buy slaves and become planters. Others left their farms to work as overseers on large plantations so that they might save money and start their own plantations. They were staunch defenders of slavery and made up the bulk of the Confederate Army after 1860.

Businessmen and professional people made up a third class. Merchants, known as "factors," were its most important members. Factors worked out of major Southern cities, and sold planters' crops for a commission. They also acted frequently as middlemen in helping planters to purchase supplies for the coming year. Many planters were constantly in debt to such merchants.

A small number of Southern manufacturers, most of them in the lumber, tobacco, textile, flour milling, or iron industries, made up a fourth group. Their role was not nearly as important as that of manufacturers in the North. Industry was less developed in the South. At the time of the Civil War, for example, the town of Lowell, Massachusetts, had as much textile manufacturing machinery as the whole South, where capital was absorbed largely in the purchase of slaves. In addition, the Southern industrialist, like the lawyer, doctor, and teacher, enjoyed less prestige than the planter.

Three kinds of people outside the mainstream of Southern life composed a final group. The first of these consisted of mountain people, who lived in isolated areas of the Appalachian and Ozark Mountains. They practiced a hardy, subsistence agriculture, spurned slavery almost entirely, and clung to traditional folkways, many of which could be traced back to Elizabethan England. These mountain people, sometimes called Southern Highlanders, were the one group that refused to support the Confederacy in the Civil War.

At the bottom of the white social ladder were the "poor whites." These "stranded frontiersmen," numbering perhaps a half million people in 1850, carried on a meager existence in squalid cabins on some of the most worn-out land in the South. Beaten down by energy-sapping diseases, such as hookworm and malaria, their most important characteristic was an unrelenting determination to keep the Negro slave in his place—at the absolute bottom of the Southern social system.

Free Negroes, who numbered about a quarter of a million before the Civil War, were most decisively outside the mainstream of Southern life. Some of them had been freed by their masters; others were descendants of freed slaves. A few had been allowed to work, save money, and purchase their own freedom. Almost all free Negroes lived hazardous lives. Laws curtailed drastically their freedom to work, move around the country, or meet together. A few free Negroes in the South prospered; some even owned slaves. But the majority lived in poverty and an atmosphere of fear and suspicion. Free Negroes had little place in a society based on Negro slavery.

The Cotton Kingdom

Agriculture provided the economic base for the Southern way of life. In the upper South, farmers raised many different kinds of crops. Virginia still grew more tobacco than any other state, but it also produced large quantities of wheat. In 1850, the South grew more than half the nation's corn and four fifths of its peas and beans. But Southern agriculture concentrated on the cultivation of staple crops for sale in the world market. Rice plantations dotted the coasts of Georgia and South Carolina. Sugar plantations flourished in lower Louisiana. Cotton, of course, was the greatest crop, with cotton fields spreading from North Carolina to Texas.

The South earned its description as "The Cotton Kingdom." In 1820, the cotton crop was 160 million pounds. In the decades that followed, more and more people in Europe and America chose cotton over woolen and linen clothing and the American cotton crop grew spectacularly. By 1860, the South grew over a billion pounds of cotton, which accounted for two thirds of all American exports.

Many of the great Southern plantations were highly efficient agricultural units, but increased cotton production resulted not from more efficient means of production, but from expanded acreage. From about 1820 until the outbreak of the Civil War, the center of the Cotton Kingdom moved steadily south and west to the new, rich soils of Alabama, Mississippi, Arkansas, and Texas. During the "Age of Jackson" speculators brought and sold land frenziedly. Nowhere was speculation more rampant than in the Southern states where men vied with each other to control valuable cotton land.

The expansion of cotton agriculture into the Southwest helped to fasten slavery even more tightly upon the South. As new lands opened to cultivation, the demand for slave labor increased. States in the upper South, such as Maryland, Virginia, Kentucky, and Tennessee, found themselves caught up in a profitable domestic slave trade with the new cotton states. Estimates suggest that almost a half million slaves were moved from the upper to the lower South in the twenty years before the war. During this period, the price of a good field slave rose as high as $1700, and about sixty percent of all slaves worked on cotton plantations.

The Economic Impact of Slavery

Was slavery economically profitable for the South? Historians have argued this question for a long time. Without any doubt some Southerners found slavery profitable. John H. Randolph bought a modest Louisiana plantation in 1841, with a down payment of $863. Before the outbreak of the Civil War, he had expanded his holdings to several thousand acres, increased his slaves from twenty-three to almost two hundred, and built an elegant fifty-one room mansion which still stands. Other Southerners enjoyed similar successes, although usually on a smaller scale. Men made fortunes buying and selling slaves. Some successful planters began as slave traders.

Against this evidence historians have argued that because the slave had no personal economic incentives he was bound to be an inefficient worker. Because his master controlled his working conditions and compensation absolutely, the slave was not encouraged to experiment with new, more efficient ways of work. He had no reason to take particular care of valuable tools or machinery, and he had to be closely supervised in even the simplest task.

The weight of evidence suggests, however, that the average, well-run plantation could make a reasonable profit. Certainly slaveholders themselves thought slavery was profitable—an important reason they defended it so tenaciously.

At the same time, slavery had an unfavorable economic impact on the South in the long run. While cotton fields expanded in the South, factories expanded in the North. While the South contributed vastly to the national wealth by producing the American commodity most in demand on the world market, it still found itself dependent on the North. As one Southerner wrote in 1857:

> The North is the Mecca of our merchants, and to it they must and do make two pilgrimages per annum—one in the spring and one in the fall. All our commercial, mechanical, manufactural, and literary supplies come from there. We want Bibles, brooms, buckets, and books, and we go to the North; we want pens, ink, paper, wafers and envelopes, and we go to the North; we want shoes, hats, handkerchiefs, umbrellas and pocket knives, and we go to the North; we want furniture, crockery, glassware and pianos, and we go to the North; we want toys, primers, school books, fashionable apparel, machinery, medicines, tombstones, and a thousand other things, and we go to the North for them all. Instead of keeping our money in circulation at home, by patronizing our own mechanics, manufacturers, and laborers, we send it all away to the North, and there it remains; it never falls into our hands again.

Hinton Rowan Helper, **The Impending Crisis of the South: How to Meet It.** New York: Burdick Brothers, 1857 p. 22.

The South depended on the North for more than manufactured goods. Many planters shipped their cotton in Northern ships through Northern harbors, and they borrowed money from Northern banks. Southern leaders before the Civil War complained about their "colonial" status with respect to the North and tried to do something about it. Southern businessmen held commercial conventions in order to stimulate development of Southern factories and investigate ways to promote direct trade between the South and Europe. In 1858, the Virginia legislature granted a charter to the Atlantic Steam Ferry Company to build four great steamships which would carry cotton directly from Southern ports to England. Like most similar proposals, this one failed. The South continued to produce most of the nation's exports and to put much of the profit from those exports into the hands of Northern businessmen.

The Psychological Effects of Slavery

Equally important as the long-run economic consequences of slavery on the South have been the psychological effects of slavery.

A twentieth-century study of the psychological impact of slavery on the slave compares the effect that slavery may have had on Negroes with the effect that concentration camps had on Hitler's prisoners during World War II. The study suggests that both forms of slavery created a kind of childish, irresponsible personality that identified with his master. Whether we accept this explanation or not, we must realize that while most white Americans learned to be ambitious and self-reliant, the slave learned that complete subservience was his best path for self-preservation. In other words, the cultural and psychological forces that shaped the lives of millions of Negro slaves before the Civil War differed radically from the forces that shaped the lives of most other Americans.

Slavery also influenced profoundly the lives of white people in the South. After about 1830, most Southern whites ceased to apologize for slavery and began to defend it fiercely: The best minds in the South attempted to show that Southern civilization based on slave labor was superior to Northern civilization based on free labor. We have read Calhoun's argument that Negro slaves, who he claimed were naturally inferior to white people, freed Southern whites from the drudgery of manual labor so that they might devote their energies to the higher arts. Southern journalists, such as George Fitzhugh, spread the idea of a separate and superior Southern civilization throughout the South. While New England writers such as Emerson and Thoreau wrote essays and poems celebrating the values of equality and individualism, Southern novelists, such as William Gilmore Simms and William Caruthers, wrote novels celebrating the aristocratic quality of Southern life.

Sir Walter Scott (1771–1832) was the most popular British writer in the South. His romantic tales of medieval English lords and ladies appealed to a people who believed that life on a Southern plantation represented the high point in American civilization. Southern planters referred to themselves as "cavaliers" after English aristocrats of the seventeenth century and copied many of the "chivalrous" traditions of the old English aristocracy. On holidays, for example, plantation owners sometimes met for contests in horsemanship and for jousting matches just as King Arthur and his knights had done hundreds of years before in England.

Southerners from lower levels of society also defended slavery. Senator Brown of Mississippi noted that Southerners without slaves supported the system as vigorously as slaveholders themselves. Many Southerners defended slavery because they were afraid. As Professor Eaton pointed out, they feared that antislavery agitation would incite slaves to revolt, and in places where slaves outnumbered whites, slave revolts might result in bloodshed and massacres. Actually there were very few slave revolts before the Civil War. The absence of slave uprisings did not allay the white Southerner's fears.

Especially strong among the lower-class white people was the fear that if Negroes were freed, their own social and economic position would be threatened. As long as slavery existed, these poor whites, no matter how miserable their own living conditions might be, could take comfort not being at the bottom of society.

Southern Attitudes Affect Civil Liberties

Because of these fears, the South took severe measures in the thirty years before the Civil War to protect itself from all criticism of slavery. Southern states passed laws making it a crime to write or speak against slavery or to possess antislavery literature. Mails were censored, and mobs frequently attacked individuals suspected of holding antislavery views and drove them from the South. Such measures were "democratic" in the sense that the great majority of Southerners supported them. At the same time, the South, because of its position on slavery, denied its citizens basic civil liberties.

The denial of these liberties also occurred, to a lesser degree, in the North. Opponents of the abolitionists mobbed antislavery meetings in attempts to break them up. Such blatant attempts to thwart the right of free assembly and free speech won for abolitionists the support of many Americans who lived outside the South.

Meanwhile, as the abolitionists grew more numerous and more vocal, Southerners retreated into angry and frightened isolation. They felt that their property was under attack. Moreover, they did not believe that they could ever live together in peace and harmony with a free Negro population. The issue of slavery became a racial problem—not only in the South. It became an American problem.

SUGGESTED READINGS

CURRENT, RICHARD, *John C. Calhoun.* This interesting brief biography describes the life of the most famous spokesman for the antebellum South.

FRANKLIN, JOHN HOPE, *The Militant South.* This interesting book emphasizes the effects of slavery on white society in the South before the Civil War.

STAMPP, KENNETH, *The Peculiar Institution.* This well written and detailed study of slavery was based largely on plantation records.

National Growth and Manifest Destiny

CHAPTER 12

STATING THE ISSUE

Two developments dominated American history in the first half of the nineteenth century. One development was the emergence of America as a mature, powerful nation, which grew economically, socially, territorially, and culturally. The other development was the increasing sectional differences between the North and the South which foreshadowed the Civil War.

During the first half of the nineteenth century, total American population increased more than thirty percent every ten years as European immigrants supplemented the rapidly growing native population. Long-established cities in the East grew at an astonishing rate, while new cities sprang up overnight in the West. The market economy, which had begun to develop after the War of 1812, expanded rapidly in the 1840's and 1850's when railroads began to link the nation together. Americans built new factories and developed new machinery which expanded economic opportunities. Products from American farms and factories played an increasingly important role in world trade.

Americans also continued the push westward. By 1820, few Americans had ventured beyond the Missouri River. In the 1840's, they launched substantial settlements on the shores of the Pacific Ocean and began to press upon the Mexican border in the Southwest and the British border in Oregon. Many Americans believed that their flag was destined to fly over the entire continent.

Yet the tremendous growth exacted a heavy price. The increase in population and industrial activity intensified differences between North and South. American settlements in the Southwest provoked a costly war with Mexico which divided Americans. Moreover, the territory acquired in the Mexican War precipitated the greatest political crisis the nation had known since the question of slavery in Missouri had been raised in 1819.

In this chapter, we will examine American growth in the three decades before the Civil War. In what ways was America becoming a great nation? What accounted for American economic growth? Why did many Americans believe that their nation should dominate the continent? How did American growth contribute to sectional differences? These are the major issues raised in Chapter 12.

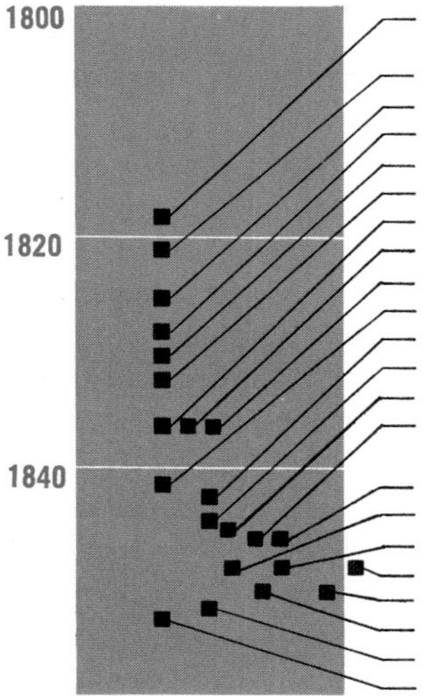

1818	United States and Britain provide for disarmament of the Great Lakes in Rush-Bagot Agreement.
1821	Americans begin settling Mexico.
1825	New York officials formally open Erie Canal.
1828	Andrew Jackson is elected President.
1830	Mexico forbids further American settlement.
1832	Cyrus McCormick successfully demonstrates his reaper.
1836	Mexican army besieges Texans at the Alamo.
1836	Sam Houston becomes president of Republic of Texas.
1836	Martin Van Buren is elected President.
1841	President William Henry Harrison dies; John Tyler becomes President.
1842	United States and Britain settle Maine boundary dispute in Webster-Ashburton Treaty.
1844	James K. Polk is elected President.
1845	Texas enters the Union.
1846	United States and Britain sign a treaty setting boundary of Oregon Territory at the 49th parallel.
1846	United States declares war on Mexico.
1848	Prospectors discover gold in California.
1848	Treaty of Guadalupe Hidalgo ends Mexican War.
1848	Zachary Taylor is elected President.
1850	President Taylor dies; Millard Fillmore becomes President.
1850	California is admitted to the Union.
1852	Franklin Pierce is elected President.
1853	Congress approves Gadsden Purchase from Mexico.

45 Westward Expansion

The western line of American settlement in the 1820's extended in an uneven line to the Missouri River. The vast prairies further west had come to the United States with the Louisiana Purchase in 1803, but their apparent barrenness and harsh climate discouraged settlers. Mexico owned most of the region in the Southwest from Texas to California. In the Northwest, both Britain and the United States claimed the Oregon Territory, which comprised the present states of Oregon, Washington, Idaho, parts of Montana and Wyoming, and parts of western Canada. By 1853, the boundaries of the continental United States had been extended to its present borders.

Settlers believed the land was barren because trees did not grow on the Great Plains. In reality, much of the soil was very fertile.

The United States gained its vast, new territories through diplomacy and war. Even before the United States acquired title to these lands, the American people had refused to be held back by geographic or political barriers. They had begun to settle in Texas as early as 1821 with the encouragement of land grants from the Mexican government. By 1830, there were 30,000 Americans in Texas, and tensions increased steadily between them and their Mexican rulers. Few Americans settled in California and New Mexico before 1848, but Yankee sea captains traded with San Francisco and western merchants carried on trade with New Mexico over the famous Santa Fe Trail. As America's interest in new western lands increased in the 1840's, many journalists and political leaders began to talk as if it were the nation's natural right—its "manifest destiny," as they called it—to acquire them.

Reading 45 presents seven short excerpts written by expansion-minded Americans during the 1830's and 1840's. In preparation for class, you are to read each passage carefully. After you have read a passage, write down in one sentence in your notebook the argument or arguments each writer makes for expansion. When you have finished all of the passages, write a hypothesis about the motives for territorial expansion which these selections suggest.

Because of the nature of this lesson, no study questions have been provided.

A Discovery Exercise

1

John L. O'Sullivan, **The United States Magazine and Democratic Review,** no. LXXV (July–August 1845), pp. 5–6, 9–10. Abridged from original.

Were other reasoning wanting in favor of elevating this question of the reception of Texas into our Union, it is surely to be found in the manner in which other nations have undertaken to intrude themselves into it for the avowed purpose of thwarting our policy and hampering our power, limiting our greatness and checking the fulfillment of our manifest destiny to overspread the continent allotted by Providence for the free development of our yearly multiplying millions. California will probably secede next. Imbecile and distracted, Mexico never can exert any real governmental authority over such a country. Already the advance guard of the irresistible army of Anglo-Saxon emigration has begun to pour down upon it, armed with the plough and the rifle, and marking its trail with schools and colleges, courts and representative halls, mills and meetinghouses. They will necessarily become independent. Their right to independence will be the natural right of self-government belonging to any community strong enough to maintain it. Away, then with all talk of balances of power on the American Continent. Whosoever may hold the balance, though they should cast into the opposite scale all the bayonets and cannon, not only of France and England, but of Europe entire, how would it kick the beam against the simple solid weight of the two hundred and fifty or three hundred millions—and American millions—destined to gather beneath the flutter of the stripes and stars, in the fast hastening year of the Lord, 1845!

Anglo-Saxon means people of English descent. As used here, Anglo-Saxon emigration refers to English-speaking Americans who were moving west.

In this context, balance of power refers to the notion of some Americans who opposed national expansion and contended that the continent should remain divided between the United States and Great Britain. Great Britain claimed the Pacific Northwest.

The author exaggerated population growth. The population of the United States in 1845 was 20,182,000, according to modern estimates by the Bureau of the Census.

2

Speech of Commodore Robert F. Stockton, who was stationed off the coast of California before the Mexican War, in **Niles National Register,** vol. XXIII, no. 21 (January 22, 1848), p. 335.

If I were now the sovereign authority, I would prosecute this war for the express purpose of redeeming Mexico from misrule and civil strife. The priceless boon of civil and religious liberty has been confided to us as trustees. I would insist, if the war were to be prolonged for fifty years, and cost money enough to demand from us each year the half of all that we possess, I would still insist that the inestimable blessings of civil and religious liberty should be guaranteed to Mexico. We must not shrink from the solemn duty. We dare not shrink from it.

The reference is to the Mexican War (1846–1848) fought between the United States and Mexico.

3

If the Creator had separated Texas from the union by mountain barriers, the Alps or the Andes, there might be plausible objections [to the annexation of Texas]; but he has planed down the whole [Mississippi] Valley, including Texas, and united every atom of the soil and every drop of the waters of the mighty whole. He has linked their rivers with the great Mississippi, and marked and united the whole for the dominion of one government and the residence of one people.

Senator Robert J. Walker, **Letter of Mr. Walker of Mississippi Relative to the Annexation of Texas in Reply to the Call of the People of Carroll County, Kentucky, To Communicate his Views on that Subject.** Washington, D.C.: Globe Office, 1844, p. 8.

In 1836, under the leadership of General Sam Houston, the Texans defeated the Mexicans and captured Santa Anna (1795–1876), the Mexican president. Santa Anna granted independence to the Texans who then requested annexation to the Union.

4

Sir, where were we two centuries ago? We were a feeble band of pilgrims on Plymouth rock, and a small band of cavaliers on the southern sands. From this small beginning, and in this short time, we have gone on, step by step, multiplying and advancing toward the Pacific, till the aborigines [Indians] of the country had disappeared before us, like the mists of morning before the sun. . . . To the Pacific ocean it is our destiny to go. The hand of Providence pointed us onward.

Shall we pause in our career, or retrace our steps because the British lion has chosen to place himself in our path [in Oregon]? Had our blood already become so pale that we should tremble at the roar of the king of beasts? We shall not go out of our way to seek a conflict with him; but if he crosses our path, and refuses to move at a peaceful command, he will run his nose in the talons of the American eagle. . . .

England's greatness rests upon her commerce. She has three hundred millions tons of shipping. We already have two hundred millions, and are gathering upon her with the strides of a swift courser. When we pass her, her downfall, by peaceable means, will be rapid and sudden. Oregon was, therefore all-important to us in a commercial point of view. It [will give] us a lever that will overturn the world. It will give us a cluster of manufacturing and navigating states on the Pacific, united to the New England States on the Atlantic. Then the inhabitants of the Mississippi Valley . . . will stretch one hand to the Eastern world through the Pacific chain, and the other to Europe through the Atlantic chain, grasping the trade of the world, as we now hold possession of the means of subsistence for the whole human family.

Representative Andrew Kennedy of Indiana in **Congressional Globe,** 29th Congress, 1st Session, pp. 180–81.

Senator Thomas Hart Benton, **Thirty Years' View or; A Short History of the Working of the American Government for Thirty Years, from 1820 to 1850.** New York: D. Appleton and Company, 1854, vol. I, p. 675.

The Brazos and the Colorado rivers are in Texas, which Congress annexed to the United States in February 1845.

5

. . . The Texan revolt has illustrated the Anglo-Saxon character, and given it new titles to the respect and admiration of the world.

It shows that liberty, justice, valor—moral, physical and intellectual power—discriminate that race wherever it goes. Let our America rejoice, let Old England rejoice, that the Brassos [Brazos] and Colorado, new and strange names—streams far beyond the western bank of the Father of Floods [Mississippi River]—have felt the impress, and witnessed the exploits of a people sprung from their loins, and carrying their language, laws, and customs, their *magna charta* and its glorious privileges, into new regions and far distant climes.

Speech by Senator Lewis Cass of Michigan, February 10, 1847, in **Congressional Globe,** 29th Congress, 2nd Session, Appendix, pp. 186–96.

6

A strong desire pervades this country, that a region, extending west of our present possessions to the Pacific Ocean, should be acquired and become part of our Confederacy. . . . It would give us a large territory, a great deal of it calculated for American settlement and cultivation, and it would connect us with the great western ocean, giving us a front along its shores in connection with Oregon of, perhaps, thirteen or fourteen degrees of latitude. It would give us also the magnificent bay of St. Francisco, one of the noblest anchorages in the world, capable of holding all the navies of the earth; and from its commanding position, controlling, in some measure, the trade of the northern Pacific. But, sir, besides these advantages, commercial and geographical, there are important political considerations, which point to extension as one of the great measures of safety for our institutions.

We want almost unlimited power of expansion. That is our safety valve. Wherever other evils betide us, we shall be free from the evils of a dense population, with scanty means of subsistence, and with no hope of advancement.

President Polk's First Annual Message to Congress, December 2, 1845, in James Richardson, ed., **A Compilation of the Messages and Papers of the Presidents.** Washington, D.C.: Government Printing Office, 1897, vol. IV, pp. 398–99. Abridged from original.

7

We must ever maintain the principle that the people of this continent alone have the right to decide their own destiny. Should any portion of them, constituting an independent state, propose to unite themselves with our Confederacy, this will be a question for them and us to determine without any foreign [intervention]. Near a quarter of a century ago the principle was distinctly announced to the world, in the annual message of one of my predecessors [President Monroe], that—

> The American continents, by the free and independent condition which they have assumed and maintained, are hence-

forth not to be considered as subject for future colonization by any European powers.

This principle will apply with greatly increased force should any European power attempt to establish any new colony in North America. Existing rights of every European nation should be respected, but it is due alike to our safety and our interests that the efficient protection of our laws should be extended over our whole territorial limits, and that it should be distinctly announced to the world as our settled policy that no future European colony or dominion shall with our consent be planted or established on any part of the North American continent.

46 Industrial Expansion

Territorial expansion was one dimension of American growth. Economic expansion was another. The industrial revolution, which had begun at the end of the eighteenth century, increased at an accelerating rate during the first half of the nineteenth century. By 1859, the value of American industrial products exceeded the value of its agricultural products for the first time.

Several factors contributed to the growth of industry during this period. A vast natural resource base had always been present. Increasing immigration from Europe supplied labor for factories. American workers readily adopted new inventions and methods of doing work. Consequently, technological changes were put to practical use more rapidly in America than in Europe. Population growth and western expansion also helped create an expanding market for American manufactured goods. Capital came from accumulated savings, foreign investors, and government subsidies.

Perhaps the transportation revolution was the greatest factor in the growth of industry. The turnpikes and canals built after the War of 1812 spurred economic growth in the 1820's by linking western farmers and merchants with manufacturers in the Northeast. In the decades that followed, western settlement, industrial growth, and the improvement of transportation facilities continued to be related closely. The most spectacular development was the building of the railroads. Railroad construction began in the United States about 1830; by 1840, the United States had 3328 miles of track, nearly double the mileage in all Europe. By 1860, this mileage had increased to over 30,000.

The first selection in Reading 46 analyzes the significance of railroads to the American economy; the second relates improvements in transportation to the growth of manufactures in the 1850's; and the third considers the impact of public education on American industry. As you read, try to answer the following questions:

1. Why did the construction of railroads increase the value of property in both country and city?
2. What connection do the authors of the second excerpt find between the growth of industry and the growth of agriculture? How did this growth affect the relationships between the North, West, and South?
3. What was the significance of the large number of new patents issued in the 1840's and 1850's?
4. In what ways did George Wallis think that public education served American industry?

The Impact of Railroads on Economic Development

I. D. Andrews prepared a Report on the Trade and Commerce of the British North American Colonies *in 1853. Portions of that Report relating to the impact of the railroads on the American economy are given here.*

Senate Executive Documents No. 112 and **House Executive Documents** No. 136, 32nd Congress, 1st Session. Washington, D.C.: Armstrong, 1853, pp. 380–84. Language simplified and modernized.

The wide distances that separate producers from consumers implies that each will have to ship his surplus products to the other. The western farmer has no local market for his wheat, as all of his neighbors have a surplus of wheat. The total surplus of the area where he lives has to be exported to consumers in the eastern United States or in Europe. In turn, the farmer has to import all of the various articles he uses which he does not produce himself.

Railroads in the United States also exert a great influence upon the value of property. The actual increase in the value of land, due to the construction of the railroads, can only be approximated. Not only do railroads affect the price of farm lands and city and village lots that lie close to the tracks, but they also influence the value of real estate in cities hundreds or thousands of miles away. The railroads of Ohio, for example, exert as much influence on raising the price of real estate in New York City as do the railroads within the state of New York.

There is no doubt that the increased value of the farm land alone through which the railroad runs is many times greater than the cost of building the railroad. It is believed that the construction of three thousand miles of railroad in Ohio will increase the value of the property of that state to at least five times the cost of the railroads.

In addition to advancing the price of farm lands, the railroads in Ohio also stimulate the growth of cities within the state. In Massachusetts, the value of property went up from $290,000,000 to $580,000,000 between 1840 to 1850—due largely to the railroads built within the state.

But even this is not the most forceful illustration of the value of the railroads. Deposits of coal and iron may be entirely useless without a railroad. With a railroad, every ton of ore is worth one, two, three, or four dollars. Without coal, our commerce, industry, and agriculture would not have grown to their present enormous size. Yet this economic growth has been achieved by a few railroads and canals in Pennsylvania which have not cost over $50,000,000. With these transportation facilities, coal can be brought into the New York market for about $3.50 per ton; without them, coal would not have been available in New York for fuel nor as a source of power.

The Impact of Machines on Economic Development

Thomas C. Cochran and William Miller are distinguished American economic historians.

Thomas C. Cochran and William Miller, **The Age of Enterprise, A Social History of Industrial America.** New York: Harper & Row, Publishers, 1961, pp. 56–59.

Men and oxen, horses and mules are plodders compared with machines. Had the United States to depend upon animal power, it would have developed at a medieval pace. The factories of the East would have choked on their goods without railroads to rush them to market. Eastern banks would have slept on their credit without the express and telegraph. The West grew a wheat crop large enough to feed the nation in 1860, but that crop would have rotted in the fields had there been no machines to harvest it. It would have overflowed the warehouses had it depended upon old-fashioned wagons and flatboats for distribution.

In 1844, Samuel F.B. Morse successfully developed the telegraph in the United States. The first telegraph message was transmitted from San Francisco to Washington, D.C., on October 24, 1861. By 1870, shortly after the merger of the Western Union Telegraph Company with the American Telegraph Company, which controlled lines in the East, thousands of miles of wire bound the nation together.

In 1840, by rivers, canals, or turnpikes, through the Gulf or up the coast, it took almost a week to go from New York to Cleveland, Cincinnati, or Louisville; two weeks to New Orleans, St. Louis, or Detroit; three weeks to Chicago or Milwaukee. By 1860 weeks had been reduced to days: St. Louis was seventy-two hours from New York; Detroit and Chicago, forty-eight; Cleveland, less than twenty-four. As early as 1851, J. D. B. De Bow declared that northern enterprise had "rolled back the mighty tide of the Mississippi and its ten thousand tributary streams until their mouth, practically and commercially, is more at New York and Boston than at New Orleans." Canals aided in this manipulation of nature, but railroads completed the job. Speedier, unimpeded by frost or low water, railroads by 1860 had joined the western granary to eastern and western fac-

J. D. B. De Bow (1820–1867) of New Orleans was a leading Southern economist and editor before the Civil War.

tories, had joined markets to the new machines, the country to the town. Communication, not production, was the key to industrialism in the United States. Settled haphazardly to suit real estate speculators rather than farmers or manufacturers, America was made up of separate economic areas, gratuitously [freely] dispersed, needlessly distant from markets or raw materials until knit by railroad and telegraph into a cohesive [unified] Union. By 1860, east of the Mississippi this cohesion had been achieved.

Farmers use a scythe to cut grass, a sickle to cut grass and grain, and a flail to thresh grain by hand.

Before turnpikes, canals, or railroads were extended into new areas, the western farmer like his eastern forebear of an earlier period ground his own flour and made his own clothes. He sowed his seed broadcast [scattered by hand], reaped with scythe and sickle, harvested with his hands, and threshed with his flail. He produced for his table and his neighbor just as the household worker in the East had spun cotton and wool, made shoes, coats, and furniture for the area around his home and shop. By the late thirties, however, as machines grew in number and regional specialization increased, this local self-sufficiency was passing; by the time of the Civil War it had virtually disappeared. . . .

By 1860 . . . [e]arly transportation facilities had made the factory possible and every subsequent advance in speed of communication and accessibility of cities had increased in "circle of the market" for manufactured goods. At the outbreak of the Civil War northern farmers had very largely abandoned household industry and had begun to concentrate on money crops while in limited specialized areas industrial production was carried on for the whole nation. The South, overladen with slaves and satisfied with the glacial [slow-moving] pace of feudal agriculture, could not so easily adapt itself to the changes going on all about it. In the East and West, however, farm and factory grew steadily in size, enlisted more and more men and machines, speeded operations many times, and by 1865 had proved the supremacy of industrial culture.

Carders combed the fibers of wool, cotton, or flax, in preparation for spinning thread. Running water turned water wheels to provide power to operate machines.

An exhibition is an organized display of the artistic and industrial products of many countries.

. . . In expanding America there was a premium on new devices, new gadgets, and 5942 new patents were issued in the 1840's; 23,140, in the 1850's. Mechanical drills and saws, steam engines, carders, water wheels, pumps—all were being improved while our new agricultural machinery was winning world supremacy. At the Paris Exhibition in 1854, six men were pitted against four different threshers for half an hour. Their respective labors yielded:

Six men with flails	60 liters of wheat
Belgian thresher	150 liters of wheat
French thresher	250 liters of wheat
English thresher	410 liters of wheat
American thresher	740 liters of wheat

In another test, an Algerian reaper cut an acre of oats in seventy-two minutes, an English reaper in sixty-six, an American in twenty-two. The job would have taken the best hand worker three times as long as the slowest machine. At the same time, water turbines were increasing factory efficiency 50 per cent. Sewing machines in carpet factories were doing the work of eight or ten men; in the boot and shoe industry and the manufacture of ready-to-wear clothes, sewing machines worked a revolution in speed and costs of production. Rapid express service after 1840 and uniform postage rates a decade later speeded and cheapened exchange. In communication of orders, in the settlement of bank balances, in determining the state of distant markets, the telegraph was like a favorable wind. Stimulated by these improvements American manufactures in 1850 passed the billion dollar mark in value. By 1860 this figure was almost doubled.

A turbine is an engine which is driven by the pressure of water or steam.

The Impact of Education on Economic Development

In 1853, the British government sent a commission to the New York Industrial Exhibition. One of the observers, George Wallis from a technical school in Birmingham, England, wrote a "Special Report," portions of which are given here.

"Special Report of Mr. George Wallis," New York Industrial Exhibition, **Parliamentary Paper,** 1854, pp. 3, 67–68. Language simplified and modernized.

The Americans display fully the versatility of an educated people. They strive constantly to overcome their shortage of skilled labor by applying mechanical power to manufacturing. An observer is impressed with the advantages of the public school systems of the New England states and Pennsylvania which educate all of the young people. In these states, where sound and systematic education has been practiced longest and where no doubt it is carried out best, the greatest manufacturing developments are found. The greatest proportion of skilled workmen in the United States are educated in these states both in fundamental knowledge and in the skillful application of their ingenuity to the practical arts and to the manufacturing industry. From these states, they spread throughout the nation, becoming the originators, directors, and, ultimately, the proprietors of factories.

There is no apprenticeship system as such, in the United States. The more useful a young man becomes to his employer, the more he profits. With a mind prepared by school discipline and education, the American working boy develops rapidly into a skilled artisan. After he has mastered one part of the business, he is not content until he has mastered it all. Doing one mechanical operation well does not satisfy either him or his employer. He is ambitious to do

England inherited its system for training craftsmen from the medieval guilds. Young men worked, usually for seven years, as apprentices to master craftsmen in order to learn a trade. They then became journeymen and worked for wages until they became masters and owners of their own shops. American systems of apprenticeship were far less rigid.

something more than one set task, and therefore, he learns all tasks. He is allowed to learn other parts of his trade as a reward for becoming master of the first. The restless activity of mind and body, the desire to improve his own branch of industry, the examples constantly before him of ingenious men who have solved economic and mechanical problems to their own profit and elevation, all stimulate and encourage the young worker. There is not a working boy in the New England states, at least, who does not have an idea for some invention or improvement in manufactures, by which, in good time, he hopes to better his position, or rise to fortune and social distinction.

The compulsory education laws of most of the states, and especially those of New England, which require the young factory worker under 14 to 15 years of age must spend three months a year in school, protects every child from the possessiveness of his parents or the neglect of the manufacturer. In order for parents or employers to profit from the child's labor during three fourths of the year, he or she must attend school regularly during the other fourth.

47 Sectional Differences in Mid-Nineteenth-Century America

Most of us today think of ourselves primarily as Americans rather than as Southerners, Iowans, or Philadelphians. Americans, in the first half of the nineteenth century, had quite different loyalties. Although the sense of American nationality grew steadily stronger after the War of 1812, many Americans continued to give their primary allegiance to their section of the country, state, or community.

Political leaders before the Civil War often debated in terms of sectional interests. Many historians explain the great controversies of the period in the same way. As the major source of conflict, they identify an agricultural South based on slave labor pitted against an industrial North based on free labor. In this confrontation, the West, composed for the most part of farmers who owned modest-sized farms, finally joined with the North.

Such an interpretation is not necessarily false, but it is not very precise. The American population and economy expanded rapidly in the two decades before the Civil War. Cities grew, industry and agriculture developed rapidly, and large numbers of Americans moved from farms to cities and from the East to the frontiers in the West.

Did these changes result in real and measurable differences among Americans living in different parts of the country? Or did people living in the three sections merely imagine themselves to be different from their fellow Americans? Today historians look to statistical data as one way to find answers to such questions. The six tables that make up Reading 45 provide some evidence which will help you make your own hypothesis about sectional differences in the United States. Because specific questions accompany each table, there are no general study questions with this reading.

1: U.S. Population Distribution by Regions, 1840–1860

This table shows the total population and the percentage of the total population living in the South, West, and Northeast in 1840, 1850, and 1860.

1. What happened to total population?
2. Which region had the smallest population?
3. Which region gained population most rapidly?
4. Might people in any of these regions have felt threatened by the population trends? Why?

U.S. Bureau of the Census, **A Compendium of the Ninth Census, June 1, 1870.** Washington, D.C.: Government Printing Office, 1872, pp. 8–9.

Year	Total U. S. Population (does not include territories)	*South*		*West*		*Northeast*	
		Population	% of total pop.	Population	% of total pop.	Population	% of total pop.
1840	17,019,641	4,749,875	27.9	4,960,580	29.1	7,309,186	42.9
1850	23,067,262	6,271,237	27.2	7,494,608	32.5	9,301,417	40.3
1860	31,183,744	7,993,531	25.6	11,796,680	37.8	11,393,533	36.5

2: Migration Within the States, 1850

The table on the following page gives data on the population of selected states based on the 1850 census.

1. To which states did Americans move in large numbers?
2. Which states received large numbers of immigrants?
3. How might these migration trends affect sectional attitudes and loyalties?

U.S. Bureau of the Census, **Statistical View of the United States; A Compendium of the Seventh Census.** Washington, D.C.: Government Printing Office, 1854, p. 61.

	Population Born in State	Population Born in Other States	Population Born Outside U.S.	Total
Northern Seaboard				
Connecticut	284,978	39,117	38,374	383,099
Massachusetts	679,624	139,419	163,598	985,450
New York	2,092,076	296,754	655,224	3,048,325
Pennsylvania	1,787,310	165,966	303,105	2,258,160
Midwest				
Illinois	331,089	399,733	111,860	846,034
Indiana	520,583	398,695	55,537	977,154
Michigan	137,637	201,586	54,593	395,071
Ohio	1,203,490	529,208	218,099	1,955,050
South				
Georgia	394,979	119,587	6,452	521,572
North Carolina	529,483	20,784	2,565	553,028
South Carolina	253,399	12,601	8,508	274,563
Virginia	813,891	57,502	22,953	894,800

U.S. Bureau of the Census, **A Compendium of the U.S. Census for 1850,** p. 40.

3: *Personal Income Per Capita by Regions, 1840–1860*

This table shows per capita personal income in percentages by region, considering the average income for the country to be 100%.

1. What does this table tell you about the distribution of wealth in the United States?
2. In which areas were people becoming more prosperous compared to those in other areas? less prosperous?
3. How might these trends in personal income affect sectional attitudes?

U.S. Census Bureau. **A Compendium of the Ninth Census, June 1, 1870.** Washington, D.C.: Government Printing Office, 1872, pp. 798–99.

Regions	1840	1860
Northeast	135%	139%
North Central	68%	68%
South	76%	72%

4: *Americans Employed in Manufacturing, 1840–1860*

This table shows the numbers of Americans employed in manufacturing in selected states.

1. Which states had the largest numbers of workers employed in manufacturing? the smallest?
2. Which states gained the most workers in manufacturing between 1840–1860? Which lost workers?
3. What does this table indicate about the American economy?
4. How might this pattern of employment affect sectional interests and attitudes?

	Persons Employed in Manufacturing		
	1840	1850	1860
Northern Seaboard			
Connecticut	27,932	50,731	64,469
Massachusetts	85,176	177,461	217,421
New York	173,193	199,349	230,112
Pennsylvania	105,883	146,766	222,132
Midwest			
Illinois	13,185	11,559	22,968
Indiana	20,590	14,440	21,295
Michigan	6,890	9,344	23,190
Ohio	66,265	51,491	75,602
South			
Georgia	7,984	8,368	11,575
North Carolina	14,322	14,601	14,217
South Carolina	10,325	7,066	6,994
Virginia	54,147	29,110	36,174

Seymour E. Harris, ed., **American Economic History.** New York: McGraw-Hill Book Company, 1961, p. 528

5: *Urban Population — Percentage of Total Population by Region*

This table shows the percentage of total population living in cities in various regions of the country.

1. What areas of the country had the largest percentage of people living in cities? the smallest?
2. Which area gained the largest percentage of urban dwellers? the smallest?
3. What do these data suggest about sectional differences?

Area	1840	1850	1860
Northeast	18.8%	27.2%	36.0%
North Central	3.9%	9.7%	13.8%
South	4.9%	7.0%	8.7%

U.S. Bureau of the Census, **Sixteenth Census of the United States Population.** Washington, D.C.: Government Printing Office, 1942, vol. I, p. 20.

6: *Regional Distribution of Wealth, 1850*

Thomas P. Kettell, **Southern Wealth and Northern Politics.** New York: George W. and John A. Wood, 1860, p. 145.

1. What does this table tell you about the comparative wealth of the three regions?
2. What does this table indicate about the American economy?
3. How might the distribution of wealth affect sectional interests and attitudes?

Property	North	West	South
Value of animals	$173,812,690	$112,563,851	$253,795,330
Capital in manufacture	382,366,732	155,883,045	94,995,674
Value in railroads	451,949,410	298,837,647	221,857,503
Value of bank capital	186,668,462	16,978,130	97,730,579
Real estate	1,835,063,613	619,154,287	1,445,008,447
Personal estate	544,718,966	195,054,073	1,385,727,523*

* Includes value of slaves

48 The Growth of America at Mid-Century

HISTORICAL ESSAY

As the American people approached the disaster of secession and Civil War, they lived in the world's most prosperous and most rapidly growing nation. This essay discusses economic, cultural, and territorial growth in that nation from about 1840 to 1860.

The annual value of manufactures in America practically doubled between 1850 and 1860. Although industry expanded spectacularly during the 1850's, it had been growing steadily throughout the century. After the War of 1812, the total annual value of manufactured goods produced in America had been less than $200 million. By 1859, the northeastern states alone produced goods worth more than one billion dollars.

Population Growth and Mobility

The rapid increase in factory production was related to the growth and mobility of the American population. During the first half of the nineteenth century, the total American population increased by over thirty percent every ten years. Moreover, the American people were on the move. Their push to the West, that had begun in earnest after the War of 1812, continued. Settlers crossed the Appalachian Mountains in such large numbers that the West grew more rapidly than any other part of the country. In 1830, more than one fourth of the total American population lived west of the Appalachian Mountains; by 1840, almost one half lived in the West.

But Americans moved not only to the western frontier; large numbers also moved to the urban frontier. Large cities sprang up in the North and West, Rural areas of New England lost population as a generation of young people abandoned the rocky soil of their parents' farms to seek new opportunities in New England manufacturing towns and cities.

In addition to the American people who moved from east to west and from country to city, substantial numbers of European immigrants arrived at American ports each year. During the 1830's only about 500,000 immigrants came to this country. During the 1840's this number tripled to over 1,500,000, and during the 1850's it climbed to about two and a half million. The great majority of the immigrants came from Ireland, a country which suffered from widespread poverty and a famine caused by failure of the potato crop, and from Germany, where in 1848 the attempt of liberals to unite the German states under a parliamentary system failed, thus creating many political refugees. Most of the Irish settled in cities on the eastern seaboard where the majority found employment as factory hands or as day laborers. Many Germans came from a middle-class background. Large numbers of them moved to the Midwest where they became farmers or merchants.

American Ingenuity and Enterprise

Population growth can weaken the economy of a country such as Ireland or India, that has limited natural and capital resources. In the United States with its vast resources, population growth spurred economic growth. More people worked to produce more goods for a constantly expanding domestic market.

The Americans' attitude toward work also helped to stimulate economic growth. The zest and ambition with which the ordinary citizen approached his job, no matter what it was, invariably impressed European travelers who visited America. Americans placed a high value on hard work. The work ethic was partly an inheritance from Protestants like the Puritans who believed that God called every person to his vocation, and therefore, all men should work hard in order to glorify God. The economic opportunities, which America offered poor people, reinforced this Puritan inheritance. As a result, regardless of their background, most European immigrants quickly picked up "the gospel of hard work."

During the 1850's, thousands of Americans decorated their parlors with a steel engraving entitled "Men of Progress" which included the portraits of American scientists and inventors, such as William Morton, a dentist who invented ether, Cyrus McCormick, who invented the reaper, Samuel Morse, the telegraph, Elias Howe, the sewing machine, Richard Hoe, the revolving printing press, and Charles Goodyear, who developed the process for vulcanizing rubber. At the end of the eighteenth century, America had been forced to rely on imported brains, such as those of Samuel Slater who left England secretly to help build textile machinery in Rhode Island. By the middle of the nineteenth century, the United States had become a world leader in many aspects of technology. At the famous London Exhibition of 1851 American machines so impressed Europeans that they sent special commissioners across the Atlantic to study American methods of manufacturing.

American technology helps to explain the expansion of American industry before the Civil War. In popular language, Americans attributed this technological success to "Yankee ingenuity" or "American know-how." Historians do not agree on a precise explanation for such a phenomenon. Most historians believe that the explosion in technology reflected the fact that the United States, unlike

Inventions and Discoveries Before 1860

Inventor or Discoverer	Date	Contribution
Eli Whitney	1793	cotton gin
	1798	interchangeable parts
Robert Fulton	1807	steamboat
Peter Cooper	1830	locomotive
Cyrus H. McCormick	1831	reaper
Charles Goodyear	1839	vulcanization of rubber
Samuel F. B. Morse	1844	telegraph
Elias Howe	1846	sewing machine
Richard Hoe	1846	rotary printing press
William Kelly	1851	Kelly process of converting pig iron into steel
Elisha Otis	1852	passenger elevator (made skyscrapers possible)
Edwin Drake	1859	oil drilling

Britain and Europe, usually had fewer workers than its industries needed. Therefore, Americans welcomed labor-saving devices. Another explanation for the innovative character of Americans argues that they placed more value on finding new ways of doing things than on adhering to traditional ways because they lived in a new country. Workmen tried to improve their tools and to invent new labor-saving machines. The English observer George Wallis believed that American education explained the efficiency and ingenuity of the American worker. Whatever the explanation, Europeans considered the tools of American carpenters and mechanics so superior to their own that artisans about to emigrate to America left their tools at home.

The growth of a national railroad system was the most spectacular aspect of the American industrial revolution before the Civil War. I. D. Andrews pointed out that the railroads expanded the market for agricultural and manufactured products and increased the value of property. The railroads also represented by far the largest industrial investment in the country before the Civil War. By 1860, private investors in America and Europe and federal, state, and local governments invested over a billion dollars in railroads. The federal government subsidized railroad construction by giving grants of federal land along the right-of-way to the railroad companies. The enormous amounts of money pumped into the American economy to construct and maintain railroads helped to spur the growth of the iron and steel industry and, in turn, to support the entire industrial enterprise.

American ingenuity and enterprise were also visible on the seas at mid-century. From 1830 to 1850, the United States led all other nations in merchant shipping. Yankee clipper ships, the fastest and most beautiful sailing vessels ever built, were a familiar sight in ports throughout the world. Beginning about 1850, the clipper ship started to give way to steamships, and America's ascendency on the seas declined. Yet, the clipper ship remained active in trade with California and the Orient, and it served as a symbol of American skill and energy.

Industrialization Creates a Working Class

We have seen that the growth, mobility, attitudes, and education of the American population influenced the development of American industry. The city and factory also worked profound changes on people's lives. In the eighteenth century, Thomas Jefferson had feared that the growth of large cities would destroy America. He envisioned an agrarian republic in which every American would be an independent farmer on his own land. He believed that, if the

American people left the land to work in factories and to live in rented houses or tenements, they would lose their independence and sense of responsibility as citizens.

Although Jefferson's fears were not realized in America during the middle of the nineteenth century, he probably would not have welcomed the changes which took place in American society. Most of the unskilled laborers and factory workers came from unsuccessful farms or from the ranks of European immigrants. The latter, especially the Irish, did most of the heavy construction work in building canals, railroads, and factories. They lived close to the bare subsistence level in crude shanties on the fringes of construction projects or in the least desirable parts of the cities. Before the tide of immigration rose in the 1840's, native born Americans did most of the skilled work in the northern factories. Two systems of labor prevailed. One, practiced in the textile mills of Lowell and Waltham, Massachusetts, employed young farm girls, provided them with supervised boarding houses, and generally agreeable working conditions. Such girls usually worked for a few years, saved their money, and then returned to their homes to get married. The second labor system employed whole families—father, mother, and young children—to tend the looms.

To modern Americans, working conditions before the Civil War seem hard and wages seem low. Men, women, and children worked 12–15 hours a day. Skilled workers earned $4–10 a week; unskilled workers, including many women and children, earned one to six dollars a week. Yet working conditions and wages in America were substantially better than in Europe as European travelers to America noted time and again.

Industrialization, nevertheless, changed American society. A distinct working class developed during the period. Class lines remained flexible, but the unpropertied industrial worker and city dweller, who had been so rare in Jefferson's time, became a normal part of American society.

An American Literature

A literary awakening accompanied growth in the economy. Educated Americans in the early part of the nineteenth century had complained that their country lacked a distinctively American literature. Americans read English writers, and most American writers tried to imitate English novels set against a background of medieval ruins and legend unlike anything which had ever existed in America. James Fenimore Cooper was really the first American novelist to concentrate on American themes, although his style was decidedly British. Such books of his as *The Last of the Mohicans* and *The*

Deerslayer dramatized the role of the pioneer and Indian in the American wilderness. Cooper's popularity, which extended to Europe, began in the 1820's, but few of his contemporaries displayed equal talent.

In 1836, the transcendentalist philosopher, Ralph Waldo Emerson, gave a famous lecture at Harvard College entitled "The American Scholar." He called for a new breed of writers, artists, and scholars who would express the unique genius of America. His call did not go unheeded, for between 1850 and 1855 some of the most famous works in the whole history of American literature appeared. Nathaniel Hawthorne wrote *The Scarlet Letter* and *The House of the Seven Gables.* Herman Melville wrote *Moby Dick.* At about the same time, Henry Thoreau wrote *Walden,* and Walt Whitman published *Leaves of Grass,* the most important volume of poetry yet written by an American.

These writers were major literary artists. Much of what they wrote criticized American society. Hawthorne and Melville, for example, expressed through their novels the fear that Americans placed too much value on individual progress and not enough on a sense of community. Thoreau and Whitman criticized the American passion for money and material possessions. None of these writers approved of slavery. They were united by a concern to make great literature out of the American experience, and a desire to uphold the values of human dignity and freedom. With the publication of their works in the 1850's, the maturing American nation expressed the cultural Declaration of Independence that Emerson had called for in the 1830's.

Territorial Expansion

Finally, the United States expanded its national boundaries between 1830 and 1850. In theory, the 30,000 American settlers living in Texas in 1830 were Mexicans, subject to Mexican law. Actually, they thought of themselves as Americans, and chafed under what they took to be Mexican restrictions upon their rights. In April 1830, the Mexican government passed a law prohibiting slavery and the further settlement of Americans in Texas. During the next few years, relationships between the colonists and the Mexican government continued to deteriorate. By 1835, the Texans asserted their right to secede from Mexico. Both sides raised armies, and in February 1836, at the famous siege of the Alamo, the Mexican army overwhelmed and massacred the Texans' tiny force. Their heroic stand and the stories, true and legendary, which grew out of the defense of the Alamo emotionally involved millions of Americans with the cause of the Texans. Later that year, the Texan army under Sam

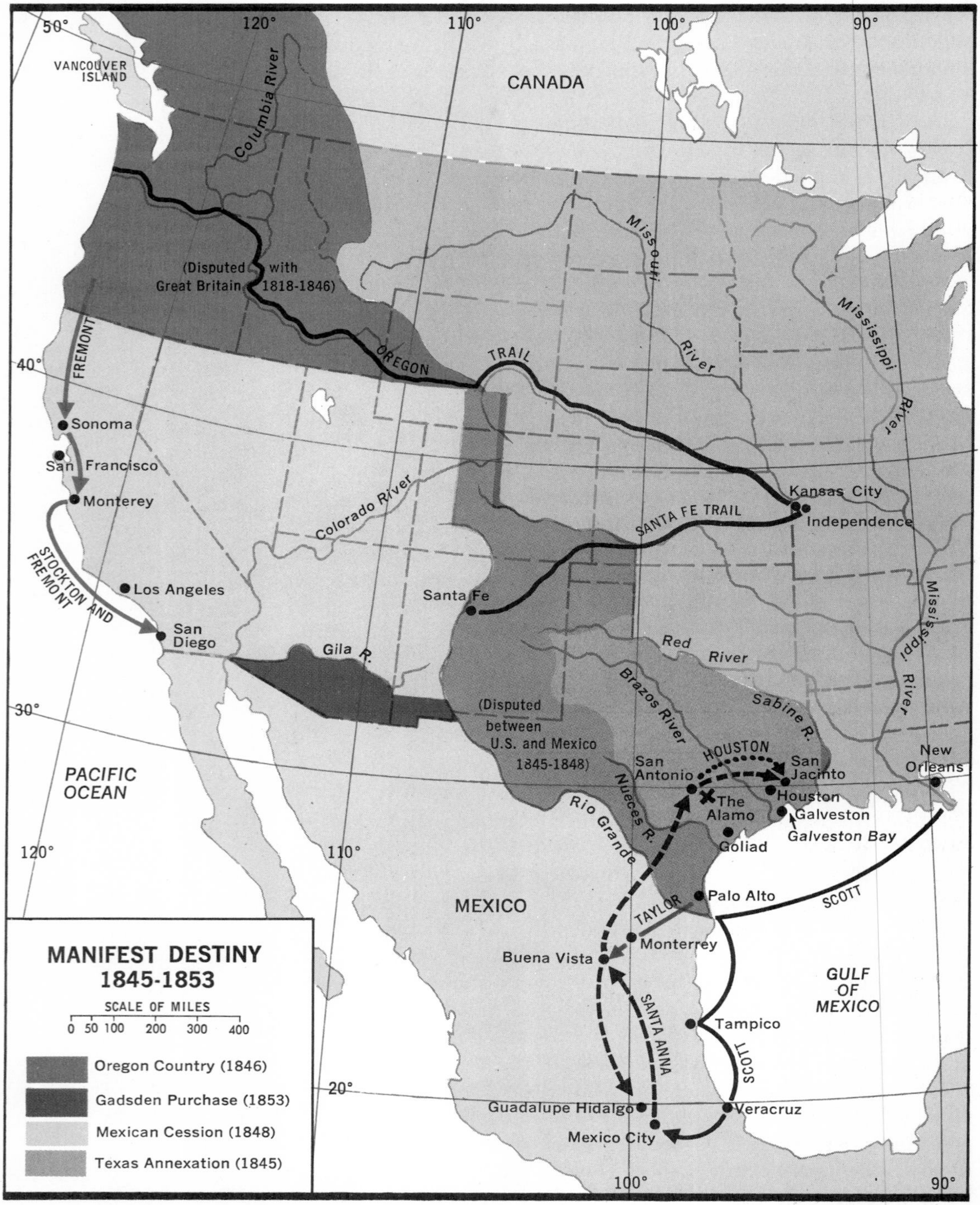
MANIFEST DESTINY
1845-1853
SCALE OF MILES
0 50 100 200 300 400
Oregon Country (1846)
Gadsden Purchase (1853)
Mexican Cession (1848)
Texas Annexation (1845)
CANADA
VANCOUVER ISLAND
Columbia River
(Disputed with Great Britain 1818-1846)
OREGON TRAIL
Missouri River
Mississippi River
FREMONT
Sonoma
San Francisco
Monterey
STOCKTON AND FREMONT
Los Angeles
San Diego
Colorado River
Gila R.
Santa Fe
SANTA FE TRAIL
Kansas City
Independence
Red River
Brazos River
Sabine R.
(Disputed between U.S. and Mexico 1845-1848)
HOUSTON
San Antonio
San Jacinto
The Alamo
Houston
Galveston
Galveston Bay
Goliad
Nueces R.
Rio Grande
New Orleans
PACIFIC OCEAN
MEXICO
Palo Alto
TAYLOR
SCOTT
Monterrey
Buena Vista
SANTA ANNA
GULF OF MEXICO
Tampico
Guadalupe Hidalgo
Veracruz
Mexico City
50°
40°
30°
20°
120°
110°
100°
90°

Houston won a decisive battle over the Mexicans at San Jacinto near Galveston Bay. In October 1836, Houston became president of the Republic of Texas. Both Texans and Americans then raised a cry for Congress to annex Texas to the United States.

The Texans' request for annexation brought the issue of American territorial expansion into politics with a vengeance. Jackson was President in 1836 when the issue was first raised. Although he personally favored annexation, he feared taking any action that might bring about a war with Mexico or divide the Democratic party. The latter was a real possibility because many people in the North believed firmly that annexation was a Southern plot to expand slave territory. For the next eight years, the Texas problem simmered. President Van Buren avoided the issue and John Tyler, who came to the Presidency in 1841 when William Henry Harrison died after one month in office, arranged with his Secretary of State, John C. Calhoun, for a secret annexation treaty with Texas. However, the Senate, with antislavery votes carrying the day, refused to ratify the treaty.

Meanwhile, Americans colonized the Far West. Since 1818, the Oregon country had been occupied jointly by the United States and Great Britain, pending final agreement on its division. Because of its remote location, Oregon had not attracted American settlers as quickly as Texas. In 1840, only a few hundred Americans lived in Oregon and most of them were missionaries and trappers. In the early 1840's, however, pioneers in substantial numbers began the long trek over the famous Oregon Trail from Independence, Missouri, to the rich farm lands in the Pacific Northwest. As American settlement in the area increased so did American interest in solving the dispute over its ownership. Both England and America had good claims to the territory. America's claim went back to the Lewis and Clark expedition of 1803–1806. The more extreme expansionists in America, such as the journalist John L. O'Sullivan, believed that America had a manifest destiny to spread its institutions the length and breadth of the continent. They insisted that the American claim be pushed as far north as the 54th parallel, several hundred miles above the present border with Canada. These expansion-minded patriots adopted the slogan "54°40′ or fight!"

Texas and Oregon

Both the Texas and the Oregon questions were very much on the public mind at the time of the 1844 election. The Whigs had become disgusted with President Tyler because of his unwillingness to support their program for a national bank, a high protective tariff, and the distribution of federal land revenues among the states. They nominated Henry Clay as their candidate. Meanwhile, the Democrats had their own internal squabbles. When neither of their two leading candidates, former President Martin Van Buren and Lewis Cass of Michigan, could get the nomination, the Democrats settled on James K. Polk of Tennessee as a compromise candidate. Polk, campaigning on a platform calling for the annexation of Texas and the insistence of American claims to Oregon, won in a very close election.

If the achievements of a President can be measured by his ability to accomplish his goals while in office, Polk was one of our most successful chief executives. A Democrat in the Jacksonian style, Polk wanted an Independent Treasury system (as opposed to a national bank), a low tariff, and lower expenditures for internal improvements. Under his leadership, these programs were all accomplished between 1844 and 1848.

President Van Buren had Congress set up an Independent Treasury system under which the government removed its funds from private banks and placed them in sub-treasuries around the country. Following the Whig victory in 1840, Congress repealed the Independent Treasury Act, which it again passed during Polk's Administration.

Polk also came into office determined to resolve the Texas and Oregon questions to the advantage of the United States. Just before his inauguration in 1845, Congress, by joint resolution, approved the admission of Texas as one of the United States. With the Texas issue apparently out of the way, Polk turned to Oregon. After the British rejected his offer of a compromise boundary along the 47th parallel, he boldly asserted America's claim to the whole Oregon territory. For a while, war between the United States and Britain over Oregon seemed likely. Finally, in June 1846, both countries agreed to a compromise that divided the territory along the 49th parallel, except for Vancouver Island which went to Britain.

War With Mexico

The settlement with Britain came at a fortunate time, for the United States was already close to war with Mexico. When Texas had declared its independence from Mexico, it claimed the Rio Grande as its western boundary. The traditionally accepted Texas boundary had been at the Nueces River, substantially to the east of the Rio Grande. When he became President, Polk sent an army to the banks of the Rio Grande, announced his determination to support the Texans' claim, and sent a minister to Mexico offering to pay certain debts the Mexican government owed Americans in exchange for the Rio Grande boundary. At the same time, he authorized the American minister to try to purchase New Mexico and California from Mexico. Mexico refused to negotiate, and after a skirmish between American and Mexican troops, in which sixteen Americans suffered casualties, the United States declared war on May 13, 1846.

Few modern American historians justify the war with Mexico. The honor and security of the United States does not seem to have been at stake. Rather the American government was determined to expand the continental boundaries of the nation. From a military standpoint, America fought a highly successful war. One American army under General Zachary Taylor, moving west from the Rio Grande into north central Mexico, gained an important victory over superior Mexican forces at Buena Vista. A second American army under General Winfield Scott landed by sea at Veracruz and, meeting little Mexican resistance, won a brilliant victory and occupied the capital at Mexico City. The Mexican military effort collapsed, and a truce followed while the two nations entered into peace negotiations. By the terms of the Treaty of Guadalupe Hidalgo formally signed February 2, 1848, and proclaimed by Polk, July 4, 1848, Mexico recognized the Rio Grande boundary and ceded New Mexico and California to the United States. The United States, in turn, agreed to pay Mexico $15 million and to assume the claims of American citizens against Mexico.

From one point of view, the acquisition of the territories of Oregon, California, New Mexico, and Texas represented a magnificent accomplishment and indicated the growth of a great nation. From another point of view it was terribly costly. The war with Mexico was not popular in the United States because thousands of Americans, mostly in the northern states, feared that any new territory won from Mexico would encourage the expansion of slavery. Economically, culturally, and geographically the nation expanded as never before, but the old sectional tensions continued to bubble under the surface of national unity. The future peace, unity, and prosperity of Americans would depend upon their ability to organize these vast new territories without letting the great debate over slavery tear the nation apart.

With the Gadsden Purchase in 1853, the United States paid Mexico $10 million for 54,000 square miles of territory along the southern New Mexico border. Since the Gadsden Purchase, the boundaries of the continental United States have remained fixed.

SUGGESTED READINGS

DE VOTO, BERNARD, *The Year of Decision, 1846.* This is an extremely well written and dramatic narrative of the experience of Americans moving to the West during the period. It covers the movements to California and to Mexican territory.

PARKER, WILLIAM N., *Commerce, Cotton and Westward Expansion, 1820–1860.* This brief volume provides a clear analysis of the various aspects of American economic growth during the period.

PARKINSON, FRANCIS, *The Oregon Trail.* This is a classic account of the adventures and hardships experienced by those nineteenth-century Americans who helped blaze the overland route from Missouri to Oregon.

The Coming of the Civil War, 1850–1860

STATING THE ISSUE

CHAPTER 13

The years between 1850 and 1860 culminated in the tragedy of Civil War. Historians have offered many explanations for the outbreak of the war. Some have argued that a conflict between two different civilizations—the Puritanical, conscience-ridden, middle-class North and the aristocratic, slaveholding South—caused the war. Others have identified the basic source of the conflict in different interpretations of the Constitution. The South maintained that the states had supreme authority; the North claimed that the national government was supreme. Still others have stressed economic differences between an industrial North, committed to high protective tariffs, and an agrarian South, committed to free trade. Some historians have called the Civil War inevitable, a "second American Revolution," and a triumph of American principles. Others have described it as our greatest national blunder and have blamed the war on the inadequacies of American political leaders.

Many forces promoted sectional conflict, but the big issues between the North and the South had been resolved, at least temporarily, through compromise. In 1850, the American people again confronted a great political crisis. The victory over Mexico had once more thrust slavery into the spotlight. Would slavery be permitted in the new territories?

Once again America's leading statesmen sought an acceptable compromise. It soon became obvious, however, that the problem of the extension of slavery into the territories would be far more difficult to resolve in the 1850's than it had been in the 1820's. Long before 1860, large areas of the West became a battleground between proslavery and antislavery forces. For the first time in their history, the American people confronted an issue they could not solve by compromise.

Chapter 13 is concerned with the compromises reached in 1850 and the most important events that destroyed those compromises. Why did the Compromise of 1850 fail? In what ways did disputes over slavery contribute to the Civil War? What might the American people have done to avoid Civil War? Was the Civil War morally justifiable from the point of view of either the North or the South? These are the major issues raised in Chapter 13.

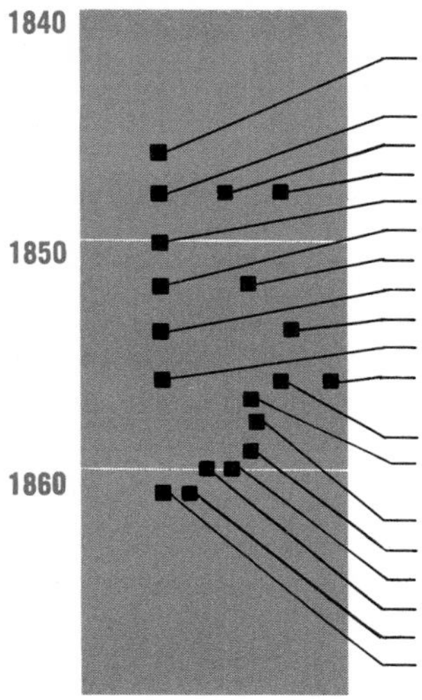

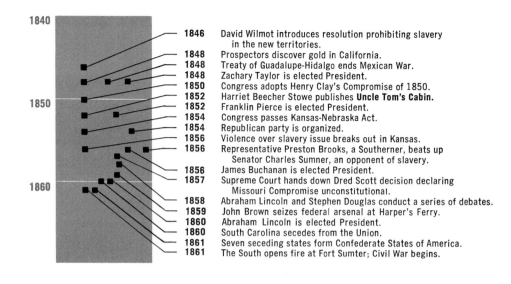

1846 David Wilmot introduces resolution prohibiting slavery in the new territories.
1848 Prospectors discover gold in California.
1848 Treaty of Guadalupe-Hidalgo ends Mexican War.
1848 Zachary Taylor is elected President.
1850 Congress adopts Henry Clay's Compromise of 1850.
1852 Harriet Beecher Stowe publishes **Uncle Tom's Cabin.**
1852 Franklin Pierce is elected President.
1854 Congress passes Kansas-Nebraska Act.
1854 Republican party is organized.
1856 Violence over slavery issue breaks out in Kansas.
1856 Representative Preston Brooks, a Southerner, beats up Senator Charles Sumner, an opponent of slavery.
1856 James Buchanan is elected President.
1857 Supreme Court hands down Dred Scott decision declaring Missouri Compromise unconstitutional.
1858 Abraham Lincoln and Stephen Douglas conduct a series of debates.
1859 John Brown seizes federal arsenal at Harper's Ferry.
1860 Abraham Lincoln is elected President.
1860 South Carolina secedes from the Union.
1861 Seven seceding states form Confederate States of America.
1861 The South opens fire at Fort Sumter; Civil War begins.

49 The Compromise of 1850

A substantial number of people in the North had opposed the Mexican War because they suspected that it was a Southern plot to extend slavery. In 1846, David Wilmot, a congressman from Pennsylvania, introduced an amendment to a bill designed to appropriate $2 million for negotiating a settlement with Mexico. Part of his amendment proposed that slavery should be barred from any territory acquired from Mexico. After bitter and prolonged debate between those who supported slavery and those who opposed it, the Wilmot Proviso, as his amendment was called, passed the House of Representatives, but failed to pass the Senate.

The theoretical issue raised by the Proviso in 1846 became a pressing, practical problem two years later. After the Mexican War, California and New Mexico belonged to the United States. In 1848, President Polk urged Northerners and Southerners to compromise their differences. He proposed extending to the Pacific the line drawn by the Compromise of 1820 at 36°30′ which separated free from slave territory. But his proposal failed to win support.

In 1848, the American voters elected the Whig candidate, Zachary Taylor, a hero of the Mexican War, to the Presidency. Meanwhile, prospectors discovered gold near Sacramento, California, setting off a rush for the gold fields. By the end of 1849, more than 100,000 prospectors and settlers had poured into California. The question of statehood could not be delayed. With the encouragement of President Taylor, Californians held a convention, drew up a constitution which prohibited slavery, and applied for immediate admission as a state.

The debate in Congress over slavery took on particular intensity because the nation consisted of fifteen free and fifteen slave states. Congressmen hesitated to upset that balance. Moreover, Northerners wanted slavery outlawed in Washington, D. C., while Southerners agitated for an effective fugitive slave law that would guarantee the return of runaway slaves. Slaves had been escaping in increasing numbers since the underground railroad had been organized in the 1830's. Runaways were a constant source of irritation to the South, especially since some of them, such as Frederick Douglass, had joined the abolitionist forces as eloquent orators and journalists.

Calhoun died in March 1850, Clay in June 1852, and Webster in October 1852.

All these issues surrounded the admission of California as one of the greatest Senate debates in American history took shape. It marked the last appearance of Daniel Webster, Henry Clay, and John C. Calhoun. Reading 49 contains portions of that debate. As you read, try to answer these questions:

1. Who would have been most likely to accept Clay's proposals: an abolitionist, a slaveholder, or a Californian? Why?
2. Why did Calhoun feel that the South was more threatened in 1850 than in earlier periods of American history? Does the evidence from Chapter 12 support his view?
3. What kind of legislation would have satisfied Calhoun?
4. What did Seward mean by "the higher law"? Can you think of any situations in which you might have to choose between established laws and "higher laws"?

Henry Clay Proposes Compromise

Henry Clay introduced proposals which he and Daniel Webster hoped would provide the basis for a compromise. His proposals, made on January 29, 1850, are given here.

Congressional Globe, 31st Congress, 1st Session, vol. 22, part I, Appendix, pp. 115–16. Language simplified and modernized.

It is desirable for the peace and harmony of the Union that all existing controversies between the states, arising out of the institution of slavery, be settled amicably upon a fair, equitable, and just basis. Therefore,

Resolved, That California ought to be admitted as a state without Congress placing any restriction on the exclusion or introduction of slavery within the boundaries of that state.

Resolved, That since slavery does not exist by law, and is not likely to be introduced into any of the territory acquired by the

United States from the Republic of Mexico, Congress ought not to provide by law either for its introduction into or exclusion from any part of that territory. Appropriate territorial governments ought to be established by Congress in all of the territory, outside the boundaries of the proposed State of California, without the adoption of any restriction or condition on slavery.

Resolved, That it is unwise to abolish slavery in the District of Columbia, while slavery continues to exist in Maryland, without the consent of that State, without the consent of the people of the District, and without just payment to the owners of the slaves within the District.

But resolved, That it is wise to prohibit within the District the slave trade of slaves brought in from states or places outside the District. They should not be sold within the District nor sent to markets outside the District of Columbia.

Resolved, That a more effective law ought to be made, according to the requirement of the Constitution, for the return of slaves who may have escaped into any state or territory in the Union.

Article 4, Section 2, Clause 3, says that nobody legally a slave in one state who escapes into a free state shall be freed as a result of the laws of the latter state. He shall be returned when his owner makes claim for him.

Resolved, That Congress has no power to promote or obstruct the slave trade between slaveholding states, but whether slaves may be admitted or excluded from a state to which they are brought depends entirely on that state's particular laws.

Calhoun Replies

John C. Calhoun prepared the answer of the extreme proslavery Southerners to the compromise that Clay had proposed. Because Calhoun's final illness had severely weakened him, the speech that he wrote was delivered to the Senate on March 4, 1850, by Senator James Mason of Virginia.

Congressional Globe, 31st Congress, 1st Session, vol. 21, part I, pp. 452–55. Language simplified and modernized.

A single section, governed by the will of the numerical majority, now controls the government and its entire powers. The North has absolute control over the government. It is clear, therefore, that on all questions between it and the South, where there are different interests, the interests of the South will be sacrificed to the North, no matter how oppressive the effects may be. The South possesses no political means by which it can resist.

Northern hostility towards the social organization of the South lay dormant a long time. The first organized movement against it began in 1835. Then, for the first time, antislavery societies were organized, presses established, lecturers sent forth to excite the people of the North, and incendiary publications were scattered over the whole South, through the mail. The South was thoroughly aroused. Meetings were held everywhere, and resolutions adopted, calling upon the North to arrest the threatened evil. But petitions poured into Congress from the North, calling upon it to abolish slavery in the District of Columbia, and to prohibit what they called the internal slave trade between the states, announcing at the same time that their ultimate object was to abolish slavery, not only in the District, but in the states and throughout the Union.

With the increase of their influence, the abolitionists extended the sphere of their action. In a short time, they had sufficient influence to get the legislatures of most of the northern states to pass acts which in effect repealed the provision of the Constitution that provides for the return of fugitive slaves. This was followed by petitions and resolutions of legislatures of the northern states and popular meetings, to exclude the southern states from all territories acquired or to be acquired, and to prevent the admission of any state into the Union which, by its constitution, does not prohibit slavery.

How can the Union be saved? There is but one way by which it can with any certainty; and that is, by a full and final settlement, on the principle of justice, of all the questions at issue between the two sections. The South asks for justice, simple justice, and less she ought not to take. She has no compromise to offer but the Constitution, and no concession or surrender to make. She has already surrendered so much that she has little left to surrender. Such a settlement would go to the root of the evil, and remove all cause of discontent, by satisfying the South, that she could remain honorably and safely in the Union. Nothing else can, with any certainty, finally and forever settle the question at issue, end agitation, and save the Union.

But can this be done? Yes, easily; not by the weaker party, for it can of itself do nothing—not even protect itself—but by the stronger. The North has only to do justice by conceding to the South an equal right in the acquired territory to do her duty by causing the constitutional provisions related to fugitive slaves to be faithfully fulfilled, to cease the agitation of the slave question, and to provide for an amendment to the Constitution. Such an amendment should restore to the South the power she possessed to protect herself, before the balance between the section was destroyed by this government.

But will the North agree to do this? It is for her to answer this question. But, I will say, she cannot refuse, if she has half the love of the Union which she professes to have, or without justly exposing herself to the charge that her love of power is far greater than her love of the Union. At all events, the responsibility of saving the Union rests on the North, and not the South.

Seward Invokes the "Higher Law"

William Seward was a senator from New York who had defended fugitive slaves in court. He expressed the sentiments of the antislavery group in this speech to the Senate, March 11, 1850.

George E. Baker, ed., **The Works of William H. Seward.** Redfield, N.Y.: 1853, vol. I, pp. 62, 74–75. Language simplified and modernized.

The honorable Senator from South Carolina, Mr. Calhoun, now says that nothing will satisfy the slave states except a compromise that will convince them that they can remain in the Union while maintaining their honor and their safety. And what are the concessions which will do that?

The terms amount to this: that the free states, which have already or may soon have a majority of the population and of the members of both houses of Congress, shall concede the unequal advantage of equality to the slave states, which have a minority in both population and representation. That is, we should change the Constitution so as to convert the government from a national democracy, based on majority rule, into a federal alliance, in which the minority could veto the wishes of the majority. This would be nothing less than a return to the original Articles of Confederation.

The Articles of Confederation required a two-thirds vote to pass measures of importance.

We must also examine this principle as it applies to the territories. They must either be held in common by the nation or be divided up by the citizens of the states. The national lands are ours. They were acquired by the valor and with the wealth of the whole nation. But we hold, nevertheless, no arbitrary power over them. We hold no arbitrary authority over anything, whether acquired lawfully or seized in war. The Constitution regulates our conduct, and the Constitution assigns the territories to the Union.

Article 4, Section 3, Clause 2, says that the Congress shall have power to dispose of and make all needful rules and regulations respecting the territory or other property belonging to the United States.

But there is a higher law than the Constitution, which regulates our authority over the public lands. The territory is a part of the common heritage of mankind, bestowed upon men by the Creator of the universe. We are His stewards, and must discharge our trust so as to secure the highest degree of happiness for mankind.

And now the simple, bold, and even awful question which presents itself to us is this: Shall we, who are founding social and political institutions for countless millions; shall we, who know by experience the wise and the just, and are free to choose them and to reject the erroneous and unjust; shall we establish human bondage, or permit it to be established? Sir, our forefathers would not have hesitated an hour. They found slavery existing here, and they left it only because they could not remove it. There is not only no free state which would now establish it, but there is no slave state, which, if it had had the free alternative we now have, would have founded slavery. Indeed, our revolutionary predecessors had precisely the same question before them in establishing a law under

The Northwest Ordinance of 1787 forbade slavery in the Northwest Territory.

which the states of Ohio, Indiana, Michigan, Illinois, and Wisconsin, have since come into the Union. They solidly repudiated and excluded slavery from those states forever. I confess that the most alarming evidence of our degeneracy, which has yet been given, is that we even debate such a question.

50 The Continuing Debate: Lincoln and Douglas on Slavery in the Territories

In September 1850, Congress passed a series of laws that admitted California as a free state, organized New Mexico without reference to slavery, made assistance to fugitive slaves a federal offense, and abolished the slave trade in the District of Columbia. These were the essential provisions of Clay's famous "Compromise of 1850."

Four years later, however, the slavery controversy flared up again with all of its old bitterness and vigor. Stephen A. Douglas, Democratic Senator from Illinois, proposed a bill to organize the Kansas and Nebraska Territories with or without slavery, depending upon the preference of the settlers. According to many Northerners, Douglas's principle of "popular sovereignty" would, in effect, repeal the Compromise of 1820 for it reopened the possibility of allowing slavery in Louisiana Territory north of parallel 36°30′.

After the Kansas-Nebraska Act became law in 1854, the political parties in the North and West reorganized. Antislavery Whigs and Democrats joined with abolitionists to found the new Republican party. Abraham Lincoln, a lawyer and Whig politician who had served in the Illinois legislature and in the House of Representatives for one term, became a Republican leader in Illinois in 1854. In 1858, he opposed Douglas as a candidate for the United States Senate. Even though Lincoln lost the election, his well-publicized debates with Douglas over the issue of slavery in the territories helped give him a national reputation.

Reading 50 gives selections from the famous Lincoln-Douglas exchange. As you read the speeches, try to answer the following questions:

1. How do you think each of the following people would have reacted to the speeches of Lincoln and Douglas: a Southern slaveholder devoted to Calhoun's principles? a New England

abolitionist? a Pennsylvania farmer about to sell his farm and move to Kansas?

2. In these speeches, did Lincoln favor the abolition of slavery? How do you account for his stand on the issue?
3. Why did Lincoln say that under the Constitution a white man in South Carolina was worth more than double a white man in Maine?
4. How did Douglas and Lincoln differ in the emphasis they put upon important events which had happened in America in 1776 and in 1787? What is the significance of their different emphases?

Douglas Argues for "Popular Sovereignty"

In the final debate held in Alton, Illinois, Douglas summarized his position and argued forcefully for his doctrine of "popular sovereignty."

Political Debates Between Hon. Abraham Lincoln and Hon. Stephen A. Douglas in the Celebrated Campaign of 1858. Columbus: Follett, Foster & Company, 1860, pp. 215–16, 222. Language simplified and modernized.

The issue between Mr. Lincoln and myself was made on three points, which we took before the people of the state. I took up Mr. Lincoln's three propositions in my several speeches, analyzed them, and pointed out what I believed to be the radical errors contained in them. First, his doctrine that this government violated the law of God, which says that a house divided against itself cannot stand. I repudiated that as a slander upon the immortal framers of our Constitution. I then said, I have often repeated, and now again assert, that in my opinion our government can endure forever, divided into free and slave states as our fathers made it.

Each state has the right to prohibit, abolish, or sustain slavery, just as it pleases. This government was made upon the great basis of the sovereignty of the states, with each state having the right to regulate its own domestic institutions to suit itself. That right was given with the understanding and expectation that, inasmuch as each locality had separate interests, each locality must have different and distinct local and domestic institutions, corresponding to its wants and interests. Our fathers knew when they made the government that the laws and institutions which were well adapted to the Green Mountains of Vermont were unsuited to the rice plantations of South Carolina. They knew then, as well as we know now, that the laws and institutions which would be well adapted to the beautiful prairies of Illinois would not be suited to the mining regions of California. They knew that in a republic as broad as this, having such a variety of soil, climate, and interest, there must necessarily be a corresponding variety of local laws—the policy and institutions of each state adapted to its condition and wants. For this reason this Union was established on the right of each state to do as it pleased on the question of slavery and every other question. The various states were not allowed to complain of, much less interfere with, the policy of their neighbors.

The whole South is rallying to the support of the doctrine that, if the people of a territory want slavery, they have a right to have it, and if they do not want it, that no power on earth can force it upon them. I hold that there is no principle on earth more sacred to all the friends of freedom than that which says that no institution, no law, no constitution, should be forced on an unwilling people contrary to their wishes. I assert that the Kansas and Nebraska Bill contains that principle. I will never violate or abandon that doctrine if I have to stand alone. I have stood immovably for that principle, fighting for it when assailed by Northern mobs or threatened by Southern hostility. I have defended it against the North and the South, and I will defend it against whoever assails it. I will follow it wherever its logical conclusions lead me. I say to you that there is but one hope, one safety, for this country, and that is to stand immovably by that principle which declares the right of each state and each territory to decide these questions for themselves. This government was founded on that principle and must be administered in the same sense in which it was founded.

Lincoln Opposes Slavery in the Territories

Lincoln made his most thorough reply to "popular sovereignty" in a speech given at Peoria, Illinois, on October 16, 1854.

John G. Nicolay and John Hay, eds., **Complete Works of Abraham Lincoln.** Lincoln Memorial University, 1894, vol. II, pp. 223–24, 227–29, 232–34.

Equal justice to the South, it is said, requires us to consent to the extension of slavery to new countries. That is to say, inasmuch as you do not object to my taking my hog to Nebraska, therefore I must not object to you taking your slave [there]. Now, I admit that this is perfectly logical, if there is no difference between hogs and Negroes. But while you thus require me to deny the humanity of the Negro, I wish to ask whether you of the South yourselves, have ever been willing to do as much?

The doctrine of self-government is right—absolutely and eternally right—but it has no just application [to the question before us]. Or perhaps I should rather say that whether it has such application depends upon whether a Negro is not, or is, a man. If he is not a man, why in that case, he who is a man may, as a matter of self-government, do just as he pleases with him. But if the

Negro is a man, is it not to that extent a total destruction of self-government, to say that he too shall not govern himself? When the white man governs himself that is self-government; but when he governs himself, and also governs another man, that is more than self-government—that is despotism. If the Negro is a man, why then my ancient faith teaches me that "all men are created equal"; and that there can be no moral right in connection with one man's making a slave of another.

Judge Douglas frequently, with bitter irony and sarcasm, paraphrases our argument by saying: "The white people of Nebraska are good enough to govern themselves, but they are not good enough to govern a few miserable Negroes!!"

Douglas had been a judge of the Illinois Supreme Court from 1841 to 1843.

Well I doubt not that the people of Nebraska are, and will continue to be as good as the average of people elsewhere. I do not say the contrary. What I do say is, that no man is good enough to govern another man, without the other's consent. . . . Allow all the governed an equal voice in the government, and that, and that only, is self-government.

Let it not be said I am contending for the establishment of political and social equality between the whites and blacks. I have already said the contrary. I am not now combating the argument of necessity, arising from the fact that the blacks are already amongst us; but I am combating what is set up as moral argument for allowing them to be taken where they have never yet been—arguing against the extension of a bad thing, which where it already exists we must of necessity, manage as we best can.

Whether slavery shall go into Nebraska, or other new territories, is not a matter of exclusive concern to the people who may go there. The whole nation is interested that the best use shall be made of these territories. We want them for homes of free white people. This they cannot be, to any considerable extent, if slavery shall be planted within them. Slave states are places for poor white people to remove from; not to remove to. New free states are the places for poor people to go to and better their condition. For this use, the nation needs these territories.

Still further: there are constitutional relations between the slave and free states, which are degrading to the latter. We are under legal obligations to catch and return their runaway slaves to them—a sort of dirty, disagreeable job which I believe, as a general rule, the slaveholders will not perform for one another. Then again, in the control of the government—the management of the partnership affairs—they have greatly the advantage of us. By the Constitution each state has two senators, each has a number of representatives, in proportion to the number of its people—and each has a number of Presidential electors, equal to the whole number of its senators and representatives together. But in ascertaining [determining] the number of the people, for this purpose, five slaves are counted as being equal to three whites. The slaves do not vote; they are only counted and so used as to swell the influence of the white people's votes.

The practical effect of this is more aptly shown by a comparison of the states of South Carolina and Maine. South Carolina has six representatives, and so has Maine; South Carolina has eight Presidential electors, and so has Maine. This is precise equality so far; and, of course they are equal in senators, each having two. Thus in control of the government, the two states are equals precisely. But how are they in the number of their white people? Maine has 581,813—while South Carolina has 274,567. Maine has twice as many as South Carolina, and 32,679 over. Thus each white man in South Carolina is more than the double of any man in Maine. This is all because South Carolina, besides her free people, has 384,984 slaves. The South Carolinian has precisely the same advantage over the white man in every other free state, as well as in Maine. He is more than the double of any one of us in this crowd. The same advantage, but not to the same extent, is held by all the citizens of the slave states, over those of the free; and it is an absolute truth, without an exception, that there is no voter in any slave state, but who has more legal power in the government, than any voter in any free state.

51 The Secession Crisis

In the Presidential campaign of 1856, the Democrats nominated James Buchanan, a Northerner with Southern sympathies, who had been Secretary of State under President Polk. He ran on a platform supporting the principles of the Kansas-Nebraska Act. The Republicans chose a famous western explorer, John C. Frémont, as their first Presidential candidate. The Republicans came out against the extension of slavery into the territories and called for the admission of Kansas as a free state. The Whigs joined forces with the anti-immigrant Know-Nothing party and nominated Millard Fillmore on a platform that avoided the slavery issue. The election revealed a deep sectional division in the nation. Buchanan carried the South, Pennsylvania, Illinois, and Indiana, thus winning a narrow victory. Frémont carried the rest of the North and West. Fillmore carried only Maryland, an outcome which marked the end of the Whigs as an important national party.

The Know-Nothing or American party began as a secret organization opposed to immigrants, particularly Irish-Catholics. With the disintegration of the established parties, the Know-Nothings won substantial victories in 1854, electing several governors, state legislators, and representatives to Congress.

During Buchanan's Administration, the breach between North and South widened. Pro- and antislavery factions in Kansas fought pitched battles with each other. Agitation over the Fugitive Slave Law continued, and in 1859, a small band of militant abolitionists under the leadership of John Brown tried to start a slave insurrection by storming the federal arsenal at Harper's Ferry, Virginia.

In this atmosphere of heightened tension, four major candidates sought the Presidency in 1860. The Republicans nominated Abraham Lincoln, who opposed the extension of slavery into the territories. Stephen A. Douglas won the Democratic nomination. He reaffirmed the party platform of 1856 which had endorsed his doctrine of popular sovereignty. Southern Democrats walked out of the Democratic convention and nominated John Breckinridge, who ran on a platform demanding slavery in the territories. John Bell was the candidate for the Constitutional Union Party which condemned sectional parties and praised the Union.

This map shows the election results.

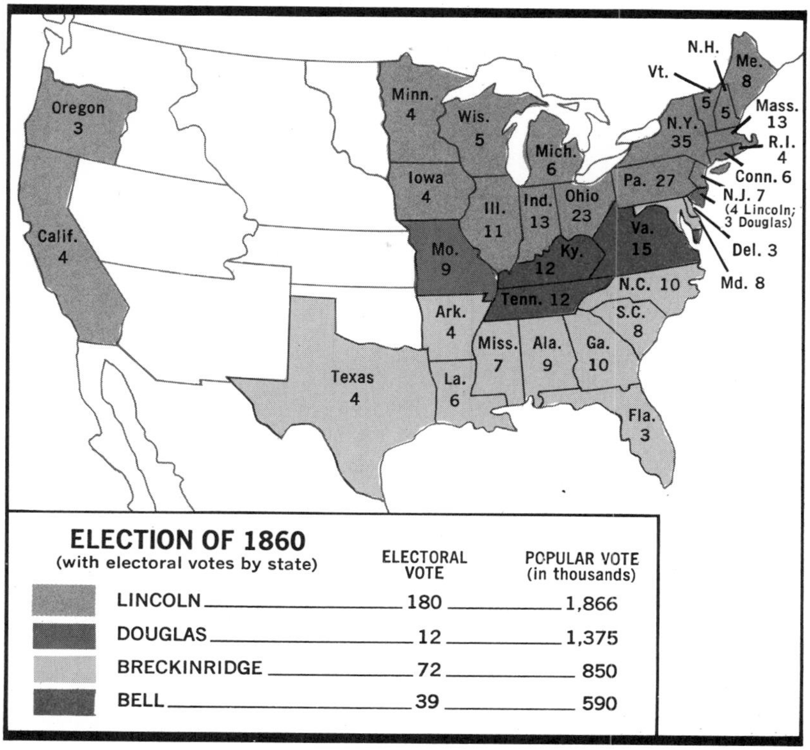

When Lincoln's electoral victory became known, South Carolina called a state convention. On December 20, 1860, the convention passed an ordinance announcing South Carolina's secession from the Union. By the time Lincoln was inaugurated, Mississippi, Florida, Alabama, Georgia, Louisiana, and Texas had followed South

Carolina out of the Union. Reading 51 examines South Carolina's reasons for secession, Lincoln's response to the crisis, and newspaper reactions to disunion. As you read, keep these questions in mind:

1. What evidence did South Carolina give to support the charge that the federal government threatened the interests of the slave states? Can you think of any other evidence?
2. How did Lincoln's conception of the federal union compare with that given in the South Carolina ordinance?
3. What do the newspaper editorials indicate about the causes of the war? Was slavery the only issue? Were all Northerners and Southerners in absolute agreement with one another?
4. Which side, if either, do you think was right? Why?

South Carolina Justifies Secession

On December 20, 1860, the South Carolina Convention voted unanimously for secession. Four days later, the Convention adopted two papers justifying secession. Parts of the "Declaration of Causes which Induced the Secession of South Carolina" follow.

Frank Moore, ed., **The Rebellion Record.** New York: G. P. Putnam, 1861, vol. I, pp. 3–4. Language simplified and modernized.

The Constitution imposed certain duties upon the several states, and restrained the exercise of certain of their powers, which necessarily implied their continued existence as sovereign states.

A compact between the states established a government with defined objects and powers, limited to the exact words of the grant.

We affirm that these ends for which this government was instituted have been defeated. The government itself has destroyed them by the action of the non-slaveholding states. Those states have assumed the right of deciding upon the propriety of our domestic institutions [slavery]. They have denied the rights of property established in fifteen of the states and recognized by the Constitution. They have denounced as sinful the institution of slavery. They have permitted the open establishment among them of abolitionist societies, whose avowed object is to disturb the peace of and to take away the property of the citizens of other states. They have encouraged and assisted thousands of our slaves to leave their homes; and those who remain, have been incited by emissaries [representatives], books, and pictures, to servile insurrection.

For twenty-five years this agitation has been steadily increasing, until it has now secured to its aid the power of the national government. A geographical line has been drawn across the Union, and all the states north of that line have united in the election of a man to the high office of President of the United States whose opinions and purposes are hostile to slavery. He is to be intrusted with the administration of the national government, because he has declared that that "government cannot endure permanently half slave, half free," and that the public mind must rest in the belief that slavery is in the course of ultimate extinction.

On the 4th of March, he will take possession of the government. He has announced that the South shall be excluded from the common territory of the nation, . . . and that a war must be waged against slavery until it shall cease throughout the United States.

We, therefore, the people of South Carolina, by our delegates in convention assembled, appealing to the Supreme Judge of the world for the rectitude [rightness] of our intentions, have solemnly declared that the Union heretofore existing between this state and the other states of North America is dissolved. The state of South Carolina has resumed her position among the nations of the world, as separate and independent state, with full power to levy war, conclude peace, contract alliances, establish commerce, and to do all other acts and things which independent states may of right do.

Lincoln's Plea for the Union

Abraham Lincoln was inaugurated on March 4, 1861. Portions of his inaugural address are given here.

James Richardson, ed., **A Compilation of the Messages and Papers of the Presidents.** Washington, D.C.: Government Printing Office, 1897, vol. VI, pp. 5–12. Abridged from the original.

Apprehension seems to exist among the people of the Southern states, that by the accession of a Republican Administration their property, and their peace, and personal security, are to be endangered. There has never been any reasonable cause for such apprehension. Indeed, the most ample evidence to the contrary has all the while existed . . . in nearly all the published speeches of him who now addresses you. I do but quote from one of those speeches when I declare that "I have no purpose, directly or indirectly, to interfere with the institution of slavery in the states where it exists. I believe I have no lawful right to do so, and I have no inclination to do so."

The proposition that . . . the Union is perpetual, [is] confirmed by the history of the Union itself. The Union is much older than the Constitution. It was formed in fact, by the Articles of Association in 1774. It was matured and continued by the Declaration of Independence in 1776. It was further matured and the faith of all the then thirteen states expressly plighted and engaged that it should be perpetual, by the Articles of Confederation in 1778. And finally, in 1787, one of the declared objects for ordaining and establishing the Constitution, was "to form a more perfect Union."

The First Continental Congress drew up a document called "The Association" in 1774. It pledged a boycott of British goods and the means to enforce the boycott. It was the first united effort by all the thirteen colonies.

It follows from these views that no state, upon its own mere motion, can lawfully get out of the Union; that resolves and ordinances to that effect are legally void, and that acts of violence, within any state or states, against the authority of the United States, are insurrectionary [rebellious] or revolutionary, according to circumstances.

I therefore consider that in view of the Constitution and the laws, the Union is unbroken; and to the extent of my ability I shall take care, as the Constitution itself expressly enjoins upon [directs] me, that the laws of the Union be faithfully executed in all the states.

Anarchy is a state of disorder resulting from the absence or ineffectiveness of government and law.

Plainly, the central idea of secession is the essence of anarchy. A majority, held in restraint by constitutional checks and limitations, and always changing easily with deliberate changes of popular opinions and sentiments is the only true sovereign of a free people. Whoever rejects it, does of necessity fly to anarchy or to despotism. Unanimity is impossible. The rule of a minority, as a permanent arrangement, is wholly inadmissible; so that, rejecting the majority principle, anarchy or despotism in some form is all that is left.

One section of our country believes slavery is right and ought to be extended, while the other believes it is wrong and ought not to be extended. This is the only substantial dispute.

I am loath to close. We are not enemies, but friends. We must not be enemies. Though passion may have strained, it must not break our bonds of affection. The mystic chords of memory, stretching from every battlefield and patriot grave to every living heart and hearthstone, all over this broad land, will yet swell the chorus of the Union, when again touched, as surely they will be, by the better angels of our nature.

Newspapers Discuss Disunion

These selections, taken from both Northern and Southern newspapers, suggest the variety of reactions to the crisis.

Vicksburg, Mississippi, Daily Whig, January 18, 1860

By mere supineness [inactivity], the people of the South have permitted the Yankees to monopolize the carrying trade [transportation of goods], with its immense profits. We have yielded to them the manufacturing business, in all its departments, without an effort, until recently, to become manufacturers ourselves. We have acquiesced in the claims of the North to do all the importing, and most of the exporting business, for the whole Union. Thus, the North has been aggrandized [enriched] in a most astonishing degree, at the expense of the South. It is no wonder that their villages have grown into magnificent cities. It is not strange that they have "merchant princes," dwelling in gorgeous palaces and reveling in luxuries transcending the luxurious appliances of the East [Orient]! How could it be otherwise? New York City, like a mighty queen of commerce, sits proudly upon her island throne, sparkling in jewels and waving an undisputed commercial scepter over the South. By means of her railways and navigable streams, she sends out her long arms.

Boston Herald, March 21, 1860

Should the South succeed in carrying out her designs she will immediately form commercial alliances with European countries who will readily acquiesce in any arrangement which will help English manufacturing at the expense of New England. The first move the South would make would be to impose a heavy tax upon the manufactures of the North, and an export tax upon the cotton used by Northern manufacturers. In this way she would seek to cripple the North. The carrying trade, which is now done by American vessels, would be transferred to British ships, which would be a heavy blow aimed at our commerce. It will also seriously affect our shoe trade and the manufacture of ready-made clothing, while it would derange [disturb] the monetary affairs of the country.

New York Herald, March 13, 1860

When it is remembered how steadily the public mind in the North has been educated in the idea that "slavery is an evil and a crime"; how for many years this has been inculcated [taught] by the school books and the churches; how under its influence the religious sects of the country, once united in their sessions and synods [church councils] have been divided and led to look upon each other as wicked; how the missionary and tract societies have been split; how the religious book concerns have been sundered into Northern and Southern organizations; how every system of moral propagandism in the North has been to a greater or lesser degree turned to the same object, and that at last political parties have come to be ranged on sectional and geographical grounds, we shall find good reason why the South should be in earnest in its present alarm.

Raleigh, North Carolina Standard, March 9, 1861

Our opinions in relation to the Chicago platform, Abraham Lincoln, and the Black Republican party are well known. We are as hostile to Mr. Lincoln and to the sectional party that elected him as any reasonable man in the South. We will never submit to the administration of the government on the principles of that party so far as they relate to slavery in the territories; but while we say this for the hundredth time, we also hold that justice should be done even to Mr. Lincoln and his party, and that he who would deliberately fan the flame of sectional strife, instead of doing all he can to put out the fires of discord which threaten to consume the temple of the Union, is guilty of an inexpiable [incapable of atonement] crime. We want peace, not war. We want Union, not disunion. We want justice for the South, but we must do justice to the North.

52 The Failure of Compromise

HISTORICAL ESSAY

Daniel Webster, who had been one of the architects of the Compromise of 1850, believed that the Compromise would bring the Whig and Democratic parties closer together. "Those who have acted together in this great crisis" he thought, could "never again feel sharp asperities [bitterness] towards one another." Many people in the country agreed; both Northern and Southern cities held street celebrations to hail the saving of the Union. Ten years later the Whig party had disappeared and the Southern states had seceded from the Union. Why did the Compromise fail?

Flaws in the Compromise: The Northern View

First, while thousands of Americans applauded Henry Clay's Compromise of 1850, thousands of others denounced it. Many Northerners bitterly resented the Fugitive Slave Law which provided for special United States Commissioners who were authorized to hold hearings, issue warrants for the arrest of suspected fugitives, and return them to their masters. The Commissioners did not allow suspected runaways, who claimed to be free citizens, to testify. The Commissioners also received a larger fee when they returned a suspect to the South, than when they set him free.

Antislavery people in the North, such as Senator Seward, found the law morally objectionable. They believed that the federal government was using its power to perpetuate slavery. Prominent Northern abolitionists and intellectuals, such as Ralph Waldo Emerson, announced publicly that they would not obey the law. Some Northern states passed "personal liberty" laws making it illegal for slaveholders to capture runaways. The total number of runaway slaves was never very great, but, whenever the commissioners arrested a suspect and gave him a hearing under the new law, the affair received publicity all over the nation.

The Fugitive Slave Law drove many Northerners to join ranks with the abolitionists because they felt the government was trying to force them to support an immoral institution. The publication of Harriet Beecher Stowe's novel, *Uncle Tom's Cabin,* in 1852 intensified Northern opposition to slavery. The book focused on the cruelty of slavery and emphasized the persecution of runaway slaves. Within a year, several hundred thousand copies of *Uncle Tom's Cabin* circulated throughout the North. The popularity of the book contributed to the growing antislavery sentiment in the North.

A Minority Region: The Southern View

Many Southerners also denounced the Compromise of 1850. Calhoun died while the Senate was still debating the issue, but other Southern leaders continued to voice his views vehemently. They pointed out that the South had become a minority area in the nation. With the admission of California the United States contained sixteen free states and fifteen slave states. In addition, population in the free states grew much more rapidly than the population of the South. Almost certainly, the territories most likely to be admitted as states (Oregon and Minnesota) would join as free states.

With the South reduced to a minority status and with slavery under attack in the rest of the nation, extremist Southern politicians, such as Robert Rhett of South Carolina, believed that the South could gain little from compromise. Such men insisted that the abolitionists be silenced and that slavery be protected everywhere in the territories. If the national government failed to do this, Southern extremists believed that secession was the only solution.

Throughout most of the 1850's, the number of Southerners who favored outright secession were a definite minority within the slave states, just as the abolitionists were a minority in the free states. The continued expansion of the world cotton market, however, strengthened the South's cause. When the country experienced a brief but rather severe depression in 1857, the North suffered much more severely than the South because the cotton market remained relatively stable. This development encouraged many Southerners to believe that they could get along outside the Union, if they had to.

Slavery in the Territories: The Kansas-Nebraska Act

Perhaps the most important reason for the failure of the Compromise was its inability to dampen the fires of controversy over slavery in the territories. The laws of 1850 applied only to territory gained by the United States through war with Mexico. The Compromise did not include the vast plains west of Missouri and Iowa which had been part of the Louisiana Purchase. In theory, slavery in that area had been prohibited by the Compromise of 1820, but the question had not arisen because the region remained unorganized.

Then in 1854, Stephen A. Douglas confused the issue further when he introduced legislation to organize the territories of Kansas and Nebraska and allow their admission to the union as states with or without slavery according to the wishes of the inhabitants. If Congress passed the bill, slavery could exist in Louisiana Purchase territory north of the 36th parallel if the settlers wanted it. The Douglas bill, in effect, repealed a critical provision of the Compromise of 1820. Douglas urged the passage of the Kansas-Nebraska bill on the grounds of "popular sovereignty." Americans had fought a revolution in order to be able to decide important matters for themselves, he said. This principle had been enshrined in the Constitution, and "popular sovereignty" was the most "American" way to solve the question of slavery in the territories.

After a furious debate, the bill became law in May 1854. If Douglas thought it would find general acceptance across the nation, he had miscalculated grievously. The South accepted the Kansas-Nebraska Act without excitement or particular interest. In the North, however, opposition was intense and immediate. The Massachusetts Senate voted unanimously to send a formal resolution of protest to Congress which was being flooded by evidence of Northern displeasure, including a petition from 3000 New England clergymen.

"Bleeding Kansas": A Rehearsal for War

The Kansas-Nebraska Act hastened the decline of the Whig party and helped create the new Republican party. Moreover, it encouraged violence in Kansas. Settlers from the North and the South poured into "Bleeding Kansas" with the goal of establishing a territorial government sympathetic to their particular views. Antislavery groups in New England raised money to support colonies of antislavery settlers. Similar organizations sprang up in the South.

Fraud and bloodshed accompanied the territorial elections which took place in 1854. Two competing territorial legislatures were established. Proslavery settlers (with the help of several thousand illegal proslavery votes from "border ruffians" who poured into Kansas from the neighboring slave state of Missouri) supported the legislators at Shawnee Mission, while antislavery settlers supported one at Topeka. By 1856, law and order had broken down completely in Kansas; civil war broke out in the state. Bands of armed

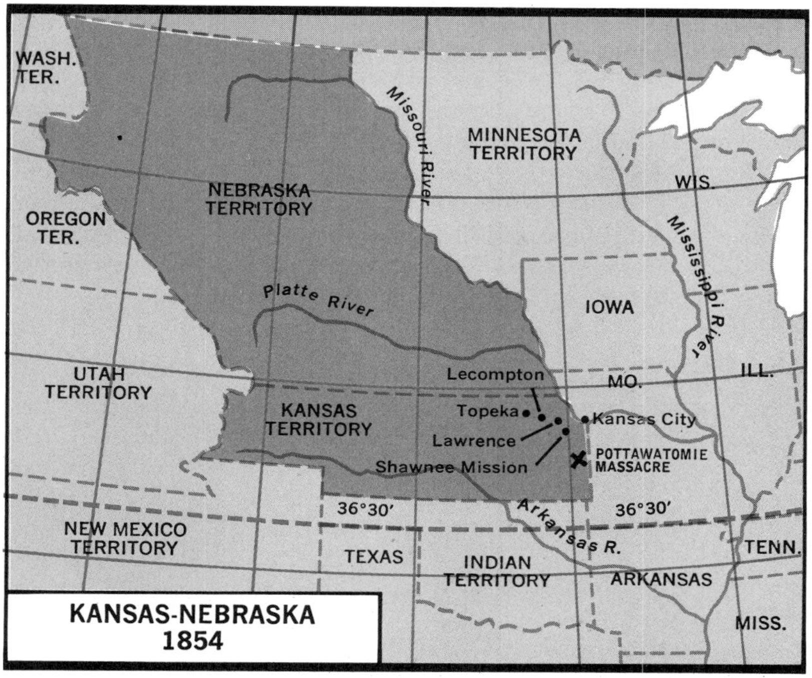

men roamed the country and pillaged and burned towns. About two hundred people died in the violent struggle. Federal troops restored temporary order in September 1856.

In 1857, the proslavery group called a constitutional convention at Lecompton. The members drew up a constitution and offered the voters a choice—the constitution with slavery or the constitution without it. Those who disliked the constitution did not vote at all, and the proslavery constitution passed. President Buchanan urged that Congress accept Kansas as a state under the Lecompton constitution, thus angering both antislavery groups and people who disliked the unfair practices. In 1855, the constitution was sent back to Kansas for a vote on accepting it. It was rejected. Kansas did not become a state until 1861. The struggle in Kansas foreshadowed the violence and bloodshed of the Civil War, and it dramatized urgently the great issue of the extension of slavery.

The Sumner-Brooks Incident

Three other events that occurred in the late 1850's helped to dramatize the slavery problem and weaken the possibilities of maintaining any kind of compromise. The first happened on the floor of the United States Senate in May 1856. Senator Charles

Sumner, from Massachusetts, was one of the most outspoken opponents of slavery in the Congress. On May 19, he made a speech bitterly denouncing the "slave power" in the South for its "crime against Kansas" and questioning the integrity of several Southern senators, including Andrew Butler from South Carolina. The next day Representative Preston Brooks, Butler's nephew, attacked and beat Sumner in the Senate chamber with a heavy cane. Sumner received severe injuries and spent two years recovering. During that period, his empty seat in the Senate symbolized to Northerners the savage unwillingness of slaveholders to tolerate criticism.

The Dred Scott Decision

The second dramatic event was a decision passed down by the Supreme Court in March 1857. The case involved a slave, Dred Scott, who had sued for his freedom after his master had taken him for a long period from the slave state of Missouri to the free state of Illinois and the free territory of Wisconsin, where the Compromise of 1820 had made slavery illegal. Chief Justice Roger Taney spoke for the majority of the Court (which was then Southern in its sympathies) when he ruled that no slave or descendant of a slave could be a citizen. Therefore, Dred Scott had no right to sue in a federal court. In addition, he said that Scott could not have been freed by the provisions of the Compromise of 1820 because that law was unconstitutional. The Court reasoned that it violated the Fifth Amendment of the Constitution which prohibited Congress from depriving persons of property without due process of law.

The Dred Scott decision marked the second time in American history that a law was declared unconstitutional. The first instance was in **Marbury** vs. **Madison** (1803).

Northerners saw in the Dred Scott decision another example of conspiracy to spread slavery throughout the nation. Taney was a Southerner from Maryland. His decision supported the Southern view that Congress had no right to pass laws about slavery in the territories. Southerners, naturally, approved of the decision, but it did not have the unifying effect which President Buchanan, among others, hoped it might have. More and more responsible people in the North began to listen attentively to the impassioned abolitionist orators who pointed to the Dred Scott decision as evidence that slaveholders had a stranglehold on the government.

This posed a dilemma for Douglas's doctrine of popular sovereignty, for if Congress could not legislate as to slavery in the territories, then the territorial legislatures authorized by Congress couldn't either. When asked by Lincoln if it were possible under the Dred Scott decision to keep slavery out of the territories, Douglas answered in his Freeport Doctrine that slavery could not exist unless legislatures passed laws to protect it.

John Brown's Raid

People in the North saw the assault on Charles Sumner and the Dred Scott decision as danger signs which symbolized Southern recklessness and Southern power. When people in the South picked up their newspapers in October 1859, to read with horror about John Brown's raid on Harper's Ferry, they believed that they saw the perfect symbol and logical result of Northern antislavery feeling.

John Brown was an abolitionist who had trained on the Kansas battleground. A man in late middle age who came from a family riddled with insanity, John Brown had been unsuccessful in several occupations before he left Ohio to join an antislavery colony in Kansas in 1855. In Kansas, Brown became captain of a local militia company. At the head of a small party, including four of his own sons, he led a raid which resulted in the massacre of five proslavery men. Upon leaving Kansas, Brown returned to the East, where he raised money with the help of leading abolitionists and organized a company of twenty-one men, including five Negroes, to liberate the slaves. On October 16, Brown and his followers seized a building in the government arsenal at Harper's Ferry, Virginia. He managed to attract very few slaves and soon found himself surrounded by federal troops. After brief fighting in which a few men were killed, Brown was captured. The state of Virginia tried him for treason, and he was hanged on December 2, 1859.

Was his the deed of a madman? Most people did not bother to ask that question. Many thoughtful Southerners believed that he attempted what the abolitionists really sought—to incite a slave insurrection and bury the South in an avalanche of blood. In the North, there was widespread disapproval of Brown's act in the press, and even some leading abolitionists such as William Lloyd Garrison were shocked by it. However, many of the most eloquent antislavery spokesmen applauded Brown. The serene way in which he had accepted his own death on a Virginia gallows impressed almost everyone. Brown became far more famous as a martyr to the antislavery cause than he had ever been when he was alive. His admirers flocked to support the new Republican party.

New Party Alignments

Since 1836, the Whig and Democratic parties had been the primary political organizations in the United States. Although the Whigs drew more strength in the northeastern states and the Democrats drew more in the South, both were national, not sectional, parties. Both bid for and attracted support in all parts of the nation. As the abolitionists grew more numerous and vocal in the 1830's and 1840's, the Whigs and Democrats faced a dilemma. To take a position on either side of the slavery controversy would mean losing important votes in either the North or the South. Consequently, the two major parties were very cautious about coming to grips with an issue that threatened to divide their supporters.

A group of Northern abolitionists became disgusted with the parties' hesitation to take a stand on slavery. They organized their own Liberty party in 1840. Out of a total of almost two and a

THE EVOLUTION OF THE TWO-PARTY SYSTEM

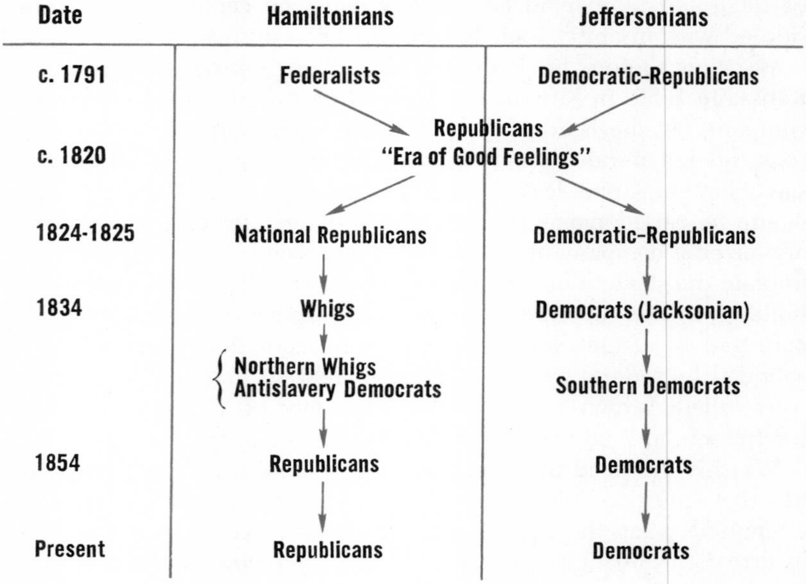

half million votes in the election of 1840, the Liberty party drew only 7069. In 1844, the Liberty party increased its vote to 62,000, but this was still about only two percent of the total popular vote. By 1848, however, the Mexican War had pushed the issue of slavery in the territories to the center of the political stage. Antislavery forces created a new Free Soil party and attracted more supporters from both Whigs and Democrats. In the election of 1848, the Free Soil candidate, Martin Van Buren, received over 291,000 votes, more than ten percent of the total number of votes cast. By taking votes away from Lewis Cass, the Democratic candidate in New York state, the Free Soil party helped swing the election to the Whig candidate, Zachary Taylor.

Date
Hamiltonians
Jeffersonians
c. 1791
Federalists
Democratic-Republicans
Republicans
"Era of Good Feelings"
c. 1820
1824-1825
National Republicans
Democratic-Republicans
1834
Whigs
Democrats (Jacksonian)
Northern Whigs
Antislavery Democrats
Southern Democrats
1854
Republicans
Democrats
Present
Republicans
Democrats

In the election of 1852 the Free Soil vote declined, largely because the Compromise of 1850 had eased political tensions over slavery temporarily. By 1856, however, the issue of slavery in the territories dominated the election. The Whigs, who had been having increasing difficulty holding together the proslavery and antislavery factions of their party, disappeared from the national scene. Two new parties emerged. One was the short-lived American party, official arm of an anti-Catholic, anti-immigrant political organization popularly known as the "Know-Nothing party." The other, a direct heir of the Free Soil movement, was the Republican party. The Republicans attracted people of antislavery sentiment from both the Whigs and Democrats and developed a platform favoring internal improvements, tariffs and a homestead law designed to appeal to both the East and the West.

Abraham Lincoln, who became one of the leaders of this party in Illinois, had begun his political career as a Whig. The Republicans took the position on the issue of slavery in the territories that Lincoln outlined in the debates he had with Douglas in 1858. The party maintained that the Constitution recognized slavery so it should be protected in the states where it already existed, but that slavery was morally wrong and should not be allowed in the territories. In the election of 1856, the combined total of Republican and American party votes exceeded the Democratic vote, but the Democrat James Buchanan won a heavy majority.

Lincoln Elected: A Northern Victory

As the antislavery position of the Republicans became more sharply defined, the Democrats fell more under the influence of extreme proslavery politicians, such as William Yancey of Alabama and Robert B. Rhett of South Carolina. By 1860, the Democrats had split into two factions, one led by Douglas with Northern support, the other dominated by Southern extremists. Because of this split Lincoln's election was almost a foregone conclusion, but Lincoln did not receive one electoral vote from a slave state.

The genius of the American political system had been its ability to absorb the disagreements of the American people and to devise compromises that had been at least effective enough to prevent open rebellion. More often than not, the differences between the major parties had not been great, but 1860 is the one year in American history when the flexibility of the political party system broke down. The South interpreted the Republican victory as a triumph for the North and for abolition.

Lincoln was not an abolitionist. He believed that slavery was wrong and he opposed its extension. At the same time he felt obligated to uphold the Fugitive Slave Law and to protect slavery in the South. Some abolitionists refused to vote for him because they believed that his position on slavery was much too moderate. The political leaders in the South, however, believed that Lincoln's election proved that the balance of political power had definitely shifted to the North and that future federal legislation would inevitably favor the North more than the South.

Mississippi, Florida, Georgia, Alabama, Louisiana, and Texas quickly followed South Carolina out of the Union. Early in February 1861, delegates from these states met in Montgomery, Alabama, where they formed a new government, the Confederate

States of America, adopted a constitution modeled after the United States Constitution, and elected Jefferson Davis President.

Secession took place during President Buchanan's last months in office. Buchanan was a Democrat, sympathetic with the grievances of the South, but unwilling to admit the right of secession. At the same time, he did not feel authorized to use force to prevent the Southern states from seceding.

The Crittenden Compromise, suggested in December 1860, was considered most seriously. Senator John J. Crittenden of Kentucky proposed that the 36°30′ line be extended to the Pacific, with slavery allowed and protected south of it and banned north of it. Lincoln was opposed to this compromise because it would have permitted the extension of slavery.

Meanwhile, eight slave states had not seceded. Men of good will from all parts of the country sought to find some compromise that would keep the Union intact. The Senate organized a special committee for this purpose. At the request of the Virginia Legislature a convention of delegates from twenty-one states met in Washington to search for a solution. All attempts at compromise failed.

Lincoln was inaugurated March 4, 1861. During the period between his election and inauguration he had remained largely silent, but had made it clear that he would not support any compromise that might encourage the further spread of slavery. In his inaugural address he said that he had no intention of interfering with slavery in the states, and urged the seceded states to return to the Union. He warned that he was sworn to uphold the Constitution and protect federal property but said there would be no violence "unless it be forced upon the national authority."

Attack on Fort Sumter: Civil War Begins

Lincoln's policy of firmness in the face of secession was put to the test almost immediately. During the previous few months the seceding states had claimed the federal institutions in their states. Southern troops had seized federal forts and arsenals in Georgia, Alabama, Florida, Louisiana, Arkansas, and Texas. In Charleston, South Carolina, Major Robert Anderson, who commanded the United States troops there, had withdrawn his garrison to Fort Sumter in Charleston Harbor. President Buchanan had dispatched an unarmed ship to provision Fort Sumter, but South Carolina shore batteries had driven the ship away. Lincoln had to decide what the federal government should do to support Major Anderson's garrison at Fort Sumter. He decided to try to provision the fort peacefully without sending armed force. This was consistent with his inaugural promise and he notified South Carolina of his decision.

Now the South had to decide what action to take. Jefferson Davis made the decision for the Confederacy. Fort Sumter was to be evacuated or captured. On April 12, 1861, South Carolina batteries opened fire on Sumter. On April 13, Major Anderson surrendered, and the next day President Lincoln declared that "insurrection" existed and called for the raising of a volunteer army in the

North. In the next weeks, Virginia, Arkansas, Tennessee, and North Carolina seceded. The Civil War had begun.

Why did the nation go to war in 1861? The societies and economies of North and South differed in significant ways. Southern political leaders argued for states' rights, while Northerners stressed a primary role for national government. Political leadership and political parties changed between 1851 and 1861. All of these factors contributed to the conflict between North and South. Yet slavery was related closely to each of these issues. More than any other thing, slavery distinguished Southern from Northern society, and slave labor also provided the basis for Southern agriculture. Many Southerners who argued most vehemently for states' rights did so knowing full well that their states could be depended upon to protect slavery. Most important of all, slavery was at the center of the major political crises of the 1850's, which contributed to the development of sectional political parties. With the political fragmentation of the nation, no machinery remained through which Northerners and Southerners could seek political solutions to the problems that divided them. Once a sectional President was elected, secession seemed the only course left to Southerners.

SUGGESTED READINGS

CURRENT, RICHARD, *Daniel Webster and The Rise of National Conservatism.* This is a brief biography of the great Whig orator who, along with Henry Clay and John C. Calhoun, played a dominant role in national politics for almost fifty years and made his last great appearances in the Senate in 1850.

HAMILTON, HOLMAN, *Prologue to Conflict: The Crisis and Compromise of 1850.* This well written account concentrates on the events surrounding the famous compromise.

MIERS, EARL SCHENCK, *Abraham Lincoln in Peace and War.* This is a balanced, well written and attractively illustrated biography of Lincoln which deals rather fully with the pre-Civil War years.

From War to Reconciliation, 1861–1877

CHAPTER 14

STATING THE ISSUE

The American Civil War, like all wars, created as many problems as it solved. For four long, bloody years, the battle raged between North and South. When the armies of the Confederacy surrendered to the North in the spring of 1865, some of the issues that had appeared and reappeared since the formation of the nation had been settled. But the war left new issues and new problems. Lincoln's assassination, shortly after the war's end, robbed the country of gifted leadership at the time when it had to confront the overwhelming problems of reconstructing the nation.

The South experienced almost total defeat. War made a shambles of Southern cities and railroads. Rich agricultural fields lay scarred by battle and untended. The slave system of labor, which Southerners had fought to preserve, was destroyed. Politically, economically, and socially, the old order in the South was torn asunder.

What were the major war aims of the North and the South? What accounted for the Union victory? What terms did the North insist upon before restoring Confederate states to full membership in the Union? What role did four million former slaves play in the reconstruction of the South? How did Northerners, Southerners, and former slaves respond to Reconstruction? These are the major issues raised in Chapter 14.

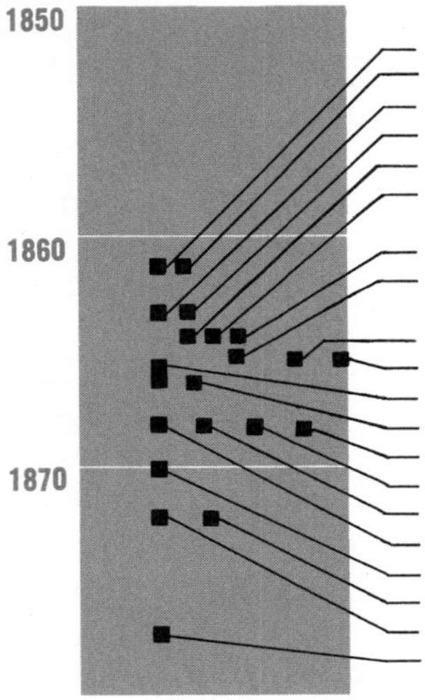

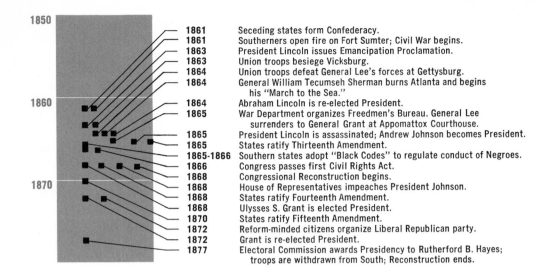

1861	Seceding states form Confederacy.
1861	Southerners open fire on Fort Sumter; Civil War begins.
1863	President Lincoln issues Emancipation Proclamation.
1863	Union troops besiege Vicksburg.
1864	Union troops defeat General Lee's forces at Gettysburg.
1864	General William Tecumseh Sherman burns Atlanta and begins his "March to the Sea."
1864	Abraham Lincoln is re-elected President.
1865	War Department organizes Freedmen's Bureau. General Lee surrenders to General Grant at Appomattox Courthouse.
1865	President Lincoln is assassinated; Andrew Johnson becomes President.
1865	States ratify Thirteenth Amendment.
1865-1866	Southern states adopt "Black Codes" to regulate conduct of Negroes.
1866	Congress passes first Civil Rights Act.
1868	Congressional Reconstruction begins.
1868	House of Representatives impeaches President Johnson.
1868	States ratify Fourteenth Amendment.
1868	Ulysses S. Grant is elected President.
1870	States ratify Fifteenth Amendment.
1872	Reform-minded citizens organize Liberal Republican party.
1872	Grant is re-elected President.
1877	Electoral Commission awards Presidency to Rutherford B. Hayes; troops are withdrawn from South; Reconstruction ends.

53 Sumter to Appomattox, 1861–1865

Most of the chapters in this book have contained three readings from historical sources followed by a historical essay. Chapter 14 is arranged differently. It opens with an essay on the Civil War, followed by two readings from historical sources and another essay on Reconstruction.

HISTORICAL ESSAY

The war aims of the North and South were diametrically opposed. The South, under the leadership of Jefferson Davis, wanted the North to recognize the independence of the Confederate states and to concede their right to legislate for themselves in all matters, including slavery. The North wanted to restore the Union; in addition many Northerners wanted to free the slaves. During the early years of the war, Lincoln insisted that his first purpose was to save the Union and "*not* either to save or destroy slavery."

Comparative Strength

Each side possessed initial advantages. The South needed only to fight defensively and maintain a stalemate to win its point. A high proportion of the best officers in the United States army were

Southerners who returned to the South after secession. The ruling classes in England and France sympathized with the South. Southern leaders hoped to exchange their cotton crops for European economic and military support.

The North had superior military capacity from the beginning. Twenty million people lived in the North as opposed to nine million (including slaves) in the South. The North had a manufacturing capacity seven times greater than that of the South, a much more extensive railroad system, most of the country's merchant marine and navy, and a near monopoly in the firearms industry.

The western part of Virginia refused to secede. In 1863, that area was admitted to the Union as the state of West Virginia.

The attack on Fort Sumter and Lincoln's call for 75,000 Union troops to put down "rebellion" forced every state to take a stand. Four wavering states in the upper South (Virginia, North Carolina, Tennessee, and Arkansas) followed their sister states out of the Union. Four border slave states (Delaware, Maryland, Kentucky, and Missouri), despite strong secessionist movements, stayed in the Union. Both Northerners and Southerners supported the initial call to arms enthusiastically.

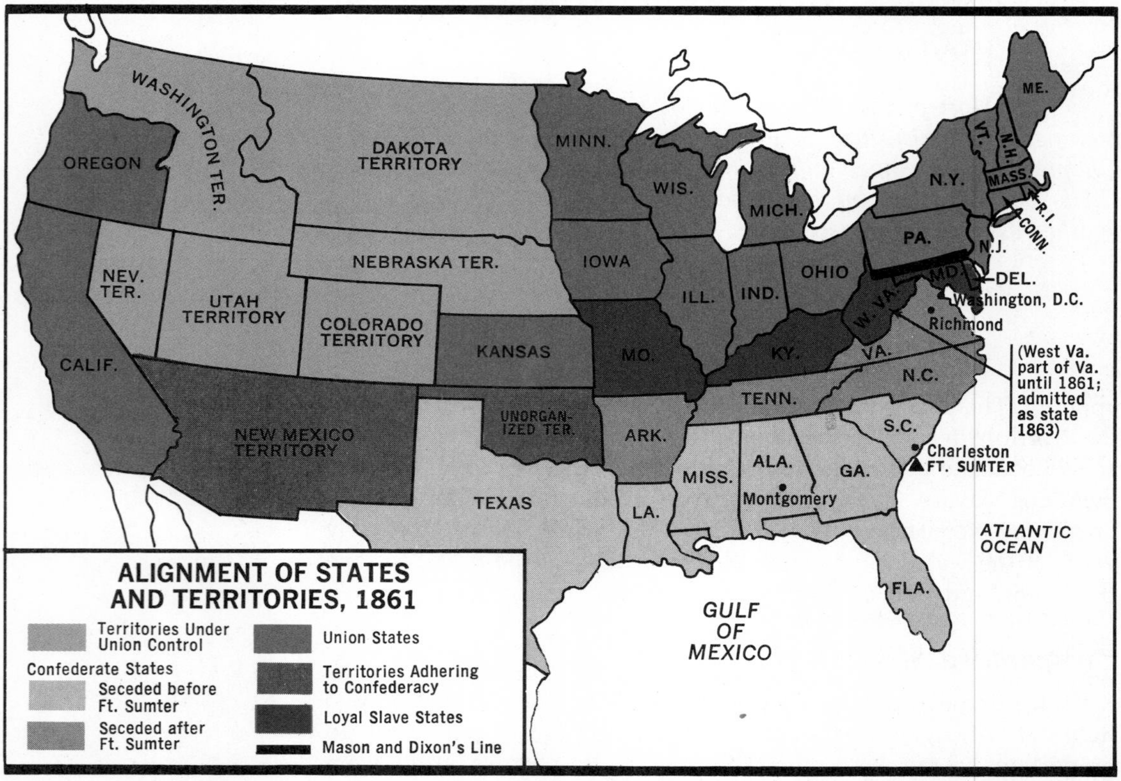

By January 1862, the North had raised an army of over 575,000 soldiers as compared to a Confederate army of about 350,000 troops. Despite the numerical superiority of its army, however, the North soon had to learn to live with defeat. In the first important battle of the war at Bull Run, Virginia (July 21, 1861), only a few miles outside of Washington, smaller Confederate forces routed a large Union army. The Confederate victory was in part due to the firm stand of General T.J. Jackson, then nicknamed "Stonewall."

The disastrous and humiliating defeat at Bull Run caused Lincoln to make the first of many changes among his generals. George B. McClellan, a retired West Point officer, replaced Winfield Scott as General-in-Chief in direct charge of the Army of the Potomac. He began a long training campaign aimed at mounting a major offensive in the Confederate capitol at Richmond, Virginia.

In May 1861, Richmond was chosen to replace Montgomery as the capital of the Confederacy.

Lincoln's Problems at Home and Abroad

Meanwhile, Lincoln encountered political and diplomatic difficulties. When the Southern states seceded and their congressmen left Washington, the control of Congress naturally fell into the hands of Northern Republicans. Within the Republican party a group of "Radicals" took over the leadership of the Congress during the early years of the War. The Radicals had strong abolitionist support, and they urged Lincoln to move more aggressively against the South to free the slaves. Under the leadership of Representative Thaddeus Stevens, they dominated the Joint House and Senate Committee on the Conduct of the War and remained a thorn in Lincoln's side throughout the conflict.

Lincoln was as anxious as anyone to bring the war to a speedy end. He believed, however, that it was his constitutional duty to direct the war effort. He was unwilling to issue a proclamation emancipating all slaves because he feared that it would encourage the South to fight to the bitter end and would particularly alienate the slaveholding border states that had reluctantly sided with the Union. Lincoln's insistence on moving cautiously against slavery caused much friction between him and the Radicals in Congress.

The diplomatic picture was not much brighter during the early years of the war. England maintained neutrality and apparently intended to consider the struggle between North and South a war, rather than a domestic rebellion. Lincoln threatened to break off diplomatic relations if England entered into official negotiations with commissioners representing the Confederacy. In November 1861, an American warship stopped the British steamer *Trent* and removed two Confederate commissioners en route to England. This interference with a British ship on the high seas inflamed British public opinion. The threat of war with Britain subsided only when Secretary of State William Seward released the Confederates.

For several months, it seemed that 1862 would repeat for the North the disappointments of the previous year. McClellan remained reluctant to engage the enemy in Virginia, and the brilliant leader of the Confederate army, General Robert E. Lee, defeated the North in a second battle at Bull Run (August 1862).

Lincoln had offered Lee the command of the Union armies. Lee, who had opposed both secession and slavery, felt his first loyalty belonged to Virginia. When Virginia seceded, he joined his state. Generals on both sides had high regard for Lee's character and ability.

The North Gathers Strength

Two events, however, made the North more optimistic. The Union mounted an effective naval blockade along the southern coastline, and Lincoln discovered that General Ulysses S. Grant could win battles. Grant was a West Point graduate who had served in the Mexican War and later retired from the army. As a civilian, he had been unsuccessful in farming and business. When the war started, he returned to military service at the head of a regiment of Illinois volunteers. In February 1862, Grant took the Confederate forts Henry and Donelson which guarded the entrance to the Cumberland and Tennessee rivers. In April, he moved south and, with heavy losses on both sides, defeated the main Confederate army in the west at Shiloh, Tennessee, near the Mississippi border. At about the same time, Union gunboats bombarded New Orleans, and Union troops moved into the city. The strategy of dividing the Confederacy along the Mississippi and Tennessee rivers began to bear fruit.

In the fall of 1862, McClellan inflicted a serious blow on Lee's army in the bloodiest fighting of the war at Antietam, Maryland. McClellan, however, failed to follow up his advantage, and Lee escaped. Lincoln dismissed McClellan from his command, but the two generals who had succeeded him, Ambrose Burnside and Joseph Hooker, were no more successful in the east than McClellan had been.

The First Strike at Slavery

Despite limited success on the battlefield, the balance of power definitely shifted to the North by 1863. On January 1, Abraham Lincoln issued the Emancipation Proclamation which declared that all slaves in areas still in rebellion were free. Because the Proclamation applied only to the Confederate States, over which the federal government had no control, it did not effectively free any slaves. It did, however, strengthen Lincoln's hand with the Radical Republicans in Congress, and it helped to influence public opinion abroad, especially in England. Now that the war had become a war to end slavery, Englishmen, proud of their own freedom, were unwilling to give either moral or material support to the South.

The Thirteenth Amendment, adopted in 1865, freed all slaves in the United States and its territories.

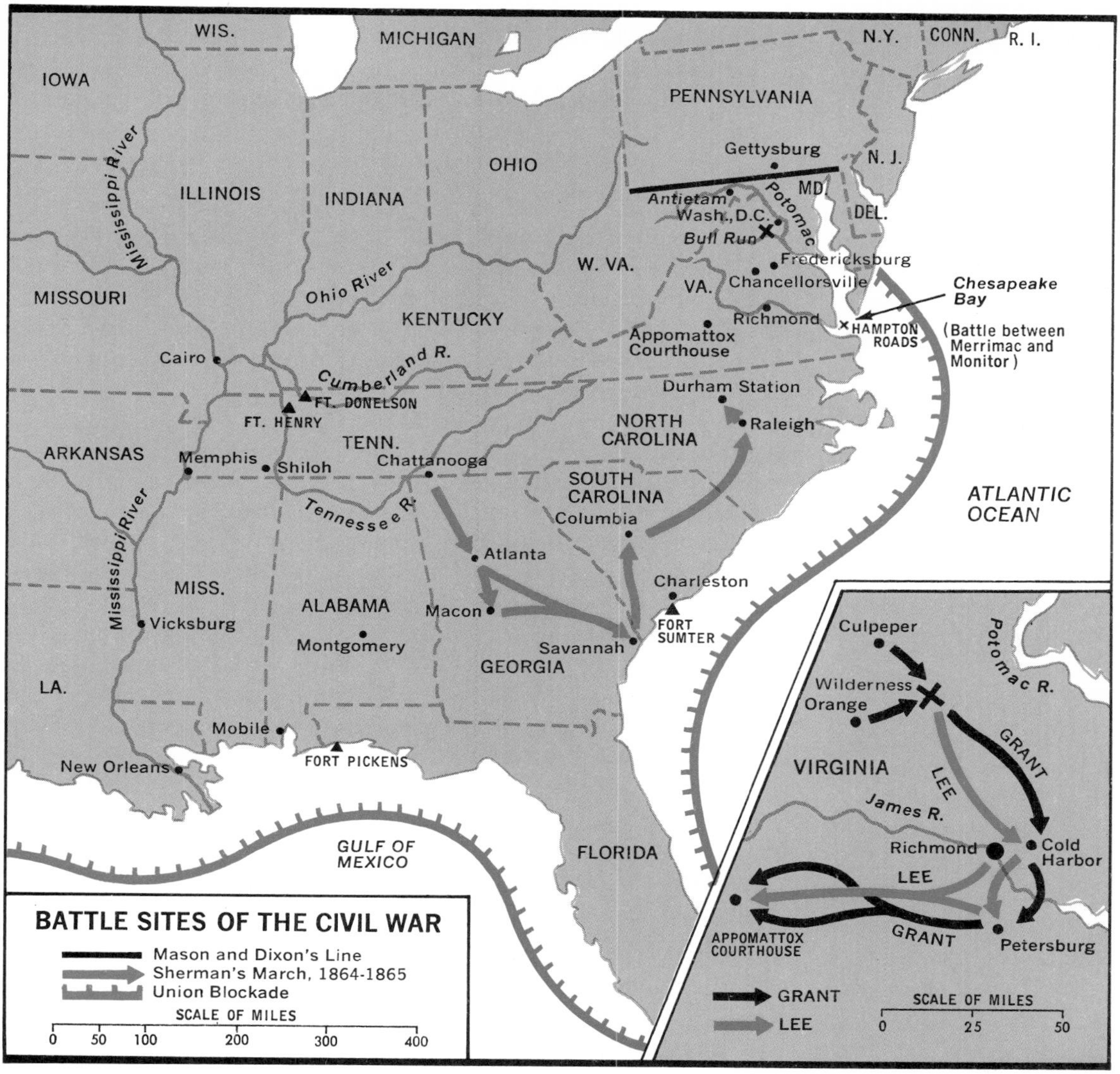

In 1863, the war to save the Union also became a war to free the slaves. Northern Negroes naturally wanted to participate in such a war. Thousands of Negroes had responded to Lincoln's call for volunteers in 1861, but they had been turned away. By the time the Union Army had begun to draft soldiers, however, Negroes were being accepted into the Northern army, and Union Negro regiments had seen action in several Southern states. More than 180,000 Negroes enrolled in the Union Army by the end of the war. Over

Appeals for volunteers did not provide the necessary manpower. In 1863, Congress passed the first draft law. One of its most resented features allowed a man to escape the draft by hiring a substitute to serve in his place or by paying a $300 fee to the authorities who in turn paid a bounty to a substitute.

38,000 Negro soldiers lost their lives in the War. Many Negro soldiers were decorated for bravery. One year after the Emancipation Proclamation, Lincoln wrote to one of his generals that Negro troops had "heroically vindicated their manhood on the field of battle."

An End in Sight

Two decisive encounters, in the spring and summer of 1863, foreshadowed the South's defeat. In May, Grant lay siege to 30,000 Confederate troops in Vicksburg, Mississippi. When Vicksburg fell on July 4, the Union gained control of the entire Mississippi River. At the same time in the east, General Robert E. Lee, after defeating numerically superior Union forces in December 1862 at Fredericksburg, and in May 1863 at Chancellorsville in Virginia, launched a final daring attempt to split the Union, by invading the North and cutting the main east-west railroads in Pennsylvania and Maryland. On July 1, Lee's army of 70,000 men attacked a Union force of 90,000 commanded by George Meade in Gettysburg, Pennsylvania. After three days of furious, bloody fighting, the Confederate forces withdrew in retreat to Virginia.

The Union victories at Vicksburg and Gettysburg introduced the final phase of the war. In March 1864, Grant assumed general command of the Union armies. He took personal command of the Army of the Potomac and began to move slowly, but relentlessly, against Lee's smaller army. At the same time, General William T. Sherman moved south and east from Chattanooga, Tennessee, into Georgia. Sherman's march through Georgia to the sea further fragmented the South, which had already been split vertically by Union victories in the river valleys of the west.

The Election of 1864

In 1864, gloom and frustration marked the public mood in the North, although the war seemed to be going better. The fighting had dragged on for three frightful years. It was an election year, and Lincoln was in trouble. On one side, Peace Democrats in the North who wanted a negotiated settlement with the South harassed the President. They drew their political strength largely from working classes in the cities, where intense resentment existed against the government's draft laws. In the summer of 1863 in New York City, this resentment had erupted into four days of rioting, pillaging, and lynching of Negroes. Union troops fresh from the battlefields at Gettysburg had been called in to restore order. On the other side, Lincoln still had trouble with the Radicals in his own party, many of whom preferred another candidate in 1864. Nevertheless, the

Republicans nominated Lincoln for re-election. General McClellan opposed him as the Democratic candidate and ran on a peace platform. Lincoln easily won in the electoral vote (212–21), but the popular vote shows how divided Northern opinion was about his leadership. Lincoln received only 2.2 million votes to McClellan's 1.8 million.

Andrew Johnson, Democrat from Tennessee and the only Southerner to remain in Congress after secession, was selected as the Republican or Union party's Vice-Presidential candidate, as a replacement for Hannibal Hamlin.

Sherman's successes in Georgia had helped to swing the election to Lincoln. By the time of Lincoln's inauguration in March 1865, the South's fate was sealed. Sherman pursued a policy of destroying factories, warehouses, bridges, railroads, and anything else that might contribute to the Confederate cause while his troops "lived off the land." He cut through Georgia to Savannah and then turned upward through the Carolinas. Columbia, South Carolina, fell in February. Two months later, Grant's relentless pounding forced Lee out of Richmond, and on April 9, Lee surrendered the tattered remains of his army at Appomattox Courthouse in Virginia. The remaining Confederate generals soon followed Lee's example; by the end of May, all military resistance had ended. The problems of the postwar nation remained, however, to haunt vanquished and victor alike.

54 Northerners and Southerners View Reconstruction

As early as 1863, Lincoln had revealed a Reconstruction plan for those confederate states—Louisiana, North Carolina, and Tennessee—then under Northern control. Lincoln wanted to pardon most Southerners willing to swear loyalty to the Union. He was willing to recognize as legal any state government in which ten percent of the 1860 electorate had taken loyalty oaths.

The mood of the Congress, however, was far less generous than Lincoln's, and the Radical Republicans in control refused to support his proposal. They believed that the South could never be reconstructed unless slaveholders lost all of their former power and prestige and the state governments protected freedmen (emancipated slaves) and encouraged them to strike out on their own.

On April 14, 1865, Lincoln was assassinated by John Wilkes Booth, a mentally disturbed actor. Andrew Johnson succeeded Lincoln to the Presidency. Like Lincoln, he assumed that the President should take the leading role in Reconstruction. Johnson adopted the essential provisions of Lincoln's plan and organized provisional governments in the Southern states, which in turn organized conventions of "loyal" citizens to amend the old state constitutions. These conventions abolished slavery, repudiated the state's war debt, and called for the election of new state governments. Johnson recognized the legality of these governments, and in December 1865, he declared the Union restored.

Congress, however, refused to seat representatives from the supposedly "reconstructed" states. Republican leaders felt that Johnson's plan was too lenient on Southern whites, while it failed to protect the rights of Negroes. Moreover, they believed that the responsibility for Reconstruction belonged to Congress rather than the President.

As 1865 drew to an end, President Johnson and the Congress were deadlocked over reconstruction policy. Meanwhile, near chaos prevailed in the South. The presence of federal troops helped maintain order, and the federal government attempted to care for the freedmen and administer abandoned property in the South through a temporary organization called the Freedmen's Bureau.

To evaluate conditions in the South at the beginning of Reconstruction, the historian must consult local laws, court records, and newspapers of the period, as well as the letters and journals of men and women who actually lived through the experience of Southern defeat. The selections in Reading 54 give two accounts of Reconstruction. The first excerpt is taken from the reports of a Northern journalist who traveled through the South in 1865. The second is from the journal of a lady in Georgia written at the same time. As you read, try to answer these questions:

1. What evidence can you cite to show that Sidney Andrews wrote from a Northern point of view? Is there any evidence that he tried to be objective in his reporting?
2. To what extent do the selections from Eliza Andrews's *Journal* support the generalizations that Sidney Andrews made about Southern attitudes toward Negroes?
3. On the basis of these selections, what do you think were the major problems of Reconstruction?

Reconstruction: A Northern View

Sidney Andrews, **The South Since the War, as Shown by Fourteen Weeks of Travel and Observations in Georgia and the Carolinas.** Boston: Ticknor and Fields, 1866, pp. 96–101 **passim.** Language simplified and modernized.

Sidney Andrews traveled through the Carolinas and Georgia in the fall of 1865 as a special correspondent for the Chicago Tribune *and the* Boston Advertiser. *Excerpts from his reports from South Carolina are given here.*

The white man and the Negro do not understand each other. Consequently, they do not work together so harmoniously as it is desirable that they should. It would seem that, one party having work to do and the other needing work done, there would be common interests that would lead to unity of purpose and action. But the fact is, that each party distrusts the other, so bickering and antagonism result.

The fault unquestionably, it appears to me, lies with the white man. Most whites assumed that it was right to keep the Negro in slavery just as long as possible, and they added the further assumption—the brutal assumption—that the Negro cannot be controlled except by fear of the lash.

There is among the plantation Negroes a widely spread idea that land is to be given them by the government, and this idea is at the bottom of much idleness and discontent. At Orangeburg and at Columbia, South Carolina, country Negroes with whom I conversed asked me, "When is de land goin' fur to be dewided?" Some of them believe the land which they are to have is on the coast; others believe the plantations on which they have lived are to be divided among themselves.

Despite the fact that nearly everybody tells me the free Negro will not work, the experience of some of the better class of planters convinces me that he will work, if he is treated like a man. He is unquestionably sensitive about his freedom—it is the only thing he has that he can call his own.

Some of the blacks are working along as before, under private arrangements with their former masters; but in most cases there is a written contract between the employer and the employed. One copy is in the hands of the planter and the other is at the Freedmen's Bureau office. I hear of very few cases in which the compensation is in money; in nearly all instances it is a part of the crop. The laborer's share ranges from one tenth to one half. On some small farms, where special privileges are given the Negroes in the way of clothing, use of land, use of a team of mules, or use of time, the share may not be over one sixth to one tenth of the regular crop. In the lower part of the state, where most of the labor is done by hand, and where there are no special privileges, the share is from one third to one half; in the upper part of the state, where horses or mules are more in use, the share is from one fourth to one third. The contracts generally expire at New Year's.

The indifference which so many of the people feel and express as to the fate of the Negro is shocking and to the last degree revolting to me. He is actually to many of them nothing but a troublesome animal; not a human being, with hopes and longings and feelings, but a mere animal, valuable, but altogether unlovable. "I would shoot one just as soon as I would a dog," said a man to me yesterday on the [railroad] cars. And I saw one shot at in Columbia as if he had been only a dog—shot at from the door of a store, and at midday! "If I can only git shet [free] of 'em I don't care what becomes of 'em," said one of my two stage companions in the ride from Columbia to Winnsboro, while speaking of the seventy Negroes on his plantation. Of course he means to "git shet of 'em" as soon as possible. There are others who will follow his example.

The whole labor system of the state is in an utterly demoralized condition. How soon it can be thoroughly reorganized, and on just what basis that reorganization will take place, are questions that are not easy to answer. The labor question, and not Reconstruction, is the main issue among intelligent thinking men of the state. Scarcely one in a dozen of the best of them have any faith in the Negro. "The experiment of free Negro labor is bound to be a failure; and you of the North may as well prepare for it first as last," is substantially the language of hundreds. And thereafter follow questions of, "What shall then be done with the Negro?" and, "Where shall we then get our labor?"

Look at the figures for a few districts. In Sumter there were, in 1860, 6857 whites and 17,012 Negroes; in Fairfield, 6373 whites and 15,736 Negroes; in Colleton, 9255 whites and 32,661 Negroes; in Beaufort, 6714 whites and 33,339 Negroes; and in Georgetown, 3013 whites and 18,292 Negroes. Is it any wonder that the white population of these districts is nervously sensitive about the Negro? The proportion of blacks is even greater now than these figures indicate; for war has taken out the whites and brought in the Negroes to such an extent that one man told me there were in his parish but twenty-two voters and over two thousand Negroes. What is to come of such a condition of affairs?

Reconstruction: A Southern View

Eliza Frances Andrews (no relation to Sidney) was the twenty-five-year-old daughter of a Georgia plantation owner. She recorded in her diary her observations and impressions of life at the end of the Civil War. Portions of her diary are given here.

Eliza Frances Andrews, **The War-Time Journal of a Georgia Girl, 1864–1865.** New York: D. Appleton and Company, 1908, pp. 286, 292–93, 314–16, 318.

June 5, 1865 It seems strange to think how we laugh and jest now over things that we would once have thought it impossible to live through. We are all poor together, and nobody is ashamed of it. We live from hand to mouth like beggars. Father has sent to Augusta for a supply of groceries, but it will probably be a week or more before they get here, and in the meantime, all the sugar and coffee we have is what Uncle Osborne brings in. He hires himself out by the day and takes his wages in whatever provisions we need most, and hands them to father when he comes home at night. He is such a good carpenter that he is always in demand, and the Yankees themselves sometimes hire him. Father says that except Big Henry and Long Dick and old Uncle Jacob, he is the most valuable Negro he ever owned.

June 7, 1865 I am afraid we shall have to part with Emily and her family. Mother never liked her, and has been wanting to get rid of her since "freedom struck the earth." She says she would enjoy emancipation from the Negroes more than they will from their masters. Emily has a savage temper, and yesterday she gave mother some impudence, and mother said she couldn't stand her any longer, and she would have to pack up and go. Then Emily came crying to Mett [Eliza's sister] and me and said that Mistis [Mrs.] had turned her off, and we all cried over it together, and Mett went and shut herself up in the library and spent the whole afternoon there crying over Emily's troubles. Mother hasn't said anything more about it to-day, but the poor darkey is very miserable, and I don't know what would become of her with her five children, for Dick can't let whisky alone, and would never make a support for them. Besides, he is not fit for anything but a coachman, and people are not going to be able to keep carriages now. I felt so sorry for the poor little children that I went out and gave them all a big piece of cake, in commiseration for the emptiness their poor little stomachs will sooner or later be doomed to, and then I went and had a talk with father about them. He laughed and told me I needn't be troubled; he would never let any of his Negroes suffer as long as he had anything to share with them, and if mother couldn't stand Emily, he would find somebody else to hire her, or see that the family were cared for till they could do something for themselves. Of course, now that they are no longer his property, he can't afford to spend money bringing up families of little Negro children like he used to, but humanity, and the natural affection that every right-minded man feels for his own people, will make him do all that he can to keep them from suffering.

June 27, 1865 The next war . . . , I think, will be against the Negroes, who are already becoming discontented with freedom, so different from what they were taught to expect. Instead of wealth and idleness it has brought them idleness, indeed, but starvation and misery with it. There is no employment for the thousands that are flocking from the plantations to the towns, and no support for those who cannot or will not work. . . . A race war is sure to come, sooner or later, and we shall have only the Yankees to thank for it. They are sowing the wind, but they will leave us to reap the whirlwind. No power on earth can raise an inferior, savage race above their civilized masters and keep them there. No matter what laws they make in his favor, nor how high a prop they build under him, the Negro is obliged, sooner or later, to find his level, but we shall be ruined in the process. Eventually the Negro race will be either exterminated or reduced to some system of apprenticeship embodying the best features of slavery, but this generation will not live to see it.

June 28, 1865 Arch has "taken freedom" and left us, so we have no man-servant in the dining-room. . . . To do Arch justice, he didn't go without asking father's permission, but it is a surprise that he, who was so devoted to "Marse Fred," should be the very first of the house servants to go.

55 The Freedmen's Views of Reconstruction

Slaves played a significant role in the Confederate war effort. At the beginning of the war, Southern officers took Negro personal servants with them. But as the fighting and the Confederate supply problems became worse, they sent their servants back home.

Although some Southern leaders wanted to arm the slaves, public opinion in the South generally opposed the idea for fear that the slaves might turn on their masters. The Confederate Army, however, used thousands of slaves as cooks, teamsters, ambulance drivers, and hospital attendants. When the Confederate government finally attempted to recruit slaves as soldiers in 1865, the war was already lost.

Even if the slaves had been armed earlier, they would probably not have been enthusiastic soldiers for the Southern cause. Although there were few actual slave uprisings during the war, evidence shows that discipline on the plantations broke down wherever Northern troops advanced in the South. Some slaves continued to be loyal to their departed masters; many others were not. They wanted freedom, and they left the plantations to search for it.

At the end of the war, all the major problems involved in Reconstruction related in some way to the status of the freed slave. Should he be given a grant of land by the federal government? Should he be apprenticed to work for former slaveholders? Should he be allowed to vote? How could his constitutional rights be protected?

The historical record is full of what white Americans had to say about these questions and of the various actions the government took. The response of the freedmen themselves, however, is not ascertained so easily. Since most of them were illiterate, they left no written record of their experiences during the period. In 1936, the Works Progress Administration of the federal government undertook to fill this gap in the historical record by recording the verbal testimony of those American Negroes who still retained memories of their experiences in slavery and during Reconstruction. Several examples of these personal narratives appear below. As you read them, try to answer the following questions:

1. On the basis of these narratives, do you think the slaves welcomed their freedom? Why?
2. If you were a historian with a pro-Southern frame of reference, what things might you be tempted to emphasize in these narratives? If you were a civil-rights advocate, what might you emphasize?
3. What special difficulties do these narratives pose for historians? How would you compare them as evidence with Stanley Andrews's report and Eliza Andrews's diary? In what ways do the three sources support each other?

Testimony of Freedmen

White and Negro workers in the Federal Writers' Project interviewed hundreds of ex-slaves in the Ohio River Valley and the South. They compiled over ten thousand pages of testimony from which B. A. Botkin selected the narratives he included in the book Lay My Burden Down. *Some of these selections which give freedmen's recollections of Reconstruction are given here.*

Over Half of Them Were Gone

B. A. Botkin, ed., **Lay My Burden Down: A Folk History of Slavery.** Chicago: University of Chicago Press, 1945, pp. 229, 241–42, 248–49.

Testimony of Harriet Robinson, 95, who had been a slave in Texas.

After the war, Master Colonel Sims went to git the mail, and so he call Daniel Ivory, the overseer, and say to him, "Go around to all the quarters and tell all the [slaves] to come up, I got a paper to read to 'em. They're free now, so you can git you another job, 'cause I ain't got no more [Negroes] which is my own." [The slaves] come up from the cabin nappy-headed, just like they gwine to the field. Master Colonel Sims, say, "Caroline (that's my mammy), you is free as me. Pa said bring you back, and I's gwine do just that. So you go on and work and I'll pay you and your three oldest children $10 a month a head and $4 for Harriet"—that's me—and then he turned to the rest and say, "Now all you-uns will receive $10 a head till the crops is laid by." Don't you know before he got halfway through, over half them [Negroes] was gone.

Nappy, in this use, means kerchief.

Then Came the Calm

Testimony of Patsy Moore, 74, who had been a slave in Mississippi.

When freedom come, folks left home, out in the streets, crying, praying, singing, shouting, yelling, and knocking down everything. Some shot off big guns. Then come the calm. It was sad then. So many folks done bad, things tore up, and nowheres to go and nothing to eat, nothing to do. It got squally [stormy]. Folks got sick, so hungry. Some folks starved nearly to death. Times got hard. We went to the washtub [did washing for others]—onliest way we all could live. Ma was a cripple woman. Pa couldn't find work for so long when he mustered out.

I Got Along Hard After I Was Freed

Testimony of Thomas Ruffin, 83, who had been a slave in North Carolina.

I got along hard after I was freed. It is a hard matter to tell you what we could find or get. We used to dig up dirt in the smokehouse and boil it and dry it and sift it to get the salt to season our food with. We used to go out and get old bones that had been throwed away and crack them open and get the marrow and use them to season the greens with. Just plenty of [Negroes] then didn't have anything but that to eat.

Even in slavery times, there was plenty of [Negroes] out of them three hundred slaves who had to break up old lard gourds and use them for meat. They had to pick up bones off the dunghill and crack them open to cook with. And then, of course, they'd steal. Had to steal. That the best way to git what they wanted.

Gourds are the bulb-shaped fruit produced by a plant belonging to a family that includes squash and pumpkins. The dried, hollowed-out shells of gourds were used as cups or storage vessels for such things as lard.

Reconstruction Was a Mighty Hard Pull

Testimony of Warren McKinney, 85, who had been a slave in South Carolina.

I was born in Edgefield County, South Carolina. I am eighty-five years old. I was born a slave of George Strauter. I remembers hearing them say, "Thank God, I's free as a jay bird." My ma was a slave in the field. I was eleven years old when freedom was declared. When I was little, Mr. Strauter whipped my ma. It hurt me bad as it did her. I hated him. She was crying. I chunked him with rocks. He run after me, but he didn't catch me. There was twenty-five or thirty hands that worked in the field. They raised wheat, corn, oats, barley, and cotton. All the children that couldn't work stayed at one house. Aunt Mat kept the babies and small children that couldn't go to the field. He had a [cotton] gin and a shop. The shop was at the fork of the roads. When the war come on, my papa went to build forts. He quit Ma and took another woman. When the war close, Ma took her four children, bundled 'em up and went to Augusta. The government give out rations there. My ma washed and ironed. People died in piles. I don't know till yet what was the matter. They said it was the change of living. I seen five or six wooden, painted coffins piled up on wagons pass by our house. Loads passed every day like you see cotton pass here. Some said it was cholera and some took consumption. Lots of the colored people nearly starved. Not much to get to do and not much houseroom. Several families had to live in one house. Lots of the colored folks went up north and froze to death. They couldn't stand the cold. They wrote back about them dying. No, they never sent them back. I heard some sent for money to come back. I heard plenty 'bout the Ku Klux. They scared the folks to death. People left Augusta in droves. About a thousand would all meet and walk going to hunt work and new homes. Some of them died. I had a sister and brother lost that way. I had another sister come to Louisiana that way. She wrote back.

Cholera is an infectious intestinal disease. Tuberculosis, an infectious disease, usually of the lungs, was commonly called consumption.

During Reconstruction, white Southerners organized the Ku Klux Klan, a secret terrorist society, to force the Negro out of politics.

I don't think the colored folks looked for a share of land. They never got nothing 'cause the white folks didn't have nothing but barren hills left. About all the mules was wore out hauling provisions in the army. Some folks say they ought to done more for the colored folks when they left, but they say they was broke. Freeing all the slaves left 'em broke.

That Reconstruction was a mighty hard pull. Me and Ma couldn't live. A man paid our ways to Carlisle, Arkansas, and we come. We started working for Mr. Emerson. He had a big store, teams, and land. We liked it fine, and I been here fifty-six years now. There was so much wild game, living was not so hard. If a fellow could get a little bread and a place to stay, he was all right. After I come to this state, I voted some. I have farmed and worked at odd jobs. I farmed mostly. Ma went back to her old master. He persuaded her to come back home. Me and her went back and run a farm four or five years before she died. Then I come back here.

Peonage

Peonage is a condition of semi-slavery. Workers cannot be sold as slaves, but work contracts compelling them to work can be sold.

Testimony of William Ward, 105, who had been a slave in Georgia.

After [Gen.] Sherman come through Atlanta, he let the slaves go, and when he did, me and some of the other slaves went back to our old masters. Old Man Governor Brown was my boss man. After the war was over, Old Man Gordon took me and some of the others out to Mississippi. I stayed in peonage out there for 'bout forty years. I was located at just 'bout forty miles south of Greenwood, and I worked on the plantations of Old Man Sara Jones and Old Man Gordon.

A levee is an embankment made of dirt and stones to prevent a river from overflowing.

I couldn't git away 'cause they watched us with guns all the time. When the levee busted, that kinda freed me. Man, they was devils; they wouldn't 'low you to go nowhere—not even to church. You done good to git something to eat. They wouldn't give you no clothes, and if you got wet you just had to lay down in what you got wet in.

And, man, they would whup [whip] you in spite of the devil. You had to ask to git water—if you didn't they would stretch you 'cross a barrel and wear you out. If you didn't work in a hurry, they would whup you with a strap that had five-six holes in it. I ain't talking 'bout what I heard—I'm talking 'bout what I done seed.

Carrying on with Free Labor

Testimony of Peter Clifton, 89, who had been a slave in South Carolina.

Yes, sir, us had a bold, driving, pushing master but not a hard-hearted one. I sorry when military come and arrest him. It was this-away: Him try to carry on with free labor, 'bout like him did in slavery. Chester [a county in South Carolina] was in military district No 2. The whole state was under that military government. Old Master went to the field and cuss a [Negro] woman for the way she was working, chopping cotton. She turned on him with the hoe and gashed him 'bout the head with it. Him pull out his pistol and shot her. Dr. Babcock say the wound in the woman not serious. They swore out a warrant for Master Biggers, arrest him with a squad, and take him to Charleston, where him had [Negro] jailors and was kicked and cuffed 'bout like a dog. They say the only thing he had to eat was cornmeal mush brought round to him and other nice white folks in a tub, and it was ladled out to them through the iron railing into the palms of their hands. Mistress stuck by him, went and stayed down there. The filthy prison and hard treatments broke him down, and when he did get out and come home, him passed over the River of Jordan [died] where I hopes and prays his soul finds rest. Mistress say one time they threatened her down there, that if she didn't get up $10,000, they would send him where she would never see him again.

56 Reconstruction and Reconciliation, 1865–1877

HISTORICAL ESSAY

In his Second Inaugural Address, Abraham Lincoln called upon his countrymen to proceed "with malice toward none; with charity for all . . . to bind up the nation's wounds" and "to do all which may achieve and cherish a just and lasting peace among ourselves, and with all nations." Six weeks later Lincoln was dead. We will never know how much difference his presence and leadership might have made during Reconstruction. We do know that the Reconstruction policy that Lincoln favored was consistent with his plea in the Second Inaugural. We know that the Congress rejected his approach and imposed a much harsher policy on the South. We know that this policy aroused a resentment among Southern whites that endured for generations. Twelve years after Appomattox, Southern whites had returned to power to preside over a society which, despite the absence of legalized slavery, resembled the old Cotton Kingdom in many ways.

The Radicals' program for Reconstruction divided the South (excluding Tennessee) into five military districts, each controlled by a general.

A New Role for the Freedmen

What were the most important problems confronting the American people as they tried to "bind up the nation's wounds"? What strategies did the political leaders pursue? Did Reconstruction work or was it a failure? This essay is built around these questions.

Many of the problems involved in Reconstruction were visible to the eye in the form of shelled cities, wrecked railroads, and abandoned fields. The Southern economy would need to be rebuilt. But who would do the building? In the past, slaves had been the work force in the South. Now slavery was abolished. What kind of work force would take its place? Thousands of freedmen wandered aimlessly around the country or camped in the cities where they were fed and cared for by the Freedmen's Bureau. Would the freedmen be given land? Could they be forced or induced to work?

Involved in all questions about the freedmen was something not so visible—the attitude of American white people toward Negroes. The South had lost the war, and most Southerners accepted the abolition of slavery as part of the price of defeat. By conviction, however, almost all of them continued to believe that Negroes were more suited for slavery than for freedom and that large numbers of whites and Negroes could never live together in peace and harmony except under white dominance.

The refusal to admit the injustice of slavery was unique to the South, but the assumption that a basic inequality existed between the races was almost universal in the country. Laws that prevented Negroes from voting in Northern states were only one example of the general prejudice against them outside the South. Widespread prejudice meant that attempts to legislate equality for the freedmen would be resisted violently in the South, and in the long run, except for a few unyielding reformers like the abolitionist Wendell Phillips, win only half-hearted support from people in the North.

Americans in the North also found it increasingly difficult to concentrate on Reconstruction during the postwar years. Reconstruction of a durable union without slavery competed for the attention and energy of the American people with enormous economic opportunities which the postwar period offered. During the war years, the Republicans had taken advantage of their control of Congress to legislate a program which served the interests of Northern farmers and businessmen. Between 1861 and 1863, Congress raised tariffs, passed a Homestead Act making free land available to farmers in the west, established a uniform national banking system, and launched a transcontinental railroad in 1862 by granting huge subsidies to the Union Pacific and Central Pacific Railroad Companies. When the war ended, the stage was set for the greatest period of economic growth and industrial expansion in American history. By the middle of the 1870's, most Americans were tired of worrying about the Negro. They wanted to believe that the problems of Reconstruction had been solved so they could concentrate on getting ahead themselves and helping to build industrial America.

These railroads received direct financial aid in the form of a loan of $60 million. Other railroads received land grants, and they often sold the land to settlers.

The President Against the Radicals

Finally, there was the problem of assigning political responsibility for Reconstruction. Lincoln had taken the position that the Confederate States rebelled against the Union for, he maintained, a state could not legally secede. The President, as Commander-in-Chief of the Army, had the right to grant pardons. Lincoln felt that the President should take the initiative in helping Southern states to resume their proper place in the Union. If ten percent of the people in a Southern state professed loyalty to the federal government and recognized the end of slavery, Lincoln was prepared to have them send representatives to Congress. Lincoln ran into trouble with Congress. The Radical Republicans in Congress felt that the President was exceeding his authority. They argued that the Confederate states were conquered provinces, subject to congressional control. They should not be readmitted to the Union until Congress was convinced that they were, in the words of Representative

Thaddeus Stevens of Pennsylvania, "republican in spirit and placed under the guardianship of loyal men." Congress was not prepared to "bind up the nation's wounds" without being sure that the infection which started the war was finally killed. Lincoln's assassination only hardened the will of the Congress in this matter, an evil foreboding to his successor.

Andrew Johnson was a former Jacksonian Democrat from eastern Tennessee, who hated slavery and slaveholders. He had been a staunch Union man during the secession crisis. Honest and courageous, he lacked Lincoln's patience and sense of the public mood. His abrasive personality and sharp tongue tended more to open new wounds than to heal old ones. When Johnson came to the White House, he faced the immediate problem of coming to an agreement with Congress on Reconstruction policy. Despite the fact that Congress had already demonstrated its unwillingness to go along with Lincoln's plan of Reconstruction, Johnson pursued a similar policy. By the end of 1865, all the Southern states had satisfied his requirements for Reconstruction, but Congress still refused to admit Southern representatives. The executive and legislative branches of government had reached a deadlock over the question of responsibility for reconstructing the Union.

Black Codes and Civil Rights

Developments in the Southern states also disturbed many congressmen. In the fall of 1865, Southern legislatures began to define the new economic position of the freedmen through a series of laws known as "Black Codes." These laws attempted to regulate the terms on which Negroes would continue to work on plantations. Although some provisions in the laws were designed to protect former slaves, the laws inhibited Negroes from leaving their plantations and moving around the country like other free men. Abolitionist Republicans in the Congress believed that Southerners designed the "Black Codes" to preserve the essential features of slavery. Therefore, they attempted to secure the Negroes' freedom by passing a Civil Rights Act (later declared unconstitutional because it violated states' rights) and by authorizing federal agents working with the Freedmen's Bureau to try persons accused of denying Negroes their rights. Both of these laws, which provided federal protection for Negroes and, at the same time, weakened the authority of Southern legislatures, were passed by Congress over the vetoes of President Johnson.

In the Congressional elections of 1866, Johnson decided to go to the voters to campaign for his Reconstruction policy. By this time he had gained the backing of Northern Democrats, but the Republicans

Most of the "Black Codes" recognized the right of Negroes to marry, to own property, and to sue and testify in court, at least in cases involving other Negroes. Most of the "Codes" also specified that Negroes could work only as farmers or domestic servants who could not change jobs without the loss of pay.

The Civil Rights Act of 1866 declared that states could not deny Negroes the right to testify in court or to own property. It made Negroes citizens and gave the federal courts jurisdiction over cases involving deprivation of rights.

opposed him solidly. Ignoring the hostility of Northern audiences, the President vehemently attacked his Republican opponents in the Congress by name. The Radicals, however, represented the public mood more accurately than Johnson did. As they piled up heavy majorities in both houses, the period of Presidential control of Reconstruction ended.

Congress Gains Control

Radical Republicans controlled Reconstruction policy from 1867 to about 1872. When Congress convened in March 1867, the Radicals commanded a two thirds vote in each house, enough to override any Presidential veto. They passed Reconstruction acts which declared existing state governments (except that of Tennessee) illegal and which divided the South into five military districts, each under the jurisdiction of a general. To qualify for readmission to the Union, these acts required states to elect delegates to new constitutional

Post Civil War Amendments

The Thirteenth Amendment ended slavery and gave Congress the power of enforcement.

The Fourteenth Amendment 1. declared that everybody born or naturalized in the United States is a citizen of both the nation and the state he lives in. A state cannot make laws limiting the rights of citizens, nor refuse due process of the law.
2. apportioned representatives on the basis of the entire population of the state (thus nullifying Article 1, Section 2, Clause 3)—except non-taxpaying Indians—and threatened to reduce the number of representatives in any state that denied the vote to male citizens over 21.
3. denied public office to most former U.S. officials who had joined the Confederacy, and repudiated the Confederate war debt.
4. gave Congress the power of enforcement.

The Fifteenth Amentment said that neither the federal nor the state government could deny the right to vote because of race, color, or previous condition of slavery. It gave Congress the power of enforcement.

conventions on the basis of universal manhood suffrage. The conventions had to guarantee Negro suffrage and to ratify the Fourteenth Amendment. This amendment had originally been proposed in June 1866, but Tennessee, already under Radical control, was the only Southern state to ratify it. Tennessee was restored to the Union on July 24, 1866.

When the South refused to organize governments under these conditions, Congress passed additional legislation requiring military commanders to enroll voters. About 700,000 Negroes and 600,000 whites were registered in this way, the great majority of whom were prepared to cooperate with the Radicals. Although the Radicals dominated the state conventions which met in 1868, Negroes also played an active role. The new constitutions drawn up by the conventions guaranteed civil rights for Negroes and disenfranchised ex-rebels. By 1870, all Confederate states were back in the Union. The Radicals were in control in all except Tennessee, Virginia, and North Carolina. In these states, where the whites were in the majority, the Democrats were able to regain control. In the same year, the Fifteenth Amendment went into effect.

In a number of Northern states, Negroes voted for the first time after the ratification of the Fifteenth Amendment.

Meanwhile, the struggle within the government between Congress and the President became critical. In order to gather a case for impeachment and to curb the powers of the executive, Congress passed, over Johnson's veto, a Tenure of Office Act forbidding the President from dismissing any important civil officer without the approval of the Senate. Johnson decided to test the constitutionality of the law and dismissed Secretary of War Edwin M. Stanton, who had cooperated frequently with the Radicals. The House of Representatives, by a vote of 126 to 47, impeached Johnson on eleven counts, including violation of the Tenure Act and trying to discredit Congress. The Senate tried the President. The vote to convict him was thirty-five to nineteen, one vote short of the two-thirds majority required for conviction by the Constitution.

President Grant Supports the Radicals

The Radicals controlled Congress, but their hold on the public opinion of the country became less secure. In the Presidential election of 1868, the Republicans nominated Ulysses S. Grant, endorsed Radical Reconstruction, and condemned Johnson. The Democrats nominated a former governor of New York, Horatio Seymour, and adopted a platform opposing Radical Reconstruction. In the election in which three Southern states did not participate and six others were under Radical control, the Republicans won by less than a ten percent majority of the popular vote. Republican political control in the South made Grant's victory possible.

During his first term, Grant supported the Radical Reconstruction effort. Congress investigated the attempt to restore white supremacy to the South through the terrorist activities of the secret Ku Klux Klan, and in 1870 and 1871 Congress passed legislation to enforce the Fourteenth and Fifteenth Amendments. By 1872, however, the Republicans themselves fell apart over the Reconstruction issue. A group of "liberal" Republicans split from the rest of the party and nominated Horace Greeley for President on a platform which opposed the corruption being uncovered in the Grant Administration and favored a more conciliatory policy toward the South. The party regulars renominated Grant who won re-election. By the time he took office for a second term, however, the balance of power in the Southern state governments had begun to slip back into the hands of Southern whites.

The Compromise of 1877

In 1874, the Democrats won a majority in the House of Representatives. The Radicals no longer controlled Congress, and they lost power to conservative Southern leaders in Arkansas, Alabama, and Texas. The election of 1876 marked the official end of Reconstruction. The two major Presidential candidates were Rutherford B. Hayes, a Republican, and Samuel J. Tilden, a Democrat. Tilden won the popular vote, but Republican-controlled election boards in Florida, South Carolina, and Louisiana claimed victory—despite higher Democratic votes—on the grounds that Negroes had been prevented from voting. Without the electoral votes of these states, Tilden had 184 undisputed votes—1 short of the majority he needed. If the disputed votes all went to Hayes, he would have the 185 to win. Congress appointed an Electoral Commission consisting of fifteen men selected from the House, Senate, and Supreme Court. By an 8–7 vote, the election was awarded to Hayes, with the understanding that federal troops would be withdrawn from the South. This so-called "Compromise of 1877" formally marked the reconciliation of North and South. The South had been "redeemed," which meant that political leadership reverted largely to members of the old planter class.

Reconstruction: Progress and Problems

Was Reconstruction a failure? The answer depends on what is meant by the question. Reconstruction succeeded in that the Union was restored without slavery. Reconstruction failed in that Negroes were not taken into the mainstream of American life on an equal basis with other citizens, and Southerners continued to feel bitter toward the North.

What accounted for the failure of Negroes to gain equality? Most Americans made a sharp distinction in their minds between the slavery and the racial discrimination. Belief in equal rights for minorities was not popular in the 1860's and 1870's. Many of the Republicans who voted for civil-rights legislation did so more because they wanted Negroes to vote Republican than because they were concerned with the Negro as a person. In addition, reports of corruption associated with Radical Reconstruction offended many people in the North. Americans associated in their minds the evidence of graft and corruption in the Reconstruction governments with the uneducated Negro. They questioned whether the Negro was prepared for the responsibilities of full citizenship.

At the end of the nineteenth and during the first half of the twentieth century, most American historians pointed out that Reconstruction was a sorry chapter in American history. They argued that it had allowed "scalawags," "carpetbaggers," and unprepared Negroes to come into power and plunder the South for personal advantage.

Scalawags were the white Southerners who cooperated with the Republicans. Carpetbaggers were Northerners who went South either to help the freedmen or to advance themselves.

There is no question that profit and corruption played a role in Radical Reconstruction. State taxes skyrocketed throughout the South, and all too often substantial revenues ended up in the pockets of unscrupulous legislators. Many Negro legislators in the South shared in the loot, but it does not appear that they were any more guilty than their white colleagues.

More recently, historians have stressed the positive side of Reconstruction. They have pointed out that graft and corruption were not peculiar to the South during the period. Scandals riddled Grant's Administration, and his Secretary of War resigned when it was disclosed that he had accepted bribes. During the same period, the infamous Tweed Ring swindled millions of dollars from the people of New York City. At about the same time, prominent congressmen were selling their political influence to the Credit Mobilier Construction Company.

William Marcy Tweed was the boss of Tammany Hall, the Democratic political organization in New York City.

The owners of the Union Pacific Railroad Company organized the Crédit Mobilier to construct the railroad. They awarded contracts to the Crédit Mobilier so as to guarantee themselves huge profits. When threatened with a Congressional investigation of their dishonest dealings, they sold Crédit Mobilier stock at a low price to influential Congressmen.

Recent historians have also noted that Negroes never dominated Reconstruction governments, never elected a governor, and held a legislative majority only in South Carolina. Negroes who did hold office seem on the whole to have been as qualified as white officeholders, and the governments which they helped to shape made lasting accomplishments, particularly in helping to bring progressive welfare legislation and free public education to the South. Some of the Negro lawmakers, such as Jonathan Gibbs in Florida and Francis Cardozo in South Carolina, were better educated than their white colleagues. Most of the Negroes active in Southern politics during this period were moderate men who sought to find a way to live together in peace and cooperation with their former masters.

John Hope Franklin, **From Slavery to Freedom,** 2nd ed. New York: Alfred A. Knopf, Inc., 1956, p. 312.

Beverly Nash, a Negro leader in South Carolina, expressed this attitude when he spoke before the state constitutional convention:

> I believe, my friends and fellow-citizens, we are not prepared for this suffrage. But we can learn. Give a man tools and let him commence to use them, and in time he will learn a trade. So it is with voting. We may not understand it at the start, but in time we shall learn to do our duty. . . . We recognize the Southern white man as the true friend of the black man. . . . In these public affairs we must unite with our white fellow-citizens. They tell us that they have been disfranchised, yet we tell the North that we shall never let the halls of Congress be silent until we remove that disability.

Did Reconstruction fail? Every student of American history must sift the evidence for himself. The problems involved were both massive and complex. In the end, Lincoln's plea for charity and justice often went unheeded. Americans restored the Union without slavery, but in 1877, the American ideal of liberty, equality, and the pursuit of happiness for all was still a long way from becoming reality.

SUGGESTED READINGS

CATTON, BRUCE, *The Battle of Gettysburg.* This detailed and dramatic account of one of the most famous and important battles in American history captures the flavor of military conflict during the Civil War.

FRANKLIN, JOHN HOPE, *Reconstruction After the Civil War.* This is a brief, well written analysis of the Reconstruction period by a leading American historian of today.

MC PHERSON, JAMES, *The Negro's Civil War.* This book describes how American Negroes in the North and South felt and acted during the war.

WILEY, BELL IRVIN, *The Plain People of the Confederacy.* In this fascinating, short history, Professor Wiley discusses the life of humble people, both white and black, during the Civil War.

The Growth of Industry

CHAPTER 15

STATING THE ISSUE

At the end of the nineteenth century, men looked back on the years since the Civil War with amazement. The entire nation seemed to have been transformed in their lifetimes. All around them were huge new cities, hosts of immigrants from Europe, a bewildering array of new machinery, a vast railroad network, and thousands of new factories, mills, and farms each whirring with machines. A new society had been born.

These dramatic changes began well before the Civil War. The textile industry had developed in New England early in the nineteenth century. In most northern states, factories, mines, and mills opened in the wake of the railroad boom of the 1840's and 1850's. After the Civil War, however, the entire economy, even in the defeated South, spurted ahead. New ways of doing things began to affect everyone, including the men and women who lived on isolated farms or in small country towns.

The new society made a profound impression on American writers. In 1889, a prominent writer on economic affairs, wrote proudly: "The economic changes that have occurred during the last quarter of a century, or during the present generation of living men, have unquestionably been more important and varied than during any former corresponding period of the world's history."

A few years later, John Dewey, America's foremost educator, told an audience: "One can hardly believe there has been a revolution in all history so rapid, so extensive, so complete." Hundreds of additional observers made similar statements. Industry was transforming America.

Chapter 15 introduces the story of this postwar revolution. What accounted for the rapid pace of economic growth? What effect did such growth have on the economy? How did it change the lives of Americans? These are the major questions with which we will be concerned in this chapter.

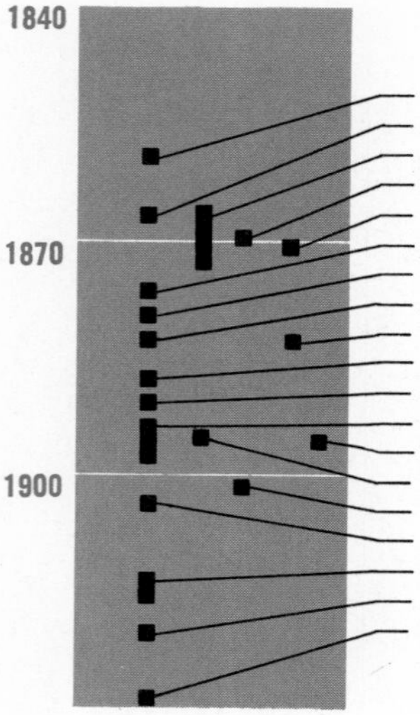

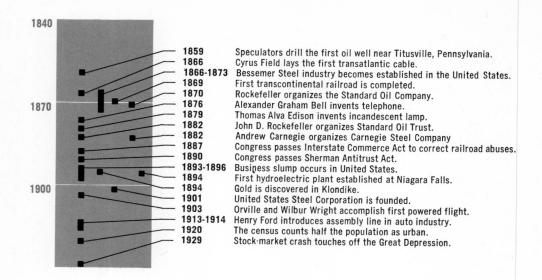

1859	Speculators drill the first oil well near Titusville, Pennsylvania.
1866	Cyrus Field lays the first transatlantic cable.
1866-1873	Bessemer Steel industry becomes established in the United States.
1869	First transcontinental railroad is completed.
1870	Rockefeller organizes the Standard Oil Company.
1876	Alexander Graham Bell invents telephone.
1879	Thomas Alva Edison invents incandescent lamp.
1882	John D. Rockefeller organizes Standard Oil Trust.
1882	Andrew Carnegie organizes Carnegie Steel Company
1887	Congress passes Interstate Commerce Act to correct railroad abuses.
1890	Congress passes Sherman Antitrust Act.
1893-1896	Business slump occurs in United States.
1894	First hydroelectric plant established at Niagara Falls.
1894	Gold is discovered in Klondike.
1901	United States Steel Corporation is founded.
1903	Orville and Wilbur Wright accomplish first powered flight.
1913-1914	Henry Ford introduces assembly line in auto industry.
1920	The census counts half the population as urban.
1929	Stock-market crash touches off the Great Depression.

57 Cold Statistics and Living Men

The revolution Dewey wrote about surrounded Americans in the year 1900. New steel mills lined river valleys, filling the air with dense clouds of smoke and dust. The smells of industry penetrated throughout American cities. Kerosene lamps and electric lights brightened long winter evenings. Immigrants from all of Europe rubbed elbows with each other and with native Americans on streetcars, at work, and in the polling places. All a man's senses told him America was changing.

Yet impressions can be misleading. Even if we could return to the late nineteenth century, our observations could provide only an incomplete picture of the changes which were transforming America. And observation consumes time and effort wastefully. Men who study contemporary societies have learned to supplement their own observations with other forms of data.

Many of the changes that had the greatest impact on the new America resulted from industrialism. These changes can be captured in statistics. But statistics are only numbers. They convey meaning only when a person who uses them looks beyond these numbers to learn their significance for men and women.

Reading 57 contains five tables and a chart about various aspects of the American economy between the end of the Civil War and the onset of the great depression of the 1930's. One or two specific questions accompany each table or chart. In addition to answering these specific questions, keep these general issues in mind as you read:

1. Which of these statistics seem to you to measure the most important changes in American life between 1865 and 1929?
2. Why should the changes implied by these statistics have involved changes in the relationships among people? Why should they have required changes in education or in daily lives?

1: Total Population and Urban Population, 1860–1930

This table lists the total population of the United States between 1860 and 1930 and the city population.

Which appeared to be growing faster, total or urban population?

Year	Total Population	Population in Cities of 25,000 or More	% of Population in Urban Areas (2500 or More)	% of Population in Cities of 25,000 or More
1860	31,400,000	3,800,000	20%	12%
1870	39,800,000	5,800,000	25%	15%
1880	50,200,000	8,700,000	28%	17%
1890	63,900,000	14,000,000	35%	22%
1900	76,000,000	19,800,000	40%	26%
1910	92,000,000	28,500,000	46%	31%
1920	105,800,000	37,800,000	51%	36%
1930	122,800,000	49,200,000	56%	40%

U.S. Bureau of the Census, **Historical Statistics of the United States, Colonial Times to 1957.** Washington, D.C.: Government Printing Office, 1960, pp. 7, 14.

2: Gross National Product, 1869–1929

It is very difficult to measure the value of all the goods and services produced in the United States. Table 2 gives figures which try to measure this value, called the gross national product, *for the years between 1869 and 1929. The figures are expressed in constant 1929 dollars, that is the worth of the goods and services at prices charged in 1929. All the figures are expressed in billions of dollars. Where more than one year is indicated, the estimate is an attempt to measure the average annual GNP during the period.*

How can you use this table and the one above to get an estimate of the real increase in the wealth of the nation?

Years	Estimate of Gross National Product
1869-1873	$ 9.11 billion
1877-1881	16.1 "
1887-1891	24.0 "
1897-1901	37.1 "
1907-1911	55.0 "
1920	73.3 "
1929	104.4 "

U.S. Bureau of the Census, **Historical Statistics,** p. 139.

3: *Number of Workers in Selected Industries, 1870–1930*

The growth in population and in gross national product involved major changes throughout American society. Table 3 measures one of these changes. It describes the number of people working at paying jobs in each of several major industries. Since not all industries have been listed, the figures do not add up to the total number of workers.

1. What appear to be the major trends described here?
2. How could such trends change the kinds of lives many Americans were accustomed to leading?

U.S. Bureau of the Census, **Historical Statistics**, p. 74.

Industrial Distribution of Gainful Workers (in thousands)

	1870	1890	1910	1930
Total Workers	12,920	23,740	36,730	47,400
Agriculture	6,430	9,990	11,340	10,180
Manufacturing	2,250	4,750	8,230	10,770
Construction	750	1,440	2,300	3,030
Education	190	510	900	1,630
Professional Services	140	350	770	1,720
Government	100	190	540	1,130

4: *Output per Man-Hour, 1869–1930*

Table 4 describes one way of explaining the increase in wealth. To compile these statistics, the author divided the value of all the goods and services produced in the United States in 1899 by an estimate of all the hours worked by Americans to produce the goods and services of this value. For convenience sake, the quotient is described as an index figure *of 100. Changes in the output per man-hour before or after 1899 can be readily described as more or less than the index figure.*

1. What does this chart show you?
2. What are the limitations of expressing the increase in productivity solely in relation to hours worked?

Seymour E. Harris, ed., **American Economic History.** New York: McGraw-Hill Book Company, Inc., 1961, p. 72.

Output/Man-hour Worked (1899 = 100)

1869-1870	61
1879-1880	67
1889-1890	82
1899-1900	100
1909-1910	125
1919-1920	151
1929-1930	243

5: Family Expenditures on Consumer Goods, 1888–1918

By consumer goods, economists mean goods, such as food and clothing, which people use to satisfy their wants.

The economic growth you have been examining meant many different things to Americans. Table 5 reports one kind of meaning. It describes the results of three studies of the income and spending habits of industrial and clerical workers in American cities between 1888 and 1919. As in Table 2, the figures are expressed in constant dollars, *in this case, constant 1950 dollars.*

1. Was the standard of living in America improving between 1888 and 1918?
2. What did people do with additional income?

	1888–1891	1901	1917–1918
Number of families surveyed	2,562	11,156	12,096
Average family size	3.9 persons	4.0 persons	4.9 persons
Average money income	$1793	$1914	$2408
Average total expenditure for goods and services	$1671	$1817	$2163
Average expenditure for food and drink	$ 797	$ 952	$ 854

U.S. Bureau of the Census, **Historical Statistics,** p. 181.

6: Number of Business Failures, 1870–1930

The growth and wealth you have measured in the previous tables has not always been smooth. Some years have been better than others; some have witnessed massive troubles in the economy. These "ups and downs" are called the business cycle. *The graph on the following page attempts to measure one dimension of the cycle. It describes the rate at which business firms have failed —gone out of business—because they could not make a profit and meet their bills.*

1. How uneven has the process of economic growth been during this time period?
2. What do you think the owners and workers do after a business has failed ?

U.S. Bureau of the Census, **Historical Statistics,** p. 570.

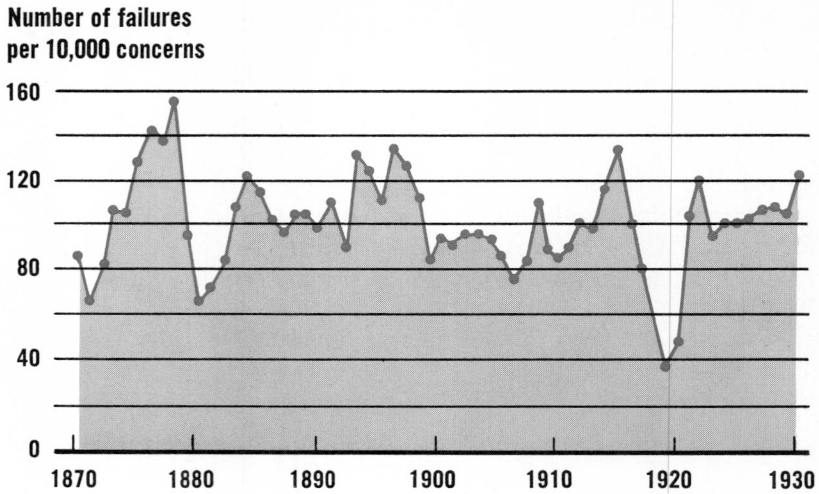

58 Two Businessmen Explain Economic Growth

Americans saw that their world was changing, and they struggled to explain why. The burden of explanation fell most heavily upon the men who seemed to have profited most from the changes, the leaders of giant business concerns. They felt called upon both to explain these changes and to justify them. The benefits of economic growth received by millions of Americans, as described in Table 5 of the previous reading, did not come close to those achieved by prosperous businessmen. Men with a great deal of new personal wealth felt compelled to justify their right to be wealthy. In the same way, businessmen, particularly in large firms, had to explain why it was all right for them to direct the working lives of laborers whom they hardly knew. As businessmen struggled with the issues posed by their own wealth and the responsibilities of leadership, they tried to answer the question, Who made the economy grow?

John D. Rockefeller and Andrew Carnegie were two of America's most successful businessmen. Competitors often accused them of being unscrupulous. Beginning in the 1860's, Rockefeller organized a giant combination of oil refineries. By 1900, this combination controlled roughly 80 percent of the refinery capacity in the United States. Rockefeller's enormous personal income and wealth exceeded the imagination of most citizens. At the time of his death in 1937, he had given almost $600,000,000 to charity.

Carnegie was born in Scotland and came to the United States as a youth. He achieved considerable success working for the Pennsylvania Railroad. At the close of the Civil War, he invested his savings in ironmaking. In the 1870's, he turned to steel production and was a major figure in the transformation of this technologically backward American industry. When he sold his interest in the Carnegie Steel Corporation in 1901, the new firm, the United States Steel Corporation, controlled half of the steel productive capacity in this country. Reading 58 gives Rockefeller's and Carnegie's explanations for the growth of the American economy. As you read, try to answer these questions:

Carnegie sold his interest to J. P. Morgan for about $440 million.

1. What were the qualities of a successful businessman according to Rockefeller and Carnegie?
2. How would Rockefeller and Carnegie have explained the economic development of the United States?
3. What do you think might be the impact upon workingmen of Carnegie's idea that an industrial plant was like a military ship? What is your opinion of his philosophy?

John D. Rockefeller Explains Business Growth

Rockefeller wrote his thoughts and observations on his life and times in his Reminiscences. *This selection from that book gives his explanation for business success.*

John D. Rockefeller, **Random Reminiscences of Men and Events.** New York: Doubleday and Company, Inc., 1933, pp. 9–11, 71–75.

It is always, I presume, a question in every business just how fast it is wise to go, and we went pretty rapidly in those days, building and expanding in all directions. We were being confronted with fresh emergencies constantly. A new oil field would be discovered, tanks for storage had to be built almost overnight, and this was going on when old fields were being exhausted, so we were therefore often under the double strain of losing the facilities in one place where we were fully equipped, and having to build up a plant for storing and transporting in a new field where we were totally unprepared. These are some of the things which make the whole oil trade a perilous one, but we had with us a group of courageous men who recognized the great principle that a business cannot be a great success that does not fully and efficiently accept and take advantage of its opportunities.

The part played by one of my earliest partners, Mr. H. M. Flagler, was always an inspiration to me. . . . It was to be expected of such a man that he should fulfil his destiny by working out some great problems at a time when most men want to retire to a comfortable life of ease. This would not appeal to my old friend. He undertook, single handed, the task of building up the east coast of Florida. He was not satisfied to plan a railroad from St. Augustine to Key West . . . but in addition he has built a chain of superb hotels to induce tourists to go to this newly developed country.

This one man, by his own energy and capital, has opened up a vast stretch of country, so that the old inhabitants and the new settlers may have a market for their products. He has given work to thousands of these people . . .

A person with a pessimistic disposition takes a gloomy, negative view of the world.

You hear a good many people of pessimistic disposition say much about greed in American life. One would think to hear them talk that we were a race of misers in this country. . . . It is by no means for money alone that these active-minded men labor—they are engaged in a fascinating occupation. The zest of the work is maintained by something better than the mere accumulation of money, and, as I think I have said elsewhere, the standards of business are high and are getting better all the time.

I confess I have no sympathy with the idea so often advanced that our basis of all judgments in this country is founded on money. If this were true, we should be a nation of money hoarders instead of spenders. Nor do I admit that we are so small-minded a people as to be jealous of the success of others. It is the other way about: We are most extraordinarily ambitious, and the success of one man in any walk of life spurs the others on. It does not sour them, and it is a libel even to suggest so great a meanness of spirit.

A libel is any written statement intended to damage, defame, or misrepresent a person or thing.

In my early days men acted just as they do now, no doubt. When there was anything to be done for general trade betterment, almost every man had some good reason for believing that his case was a special one, different from all the rest. For every foolish thing he did, or wanted to do, for every unbusinesslike plan he had, he always pleaded that it was necessary in his case. He was the one man who had to sell at less than cost, to disrupt all the business plans of others in his trade, because his individual position was so absolutely different from all the rest. It was often a heart-breaking undertaking to convince those men that the perfect occasion which would lead to the perfect opportunity would never come, even if they waited until the crack o' doom.

Then, again, we had the type of man who really never knew all the facts about his own affairs. Many of the brightest kept their books in such a way that they did not actually know when they were making money on a certain operation and when they were losing. This unintelligent competition was a hard matter to contend with. Good old-fashioned common sense has always been a mighty rare commodity. When a man's affairs are not going well, he hates to study the books and face the truth. From the first, the men who managed the Standard Oil Company kept their books intelligently as well as correctly. We knew how much we made and where we gained or lost. At least, we tried not to deceive ourselves.

My ideas of business are no doubt old-fashioned, but the fundamental principles do not change from generation to generation, and sometimes I think that our quick-witted American businessmen, whose spirit and energy are so splendid, do not always sufficiently study the real underlying foundations of business management. . . . [M]any people assume that they can get away from the truth by avoiding thinking about it, but the natural law is inevitable, and the sooner it is recognized, the better.

Rockefeller is probably referring to the natural law of competition. Economic and social thinkers transferred Charles Darwin's theory of survival of the fittest from the field of biology to the field of economics. Human struggle was seen as a struggle for livelihood, and those who succeeded in business overcame all competition because they were most fit.

One hears a great deal about wages and why they must be maintained at a high level, by the railroads, for example. A laborer is worthy of his hire, no less, but no more, and in the long run he must contribute an equivalent for what he is paid. If he does not do this, he is probably pauperized [made very poor] and you at once throw out the balance of things. You can't hold up conditions artificially, and you can't change the underlying laws of trade. If you try, you must inevitably fail. All this may be trite and obvious, but it is remarkable how many men overlook what should be the obvious. These are facts we can't get away from—a businessman must adapt himself to the natural conditions as they exist from month to month and year to year. Sometimes I feel that we Americans think we can find a short road to success, and it may appear that often this feat is accomplished; but real efficiency in work comes from knowing your facts and building upon that sure foundation.

Andrew Carnegie Explains Business Growth

Andrew Carnegie wrote several books describing his views of life, money-making, democracy, and the responsibilities of wealth. The following selection is from his Autobiography, *published in 1920, a year after his death.*

Autobiography of Andrew Carnegie. Boston: Houghton Mifflin Company, 1920, pp. 135–36, 202, 204. Reprinted by permission.

As I became acquainted with the manufacture of iron I was greatly surprised to find that the cost of each of the various processes was unknown. Inquiries made of the leading manufacturers of Pittsburgh proved this. It was a lump business, and until stock was taken and the books balanced at the end of the year, the manufacturers were in total ignorance of results. I heard of men who thought their business at the end of the year would show a loss and had found a profit, and vice-versa. I felt as if we were moles burrowing in the dark, and this to me was intolerable. I insisted upon such a system of weighing and accounting being introduced throughout our works as would enable us to know what our cost was for each process and especially what each man was doing, who saved material, who wasted it, and who produced the best results.

To arrive at this was a much more difficult task than one would imagine. Every manager in the mills was naturally against the new system. Years were required before an accurate system was obtained, but eventually, by the aid of many clerks and the introduction of weighing scales at various points in the mill, we began to know not only what every department was doing, but what each one of the many men working at the furnaces was doing, and thus to compare one with another. One of the chief sources of success in manufacturing is the introduction and strict maintenance of a perfect system of accounting so that responsibility for money or materials can be brought home to every man. Owners who, in the office, would not trust a clerk with five dollars without having a check upon him, were supplying tons of material daily to men in the mills without exacting an account of their stewardship by weighing what each returned in the finished form.

The Siemens Gas Furnace, introduced in 1868 by Karl Wilhelm Siemens, was used in the open-hearth method of making steel. The high temperatures attained by the open-hearth furnace break down the elements of the iron so thoroughly that low-grade ore and scrap can be used.

The Siemens Gas Furnace had been used to some extent in Great Britain for heating steel and iron, but it was supposed to be too expensive. I well remember the criticisms made by older heads among the Pittsburgh manufacturers about the extravagant expenditure we were making upon these new-fangled furnaces. But in the heating of great masses of material, almost half the waste could sometimes be saved by using the new furnaces. The expenditure would have been justified, even if it had been doubled. Yet it was many years before we were followed in this new departure; and in some of those years the margin of profit was so small that the most of it was made up from the savings derived from the adoption of the improved furnaces.

An auditor is a person who examines and verifies financial accounts and records.

The mills were at last about ready to begin [1874] and an organization the auditor proposed was laid before me for approval. I found he had divided the works into two departments and had given control of one to Mr. Stevenson, a Scotsman who afterwards made a fine record as a manufacturer, and control of the other to a Mr. Jones. Nothing, I am certain, ever affected the success of the steel company more than the decision which I gave upon that proposal. Upon no account could two men be in the same works with equal authority. An army with two commanders-in-chief, a ship with two captains, could not fare more disastrously than a manufacturing concern with two men in command upon the same ground, even though in two different departments. I said:

"This will not do. I do not know Mr. Stevenson, nor do I know Mr. Jones, but one or the other must be made captain and he alone must report to you."

The decision fell upon Mr. Jones and in this way we obtained "The Captain," who afterward made his name famous wherever the manufacture of Bessemer steel is known.

The Bessemer process for producing steel cheaply was invented independently by a Kentuckian, William Kelly, and an Englishman, Henry Bessemer, in the middle of the nineteenth century. A blast of hot air forced through the molten iron removed impurities. The open-hearth method of steel manufacture replaced the Bessemer process.

Our competitors in steel were at first disposed to ignore us. Knowing the difficulties they had in starting their own steel works, they could not believe we would be ready to deliver rails for another year and declined to recognize us as competitors. The price of steel rails when we began was about seventy dollars per ton. We sent our agent through the country with instructions to take orders at the best prices he could obtain; and before our competitors knew it, we had obtained a large number—quite sufficient to justify us in making a start.

So perfect was the machinery, so admirable the plans, so skillful were the men selected by Captain Jones, and so great a manager was he himself, that our success was phenomenal. I think I place a unique statement on record when I say that the result of the first month's operations left a margin of profit of $11,000. It is also remarkable that so perfect was our system of accounts that we knew the exact amount of the profit. We had learned from experience in our iron works what exact accounting meant. There is nothing more profitable than clerks to check up each transfer of material from one department to another in process of manufacture.

59 An Innovating People

Both Rockefeller and Carnegie credited businessmen for the rate at which American industry grew. Businessmen systematically assembled natural, capital, and human resources in efficient ways based on the latest knowledge. They built a new transportation system, assembled money to build mills and factories, pioneered in new ways to market goods, and quickly adopted the latest technology. No one denies the key role which businessmen played in the process of industrialization.

But the few hundred businessmen who owned and ran major companies, such as Standard Oil and Carnegie Steel, could not have succeeded alone. If American customers had been wedded to the past, they would have refused to buy new products or try new ways, just as many peasants in villages in underdeveloped Asian and African countries, such as India, have done today. If the sons and daughters of farmers—American born and immigrant alike—had remained on the farm, no one would have been available to man the new machines. And if American mechanics had been satisfied with accepted ways to do things, new machines would never have been invented.

Modern attempts to speed economic growth by shipping new machines to underdeveloped countries often produce little change. People get in the way. They like established ways of doing things. They lack the skill to operate and repair the new machines. And they lack incentive to advance. All of these attitudes retard growth. None of them characterized typical Americans of the late nineteenth century.

Reading 59 contains three excerpts from foreigners who wrote about the United States. Each of these commentators was struck in one way or another by characteristics of Americans which seemed to set them off from their European contemporaries. As you read, think about the following questions:

1. What characteristics of Americans made the most marked impression on these European visitors?
2. How may these characteristics have been related to the ability of American industry to grow so rapidly?
3. How reliable do you think these accounts are? What sort of evidence would you need to check the validity of these statements?

Judges of the London World's Fair View American Manufactures

In 1862, there was a great international exhibition, a world's fair, held in London. Judges compared machines, tools, and products from many different nations and awarded prizes. There were, unfortunately, no entries from the United States in Class XXXI, "Manufactures in Iron, Copper and General Hardware." The judges, nevertheless, made the following comment.

International Exhibition, 1862, **Reports by the Juries.** London: William Clowes and Sons, 1863, Class XXXI, p. 3. Language simplified and modernized.

Unfortunately we are without any direct means of comparing the European manufactures of Class XXXI with those of the United States, because there are no American exhibitors at the present time. Yet it is only just to state that those articles which find their way across the Atlantic (often to be copied and reproduced in Europe) exhibit great ingenuity and successful effort on the part of the inventors to provide machines to replace manual labour for every purpose of domestic life. They are also constructed so as to be produced by labour-saving machinery and are sure, as soon as they are invented, to be received favourably and adopted by the American public. Until the Civil War, Americans, occupied with the development of their agriculture, mineral riches, and trade, were ready to use every plan or machine which might spare the services or reduce the labour of domestic servants.

In the North American States, public feeling is the reverse of ours. There is little desire for trade-unions, and change and novelty in everything seem to be the desire of all classes. Manufacturing companies are in great favour, and provide an abundance of capital for the trial of countless new projects. Many of these have failed, but many others have eventually proved profitable to the shareholders.

In the early nineteenth century, some skilled workers had organized local craft unions. In 1834, trade-union members organized the National Trades' Union which grew rapidly for a few years. Membership declined sharply after the Panic of 1837, and the trade union movement was not revived until after the Civil War.

The willingness of the American public to buy what is offered them, if it can in any way answer the purpose, has given a great advantage to the North American manufacturer over his European competitor, who has to contend with centuries-old habits and prejudices. The demand in the states during the last few years for hardware has been enormous. By choosing the best shapes and sizes of goods in large demand, and erecting machinery to produce them cheaply and quickly, by special workmen and tools, an American manufacturer can sell very large quantities of one kind or shape. He is sure to beat the European manufacturer, who employs general workmen and has to contend against a heavy import duty and against competitors who have the advantage of being on the spot where the consumption of the article takes place.

In every country useful inventions are first made to supply the wants of its own population. On proof of their utility, they are afterwards adopted elsewhere in the world. The United States have long been recognized by inventors as the proper field for the birth and manufacture of every species of labour-saving machine that could supply enormous local wants. Artisans from all countries have taken their new ideas and technical skill to America to reap the rich harvest jointly with the natives. Newly invented goods are crude, when first brought before the public, and are only perfected by successive modifications, suggested by experience. They are also generally expensive at first, and become gradually cheaper, as better methods of manufacture are discovered, and they begin to be produced in larger quantities.

Americans overlook defects more than Europeans do. They are satisfied if a machine intended to supersede domestic labour will work even imperfectly. However, we insist upon its being thoroughly well made and efficient.

It is very difficult to introduce new articles into families in England and other countries where domestic servants and workpeople are abundant and trained to supply every want. Inventions are received with a certain degree of apathy, and manufacturers—only meeting with a small demand—must ask a high price, which limits consumption. In the United States, on the contrary, the manufacturer of a new article or author of any improvement is listened to at once; and, encouraged by a brisk demand for his goods, he at once erects labour-saving machinery.

An Englishman Views American Growth

This selection comes from an Englishman's attempt to understand the sources of American economic growth.

Sidney J. Chapman, **Work and Wages.** London: Longmans, Green, and Company, 1904, Part I, pp. 175–78. Language simplified and modernized.

The keenness and originality of the American captains of industry have caused a steady advance in the productive capacity of American industry. The American workman has secured his share of the gains in production. Even in industries in which no improved methods have been introduced wages have naturally tended to rise. The employer has therefore had to save labour by devising labour-saving methods.

That dash in economic affairs should be exhibited in a comparatively new country is not astonishing. American energy has, in addition, been stimulated by a growing market. When the market grows rapidly and steadily, an employer is constantly confronted with the idea of expanding his operation. In thinking of change, he thinks naturally of possible improvements. Further, there is always room for new businesses, and new businesses use the newest machines and methods. In beginning a business, men seek naturally for the best plans and appliances available; apathy comes only with old habits. Wherever the proportion of new businesses to old ones is large, the industry of which they are parts will tend to develop fast.

The market for American textiles has grown faster than ours, for America has had, and in some degree still has, her home market to win, and in addition her international trade to develop. And her home demand has been expanding rapidly, partly through the natural increase of the American people, partly through immigration and the expansion of the country, and partly through increasing wealth.

The apparent ease with which experiments can be conducted and changes made in factory organization in the United States at once suggests that the employer there is less hampered than his English rival by interference from his workers. Of this there seems to be little doubt. The American workman is readier to face new situations and expects less permanence in the nature of his economic surroundings. If he is an immigrant this is understandable, for he is probably enterprising, and he has already made a change. If he is an American, he has lived in an atmosphere of change. As things move faster in a rapidly developing country, every American has learned to take the ups and downs of life as normal, and the new experience is upon him before the old is forgotten. Therefore, the thought of resisting or impeding advance is seldom so seriously entertained in America as in England. Besides, the American cotton workers are not so strongly organized as the English. And, in addition, there seems to be little doubt that the American workman's experience has not led him to fear new conditions. An English workman finds it almost impossible to imagine that the adoption of labour-saving methods could result in higher wages and more employment. But the American knows that an increased demand for labour has followed the recent improvements in the cotton industry in his own country. Some 85,000 automatic looms have been set running in the United States in the last few years, and yet the demand for weavers and all cotton workers is greater than ever. Wages in the northeastern states have risen fast.

In the cotton industry, most American wages are now much higher than English wages. As an immigrant weaver put it, "This is the right side of the water . . . better for making money."

A Russian Views American Growth

Peter A. Demens left Russia for America in the late 1870's. In the United States, he established a number of businesses and wrote a book Sketches of the North American United States. *He explains some of the ways Americans expanded their businesses in the selections from that book which follow.*

Peter A. Demens [Tverskoy, pseud.], **Sketches of the North American United States,** St. Petersburg: I.N. Skorokhdov, 1895, as cited in **This Was America** by Oscar Handlin, ed. Harvard University Press, 1949, pp. 351–52, 361–62.

Huge sums are spent in advertising of every kind. Nowhere in the world is there such a mass of newspapers; in the majority of cases these hold almost nothing but advertisements. There are also many other methods [of advertising]. All the fences, the sides of buildings, and often the roofs are inscribed with signs. Many commercial houses have specially organized publicity departments which spend tens of thousands of dollars annually; the mails are choked with the circulars, throw-aways, and brochures of these enterprising men of letters. Frequently visited public places are equipped with billboards which command a high price. In buses, trolleys, and at railroad stations, the ceilings and walls are written over with these advertisements, frequently in rich frames and adorned with luxurious pictures and huge letters. About two months ago an enterprising soap dealer paid $17,000 at an auction sale for the right to advertise one year on the wall of the main entrance of the suspension bridge across the East River [in New York]. The New York elevated trains annually receive more than $100,000 for the [advertising] rights to their stations. And, most recently, shrewd speculators have reached the point where they hire special railroad cars, cover the outside walls with praises of their goods, and send them traveling over the whole Union.

In 1867, Colonel Charles T. Harvey built an experimental one-track elevated line on the outskirts of New York. The elevated tracks are held up by strong steel beams. The railroad gets its power from a third rail running parallel to the track via a metal plate which slides along the rail and connects to the motor.

But the most expensive, the most widespread, and the most unpleasant means of advertising is the dispatch of special people, called "drummers." These are clever, brash, nimble-tongued young gentlemen, usually foppishly [flashily] dressed, uninhibited in manners, and supplied with an inexhaustible fund of shrewdness and impudence. The drummer is provided with great trunks of samples of the goods he sells. Sometimes he works for a commission, but more often for a fixed salary, and his boss pays all expenses. Such a migratory young man costs a commercial house no less than $3000 a year; the smart ones may even cost $5000 and especially good ones get up to $15,000. I myself know many firms which support as many as ten or fifteen such traveling salesmen, and know dozens of companies the advertising costs of which exceed $100,000 a year.

The unusual mobility of the American people and their passion for change of residence also foster in strong measure both the diffusion of knowledge and the spirit of general equality. Tens of thousands of people, artisans for the most part, constantly move around over the whole Union. On the road and in the new places, as a result of the national quality of quickness in acquaintanceship, they constantly come in contact with new people, new ideas, and new impressions, which they assimilate very rapidly. I have often been amazed at the many-sidedness and knowledge of my own workers. Where have they not been, what have they not done, in what positions have they not found themselves? It would seem that there is nothing in the world of which they have not heard, nothing they have not seen.

Several Germans and Englishmen always worked for me. Although they were excellent workmen and perhaps in cleanliness and fineness of work surpassed the Americans, they were inferior to the latter in every other way—difficult at making a beginning, extremely conservative in their mode of work, and always exceedingly specialized. The Europeans knew a certain part of the job; nothing else interested them. In the great majority of cases they learned nothing else; as they left their training, so will they die.

60 A Recipe for Economic Growth

HISTORICAL ESSAY

The spectacle of American economic growth excites everyone's interest and envy. We live in a world with a few rich nations and a host of poor ones. The poor would like to become rich. How, they ask, did Americans, the richest of all, do it? The readings in Chapter 15 suggest a partial answer to this vital question. We can say, for example, that Americans did it because they were a certain kind of people—ready to change, interested in innovation, anxious to get ahead. Although not all Americans shared these characteristics, a large number did, including most of the small group of leaders who dominated industry during the nineteenth century. These leaders found support among consumers who were willing to abandon an old product for a new one and from workers who were willing to try new ways to do things.

To a poor nation, "We did it because we were like that," is not an entirely satisfactory answer. First, this answer does not indicate how we got to be that way. Why were Americans relatively unafraid to change? Second, this answer does not reveal what an inventive people must do to generate steady economic growth. This essay, therefore, examines the steps that innovating Americans took to promote the enormous growth apparent in the statistics in Reading 57.

Goods (such as food, clothing, or tools) and services (such as medical care or education) come from a combination of natural, capital, and human resources. Any careful investigation of economic growth must begin with an analysis of each of these components. Natural resources make a convenient starting place.

The Importance of Natural Resources

During the half century after the Civil War, American industry tapped vast new deposits of precious raw materials. As iron ore mines in Pennsylvania began to run out in the 1870's, steelmen began to exploit new fields near Lake Superior. In the 1800's, the iron-and-steel industry opened rich iron ore deposits stretching from Birmingham, Alabama, to Chattanooga, Tennessee. During these same decades, steelmakers who had learned to manufacture coke from bituminous coal began to exploit a vast coalfield extending from northern Alabama to Lake Erie. In 1859, enterprising speculators drilled the first oil well near Titusville, Pennsylvania, and rapidly expanded drilling to new fields as they were discovered. Year after year, fresh deposits of copper, lead, gold, silver, and other minerals came to light, particularly late in the century in the Rocky Mountain region. Great timberlands in the Midwest, the west coast, and the South supplied a variety of woods to American industry. All the natural resources essential for a modern economy flowed freely from beneath America's rich soils.

Coke is a hard, grayish substance that remains after soft coal is heated in an airtight oven at about 2000° F.

Natural resources are gifts from nature, which blessed the United States with vast acres of fertile soil, rich mineral deposits, and abundant supplies of energy resources such as water. Until 1898, when the United States acquired Hawaii, the resource base of the American economy increased steadily as the nation acquired new land. Since that date, the total amount of resources available to the nation has not increased. Newly developed techniques to find deposits of raw materials, to extract them from the ground, and to process them into usable form have, however, steadily increased the quantity of known deposits of many minerals. In addition, fertilizers and irrigation have improved crop yields, and new technology has made it possible to turn uranium into energy in atomic reactors. These examples illustrate the application of capital and human resources to the natural resource base. They do not alter the basic conclusion that the quantity of natural resources has been fixed by nature and therefore cannot explain economic growth.

The Growth of Capital Resources

Capital resources, however, can be increased. In fact, the long-run growth rates of most major countries parallel roughly the proportion of their gross national product which they invest in capital goods. Throughout the nineteenth century, the United States was a high-saving and high-investing economy. During the whole period of development since the Civil War, for which we have reasonably accurate figures, the level of saving in the United States has remained relatively constant. Approximately 12 percent of the gross national product has been saved and invested every year. This statement does not mean, of course, that the rate of savings in every year has been 12 percent. In some years, savings have been higher, and in other years lower. In addition, there has been one small but still significant general shift from the 12 percent figure. The rate of saving was probably highest in the few decades after the Civil War and since then has shown a slight tendency to decrease. Since the 1890's, Americans have saved less and invested a smaller proportion of their income in machines.

To invest means to use money for the purchase of properties, stocks, or a business with the expectation of making a profit. To save means to set aside money for future use. Hence, money can be saved which is not invested, although typically people save money by investing it.

During the last decades of the nineteenth century, industrialists financed capital expansion in three ways. First, dozens of large businesses grew through reinvested profits. The income tax levied during the Civil War was repealed in 1871, and businessmen contributed comparatively little to support either their local or national governments. Special conditions permitted them to keep costs low. Since few unions existed, employers could simply fire their workers when times were bad without contributing to their support. When a boom developed, both former farmhands and immigrants from Europe lined up before employment offices and willingly worked overtime at regular hourly rates. In addition, new technical developments often gave an individual entrepreneur a temporary economic advantage which he exploited to the utmost. Prudent men such as Carnegie and Rockefeller financed most of their programs of expansion out of reinvested profits. Because profits were high, some of America's largest firms were owned by individual proprietors.

Capital means any type of wealth that is used to produce more wealth, including factories, machines, tools, etc. Capital expansion is thus an attempt to increase the amount of property a business already has.

An entrepreneur is one who assumes full control and liability in starting a business enterprise.

Many businesses, however, required larger sums than one man could accumulate. Hence, a second way of financing capital expansion developed. It involved the growth of large financial institutions such as the banking house of J. P. Morgan, which made loans to finance new ventures or to expand going concerns. These financial firms also negotiated large sales of stocks or bonds to smaller investors, providing a way in which the savings of people all over the nation could be used to expand industry. In addition, many foreigners bought shares in American industry. Increasingly, businessmen turned from the individual proprietorships or partnerships to corporations in order to raise capital and to protect themselves from the risks inherent in single ownership.

Corporations, unlike individually owned businesses and partnerships, are considered to be separate "beings" having independent legal existence. Shareholders who have invested in corporations are not personally responsible for the corporation's debts whereas individual owners and business partners are.

Finally, government helped to finance some business ventures. The federal government gave millions of acres of land along rights-of-way to railroads in order to encourage them to build tracks into areas where business might develop only after many years had elapsed. In some cases, local governments bought bonds or shares of stock from railroads in order to persuade them to build through their towns. The government, however, was a relatively minor source of capital.

Investors in corporations can lose only their initial investment. Corporations have an additional advantage over individual proprietorships or partnerships because they do not dissolve when the original founders or owners die.

Although the rate of saving and investment declined from the 12 percent figure, the productivity rate increased, particularly after 1914. Every year, as the figures in Reading 57 suggested, Americans through a combination of their own skill and the machines with which they worked produced more and more goods for every hour of labor. The rate of increase accelerated after World War I. How can we account for this increase when the natural resource base did not change and the rate at which Americans invested in machines tended to slow somewhat?

The Nation's Unusual Human Resources

The answer to this question probably lies in the way in which we keep accounts of what is saving and what is investment. If Americans put their money in a bank and the bank then invests this money in a machine, it is counted as investment. If instead of putting money in a bank, they spend it to educate themselves or their children or to improve their health, it is counted as consumption—as using wealth rather than saving it. This accounting procedure can be deceptive. Investment in human resources (which our accounting procedure calls consumption) has become the major ingredient of economic growth. Looked at another way, better education and improved health are investments in human resources which pay dividends later.

Four factors affect the quality of human resources: numbers, education, health, and attitude. Clearly, the more workers an economy has, the larger the pool of human resources which becomes available. So long as the number of people does not become too great for the natural and capital resource base, numbers increase growth. Throughout the entire period from 1860 to 1930, as Table 1 indicates, the population of the United States grew from 31 million to 123 million, roughly a fourfold increase. Part of the growth in population represents natural increase; the remainder stemmed from immigration. During these seventy years, more than 30 million immigrants entered the United States, largely from Europe. The labor of these new Americans contributed substantially to overall economic growth, particularly since most of them came as adults who had been educated through the unproductive years of childhood at Europe's expense. But during these same years, the gross national product increased from less than $9 billion to more than $100 billion, roughly eleven times. And during this entire span of years, Americans continued to invest at a steady rate of about 12 percent of their gross national product each year.

More and better education accounts for some of the growth. Individually and collectively, Americans made decisions to improve themselves as productive tools. Of the children between 5 and 17 years old in 1870, 57 percent were enrolled in public schools. In 1900, of the children in this age group 72.4 percent were enrolled; in 1920, 77.8 percent. These figures minimize the number of children in school because they do not include parochial schools which, although they were relatively few in 1870, absorbed a great many children into their classrooms after 1900. In 1870, 2 percent of the 17-year-olds in the United States had graduated from high school; in 1900, 6.4 percent were graduates; in 1920, this figure had leaped to 16.8 percent. In 1870, only 1.68 percent of students between 18 and 21 years of age were enrolled in institutions of higher education. By 1920, 8.09 percent were enrolled.

Improved schools are only one dimension of investment in human resources which helps to explain the growth of the American economy. Training programs in business firms are another. Unfortunately we do not have good statistics about these training programs. They were probably increasing at least as rapidly as public expenditures upon schools. Indeed, they may have been rising at a faster rate. One of the reasons that businessmen in the late nineteenth century tended to support the development of public high schools was because they hoped that schools would take over some of the burdens of training the skilled workers that they needed.

Improved health also raised the quality of the nation's human resources. The death rate of the American population remained stable between 1860 and 1900, that is, the number of people who died each year was relatively constant compared to total population. After 1900, however, the rate of death dropped rapidly, for two major reasons. First, infant mortality declined. For every 1000 children born in 1900, in the state of Massachusetts, 141 died. In 1920, only 78 died; in 1940, 34 died. The second source of this change came from a less striking but very important decline in the death rate of

Figures are available for Massachusetts because it was the first state to establish a state board of health (1869) which, among other tasks, kept such statistics.

adults. For every 1000 Americans in the age group 35 to 44 in 1900, there were 10.2 deaths; in 1920, this figure was down to 8.1, in 1940, it dropped to 5.2, and in 1950, to 3.6. Moreover, adults had fewer illnesses as time passed by. This improvement in American health meant that more people lived into their productive years so that resources invested in training them were not wasted either through an early death or through losing hours on the job because of sickness.

In addition to numbers, education, and health, the attitudes of people affect their quality as human resources. A large number of healthy and well-educated men and women will produce nothing unless they are willing to work. Americans were. European travelers constantly marveled at the energy and dedication of Americans. Moreover, Americans were willing to use part of their income to purchase capital equipment which helped to make a steady increase in productivity per man possible in the future. Finally, Americans accepted change willingly. They believed in progress. They thought that every man should strive valiantly to get ahead. All of these attitudes contributed to a rapid growth rate.

Rockefeller and Carnegie would probably have agreed with this analysis of the role of human resources in economic development. They both recognized that their particular contribution to the economy involved the application of knowledge and systematic methods of analysis to business problems. In later life, both men left parts of their fortunes to found new institutions of higher learning—Carnegie to what is now Carnegie-Mellon University, and Rockefeller to the University of Chicago. Countless other businessmen left fortunes to colleges or encouraged public education.

Increasingly during the last decades of the nineteenth century, manufacturing took place in a new industrial setting characterized by large-scale enterprises. A vast transportation and communication system grew up to link deposits of raw materials to factories and mills and to speed messages between them. The railroads also distributed finished products over the length and breadth of the land. Within thirty years after 1869, when a golden spike linked the east and west sections of the Union Pacific Railroad at Promontory Point in Utah, four additional transcontinental railroads spanned the continent. During the entire period between the end of the Civil War and 1930, American railroad companies built 395,000 miles of track. The telegraph spread rapidly. So did cables across the Atlantic and the number of telephones, particularly in large cities. All these developments helped to spur economic growth by speeding goods around the country. They also made giant enterprise practical. The chart on page 388 shows some key inventions of the era.

As the size of the market increased, the scale of production grew proportionally. So long as inexpensive transportation was available,

Inventions and Discoveries

Inventor/Discoverer	Date	Contribution
Edwin Drake	1859	oil drilling
George Pullman	1864	railroad sleeping car
Cyrus Field	1866	transatlantic cable
Christopher Sholes	1867	typewriter
George Westinghouse	1872	air brake
Alexander Graham Bell	1876	telephone
Thomas Alva Edison	1878	phonograph
	1879	incandescent light bulb
	1891	radio
George B. Selden	1879	first automobile patent
Ottmar Mergenthaler	1884	Linotype printing machine
C. Francis Jenkin and Thomas Armat	1896	motion-picture projector
Orville and Wilbur Wright	1903	first powered flight
Adolphus Busch	1898	first Diesel engine
Robert H. Goddard	1914	liquid fuel rocket
Peter C. Hewitt and F. B. Crocker	1918	helicopter

industrialists could locate factories in places where the supply of raw materials, the presence of a skilled labor force, or some other factor contributed to low unit costs. Hence, factories grew larger and larger, and the jobs within a factory became more and more subdivided. When one complex job became divided into a number of more simple operations, relatively unskilled men could learn them quickly, do them well, and command less pay than a skilled craftsman.

The idea of interchangeable parts and the introduction of the assembly line became essential to the new production methods. The assembly line became the most famous product of the division of labor. On an assembly line, a product moved on a continuous belt past rows of workers each of whom performed one simple function. Assembly lines had been used extensively in meat packing even before the Civil War. They took on a kind of mythical value as a symbol of American industry when Henry Ford introduced them into the automobile industry just before World War I. Actually, assembly lines organized around a continuous belt affected only a relatively small group of American workers. Still, most industrial laborers felt the effects of division of labor throughout the late nineteenth and earlier twentieth centuries. And the economy benefited through increased productivity per man.

Eli Whitney, the inventor of the cotton gin, had introduced the concept of interchangeable parts during the American Revolution in manufacturing firearms. His system allowed any part to fit any gun. Replacements for broken parts could be made from stock items. The practice of making interchangeable parts made the assembly line possible.

By 1818, a meat-packing industry had developed in Cincinnati. By 1860, Chicago had become the leading center for this industry.

Particularly after 1900, the quality of American machines improved. An investment of $5000 in a lathe that operates twice as fast as its predecessor makes a larger contribution to economic growth than that same $5000 invested in a slower machine. Large-scale factories and minute subdivision of labor encouraged technical improvements. When technology improves, the quality of capital resources goes up. Since World War II, technical change has been particularly rapid.

One additional factor which may help to account for rapid economic growth remains to be considered: the development in the United States of a mixed economy which prizes and rewards individual initiative and private enterprise. America's economic, social, political, and religious atmosphere clearly favored individual initiative, the pursuit of material rewards, and hard work. The children of successful businessmen, if not the tycoons themselves, quickly climbed to high rungs on the status ladder. The society, in other words, placed a premium on economic success and stamped its approval on a man who would make substantial contributions to economic growth.

A mixed economy is an economic system characterized by free enterprise, private ownership, and government intervention. In the United States, the government owns very few businesses, and intervenes in the economy to regulate business competition and trade, and to protect consumers and workers.

At the same time, government was friendly to business and promoted economic growth. The constitutional protection of patents encouraged inventors. High tariffs protected American industry from foreign competition. Grants of land helped finance many railroads. Government support of agricultural experiment stations and of land-grant colleges contributed to improved technology and better human resources. In addition, government maintained peace and order, protected property rights, and provided essential services such as roads and schools. All these activities provided a firm base for economic growth. Without this rapid growth, the United States would be an entirely different society from what it is today.

Article 1, Section 8, Clause 8 gives Congress the power to issue copyrights and patents.

SUGGESTED READINGS

DAVIS, LANCE E., *The Growth of Industrial Enterprise, 1860–1914.* This short and easy-to-read booklet describes the American economy during the period covered by Chapter 15.

KIRKLAND, EDWARD C., *Dream and Thought in the Business Community, 1860–1900.* This volume contains a sympathetic account of the ways in which businessmen strove to understand the revolution they were making.

NORTH, DOUGLAS, *Growth and Welfare in the Past: A New Economic History.* North's book presents a particularly clear statement about major issues in the history of economic growth.

CHAPTER 16

The American Farm: Change and Discontent

STATING THE ISSUE

An agricultural revolution accompanied and, to some extent preceded, industrial growth. If American farmers had been unable to feed the new industrial workers, men could not have moved into the cities to work in factories. In turn, factory-produced tools and machinery, together with new scientific knowledge about soil, seeds, fertilizers, and animals, increased farm productivity.

Before 1850, the productivity of America's farms kept pace with the growth of population. The same amount of food was available for each person each year. After 1850, agriculture production in the United States increased rapidly. More food was available for each American while great shiploads of grain, cotton, and cattle were exported.

The American farmer, like the American factory worker, was willing to innovate. If new methods would yield new profits, they were worth trying. Because land was cheap and abundant and labor was scarce, farmers turned to a vast array of new machinery to work the soil and to harvest the crops. The United States soon had more machines per farmer than any other nation in the world. Americans also developed new ways to market crops. Farmers urged the construction of a network of turnpikes, canals, and railroads to speed their products to eastern customers. They also developed new kinds of organizations to improve their lives and work for legislation.

By 1900, American agriculture was the envy of the world. Delegations came from other nations to examine both farming methods and the system of railroads, warehouses, shipping agencies, and banks that serviced farmers. American farmers, however, were not always satisfied. Chapter 16 examines the transformation of American agriculture and the reaction of many farmers to it. How did the American farm change between 1870 and 1929? Why were some farmers dissatisfied with the revolution they had helped to make? What solutions did farmers seek for their problems? Did farmers understand the new mechanical world? These are the major issues raised in this chapter.

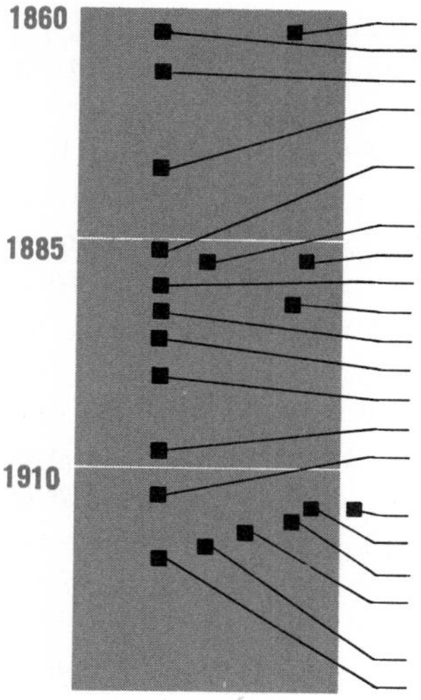

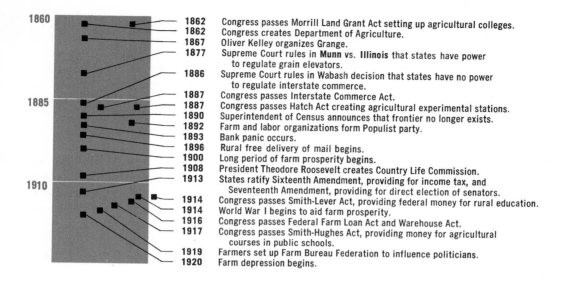

1862 Congress passes Morrill Land Grant Act setting up agricultural colleges.
1862 Congress creates Department of Agriculture.
1867 Oliver Kelley organizes Grange.
1877 Supreme Court rules in **Munn** vs. **Illinois** that states have power to regulate grain elevators.
1886 Supreme Court rules in Wabash decision that states have no power to regulate interstate commerce.
1887 Congress passes Interstate Commerce Act.
1887 Congress passes Hatch Act creating agricultural experimental stations.
1890 Superintendent of Census announces that frontier no longer exists.
1892 Farm and labor organizations form Populist party.
1893 Bank panic occurs.
1896 Rural free delivery of mail begins.
1900 Long period of farm prosperity begins.
1908 President Theodore Roosevelt creates Country Life Commission.
1913 States ratify Sixteenth Amendment, providing for income tax, and Seventeenth Amendment, providing for direct election of senators.
1914 Congress passes Smith-Lever Act, providing federal money for rural education.
1914 World War I begins to aid farm prosperity.
1916 Congress passes Federal Farm Loan Act and Warehouse Act.
1917 Congress passes Smith-Hughes Act, providing money for agricultural courses in public schools.
1919 Farmers set up Farm Bureau Federation to influence politicians.
1920 Farm depression begins.

61 The Farmer Is Not To Blame

The vast increase in agricultural production in the decades after the Civil War resulted primarily from the application of new knowledge, organization, and machinery in established farming areas. Prior to the Civil War, cotton had certainly been king in the South, but annual production increased fourfold between 1860 and 1914. The corn belt, which extended from Ohio to eastern Nebraska, had been settled before the Civil War, but production had been less than a third of what it became by 1914. The enormous expansion of commercial canning and the introduction of refrigerated railroad cars allowed local fruit producers in California, Florida, and many other areas to expand their farms and orchards in order to enter nationwide markets.

The dominance of already established areas in the agricultural revolution emphasizes the changing way of life for farmers. Farmers did not move far away to do things in new ways; change came to them on their old homesteads. New machines altered the farmer's daily activities and increased his productive capacity. By 1900, the limits of efficient animal or even steam power seemed to have been reached. In 1905, the first gasoline tractors appeared in America.

New marketing organizations and techniques also appeared after the Civil War. "East of the Rockies," one economic historian writes, "the business of assembling, handling, financing, and transporting grain was vastly superior to that of any other nation." Farmers severely criticized grain-elevator owners for paying them low prices for their grain at harvest time and then storing the grain until prices

A grain elevator is a large structure for storing grain.

went up before reselling it to flour mills. Nevertheless, such middlemen performed an important marketing function in the complex process of distributing food products to consumers.

Yet many farmers took a pessimistic view of the changes they had helped to bring about. Reading 61 is taken from a book by William A. Peffer, a participant in the American agricultural revolution at which the world marveled. Peffer had been born in Pennsylvania, and had farmed in Indiana, Missouri, and Illinois. While serving in the Union Army, he studied law and later set up practice in Tennessee. From Tennessee he moved to Kansas where he became the editor of two local newspapers and a leading farm journal. He was elected to the State Senate in Kansas in 1874 and later to the United States Senate as a representative of the People's party. As you read Peffer's analysis of the farm problem, keep these questions in mind:

Discontented farmers organized the People's, or Populist, party as a national political party in 1892.

1. What changes occurred on the American farm? How did Peffer explain this revolution?
2. How did he account for the farmers' problems?
3. Based on Peffer's analysis of the problems facing farmers, what solutions do you think he would seek?
4. In what ways would the introduction to this reading have been different had Peffer written it?

The Farmer's Side

In 1891, the year he was elected to the United States Senate, William Peffer published The Farmer's Side, His Troubles and Their Remedy *from which this selection is taken.*

William Peffer, **The Farmer's Side, His Troubles and Their Remedy.** New York: D. Appleton and Company, 1891, pp. 56–60, 64, 67. Language simplified and modernized.

The American farmer of today is altogether a different sort of a man from his ancestor of fifty or a hundred years ago. A great many men and women now living remember when farmers were largely manufacturers; that is to say, they made a great many implements for their own use. Every farmer had an assortment of tools with which he made wooden implements, as forks and rakes, handles for his hoes and plows, spokes for his wagon, and various other implements made wholly out of wood. Then the farmer produced flax and hemp and wool and cotton. These fibers were prepared upon the farm; they were spun into yarn, woven into cloth, made into garments, and worn at home. Every farm had upon it a little shop for wood and iron work, and in the dwelling were cards and looms; carpets were woven, bed-clothing of different sorts was prepared; upon every farm geese were kept, their feathers used for supplying the home with beds and pillows, the surplus being disposed of at the nearest market town. During the winter season wheat and flour and

Cards are toothed instruments used to comb flax, wool, and cotton in preparation for spinning. A loom is a machine for weaving thread or yarn into cloth.

cornmeal were carried in large wagons drawn by teams of six to eight horses a hundred or two hundred miles to market, and traded for farm supplies for the next year—groceries and dry goods.

Besides this, mechanics [skilled workers] were scattered among the farmers. During winter time the neighborhood carpenter prepared sashes and blinds and doors and molding and cornices for the next season's building. When the frosts of autumn came, the shoemaker went to the farmers' dwellings, and there, in a corner set apart to him, he made up shoes for the family during the winter.

Sashes are the movable frameworks of windows in which panes of glass are set. A molding is a decorative outline made of strips of wood and placed around doors and windows and between walls and floors. A cornice is a molding placed between walls and ceiling.

When winter approached, the butchering season was at hand; meat for family use during the next year was prepared and preserved in the smokehouse. The orchards supplied fruit for cider, for apple butter, and for preserves of different kinds, amply sufficient to supply the wants of the family during the year, with some to spare.

A smokehouse is a small building in which meats are preserved by exposing them to smoke.

One of the results of that sort of economy was that comparatively a very small amount of money was required to conduct the business of farming. Because so much was paid for in produce, a hundred dollars average probably was as much as the largest farmers of that day needed in the way of cash to meet the demands of their farm work, paying for hired help, repairs of tools, and all other incidental expenses.

Coming from that time to the present, we find that everything nearly has been changed. All over the West particularly, the farmer thrashes his wheat all at one time. He disposes of it all at one time, and in a great many instances the straw is wasted. He sells his hogs, and buys bacon and pork; he sells his cattle, and buys fresh beef and canned beef or corned beef, as the case may be; he sells his fruit, and buys it back in cans. Indeed, he buys nearly everything now that he produced at one time himself, and these things all cost money.

Besides all this, and what seems stranger than anything else, in the earlier time the American home was free and unencumbered. Not one in a thousand homes was mortgaged to secure the payment of borrowed money. But a small amount of money was then needed for actual use in conducting the business of farming, and there was always enough of it among the farmers to supply the demand. Now, when at least ten times as much money is needed, there is little or none to be obtained. Nearly half the farms are mortgaged for as much as they are worth, and interest rates are exorbitant.

Unencumbered means not mortgaged, that is, property which has not been used as security for a loan.

As to the cause of such wonderful changes in the condition of farmers, nothing more need be said than that the railroad builder, the banker, the money changer, and the manufacturer undermined the farmer. The matter will be further discussed as we proceed. The manufacturer came with his woolen mill, his carding mill, his broom factory, his rope factory, his wooden-ware factory, his cotton factory,

Exorbitant means excessively high. Money lenders charged interest rates as high as 20 percent. They justified charging farmers higher rates than they charged other borrowers on the grounds that farming was riskier than business or industry.

his pork-packing establishment, his canning factory, and fruit-preserving houses. The little shop on the farm has given place to the large shop in town; the wagon-maker's shop in the neighborhood has given way to the large establishment in the city where men by the thousand work and where a hundred or two hundred wagons are made in a week. The shoemaker's shop has given way to large establishments in the cities where most of the work is done by machines; the old smokehouse has given way to the packing house, and the fruit cellars have been displaced by preserving factories.

A fruit cellar is an underground room used for storing fruit.

The farmer now is compelled to go to town for nearly everything that he wants; even a hand rake to clean up the door-yard must be purchased at the city store. And what is worse than all, if he needs a little more money than he has about him, he is compelled to go to town to borrow it. But he does not find the money there; he finds instead an agent who will "negotiate" a loan for him. The money is in the East, a thousand or three thousand or five thousand miles away. He pays the agent his commission, pays all the expenses of looking through the records and furnishing abstracts, pays for every postage stamp used in the transaction, and finally receives a draft for the amount of money required, minus these expenses. In this way the farmers of the country today are maintaining an army of middlemen, loan agents, bankers, and others, who are absolutely worthless for all good purposes in the community, whose services ought to be, and very easily could be, dispensed with, but who, by reason of the changed condition of things, have placed themselves between the farmer and the money owner. In this way they absorb a livelihood from the people.

A commission is a sum of money, usually determined on a percentage basis, allowed to an agent for his services. Farmers had to pay the agent's commission, as well as the interest on the loan.

Abstracts are legal documents which give a condensed history of the title to land. They contain summaries of all transfers of the property from one owner to another and of any liens or charges against the property.
A bank draft is a written order that authorizes a bank to give money to someone.

It will be urged that the farmers themselves are at fault in this matter; that they are responsible for many of the changes in their habits and condition which have worked against them. This is doubtless true. Seamen might have continued the use of old-fashioned wooden ships, and we might all be traveling in stage-coaches. So might farmers still use the steel and flint to start their fires with; they might be using the sickle to cut their grain, and have the wheat kernels trodden from the straw by horses' hoofs. So, too, farmers might be spinning yarn and weaving cloth and tanning leather and making ropes and rakes. But does anybody believe such things either desirable or practicable? What would be the common estimate of a man whose farm is conducted like that of his grandfather before the age of railroads?

Tanning is the process of converting hides or skins into leather.

Like other men, the farmer was moved ahead by a current which was moving all men. His habits and his methods have changed, not because he desired it or worked for it, but because conditions forced it. Whether for better or worse, the whole business world has changed, and methods, like machines, have changed in all departments of industry. It is apparent that had he been less progressive, and had he not adopted all labor-saving devices which were brought to him, he would be still farther behind than he is.

It is expensive to supply a farm with improved utensils and machinery, but that is not a good reason why we should go back to the wooden moldboard and brush-harrow, to the flail, the flax-break, and hand loom. The truth is, farmers can and do produce vastly more now than they did or could produce under the old regime with an equal amount of labor.

The moldboard of a plow is the curved board that turns over the earth. Metal moldboards replaced those made of wood. A brush-harrow is a piece of brush drawn over plowed ground to break up clods of earth. Implements made with iron teeth replaced crude wooden harrows. A flax-break was used to remove the woody portion of flax from the fibers. More complex, efficient machines replaced the flax-break.

Transportation brings the farm and the factory close together; transportation makes it possible for men of different callings to serve one another, no matter how far apart they may be. The manufacturer supplies the tools, the machinery, and the oil to keep the farm and the railroad moving. In truth, the farmer, the carrier, and the manufacturer are natural allies, and some day they will so understand it. One reason why the farmer is behind in the race is because his forces are scattered while theirs are consolidated.

Thousands of individual farmers operated farms, while a few large companies manufactured goods and a few railroads transported goods.

The railroad employs large numbers of men; so does the factory, and these men, in political matters, are largely under the influence of their employers. This gives great social influence to the millionaires—enough, when combined with the power of the money they control, to dictate legislation in their favor. They are close to the governing agencies of the people. Lawmakers listen to the men that speak, and these are they who do the talking. Farmers have ceased to be congressmen and senators. Lawyers, bankers, railroad officers—they compose our legislative bodies largely now, and it is men of their classes that ask and obtain laws to further or protect their interests.

62 The Populist Attack

The many changes which Peffer described encouraged farmers to join together in an attempt to solve their common problems. Organizations of farmers during the post-Civil War decades dealt with a broad range of issues. The National Grange, organized in 1867 by Oliver Hudson Kelley as a social and educational society of farmers, led the attack on the railroads. In a number of midwestern states and in California, the Grangers promoted legislation to regulate freight rates within the state.

Railroad companies contested the legality of the "Granger laws." In a series of decisions, the most important of which was **Munn vs. Illinois** (1877), the Supreme Court ruled that state legislatures could regulate businesses that affected the public. This principle was applied to railroads. In 1886, in the Wabash Case, the Court modified its position by ruling that state legislatures could not regulate railroads which ran between states. Only Congress had the authority to regulate interstate commerce.

Several farmer organizations urged programs to deal with the complex issues of money and credit, which bothered Peffer so deeply. There were three related elements in the farm complaints: agricultural prices were falling more rapidly than the prices of manufactured goods, railroad and warehouse companies and other middlemen were charging too much for their services, and agricultural credit was both too difficult to get and too expensive. These three complaints provided the program for a series of organizational efforts.

Farmer organizations proposed remedies similar to those proposed in the mid 1780's. They wanted the government to increase the supply of money. The government had issued paper money, called *greenbacks,* during the Civil War, but had withdrawn some greenbacks at the end of the war. The Greenback party, organized in the mid 1870's, proposed that the government again increase the supply of paper money. Although the party soon disappeared, the Farmers' Alliances, organized both in the North and the South in the 1880's, took up the notion that farmers' problems could be solved through inflation.

In 1875, the Resumption Act required the government to pay specie (money in the form of metal) for greenbacks. This measure made them worth the same as gold-backed paper money. In 1879, the government again resumed withdrawing greenbacks from circulation.

Coinage of silver also became an issue during the 1870's. In the Coinage Act (1873), Congress had voted to stop coining silver dollars because of a shortage of silver. Within a few years, many silver mines were discovered in the West. Mine owners joined with farmers to demand the coinage of silver. They succeeded in 1878.

In 1878, Congress passed the Bland-Allison Act, which authorized the Secretary of the Treasury to buy \$2–4 million worth of silver monthly for coinage. In 1890, Congress passed the Sherman Silver Purchase Act, which authorized the purchase of 4½ million ounces of silver a month—almost all the silver produced in the United States.

In 1892, after preliminary meetings in St. Louis, Missouri; Ocala, Florida; and Cincinnati, Ohio, representatives of the Alliances and of other farm and labor organizations met in St. Louis to form a new political party. In July, this new People's, or Populist, party nominated General James B. Weaver of Iowa for President of the United States and proclaimed a platform reflecting the full range of farmer interests. Weaver received roughly a million votes, although he did not gain universal farmer support. Farmers who felt confident of their ability to get on in the new mechanized world, particularly those in areas where they raised more than one cash crop, voted for the candidates of the two major parties.

In 1896, in the midst of a depression, angry farmers in the Midwest, encouraged by western silver producers, focused their attention on the money issue and convinced the main faction of the Democratic party to urge expansion of the currency. Free-silver Democrats and Populists, to the dismay of many southern Populist leaders, joined in nominating a single candidate, William Jennings Bryan of Nebraska. Democrats who wanted gold nominated John Palmer. William McKinley, the Republican candidate, won a decisive victory.

Congress repealed the Sherman Silver Purchase Act in 1893 because of a bank panic that year. The repeal split the Democratic party.

Reading 62 describes the Populist view of farm problems and their proposed solutions to these problems. As you read, keep these questions in mind:

1. What did Peffer think caused the farmers' problems?
2. Why did Peffer believe that the Grange and the Farmers' Alliance were important organizations?

3. According to Peffer, why did farmers organize an independent political party? Why do you think Populist proposals appealed only to certain sections of the farm population? Which of their proposals have been realized today?

How We Got Here

This selection is also from Peffer's The Farmer's Side.

Peffer, **The Farmer's Side, His Troubles and Their Remedy,** pp. 121–23, 148–61. Abridged and language simplified and modernized.

The reader need have no difficulty in determining for himself "how we got here." The hand of the money changer is upon us. Money dictates our financial policy; money controls the business of the country; money is plundering [robbing] the people.

Here in the very heart of the best civilization on earth, at the very center of business life and activity, living in luxury and ease, renting costly pews in splendid churches, are men with millions of dollars at their call, governments at their command, and a loyal people in their service. These men produce nothing, add not a dollar to the nation's wealth, and fatten on the failures of other men. These men masquerade as philanthropists and patriots while they plunder a nation and rob the poor. These are the men who engineered the train that brought us where we are.

A philanthropist is one who displays his love of mankind by performing benevolent deeds, such as giving money to charitable or educational institutions.

This dangerous power which money gives is fast undermining the liberties of the people. It now has control of nearly half their homes, and is reaching out its clutching hands for the rest. This is the power we have to deal with. It is the giant evil of the time. Money is the great issue—all others pale into insignificance before this, the father of them.

Here, Peffer is referring to the fact that half the farms in Populist states were mortgaged.

The great thing, the essential matter, that overshadowing all others, and before which everything else pales, is the money power. That must be dealt with and disposed of at all hazards. Not that there is to be any destructive method; not that there is to be any anarchistic philosophy about it. Not that there is any inclination on the part of farmers or any considerable portion of the working masses to take away any man's property, or to distribute the existing wealth of the country among the people. Not that there is any desire to repudiate debts, to get rid of honest obligations, to rashly change existing forms or customs, or to indulge in any sort of disloyalty. Simply the influence of money as a power in society must be neutralized in some way.

Anarchistic means in a state of political and social disorder due to the absence of government.

The first step necessary in reaching equality in profits is for the persons interested in the movement to organize themselves into a political force. This can not be done at once. It must come through the formation of local bodies organized at first for purposes of mutual improvement and social benefits. This brings men and women into closer social relations with one another in communities. It is one of the best educating agencies ever adopted in any stage of social advancement.

Here, then, is the beginning of the great work that the farmers and their fellow-workers have to accomplish. Fortunately, this has been already largely begun. The Patrons of Husbandry, commonly known as the Grange, began their organization about twenty-four years ago in the city of Washington. "Granger" railroad legislation established in our laws the principle that transportation belongs to the people, that it is a matter for them to manage in their own way, and that the Congress of the United States is authorized and empowered by the Constitution to regulate commerce among the several states as well as with foreign nations.

Aside from the political influence of the Grange, it has been a powerful factor in the social development of farmers. Go into a Grange neighborhood, any place where the members have maintained their organization during all the troublesome, trying years that followed their first organization, and you find a neighborhood of thrifty, intelligent, well-advanced farmers. Their wives and daughters enjoy all of the comforts and conveniences which have been brought into use through the multiplication of inventions for the saving of labor and the production of wealth.

The Farmers' Alliance is a body in many respects quite similar to that of the Grange. In both bodies, women are equal with men in all of the privileges of the association. They are fast training women in political thought. Many of the best essays and addresses read and delivered in their meetings are prepared by women. It is beginning to dawn upon the minds of men, long incrusted by custom and usage, that the women who were chosen in early life as partners and companions are quite as capable of looking after the interests of adults as they are of infants. These social bodies of farmers, where men and women are at last made equal in public affairs, even though to a limited degree, are fast, very fast, educating the rural mind to the belief that women are as necessary in public affairs as they are in private affairs.

Except in Colorado, Idaho, Utah, and Wyoming, women could not vote before 1900.

The lesson learned by the movement of Alliance men in Kansas in 1890 has been one of very great profit to members in other parts of the country. They discovered in Kansas that political party machinery was so completely in the hands of a few men as to make party policy simply what was dictated by the little circle of leaders. It was evident that they were completely wedded to the power which has been absorbing the toilers.

They found that it was practically impossible to control the course of political parties. The machinery was in the hands of men living in the towns who were connected in one way or another with railroads, with corporations engaged in lending money for people in the East, real-estate transactions, and with other matters that were opposed to the interests of the farmers. Looking the situation over carefully and deliberately, the Alliance men came to the conclusion that the best way out of their troubles was through an independent political movement.

An article in the *Cosmopolitan Magazine* for April 1890, describes the Kansas campaign:

> Three party tickets were actively supported, Republican, Democratic, and the People's. All the trained stump speakers were with the old parties; they discussed old party issues, while farmers, mechanics, and laborers, with a few preachers, doctors, and editors, took up things of present and pressing interest to the people as they were outlined in their platform. Men, women, and children by thousands met in groves, and by hundreds in school-houses and halls, to listen to people of their own class and grade who talked about these new issues. Meetings of five thousand and six thousand people were common, and frequently as many as ten thousand persons met at one time and place to hear the "new gospel" taught. This outpouring of the masses, however, was limited to the People's party. The old party meetings were generally small, often discouragingly so; the most distinguished speakers failed to draw large audiences.

A stump speaker is a person who gives political speeches in support of a cause or a candidate during an election campaign.

The result in Kansas encouraged farmers in other states. Soon a movement was set on foot aimed at organizing an independent political movement covering the whole country. The first step in that direction was the National Union Conference, held at Cincinnati May 19, 1891, composed of nearly 1500 delegates representing thirty-two states and two territories.

That Cincinnati conference adopted the following resolutions:

1. That in view of the great social, industrial, and economical revolution now dawning on the civilized world and the new and living issues confronting the American people, we believe that the time has arrived to crystallize the political reform forces of our country and to form what should be known as the People's Party of the United States of America.

2. That we most heartily endorse the demands of the platforms as adopted at St. Louis, Mo., in 1889, Ocala, Fla., in 1890, and Omaha, Neb., in 1891, by industrial organizations there represented, summarized as follows:

Representatives of labor unions were invited to join the Populists in an attempt to link "the organized tillers and the organized toilers" of the nation.

a. The right to make and issue money is a sovereign power to be maintained by the people for the common benefit. Hence we demand the abolition of national banks as banks issuing money. As a substitute for national-bank notes we demand that legal-

The National Bank Acts of 1863 and 1864 provided for a system of banks that had federal charters although they were privately owned. **Notes** are certificates which serve as money. **Legal tender** is any form of currency which may be offered lawfully in payment of debts and which may not be refused by creditors.

Syndicates are combinations of businessmen or bankers organized to carry out some project requiring large amounts of capital.

In the nineteenth century, property taxes were a major source of government revenue. Farmers' land, buildings, and animals could be seen more easily by a tax assessor than bankers' or industrialists' stocks and bonds. Hence, farmers believed they bore an unfair tax burden.

A graduated income tax is a tax on income scaled so that the tax rate increases as income increases. The federal government had passed such a tax during the Civil War. In 1895, the Supreme Court ruled that a federal income tax was unconstitutional. The Sixteenth Amendment (1913) made it legal.

The Seventeenth Amendment (1913) provided for direct election of senators. That amendment changed Article 1, Section 3, Clause 1, of the Constitution, which said that the state legislature would choose the senators.

Wall Street, located in the financial center of New York City, often symbolizes financial power in America.

tender treasury notes be issued in sufficient volume to transact the business of the country on a cash basis without damage or especial advantage to any class or calling. Such notes shall be legal tender in payment of all debts, public and private, and such notes, when demanded by the people, shall be loaned to them at not more than 2 percent interest per annum [a year].

b. We demand the free and unlimited coinage of silver.

c. We demand the passage of laws prohibiting alien ownership of land. Further we demand that Congress take prompt action to obtain all lands now owned by alien and foreign syndicates, and that all land held by railroads and other corporations, in excess of such as is actually used and needed by them, be reclaimed by the government, and held for actual settlers only.

d. Believing the doctrine of equal rights to all and special privileges to none, we demand that taxation—national, state, or municipal—shall not be used to build up one interest or class at the expense of another.

e. We demand that all revenue—national, state, or county—shall be limited to the necessary expenses of the government, economically and honestly administered.

f. We demand a just and equitable system of graduated tax on income.

g. We demand the most rigid, honest, and just national control and supervision of the means of public communication and transportation. If control and supervision do not remove the abuses now existing, we demand the government ownership of such means of communication and transportation.

h. We demand the election of President, Vice-President, and United States senators by a direct vote of the people.

63 A New Rural Life

Peffer's view of farmers' problems suggested that men hiding in some dark corner of Wall Street conspired against the farmer. In many ways, Peffer presented an overly simplified view of complex economic changes that were occurring in America. The whole economy was being transformed, and the farmers' problems were part of that transformation.

Peffer's opponents held similarly oversimplified views of the farmer, his problems, and his proposed solutions to those problems. Plans to change the banking or monetary system, for example, were interpreted as great conspiracies. Theodore Roosevelt, who later became President, described the Populists as men "plotting a social revolution and the subversion of the American Republic." He said that an example should be made of twelve of their leaders by putting them against a wall and shooting them.

A great many changes in the early twentieth century worked to close the gap between farm and city. Farmers' protests died out, in part because farm prices rose. New gold discoveries in Alaska, South Africa, and Australia relieved the money shortage of which farmers had complained so bitterly. The major political parties adopted and secured the passage of a number of Populist reform proposals, such as the direct election of senators, the initiative and referendum, regulatory legislation for railroads, and an income tax. With funds from the federal government, the land-grant colleges sent extension agents into rural areas to give farmers and their wives new knowledge about farming methods and home economics. The automobile, the radio, and mail-order houses, such as Sears Roebuck, drew the farmer and the city dweller closer together.

Initiative is a procedure by which a specified number of voters may propose a law or constitutional amendment and compel a popular vote on its adoption. **Referendum** is a procedure for referring laws already passed by a legislature to the voters for their approval or rejection.

Reading 63 contains one early attempt to study rural life. In 1908, President Theodore Roosevelt asked a group of men who had concerned themselves deeply with the problems of the farm to report to him "upon the present conditions of country life, upon what means are now available for supplying the deficiencies which now exist, and upon the best methods of organized permanent effort in investigation and actual work along lines I have indicated." These men, organized as the Country Life Commission, submitted a report which revealed many widely shared assumptions about the value of the farm and the differences between farm and city. As you read these selections from the report, keep these questions in mind:

1. What impression of rural life do you get from the Missouri farmer? What attitudes and values did he express?
2. According to the report, why did farmers move to towns?
3. What suggestions did the Commissioners make for improving rural life? Why did they stress order, stability, and planning?
4. How did the Commission's report compare and contrast with Peffer's evaluation of farm life? In your opinion, what conditions are necessary for the "good life"?

A Missouri Farmer's View of Country Life

This selection is from President Theodore Roosevelt's introduction to the Report of the Country Life Commission.

Report of the Country Life Commission, Senate Document No. 705, 60th Congress, 2nd Session. Washington, D.C.: Government Printing Office, 1909, pp. 10–11. Abridged and language simplified and modernized.

One of the most illuminating—and incidentally one of the most interesting and amusing—series of answers sent to the commission was from a farmer in Missouri. He stated that he had a wife and eleven living children. He and his wife were each 52 years old. They owned 520 acres of land without any mortgage hanging over their heads. He had himself done well, and his views as to why many of his neighbors had done less well deserve consideration. These views are expressed in terse and vigorous English; they cannot always be quoted in full. He states that the farm homes in his neighborhood are not as good as they should be because too many of them are mortgaged; that the schools do not train boys and girls satisfactorily for life on the farm, because they allow them to get an idea in their heads that city life is better. To remedy this he thinks practical farming should be taught.

To the question whether the farmers and their wives in his neighborhood are satisfactorily organized, he answers: "Oh, there is a little one-horse grange gang in our locality, and every darned one thinks they ought to be a king." To the question, "Are the renters of farms in your neighborhood making a satisfactory living?" he answers: "No; because they move about so much hunting a better job." To the question, "Is the supply of farm labor in your neighborhood satisfactory?" the answer is: "No; because the people have gone out of the baby business"; and when asked as to the remedy he answers, "Give a pension to every mother who gives birth to seven living boys on American soil." To the question, "Are the conditions surrounding hired labor on the farm in your neighborhood satisfactory to the hired men?" he answers: "Yes, unless he is a drunken cuss," adding that he would like to blow up the stillhouses and root out whisky and beer. To the question, "Are the sanitary conditions on the farms in your neighborhood satisfactory?" he answers: "No; too careless about chicken yards (and the like) and poorly covered wells. In one well on a neighbor's farm I counted 7 snakes in the wall of the well, and they used the water daily. His wife is dead now and he is looking for another." He ends by stating that the most important single thing to be done for the betterment of country life is "good roads."

Stillhouses or "stills" are buildings containing distilling apparatus for making alcoholic beverages. "Home brew" violates federal and state tax laws on alcoholic beverages.

Report of the Country Life Commission

This selection is drawn from the report itself.

Report of the Country Life Commission, pp. 19–21, 48–65. Abridged and language simplified and modernized.

Upon the development of a new and distinctively rural civilization rests ultimately our ability to continue to feed and clothe the hungry nations; to supply the city with fresh blood, clean bodies, and clear brains that can endure the strain of modern urban life; and to preserve a race of men in the open country that, in the future as in the past, will be the stay and strength of the nation in time of war and its guiding and controlling spirit in time of peace.

Broadly speaking, agriculture in the United States is prosperous, and the conditions in many of the great farming regions are improving. There has never been a time when the American farmer was as well off as he is today, when we consider not only his earning power, but the comforts and advantages he may secure. Yet there is a widespread tendency for farmers to move to town. It is not advisable, of course, that all country persons remain in the country; but this general desire to move is evidence that the open country is not satisfying as a permanent home. In difficult farming regions, and where the competition with other farming sections is most severe, the young people may go to town to better their condition.

Around the turn of the century, farm prices had risen substantially, in part because of an increased demand for farm products.

Nearly everywhere there is a townward movement in order to secure educational advantages for the children. This tends to destroy the open country and to lower its social status.

The social disorder is usually unrecognized. If only the farms are financially profitable, the rural condition is commonly pronounced good. Country life must be made thoroughly attractive and satisfying, as well as profitable and able to hold the center of interest throughout one's lifetime. With most persons this can come only with the development of a strong community sense of feeling.

The cohesion [sticking together] that is so marked among the different classes of farm folk in older countries cannot be reasonably expected at this period in American development. We are as yet a new country with undeveloped resources, and many far away pastures which, as is well known, are always green and inviting. Our farmers have been moving, and numbers of them have not yet become so well settled as to speak habitually of their farm as "home."

The middle-aged farmer of the Central States sells the old homestead without much hesitation or regret and moves westward to find greater acreage for his sons and daughters. The farmer of the Middle West sells the old home and moves to the Mountain States, to the Pacific coast, to the South, to Mexico, or to Canada.

Even when permanently settled, the farmer does not easily combine with others for financial or social betterment. The training of generations has made him a strong individualist, and he has been obliged to rely mainly on himself.

He does not as a rule dream of a rural organization that can supply as completely as the city the four great requirements of man—health, education, occupation, society. While his brother in the city is striving by moving out of the business section into the suburbs to get as much as possible of the country in the city, he does not dream that it is possible to have most that is best of the city in the country.

The correctives for the social barrenness of the open country are already in existence or under way. The regular agricultural departments and institutions are aiding in making farming profitable and

Free delivery of letters and packages to mailboxes in rural areas was established in 1896. Before that, people in those areas had to go to the nearest post office—sometimes at a considerable distance—to get their mail. Pressure from the Grange influenced Congress to provide free rural delivery.

Groups of farmers organized cooperative associations to bypass middlemen. Producer cooperatives processed farm products, such as milk, which was marketed directly to consumers. Farmers also organized consumer cooperatives—retail stores that sold such items as farm machinery and clothing—at cost to the members of the cooperative.

With the Smith-Hughes Act of 1917, Congress provided money for vocational education in public schools, including courses in agriculture and home economics.

The word **patrons** in this sentence refers to the members of cooperative associations.

Grading means classifying products, such as eggs or fruit, according to size and quality. Graded products can be marketed to the greater advantage of both seller and buyer.

attractive, and they are also giving attention to the social and community questions. There is a widespread awakening, as a result of this work. This awakening is greatly aided by the rural free delivery of mails, telephones, the gradual improvement of highways, farmers' institutes, cooperative creameries and similar organizations, and other agencies.

In every part of the United States there seems to be agreement, on the part of those capable of judging, on the need to redirect the rural schools. The schools are held to be largely responsible for ineffective farming, lack of ideals, and the drift to town. It is probable that the farming population will willingly support better schools as soon as it becomes convinced that the schools will really be changed in such a way as to teach persons how to live.

The feeling that agriculture must influence rural public schools is beginning to express itself in the interest in nature study, in the introduction of agriculture classes in high schools and elsewhere, and in the establishment of separate or special schools to teach farm and home subjects. These agencies will help to bring about the complete reconstruction of rural life.

It is of the greatest importance that the people of the open country should learn to work together. This effort should be a genuinely cooperative or common effort in which all the associated persons have a voice in the management of the organization and share proportionately in its benefits. Many of the so-called "cooperative" organizations are really not such, for they are likely to be controlled in the interest of a few persons rather than for all and with no thought of the good of the community at large. Some of the societies that are cooperative in name are really strong centralized corporations or stock companies that have no greater interest in the welfare of the patrons than other corporations have.

At present the cooperative spirit works itself out chiefly in business organizations devoted to selling and buying. The commission has found many organizations that seem to be satisfactorily handling the transporting, distributing, and marketing of farm products. With some crops, notably cotton and the grains, it is advantageous to provide cooperative warehouses in which the grower may hold his products till prices rise, and also in which scientific systems of grading of the products may be introduced.

Organized cooperative effort may take on special forms. It is probable, for example, that cooperation to secure and to employ farm labor would be helpful. It may have for its object the securing of telephone service (which is already contributing much to country life, and is capable of contributing much more), the extension of electric lines, the improvement of highways, and other forms of betterment.

While it is of course necessary that the farmer receive good compensation for his efforts, it is nevertheless true that the money consideration is frequently too exclusively emphasized in farm homes. Teachers of agriculture have placed too much relative emphasis on the income and production sides of country life. Money hunger is as strong in the open country as elsewhere, and as there are fewer opportunities and demands for spending this money for others and for society, hoarding and a lack of public spirit that is disastrous to the general good often develop. So completely do financial considerations often control motives that other purposes in farming often remain dormant [inactive]. The complacent contentment in many rural neighborhoods is itself evidence of social incapacity or decay.

The farming country is by no means devoid of leaders, and is not lost or incapable of helping itself, but it has been relatively overlooked by persons who are seeking great fields of usefulness. It will be well for us as a people if we recognize the opportunity for usefulness in the open country and consider that there is a call for service.

64 Farm Complaints and the Process of Change

HISTORICAL ESSAY

American farmers complained bitterly throughout the last forty years of the nineteenth century. They carried their complaints into the political arena, organizing one short-lived reform movement after another. Around 1900, however, the fortunes of farmers took a turn for the better. During World War I, they enjoyed enormous prosperity. Then at the end of the war, an agricultural depression set in which worsened during the 1930's and ended only with the arrival of World War II. Talk about the fortunes of farmers in the United States during those seventy years filled the newspapers and occupied the attention of Congress. Much of this talk displayed ignorance of basic economic principles.

The Economic Setting of Agriculture

Economists classify agriculture as a purely competitive industry. In order to be purely competitive, an industry must have:

1. a very large number of producers, each so small in relation to the total size of the market that his production will make no real difference in the market price or the quantity produced;

2. an identical product marketed by these producers so that the consumer has no preference about which one he buys from;
3. easy entrance into this field of production, and easy exit for those who fail in it; and,
4. an absence of any collusion (secret agreements) among producers on the price, quantity, or quality of goods sold.

The wheat industry may serve as an example of pure competition. Throughout this entire period, hundreds of thousands of farmers raised wheat. Not a single farmer raised as much as one tenth of one percent of a year's wheat crop; hence, if an individual farmer refused to sell his wheat, the price would neither rise nor fall. Millers who bought wheat to make flour for bread had no reason to prefer grain from any particular farmer. It was easy to enter the wheat industry; a farmer who raised corn could quickly shift to wheat in many parts of the country. It was also easy to leave; a farmer could simply plant another crop or abandon farming. Finally, because farmers scattered all over the nation raised wheat, they could not get together to work out and enforce agreements to limit production or set prices.

Pure competition made the individual farmer helpless in an impersonal market. Again an example may help to clarify the problem. In 1867, farmers produced about 211,000,000 bushels of wheat on almost 17,000,000 acres; the average price per bushel was $2.01. Because prices were so high, farmers used savings or borrowed money to buy additional land and machinery. They harvested 246,000,000 bushels on more than 19,000,000 acres during 1868; the price fell to $1.46 per bushel. But instead of planting fewer acres the next year, farmers planted 2,000,000 acres more and harvested almost 290,000,000 bushels; the price fell to $.92 a bushel, less than half of what it had been two years before.

An examination of these figures reveals that the total value of the wheat crop to farmers had dropped $6.5 million between 1867 and 1868, and another $9 million by 1869.

To understand what happened, we must try to see the world from the point of view of the individual farmer. "Returns are high. I'll borrow $1000 to buy more land and some new machinery," a farmer might have said in 1867. "I grow about thirteen bushels an acre. Wheat sells for $2.00. If I plant ten more acres, I will harvest 130 additional bushels and my income will increase by about $260 each year. In five years, I'll be able to repay the $1000, pay the interest on this money, and have some left over." When prices fell the next year and the loan still had to be repaid, the farmer persuaded himself to plant more wheat, not less, so that even though he received fewer dollars per bushel, his total income would remain constant.

Hundreds of other farmers thought the same way. Wheat flooded the market, and prices fell still further. Moreover, their fortunes were affected by international conditions since grains, cotton, meat, and many other products sold on a worldwide market. A bumper crop of wheat in the Ukraine or of cotton in India or Egypt could bankrupt American farmers. This competitive situation eventually forced inefficient farmers out of business, a development which kept the industry efficient and provided food to consumers at the lowest possible cost, but which also created severe agricultural discontent. Farmers paid the human costs of a purely competitive system.

The Growth of Productivity

Settlers occupied the last of the excellent farm lands in the United States about 1890, according to historians, the date which marks the end of the advancing frontier. Although more than a million additional farms existed ten years later, the growth in both the number of farms and in farm acreage clearly slowed down after that, as Table 1 indicates.

In his annual report for 1890, the Superintendent of the Census stated that there was no longer a frontier line in the United States. Historian Frederick Jackson Turner noted the disappearance of the frontier in a paper entitled "The Significance of the Frontier in American History." Turner's thesis was that the frontier experience had created a distinct American character and way of life.

TABLE 1 Number of Farms, Farm Acreage, and Value of Farms, 1870–1930

Year	Number of Farms	Farm Acreage	Farm Lands and Buildings: Total Value	Farm Lands and Buildings: Average Value/acre
1870	2,660,000	408,000,000	$ 7,444,000,000	$18.26
1880	4,009,000	536,000,000	10,197,000,000	19.02
1890	4,565,000	623,000,000	13,279,000,000	21.31
1900	5,737,000	839,000,000	16,615,000,000	19.81
1910	6,362,000	879,000,000	34,801,000,000	39.60
1920	6,448,000	956,000,000	66,316,000,000	69.38
1930	6,289,000	987,000,000	47,886,000,000	48.52

U.S. Bureau of the Census, **Historical Statistics of the United States, 1789–1945.** Washington, D.C.: Government Printing Office, 1949, p. 95.

Between 1870 and 1900, farmers put an additional 10,000,000 to 20,000,000 acres under cultivation each year. Then the rate of growth slowed drastically. The size of the farm labor force reflects this trend. Table 2 has the figures.

TABLE 2 Total Population and Farm Labor Force, 1870–1930

Year	Total Population	Farm Labor Force
1870	39,818,449	6,849,772
1880	50,155,783	8,584,810
1890	62,947,714	9,938,373
1900	75,994,575	10,911,998
1910	91,972,266	11,591,767
1920	105,710,620	11,448,770
1930	122,775,046	10,471,998

U.S. Bureau of the Census, **Historical Statistics,** p. 63.

Although total population grew steadily, the size of the farm labor force increased very slowly after 1900 and began to fall between 1910 and 1920. Together Tables 1 and 2 show that after 1900 a stationary farm labor force tilling about the same number of acres was able to feed a rapidly growing population. Each farmer produced more food. No wonder that the average value of farm lands and buildings per acre, after remaining almost unchanged between 1870 and 1900, began to climb rapidly (see Table 1).

A short ton equals 2000 pounds.

Tables 3 and 4 contain data which help to explain what happened.

TABLE 3 Value of Farm Implements and Machinery, 1870–1930

1870	$ 271,000,000
1880	407,000,000
1890	494,000,000
1900	750,000,000
1910	1,265,000,000
1920	3,595,000,000
1930	3,302,000,000

TABLE 4 Short Tons of Commercial Fertilizer Consumed in the United States, 1870–1930

1870	321,000
1880	753,000
1890	1,390,000
1900	2,730,000
1910	5,547,000
1920	7,296,000
1930	8,425,000

U.S. Bureau of the Census, **Historical Statistics**, p. 100. (both tables)

Instead of plowing additional acres or adding more men and women to the agricultural labor force, farmers bought more and better machines and used more fertilizer, particularly after 1900. Hence, productivity per man rose.

A combine is a harvesting machine that reaps, threshes, and cleans grain.

Farmers began to alter their traditional tools long before 1860. By 1870, mechanical reapers, binders, threshers, combines, gang plows, harrows, seeders, and cultivators were all widely used. After 1870, virtually every year saw a new or an improved machine on the market. Until World War I, horses provided most of the power on farms although steam tractors pulled huge machines through large western wheat fields. In 1910, there were only about 1000 gasoline-powered tractors on American farms; by 1930, there were 920,000. Mechanization had taken command.

The Morrill Land Grant Act of 1862 granted public lands to the states and territories to be used to establish agricultural and mechanical colleges. Many of today's state universities began as land-grant colleges. The Hatch Act of 1887 provided federal money for agricultural experimental stations and farms. The Smith-Lever Act of 1914 provided federal money for county extension agents to act as intermediaries between the colleges and experimental stations and the farmers.

Education and research also contributed to farm productivity. In May 1862, President Lincoln had established the Cabinet-level Department of Agriculture with an appropriation of $64,000, part of which was to be used to supply farmers with information about a number of practical subjects. Soon afterwards, Congress passed the Morrill Act granting every state then in the Union 30,000 acres of federal land for each senator and representative in Congress at the time. This money was to be used to endow at least one college which would teach agriculture and the "mechanic arts" in every state. By 1916, the states had founded 69 land-grant colleges. In 1887, the Hatch Act added agricultural experiment stations to the land-grant colleges. Both federal and state governments also developed extension work to educate farmers through lectures, county fairs, publications, and correspondence. All of these activities contributed to the agricultural revolution by developing excellent seeds, new fertilizers, and better machinery and by educating farmers to use them well.

The Farmers' Complaints

In retrospect, the causes of agricultural complaints in the hundred years since 1870 seem plain. They were not at all plain to farmers. The farm organizations described in Readings 61 and 62 launched vigorous attacks on a number of problems. Perhaps the inability to change basic laws of supply and demand encouraged them to seek out problems which could be solved, even if they were of secondary importance. History textbook writers have sometimes added to the confusion. Some of them have written as if all farmers stood together and as if all of them were equally affected by the same troubles. In fact, there were dozens of different kinds of farmers with quite different problems. Farmers in the South may serve as an example.

Southern farmers grew a variety of crops. By 1879, the cotton crop was larger than in any prewar year and continued to increase rapidly in size as farmers opened new fields in Texas, Arkansas, and Oklahoma; by 1914, total productivity exceeded three times the

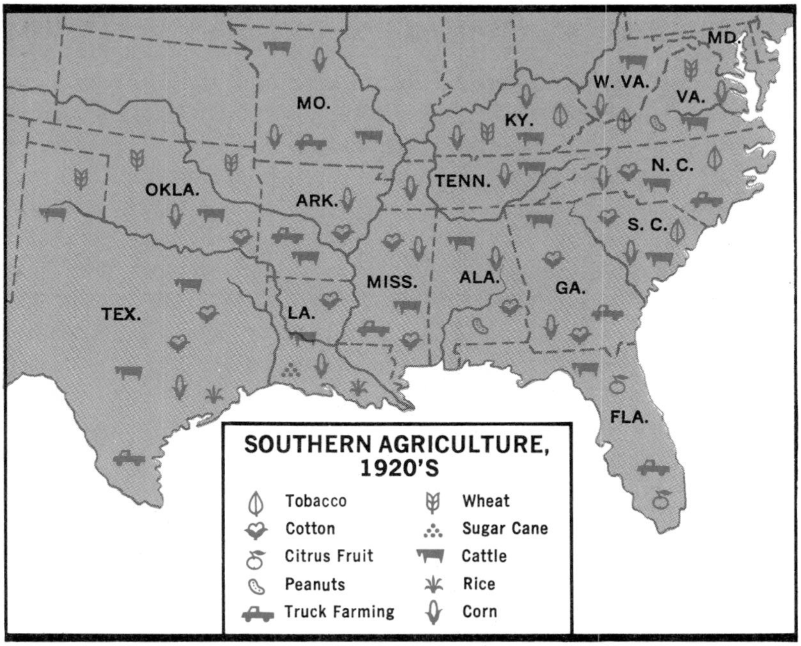

prewar crop. Most cotton was raised by the sharecropping system. A landlord loaned part of his land to a former slave or a poor white, and provided seed, fertilizer, equipment, and even food and clothing in return for a share of the crop. The impoverished tenants were constantly in debt to landlords and to owners of country stores who gave credit at high interest rates. For cotton farmers, tenantry combined with the low price of cotton became major political issues.

Truck farming is the growing of fresh vegetables for market. These vegetables are usually transported to the cities by truck.

Rice and sugar cane growers left the east coast for Louisiana where they assembled large holdings and invested heavily in machinery. These farmers demanded protection against foreign competition and worried about adequate loans to buy machinery. Tobacco growers, increasingly located in Kentucky, Tennessee, Virginia, and North Carolina, lived on small family farms either owned by the farmer or rented on a sharecrop basis. Prices and tenantry were their main concerns. Towards the end of the nineteenth century, a number of farmers began truck farming near the cities or developed apple, peach, or citrus orchards. Their prosperity fluctuated with the weather and, in the case of fruit growers, the availability of labor at harvest time. No one issue, such as railroad rates or the tariff, united all these farmers. This same generalization holds true for farmers from the remainder of the country.

Particularly during the four decades after 1870, farm organizations set forth a number of complaints. They pointed out, for example, that farm prices fell more rapidly than prices as a whole, putting the farmer who bought machinery and sold wheat at a disadvantage. Between 1864 and 1900, the index of wholesale prices for all products fell 59 percent; the index for agricultural products alone dropped 65 percent. Hence, many farmers favored measures which they thought would halt the price drop, particularly measures to increase the money supply by issuing greenbacks or coining silver. They also pressed for laws to reduce the price of what they bought by regulating railroad rates or controlling the profits of middlemen.

Although these grievances were genuine, they were not overwhelming, nor were they universal. During the last half of the nineteenth century, exports of food products boomed, increasing almost tenfold in dollar value between 1866 and 1899. In addition, between 1870 and 1900, the population of the nation almost doubled. Partly as a result of the increased demand for food to feed these people, total farm income increased about 80 percent during these years. The number of persons engaged in agriculture, however, increased only about 60 percent. These figures indicate a real per capita increase in farmers' incomes. Moreover, prices fell throughout this period. A farmer who had borrowed money when prices were high, such as the hypothetical farmer described earlier in this chapter, suffered during deflation because he had to repay the loan when the

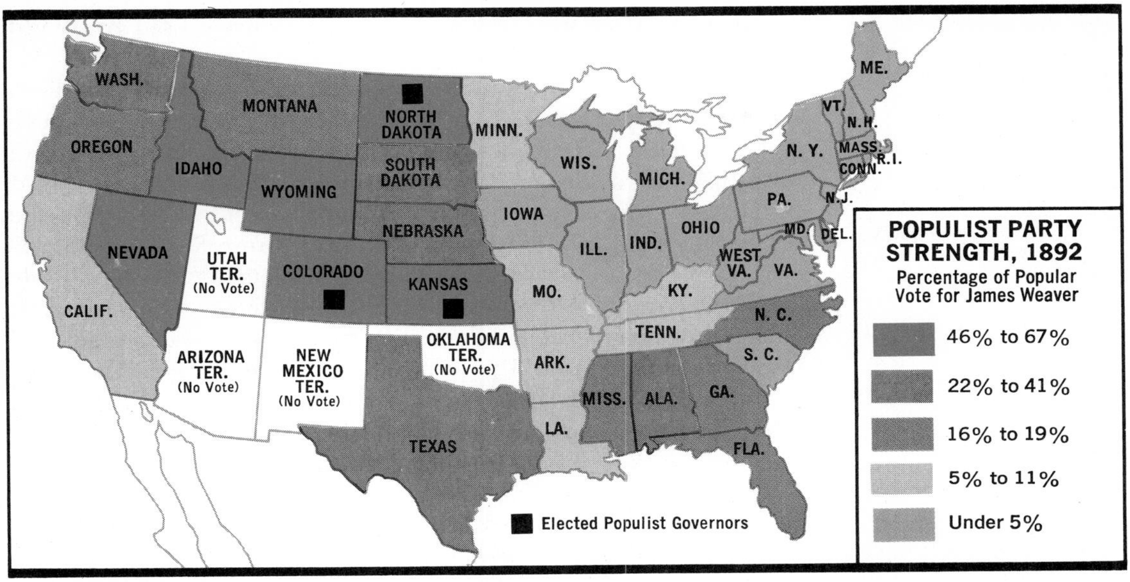

prices he received per bushel of wheat had fallen. But farmers who were not in debt at the beginning of this period of deflation probably had a slow but steady rise in their standard of living.

The Granger movement of the 1870's focused in the wheat and corn growing areas of Illinois, Wisconsin, Minnesota, and Iowa. Here farmers had gone into debt to buy land and machinery and were caught when the price of wheat fell from more than $2.00 to less than $1.00 in two years. Twenty years later, the center of wheat and corn cultivation had shifted to Kansas, Nebraska, the Dakotas, and western Minnesota, the heart of Populist country, where more than half the farms were mortgaged. Southern cotton farmers suffering under the sharecropping system also joined the Populists. The remaining American farmers did not flock overwhelmingly to the Populist standard, possibly because they were not in the same difficulties as wheat, corn, and cotton farmers.

The Farmer's Lot Improves

After 1900, agricultural conditions improved steadily for twenty years. The discovery of gold in Alaska and South Africa increased the money supply and reversed the trend of prices. Population grew steadily while the growth in the number of acres cultivated slowed since all the good western lands were already occupied. As a result, the wholesale price index of all farm products rose almost 50 percent between 1900 and 1910 while the index of products which farmers bought rose less than 20 percent. A new day had seemingly arrived.

American farmers supplied war-torn Europe with food for three years before America's entry in the war in 1918. Between 1914 and 1917 the value of wheat exported increased from $88,000,000 to almost $300,000,000. When the war began, a bushel of wheat sold for less than $1.00; by 1918, the price had risen to $3.00.

These trends continued to 1915, when the boom caused by World War I skyrocketed farm prices.

European demand for American food revolutionized the farm economy for four years. Total farm production did not rise above the 1915 level, despite a substantial increase in acreage planted, until 1920. But as demand increased, prices shot up. Prices received by farmers more than doubled during these four years while the prices they paid including interest and taxes rose less than 90 percent. Then the war ended. In 1920, Europe's demands dropped while a temporary postwar slump that placed about five million Americans among the unemployed cut domestic demand. At the same time, total farm productivity rose 5 percent, and prices collapsed. The index of prices received by farmers fell from 215 in 1919, to 124 in 1921, while the prices of what they bought fell far less. Although conditions on the farm improved after 1923, farm income remained low throughout the 1920's. Farmers who had borrowed during the war to buy more land and machinery were hit particularly hard by this new wave of deflation.

Frank Woolworth opened his first store in Utica, New York, in 1879 and sold only low-priced goods. At first he was barely able to break even, but several years later with help from partners, he succeeded in opening "chains" of stores.

In 1872, Aaron Montgomery Ward started a mail-order house in Chicago to meet the needs of the Grangers. In 1895, Sears, Roebuck and Company was formed.

While these economic developments took place, the entire nature of farm life was changing. A great network to distribute goods and services spread out from the cities. General stores became small department stores. Woolworth's and other chain stores appeared in one country town after another. Mail-order houses grew rapidly, encouraged by the free delivery of rural mail which began in 1896 and by the growth of the national parcel post service. Mail-order sales were $31 million in 1899; they reached $543 million in 1919.

Farmers learned to work together more effectively. Early in the twentieth century, they formed many organizations such as those described by the Country Life Commission to help solve their problems. They established cooperatives to market goods without the intervention of middlemen; they pooled their resources to gain credit. In 1919, they founded the Farm Bureau Federation to influence political leaders and to hire experts who could bring business methods to the farm.

The farm organizations achieved a few notable successes during the first two decades of the twentieth century. In 1916, Congress passed the Federal Farm Loan Act and the Warehouse Act which permitted the federal government to store produce such as wheat and to offer loans to farmers until the price of their crops rose. In addition, the federal government expanded its support of scientific agriculture by enlarging its staffs of county agents who toured rural districts to teach new agricultural techniques. The government also gave grants to public schools that offered agricultural education.

Many farmers did not share in the benefits of rising prices, the movement of city life to the farm, or the support of the government.

Farmers with little land or machinery and farm laborers with no land at all hardly benefited from the new prosperity. In the 1920's, when the prices of major crops dropped, farm organizations dominated by large farmers asked the government to offer price supports. Although Congress approved several of these schemes, President Coolidge vetoed them. But even if they had passed, they would not have helped the little man.

Under a program of price supports, the federal government assigns a "base" period for the prices of farm products, a period when farmers were relatively prosperous and received good prices for their crops. When farm prices drop below the figures for the base period, the government gives the farmers "loans" to make up the difference in price.

By the end of the 1920's with the Depression hard upon him, the American farmer faced a bleak future despite the steady improvement in his lot. The development of superior machines, new seeds, and new agricultural techniques enabled efficient farmers to produce more and more each year with fewer and fewer hands. So long as the nation was prosperous and displaced farmers could get jobs in factories, the shock of transition could be eased somewhat. But once the Depression hit, there was nowhere to go. Social tragedy lay ahead in the bleak decade of the 1930's.

SUGGESTED READINGS

CURTI, MERLE, *Making of an American Community: A Case Study of Democracy in a Frontier County.* This is a detailed account of the meaning for one Wisconsin county of the changes described by Peffer.

RÖLVAGG, O.E., *Giants in the Earth.* A deeply touching novel of the immigrant experience on the rural frontier; this book has become an American classic.

TINDALL, GEORGE B., ed., *A Populist Reader.* Tindall has collected a fascinating group of writings primarily written by leaders of the Populist movement.

CHAPTER 17

Negroes and Whites in the Southern States

STATING THE ISSUE

During the late nineteenth century, the South remained a poor region committed to staple agriculture. Few people lived in cities, and few worked in industry. The South faced a host of problems, such as transforming agriculture, improving education, speeding the growth of industry, and freeing the region from excessive dependence on the North. These problems would have been difficult if southern society had not been divided by racial antagonisms.

But the South was divided. Hence, each of the complex issues of regional development was shaped by the bitter fruits of slavery, coercion, and fear. Before the Civil War, whites and blacks had lived together as master and slave. Because a sharp line drawn by the overwhelming power in the hands of the whites had divided the races, whites were able to deal with Negroes frequently and casually. White and black rode in the same railway car or wagon and sometimes ate at the same table. Although rarely formally married, members of the two races often had children together.

Emancipation and reconstruction destroyed the patterns of race relations which had existed under slavery. As we learned in Chapter 14, however, these developments did not set the South firmly on the path toward equality. Few people in the North were willing to grant or fight for true racial equality, and white southerners certainly were not willing to do so. Lacking white allies, blacks who demanded freedom had little chance of success. Since slavery could not be reimposed and since whites were unwilling to grant equality, the South had to develop a system between these two extremes.

For a time after conservative southerners regained control of their state and local governments, relations between the races were in a state of flux. Twenty years of debate preceded the decision to suppress Negro rights and to legislate rigid inequality. Chapter 17 focuses on this debate and on the critical decisions white southerners made in the last two decades of the nineteenth century about their relations with black citizens. What attitudes did white southerners display toward Negroes? Why were Negroes suppressed? How did Negroes react? How did the rest of the nation react? These are the major issues raised in this chapter.

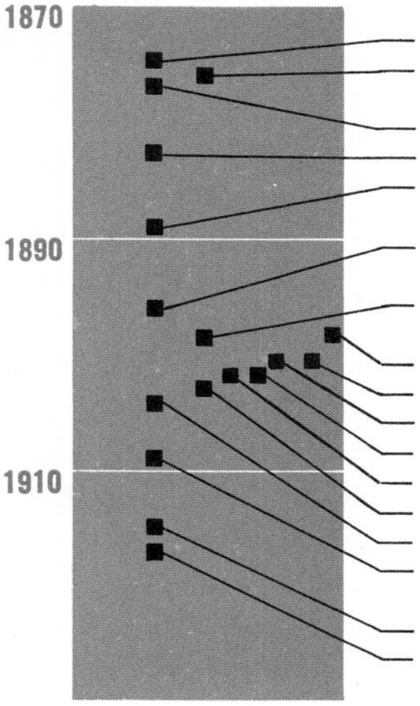

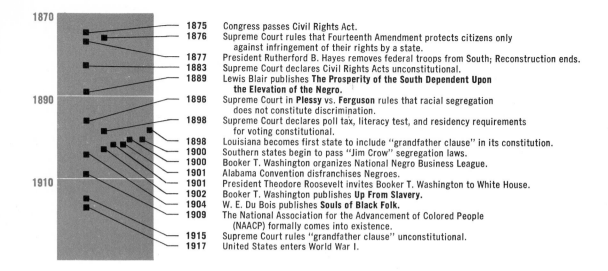

1875	Congress passes Civil Rights Act.
1876	Supreme Court rules that Fourteenth Amendment protects citizens only against infringement of their rights by a state.
1877	President Rutherford B. Hayes removes federal troops from South; Reconstruction ends.
1883	Supreme Court declares Civil Rights Acts unconstitutional.
1889	Lewis Blair publishes **The Prosperity of the South Dependent Upon the Elevation of the Negro.**
1896	Supreme Court in **Plessy** vs. **Ferguson** rules that racial segregation does not constitute discrimination.
1898	Supreme Court declares poll tax, literacy test, and residency requirements for voting constitutional.
1898	Louisiana becomes first state to include "grandfather clause" in its constitution.
1900	Southern states begin to pass "Jim Crow" segregation laws.
1900	Booker T. Washington organizes National Negro Business League.
1901	Alabama Convention disfranchises Negroes.
1901	President Theodore Roosevelt invites Booker T. Washington to White House.
1902	Booker T. Washington publishes **Up From Slavery.**
1904	W. E. Du Bois publishes **Souls of Black Folk.**
1909	The National Association for the Advancement of Colored People (NAACP) formally comes into existence.
1915	Supreme Court rules "grandfather clause" unconstitutional.
1917	United States enters World War I.

65 The Indivisible South

The Civil War had devastated the South. A quarter of a million men and hundreds of thousands of animals had died. Farm buildings had been ruined in a way that resembled city blocks following an air raid. Railroad tracks were torn up, locomotives gutted, and factories burned to the ground.

Destruction of physical resources, as great as it may be, can be overcome if human resources remain intact. The South made an amazing recovery from the blows of war. By 1875, southern agriculture had practically returned to its prewar level; in 1880, cotton production surpassed all prewar records. Merchants and bankers, who before the war had provided services only in a few large southern cities, established businesses in smaller cities throughout the region. After the economic decline of the mid 1870's, northern financiers invested in southern railroads, timber, and iron and steel plants.

The men who won political control in the South at the end of Reconstruction adopted the images of the old slaveholding elite. They boasted of their respect for southern traditions. Even the name applied to them, "Southern Bourbons," recalled a past of plantations, fox hunts, and an elegant way of life. These Bourbons, despite their reliance on tradition, hoped to transform southern life through rapid economic growth. They wanted a South dotted with new steel mills and tied together by railroads. Many of these economic leaders entered the political arena. Corporation lawyers and industrialists held leading positions in the governments of Mississippi, Georgia, and Tennessee during most of the late nineteenth century.

The Bourbons are a royal family in Europe. In the antebellum South, the term was used to designate the class of wealthy white plantation owners who set the style. After the war, the term had no distinct significance and was used by many politicians, usually liberals, to describe those people who opposed them.

Southern industrialists looked to the North for models of economic development. They wanted to enrich themselves and their region by encouraging manufacturing and mining. They believed that economic development depended upon cheap labor, freedom from government regulation of business, a stable society that supported property rights, and low taxes. Bourbon leaders even cut the budgets of public schools established during Reconstruction in order to save tax money.

Not all southern leaders believed that these policies were realistic or wise. Lewis Blair, a member of one of the oldest and most prominent Virginia political families, challenged the idea that economic development could be achieved without a revolution in race relations. As you read Blair's arguments, consider these questions:

1. What were Blair's assumptions about southern society?
2. Why did he believe the white South would have to change?
3. What changes in southern white attitudes would have been necessary for the success of Blair's program? What means could have been used to modify attitudes?
4. Do you think southern whites would have granted Negroes an equal place in society if they had been convinced that unequal treatment of Negroes would hurt them?

A Proposal for Southern Prosperity

In 1889, Lewis H. Blair published his proposal for southern prosperity, entitled The Prosperity of the South Dependent Upon the Elevation of the Negro. *Here are some of Blair's arguments.*

Lewis Blair, **The Prosperity of the South Dependent upon the Elevation of the Negro.** Richmond, Va.: Everett Waddey, 1889, pp. 9–11, 28–29, 43–45, 50–51. Republished as **A Southern Prophecy.** Boston: Little, Brown and Company, 1964, pp. 25–27, 48–49, 67–68, 69, 75, 77.

There are many causes for the poverty of the South, the principal of which are a widespread ignorance, a general disregard of human life, a general lack of economy and self-denial. But great as these causes are, a greater and more far-reaching cause of all is the degradation of the Negro, who, being our principal source of labor, is our principal source for prosperity.

Each of these causes would greatly retard the prosperity of the South, or indeed of any country. But all of them combined, destructive as they would necessarily be to prosperity, are not as serious and as fatal as the last cause, namely: the degradation of the Negro. Like a deadly cancer which poisons the whole system, this degradation seems to intensify all the other drawbacks under which we labor. Thus general ignorance is intensified by the gross ignorance of all the blacks and of the whites nearest them in social and financial condition. The general disregard of human life is intensified by the slight regard in which a Negro's life is held. The whites, regarding the Negro's life of little value, naturally regard all life as of little value, and therefore they freely take each other's life. The general lack of economy and self-denial is naturally intensified by the careless, wasteful and negligent manner in which the Negro, upon whom we are mainly dependent for labor, usually does his work. The Negro is an extremely defective tool, and no man, whether planter, carpenter, or whatnot, can continue constantly to use wretched implements without becoming wasteful and negligent himself, and without disregarding economy. Just as we would urge the South to improve its animals, tools, methods of planting, etc., so that it may derive the more good from their labor and capital, so we urge the elevation of the Negroes, because the better men and citizens they are the more we, the whites, can in the end make out of them.

But the question will be very generally asked, Why elevate the Negro at all? Is he not now good enough to obey us dutifully, and to make our corn, our cotton, our tobacco, our rice, and our sugar? What more do we want of him? The reply is that if the Negro is forever to remain simply the instrument for doing our menial and manual work, for plowing and sowing, for driving mules, for worming tobacco, and picking cotton, he is already too elevated, and he should be still further humbled and degraded. In his present condition he has some of the ideas and aspirations of a freeman, some desires for education, and he has almost entire control of his personal movements. He works when it suits him, but then he may idle at the crisis of a crop; but as we cannot compel him with the lash to work, he is on the whole not a profitable laborer either for himself or for an employer. To make him efficient, and to make him work the crop at the proper time, in spite of the attractions of political and religious gatherings, the overseer with the lash must be ever before his eyes. To allow the Negro to remain as he is, is for him a still "lower deep" in the social scale, and in his descent he drags us down with him.

But if the Negro is to become an intelligent voter, is to be a citizen capable of taking a sensible part in the affairs of his community, and to be a valuable co-worker in adding to the wealth of the state, then we have a vast deal to do in order to elevate him. To make him *our* assistant in the production of wealth, the Negro must be made to work, or he must be induced by ambition, by the hope of enjoying in full the fruits of his labors, to work steadily and intelligently. If we are not willing to elevate him, we should set to work resolutely and deliberately to fetter [chain] both his mind and limbs, and to cow [frighten] him, so that a little white child shall control a thousand. We will then at least get enough out of him to supply his few physical wants and to enable us to live in idleness and comparative comfort, which is not now the case. But if there is no hope of our ever being able to do this, what is the next best thing for

Serfdom was a condition of most peasants under feudalism. Serfs were bound to the land and could not leave the land without their lord's permission. They held low status in the social structure.

us to do for our own good? Make a man of him. But this can be done only by means of education and other fostering influences, by cultivating his self-respect, by inspiring his hope, by letting him see that the land of his birth is as much his country as it is that of the wealthiest and haughtiest white. Now he is not only an alien, but an inferior—in reality a serf, in the land of his nativity.

We must trample, or we must elevate; to maintain the *status quo* [present situation] is impossible. To trample is to perpetuate and intensify the poverty and stagnation under which we groan; to elevate is to make the South rich, happy and strong. What are we going to do? Shall we oppose, or shall we drift and take chances of killing or curing, or shall we promote the Negro's progress? Prejudice counsels the first, timidity the second, common sense the third; so what shall we do?

The majority will probably say, Wait; why take any steps to correct any abuses or to counteract any injurious consequences associated with his present degraded condition, for (say they) evils will in time cure themselves. But although history and observation abundantly prove that evils do not always work their own cure, but as often or oftener effect the ruin of the patient, we will admit that time will happily effect a solution of the Negro problem. But then we must remember that time is not only a very uncertain, but also a very long, something, and while we are waiting for this time we will be really suffering all the evils and disadvantages of actual poverty.

The measures necessary for the elevation of the Negro cannot be carried out summarily or by simple act of legislation, but they require time, care, wisdom and patience, and are impossible without the acquiescence [acceptance] and cordial cooperation of the whites. Great as is the power of the national government, it cannot elevate the Negroes itself, nor can it force the whites to do so. The question is, we may say, absolutely within control of the whites. They can keep the Negro in his present degraded condition, but they cannot do so without at the same time laying the axe at the root of their own welfare; and they can crush, but while doing this, they will be destroying themselves.

The whites cannot see this now, for they are dominated by a great apprehension—namely that the elevation of the Negro means the degradation of the whites. Until this fear is put to rest by showing them that little probable harm can come to them thereby, it will be like appealing to the winds to urge them to steps leading to the complete elevation and enfranchisement of the Negro. In spite of all advice to love our neighbor as ourself, human nature will persist in loving itself better than its neighbor, and so, as long as the Southern people believe that the complete elevation of the Negro will be an injury to them, they cannot be expected to take kindly, or even to take at all, to the idea. Show one that his interest lies in a certain direction, and there is little difficulty in getting him to go that way. So to elevate the Negro, we must show the whites that his elevation will be no disadvantage to them.

The South is truly a land of caste, and its chains hang heavily upon those of the lowest caste. Southern society is now virtually divided into two castes. In the first caste are merged gentleman, farmer, overseer, poor white, and each and every one of these, regardless of education, worth, refinement, decency, or morality, belongs to this class simply by reason of a white skin. The second caste is composed of all who have a black skin and all related to them, however remotely. All who are thus marked, however cultured and refined they may be, however able and however excellent, are confined as by fate to this caste. They are not permitted to throw off their galling chains; and society, by its unalterable verdict, decrees that the meanest, lowest, and most degraded of the first caste are the irreversible and permanent superiors of the best, highest and ablest of the second caste.

A caste system rigidly divides members of society into groups on the basis of birth, wealth, or religion. No social mobility takes place within a caste system.

Hope cannot exist, certainly cannot flourish, under such a weight. If he is to remain forever a "nigger," an object of undisguised contempt, even to the lowest whites, the Negro will naturally say to himself, Why strive, why labor, why practice painful self-denial in order to rise, if I am to derive no good from my effort? On the contrary, he will not exert himself, but will sink into despondency.

66 "They Cannot Be Equal"

Lewis Blair was not the only leader in the New South who urged the elevation of Negroes. Even if they did not advocate Negro equality, many conservative leaders of the 1870's and 1880's believed that Negroes could not be barred from the political life of the region. In fact, they looked to Negro voters to help defeat whites who challenged their leadership. In return for their support, Negroes received minor offices in government and other jobs. Although Negroes often lived in fear of reprisals from the terrorist Ku Klux Klan, they were not segregated legally from the white community.

This delicate balance in race relations was shattered in the last decade of the nineteenth century. Beginning with Mississippi in 1890, state after state passed laws to prevent Negroes from voting. Following disfranchisement, southern states adopted policies to segregate the races. Between 1900 and 1911, most states passed "Jim Crow" laws, which required Negroes and whites to sit separately in railroad cars, trolleys, ferries, and steamboats. Many southern cities adopted

The origin of the term "Jim Crow" is uncertain. It may have come from a character or a song in a musical. Sometimes the term is used to mean "Negro," but more often it means "discriminating against Negroes."

rules requiring whites to live in separate neighborhoods. Even southern reformers, fighting for progressive farm measures, urged that Negro and white farmers should take up segregated farm lands.

Many northerners, who had been friendly to Negroes consented to this policy of segregation. Even the Supreme Court of the United States endorsed it. In 1896, the Court decided in the case of *Plessy* vs. *Ferguson,* that a Louisiana law requiring Negroes and whites to travel in separate railroad cars did not violate equal protection of the laws under the Fourteenth Amendment. The Court held that segregation did not mean discrimination. As long as the railroad cars were of equal quality, the constitutional rights of the Negroes were not violated, it said. The extension of this doctrine of "separate but equal" to public schools allowed southerners to build black and white schools, which while separate were rarely equal.

Historians do not understand fully why the South segregated Negroes. The easiest explanation contends that it took a while for traditional patterns of behavior to be cemented into law. But such an explanation fails to take into account the alternative policies which southerners considered. The white Populists, for example, tried to attract Negro support in the 1890's in order to defeat conservative Bourbon leaders. Whites in the South's new industrial cities began to feel that they had lost status by taking factory jobs, and this changed attitude toward themselves may have influenced their attitudes toward blacks.

Reading 66, drawn from the debates in the Alabama convention of 1901, which deprived Negroes of the vote, will help you understand why the South adopted segregation. As you read, try to answer these questions:

1. What are the arguments given here for denying the vote to Negroes? What are the arguments for permitting all white men to vote?
2. What role did these speakers want the Negro to play in southern life? Does this concept of the Negro's role imply Jim Crow laws?
3. Can you justify denying the vote to members of a particular race? to members of a particular religious group? to women? to criminals? to the insane? to the uneducated?

The Alabama Convention Disfranchises Negroes

The Democratic Party platform prior to the Alabama convention of 1901 promised that no whites would be disfranchised. A minority in the convention, however, objected to open discrimination in violation of the United States Constitution and argued for educational and property qualifications. The following selections state the majority position.

Official Proceedings of the Constitutional Convention of the State of Alabama (May 21, 1901 to September 3, 1901), vol. III, pp. 2839–48. Adapted.

MR. GRESNER WILLIAMS: How can you have a progressive and enlightened state unless white men rule it? It does not insult the white men of Alabama, nor do you put the slave of your father above him, when you require the slave to have a qualification that the white man does not. Gentlemen of the Convention, God Almighty Himself put the seal on the white man, and He put it upon the negro. He has made the distinction and we only ask you to stand by your own people. I was fortunate when I was born in that my father had a competency [good living] after the dreadful Civil War. I know young men, however, who were the playfellows of my elder brothers and of myself whose fathers before the war were wealthy men. These young men today can scarcely write their names, and after it is written for them can scarcely read it, though printed in the boldest of letters. Would you disfranchise those men, or the children of those men, who were denied opportunities, because of the scourges [sufferings] of war, to get an education? Does not this section guarantee the right to vote to these men, grown to manhood, and now having children of their own, and who have been so unfortunate as not to have been able to attend school? Are you not willing to guarantee the ballot to those who will not be able to give to their children's children as much education as will be necessary to compete with the negro child whose blood has possibly mingled with the Caucasian? It is an absurdity to me that any man who has seriously watched the current of events through their boyhood and young manhood and seen changed conditions sweep over this country, that they cannot realize and see that our country demands the enfranchisement of every man with pure white blood in his veins in this state.

Many southern states included a "grandfather clause" in their constitutions. This clause exempted from the literacy tests and poll taxes anyone who had been eligible to vote on January 1, 1867, or whose parents or grandparents had been eligible to vote at that time. This clause thus gave the vote to many uneducated, poor whites while denying it to Negroes.

They say that this device is invalid. I shall not discuss that proposition now, because it is a proposition which has been tried and has not been found wanting. I think delegates to this Convention will see when this matter is tested that it is not found wanting in the State of Alabama. It has been said that a race war is possibly imminent [about to take place] in Alabama. I don't believe it, but for the sake of argument I will admit it. Should a race war come, will not delegates to this Convention want the lowliest white man that plows the cotton row in south Alabama or the corn row in north Alabama, who works and delves in the mines, whether they are able to read or write, will you not want him to shoulder the musket and go out against the black? I say, put the test: white man against negro. And we ask you in this majority report to place the white man, be he ever so lowly, against [above] the negro, be he ever so high and exalted among his own people. We are tired . . .

THE PRESIDENT: The time of the gentleman has expired.

MR. WILLIAMS: And I am tired also.

The speaker is referring to Adam and Eve and their fall from innocence in the Garden of Eden.

MR. J. THOMAS HEFLIN: Since man tasted the supernatural joys of Paradise and lost that high estate, he has been wandering in search of an ideal country. It was here [in the United States], Mr. President, that the Caucasian race hewed [carved] out a Republic. It was here that the representatives of the proudest race that ever lived established a government that will never fall. It was here that the white man drove the red man from his home in the forest, and took possession of this land. We find in the Bible that God gave His servants command, to go up and possess the land. I believe he reserved America, this section of the western world, for the permanent settlement of the Caucasian race. Here by mutual consent, they came together and by mutual consent established a government for the good of all the people.

In the course of time, gentlemen of the Convention, slaves were hunted out in Africa. The negro wandered through the woods like a beast of the field, and was brought here to do what? To be put upon the block and sold to the highest bidder, to be the servant of his superior, the white man in this country. I believe as truly as I believe that I am standing here, that God Almighty intended the negro to be the servant of the white man. I believe that the Scripture will sustain my position on that question. I know he is inferior to the white man, and I believe that delegates of this Convention believe him to be inferior. He knows it himself.

Here the speaker was in error. The Emancipation Proclamation freed those slaves living in states under Confederate control. In essence, President Lincoln had no jurisdiction over these states as they had seceded from the Union and had set up their own government. It was the Thirteenth Amendment that freed the slaves.

"Kill his will" means that each Negro vote would cancel out a vote cast by a white southerner.

After remaining here the servant of the white man for years and years, finally upon a question of state rights, and not on the question of slavery, the greatest civil conflict in human history was enacted in our country. Great men were arrayed upon opposing sides. For four years the undaunted sons of the South illustrated to the world the bravest spirit that has ever throbbed beneath God Almighty's sun. They fought for home rule, and for self-government, and what occurred? The President of the United States issued a proclamation freeing the slaves of the South, taking from the slaveowners that which they had bought and paid for with their own money, snatching from them this property that they had bought in the market, and which belonged to them. This was a military blow at the labor system of the South. Later on they said to this mass of ignorant slaves, untutored and uncultured, "you may walk side by side with your master of yesterday and cast your vote and kill his will." Unfit for the responsibilities of Government they were turned loose upon the people of the South and marched side by side with the chivalric [gallant] sons of our country up to the ballot box. They voted like the high-spirited, freeborn Americans of our land, like the men who fought the battles of this country, the men who bought it with their blood, and who with their arms bravely and undauntedly secured American independence. Why, Mr. President, the striking from him of the title slave, and placing in his hand the ballot was the most diabolical [devilish] piece of tyranny ever visited upon a proud though broken people.

Mr. President, this was the only instance in history where a race which you might say was physically prohibited from amalgamating or assimilating with another race, was given equal rights and privileges by the law with that other race in the same community. You can't trace history back to a single recorded instance where two such opposite races were ever brought together under the same laws affecting both alike. There is nowhere a single recorded instance where African and Caucasian races, impossible of mutual absorption or amalgamation, were given the same political, legal and social rights under the same government. Where two races are thrown together the stronger will dominate. That is true, and the white man is going to dominate here.

The speaker is inaccurate here. For example, as far back as the eighteenth century B.C. in Egypt, both Negroes and whites held positions of honor and influence in the government.

Mr. President, we have told the people of Alabama for years that we wanted to disfranchise the negro. He has been about the ballot box like sheep in the market for sale to the highest bidder. The white people who love the ballot, who love the sanctity of their fireside, who love the government of their homes and of their States, want to exercise that great weapon in the defense of things that are right and sacred. We want to take it out of the hands of men whom you can purchase for twenty-five cents and a drink of whisky. We want the white men who once voted in this State and controlled it, to vote again. We want to see that old condition restored. Upon that theory we took the stump in Alabama, having pledged ourselves to the white people of Alabama, upon the platform that we would not disfranchise a single white man. It is our purpose to disfranchise every negro in the State and not a single white man.

Mr. President, I love to think of how faithful the Negroes were during the war. The gentleman from Montgomery [Mr. Oates] spoke about how they protected our homes, and how they looked after our affairs. That, Mr. President, was the old-time slave of over thirty years ago. That, Mr. President, was the negro that had been brought up in the kitchen and in the backyard, and brought up to reverence and respect his master. There was a spirit of fear that went about him; reverence for his superior, and a feeling of humility and obedience on occasions like that was innate [inborn], and we are glad that they did so well. I am not an enemy to the negro. I am a friend to him in his place. My father owned more slaves than any man in Randolph County. I love the old-time Southern negro. He was in his place as a slave, and happy and contented as such. And, Mr. President, I love to think of the old black mammy. As Governor Taylor says; I believe the day will come when the South will erect a monument to the old black mammy for the lullabies she has sung. We like to think of all these things. We like to think of old Ephraim, sitting around the fire place picking his banjo and eating roasted potatoes, and "sich" [such]. We love to go back and bring them back to memory.

But you take the young negro of today, and put them in the same position that their fathers were in, and, gentlemen, a quarter of a century from now you would not be on a floor like this singing their praises. I tell you that the old negroes are passing out and the young bucks that are coming on have got to be attended to. I like to think of the negro from the old-fashioned Southern standpoint. I like to tell him you do this, or you do that John, and here is a quarter. You black my shoes, or catch my horse, and you go do this and that, and all is well. But I don't like it when I have to walk up to him and say, "John, come down off of that telegraph pole where you are setting telegraph wires through the city, come down, I want to talk to you about the tariff question," and sit down with him at my side, just light up our cigars and talk. We are equal in the light of the law, and I have got to sit down by you and ask you to vote my way, not because you are my equal, for God Almighty never made you so, but because under the operation of a law that was born in hate and malice, makes it so. Under it you are entitled to hear me and be persuaded by me to vote for me, or to vote against me. Is not that a sad state of affairs?

A stereotype is a simple, standardized mental picture of a racial or nationality group or of an issue or event. This description of a Negro is an example of a stereotype formerly held by prejudiced white people.

Why, Mr. President, I saw this morning a little fellow coming down the street as happy as could be, with a piece of watermelon in one hand and a set of cane quills [hollow reeds] from the swamp tied together with a string, in the other, blowing "Boogoo Eyes." You see them now and then in a blacksmith shop, with a squeaking bellows, and with the hammer and anvil making music sweet. That is his home; that is where he ought to be, and that is where he must be.

A bellows is an accordion-like instrument that draws in air by expanding and contracting. It is used to fan fires.

Mr. President, so far as I am concerned, I am opposed to the disfranchisement of any white man, I care not whether he is learned or unlearned, whether he wears the purple robes of good fortune, or the tattered garments of poverty and want. I care not whether he is in a little hut on the hillside or dwells in a mansion on the mountain top. He is a descendant of those who fought for our freedom.

The color purple is frequently worn by royal or imperial rulers. It signifies rank and authority.

In conclusion, I want to say to the gentlemen who compose the minority of the Committee: You will live to see that we are right, and that you are wrong, and the people of Alabama, whom we represent here today in this supreme body, will endorse our action and repudiate yours. I thank the Convention for their attention.

67 A Choice Of Paths

The Negro population reacted in many different ways to widespread suppression in the South. As time went on, more and more Negroes saw the white southerner as an enemy, rather than a potential friend. Negroes had good reasons for this view. Not only were they barred from the political life of the South, but they were also driven from skilled trades at which many had previously worked. Whites excluded them from jobs in new factories, except to use them as strikebreakers. In rural areas, Negroes became tenant farmers or sharecroppers, who owed large debts to farm owners. By 1900, only a quarter of the black farmers in the South owned their land.

When Negroes protested against their plight or ran afoul of the law, they faced the threat of violence. Between 1884 and 1900, at least 2500 blacks were lynched in the South. The nineteenth century closed with a race riot against Negroes in Wilmington, North Carolina. In 1906, white mobs pillaged and murdered in the Negro districts of Atlanta.

During this period of repression, Negro leadership faced almost insurmountable difficulties. The largely illiterate black population, scattered throughout the rural South, was hard to reach and even harder to organize. Leadership depended largely upon the ability to mobilize relatively small Negro groups and often upon the consent and support of the white community.

Black leadership proposed two sharply different responses to the plight of Negroes. Booker Taliaferro Washington represented the response that most whites preferred. Washington had been born a slave. He obtained an education after the Civil War by working as a school janitor, and in 1881 he became the principal of an industrial training school for Negroes in Tuskegee, Alabama. With the help of northern philanthropists, he transformed Tuskegee into a model institution which combined formal education, self-help, and vocational training. President Theodore Roosevelt invited him to dinner at the White House in 1901, an act which confirmed Washington's status as the most celebrated Negro in the United States.

White southern racists violently protested Washington's visit to the White House.

William Edward Burghardt Du Bois, who had been born free in Massachusetts, offered a different solution. W. E. B. Du Bois's academic success won him scholarships to Fisk and Harvard universities. He earned a Ph.D. from Harvard, and he also studied in Germany. In the last years of the nineteenth century, he examined the sociological and economic life of Negro communities in both the North and the South. In 1905, he called for an organization of men who believed in "Negro freedom and growth." Twenty Negroes responded and met at Niagara Falls. This group held several subsequent meetings and rallies in various cities. In 1909, they merged with an organization of white liberals to form the National Association for the Advancement of Colored People (NAACP). Du Bois became the Association's director of publicity and research, and he edited its magazine, *The Crisis.* As you read Washington's and Du Bois's arguments, try to answer these questions:

1. What did Washington mean by "cast down your bucket"? How did he think the condition of Negroes could be improved? What assumptions did he seem to make about both Negroes and whites?
2. In what ways did Du Bois disagree with Washington?
3. Which man seemed to give the more realistic appraisal of southern policies? Why?
4. Which man seemed to give the more realistic appraisal of the possibilities for change? Why?

The Atlanta Exposition Address

In 1895, Booker T. Washington spoke at the Atlanta Cotton States and Industrial Exposition. Both northern and southern whites praised the speech, portions of which are given here.

Booker T. Washington, **Up From Slavery, An Autobiography.** New York: Doubleday, Page and Company, 1902, pp. 219–24.

A ship lost at sea for many days suddenly sighted a friendly vessel. From the mast of the unfortunate vessel was seen the signal: "Water, water, we die of thirst." The answer from the friendly vessel at once came back, "Cast down your bucket where you are." A second time the signal, "Water, water, send us water," ran up from the distressed vessel and was answered, "Cast down your bucket where you are," and a third and fourth signal for water was answered, "Cast down your bucket where you are." The captain of the distressed vessel, at last heeding the injunction, cast down his bucket and it came up full of fresh, sparkling water from the mouth of the Amazon River.

In 1822, the state of Liberia, in Africa, was bought as a home for freed slaves who wanted to relocate in Africa. Although some ex-slaves emigrated, the "back-to-Africa" movement declined. It was revived several times after the Civil War.

To those of my race who depend on bettering their condition in a foreign land or who underestimate the importance of cultivating friendly relations with the southern white man, who is their next-door neighbor, I would say: "Cast down your bucket where you are." Cast it down in making friends, in every manly way, of the people of all races by whom you are surrounded. Cast it down in agriculture, in mechanics, in commerce, in domestic service, and in the professions.

Our greatest danger is that in the great leap from slavery to freedom we may overlook the fact that the masses of us are to live by the production of our hands, and fail to keep in mind that we shall prosper in proportion as we learn to dignify and glorify common labor and put brains and skill into the common occupations of life. It is at the bottom of life we must begin, and not at the top. Nor should we permit our grievances to overshadow our opportunities.

To those of the white race who look to immigrants for the prosperity of the South, were I permitted, I would repeat what I say to my own race, "Cast down your bucket where you are." Cast it down among the eight millions of Negroes whose habits you know, whose fidelity and love you have tested. Cast down your bucket among these people who have, without strikes and labor wars, tilled your fields, cleared your forests, built your railroads and cities, brought forth treasures from the bowels of the earth, and helped make possible this magnificent representation of the progress of the South. Casting down your bucket among my people, helping and encouraging them as you are doing on these grounds, and to education of head, hand, and heart, you will find that they will buy your surplus land, make the waste places in your fields blossom, and run your factories. While doing this, you can be sure in the future, as in the past, that you and your families will be surrounded by the most patient, faithful, law-abiding, and unresentful people that the world has seen. In all things that are purely social we can be as separate as the fingers, yet one as the hand in all things essential to mutual progress.

The wisest among my race understand that the agitation of questions of social equality is the extremest folly, and that progress in the enjoyment of all the privileges that will come to us must be the result of severe and constant struggle rather than of artificial forcing. No race that has anything to contribute to the markets of the world is long in any degree ostracized [excluded]. It is important and right that all privileges of the law be ours, but it is vastly more important that we be prepared for the exercises of these privileges. The opportunity to earn a dollar in a factory just now is worth infinitely more than the opportunity to spend a dollar in an opera-house.

Up from Slavery

In 1901, Washington published his autobiography, Up From Slavery, *from which this selection comes.*

Washington, **Up From Slavery,** pp. 234–36.

I am often asked to express myself more freely than I do upon the political condition and the political future of my race. My own belief is, although I have never before said so in so many words, that the time will come when the Negro in the South will be accorded all the political rights which his ability, character, and material possessions entitle him to. I think, though, that the opportunity to freely exercise such political rights will not come in any large degree through outside or artificial forcing. Southern white people will give the Negro such rights, and they will protect him in the exercise of those rights, as soon as the South gets over the old feeling that it is being forced by "foreigners," or "aliens," to do something which it does not want to do.

I believe it is the duty of the Negro—as the greater part of the race is already doing—to conduct himself modestly in regard to political claims. He should depend upon the slow but sure influences that proceed from the possession of property, intelligence, and high character for the full recognition of his political rights. I think that the full exercise of political rights is going to be a matter of natural, slow growth, not an overnight affair. I do not believe that the Negro should cease voting, for a man cannot learn the exercise of self-government by ceasing to vote, any more than a boy can learn to swim by keeping out of the water. But I do believe that in his voting he should more and more be influenced by those of intelligence and character who are his next-door neighbors.

In my opinion, the time will come when the South will encourage all of its citizens to vote. It will see that it pays better, from every standpoint, to have healthy, vigorous life than to have that political stagnation which always results when one half of the population has no share and no interest in the Government.

Du Bois Answers Washington

In 1903, W.E.B. Du Bois published a series of essays, The Souls of Black Folk, *in which he criticized Washington's philosophy.*

W.E.B. Du Bois, **The Souls of Black Folk.** Chicago: A.C. McClurg & Company, 1904, pp. 50–58.

Civil rights means those freedoms and privileges given to all members of a community, state, or nation by law. They include freedom of press, religion and speech; equal protection of the laws; fair trial; and the right to own property and to vote. Since the Civil War, the term has referred especially to the extension of these rights to Negroes.

Mr. Washington represents in Negro thought the old attitude of adjustment and submission. He distinctly asks that black people give up, at least for the present, three things: political power, insistence on civil rights, and higher education of Negro youth. He asks Negroes to concentrate all their energies on industrial education, the accumulation of wealth, and the conciliation of the South.

In the fifteen years he has advocated this policy, these things have occurred: 1) the disfranchisement of the Negro, 2) the legal creation of a distinct status of civil inferiority for the Negro, 3) the steady withdrawal of aid from institutions for the higher training of the Negro. These movements are not, to be sure, direct results of Mr. Washington's teachings; but his propaganda has, without a shadow of doubt, helped their speedier accomplishment.

Mr. Washington thus faces three contradictions: 1) he is striving nobly to make Negro artisans [craftsmen], businessmen, and property-owners; but it is utterly impossible, under modern competitive methods, for workingmen and property-owners to defend their rights and exist without the right to vote, 2) he insists on thrift and self-respect, but at the same time counsels a silent submission to civic inferiority, such as is bound to sap the manhood of any race in the long run, 3) he advocates common-school [public school] and industrial training, and belittles institutions of higher learning. But neither the Negro common-schools, nor Tuskegee itself, could remain open a day were it not for teachers trained in Negro colleges, or trained by their graduates.

In 1900, there were 99 Negro colleges in the United States and 2624 Negroes enrolled in schools of higher learning.

Two classes of colored Americans criticize Mr. Washington's position. One class hates the white South blindly and thinks that the Negro's only hope lies in emigration beyond the borders of the United States. The other class of Negroes has hitherto said little aloud. Its members feel, in conscience, bound to ask three things of this nation: the right to vote, civic equality, and the education of youth according to ability. They acknowledge Mr. Washington's invaluable service in counseling patience and courtesy in such demands. They know that the low social level of the mass of the race is responsible for much discrimination against it, but they also know, and the nation knows, that relentless [unceasing] color-prejudice is more often a cause than a result of the Negro's degradation.

This group of men honor Mr. Washington for his attitude of conciliation toward the white South. But they insist that the way to truth and right lies in straightforward honesty, not in indiscriminate flattery. They are absolutely certain that the way for a people to gain their reasonable rights is not by voluntarily throwing them away and insisting that they do not want them; that the way for a people to gain respect is not by continually belittling and ridiculing themselves. On the contrary, Negroes must insist continually that voting is necessary to modern manhood, that color discrimination is barbarism, and that black boys need education as well as white boys.

The growing spirit of kindliness and reconciliation between the North and South after the frightful differences of a generation ago ought to be a source of deep congratulation to all and especially to those [the slaves] whose mistreatment caused the war. But if that reconciliation is to be marked by the industrial slavery and civic death of those same black men, by permanently legislating them into a position of inferiority, then those black men, if they are really men, are called upon by every consideration of patriotism and loyalty to oppose such a course by all civilized methods, even though such opposition involves disagreement with Mr. Booker T. Washington. We have no right to sit silently by while the inevitable seeds are sown for a harvest of disaster to our children, black and white.

While it is a great truth to say that the Negro must strive and strive mightily to help himself, it is equally true that unless his striving be not simply seconded, but rather aroused and encouraged, by the initiative of the richer and wiser group, he cannot hope for great success.

In his failure to realize and impress this last point, Mr. Washington is especially to be criticized. His doctrine has tended to make the whites, North and South, shift the burden of the Negro problem to the Negro's shoulders and stand aside as critical and rather pessimistic spectators. In fact, the burden belongs to the nation, and the hands of none of us are clean if we do not bend our energies to righting these great wrongs.

We cannot settle this problem by diplomacy and suaveness, by policy alone. If worse come to worst, can the moral fiber of this country survive the slow throttling and murder of nine millions of men?

68 "In the Same Ditch"

HISTORICAL ESSAY

The debate over Negro rights in the South during the last decades of the nineteenth century was part of a broader discussion of political power and economic development. Southern political leaders hoped to copy the economic success of the North. Success, they thought, required the promotion of industrial enterprise combined with freedom for enterprising businessmen to start and run new ventures. These leaders resisted all attempts to tax corporations or to disturb the rights of property. They urged men to construct railroads and other internal improvements, often asking the help of the federal government. They invited northern businessmen to locate factories in the South and offered them financial aid and tax advantages. Despite strong pressure from farmers, southern representatives did not seriously challenge the federal government's hard-money policy. They resisted allying the South with western farmers who favored a large increase in the supply of money.

Problems of the Southern Economy

This attempt to make the South over in the image of the North involved several problems. After northern businessmen had invested in the South, southerners found that they had given up some control over their own affairs. They charged that northern businessmen were imperialists who treated the South like a colony. Although northern investors could not help being "outsiders," the charge had considerable truth to it. In the steel industry, for example, northern steelmakers developed new plants in Birmingham, Alabama. They insisted, however, that charges for transportation on all steel shipped from these plants to nearby markets should be the same as if it had been shipped from Pittsburgh, the center of the northern steel industry. "Pittsburgh plus" prices prevented southern mills from taking advantage of selling steel cheaper to nearby customers.

The South's failure to achieve rapid economic growth was not, however, primarily due to northern oppression. Although southern political leaders tried to copy the North, they failed to understand why the North had grown so rapidly. They were impressed with the North's railroads, steel mills, and textile factories, and they encouraged the growth of such enterprises in the South. But they did not see that the North's development depended on both the ability of the agricultural areas to feed industrial workers and the willingness of industrialists and farmers to take risks with new methods.

One important group of southerners did see this situation, but they encountered the violent opposition of conservative business-oriented southern leaders. The group was composed of relatively successful southern farmers with training and income enough to see the problems of the South in a large perspective. They organized the several farm organizations described in Chapter 16 and insisted throughout the 1880's and 1890's that economic development in the South had to be based upon agricultural prosperity. They supported progressive taxation and expanded educational programs. They also asked for fundamental changes in the banking system.

As cotton prices fell in the decades after the Civil War, southern farmers had to borrow money. In the absence of adequate banking facilities, they borrowed from what were called "lien merchants," that is, town shopkeepers who lent cash to the farmer. The loan was protected by the farmer's promise to pay with the proceeds of his next crop. The farmer was forced to buy goods from the lien merchant in the meantime. Naturally the prices were high. The farmer faced a dreary prospect; he had to pay high interest rates and high prices while being forced to produce more and more cotton despite declining prices. With next year's harvest—and sometimes those for two and three years ahead—promised to the merchant, he could not experiment with new crops that might replenish his land. Only some new means of financing agricultural production could break the paralyzing grip of the lien merchant.

When farmers borrowed money, their property and ungrown crops were put up as security for the loan. A lien, or mortgage, was thus placed on the farmer's property, and the property could then be seized as payment if the debt was not paid.

Since cotton was a sure money crop, farmers planted cotton year after year, despite the fact that cotton robs the soil of valuable minerals. The reduced yield from the mineral-poor soil was one cause of the South's agrarian poverty shortly after the war.

Southern farmers could not outline a clear alternative policy for economic development. Whenever a political attack on their power was raised in the South, conservative leaders argued that all good men must stay with the "white man's party." If white men were divided, they insisted, Negroes would take advantage of the situation. This insistence upon white solidarity stifled the expression of political differences and favored existing leaders. Negro-white relationships lay at the heart of southern politics.

The Progress of Negroes

In 1870, the total population of the South was about 12,200,000 of whom 7,800,000 were white and 4,400,000 were Negro. In 1930, the total population of the South reached 37,800,000 of whom 28,400,000 were white and 9,400,000 were Negro. In the meantime, the Negro population of the remainder of the country rose from about 450,000 in 1870 to about 2,500,000 in 1930 as Negroes emigrated from their southern birthplaces toward the North. Few of the immigrants who crossed the oceans from both Europe and the Far East settled in the South. Most ports of entry were in the Northeast or on the west coast. But more important, a relatively stagnant economy and bitter race relationships made the area unattractive to men and women seeking economic opportunities and the advantages of a free society. The South lagged steadily behind the remainder of the nation.

At the end of the Civil War, the nation seemed committed to equality for freedmen. During the war and the period of Reconstruction, the government passed the thirteenth, fourteenth, and fifteenth amendments and several civil-rights acts to insure that equality. The commitment was soon betrayed by both North and South. Laws providing for discrimination passed the legislatures of several northern cities. Northern labor unions discriminated against Negro members. In the South, after more than two decades of relatively good relations, the number of lynchings began to rise steadily. More than 2500 Negroes were lynched between 1882 and 1902. Segregation in the South became absolute, the Democratic party ruled unopposed, and Negroes were denied the vote. Southern states adopted poll taxes, literacy tests, property qualifications, and lengthy residence requirements in order to keep Negroes from voting. Between 1896 and 1915, Negroes were excluded from voting in the Democratic primary (which, in effect, was the deciding election). But because these restrictions affected whites as well as Negroes, many states, starting with Louisiana in 1898, adopted "grandfather clauses," which allowed any male to vote whose father or grandfather had voted on January 1, 1867.

A poll tax is a tax levied by some states on their voters. Although Massachusetts and Indiana levied such taxes, this device was primarily used by southern states to disfranchise Negroes. The Twenty-Fourth Amendment (1964) forbids the use of a poll tax in federal elections.

Despite this grim history, a significant number of Negroes made dramatic achievements during this period. Former slaves resisted attempts to keep them on plantations as a servile labor force. Many were able to establish stable families and to win a place in the economy. Rather than work for wages, former field hands became sharecroppers or bought land of their own. By 1890, about 120,000 Negroes were landowners, a remarkable achievement for a people who had been slaves twenty-five years before. To win a place in a market economy, they had to learn how to buy and sell goods, how to make contracts of a number of kinds, and how to work without the supervision to which they had been accustomed. They also had to learn to resist the careless habits which many had acquired during slavery when they toiled only for someone else's benefit.

A few Negroes began to emigrate to the cities, to rich lands in the Mississippi delta, and to the Southwest. A large number of ex-slaves who had been craftsmen on the plantations began to practice their trades in towns all over the South. Shortly after the war, Negro artisans were said to outnumber whites by five to one. A few began small businesses. An even smaller number became teachers or ministers, the only two professions open to black men. In 1900, Booker T. Washington organized the National Negro Business League to increase Negro participation in business and manufacturing and to provide Negro businessmen with an opportunity to exchange ideas.

Deltas are fan-shaped plains of rich fertile soil formed at the mouths of rivers. The Mississippi delta, around New Orleans, is especially suited for growing rice and cotton.

World War I, which promoted a boom in the economy at the same time that it reduced European immigration, attracted Negroes to the North. Between 1910 and 1920, more than 300,000 blacks left the states of the former Confederacy for better opportunities in northern cities. This stream of internal migration increased during the 1920's, and has not stopped since then. Negro citizens consistently sought to better themselves. Although the majority stayed in the South and remained on farms, the hundreds of thousands who bought their own land, established businesses, or left for better opportunities elsewhere testify to the vitality and ambition of a people anxious to break the bonds of slavery and share fully in the American dream.

Negroes and Southern Politics

For a decade or so after the end of Reconstruction, whites and Negroes cooperated to a degree in southern politics primarily because white conservatives needed Negro support to stay in power. In 1877, President Rutherford B. Hayes had told southern Negroes that their rights and interests would be safer if the government left southern whites to run their own affairs. He appointed southern Democrats to office, hoping to enlist their support for the Republican party. In an attempt to reconcile northern and southern whites, Hayes and his successors abandoned Negroes. Conservative Democrats adopted them temporarily.

Southern conservatives genuinely wanted to protect Negro rights as these conservatives defined rights. They thought Negroes were inferior human beings who should be satisfied with a subordinate status. Because they needed protection and support when they were abandoned by the North, Negroes turned to the conservatives. Southern politicians such as L.Q.C. Lamar of Mississippi, Wade Hampton of South Carolina, and Alexander H. Stephens of Georgia solicited votes from Negroes and supported their right to the ballot.

L.Q.C. Lamar was well known for his attempts to restore relations between the North and the South. He served in Congress, President Cleveland's Cabinet, and on the Supreme Court.
Wade Hampton was a Confederate general, governor of South Carolina, and after 1879, the state's senator.
Alexander Stephens was Vice-President of the Confederacy, a United States congressman, and governor of Georgia.

Wade Hampton, a Democrat was elected governor in 1876 and again in 1878.

Negroes continued to vote throughout the South for two decades after the end of Reconstruction. Except for one term, they kept at least one Negro in the House of Representatives. Many Negroes held state and local offices; Wade Hampton alone appointed eighty-six Negroes to office during his governorship in South Carolina. Although Negroes broke away from white churches to establish their own congregations after the war, separation did not extend to transportation or to public services generally. Whites did, however, prevent Negroes from attending white schools. Communities usually allotted less money per pupil for Negro schools than for white.

In the meantime, the Supreme Court and a number of subordinate courts undermined the legal provisions that had been passed during and immediately after the Civil War to insure equal status for Negroes. In *United States* vs. *Cruikshank* (1876), the Court declared that the Fourteenth Amendment protected citizens only against infringement of their rights by a state. This decision removed the Court's protection of rights that were violated by individual citizens. In the Civil Rights Cases of 1883, the Court declared that the Civil Rights Act of 1875 was unconstitutional. This act had forbidden segregation in public facilities such as transportation, hotels, and theaters. In 1896, the case of *Plessy* vs. *Ferguson* sanctioned segregation so long as "separate but equal" facilities were provided for the two races. Two years later, in the case of *Williams* vs. *Mississippi*, the Court approved a law that deprived Negroes of the ballot by combining a poll tax with a literacy test and residency requirements. In 1915, the Court declared "grandfather clauses" unconstitutional.

The Populist Period

During the 1890's, under the growing pressure of the business depression, many southern farmers took what was to them an awesome step; they entered the new People's (Populist) party, breaking the front of white solidarity and Democratic voting. The southern Populists achieved much greater success than their midwestern colleagues. Their strength was remarkable because their victories were achieved against tremendous obstacles. They were charged with being "traitors" to their race. If they owed money on their land, they were threatened with eviction. Many lost their jobs. They were shunned by the leaders of their churches. They were denied credit. If they succeeded in bringing voters to the polls, corrupt officials cheated them when the ballots were counted. Many Populists were thrown into jail on false charges and then dragged from the jailor's hands by a mob and killed.

In response to this attack, the Populists sought an alliance with the Negroes. They were not willing to grant Negroes full equality.

"This is a white man's country and always will be controlled by the whites," a Virginia Populist wrote in an introduction to his essay urging increased rights for Negroes. Nevertheless, the Populists did understand that Negro and white farmers had common interests and common problems or, as one put it, "they are in the ditch just like we are." Tom Watson, the major Populist leader in Georgia, advised his fellows: "Let it once appear plainly that it is to the interest of a colored man to vote with the white man, and he will do it." He argued that "the accident of color can make no difference in the interest of farmers, croppers, and laborers." "You are kept apart," he lectured both races, "that you may be separately fleeced of your earnings."

The Populists proposed a comprehensive program for southern economic development. Unlike the midwestern and mountain-state Populists, who fastened on the issue of the expansion of the currency, the southern Populists insisted that fairer loans for farmers, education, and progressive taxes were more important than an expansion of the money supply. Southerners resisted the tendency in 1896 to focus the whole Populist program around the issue of money and to agree to a coalition with the Democrats. A national coalition of Populists and Democrats rankled them because they had invested so much effort in 1892 in their break with the local Democratic party. Nevertheless, the South voted strongly for William Jennings Bryan, the Democratic candidate, in 1896.

After the election of 1896 and Bryan's defeat, the Populist party was destroyed in the South. The remnants of the southern Populists movement continued to insist that change would have to come about with a new comprehensive program for economic development. After the 1896 election, because the failure of their attempt to unite white and Negro farmers had been successfully used against them in local elections, the Populists turned with vengeance upon Negroes. Tom Watson reasoned that the only way to destroy racial equality as an issue in southern politics was to suppress Negroes entirely. Men who in the early 1890's had reached out their hand to Negroes became the worst Negro-baiting politicians in the South. They hoped to prove their loyalty to the white race, remove the issue of equality for Negroes as a charge against them, and achieve political success.

Jim Crow Laws

During the two decades after 1890, the major accomplishments of the Reconstruction period were undone. By 1900, all southern states had segregated railroad cars. Later, segregation extended to railway stations, streetcars, public parks and buildings, prisons, sports events, and even cemeteries. Following Mississippi's example, one state after another took away the vote and dropped Negroes from public offices where so many of them had served so well. The last southern Negro congressman left Washington in 1901. The steady encroachment on Negro rights was supported by violent repression. During the 1890's, lynchings averaged almost 190 a year of which 82 percent were in the South. The great majority of the victims were Negroes. Both equality and freedom had fallen victim to racism. The attitude of many whites to Negroes can be seen in the debates of the Alabama State Convention which appeared in Reading 66.

The word "racist" describes people or ideas that employ information—or misinformation—about race in an attempt to prove that one race is superior to another.

It is not surprising that under these circumstances, Negroes followed the path indicated by Booker T. Washington in his famous Atlanta speech. As late as 1900, 75 percent of Negro farmers in the South were still sharecroppers or tenants. Employers had consistently discriminated against Negro artisans, and all-white trade unions had helped to squeeze them out of better-paid jobs. Hence, most Negroes remained poorly paid and subservient. The small Negro middle class, which consisted mainly of business and professional people, dominated Negro society. Fearing to offend whites and thus lose what they had gained, they embraced Washington's advocacy of industrial training and his rejection of demands for an integrated society. Washington was able to attract money from philanthropists to support his work. His advocacy of hard work, friendship to whites, and subservience offend most modern blacks. But Washington dealt with the reality of an oppressive period, and he carefully avoided speaking of his ultimate objectives for Negroes. This brilliant and sensitive man might have taken an entirely different position under more fortunate circumstances.

The South as a Colonial Area

The economy of the South made significant advances, but not enough to catch up to the North. Between 1880 and 1890, railway mileage in the South increased by 135 percent, 50 percent faster than the national rate. Between 1876 and 1901, pig-iron production increased by seventeen times in the South compared to eight times in the nation at large. The South developed new techniques to manufacture tobacco, which revitalized the entire tobacco industry. It attracted large numbers of cotton mills to the source of supply. But the South remained essentially a raw materials producing area. Final processing of many of its products, such as cotton, sugar, liquor, naval stores, and rice, still took place predominately in the North.

Pig iron is the crude iron that results when iron ore is smelted in blast furnaces to free it of certain impurities. The iron leaves the furnace in a molten stage and is poured into molds or bars called "pigs."

The South was an outpost of northern industry still suffering from a backward economy based on agriculture. In 1860, the income of the average southerner was roughly 72 percent of the national average; in 1880, it was 51 percent; in 1900, it was also 51 percent. It rose to 62 percent by 1920 but fell again to 55 percent a decade later. In 1900, less than 10 percent of the population of the South Atlantic states south of Maryland were classified as urban; on the other hand, almost 60 percent of the people in the North Atlantic states from Pennsylvania north had become urban.

The South also lost political power during this period. Southerners had held the Presidency for fifty years and the position of Chief Justice for sixty years during the seventy-two years between Washington and Lincoln. The South also furnished about half of the Supreme Court Justices, important diplomatic representatives, Speakers of the House of Representatives, and Cabinet members. During the next half century, Andrew Johnson was the only southern President or Vice-President, and southerners filled only about 10 percent of the important political positions listed above. Although the South did a little better after 1900—Woodrow Wilson was a southerner—it remained a northern satellite well into the twentieth century.

Woodrow Wilson was born in Virginia, spent his youth in Georgia, and studied law at the University of Virginia. At the time of his nomination for President, however, he was governor of New Jersey.

SUGGESTED READINGS

DU BOIS, WILLIAM E., *Souls of Black Folk*. Du Bois wrestles in this book with the problems of both group and national identity and action.

MEIER, AUGUST, and ELLIOTT RUDWICK, *The Making of Black America*. 2 vols. This collection of essays reflects the best of recent scholarship.

WASHINGTON, BOOKER T., *Up From Slavery*. Even if one disagrees with Washington's views, his work and character cannot help but command respect.

WOODWARD, C. VANN, *The Strange Career of Jim Crow*. The leading historian of the postbellum South has published several worthwhile books. This is the simplest but the others, notably *The Origins of the New South, 1877–1913*, are also worth reading.

The New Immigrants

STATING THE ISSUE

CHAPTER 18

Between 1815 and 1920, roughly 35 million men, women, and children emigrated from Europe to the United States in search of homes, jobs, and freedom. Before about 1880, most immigrants came from western Europe, primarily from the British Isles, Scandinavia, and Germany. After 1880, an increasing number of immigrants left their homes in southern and eastern Europe—in Italy, the Austro-Hungarian Empire, and Poland—to begin the long and difficult journey to America.

These new immigrants came from a part of the world that seemed both distant and unfamiliar to most Americans. Moreover, they came in greater numbers than any previous wave of newcomers. By the first two decades of the twentieth century, the number of immigrants arriving each year had more than doubled that of the biggest year preceding 1880.

Such a mass of people jammed together in cities would have presented enormous problems even if they had been much like the Americans among whom they settled. But they were not. They came from societies very different from the America of 1900. Their peasant backgrounds prepared them poorly for life in an urban, industrial environment. Their clothing, languages, and, in some instances, their religious beliefs and practices seemed strange—even threatening—to many native Americans.

Chapter 18 examines the backgrounds of these immigrants, their difficulties in establishing new lives in America, and Americans' responses to them. How did the societies that the new immigrants left compare with the American society they entered? How did the move to a new society affect the immigrants' manner of living and working in America? How did Americans respond to the immigrants? Which one or which combination of the four social processes—extermination, accommodation, assimilation, or amalgamation—took place between the new immigrants and the native Americans? These are the major issues raised in Chapter 18.

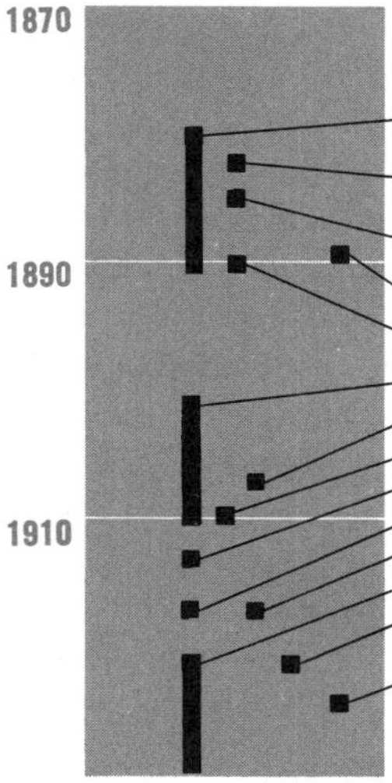

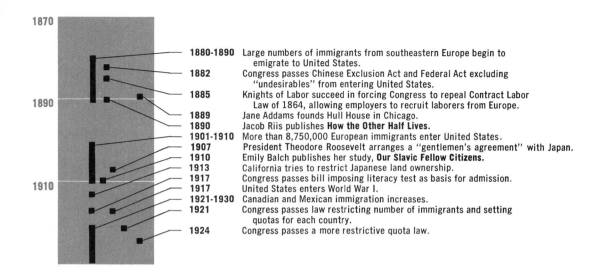

1880-1890	Large numbers of immigrants from southeastern Europe begin to emigrate to United States.
1882	Congress passes Chinese Exclusion Act and Federal Act excluding "undesirables" from entering United States.
1885	Knights of Labor succeed in forcing Congress to repeal Contract Labor Law of 1864, allowing employers to recruit laborers from Europe.
1889	Jane Addams founds Hull House in Chicago.
1890	Jacob Riis publishes **How the Other Half Lives.**
1901-1910	More than 8,750,000 European immigrants enter United States.
1907	President Theodore Roosevelt arranges a "gentlemen's agreement" with Japan.
1910	Emily Balch publishes her study, **Our Slavic Fellow Citizens.**
1913	California tries to restrict Japanese land ownership.
1917	Congress passes bill imposing literacy test as basis for admission.
1917	United States enters World War I.
1921-1930	Canadian and Mexican immigration increases.
1921	Congress passes law restricting number of immigrants and setting quotas for each country.
1924	Congress passes a more restrictive quota law.

69 "The Old Country"

Immigrants from eastern and southern Europe spoke so many unfamiliar languages that most Americans had difficulty learning about the lives and values of their new neighbors. They thought of the newcomers in simple, stereotyped terms: one nationality group had a hot temper, another was placid, another crafty, and so on.

Those Americans who reached out to the new immigrants found that such stereotyped, simple images did not fit the men and women they came to know. They failed to find a group of ignorant, dirty people bent on undermining American society. They found instead lonely, often confused, men and women clinging desperately to their own values and images of the good life.

Many of the people who tried to reach the new immigrants worked in settlement houses—what we now call community centers—which were scattered through immigrant sections of many cities. Such houses flourished in the 1890's and in the first decades of the twentieth century. Unlike present-day centers staffed by professional social workers who frequently live outside the neighborhood, the settlement houses became temporary homes for middle-class residents who came both to learn about the immigrants and to help introduce them to American society. The residents of the settlement houses dealt, at least in theory, with the people of the community as "neighbors," not as "clients" or "cases," as the modern social worker often does.

A sense of religious mission inspired many of the first settlement workers who came from devout, Protestant families and who were often ministers themselves. A recent historian of the movement writes that for most of these settlement workers, "the decision to live in the slums was somehow related to the desire to apply the Christian idea of service to the new challenges and the new problems of the city." After 1900, graduate students in the social sciences, reformers, novelists, and journalists, in increasing numbers, filled the rooms in the settlement houses formerly occupied by ministers.

In 1890, Jacob Riis, himself an immigrant, published **How the Other Half Lives,** a shocking description of slum life among New York City immigrants.

All settlement workers shared a dual mission: to tell immigrants about American society outside their neighborhood, and to tell other Americans about the immigrants. Unlike early reporters, such as Jacob Riis, who made judgments as they described life in the ghettos, the settlement investigators tried to cultivate an analytical objectivity, which they hoped would increase the effectiveness of their message. Reading 69 is drawn from the writings of one such investigator, Emily Green Balch, who studied Slavic immigrants. As you read, try to answer these questions:

Slavic peoples are those who speak any of the Slavic languages, such as those spoken in modern Czechoslovakia, Bulgaria, Yugoslavia, Poland, and parts of the U.S.S.R.

The Austro-Hungarian Empire (1867–1914) included all of present-day Austria, Hungary, and Czechoslovakia, and parts of Romania, Yugoslavia, Poland, and Italy.

1. What had been the peasant's traditional position in the social structure of the Austro-Hungarian Empire?
2. What changes took place during the nineteenth century in the old peasant economy? How did these changes affect the peasant's social status?
3. What relationship did Miss Balch see between economic and social changes in Europe and Slavic emigration?
4. How well prepared do you think the Slavic immigrant was for life in urban, industrial America? Which of the four social processes—amalgamation, assimilation, accommodation, or extermination—do you think would take place between Slavic immigrants and most native Americans?

The Slavic Homeland

Emily Balch, **Our Slavic Fellow Citizens.** New York: Charities Publication Committee, 1910, pp. 37–54 **passim.**

Emily Balch was an associate professor of economics at Wellesley College at the time she wrote Our Slavic Fellow Citizens. *In collecting data for the book, she traveled extensively in Austria-Hungary, the area of Europe from which most Slavs emigrated. This reading contains selections from her work in which she explains the European background of the Slavic immigrants.*

Bohemians were Slavic-speaking people who lived in Bohemia, a province of modern Czechoslovakia. Between 1848 and about 1860, many political refugees left Bohemia for the United States. Most of these immigrants were skilled craftsmen.

One of the most important general facts about our Slavic immigrants is that apart from the early Bohemian movement they for the most part represent the peasant class. There is, I think, much misunderstanding in America as to what this means. A peasant seems to be understood as a synonym for a member of the lowest possible social class; a being devoid of all claims to respect who takes a great

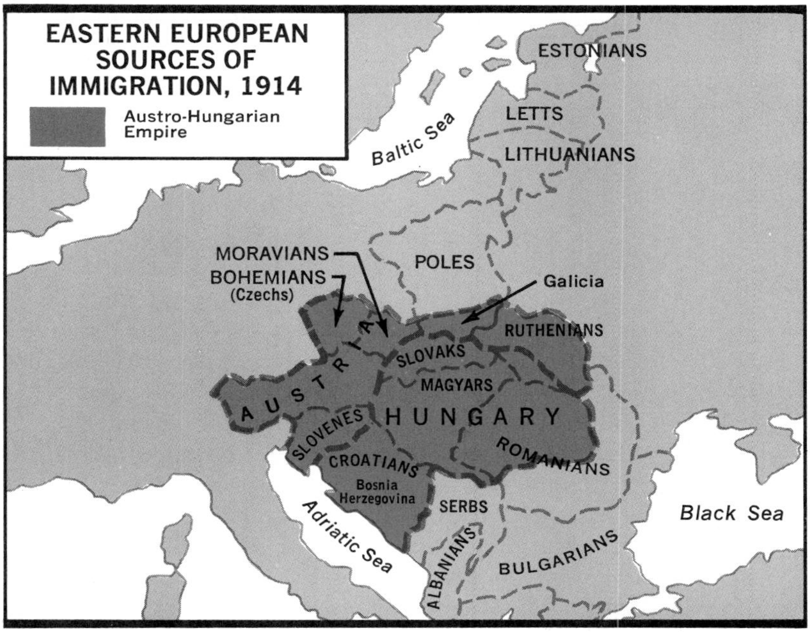

step up when he becomes a factory employee. Such views rest on a serious misconception. The peasant is a landholder, more nearly comparable to the American farmer than to any other class among us, and at home is far from being at the bottom of the social ladder. The old peasant life . . . which still largely subsists [exists now] in Austria and Hungary was once universal throughout feudal Europe, passing away in some countries earlier, in others later. In Austria, up to 1848, medieval conditions were comparatively little changed. . . . [L]egal ownership of land was still vested in the lords or landed class; . . .

The peasant holding involved very definite duties and rights. In return for his land the peasant had to do a certain amount of work for his lord, and these labor dues . . . were often very oppressive.

In 1848 serfdom, in the sense in which it still existed, was abolished in Austria, and also in Hungary where the conditions had been similar to those in Austria. The peasant became a free peasant proprietor. . . .

While it is nearly two generations since the old agrarian system, resting on an unfree peasant class, was legally abolished, its results are by no means a thing of the past. . . .

A peasant is then something quite distinct from anything that we know in America. On the one hand, he is a link in a chain of family inheritance and tradition that may run back for centuries, with a

In 1848, mass uprisings broke out in France, Italy, Germany, and the Austrian Empire. The revolutionaries in these countries demanded constitutional governments, national independence and unification, and an end to serfdom. In 1781, Emperor Joseph II had abolished serfdom in Austria, but it continued in many provinces until 1848.

name, a reputation, and a posterity. On the other hand, he is confessedly and consciously an inferior. It is part of his world that there should be a God in heaven, and masters . . . on the earth.

The typical village has one considerable gentleman's estate and a number of small properties. So the peasant takes off his cap to those dressed like gentlefolk, known or unknown. He bears himself toward them with an inherited respect. At the same time there is a sense of profound and hardly bridgeable difference between himself and gentlemen, a feeling which may be friendly, but is sometimes colored by distrust or intense antagonism.

On the other hand, if the peasant has his superiors, he also has recognized inferiors, and in many places three classes of them. First is the cottager or cottier, . . . the man who, with a house and bit of field, has yet no pretensions to getting his living off his land.

Secondly, there are the day laborers, who often live in cottages belonging to their employer, and may be paid partly in cash, partly in kind [goods they produced].

Thirdly, there are the "farm servants," not servants in the American sense, but rather what we should call "farm hands." There are both men and girls, and are generally hired by the year, and boarded by their employer. You will often find peasants living so wretchedly that we should consider them on the brink of misery, who yet are worlds above their servants housed more like animals than people. . . .

In his circumstances the peasant may be not only prosperous but rich—very rich, even, if one takes his way of living and aspirations into account. But he is more likely to be hard pressed with work, with care, perhaps with debt. His roof may leak, his meal [ground grain] chest show the bottom, his crop be sold to the usurer before it is sown,—he is still a property owner, a taxpayer, a permanent constituent of an old social order, known to and knowing all his associates, and enjoying a respect adjusted to his acres and family.

A usurer is a person who lends money to others, usually at a high interest rate.

The peasant is an entirely different type from the workingman. He has not the workingman's quickness, nor all that he has gained in intelligence and self-reliance through competition, frequent change of place, and the trituration [grind] of city and factory life. On the other hand, he has the conservatism, the solidity, the shrewdness, the self-respect that go with property, independence, and an assured social position. He is likely to be hard and niggardly [stingy]; this is perhaps the ugliest side. . . .

Yet along with all this, and seemingly contradicting it, the Slavic peasant has created a world of fancy, of song, of tradition, a whole code of dress, manners, morals. . . .

[The] old self-sufficient household economy was, however, gradually broken in upon from many sides as industry developed at the expense of agriculture. Even in places where no industry arose, the effect of that which was growing up in other countries, afar or nearby, made itself powerfully felt. As a "money economy," with purchase and sale, extended, the dependence on household production diminished. Money was needed for taxes. The obvious economy of cheap factory textiles, the superiority of iron pots to earthen ones, indeed the temptation of novel wares of various kinds at low prices, all made new demands for money. With these changes went a rise in standards of living; new goods were available and new desires were contagious.

At the same time with this rise in demands, growth of population without growth of industry made an increased pressure on the land.

The old peasant economy had represented a fairly stable economic equilibrium [balance]. Population was kept more or less at a level by it, since only one son could take his father's place, and consequently it was difficult for more than one to establish a family, unless, indeed, he went away "to seek his fortune." It was the expectation that everything should go on as it had done. That is the essence of custom, and the peasant world is the world of custom.

The results of the breakup of the old system of landholding were often disastrous. The peasant being free to divide his land and feeling that his children all had equal claims, cut up land which was only sufficient to support one household among a number of descendants. The landholder unable to support himself from his own plot sought to eke out his living by working for wages in a population where few could afford to hire labor. In some districts debts, contracted under circumstances which put the borrower at the mercy of a creditor, worked havoc.

Thus the peasant with mortgage payments which he could not meet or with children for whom he could not provide an adequate patrimony [inheritance], saw himself face to face with an intolerable decline of social status for himself or for his children; namely, reduction to the position of a propertyless day laborer. This is the sting which induces many a man among the Slovaks, the Poles, the Ruthenians, to fare over seas or to send out his son to the new land from which men come back with savings.

While the grounds of emigration are in the main economic, it is a mistake to suppose that poverty is its cause in the sense that the greater the poverty of a man or district, the greater the impulse to emigration.

It is when the habitual balance of family budgets is disturbed that a sense of poverty incites to emigration. The misadjustment may be due to a cutting down of income by some disaster, or it may be due to an increase of wants. The result is the same. And this awakening of new wants is a characteristic of our time, affecting one backward and lethargic [sluggish] region after another. It is extremely contagious, and the news that it is anywhere possible to earn more and to live better calls slumbering forces of energy and unrest into sudden life. Emigration will then result if there is any opening which promises improved circumstances.

Military service is another direct and continuing cause of emigration. Every man in Austria and Hungary, with certain exceptions, must serve his three years, and he is forbidden to marry till after his liability to this service is past. Undoubtedly the interruption of work caused by the time in the army is in many cases felt as a grievous burden, and many emigrate to escape it, . . .

Another complicating cause is political unrest. Many of our Slavic immigrants come from groups which are more or less in the position of the underdog. . . . I was told, for instance, that immigrants . . . who seem to have no economic reason for leaving home, when asked why they go, say, . . . "We go to see if there is still justice in the world." Generally, however, I think that the effect of such conditions is less to initiate emigration than to cause the emigrant who returns to his old home to feel himself a misfit there, and to decide to take up his permanent residence in America.

Another "cause" of emigration is the advertising and solicitation of transportation agencies. My impression is that the less direct and concrete knowledge of the matter a man has, the more weight he lays on this factor. . . .

To encourage Europeans to emigrate, steamship companies advertised in Europe describing economic opportunities in the United States. Eventually, transportation agencies developed to assist emigrants. Immigrants helped fill American industry's demand for cheap labor, steamship companies' increasingly competitive need for passengers, and the railroads' desires to sell land along government-granted rights of way.

The general causes at work are intensified at given places and at given times, by all sorts of occurrences. A flood, a conflagration [fire], a new American tariff, an outbreak of phylloxera [plant lice] in the vineyards, or a treaty admitting Italian wine at a lower rate—all these have been actual stimulants of Slavic inflow.

As in any mass movement, the individual is more conscious of the purely personal and special motives which have moved him than of the general causes at work. Men emigrate to avoid family friction, to escape a scandal, to see new scenes, to join relatives, because others have gone, and for a thousand other unclassifiable reasons.

70 Preserving and Changing

New immigrants did not seek to change their way of life overnight. Some even planned to return to their native lands. As Emily Balch described in the previous reading, they had been caught in a conflict between old and new ways of life in their homelands. In the United States, they were caught in a similar and even greater dilemma. On the one hand, they had to find new homes, different kinds of jobs, and new patterns of behavior in an unfamiliar, urban environment. On the other hand, they had to find a meaning to life in terms of the values and customs of their native lands. The process of fitting into American society wrenched their lives.

Many immigrants retained much of their old language, dress, behavior, values, and beliefs. At the beginning of the twentieth century, sympathetic observers, such as Emily Balch, often spoke of the American "melting pot." They envisioned that in the future—how distant in the future they did not say—all Americans would appear to be very much alike and would share similar attitudes and values. Assimilation and amalgamation, they believed, would blur ethnic differences.

Ethnic refers to a group of people related by race, language, or nationality, who share a common, distinctive culture, or tradition.

Amalgamation may take place completely at some future date. Among the children, grandchildren, and even great-grandchildren of the immigrants of 1900, however, some differences still persist. In large American cities, ethnic neighborhoods, each with its own social and religious organizations, bear evidence that ethnic groups continue to be distinguished from one another. American politicians still recognize the importance of ethnic loyalties as they appeal consciously for the "Polish" vote, the "Jewish" vote, and the votes of other groups.

Reading 70 describes the immigrants' dual process of reaching out for a new life in America while at the same time clinging to the old. As you read, try to answer these questions:

1. According to Miss Balch, what were the most important ways in which new immigrants became Americans?
2. In what ways did immigrants try to retain their ethnic identities?
3. How did the author's own values influence her description of the process of change in the immigrant community?
4. In the process of change described, what balance was struck among accommodation, assimilation, and amalgamation?

"What Are Americans?"

Emily Balch worked actively throughout her life to promote international understanding for which she received the Nobel Peace Prize in 1946. In this selection from her book Our Slavic Fellow Citizens *she describes the immigrants' experiences in America.*

Balch, **Our Slavic Fellow Citizens,** pp. 419, 424, 45, 58–60, 378–79, 381, 383–85, 412–15, 398–99.

"My people do not live in America, they live underneath America. America goes on over their heads. America does not begin till a man is a workingman, till he is earning two dollars a day. A laborer cannot afford to be an American."

These words, which were said to me by one of the wisest Slav leaders that I have ever met, have rung in my mind during all the five years since he spoke them. Beginning at the bottom, "living not in America but underneath America," means living among the worst surroundings that the country has to show, worse, often, than the public would tolerate, except that "only foreigners" are affected.

. . . [C]oming to America they are cut off from the life of their old country, without getting into contact with the true life of their new home, from which they are shut off by language, by mutual prejudice, by divergent ideas. To them, both parents are dead, the fatherland that begot them and the foster-mother that supports without cherishing them.

[I]mport a . . . peasant into America. The courtesy which rested on acceptance of a fixed class station disappears as he realizes that he is not expected to regard himself as an inferior. On the other hand, he loses that standing which largely gave him his old form of self-respect and self-consciousness.

. . . "Does the individual emigrant gain?" . . . In the first place, emigration always involves pain; pain to those who go, and, above all, pain to those who are left behind. . . . [I]mmigrants are inevitably to some extent exiles, separated from the old familiar scenes for which everyone sometimes yearns, and divided, even if the more immediate family has all been brought together, from some of those near and dear to them.

What it means to be in a country where one cannot speak the language is, as many a traveler can testify, a feeling that must be experienced to be understood. . . . [A] sort of inhibition of all expression sets in; it seems as useless to gesticulate [gesture] or smile as to speak. It is almost as if one could not even think, so pervasive and numbing is the sense that the channels of communication are blocked.

I get the impression that the women are more apt to be homesick than the men. . . . As a matter of fact, I think the women both lose more and gain less by the change than the men. They do not like the iron stoves, which do not bake such sweet bread as their old ovens. They miss, I think, the variety of work, employment within doors alternating with field work . . . and most of all the familiar, sociable village life where everyone knows everyone else, and there are no uncomfortable superior Yankees to abash [embarrass] one, and where the children do not grow up to be alien and contemptuous.

The men live more out in the world. They get more from America and perhaps had less to lose in the old conditions. In spite of the undemocratic treatment of immigrants which is too common in the United States, and which sometimes makes one's blood boil, they do get in America a sense of being more regarded, of being equals, that is new and dear to them. To the men it often means expansion.

One of the most surprising facts in the life of Slavs in America is the degree to which they are organized into societies.

Many of their associations are small local affairs of the most various sorts. In a New York Bohemian paper I found a list of 95 local societies among this group of perhaps 35,000 people.

Each of the main Slavic nationalities in the United States has one or more . . . national societies, all apparently organized on much the same plan, with a central co-ordinating committee and numerous branches, founded primarily for the object of mutual insurance but also serving many other purposes, and with a membership defined by national or national-religious lines.

In addition to church-related societies, immigrants organized a wide variety of associations, such as loan societies, cooperative stores, patriotic organizations associated with political activities in their native countries, educational and cultural societies, and insurance organizations.

When one considers the scattered groups of poor and ignorant immigrants, totally unused to organization and foreign to all ideas of parliamentary procedure, from which these societies must draw a large part of their membership it is remarkable how rapidly they have grown, how highly developed and successful they are.

When men are scattered in a strange country, the "consciousness of kind" with fellow countrymen has a very special significance. . . . [T]o many an immigrant the idea of nationality first becomes real after he has left his native country; at home the contrast was between peasants as a class and landlords as a class. In America he finds a vast world of people, all speaking unintelligible tongues, and for the first time he has a vivid sense of oneness with those who speak his own language, whether here or at home.

But it is not only common speech and ways, and in some cases common political aims, that draw the different groups of immigrants together, but also the sense of economic weakness. The especially dangerous character of the work in the mines and foundries which employ so many Slavs is calculated to enhance their appreciation of the advantages of mutual aid.

A foundry is a plant where molten metal is cast or shaped in molds.

Closely connected with the societies are the newspapers, which also have attained a surprising development here. Among the Slovaks, and perhaps among some other nationalities, the circulation of papers in their own language is greater in America than it is at home.

If the spontaneous and luxuriant growth of private organizations among the Slavs in America is a surprising fact, it can of course be no surprise that they organize, or are organized, for religious purposes in this country as in the old.

A condition in America which doubtless strikes as strange all these newcomers equally, and which it takes them some time to understand, is the disassociation [separation] here of church and state. . . . Of course, the independence of church and state means to the newcomers the unaccustomed burden of building their own churches and meeting all the cost of maintaining their services. In general, these new demands seem to make for more devotion rather than for less, and it is astonishing to see the number and magnificence of the churches which these laborers have sown in so few years.

Many immigrants, including the Slavs, came from countries in which the government gave financial support to the established religion.

The recent Slavic immigrants, Poles and others, have . . . formed considerable colonies, and their hearts are set, with a strength of desire which we can hardly conceive, on having their children speak their own language as their proper tongue. . . . I have heard of graduates of Polish schools in Chicago and Baltimore who do not understand English. I have been in a Polish "sisters'" school where the children were singing Polish songs.

> "We are little exiles;
> Far from our dear home
> We weep night and day,"

or something like that, the little round-cheeked boys just in from play on a Chicago sidewalk were chanting.

A thousand more items to show the separateness of the foreign life in our midst might be piled together, and in the end they would all be as nothing against the irresistible influence through which it comes about that the immigrants find themselves the parents of American children. They are surprised, they are proud, they are scandalized, they are stricken to the heart with regret,—whatever their emotions they are powerless.

The prestige of America and the hatred of children for being different from their playmates is something the parents cannot stand against. . . .

With the acquisition of English the children are apt to lose their parents' language. Against this the parents strive. It is very common, for instance, for the parents to endeavor to have the children speak only the old language until they go to school, knowing that this is their one opportunity to acquire it, and foreseeing that after the children have entered school, they will speak English not only outside of the home but within it, too, so that it will be impossible to keep English from becoming also the family language. Henceforth the parents must talk with their own children in a foreign medium in which they are consciously at a disadvantage.

. . . One of the great evils among the children of foreigners, as every one who knows them realizes, is the disastrous gulf between the older and the younger generation. Discipline, in this new freedom which both parents and children misunderstand, is almost impossible; besides which, the children, who have to act as interpreters for their parents and do business for them, are thrown into a position of unnatural importance, and feel only contempt for old-world ways, a feeling enhanced by the too common American attitude. One hears stories of Italian children refusing to reply to their mother if spoken to in Italian.

One comes sometimes with a sense of shock to a realization of points of view strange to one's own. Take, for instance, a conversation that I once had with a Polish-American priest. I had said something about "Americans," that they were not apt to be interested in Polish history, or something of the sort. Instantly he was on fire.

"You mean English-Americans," he said. "You English constantly speak as if you were the only Americans, or more Americans than others." I remarked that if I went to Poland he would not consider me a Pole.

"No, that is different," was his reply. "America was empty, open to all comers alike. There is no reason for the English to usurp [seize] the name of American. They should be called Yankees if anything. That is the name of English-Americans. There is no such thing as an American nation. Poles form a nation, but the United States is a country, under one government, inhabited by representatives of different nations. . . . For myself, I do favor one language for the United States, either English or some other, to be used by everyone, but there is no reason why people should not also have another language; that is an advantage, for it opens more avenues to Europe and elsewhere."

The writer is dealing with two different meanings of "nation." According to the older meaning, a nation is a group of people with a common language and tradition, not necessarily organized in a political state. The more modern concept of nation is a politically united group under one government, which may contain several nations of the first type. The United States is a nation of the second type.

71 Training Immigrant Children

The attempts of the immigrants to preserve their old ways of life often led to unexpected adjustments to America. As they came together in their communities and through their social and religious organizations, they dropped much of their loyalty for their native villages. In its place, they developed a strong sense of national identity. In the old country, they had been accustomed to small organizations in their local communities. In America they learned to manage remarkably complex mutual-aid organizations with large amounts of capital, complicated accounting, officers, and elections.

If the results of the immigrants' behavior were often unexpected, the same must be said of the American response to the immigrants. As Emily Balch emphasized, the child was the most important agent of change within the immigrant community. He stood between two worlds—the old world of his parents and the new world of their adopted home. The public schools tried, sometimes gently, sometimes forcibly, to bring the immigrant child into the mainstream of American society. The schools taught him the English language and trained him for citizenship and loyalty to the American way of life.

Not all Americans, however, were satisfied with the performance of the public schools. At the turn of the century, Miss Jane Addams was undoubtedly the most respected settlement-house worker in the United States. She had helped found Hull House in Chicago and was an active participant in almost every major movement to benefit the disadvantaged and to promote international peace. Like many other settlement workers, Miss Addams saw the school as a major institution for personal and community development. With considerable success, settlement workers campaigned actively for school improvements, such as hot lunches, school nurses, adult education, after-school playgrounds, kindergartens, and vocational training and guidance. They also wrestled, with less success, with the inadequacies of the educational program taught in the classroom. Schools, Jane Addams believed, tried to teach children American values, but the values taught were often not those intended. Reading 71 gives her criticism of the public schools and some of her suggestions for their reform. As you read, try to answer these questions:

1. What is the heart of Miss Addams's criticism of the schools she had visited? Does it make sense to you in terms of what you have learned about the new immigrants?
2. What were her ideas for reform? Do they seem reasonable?
3. On the basis of your own experience or from what you have read, does Miss Addams's criticism still apply to American education? If so, do you think her proposals would provide appropriate remedies?

National Education Association, **Journal of Proceedings and Addresses of the Thirty-Sixth Annual Meeting Held at Milwaukee, Wisconsin, July 6–7, 1897.** Chicago: University of Chicago Press, 1897, pp. 104–12 **passim.** Language simplified and modernized.

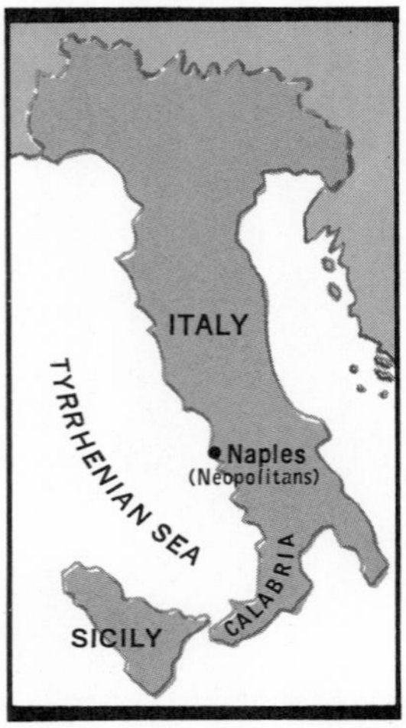

American Schools and the Immigrant Child

Jane Addams gave a speech to the National Education Association in 1897 in which she described the impact of the schools upon the immigrant children she knew in Chicago.

I have had unusual opportunities for seeing the children of immigrants during and after the period of their short school life. These observations are confined to the children of the Italian colony lying directly east of Hull House, in the nineteenth ward of Chicago, although what is said concerning them might be applied, with certain modifications, to the children of Chicago's large Bohemian and Polish colonies.

The members of the nineteenth ward Italian colony are largely from south Italy, Calabrian and Sicilian peasants, or Neapolitans, from the workingmen's quarters of that city. They have come to America with a distinct aim of earning money, and finding more room for the energies of themselves and their children. In almost all cases they mean to go back again, simply because their imaginations cannot picture a continuous life away from the old surroundings. Their experiences in Italy have been that of simple, out-door activity, and the ideas they have have come directly to them from their struggle with nature, such a hand-to-hand struggle as takes place when each man gets his living largely through his own cultivation of the soil, with tools simply fashioned by his own hands. The women, as in all primitive life, have had more diversified activities than the men. They have cooked, spun, and knitted, in addition to their almost equal work in the fields.

The entire family has been upheaved, and is striving to adjust itself to its new surroundings. The men for the most part work on railroad extensions through the summer.

During warm weather, railroads hired gangs of Italian laborers from the cities to maintain tracks throughout the country. They lived in old box cars, cooked their own food, and were often gone from their families for months.

The first effect of immigration upon the women is that of idleness. All of those outdoor and domestic activities, which she would naturally have handed on to her daughters, have slipped away from her. The domestic arts are gone, with all their absorbing interests for the children, their educational value and incentive to activity.

The child of these families has little or no opportunity to use his energies in domestic manufacture, or, indeed, constructively, in any direction. No activity is supplied to take the place of that which, in Italy, he would naturally have found in his own home, and no new union is made for him with wholesome life.

Italian parents count upon the fact that their children learn the English language and American customs before they themselves do. The children act not only as interpreters of the language about them, but as buffers between them and Chicago, and this results in a certain, almost pathetic dependence of the family upon the child. When a member of the family, therefore, first goes to school, the event is fraught with much significance to all the others. The family has no social life in any structural form, and can supply none to the child. If he receives it in the school, and gives it to his family, the school would thus become the connector with the society about them.

Let us take one of these boys, who has learned in his six or eight years to speak his native language, and to feel himself strongly identified with the fortunes of his family. Whatever interest has come to the minds of his ancestors has come through the use of their hands in the open air. Yet the first thing that the boy must do when he reaches school is to sit still, at least part of the time, and he must learn to listen to what is said to him, with all the perplexity of listening to a foreign tongue. The peasant child is perfectly indifferent to showing off and making a good recitation.

Maria Montessori (1870–1952), an Italian educator, developed what is now known as the Montessori method for the preschool child. Under this method, the child learns through discovery and freedom of action. The teacher acts as a supervisor and guide.

I venture to assert that if the little Italian lad were supplied, then and there, with tangible and resistance-offering material upon which to exercise his muscle, he would go bravely to work. He would probably be ready later to use the symbols of letters and numbers to record and describe what he had done; and might even be encouraged to read to find out what other people had done.

Too often the teacher's notion of her duty is to transform the child into an American of a somewhat smug and comfortable type. She insists that the boy's powers must at once be developed in an abstract direction, quite ignoring the fact that his parents have had to do only with tangible things. She has little idea of the development of Italian life. Her outlook is national and not racial, and she fails, therefore, not only in knowledge of, but also in respect for, the child and his parents. She quite honestly estimates the child upon an American basis. The contempt for the experiences and languages of their parents which foreign children sometimes exhibit, and which is most damaging to their moral as well as intellectual life, is doubtless due in part to the overestimation which the school places upon speaking and reading in English. This cutting into his family loyalty takes away one of the most valuable traits of the Italian child.

If we admit that in education it is necessary to begin with the experiences which the child already has, through his spontaneous and social activity, then the city street begins this education for him in a more natural way than does the school.

Some states had passed laws regulating child labor. In 1916, Congress passed the Keating-Owen Act which forbade interstate shipping of products from factories employing children under age 14 or from mines employing children under 16. The Supreme Court declared the law unconstitutional.

Leaving the child who does not stay in school, let us now consider the child who does faithfully remain until he reaches the age of factory work, which is, fortunately, in the most advanced of our factory states, fourteen years. Has anything been done up to this time, has even a beginning been made, to give him a consciousness of his social value? Has the outcome of the processes to which he has been subjected adapted him to deal more effectively and in a more vital manner with his present life? May we not charge it to the public school that it has given to this child no knowledge of the social meaning of his work?

He finds himself in the drudgery of a factory, senselessly manipulating unrelated material, using his hands for unknown ends, and his head not at all. Owing to the fact that during his years in school he has used his head mostly, and his hands very little, nothing bewilders him so much as the suggestion that the school was intended as a preparation for his work in life.

Foreign-born children have all the drudgery of learning to listen to, and read and write an alien tongue. Many never get beyond this first drudgery. I have interrogated [questioned] dozens of these children who have left school from the third, fourth, and fifth grades, and I have met very few who ever read for pleasure.

From one point of view the school itself summarizes the competitive system of the factory. Certain standards are held up and worked for; and, even in the school, the child does little work with real joy and spontaneity. The pleasure which comes from creative effort, the thrill of production, is only occasional, and not the sustaining motive which keeps it going. The child in school often contracts the habit of expecting to do his work in certain hours, and to take his pleasure in certain other hours; quite in the same spirit as he later earns his money by ten hours of dull factory work, and spends it in three hours of lurid and unprofitable pleasure in the evening. Both in the school and the factory, his work has been dull and growing duller, and his pleasure must constantly grow more stimulating. Only occasionally has he had the real joy of doing a thing for its own sake.

Miss Addams is referring to the effects of the division of labor. Workers found they were repeatedly making one part, rather than an entire finished product in which they could take pride.

Those of us who are working to bring a fuller life to the industrial members of the community, who are looking forward to a time when work shall not be senseless drudgery, but shall contain some self-expression of the worker, sometimes feel the hopelessness of adding evening classes and social entertainments as a mere frill to a day filled with monotonous and deadening drudgery. We sometimes feel that we have a right to expect more help from the public schools than they now give us.

Evening classes in subjects such as English, history, and government helped immigrants to adjust to life in America and also to prepare for their naturalization tests. In order to become citizens, immigrants had to read and write English and to demonstrate a knowledge of American history and government.

We have a curious notion, in spite of all our realism, that it is not possible for the mass of mankind to have interests and experiences of themselves which are worth anything. We transmit to the children of working people our own skepticism regarding the possibility of finding any joy or profit in their work. We practically encourage them to get out of it as soon as possible.

I am quite sure that no one can possibly mistake this paper as a plea for trade schools, or as a desire to fit the boy for any given industry. Such a specializing would indeed be stupid when our industrial methods are developing and changing, almost day by day. But it does contend that life, as seen from the standpoint of the handworker, should not be emptied of all social consciousness and value. The school could make the boy infinitely more flexible and alive than he is now to the materials and forces of nature which, in spite of all man's activities, are unchangeable.

Trade schools train students for a skilled trade, such as carpentry or mechanics.

The isolation of the school from life—its failure to make life of more interest, and show it in its larger aspects—the mere equipping of the children with the tools of reading and writing, without giving them an absorbing interest concerning which they wish to read and write, certainly tends to defeat the very purpose of education.

72 Our Grandfathers Inside Us

HISTORICAL ESSAY

Ethnic background remains one of the most potent factors in American life. For many Americans, it continues to influence whom one marries, votes for, invites to dinner, or worships with. The hoped-for day when all Americans will amalgamate into one indistinguishable people, heralded in *The American Farmer* by Hector St. Jean de Crévecoeur in the 1780's and by another naturalized New Yorker, Israel Zangwill, in a play entitled *The Melting Pot* in 1907, has not yet come to pass. In the last half of the twentieth century, the American people seem to be dividing into four major groups: Catholics, Jews, white Protestants, and Negroes. The reasons for this development lie buried deep in the history of the immigrants who have flocked to the "land of the dollar" from every nation.

American Population Growth

Before the Civil War, the population of the United States grew rapidly. Each year 103 Americans lived where only 100 had been twelve months before. Every twenty-five years the population doubled. This high growth rate is understandable. Since food was plentiful, Americans survived childhood better and lived a little longer than most Europeans. Moreover, because large families helped farmers wrestle with a shortage of labor, the birth rate remained high.

After 1850, Americans stopped having as many babies as they had had previously. Large families were no longer so beneficial to parents, particularly in the cities. Farm children were easy to house and feed and did substantial amounts of work around the farm. But in the city, children crowded small apartments, strained their parents' slender incomes, and were seldom able to find useful work. Moreover, city children required many years of expensive education.

The decline in the birth rate contributed to a slow but dramatic change in the age level of the American people. In 1790, the median age of white males was about 16 years. The median age rose steadily for the next century and a half; by 1950, it had passed 30, almost double the 1790 figure. Many of the people in the 1950 total were the children and grandchildren of immigrants.

A median is a number exactly in the middle. In this case, it means that there were just as many people under the age of 16 as there were people over the age of 16 in the United States in 1790.

The decline in the American birth rate increased the national shortage of labor and spurred demands for immigrants from abroad. Who came and from where depended upon several factors. A long-run change in the social and economic structure of Europe played the primary role. As Emily Balch noted, European agriculture and industry were being transformed. As farms were subdivided among several sons, holdings eventually became too small to support a man and his family. Sooner or later, he cut his ties to his peasant past to move to a nearby city or even risk a new life abroad. At the same time, village artisans, forced to compete with machine-made products, eventually gave up the unequal struggle and shipped out for better economic opportunities in the New World. Emigration was cumulative. The daring souls who first braved the Atlantic crossing saved money and accumulated experience to help their more timid friends and relatives who followed. In addition, the spread of the railway network eastward into Europe made the land journey easier, and the development of better steamships decreased the hardships of the ocean voyage. By 1900, a steerage ticket cost from nine to fifteen dollars. Occasionally, religious persecution, a desire to escape military service, or a similar temporary event triggered emigration.

Steerage was the kind of ship transportation available for people paying the lowest fares. Steerage passengers usually occupied the forward lower decks of a passenger ship where conditions were crowded and unsanitary.

Through the 1860's, these factors attracted immigrants primarily from England, Germany, and Ireland. Between 1847 and 1857, more than 200,000 immigrants landed each year, with a peak of over 400,000 in 1854. A second wave developed after the Civil War. Increasing numbers of Scandinavians joined the earlier groups, and in the 1880's people from southern and eastern Europe added to the influx. Annual immigration exceeded 400,000 for fifteen of the thirty-five years between 1865 and 1900. The 1900 census revealed that a third of the nation was either foreign born or the children of the foreign born. The third and largest wave of immigration came between 1901 and 1924. Table 1 presents the story statistically.

TABLE 1 The Source of European Immigration, 1861–1930

Period	Total Immigrants Admitted	Northern and Western Europe		Southern and Eastern Europe	
1861-70	2,314,824	2,031,624	87.8%	33,628	1.4%
1871-80	2,812,191	2,070,373	73.6	201,889	7.2
1881-90	5,246,613	3,778,633	72.0	958,413	18.3
1891-1900	3,687,564	1,643,492	44.6	1,915,486	51.9
1901-10	8,795,386	1,910,035	21.7	6,225,981	70.8
1911-20	5,735,811	997,438	17.4	3,379,126	58.9
1921-30	4,107,209	1,284,023	31.3	1,193,830	29.0

U.S. Bureau of the Census, **Historical Statistics of the United States, Colonial Times to 1957.** Washington, D.C.: Government Printing Office, 1960, pp. 56–58.

Table 2 indicates that a shift also occurred in the source of immigrants from Asia and North America.

TABLE 2 Immigrants from China, Japan, Canada, and Mexico, 1861–1930

Period	China	Japan	Canada	Mexico
1861-70	64,301	186	153,878	2,191
1871-80	123,201	149	383,640	5,162
1881-90	61,711	2,270	393,304	1,913 [2]
1891-1900	14,799	25,942	3,311 [1]	971 [2]
1901-1910	20,605	129,797	179,226	49,642
1911-1920	21,278	83,837	742,185	219,004
1921-1930	29,907	33,462	924,515	459,287

[1] *The actual figure is higher because good records are not available for 1892 and 1893.*
[2] *The actual figure is higher because no figures are available from 1886–1893.*

U.S. Bureau of the Census, **Historical Statistics**, pp. 58–59.

The Chinese Exclusion Act also denied American citizenship to people born in China. Chinese students and other specific groups were, however, allowed to enter the United States.

A total of 129,797 Japanese arrived in the United States between 1901 and 1910. In 1906, the San Francisco School Board declared that Oriental students must attend segregated public schools. President Theodore Roosevelt persuaded the board to cancel this order. In a series of notes (1907–1908), he reached a "gentleman's agreement" with the Japanese government to stop the emigration of Japanese laborers to the United States.

Between 1854 and 1883, substantial numbers of Chinese came to the United States to seek better economic opportunities. In 1882, almost 40,000 Chinese entered the country, and many took jobs building railroads in the West. In 1882, Congress barred further immigration of Chinese for ten years. This prohibition was renewed each decade until the close of World War II. After 1883, Japanese began to emigrate in larger numbers. In order to prohibit Japanese immigration, the United States government, after considerable controversy and diplomatic negotiations, persuaded the government of Japan to prohibit the emigration of laborers to the United States. Both of these restrictive acts had been promoted by western states, particularly by labor unions in the West. They feared competition from Oriental workers and claimed that Chinese and Japanese were an alien race in a land peopled primarily by Caucasians.

After 1900, both Canadians and Mexicans began to arrive in the United States in substantial numbers. In the decade after 1910, about one million English-speaking and 500,000 French-speaking Canadians crossed the border. This population traffic, however, went both ways. Between 1890 and 1914, almost a million Americans emigrated to Canada, particularly into the provinces bordering the states from Minnesota to Montana. In addition, the census revealed that in 1930 about 750,000 Mexicans lived in the United States, where they were concentrated in Texas, New Mexico, Arizona, and California. Mexican immigrants were usually poor and illiterate. They worked primarily as farm laborers and became involved in difficult problems of labor and ethnic relations which have only begun to be resolved in our own day.

The Characteristics of the Immigrants

At the time of each immigrant's entry, officials asked him to state his occupation. Table 3 was compiled from immigrants' answers.

Ernest Rubin, "Immigration and Economic Growth of the U.S.: 1790–1914," Conference on Research in Income and Wealth, September 4–5, 1957, National Bureau of Economic Research, p. 8, as cited in Seymour E. Harris, ed., **American Economic History.** New York: McGraw-Hill Book Company, Inc., 1961, p. 269.

TABLE 3 The Occupations of Immigrants to the United States at Entry, 1860–1910

Decade	Agriculture	Skilled labor	Unskilled labor	Domestic service	Professional	Misc.
1861-70	17.6%	24.0%	42.4%	7.2%	0.8%	8.0%
1871-80	18.2%	23.1%	41.9%	7.7%	1.4%	7.7%
1881-90	14.0%	20.4%	50.2%	9.4%	1.1%	9.4%
1891-1900	11.4%	20.1%	47.0%	15.1%	0.9%	15.1%
1901-10	24.3%	20.2%	34.8%	14.1%	1.5%	14.1%

As Emily Balch noted, many uprooted peasants had moved to cities in their native lands where they had taken jobs in industry before coming to the United States. How deeply this experience had penetrated, and how many people were accustomed to factory work before coming to the United States, we do not know.

Nor do we know how the immigrants differed from those who stayed behind. More than sixty percent of the immigrants were males, and most were young adults. Hence most immigrants could work for many years, and few would have to be supported by others. Some scholars think that emigrants had in common a sense of adventure and were drawn from the most free and modern segments of the population. Nobody can be sure of this conclusion. Intensive comparison of a few areas in Italy, for example, suggests that immigrants came from traditional villages where ancient ways were firmly embedded.

Adjusting to American Society

Once within the United States, the changes in immigrants sketched by Emily Balch seem to have been almost universal. The experience of emigration weakened attachments to European villages or towns and increased identification with the national state. Groups whose life had focused around the family developed a wide range of formal organizations, such as mutual-benefit societies. A vigorous press grew up among peoples who had hardly seen a newspaper before. In every group children confronted parents with conflicts between old cultures and new.

This experience was not quite the same for every immigrant group. For each it involved slightly different opportunities, choices, and difficulties. The eastern Europeans, for example, included approximately the one and a half million Jews. Since Jews had been forbidden by law to own land in eastern Europe and had not been permitted to participate fully in society, they lived differently from eastern European peasants. Most of them earned their livings as artisans or merchants. They were accustomed to being treated as aliens in a strange and often hostile land. Jews placed a high premium on knowledge and achievement as measures of individual worth. In addition, their own traditional culture had been changing for several centuries. Young men had become excited by ideas of "enlightenment" and nationalism. Released from the constraints of the Russian, Polish, or Hungarian village when they emigrated to Vienna or New York, Jews moved rapidly into the mainstream of modern life.

On the American side of the Atlantic, Jews quickly developed the sort of community institutions that Miss Balch described to give them mutual protection and help them accommodate to American society. They achieved unusual personal successes. By the first decade of the twentieth century, sons of Jewish immigrants who

"Enlightenment" refers to a belief in progress, natural law and natural rights, and reason. Young enlightened men scorned tradition and believed that each generation would, by its endeavors, contribute a better life for the next generation. The years immediately following the French Revolution of 1789 were known as the Age of Enlightenment.

entered the United States in 1890 were protesting against discrimination in college admission procedures. This personal success had a twofold effect upon the institutions which first-generation immigrants had set up. On the one hand, successful men and women provided a large fund of capital and of trained personnel for community purposes. On the other hand, success by American standards challenged, more rapidly than in other groups, the adequacy of group identification and pride as a way of participating in American life. Jews have, at one and the same time, been vigorous spokesmen for "cultural pluralism"—the idea that there are many American cultures, each to be respected—and of full assimilation into America.

Jews have not been entirely unique. The Oriental communities of the west coast showed many of the same traits of enterprise and emphasis upon achievement and intellectual accomplishment. Both Orientals and Jews met greater discrimination as they became more successful by American standards. For example, California tried to restrict Japanese land ownership at a time (1913) when Japanese immigrants threatened to take over large stretches of land, such as the San Joaquin Valley. And, like Jews, Orientals have contributed a disproportionately large number of intellectuals and professional people to the society.

The differences which developed among immigrant groups between the early twentieth century and today did not grow exclusively from the values which immigrants brought with them to this country. Differences also stemmed from the American experience. Each group tended to cluster in a special set of industries or occupations. The initial concentration was in part accidental, depending upon the most active employers at the time when a particular immigrant group first entered the country. Later, clustering was not so accidental. The first entrants, with the support of their employers, encouraged their countrymen to move to the firm or industry with which they were familiar. The census of 1910 showed the effects of this clustering behavior. Though foreign-born males comprised only 20.5 percent of all male industrial workers, in twenty-three industries they formed between 40 and 76 percent of the work force. Several of these industries, particularly in individual cities, were dominated by single groups such as Irish in construction, Jews in clothing manufacturing, and Slavs and Magyars in steel.

A Magyar is a person who speaks the main language of what is now Hungary.

The industry where members of an ethnic group first found employment strongly affected its future development. Groups working in industries with few highly paid jobs requiring education have shown relatively little social mobility. Industries that offered more opportunities for advancement helped immigrant groups who worked there to push up the social ladder. Behavior that people used to attribute to ethnic background appears on closer examination to have resulted from conditions in particular industries. When Italians took jobs in the textile industry, where they were largely unskilled or semi-skilled workers, union leaders argued that they could not be unionized. But Italians in the building trades, where it was relatively easy to organize because skilled workers there had more bargaining power, joined unions readily. In general, the ability to form unions and gain higher wages depended more on the amount of skill people needed than on ethnic background.

Since it is difficult to obtain good, skilled labor, skilled laborers are in better position to bargain with their employers than unskilled laborers.

Immigration Restriction

The era of mass immigration closed during the 1920's. Since the first onset of heavy Irish immigration in the 1840's, "native" Americans had responded ambiguously to the newcomers. Some welcomed them. Others feared for American values and greeted the newcomers with hostility. In the 1840's and 1850's, this hostility, compounded with anti-Catholicism, was probably the most important political issue through most of the northeastern United States. Anti-Catholic riots broke out in most major cities and the Know-Nothing Party became a major political force. If there had been a public-opinion poll at the time, the number one issue on people's minds would probably have been "nativism" rather than slavery.

The Know-Nothing, or American, party began as a secret organization opposed to immigrants, particularly Catholics. With the disintegration of the established parties, the Know-Nothings won substantial victories in 1854 and elected several governors, state legislators, and representatives to Congress.

Nativism did not die after the Civil War, though for a time other issues seemed more important. In the 1880's and 1890's, however, three events helped it gain strength. The first was the increase in the proportion of eastern and southern European immigrants. Native-born Americans—whose ancestors came from northern and western Europe—claimed that the newcomers came from less desirable backgrounds. Second, the old immigrants were beginning to take part in American political life. Several eastern cities elected their first mayors of Irish descent. Germans insisted that public schools should teach German and that beer gardens should be allowed to remain open on Sunday. Many older groups resented the new power of recent immigrants. Third, the increasing economic growth and urbanization of the country, threatened the self-images and traditions of many people. The immigrants, so much a part of the new age, became scapegoats for the tensions it generated.

This renewed nativism showed its first important fruits in the 1890's. Local communities throughout the country redoubled their efforts to make everyone more patriotic. They passed laws insisting upon English as the only language of instruction in the schools and prohibiting some of the "immoral" practices associated with immigrants, especially in matters, such as gambling and liquor sales, that conflicted with religious attitudes of native groups.

Nativists also led a movement to restrict immigration. During the first three quarters of the nineteenth century, states that were the ports-of-entry for a large number of immigrants had attempted through the police power to exclude diseased persons, paupers, and criminals. In 1882, Congress excluded convicts, idiots, and persons likely to become public charges, and imposed a head tax of fifty cents on each immigrant admitted. In a series of later acts, Congress excluded additional groups, increased the head tax, and forbade contract labor. These acts, based on the principle that the government should select the types of persons to be admitted, did not noticeably decrease the total flow of immigrants. A demand for stricter selection and for restricting the total to be admitted built up steadily, particularly among union members.

In 1864, Congress had passed a Contract Labor Law which allowed employers to recruit laborers from Europe. Workers signed contracts agreeing to work for one employer for a specified period of time for specified wages. Workers could not legally leave the job during the contract term. American laborers objected to the law, and Congress repealed it in 1885.

The "Literacy Test Act" required aliens over the age of 16 to read "not less than thirty nor more than eighty words in ordinary use" in either English or some other language.

A bill providing for a literacy test in any language as a basis of admission passed one house of Congress thirty-two times and on four occasions passed both houses, only to be vetoed by the President (Cleveland and Taft once each and Wilson twice). In 1917, however, the bill passed over Wilson's veto. In theory selective, this act was in fact also restrictive because a large proportion of the immigrants from southern and eastern Europe could not read. Fearing a flood of immigrants in the years following World War I despite the literacy test, Congress passed another restrictive law in 1921 limiting annual immigration to 357,802 and setting a quota for each nation computed by taking 3 percent of the total number of persons of that nationality residing in the United States in 1910. The quota favored northern and western Europe.

In 1924, the law was toughened. It provided that after 1927 total immigration in any one year would be limited to 150,000. To make up this total, a quota was allocated to each country according to the proportion of its natives in the population of the United States in 1920. The quota allocated to each group had no relationship to the number of people who actually wanted to come to the United States. The quota for England, which was very large, was unused while the quotas for eastern and southern European nations were small in comparison to the number who wanted to emigrate. This quota system implied that the newer immigrants were less desirable than those from northern and western Europe.

Since 1968, the United States admits 120,000 immigrants from the Western Hemisphere and 170,000 from elsewhere each year. Preference is given to those who are scientists, professionals, or victims of political oppression, and to those having relatives in the United States. There are no longer any strict national quotas.

The Contributions of Immigrants

Textbooks often contain long lists of immigrants who made important contributions to American society. The lists are usually filled with names of famous men and women: political leaders, authors, musicians, inventors, athletes, soldiers, and so forth. Without exception, every immigrant group has distinguished candidates for such a list. But a list of people who became successful does not begin to indicate the major contributions of immigrants to American life. A walk through any major city offers far richer data.

Look at the New York subways, built largely by the labor of Irish and Italians. Look at the restaurants, with food whose recipes came in the holds of ships from ports around the world. Observe the architecture, reminiscent of Europe, Asia, or the Middle East, of churches, stores, and houses. Enter the shops of importers who travel to their homelands each year to buy fresh stock. Watch the billboards advertising dance troupes and orchestras filled with foreign-born artists. Most of all, look at the people: brunettes, blondes, and red-heads; skins from ebony to ivory; long faces and broad ones; five-footers next to men seven feet tall; eyes of every color; features of every type. We are all immigrants and the offspring of immigrants, and we have all contributed to the infinite variety and richness of our nation.

Many of the most important contributors have been unknown people who lived quiet, happy lives, doing an ordinary job well and raising a family. Most of the first generation of immigrants, like those described by Emily Balch, struggled to stay alive and to find a new meaning to life in a strange land. Partly because they clung to the ways of their homeland, many of their children scorned them and refused to speak their parents' language. But the third generation, secure in an America which was their home, often moved to the suburbs, learned their ancestral languages in high school or college, and asked their grandparents endless questions about their birthplaces and the long trip to the New World. As the readings in this chapter indicate, the struggle to survive was seldom easy. This was no mean contribution: to raise children and grandchildren each proud in his own way of his nation and his heritage and each struggling successfully to find a place within both.

The immigrants contributed to the social mobility which has characterized the United States. They usually entered the labor force at the bottom, taking the unskilled and semi-skilled jobs. This development often pushed older American groups up the economic ladder into skilled crafts and supervisory positions. More money and more responsibility often encouraged people to educate their children better, thus giving them even greater opportunities than their parents had for advancement. The immigrants actually created new and better jobs for native Americans, although this phenomenon was not always obvious.

Amalgamation, Accommodation, Assimilation

No single pattern of adjustment emerged among American immigrants. The descendants of English, Scotch, Dutch, Scandinavian, and German immigrants who came to the New World in the eighteenth and early nineteenth centuries amalgamated to the point that distinguishable group lines largely disappeared. With these groups, the concept of the melting pot is valid. To a greater or lesser degree, all immigrant groups became partly assimilated. They adopted a common language, common clothing, common norms of behavior, and many other traits. But many groups came closer to accommodation than to assimilation. They retained exclusive social organizations, such as mutual aid societies, and separate religious congregations.

Instead of amalgamating into one homogeneous people, modern Americans seem to have clustered into four major groups separated by religious and racial lines: Catholics, Jews, white Protestants, and Negroes. Marriage statistics indicate that, although numerous exceptions can be cited, members of each major religious group tend to marry within the group. Irish Catholics marry Italian Catholics much more than Catholics marry Protestants or Jews. One scholar called this development a "triple melting pot" characterized by religious affiliation. A fourth group, black Americans, makes the pot quadruple. Rather than give an ethnic identification, many modern Americans, when asked who or what they are, respond by giving their occupation, their religion, and their race.

Strong feelings about religion and race do exist. Some Catholics, some Jews, some Protestants, and some Negroes would still be deeply distressed if one of their children married someone of another religious faith or race. But large numbers of people in all of these groups would not. Moreover, they are bound together with a common adherence to a democratic way of life. In the future, the dream of Crèvecoeur and Zangwill, a French Catholic and a British Jew of Russian origins, may come true for us all—black, white, red, and yellow; Protestant, Catholic, Jew.

SUGGESTED READINGS

GLAZER, NATHAN, and DANIEL P. MOYNIHAN, *Beyond the Melting Pot: The Negroes, Puerto Ricans, Jews, Italians and Irish of New York City.* This account carries the story of immigrants beyond the first generation into the present.

HANDLIN, OSCAR, *The Uprooted.* This book contains a moving view of social upheaval, primarily from the perspective of the "new immigrants" from eastern and southern Europe.

HERBERG, WILL, *Protestant—Catholic—Jew: An Essay in American Religious Sociology.* This excellent volume traces the development of the triple melting pot.

HIGHAM, JOHN, *Strangers in the Land.* An account of the nativist sentiment which led in the 1920's to the restriction of immigration, Higham's book traces an unpleasant theme in American history.

Work and Organization

CHAPTER 19

STATING THE ISSUE

A major change in the kinds of work people did took place after the Civil War. The change affected native Americans and immigrants, blacks and whites, and it accompanied a population shift from the farms to the cities. But many of the people whose efforts helped industrialize America never entered a manufacturing plant.

Some workers built the houses, streets, sewers, and other structures for the growing cities. Others, who worked in trade, finance, real estate, transportation, and public utilities, increased in number more rapidly between 1880 and 1920 than those who worked in manufacturing. In addition, the cities' demands raised the proportion of teachers, doctors, lawyers, accountants, and other professionals. Nevertheless, the most fundamental changes in work methods and organization occurred in mills, mines, and factories.

What did these changes mean to the workers? Economists can discuss an economy in terms of gross national product and average per capita income. It is more difficult for them to determine actual cash income for workers. Recent estimates of what a worker could buy with his income during the 1890–1914 period indicate that increases occurred in irregular spurts. But while increases took place, the gap widened between the high incomes of manufacturers and bankers and the low incomes of unskilled workers.

Work, however, involves more than a source of income for the worker and the production of goods for the market. Work is also a system of complex social relationships among men laboring together on a job, between employees and employers, men and their families, and workers and the rest of society. The readings in Chapter 19 focus on these relationships in the steel industry. The underlying changes in patterns of work described in these readings apply to other manufacturing jobs and other industries. How did work within the steel industry change? How did the changes influence relationships among workers? between employers and employees? between workers and their families? between workers and the community? How did the movement for collective bargaining influence management and labor? What role did government play in the union movement? These are the major issues raised in Chapter 19.

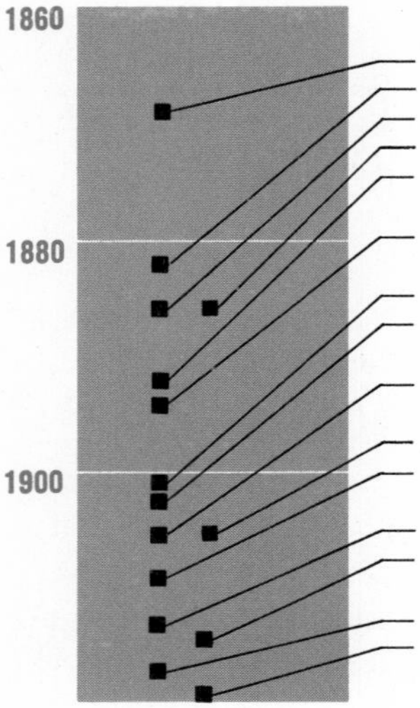

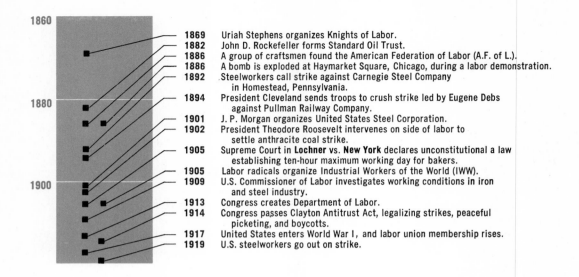

1869 Uriah Stephens organizes Knights of Labor.
1882 John D. Rockefeller forms Standard Oil Trust.
1886 A group of craftsmen found the American Federation of Labor (A.F. of L.).
1886 A bomb is exploded at Haymarket Square, Chicago, during a labor demonstration.
1892 Steelworkers call strike against Carnegie Steel Company in Homestead, Pennsylvania.
1894 President Cleveland sends troops to crush strike led by Eugene Debs against Pullman Railway Company.
1901 J. P. Morgan organizes United States Steel Corporation.
1902 President Theodore Roosevelt intervenes on side of labor to settle anthracite coal strike.
1905 Supreme Court in **Lochner** vs. **New York** declares unconstitutional a law establishing ten-hour maximum working day for bakers.
1905 Labor radicals organize Industrial Workers of the World (IWW).
1909 U.S. Commissioner of Labor investigates working conditions in iron and steel industry.
1913 Congress creates Department of Labor.
1914 Congress passes Clayton Antitrust Act, legalizing strikes, peaceful picketing, and boycotts.
1917 United States enters World War I, and labor union membership rises.
1919 U.S. steelworkers go out on strike.

73 Work and Participation

In 1880, observers who compared the American with British, German, and French iron industries recognized that American methods for producing iron and steel had fallen behind. American mill owners had failed to take advantage of new manufacturing techniques discovered in the previous twenty years. American manufacturers still heated pig iron in large crucibles. Men called "puddlers" then stirred cinders into the molten metal until it formed crystallized balls which could be squeezed and rolled. The entire process required physically strong workers who could exercise a great deal of individual judgment about the properties of metal as it passed from one stage to another. Moving great batches of metal manually within the mill also required strong men, although they made fewer decisions based on judgment.

A crucible is a pot made of heat-resistant material such as clay or porcelain.

The American iron and steel industry soon caught up with its European competitors. In rapid succession, manufacturers switched from the crucible to the Bessemer and then to the open-hearth process for making steel. The Bessemer converter blew hot air rapidly through molten pig iron to burn out major impurities. The open-hearth system, involving huge furnaces which heated the metal to extremely high temperatures, allowed for better control of the quality of the metal. Both methods reduced the hot back-breaking work men had performed previously in iron and steel production. But as these new methods replaced the old, fewer skilled workers were needed. Semiskilled and unskilled workers entered the industry in increasing numbers.

Skilled craftsmen, such as carpenters and plumbers, perform work that requires special training or experience. Semiskilled workers perform less-specialized tasks which require less training. Unskilled workers hold jobs that require little or no special training.

As production processes changed, changes also took place in the relationships among workers and in their relationships with their employers. Reading 73 examines some of these changes. As you read, try to answer these questions:

1. How did changes in the production process affect the kinds of workers employed in the iron and steel industry?
2. How did the transformation of the labor force affect workers' relationships with each other? What implications do you think these new relationships had for effective union organization?
3. How did changes in the ownership of steel mills influence employer-employee relationships?
4. What were the steelworkers' work schedules? How would such schedules affect the worker and his relationship with his family?

Employment Conditions in the Iron and Steel Industry

In 1909, the United States Commissioner of Labor began an extensive investigation of working conditions in the iron and steel industry. Portions of his report follow.

Report on Conditions of Employment in the Iron and Steel Industry, Senate Document No. 110, 62nd Congress, 1st Session. Washington, D.C.: Government Printing Office, 1913, vol. III, pp. 36–37, 109–11, 159–60.

Some conception of the tremendous increases in productive efficiency [of the American steel industry] may be given by the statement that in the 40 years from 1869 to 1909 the annual output of the blast furnaces increased from 66.5 tons per man to 596.4 tons. The average annual product per man in 1909 was therefore nine times as great as in 1869. Similarly in the steel works and rolling mills the annual production of finished products increased from 28.3 tons per man to 102.4 tons. In this branch of the industry therefore the production per employee in 1909 was three and a half times as great as in 1869.

Rolling mills contain machinery for rolling iron and steel into sheets and for shaping the metal into bars.

In every case the change in [production] processes has carried with it the elimination of much heavy manual labor done under conditions of exhausting heat, and at the same time the decrease in the proportion of skilled men and their replacement either by unskilled workmen or by semiskilled machine operators of various kinds.

In 1890, while all the important methods of producing steel were in use, the development of mechanical methods of handling materials and of regulating processes had hardly begun. The iron and steel industry therefore required a very much larger proportion of highly skilled and specially trained men than at the present time [1909–1913]. The supply of such workmen was limited and could not be increased at will as is the case with unskilled labor, which can readily be recruited either from other industries or from Europe by slightly increasing the rate of wages. Such a situation assured the skilled workmen a considerable degree of independence and of control over their working conditions.

The introduction of mechanical processes has to a large degree displaced these men either with unskilled laborers or with semi-skilled workmen who can be recruited by the thousands whenever it is necessary. Similarly, although in 1890 there was a large proportion of foreign-born employees in the industry, they were principally English, Irish, Welsh, and Germans, and were therefore largely familiar either with the iron and steel industry or with some other industry organized along similar lines. At present more than half the working force of the industry is drawn from the farms of eastern and southern Europe, and is therefore accustomed to the position of tenant or farm laborer and unacquainted with the wage system of industry. Apart from the unwillingness of the English-speaking workmen to associate with these immigrant employees, the working force is at present divided into two groups which are unable to communicate except by signs or through an interpreter.

Great Britain and Germany were two of the leading steel-producing countries. Making iron was an important industry around Dublin, Ireland, and steelworks constituted a major part of the industrial wealth of Wales. Thus, these immigrants had the experience of working in the iron and steel industries.

In 1890, although there were a number of companies with comparatively large capital, the typical establishment was of small size and was owned by an individual or a partnership rather than by a corporation. The skilled workmen, on the other hand, were largely banded together in one strong organization, the Amalgamated Association of Iron and Steel Workers, and so successful had it been in extending its influence and membership that many of the manufacturers expected that it would within a short time reach such a position that it would have to be dealt with by the manufacturers acting through some form of organization. It was suggested at this time that to avoid the losses from strikes and other labor disturbances, voluntary arbitration should be submitted to and some form of profit sharing generally introduced which would tend to identify more closely the interests of the skilled workmen with those of the manufacturers.

The Amalgamated Association of Iron and Steel Workers had been organized in 1876 when three separate iron and steel unions united.

Strikes are work stoppages called by unions either to try to force an employer to meet their demands or to protest against conditions imposed by an employer. Profit sharing is a system in which workers receive a share of the business profits in addition to their wages.

The consolidation of manufacturing interests has been achieved to a degree which in 1890 was not believed to be possible. But instead of the strong organizations of workmen expected, the end of 20 years sees the employees not only without strong unions, but completely unorganized in all except two minor branches of the industry, and even there the union is extremely weak. Not only is there no arbitration of questions involving wages and working conditions between two strongly organized parties to the dispute, but it is generally insisted that the employees shall accept whatever wages are offered without dispute or argument. In many companies

Consolidation is the formation of a larger business from several smaller ones.

no committees are received even to present the case of unorganized men, the management dealing only with the individual workman. Instead of the identification of the interests of the employers and employed by a wide extension of profit sharing, only two companies have made any efforts in this direction, and these so recently that no effects in the direction hoped for can be perceived.

The consolidation of the manufacturing interests has been progressing steadily since 1890 and has now reached the point where a single corporation [United States Steel] with a total outstanding capitalization, including stocks and bonds, of one and a half billion dollars, controls one half the industry, and a half dozen other large corporations with a total outstanding capitalization of three hundred and sixty millions owns more than one third of the productive capacity of the other half of the industry.

The steel industry proper, therefore, is largely in the hands of a small number of large and powerful corporations. In addition to this centralized ownership, the steel manufacturers are held together by the social forces of such organizations as the American Iron and Steel Association and the American Iron and Steel Institute. While these organizations have special purposes quite far removed from the promotion of common action in labor disputes, the result of the close association of the most prominent men in the industry is conducive [leading] to a common attitude toward labor and labor organizations.

All of these large companies and corporations, with two exceptions, insist upon dealing with their workmen as individuals. Furthermore, the two large corporations, which employ union men, have them only in their puddling mills and small rolling mills, which branches constitute only a small part of their business.

In contrast to this great aggregation [massing] of power on the part of the manufacturers, the two unions of iron and steel workers had in 1911 a total membership of less than 6000 of the 275,000 men employed in the manufacturing plants of the industry. In no branch of the industry, except perhaps in puddling, do these unions include a majority of the skilled workmen. There is only one open-hearth steel plant in the United States for which a wage scale is signed by organized workmen and no Bessemer steel plant. Not only is there a lack of any formal organization in these departments, but . . . there are strong forces working to increase the state of disorganization in which the workmen in this industry have been practically since the early nineties.

[T]he greater part of the workmen in the iron and steel industry [work] . . . unusually long hours with an alternation of day and night work and with frequent extended periods of overtime. Approximately one half of the employees in the iron and steel in-

Some businesses were consolidated to reduce cutthroat competition. Rival businessmen formed mergers by combining their firms into a single company. **Trusts** were organized so that one board of "trustees" ran several companies in related industries and controlled a majority of the stock in each company. After the Sherman Anti-Trust Law outlawed trusts in 1890, **holding companies** and **interlocking directorates** replaced them. A **holding company** owns the stock and hence controls other firms in related industries. **Interlocking directorates** are formed when the same men serve on the board of directors of several firms in related industries. Sometimes businessmen in similar industries arranged **pools** whereby they divided the market and agreed upon a fixed price for their products.

The American Iron and Steel Association was formed during the Civil War and was absorbed by the American Iron and Steel Institute in 1913. The purpose of the Institute is to collect and exchange information, to promote the interests of the industry, and to engage in scientific research.

dustry have a regular working-day of 12 hours, usually from 6 A.M. to 6 P.M. when on the day shift and from 6 P.M. to 6 A.M. when on the night shift. Every week or two weeks practically all of these 12-hour workmen change from the day shift to the night shift, or vice versa, and must consequently accustom themselves to the changed conditions of eating and sleeping. Apart from the difficulty of making this periodic readjustment of habits, to which all of the workmen interviewed testified, there is in the case of the married employees the added hardship of almost complete separation from their wives and children. Furthermore, at the end of the 12-hour day, whether on the day shift or the night shift, the workmen are, as is shown elsewhere, liable to be called upon to work 12 hours more in place of absent workmen, or to work for several hours until some repair job is completed. Many cases were encountered in the investigation where workmen were on duty continuously for 36 hours, often without an hour's sleep or rest and sometimes without even hot food. Moreover, a large number of the employees work every day in the week, including Sunday, and, at the time the shifts are changed from day to night, these workmen are on duty continuously for either 18 or 24 hours. In May 1910, 30 percent of the employees worked 7 days a week, but during the past year [1911–1912] a number of companies have made such arrangements that none of their employees is permitted to work more than 6 days per week. Between 40 and 50 percent of the employees formerly working 7 days per week have been affected by these arrangements for 6-day work, but this still [August 1912] leaves more than 15 percent of the employees in the industry generally and more than 50 percent of the blast-furnace workmen on a regular schedule of 7 days a week with a long turn of 18 or 24 hours at the change of shift.

74 The Limits of Welfare

In the 1880's, many American steelworkers belonged to unions. By 1892, members of the Amalgamated Association of Iron and Steel Workers held approximately half the jobs in the industry. The Amalgamated bargained with employers about wages and rules of employment and work.

An ultimatum is a final demand which if rejected will end negotiations and result in some direct action, usually force.

In 1892, at the Homestead mills just outside of Pittsburgh, the Carnegie Corporation gave the union an ultimatum—accept the company wage offer or be totally excluded from the mills. The union refused to accept terms that made negotiations with the company impossible. It called a strike and occupied the plant to support its claim that workers had "property" rights in their jobs, which they believed could not be taken away without compensation.

The company denied this claim. "The question at issue is a very grave one," one of Carnegie's associates argued. "It is whether the Carnegie Company or the Amalgamated Association shall have absolute control of our plant." The strike collapsed after five months, and in the decade following the Homestead Strike, Carnegie and other companies vigorously asserted the right to "absolute" control of their "property." One of Andrew Carnegie's partners briefly described the reasoning for their policy, "The Amalgamated placed a tax on improvements, therefore the Amalgamated had to go."

In order to be successful, however, such a policy could not be confined to the organization of the industrial plant itself. In 1892, the union was a power in the local community of Homestead as well as in the mills. The police and a large part of the clergy sympathized with the workers. Businessmen extended credit to the striking workmen, and the local newspapers reported favorably on the workers' activities. In order to gain control of its plants, the company had to revolutionize community life.

The new forms of work, employer-employee relations, and community life in industrial society disturbed social critics in the decades surrounding the turn of the century. While many critics released emotional blasts at what they thought were unwelcome aspects of the new society, others realized that a thorough knowledge of that complex society was required in order to change it. Reading 74 comes from a volume in *The Pittsburgh Survey,* one comprehensive attempt to analyze the way in which the transformation of work and employer-employee relations affected community life. As you read, try to answer these questions:

1. What sorts of communities were the companies, notably United States Steel, trying to establish? What benefits did they offer through their extensive welfare work?
2. What were the limitations of the company's notion of community change? of employer-employee relations?
3. Why did the workers agree to company policies? What real alternatives did they have?
4. What were the values of the author of the survey? How would you evaluate his methods for collecting information?

Life in Steelworkers' Communities

Shortly after 1900, a group of Pittsburgh charitable organizations realized that to work effectively they had to know more about their own communities. With the support of the Russell

John A. Fitch, **The Steel Workers.** New York: Charities Publication Committee, 1910, pp. 192–94, 196, 198–204, 207, 210, 212–14, 216, 219. Language simplified and modernized.

Sage Foundation of New York, they commissioned an intensive investigation of the life of industrial workers in Pittsburgh and its suburbs. Portions of the findings follow.

Paternalistic means that persons in authority treat those under them in a fatherly way by regulating their conduct and supplying their needs.

Entirely apart from unionism or non-unionism are certain arrangements which may be termed employees' benefit policies. A paternalistic spirit appeared early in the history of the Carnegie Steel Company. The arrangement has become general in the Carnegie mills of delivering coal to employees at cost. A more considerable plan has been that of loaning money to employees for the purpose of building homes. It is an advantage to a mill-town employer to have property-owning employees. The labor force is more stable and there is less likelihood of a strike. The employees do not wish to jeopardize their positions after a house has been acquired, lest they have to move.

In Homestead and Munhall, where the Carnegie Company owns a number of houses, it has proved itself a good landlord in comparison with some of the small owners of rented properties in these boroughs. The company rents these houses at a figure 30 to 40 percent below that charged by other landlords.

Hazards of industry refers to accident compensation which involves payment for injuries received on the job.

This year [1910] the United States Steel Corporation has announced two important developments in the way of a relief plan and a pension system. As long as a man remains an employee, the company will help protect his family against the hazards of industry and will make some provision toward his old age. A man will think twice before giving up a job with a pension attachment for something immediately better. He will be reluctant, especially as he gets along in service, to risk discharge; he will not join a union, offhand at least, if joining means discharge. United States Steel Corporation is pushing forward a positive, constructive policy of safeguarding machinery and reducing the possibilities of accidents as far as possible.

These plans illustrate the administrative and, to a degree, the human advantages which have come with consolidating the ownership of steel industry. In the first place, as illustrated by the safety work, inventions and adaptations instituted in one plant may at once be introduced in many. An expert staff can be set at the exact study of difficult problems with all of the corporation's mills as their laboratory. Standards once adopted, whether of safety inspection, accident compensation, or surgical service, may be enforced by executive act so as to affect 200,000 men instead of waiting for such programs to be introduced by a hundred independent managers. Again, the private owners of the 1890's faced a wracking competition, but profits went wholly into their own pockets. The directors and executive officials of the Steel

Corporation bear a different relation to the year's profits. Their personal incomes are not affected by starting a relief fund, for example.

A director of a corporation is usually a large stockholder and receives a fee for attending Board of Directors' meetings. Officials of the company who carry out the day-to-day business are salaried. Therefore, their annual salaries would not be affected by setting up a relief fund, nor would any one stockholder's earnings. Individual owners of companies do receive the profits that are not reinvested. If a relief fund were set up, profits would be lower.

As already indicated, the break with unionism had no direct bearing on the policies which have thus far been cited. Some of them were initiated by the employers during the time of greatest union strength. But there are other conditions which have come into being that would certainly have been opposed if the men had retained their collective power.

One of these is that internal organization of the industry which, in eliminating waste of all kinds and introducing mechanical changes, has also put the entire control of the mills back into the hands of foremen and superintendents. In this way the labor force is coordinated so as to make it most easy to control and most difficult to unionize. Another is the wage policy, which, while advancing the wages of common labor, has brought down the earnings of men of highest skill. Cuts in pay have accompanied increased output. The whole wage movement, unprodded by union demands, lags behind the rise in prices of family necessities.

Steelworkers were paid according to the amount of steel they produced rather than according to a set hourly rate. Such a method is known as piece work.

With the employers no longer penalized by having to pay extra for overtime, the day's, the week's, and the year's work has been lengthened. Now the twelve-hour day is the working schedule for the majority. At least 20 percent of all employees work seven days a week, and the twenty-four hour shift comes once every two weeks for large numbers of workers.

Steelworkers worked days for two weeks and then nights for two weeks. They worked without interruption for twenty-four hours when they moved from the day to the night shift and had twenty-four hours free two weeks later.

Added to these adverse conditions is the speeding up system. "Pushers" drive the common laborers, and cash rewards go to foremen and superintendents for helping to keep up the tension. Finally, cuts from time to time in the rate of pay per ton of steel produced make the men put forth the last ounce of energy to prevent a wage loss. All these, together with the heat and the danger of accident, result in overstrain and mental and physical exhaustion.

Let us look at the situation as it is reflected in the everyday life of the men. The immediate effect of such a working schedule is on the home. Many a steelworker has said to me with grim bitterness, "Home is just the place where I eat and sleep. I live in the mills." The steelworkers are united in saying that "on the night shift you can't do anything but work, eat, and sleep anyhow." So home pleasures and social pleasures alike are entirely lacking during a full half of the time. Whatever opportunity for enjoyment of the home there may be, must come in the alternate weeks on day shift.

The wife of the steelworker, too, has a hard day, and even a longer one than her husband's. To prepare a breakfast by six in the morning she must rise not later than half past five. The family cannot sit down at the supper table until seven or later, and after that the dishes must be washed. There is little time for husband and wife to have each other's company. It is only by an extra exertion that they can spend an evening out together, and the evening at home is robbed of much of its charm by the projection of the domestic duties beyond the time that would be required if the meal were served earlier. The father, too, has little time with his children. If they are quite small, he may go for weeks without seeing them except in their cribs.

Andrew Carnegie believed that millionaires should administer their surplus wealth for the benefit of the public. Before his death, Carnegie had given away over $350 million to set up libraries, schools, colleges, research institutes, and foundations for the advancement of peace.

Not only is home life threatened, but other healthy influences in the mill towns feel the blighting effect of the twelve-hour day. Opportunity for mental culture would seem to be ample in the mill towns. Each has its Carnegie Library. Each has its auditorium and music hall with a fine pipe organ, where lectures and concerts of high grade are held. But the steelworkers seldom make use of these privileges. The trouble is the same as that which has already spoiled half of the home life. There is not enough energy left at the end of a twelve-hour day to enable the average man to read anything of a very serious nature, and the reading done by even the most intelligent does not extend much beyond the limits of the daily paper. As for lectures and concerts—to attend them would necessitate a change of clothing and a preparation for which a weary twelve-hour man has little heart. The difficulties that must be met before these cultural opportunities can be enjoyed are usually too great to be overcome.

It now becomes necessary to discuss the reasons for the apparent acquiescence [agreement] of the steelworkers in existing conditions. The obvious obstacle to collective action on their part is the fact that they are non-union. But that merely suggests the question: Why don't they organize? To understand the absence of united action and resistance to the policies of the companies one must understand the obstacles that stand in the way.

Corporations offer different kinds of stock to people who buy shares in the company. Preferred stockholders receive a set dividend (income from stock) every year, and they are paid before common stockholders if the company goes bankrupt or is dissolved, but they cannot vote at stockholders' meetings. Common stockholders receive dividends based on the corporation's profits.

In the first place, there is the so-called profit-sharing system of the United States Steel Corporation. Beginning in 1903, the corporation has set aside shares of preferred stock. Each employee can subscribe to as many shares as he wishes within limits depending upon his annual salary.

There can be no doubt of the value to the employees of the stock-issue plan as a business proposition. An average net return on an investment of 17 to 25 percent per year, for the first five years, and after that 7 percent, is not bad.

The stock-issue system, however, brings those employees who invest in stock more surely under the domination of the Corporation. The bonus paid each year for five years is to go to those who have shown "a proper interest in the welfare and progress" of the corporation and the extra dividends at the end of the five-year period are awarded to those whom the corporation finds "deserving thereof." There is nothing to prevent an employee of the corporation purchasing stock on the same basis as the outsider, but in that case he will receive only ordinary dividends. The extraordinary return received by the holder of employees' stock is based on his acquiescence as an employee.

A bonus is a sum of money or some other form of compensation which an employer gives an employee in addition to regular wages.

But the positive influence of these systems of rewards, which binds the working force to the company, is supplemented by the negative influence, far more sinister, of a system of espionage.

I doubt whether you could find a more suspicious body of men than the employees of the United States Steel Corporation. They are suspicious of one another, of their neighbors, and of their friends. I was repeatedly suspected of being an agent of the corporation, sent out to sound out the men's attitudes toward the corporation and toward unionism. The fact is, the steelworkers do not dare openly express their convictions. They do not dare assemble and talk over affairs pertaining to their welfare as mill men. They feel that they are living always in the presence of a hostile critic. They are a generous, open-hearted set of men, upon the whole; the skilled men are intelligent and are able and glad to talk upon a variety of subjects. But let the conversation be shifted to the steel works, and they immediately become silent. It is safe to talk with a stranger about the price of groceries, or the prospect of war with Japan, but not about the steel industry.

This self-repression, this evident fear of a free expression of personality, shows itself in other ways besides a hesitancy to talk with strangers. The men do not talk much with each other about mill conditions. There is little discussion of politics—that, too, could easily bring a man into dangerous waters.

All of the steel companies have effective methods of learning what is going on among the workmen. The Jones and Laughlin Company has some organization that keeps it sufficiently informed as to the likelihood of disorder breaking out. The United States Steel Corporation has regular secret-service departments. Its agents are thought by the men to be scattered through all of the mills of the corporation, working shoulder to shoulder at the rolls or furnaces with honest workmen, ready to record any "disloyal" utterances or to enter into any movement among their fellows. The workmen feel this espionage. They believe it exists, but they do not know who the traitors are. It may be that the friend of long standing who works at the next furnace is one of them, or, possibly, the next-door neighbor at home; they do not know. Is it any wonder, therefore, that they suspect each other and guard their tongues?

75 Strike!

In 1917, the United States entered World War I. President Woodrow Wilson told the American people that they were involved in a great international struggle to preserve democracy. American steelworkers expected to benefit from this struggle. They hoped at war's end to find a new democratic atmosphere in their communities. Although workers had derived many benefits from company welfare policies before the war, they had been denied participation in all company and many community decisions. Wilson's words seemed to signal a new day. They demanded a hearing.

On September 22, 1919, nearly a year after the war had ended, the steelworkers struck. Although the steel strike of 1919 was a complex affair, the real issue focused on the workers' demand that the steel companies deal with them collectively. The officers of the companies agreed to talk to any individual worker who wanted to complain about his wages or his conditions of work. The workers insisted, however, that the companies must deal with them through a few leaders chosen by the workers to discuss terms for them all. This is what "collective bargaining" meant.

In 1881, at a meeting in Pittsburgh, Samuel Gompers organized several craft unions into the Federation of Organized Trades and Labor Unions of the United States and Canada. In 1886, the Federation called a conference, formed the American Federation of Labor and broke all ties with the Knights of Labor, urging all skilled workers to do the same. By 1890, the A. F. of L. numbered 550,000 members

The American Federation of Labor, an alliance of established trade unions, aided the steelworkers in their struggle. Despite this assistance, the strike required strenuous efforts and sacrifices from the steelworkers themselves. In many ways, they had to readjust their own picture of themselves. Unskilled immigrant workers and skilled, often native-born, workers had to cooperate. They had to recognize that industrial changes had put them in "the same ditch."

The steel companies also faced a readjustment. To accept collective bargaining meant accepting a powerful, rival voice in the process of deciding the wages they would pay and in determining the organization of work and community life. The companies resisted this adjustment. With the help of the federal, state, and local governments, the press, and many of the churches, the companies finally defeated the workers' efforts to unionize the industry.

After the strike, a group of Protestant clergymen investigated the causes of the strike and the reasons for its failure. Reading 75 is from their report. As you read, try to answer these questions:

1. In what ways was the steel strike more than just a labor-management dispute?
2. Why do you think the companies fastened on the charge that Communists were behind the strike?
3. What means were used to break the strike? What do you think the ultimate effects of such methods would be for the companies?
4. What policies might have been better for management?

The Immigrant Asserts Himself

The Interchurch World Movement represented several Protestant denominations working together to help solve the social problems of industrial society. During the strike, the leaders of the movement worked to arrive at a peaceful solution. After it was over, they investigated the strike. This portion of their report analyzes some of the sources of strikers' discontent.

The Commission of Inquiry of the Interchurch World Movement, **Public Opinion and the Steel Strike.** New York: Harcourt, Brace & World, Inc., 1921, pp. 239–41. Abridged. Reprinted by permission of Harcourt, Brace & World, Inc.

The determination of the immigrant worker to assert himself . . . was the chief reason why the foreign and the English press, and especially the "American" [native-born] elements of society, considered the strike as having deeper motives than mere demands of ordinary trade unionism. Not only the mill managers, but all the governing classes in steel towns were accustomed to seeing the immigrant docile [manageable] and submissive; to them any strike was indeed a revolution. Formerly the immigrant obeyed orders without questioning. He did the unpleasant work, the heavy and exhausting work, and never asked the reason why.

He had submitted for years to militaristic mill discipline. In the community he had acted in the same way. He had lived his life away from the others, at first purposely keeping out of their way. Then as he became "Americanized," he began in recent years to assert himself as a member of the community. As one "American" minister explained it, "The foreigner wants too much; he owns the largest churches in the community, is buying up the property, and is now even running his own candidates for political office."

Most important, the immigrant in the steel mills had tasted better conditions during the war. He had had an opportunity to earn more by working on the better-paying jobs, for the first time he had been treated considerately by the foreman, etc. In the community, he had also been looked upon differently, that is either as an "American" or as a worthy ally. At "home," his fellow countrymen were becoming free citizens in nations rid of autocrats.

An autocrat is a ruler with absolute or unlimited power.

The immigrant worker took these new developments seriously and was very much disillusioned after the signing of the armistice when the employers and the dominant elements in the community took the attitude that, now the war was over, it was time to return to all the old conditions. The immigrant was again a "hunkie." This was the last straw. Thereafter he waited for anybody to lead him into the promised land. . . .

"Hunkie" was a derogatory term applied to unskilled workmen of foreign birth, especially those from Hungary.

It was because the immigrant's deepest emotions and instincts were stirred that this huge and unprecedented strike was possible. The immigrant wanted not only better wages and shorter hours. He resented being treated as a chattel [possession] or a "hunkie."

Not Unionism, but Americanism

One portion of the clergymen's report contained an interview between Bishop J. McConnell and Dr. Daniel A. Poling, who represented the Interchurch World Movement and Judge Elbert H. Gary, Chairman of the Executive Committee of the United States Steel Corporation. Selections from that interview follow.

Public Opinion and the Steel Strike, pp. 336–38.

Mr. Gary insisted that the point at issue was not now unionism as such, but whether the American government should be supported and American institutions upheld. He insisted that the whole movement of the steel strike was a movement of red radicals [Communists]. He repeatedly avowed his belief that the only outcome of a victory for unionism would be Sovietism in the United States "and forcible distribution of property." "And, therefore," he said, "my positive word is a declination [refusal] to arbitrate."

Sovietism refers to the system of government in the Union of Soviet Socialist Republics.

The Chairman then said, "Judge Gary, you are on record in your own testimony as being in favor of collective bargaining. Would you look with favor upon an organization in your shops in which the workers should choose their own representatives to state any grievances to the authorities that they might have?"

Judge Gary replied that he was heartily in favor of such an organization, "provided it be the right kind of organization."

The Chairman then called attention to the fact that the testimony gathered by our investigators and by the members of the Commission themselves showed that, while Mr. Gary's statement might favor collective bargaining, as a matter of fact the men could not get their grievances beyond the foremen.

Mr. Gary then rather closely cross-questioned the Chairman and Mr. Poling on the type of men whom the Commission had interviewed, insisting that it could only have been men to whom we were directed by red radicals.

The Chairman then asked Judge Gary this question: "Supposing all the men have gone back and the strike has failed in the sense that the men have returned to work with a consciousness of failure, with the feeling that they have been beaten, what kind of a situation is produced by the presence of men in such a temper in the mills?"

Mr. Gary replied that this statement was not adequate to the real situation, that the men were contented and had been intimidated [frightened] into going out. . . . [A]s soon as adequate police force and United States soldiers arrived on the scene they voluntarily returned and they returned all the more willingly because Mr. Gary himself had stated to his officials that the strike was not voluntary and that they must see that the families even of the strikers suffered no lack of food or other necessities while they were out. Mr. Gary stated positively, "We fed the families of strikers."

Mr. Gary insisted that the issue was not unionism but fundamental devotion to American institutions. He spoke quite strongly that "there had been red organizations in Pittsburgh known to the officers of the government which the government had not broken up."

Mr. Gary said that of course this Commission could make any public statement that it pleased, but he warned us "to bear in mind that the very foundations of the American government were involved in the matter."

Breaking the Strike

This selection, also from the Interchurch World Movement, describes the companies' strike-breaking efforts.

The Commission of Inquiry of the Interchurch World Movement, **Report on the Steel Strike of 1919.** New York: Harcourt, Brace & World, Inc., 1920, pp. 238–44. Abridged. Reprinted by permission of Harcourt, Brace & World, Inc.

Great numbers of workers came to believe—

that local mayors, magistrates and police officials try to break strikes;

that state and Federal officials, particularly the Federal Department of Justice, help to break strikes, and that armed forces are used for this purpose;

that most newspapers actively and promptly exert a strike-breaking influence; most churches passively.

The steel strike made tens of thousands of citizens believe that our American institutions are not democratic or not democratically administered.

The basis of such beliefs will be hastily summarized here.

Local magistrates, police authorities, etc., around Pittsburgh were very frequently steel mill officials or relati[ves] of mill officials.

When a striker was taken before mill-official public-officials he was likely to suspect connections between his fate and the steel company's desires. In many other cases officials of mills only, personally, gave the orders for arrests, and the decisions as to whether the arrested should be jailed or not, generally after learning whether the striker would return to work or not.

The charges on which strikers were arraigned before local magistrates, then imprisoned or fined, were often never recorded and never learned by the prisoners.

Arraigned means that a person has been called before a court to answer a charge or an accusation.

Arrested men were frequently taken, not to jail, but inside the steel mill and held there. The charges of beatings, [and] clubbings, often substantiated by doctors' and eye-witnesses' affidavits [sworn statements], were endless and monotonous; in most communities the only public official to appeal to turned out to be a mill official.

Federal officials' active intervention concerned chiefly (1) the Department of Justice, and (2) the U. S. Army. Both cases contributed to steelworkers' beliefs about strike-breaking activities.

The principal use of armed forces outside of Pennsylvania was at Gary, Indiana, occupied first by the state militia, then by the U. S. Army under General Leonard Wood.

Picketing is the practice strikers use of stationing union members, who usually carry signs, around a struck firm to persuade workers or shoppers not to enter the building during a strike.

General Wood declared that "the army would be neutral." He established rules in regard to picketing. These rules were so interpreted and carried out as to result in breaking up the picket line. The picket line thus dwindled, and its disappearance signaled to the Gary workers that the strike was breaking. Army officers sent soldiers to arrest union officers in other trades, for example, for threatening to call a strike on a local building operation. Workers throughout the city believed that the federal government opposed them and that the [army] regulars would stay as long as the steelworkers remained on strike. The army was not withdrawn until the strike was declared off.

The feeling of the steelworkers, then, might be summed up thus: that local and national government not only was not their government (*i.e.*, in their behalf) but was government in behalf of interests opposing theirs; that in strike times government activities tended to break strikes.

Finally the press in most communities, and particularly in Pittsburgh, led the workers there to the belief that the press lends itself instantly and persistently to strike breaking. They believed that the press immediately took sides, printed only the news favoring that side, suppressed or colored its records, printed advertisements and editorials urging the strikers to go back, denounced the strikers and incessantly misrepresented the facts. All this was found to be true in the case of the Pittsburgh papers. Foreign-language papers largely followed the lead of the English papers. The average American-born discriminating citizen of Pittsburgh could not have obtained from his papers sufficient information to get a true conception of the strike; basic information was not in those papers.

Discriminating has several meanings. In this case it means "able to make careful distinctions based on good judgment."

To sum up the social consequences of a non-union labor policy, especially that of the Steel Corporation, is plainly difficult; the manifestations were so wide and so various. The beaten steelworker displayed little interest in governmental institutions; instead he had acquired a rather active distrust of them. While many of the "foreigners" began piling up money to get themselves out of America, the great majority began waiting for "the next strike." That was the only resource thoughtfully provided for them among the democratic American institutions.

sonality. Size also brought new problems involved in controlling production since no one man could supervise the work of 4000.

There were few trained managers. Before the Civil War, only the Rensselaer Polytechnic Institute, founded in 1824, concentrated on training men for industry. Massachusetts Institute of Technology, which opened in 1865, trained many scientists and placed secondary emphasis upon engineers. Soon additional colleges and universities entered the field. During the late nineteenth century, however, most managers were trained on the job.

In order to organize a large plant, these managers gave substantial amounts of power to foremen. The foreman was often almost a sub-contractor working within a plant. Management gave him raw materials and cash and made him responsible for hiring and firing workers and controlling production. Often he became a petty tyrant. But as the production process became more complicated, managers deprived foremen of powers like these in order to coordinate production.

A contractor is one who agrees to supply materials on a large scale or to perform certain tasks for a fee. A sub-contractor is a third party who agrees to carry out the provisions of all or a part of the original contract for a set fee.

Increasingly after 1900, professional managers ran American industry. They were hired by stockholders to produce goods and make a profit. This development tended to democratize American business since men who did well in business or engineering school were often men without family connections in business.

As enterprises grew larger, managers subdivided the work process into smaller and smaller steps. Sometimes, subdivision got out of hand. Goods stockpiled in one part of a factory were needed in another. Parts arrived at the assembly line too late or too early, slowing production or even bringing it to a halt. Forced to perform one monotonous task for long hours, workers rebelled. They eith struck or refused to work at the pace supervisors demanded.

Techniques employed by trained managers often increas worker dissatisfaction. In the twentieth century, a school of scientific management grew up led by men who went to great lengths to improve efficiency. They hired men to make time-and-motion studies of each step in the process of production. A man with a stop watch timed every move that a worker made and established norms for production. Often he would recommend that a certain step in the production process should be further subdivided in order to increase efficiency. He might also suggest that workers who could not meet the norms he established should be fired. Naturally, many workers resented the impersonal atmosphere—and the human tragedy—which sometimes resulted.

Frederick W. Taylor is credited with the idea of scientific management as well as "time-and-motion" studies.

In order to counter worker resentment and to undercut the growing power of unions, many managers turned periodically to welfare capitalism. They offered a number of welfare programs such as those described in Reading 74 to their workers. Some owners even formed company unions dominated by men sympathetic to management in order to give their men a feeling that they had a real share in making important decisions. But workers demanded a genuine voice in their own destiny. An independent union free from management influence provided one way to get such a voice.

Why Unions Were Small

The labor movement grew slowly between 1870 and 1930 as the following table indicates.

U.S. Bureau of the Census, **Historical Statistics of the United States, Colonial Times to 1957.** Washington, D.C.: Government Printing Office, 1960, pp. 72, 98.

TABLE 1. Union Membership, 1870–1930

Year	Average annual union membership	Number of workers, 10 years and over, excluding agricultural workers	Union membership as a percentage of the total number of workers outside agriculture
1870	300,000*	6,075,000	4.9%
1880	200,000*	8,807,000	2.3%
1890	372,000*	13,380,000	2.7%
1900	868,000	18,161,000	4.8%
1910	2,140,000	25,779,000	8.3%
1920	5,048,000	30,985,000	16.3%
1930	3,393,000	38,358,000	8.8%

* *Figures for 1870, 1880, and 1890 are estimates.*

Repression by the government was largely responsible for low union membership. Both state and national laws had long been hostile to labor unions. Early in the nineteenth century, the courts frequently treated unions as if they were criminal conspiracies organized to raise wages "unnaturally." The courts often held unions responsible for harm to the property of their employers during strikes, for encouraging employees to break contracts, or for encouraging consumers to boycott the products of anti-union employers. Judges frequently issued injunctions that forbade strikes or boycotts. Police, militia, and the regular army enforced these court orders. Not until the famous case of *Commonwealth* vs. *Hunt* (1842) was the legality of unions assured.

An injunction is a court order issued by a judge without a jury trial requiring that a certain party refrain from taking a certain action.

The most famous case combining the use of the injunction and armed force occurred in the Chicago area in 1894. A strike of men who built Pullman cars for railroads spread to the railway workers themselves. The federal government intervened to ask for an injunction forbidding strikers to interfere with the movement of the mails. A federal court responded with a general prohibition against strike activity. The order restrained any persons from:

George Pullman was the first person to build a railroad sleeping car. He also developed the idea of dining and parlor cars to make rail travel more comfortable.

> . . . interfering with, hindering, obstructing, or stopping any mail train, express train or other trains, whether freight or passenger, engaged in interstate commerce . . . and from in

any manner interfering with, injuring, or destroying any of the property of any of said railroads engaged in or for the purpose of, or in connection with, interstate commerce, or the carriage of the mails of the United States.

The union refused to obey the order. Over the protests of John Altgeld, the Governor of Illinois, federal troops intervened and forcibly crushed the strike. The strike leader, Eugene Victor Debs, and his associates, were sentenced to six months in prison.

During World War I, unions grew rapidly. President Theodore Roosevelt had established a precedent for dealing fairly with unions when he intervened on the side of labor in the 1902 anthracite coal strike. President Wilson had created a Department of Labor with a secretary of cabinet rank in 1913. The Clayton Antitrust Act, passed in 1914, seemed to exempt labor from antitrust action; legalized strikes, peaceful picketing, and boycotts; and forbade use of injunctions in labor disputes "unless to prevent irreparable injury." But the war emergency, rather than a friendly voice within the administration, contributed most to labor's cause. During and immediately after the war years, union membership doubled. President Wilson set up administrative boards to regulate relations between capital and labor and to fix wages in key industries without risking strikes or lockouts. With government showing a friendly attitude and industry unable to discriminate against workers who joined unions, union membership rose rapidly.

The courts frequently used the "irreparable injury" clause to grant injunctions against labor unions. Thus, the Clayton Act was not much benefit to labor.

A lockout is the closing of a company by the employer until the union or the workers accept management's terms.

The steel strike of 1919, which you studied in Reading 75, brought to a dramatic close this period when unions succeeded relatively well. Companies fought unions, and the gains of the war years faded quickly. Government reverted to its customary role. Courts issued injunctions against unions and declared that laws to prohibit child labor or set minimum wages for women were unconstitutional. Simultaneously many corporations established company unions and increased their welfare activities while discharging free union workers. The history of the labor movement from 1914 through 1930 supports the conclusion that the attitude of government played the major role in determining whether or not unions would enroll a large number of workers. The history of the labor movement in the 1930's was soon to confirm this.

In 1905, the Supreme Court in **Lochner** vs. **New York,** declared unconstitutional a New York law fixing a 10-hour maximum working day for bakers. The Court argued that such legislation deprived the proprietors of their property without due process of law and violated the right of contract between employer and employee. When an employee accepted employment, he was, according to the Court, making a contract with his employer.

The Labor Movement

Faced by hostile laws and hostile courts, union workers of the late nineteenth and early twentieth centuries wrestled with two important decisions:

1. What is the appropriate scale of union activity? Should unions focus their activity on the individual plant, trade, or industry, or

should they concentrate on organizing large masses of people to influence city, county, state, or national politics?

2. What should be the range of union interests? Should unions concern themselves with bread-and-butter issues on the job, such as wages and working conditions, or should they focus on the broadest issues of social organization and reform?

The history of the union movement can be viewed as an interaction among men with different answers to these questions.

There were three important lines of response. The first was characteristic of an organization called the Noble and Holy Order of the Knights of Labor, founded by Uriah Stephens, which began to recruit members in 1869. The Knights tried to appeal to "all who toiled." It concentrated, however, on local assemblies composed primarily of already organized skilled workers and semiskilled workers with little previous union experience. The initial position of the Knights followed the tradition of the urban reform movements of the 1830's and 1840's. Strikes were discouraged, while long platform statements marshalled support for a host of political measures: paper money, the eight-hour day, a national income tax, the abolition of child labor, prohibition, cooperatives, and so on. In the mid 1880's the Knights prospered, rising to 700,000 members in 1886, and struck more frequently. The national leadership, dominated by Terence V. Powderly, remained convinced, however, that only minor advantages could be obtained directly by wresting concessions from individual employers. "Toiling men" (which excluded lawyers, bankers, brokers, gamblers, and liquor dealers) must reshape their local communities and the national government, Powderly argued. To reach these goals, he supported political activity and the development of cooperatives.

The Knights collapsed after the Haymarket Affair. At a labor demonstration in Haymarket Square, Chicago, in May 1886, a bomb thrown into the crowd killed seven persons. The public hysteria against labor militants which followed was in many places directed against the Knights. By 1890, they had barely 100,000 members.

Eight men were arrested. Seven men were sentenced to death; the eighth was given a 15-year sentence. Four were hanged, one committed suicide, and the other three were pardoned by Governor Altgeld in 1893. The actual bomb thrower was never identified.

The Haymarket Affair was probably not quite so important to the collapse of the Knights as it seemed at the time to have been. The Knights of Labor attempted an enormous task of organizing all workers—skilled and unskilled—with a limited amount of money, inexperienced leaders, and a program that tried to accomplish too much at once. The Knights' goal of making "every man his own master, every man his own employer" was inconsistent with the developing scale of enterprise in the American economy which was moving toward larger and larger plants owned by corporations and not by the workers themselves. Even without the hostility aroused by Haymarket, the Knights would probably have collapsed.

The second response to the question of appropriate scale and range of interests came from a varied group of men working in the socialist tradition. Today when a great many measures advocated by socialists at the beginning of the twentieth century have become accepted public policy, few Americans describe themselves as socialists. In 1900, however, substantial groups of native Americans and immigrants proudly wore the socialist label. They urged a wide range of programs: public ownership of the means of production, regulation of industry, redistribution of wealth through an income tax, and many similar proposals. In addition to workers, the ranks of the socialists included intellectuals, many farmers, particularly in the corn and wheat belts, and middle-class people who felt that a competitive, free-enterprise economy which pitted man against man was immoral.

In 1912, the Socialist Party offered Eugene Debs as its candidate for President. He received 897,000 votes, 6 percent of those cast. But as the Democratic and Republican parties took over planks from the Socialist platform, the appeal of the third party diminished. Attacks on the Socialist Party during World War I, when Eugene Debs and other leaders were jailed for opposing the war, helped to undermine its appeal. After the election of 1920, when Debs ran for President from a cell in an Atlanta prison and received almost a million votes, the party's vote-getting ability faded steadily.

These planks included demands for a graduated income tax, government regulation of the railroads, and government protection of the consumer.

The most important union in the socialist tradition was the Industrial Workers of the World, popularly known as the "Wobblies." The IWW had its principal base among migratory workers in lumber, mining, and agriculture. Cut off from their families and often unable to vote, these men worked long hours at dangerous jobs for low pay. They became convinced that they would have to win complete control of industry through worker ownership in order to make fundamental improvements in their working lives. They became revolutionaries advocating forcible overthrow of the government and sabotage. When conditions became desperate in industries such as textiles, the IWW often led dramatic strikes largely of unskilled immigrants. The immigrants, alarmed at talk of revolution, usually did not become permanent IWW members. The IWW collapsed during World War I when government repression deprived it of its leaders and relative prosperity turned the minds of workers away from thoughts of radical change.

The third response to the questions of scale and range has had a permanent life. In several steps during the 1880's, the existing unions of skilled workers, many of which had been organized since the Civil War, joined together in a national federation which came in 1886 to be called the American Federation of Labor. In that same year, Samuel Gompers, a leader of the International Cigar Makers Union, was elected president. Except for one year when he fell before a socialist revolt, Gompers remained president until his death in 1924.

The A.F. of L. was a loose alliance composed primarily of craft unions. A craft union enrolled only men who worked at an individual trade. Plumbers joined one union, carpenters a second, and bricklayers a third, for example, despite the fact that all three groups as well as members of many additional unions, worked on the same building. Each union went its own way to work for the welfare of its members. Gompers believed in "bread-and-butter" unionism. He thought that labor should work primarily for higher wages, shorter hours, and better working conditions. Instead of aligning labor with a particular political party, he believed that workers should reward friendly legislators of all parties with votes and punish the enemies of labor, no matter what their party affiliation, by working against them. He staunchly opposed talk of revolution or the use of violence. Most of the A.F. of L. unions were composed of skilled workers who could wrest concessions from their employers because they had bargaining power; that is, they had the power to stop production in an industry because it could not run without the skills of union members.

Each of the individual unions—the plumbers, machinists, or stonecutters, for example—which were federated in the A.F. of L. concentrated on the welfare of its own members. These unions did not press for a great class alliance of all working men. They operated on a small scale and focused on a narrow range of issues. And they were successful. As a result, most of the men who belonged to A.F. of L. unions made wages far above the national average. The workers in the railroad brotherhoods, whose unions did not join the A.F. of L., were similar in their characteristics to A.F. of L. members. Unskilled workers called the A.F. of L. the aristocracy of labor. Radicals called its leaders labor fakers. The great mass of unskilled and semiskilled workers in mass production industries such as steel, automobiles, rubber, and textiles remained outside union ranks despite occasional valiant attempts, such as the 1919 steel strike, to organize them.

The railroad brotherhoods which include the conductors, brakemen, clerks, carmen, and firemen were organized in the 1860's and 1870's. Today, most brotherhoods belong to the A.F. of L.-C.I.O.

The unions in the A.F. of L. grew up in the decades after the Civil War when skilled workers dominated production processes in small factories. The way in which the A.F. of L. answered the questions of scale and size made sense for the 1870's and 1880's. But American industries grew rapidly. Both vertical and horizontal integration led to giant corporations valued at hundreds of millions of dollars. Huge plants employing thousands of workers subdivided the productive process and undermined the positions of skilled workers. Focusing on the wages, hours, and working conditions of these skilled men through craft unions which did not enroll the unskilled provided no answer to the needs of men and women in mass production industries. Until government changed its attitude and supported the rights of unskilled workers to join unions without reprisals from their employers, the history of the 1919 steel strike would be repeated over and over again.

A federation of industrial unions, the Committee for Industrial Organization (C.I.O.), was formed in 1935.

SUGGESTED READINGS

BRODY, DAVID, *Labor in Crisis, the Steel Strike of 1919.* Brody's book further details the story described in the readings.

DAVID, HENRY, *History of the Haymarket Affair.* An authoritative account of this famous incident, this volume is also good on its social and intellectual context.

PELLING, HOWARD, *American Labor.* This useful survey identifies the history of "labor," with that of "labor unions."

CHAPTER 20

Wild West and Wild Cities

STATING THE ISSUE

During the late nineteenth century, the United States expanded on two frontiers. Cattlemen, farmers, lumbermen, and miners opened one frontier on the vast stretch of land west of Kansas and Nebraska. American and European ex-farmers with a few European city dwellers opened the other on the streets of the nation's rapidly growing cities. On the surface, the western and the urban frontiers seem different. Yet their problems had much in common.

Settlers on both frontiers had to make new rules for owning and controlling land, for example. In medieval Europe, land ownership had involved an elaborate network of social privileges and responsibilities. Over the centuries that followed, the concept of property had become restricted to mean primarily the owner's right to use a piece of real estate freely. In every new situation, however, the rights and privileges of owners had to be redefined as new questions arose. In the West, did ownership of land imply a right of access to water, a right to build a fence across a cattle trail, or a right to cultivate soil freely, even if cultivation led to erosion? In the new cities, could a property owner do anything he wanted to on his land—slaughter animals, throw clouds of smoke and soot into the air, crowd tenants into a room, dump sewage in his yard?

A second important question the men and women of both frontiers confronted involved maintaining law and order in their societies. In the new West, for example, who would stand for law and order in an area where everyone was a stranger and where settlements were too sparse to support elaborate law enforcement and judicial systems? In the cities, rapid growth and crowding strained the traditional patterns and insitutions of justice even more severely. Chicago was probably a more dangerous place in the late nineteenth century than Cheyenne or Dodge City.

Chapter 20 examines the responses of western and urban frontiersmen to these and other problems in two seemingly different worlds. How did the problems of the wild West differ from those of the wild cities? In what ways were they similar? How did men respond to the new challenges of the West and of the cities? Was there any pattern to their responses? These are the major issues raised in Chapter 20.

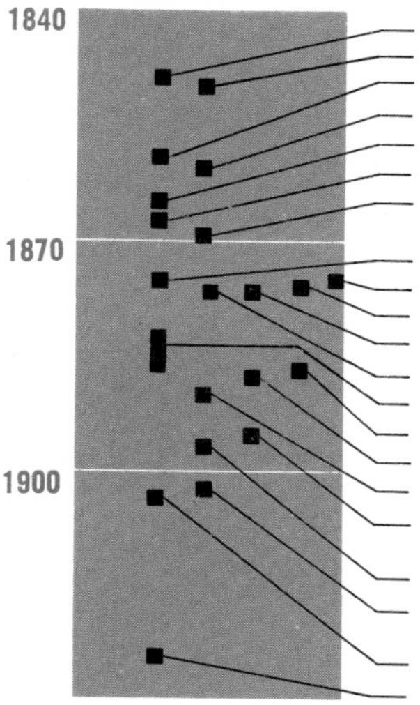

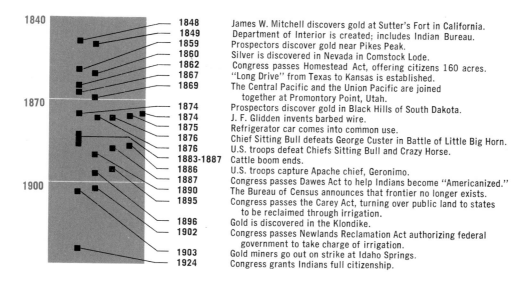

1848	James W. Mitchell discovers gold at Sutter's Fort in California.
1849	Department of Interior is created; includes Indian Bureau.
1859	Prospectors discover gold near Pikes Peak.
1860	Silver is discovered in Nevada in Comstock Lode.
1862	Congress passes Homestead Act, offering citizens 160 acres.
1867	"Long Drive" from Texas to Kansas is established.
1869	The Central Pacific and the Union Pacific are joined together at Promontory Point, Utah.
1874	Prospectors discover gold in Black Hills of South Dakota.
1874	J. F. Glidden invents barbed wire.
1875	Refrigerator car comes into common use.
1876	Chief Sitting Bull defeats George Custer in Battle of Little Big Horn.
1876	U.S. troops defeat Chiefs Sitting Bull and Crazy Horse.
1883-1887	Cattle boom ends.
1886	U.S. troops capture Apache chief, Geronimo.
1887	Congress passes Dawes Act to help Indians become "Americanized."
1890	The Bureau of Census announces that frontier no longer exists.
1895	Congress passes the Carey Act, turning over public land to states to be reclaimed through irrigation.
1896	Gold is discovered in the Klondike.
1902	Congress passes Newlands Reclamation Act authorizing federal government to take charge of irrigation.
1903	Gold miners go out on strike at Idaho Springs.
1924	Congress grants Indians full citizenship.

77 Planning the Land and Water

Americans who moved beyond the ninety-ninth meridian in western Kansas took with them laws and patterns of behavior which had been developed in the settled areas of the East, where rain and timber were plentiful. Under the Homestead Act of 1862, the federal government offered to give farmers one hundred sixty acres of the public lands if they would live on the land and raise crops for five years. As a result, small farms spread across the countryside where there was adequate water for crops from rain or brooks and enough timber for houses, barns, and fences.

The Great Plains west of the ninety-ninth meridian lacked both adequate water and timber. This fertile but arid area challenged traditional methods of farming. Breaking up the tough sod of the plains demanded new, expensive plows; acquiring water for animals and crops required complicated equipment to drill wells two or three hundred feet deep. Without wood, settlers either built sod houses, which they heated with dried buffalo dung, or imported lumber and fuel from the East.

A meridian is half of a circle passing through the north and south poles. On a map the meridian is represented by lines of longitude running north and south.

Wheat farmers and cattle ranchers who moved into the area had to adapt their accustomed ways of doing work and organizing the land to these new conditions. The expense of breaking up the soil, drilling wells, irrigating and fencing the land, and constructing homes and farm buildings kept poor settlers from farming the plains profitably. Farmers with larger amounts of capital found 160 acres too little to justify investing in tools and machines. Ranchers required larger grazing areas for their animals.

On the frontiers of Montana and Wyoming, cattle grazers allowed enormous herds to roam freely over public lands. They often tried to fence off their own private preserves. Faced with an unsatisfactory land system, they resorted to evasion, fraud, and often violence. In 1885, William Andrew Jackson Sparks, a Federal Land Commissioner, confronting this pattern of illegal behavior, attempted to enforce the laws and to safeguard millions of acres of public land from what he considered to be greedy cattlemen and lumbermen. Westerners responded bitterly and attacked "King" Sparks, who, they argued, dealt ignorantly with a complex situation. Reading 77 examines the controversy between Sparks and Governor Warren of Wyoming. As you read, consider these questions:

1. According to Sparks, how were federal laws violated? What evidence was there that the laws had not been made wisely?
2. Why did Governor Warren believe that the development of the new territory should proceed rapidly?
3. Why was there a lag before Americans adjusted their laws to the new requirements of the western environment?
4. How do you think conflicts between private and public interests should be resolved?

A Federal Land Commissioner's Report

William Andrew Jackson Sparks investigated the ways in which some individuals acquired public lands. Sparks believed that the practices he found prevented genuine settlers from getting land. Parts of his report to the Secretary of the Interior follow.

Report of the Secretary of the Interior. Washington, D.C.: Government Printing Office, 1885, vol. I, pp. 205–15 **passim.** Language simplified and modernized.

In preparing this report, I had before me the records of special agents, inspectors employed by the surveyors-general, and local land offices, communications from United States attorneys and other officials, and letters from public men and private citizens throughout the country. All pointed to a common story of widespread, persistent land robbery committed under the guise [mask] of various forms of public land entry.

A public land entry was the application a settler made to secure legal title to public lands.

In many sections of the country, particularly throughout regions west of the ninety-ninth meridian which are dominated by cattle-raising interests, the investigations showed public land entries were chiefly fictitious and fraudulent. The entries were made largely through methods adopted by organizations that parceled out land among themselves and that maintained possession of unentered lands with armed riders. Systems of espionage and intimidation kept out settlers.

In farming regions near the cattle belt, speculation by individuals was covering whole townships of agricultural land. Entries were made for the purpose of selling the claims to others or for acquiring large parcels of land.

In timbered regions, the forests were being appropriated by domestic and foreign corporations through fraudulent entries that evaded the law. Newly discovered coal fields were seized and possessed in a similar way.

The following extracts from general reports of officers of this department disclose the customary methods of fraudulent appropriation of land and indicate the extent to which it is carried on.

From A. R. Greene, Inspector, November 3, 1884

Generally speaking, I believe that fraudulent entries of the public lands include a large percent of the whole number.

The idea prevails almost universally that, because the government in its generosity has provided for the donation of the public domain to its citizens, strict compliance with the conditions imposed is not essential. Men who would scorn to commit a dishonest act toward an individual, even if he were a total stranger, eagerly listen to every scheme for evading the settlement laws. In a majority of instances, I believe they practice such schemes.

Our land officers share this feeling in many instances. This is especially true with entries made under the Timber-Culture Law. At the very best, this law was a doubtful experiment at the start. The greater portion of the lands upon which planted groves of trees could be grown without irrigation had passed from the government before it was enacted. Climate and neglect together have made its success impossible.

The Timber-Culture Law passed in 1873 offered an additional quarter section (160 acres) to a settler who would plant forty acres of it in timber.

The question is not to encourage greater productivity from a climate and soil favorable to forest growth. Rather it is a question of trying to make forests grow on uncongenial [unfriendly] soil amidst blighting winds. The experiment had about as much chance of success as an effort to make water flow uphill. I doubt if the trees standing on any timber-culture entry west of the one hundredth meridian would retard a mild breeze.

I have seen small patches of land, possibly five acres, where the prairie had been furrowed and an occasional sickly cottonwood sprout stands two or three feet high. In other cases, the land had evidently been honestly plowed at some time, but through neglect had grown up again to grass. The trees were holding up their tiny branches in mute protest against the absurdity of the law.

A more vicious system of fraudulent entries has been practiced successfully by and in the interest of cattlemen and stock corporations. If the law had been enacted solely for their benefit it could scarcely have been more successful. A "cattle king" employs a number of cowboys. The herd is located on a favorable portion of the public lands where grass, water, and shelter are convenient. Each cowboy is required to make a timber-culture entry of lands along the stream. These entries often very nearly, if not quite, occupy all the watered lands in a township and make the remainder undesirable for actual settlement for farming purposes. Settlers avoid such localities as they would districts stricken with a plague.

From Special Agent T. H. Cavenaugh, Olympia, Washington Territory, November 8, 1884

The country lying west of the Cascade Range of mountains and north of the Columbia River in Washington Territory is a vast and almost impenetrable forest. The frauds attempted in this district are prompted solely by a desire to secure the valuable timber lands for lumbering purposes.

The Timber and Stone Act of 1878 offered for sale 160 acres of timber land in California, Nevada, Oregon, and Washington at $2.50 an acre.

A notary public is an official authorized to notarize, or certify, legal documents.

A deed is a notarized document that records a transfer of property from one owner to another.

The way to secure lands under the Act of 1878, is for a party interested in acquiring timber to be appointed a notary public for Washington Territory, which authorizes him to act in any county in the territory. He then establishes himself close to the lands which he intends to secure. All papers pertaining in any way to entries are made before him. All the papers, acts, and facts concerning the entries are in his possession. Notaries public in this territory are not by law required to keep a record of their official acts. Therefore, there can be no inspection to prove or to determine the rate of the entry, acknowledgment of deeds, mortgages, etc.

A Governor's Protest

In 1886, Wyoming was not yet a state. The President appointed the governor, who closely represented the interests of the area's ranchers. Portions of Governor Francis E. Warren's protest to Sparks's report follow.

Report of the Secretary of Interior, vol. II, pp. 1007–09. Language simplified and modernized.

Efforts of the General Land Office to protect the public domain of the United States for actual settlers and to prevent frauds are commendable. But if an overzealous [overenthusiastic] course is pursued and the acquisition of land by *bona fide* [genuine] entrymen is made too difficult, very great injury is done to the class of people which such efforts are intended to benefit.

The public lands of the United States should pass as rapidly as possible into the hands of private owners, provided always it is through lawful settlement and improvement. The growth and success of our country largely depend upon the development of new territory.

Land proofs were evidence that the applicant for public lands had complied fully with the requirement for obtaining title to the land. Such requirements might include improvement of or settlement on the land or the payment of legal fees or purchase money.

From close observation, it is estimated that more than three fourths of the rejected land proofs today affect the poorer classes.

The entries are made in good faith and are entirely free from fraud or double dealing. But, in many cases, men are unable on this arid land to support their families, make necessary improvements on their homesteads, and confine themselves entirely upon their land as the law requires. The settler frequently must leave his land to work for wages in order to secure food and the necessary means to make his improvements.

If this is so, should not the Land Office display greater leniency and liberality? It must be remembered that Wyoming is not a natural garden spot. Unlike the lands of Iowa, Nebraska, Kansas, and other states, where every acre requires but to turn the sod to grow abundant crops, in this territory agricultural products, aside from the sparse native grasses—fit only for grazing—cannot be produced except through expensive, long-term irrigation. In fact, months of patient labor must be expended in getting water upon the land. Perhaps years must then elapse before agricultural crops can be produced, if at all.

It should be borne in mind that the laws framed to cover the fertile lands of the older eastern states are not applicable to the arid lands of Wyoming. They should be made more generous to the settler and applicable to the arid condition of this country.

It is true that settlers are not compelled to settle upon public lands, and the Government can afford to hold them. But it is nevertheless true that the Government is of the people and for the people, and these lands belong to the settler under traditional rights, subject only to legal and proper rules and regulations. It is submitted as a principle, that an entryman should receive the benefit of a doubt in making final proof of his land claim. He should not be subject to the arbitrary rule that all doubts shall be held against him and that he shall be considered dishonest until he proves himself honest.

78 Planning the Sewers

Cities grew in all regions of the United States during the late nineteenth century. New cities developed close to established urban areas in the East. Marketing towns sprang up across the countryside with the increase of crops raised to be sold. From the beginning, the mining industries of the Rocky Mountain States were centered in cities. By 1910, every region of the country, except the Southwest, included a city with more than 100,000 people. The urban giants—New York, Chicago, and Philadelphia—had grown at a rate unknown in all previous history.

The enormous concentration of people in the new cities posed innumerable, interrelated problems. In large mid-nineteenth-century cities, for example, men and women moved about either on foot or in horse-drawn buses. Only a very small percentage of the population enjoyed the privilege of private, horse-drawn transportation. As urban population mushroomed, limited transportation systems required changes in land use and patterns of life. If cities were to support large-scale industry, either people had to be housed densely near centrally located factories or industry had to spread throughout the city so that people could get to work easily.

As each city grew, a balance was struck between these solutions. In Philadelphia, small, privately-owned row houses spread across the metropolis, and industrial centers spread with them. In Boston, four-story houses concentrated the labor force, and in New York, five-story tenements became the main form of workers' housing.

The housing patterns in each city changed with the introduction of new methods of transportation. The largest cities built elevated, and in a few cases, underground railroads, which allowed the population to spread out. Electric streetcars were even more common. By 1895, there were 10,000 miles of trolley lines operating in American cities. Settlements stretched along the trolley tracks.

A city is a complex system of interrelated parts. Almost any urban problem involves complex relationships with other problems. Reading 78 focuses on the problem of water and waste removal in two cities. As you read, try to answer these questions:

1. How were sewage problems related to housing patterns? to transportation systems? to the use of the land?
2. How did the sewage problems of San Francisco and Philadelphia compare with the problems of land and water in the West?
3. Why weren't the sewer systems better planned and maintained? Were the reasons similar to those that account for the lag between laws and the requirements of the western environment?
4. How do these problems compare with those of cities today?

Sewer Systems in Two American Cities

These selections are drawn from the first comprehensive survey of American cities prepared as part of the 1880 census.

Department of the Interior Census Office, **Report on the Social Statistics of Cities,** compiled by George E. Waring, Jr., Washington, D.C.: Government Printing Office, 1887, vol. I, pp. 823, 825, 830, and vol. II, p. 807.

San Francisco, California

The total length of sewers constructed up to 1880 is about 126 miles. Of these, about 75 miles had been constructed at the time of the preparation of a complete sewer plan (1876) by William

P. Humphreys, city and county surveyor. Mr. Humphreys describes the condition of the sewers existing at that time as follows:

"The greater portion of these sewers are of brick, but their cost has been excessive, because, among other reasons, they have been unnecessarily large. Most of the streets in the older portion of the city have brick sewers, which extend up the hillsides to irregular distances. Where these sewers approach the lower portions of the city, where the foundation is not sufficiently solid to sustain a brick sewer without pilings, the sewers are of wood, and are generally level, or nearly level. Being down, or nearly down, to low water, the tide rises and falls in them, so checking their outflow that most of them are today nothing more than long cesspools badly choked with offensive sewage matter. This evil must go on increasing from year to year until some change is made.

Pilings are heavy timbers or beams driven into the ground to support bridges, docks, buildings, or sewers.

A cesspool is an underground pit or basin that collects drainage and other household filth.

"In fact, the existing sewers in the city have been built without regard to a system of any kind which looks to the general drainage of the city. Each sewer appears to have been built independent of all others and without regard to the duty it has to perform. Some of the alleys and short streets in the city, for instance, where there are only a few houses, have sewers of the same size as those in the larger streets. A foot earthenware pipe, at one fifth the cost of the great brick sewer, would have afforded much more efficient drainage for all such alleys and short streets."

"San Francisco Bay with its great size and its strong tidal currents, affords great facilities for getting rid of the city's sewage. But to make the Bay useful the sewers must be carried out to points where there are strong currents. If they stop short, the lower parts of the city must always remain in an offensive and unhealthy condition.

"Along the busy waterfront of the city some of the sewers do not extend out into the Bay. They stop short, ending inside of the rubble-stone bulkhead, where the offensive solid matter is deposited, and the liquid matter allowed to escape as best it can, rendering the slips between the wharves at times offensive to the last degree of endurance. All of these sewers should be carried out to the ends of the wharves, discharging their contents through a bent hood, leading from the outer end of the sewer down below the level of low water. The tide will then speedily remove the sewage matter away from the city, and there will be no offensive smell about the wharves."

A bulkhead in a harbor is a wall or embankment built to hold back the water. A slip is a place between piers for a ship to enter.

Philadelphia, Pennsylvania

There is no system of inspection of sewers in Philadelphia. Few persons have ever been in them except workmen to make the necessary repairs, and these only at rare intervals, for repairs and connections are almost invariably made from the outside. Hence the condition of the inside of sewers is unknown and appears to be uncared for, so long as water turned into them gets away and does not come back to the surface or flow into cellars or basements. When, therefore, anybody proposes to go into a sewer for no other purpose than to find out its sanitary defects and condition, he is met with looks and expressions of genuine astonishment and surprise on the part of the city officials.

The first indication that a sewer is out of order is that the street caves in. The break is mended and the street and pavement are restored, but what becomes of the rubbish, bricks, and paving stones that have fallen into the sewer nobody knows or cares. It is supposed, and confidently asserted, that these are washed away by the water. But when one walks through a sewer he learns better. Even in large mains [main pipes] where there is a great rush of storm-water, the heavier rubbish, such as brick-bats [loose bricks] and paving stones, are met farthest down stream, and behind these accumulate the different grades of pebble, gravel, sand, and mud, while the slackwater backed up behind all shows the deposits still to be in progress.

Several things impress themselves very forcibly on the mind of any person who goes into the sewers of Philadelphia.

First. The necessity for a system of maintenance and repairs to keep the interior clear of the rubbish, bricks, paving-stones, and debris falling in from the many breaks constantly recurring all over the city. It may be assumed that any system of public works worth building is worth maintaining in repair when it is built. If it is worthwhile to expend $14,000 to $15,000 a mile to build branch sewers, it is also worthwhile to pick up and remove the building refuse and rubbish left in them by the masons and workmen, so that the water may have some chance to flow through when they are done. There are about 200 miles of public sewers in Philadelphia, and in them about 400 to 500 breaks occur every year, or on the average not far from one break per year for every half mile of sewer. Hence it seems quite essential that the rubbish and debris from so many places should be taken out before the whole system of underground work gets filled up.

Masons are skilled craftsmen who build structures with bricks or stones.

Second. The sewers of Philadelphia are obliged to carry almost everything which a great population wants to get rid of. Probably it is quite unavoidable that much kitchen waste, garbage, and swill [liquid garbage] should find its way into the sewers. But there seems to be no good reason why they should be filled up with ashes and cinders, cast-off clothing, boots and shoes, broken dishes and glass, nor why they should be expected to carry off the waste products from slaughter-houses and markets, or the steam and hot water from factories and machine shops.

The Philadelphia sewer system presents many serious difficulties. At present the sewage is discharged at different points along the river front, mainly into the Delaware River, a stream which flows back and forth with a strong tide. The river cannot be expected to dispose completely and properly of the sewage of the enormous population. The great extension of the area of the city, with hundreds of acres being covered by small houses occupied by single families, presents difficulties when we consider gathering together and transporting to a proper outlet the immense volume of foul sewage. The working classes of New York and other large cities are concentrated in limited areas. Tenement houses of five and six stories, with four families on each floor (25 by 80 feet), are not as satisfactory as the houses occupied by the same class of people in Philadelphia, where each family has its own house, open both front and rear to the light and air. However, the removal of liquid wastes is a simple proposition in New York compared with the problem of providing all of Philadelphia's thousands of scattered houses with proper connections with a proper sewer system.

This brief account of the house-drainage and sewer system of Philadelphia, while far from complete, indicates clearly the general character of the existing sewers and those still being constructed.

The work done includes some well-planned and well-constructed main sewers. The system as a whole, however, is totally and inexcusably bad, violating nearly every accepted principle of sanitary engineering and inevitably counteracting those natural influences which are so conducive [favorable] to the health of a population. It is, however, proper to call attention to the generally accepted and doubtless correct statement that the death rate of Philadelphia is lower than that of other cities which have fewer obvious defects in their public and private sanitary works. This low death rate can be ascribed only to the very favorable conditions under which the working classes of the population live. As a general rule—and this is a very marked and most interesting feature of Philadelphia—every family lives in its own house, and every individual lives and sleeps in a room well lighted and ventilated by outer windows. This condition removes the most important feature of "overcrowding," to which is due so much of the mortality of large cities the world over.

If a proper system for the removal of household wastes could be extended to all parts of the city of Philadelphia, it might reasonably be hoped that this city would have a lower death rate, even much lower than that of any other city of the world.

The question of the universal sanitary improvement of the city is one of the greatest importance. There are about 2000 miles of streets in the city, and population is rapidly extending in every direction. There are at this time [1880] less than 200 miles of sewers, all told, and a very large proportion are entirely unsuited for the use for which they were intended.

To construct proper sewers throughout the city, to secure the needed remodeling of house-drainage, and to provide for the permanent unobjectionable disposal of the city's filth, would involve an expenditure of money and an application of engineering skill hardly called for in any other city of the civilized world.

79 Law and Violence in the Cities and the West

From the very beginnings of American history, violence has been associated with frontier settlements. The image of frontier violence, however, is a combination of a realistic appraisal of the facts with myths created in the minds of men. People back home in the old settlement wanted—half in fear, half in envy—to believe that the frontier was an exciting place where the rules of civilization were relaxed. In their minds, man and nature were both magnificent and untamed.

Each frontier—the Appalachian fringes of the early settlements, the Kentucky wilderness, the Mississippi backcountry, and the Texas, Wyoming, and Montana cattle frontiers—has enjoyed a reputation for rough-hewn violence. In the popular imagination of today, only the cattle frontiers retain the image, magnified by movies and television into the major violent American experience.

Since the eighteenth century, large cities throughout Europe and America have also had a reputation for danger, although without the same exciting overtones the West enjoyed. While medieval European cities had symbolized personal safety, few people thought of eighteenth-century Paris or London as places of personal security. When Thomas Jefferson warned Americans of the dangers inherent in the growth of cities, he was, among other things, warning of riots, robberies, and murders. Alexis de Tocqueville's account of the United States in the early 1830's indicated his fear that New York and Philadelphia might be overtaken by unruly mobs. Violence was common in American cities around 1900.

The historical image of cities as centers of violence and danger has been largely lost. As a result, discussions of today's high crime rates or riots confuse our perspective on the present. Superficial commentators on the American scene today tell us that we were once secure, but are now sliding into an abyss of urban violence.

The crime rate in the nineteenth century was probably higher than it is today.

Reading 79 looks at nineteenth-century cities through an examination of the police as a source of violence in New York City in the 1890's and labor disputes as sources of violence on the western frontier. As you read, try to answer these questions:

1. What were the causes of the violence described in each selection? Have these causes been eliminated today? If so, how?
2. Why did some Americans believe that police departments and courts were taking sides in a war between social groups rather than acting as fair exponents of justice?
3. Under what conditions are men willing to see the law used impartially?
4. In finding solutions to present-day problems of law and order, what are the implications of either "forgetting" history or of considering violence as simply part of "the American character"?

Police Brutality, 1895

The Democratic party usually controlled New York City government, while the Republicans normally held a majority of the seats in the New York State Legislature. Every once in a while, Republicans in the legislature decided to show "just how badly" the city Democrats were doing. This selection is from a report of a legislative committee on New York City police, prepared in 1895.

Report and Proceedings of the Senate Committee Appointed to Investigate the Police Department of the City of New York. Albany: James B. Lyon, 1895, vol. I, pp. 25–32. Language simplified and modernized.

Persons in the humbler walks of life were subjected to appalling outrages. They were abused, clubbed, and imprisoned, and even convicted of crime on false testimony by policemen and their accomplices. Men of business were harassed and annoyed in their affairs. They too, were compelled to bend their necks to the police yoke, in order that they might share that so-called protection which seemed indispensable to their affairs. People from all walks of life seemed to feel that to antagonize the police was to call down upon themselves the swift judgment and persecution of an invulnerable force. Strong in itself, banded together by self-interest and the common goal of unlawful gain, the Police Department is so thoroughly entrenched in the municipal government as to defy ordinary attacks.

The poor, ignorant foreigner residing on the great east side of the city has been especially subjected to a brutal and infamous rule by the police. In the administration of the local inferior [lower] criminal courts, it is beyond a doubt that innocent people who

Extortion is the practice of obtaining money through threats, violence, or misuse of authority.

have refused to yield to criminal extortion, have been clubbed and harassed and confined in jail.

It is generally conceded that the municipal police are zealous [eager] and unsurpassed in efficiency and desire to protect life and property upon New York streets.

It is a significant fact that but little corruption has been traced into the pockets of the ordinary patrolman. Such sins as may be laid at his door, largely consist in abuse of physical force, infringement upon the rights and privileges of private citizens, and failure to disclose the criminal conduct of his superiors.

It was proven by a stream of witnesses who poured continuously into the sessions of the committee, that many of the members of the force, and even superior officers, have abused the physical power which has been provided for them. In making arrests and in restraining disorder, they gratify personal spite and brutal instincts by reducing their victims to a servile condition. Even in the eyes of our foreign-born residents our institutions have been degraded. Those who have fled from oppression abroad have come here to be oppressed in a professedly free and liberal country.

It appears, therefore, that the police formed a separate and highly privileged class, armed with the authority and the machinery for oppression and punishment. But they are practically free themselves from the operation of the criminal law.

We emphasize finding police brutality because it affects every citizen, whatever his condition, because it shows an invasion of constitutional liberty by one of the departments of government, whose supreme duty it is to enforce the law, and because it establishes a condition gravely imperiling safety and welfare.

Violence on the Mining Frontier

In many places on the timber and mining frontiers of the West, a small number of employers dominated local business and government. Workers in these areas often felt that they had little control over either their working lives or their political fortunes. The labor unions formed by miners and loggers frequently expressed the idea that democracy was a sham, cloaking the power of a few rich men. Meetings between angry union members and powerful employers often led to violence. This selection is from a report on a bitter strike in Idaho Springs, Colorado.

A Report on Labor Disturbances in the State of Colorado, From 1880 to 1904, Inclusive, Senate Document No. 122, 58th Congress, 3rd Session, Washington, D.C.; Government Printing Office, 1905, pp. 151–59. Language simplified and modernized.

In the spring of 1903, there was a strike of gold miners at Idaho Springs in Clear Creek County. They struck for a working day of eight hours, with no reduction of wages.

The Sun and Moon mine, which had employed about 125 men before the strike, resumed operations, on June 8, with a small non-union force and by July 1 had about 70 employees.

Shortly after 11 o'clock on the night of July 28 there was a terrific explosion at the Sun and Moon mine. It was caused by kegs of powder or dynamite, which, being rolled down the hillside, wrecked the transformer house. As it happened, the only loss of life was one of the dynamiters, a union man.

A transformer is an apparatus used in telephones, radios, and common electrical appliances, for the purpose of increasing or decreasing the voltage of an electric current.

Deputy sheriffs began scouring the hills for the dynamiter or dynamiters. Meanwhile other deputy sheriffs visited the homes of officers and members of the miners' union, placed them under arrest, and confined them in jail. Thirteen were arrested during the night and others the next day.

An indignation meeting to denounce the crime was called by the Citizens' Protective League. This was an association of mine owners and businessmen which had been organized since the beginning of the strike at Idaho Springs.

Lafayette Hanchette, manager of the Lamartine mine and president of the First National Bank of Idaho Springs, said: "Don't do anything unlawful, but we can't have bad citizens among good ones, and we must get rid of them. I now move that it is the sentiment of this meeting that we go to the jail and there take the prisoners and escort them to the edge of the city limits and tell them firmly to go and never return."

The chairman then put the motion, which was carried with a shout. The meeting broke up and the people started for the county jail. The crowd was composed of about 500 citizens, including many businessmen and professional men. On reaching the jail they demanded the prisoners. The three guards were required to give up the keys and the door was unlocked. Fourteen of the twenty-three men in the jail were ordered out. All of these men were members of the Western Federation of Miners.

The Western Federation of Miners was organized in 1893 in the Rocky Mountain area. Its goals were higher wages, an eight-hour day, and laws establishing safety regulations for the mines. From the start, the union became involved in a long series of strikes. Leaders of the Western Federation of Miners helped to organize the Industrial Workers of the World (Wobblies).

With the fourteen union men in advance the crowd moved down the main street to the extreme eastern end of the city, more than a mile away. At that point Lafayette Hanchette told the fourteen men that the citizens of Idaho Springs would not condone violence; that they were satisfied that at least some of the men had instigated the plot to dynamite the Sun and Moon mine, and also planned to assassinate certain mine managers. He said that the citizens had decided that these men must leave and never return. "Never show your faces in Clear Creek County again," he said, "for if you do we will not be responsible for what may happen to you. A very considerable element here has been for hanging you men, but the conservative citizens have prevailed. They expect you to keep moving until you get out of the state.

Don't stop in Denver except long enough to get aid from your Federation."

On July 30, the executive committee of the Citizens' Protective League issued the following statement: "The members of the union were given to understand from the first that so long as they were agitators of socialistic principles we would hold them responsible should any damage be done to any property in the district. The people of Idaho Springs had reached the limit of endurance. This has never been a union stronghold, and our people believe that they would rather give up their homes and businesses than submit to policies of tyranny which have threatened our public and private institutions and the lives of our citizens for the past six months. The action of last night shows that the people will not submit to the dictation of a few imported union agitators. There may be some people who believe that the action was too radical, but for each of them, there are two others who believe it was not radical enough."

On July 31, four additional union men were deported from Idaho Springs, and on the next day one more. On August 4, there was a meeting of the Citizens' Alliance at Denver with about five hundred present. Resolutions were adopted and the following is quoted from the preamble:

> Our attention has been called to the recent action of the Citizens' Protective League of Idaho Springs, which, while technically speaking, was without due process of law, yet, nevertheless, from the standpoint of expediency and self-defense, was calculated to save lives, liberty, and property.
>
> Now, therefore, we, the Citizens' Alliance of Denver, believe that the business men of Idaho Springs acted within that higher and unwritten code of self-preservation to which resort must always be had by men when there is no speedy and adequate remedy at law.

The Fifth Amendment guarantees that no person shall be "deprived of life, liberty, or property without due process of law." The Fourteenth Amendment contains a similar clause, binding on the states.

On application of the attorney of the deported men, on August 10, 1903, Judge Frank W. Owers, sitting in the district court at Georgetown, granted an injunction restraining each and every member of the Citizens' Protective League from interfering with the deported men or preventing their return to their homes and business.

Eight of the deported men returned to Idaho Springs on August 11. On the complaint of Manager H. N. Sims, of the Sun and Moon mine, a police officer issued warrants for the arrest of the eight men on the charge of destroying the transformer house, and they were, on the same day, confined in the city jail.

On complaint of the deported men, by their attorney, Judge Owers issued bench warrants for 129 citizens of Idaho Springs, charging them with rioting, making threats, and assault. Most of these men were arrested, and gave bond for their appearance in the sum of $500 each. The deported men who had been reimprisoned were also released on bail.

To give bond means to pledge money or property as bail which releases an arrested person temporarily on assurance that he will appear in court at an appointed time for a trial.

In December 1903, John E. Chandler, financial secretary and business agent of the Federation in Idaho Springs, Foster Milburn, Ralph Sanborn, Frank Napoli, and Joseph Carbonetti were tried at Georgetown, Clear Creek County, on the charge of conspiracy to blow up the transformer house of the Sun and Moon mine. They were acquitted [found not guilty], but were rearrested immediately, and brought to Central City, Gilpin County. They were charged with malicious mischief in blowing up the transformer house. In the trial at Central City, Chandler was acquitted in June 1904, and Milburn was acquitted in July 1904, after which the district attorney dropped the cases against Sanborn, Napoli, and Carbonetti.

A district attorney is a lawyer elected or appointed in a specified district who serves as the prosecutor for the state in criminal cases.

In the district court at Georgetown on February 8, 1904, District Attorney H. G. Thurman entered a *nolle prosequi* in each of the cases against the citizens charged with rioting and making threats and assaults when they drove union miners away from Idaho Springs. F. F. Richardson, who had been engaged to aid in the prosecution, severely criticized the action of the district attorney. Mr. Richardson said that it seemed that pressure had been brought to bear, and as though there was one law for influential citizens and another for poor people. He further declared that in his whole experience at the bar he had never known a case to be dropped with the evidence so clear and convincing.

A **nolle prosequi** is a formal notice made by a prosecutor that he will proceed no further in the prosecution of a criminal case.

After the union miners were deported from Idaho Springs only non-union men were able to secure employment in the mines there.

80 Taming the Frontier

HISTORICAL ESSAY

During the period between 1860 and 1890, the most important American frontier lay in the West. Miners, cattlemen, and farmers closed in from both the East and from California on the Great Plains and the Rocky Mountain region. By 1890, the Bureau of the Census proclaimed that a clear frontier line no longer existed. Isolated spots of settlement now dotted every area of the nation. Settlement of the West continued for several decades after 1890. During this decade, however, a larger number of people moved from the countryside to the city than from the settled areas into

Two of the Pacific coast states —California and Oregon— became states before the Civil War. The "last West," or last frontier, was the remaining area west of the states forming a line from Louisiana to Minnesota. The Census Bureau defined a frontier as any area having more than two persons but less than six persons per square mile.

the West. The cities became America's most important frontier. This essay, however, concentrates on the events that took place on the western frontier, making only a few comparisons with what happened in the cities. Reading 84 will trace the development of the modern urban frontier in greater detail.

The Indians

In the 1840's, farmers reached the eastern edge of the Great Plains, roughly at the ninety-ninth meridian (see map, opposite). Then, instead of moving steadily westward, the line of settlement jumped to the Pacific Coast, where tales of gold and rich lands drew settlers by the thousands. Fifteen hundred miles of plains and mountains, including roughly one fifth of the total land area of the United States, stretched between these two settled areas. On this land lived about 225,000 Indians, a formidable obstacle to white settlement.

The Spanish explorer Francisco Vásquez de Coronado had first described the Indians of the plains in the sixteenth century. According to his account, they dressed in leather, lived in tepees, ate buffalo meat, and followed the buffalo herds on which their livelihood depended. Coronado admired these fearless men who could creep close to a buffalo herd on their hands and knees, covered with a wolf skin as a disguise, and bring down a giant animal with a single shot from a bow and arrow.

War played a vital role in the lives of these Indians. A warrior who struck an enemy in hand-to-hand combat won honor among his fellows and elevation to a position as a chief. In some tribes, the number of scalps taken in battle determined a man's prestige. By the time white American settlers reached the Great Plains, the fighting spirit of these Indians had been bolstered by the acquisition of horses and guns.

Horses had become extinct in the Americas. Then the Europeans brought them. At first most Indians ignored horses or killed them with their riders. Early in the seventeenth century, the Apaches realized that horses were valuable for hunting, fighting, and traveling. Horses acquired through purchase or trade began to pass northward from tribe to tribe. They changed the traditional manners of living among most of the Indian tribes.

Although white settlers considered all the Indians of the plains as one group, the Indians considered themselves Cheyenne, or Sioux, or Apache, and not part of a larger group called Indians. They spoke different languages, had separate ancestries, and, until the mid-eighteenth century, shared no substantial common culture. Since the various tribes often fought each other, it was unlikely that they would unite against a common enemy.

But even in small numbers, the Plains Indians were worthy foes. Their fearlessness, their determination to maintain their way of life, and their aroused anger when whites broke treaties and sent hunters and settlers to slaughter the buffalo upon which their livelihood depended all inspired them to resist. They battled bravely for their homelands against a ruthless enemy with a supe-

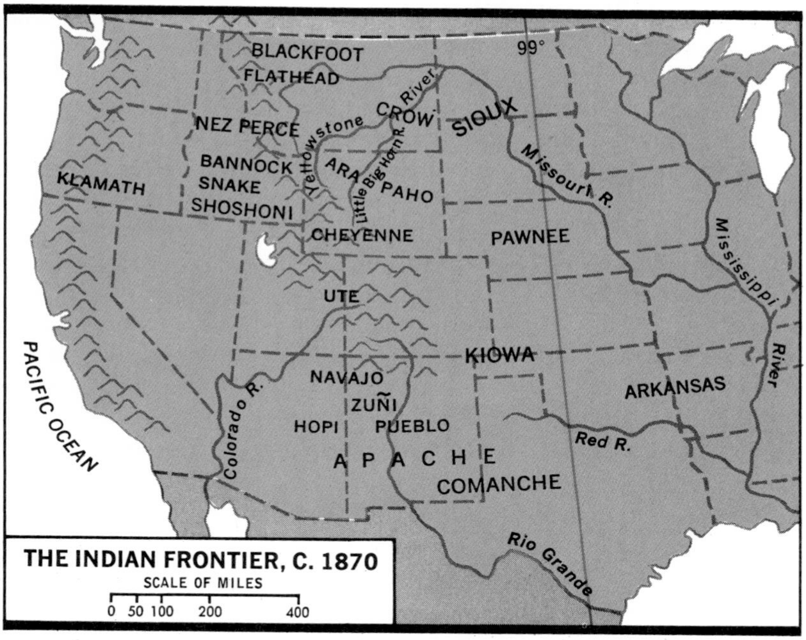

rior technology who was determined to exterminate them or to shut them up in reservations.

The first serious invasions of Indian areas in the West came in California. In 1850, about 100,000 Indians lived in California; ten years later, only about 35,000 remained. White miners pushed the Indians from one valuable mining site after another. Penniless, starving, and homeless, they died off. The Commissioner of Indian Affairs described the process: "[D]espoiled [robbed] by irresistible forces of the land of their fathers; with no country on earth to which they can migrate; in the midst of a people with whom they cannot assimilate; they have no recognized claims upon the government and are compelled to become vagabonds—to steal or to starve." As miners pushed into the mountains and cattlemen and settlers invaded the Great Plains, this process was often repeated.

Before the Civil War, the Indians had fought intermittently with white settlers. Skirmishes increased in number during the war itself. In 1862, the Sioux tribes in the Dakotas went on the warpath massacring almost a thousand settlers in Minnesota. Revenge fell swiftly upon innocent and guilty alike. Whites exacted a similar vengeance for attacks by the Cheyenne in Colorado in 1864. When the Civil War ended, the government sent 25,000 veteran troops to the frontier. During the next twenty or so years, warfare raged constantly. Occasionally, Indians would win an engagement such as the famous victory in 1876 when the Sioux, led by Chiefs Sitting Bull and Crazy Horse, wiped out General George Custer's command of 264 men on the Little Big Horn. But numbers and superior technology eventually won out. The capture of the Apache chief, Geronimo (1886) marked the virtual end of Indian resistance.

Treaties that the American government made with the various tribes were often complicated by cultural differences. For example, many tribes did not understand the concept of owning land, and not all chiefs had the right to make treaties for their people.

The entire process by which the Indians were deprived of their lands or killed if they resisted invasion was filled with deceit and trickery. Treating each Indian tribe as if it were a sovereign nation like Great Britain or Germany was clearly unrealistic. Indians often did not understand the terms of treaties they signed, and men who negotiated these treaties often failed to explain them clearly. Railroads cheated tribes of their lands. Frontiersmen and soldiers subscribed widely to the notion that the only good Indian was a dead Indian. In 1877, President Rutherford B. Hayes summed up this inglorious history in his Annual Message to Congress:

> The Indians were the original occupants of the land we now possess. They have been driven from place to place. The purchase money paid to them in some cases for what they called their own has still left them poor. In many instances, when they had settled down upon lands assigned to them by compact and begun to support themselves by their own labor, they were rudely jostled off and thrust into the wilderness again. Many, if not most, of our Indian wars have had their origin in broken promises and acts of injustice on our part.

A Century of Dishonor was written to protest the government's injustices toward the Indians.

The conscience of the nation, or at least of easterners who were not actively involved in the advancing frontier, was at last aroused. Stirred partly by Helen Hunt Jackson's book *A Century of Dishonor*, Congress in 1887 passed the Dawes Act, which established policy toward the Indians for a half century. The Dawes Act dissolved the tribes as legal units and divided a tribe's land among its members. For twenty-five years, the Indians were forbidden to sell the land they had acquired in this way. Then they were to receive full legal rights to their land as well as citizenship. In 1924, Congress finally granted full citizenship to all Indians, whether they had land or not.

The American Indian was considered to be a "ward" of the federal government and a citizen of his reservation. The Fourteenth Amendment which defined citizenship was never interpreted to include the Indian.

The Bureau of Indian Affairs was set up in 1836 by President Jackson. In 1849, the Department of Interior was created, and the Indian Bureau became part of that department.

Hailed as the Indian Emancipation Act, the Dawes Act instead proved to be a disaster for redmen. Within fifty years after its passage, lands owned by Indians decreased from 138 to 48 million acres, many of which were virtually worthless. Rather than protect its charges, the Indian Bureau sometimes helped to rob them of their heritage. The low point may have been reached in the 1920's when Secretary of the Interior Albert B. Fall tried to take away oil lands belonging to the Navajos. The Indians were finally pushed onto reservations where they lived on government handouts while their culture crumbled around them. What a fate for the offspring of a proud and free people! They had committed a great sin. They had made their homes in the path of western expansion.

The Mining Frontier

Miners opened the first frontier of the last West. The map below shows the most important mining areas. The discovery of gold at Sutter's Fort in 1848 pulled a throng of miners to California. In 1859, a new strike near Pikes Peak in Colorado started a rush to the eastern edge of the Rockies. By 1860, the Territory of Jefferson, whose name was later changed to Colorado, had a population of 35,000. In that same year, Nevada was carved out of Utah after the discovery of the Comstock Lode, the world's richest vein of silver, in the mountains near Lake Tahoe. Within twenty years, the Comstock Lode alone yielded more than $300 million in silver. Gold was also discovered in 1860 in eastern Washington and in Idaho and Montana, leading to the settlement of a few thousand miners who took $100 million in gold from Montana alone within a decade. In the 1880's, William Clark opened the Anaconda Mine near Butte, Montana, from which miners extracted more than $2 billion dollars in copper during the next fifty years. The last gold rush within the continental United States took

A lode is a mineral deposit that fills a vein or a crack in a rock.

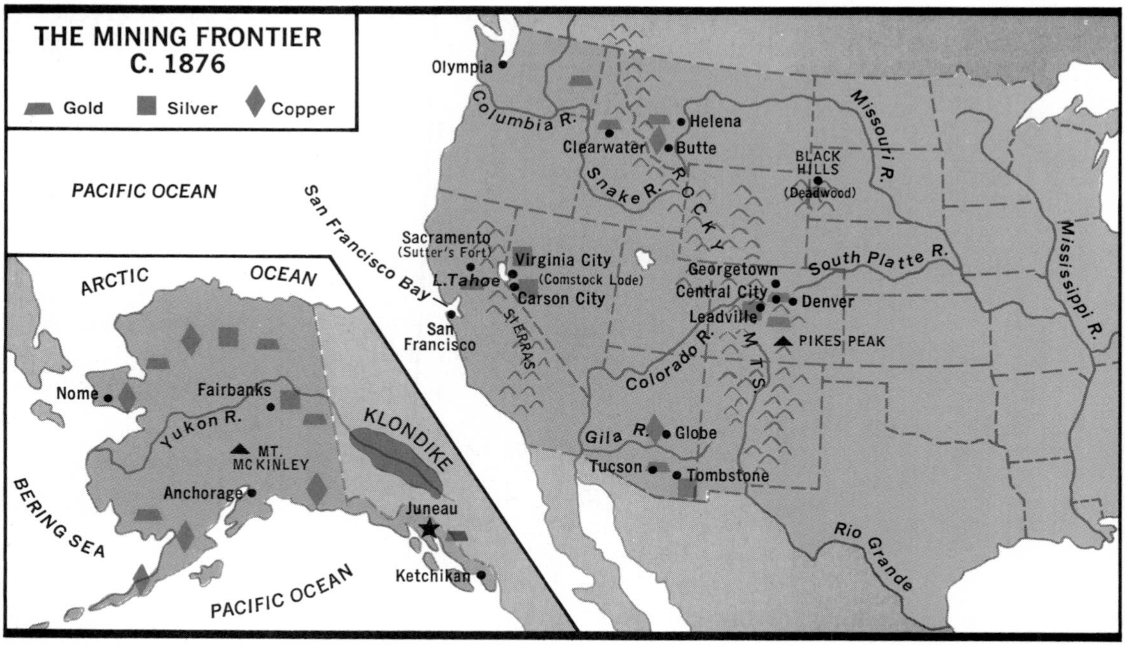

place in the mid 1870's when miners rushed into the Black Hills of the Dakotas. Finally, a strike in the Klondike region of Alaska in 1896 brought miners who in two years numbered 30,000.

The miners' frontier had a short history—about forty years in all—but the miners played a vital role in the settlement of the West. They advertised the area's magnificent resources. They forced the government to do something about the Indians, opening the way for the cattlemen and farmers who were to follow. Between 1860 and 1890, they mined about $2 billion in gold and silver. And they added to the lore of the West, producing a number of the gunmen, sheriffs, dancehall girls, and prospectors who have become the stock in trade of Western novelists and moviemakers. No mean heritage this!

Texas cattlemen and cowboys used to drive the cattle northward over a thousand miles of plains to the nearest railroad towns, usually in Kansas. There the cattle would be shipped to the stockyards of Kansas City and Chicago. A head of cattle was worth about $4 in Texas, $40 in Chicago.

The Day of the Cattlemen

The Day of the Cattlemen dawned in 1867 when the "long drive" north from Texas became established and the town of Abilene, Kansas, shipped its first herd of cattle over the Kansas Pacific Railroad. The map on this page shows the main trails and the cattle towns. Its sun set in the two terrible winters of 1885–1886 and 1886–1887, which destroyed thousands of cattle on the open range. The twenty years between these dates marked the develop-

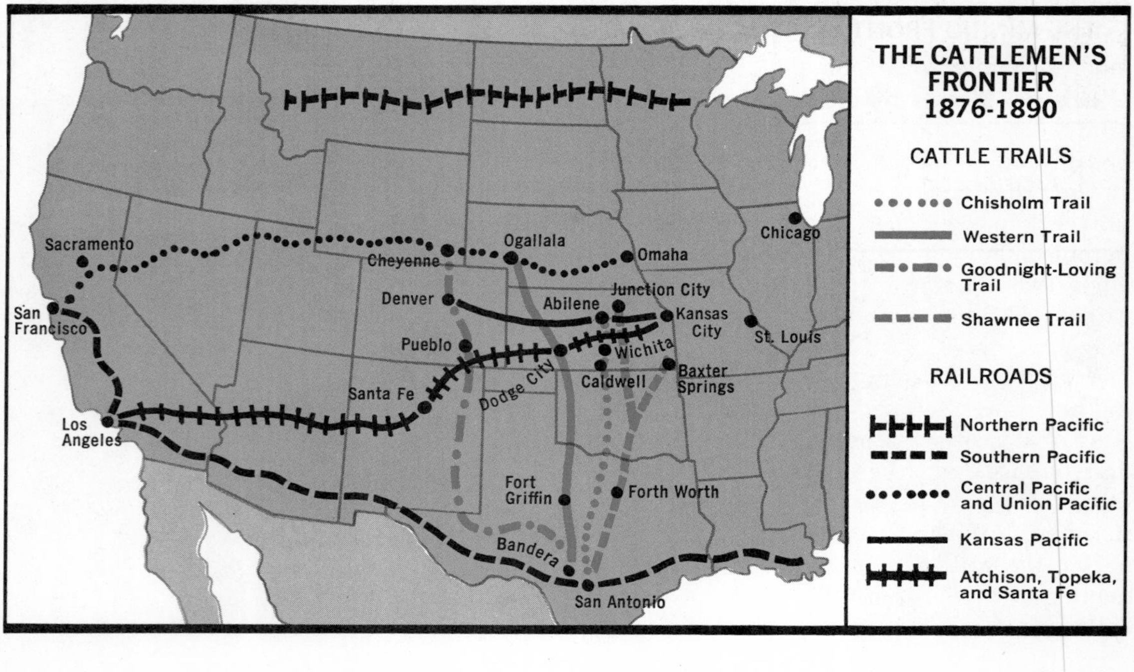

ment of America's most romanticized industry, recorded in songs, films, and novels as the age when cowboys, rustlers, cattle barons, Indians, lawmen, and soldiers wrestled to dominate raw towns.

A number of developments combined to make the cattlemen's frontier possible. The government opened the public domain after the Civil War. The army relentlessly killed off the Indians. Soldiers, settlers, and professional hunters annihilated the buffalo which had long fed on the vast grasslands. Railroads stretched out onto the prairies. Meat-packing centers grew up in Kansas City, Chicago, and elsewhere. They shipped meat all over the nation by the newly developed refrigerator car, which came into common use about 1875. Finally, the consumption of meat increased in the East at the same time that production of cattle and sheep declined.

The Union Pacific and the Central Pacific were joined together at Promontory Point, Utah, in 1869. The Atchison, Topeka and Santa Fe reached Colorado by 1872 and Los Angeles by 1883. The Southern Pacific Railroad reached El Paso by 1881.

Longhorn cattle, the descendants of Spanish herds, had grazed for centuries on the rich prairie grasses of Texas. In 1846, cowboys drove the first herd of these semi-wild creatures to Ohio. Ten years later, a herd of Texas cattle reached Chicago. By the end of the Civil War, the "long drive" had ceased to be only an experiment. In such towns as Abilene and Dodge City in Kansas, cowboys loaded hundreds of thousands of cattle, which had traveled up the Chisholm and Goodnight trails, onto railroad cars bound for slaughtering centers such as Chicago. Later, the long drive extended farther north, to the Union Pacific and Northern Pacific railroads which crossed the northern grasslands where cattle fattened at the end of their long trip north. Between 1866 and 1888, about six million head of cattle were driven from Texas to winter in Colorado, Wyoming, or Montana.

This new industry challenged the settled institutions imported from the East. What good was a 160-acre homestead to a cattleman? What good was land to anyone if cattlemen owned the banks of streams that determined people's access to water? What could a farmer do when a huge herd of wild cattle driven by tough cowboys trampled through his wheat field? And who would settle disputes when two or more cattle barons vied for the same land or when cattlemen and sheepmen tried to pasture their animals on the same range?

The railroads that brought cattle to market also brought sheep to the Great Plains area. Sheepherders would break up the "open range," where the cattle fed, into farms surrounded by barbed wire. Sheep eat the grass much closer to the ground than cattle do; therefore, the two animals could not pasture together.

A state like Wyoming, whose vast acres were unsuited for farming but superb for large-scale ranching, typified some of the problems of this new way of life. Cattlemen seized both Indian lands and public lands there. For almost two decades, the Wyoming Stock Growers' Association practically ran the state, writing laws as it saw fit. When sheepherders moved into the territory in the 1870's, the cattlemen wiped out entire flocks, and only the intervention of the United States Army blocked the outbreak of a full-scale war. Hence, the recommendations of men like Sparks.

The cattle boom reached its peak in 1885. The two terrible winters that followed wiped out thousands of head of cattle on the northern ranges. But even without bad weather, the long drive was falling victim to the advance of settlement. Railroads blocked the trails. So did the barbed-wire fences of men who established settled ranches and farmers who tried to protect their fields from the cattle herds. Cattle diseases had led to state quarantine laws which complicated interstate drives. Cattlemen began to fence off their lands. The ranch replaced the long drive across the public domain. The cowboys lingered on, domesticated on ranches. The glamorous days of the cattle wars, the strong silent cowboy, the rancher's daughter, and the dancehall girl faded into history.

The Farmers' Last Frontier

More than any other factor, the rush of farmers into the West ended the picturesque days of the miners and cattlemen. A number of factors help to account for this movement. Tales of rich lands and fantastic yields per acre whetted the appetites of easterners. Immigrants from Europe were willing to purchase farms in more settled areas. The railroads provided transportation to the West, a way to market crops, and encouragement to settle through offers of their land at cheap prices. The invention of barbed wire by J. F. Glidden, in 1874, solved the fencing problem in a land where trees were scarce. Deep wells and windmills provided a supply of fresh water on the semi-arid plains. Dry-farming techniques permitted farmers to grow grains in semi-arid regions. Finally, the growth of new markets in eastern cities and in Europe provided an outlet for the rich harvests of the new West.

Immigrants did not know how to farm on the frontier where they had to cope with either a dense forest or the thick sod of the prairie. Hence, they moved in behind frontier farmers.

Men came by the millions. The population of the area west of the Mississippi rose from 6,877,000 in 1870 to 16,775,000 in 1890. The center of the corn and wheat belts shifted from the old Granger states of the 1870's to the Populist states—Kansas, Nebraska, the Dakotas, and western Minnesota—in the 1890's. The agricultural revolution traced in Chapter 16 followed. Although a million new farms opened in the decade of the 1890's, there was no longer an identifiable frontier line. If farmers were to increase productivity during the twentieth century, they had to do so by using additional tools and better farming techniques, not by moving onto new soil.

Millions of acres of arid lands could be made productive with irrigation, however. Congress passed the Carey Act in 1895 and the Newlands Reclamation Act in 1902 to open these acres. By 1910, about fourteen million acres of western land were being irrigated mainly with waters impounded behind government-owned dams. By 1930, more than five million additional acres had been added.

The Carey Act authorized the President to cede to any state up to one million acres of land owned by the federal government for the purposes of cultivation, irrigation, and settlement. The Newlands Reclamation Act authorized the federal government to use the money raised from the sale of land in 16 western states to build irrigation projects such as dams.

Political Organization

The chart on this page shows the political results of this last surge of settlement. Fifteen new states, all except West Virginia from beyond the Mississippi, were added to the union between the admission of Kansas in 1861 and of New Mexico and Arizona in 1912. They embraced more than a third of the territory of the nation. Of our present fifty states, only Hawaii and Alaska, neither having common borders with the other forty-eight, remained beyond the fold when World War I broke out.

The Formation of New States, 1861-1959

State	Date of Admission	Area in Square Miles
Kansas	1861	82,276
West Virginia	1863	24,181
Nevada	1864	110,540
Nebraska	1867	77,237
Colorado	1876	104,247
North Dakota	1889	70,665
South Dakota	1889	77,047
Montana	1889	147,138
Washington	1889	68,192
Idaho	1890	83,557
Wyoming	1890	97,914
Utah	1896	84,916
Oklahoma	1907	69,919
New Mexico	1912	121,666
Arizona	1912	113,909
Alaska	1959	586,400
Hawaii	1959	6,435

Utah was denied statehood several times because it permitted men to have more than one wife (polygyny). Congress had passed laws in 1862, 1882, and 1887 forbidding this practice. In 1890, the Mormon Church ratified an edict advising its members to refrain from practicing polygyny.

The constitutions of these new states were much like those of the older ones. Wyoming and Utah permitted women to vote in their constitutions, and other western states imitated this precedent by law a few years later. Most of the new states provided for regulation of railroads in their constitutions and some had provisions for direct democracy, such as the initiative, referendum, and recall. But on the whole, they wrote constitutions much like those of the more established eastern states. That American democracy is a product of the unsettled frontier is one of the myths which Americans cling to despite evidence to the contrary. The vigilantes of frontier towns, the summary justice of the sheriff, his posse, and his rope, the cruel slaughter of the Indians, and the gunshot justice of cattle barons contributed more to the American tradition of violence than they did to justice and free choice.

A vigilante is a member of a self-appointed group that makes itself responsible for interpreting and enforcing the law and preventing crime. Law-enforcement agencies as we know them today generally did not exist in the West.

Adjusting Institutions on the Last Frontier

The American people were forced to adjust their institutions to the demands of the new environment in the West. Three conditions affected this adaptation. First, the federal government maintained a considerable amount of centralized control both of land and of natural resources, such as water. The following table shows what had happened to the public domain by 1904.

The Disposal of the Public Domain by 1904

Disposition	Number of Acres
Purchased by individuals	278,000,000
Granted to states or railroads	273,000,000
Acquired by or available to individuals free of charge	147,000,000
Unappropriated	474,000,000
Reserved explicitly to the government	209,000,000

Between 1904 and 1920, an additional 175,000,000 acres were reserved to the government, primarily in new or expanded national parks. About 200,000,000 acres intended for disposition to citizens still lay vacant. The government was by far the largest landowner in the West.

Second, policies that were poorly adapted to the new environment often brought disaster in their wake. Cattle by the thousands died in the blizzards of the 1880's in Wyoming. Thousands of acres of semi-arid lands in western Kansas, Nebraska, and Oklahoma blew away in the dust storms of the 1930's. Careless disposal of wastes from mines ruined hundreds of streams in the West.

Finally, scientific knowledge developed rapidly to cope with the challenges of the new environment. Scientists, many of whom worked for state or national governments, developed new methods of dry farming, irrigation, and animal husbandry. Engineers built new dams and developed new techniques to irrigate vast areas of semi-arid soil. The refrigerator car, the windmill, and barbed wire made farming and ranching on the Great Plains possible.

American cities during the period between 1870 and 1930 faced similar problems of adjusting institutions to a new environment. Unlike the federal government in the West, however, cities controlled little land. They had given most of it to private individuals early in the century. They had to buy it back at high prices to build parks, streets, or other public facilities. Moreover, the taxation system, which required owners of adjoining property to pay special assessments for sewers, streets, sidewalks, and so forth, made centralized planning almost impossible. Real political power

Only Congress can designate national parks. It usually chooses sites that are distinguished for their scenic beauty, scientific interest, or historic significance. The National Parks System in the Department of Interior administers these parks. The first national park was Yellowstone, established in 1872.

The story of these "Okies" and their trek from the Dust Bowl to California is realistically described in John Steinbeck's novel, **The Grapes of Wrath,** written in 1936.

Theodore Roosevelt was the first President to awaken the public, Congress, and state governments to the need for conservation. During his Administration, the Newlands Reclamation Act was passed. In 1908, he called a conference at the White House of governors, judges, congressmen, scientists, and prominent citizens to discuss the problem. As a result, the National Conservation Commission was set up, as well as conservation agencies in forty-one states.

was decentralized in cities, and most developmental decisions were made by private citizens. So, as we have seen, were the major political decisions in Wyoming when cattle barons ran the state. Both New York City and Wyoming had to develop new governmental institutions to cope with these new problems.

Just as they did in the West, policies poorly adapted to the environment brought disaster in the cities. Bad sewers spread disease. Poor planning of streetcar lines and roads provoked impossible traffic jams. The spread of telephone poles turned cities into ugly nests of overhead wires.

Like westerners, citizens in cities turned to scientists to help them solve their problems. With their engineering allies, scientists developed streetcars, subways, elevated lines, automobiles, and trucks to solve the transportation problem. The cable, telegraph, and telephone helped to speed communications. Scientific knowledge and engineering skill provided the means to purify water and dispose of waste. But scientists and engineers also perfected skyscrapers and built four- and five-story tenements, making it possible to concentrate urban dwellers in crowded slums. And no one could solve all the problems of modern cities with obsolete governments designed for simple farming and trading communities. Chapter 21 describes the attempts of Americans during the first decades of the twentieth century to cope with the problems of city life that sprang from this new urban environment.

SUGGESTED READINGS

MANDELBAUM, SEYMOUR J., *Boss Tweed's New York.* This volume presents an extension of the frontier image to the urban environment.

OSGOOD, E.S., *Day of the Cattleman.* Here is a detailed but fast-moving account of the Montana and Wyoming frontiers.

WEBB, WALTER P., *The Great Plains.* This classic statement analyzes the meaning of the expansion into the plains for those who participated in it and those who simply watched.

The Progressives and the New City

STATING THE ISSUE

CHAPTER 21

During the last decades of the nineteenth century, the United States became steadily more urban. Although towns and cities had played important roles in American life since the first settlers landed along the Atlantic coast, the majority of American citizens had lived in rural areas and made their livings from the soil. The census of 1900, however, revealed that 40 percent of the nation's people lived in towns or cities of more than 2500 people; in 1920, more than half of the nation's population was urban. The problems of these urban areas, and particularly of the great cities, growing apace throughout the country, quickly drew the attention of a host of critics and reformers.

Ordinary citizens joined the chorus calling for change. Some residents of cities wanted parks; others demanded tree-lined boulevards; still others asked for changes in the way in which members of boards of education or city councils were chosen. Some demanded regulation of public transportation or public ownership of utilities; others concerned themselves with aid to workingmen struck down by industrial accidents. A few insisted that the most pressing issue of the day was the control of housing to reduce overcrowding; other reformers called for regulating the labor of women and children. A few people were actively concerned with all these great issues. Many more pressed for only one or two of them but identified themselves as progressive men of action linked to others by their common interest in reform.

Many historians have argued that a great progressive movement for reform developed during the late nineteenth and early twentieth centuries. Chapters 21, 22, and 24 examine this argument and raise some serious questions about it. They raise a key issue: whether or not the efforts to plan and control the environment were too complex to be brought together in a single comprehensive social movement.

Chapter 21 focuses on progressivism in the new city. What changes did reformers wish to bring about? Did they share common goals? How did they propose to make changes? What obstacles stood in their way? To what degree were they successful? These are the major issues raised in Chapter 21.

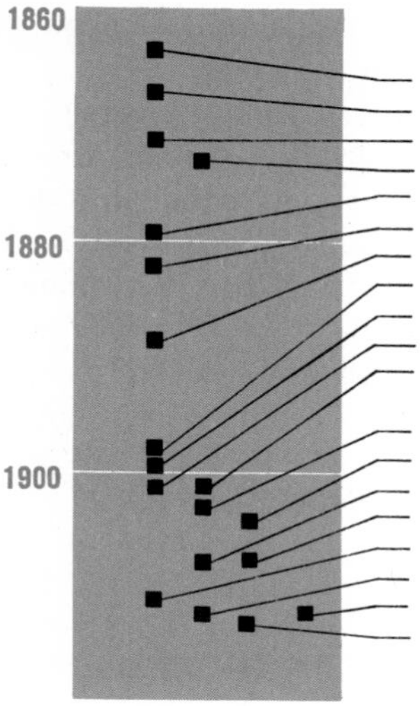

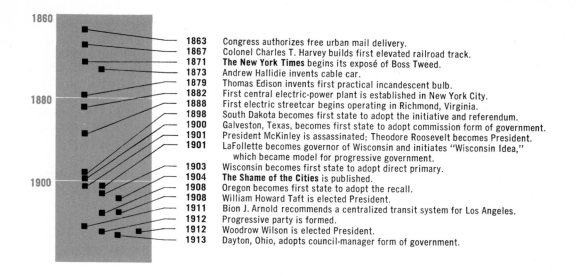

1863	Congress authorizes free urban mail delivery.
1867	Colonel Charles T. Harvey builds first elevated railroad track.
1871	**The New York Times** begins its exposé of Boss Tweed.
1873	Andrew Hallidie invents cable car.
1879	Thomas Edison invents first practical incandescent bulb.
1882	First central electric-power plant is established in New York City.
1888	First electric streetcar begins operating in Richmond, Virginia.
1898	South Dakota becomes first state to adopt the initiative and referendum.
1900	Galveston, Texas, becomes first state to adopt commission form of government.
1901	President McKinley is assassinated; Theodore Roosevelt becomes President.
1901	LaFollette becomes governor of Wisconsin and initiates "Wisconsin Idea," which became model for progressive government.
1903	Wisconsin becomes first state to adopt direct primary.
1904	**The Shame of the Cities** is published.
1908	Oregon becomes first state to adopt the recall.
1908	William Howard Taft is elected President.
1911	Bion J. Arnold recommends a centralized transit system for Los Angeles.
1912	Progressive party is formed.
1912	Woodrow Wilson is elected President.
1913	Dayton, Ohio, adopts council-manager form of government.

81 Demands of Interdependence

During the middle and late nineteenth century, American cities suffered from decentralized government. Sewers were built bit by bit with little centralized direction or control. Local police captains administered the law with little regard for either police commissioners or constitutional guarantees. Boards elected at the neighborhood level often ran public-school systems. Yet problems such as the control of waste, the protection of lives and property, and education extended throughout the entire city.

Observers of the American scene claimed that cities were run by all-powerful bosses who controlled every aspect of city life. Although many of these bosses did manage to exploit almost everyone, none of them exercised universal power. Nineteenth-century cities suffered from too little government, not too much.

A concerted movement demanding more central control of urban development grew slowly toward the end of the nineteenth century. In one city after another, public commissions recommended public control, regulation, and planning of vital services such as transportation, public utilities, waste disposal, or schools. Countless plans for broad, tree-lined boulevards or for regulating bodies designed to control the distribution of electricity or gas emerged.

The need for coordinated planning seemed particularly acute in Los Angeles, a new city which sprouted from a tiny town in 1870. By 1880, the population had reached only 11,000; by 1900, the metropolitan area housed 190,000 persons; ten years later, almost 500,000 people lived there. Moreover, the city was already begin-

A metropolitan area contains a central city and the area surrounding it. The United States government defines it as a region with at least one city having a minimum population of 50,000, as well as the entire county in which the city is located.

ning to sprawl over a vast land area where a number of independent municipal governments sprang up.

In 1911, Los Angeles asked a traffic expert, Bion J. Arnold, to recommend plans for a coordinated transportation system for the city. As you read parts of his report, think about these questions:

1. What recommendations did Arnold make? Do these recommendations seem reasonable?
2. What sort of governmental structure would be required to carry out the recommendations? Could a decentralized system of government do the job?
3. Who would benefit most if these recommendations were carried out? Who would have most to lose?

An Expert Analyzes Transportation Problems in Los Angeles

At the time he was asked to study the transportation problems of Los Angeles, Bion J. Arnold was Chief Engineer of the municipal transportation system of Chicago. He had helped to plan the street railways of Chicago and Pittsburgh and the subway system of New York. His study of Los Angeles began when a group of businessmen became concerned about transportation to the harbor, which they expected to grow rapidly with the scheduled completion of the Panama Canal in 1914.

"The Transportation Problem of Los Angeles," **The California Outlook, A Progressive Weekly,** vol. XI, no. 19 (November 4, 1911). Language simplified.

The transportation of both passengers and freight is the very life blood of the Los Angeles district. Unless passengers and freight flow freely to every part of the community, the city's growth will be restricted. On the other hand, if we provide transportation facilities too far in advance of actual needs, we will invest large sums of money without adequate financial returns. Ideally we should be able to find a halfway point which will meet the increasing demands for transportation without providing too much in one year and not enough in others. The development of transportation must go forward steadily. Nothing more directly affects the cost of living than transportation. The welfare of the people of any district depends largely on their ability to obtain adequate transportation at minimal cost.

Municipal Railroad The city needs a municipal railroad to connect the main business section of Los Angeles, which is twenty miles inland from the Pacific Ocean, with the new city-owned harbors at Wilmington and San Pedro. Such a railroad will be easy to locate and construct. The terrain between Los Angeles and the sea presents no significant engineering difficulties. The right-of-way for the railroad should be at least 250 feet wide in order to provide for eight railroad tracks and two highways. In fact, the entire enterprise appeals strongly because of the possibilities for highways.

Automobile trucks are now being developed rapidly. A large part of the tonnage between the harbor and local delivery and collection points may soon be handled by means of trucks. When the distance is comparatively short, the largest part of the cost of transportation comes in the cost of handling freight at terminals. Trucks will make it possible to deliver goods from wharf or warehouse directly to stores or factories and thus eliminate the expense of intermediate transfers. The already extensive use of trucks in the Los Angeles area proves the practicality of this suggestion.

Local Street Railways A large part of the streetcar system in Los Angeles and its immediate vicinity operates independently of the streetcar lines which serve the surrounding towns and communities. The urban and inter-urban [between-cities] systems use different gauges of track. In the city proper, Mr. H. E. Huntington, who controls the streetcar lines, uses a narrow gauge system and supplies a liberal amount of up-to-date and well maintained equipment. As a result, travel upon the city tracks approximates nearly one ride for each inhabitant per day; other cities of a similar size have a ratio of about one ride to two inhabitants. Los Angeles street railways have already introduced a system of universal transfers. People can travel over the entire city for one fare and often follow "through routes." Many cities do not have these benefits.

Gauge is the distance between rails in a railroad track. The standard gauge in the United States is now 4 feet, 8½ inches.

Three problems concerning transportation requirements face the city: to do away with present and future congestion in the business district; to plan future extensions including the building of crosstown and outside circuit lines; and to provide better pavement between and next to the rails.

The street railway system lacks crosstown and circuit lines, particularly inside the four-mile circle at the center of the city. Lines which radiate out from the center of the city have been built liberally. Even extensions into the outlying districts have been built, although the long haul and the small amount of business has meant a loss to the company. However, the cross connecting lines, which could join two outlying districts to each other and are usually considered as desirable parts of a system of this size, have been neglected.

Two results should be sought in planning these circuit routes. First, the city should try to get a route—and eventually more than one route—entirely around the city outside of the downtown congested district. Secondly, the city should try to use crosstown lines to connect lines which radiate out from the city center. Eventually, crosstown lines could form a series of outside loops which will make it possible to get around the city without returning each time to the center of town.

This inter-urban system should be laid on level ground. It should eliminate almost all city stops. If these plans are carried out, high-powered cars should reach the circle five miles out from the center of the city in from ten to twelve minutes. In thirty minutes cars should reach centers fully twelve to fifteen miles from the business district. Beyond a certain distance from the city's center, it is clear that the territory can be best served by a high-speed system.

Development of high-speed terminals in the inter-urban systems will affect the business center of Los Angeles. With good rapid transit, the 35,000 people living in Pasadena could get to the shopping center of Los Angeles as rapidly as the residents of the city who live between three and four miles from the center of the city do now. There is no other way for Los Angeles to extend the area it serves both for pleasure and for business than to have an excellent inter-urban system. The rides per capita of people in this district are already very high. Every improvement will make it still easier to travel from one center to other centers and will further increase the riding habit. Towns and cities have been built up in this district at remarkable speed. The prosperity of the community paralleled the activity of its people which was made possible by electric-car service. These conclusions can only point to still greater extensions of the service. Of all possible improvements, building a comprehensive Los Angeles city terminal for the inter-urban system would be the most important.

Pasadena is a suburban residential city, eight miles northeast of Los Angeles.

Immediate Relief from Main Street Congestion The first step to be taken to improve transit conditions in Los Angeles and vicinity involves the relief of congested traffic because of the operation of both inter-urban and local surface cars on Main Street. During rush hours each day, as many as 40,000 riders on both systems are delayed for between five and forty minutes. As many more riders are inconvenienced in non-rush hours because of crowding along Main Street.

The first electric streetcar began to operate in Richmond, Virginia, in 1888. The current, generated from a power house, passes through copper wires. The streetcar is attached to the overhead line by a long trolley pole which conducts the current to the motors under the car.

City and District Planning Greater Los Angeles can grow by unifying the present city with its satellite communities which lie within a radius of perhaps 25 miles from the present center. An enlarged district such as this, however, could not reach its greatest potential for civic development under the present form of city government. The city needs some form of consolidation such as a borough system to unite the present metropolitan center with sur-

Satellite communities grow up around a larger city, such as Los Angeles, and become secondary centers of industrial activity.

A borough is a unit of local government. It is chartered by the state and usually has its own police force, fire department, school system, and governing board.

rounding communities so that common problems of transportation, water supply, sewage, and street plans can be coordinated and centrally controlled. In this way, the more strictly local problems such as street cleaning and lighting, fire and police protection, and so forth, can be administered by each individual locality.

This report is not a city plan; it would be better for both transportation and city planning, however, if the city could solve both problems—that is, transportation and governmental reform—at once.

Every community naturally tends to develop around centers. Every city has its business center. Even within the business center certain kinds of businesses are to be found together. Hence, we have a wholesale district, a manufacturing district, a retail district, and sometimes a financial district. City planning should recognize this tendency toward centralization and establish centers of amusement and recreation, of art, of education, of conventions and assemblies, and so forth. Once this development has taken place, the transportation system can be built to carry people most effectively between their homes and these common meeting points.

City and district planning, therefore, should start by adopting this principle of centers. It should also recognize that the development about any center—even the original one—may become too large. For this reason, subcenters will develop. The location and the character of such subcenters should be controlled by natural influences. Artificial development of subcenters will not work. Transportation will play the key role in developing the district and its subcenters by providing a rapid, comfortable, and economic system of communication among them. Citizens should be able to reach each center, to pass through it, or to avoid it entirely by a convenient by-pass. As centers grow, they each will need an individual collecting and distributing streetcar system. Such a system will contribute to the effectiveness of main rapid-transit lines by providing additional cars which make local stops. Thus the inter-urban lines can confine service to the stops at centers.

82 The Machine: An ABC of Politics

Bion J. Arnold wrote a reasoned and sensible call for comprehensive regional development. He saw clearly the ways in which the welfare of various parts of a metropolitan area were related to each other. He also saw the relationship between successful planning for a regional transportation system and the reorganization of local governments. Like Arnold, many other reformers argued that America's cities needed efficient, centralized, "scientific" government if they were to solve basic problems.

Lincoln Steffens wrote many articles for magazines exposing municipal corruption. These articles were collected and published as **The Shame of the Cities** in 1904.

At the same time, reformers denounced the corrupt alliance of businessmen and city bosses who were said to rule America's metropolitan areas with iron hands. Throughout the first decade of the twentieth century, newspapers and magazines were filled with articles that denounced this alliance. Lincoln Steffens, the most famous of the urban journalists of the time, called toleration of this corrupt coalition "the shame of the cities." What chance would centralization have unless corruption could be eliminated? Hence, the reformers attacked corrupt bosses and urged a return to freedom, honesty, and democratic government.

Tammany Hall, named after an Indian chief, was formed in 1789 as a patriotic and social club. After 1854 and until the inauguration of Mayor Fiorello LaGuardia, a Republican, in 1934, it controlled New York City politics most of the time. The bosses in Tammany Hall nominated candidates, got them elected, and handed out municipal jobs and contracts. Although still in existence, it has lost its power.

The reformers seemed to be urging contradictory policies. On the one hand, they demanded centralization to solve problems involving a large geographic area. On the other, they denounced the existing central governments as corrupt and they demanded that control of the government be returned to the people. Much of their attack on existing governments centered on the political boss.

Cities are divided into wards for purposes of voting, representation, and administration.

Reading 82 examines the role of the boss in municipal government. Around 1900, George Washington Plunkitt, a local political leader in New York, gave his views about what made municipal government run to a reporter named William Riordan. Although he was an official in Tammany Hall, New York's Democratic party machine, Plunkitt was neither a party leader nor a mayor. He saw politics from the bottom up and knew their base at the ward level as well as any man in the country. Many of the reformers recognized the valuable functions that men like Plunkitt performed, as the second excerpt, written by a Boston settlement worker, indicates. As you read these two excerpts, think about these questions:

Constituents refer to the voters who live in the district Plunkitt controlled.

1. What services did Plunkitt provide for his constituents? Where did he get the money to provide these services? What sort of institutions would the city have to organize before the services that Plunkitt offered could be replaced?
2. Why did Woods think that opposition to a local boss was futile? What did reformers lack which men like Plunkitt had?
3. Suppose you were trying to build a regional transportation system, what would your attitude to men like Plunkitt be?

Plunkitt of Tammany Hall

In the first part of this selection, Riordan tries to capture the flavor of Plunkitt's own speech. The second part represents his observations of a typical day in Plunkitt's busy life. The third section contains Plunkitt's analysis of "honest graft."

Reformers Only Mornin' Glories

William L. Riordan, **Plunkitt of Tammany Hall.** New York: Alfred A. Knopf, Inc., 1948, pp. 22, 25–27, 121, 123–26, 131–32.

College professors and philosophers who go up in a balloon to think are always discussin' the question: "Why Reform Administrations Never Succeed Themselves!" The reason is plain to anybody who has learned the ABC of politics.

This chapter is based on extracts from Plunkitt's diary and on my daily observation of the work of the district leader.—W. L. Riordan

The fact is that a reformer can't last in politics. He can make a show for a while, but he always comes down like a rocket. Politics is as much a regular business as the grocery or the dry-goods or the drug business. You've got to be trained up to it or you're sure to fall. Suppose a man who knew nothing about the grocery trade suddenly went into the business and tried to conduct it according to his own ideas. Wouldn't he make a mess of it? He might make a splurge for a while, as long as his money lasted, but his store would soon be empty. It's just the same with a reformer. He hasn't been brought up in the difficult business of politics, and he makes a mess of it every time.

You can't begin too early in politics if you want to succeed at the game. I began several years before I could vote, and so did every successful leader in Tammany Hall. When I was twelve years old I made myself useful around the district headquarters and did work at the polls on election day. Later on, I hustled about gettin' out voters who had jags on [were drunk] or who were too lazy to come to the polls. There's a hundred ways that boys can help, and they get an experience that's the first real step in statesmanship. Show me a boy that hustles for the organization on election day, and I'll show you a comin' statesman.

That's the ABC of politics. It ain't easy work to get up to Y and Z. You have to give nearly all your time and attention to it. Of course, you may have some business or occupation on the side, but the great business of your life must be politics if you want to succeed in it.

Do you understand now, why it is that a reformer goes down and out in the first or second round, while a politician answers to the gong every time? It is because the one has gone into the fight without trainin', while the other trains all the time and knows every fine point of the game.

In boxing, the timekeeper rings a gong to start and end rounds of fighting. A rest period occurs between rounds. A fighter loses if he cannot "answer the gong" at the end of a rest period.

Strenuous Life of the Tammany District Leader

This is a record of a day's work by Plunkitt:

2 A.M. Aroused from sleep by the ringing of his door bell; went to the door and found a bartender, who asked him to go to the police station and bail out a saloon-keeper who had been arrested for violating the excise law. Furnished bail and returned to bed at three o'clock.

6 A.M. Awakened by fire engines passing his house. Hastened to the scene of the fire, according to the custom of the Tammany district leaders, to give assistance to the fire sufferers, if needed. Met several of his election district captains who are always under orders to look out for fires, which are considered great vote-getters. Found several tenants who had been burned out, took them to a hotel, supplied them with clothes, fed them, and arranged temporary quarters for them until they could rent and furnish new apartments.

8:30 A.M. Went to the police court to look after his constituents. Found six "drunks." Secured the discharge of four by a timely word with the judge, and paid the fines of two.

9 A.M. Appeared in the Municipal District Court. Directed one of his district captains to act as counsel for a widow against whom dispossess proceedings had been instituted and obtained an extension of time. Paid the rent of a poor family about to be dispossessed and gave them a dollar for food.

Between 1900 and 1914, the cost of food increased greatly. Eggs went from 21 cents to 35 cents a dozen, milk from 7 to 9 cents a quart, steak from 13 to 24 cents a pound. At these prices, a dollar could feed a family for a day or two.

11 A.M. At home again. Found four men waiting for him. One had been discharged by the Metropolitan Railway Company for neglect of duty, and wanted the district leader to fix things. Another wanted a job on the road. The third sought a place on the subway and the fourth, a plumber, was looking for work with the Consolidated Gas Company. The district leader spent nearly three hours fixing things for the four men, and succeeded in each case.

Plunkitt is referring to the ferry from Manhattan to Staten Island.

3 P.M. Attended the funeral of an Italian as far as the ferry. Hurried back to make his appearance at the funeral of a Hebrew constitutent. Went conspicuously to the front both in the Catholic church and the synagogue, and later attended the Hebrew confirmation ceremonies in the synagogue.

7 P.M. Went to district headquarters and presided over a meeting of election-district captains. Each captain submitted a list of all the voters in his district, reported on their attitude toward Tammany, suggested who might be won over and how they could be won, told who were in need, and who were in trouble of any kind and the best way to reach them. District leader took notes and gave orders.

8 P.M. Went to church fair. Took chances on everything, bought ice-cream for the young girls and the children. Kissed the little ones, flattered their mothers and took their fathers out for something [to drink] down at the corner.

9 P.M. At the club-house again. Spent $10 on tickets for a church excursion and promised a subscription for a new church-bell. Bought tickets for a baseball game to be played by two nines from his district. Listened to the complaints of a dozen pushcart peddlers who said they were persecuted by the police and assured them he would go to Police Headquarters in the morning and see about it.

10:30 P.M. Attended a Hebrew wedding reception and dance. Had previously sent a handsome wedding present to the bride.

12 P.M. In bed.

That is the actual record of one day in the life of Plunkitt. He does some of the same things every day, but his life is not so monotonous as to be wearisome.

By these means the Tammany district leader reaches out into the homes of his district, keeps watch not only on the men, but also on the women and children; knows their needs, their likes and dislikes, their troubles and their hopes, and places himself in a position to use his knowledge for the benefit of his organization and himself. Is it any wonder that scandals do not permanently disable Tammany and that it speedily recovers from what seems to be crushing defeat?

Honest Graft and Dishonest Graft

Everybody is talkin' these days about Tammany men growin' rich on graft, but nobody thinks of drawin' the distinction between honest graft and dishonest graft. There's all the difference in the world between the two. Yes, many of our men have grown rich in politics. I have myself. I've made a big fortune out of the game, and I'm gettin' richer every day, but I've not gone in for dishonest graft—blackmailin' gamblers, saloon-keepers, disorderly people, etc. —and neither has any of the men who have made big fortunes in politics.

There's an honest graft, and I'm an example of how it works. I might sum up the whole thing by sayin': "I seen my opportunities and I took 'em."

Just let me explain by examples. My party's in power in the city, and it's goin' to undertake a lot of public improvements. Well, I'm tipped off, say, that they're going to lay out a new park at a certain place.

I see my opportunity and I take it. I go to that place and I buy up all the land I can in the neighborhood. Then the board of this or that makes its plan public, and there is a rush to get my land, which nobody cared particular for before.

Ain't it perfectly honest to charge a good price and make a profit on my investment and foresight? Of course, it is. Well, that's honest graft.

Or supposin' it's a new bridge they're going to build. I get tipped off and I buy as much property as I can that has to be taken for

An approach is a small road by which a main roadway or bridge can be reached.

approaches. I sell at my own price later on and drop some more money in the bank.

Wouldn't you? It's just like lookin' ahead in Wall Street or in the coffee or cotton market. It's honest graft, and I'm lookin' for it every day in the year. I will tell you frankly that I've got a good lot of it, too.

I'll tell you of one case. They were goin' to fix up a big park, no matter where. I got on to it, and went lookin' about for land in that neighborhood.

I could get nothin' at a bargain but a big piece of swamp, but I took it fast enough and held on to it. What turned out was just what I counted on. They couldn't make the park complete without Plunkitt's swamp, and they had to pay a good price for it. Anything dishonest in that?

A watershed is that area of land from which water drains into a river, lake, or city water supply.

Up in the watershed I made some money, too. I bought up several bits of land there some years ago and made a pretty good guess that they would be bought up for water purposes later by the city.

Condemnation commissioners declare what property will be taken for public use. The government pays the owner a just compensation for his property.

Somehow, I always guessed about right, and shouldn't I enjoy the profit of my foresight? It was rather amusin' when the condemnation commissioners came along and found piece after piece of the land in the name of George Plunkitt of the Fifteenth Assembly District, New York City. They wondered how I knew just what to buy. The answer is—I seen my opportunity and I took it. I haven't confined myself to land; anything that pays is in my line.

A Settlement-House Worker Analyzes the Role of the Local Boss

Robert Woods found he could work comfortably with the local leader in the South End of Boston, "Honorable Jim" Donovan. They cooperated to gain a series of public improvements for their district. The settlement-house worker was a useful ally in a battle against Donovan's political opponents and encouraged the "better elements" of the district to support Donovan.

Robert Woods, "Settlement Houses and City Politics," **Municipal Affairs,** IV (June 1900), pp. 396–97.

In nearly all cases it is idle for the settlement to attempt to win away the following of local politicians. To make such an attempt is to leave out of account the loyalties of class, race, and religion which bind the people of the crowded wards to their political leaders. The notion that the young university man by living in such a ward a few years and dispensing kindness around, can become political master of the situation, is one that belongs to the story books. The successful political leader is the man to the local manner born, who enters instinctively into the ambitions and passions of his people, and to whom they return even after he has been untrue to them, as one does to a blood relation. No ready-made attachment can take the place of such a bond as this.

The method of the boss in organizing his local power, however, has two fatal defects. The awarding of his favors has the uncertainty of a game of chance; after election he may not have favors to award. It has in addition a great deal of unfairness and partiality. The strength of the method of the boss lies in the fact that it has to do with supplying tangible benefits to meet keenly felt, unrelenting human needs such as are characteristic of his constituency. He controls some of the best avenues to livelihood; the winning of a job or a license depends on him. A man in need may through him reach the resources of charity. A wrongdoer may through him find immunity from punishment.

83 The Reform of Urban Politics

Many people agreed that major political changes had to precede the sort of reforms that men like Bion Arnold described for Los Angeles. Reformers urged many different proposals upon cities and states across the country. They suggested that people should be permitted to vote directly upon many public issues in a popular referendum. They proposed the adoption of rules which would make it possible to recall a public official who had betrayed his trust; a large group of citizens could require him to stand for re-election before his normal term of office was over. They urged the adoption of commission governments or the appointment of city managers who reported to elected boards.

All these plans seemed to provide ways to undercut the power of the bosses. The initiative and referendum gave citizens a chance to pass legislation which could not be vetoed by a boss-controlled council. Recall provided a method to remove a dishonest boss from power. Professional managers or commissions elected at large deprived a local boss like Plunkitt of his base of operations.

Voting for candidates at large means that all voters elect the members of a governing unit instead of voters in each district electing people to represent only their district.

Reading 83 contrasts two progressive views of the needs of urban government. The first selection comes from a speech given by the mayor of Oakland, California, to a citizens' group in Los Angeles in 1911, the same year as the Arnold report. The second excerpt describes Jane Addams's rationale for political activity. Miss Addams was one of the leading figures in the establishment of Chicago's Hull House, one of the first and most famous settlement houses. As you read the excerpts, think about these questions:

1. Why did Mayor Mott want to change municipal government? Who would benefit from the changes he proposed?
2. Why did Miss Addams disagree with Robert Woods? Did she have the same interests as Mayor Mott?
3. Would a government by experts supervised primarily by upper-class people elected from the city at large be likely to eliminate the abuses Miss Addams complained of? Why, or why not?

Mayor Mott Discusses Commission Government

In the summer of 1911, Oakland, California, adopted a commission form of government. Mayor Frank K. Mott traveled to Los Angeles in October to discuss with a group of businessmen the advantages and possible disadvantages of the new system.

Mayor Frank K. Mott, "Suggestions for Municipal Government," **The California Outlook,** vol. XI, no. 19 (November 4, 1911), pp. 11–12, 15–16. Language simplified.

Widespread unrest has spread through American cities. Everyone deplores the lack of business methods in government. No one seems confident that taxes have been spent wisely and economically in the public interest. As a result, we see numerous attempts to break away from old forms of municipal government in the name of greater democracy and more efficiency. Greater democracy leads to demands for the recall, the initiative, and the referendum; to get more efficiency, citizens recommend the so-called commission form of government.

Sound business principles like those of great industrial and mercantile establishments combined with better education of the people are indispensable to efficiency and progress in municipal affairs. We customarily point with pride to the growth of population in our cities and to our great engineering works. If by chance a visitor from Europe suggests that some municipal matters are poorly run, we reply that we are young and that Europe started to solve municipal problems many centuries before we did.

But the continental cities of Europe have grown as fast as ours. Many of those cities are far ahead of us in ways to solve municipal problems which are as new to them as they are to us. At the same time, they have provided the benefits of modern technology on which we pride ourselves far more economically and perfectly than we have. We should study their methods in order to adapt the underlying principles to American conditions.

Politicians should be the leaders and teachers of the people. We must no longer shut our eyes to the hideousness of much of our architecture, to our haphazard care of streets, to the absence of parks and playgrounds, to the lack of shade trees along our thoroughfares, to the unsightly and dangerous array of poles which shut out the sky by networks of wires. At the same time we must strive for better sanitary conditions, for better transportation, for purer and more abundant water, for better gas and electric service for domestic and industrial uses, for more and better schools, and for the development of business interests.

One of the most obvious characteristics of German cities is the composition of the administrative body called the magistracy. The burgomaster is the head of this body. It is an administrative body, responsible to the municipal council. In reality these German cities practically have a commission form of government somewhat similar to that proposed for American cities. The magistracy is a body of immense authority and dignity, compact and always ready for action. It has both paid and unpaid members. The former, experts in their fields, are chosen for their technical skill or their previous experience. The unpaid members are required to be men of general capacity and experience in public affairs. The German system is not a government by experts nor a government of experts. The system makes use of experts very well. But every group within the society takes an active part in controlling the work of the experts.

In all lands experts are usually specialists who can be carried away by professional zeal for their specialty. They can easily lose their sense of proportion. They can allow other interests to suffer in their ardent pursuit of things dear to their own hearts. In America, several conditions seem to prevent anything like a government in which experts play the principal part.

No doubt it would be best if citizens elected to office men who have had experience and would employ men with high technical skills in administration. But we cannot count on the electorate to choose experts. Personal popularity is still the major criterion for election to office. Surely citizens should be educated to see the advantages to themselves of having experienced and trained men at the head of their municipal governments. But unless only trained candidates become eligible for office, we cannot expect this outcome. Reason, judgment, and principle influence only a minority of the electorate. In addition, a good specialist or expert would seldom be a good vote getter. He would usually be unwilling to spend his time in a strenuous campaign for an office which lasted only a short term. A long tenure of office is unpopular in America. How then shall the situation be met?

There is no real problem with subordinate officeholders. We can develop a suitable system of awards and demerits for them. The heads of departments must be kept alert by other means.

The spirit of the German system may be captured by the hoped-for efficiency of the commission form of government to which some of our cities are now committed. Let us have an official council drawn from voluntary bodies such as the Chamber of Commerce, taxpayers' associations, improvement clubs, and so forth, as well as representatives from among citizens at large.

A body like this would be non-partisan and representative of the varied interests of the city. It would serve as a sensitive medium to test public opinion. Members could carry discussion of every question into the homes of the people. Their approval would strengthen the administration and leave it free to carry on important works for the public good. Under such conditions it would be safe to enlarge the tasks which city governments might do. The city charter might become a true constitution for the city government, a statement of broad principles and a grant of wide discretionary power. If citizens chose for elective office only people who had served a year on the citizens' council, a degree of expertness would come to the administrative body. The commission should appoint no one but experts to important positions and make fitness for office the criterion for appointment or promotion in all cases.

Jane Addams Attacks a Boss

Jane Addams, "Ethical Survivals in Municipal Corruption," **International Journal of Ethics,** VIII (April 1898), pp. 278–79, 288–89.

Unlike Robert Woods, Jane Addams was unable to work successfully with her local councilman, Johnny Powers. This selection is an attack on Powers and his "system." Powers, in turn, insisted that "the trouble with Miss Addams is that she is just jealous of my charitable work in the ward." He promised that Hull House would be driven from his territory.

An alderman is a member of the governing council of a ward, district, or city.

Padrones were men who would contract employment for Italian immigrants and also handle their money for them as well as advance them loans, usually at a large profit. Civil-service jobs were a threat to their income.

Of a like blighting effect upon public morals was the alderman's action in standing by an Italian *padrone* of the ward when he was indicted for violating the Civil Service law. The Commissioners had sent out notices to certain Italian day-laborers who were upon the eligible list that they were to report for work at a given day and hour. One of the *padrones* intercepted these notifications and sold them to the men for five dollars apiece, making also the usual bargain for a share of the wages. The *padrone's* entire arrangement followed the custom which had prevailed for years before the enactment of the Civil Service law. Ten of the laborers swore out warrants against the *padrone,* who was convicted and fined seventy-five dollars. This sum was promptly paid by the alderman; and the *padrone,* assured that he would be protected from any further trouble, returned triumphant to the colony. The simple Italians were much bewildered by this show of a power stronger than that of the Civil Service law which they had trusted as they did that of Italy. This was one of the first violations of its authority, and various sinister acts have followed, until no Nineteenth-Ward Italian feels quite secure in holding his job unless he is backed by the friendship of the alderman. According to the Civil Service law, a laborer has no right to a trial; many are discharged by the foreman, and find that they can be reinstated only upon the aldermanic recommendation. The alderman thus practically holds his old power over the laborers working for the city, and the popular mind is convinced that an honest administration of the Civil Service is impossible, and that it is but one more instrument in the hands of the powerful. It will be difficult to establish genuine Civil Service among these men who learn only by experience. To their minds it is "no good."

The positive evils of corrupt government are bound to fall heaviest upon the poorest and least capable. When the water of Chicago is foul, the prosperous buy water bottled at distant springs; the poor have no alternative but the typhoid fever which comes from using the city's supply. When the garbage contracts are not enforced, the well-to-do pay for private service; the poor suffer the discomfort and illness which are inevitable from a foul atmosphere. The prosperous businessman has a certain choice as to whether he will treat with the boss politician or preserve his independence on a smaller income; but to an Italian day-laborer it is a choice between obeying the commands of a political boss or practical starvation. Again, a more intelligent man may philosophize a little upon the present state of corruption, and reflect that it is but a phase of our commercialism, from which we are bound to emerge. At any rate, he may solace himself with the ideals of literature and history. But the more ignorant man who lives only in the narrow present has no such resource. Slowly the conviction enters his mind that politics is a matter of favors and positions, that self-government means pleasing the boss and standing in with the gang. This slowly acquired knowledge he hands on to his family. During the month of February his boy may come home from school with rather incoherent tales about Washington and Lincoln, and the father may for the moment be fired to tell of Garibaldi, but such talk is only periodic, and the long year round the fortunes of the entire family, even to the opportunity to earn food and shelter, depend upon the boss.

Guiseppe Garibaldi (1807–1882) was an Italian nationalist and military leader who helped to bring about the unification of Italy.

This lowering of standards, this setting of an ideal, is perhaps the worst of the situation, for daily by our actions and decisions we not only determine ideals for ourselves, but largely for each other. We are all involved in this political corruption, and as members of the community stand indicted. This is the penalty of a democracy—that we are bound to move forward or retrograde [backward] together. None of us can stand aside, for our feet are mired in the same soil, and our lungs breathe the same air.

84 The American City

HISTORICAL ESSAY

During the colonial period, only a few towns, mainly centers for international trade, dotted the Atlantic coast. These towns grew slowly but steadily. After the War of 1812, a number of urban centers sprang up in the interior, particularly along major rivers. By far the greatest growth period for urban areas in the United States, however, was the fifty years between 1860 and 1910. In 1860, four times as many people lived in rural as in urban areas; by 1910 urban and rural population were almost equal; the 1920 census indicated that the balance had swung to cities and towns. This shift from rural areas to towns and cities had an enormous impact on the lives of the American people. No one can understand the American past who has not studied urban growth.

The Development of Cities

Table 1 describes the development of urban population between 1860 and 1930.

U.S. Bureau of the Census, **Historical Statistics of the United States, Colonial Times to 1957.** Washington, D.C.: Government Printing Office, 1960, p. 14.

TABLE 1. Number of Cities, by Population, 1860–1930

Year	Rural Population	Urban Population	Number of Urban Places	100,000 or more No.	100,000 or more Population
1860	25,226,803	6,216,518	392	9	2,638,781
1870	28,656,010	9,902,361	663	14	4,129,989
1880	36,026,048	14,129,735	939	20	6,210,909
1890	40,841,449	22,106,265	1,348	28	9,697,960
1900	45,834,654	30,159,921	1,737	38	14,208,347
1910	49,973,334	41,998,932	2,262	50	20,302,138
1920	51,552,647	54,157,973	2,722	68	27,429,326
1930	53,820,223	68,954,823	3,165	93	36,325,736

Year	50,000 to 100,000 No.	50,000 to 100,000 Population	5,000 to 50,000 No.	5,000 to 50,000 Population	2,500 to 5,000 No.	2,500 to 5,000 Population
1860	7	452,060	213	2,531,162	163	594,515
1870	11	768,238	329	3,917,805	309	1,086,329
1880	15	947,918	437	5,352,959	467	1,617,949
1890	30	2,027,569	636	8,103,729	654	2,277,007
1900	40	2,709,338	827	10,343,072	832	2,899,164
1910	59	4,178,915	1,093	13,789,685	1,060	3,728,194
1920	76	5,265,408	1,323	17,077,334	1,255	4,385,905
1930	98	6,491,448	1,642	21,420,049	1,332	4,717,590

Observers of the rise of the city commented most frequently upon the growth of giant cities along the eastern seaboard. In reality, cities of all sizes grew rapidly throughout the nation except in the South, which remained primarily rural. The South lagged about fifty years behind the rest of the country in the proportion of its population that lived in cities. In 1900, only 15.2 percent of the South's population was urban; the national figure for the percentage of people in urban areas had been 15.3 percent in 1850. The South excepted, however, the move to the cities swept the entire nation.

Fundamental economic changes spurred city growth. Specialization of labor in factories and mills resulted in the development of trade and manufacturing centers to make and exchange goods. Cities grew in several different types of locations. Many developed around ports which also became centers of manufacturing, such as New York City, Boston, San Francisco, Baltimore, or Philadelphia. Some grew where special technological or economic developments took place: Schenectady, New York, became the home of the General Electric Company; Hershey, Pennsylvania, manufactured chocolate; Milwaukee, Wisconsin, brewed beer; Holyoke, Massachusetts, made paper, and Memphis, Tennessee, processed cottonseed oil. Some towns and cities, such as Butte, Montana; Scranton, Pennsylvania; or Tulsa, Oklahoma, grew up around mines or near oil wells. Dozens of cities developed along, or in anticipation of, railroad lines, an almost indispensable ingredient of rapid growth. A few—Washington, D.C., and several state capitals—grew primarily because they were governmental centers. Nevertheless, the location of American towns and cities at places like these indicates the close ties between city growth and economic change.

Promoters played a key role in the development of most nineteenth-century cities. Often stressing the prosperity which would follow close after a railroad or a mining strike, promoters advertised the advantages of townsites so widely that they drew investors from as far away as Europe. Although some of these grandiose schemes failed completely, others were remarkably successful. The rapid development of cities such as Los Angeles, California; Seattle, Washington; and Wichita, Kansas, were all spurred by the work of promoters. Without economic advantages, however, cities failed to grow no matter what promotional activities supported them.

More People, More Problems

Urbanization transformed American civilization. Between 1860 and 1910, American cities increased about seven times in population. With this vast increase came new technological developments which remade daily life. To draw people and technology together, new institutions developed and old ones dissolved. Torn from accustomed ways of living in European villages or on American farms, new city dwellers were forced to remake their lives in relatively impersonal environments where the timeclock, instead of the sun, governed every moment of life from sunrise to bed.

City dwellers came from four major sources. Almost twelve million people who lived in cities in 1910 were not living there in 1900. Of these twelve million people, about 41 percent were immigrants from abroad, 29.8 percent had come from American rural areas, 21.6 percent had been born in cities since the 1900 census, and 7.6 percent had lived in towns which cities had incorporated within their boundaries during the decade. These figures indicate that high birth rates in rural areas in both Europe and the United States sustained the growth of American cities. The application of knowledge to rich resources had raised the productivity of the American wheat farmer eighteen times between 1830 and 1900. At the same time, industrial growth opened new jobs in cities to lure the sons and daughters of farmers from the family homestead.

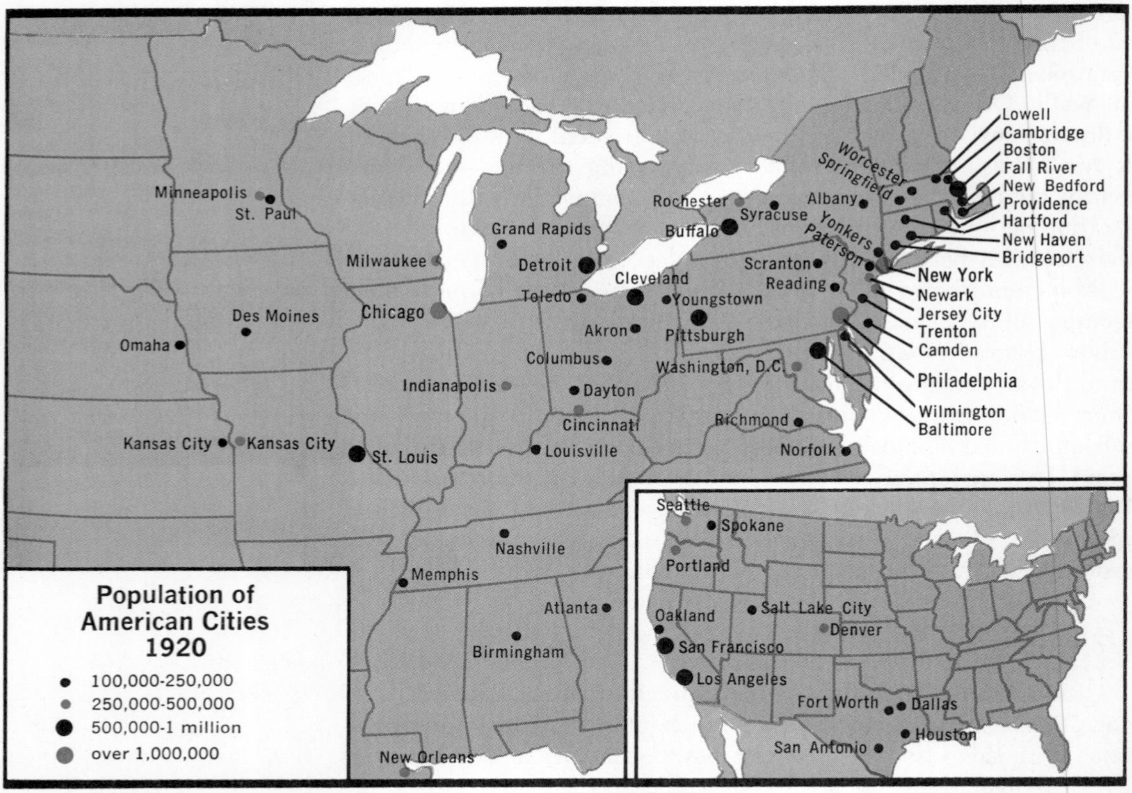

Population of American Cities 1920

American migrants often moved first to a nearby town, then to a larger regional city, and finally to one of the giants, such as Chicago or New York. Immigrants from abroad frequently moved immediately to large cities. They avoided both cities in the South and interior cities such as Indianapolis or Kansas City.

The growth of urban areas demanded a new technology to cope with problems such as transportation, communication, water supply, waste disposal, housing, roads, lighting, and sewage. Before the Civil War, the horse-drawn bus, the steam railroad, and the horse-drawn railway car had been developed to allow for rapid movement through cities. New York built an elevated line for steam railroads just after the Civil War. A few years later, a number of cities, including New York, Philadelphia, and San Francisco, pioneered in the use of cable cars. The most important innovation, however, took place in the 1880's and 1890's when the electric-powered railway, or streetcar, made its appearance. Streetcars spread rapidly throughout the nation. Their development made the use of the subway possible; experiments in both Boston and New York City around 1900 proved the practicality of this new development. Bridges, developed on new principles during the 1870's, helped link parts of the new cities, many of which were located on rivers or harbors. Automobiles and buses began to appear in cities in large numbers around World War I.

Better communication systems accompanied improvements in transportation. The telegraph did little to speed messages within a city. In 1863, however, free urban mail delivery was established in New York City and spread rapidly to other metropolitan centers. The telephone eventually revolutionized urban communication. In 1880, 148 telephone companies in 85 cities had fewer than 50,000 subscribers. By 1900, nearly 800,000 telephones were in use, and their numbers continued to increase rapidly.

Additional technological developments helped to make life in the cities more attractive. Experiments with bricks, stone blocks, and wood eventually led to the development of inexpensive asphalt paving, which solved the problem of an efficient road-building material. In the 1880's, the electric carbon arc lamp began to replace less satisfactory gas and kerosene lamps. The development of the incandescent electric light and of the first central power system (1882) revolutionized lighting and paved the way for the development of the electric motor, an invention which worked dramatic changes in industry. New ways to filter water and to dispose of sewage were developed between 1890 and 1910. Finally, the invention of the steel skeleton and the elevator made it possible to erect tall buildings of the sort which now grace the skyline of every major American city.

The cable car was invented in 1873 by Andrew Hallidie to travel the steep hills of San Francisco. A cable running through a trench in the ground's surface pulls the car. A gripping device attaches the car to the cable.

One new idea was that of the suspension bridge which hangs on parallel cables made of twisted steel wire, fastened to high towers. This type of bridge is not as expensive as others. The idea was perfected by John Roebling, who designed the Brooklyn Bridge.

Light is produced in an electric carbon arc lamp when a current of electricity leaps from one end of an electrode to another. The current causes the electrode, usually a pointed rod made of carbon, to turn to glowing vapor and waste away.

The incandescent electric light, developed by Thomas Edison, gives off light when an electric current flows through a metal filament such as one made of tungsten. It lasts much longer than a carbon-arc light.

All these developments helped to crowd more people into less and less space. The four- and five-story tenements in which workers in New York lived in the late nineteenth century were unbelievably crowded. Windowless except in the front and rear, and without plumbing or heat, some packed as many as 800 people into a building erected on a lot that measured 245 feet by 35 feet. In the 1880's, builders developed the dumbbell tenement which at least provided interior ventilation. Built five or six stories high with fourteen rooms to a floor, and covering most of a standardized 25 foot by 100 foot New York City lot, the dumbbell had a narrow indentation on both sides at the center of the building which permitted windows to open on an air shaft. Four families lived on one floor. The ten dumbbells on one block often housed as many as 4000 people. Imagine how a farmer from either a European village or an American farm would feel, packed with his family into three or four rooms in one of these buildings. And how could people live in them unless everyone spoke the same language and shared the same outlook on the world? The buildings themselves helped to create the patchwork of immigrant colonies, each containing within its own boundaries its own stores, banks, clubs, and churches. No other city was quite so crowded as New York, but high population densities existed almost everywhere. Even new suburban developments built around trolley lines frequently included block after block of multi-story buildings.

This new environment brought a host of problems in its wake. How could a stranger find his way in this new world? What could be done to make the new environment less harsh? What reforms should the government sponsor to solve the most pressing problems of the society? Much of American local politics revolved around these issues from the end of the Civil War to 1930.

Municipal Government

Rapid urban growth in the early decades of the nineteenth century overwhelmed the political and governmental structures of cities. The 1880 census testified to the continued weakness of all efforts requiring coordinated planning. Some historians trace this weakness to the decline in the number of prominent businessmen and social leaders who devoted themselves to public life. "Good" men simply didn't go in for politics, and so a scorned profession attracted incompetents.

Other historians are less interested in the actual leaders than the leadership roles. The rapid growth of cities made it difficult to achieve any public consensus on policy. The very organization of city government made action difficult. City charters called for elaborately divided and extremely limited powers. Cities had to appeal constantly to state legislatures for additional powers or to call on states to provide essential services. Budgets were surprisingly small. In 1810, New York City's budget was only $100,000—one dollar for each citizen. Voluntary associations took care of the poor; volunteer fire companies served without pay; there were no uniformed policemen in most cities until about 1850.

New York City's budget for 1969–1970 amounted to $6.6 billion.

Government became more complicated as new functions and powers were added bit by bit. New semi-independent offices and boards were created. At one time, Philadelphia's city government included thirty boards, each responsible for a separate function, such as supervising health or running the schools. In the meantime, state governments interfered constantly to amend city charters or pass laws for cities, often at the request of special-interest groups. The New York State Legislature, for example, passed thirty-nine laws for the city of Brooklyn in a single year—1870.

In 1898, Brooklyn became a borough of New York City. Brooklyn now has three different forms of local government. It has its own borough president with local responsibilities. He sits with nine other representatives from Brooklyn on the New York City Council. As a county, Brooklyn elects its own district attorney, county clerk, and county judges.

Although city governments became more complicated and more subject to interference from states, they also became more important. By mid-century, large cities had started municipally owned water works to replace private wells. By 1870, all major cities had a Board of Education. Around the 1870's, cities began to set up Boards of Health with inspectors to enforce laws, clean up the slums, and require that tenements have windows in every bedroom. A modern, uniformed police force was organized in New York in 1845, and the practice spread rapidly to other cities. In the 1850's, paid firemen began to replace volunteer companies. Between 1850 and 1870, most cities began to build public sewers, to collect garbage and trash, and to sweep the streets. At about the same time, they began to purchase land for public parks. All these developments cost money. In New York City, per capita expense for government quadrupled between 1850 and 1900. Many cities went heavily into debt to finance municipal improvements.

In most cities, franchises granted to utility companies failed to help solve financial crises. Because cities were anxious to have streetcar lines or electric-power facilities built, they granted generous terms to private companies. Some franchises gave privileges for fifty or even a hundred years. Instead of returning money to the city, franchises sometimes cost them cash. Moreover, because franchises were so profitable, their owners began to bribe legislators until owners became so powerful that they dominated a number of governments.

A franchise is the right or privilege granted to a company by the city government to carry on a business with little or no competition.

The Rise of the Bosses

Political organizations of the sort described by George Washington Plunkitt and both criticized and praised by Jane Addams and

Instead of paying a bribe beforehand to a boss, companies that received contracts would give the boss a certain percentage of the fees they charged the city.

In 1871, **The New York Times** began an expose of the corrupt regime of Boss William Marcy Tweed. The cartoons of Thomas Nast in **Harper's Weekly** did much to enrage public opinion. In 1872, Tweed was convicted of having robbed New York City of $75–200 million.

Robert Woods played an important role in city development. At the level of the neighborhood, Plunkitt and men like him provided a variety of services: jobs and food when men were down on their luck, or help with the police when trouble arose. At the city-wide level, political parties provided a chain across the divided maze of government agencies and contending publics. The links in the chain were the combined power of jobs and money. Government jobs were distributed by party leaders. Companies holding city franchises graciously provided jobs for the machine's supporters. Money for all these services came from a variety of sources, as Plunkitt's memoirs revealed. Many companies that won contracts or franchises from the city kicked back a portion of their fee to the city leaders. Although reform groups occasionally ousted bosses, as New York reformers did to William Marcy Tweed in 1871, they or their heirs often won control again within a few years.

Political parties depended ultimately upon their ability to attract votes. Men like Plunkitt devoted all of their waking hours to the business of politics. Amateur reformers were not likely to replace them permanently by devoting an evening or two each week to their constituents. The bosses were talented men. Many sprang from the poor who gave them votes, and they symbolized success to the new urban immigrants. The poor looked to them as if they were Robin Hoods, caring for the poverty-stricken with money taken from the rich and well born. What difference if some of the money that fed one's starving children was tainted!

Reform in City Governments

Agitation for the reform of city governments grew in the 1870's. By the end of the 1880's, reform talk was in the air in every American city. During the next few decades, a number of key reform demands turned up in one city after another. They included demands for home rule free from state interference, an increase in the authority of the mayor, a demand for simplified government, a movement to separate city politics from state and national elections, an attempt to coordinate reform in a number of cities into one concerted movement, and the development of two new proposals for city government—the city-manager and commission plans.

The proposal for commission government, which Mayor Mott of Oakland described in Reading 83, flourished after it was first adopted in Galveston, Texas, in 1900. A hurricane and tidal wave had devastated the city. Responding to this disaster, the state legislature temporarily replaced the city government with a five-man commission. The group worked so well that it was made a permanent government in 1903. By 1917, about five hundred small and medium-size cities had adopted commission governments.

Another group of cities adopted a variation of the commission plan. They hired city managers to coordinate all of the administrative work of the municipality and report to elected officials. At least in theory, the manager was an expert in municipal affairs who was free of political ties. By the mid 1920's, more than three hundred cities had hired managers, including a few large metropolitan centers such as Cleveland and Cincinnati, Ohio; and Kansas City, Missouri.

Most large cities, however, did not adopt an entirely new form of government. Each of them, however, took important steps to centralize authority, usually in the hands of the mayor, and to make public service more professional. By the end of the 1920's, most cities had adopted some form of municipal civil service. They employed engineers in many departments and retained professional planners to develop comprehensive development programs. The plans drawn up for public transportation in Los Angeles, which you studied in Reading 81, represent the sort of work that many of these experts did. Even local school boards were replaced by city-wide boards elected from the city at large so that each district no longer had its own representative. In many cities, all members of the city council were also chosen at large rather than on a district-by-district basis.

These developments tended to exclude the lower classes from an active role in municipal politics. Men with high social and business status led many municipal reform movements. They tended to take a metropolitan view of urban problems and to emphasize the importance of expert knowledge. In Pittsburgh, for example, the Voters' League argued that ". . . small shopkeepers, clerks, [and] workmen at many trades, . . . could not, however honest, be expected to administer properly the affairs of an educational system, requiring special knowledge, and where millions are spent each year." In 1911, a new charter in Pittsburgh provided for at-large election of both the City Council and the School Board. In practice, this government, and particularly the School Board, began to represent the point of view of the business and social elite of the city.

Some of the products of these "reforms" have been unusually praised; others are more controversial. On the one hand, expenditures for public health increased six or seven times between 1900 and 1910 alone, and infant mortality began to drop rapidly as a result. New parks and boulevards began to grace many urban landscapes. In several large cities, fire and sanitation departments were among the best in the world. By the end of the 1920's most cities had established minimal standards for housing and for controlling the use of land through zoning ordinances.

Zoning is the practice of dividing a city into districts or zones, specifying what each district may be used for. Zoning provides for industrial districts, local business districts, and residential districts. It also restricts the height of buildings, and segregates different types of residences (one-family houses, apartments) or industries (factories, stores).

When the New York City Board of Education gave in February 1968, communities the right to control their own schools, the school boards dismissed several white teachers. According to established city law, these teachers had passed the qualifying tests and had taught long enough to be permanent employees who could not be dismissed without due process. The city board had failed to establish clearly what power local boards did and did not have. The local boards claimed they did have the right to dismiss teachers they considered unsuitable for local students. All city teachers went on strike the following fall to protest the threat they saw to their jobs, and some local boards hired outside teachers. The strike was not settled until the city set up clear rules that protected both the teachers' rights and the rights of the local boards.

On the other hand, the new governments devoted more attention and more money to transportation than to housing. Within the housing field, more effort was expended on middle-class accommodations than on the housing of the poor. Zoning laws often kept poor people out of "good" neighborhoods by requiring that houses there use more land than the poor could afford. As a result, segregation of poor from well-to-do groups increased. Realtors often supported new zoning laws in order to bring this situation about because middle-class citizens often wished to separate themselves from the poor, particularly if the poor were also black or immigrants. Finally, although the health of all classes improved, that of richer people improved more rapidly than that of the poor.

One unexpected result of the progressive reforms in cities was the alienation of many citizens from their municipal governments. Lower-class urbanites, in particular, complained to interviewers in the 1920's and 1930's that the new experts and commissions were not as approachable as the old politicians. Not until the 1960's, however, was the basic premise of the progressive period essentially challenged. In the early part of this century it seemed clear that professionalism and expertise were ways for urban dwellers to gain control of their destinies. Recently, however, political conflicts over the organization of schools, police, and social-welfare agencies have raised a set of new questions: Have expert professionals exaggerated their expertise and isolated themselves unduly from the public they serve? What new forms of political control and public service are necessary to re-establish the connection between urban governments and their citizens?

SUGGESTED READINGS

ADDAMS, JANE, *Twenty Years at Hull-House.* A deeply committed woman pictures life in the inner city in this famous book.

WARNER, SAM B., JR., *Streetcar Suburbs: The Process of Growth in Boston, 1870-1900.* An excellent picture of the pattern of suburban expansion at the turn of the century comes from these pages.

WIEBE, ROBERT, *Search for Order, 1877-1920.* Wiebe's book describes a general framework in which urban change can be placed.

National Politics

CHAPTER 22

STATING THE ISSUE

During the 1850's and 1860's, national attention focused on the activities of the government in Washington, D.C. Throughout the 1850's, the halls of Congress echoed with the sounds of debate about the future of the Union and of the slaves, whose presence threatened to tear that Union asunder. During the 1860's, the progress of the Civil War and subsequent attempts to remake the South sustained attention on the nation's capital. The large grants of land given to encourage the development of railroads and the public colleges also reminded citizens that their government played an important role in their lives.

Then for more than thirty years, national politics faded from its former position of prominence. The telegraph, telephone, and electric power networks grew without government support. Washington ignored the growth of public high schools, the most important educational development of the period. The abuses of railroad magnates and the officers of trusts went on with only an occasional slap on the wrist from Washington. Most administrations during the last three decades of the nineteenth century were content to keep down civil disorder at home, negotiate with representatives of foreign nations, and interfere as little as possible with the "natural laws" which were thought to govern the economy.

A new era seemed to dawn when Theodore Roosevelt succeeded to the Presidency in 1901 after an assassin killed President William McKinley. A champion of the strenuous life, Roosevelt seemed determined to carve out a new and vigorous role for the federal government. Woodrow Wilson, who came to the Presidency four years after Roosevelt left it, seemed to be cast in a similar mold. Yet despite the efforts of these two men, the national government made few far-reaching changes in the balance of power between the public and private sectors of the economy.

What accounts for the relative inactivity of the national government between the end of the Civil War and the onset of the Great Depression? What were the major political issues that occupied the time of officials in the American government? What does the nature of national politics reveal about American society during this period? These are the major issues of Chapter 22.

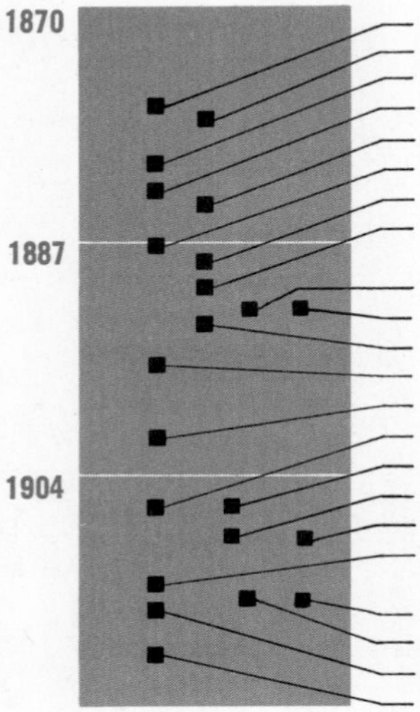

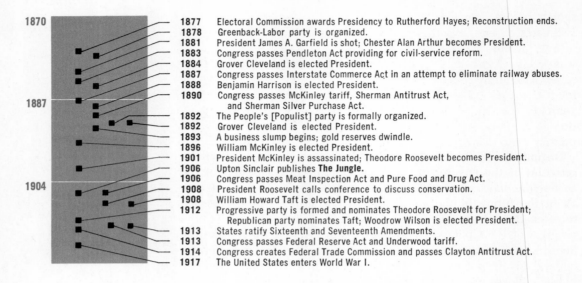

1877 Electoral Commission awards Presidency to Rutherford Hayes; Reconstruction ends.
1878 Greenback-Labor party is organized.
1881 President James A. Garfield is shot; Chester Alan Arthur becomes President.
1883 Congress passes Pendleton Act providing for civil-service reform.
1884 Grover Cleveland is elected President.
1887 Congress passes Interstate Commerce Act in an attempt to eliminate railway abuses.
1888 Benjamin Harrison is elected President.
1890 Congress passes McKinley tariff, Sherman Antitrust Act, and Sherman Silver Purchase Act.
1892 The People's [Populist] party is formally organized.
1892 Grover Cleveland is elected President.
1893 A business slump begins; gold reserves dwindle.
1896 William McKinley is elected President.
1901 President McKinley is assassinated; Theodore Roosevelt becomes President.
1906 Upton Sinclair publishes **The Jungle.**
1906 Congress passes Meat Inspection Act and Pure Food and Drug Act.
1908 President Roosevelt calls conference to discuss conservation.
1908 William Howard Taft is elected President.
1912 Progressive party is formed and nominates Theodore Roosevelt for President; Republican party nominates Taft; Woodrow Wilson is elected President.
1913 States ratify Sixteenth and Seventeenth Amendments.
1913 Congress passes Federal Reserve Act and Underwood tariff.
1914 Congress creates Federal Trade Commission and passes Clayton Antitrust Act.
1917 The United States enters World War I.

85 Politics: A Statistical Account

Traditional accounts of national politics in the United States move from one election campaign to another describing the issues debated by the candidates and then the results of each election. These accounts suggest that in each two- or four-year period, American voters make up their minds on a number of issues, most of them economic, and decide who shall be their President or their representatives in Congress. The votes of citizens determine which candidate and party control the country.

Accounts like these have never been accurate no matter what period of American history is concerned. The great Democratic-party majority of the first half of the nineteenth century was composed of many smaller groups and contained such diverse people as northern abolitionists and southerners who defended slavery to the last. Even after leading the nation to victory in the Civil War, the new Republican party was so torn internally that it maintained control through Reconstruction only with the votes of southern representatives and senators. A majority of members of one party in the Senate and the House has never guaranteed effective control of Congress unless the majority was substantial and the party united.

Reading 85 carries the story of American Presidential elections from 1876 to 1920. These were years during which the Granger and the Populist movements agitated farmers. At the same time, American industry grew rapidly with all the new problems that industrialization brought in its wake. One of these problems, for example, was a serious depression that struck the nation in 1894, shortly before Grover Cleveland entered office for his second term. Estimates of the proportion of unemployed ran as high as one out of five. "Armies" of unemployed workers, the most famous of which was led by Jacob S. Coxey, marched on Washington to demand relief. Although these demonstrators were generally peaceful, President Cleveland warned ominously of the danger of mob rule and anarchy. This long and serious depression, together with the agitation of the Populists, eventually began to have an effect on national politics. So did World War I, which America entered in 1917.

Reading 85 consists of four tables and an excerpt from the Inaugural Address of President Grover Cleveland. Specific questions accompany each section of the reading.

1: *Presidential Elections, 1876–1920*

This table lists the major candidates for President in every election from 1876 to 1920. The winner's name appears first in each group and in capital letters. In some instances, the total is less than 100% because some small political parties are omitted.

1. How close were these elections? Is there any difference in the margin of victory between the first five and next four elections?
2. What difference would it make in the ability to pass sweeping legislation if margins of victory had been larger? smaller?

U.S. Bureau of the Census, **Historical Statistics of the United States, Colonial Times to 1957.** Washington, D.C.: Government Printing Office, 1960, p. 682.

Year	Candidates	Party	% of Popular Vote
1876	RUTHERFORD B. HAYES	Republican	48.0
	Samuel J. Tilden	Democratic	51.0
1880	JAMES A. GARFIELD	Republican	48.5
	Winfield S. Hancock	Democratic	48.1
	James B. Weaver	Greenback-Labor	3.4
1884	GROVER CLEVELAND	Democratic	48.5
	James G. Blaine	Republican	48.2
	Benjamin F. Butler	Greenback-Labor	1.8
	John P. St. John	Prohibition	1.5
1888	BENJAMIN HARRISON	Republican	47.9
	Grover Cleveland	Democratic	48.6
	Clinton B. Fisk	Prohibition	2.2
	Alson J. Streeter	Union Labor	1.3
1892	GROVER CLEVELAND	Democratic	46.1
	Benjamin Harrison	Republican	43.0
	James B. Weaver	Populist	8.5
	John Bidwell	Prohibition	2.2

The Greenback-Labor party, formed in 1878, supported the unlimited coinage of silver, minimum hours for workers, an end to immigration of Chinese workers, woman's suffrage, a graduated income tax, and federal regulation of interstate commerce.

The Prohibition party was organized in 1869, when the Democratic and Republican parties refused to support prohibition.

The Union Labor party was organized in 1887 by Grangers, Greenbackers, and members of the Knights of Labor.

In 1896, the Populist party supported the Democratic candidate, William Jennings Bryan, an advocate of free silver.

The Progressive party, the liberal element of the Republican party, was also referred to as the "Bull Moose" party.

The Farmer-Labor party, founded in 1920, called for government ownership of railroads, mines, and natural resources, and advocated social security legislation and laws to protect farmers and union members.

1896	WILLIAM McKINLEY	Republican	51.1
	William J. Bryan	Democratic	47.7
1900	WILLIAM McKINLEY	Republican	51.7
	William J. Bryan	Democratic; Populist	45.5
	John G. Woolley	Prohibition	1.5
1904	THEODORE ROOSEVELT	Republican	57.4
	Alton B. Parker	Democratic	37.6
	Eugene V. Debs	Socialist	3.0
	Silas C. Swallow	Prohibition	1.9
1908	WILLIAM H. TAFT	Republican	51.6
	William J. Bryan	Democratic	43.1
	Eugene V. Debs	Socialist	2.8
	Eugene W. Chafin	Prohibition	1.7
1912	WOODROW WILSON	Democratic	41.9
	Theodore Roosevelt	Progressive	27.4
	William H. Taft	Republican	23.2
	Eugene V. Debs	Socialist	6.0
	Eugene W. Chafin	Prohibition	1.4
1916	WOODROW WILSON	Democratic	49.4
	Charles E. Hughes	Republican	46.2
	A. L. Benson	Socialist	3.2
	J. Frank Hanly	Prohibition	1.2
1920	WARREN G. HARDING	Republican	60.4
	James M. Cox	Democratic	34.2
	Eugene V. Debs	Socialist	3.4
	P. P. Christensen	Farmer-Labor	1.0

2: Votes for President in Four New York Counties, 1888–1900

This table presents the votes for President in two urban and two rural New York counties for the four Presidential elections between 1888 and 1900. The two rural counties had the highest percentage of Democratic votes of all the rural counties in the state.

1. Where did support for Republicans seem to come from, urban areas, rural areas, or both?
2. How do you account for the rise in Republican strength in cities in the 1896 election?

Lee Benson, "Research Problems in American Political Historiography," in Mirra Komarousny, ed., **Common Frontiers of the Social Sciences.** Glencoe, Illinois: 1957, p. 168.

	New York County (urban)		Kings County (urban)		Schoharie County (rural)		Seneca County (rural)	
Year	*Dem.*	*Rep.*	*Dem.*	*Rep.*	*Dem.*	*Rep.*	*Dem.*	*Rep.*
1888	60.1	39.9	53.7	45.6	56.1	41.4	49.8	48.1
1892	61.5	34.7	56.8	40.0	55.3	39.5	47.7	46.4
1896	44.0	50.8	39.7	56.3	51.0	46.6	44.6	53.5
1900	52.2	43.9	48.3	49.6	51.6	46.2	46.8	51.2

3: Party Control of the Executive and Legislative Branches, 1875–1921

Voters in national elections also elected representatives. Until 1916, they elected senators indirectly since state legislatures continued to choose senators until that date when the Seventeenth Amendment provided for their election directly by voters. The following table shows the results of these decisions by voters.

1. Which party controlled the Presidency, the House, and the Senate from 1875 to 1895? from 1895 to 1911? from 1911 to 1920?
2. What effect would these alignments have on the ability of a President to push through an imaginative program of legislation?

Year	President's Party Affiliation	Majority Party and Margin: House of Rep.	Senate
1875-1877	R	D (60)	R (16)
1877-1879	R	D (13)	R (3)
1879-1881	R	D (19)	D (9)
1881-1883	R	R (12)	even
1883-1885	R	D (79)	R (2)
1885-1887	D	D (43)	R (9)
1887-1889	D	D (17)	R (2)
1889-1891	R	R (7)	R (2)
1891-1893	R	D (147)	R (8)
1893-1895	D	D (91)	D (6)
1895-1897	D	R (139)	R (4)
1897-1899	R	R (91)	R (13)
1899-1901	R	R (22)	R (27)
1901-1903	R	R (46)	R (24)
1903-1905	R	R (30)	R (22)
1905-1907	R	R (114)	R (22)
1907-1909	R	R (58)	R (30)
1909-1911	R	R (47)	R (29)
1911-1913	R	D (67)	R (10)
1913-1915	D	D (164)	D (7)
1915-1917	D	D (34)	D (16)
1917-1919	D	D (6)	D (11)
1919-1921	D	R (50)	R (2)

U.S. Bureau of the Census, **Historical Statistics of the United States, Colonial Times to 1957.** Washington, D.C.: Government Printing Office, 1960, p. 691.

4: Federal Government Finances, 1876–1920

Table 4 shows the receipts, expenditures, quantity of surplus or deficit, and total gross debt of the federal government for every fifth year from 1876 to 1920. You may gain perspective on *this budget when you realize that the 1969 budget for the federal government was $201.7 billion, the deficit was $8 billion, and the total estimated national debt was $387.2 billion.*

1. Did government expenditures from 1876 to 1920 follow any set trend? What evidently happened to expenditures during the World War I period (1915–1920)?
2. What does the size of the budget indicate about the attitudes of government officials toward the federal government?

U.S. Bureau of the Census, **Historical Statistics,** p. 711.

Year	Receipts	Expenditures	Surplus or Deficit	Total Gross Debt	Estimated Population
1876	$ 294,096,000	$ 265,101,000	$ 28,995,000	$ 2,130,846,000	46,107,000
1880	333,527,000	267,643,000	65,884,000	2,090,909,000	50,262,000
1885	323,691,000	260,227,000	63,464,000	1,578,551,000	56,658,000
1890	403,081,000	318,041,000	85,040,000	1,122,397,000	63,056,000
1895	324,729,000	356,195,000	—31,466,000	1,096,913,000	69,580,000
1900	567,241,000	520,861,000	46,380,000	1,263,417,000	76,094,000
1905	544,275,000	567,279,000	—23,004,000	1,132,357,000	83,820,000
1910	675,512,000	693,617,000	—18,105,000	1,146,940,000	92,407,000
1915	697,911,000	760,587,000	—62,676,000	1,191,264,000	100,549,000
1920	6,694,565,000	6,403,344,000	291,222,000	24,299,321,000	106,466,000

The Political Philosophy of Grover Cleveland

Of the nineteenth-century Presidents after Abraham Lincoln, only Grover Cleveland has won a good reputation. Although he did not pioneer for new ways to do things, at least he was honest and purposeful. The excerpt from his Second Inaugural Address which follows illustrates Cleveland's political philosophy.

1. What was Cleveland's conception of the role of the federal government in relationship to the economy?
2. What relationship do you see between Cleveland's philosophy and the budget figures in Table 4?

Inaugural Addresses of the Presidents of the United States from George Washington 1789 to Harry S Truman 1949, House Document No. 540, 82nd Congress, 2nd Session, Washington, D.C.: Government Printing Office, pp. 153–57. Language simplified and modernized.

Every American citizen must look with utmost pride and enthusiasm upon the growth and expansion of our country, the ability of our institutions to withstand violence, the wonderful thrift and enterprise of our people, and the demonstrated superiority of our free government. Nevertheless, we must constantly watch for every symptom of weakness that threatens our national vigor.

Paternalism ruins republican institutions and imperils government by the people. It degrades the plan of rule our fathers established and handed on to us. It corrupts the patriotic sentiments of our countrymen and tempts them to try to find ways to get the government to support them. It undermines self-reliance and substitutes in its place dependence upon governmental favors. It stifles the spirit of true Americanism. While the people should patriotically and cheerfully support their government, the government should not support the people.

Under our scheme of government, wasting public money is a crime against citizens. The contempt of our people for economy and thrift in personal affairs deplorably saps the strength of our national character. It is a plain principle of good government that public expenditures should be limited by public necessity. Necessity, in turn, should be measured by the rules of strict economy. It is equally clear that thrift among the people will best guarantee support of free institutions.

One way to avoid misappropriation of public funds is to appoint good and efficient workers to government jobs instead of appointing people whose major claim to office is that they have been the political supporters of the official who appoints them. To get better people appointed to office, civil service reform has found a place in our public policy.

Cleveland referred here to the passage of the Pendleton Civil Service Act in 1883.

The growth of combinations of business interests [trusts] formed to limit production and fix prices is inconsistent with a free enterprise system. Competition in business should not be replaced by trusts that have the power to destroy competition. Nor should the people lose the benefit of lower prices which usually results from wholesome competition. These combinations of business firms frequently constitute conspiracies against the interests of the people. They are unnatural and opposed to our American sense of fairness. To the extent that they can be restrained by federal power, the government should relieve our citizens from their interference with competition.

The people of the United States have decreed that on this day, the control of their government in its legislative and executive branches shall be given to a political party pledged in the most positive terms to the accomplishment of tariff reform. They have thus spoken in favor of a more just and fair system of federal taxation. This Administration is, therefore, determined to devote itself to tariff reform.

In his campaign, Cleveland pledged to lower the McKinley tariff passed by the Republicans in 1890. The Wilson-Gorman tariff, passed in 1894, although lower, was still thoroughly protective. Therefore, Cleveland allowed it to become law without his signature.

Above all, I know there is a Supreme Being who rules the affairs of men and whose goodness and mercy have always supported the American people. I know He will not turn from us now if we humbly and reverently seek His powerful aid.

86 Roosevelt and Wilson Discuss the Role of Government

Throughout the closing decades of the nineteenth century, most political leaders, like President Grover Cleveland, advocated limited governmental intervention in the economy. At the same time, they supported special subsidies for particular interests such as railroads, which received large grants of land from the government. Belief in limited government, however, caused politicians to look skeptically at suggestions that the government should try to control unemployment, develop national resources in a comprehensive way, or pass extensive social-welfare legislation.

Support for restricting the amount of government intervention—sometimes loosely called laissez-faire—had many roots. In part, it came from the desire of businessmen to be left alone, free of what they felt was government incompetence. This desire received support from the works of many nineteenth-century economists who, like the pioneer Scottish economist Adam Smith, believed in the principles of a competitive economy. Late in the nineteenth century, philosophers called Social Darwinists began to combine Smith's ideas with biological concepts.

Darwinism was also used to justify ruthless business practices used by such "captains of industry" as Rockefeller and Vanderbilt on the grounds that big business was a jungle world where only the fittest survived.

Charles Darwin, the famous English naturalist, had argued that in the struggle to survive among plants and animals the "fittest" specimens were able to adjust to the environment while the weaker and less fit died off. This process, Darwin thought, improved the species because the better-adapted creatures survived. Darwin, however, never applied his theory to human society.

Social Darwinists, the most notable of whom was Herbert Spencer, made this application. Government or even private organizations, they said, should not interfere with "natural laws." If government provided jobs, passed laws to regulate working conditions, or gave poor relief, some of the "less fit" might survive and drag down the rest of the society. For this reason, they said, government should refrain from interfering with the economy and permit the "natural laws" to operate. The new forces of an urban-industrial society, however, demanded government action.

Presidents Theodore Roosevelt (1901–1909) and Woodrow Wilson (1913–1921) represent men of change. Neither broke completely with the past, but both tried new ways. As you read excerpts from their speeches, think about the following questions:

1. What did Roosevelt and Wilson think was the responsibility of the federal government in relationship to the welfare of the American people? Why did they take their particular stands?

2. What were the origins of the problems each man discussed?
3. How could the government fulfill the goals set by these two men? Do the problems they described exist today?

Theodore Roosevelt on the New Nationalism

After two terms as President, Theodore Roosevelt took a long hunting trip to Africa. On his return, he broke with his hand-picked successor, William Howard Taft. He gave the speech which follows before veterans of the Grand Army of the Republic gathered at Osawatomie, Kansas, in 1910.

Theodore Roosevelt, **The New Nationalism.** New York: Outlook Company, 1911, pp. 3–33. Abridged and language simplified and modernized.

One of the main objectives in every wise struggle for human betterment has been to achieve equality of opportunity. In the struggle for this goal, nations rise from barbarism to civilization. Through it people press forward from one stage of enlightenment to the next. The destruction of special privilege is one of the chief factors in progress. The essence of any struggle for liberty has always been, and must always be, to take from some men the right to enjoy power, wealth, position, or immunity which has not been earned by service to their fellows.

When we achieve it, equality of opportunity for all citizens will have two great results. First, every man will have a fair chance to reach the highest point to which his capacities can carry him, unassisted by special privilege and unrestricted by special privileges of others. Second, the society will get from every citizen the highest service he is able to contribute.

I stand for the square deal. When I say that I am for the square deal, however, I do not mean merely that I stand for fair play under the present rules of the game. I stand for having those rules changed to work for greater equality of opportunity and reward.

This philosophy means that our national and state governments must be freed from the sinister influence or control of special interests. Every special interest is entitled to justice—full, fair, and complete. If there were any attempt by mob-violence to do harm to a special interest or a wealthy man, I would fight for him, and you would if you were worth your salt, even if you disliked him. He should have justice. Every special interest is entitled to justice. But no person or interest is entitled to a vote in Congress, to a voice on the bench, or to representation in any public office. The Constitution guarantees protection to property, and we must make that promise good. It does not, however, give the right of suffrage to any corporation.

The absence of effective state and national controls over unfair money-getting has tended to create a small class of enormously wealthy and economically powerful men whose chief object is to hold and increase their power. We must change the conditions which enable these men to accumulate power which they can use against the general welfare. They should have power only so long as it benefits the community. This conclusion implies more active governmental interference with social and economic conditions in this country than we have yet had. I think we must face the fact that such an increase in governmental control is now necessary.

I think we may go still further. Everyone admits that government has the right to regulate the use of wealth in the public interest. Let us also concede that government has the right to regulate the conditions of labor in the interest of the common good. Every man should have a chance to reach a position in which he will make the greatest possible contribution to the public welfare. Give him a chance; don't push him up if he will not be pushed. Help any man who stumbles; if he is a worthy man, try your best to see that he gets a chance to show the worth that is in him. No man can be a good citizen unless he earns more money than he requires to cover the bare cost of living, and has hours of labor short enough so that he will have time and energy to bear his share in the management of the community after his day's work is done. We prevent many men from being good citizens by the conditions of life under which we force them to live. We need comprehensive workmen's compensation acts, both state and national laws to regulate child labor and the work of women, and practical training for daily life and work to supplement book-learning in public schools. We need to provide better sanitary conditions for our workers and to extend the use of safety appliances in industry and commerce. In the interest of the working man himself we need to set our faces like flint against mob-violence just as we do against corporate greed; against violence and injustice and lawlessness by wage-workers, just as much as against lawless cunning, greed, and selfish arrogance by employers.

I do not ask for too much power for the central government, but I do ask that we work in a spirit of broad and far-reaching nationalism. We are all Americans. Our common interests are as broad as the continent. The National Government belongs to the whole American people. Where the whole American people are interested, that interest can be guarded effectively only by the National Government.

The American people rightfully demand a New Nationalism, without which we cannot hope to deal with new problems. The New Nationalism puts the national need before sectional or personal advantage. It is impatient of the confusion which comes when local legislatures attempt to treat national issues as local issues. It is still more impatient of the lack of power which springs from dividing governmental powers widely, making it possible for local selfishness or legal cunning, hired by wealthy special interests, to bring national activities to a deadlock. This New Nationalism regards the executive power as the guardian of the public welfare. It demands that the courts shall be interested primarily in human welfare rather than in property. It demands that legislatures shall represent all the people rather than any one class or section of the people.

Woodrow Wilson on the New Freedom

When the Republican party split in 1912 over the rival candidacies of William Howard Taft and Theodore Roosevelt, Woodrow Wilson won the Presidency. His Inaugural Address opened a remarkable period of legislative activity in the Congress. Major legislation followed quickly in the three fields he mentioned in his Address: banking, tariff reduction, and the regulation of business activity.

A Compilation of the Messages and Papers of the Presidents Prepared Under the Direction of the Joint Committee on Printing, of the House and Senate. New York: Bureau of National Literature, Inc., vol. XVII, pp. 7868–70. Abridged and language simplified and modernized.

There has been a change of government. What does the change mean? That is the question which is uppermost in our minds today.

It means much more than the mere success of a party. The success of a party means little except when the nation is using that party for a large and definite purpose. No one can mistake the purpose for which the nation now seeks to use the Democratic party. It seeks to use it to interpret a change in its own plans and point of view.

Nowhere else in the world have noble men and women shown more sympathy and helpfulness in their efforts to rectify [right] wrong, ease suffering, and give the weak strength and hope. We have built up a great system of government, which has become a model for those who seek to set liberty upon foundations that will endure. Our life contains every great thing, and contains it in rich abundance. But evil has come with the good, and much fine gold has been corroded. With riches has come inexcusable waste. We have wasted a great part of what we might have used, and have not stopped to conserve the bounty of nature, without which our genius for enterprise would have been worthless and impotent. We have been proud of our industrial achievements, but we have not stopped thoughtfully enough to count the human cost, the cost of lives snuffed out, of energies overtaxed and broken, the fearful physical and spiritual cost to men, women, and children upon whom the burden has fallen. The groans and agony of it all has not yet reached our ears. The great government we loved has too often been used for private and selfish purposes, and those who used it had forgotten the people.

At last we have a vision of our life as a whole. We see the bad with the good. With this vision we approach new problems. Our duty is to cleanse, to reconsider, to restore, to correct evil without harming the good, to purify and humanize every part of our life without weakening or sentimentalizing it. There has been something crude, heartless, and unfeeling in our haste to succeed and be great. We said, "Let every man look out for himself, let every generation look out for itself," while we built giant machinery which made it impossible for anyone except those who stood at the controls to have a chance to look out for themselves. We had not forgotten our morals. But we were very heedless and in a hurry to be great.

We have come now to a sober second thought. We have made up our minds to measure every process of our national life against the standards we so proudly set up at the beginning and have always carried in our hearts. Our work is a work of restoration.

We have itemized the things that ought to be altered and here are some of the chief items: A tariff which cuts us off from our proper part in the commerce of the world, violates just principles of taxation, and makes the government an instrument in the hands of private interests; a banking and currency system based upon outmoded financial principles which result in concentrating cash improperly and restricting credits; an industrial system which holds capital in check, restricts the liberties and limits the opportunities of labor, and exploits the natural resources of the country; a body of agricultural activities less efficient than big business, handicapped because science has not served the farmer directly enough, and crippled because the system of credit does not serve it well; watercourses undeveloped, waste places unreclaimed, forests untended, fast disappearing without plan or prospect of renewal, unregarded waste heaps at every mine. We have studied as perhaps no other nation has the most effective means of production, but we have not studied cost or economy as we should.

Nor have we studied and perfected the means by which government may be put at the service of humanity to safeguard the health of the nation. This is no sentimental duty. The basis of government is justice, not pity. These are matters of justice. There can be no equality of opportunity, the first essential of justice, if men and women and children are not shielded from the consequences of great industrial and social processes which they can not alter, control, or cope with by themselves. Society must not crush, weaken, or damage its own constituent parts. Law must keep sound the society it serves. Sanitary laws, pure food laws, and laws setting up conditions of labor which individuals are powerless to determine for themselves are intimate parts of the business of justice and legal efficiency.

These are some of the things we ought to do. We must not, however, leave the others undone, the old-fashioned, never-to-be-neglected, fundamental safeguarding of property and of individual rights. This is the high enterprise of the new day: to lift everything that concerns our life as a nation to the light that shines from every man's conscience and vision of the right.

87 War and the Image of Government

Neither the hopes of Roosevelt's New Nationalism nor those of Wilson's New Freedom were wholly fulfilled. Both men made significant contributions to both the philosophy and practice of government, but neither was able to push his entire program through Congress nor conceive of a role for government on the scale to which we are accustomed. Then, World War I dramatized a new concept of an enlarged governmental role in the economy.

Following the defeat of Napoleon in 1814, Europe enjoyed a century of peace. No general war involved all the great powers. Since no single power threatened to dominate the entire European continent, American interests were safeguarded with little or no expenditure of funds. Americans enjoyed what one historian has called "free security," which enabled them to avoid any large-scale appropriations for military preparedness or for foreign warfare. It encouraged many Americans to think that they did not really have to worry about the safety of the nation. But World War I broke out in 1914, and the United States became a belligerent in 1917.

A belligerent is a nation participating in a war.

In the first months of World War I, lack of experience with major governmental enterprise yielded disastrous results. The production of heavy guns was completely confused. Many assembly lines worked effectively only after the war was over. At the beginning of the war, one general complained the "birds were still nesting in the trees from which the great wooden fleet was to be made." It was hard to get the birds out of the trees. The first vessel did not emerge from the largest government shipyard until after the war was over. The railroad lines were totally disorganized, freight cars were scarce, and the government finally took over the railroads.

Thousands of regulations flowed out of Washington. Elevator operators were told they could make so many stops and no more. Traveling salesmen were told that they could not carry more than two trunks. Everyone in the nation was given just so much coal and oil and no more. Factories that were not working in the war effort were closed down for a week. The railroad administration ran the nation's railroads as a single system. The National War Labor Board guaranteed that the rights of working men would be safeguarded if they promised not to strike. Collective bargaining was introduced into many industries where it had been unknown.

In another area of the economy, Herbert Hoover made a national reputation for himself as the leader of the Food Administration. In order to insure that both the American population and its allies would be adequately fed, he bought grain and distributed wheat. He set hog prices so that farmers would double their production. Sugar was rationed. Shark steak and whale meat appeared on restaurant menus to enlarge the sources of protein. The United States shipped three times as much food to the allied countries during the war as it had before the beginning of hostilities.

The next two selections attempt to see peacetime implications of this experience. As you read, think about these questions:

1. What new elements did the war introduce into the government? What did Bernard Baruch think should be done?
2. What were the lessons of the war for John Dewey?
3. If the changes suggested by these two writers were to take place, what would be the implications for the national budget? for the role of a President and his party? for an expanded executive branch which might be responsible for public planning?

Bernard Baruch on the Peacetime Implications of the War

As a young man, Bernard M. Baruch (1870–1965) made a fortune in the stock market. In later life, he became an adviser to a number of American Presidents. The selection that follows has been taken from the Final Report of the War Industries Board, the central planning agency responsible for mobilizing the civilian war effort. Baruch was the chairman of the W. I. B.

Bernard M. Baruch, **American Industry in the War—A Report of the War Industries Board.** Washington, D.C.: Government Printing Office, 1921, pp. 98–100. Abridged and language simplified and modernized.

The experience of the War Industries Board in controlling American industry leads its members to make a further suggestion, which has less to do with war than with the normal practices of business during peacetime.

During the past few decades, American businessmen and technical experts have, through the control of great masses of capital, made extraordinary strides in converting the natural resources of this country into goods useful for human comfort and satisfaction. In the process, the older and simpler relations of government to business have been gradually forced to give way. We have been compelled to drift away from two old doctrines of Anglo-American law: that government activity should be limited to preventing breach of contract, fraud, physical injury, and injury to property; and that government should protect only non-competent persons. Modern industry has made it necessary for the government to reach out its arm to protect competent individuals against the practices of mass industrial power. We have already evolved a system of government control over our railroads and over our merchant fleet. We continue to argue, however, that competition can be preserved in all other industries so that the interests of the public will be served and efficiency and wholesome growth in the development of natural wealth will take place. With this end in view, the Sherman and Clayton Acts have forbidden combinations in restraint of trade, monopolies, and many other vices which develop when individuals control great masses of capital. This legislation represents little more than a moderately ambitious effort by the government to make business conform to the simpler principles which worked satisfactorily in the past.

A breach of contract occurs when a party to an agreement violates the terms of that agreement or contract. Contracts are enforceable by law.

The war introduced a new element into this situation. The Sherman Act had broken many large companies into smaller ones. Many of these smaller companies grew during the war until some of them have become larger than the original parent company. The conditions of war made developments like these desirable. The war brought an absolute demand for goods no matter what they cost or how difficult they were to acquire. An absolute shortage of some goods developed, and most goods were in short supply for a time, at least. Group action, industry by industry, accompanied by government control of prices and distribution, was the only solution.

During the war, hundreds of trades were organized for the first time into national associations, each responsible for its component companies. They were organized on the suggestion and under the supervision of the government. Practices aimed at efficient production, price control, conservation of scarce materials, control of the quantity of production, and so forth began everywhere. As a result, many businessmen experienced the tremendous advantages to themselves and the general public, of combination, cooperation, and common action with their natural competitors. To restore through new legislation the competitive situation which immediately preceded the war will be very difficult. On the other hand, to leave business combinations without adequate supervision and attention by the Government will tempt businessmen to run businesses for private gain with little reference to public welfare.

These associations can be beneficial to the general public. They can eliminate wasteful practices which result from producing a large number of different brands or types of the same articles. They can help to cultivate the public taste for excellent commodities. They can exchange information to eliminate wasteful methods of production and distribution. They can localize production in places where goods can be produced most economically. By exchanging information about purchasers and goods, they can balance supply and demand more economically. In an emergency, these associations would be of incalculable aid to the government.

These combinations are also capable of doing great harm to the public. They can keep production just short of current demand and thus cause prices to rise steadily. They can set up agreements about prices to keep them abnormally high. They can favor one buyer over another. Nearly every businessman in the country learned during the war that a slight shortage of his product helped him because he could then charge more for it and make larger profits. Trade associations can influence management to produce just enough goods to keep prices high.

The question, then, is what kind of government organization can be devised to safeguard the public interest while these associations continue to carry on the good work of which they are capable. The country will quite properly demand the vigorous enforcement of all proper measures for the suppression of unfair competition and unreasonable restraint of trade. But this essentially negative policy of curbing vicious practices should, in the public interest, be supplemented by a positive program. To this end the experience of the War Industries Board points to the desirability of giving some government agency constructive as well as investigatory powers. This agency should encourage, under strict government supervision, cooperation and coordination in industry to increase production, eliminate waste, conserve natural resources, improve the quality of products, promote efficiency in operation, and thus reduce costs to the ultimate consumer.

John Dewey Reflects upon the Wartime Experiences

John Dewey was one of America's best-known philosophers and educators. Unlike many intellectuals, he supported the war effort. In the article that follows, he predicted what some of the consequences of the war would probably be.

John Dewey, **Characters and Events—Popular Essays in Social and Political Philosophy.** New York: Holt, Rinehart and Winston, Inc., 1929, vol. II, Book 4, Section 1, pp. 551–57. Abridged and adapted.

The first result of the war which I see is the more conscious and extensive use of science for community purposes in the postwar world. Changes produced by new mechanical inventions and appliances endure. The transformation brought about first in industry and then in general social and political life by the steam engine, the locomotive, and the gasoline engine have remained with us, while matters which in their day absorbed much more conscious attention have disappeared. Mechanically speaking, the greatest achievements of the year have been the submarine and airplane. Is it not likely that the combined effects of the two will do more to displace war than all the moralizing in existence?

In addition to specific inventions, the war has made it customary to utilize the collective knowledge and skill of scientific experts in all lines, organizing them for community ends. We shall probably never return wholly to the old divorce of knowledge from the conduct of public life, a divorce which made knowledge abstract and left public affairs in the hands of men who ruled by routine, vested interest, and skilled manipulation. Used for the ends of a democratic society, the social mobilization of science should bring about changes in the practice of government which may eventually develop into a new type of democracy. With respect to this development, as with respect to the airplane, we are more likely to underestimate than to exaggerate the consequences which will follow.

In every warring country, people have demanded that production for profit should be subordinated to production for the public good. Legal restrictions and individual property rights have had to give way before the good of the society. The old conception of the absoluteness of private property has received a blow from which it will never wholly recover. The control of an individual or group over their "own" property has become relative to public needs. Public requirements may at any time be given precedence over private desires by public machinery devised for that purpose.

Ways have been developed to regulate or control every part of our national life. Banking, finance, and new corporations have been affected by regulations to various degrees in all countries. The demand for food during the war has made clear to everyone the social meaning of all the occupations related to the food industry. Consequently, the question of the control of land for use instead of for speculation has become acute. Regulations have also been passed to control the transportation and distribution of food, fuel, and metals such as steel and copper which play a vital role in war.

Not every agency developed during the war to protect the public interest will last. Many of them will melt away when the war comes to an end. But it must be borne in mind that the war did not create the inter-dependent interests which have given social significance to enterprises which were once private and limited in scope. The war only revealed the state of affairs which the application of steam and electricity to industry and transportation has already brought about. It offered an impressive object lesson about what had occurred, and made it impossible for men to proceed any longer by ignoring the revolution which has taken place.

88 Fifty Years of National Politics

HISTORICAL ESSAY

Throughout the period before the Civil War, the activities of the national government had relatively little effect on the daily lives of American citizens. The national capital seemed far away. Men and women worked hard to wrest a living from the soil, from trade, or from manufacturing. Local and state governments built roads, educated children, and passed the majority of laws. Officials of these governments frequently came into direct contact with citizens.

Many of the political issues that arose between 1789 and 1860, however, had national implications. In particular, the slavery issue aroused men and women all over the country. For many years, great Presidents such as Washington, Jefferson, and Jackson drew the attention of voters to national affairs. Then the Civil War settled the nation's two most divisive issues—the preservation of the Union and the legal status of blacks—and an assassin's bullet ended the life of the last of the nineteenth century's great Presidents, Abraham Lincoln. For almost seventy years after these events until the inauguration of Franklin D. Roosevelt in 1933, most of the important developments in American life took place outside the arena of national politics, except for a brief flurry of activity during the Administrations of Theodore Roosevelt (1901–1909) and Woodrow Wilson (1913–1921) and of greater significance, the enlarged role forced on the government by World War I.

Why the National Government Was Weak

Six major factors help to explain the relative weakness of the national government between the end of the Civil War and the

Administration of Franklin D. Roosevelt. The first is mediocre leadership. With the exceptions of Woodrow Wilson, Theodore Roosevelt, and Grover Cleveland, American Presidents throughout this period ranged from failures to average. In 1948, fifty-five prominent American historians were asked to rank American Presidents. The list below includes their composite ranking of all American Presidents to that date. The Presidents between Ulysses S. Grant and Herbert D. Hoover have been set off in capitals, with the dates of their administrations in bold-face type.

For a discussion of these Presidents by Arthur M. Schlesinger, see **Life**, vol. 25, no. 18 (November 1, 1948), pp. 65–74.

The Quality of American Presidents, 1789–1932

Great	Near Great
Lincoln Washington F. D. Roosevelt WILSON **(1913-1921)** Jefferson Jackson	T. ROOSEVELT **(1901–1909)** CLEVELAND **(1885-1889, 1893-1897)** J. Adams Polk
Average	**Below Average**
J. Q. Adams ARTHUR **(1881-1885)** Monroe McKINLEY **(1897-1901)** HAYES **(1877-1881)** A. Johnson Madison HOOVER **(1929-1933)** Van Buren B. HARRISON **(1889-1893)** TAFT **(1909-1913)**	Tyler COOLIDGE **(1923-1929)** Fillmore Taylor Buchanan Pierce **Failures** GRANT **(1869-1877)** HARDING **(1921-1923)**

Not Listed

GARFIELD **(1881)**
W. H. Harrison **(1841)**

These two Presidents were not in office long enough to be evaluated. William Henry Harrison died of pneumonia one month after his inauguration. James Garfield was fatally shot almost four months after his inauguration.

Why mediocre men? A number of elements seem to have been involved. The greatest opportunities during most of these years lay in business, a field that attracted a host of talented men. Those businessmen who wished to make changes in government worked primarily in local or state politics where more was happening and where there was an opportunity to make a constructive contribution in a few years. Outstanding men, for example Roscoe Conkling of New York, James G. Blaine of Maine, or John Sherman of Ohio, usually found their rivals pitted against them at nominating conventions. Usually a "dark horse" emerged who was more or less acceptable to everyone—and usually mediocre as well. Until the twentieth century, most candidates were ex-Civil War generals or relatively undistinguished lawyers. Between 1870 and 1890, elections hung on the results in five states—Connecticut, New York, Indiana, Nevada, and California. Sixteen states always voted Re-

Roscoe Conkling (1829–1888) led a faction of the Republican party known as the "Stalwarts" or "Old Guard," who favored harsh Reconstruction policies and opposed reform. The "Half-Breed" wing of the party, led by Speaker of the House James G. Blaine (1830–1893) and by John Sherman (1823–1900), supported some reform.

When a convention deadlocks and cannot agree on a candidate, it may turn to an unknown or non-controversial figure as a compromise. James K. Polk was the first "dark-horse" Presidential candidate.

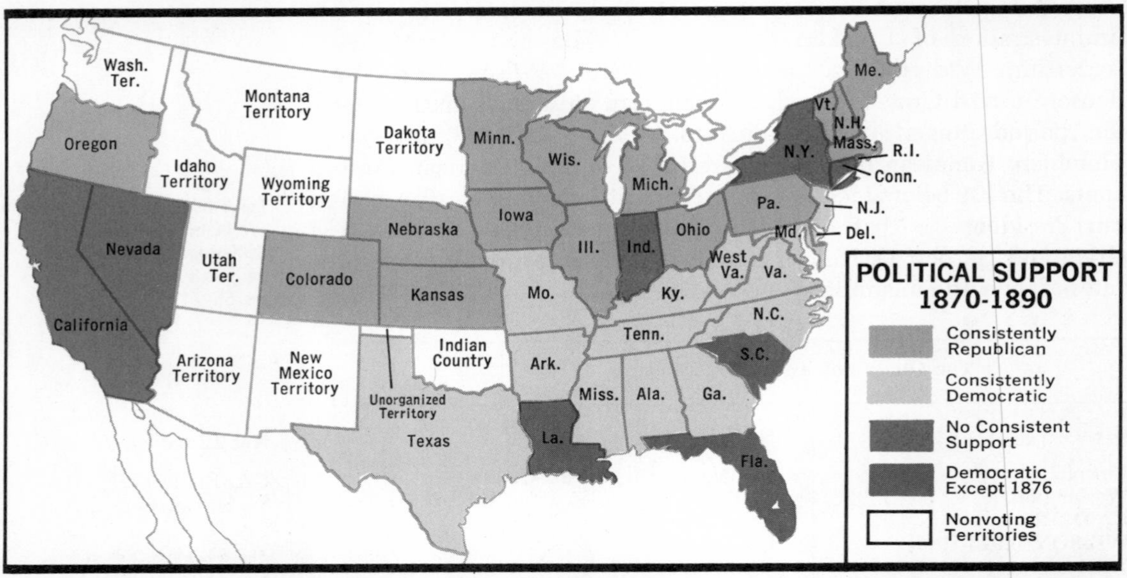

publican and fourteen Democratic, as the accompanying map shows. Three additional southern states voted Republican only under Reconstruction governments. During the entire period from 1872 to 1932, Herbert Hoover was the only Republican to carry a state in the "solid South," and he ran against Governor Al Smith, of New York, of Irish descent, Catholic, and a foe of Prohibition.

Most Presidents during the entire period from Grant through Hoover had a narrow conception of the role of the Presidency. To many of them, that government was best which governed least. Many had been influenced by the ideas of the Social Darwinists. Rather than press for reforms, they permitted legislative leadership to fall into the hands of senators and representatives. Only Theodore Roosevelt and Woodrow Wilson of all these men seemed to have grasped the possibilities of national leadership inherent in the office of the President.

Nevertheless, interest in politics remained high. During national campaigns, Republican orators in the North "waved the bloody flag of the rebellion." Torchlight parades and flamboyant oratory attracted crowds to political rallies. In addition, local bosses in both urban and rural areas kept in close contact with voters whose vital interests they served. The percentage of people who voted in elections kept pace with the rise in population through the last decades of the nineteenth century. A base for dramatic political action did exist. But no one managed to put together a firm coalition of voters willing to support an active administration.

It was difficult to set a consistent direction to national legislative action without a Congress that would work closely with the President. During the late nineteenth century, the two major parties received roughly similar numbers of votes at national elections. Of all the Presidents between Hayes and Roosevelt, only McKinley received more than 50 percent of the popular vote. Two Presidents (Hayes and Benjamin Harrison) received fewer popular votes (although more electoral votes) than one of their rivals. Presidents usually found Democrats in the majority in the House of Representatives during these years. Republicans usually controlled the Senate. Between 1896 and 1911, however, Republicans did control both Houses of Congress and the Presidency, and usually by generous margins. But the Republican party was divided between the progressive wing, led by Theodore Roosevelt, and a more conservative group to which many prominent senators belonged. Hence, no President could push a legislative program through the Congress without running into major opposition from powerfully entrenched men. Since most Presidents had no well formulated legislative program, effective political leadership often fell to the Congress.

The Senate at this time was referred to by many as the "Millionaires' Club." In 1906, David Phillips in a series of articles entitled "The Treason of the Senate" charged that 75 of the 90 senators represented the interests of railroads and the trusts.

In addition to relatively weak Presidents and the failure of one united party to win control of Congress, the lack of a national consensus on major political issues hampered political action. A President needed a stable and firmly committed bloc of voters willing to elect congressmen who would support him if he wanted substantial changes. But how could he get such support? Local political leaders rallied voters to their own banners and tried through the use of patronage and the other devices of local political bosses to weave a web of personal loyalty instead of developing bonds that tied voters to a national party. A reforming national administration had to raise the voters' sights from battles over local issues which affected people's lives directly to less personal problems on the national level.

Except for momentous national issues such as wars, however, citizens of the United States did not yet have enough in common to support comprehensive national political action. Early in the twentieth century, large daily newspapers and magazines began to serve a substantial national public. Journalists, whom President Theodore Roosevelt called "muckrakers," used these newspapers and magazines to inform readers of the "reality"—usually the "harsh reality"—of the new industrial society. Journalists could not create a political revolution alone. Although illiteracy had been reduced to 10 percent by 1910, most Americans had never been within the walls of a high school. Reforming magazines such as *The Saturday Evening Post,* which had a circulation of about two million in 1914, served the enlarged middle class, but hardly touched the minds of most Americans. Only great events like war or the depression of the 1930's sharply affected the lives of most

Muckrakers began to achieve prominence shortly after 1900 with the publication of such popular magazines as **McClure's, Cosmopolitan,** and **Collier's.** Prominent muckrakers included Upton Sinclair who wrote **The Jungle,** Lincoln Steffens, author of **The Shame of the Cities,** and Ida Tarbell who exposed the corrupt business dealings of Rockefeller in **The History of the Standard Oil Company.**

President Roosevelt frequently used the radio to deliver his "fireside chats." These informal radio talks helped restore the confidence of the American people during the Depression crisis and enabled them to understand the Administration's policies.

citizens. By the 1930's, the radio helped a reforming President like Franklin D. Roosevelt to rally support directly from voters. After World War II, television began to play a similar, and far more important, role. But in the progressive decades of Theodore Roosevelt and Woodrow Wilson, a national constituency was only beginning to form, and its members were largely middle-class people.

A fourth reason for the relative inactivity of the national government was the active part played by state and local governments in dealing with the major political issues of the day. The first important laws to regulate railroads were passed by state legislatures in the 1870's. The early progressives made their most significant gains on the state and local levels where mayors such as Tom Johnson (Cleveland, Ohio), Brand Whitlock (Toledo, Ohio), Emil Seidel (Milwaukee, Wisconsin), Mark Fagan (Jersey City, New Jersey), and Fremont Older (San Francisco, California) fought against bosses and for reform legislation with equal vigor. On the state level, men such as Robert M. La Follette of Wisconsin, Hazan Pingree of Michigan, Hiram Johnson of California, and Albert Cummings of Iowa organized powerful reform efforts which succeeded far more rapidly than any similar movement on a national scale. Eventually, these reformers learned that many of the issues with which they were concerned, such as railroad regulation, the control of trusts, or the regulation of child labor, could only be settled on a national level. But in the meantime, they drew attention from the White House to mayors' and governors' offices.

Even if attention had been focused on Washington, a national consensus had emerged, one united party had dominated the Congress, and the Presidents had been powerful leaders, the national government could have done little effective work without more money. American society starved its government for decades. The federal government's expenditures amounted to about 5% of the gross national product. (By comparison, in the 1950's, the federal government was spending about 15% of the gross national product.)

For a definition of GNP, see page 369.

Citizens asked government to take on a host of new tasks, but they did not provide the money. Lack of money helps to explain both the failure to start new programs and the inability to enforce ones which were already on the books. In September 1914, for example, Congress passed the Federal Trade Commission Act, followed one month later by the Clayton Antitrust Act. The Federal Trade Commission was empowered to gather information on business activities and to ". . . prevent persons, partnerships, or corporations . . . from using unfair methods of competition." The Clayton Antitrust Act listed many activities which were to be considered restraints of trade under the original antitrust legislation, the Sherman Act (1890). But the FTC never got enough funds to do its job. The Antitrust Division of the Justice Department, which administered antitrust cases, never included more than eighteen lawyers during Wilson's Administration. Experience during the 1930's indicated that the Department required a staff at least ten times that large to check abuses adequately.

Because funds for thorough investigations were not provided and staffs were small, government officials often had to depend on information provided by the industries they were regulating as a basis of action. Naturally, they did not always learn what they needed for effective control. By controlling the flow of information, businesses were subtly able to shape regulations to their own liking. Aroused by muckraking books such as Upton Sinclair's *The Jungle* (1906), an exposure of abuses in the meat-packing industry, Congress moved to regulate packing houses. Big packers were anxious to establish standards high enough to protect them against the competition of small, local packers. The Pure Food and Drug Act and the Meat Inspection Act passed easily, partly because the major packers supplied data in support of regulation, and partly because Roosevelt avoided a battle with these industrialists by taking money for inspection out of general tax funds instead of asking for a special fee to be paid by packers themselves. No acts, no matter how excellent their intention, could serve the public effectively without strong provisions for enforcement backed by congressional appropriations. Not until 1913, when the adoption of the Sixteenth Amendment legalized the income tax, did the government have a practical way to raise the huge funds that expanded federal services were soon to require.

In 1894, as part of the Wilson-Gorman tariff, Congress passed a two percent tax on incomes over $4000. The following year, the Supreme Court ruled the tax unconstitutional on the grounds that it was a direct tax not apportioned among the states according to population as specified in Article 1, Section 2, Clause 3.

The sixth major factor that helps to account for the relative weakness of the federal government was lack of reliable knowledge about the nation. Late in the nineteenth century, the executive branch began to improve its facilities for gathering data. The census of 1880 had been a massive attempt to gather a huge amount of information. The result of this effort filled twenty-five volumes. But when the census was finished, the staff was dispersed and had to be gathered anew in both 1890 and 1900. In 1902, the Bureau of the Census was finally established with a permanent staff which worked constantly instead of once every ten years. New series of statistics, begun during the first decades of the twentieth century, later played a vital part in guiding legislation. In the meantime, social scientists developed new theoretical models of the social and economic structure of the nation. In the 1920's and 1930's, the concept of the gross national product became important among economists who began to develop techniques by which the government might control inflation and depression and insure steady economic growth. Even if they had wanted to do something to stabilize the economy, American Presidents as late as the 1920's lacked both the theoretical knowledge and the statistical data on which a full-scale attack on a depression could have been based.

National Legislation

Four issues dominated the national politics between 1872 and 1920. They were the regulation of business, the control of the money supply, the regulation of the tariff, and the development of ways to eliminate corruption in government and to make government more directly responsive to the wishes of voters. Occasionally other issues occupied the attention of legislators. Congress set up land-grant colleges, agricultural experiment stations, and county extension programs. Particularly under President Theodore Roosevelt, the federal government established irrigation projects and set aside land for national parks. Under Woodrow Wilson, the government established the Department of Labor and passed such measures as the La Follette Seaman's Act (1915) establishing minimal working conditions on steamships, the Adamson Act (1916) establishing the eight-hour day on interstate railroads, a Child Labor Act (which was later declared unconstitutional) establishing minimal working

Federal Legislation Regulating Industry, 1887–1920

Name of Act	Date	Provisions
Interstate Commerce Act	1887	Created Interstate Commerce Commission (I.C.C.) of five members to regulate and investigate railroads. Required railroads to charge "reasonable and just rates" and give 10-day notice and public posting of new rates. Forbade pooling, charging more for a short haul than a long haul, and discriminating by allowing special favors or rebates.
Sherman Antitrust Act	1890	Declared all combinations in the form of trusts or conspiracies "in restraint of trade" illegal.
Elkins Act	1903	Forbade shippers, railway officials, and agents from giving or receiving rebates. Made railroads charge only the published rates.
Hepburn Act	1906	Forbade railroads from granting free passes. Increased I.C.C. to seven members and gave it authority to fix maximum rates and to regulate express and sleeping-car companies, oil pipelines, ferries, bridges, and railroad terminals.
Pure Food and Drug Act	1906	Prohibited the manufacture, sale, and transportation of adulterated or mislabeled goods and drugs. Required manufacturers of patent medicines to label containers indicating contents.
Meat Inspection Act	1906	Provided for federal inspection of all companies selling meat between states.
Mann-Elkins Act	1910	Authorized I.C.C. to regulate telephones, telegraphs, and cables.
Clayton Antitrust Act	1914	Prohibited price discrimination, interlocking directorates over $1 million, and the acquisition of another company's stock in order to create a monopoly.
Federal Trade Commission Act	1914	Set up Federal Trade Commission (F.T.C.) of five members to investigate companies and prevent unfair business practices such as false advertising and mislabeling.
Esch-Cummins Act	1920	Authorized I.C.C. to fix minimum and maximum rates and to approve railroad consolidations.

Money and Banking Legislation, 1863–1913

Name of Act	Date	Provisions
National Banking Act	1863	Permitted five or more people with capital of $50,000 to secure charter and set up national bank. Required banks to invest one third of capital in government bonds and to issue bank notes up to 90% of face value of bonds.
Coinage Act	1873	Ended coinage of silver dollars.
Resumption Act	1875	Agreed to redeem greenback dollars in gold if presented to Treasury on or after January 1, 1879.
Bland-Allison Act	1879	Required Treasury to buy and mint $2–4 million silver a month.
Sherman Silver Purchase Act (repealed 1893)	1890	Required Treasury to purchase 4.5 million ounces of silver each month at the market price and to pay for it with paper money redeemable in either gold or silver.
Gold Standard (Currency) Act	1900	Made gold the standard unit of value backing the dollar. Provided gold reserve of $150 million for redemption of paper money.
Aldrich-Vreeland Act	1908	Authorized national banks to issue emergency money to be backed by commercial paper and state and local bonds.
Federal Reserve Act	1913	Divided United States into 12 districts, each to be served by a federal reserve bank, all supervised by Board of Governors appointed by President for 14 years. Required federal reserve banks to serve district banks by clearing checks, lending money, rediscounting loans, issuing paper money (federal reserve notes) backed by gold and commercial paper, and transferring money between districts in emergencies. Required all national banks to join, keep a certain percentage of deposits in reserve bank, and buy a percentage of bank's stock.

standards for children, the Federal Farm Loan Act which set up flexible ways for farmers to get credit, and the Rural Post Roads Act which established a precedent for federal aid to highway construction. But legislation like this was unusual.

The chart on page 562 shows the major laws which regulated business. The growth of industry made these laws necessary. Many of them were directed at the abuses of railroads against which farmers had protested so vigorously for decades. Others tried to assure competition in industry by controlling the activities of pools, trusts, and giant corporations which threatened to win monopolistic control of many industries. These laws were minimally successful. In many cases, the Supreme Court undermined them by decisions that restricted the power of administrators to do what legislators had seemingly wished them to do. Because government agencies were underfinanced and understaffed, they were unable to prosecute business as vigorously as they should have done. Finally, a number of proposals which might have led to more effective legislation were defeated or watered down in Congress by legislators who were firm believers in laissez-faire and beholden to business.

Until the passage of the Federal Reserve Act under Woodrow Wilson in 1913, debate over the money supply and banking regulations occupied an enormous amount of attention. Farmers in particular pressed for an expanded money supply in order to combat the long-run deflationary trend which extended through most of the 1870's, 1880's, and 1890's. During the Populist campaign of 1892, and the 1896 contest which pitted the Republican William McKinley against William Jennings Bryan, the nominee of both the Democrats and the Populists, the proposal to coin silver in unlimited amounts in order to expand the money supply dominated political debate. Although an influx of gold from Alaska and South Africa halted the inflationary spiral and drove the issue of an expanded currency out of politics, the Federal Reserve Act was still needed, as the list of legislation on page 563 explains, to keep currency flexible.

Tariff legislation also occupied the attention of almost every administration. The graph on this page traces the history of the major laws. Advocates of high tariffs won support from industry whose managers argued that high tariffs protected American employers and workers from the competition of foreign goods produced by workers earning lower wages than Americans. Foes of the tariff pointed out that high tariff rates permitted inefficient producers to charge higher prices because tariff walls protected them from competition by efficient foreign firms. Tariffs also hurt farmers, they argued, by raising prices on manufactured goods with no compensating increase in the price of foodstuffs which farmers raised. Because business exerted such an enormous influence over large numbers of senators and representatives, tariffs tended to be high despite the barrage of excellent arguments leveled by economists against them.

The final issue that occupied the attention of President and Congress concerned corruption in government and government re-

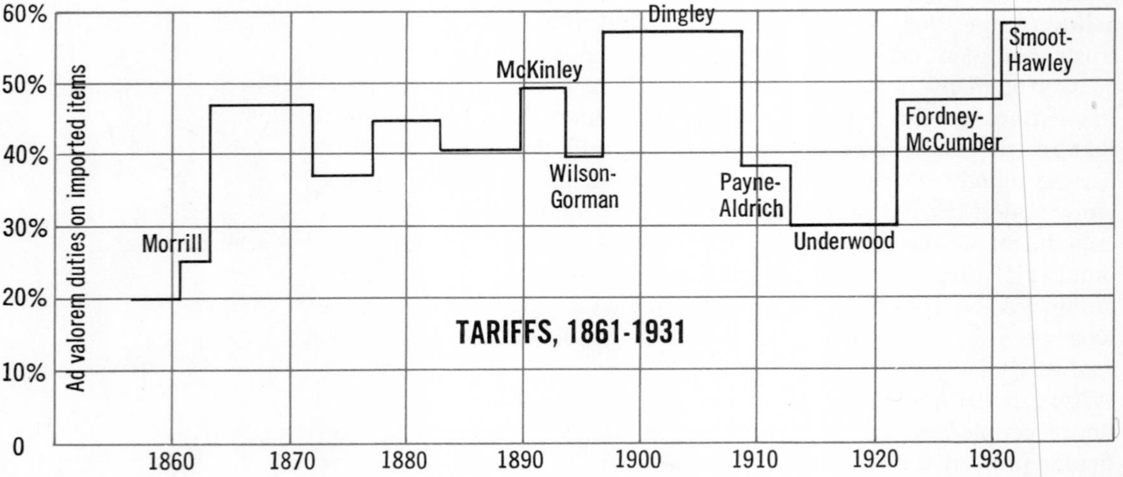

Making Government More Democratic, 1880–1920

Name of Act	Date	Provisions
Pendleton Civil Service Act	1883	Set up three-man Civil Service Commission to draw up and administer competitive examinations for certain federal jobs. Forbade political party in power from asking for campaign contributions.
Publicity Act	1910	Required congressional representatives to file statements of campaign contributions.
Seventeenth Amendment	1913	Called for popular election of senators.
Nineteenth Amendment	1920	Provided for woman suffrage.

sponsiveness to the demands of citizens. During the Grant Administration, corruption ran rampant through a number of administrative departments, leading eventually to the discharge of a number of Grant's appointees. In later administrations the spoils system led to a wholesale turnover of federal appointees whenever the Presidency changed hands from one party to another. Several Presidents complained that most of their time was spent in the tiresome task of interviewing applicants for federal jobs, such as postmasters. Finally, after a disappointed office-seeker assassinated President James A. Garfield in 1881, Chester Alan Arthur, who succeeded him, pushed through the Pendleton Civil Service Act, whose provisions can be found in the chart on this page. The other major developments on the national scene were the passage of the Seventeenth Amendment (1913), which provided that United States Senators should be elected directly by voters instead of by the members of state legislatures who had chosen Senators since 1789, and the passage of the Nineteenth Amendment extending the franchise to women.

Secretary of the Treasury, Benjamin H. Bristow, discovered that a "whiskey ring," which included the Supervisor of Internal Revenue, was robbing the federal government of $1 million annually by not turning over revenue taxes collected on distilled liquors and fines placed on tax-evading distillers. Secretary of War, William E. Belknap, was forced to resign when it was revealed that he had accepted $24,000 in bribes from a trader in Oklahoma. The Secretary of the Navy "sold" contracts to shipbuilders; and the Secretary of the Interior was found to be working closely with land speculators.

The Place of National Politics in History

"History is past politics," a famous historian once said. This point of view seems narrow—even inaccurate—to most contemporary historians. The history of the United States involves all its people and all of their lives—where they came from, what they thought, how they made a living, and how they got along with each other and with people from other nations.

Most of us view our lives differently from the way we look at the history of our nation. Our personal lives involve the cycle of birth, growth, marriage, work, child-rearing, aging, and death. Occasionally an event in national politics affects us personally. A war breaks out and families are disrupted; Congress passes a new tax, and our pay checks are smaller. But most of the days of our lives, even in an age when television fills the airwaves with news from Washington, pass by without direct, personal knowledge of the way in which national politics have affected us.

Yet national politics reveal a great deal about the past. In a way, they reflect our collective conscience. What troubles the nation greatly eventually troubles Congress. We can learn much about ourselves and about our ancestors by watching what our representatives and theirs have done. But this conclusion does not indicate that we ought to organize a history book around national politics. Thomas Edison probably had a more significant impact on American society than any nineteenth-century senator. Most high school and college history textbooks are still organized around a "Presidential synthesis," that is, the events of our history have been related to various administrations as if Presidents bound our past together. During the period between the end of the Civil War and the first Administration of Franklin D. Roosevelt, this tie was not nearly so important to the future of the nation as many others: the development of American industry, the dramatic changes taking place in agriculture, the shift of people from rural areas in Europe and the United States to great new cities, the development of new frontiers in the West and on the streets of urban areas, and even the events which took place in the council chambers of city governments. After 1933, however, the federal government began to sponsor a series of new programs which eventually touched the life of every American virtually every day.

SUGGESTED READINGS

BLUM, JOHN MORTON, *The Republican Roosevelt* and *Woodrow Wilson and the Politics of Morality*. These books contain telling, brief portraits of the two key figures in the "progressive movement."

GLAD, PAUL W., *McKinley, Bryan and the People*. This volume is a useful introduction to the controversial politics of the 1890's.

HOFSTADTER, RICHARD, *The Age of Reform, From Bryan to F.D.R.* Subtle and often confusing—and perhaps confused—this book presents the central statement around which much of contemporary writing has grouped itself.

The United States Becomes a World Power, 1898–1920

CHAPTER 23

STATING THE ISSUE

Throughout most of the nineteenth century, Americans had been preoccupied with expanding their continental frontiers, settling a vast new land area, developing agriculture and industry, building roads, canals, and railroads, and dealing with sectional conflicts that were sharpened by the Civil War. After the War of 1812, most Americans gave little attention to their nation's role in the world. Then between 1898 and 1920, the United States became one of the strongest and most influential nations in world affairs. The change from continental nation to world power took both Americans and citizens of other countries somewhat by surprise. That change also made profound differences in international relationships.

In 1898, the United States, exasperated by a long, bloody revolution in Cuba, declared war on Spain in order to end the revolt. The three-month war left Cuba independent. It also left the United States in control of Puerto Rico and the Philippine Islands.

During World War I, the United States gave vital assistance to Great Britain, France, and their allies and helped to defeat Germany and its supporters. Americans fought German armies on French soil and German submarines on the seas. So great was American influence at the end of the war that President Woodrow Wilson played the leading part in the conference that wrote a peace treaty and created an international organization to keep peace.

While many Americans cheered the advance of the flag into the far Pacific and the Caribbean and many acclaimed the League of Nations, others disapproved strongly of the nation's expanded role abroad. Because Americans themselves differed over their national goals, other countries found it difficult to know what to expect of the United States in international affairs.

Chapter 23 examines the growth of the worldwide power and influence of the United States. Why did America become a world power? Why did Americans disagree over the role their nation should take in international affairs? What were the consequences of America's new power for the United States? for other nations? What were the consequences of Americans' disagreements over the appropriate use of that power? These are the major issues raised in Chapter 23.

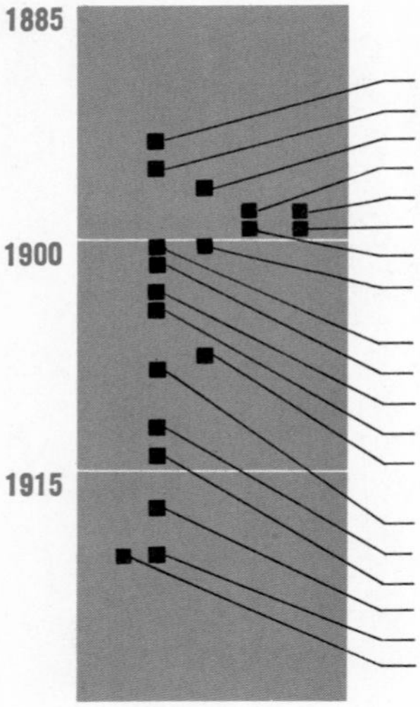

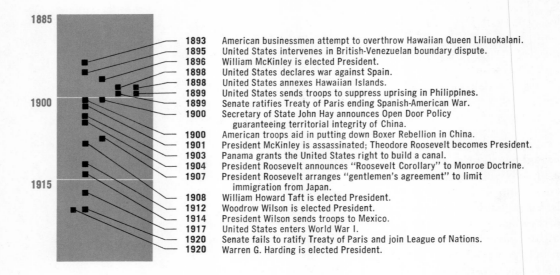

1893 American businessmen attempt to overthrow Hawaiian Queen Liliuokalani.
1895 United States intervenes in British-Venezuelan boundary dispute.
1896 William McKinley is elected President.
1898 United States declares war against Spain.
1898 United States annexes Hawaiian Islands.
1899 United States sends troops to suppress uprising in Philippines.
1899 Senate ratifies Treaty of Paris ending Spanish-American War.
1900 Secretary of State John Hay announces Open Door Policy guaranteeing territorial integrity of China.
1900 American troops aid in putting down Boxer Rebellion in China.
1901 President McKinley is assassinated; Theodore Roosevelt becomes President.
1903 Panama grants the United States right to build a canal.
1904 President Roosevelt announces "Roosevelt Corollary" to Monroe Doctrine.
1907 President Roosevelt arranges "gentlemen's agreement" to limit immigration from Japan.
1908 William Howard Taft is elected President.
1912 Woodrow Wilson is elected President.
1914 President Wilson sends troops to Mexico.
1917 United States enters World War I.
1920 Senate fails to ratify Treaty of Paris and join League of Nations.
1920 Warren G. Harding is elected President.

89 American Goals Abroad, 1893–1898

Several times during the 1890's Americans faced the question of whether to extend their nation's power into weak foreign lands. During the nineteenth century, European countries had carved up Africa, and, together with Japan, had taken control of rich or strategic parts of China. In the Middle East and in Southeast Asia, European rivals competed for territory and influence.

The United States showed a flickering interest in the competition. In 1867, it purchased Alaska from Russia; in 1878, it joined Britain and Germany to establish a joint protectorate over the Samoan Islands in the South Pacific. Later, the United States acquired a naval base at Pearl Harbor in Hawaii.

Under a protectorate, a weak nation allows a stronger nation to control its trade and its relations with other nations in return for military protection. Protectorates are supposedly more independent than colonies.

But the relationship between the United States and Latin American countries shows more typical American attitudes toward overseas expansion. Except during the Mexican War, the United States sent neither armies nor navies to try to gain territory or win influence in Latin America, in spite of many opportunities to take advantage of the political instability of the area. Most Americans neither wanted their country to expand south of the border nor wished to deprive other American republics of their independence.

Two events in the 1890's—a revolt in Hawaii and a revolt in Cuba—tested America's tradition of international restraint. Europeans and Americans who had sugar plantations and other interests in Hawaii rebelled in 1893, when the Hawaiian Queen Liliuokalani declared that she intended to rule as an absolute monarch in order to keep political power in the hands of the native population. The businessmen and planters considered this move a threat to their interests and their power. They formed a revolutionary government and asked the United States to annex the islands. President Cleveland refused, and the annexation issue died down until 1898.

After struggling for decades to suppress Cubans who demanded self-government, the Spanish government sent General Valeriano Weyler to crush the revolt which had again broken out in 1895. General Weyler aroused Americans' indignation by placing hundreds of Cubans in concentration camps. Sensational newspapers played a major role in inflaming public opinion by printing sensational stories. The *New York Journal* managed to get and print a private letter written by the Spanish minister to Washington, Dupuy De Lôme, which made unflattering comments about President McKinley. At about the same time, the American battleship *Maine*—stationed in Havana harbor for the stated purpose of protecting Americans and their property there after riots earlier that year—exploded mysteriously and sank in the harbor. The newspapers played up the story, and the cry "Remember the Maine" swept America.

Reading 89 presents some of the reasons American expansionists wanted to annex Hawaii and gives President McKinley's reasons for war against Spain. As you read, try to answer these questions:

By the end of the nineteenth century, Spain had lost most of its empire, which at one time included a large portion of Latin America. The only major Spanish colonies remaining were Cuba and Puerto Rico, in the Caribbean, and the Philippine Islands and Guam, in the Pacific.

By the 1890's, the New York **World** published by Joseph Pulitzer, and the New York **Journal,** owned by William Randolph Hearst, were engaged in a battle for circulation. Each newspaper sought to outdo the other with screaming headlines and scandalous stories. The use of excessive sensationalism to sell newspapers is known as "yellow journalism."

The term "Jingo" was often used to mean warlike patriotism. The press was often called a jingo press.

1. What arguments for annexation of Hawaii appeared in the newspaper editorials?
2. Using only these editorials, what statements can you make about international relations in the late nineteenth century? about the position of the United States in the world?
3. Why did the United States choose to exert its power in a war in 1898?
4. Do nations have moral obligations to intervene in other nations to prevent war or bloodshed? Does the belief that its civilization is more advanced give a nation the responsibility to rule other nations?

The United States and Hawaii

The United States minister to Hawaii, John L. Stevens, aided the conspiracy against the Hawaiian Queen Liliuokalani. He called in United States marines, who stood by with artillery pieces while the businessmen-revolutionaries ousted the queen and her government. The four newspaper editorials that follow appeared before these details about the rebellion became public in the United States. The political leaning of each paper is noted.

New York Commercial Advertiser (Independent), February 18, 1893

In dealing with a partly barbarous country, the United States is not amenable to the same demands of justice which a civilized country might properly make of us. The native population is entitled to humane treatment, but the underlying principle in the negotiations is that law and order must be insisted upon by the nations of the earth. When a people proves itself unable to maintain a stable government, it is the province of a higher civilized nation to step in and supply the need. The Hawaiians are to be treated kindly, firmly as children. The time has passed for seriously regarding them as competent to govern themselves, or to tell others how to govern them. President [Benjamin] Harrison has more wisely taken his counsel from superior, trustworthy Anglo-Saxons. Then, his duty clear, he ceased to talk, and acted. The Anglo-Saxons are the nation-builders of the world. To lavish sympathy on the poor, dying contingent of an aboriginal [native] race is permissible, but to prate [talk at length] of the "justice" of temporizing with them, when decisive action is called for, is to forget the history of nations in all times under the grim but beneficent law which confers on highly civilized States the prerogatives [rights] of government.

Washington Post (Independent), February 1, 1893

The Hawaiian question is a National question. It is one of patriotic feeling and plain common sense. Shall we take Hawaii, and thereby prosper and magnify ourselves, or shall we let England take it, and thereby enfeeble and humiliate us? If we be a great nation, with pride and purpose and intelligence, we shall seize the opportunity. If we are inert, cowardly and stupid we'll keep quiet and let England complete the chain of her hostile environment. . . .

This is an affair for us to settle for ourselves. Hawaii is the natural and logical outpost of the United States in the Pacific. Its possession would mean the saving of incalculable millions in coast defense and the control of the commercial pathways of more than half the salt water on the globe. The Hawaiians have come to us for protection and help, and in responding to their petition we shall immeasurably strengthen and enrich ourselves. Shall we do it? That is the only question. England's protests are not to be considered. We do not need Great Britain's approval in our National affairs, and, even if we did, that is the last thing we should get where our advantage lay. Leave England out of the question, and let us consider only what is our profit and honor in the case. If England ventures to interfere or to throw obstacles in the way of our will and pleasure, let England look to herself. This country has grown since 1776.

Denver News (Democrat), January 29, 1893

There can be little doubt of the great importance which the acquisition of the [Hawaiian] islands will prove to the Pacific coast cities. Their ownership would at once give strength to the naval force of this Government and a most commanding position in the event of a naval war between the United States and France, England or Germany.

Boston Traveller (Republican), February 13, 1893

Is Hawaii worth annexing, or should the United States abandon it to itself and leave it to work out its own destiny? There are facts and figures worthy [of] consideration. In the fiscal year ending June 30, 1892, the United States alone received Hawaiian products, chiefly sugar, to the value of $8,075,881. That is an astonishing amount of merchandise for 85,000 people, many of them hampered by the indolence [laziness] common to natives of tropical countries, to be able to sell for export in a single year, and, of course, the surplus products of Hawaii were not all marketed in the United States. The total exports were about $9,000,000, or over $100 for every man, woman or child in the Hawaiian Islands. A similar export trade in proportion to the population of the United States would make the annual shipments of merchandise from this country about $6,500,000,000 or about six times as much as they have ever been in the history of the nation. Such a foreign commerce, maintained by a country with only a semi-civilized system of government, is at once a proof of almost phenomenal natural resources.

A fiscal year is a full year for keeping financial records. The federal government's fiscal year runs from July 1 of one year to June 30 of the following year. States, big companies, and other organizations establish their own fiscal years to suit their particular financial patterns.

The United States and Cuba

An immediate investigation failed to explain the explosion of the Maine *satisfactorily. Pressures on President McKinley to ask Congress to declare war on Spain mounted, as diplomats worked to get Spain to accept a series of demands for reforms in Cuba. Two days after the Spanish government had agreed to all of the demands of the State Department, McKinley delivered a war message.*

Papers Relating to the Foreign Affairs of the United States, with the Annual Message of the President Transmitted to Congress, December 5, 1898. Washington, D.C.: Government Printing Office, 1901, pp. 757–58.

The grounds for such [American] intervention [in Cuba] may be briefly summarized as follows:

First. In the cause of humanity and to put an end to the barbarities, bloodshed, starvation, and horrible miseries now existing there, and which the parties to the conflict are either unable or unwilling to stop or mitigate [reduce]. It is no answer to say this is all in another country, belonging to another nation, and is therefore none of our business. It is specially our duty, for it is right at our door.

Second. We owe it to our citizens in Cuba to afford them that protection and indemnity [security against loss or damage] for life and property which no government there can or will afford, and to that end to terminate the conditions that deprive them of protection.

Third. The right to intervene may be justified by the very serious injury to the commerce, trade, and business of our people, and by the wanton destruction of property and devastation of the island.

Fourth, and which is of the utmost importance. The present condition of affairs in Cuba is a constant menace to our peace, and entails [obliges] upon this Government an enormous expense. With such a conflict waged for years in an island so near us and with which our people have such trade and business relations; when the lives and liberty of our citizens are in constant danger and their property destroyed and themselves ruined; where our trading vessels are liable to seizure and are seized at our very door by war ships of a foreign nation, . . . —all these and others that I need not mention, with the resulting strained relations, are a constant menace to our peace, and compel us to keep on a semiwar footing with a nation with which we are at peace.

These elements of danger and disorder already pointed out have been strikingly illustrated by a tragic event which has deeply and justly moved the American people. I have already transmitted to Congress the report of the naval court of inquiry on the destruction of the battleship *Maine* in the harbor of Havana during the night of the 15th of February. The destruction of that noble vessel has filled the national heart with inexpressible horror. Two hundred and fifty-eight brave sailors and marines and two officers of our Navy, reposing in the fancied security of a friendly harbor, have been hurled to death, grief and want brought to their homes, and sorrow to the nation.

The naval court of inquiry, which, it is needless to say, commands the unqualified confidence of the Government, was unanimous in its conclusion that the destruction of the *Maine* was caused by an exterior explosion, that of a submarine mine. It did not assume to place the responsibility. That remains to be fixed.

In any event the destruction of the *Maine*, by whatever exterior cause, is a patent [clear] and impressive proof of a state of things in Cuba that is intolerable. That condition is thus shown to be such that the Spanish Government can not assure safety and security to a vessel of the American Navy in the harbor of Havana on a mission of peace, and rightfully there.

90 The Issue of Imperialism, 1898–1900

When Commodore George Dewey's ships blasted a rickety Spanish fleet out of the water in Manila Bay in the Philippines in 1898, the most perplexing question to grow out of the Spanish-American War became apparent: Should the United States rule a distant land that contained people with an alien culture? This, of course, was the same question that had been raised by the Hawaiian issue earlier, but the Philippine question was more complicated.

Many Filipinos wanted independence, which they expected the United States to grant them once the Spanish had been driven out. When the Filipinos became convinced that the United States did not intend to grant them immediate independence, they began a guerrilla insurrection against the new American authority. To suppress the revolt, American soldiers finally resorted to tactics similar to those for which Americans had condemned the Spanish in Cuba.

Before the outbreak of the Spanish-American War, a group of Filipino guerrillas, led by Emilio Aguinaldo, had been fighting for their independence from Spain. After the war, when they discovered that the United States did not intend to grant independence, they redirected their battle against the United States.

Not since the United States had won the Southwest from Mexico in 1848 had the issue of territorial expansion generated such controversy among the American people. The anti-imperalist movement, which lacked effective organization and leadership, included social reformers, such as Jane Addams, political reformers, such as Carl Schurz, two former Presidents, Republican Benjamin Harrison and Democrat Grover Cleveland, industrialist Andrew Carnegie, and some of America's most distinguished college professors and literary artists. But President McKinley studied American opinion closely, consulted his own judgment, and decided to annex the Philippine Islands. He instructed his diplomats who were discussing a peace treaty with Spain in Paris to insist upon American ownership of not only the Philippines, but of Guam in the Pacific and Puerto Rico in the Caribbean as well. Although Americans never voted directly on the issue of keeping the Philippines, President McKinley won re-election easily in 1900, in a campaign in which his Democratic opponent, William Jennings Bryan, strongly opposed "imperialism." In spite of vocal opposition to annexation, most Americans probably approved of the President's decision.

A selection by Jane Addams, the social worker, appeared in Reading 83. Carl Schurz, a distinguished immigrant from Germany, was a liberal Republican, Secretary of the Interior under President Hayes, and a leader in the movement to develop a merit system in civil service jobs.

Reading 90 gives the major arguments used by those who supported and those who opposed annexation of the Philippines. As you read, consider these questions:

1. Why was McKinley not sure what to do with the Philippines?
2. Considering that the great powers spent more and more money on armies and navies after 1900, were Carnegie's arguments against annexation valid?

3. How did Beveridge's and Mason's views of American democracy differ? Which writer more closely represents your view of American democracy? Why?
4. How do these four statements help to describe the values of Americans in 1900?

President McKinley Decides To Annex the Philippines

This selection, taken from a biography of President McKinley, describes his thoughts about annexing the Philippine Islands, as he reported them to a committee of men interested in Christian missionary work that visited him.

Charles S. Olcott, **The Life of William McKinley.** Boston: Houghton Mifflin Company, 1916, vol. II, pp. 110–11.

Manila is the largest city of the Philippine Islands. It is situated on the largest island, Luzon.

"When . . . I realized that the Philippines had dropped into our laps I confess I did not know what to do with them. I sought counsel from all sides—Democrats as well as Republicans—but got little help. I thought first we would take only Manila; then Luzon; then other islands, perhaps, also. I walked the floor of the White House night after night until midnight; and I am not ashamed to tell you, gentlemen, that I went down on my knees and prayed Almighty God for light and guidance more than one night. And one night late it came to me this way—I don't know how it was, but it came: (1) That we could not give them back to Spain—that would be cowardly and dishonorable; (2) that we could not turn them over to France or Germany—our commercial rivals in the Orient—that would be bad business and discreditable; (3) that we could not leave them to themselves—they were unfit for self-government—and they would soon have anarchy and misrule over there worse than Spain's was; and (4) that there was nothing left for us to do but to take them all, and to educate the Filipinos, and uplift and civilize and Christianize them, and by God's grace do the very best we could by them, as our fellow-men for whom Christ also died. . . ."

"The March of the Flag"

Albert J. Beveridge, an Indiana Republican, was elected to the Senate in 1899. This selection comes from a speech he made on the Philippine issue in 1898.

Albert J. Beveridge, "The March of the Flag," in **Modern Eloquence,** edited by Ashley H. Thorndike. New York: Modern Eloquence Corporation, 1923, vol. 10, pp. 359–63 **passim.**

. . . [I]n this campaign, the question is larger than a party question. It is an American question. It is a world question. Shall the American people continue their resistless march toward the commercial supremacy of the world? Shall free institutions broaden their blessed reign as the children of liberty wax [grow] in strength, until the empire of our principles is established over the hearts of all mankind? And shall we reap the reward that waits on our discharge of our high duty as the sovereign power of earth; shall we occupy new markets for what our farmers raise, new markets for what our factories make, new markets for what our merchants sell—aye, and, please God, new markets for what our ships shall carry?

The opposition tells us that we ought not to govern a people without their consent. I answer: The rule of liberty, that all just government derives its authority from the consent of the governed, applies only to those who are capable of self-government. I answer: We govern the Indians without their consent, we govern our territories without their consent, we govern our children without their consent. I answer: How do you assume that our government would be without their consent? Would not the people of the Philippines prefer the just, humane, civilizing government of this republic to the savage, bloody rule of pillage [looting] and extortion from which we have rescued them?

[The opposition asks] us how we will govern these new possessions. I answer: Out of local conditions and the necessities of the case, methods of government will grow. If England can govern foreign lands, so can America. If Germany can govern foreign lands, so can America. If they can supervise protectorates, so can America. Why is it more difficult to administer Hawaii than New Mexico or California? Both had a savage and alien population; both were more remote from the seat of government when they came under our dominion than Hawaii is to-day.

Will you say by your vote that American ability to govern has decayed; that a century's experience in self-rule has failed of a result? Will you affirm by your vote that you are an infidel to [nonbeliever in] American vigor and power and practical sense? Or, that we are of the ruling race of the world; that ours is the blood of government; ours the heart of dominion; ours the brain and genius of administration? Will you remember that we do but what our fathers did—we but pitch the tents of liberty farther westward, farther southward—we only continue the march of the flag. . . .

Fellow Americans, we are God's chosen people. Yonder at Bunker Hill and Yorktown His providence was above us. At New Orleans and on ensanguined [blood-covered] seas His hand sustained us. Abraham Lincoln was His minister, and His was the Altar of Freedom the boys in blue set on a hundred battlefields. His power directed Dewey in the East, and delivered the Spanish fleet into our hands on the eve of Liberty's natal [birth] day. . . . We cannot fly from our world duties; it is ours to execute the purpose of a fate that has driven us to be greater than our small intentions. We cannot

Beveridge was referring to sites of battles in the American Revolution (Bunker Hill and Yorktown), the War of 1812 (New Orleans), the Civil War, and the Spanish-American War.

retreat from any soil where Providence has unfurled our banner; it is ours to save that soil for liberty and civilization. For liberty and civilization and God's promise fulfilled, the flag must henceforth be the symbol and the sign to all mankind—the flag!

Andrew Carnegie Cautions Against Expansion

Andrew Carnegie, the steel magnate, gave his views of American expansion in an article published in The North American Review *in 1898. Portions of that article follow.*

Andrew Carnegie, "Distant Possessions—the Parting of the Ways," **The North American Review,** vol. CLVII (August 1898), pp. 246–47.

If we are to compete with other nations for foreign possessions we must have a navy like theirs. It should be superior to any other navy, or we play a second part. . . .

What it means to enter the list of military and naval powers having foreign possessions may be gathered from the following considerations. First, look at our future navy. If it is only to equal that of France it means 51 battleships; if of Russia, 40 battleships. If we cannot play the game without being at least the equal of any of our rivals, then 80 battleships is the number Britain possesses. We now have only 4, with 5 building. Cruisers, armed and unarmed, swell the number threefold, Britain having 273 ships of the line [large warships] built or ordered, with 308 torpedo boats in addition; France having 134 ships of the line and 269 torpedo boats. All these nations are adding ships rapidly. Every armor and gun making plant in the world is busy night and day. Ships are indispensable, but recent experience shows that soldiers are equally so. While the immense armies of Europe need not be duplicated, yet we shall certainly be too weak unless our army is at least twenty times what it has been—say 500,000 men. . . .

This drain upon the resources of these countries has become a necessity from their respective positions, largely as graspers for foreign possessions. The United States, happily, to-day has no such necessity, her neighbors being powerless against her, since her possessions are concentrated and her power is one solid mass.

"I Ask Only an Endorsement of the Declaration of Independence"

Senator William E. Mason of Illinois, a leader in the Senate in the fight against annexation of the Philippines, offered the following resolution and supporting argument.

Whereas all just powers of government are derived from the consent of the governed: Therefore, be it

Resolved by the Senate of the United States, That the Government of the United States of America will not attempt to govern the people of any other country in the world without the consent of the people themselves, or subject them by force against their will.

Congressional Record, 55th Congress, 3rd Session, vol. 32, part 1, pp. 528–29, 531, 533 **passim.**

[Mr. Mason] . . . Mr. President, I ask only an indorsement of the Declaration of Independence. Surely American gentlemen will not sneer at my simplicity. Surely American gentlemen have not outgrown this document; and if they have, they will have to pardon me that I have not mentally, morally, and loyally kept pace with them in their wonderful growth. . . .

Mason was addressing the President **pro tempore** of the Senate. President McKinley's death had made Theodore Roosevelt President and had left the country without a Vice-President.

I am for the independence of the people of the Philippine Islands, as I am for independence of the people of Cuba. Mr. President, let us say to them, as we have said to Cuba, "Go on your way; learn by evolution"—for that is the only way. Give them the independence they plead for, and we shall have kept our promise with the people of the world.

The last clause of the war resolution against Cuba stated that the United States had no intention of ruling Cuba and that, after the war, the Cubans could govern themselves. The statement, known as the Teller Amendment, denied any imperialist motive on the part of the United States.

[O]ur Government was builded right. The just powers of the Government have been derived from the consent of the people. It is builded on a rock that can not wash away. It has within itself the wellspring of eternal youth.

And why, Mr. President, in the name of all that is generous, should we refuse the Filipino the privilege of lighting his feeble taper at the light and heat of our flaming torch?

Mr. President, who wants to govern the Philippines, let me ask in conclusion? Where is the ambitious Senator who wants to make laws at this desk to govern people 10,000 miles away? Who is the kindhearted statesman? You can not speak their language. You do not know their schools. You can not read their newspapers. You do not know their religion. I never even saw one of their papers.

I have an idea that their homes are sacred, that their children are beloved, that they love their soil, and that they have their songs; that the father has his prayer, that they have a hearthstone of some kind, and that the mother has a lullaby for her babe. Who wants to govern them here? In the name of God, who wants to do it? Who craves the power to make laws for men 10,000 miles away whom you never saw?

Ah, Mr. President, the fever has run high, the temperature has been almost beyond our power to withstand. The war made heroes of all of us—some of us in our minds, some of us on the field. In the contemplation of the heroic work of Dewey and the Army and Navy we have grown so heroic that we know not where to stop; and in love of power we have forgotten the high purpose and the lofty plan upon which the declaration of war was founded.

91 The Question of International Responsibility, 1919–1920

With the decision to expand beyond its continental frontiers, the United States became increasingly involved in international politics. In the early years of the twentieth century, the United States extended its political, economic, and military influence into several Latin American countries and joined with other world powers in working out policies for Asia. On April 6, 1917, when the United States joined World War I, it achieved the position of a leading world power. The victory of the Allied forces over Germany and its allies in 1918, however, posed a new problem for Americans. What actions should their country take to help ensure that so devastating a war could not happen again?

Most Americans had not considered this question before. Prior to World War I, only a few idealistic reformers had thought about ways to prevent war. No large-scale international war had been fought for a century, and many persons did not believe that civilized people would again stake the existence of their nations and the lives of their young men in major conflicts. The twenty million deaths in war between 1914 and 1918 dealt a devastating blow to such confidence, and convinced many Europeans and Americans that some way had to be found to maintain international peace.

In his declaration of war aims, called the Fourteen Points, President Woodrow Wilson called for the creation of a League of Nations as one of the United States' war goals. Thousands of European men and women hailed him as the inspired prophet of a new day in international relations. Wilson insisted, sometimes against the wishes of other allied leaders, that the framework of a League of Nations be built into the peace treaty with Germany and that the League be given authority to take military action in international disputes.

Many Americans, still caught up in patriotic enthusiasm for the war, applauded the League. Others did not want the United States to yield any of its power to an international organization. When the peace treaty, which included the plan for the League, reached the Senate for ratification, debate focused on the most controversial provision of the Covenant, Article 10, which pledged members of the League to defend each other against attack. Reading 91 examines Article 10 and the arguments two Americans made for and against the League. As you read, try to answer these questions:

1. Why did Lodge see Article 10 as a trap for the United States?
2. If, as Wilson said, the United States could use a negative vote in the Council to keep the League from calling on American forces,

did the pledge of action in Article 10 really mean anything? Did Wilson think so? Did Lodge?

3. What did the United States' refusal to join the League mean, in terms of the nation's role in the world? in terms of the extension of American influence and power?

Article 10

The text of the controversial Article 10 of the Covenant of the League of Nations follows.

The Members of the League undertake to respect and preserve as against external aggression the territorial integrity and existing political independence of all Members of the League. In case of any such aggression or in case of any threat or danger of such aggression the Council shall advise upon the means by which this obligation shall be fulfilled.

Territorial integrity means the undestroyed original condition of a country and its boundaries.

The League of Nations required a unanimous vote by its members before any action could be taken.

Senator Lodge Attacks Article 10

Senator Henry Cabot Lodge, Republican from Massachusetts and chairman of the Senate Foreign Relations Committee had been an outspoken advocate of American territorial expansion at the turn of the century. He later led the Senate fight against the League of Nations. Excerpts from one of his Senate speeches follow.

Congressional Record, 66th Congress, 1st Session, vol. 58, part 4, pp. 3780, 3783.

. . . In article 10 the United States is bound on the appeal of any member of the league not only to respect but to preserve its independence and its boundaries, and that pledge, if we give it, must be fulfilled. . . . The following dispatch appeared recently in the newspapers.

Hejaz Against Bedouins

> The forces of Emir Abdullah recently suffered a grave defeat, the Wahabis attacking and capturing Kurma, east of Mecca. Ibn Savond is believed to be working in harmony with the Wahabis. A squadron of the royal air force was ordered recently to go to the assistance of King Hussein.

The Bedouins and other desert tribes were nomads who did not live within settled tribal boundaries. Emir Abdullah was the son of King Hussein, who unsuccessfully fought for control of Hejaz, a mountainous region in northwest Saudi Arabia.

Hussein I take to be the Sultan of Hejaz. He is being attacked by the Bedouins, as they are known to us, although I fancy the general knowledge about the Wahabis and Ibn Savond and Emir Abdullah is slight and the names mean but little to the American people. Nevertheless, here is a case of a member of the league—for the King of the Hejaz is such a member in good and regular standing and signed the treaty by his representatives Mr. Rustem Haidar and Mr. Abdul Havi Aouni.

Under article 10, if King Hussein appealed to us for aid and protection against external aggression affecting his independence and the boundaries of his kingdom, we should be bound to give that aid and protection and to send American soldiers to Arabia. . . . I am unwilling to give that right to King Hussein, and this illustrates the point which is to me the most objectionable in the league as it stands—the right of other powers to call out American troops and American ships to go to any part of the world, an obligation we are bound to fulfill under the terms of this treaty. I know the answer well—that of course they could not be sent without action by Congress. Congress would have no choice if acting in good faith, and if under article 10 any member of the league summoned us, or if under article 11 the league itself summoned us, we should be bound in honor and morally to obey. There would be no escape except by a breach of faith, and legislation by Congress under those circumstances would be a mockery of independent action. Is it too much to ask that provision should be made that American troops and American ships should never be sent anywhere or ordered to take part in any conflict except after the deliberate action of the American people, expressed according to the Constitution through their chosen representatives in Congress?

Article 11 states that war or the threat of war concerned all members, not just those involved directly. Every member had the right to demand that the crisis be considered by the council, and, if necessary, to insist on a council meeting.

Those of us, Mr. President, who are either wholly opposed to the league, or who are trying to preserve the independence and the safety of the United States by changing the terms of the league, and who are endeavoring to make the league, if we are to be a member of it, less certain to promote war instead of peace have been reproached with selfishness in our outlook and with a desire to keep our country in a state of isolation. So far as the question of isolation goes, it is impossible to isolate the United States. I well remember the time, 20 years ago, when eminent Senators and other distinguished gentlemen who were opposing the Philippines and shrieking about imperialism sneered at the statement made by some of us, that the United States had become a world power. I think no one now would question that the Spanish war marked the entrance of the United States into world affairs to a degree which had never obtained before. It was both an inevitable and an irrevocable step, and our entrance into the war with Germany certainly showed once and for all that the United States was not unmindful of its world responsibilities. We may set aside all this empty talk about isolation. Nobody expects to isolate the United States or to make it a hermit Nation, which is a sheer absurdity. But there is a wide difference between taking a suitable part and bearing a due responsibility in world affairs and plunging the United States into every controversy and conflict on the face of the globe. By meddling in all the differences which may arise among any portion or fragment of human-

Isolation is the policy of keeping out of the affairs of other nations by avoiding treaties, alliances, and other political and commercial dealings.

kind we simply fritter away our influence and injure ourselves to no good purpose. We shall be of far more value to the world and its peace by occupying, so far as possible, the situation which we have occupied for the last 20 years and by adhering to the policy of Washington and Hamilton, of Jefferson and Monroe, under which we have risen to our present greatness and prosperity. The fact that we have been separated by our geographical situation and by our consistent policy from the broils [conflicts] of Europe has made us more than any one thing capable of performing the great work which we performed in the war against Germany, and our disinterestedness is of far more value to the world than our eternal meddling in every possible dispute could ever be.

President Wilson Defends Article 10

Opponents of the League in the Senate were divided between irreconcilables, who opposed the United States joining the organization under any circumstances, and reservationists, led by Henry Cabot Lodge, who favored joining the League with reservations that would limit America's commitment. President Wilson opposed compromises, and in the fall of 1919 he took his case directly to the American people. At the end of a twenty-two day speaking trip, he collapsed on September 25 after a speech in Pueblo, Colorado. A few days later he suffered a stroke from which he never recovered fully. This selection is from his Pueblo speech.

Selected Literary and Political Papers and Addresses of Woodrow Wilson. New York: Grosset and Dunlap, Inc., 1926, vol. II, pp. 378–79, 381–82, 389–90.

When you come to the heart of the Covenant, my fellow citizens, you will find it in article ten, and I am very much interested to know that the other things have been blown away like bubbles. There is nothing in other contentions with regard to the league of nations, but there is something in article ten that you ought to realize and ought to accept or reject. Article ten is the heart of the whole matter. . . . Article ten provides that every member of the league covenants [pledges] to preserve the territorial integrity and existing political independence of every other member of the league as against external aggression. Not against internal disturbance. There was not a man at that table who did not admit the sacredness of the right of self-determination, the sacredness of the right of any body of people to say that they would not continue to live under the Government they were then living under, and under article eleven of the Covenant they are given a place to say whether they will live under it or not. For following article ten is article eleven, which makes it the right of any member of the League at any time to call

Self-determination is the right of people to decide for themselves whether they will have an independent government or will be part of another nation.

attention to anything, anywhere, that is likely to disturb the peace of the world or the good understanding between nations upon which the peace of the world depends.

But you will say, "What is the second sentence of article ten? That is what gives very disturbing thoughts." The second sentence is that the council of the League shall advise what steps, if any, are necessary to carry out the guaranty of the first sentence, namely, that the members will respect and preserve the territorial integrity and political independence of the other members. I do not know any other meaning for the word "advise" except "advise." The council advises, and it cannot advise without the vote of the United States. Whether we use it wisely or unwisely, we can use the vote of the United States to make impossible drawing the United States into any enterprise that she does not care to be drawn into.

Yet article ten strikes at the taproot of war. Article ten is a statement that the very things that have always been sought in imperialistic wars are henceforth forgone by every ambitious nation in the world. . . . I ask you this: If it [the League] is not an absolute insurance against war, do you want no insurance at all? Do you want nothing? Do you want not only no probability that war will not recur, but the probability that it will recur? The arrangements of justice do not stand of themselves, my fellow citizens. The arrangements of this treaty are just, but they need the support of the combined power of the great nations of the world. And they will have that support. Now that the mists of this great question have cleared away, I believe that men will see the truth, eye to eye and face to face. There is one thing that the American people always rise to and extend their hand to, and that is the truth of justice and of liberty and of peace. We have accepted that truth and we are going to be led by it, and it is going to lead us, and through us the world, out into pastures of quietness and peace such as the world never dreamed of before.

92 The Uses of American Power and Influence

HISTORICAL ESSAY

Between 1815 and 1875, Americans threw vast energy into acquiring, exploring, and settling the trans-Mississippi West, developing their economy, and resolving the slavery issue. They played only a minor role in international politics. The United States formed neither diplomatic nor military alliances with other nations. It fought its only foreign war against an American neighbor, Mexico. It sought no territory outside North America.

Yet lack of political involvement did not mean isolation. American businessmen, ships, and seamen expanded the nation's foreign trade. American diplomats served in the far places of the world. And when the United States chose to act, it commanded some respect. An American naval squadron under Commodore Matthew C. Perry, paying a visit in 1853 that combined diplomacy, commerce, and a show of strength, persuaded Japan, which had been isolated by choice, to open its ports to foreign traders and modernize its society.

The Monroe Doctrine

Americans displayed considerable interest in the countries of Latin America, especially the lands rimming the Gulf of Mexico and the Caribbean Sea. Concerned with their own national security, Americans had always tried to keep European powers from establishing new footholds in the Western Hemisphere. As the nineteenth century passed, the United States succeeded in holding European influence in the Americas to a minimum. In 1864, during the Civil War, for example, France sent troops to Mexico to establish an empire headed by an Austrian archduke, Maximilian. In 1865, when large Union armies finally defeated the Confederacy, Secretary of State William Seward warned France forcefully against maintaining its puppet state. French soldiers withdrew, and the empire of Maximilian collapsed in 1867. By 1900, the United States had estabished predominance in the New World so firmly that no European nation willingly risked challenging American wishes in the area.

As the power of the United States grew, relationships with its old enemy, Great Britain, improved. Fortunately for both Anglo-American harmony and the integrity of the Monroe Doctrine, Britain

The Monroe Doctrine was enforceable in 1823, when it was issued, only because Britain stood behind it. As the United States grew, it found that its own power would deter European nations from interfering in the New World. In return, the United States kept out of European affairs as much as possible.

In 1861, Great Britain, Spain, and France sent an expedition to Mexico to collect a debt. After payment, both Britain and Spain withdrew. Napoleon III of France, however, refused to remove his troops. He hoped that by creating a Mexican Empire, he could restore France's prestige and regain favor with his people.

Treaties Between Great Britain and United States

Name	Date	Provisions
Rush-Bagot	1817	Agreed to naval disarmament of the Great Lakes.
Webster-Ashburton	1842	Settled the boundary between Maine and New Brunswick.
Aberdeen Proposal	1846	Fixed boundary between United States and British territory in Oregon at the 49th parallel.
Clayton-Bulwer	1850	Agreed to a joint control of any canal built across Central America and guaranteed that such a canal would be unfortified and neutral.
Treaty of Washington	1871	Agreed to arbitration by an international tribune of damages claimed by United States against British shipbuilders for Civil War losses.
Hay-Pauncefote	1901	Cancelled Clayton-Bulwer Treaty; United States could build and control the canal but canal was to be free and open to all nations.

chose to support independent Latin American republics rather than join a contest among the great powers for territory and influence in Latin America. Both the United States and Great Britain wanted to avoid war. They were each others' best customers, and the British had invested heavily in the development of American agriculture and industry. The British knew that Canada would be hard to defend; in turn the United States knew that the British navy could ruin American ocean commerce in case of war. Finally, Britain left naval leadership in the Caribbean to the United States, calling many warships back to home waters to counter naval competition from the German Empire after about 1900.

Expansion of American Power and Influence

The same forces that compelled European nations and Japan toward expansion also affected the United States. The nineteenth century had witnessed a surge of nationalistic feelings. People in Western nations and in Asia took increased pride in national cultures, languages, and traditions. As countries competed for control of lands and people in Africa, Asia, and ocean islands, national rivalries sharpened. Consequently most armies and navies grew.

Western nations found new ideologies to explain and justify national competition. In *The Origin of Species*, the great English naturalist, Charles Darwin, had argued that the species of plants and animals that survived and multiplied were the ones best adapted to their physical and social environments; others dwindled or were exterminated. European and American writers and politicians quickly applied Darwin's term "natural selection," or "the survival of the fittest," to explain the successes of some nations over others, the conquest by white peoples of black, brown, red, and yellow peoples, or even the growth of Christianity at the expense of other religions. But different human groups were not different species.

Race can be defined scientifically as a group of humans having common ancestry. Three basic races have been identified; Caucasoid, Mongoloid, and Negroid. Each is distinguished by a set of physically inherited characteristics, including pigmentation and body proportions. No evidence exists to indicate that any one race is superior in intellectual potential to other races. Moreover, differences that are not physically inherited such as language, religion, nationality, customs, or values, are not racial differences.

In mentioning groups of humans, writers and politicians made free use of the vague term "race." They employed this all-purpose word to describe color ("the yellow race"), language or culture ("the French race"), religion ("the Jewish race"), or geography ("the African race"). Their failure to define "race" precisely mattered little to them. Their rapid expansion convinced Westerners that their "race" was superior to those of their victims.

The influence of racist ideas in the United States can be seen in such works as *Our Country,* written in 1885 by Josiah Strong, a Congregationalist minister interested in Christian missionary activities abroad. Strong told readers in his widely sold book that the Anglo-Saxon peoples—at least those who spoke English—were destined to win the competition of nations and races. They alone, he said, possessed the keys to success: true Protestant Christianity and democracies. Such racist ideas filled many articles and speeches.

Dominance in the Caribbean

In the 1890's, the United States, intent on securing its supremacy in the Americas, embarked on more aggressive policies. In 1895, Great Britain and Venezuela disagreed over the border between Venezuela and British Guiana [now Guyana]. The United States virtually threatened war to support the demand that Britain submit the dispute to arbitration. Britain agreed.

Arbitration is the settling of a dispute by uninvolved parties who are acceptable to all parties in the dispute.

The United States took a giant step toward further control of the Caribbean and involvement in world affairs when it declared war against Spain in 1898. In some ways Americans reached this decision reluctantly. Despite their disapproval of harsh Spanish attempts to repress rebellions in Cuba and their concern over destruction of sugar plantations owned by Americans, neither President Grover Cleveland nor his successor, William McKinley, wanted to intervene. American businessmen, too, generally opposed intervention, fearing Spanish attacks on American shipping and ports.

Then the unexplained sinking of the American battleship *Maine* in Havana harbor in February 1898, with the loss of 260 lives, aroused American indignation. The resulting furor in metropolitan

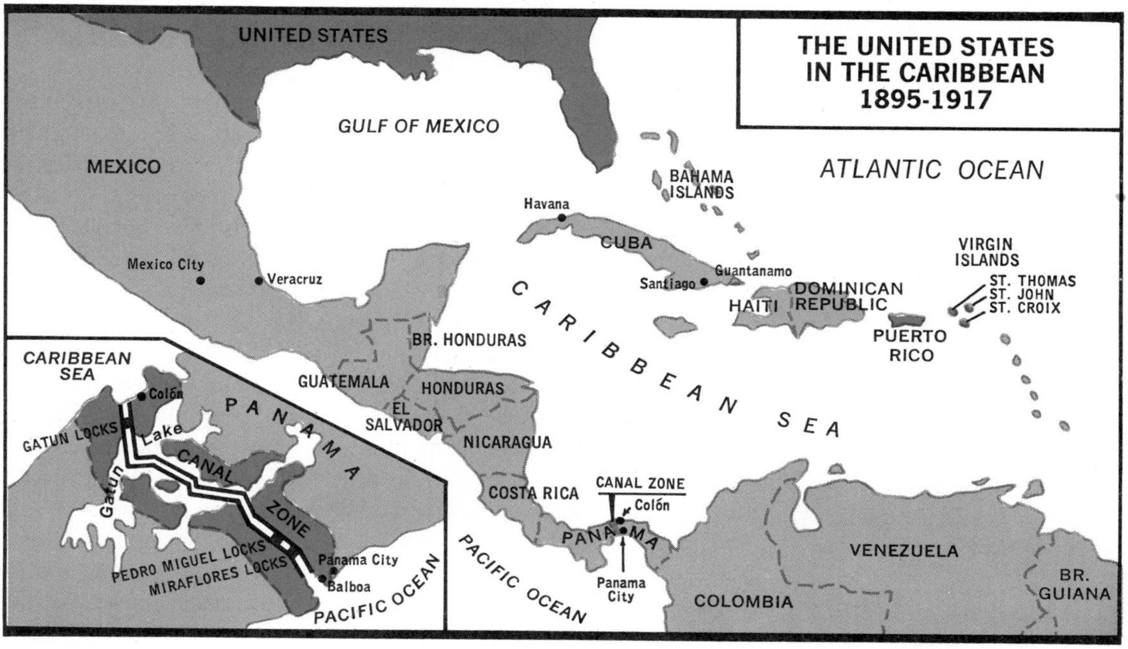

Hearst sent the artist Frederic Remington to Cuba to sketch the atrocities taking place there for publication in the **World.** When the artist reported that conditions were not so bad, Hearst is alleged to have answered, "You furnish the pictures and I'll furnish the war."

During the treaty negotiations ending the Spanish-American War, Spain agreed to cede the Philippines to the United States in return for $20 million.

A deranged anarchist assassinated President McKinley at a reception at the Pan American Exposition in Buffalo. Leon Czolgosz, the assassin, had concealed the gun in his bandaged hand.

In 1913, after a period of internal disorder, Victoriano Huerta, a military strongman, gained control of Mexico. President Wilson refused to recognize the new government, claiming that the Huerta regime did not have the support of the masses, and initiated a policy of "watchful waiting." In 1914, when Huerta's men arrested some American sailors and at the same time a German boat landed in Veracruz with military supplies for Huerta, President Wilson ordered the marines to seize Veracruz. Wilson then accepted an invitation from the ABC powers (Argentina, Brazil, and Chile) to mediate Mexican-American differences. As a result, Huerta resigned. In 1916, American troops led by General John J. Pershing were again sent to Mexico to capture Pancho Villa, who was responsible for the murder of several Americans.

newspapers, some of which manufactured stories of Spanish atrocities to attract readers, helped to inflame public opinion. By April both President McKinley and Congress sensed that the public really wanted war. They overlooked the importance of concessions to American demands made by the Spanish government in early April that amounted to sweeping changes in policies in Cuba. McKinley asked Congress for intervention in Cuba on April 11; Congress declared war on April 20.

The fighting lasted only three months. Commodore George Dewey's squadron destroyed Spanish naval power in the Philippines on May 1, and American ships destroyed a Spanish fleet at Santiago, Cuba, on July 3. Spanish land forces surrendered by mid-August, and the two nations agreed to discuss peace terms. The treaty gave Cuba independence as Congress had promised in the Teller Amendment, and granted the Philippines, the islands of Guam and Midway in the Pacific, and Puerto Rico to the United States.

Theodore Roosevelt, who gained fame from the war, came to symbolize American expansion and a vigorous foreign policy. Roosevelt, a New Yorker who had had ranching experience in the west, resigned his position as Assistant Secretary of the Navy to organize a group of volunteer cavalrymen ("Rough Riders") to fight in Cuba. The publicity given his courageous leadership helped him to win the governorship of New York in 1898 and the Vice-Presidency of the United States in 1900. He succeeded to the Presidency in September 1901, when an anarchist assassinated McKinley.

Two episodes reveal Roosevelt's approach to Latin America. In 1904, European creditors to whom the Dominican Republic owed money threatened that their governments would intervene to collect the debts. Roosevelt responded in his annual message by promising American intervention in Latin American countries in order to preserve order and to provide for the payment of such debts. Under this "Roosevelt Corollary" to the Monroe Doctrine, the United States ran the Dominican Republic's customs service for two years. The United States also used police power in Nicaragua in 1911 under President William H. Taft, in Mexico from 1914 to 1917, in Haiti in 1915, and in the Dominican Republic again in 1916, all under President Wilson. Not until the statement of the "Good Neighbor policy" in 1933 did the United States formally give up its role as policeman in the internal affairs of Latin American countries.

Roosevelt recognized the importance of navies in international politics. He and other leaders also realized that a canal connecting the Caribbean and the Pacific would give a tremendous advantage to the United States in war or peace. It would reduce the time and risk of shipping between the east and west coasts, and would eliminate the need for separate American fleets in the Atlantic and Pacific. But unless the canal was American-owned, it could put shipping at the mercy of unstable or unfriendly governments.

The United States and Britain signed the Hay-Pauncefote Treaty in 1901. In it, Britain agreed to yield any control over building a canal. A French company had attempted to build a canal across the Isthmus of Panama—then part of Colombia—and had failed financially. The United States agreed to buy the French rights for $40 million, but Colombia stalled, hoping to get more money if it waited until the French time limit was up. Then in November 1903, a revolt broke out in Panama, and a group of Panamanians, supported by the canal company, declared Panama's independence.

Several attempts had been made earlier by the United States to build a canal through Nicaragua, which many engineers think would have provided a better route. American investors in the Panama Canal, however, helped convince the government to favor Panama.

Roosevelt, who knew of the likelihood of a revolt, took full advantage of it. He sent an American warship, the *Nashville*, to Colon, Panama. The *Nashville* appeared on November 2. The insurrection broke out on November 3, but the *Nashville* prevented the landing of Colombian troops to reach the fighting. The United States recognized the independence of Panama only three days after the revolt began and signed the Hay–Bunau-Varilla Treaty twelve days later. It guaranteed Panama's independence and gave the United States the right to build a canal and a 99-year lease on a ten-mile-wide strip of land. Columbia's protests were ignored; the canal was built.

Thrust Into the Pacific

The American decision to take Hawaii and the Philippines obligated the United States to use its army and navy to protect its new interests in the far Pacific. The re-election of McKinley in 1900 allowed his Administration and that of Roosevelt to suppress the Philippine independence movement led by Emilio Aguinaldo. Stamping out the revolt took three years. But the United States promptly embarked upon policies to increase literacy, build roads, and promote self-government and eventual independence for the Philippines.

Hawaii became a territory of the United States in the spring of 1900. President Cleveland had opposed the annexation, but President McKinley was for it, especially after the battles in the Pacific during the Spanish-American War demonstrated its strategic location as a naval base.

Following a military defeat by Japan (1894–1895), China was in no position to resist the imperialist demands of European powers for political and economic concessions. In its new international role, the United States tried to prevent the breakup of China. In 1899, Secretary of State John Hay sent a letter to six great powers asking them to agree to preserve free trade in China rather than assume special privileges over trade in spheres of influence they controlled. Although the answers to his letters were evasive, Hay announced in 1900 that the powers had agreed. This so-called "open door policy", however, did little to maintain China's territorial integrity. In 1900, American troops took part in an international force which helped China put down a rebellion launched by a militant band of anti-foreigners, known as the Boxers. Hay took this opportunity to notify

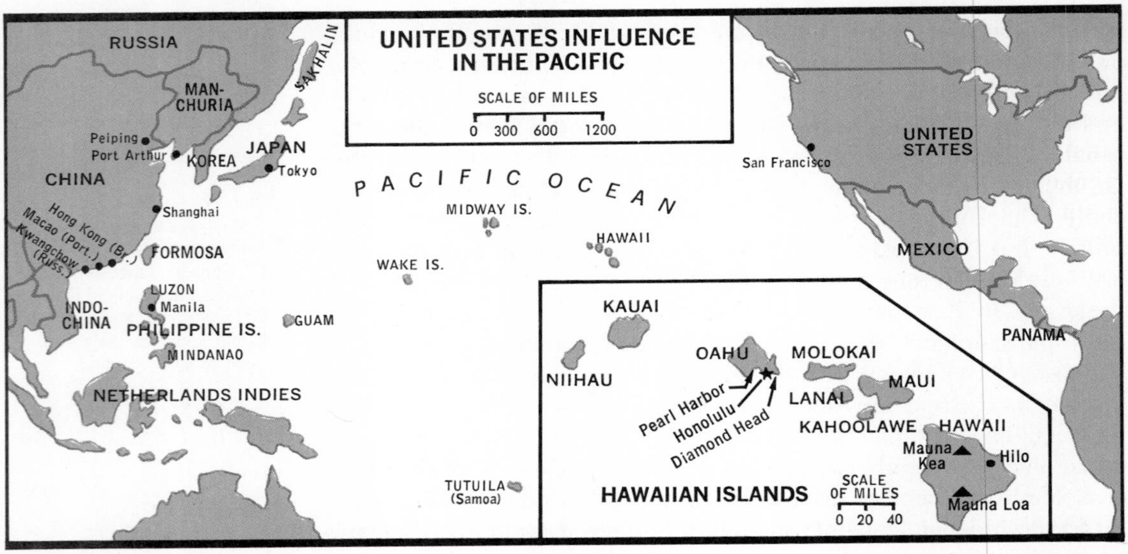

the great powers that the United States desired to maintain Chinese "territorial and administrative entity," or independence. Nobody paid much attention. Russia seized part of the Chinese province of Manchuria shortly afterward, and the United States itself tried unsuccessfully to obtain territory for a naval base on the coast of China. Later attempts by the United States government, during President Taft's Administration, to encourage American businessmen to invest in China to increase American influence were unsuccessful.

If America's China policy showed little more than unrealistic good intentions, American policy towards Japan revealed a somewhat more realistic attitude. Presidents Roosevelt, Taft, and Wilson understood that the American people were simply not prepared to exert military force in the far Pacific in order to impose American ideas about territorial changes there. In 1904–1905, Japan defeated Russian forces and seized Manchuria and other parts of China controlled by Russia. The United States and Japan then made the secret Taft-Katsura agreement that gave Japan a free hand in Korea in return for a Japanese promise to keep out of activities in the Philippines. The Root-Takahira Agreement of 1908 furthered the two nations' policies of respecting each others' possessions in the Pacific. Even though these two actions were executive agreements made by the Roosevelt Administration, rather than treaties ratified by Congress, they were respected by subsequent administrations.

The attitudes and actions of some Americans who lived on the West Coast threatened good relations with Japan. In 1906, these Americans wished to exclude Japanese immigrants and to establish segregated public schools for Oriental children. Japan protested the segregation vigorously. President Roosevelt pressured San Francisco's leaders to halt school segregation in return for his promise to reduce Japanese immigration. He blocked the entry of Japanese immigrants from other countries and concluded a "gentlemen's agreement" according to which Japan promised to keep laborers from emigrating to the United States. In part to show Japan that the United States would make no concessions out of fear or weakness, Roosevelt sent the American navy's sixteen battleships on a trip around the world. They stopped in Japan in order to emphasize the fact that the strength of the United States navy had grown until it was second only to that of Great Britain.

American Power and Europe

Only in very minor ways had the United States departed from the Monroe Doctrine's pledge of non-intervention in European affairs. The United States had cooperated in submitting certain disputes with other powers to the arbitration of international commissions, especially the Hague Tribunal. Theodore Roosevelt, acting at the request of Germany, had helped to bring about an international conference at Algeciras, Spain, in 1906 to settle a crisis which had arisen over French-German competition in Morocco, a country in North Africa. The Senate had ratified the international agreement about Morocco, but added that such action should not be interpreted as a departure from traditional American non-intervention in the affairs of European nations.

An international conference was called in 1899 at the Hague, a city in the Netherlands. The conference set up a Permanent Court of Arbitration, sometimes called the Hague Tribunal, to encourage nations to settle their disputes through mediation.

This tradition ended when America entered World War I in 1917. The war in Europe had begun in 1914, after a Serbian nationalist assassinated an Austrian archduke. European countries were so deeply involved in alliances that Britain, France, Russia, and Italy found themselves fighting with Serbia against Germany, Austria, and the Ottoman Empire. Since America considered it a European war, it maintained neutrality. American companies, however, were selling supplies and making loans to both sides, but chiefly to the Allies (Britain and its allies). Britain and Germany struggled desperately for control of the seas; both interfered with American commerce. Britain blockaded ports supplying Germany.

Serbia is now part of Yugoslavia.

In 1915, Germany, using its new war vessels, submarines (called U-boats), announced it would sink any boats going with supplies into the war zone it proclaimed around Britain. Americans were shocked when a U-boat sank a British liner, the *Lusitania*, and caused the deaths of nearly 1200 passengers, including over a hundred Americans. President Wilson sent Germany a strongly worded note. Eventually, after several exchanges of notes and the sinking of another British liner, the *Arabic*, Germany agreed to

Germany claimed that the **Lusitania** was carrying rifles and ammunition.

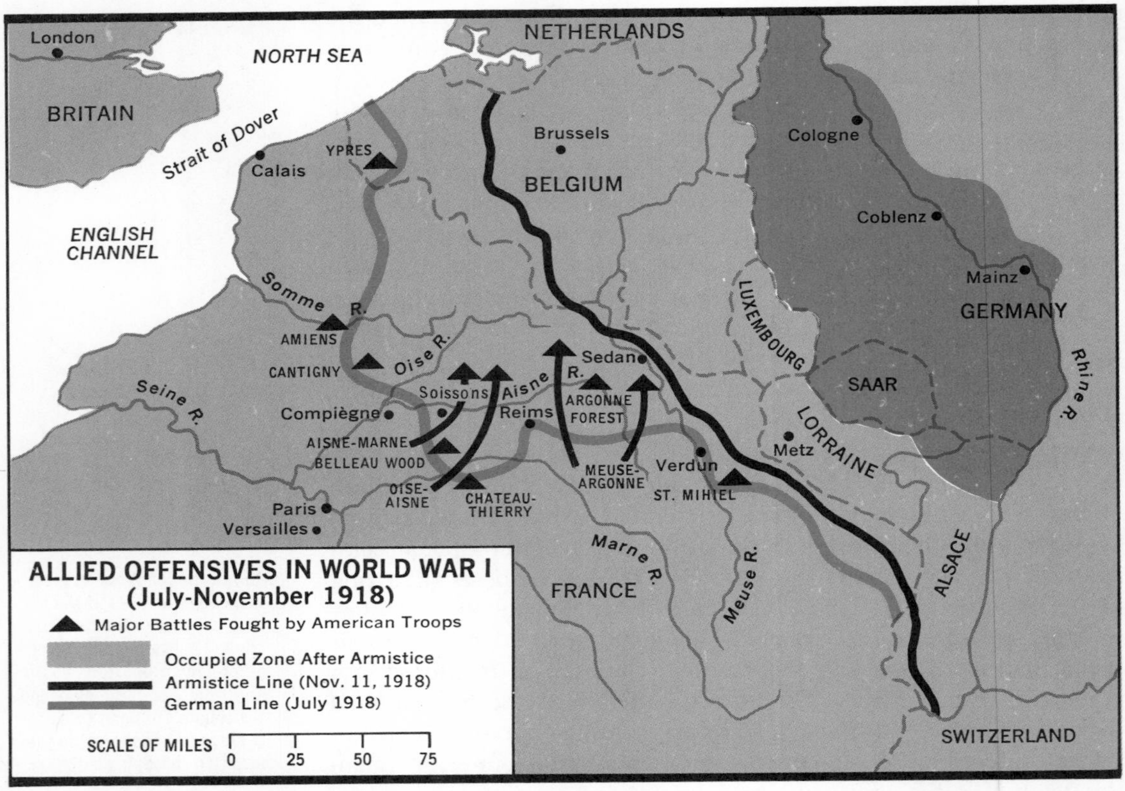

suspend submarine warfare against passenger ships. In 1916, Wilson attempted in vain to negotiate a peace in Europe.

Then early in 1917, Germany, threatened by loss of the war, announced it would resume submarine warfare. American opinion, already hostile to Germany, rose quickly. It was further influenced by the Zimmermann Note. The British had intercepted a coded note from the German Foreign Secretary Zimmermann to the German minister in Mexico. In it he promised that if the United States entered the war on the side of the Allies and Mexico, in turn, entered on Germany's, Germany would help reconquer Texas and the territories lost in 1848. The telegram was made public March 1, 1917.

The last hope of averting war lay in German restraints on their U-boats. But in March the submarines sank four unarmed American merchant ships. On April 2, President Wilson asked Congress to declare war, and after two days of debate, Congress complied.

Other factors had caused the United States to sympathize with Britain, France, and their Allies. Americans remembered France as an invaluable friend during the American Revolution. Anglo-

American friendship was at its highest point since 1815. Germany, on the other hand, had invaded Belgium ruthlessly, and British propaganda, some of it false or exaggerated, helped to convince many Americans that German troops committed atrocities there. The United States discovered that Germany and its ally, Austria, were trying to sabotage arms production in the United States and that Germany had tried to encourage Mexico to make war on the United States. Finally between 1914 and 1917, the American economy became more and more committed to Allied victory.

American soldiers arrived in Europe at a crucial time in the spring of 1918, as German armies pushed back weary French and British forces. Within months fresh American troops, who eventually numbered two million, helped to stop and drive back the Germans. At the same time, the American navy, by organizing an effective convoy system, cut losses of ships to German submarines. The fighting ended with an armistice on November 11, 1918.

The Allied victory marked the peak of American power and influence. But were Americans willing for any reason to continue such influence in European affairs? President Wilson had denounced the system of alliances that had led so much of the world into war. Knowing that few Americans favored committing their nation to further military alliances, he worked desperately for his ideal of an international peace-keeping organization.

The peace treaty that the President submitted to the Senate in 1919 disappointed Americans in some ways. Wilson, in his "Fourteen Points" statement of war goals in 1918, had promised that the United States would not fight for territorial gains. Obviously, however, Germany had lost its colonies to the European Allies, and Japan had encroached further upon China in taking over German holdings there. The goal of freedom of the seas was also not ensured. But generally Americans supported the treaty.

Woodrow Wilson's Fourteen Points

1. an end to secret treaties
2. freedom of the seas in peace and war
3. removal of restrictions on international trade
4. disarmament
5. adjustment of colonial claims

6–13. evacuation and self-determination of certain nations; readjustment of European boundary lines

14. establishment of a general association of nations to guarantee political independence and territorial integrity

The Senate refused to ratify the Treaty of Versailles, which required Germany to admit guilt for the war, give up colonies, pay reparations (which amounted to $56 billion), and maintain disarmament. Instead of signing the treaty, Congress passed a joint resolution in 1921 declaring the war between the United States and Germany was over.

The League of Nations, included as part of the treaty, was far more popular; it suited American ideals about an impartial way to keep order in the world. Yet, ironically, it was the issue of the League that prevented Senate ratification of the treaty. Senators fighting the treaty, led by Henry Cabot Lodge of Massachusetts, offered amendments which would have restricted American participation in the League. They thought Wilson would not accept such restrictions, and they were right. The President, embittered by their opposition, refused to accept any important amendments, and the treaty did not receive the necessary two-thirds vote in the Senate. By a margin of seven votes, the United States failed to join the League of Nations. When the Republican party swept the Democrats out of office in the Presidential election of 1920, President Warren G. Harding took the election results as an American rejection of membership. The issue never again rose seriously.

Thus in the early twentieth century the United States extended its power vigorously but uncertainly. Its ventures into Latin America gave it an unprecedented amount of control over its neighbors, but aside from a naval base in Cuba, its control of the ten-mile-wide Panama Canal Zone, and its purchase of the Virgin Islands from Denmark in 1917, it obtained no territory. It continued to refuse to make alliances with Latin American as well as other nations. In the Pacific, the United States obtained no further territory after 1898. Instead it used its influence, without much effect, to try to maintain the status quo [situation as it was] in Asia. And in Europe the United States withdrew its forces at the end of World War I and refused to make either military or political commitments to guarantee the peace it had helped to establish.

SUGGESTED READINGS

BAILEY, THOMAS A., *Woodrow Wilson and the Lost Peace* and *Woodrow Wilson and the Great Betrayal.* These two sharply critical studies emphasize the impact of politics and personality on the ending of World War I and the failure of the U.S. to join the League of Nations.

BEALE, HOWARD K., *Theodore Roosevelt and the Rise of America to World Power.* Beale's book is a perceptive study of the relationship between a strong, internationally minded President and American foreign policy.

MAY, ERNEST R., *The World War and American Isolation, 1914–1917.* May analyzes America's entry into World War I.

MILLIS, WALTER, *The Martial Spirit.* This is a lively account of the war with Spain in 1898.

The 1920's: A Normal America?

CHAPTER 24

STATING THE ISSUE

Your grandparents probably look upon the 1920's as a very special period. The great effort of World War I was over. The difficult times of the Great Depression were yet to come. Not everyone was well off in the 1920's, but signs of prosperity appeared on every side. Partly because the Presidents and politics of the period were dull, nothing detracted from the business of enjoying new-found wealth.

By every standard, the 1920's was an exciting decade. Fashionable girls, called flappers, wore their skirts above their knees and to emphasize their freedom cut their hair in a close, boyish style. The nation had decided to outlaw the drinking of alcohol, but prohibition seemed to make liquor more exciting than it had ever been before. Saloons sprang up everywhere and were patronized by some of the "best people." The automobile freed young couples from the front-porch swing and opened a whole new world of adventure to millions of Americans.

The nation played. College students danced the Charleston and the Black Bottom, and everyone throbbed to jazz rhythms discovered in the Negro districts of New York and New Orleans. The nation also watched its golden heroes play for it. Babe Ruth swung his famous bat, and the New York Yankees, a failing baseball team, became the masters of the game. A young aviator, named Charles A. Lindbergh, flew alone across the Atlantic Ocean to return the most celebrated hero of the decade. The whole world became a new and exciting place for young men and women.

Students of today may look on the 1920's in a different light. What seemed glamorous and new in 1925 may seem quite commonplace in the 1970's. The knowledge that the Depression struck in 1929 also influences our picture of that decade. What were the major developments in society during the 1920's? What political developments took place? How were the developments that took place in the private lives of citizens related to the events in public life, particularly national politics? These are the major issues of Chapter 24.

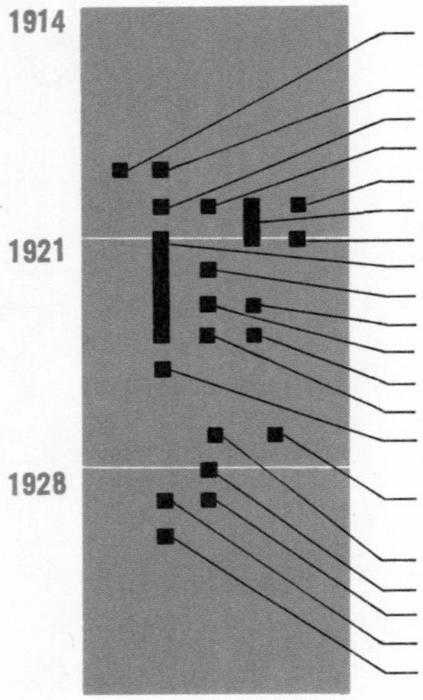

1919	"Red Scare" begins as Attorney-General Mitchell Palmer begins massive arrests of suspected anarchists, socialists, and communists.
1919	States ratify Eighteenth Amendment, providing for prohibition.
1920	KDKA, first commercial radio station, begins broadcasting in Pittsburgh.
1920	States ratify Nineteenth Amendment, granting women the vote.
1920	Warren G. Harding becomes President.
1920-1921	United States suffers a postwar depression.
1921	Nicola Sacco and Bartolomeo Vanzetti, Italian anarchists, are convicted of murder.
1921-1924	Congress passes legislation restricting immigration.
1922	Congress passes Fordney-McCumber tariff.
1923	Newspapers begin exposés of Ku Klux Klan.
1923	Warren G. Harding dies suddenly; Calvin Coolidge becomes President.
1924	Congressional committees disclose Teapot Dome oil scandal.
1924	Calvin Coolidge is elected President.
1925	A Tennessee court convicts John Scopes of teaching evolution in public high school.
1927	Charles A. Lindbergh makes first solo flight across Atlantic, nonstop from New York to Paris.
1927	Warner Brothers releases **The Jazz Singer,** first "talkie."
1928	Herbert Hoover is elected President.
1929	Stock market crashes; the Great Depression begins.
1929	Robert and Helen Lynd publish **Middletown.**
1930	Congress passes high protective Smoot-Hawley tariff.

93 Parents and Children in a Midwestern City

A sociologist is a person who studies human society, its institutions, and the relationships among different groups in the society.

In the middle of the 1920's, two young sociologists, Robert and Helen Lynd, decided to study a city which they hoped would be as representative as possible of contemporary American life. They chose a city of 35,000 people, small enough to allow them to analyze it in what they called a "total situation study." They called their town "Middletown"; it was, in fact, Muncie, Indiana, a town that had grown from 11,000 inhabitants in 1890. Most of its citizens were white native Americans.

Although the Lynds made no claims that Middletown was typical of America, they had sought a place with many of the characteristics which a "typical" town might have. Muncie had a temperate climate. Since its population had more than tripled in thirty-five years, it had acquired an assortment of growing pains similar to those that accompanied social change all over the United States. Muncie had a number of factories with no single one large enough to make the city a "company town." Modern, high-speed machine production had brought many of the aspects of an industrial culture to the city. This machine culture was balanced by an abundant artistic life. Moreover, Muncie had no outstanding peculiarities or severe local problems to set it off from other American towns.

An anthropologist usually studies a society by living for a time in the community, interviewing people who live there, and observing the variety of social and religious functions practiced there.

Assisted by a staff of three additional researchers, the Lynds moved to Muncie for more than a year. They used the methods of a social anthropologist to investigate every phase of the city's life.

They chose 1890 as a base line from which to assess the changes that had been taking place in the culture. They finished the process of gathering data in 1925; in 1929, they published the results of their study.

The three readings in Chapter 23 have all been taken from *Middletown*. As you study the excerpts in this first reading, think about the following questions:

1. What social forces had been influencing family life in Middletown? How many of these forces seem to have developed since 1890?
2. What norms of behavior were changing? What caused these changes?
3. How did parents and children try to cope with the new problems that came with changing conditions?
4. Were the problems of parent and child in Middletown similar to those in your own life? How "modern" was Middletown in the 1920's?

A norm is a standard model of behavior or practices among a given group of people.

Child-Rearing in Middletown

Robert S. Lynd and Helen Merrell Lynd, **Middletown: A Study in American Culture.** New York: Harcourt, Brace & World, Inc., pp. 131–52. Abridged.

Families of six to fourteen children, upon which the grandparents of the present generation prided themselves, are considered as somehow not as "nice" as families of two, three, or four children. With increasing regulation of the size of the family, emphasis has shifted somewhat from child-bearing to child-rearing.

Middletown parents are wont [accustomed] to speak of many of their "problems" as new to this generation, situations for which the formula[s] of their parents are inadequate. Even from the earliest years of the child's life the former dominance of the home is challenged; the small child spends less time in the home than in the ample days of the nineties. Shrinkage in the size of the yard affords less play space. "Mother, where can I play?" wailed a small boy of six, as he was protestingly hauled into a tiny front yard from the enchanting sport of throwing ice at passing autos. The community has recently begun to institute public playgrounds, thereby hastening the passing of the time when a mother could "keep an eye on" the children in the home yard. The taking over of the kindergarten by the public schools in 1924 offers to children of four and five an alternative to the home. "Why, even my youngster in kindergarten is telling us where to get off," exclaimed one bewildered father. "He won't eat white bread because he says they tell him at kindergarten that brown is more healthful!"

Nor can parental authority reassert itself as completely as formerly by the passing on of skills from father to son. Less often does a son learn his trade at his father's workbench, perhaps being apprenticed under him, nor do so many daughters learn cooking or sewing at their mothers' side; more than a few of the mothers interviewed said unhappily that their daughters, fresh from domestic science in school, ridicule the mothers' inherited rule-of-thumb practices as "old-fashioned."

With entry into high school, the agencies drawing the child away from home multiply. Athletics, dramatics, committee meetings after school hours demand his support; Y.M.C.A., Y.W.C.A., Boy Scouts, Girl Reserves, the movies, auto-riding—all extra-neighborhood concerns unknown to his parents in their youth—are centers of interest; club meetings, parties or dances, often held in public buildings, compete for his every evening.

"I've never been criticized by my children until these last couple of years since they have been in high school," said one business class mother, "but now both my daughter and older son keep saying, 'But, Mother, you're so old-fashioned.'" "My daughter of fourteen thinks I am 'cruel' if I don't let her stay at a dance until after eleven," said another young mother. "I tell her that when I was her age I had to be in at nine, and she says, 'Yes, Mother, but that was fifty years ago.'"

The first four sources of disagreement with their parents indicated by the boys were over the following issues: 1) the hours they must come home, 2) the number of evenings they may stay out late, 3) school grades, and 4) the amount of spending money.

Use of the automobile ranks fifth among the boys and fourth among the girls as a source of disagreement. The extensive use of this new tool by the young has enormously extended their mobility and the range of alternatives before them; joining a crowd motoring over to dance in a town twenty miles away may be a matter of a moment's decision, with no one's permission asked. Furthermore, among the high school set, ownership of a car by one's family has become an important criterion of social fitness; a boy almost never takes a girl to a dance except in a car; there are persistent rumors of the buying of a car by local families to help their children's social standing in high school.

The more sophisticated social life of today has brought with it another "problem" much discussed by Middletown parents, the apparently increasing relaxation of some of the traditional prohibitions upon the approaches of boys and girls to each other's persons. Here again new inventions of the last thirty-five years have played a part; in 1890 a "well-brought-up" boy and girl were commonly forbidden to sit together in the dark; but motion pictures and the automobile have lifted this taboo, and, once lifted, it is easy for the practice to become widely extended. Buggy-riding in 1890 allowed only a narrow range of mobility; three to eight were generally accepted hours for riding, and being out after eight-thirty without a chaperon was largely forbidden. In an auto, however, a party may go to a city halfway across the state in an afternoon or evening, and unchaperoned automobile parties as late as midnight, while subject to criticism, are not exceptional.

The relaxing of parental control combines with the decrease in group parties to further the greater exclusiveness of an individual couple. In the nineties, according to those who were in high school then, "We all went to parties together and came home together. If any couple did pair off, they were considered rather a joke." Today the press accounts of high school club dances are careful to emphasize the escort of each girl attending. The number of separate dances at a dance is smaller and there is much more tendency for each individual to dance with fewer partners, in some cases to dance the entire evening with one person. "When you spend four or five dollars to drag a girl to a dance," as one boy put it, "you don't want her to spend the evening dancing with everyone else."

Mothers of both working and business class, whether they lament the greater frankness between the sexes or welcome it as a healthy sign, agree that it exists and mention the dress and greater aggressiveness of girls today as factors in the change. Such comments as the following from the mothers of both groups are characteristic:

> "Girls aren't so modest nowadays; they dress differently." "It's the girls' clothing; we can't keep our boys decent when girls dress that way." "Girls have more nerve nowadays—look at their clothes!" "Girls are far more aggressive today. They call the boys up to try to make dates with them as they never would have when I was a girl."

A natural reaction to these various encroachments upon parental dominance and shifts in the status of children is the vigorous reassertion of established standards. And in Middletown the traditional view that the dependence of the child carries with it the right and duty of the parents to enforce "discipline" and "obedience" still prevails.

The term "shifts in status" here refers to the fact that children in Middletown had become less dependent on their parents and more critical of them.

And yet not only are parents finding it increasingly difficult to secure adherence to established group sanctions, but the sanctions themselves are changing; many parents are becoming puzzled and unsure as to what they would hold their children to if they could. As one anxious business-class mother said:

Sanctions are rewards or punishments a group uses to obtain conformity to its standards.

> "You see other people being more lenient and you think perhaps that it is the best way, but you are afraid to do anything very different from what your mother did for fear you may leave out something essential or do something wrong. I would give anything to know what is wisest, but I don't know what to do."

A more democratic system of relationships with frank exchange of ideas is growing up in many homes: "My mother was a splendid mother in many ways, but I could not be that kind of mother now. I have to be a pal and listen to my children's ideas," said one of these mothers.

Not all of the currents in the community are set in the direction of widening the gap between parents and children. It is the mother who has the chief responsibility in child-rearing, and many Middletown mothers, particularly among the business class, are devoting a part of their increasing leisure to their children. Such comments as the following represent many of the business-class wives interviewed:

> "I accommodate my entire life to my little girl. She takes three music lessons a week and I practice with her forty minutes a day. I help her with her school work and go to dancing school with her."

By both groups, the author means working-class and business-class parents.

The attitude that child-rearing is something not to be taken for granted but to be studied appears in parents of both groups. One cannot talk with Middletown mothers without being continually impressed by the eagerness of many to lay hold of every available resource for help in training their children.

And yet a prevalent mood among Middletown parents is bewilderment, a feeling that their difficulties outrun their best efforts to cope with them:

> "Life was simpler for my mother," said a thoughtful mother. "In those days one did not realize that there was so much to be known about the care of children. I realize that I ought to be half a dozen experts, but I am afraid of making mistakes and usually do not know where to go for advice."

The following discussion among eighteen high school boys and girls at a young people's meeting in a leading church on the general topic, "What's Wrong With the Home?" reveals the parents' perplexity as seen by the children:

Boy. "Parents don't know anything about their children and what they're doing."

Girl. "They don't want to know."

Girl. "We won't let them know."

Boy. "Ours is a speedy world and they're old."

Boy. "Parents ought to get together. Usually one is easy and one is hard. They don't stand together."

Boy. "Parents ought to have a third party to whom they could go for advice." [Chorus of "Yes."]

Boy. "This is the first year I've wanted to dance. Dad wanted me to go to only two this Christmas. [Triumphantly.] I'm going to five and passing up four!"

One shrewd businessman summarized the situation: "These kids aren't pulling the wool over their parents' eyes as much as you may think. The parents are wise to a lot that goes on, but they just don't know what to do, and try to turn their back on it."

94 The High School Comes of Age

In many contemporary high schools, more than half the graduating class enrolls in college or some other form of post-high school education. College is becoming an expected part of the education of millions of young people. In the 1920's, high schools were in the position that colleges are today: they were becoming a part of the educational experience of most young people. This new trend marked a major revolution in the world. In no other nation did such a large percentage of teen-aged youth go to school, instead of work for a living.

Between 1910 and 1920, secondary-school enrollment more than doubled. In 1920, 2,199,000 students were enrolled; in 1930, 4,399,000. The automobile and school bus made it possible to close down some one-room schoolhouses as rural children were transported to better-equipped consolidated schools. Many communities organized junior high schools to include the seventh, eighth, and ninth grades, thus reducing senior high school to three years.

The Lynds were strikingly impressed by the change in the role of the school in Middletown's society between 1890 and 1925. The curriculum had been expanded to meet the needs of a new day. More and more children went to school for longer and longer periods of time. The school became an important center of town life with considerable local pride involved in the triumphs of its students both in the classroom and on the athletic field.

The following selection from *Middletown* describes these changes. As you read, think about the following questions:

1. What roles did the schools play in the life of Middletown? How many of these roles were relatively new ones? Why had they become necessary?
2. What subjects did the school stress? Why these subjects and not others? Why did the schools attempt to teach more?
3. What did parents think of the schools?
4. How does this analysis of education compare with your own schools? How much has education changed since 1925?

Schooling in Middletown

Abridged from **Middletown**, pp. 181–220.

When the child is six the community for the first time concerns itself with his training.

Prior to 1897 when the first state "compulsory education" law was passed, the child's orientation to life might continue throughout as casually as in the first six years. Even after the coming of compulsory schooling only twelve consecutive weeks' attendance each year between the ages of eight and fourteen was at first required. During the last thirty years, however, the tendency has been not only to require more constant attendance during each year, but to extend the years that must be devoted to this formal, group-directed training both upward and downward. Today, no person may stop attending school until he is fourteen, while by taking over and expanding in 1924 the kindergartens, hitherto private semi-charitable organizations, the community is now allowing children of five and even of four, if room permits, to receive training at public expense.

In 1889–1890, there were 170 pupils in the high school, one for every 67 persons in the city, and the high school enrollment was only 8 percent of the total school enrollment, whereas in 1923–1924 there were 1,849 pupils in high school, one for every 21 persons in the city, and the high school enrollment was 25 percent of the total school enrollment. In other words, most of Middletown's children now extend their education past the elementary school into grades nine to twelve.

Equally striking is the pressure for training even beyond high school. Of those who continue their training for twelve years, long enough to graduate from high school, over a third prolong it still further in college or normal [teacher-training] work.

In the culture of thirty-five years ago it was deemed sufficient to teach during the first seven years of this extra-home training the following skills and facts, in rough order of importance:

a. The various uses of language. (Overwhelmingly first in importance.)

b. The accurate manipulation of numerical symbols.

c. Familiarity with the physical surroundings of peoples.

d. A miscellaneous group of facts about familiar physical objects about the child—trees, sun, ice, food, and so on.

e. The leisure-time skills of singing and drawing.

Today the things for which all children are sent to school fall into the following rough order:

a. The same uses of language.

b. The same uses of numerical figures.

c. Training in patriotic citizenship.

d. The same familiarity with the physical surroundings of peoples.

e. Facts about how to keep well and some physical exercise.

f. The same leisure-time skills of singing and drawing.

g. Knowledge and skills useful in sewing, cooking and using tools about the home for the girls, and, for the boys, an introductory acquaintance with some of the manual skills by which the working-class members get their living.

The school training of a generation ago appears to have been a more casual adjunct of the main business of "bringing up" that went on day by day in the home. Today, however, the school is relied upon to carry a more direct, if at most points still vaguely defined, responsibility.

The high school has been more adaptable than the lower school. Here group training no longer means the same set of facts learned on the same days by all children of a given grade. The freshman entering high school may plan to spend his four years following any one of twelve different "courses of study."

The most pronounced region of movement appears in the rush of courses that depart from the traditional dignified conception of what constitutes education and seek to train for specific tool and skill activities in factory, office, and home. A generation ago a solitary optional senior course in bookkeeping was the thin entering wedge of the trend that today controls eight of the twelve courses of the high school and claimed 17 percent of the total student hours during the first semester of 1923–1924 and 21 percent during the second. At no point has the training prescribed for the preparation of children for effective adulthood approached more nearly actual preparation for the dominant concerns in the daily lives of the people of Middletown. This pragmatic [practical] commandeering of education is frankly stated by the president of the School Board: "For a long time all boys were trained to be President. Then for a while we trained them all to be professional men. Now we are training boys to get jobs."

Second only in importance to the rise of these courses addressed to practical vocational activities is the new emphasis upon courses in history and civics. These represent yet another point at which Middletown is bending its schools to the immediate service of its institutions—in this case, bolstering community solidarity against sundry [various] divisive tendencies. A generation ago a course in American history was given to those who survived until the eighth grade. Today, separate courses in civic training and in history and civics begin with the first grade for all children and continue throughout the elementary school, while in high school the third-year course in American history and the fourth-year course in civics and sociology are, with the exception of the second-year English course, the only courses required of all students after the completion of the first year.

Evidently Middletown has become concerned that no child shall be without this pattern of the group. Precisely what this stamp is appears clearly in instructions to teachers:

"History furnishes no parallel of national growth, national prosperity and national achievement like ours," asserts the State Manual for Secondary Schools for 1923. "Practically all of this has been accomplished since we adopted our present form of government, and we are justified in believing that our political philosophy is right, and that those who are today assailing it are wrong. To properly grasp the philosophy of this government of ours, requires a knowledge of its history."

Further insight into the stamp of the group with which Middletown children complete their social studies courses is gained through the following summary of answers of 241 boys and 315 girls, comprising the social science classes of the last two years of the high school, to a questionnaire:

Statement	Percentage answering "True"		Percentage answering "False"		Percentage answering "Uncertain"		Percentage not answering	
	Boys	Girls	Boys	Girls	Boys	Girls	Boys	Girls
The white race is the best race on earth	66	75	19	17	14	6	1	2
The United States is unquestionably the best country in the world	77	88	10	6	11	5	2	1
Every good citizen should act according to the following statement: "My country—right or wrong!"	47	56	40	29	9	10	4	5
A citizen of the United States should be allowed to say anything he pleases, even to advocate violent revolution, if he does no violent act himself	20	16	70	75	7	7	3	2
The Allied Governments in the World War were fighting for a wholly righteous cause	65	75	22	8	11	14	2	3
Germany and Austria were the only nations responsible for causing the World War	22	25	62	42	15	31	1	2
The Russian Bolshevist government should be recognized by the United States Government	8	5	73	67	17	24	2	4
A pacifist in war time is a "slacker" and should be prosecuted by the government	40	36	34	28	22	28	4	8
The fact that some men have so much more money than others shows that there is an unjust condition in this country which ought to be changed	25	31	70	62	4	5	1	2

Accompanying the formal training afforded by courses of study is another and informal kind of training, particularly during the high school years. The high school, with its athletics, clubs, sororities and fraternities, dances and parties, and other "extracurricular activities," is a fairly complete social cosmos [world] in itself. This informal training is not a preparation for a vague future that must be taken on trust, as is the case with so much of the academic work; to many of the boys and girls in high school this is "the life," the thing they personally like best about going to school.

This whole spontaneous life of the school becomes focused, articulate, and even rendered important in the eyes of adults through the medium of the school athletic teams—the "Bearcats." The businessman may "lay down the law" to his adolescent son or daughter at home and patronize their friends, but in the basket-ball grandstand he is if anything a little less important than these youngsters of his who actually mingle daily with those five boys who wear the colors of "Magic Middletown."

The relative disregard of most people in Middletown for teachers and for the content of books, on the one hand, and the exalted position of the social and athletic activities of the schools, on the other, offer an interesting commentary on Middletown's attitude toward education. And yet Middletown places large faith in going to school. The heated opposition to compulsory education in the nineties has virtually disappeared. And yet when one looks more closely at this dominant belief in the magic of formal schooling, it appears that it is not what actually goes on in the schoolroom that these many voices laud. Literacy, yes, they want their children to be able to "read the newspapers, write a letter, and perform the ordinary operations of arithmetic," but, beyond that, many of them are little interested in what the schools teach. This thing, education, appears to be desired frequently not for its specific content but as a symbol—by the working class as an open sesame that will mysteriously admit their children to a world closed to them, and by the business class as a heavily sanctioned aid in getting on further economically or socially in the world.

Rarely does one hear a talk addressed to school children by a Middletown citizen that does not contain in some form the idea, "Of course, you won't remember much of the history or other things they teach you here. Why, I haven't thought of Latin or algebra in thirty years! But . . ." And here the speaker goes on to enumerate what *are* to his mind the enduring values of education which every child should seize as his great opportunity: "habits of industry," "friendships formed," "the great ideals of our nation." Almost never is the essential of education defined in terms of the subjects taught in the classroom. One member of Rotary spoke with pitying sympathy of his son who "even brought along a history book to read on the train when he came home for his Christmas vacation —the poor overworked kid!"

Rotary Clubs are men's clubs devoted to community service.

95 The Reach of Technology

In the election campaign of 1960, a television debate was held between the two major candidates—Kennedy and Nixon. Many observers felt that such non-political factors as personal appearance and the ability to project personality across a TV screen, apparent in the debate, swayed the election.

Television has changed life in America since World War II. It has provided evenings when the entire family clustered before a favorite program. It has had a marked influence on politics; one television debate may have tipped enough votes from Richard Nixon to elect John F. Kennedy in 1960. It has helped to catapult professional football into its new status as the national game. New inventions have often had a similar strong influence on the daily lives of people who make and use them.

The three major inventions that affected life in Middletown in the 1920's were the automobile, the movies, and radio. The Lynds had sought a town relatively free from dependence upon a nearby metropolis. But once on the scene, they learned that the impact of the city had made itself felt through modern transportation and communication. No longer could most American parents raise their children in cultural isolation. Through technology, Chicago and Indianapolis, New York, and Hollywood became a part of the lives of young people in Middletown.

As you read the following excerpts, think about these questions:

1. What had the automobile, the movies, and the radio done to the culture of Middletown? How had they affected the imagination?
2. How did these inventions affect the parents' ability to control the experiences of young people? How could parents shield young people from new influences? How could they use these new inventions to widen the horizons of their children?
3. Except for television, have any technological developments played a role in the lives of modern teenagers similar to the role played by the automobile, movies, and radio in the 1920's? How modern was Middletown?

Technology's Effect on Middletown

Abridged from **Middletown**, pp. 251–71.

"Why on earth do you need to study what's changing this country?" said a lifelong resident and shrewd observer of the Middle West. "I can tell you what's happening in just four letters: A-U-T-O!"

The first real automobile appeared in Middletown in 1900. About 1906 it was estimated that "there are probably 200 in the city and county." At the close of 1923 there were 6221 passenger cars in the city, one for every 6.1 persons, or roughly two for every three families. As, at the turn of the century, business-class people began to feel apologetic if they did not have a telephone, so ownership of an automobile has now reached the point of being an accepted essential of normal living.

No one questions the use of the auto for transporting groceries, getting to one's place of work or to the golf course, or in place of the porch for "cooling off after supper" on a hot summer evening; however much the activities concerned with getting a living may be altered by the fact that a factory can draw from workmen within a radius of forty-five miles, or however much old labor-union men resent the intrusion of this new alternate way of spending an evening, these things are hardly major issues. But when auto riding tends to replace the traditional call in the family parlor as a way of approach between the unmarried, "the home is endangered," and all-day Sunday motor trips are a "threat against the church"; it is in the activities concerned with the home and religion that the automobile occasions the greatest emotional conflicts.

Group-sanctioned values are disturbed by the inroads of the automobile upon the family budget. A case in point is the not uncommon practice of mortgaging a home to buy an automobile. According to an officer of a Middletown automobile financing company, 75 to 90 percent of the cars purchased locally are bought on time payment, and a working man earning $35.00 a week frequently plans to use one week's pay each month as payment for his car.

In borrowing money to buy a car, a person would transfer the mortgage or ownership of his house to the lender with the condition that the transfer would not be effective if the borrower paid back the money.

Many families feel that an automobile is justified as an agency holding the family group together. "I never feel as close to my family as when we are all together in the car," said one business-class mother, and one or two spoke of giving up Country Club membership or other recreations to get a car for this reason. "We don't spend anything on recreation except for the car. We save every place we can and put the money into the car. It keeps the family together," was an opinion voiced more than once. Sixty-one percent of 337 boys and 60 percent of 423 girls in the three upper years of the high school say that they motor more often with their parents than without them.

But this centralizing tendency of the automobile may be only a passing phase; sets in the other direction are almost equally prominent. "Our daughters [eighteen and fifteen] don't use our car much because they are always with somebody else in their car when we go out motoring," lamented one business-class mother. And another said, "The two older children [eighteen and sixteen] never go out when the family motors. They always have something else on." "In the nineties we were all much more together," said another wife. "People brought chairs and cushions out of the house and sat on the lawn evenings. We rolled out a strip of carpet and put cushions on the porch step to take care of the unlimited overflow of neighbors that dropped by. We'd sit out so all evening. The younger couples perhaps would wander off for half an hour to get a soda but come back to join in the informal singing or listen while somebody strummed a mandolin or guitar." "What on earth *do* you want me to do? Just sit around all evening!" retorted a popular high school girl of today when her father discouraged her going out motoring for the evening with a young blade in a rakish [sporty] car waiting at the curb. "The desire of youth to step on the gas when it has no machine of its own," said the local press, "is considered responsible for the theft of the greater part of the [154] automobiles stolen from [Middletown] during the past year."

Sharp, also, is the resentment aroused by this elbowing new device when it interferes with old-established religious habits. The minister must compete against the strong pull of the open road strengthened by endless printed "copy" inciting to travel. Preaching to 200 people on a hot, sunny Sunday in midsummer on "The Supreme Need of Today," a leading Middletown minister denounced "automobilitis—the thing those people have who go off motoring on Sunday instead of going to church. If you want to use your car on Sunday, take it out Sunday morning and bring some shut-ins to church and Sunday School; then in the afternoon, if you choose, go out and worship God in the beauty of nature—but don't neglect to worship Him indoors too."

But if the automobile touches the rest of Middletown's living at many points, it has revolutionized its leisure; more, perhaps than the movies or any other intrusion new to Middletown since the nineties, it is making leisure-time enjoyment a regularly expected part of every day and week rather than an occasional event. The readily available leisure-time options of even the working class have been multiplied many-fold. As one working-class housewife remarked, "We just go to lots of things we couldn't go to if we didn't have a car." Beefsteak and watermelon picnics in a park or a nearby wood can be a matter of a moment's decision on a hot afternoon.

Use of the automobile has apparently been influential in spreading the "vacation" habit. The custom of having each summer a respite [rest], usually of two weeks, from getting-a-living activities, with pay unabated [continuing], is increasingly common among the business class, but it is as yet very uncommon among the workers. "Vacations in 1890?" echoed one substantial citizen. "Why, the word wasn't in the dictionary!"

Like the automobile, the motion picture is more to Middletown than simply a new way of doing an old thing; it has added new dimensions to the city's leisure. To be sure, the spectacle-watching habit was strong upon Middletown in the nineties. Whenever they had a chance people turned out to a "show," but chances were relatively fewer. Fourteen times during January 1890, for instance, the Opera House was opened for performances ranging from *Uncle Tom's Cabin* to *The Black Crook,* before the paper announced that "there will not be any more attractions at the Opera House for nearly two weeks." In July there were no "attractions"; a half dozen were scattered through August and September; there were twelve in October.

Today nine motion-picture theaters operate from 1 to 11 P.M. seven days a week summer and winter. The decentralizing tendency of the movies upon the family, suggested by this last, is further indicated by the fact that only 21 percent of 337 boys and 33 percent of 423 girls in the three upper years of the high school go to the movies more often with their parents than without them. On the other hand, the comment is frequently heard in Middletown that movies have cut into lodge attendance, and it is probable that time formerly spent in lodges, saloons, and unions is now being spent in part at the movies, at least occasionally with other members of the family. Like the automobile and radio, the movies, by breaking up leisure time into an individual, family, or small group affair, represent a counter movement to the trend toward organization so marked in clubs and other leisure-time pursuits.

A lodge is the local branch or chapter of a national fraternal organization engaged in social and charitable functions.

How is life being quickened by the movies for the youngsters who bulk so large in the audiences, for the punch-press operator at the end of his working day, for the wife who goes to a "picture" every week or so "while he stays home with the children," for those business-class families who habitually attend?

A punch press is a machine that is used to stamp, cut, and shape metal.

"Go to a motion picture . . . and let yourself go," Middletown reads in a *Saturday Evening Post* advertisement. "Before you know it you are *living* the story—laughing, loving, hating, struggling, winning! All the adventure, all the romance, all the excitement you lack in your daily life are in——Pictures. They take you completely out of yourself into a wonderful new world. . . . Out of the cage of everyday existence! If only for an afternoon or an evening—escape!"

As in the case of the books it reads, comedy, heart interest, and adventure compose the great bulk of what Middletown enjoys in the movies. "Middletown is amusement hungry," says the opening sentence in a local editorial; at the comedies Middletown lives for an hour in a happy sophisticated make-believe world that leaves it, according to the advertisement of one film, "happily convinced that Life is very well worth living."

Actual changes of habits resulting from the week-after-week witnessing of these films can only be inferred. Young Middletown is finding discussion of problems of mating in this new agency that boasts in large illustrated advertisements, "Girls! You will learn how to handle 'em!" and "Is it true that marriage kills love? If you want to know what love really means, its exquisite torture, its overwhelming raptures, see ——."

> "Sheiks and their 'shebas'," according to the press account of the Sunday opening of one film, ". . . sat without a movement or a whisper through the presentation. . . . It was a real exhibition of love-making and the youths and maidens of [Middletown] who thought that they knew something about the art found that they still had a great deal to learn."

Some high school teachers are convinced that the movies are a powerful factor in bringing about the "early sophistication" of the young and the relaxing of social taboos. One working-class mother frankly welcomes the movies as an aid in child-rearing, saying, "I send my daughter because a girl has to learn the ways of the world somehow and the movies are a good safe way." The judge of the juvenile court lists the movies as one of the "big four" causes of local juvenile delinquency, believing that the disregard of group mores [moral attitudes] by the young is definitely related to the witnessing week after week of fictitious behavior sequences that habitually link the taking of long chances and the happy ending.

Though less widely diffused [spread] as yet than automobile owning or movie attendance, the radio nevertheless is rapidly crowding its way in among the necessities in the family standard of living. Not the least remarkable feature of this new invention is its accessibility. Here skill and ingenuity can in part offset money as an open sesame to swift sharing of the enjoyments of the wealthy. With but little equipment one can call the life of the rest of the world from the air, and this equipment can be purchased piecemeal at the ten-cent store. Far from being simply one more means of passive enjoyment, the radio has given rise to much ingenious manipulative activity. In a count of representative sections of Middletown, it was found that, of 303 homes in twenty-eight blocks in the "best section" of town, inhabited almost entirely by the business class, 12 percent had radios; of 518 workers' homes in sixty-four blocks, 6 percent had radios.

As this new tool is rolling back the horizons of Middletown for the bank clerk or the mechanic sitting at home and listening to a Philharmonic concert or a sermon by Dr. Fosdick, or to President Coolidge bidding his father good night on the eve of election, and as it is wedging its way with the movie, the automobile, and other new tools into the twisted mass of habits that are living for the 38,000 people of Middletown, readjustments necessarily occur.

Dr. Harry Emerson Fosdick (born 1878), a clergyman, was a spokesman in the 1920's for liberal theology against Fundamentalism. His sermons were impressive and practical and were nationally broadcast until his retirement in 1946.

The place of the radio in relation to Middletown's other leisure habits is not wholly clear. As it becomes more perfected, cheaper, and a more accepted part of life, it may cease to call forth so much active, constructive ingenuity and become one more form of passive enjoyment. Doubtless it will continue to play a mighty role in lifting Middletown out of the humdrum of every day; it is begining to take over that function of the great political rallies or the trips by the trainload to the state capital to hear a noted speaker or to see a monument dedicated that a generation ago helped to set the average man in a wide place. But it seems not unlikely that, while furnishing a new means of diversified enjoyment, syndicated newspapers, and other means of large-scale diffusion, as yet another means of standardizing many of Middletown's habits. Indeed, at no point is one brought up more sharply against the impossibility of studying Middletown as a self-contained, self-starting community than when one watches these space-binding leisure-time inventions imported from without—automobile, motion picture, and radio—reshaping the city.

Syndicated newspapers refer to a group of newspapers using the same lead articles, comic strips, political cartoons, and editorials. These newspapers subscribe to certain "syndicates" and news-reporting services such as the Associated Press (AP) and the United Press International (UPI) to obtain the news, and special features.

96 A Decade of Transition

HISTORICAL ESSAY

Three trends marked the decade of the 1920's. First, except in agriculture and a scattering of depressed industries, the economy pushed steadily ahead to new heights of prosperity after a postwar dip. Second, politics saw little constructive legislation as three lackluster Presidents, all from small towns or rural areas, presided over an urban-industrial society which they did not understand. Beneath the surface, however, men laid the foundations of a political realignment which was to result in a new majority for the Democratic party. Finally, the new prosperity contributed to changing patterns of behavior, some of which were described in the three readings from *Middletown*. In addition to the developments noted there, the 1920's marked a new step in female emancipation, saw the deterioration of the family accompanied by a wave of delinquency and crime, and witnessed militant attacks against foreigners, Catholics, Jews, blacks, and radicals.

The Economy

The transparencies accompanying Chapter 25 will analyze the economy of the 1920's in detail. No one can understand what happened to society in that decade, however, without some knowledge of trends in its economic life. After World War I ended in November 1918, a postwar boom set in. This boom collapsed in 1920. As many as 5 million workers may have been unemployed in 1921 during the depths of the depression. Almost half a million farmers lost their farms, and bankruptcies in business topped the 100,000 mark. By the middle of 1923, however, the economy had recovered completely, and for the next seven years, a constantly expanding boom pushed production to new heights.

Durable goods are items such as cars, machines, and household appliances, that may be used for several years.

The boom grew primarily through two sources: investments in a number of new industries and purchases of large quantities of new consumer durable goods. A housing boom, following a period during the war when little new housing had been produced, supported expansion in the construction industry until the middle of 1927. The rise of the automobile industry created huge investments in new plants and equipment. Other industries, such as electric power, aluminum, radios, and refrigerators, also spurred growth. Only a few industries, such as textiles (in New England) or coal mining, lagged behind. But agriculture was in decline as worldwide competition flooded the market with foodstuffs after the war. Farm population dropped by a million persons during the decade, and 13 million acres of farmland were abandoned. Nor did labor prosper as much as the owners of capital. Under constant attack from industry, the American Federation of Labor lost about one million members during the decade while wages generally rose more slowly than rents, interest, and dividends. In the meantime, a boom in stock prices pushed the market to unprecedented heights. During an eighteen month period, for example, United States Steel doubled in price while G.E. and Westinghouse tripled. This boom led to a general belief that prosperity in America would last forever.

Local Politics

On local and state levels, reform activities continued on a reduced scale throughout the 1920's. Much of the reform activity failed to draw the attention of newspaper and magazine writers, as it had done just after 1900. The reformers who first founded settlement houses or warred on the bosses made a great deal of noise. By the 1920's, men and women in similar roles had often studied social work or urban planning in college, and they approached their jobs from a perspective which did not value the emphasis which earlier reformers had placed on publicity.

The reformers of the first decade of the century had called for a change in the entire society. In the 1920's, reformers were more likely to work for changes in individuals rather than for full-scale societal reform. They expected the poor to adjust to their condition and to learn to solve personal emotional problems which distressed them. Professional social workers stuck to their tasks; they left overall social reform to amateurs, or to professional politicians.

Many of the reform measures pioneered in the early 1900's spread rapidly in the 1920's, however. The city-manager and commission forms of government were adopted in hundreds of cities. Many cities used zoning ordinances to control the use of land for public purposes. More and more states adopted industrial insurance. But, despite these reforms, the pace of change in the cities declined during the 1920's. Between 1900 and 1930, the proportion of people in 13 large metropolitan areas, who lived in the central cities of these areas declined from 69.1 percent to 63.7 percent. It is easy to understand what happened. First the streetcar and then the automobile made it easy for people to move out of central cities. In 1911, manufacturers sold 199,000 automobiles in the United States; in 1917, they sold 1,746,000; in 1923, 3,624,717; in 1929, 4,587,400. The ability to move to the suburbs allowed many Americans to leave the problems of central cities behind them. Rather than work to change the urban environment, millions of educated, ambitious, middle-class people moved out. With them went much of the dynamism which had been changing cities during the progressive era. They poured this energy into suburban schools, suburban libraries, suburban social services, and suburban police. Gradually, and then at an increasing rate, the quality of life in the central city and its suburbs grew apart.

See pages 525–28, 536–37.

Particularly during the 1960's, Americans began to realize that people who had moved to the suburbs had not left urban problems behind them completely. A metropolitan region makes up an interdependent unit. People who live in central cities and the suburbs which surround them must work together to solve the problems they have in common. Dwellers in suburbia can no more ignore the problems of the city than the United States can live isolated from the rest of the world. But during the 1920's, flight to the suburbs seemed to be an escape from an entanglement of problems that were becoming increasingly perplexing.

See page 515.

National Politics

Three Republicans won the Presidency during the 1920's; the Republican party maintained substantial majorities in both the Senate and the House of Representatives. Table 1 on the following page shows the popular vote in Presidential elections between 1920 and 1928. Table 2 demonstrates Republican dominance in the House and Senate during this period.

U.S. Bureau of the Census, **Historical Statistics of the United States, Colonial Times to 1957.** Washington, D.C.: Government Printing Office, 1960, p. 682.

Table 1. The Elections for President, 1920-1928

Year	Candidates	Party	% of Popular Vote
1920	WARREN G. HARDING	Republican	60.4
	James M. Cox	Democratic	36.2
	Eugene V. Debs	Socialist	3.4
	P. P. Christensen	Farmer-Labor	1.0
1924	CALVIN COOLIDGE	Republican	54.
	John W. Davis	Democratic	24.5
	Robert La Follette	Progressive	16.6
1928	HERBERT HOOVER	Republican	58.2
	Alfred E. Smith	Democratic	40.9

Historical Statistics, p. 691.

Table 2. Party Control of the Executive and Legislative Branches of Government, 1921-1931

Year	President's Party	Majority Party and Margin: House of Rep.	Majority Party and Margin: Senate
1921-1923	R	R (172)	R (22)
1923-1925	R	R (20)	R (8)
1925-1927	R	R (64)	R (17)
1927-1929	R	R (42)	R (3)
1929-1931	R	R (100)	R (17)

President Harding, although not involved in any scandals, appointed dishonest, undeserving men to office. Harry Daugherty, Attorney-General, used his office to protect violators of the prohibition law. Charles F. Forbes, Director of Veteran's Bureau, robbed his agency of about $250 million. Thomas W. Miller obtained $50,000 by fraudulently selling foreign-owned properties seized by the United States government during World War I.

The issues which had dominated national legislation for fifty years—money and banking, the tariff, business regulation, and efficiency in government—continued into the 1920's, but they no longer occupied the center of the stage. No significant banking legislation was passed. The Fordney-McCumber Tariff (1922) and the Hawley-Smoot Tariff (1930) reversed the trend set by the Underwood Tariff (1913) by raising rates substantially and placing new ones on many agricultural products. Trusts and holding companies grew at a rapid rate, but Congress failed to pass significant legislation to control them. Scandals during the Harding Administration, most of them involving cronies of the President who held important administrative positions, failed to arouse the nation sufficiently to bring a change in administration. Throughout the decade, men like Herbert Hoover in the Commerce Department and Andrew Mellon in the Treasury Department insisted on efficiency in government and kept expenditures to a minimum. Rather than these traditional issues, immigration restriction, already discussed in Chapter 18, and prohibition occupied the center of the political stage during the 1920's. In one way or another, both had been vital factors in American politics since the 1890's.

Twenty-six states had already adopted prohibition laws by 1917. During World War I, Congress first prohibited the manufacture or sale of intoxicating liquors and then passed the Eighteenth Amendment, which placed this prohibition into the Constitution. Ratified in 1919, the amendment went into effect in 1920 together with the Volstead Act, which provided means to enforce it. Americans, by the millions, violated the prohibition laws. Newspapers during the 1920's were filled with stories of rum-runners and gangsters who supplied rich and poor alike with illegal liquor. Prohibition agents tried in vain to enforce a law which a substantial number of citizens broke willingly.

The Volstead Act (1919) defined an alcoholic beverage as one containing ½ of 1 percent alcohol and placed the enforcement of the law under the Bureau of Internal Revenue. Any person manufacturing or selling liquor was to be fined not more than $1000 or imprisoned not more than six months for a first offense and receive more severe punishments for succeeding offenses.

Conventional political histories of the 1920's often describe the way in which business reasserted its power in the national government, reversing many of the trends evident during the progressive period. In 1920, President Warren G. Harding, a resident of Marion, Ohio, spoke of a "return to normalcy" and an end to "wild experiments." He died in 1923, as scandals were erupting in his Administration. His successor, Vermont-born Calvin Coolidge, was an even more determined advocate of the American business system. "The business of the country is business," he once said. His successor, once an Iowa farm boy, named Herbert Hoover, returned to an early Wilsonian idea of the role of government in the economy. During his second term, Woodrow Wilson had turned toward government aid to agriculture, the regulation of the length of the working day, and similar positive governmental measures. Hoover, however, attacked relief programs for the farmer, public ownership or control of electric power facilities, and even the development of a state liquor monopoly as measures which "would impair the very basis of liberty and freedom." Table 1 on page 612 indicates what happened to the forces of progressivism when they attempted to challenge this defense of limited government in 1924.

The most famous scandal was the Teapot Dome scandal. Secretary of the Interior, Albert B. Fall, had persuaded Secretary of the Navy, Edwin C. Denby to transfer his department's jurisdiction of certain oil reserves to the Interior Department. In 1922, Fall secretly leased the reserve at Teapot Dome, Wyoming, to Harry F. Sinclair, and the reserve at Elk Hills, California, to Edward L. Doheny. A Senate investigation revealed that the two oil speculators had "loaned" Fall about $350,000. All three men were indicted for conspiracy and bribery but only Fall was convicted.

Emphasizing Republican dominance and support of business in national politics during the 1920's obscures a more vital matter. The 1920's saw a number of conflicts arise over the fundamental nature of American society and American politics. A whole set of conflicting images became compressed under the labels "wet" and "dry"; Protestant or Catholic; country town and farms, or big city; old immigrants now long removed from Europe or new immigrants still caught up in values of lands across the water.

Because it contained roughly equal representation of people favoring both images, the Democratic party became the center of this conflict. A resolution attacking the Ku Klux Klan as un-American divided the Democratic Convention in 1924. The resolution lost by a narrow vote (546–541) and was replaced by a compromise plank in the platform condemning religious and racial antagonisms. The

The old Ku Klux Klan, defunct for many years after the Civil War, was revitalized in 1915. By 1925, the Klan was operating in the North and South and numbered between 4 and 5 million members.

battle over the platform carried over into the nominating procedure. The South supported W. G. McAdoo, formerly Wilson's Secretary of the Treasury; the North supported Governor Alfred E. Smith of New York, a second-generation Irish Catholic who advocated repeal of prohibition. Supporters of the two men battled stubbornly through 102 ballots before an exhausted convention settled on a compromise candidate, John W. Davis, a New York corporation lawyer who had been raised in West Virginia.

Smith won the nomination more easily in 1928 only to have normally Democratic voters turn against him. Although Hoover dissociated himself from an ugly anti-Catholic campaign, the contrasts in the two men stood out vividly. Excerpts from two of their speeches capture the essence of the images they presented:

The New Day, Campaign Speeches of Herbert Hoover, 1928. Stanford: Stanford University Press, 1929, p. 48.

> There is no imprint upon our minds so deep as those of early boyhood. Mine are the joys of Iowa—the glories of snowy winter, the wonder at the growing crops, the joining of the neighbors to harvest, the gathering of apples, the pilgrimage to the river woods for the annual fuel and nuts, the going to school, the interludes from work, in the swimming hole, fishing in creeks, the hunting for prairie chickens and rabbits in the hedges and woods. It is the entry to life which I could wish for every American boy and girl.

Campaign Addresses of Governor Alfred E. Smith, Democratic Candidate for President, 1928. Washington, D.C.: Democratic National Committee, 1929, pp. 121–22.

> The Republican party [of New York State] about three or four days ago adopted a platform that is as meaningless as anything I ever saw in my life.
>
> Personally, after looking at it, I could get more comfort from a Chinese laundry ticket.
>
> It brought me back over some thirty-five years. All you have to do is pick it up, and you would imagine that you were in the Fulton [Fish] Market in the dead of winter, picking up a fish.

Most Americans still identified with Iowa farms rather than with Chinese laundry tickets and fish markets. Hoover broke the Democratic dominance of the South, capturing Florida, North Carolina, Tennessee, Texas, and Virginia. Smith carried only the remaining states of the old Confederacy and two New England states, Massachusetts and Rhode Island.

Beneath this massive Republican victory lay an important shift in the electorate which was not immediately clear. The Republican majority had been fashioned in the 1890's around a coalition of farmers and small- and big-city voters who joined in a common image of the good life. In the 1920's, this coalition was breaking apart. Tables 3 and 4 tell much of the story.

Table 3. Presidential Votes in
Cities with Fifty Percent or More Immigrant Stock

Carl N. Degler, "American Political Parties and the Rise of the City: An Interpretation," in **Journal of American History,** vol. LI (June 1964), pp. 53–56.

City	Democratic Vote in nearest thousand		Percent Change	Republican Vote in nearest thousand		Percent Change
	1920	*1928*		*1920*	*1928*	
Boston	68	205	202	108	99	—7.7
Buffalo	40	126	215	100	145	45.0
Chicago	197	716	266	635	812	27.8
Cleveland	71	166	132	149	195	30.7
Detroit	52	157	201	221	265	19.9
Jersey City	63	153	143	102	100	—1.9
Los Angeles	56	210	275	178	514	189.0
Milwaukee	25	111	344	73	82	12.2
Minneapolis	143	396	178	519	561	8.1
Newark	41	118	188	116	169	45.6
New York	345	1,168	239	786	715	—9.1
Oakland	21	61	190	73	119	63.2
Philadelphia	90	276	209	308	420	36.5
Pittsburgh	40	161	301	139	216	55.5
Providence	46	97	112	80	86	7.5
Rochester	29	74	156	74	100	35.2
St. Paul	21	57	171	40	53	32.5
San Francisco	33	97	195	96	96	0.0
Seattle	17	47	176	59	96	62.9

Table 4. Presidential Votes in
Cities with Less than Fifty Percent of Immigrant Stock

Degler, pp. 53–56.

City	Democratic Vote in nearest thousand		Percent Change	Republican Vote in nearest thousand		Percent Change
	1920	*1928*		*1920*	*1928*	
Akron	28	32	14.3	44	79	79.5
Atlanta	9	7	—22.5	3	6	100.0
Baltimore	87	126	44.8	126	135	7.3
Birmingham	25	17	—32.0	7	18	157.0
Cincinnati	78	110	41.0	113	148	31.0
Columbus	48	47	—2.3	60	92	53.2
Dallas	14	17	21.4	5	27	440.0
Denver	23	41	78.5	44	74	68.1
Houston	15	22	47.7	8	27	237.0
Indianapolis	61	73	19.7	80	110	37.4
Kansas City, Mo.	77	97	26.0	80	127	58.6
Louisville	56	64	14.3	68	98	44.3
Memphis	16	18	12.5	9	12	33.3
New Orleans	33	56	70.0	18	14	—22.2
Portland, Ore.	28	45	60.5	45	76	68.8
St. Louis	106	176	66.0	163	162	—0.68
Toledo	30	45	50.0	52	78	50.0

Ethnic identification and urban residence lay at the center of political shifts in the 1920's: Politicians did not turn their backs on all the reform concerns of the past decades. Instead, they wrestled with two of the chief issues of the era, prohibition and immigration restriction. These issues had turned up in the 1890's; by the 1920's they had become dominant political themes. America was far more urban in 1920 than it had been thirty years before. In addition, the way of life in small towns became much more like that in a metropolis because of the influence of the automobile, radio, and movies.

The first commercial radio station—KDKA—began broadcasting in Pittsburgh in 1920. Radio broadcasting grew rapidly in the 1920's. Until 1927, movies had all been silent films. **The Jazz Singer** was the first motion picture to use sound.

As long as the country was prosperous, Hoover's image remained attractive to many voters. It was not, however, an image that could capture the imagination of the urban masses. Nor could it long retain the allegiance of poor blacks, although they continued out of loyalty to a party that had freed the slaves, to vote Republican into the 1930's. The dramatic shift to the Democratic party in the votes of the foreign-born and the children of foreign-born parents living in large cities between 1920 and 1928 was an omen of what was to come.

Hoover's image and the policies of the Republican party could not even hold the farm vote once the Depression struck after 1929. Hoover described a rural America of a bygone day. Throughout the 1920's, American farmers suffered a sharp reversal in their fortunes. Between 1921 and 1924, the farm bloc in Congress, which represented mainly large and relatively prosperous farmers, pushed through a series of measures to supply credit, limit imports, regulate speculation in farm products, and control the activities of meatpackers and stockyards. When these measures failed to restore farm prosperity, the farm bloc pushed for expanded government aid in the form of a price support plan called the McNary-Haughen Bill. Coolidge vetoed the measure just as he resisted demands for the public development of power in the Tennessee Valley. Hoover echoed Coolidge's policies. Farmers stirred restlessly. Then the collapse of farm prices at the onset of the Depression in 1929 added this farm discontent to the urban and ethnic unrest which were building a new political coalition for the Democratic candidate, whomever he might be.

The McNary-Haugen Bill of 1924 proposed a federal Farm Board to buy farm surpluses and either store them until prices rose or sell them abroad at the international price. The Bill suffered successive defeats in both houses, was finally passed in 1927, only to be vetoed by President Coolidge.

The Society

To a marked degree, the people described in *Middletown* shared many of the trends taking place in American society during the 1920's despite the fact that Muncie, Indiana, was a small town. Industry, the radio, the movies, and the automobile were slowly forging a national culture. No one was immune to these new trends, not even people on farms. Like everyone else, they were caught up in a machine age where developments such as mail-order houses, free mail delivery, the film, and the radio brought the city to their doorsteps each day.

The shift from a rural to an urban society and from agriculture to industry changed the American family. For every five marriages during the 1920's there was almost one divorce. Women had become far more independent. The number of female wage earners had been rising steadily, and it continued to rise during the 1920's. With the passage of the Nineteenth Amendment in 1917, women won the vote. A new attitude to sex developed, spurred by the automobile, the glamor of illegal liquor, a knowledge of psychology, and a higher educational level. Rather than submit to abuses from their husbands, many women preferred divorce and freedom.

Children also tended to drift from home. Movies and the radio gave them new models to imitate. The automobile freed them from the restraints of their parents and opened a new and exciting world to explore. New courses taught in the schools also gave many children a glimpse of a new culture. Large numbers of them revolted, particularly during the college years.

In response to these trends, another segment of the public reasserted the value of old-time morality. Prohibition was one indication of this counterattack. So was fundamentalism. Revivalists such as the former major-league baseball player, Billy Sunday, appeared before enormous crowds throughout the decade to preach the virtues of religion and strict moral standards. A Tennessee court convicted a high school biology teacher, John T. Scopes, of disobeying a law, passed overwhelmingly by the state legislature, which forbade the teaching of Darwinism in the public schools. And then there were the attacks on radicals, real and pretended.

Fundamentalism is a conservative Protestant movement that emphasizes the belief in the literal truth of the Bible.

Tennessee law prohibited the teaching of evolution because of the fundamentalist claim that it contradicted the Bible. Scopes was arrested and his trial attracted national attention, largely because William Jennings Bryan, the former Presidential candidate, argued for the prosecution and Clarence Darrow, a lawyer of national prominence, defended Scopes.

In 1919, a full-scale Red Scare broke out, led by A. Mitchell Palmer, Attorney-General under Woodrow Wilson. In the midst of the hysteria, which came in the wake of the communist revolution in Russia, the government jailed thousands of men and women on trumped-up charges and deported hundreds of them. After 1920, the modern Ku Klux Klan, which had been reorganized in 1915, began to grow rapidly, attacking radicals, Catholics, Jews, and Negroes, particularly in the midwestern states. The Klan advocated racist doctrines and claimed to protect "Americanism." Its power declined around the middle of the decade, particularly after the corruption of some of its officers was exposed. In the meantime, the entire country had become involved in the trial of two anarchists, Nicola Sacco and Bartolomeo Vanzetti, who were accused of murdering a payroll guard in Braintree, Massachusetts. Although the two men were convicted in 1921, they were not executed until 1927 while appeals crept through the courts and much of the

The trial of Sacco and Vanzetti attracted national attention. Many people believed that anti-immigrant and anti-radical feelings were primarily responsible for their conviction.

nation's intellectual elite rallied to their defense on the grounds that their trial had been grossly unfair.

The 1920's tumbled new and old America together in bewildering combinations. Families drove to old-time revival meetings in their new Model T Fords. Republican Presidents used the magic of radio to appeal to classic virtues, such as thrift and individualism. In politics, prohibition and immigration restriction looked back to days long past while measures to support agricultural prices anticipated the reforms of the New Deal. Then in October 1929, came the stock-market crash which heralded the advent of the Great Depression. America would never be the same again.

SUGGESTED READINGS

ALLEN, FREDERICK L., *Only Yesterday.* Allen argues in a lively manner that the twenties were a trauma induced by battle fatigue.

HANDLIN, OSCAR, *Al Smith and His America.* This brief biography contains a sympathetic story of the man whose presidential candidacy reflected enormous changes in American life.

LYND, ROBERT and HELEN, *Middletown.* Here is a full account of the selection you sampled in the chapter. *Middletown in Transition* carries the story into the 1930's.

CHAPTER 25

The Depression and the New Deal

STATING THE ISSUE

In October 1929, prices on the New York Stock Exchange collapsed. For six years, the prices of common stock had risen steadily, despite an occasional dip. They reached unprecedented heights in the fall of 1929 amid predictions that they would continue ever upward. Then came the crash, with the Depression following hard on its heels. For month after dreary month, the economy spiraled downward. No other development had such a profound impact on American society during the 1930's.

The Depression ended the political ascendancy of the Republican party, an ascendancy which had begun in the 1890's. During the 1920's, the basis of a new political alignment had been formed among the people of foreign stock in urban areas and the farmers who had never shared in full the prosperity of the 1920's. Franklin D. Roosevelt, the Democratic standard bearer in 1932, welded the elements of this new coalition together. For more than twenty years, the Democrats ruled supreme in Washington. Not once during these two decades were the Republicans so much as able to win control over one of the houses of Congress.

For most of his first two terms in office, Roosevelt struggled with the crisis caused by the Depression. By the time of his inauguration in March 1933, between 20 and 25 percent of the labor force was unemployed. Relief, recovery, and reform became the order of the day. During the first one hundred days of the new Administration, Roosevelt attacked each of these three problems as he promised a New Deal to the American people. For the next eight years, domestic politics occupied most of the energy and thought of the new administration until World War II solved the unemployment problem at the same time that it made international affairs overwhelmingly important.

What caused the Depression which began in 1929 and lasted more than a decade? What effects did the Depression have on the American people? What did private citizens and the government do to combat the effects of the Depression and to prevent another one from happening in the future? These are the major issues of Chapter 25.

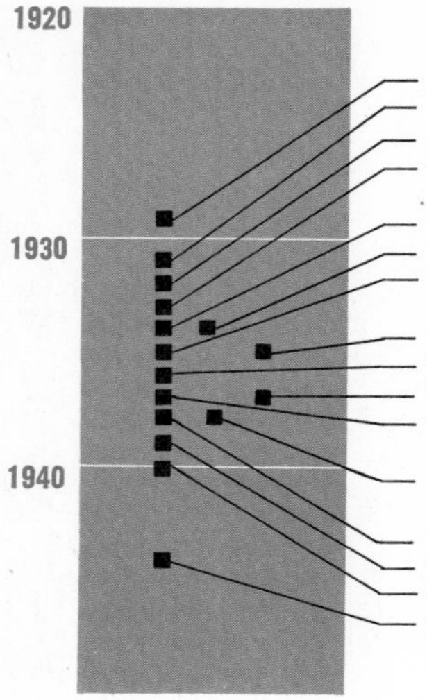

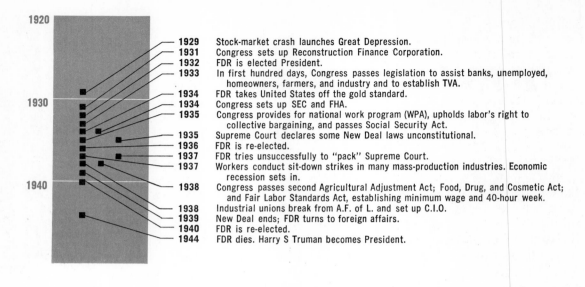

1929	Stock-market crash launches Great Depression.
1931	Congress sets up Reconstruction Finance Corporation.
1932	FDR is elected President.
1933	In first hundred days, Congress passes legislation to assist banks, unemployed, homeowners, farmers, and industry and to establish TVA.
1934	FDR takes United States off the gold standard.
1934	Congress sets up SEC and FHA.
1935	Congress provides for national work program (WPA), upholds labor's right to collective bargaining, and passes Social Security Act.
1935	Supreme Court declares some New Deal laws unconstitutional.
1936	FDR is re-elected.
1937	FDR tries unsuccessfully to "pack" Supreme Court.
1937	Workers conduct sit-down strikes in many mass-production industries. Economic recession sets in.
1938	Congress passes second Agricultural Adjustment Act; Food, Drug, and Cosmetic Act; and Fair Labor Standards Act, establishing minimum wage and 40-hour week.
1938	Industrial unions break from A.F. of L. and set up C.I.O.
1939	New Deal ends; FDR turns to foreign affairs.
1940	FDR is re-elected.
1944	FDR dies. Harry S Truman becomes President.

97 Facing the Depression Crisis

Herbert Hoover took office in March 1929. Seven months later, the stock market crash echoed down the narrow canyons of Wall Street. Despite optimistic statements from government officials and business leaders, conditions grew steadily worse. Hoover tried to restore confidence by proclaiming that the economy was essentially sound. He held a number of meetings with leaders of business, labor, and farmers to rally support for voluntary programs designed to combat the economic crisis. When voluntary support failed, Hoover pressed through a tax cut and asked Congress for an increase of $423 million in appropriations for public works. He also pushed through the Smoot-Hawley Tariff which raised rates to new heights, a measure which helped to undermine the effects of a one-year moratorium on war debt payments designed to help European economies. These measures excepted, Hoover placed his faith in voluntary efforts to end the economic decline.

As a result of World War I, European nations owed the United States $10 billion. In 1931, due to the world-wide depression, President Hoover announced a one-year moratorium or postponement of the payment of war debts.

In 1930, the Democrats won control of the House of Representatives by a narrow margin. Combined with progressive Republicans, they had effective control of the Senate. Economic conditions had reached crisis proportions by the time that the new Congress met in March 1931. Hence, Hoover abandoned his reliance on voluntary measures. In January, Congress passed a measure setting up the Reconstruction Finance Corporation which loaned $1.5 billion during 1932 to support banks, businesses, and railroads. Hoover also signed a bill which authorized the Reconstruction Finance Corporation to loan $1.5 billion for the building of public works, such as dams that could generate electric power, which would eventually earn enough money to pay for themselves. The government also appropriated $300 million for direct relief. On the whole, however, Hoover believed that feeding people and keeping them warm was the responsibility of private charity and local government, not of Washington.

The readings which follow illustrate Hoover's philosophy and indicate what some Americans did to cope with the crisis that the Depression brought to their lives. As you read, think about the following questions:

1. What was Hoover's attitude toward the role of the government in the Depression crisis? Was this attitude realistic?
2. How did individuals try to cope with the crisis that the Depression brought to their lives?
3. What were the human costs of the Depression?
4. Should government try to stop depressions from happening? What might be the costs of preventing depressions?

Herbert Hoover Emphasizes Self-Reliance

Herbert Hoover feared that expansion of federal power into relief activities might undermine individualism and self-reliance. The following statement, typical of many he made, shows his position clearly.

Press Statement, February 3, 1931.

This is not an issue as to whether people shall go hungry or cold in the United States. It is solely a question of the best method by which hunger and cold shall be prevented. It is a question as to whether the American people on one hand will maintain the spirit of charity and mutual self-help through voluntary giving and the responsibility of local government as distinguished on the other hand from appropriation out of the Federal Treasury for such purposes. My own conviction is strongly that if we break down this sense of responsibility of individual generosity to individual and mutual self-help in the country in times of national difficulty and if we start appropriations of this character we have not only impaired something infinitely valuable in the life of the American people but have struck at the roots of self-government. Once this has happened it is not the cost of a few score millions but we are faced with the abyss of reliance in the future upon government charity in some form or other. The money involved is indeed the least of the costs to American ideals and American institutions. . . .

During World War I, Hoover was chairman of the American Relief Commission in London and later the Belgian Relief Commission. When the United States entered the war, he was appointed Food Administrator with power to set controls on the production and consumption of food and fuel. He served as Secretary of Commerce from 1921 to 1928.

I have indeed spent much of my life in fighting hardship and starvation both abroad and in the southern states. I do not feel that I should be charged with lack of human sympathy for those who suffer but I recall that in all the organizations with which I have been connected over these many years, the foundation has been to summon the maximum of self-help. I am proud to have sought the help of Congress in the past for nations who were so disorganized by war and anarchy that self-help was impossible. But even these appropriations were but a tithe [tenth] of that which was coincidently mobilized from the public charity of the United States and foreign countries. There is no such paralysis in the United States and I am confident that our people have the resources, the initiative, the courage, the stamina, and kindliness of spirit to meet this situation in the way they have met their problems over generations.

I will accredit to those who advocate federal charity a natural anxiety for the people of their states. I am willing to pledge myself that if the time should ever come that the voluntary agencies of the country together with the local and state governments are unable to find resources with which to prevent hunger and suffering in my country, I will ask the aid of every resource of the federal government because I would no more see starvation amongst our countrymen than would any senator or congressman. I have the faith in the American people that such a day will not come.

Two Families Face Starvation

Some families, too proud to beg or go on relief, preferred to starve. Although people such as these were exceptions, their stories indicate one response to the Depression.

MIDDLETOWN, N.Y., Dec. 24—Attracted by smoke from the chimney of a supposedly empty summer cottage near Anwana Lake in Sullivan County, Constable Simon Glaser found a young couple starving. Three days without food, the wife, who is 23 years old, was hardly able to walk.

The couple, Mr. and Mrs. Wilfred Wild of New York, had been unemployed since their formerly wealthy employer lost his money, and several days ago they invested all they had, except 25 cents for food, in bus fare to this region in search of work. Finding none, they went into the cottage, preferring to starve rather than beg. They said they had resigned themselves to dying together.

An effort is being made to obtain employment for them, but if this fails they will be sent back to New York.

DANBURY, CONN., Sept. 6.—Found starving under a rude canvas shelter in a patch of woods on Flatboard Ridge, where they had lived for five days on wild berries and apples, a woman and her 16-year-old daughter were fed and clothed today by the police and placed in the city almshouse.

The New York Times, September 7, 1932. Copyright © 1932 by The New York Times Company.

The woman is Mrs. John Moll, 33, and her daughter Helen, of White Plains, N.Y., who have been going from city to city looking for work since July 1931, when Mrs. Moll's husband left her.

When the police found them, they were huddled beneath a strip of canvas stretched from a boulder to the ground. Rain was dripping from the improvised shelter, which had no sides.

College Graduates Help Each Other

Unemployment was no respecter of education. The following short article indicates what graduates of one group of distinguished colleges did in the midst of the Depression crisis.

Organization of the Association of Unemployed College Alumni was announced yesterday after a meeting of graduates of nine eastern colleges at the offices of the League for Industrial Democracy. Estimating the number of unemployed alumni in this city alone at more than 10,000, the association made public a plan of action designed to enlist members throughout the country.

The New York Times, July 27, 1932. Copyright © 1932 by The New York Times Company.

The League for Industrial Democracy, founded in 1905, is made up of educators, labor union officials, journalists, and students. It sponsors lectures, radio broadcasts, and public affairs conferences.

In a statement prepared at the meeting the group pointed out that since June 1929, it had become increasingly difficult for university graduates to obtain positions. Distress consequent upon unemployment was more acute among college-trained men and women, according to the announcement, because of their relatively high standards of living and education. . . .

Colleges represented at the meeting included Columbia, Harvard, New York University, Vassar, Hunter. City College, Swarthmore, Columbia Law School and New York Dental School.

An Unemployed Seaman Looks for a Place to Sleep

Rather than move into the shantytowns which grew up in every city, some men tried a variety of alternatives of which the following instance is a good example.

Somewhere in Tin Mountain, the four-acre jungle on the Red Hook waterfront in Brooklyn, Louis Bringmann put down his old sea chest last night and looked about him for a place to sleep. He was 60 years old, penniless, friendless, and jobless.

The New York Times, July 9, 1932. Copyright © 1932 by The New York Times Company. Reprinted by permission.

Up to 9 A.M. yesterday, Louis Bringmann had had a home on the top landing of the Atlantic Theatre, at Flatbush Avenue and Dean Street, but the Fire Department inspector on his monthly round discovered it.

Patrolman Richard Palmay of the Bergen Street police station climbed the fire-escape stairs at 8 A.M. with orders to "remove the fire hazard." At the top landing he peered over the walls of corrugated cardboard which Bringmann had built around the grill-work. The tenant was fast aseep.

On the cardboard wall was a neat sign, done in old-school flourishes and shading:

> NOTICE
>
> Please be kind enough not to destroy or take anything from this resting place. I am out of work and this is all I have. I have no money and I can't find a job, so please leave me alone. I'll appreciate your kind consideration and
>
> THANK YOU.

Patrolman Palmay looked down on the tired old face, the slight figure outlined beneath the worn but clean-looking blankets, at the socks and spotless shirt fluttering in the breeze on the short clothes-line overhead. He had his orders, but—

An hour later, doubling back on his post, Palmay saw Louis Bringmann leaving his cardboard shelter. He watched him as he dipped into the rain barrel he had fixed under the copper leader, to make his morning ablutions [washing]. Then he walked over.

"You'll have to move, old man." He hated the job.

"I can't stay? I'm not bothering any one. And they don't use the theatre in the summer time. I keep everything clean. I—"

"They gave me orders," replied Palmay. "It's against the fire laws."

The snow-white head nodded. Louis Bringmann was too patient a man to vent his bitterness in vain argument.

He rolled his blankets carefully and dressed. He took his little sea chest under one thin arm. The other meager chattels [possessions] dangled from his white fingers. He started to move.

Palmay thrust a half dollar into the free hand and walked away. . . .

The white-haired Bringmann plodded up the avenue, immaculate in his worn brown trousers and blue jacket, heading toward the river.

He had known of Tin Mountain before, but he was proud. In Tin Mountain, a sprawling village of tin huts and makeshift dugouts at the foot of Henry Street, are all types of men—brawny Scandinavian seamen, husky Irish longshoremen—good men, but a bit rough. One of its streets has the bitter legend on a placard, "Prosperity Boulevard."

Late in the afternoon he was still sitting on the little chest that contains the meager souvenirs of better days—a few faded menus he had made up when he was head chef of one of the big Manhattan hotels. He wouldn't tell which one.

"The past," said Louis Bringmann, "is a turned-over page. When I read it I read alone. They tell me now that I'm even too old for dishwashing—that's the whole story. I have no friends and my money is gone."

98 A Case History of a Depression Family

No typical experience can capture the effect of the Depression on American families. Some families lived through the entire Depression decade with their pattern of living relatively unchanged. Others found their entire way of life disrupted. For the majority of families, the Depression meant a reduced standard of living, but no drastic change in accustomed patterns of life.

Cases of extreme want have become part of American folklore. The Okies, farmers from the Great Plains who were driven off their lands by a series of dust storms, became famous through John Steinbeck's novel, *The Grapes of Wrath.* Unemployed men who left their homes to seek work elsewhere often lived in shantytowns on the edges of cities. By calling these temporary communities Hoovervilles, they added a new word to the language. Everyone who lived through the 1930's remembers the breadlines outside soup kitchens and the proud men who sold apples on street corners rather than beg or go on relief.

During the Depression, local charities set up "soup kitchens" to distribute soup, broth, and bread to the starving.

State, local, and federal governments all sponsored relief projects. The two most famous were the Works Progress Administration (WPA) and the Public Works Administration (PWA). Designed for somewhat different objectives, these two programs kept millions of Americans alive during the worst days of the Depression. With one person in four unemployed, projects sponsored by these agencies often enlisted unskilled laborers, skilled mechanics, and college graduates, working side by side and united by a common bond of misfortune.

Reading 98 traces the history of one family through the Depression crisis. As you read it, think about the following questions:

1. What did the Park family do to live through the Depression years? How do you think these experiences may have affected their image of themselves? their attitude toward the role of the government in the economy?
2. How much money did the Parks have in a typical Depression year? What did the organization of the federally supported public works projects mean to them?
3. What, if anything, should the government do to try to prevent depressions? to take care of people if depressions do occur?

The Claud Park Family Faces the Depression

During 1938–1939, the Works Progress Administration made a survey in Dubuque, Iowa, of 103 Depression families. The WPA published 45 case histories in mimeographed form. The Claud Park family was as typical as any of the others. The history of the Parks indicates the impact of the Depression on one working-class family.

Jessie A. Bloodworth, ed., **The Personal Side.** Washington, D.C.: Works Progress Administration, Division of Research, 1939, pp. 13–18.

PARK	
Mr. Park	32
Mrs. Park	31
Claud, Jr.	11
Mary	9
Dorothy	4

Interviewing completed January 2, 1938

When Claud Park was granted a pay raise a year ago at the Mississippi Milling Company, where he had been hired in August 1935 after 4 years of unemployment, the Parks thought the Depression was ended for them. Now, however, with working hours reduced to 25 a week, the Park family fear that they are "getting right back" where they were 5 or 6 years ago.

At 32, Claud is weatherbeaten in appearance and shows the effects of worry and anxiety. Though frank and spontaneous, he is slow of speech and drawls out his words as he discusses the family's Depression experiences. After the long siege of unemployment and dependency on either direct relief or work projects, Claud considers himself an "authority on the Depression."

The Parks live in a rented five-room brick house in a neighborhood of small homes in the north end of town. Martha Park, the mother of three children, has found time to take an active part in the Parent Teachers Association and the Mothers Club of the church, despite her desperate struggle to make ends meet on a limited budget. She considers that her high school courses, especially home economics, have stood her in good stead in managing her household on a limited budget. Believing that the family's depressed circumstances should not be permitted to interfere with the proper rearing of the children, she has always taken advantage of anything that would help her to become a more understanding mother and homemaker. Claud Jr., 11 years old, is in the sixth grade and Mary, 9, is a fourth-grader. Dorothy, 4, a "Depression baby," is the pet of the family.

Claud and Martha Park "grew up" in a small town in southern Minnesota, but have lived in Dubuque during most of the 13 years of their marriage. Claud's education was cut short when he had to leave school after completing the eighth grade to help his father support a large family.

The Parks moved to Dubuque immediately after their marriage in 1924, when Claud, through a relative, got a job as a spray painter at the Iowa Foundry. His entrance rate was 45¢ an hour and he worked 54 hours a week. After 2 years, Claud was advanced to the position of foreman of the paint department; his rate of pay was increased to 50¢ an hour. The paint did not agree with him, however, and after he had lost considerable weight and suffered from ulcers of the throat, he decided to quit early in 1927 and go to Chicago where he had heard of a chance to "get on" as a janitor in a new building at $200 a month. Soon after the Parks arrived in Chicago, they both came down with typhoid fever; by the time Claud had recovered, all jobs in the new building had been filled. He found a janitorial job in another building, but it paid only $100 a month. After having worked at this job for about 2 years, he decided that with the higher cost of living in Chicago, he would be better off working at the foundry in Dubuque.

On his return to Dubuque, he worked at the Iowa Foundry for a year before he was laid off during the general reduction in force in February 1931. From February 1931 to the fall of 1932 he worked irregularly for a barge line and at an insulating plant, averaging from $5 to $25 a week, depending on the amount of work available. The family began running in debt and it was necessary for Claud to borrow $200 from his "folks." When this was exhausted. $80 was borrowed on a $1,000 insurance policy, which was later allowed to lapse. Claud regrets very much losing his only insurance policy. On their return from Chicago, the Parks lived in a five-room house for which the rent was $18 a month, but as circumstances became more strained, they moved to a small four-room house for which they paid only $10.

During the Depression, it was common for individuals to borrow money from their insurance companies using the insurance policy as security for the loan. One could usually borrow up to the cash value of the policy and still remain insured while the loan was outstanding.

By December 1932, the situation had become desperate. The temperature was below zero, and there was little fuel or food left. As the Parks owed a coal bill of $40 and a grocery bill of $25, they expected credit to be discontinued at any time. To add to the seriousness of their plight, Mrs. Park was pregnant. After talking things over one night they could see no alternative except to apply for relief; yet they both felt that they would be "disgraced." Mrs. Park bitterly opposed going on relief, but during the night Claud got "scared about the kids," and thought "we can't let the kids starve just because we are proud." The next morning, without telling his wife his intentions, he went to the courthouse to make application for relief. When he arrived at the courthouse he couldn't go in. "I must have walked around the block over a dozen times—it was 10 below zero, but I didn't know it." Finally he got up sufficient courage to make his application.

The family was "investigated" and after about 2 weeks "a lady brought out a grocery and coal order." This was just in the "nick of time" as they were completely out of provisions. Mr. Park considered that they got along very nicely on the weekly grocery order. Part of the time they were also allowed milk from the milk fund and "this helped a lot." The Parks feel that they were well treated by the relief office and did not find the routine investigations obnoxious. "It's part of the system and when you ask for relief, of course you have to cooperate." "The questions didn't bother us so much as the idea of being on charity."

Mrs. Park's confinement created less hardship than the Parks expected, as Mr. Park did all of the housework and a visiting nurse came in once a day to care for Mrs. Park.

Claud Park "never felt right about accepting the relief slip." He says, "Later, when they let me do some work for it, I felt better." The relief office allowed only $7.50 a month for rent and Claud did odd jobs for the landlord to make up the difference. In the fall of 1933 he was placed on a CWA road construction project at $80 a month. He was delighted to be paid in cash and didn't feel that he was "getting something for nothing." At the close of CWA in the spring of 1934, he was placed by the public employment office on the lock and dam project, and his wages were cut to $50 a month and later to $48. He was intermittently employed on emergency work projects until August 31, 1936, when he got a job as a benchman finishing sashes at the Mississippi Milling Company. Claud had made application at all the factories in town, but he feels that he would never have been taken on at the Mississippi Milling Company had not an old employee there spoken for him.

During the winter of 1934, the Civilian Works Administration (CWA) created for 4 million men such jobs as resurfacing highways, painting, and building or repairing playgrounds, schools, and airports. When President Roosevelt saw how much the program cost ($1 billion), he discontinued it.

The Parks kept a detailed monthly account of their income from all sources, including work relief, direct relief, and odd jobs, from 1933 through 1935. The total income in 1933 was $450.96, and for 1935 it was $698.64. Included in these amounts is work for back rent totaling $85.15 in 1933 and $107.25 in 1935. The Parks feel that 1932 and 1933 were their "hardest years." After Claud started to work on emergency projects, the family had "a little more to live on."

During the lean years of the Depression the Parks barely "subsisted," and Claud feels that it would be impossible "even to subsist" on this low income over an extended period as clothing and furniture would have to be replaced. The Parks thought they were very economical in 1926, when their total expenditures were $1,095.15, including payments on furniture, medical bills, insurance, and a move to Chicago. At that time, there were only three in the family, but in 1933 there were five. The Parks are keeping the calendars on which they marked every item of income for the depression years as "relics" to look at when they are old, and, Claud hopes, "better off."

At the Mississippi Milling Company, Claud had worked 9 hours a day, 5½ days a week, for about 7 months. The time was then reduced to 35 hours a week, and about 2 months ago, a 25-hour week went into effect. His entrance rate was 45¢ an hour, but when he requested a raise a few months after starting work, his rate was increased to 47¢ an hour. At present, the weekly pay check amounts to only $11.75, and the family is again getting behind with bills. Because of the uncertainty of the working hours at the mill, it is impossible for Claud to "fill in" with odd jobs. He feels that there is no use to look for more regular work in other factories, for in most of them work is just as irregular as at the Mississippi Milling Company. Then, too, if he quits to take another job, he might never be able to get on again at the Mississippi Milling Company.

After Claud's pay raise, "things began to look bright again," and the family moved to their present home where the rent is $17 a month. Mrs. Park felt that the overcrowding in the other house was bad for the children. After paying up back bills, she had even started some long-needed dental work, which she discontinued before completion when Claud went on short hours. She told the dentist he could keep the bridge he had finished in his safe, but he said that it was of no use to him and he was willing to trust the Parks.

In an attempt to make ends meet with the reduced income, the Parks now take 1 quart of milk for the children instead of 2, and buy meat only once a week. They have enough canned and dried vegetables from their garden on "the island" to last through the winter. The biggest problem is warm clothing for the children. Claud Jr. and Mary both need shoes, overshoes, and winter underwear, but so far it has been impossible for the Parks to do more than buy food and pay the rent, gas, and electric bills. In bad

In order to have enough to eat during the Depression, many families supplemented their meager groceries by keeping fruit and vegetable gardens.

weather "the children will have to be kept home from school," and Mrs. Park "feels terrible" about that. She thinks "employers don't begin to realize how much hardship they cause by reducing the paychecks of the workers."

99 The Philosophy of Franklin D. Roosevelt

In 1932, the American people overwhelmingly elected Franklin D. Roosevelt to the Presidency. Herbert Hoover, nominated without much enthusiasm for a second term by the Republicans, received 15,800,000 popular votes to his rival's 22,800,000. Hoover received the electoral votes of only Pennsylvania, Connecticut, Delaware, Vermont, New Hampshire, and Maine. The Democrats won control of both houses by overwhelming majorities.

Roosevelt was the only child of James and Sara Delano Roosevelt, a wealthy family of an illustrious lineage who owned estates at Hyde Park, New York. He was educated first by tutors and governesses, then at Groton, and finally at Harvard. Although he later studied at Columbia Law School, he failed to get a degree there. Elected to the New York State legislature in 1910, Roosevelt aligned himself with the progressive wing of his party.

Roosevelt became Assistant Secretary of the Navy under Woodrow Wilson during World War I. In 1920, he was the Democratic candidate for Vice-President during the campaign when Warren G. Harding swept to victory. Then in 1921, polio struck him down and left him a cripple, able to walk with braces and crutches and then only with great difficulty. Rather than succumb to this personal tragedy, Roosevelt fought back. In 1928, he became Governor of New York, establishing an outstanding record as a man who could cope humanely with the Depression crisis. At his insistence, the New York State legislature in 1931 established the Temporary Emergency Relief Administration which became a model for other states and eventually for a federal relief program.

In 1931, Governor Roosevelt set up the Temporary Emergency Relief Administration, the first of its kind in any state, to provide local agencies with state aid to use for cash handouts or to set up work projects. Roosevelt also found work for many New Yorkers on state conservation projects.

During his campaign in 1932, Roosevelt promised something to each of the main groups of American voters. Some of his promises were contradictory. He pledged himself, for example, to cut federal expenditures by 25 percent and balance the budget at the same time that he called for increased government activity which would be certain to raise expenditures. But Roosevelt's easy-going manner and his optimistic tone won America's confidence.

Despite his contradictory statements and his pragmatic ways, Roosevelt brought a new philosophy to the Presidency. No American President since Roosevelt's death has been able to ignore the major points of FDR's philosophy. As you read the following excerpts from his Inaugural Address and the most notable speech of the 1932 campaign, think about the following questions:

1. What do you think was the psychological purpose of the first and last paragraphs of Roosevelt's Inaugural Address? How do you think unemployed people would have responded to it?
2. According to Roosevelt, how had the government helped the economy to grow in the past? What brought this phase of growth to an end?
3. What changes in American society called for a new role for the federal government, according to this speech?
4. What rights did Roosevelt support? To what groups of people would ideas like these appeal in 1932?

Roosevelt Rallies the American People

President Roosevelt's First Inaugural Address rallied the Congress and the nation during the dark days of March 1933. The first paragraph and the last three paragraphs convey the tone of the entire address.

Basil Rauch, ed., **The Roosevelt Reader, Selected Speeches, Messages, Press Conferences, and Letters of Franklin D. Roosevelt.** New York: Holt, Rinehart and Winston, Inc., 1957, pp. 90, 95.

I am certain that my fellow Americans expect that on my induction into the Presidency I will address them with a candor [openness] and a decision which the present situation of our Nation impels. This is preeminently the time to speak the truth, the whole truth, frankly and boldly. Nor need we shrink from honestly facing conditions in our country today. This great Nation will endure as it has endured, will revive and will prosper. So, first of all, let me assert my firm belief that the only thing we have to fear is fear itself—nameless, unreasoning, unjustified terror which paralyzes needed efforts to convert retreat into advance. In every dark hour of our national life a leadership of frankness and vigor has met with that understanding and support of the people themselves which is essential to victory. I am convinced that you will again give that support to leadership in these critical days. . . .

We face the arduous [difficult] days that lie before us in the warm courage of national unity; with the clear consciousness of seeking old and precious moral values; with the clean satisfaction that comes from the stern performance of duty by old and young alike. We aim at the assurance of a rounded and permanent national life.

We do not distrust the future of essential democracy. The people of the United States have not failed. In their need they have registered a mandate that they want direct, vigorous action. They have asked for discipline and direction under leadership. They have made me the present instrument of their wishes. In the spirit of the gift I take it.

In this dedication of a Nation we humbly ask the blessing of God. May He protect each and every one of us. May He guide me in the days to come.

Roosevelt's Creed

Roosevelt was not a distinguished political philosopher. The following excerpts from a 1932 campaign speech contain the most important statement of his philosophy that Roosevelt ever made.

The Roosevelt Reader, pp. 74–85. Reprinted by permission of the National Archives and Record Service, Franklin D. Roosevelt Library, Hyde Park, New York.

The Commonwealth Club is a men's civic organization in San Francisco.

I count it a privilege to be invited to address the Commonwealth Club. It has stood in the life of this city and state, and it is perhaps accurate to add, the nation, as a group of citizen leaders interested in fundamental problems of government, and chiefly concerned with achievement of progress in government through nonpartisan means. The privilege of addressing you, therefore, in the heat of a political campaign, is great. I want to respond to your courtesy in terms consistent with your policy.

The issue of government has always been whether individual men and women will have to serve some system of government or economics, or whether a system of government and economics exists to serve individual men and women. This question has persistently dominated the discussion of government for many generations. On questions relating to these things men have differed, and for time immemorial it is probable that honest men will continue to differ.

Congress granted 158,000,000 acres of land to subsidize railroad construction before 1871, the year in which such grants were discontinued.

During this period of expansion [of industry during the last decades of the nineteenth century], there was equal opportunity for all and the business of government was not to interfere but to assist in the development of industry. This was done at the request of businessmen themselves. The tariff was originally imposed for the purpose of "fostering our infant industry," a phrase I think the older among you will remember as a political issue not so long ago. The railroads were subsidized, sometimes by grants of money, oftener by grants of land; some of the most valuable oil lands in the United States were granted to assist the financing of the railroad which pushed through the Southwest. A nascent [beginning] merchant marine was assisted by grants of money, or by mail subsidies, so that our steam shipping might ply the seven seas. Some of my friends tell me that they do not want the government in business.

With this I agree; but I wonder whether they realize the implications of the past. For while it has been American doctrine that the government must not go into business in competition with private enterprises, still it has been traditional particularly in Republican administrations for business urgently to ask the government to put at private disposal all kinds of government assistance. The same man who tells you that he does not want to see the government interfere in business—and he means it, and has plenty of good reasons for saying so—is the first to go to Washington and ask the government for a prohibitory tariff on his product. When things get just bad enough—as they did two years ago—he will go with equal speed to the United States government and ask for a loan; and the Reconstruction Finance Corporation is the outcome of it. Each group has sought protection from the government for its own special interests, without realizing that the function of government must be to favor no small group at the expense of its duty to protect the rights of personal freedom and of private property of all its citizens.

See pages 620–21.

In retrospect we can now see that the turn of the tide came with the turn of the century. We were reaching our last frontier; there was no more free land and our industrial combinations had become great uncontrolled and irresponsible units of power within the state. Clear-sighted men saw with fear the danger that opportunity would no longer be equal; that the growing corporation, like the feudal baron of old, might threaten the economic freedom of individuals to earn a living. In that hour, our antitrust laws were born. The cry was raised against the great corporations. Theodore Roosevelt, the first great Republican progressive, fought a Presidential campaign on the issue of "trustbusting" and talked freely about malefactors [evil-doers] of great wealth. If the government had a policy it was rather to turn the clock back, to destroy the large combinations and to return to the time when every man owned his individual small business.

A glance at the situation today only too clearly indicates that equality of opportunity as we have known it no longer exists. Our industrial plant is built; the problem just now is whether under existing conditions it is not overbuilt. Our last frontier has long since been reached, and there is practically no more free land. More than half of our people do not live on the farms or on lands and cannot derive a living by cultivating their own property. There is no safety valve in the form of a Western prairie to which those thrown out of work by the Eastern economic machines can go for a new start. We are not able to invite the immigration from Europe to share our endless plenty. We are now providing a drab living for our own people.

The historian, Frederick Jackson Turner (see margin note, page 407), believed that the American frontier was a safety valve. The availability of free land provided Americans with an escape from the economic and social unrest in the factories in the East, he contended. Most modern historians reject the safety valve thesis.

Here Roosevelt is referring to the Smoot-Hawley Tariff (1931) discussed on page 620.

Our system of constantly rising tariffs has at last reacted against us to the point of closing our Canadian frontier on the north, our European markets on the east, many of our Latin American markets to the south, and a goodly proportion of our Pacific markets on the west, through the retaliatory tariffs of those countries. It has forced many of our great industrial institutions who exported their surplus production to such countries, to establish plants in such countries, within the tariff walls. This has resulted in the reduction of the operation of their American plants, and opportunity for employment.

Roosevelt is referring to President Woodrow Wilson's statement that the small businessman would find himself "either squeezed out or obliged to sell and allow himself to be absorbed."

The Senate Committee on Banking and Currency estimated that the banking house of J.P. Morgan, for example, controlled directly or indirectly one-fourth the total corporate assets in the United States or roughly $74 billion.

Just as freedom to farm has ceased, so also the opportunity in business has narrowed. It still is true that men can start small enterprises, trusting to native shrewdness and ability to keep abreast of competitors; but area after area has been pre-empted [taken over] altogether by the great corporations, and even in the fields which still have no great concerns, the small man starts under a handicap. The unfeeling statistics of the past three decades show that the independent businessman is running a losing race. Perhaps he is forced to the wall; perhaps he cannot command credit; perhaps he is "squeezed out," in Mr. Wilson's words, by highly organized corporate competitors, as your corner grocery man can tell you. Recently a careful study was made of the concentration of business in the United States. It showed that our economic life was dominated by some six hundred odd corporations who controlled two-thirds of American industry. Ten million small businessmen divided the other third. More striking still, it appeared that if the process of concentration goes on at the same rate, at the end of another century we shall have all American industry controlled by a dozen corporations, and run by perhaps a hundred men. Put plainly, we are steering a steady course toward economic oligarchy, if we are not there already.

Clearly, all this calls for a reappraisal of values. A mere builder of more industrial plants, a creator of more railroad systems, an organizer of more corporations, is as likely to be a danger as a help. The day of the great promoter or the financial Titan [giant], to whom we granted anything if only he would build, or develop, is over. Our task now is not discovery or exploitation of natural resources, or necessarily producing more goods. It is the soberer, less dramatic business of administering resources and plants already in hand, of seeking to re-establish foreign markets for our surplus production, of meeting the problem of underconsumption, of adjusting production to consumption, of distributing wealth and products more equitably, of adapting existing economic organizations to the service of the people. The day of enlightened administration has come. . . .

As I see it, the task of government in its relation to business is to assist the development of an economic declaration of rights, an economic constitutional order. This is the common task of statesman and businessman. It is the minimum requirement of a more permanently safe order of things. . . .

Every man has a right to life; and this means that he has also a right to make a comfortable living. He may by sloth [laziness] or crime decline to exercise that right; but it may not be denied him. We have no actual famine or dearth; our industrial and agricultural mechanism can produce enough and to spare. Our government formal and informal, political and economic, owes to every one an avenue to possess himself of a portion of that plenty sufficient for his needs, through his own work.

Every man has a right to his own property; which means a right to be assured, to the fullest extent attainable, in the safety of his savings. By no other means can men carry the burdens of those parts of life which, in the nature of things, afford no chance of labor: childhood, sickness, old age. In all thought of property, this right is paramount; all other property rights must yield to it. If, in accord with this principle, we must restrict the operations of the speculator, the manipulator, even the financier, I believe we must accept the restriction as needful, not to hamper individualism but to protect it.

These two requirements must be satisfied, in the main, by the individuals who claim and hold control of the great industrial and financial combinations which dominate so large a part of our industrial life. They have undertaken to be, not businessmen, but princes—princes of property. I am not prepared to say that the system which produces them is wrong. I am very clear that they must fearlessly and competently assume the responsibility which goes with the power. So many enlightened businessmen know this that the statement would be little more than a platitude, were it not for an added implication.

This implication is, briefly, that the responsible heads of finance and industry instead of acting each for himself, must work together to achieve the common end. They must, where necessary, sacrifice this or that private advantage; and in reciprocal self-denial must seek a general advantage. It is here that formal government—political government, if you choose, comes in. Whenever in the pursuit of this objective the lone wolf, the unethical competitor, the reckless promoter, the Ishmael or Insull whose hand is against every man's, declines to join in achieving an end recognized as being for the public welfare, and threatens to drag the industry back to a state of anarchy, the government may properly be asked to apply restraint. Likewise, should the group ever use its collective power

In the Bible, Ishmael was the son of Abraham and his Egyptian servant, Hagar. When Isaac was born to Abraham's wife, Ishmael and his mother were exiled. This prophecy appears in the Bible (**Genesis** 16:12) about Ishmael: "His hand will be against every man, and every man's hand against him." Samuel Insull (1859–1938) was a public utilities financier. He controlled diverse business enterprises through a mammoth interlocking directorate, serving as chairman of the board for 65 companies. In 1932, his empire collapsed and he faced charges of embezzlement and stock fraud.

contrary to the public welfare, the government must be swift to enter and protect the public interest.

The government should assume the function of economic regulation only as a last resort, to be tried only when private initiative, inspired by high responsibility, with such assistance and balance as government can give, has finally failed. As yet there has been no final failure, because there has been no attempt; and I decline to assume that this nation is unable to meet the situation.

The final term of the high contract was for liberty and the pursuit of happiness. We have learnt a great deal of both in the past century. We know that individual liberty and individual happiness mean nothing unless both are ordered in the sense that one man's meat is not another man's poison. We know that the old "rights of personal competency"—the right to read, to think, to speak, to choose and live a mode of life, must be respected at all hazards. We know that liberty to do anything which deprives others of those elemental rights is outside the protection of any compact; and that government in this regard is the maintenance of a balance, within which every individual may have a place if he will take it; in which every individual may find safety if he wishes it; in which every individual may attain such power as his ability permits, consistent with his assuming the accompanying responsibility. . . .

Faith in America, faith in our tradition of personal responsibility, faith in our institutions, faith in ourselves demands that we recognize the new terms of the old social contact. We shall fulfill them, as we fulfilled the obligation of the apparent Utopia which Jefferson imagined for us in 1776, and which Jefferson, Roosevelt and Wilson sought to bring to realization. We must do so, lest a rising tide of misery engendered by our common failure, engulf us all. But failure is not an American habit; and in the strength of great hope we must all shoulder our common load.

Utopia is an imaginary land where economic and social conditions are perfect, described in a book by that name written by Sir Thomas More in 1516.

100 FDR and the New Deal

HISTORICAL ESSAY

A few years ago, an eighty-year-old man entered a home for the aged. He took with him three personal treasures: a family photograph album, a package of letters collected through a lifetime, and a framed picture of Franklin Delano Roosevelt. Millions of Americans felt close to FDR. The issues he dramatized during the

New Deal years may seem irrelevant to today's high school students, who take social security and insured bank accounts for granted. But to people who were adults in the 1930's, when a fourth of the nation was unemployed and children went hungry, Roosevelt remains a potent symbol—for some, an enemy of all the sacred ways, for others, the savior of a nation.

The Onset of the Depression

October 1929 dramatized the end of the prosperity of the 1920's. Through September, prices in the stock market had wavered up and down. Then on October 24 and again on 29, a deluge of sell orders sent prices tumbling. The stock-market crash accentuated weaknesses throughout the economy. The long, dismal spiral into the Depression had begun.

The crash wiped out the savings of small investors who had had hopes of quick and easy gains. Their confidence gone, they clung to the rest of their money rather than spend it on consumer goods. Sales, and hence production, fell off rapidly. But prices, controlled in part by large corporations, fell less rapidly than wages. The industrial depression aggravated an already serious agricultural situation, and prices of farm products continued to fall. In the whole economy, investment in factories and tools fell from $10 billion in 1929 to $1 billion in 1932. By 1932, about one in every four workers was unemployed.

Although he was intelligent and an experienced businessman and administrator, Herbert Hoover made a poor depression President. He offended politicians because he was rigid, and he failed to attract public support because he seemed so aloof to suffering. He placed faith in his powers to persuade Americans to accept policies he suggested and in the ability of state and local governments to deal with the depression crisis. His overemphasis on a balanced budget, his refusal to permit the federal government to sponsor relief programs, and his support for the protective Smoot-Hawley Tariff cost the country dear and hurt his party. As the election drew near in November 1932, Hoover seemed pessimistic and defeated, and his occasional announcements that prosperity lurked around the corner rang hollow in the ears of hungry millions.

In an attempt to reassure the American public, President Hoover made several optimistic public statements.

The Hundred Days

In November 1932, Roosevelt swept to an impressive victory. Hoover had won forty states in 1928; he now carried only six. During the months between the election and Roosevelt's inauguration on March 4, the economy reached low ebb. Hoover hesitated to experiment without Roosevelt's approval; FDR refused to accept

Legislation and Agencies of the New Deal—First Hundred Days

Name	Date	Provisions
Emergency Banking Relief Act	3/9/33	Authorized President to regulate banking transactions and foreign exchange. Forbade any bank to reopen until it proved solvency to Treasury Department.
Civilian Conservation Corps (CCC)	3/31/33	Set up work camps employing 18–25-year-old men in conservation tasks.
Federal Emergency Relief Act (FERA)	5/12/33	Authorized federal money to be given to states for direct relief.
Agricultural Adjustment Act (AAA)	5/12/33	Limited farm surplus by curtailing production. Provided farm subsidies raised by taxing food processors. Set up Federal Land Banks to lend money at low interest rates.
Tennessee Valley Authority (TVA)	5/18/33	Set up publically owned corporation to develop resources of the area.
Federal Securities Act (Truth-in-Securities Act)	5/27/33	Compelled promoters to give investors complete and truthful information about new securities.
Home Owners' Loan Corporation (HOLC)	6/13/33	Provided mortgage loans at low interest to refinance mortgages on non-farm homes.
National Recovery Administration (NRA)	6/16/33	Suspended antitrust laws. Helped industry set up fair codes of cooperation. Gave labor right of collective bargaining.
Public Works Administration (PWA)	6/16/33	Set up public-works projects to provide employment and increase business activity.

Banks rarely keep much cash on hand. Most of the depositors' money is invested in mortgages, stocks, etc. When an unusually large number of people tried to withdraw money, the banks could not supply it. In addition, many investments had declined in value leaving banks with little or no assets.

leadership until he took office. The nation drifted. Then the banking system collapsed. As citizens rushed to withdraw money, one institution after another ran out of cash and turned depositors away. By March 4, four fifths of the states had suspended banking.

Roosevelt's inaugural speech, delivered on a bleak March day, captured the faith of the American people. For a hundred days, Congress passed measures that Roosevelt requested, as the chart above indicates. Four types of activities were particularly important.

First came a series of measures to untangle the national financial mess. On the day after his inauguration, Roosevelt declared a national bank holiday and forbade anyone to export gold. Supported by Congress, the Administration developed a plan to reopen banks after a Treasury Department inspection testified to their soundness. Congress established the Federal Deposit Insurance Corporation which insured bank deposits against failure, established the Home Owners' Loan Corporation, and made other banking reforms. By

The FDIC at first insured bank deposits up to $2500; coverage was increased to $5000 in 1934, to $10,000 in 1950, and to $15,000 in 1967.

the Federal Securities Act, Congress required promoters to give explicit information about new issues of stocks and gave the Federal Trade Commission the power to regulate stock issues. Finally, Roosevelt took the nation off the gold standard and later fixed the price of gold at $35 an ounce in an attempt, largely unsuccessful, to raise prices.

Second, the Administration pushed through measures designed to stimulate the economy. The practice of pumping federal funds into the economy was known as "pump priming." The object was to help business revive and employ more people who would then spend more money. An appropriation of $500 million launched the Civilian Conservation Corps. Then the National Industrial Recovery Act opened a three-pronged attack on the Depression. It created the Public Works Administration with an appropriation of $3.5 billion to provide work such as building schools and roads. It also set up the National Recovery Administration to draw up industry-wide codes of fair business practices in order to limit production and raise prices. In addition, the codes established minimum wages and maximum hours, an important precedent. Finally, Section 7A of the Act set up boards to conduct elections in order to determine whether or not workers wished to be represented by a union. As a result, the membership of labor unions spurted rapidly, especially the newly formed Committee for Industrial Organization.

Third, the Agriculture Adjustment Act of May 1933, launched the agricultural reforms of the New Deal era. The act aimed to raise farm prices to "parity" with the goods which farmers bought. Farmers who withdrew part of their acres from cultivation received cash payments from the government. Reduced acreage, combined with a drought, raised prices substantially within the next few years. Roosevelt chose Henry A. Wallace to administer this program.

Finally, the Administration launched the Tennessee Valley Authority to develop hydroelectric power, establish nitrate plants to make fertilizer, inaugurate a system of flood control and improved navigation, and coordinate efforts at reforestation, soil conservation, and industrialization in a huge area covering all or part of seven states. Despite opposition from private power interests, the TVA forged steadily ahead, substantially improving the standard of living of millions of people.

No over-all philosophy guided this emergency legislation. Some measures that Congress passed were contradictory or worked against each other. But despite vague pronouncements, contradictory measures, and all the things that remained to be done, it was obvious that a fresh spirit had entered American politics. It combined elements of Populist opposition to financiers, Theodore Roosevelt's New Nationalism, and techniques employed by the World War I

The Glass-Steagall Banking Act, which set up the FDIC, also restricted the use of bank credit for speculative purposes, expanded the Federal Reserve System to include banks previously excluded, and separated commercial and investment banks.

In 1935, A.F. of L. leaders who headed industrial unions, formed the Committee for Industrial Organization and began unionizing workers in mass-production industries. When the A.F. of L. refused to accept industrial unions, the C.I.O. became independent, changed its name to the Congress of Industrial Organizations, and rivaled the A.F. of L. in size. In 1955, they merged into the AFL-CIO.

Parity means equality; here it refers to the ratio between the prices a farmer receives when he sells his products and the prices he pays for industrial goods. The government through cash bounties insures that the farmer will always have favorable purchasing power no matter what the price of his crop.

Since World War I, the government had owned a dam and nitrate plant at Muscle Shoals on the Tennessee River. FDR used this as the focus of a comprehensive experiment in government ownership.

President Roosevelt surrounded himself with a small group of liberal intellectuals, predominately young college professors and lawyers known as his "Brain Trust." These men wrote many of his speeches as well as much of the New Deal legislation. Roosevelt also appointed a number of Negroes to top government posts. Other Negroes, mostly college professors, served as specialists or advisors to government agencies.

War Labor Board to rally the economy. A host of bright, energetic men and women enlisted in the Administration and brought a new flavor to national political life. The public seemed convinced that Roosevelt cared and that he wanted to improve everyone's life. Voters seemed ready to label the New Deal a success and to ask for more.

Despite the fact that 4 million men remained unemployed, the Democrats picked up seats in both the Senate and the House of Representatives in 1934. Two measures to fight unemployment may have rallied some of this support. In May 1933, Congress had appropriated $500 million to be given to state relief organizations through the Federal Emergency Relief Administration. Harry Hopkins, the Director of the FERA, insisted, however, that unemployed men needed jobs rather than handouts. He persuaded Roosevelt to establish the Civil Works Administration late in 1933. Although FDR permitted the CWA to die, he continued a public works program during 1934 through the FERA.

In May 1935, Roosevelt put Hopkins in charge of a new federal agency, the Works Progress Administration. In eight years, the WPA employed about 8.5 million people and spent about $11 billion. In addition to public works, the WPA also sponsored projects to employ actors, writers, and artists and organized the National Youth Administration which created part-time jobs for about 2 million young people. But the WPA did not reach enough of the unemployed, pay high enough wages, or undertake large enough projects to provide the massive stimulus the economy needed.

Attacks from Right and Left

Three movements threatened the Democratic ascendancy during these years. Senator Huey Long of Louisiana at first supported Roosevelt, but later broke with him and threatened to start a new party, partly to further his own ambitions and partly because he thought Roosevelt was too conservative. The "Share-Our-Wealth" movement that Long started proposed to distribute money taken from the rich among the masses. Long's program had widespread appeal among the poor.

Father Charles E. Coughlin of Detroit had even wider influence. A Catholic priest who made nationwide radio broadcasts, Coughlin changed from an avid New Deal supporter to one of its most formidable opponents in 1935. He began to attack bankers, the farm program, and government planning. He accused the Administration of communist sympathies. Coughlin's National Union for Social Justice appealed primarily to Catholics, although many Americans of other faiths also joined.

In later years, Coughlin's pro-Fascist sympathies and anti-Semitic overtones alienated many of his followers.

The third movement formed behind a crackpot scheme to pay a

monthly pension of $200 to people over sixty on the condition that they would spend the entire sum within thirty days. A retired California physician, Dr. Francis E. Townsend, spearheaded this movement. About half the national income would have been needed to make these payments, but Townsend and his followers pressed on. His weekly newspaper, which reached a circulation of 200,000, appealed to a substantial segment of the Roosevelt coalition.

These threats to his political base, the increasing alienation of the business community, and the influence of trusted advisors, such as Louis Brandeis and Felix Frankfurter, combined to push Roosevelt in a new direction. In May 1935, the Supreme Court declared the NIRA unconstitutional in the case of *Schecter* vs. *U.S.* A month later, Roosevelt called on Congress to pass a series of new laws, launching the "Second New Deal" in the process (See chart on page 642).

Louis D. Brandeis (1856–1941), a Boston lawyer who defended the public against big business in cases involving public utility rates and the constitutionality of work laws, was appointed to the Supreme Court by President Wilson. Throughout his years on the bench (1916–1939), he maintained an attitude of judicial liberalism.
Felix Frankfurter, born 1882, was appointed to the Supreme Court in 1939 by President Roosevelt. He had previously been a professor at Harvard Law School and had served intermittently at various government posts.

The Second New Deal

Among the most important of these new laws was the National Labor Relations Act, often called the Wagner Act. This legislation gave workers the right to bargain collectively and prohibited employers from interfering with the attempts of unions to organize workers. It established the National Labor Relations Board which was authorized to supervise elections and indicate which union, if any, had a right to represent the workers. The NLRB also got power to investigate charges of unfair labor practices.

These two rights had been included in the National Industrial Recovery Act (NIRA) which had been declared unconstitutional.

In August 1935, Congress passed the Social Security Act which insured workers against unemployment and old age. Taxes on workers and their employers financed social security. Although many workers, particularly farmers and the self-employed were not covered, and the payments were small, this law marked a vital beginning.

Four additional measures of the Second New Deal also marked significant turning points. The Public Utility Holding Act forbade holding companies to buy up the stock of operating companies and gave various federal agencies powers to regulate the utility industry. A new banking act reorganized the Federal Reserve System and gave its board of governors new regulatory powers. The Rural Electrification Administration brought electricity to American farmers, only one in ten of whom had electricity in 1935. Finally the Wealth Tax Act raised taxes on high incomes, gifts, and estate taxes, an important precedent for later legislation that shifted American taxation more and more toward the rich.

Under the REA, farmers were encouraged to form associations subsidized by low-interest loans from the REA to erect light and power lines to furnish electricity to those people not receiving central-station service.

This spate of new legislation affected American voters. It almost certainly helped to draw support away from men like Long, Coughlin, and Townsend. On the other hand, it enraged American conservatives who denounced "That Man" in the White House.

Legislation and Agencies of the New Deal, 1934–1938

Name	Date	Provisions
Gold Reserve Act	1/30/34	Gave federal government control over dollar devaluation.
Securities and Exchange Commission (SEC)	6/6/34	Set up commission to supervise issuance of new securities and to supervise stock exchanges.
Reciprocal Trade Agreements Act	6/12/34	Authorized President to raise or lower tariffs by as much as 50% without Senate's consent.
Federal Housing Administration (FHA)	6/28/34	Insured banks against commercial loans for construction and repair of houses and business properties.
Works Progress Administration (WPA)	4/8/35	Provided for large-scale national work programs.
Rural Electrification Administration (REA)	5/11/35	Set up to provide isolated rural areas with low-cost electricity.
National Youth Administration (NYA)	6/26/35	Provided part-time work for needy students.
National Labor Relations Act (Wagner-Connery Act)	7/5/35	Set up National Labor Relations Board (NLRB) to arbitrate employer-employee differences. Upheld labor's right of collective bargaining.
Social Security Act	8/14/35	Provided unemployment compensation, old-age security, and social services.
United States Housing Authority (USHA)	9/1/37	Authorized loans of federal funds to local agencies for slum clearance and housing projects.
Agricultural Adjustment Act (Second AAA)	2/16/38	Provided for production quotas through soil-conservation programs, marketing quotas, and parity payments.
Food, Drug, and Cosmetic Act	6/24/38	Prohibited misbranding and false advertising. Required manufacturers of foods, drugs, and cosmetics to list ingredients.
Fair Labor Standards Act	6/25/38	Set up minimum wages and maximum hours for workers in interstate trade. Prohibited child labor under 16.

The End of an Era

Three candidates competed for public favor in 1936. The Democrats nominated Roosevelt by acclamation. The Republicans chose a moderately liberal governor, Alfred M. Landon of Kansas. Dissatisfied elements, such as those who followed Coughlin and Townsend, organized the Union Party with Congressman William Lemke of North Dakota as its candidate. But the extremists were losing ground. Long had been assassinated in September 1935, and the legislation of the Second New Deal cut the ground from under the Townsendites. Roosevelt's attacks during the campaign on "economic royalists" appealed to the underprivileged. Roosevelt's Administration had been remarkably free of racial prejudice, and the economic reforms of the New Deal which had helped black voters shifted that block of votes to FDR. Farmers supported Roosevelt because of AAA; labor supported him because of the Wagner Act; the elderly appreciated Social Security; homeowners blessed him for HOLC; a slight upturn in the economy played into his hands. For all these reasons, Roosevelt carried every state except Maine and Vermont.

In September 1935, at the new state capitol building, Huey Long was assassinated by Dr. Carl A. Weiss, the son-in-law of one of his political opponents. Long's bodyguards immediately killed the assassin.

Noting in his inaugural address that a third of the nation remained "ill-housed, ill-clad, and ill-nourished," Roosevelt seemed set for a further wave of reforms. But the Supreme Court stood in his way. Four of the nine judges staunchly opposed his new trends; three often supported his proposals; two, including Chief Justice Charles Evans Hughes, wavered depending on the issue. The Court had invalidated the first AAA, the NIRA, and laws establishing minimum wages at both state and national levels. Some of its members seemed intent on destroying the entire New Deal.

The Constitution provides for a Supreme Court but does not specify the number of justices. Congress has varied the number of judges from five to ten. Since 1869, the figure has been set at nine. President Roosevelt asked Congress for the power to appoint an additional judge for each judge who did not retire upon reaching seventy years of age.

Roosevelt tried to increase the size of the Court. He asked for permission to appoint additional judges. A public outcry broke out; the balance among the three branches of government seemed threatened. After a long battle, Congress defeated the measure. But the Justices began to interpret the Constitution less strictly. As Justices retired, Roosevelt appointed men who shared his point of view, and the conservatives abandoned the fight. But Congress never again responded enthusiastically to his domestic program.

President Roosevelt appointed seven justices within the next four years. He appointed such men as Senator Hugo L. Black, Felix Frankfurter, and William O. Douglas who appeared to be more sympathetic to New Deal legislation.

Three developments, coming atop the Supreme Court fight ended the New Deal. First, a rash of sit-down strikes which marked the organizing drives of the C.I.O. in 1937 frightened many middle-class people. Instead of leaving factories, workers in industries such as automobiles and rubber sat down at their machines in order to wrest concessions from their employers. Afraid to resort to force, management conceded, usually granting union recognition, the forty-hour week, and pay raises. In a few instances, violence did break out, particularly in the steel and automobile industries. These new tactics and reports of clashes between strikers and the police cooled the ardor for reform.

In the midst of the Court fight and the sit-down strikes, economic recession set in. Roosevelt had cut the relief program sharply in June 1937; within five months, unemployment rose by two million. Not until April 1938, did he urge Congress to pass a $3.75 billion public works program. He also sponsored a new AAA measure.

The Second AAA (1938) provided farmers with cash benefits proportionate to acreage withheld from production to use for plant-conserving crops. If two-thirds of the farmers producing a certain commodity consented, the government could assign marketing quotas limiting the amount that the farmers could sell. If surpluses still existed, the farmers could store them in government warehouses. With the crops as security, the government would grant the farmers "commodity loans." When the market price of the stored items rose, the farmers would sell the surplus and pay back the government.

Finally, he pushed through the Fair Labor Standards Act which established a 40-hour week and a minimum wage of 40 cents an hour. These three measures further alienated conservative voters, but they did not effect the economy.

Then Roosevelt committed a major political blunder. Southern congressmen had increasingly resisted reform measures. In the 1938 election, Roosevelt set out to get rid of them. He failed. His major targets won in the primaries and returned to Washington prepared for vengeance. In addition, Republicans picked up seats in the House and the Senate. Combined with conservative southern Democrats, they were able to effectively brake further reform. By 1939, Roosevelt was so involved in foreign affairs that domestic matters seemed relatively unimportant.

The Meaning of the New Deal

The New Deal failed to overcome the Depression. Only a wave of war orders from the allied nations finally put the remainder of the unemployed back to work. But the New Deal left a vital legacy. It convinced Americans that their government should accept responsibility for the nation's economy and should protect its people from old age and unemployment. Farmers, industrial workers, bank depositors, stock buyers, homeowners, and others benefitted. TVA and REA made farm life far more pleasant. A serious endeavor to appoint blacks to public office started this long abused minority on the long road to equality in American society. Finally, the New Deal brought a new spirit into American life and helped to change a people defeated by economic catastrophe.

SUGGESTED READINGS

PERKINS, DEXTER, *The New Age of Franklin D. Roosevelt, 1932–1945.* This brief general history chronicles the entire period of Roosevelt's greatest influence.

PERKINS, FRANCES, *The Roosevelt I Knew.* Miss Perkins, Roosevelt's Secretary of Labor, has left this sympathetic yet accurate account of Roosevelt's life.

SCHLESINGER, ARTHUR M., JR., *The Coming of the New Deal.* Schlesinger's volume contains the best account of the early New Deal period and its antecedents, although his interpretation has recently come under attack.

Years of Peace and War, 1921–1945

CHAPTER 26

STATING THE ISSUE

During the 1920's, Americans concentrated on what President Harding called a return to "normalcy." Presumably, they meant the expansion of business and industry and the pursuit of personal prosperity and well-being. Then came the Crash of 1929 followed by the "abnormal," but grimly real, depression of the 1930's. During these two decades, Americans focused attention on their own affairs.

In the meantime, fateful changes took place in Europe and Asia. Japan came under military rule and attacked China. Militaristic, anti-democratic dictators came to power in Italy and Germany.

At first American leaders, supported by the great majority of the people, believed that the rise of dictators in Europe and Asia did not concern the United States directly. American soldiers had fought in Europe in 1918 to "make the world safe for democracy." Many Americans believed that their efforts had been in vain. They did not want to sacrifice American lives and resources again.

As the 1930's continued, however, Americans increasingly questioned the effectiveness and morality of their nation's policies of isolation and strict neutrality. President Franklin D. Roosevelt gradually formulated policies based on two assumptions: that Americans had a moral stake in world events, and that the security of the United States was very much involved in the struggle between democratic and totalitarian nations. Americans, however, remained divided over the role their country should take in that struggle.

Finally, after Europe had been at war for two years, Japan attacked Pearl Harbor on December 7, 1941. Americans united quickly behind their government, as it went to war against Japan. Germany immediately entered the war with Japan against the United States.

For almost four years, the barbarism of total war continued. Finally, after the United States employed the atomic bomb, peace returned, bringing a revolutionary new world with a multitude of new problems. Chapter 26 examines America's role in world affairs between 1921 and 1945. How did the United States respond to problems of international relations following World War I? What caused isolationism? In what ways did totalitarian aggression threaten American security? What new kinds of world problems did the Allied victory create? These are the major issues of Chapter 26.

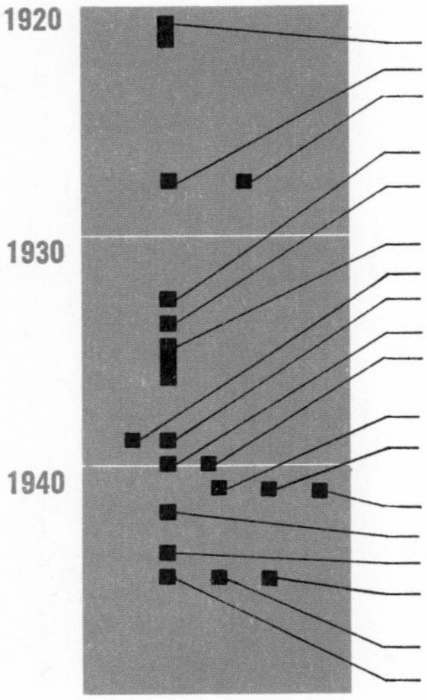

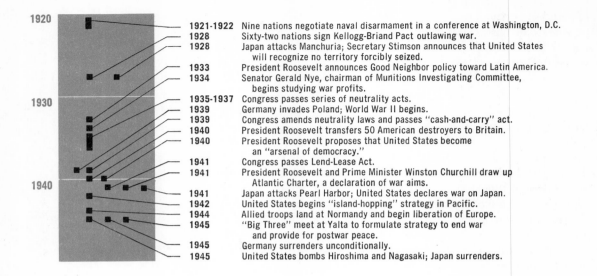

1921-1922	Nine nations negotiate naval disarmament in a conference at Washington, D.C.
1928	Sixty-two nations sign Kellogg-Briand Pact outlawing war.
1928	Japan attacks Manchuria; Secretary Stimson announces that United States will recognize no territory forcibly seized.
1933	President Roosevelt announces Good Neighbor policy toward Latin America.
1934	Senator Gerald Nye, chairman of Munitions Investigating Committee, begins studying war profits.
1935-1937	Congress passes series of neutrality acts.
1939	Germany invades Poland; World War II begins.
1939	Congress amends neutrality laws and passes "cash-and-carry" act.
1940	President Roosevelt transfers 50 American destroyers to Britain.
1940	President Roosevelt proposes that United States become an "arsenal of democracy."
1941	Congress passes Lend-Lease Act.
1941	President Roosevelt and Prime Minister Winston Churchill draw up Atlantic Charter, a declaration of war aims.
1941	Japan attacks Pearl Harbor; United States declares war on Japan.
1942	United States begins "island-hopping" strategy in Pacific.
1944	Allied troops land at Normandy and begin liberation of Europe.
1945	"Big Three" meet at Yalta to formulate strategy to end war and provide for postwar peace.
1945	Germany surrenders unconditionally.
1945	United States bombs Hiroshima and Nagasaki; Japan surrenders.

101 Neutrality and the Reaction Against World War I

In his inaugural address in 1921, President Harding spoke for the great majority of the American people when he said, "We seek no part in directing the destinies of the world." Harding interpreted his election as a mandate to close the issue of American participation in the League of Nations; most of his countrymen agreed. American foreign policy in the 1920's was isolationist.

In order to achieve its foreign policy goals in the 1920's, the United States relied upon other nations' promises and good will, rather than upon agreements supported by military power. At the Washington Naval Conference in 1922, the United States persuaded major world powers to agree to limit the size of their navies and to accept in principle the traditional American policy of an independent China. In 1928, the United States played a leading part in drawing up the Kellogg-Briand Pact in which sixty-two nations agreed to renounce war as a way to settle international disputes. There were no means to deal with nations that violated the pacts.

The United States also relied on a "businessmen's" approach to foreign policy. Americans invested heavily in "friendly" governments, such as the German Republic, Japan, and certain South American governments. American attitudes toward the war debts piled up by the Allies during World War I also reflected the "business" approach to foreign policy. Both Presidents Harding and Coolidge interpreted the debts strictly as business transactions and

During the war, the U.S. lent the Allied nations a total of over $10 billion, at reduced interest rates, payable over a long period of time.

demanded repayment. The Allies argued that the blood they had expended in battle balanced the money that Americans had contributed. The controversy over war debts reinforced the opinion of many Americans that their country's participation in World War I had been a colossal blunder—one that must never be repeated.

During the early 1930's, war again threatened the world as dictators began their aggressive march. In 1931, Japan invaded Manchuria. Four years later Hitler began to raise an army in violation of the Versailles Treaty, and Italy under Mussolini invaded Ethiopia.

How should the United States respond to such threatening changes in the world? Many Americans believed that their country should follow a course of absolute neutrality. Reading 101 examines reasons for this attitude. As you read, consider these questions:

1. According to the authors of the Nye Report and Senator Clark, why did the United States entered World War I?
2. According to Clark, what were the long-term effects of the war on the United States?
3. What kind of neutrality policy did Senator Clark support?
4. Are you convinced by the arguments of the Nye Committee and Senator Clark? Explain. For what kinds of reasons might you advocate that your country go to war?

The Nye Report

Senator Gerald P. Nye of North Dakota chaired the Senate Munitions Investigating Committee which, between 1934 and 1936, gathered evidence about the reasons the United States entered the war. This selection comes from the committee report.

United States Congress, **Senate Reports,** V, No. 944, 74th Congress, 2nd session, pp. 8 ff.

The Committee wishes to point out most definitely that its study . . . is in no way a criticism, direct or implied, of the sincere devotion of the then President, Woodrow Wilson, to the high causes of peace and democracy. Like other leaders in government, business and finance, he had watched the growth of militarism in the pre-war years. Militarism meant the alliance of the military with powerful economic groups to secure appropriations on the one hand for a constantly increasing military and naval establishment, and on the other hand, the constant threat of the use of that swollen military establishment in behalf of the economic interests at home and abroad of the industrialists supporting it. It meant the subjugation of the people of the various countries to the uniform, the self-interested identification of patriotism with commercialism, and the removal of the military from the control of civil law. After the war had begun President Wilson and a great number of leading Ameri-

During its period of neutrality, the U.S. lent the Allies $2.3 billion and Germany only $27 million. In 1914, the U.S. sold over $6 million worth of explosives to the Allies; in 1917, more than $8 million. Iron and steel exports increased in that same period from $25 million to over $1 billion. The British blockade of the seas prevented any armaments from being shipped to Germany and Austria-Hungary.

cans became convinced that the war was the logical outcome of militarism, and that the success of militarism anywhere was a constant threat to the democracies of the world. All the members of the Committee and its staff shared that conviction.

This belief was also shared by munitions makers, bankers, exporters and producers in this country who had enormous profits at stake in the war. In the unrestricted pursuit of these profits they became involved in a situation which made it to their interest to support the allies and to favor war against Germany. Public opinion became so powerful that it threatened the existence of the party in power and the prestige of the President of the United States. President Wilson was personally impelled by the highest motives and the most profound convictions as to the justice of the cause of our country and was devoted to peace. He was caught up by a situation created largely by the profit-making interests in the United States, and such interests spread to nearly everybody in the country. It seemed necessary to the prosperity of our people that their markets in Europe remain unimpaired.

President Wilson, himself, stated that he realized that the economic rivalries of European nations had played their part in bringing on the war in 1914. After the war had started the great democracies, England and France, were fighting for their very lives. No reflection of any kind on them in their hour of need is intended by discussion of the terms which they found it necessary to offer other powers in return for support. The Committee's interest in those terms revolved around their function in a war which we entered for purposes of establishing our neutral rights by force of arms and which finally failed to secure acknowledgment throughout the world of those neutral rights, even after the war had been successfully concluded.

While the Committee's function is to discuss the adequacy of existing legislation in the light of the most immediate experience available, which in this case has been the World War, the Committee wishes to go out of its way to pay tribute to those soldiers, dead, wounded, or otherwise suffering from the results of that war, who accepted the ideal of making the world safe for democracy, and of regretting to them that there has not been the will or power or cooperation between nations to have accomplished that ideal.

Senator Clark Argues for Neutrality Legislation

Democratic Senator Bennett Champ Clark from Missouri published an article in Harper's Magazine *in 1935 in which he argued for legislation to keep America out of future wars.*

. . . At the present the desire to keep the United States from becoming involved in any war between foreign nations seems practically unanimous among the rank and file of American citizens; but it must be remembered there was an almost equally strong demand to keep us out of the last war. In August 1914, few could have conceived that America would be dragged into a European conflict in which we had no original part and the ramifications of which we did not even understand. Even as late as November 1916, President Wilson was re-elected because he "kept us out of war." Yet five months later we were fighting to "save the world for democracy" in the "war to end war."

Senator Bennett Champ Clark, "Detour Around War," **Harper's Magazine,** vol. CLXXII (December 1935), pp. 1 ff. Reprinted by permission of Violet Hemming Clark.

In the light of that experience, and in the red glow of war fires burning in the old countries, it is high time we gave some thought to the hard, practical question of just how we propose to stay out of present and future international conflicts. No one who has made an honest attempt to face the issue will assert that there is an easy answer. But if we have learned anything at all, we know the inevitable and tragic end to a policy of drifting and trusting to luck. We know that however strong is the will of the American people to refrain from mixing in other people's quarrels, that will can be made effective only if we have a sound, definite policy from the beginning.

Such a policy must be built upon a program to safeguard our neutrality. No lesson of the World War is more clear than that such a policy cannot be improvised after war breaks out. It must be determined in advance, before it is too late to apply reason. I contend with all possible earnestness that if we want to avoid being drawn into this war now forming, or any other future war, we must formulate a definite, workable policy of neutral relations with belligerent nations. . . . The United States cannot turn back to a policy of so-called neutrality that finally pulls us into conflict with one or all of the belligerents. Surely it is obvious that the legislation forcing mandatory embargoes upon war materials will serve to check the growth of another vast munitions trade with warring powers and the dangers that follow a swing of our foreign trade in favor of our munitions customers and against those who cannot purchase the munitions. . . .

The Neutrality Act of 1935 prohibited the sale of munitions to belligerent countries and allowed the President to forbid Americans from traveling on belligerent ships except at their own risk. The embargo did not, however, include such items as oil, steel, and copper.

Let us foresee that under conditions of modern warfare everything supplied to the enemy population has the same effect as supplies to the enemy army, and will become contraband. Food, clothing, lumber, leather, chemicals—everything, in fact, with the possible exception of sporting goods and luxuries (and these aid in maintaining civilian "morale")—are as important aids to winning the war as are munitions. Let us foresee also that our ships carrying contraband will be seized, bombed from the air or sunk by sub-

Contraband is anything that is smuggled or sold illegally.

marines. Let us not claim as a right what is an impossibility. The only way we can maintain our neutral rights is to fight the whole world. If we are not prepared to do that we can only pretend to enforce our rights against one side, and go to war to defend them against the other side. We might at least abandon pretense.

On the matter of loans and credits to belligerents, the train of events which pulled us into the World War is equally significant. Correspondence which our Munitions Investigation Committee discovered in the files of the State Department offers illuminating proof that there can be no true neutrality when our nation is allowed to finance one side of a foreign war. One letter, written by Secretary [of State] Robert Lansing to President Wilson, dated September 5, 1915, lucidly [clearly] points out that loans for the Allies were absolutely necessary to enable them to pay for the tremendous trade in munitions, war materials generally, food stuffs, and the like, or else that trade would have to stop. He declared that the Administration's "true spirit of neutrality" must not stand in the way of the demands of commerce. About one month later the first great loan—the Anglo-French loan of $500,000,000—was floated by a syndicate headed by J. P. Morgan and Company. This company had been the purchasing agents for Allied supplies in the United States since early in 1915. Other loans to the Allied powers quickly followed. . . .

Just who profited from the last war? Labor got some of the crumbs in the form of high wages and steady jobs. But where is labor today with its fourteen million unemployed? Agriculture received high prices for its products during the period of the War and has been paying the price of that brief inflation in the worst and longest agricultural depression in all history. Industry made billions in furnishing the necessities of war to the belligerents and then suffered terrific reaction like the dope addict's morning after. War and depression—ugly, misshapen inseparable twins—must be considered together. Each is a catapult [launching device] for the other. The present world-wide depression is a direct result of the World War. Every war in modern history has been followed by a major depression.

Therefore I say, let the man seeking profits from war or the war-torn countries do so at his own risk. . . .

If there are those so brave as to risk getting us into war by traveling in the war zones—if there are those so valiant that they do not care how many people are killed as a result of their traveling, let us tell them, and let us tell the world that from now on their deaths will be a misfortune to their own families alone.

The profiteers and others who oppose any rational neutrality shout: "You would sacrifice our national honor!" Some declare we are about to haul down the American flag, and in a future war the belligerents will trample on our rights and treat us with contempt. Some of these arguments are trundled [dragged] out by our naval bureaucracy. The admirals, I am told, objected strenuously when the State Department suggested a new policy of neutrality somewhat along these lines.

I deny with every fiber of my being that our national honor demands that we must sacrifice the flower of our youth to safeguard the profits of a privileged few. I deny that it is necessary to turn back the hands of civilization to maintain our national honor. I repudiate any such definition of honor. Is it not time for every lover of our country to do the same thing?

102 Moving Away From Neutrality

Congress responded to the call for neutrality in the mid-1930's. It passed a series of laws that authorized the President to forbid arms shipments and to restrict loans to belligerent nations, to forbid American ships from entering war zones, and to prohibit American citizens from traveling on the vessels of belligerent nations, except at their own risk.

The international situation deteriorated rapidly in the late 1930's. The groups that had attained power in Germany, Italy, and Japan were aggressive and militaristic. In Germany, Adolph Hitler's Nazi party believed so strongly in the natural superiority of the German "race" that he began massive persecutions against all Jews, many Catholics, and most other people in the country who were unwilling to recognize Germans as a "master race." In Italy, the Fascists, led by dictator Benito Mussolini, tried to establish "law, order, and morality" with a repressive government. In Japan, a militaristic regime used the traditional emperor worship to pursue aggression.

In March 1938, Hitler annexed Austria. A year later, while Mussolini seized Albania, Hitler invaded Czechoslovakia and threatened Poland. Britain and France, pledged to guarantee Poland's independence, declared war when Germany invaded Poland on September 1, 1939.

Most Americans initially reacted to the war in Europe with guarded sympathy for the Allies. President Roosevelt, however, spoke for the masses of Americans when he announced his determination to maintain neutrality. No one, however, was prepared for the incredible scope and rapidity of German victories in the first years of the war. Poland fell in less than a month. In April 1940, Germany attacked Denmark and Norway and in May moved

The major Allies were Britain and France and eventually the U.S., and the U.S.S.R. Many smaller countries later joined them. Their enemy was known as the Axis: Germany, Italy, and Japan. A few smaller countries sided with them.

through Belgium and the Netherlands into France. On June 22, France surrendered. In September, Germany concluded a military alliance with Italy and Japan. England stood alone, the last bastion of democracy.

Confronted with potential aggressors in both Europe and Asia, the United States began to modify its neutrality policies. Soon after the war began, Congress revised the neutrality legislation in order to allow belligerents to purchase war materiel in the United States provided they paid cash and carried the goods away in their own ships. Expanded defense plans provided for a two-ocean navy and an enlarged air force. In September 1940, President Roosevelt leased fifty old destroyers to Britain in exchange for the right to lease naval and air bases on British possessions in the Western Hemisphere and Congress passed the first peacetime draft law.

Materiel is military equipment, clothing, and supplies.

Roosevelt continued to press his countrymen to support the Allies even more actively, while a vocal group of American isolationists organized the America First Committee, whose most popular spokesman was Charles A. Lindbergh, the national hero of the 1920's. Reading 102 examines Roosevelt's and Lindbergh's conflicting arguments about the most appropriate way to guarantee American security. As you read, try to answer these questions:

Charles A. Lindbergh, in 1927, became the first man to fly solo over the Atlantic Ocean from New York to Paris. His flight took 33 hours and 39 minutes. In 1938, Lindbergh inspected European air forces and became convinced of German superiority in that field. He returned to the United States advocating isolation.

1. Why did Roosevelt believe that the United States could not allow Great Britain to be defeated? What was Lindbergh's attitude toward a British defeat?
2. What did Roosevelt mean when he said the United States should become "the great arsenal of democracy"? How do you think Lindbergh reacted to Roosevelt's speech?
3. Which of the two policies do you think was the more realistic? Which would you have supported? Why?

Roosevelt Calls for an "Arsenal of Democracy"

U.S. Department of State, **Peace and War: United States Foreign Policy, 1931–1941,** Department of State Publication 1933. Washington, D.C.: Government Printing Office, 1943, pp. 600–07 **passim.**

President Roosevelt delivered a radio address to the American people on December 29, 1940, in which he alerted them to the peril of a British defeat and offered a way to prevent it.

Germany, Italy, and Japan signed the Rome-Berlin-Tokyo Pact, a 10-year military and economic alliance pledging mutual assistance in the event of attack by a country not yet involved in the European War or in the Chinese-Japanese conflict. Japan recognized the leadership of Germany and Italy in Europe in return for leadership in east Asia.

. . . [O]n September 27, 1940, by an agreement signed in Berlin, three powerful nations, two in Europe and one in Asia, joined themselves together in the threat that if the United States interfered with or blocked the expansion program of these three nations—a program aimed at world control—they would unite in ultimate action against the United States.

The Nazi masters of Germany have made it clear that they intend not only to dominate all life and thought in their own country but also to enslave the whole of Europe, and then to use the resources of Europe to dominate the rest of the world.

Three weeks ago their leader [Hitler] stated, "There are two worlds that stand opposed to each other." Then in defiant reply to his opponents, he said this: "Others are correct when they say: 'With this world we cannot ever reconcile ourselves.' . . . I can beat any other power in the world." So said the leader of the Nazis.

In other words, the Axis not merely admits but proclaims that there can be no ultimate peace between their philosophy of government and our philosophy of government. . . .

Some of our people like to believe that wars in Europe and in Asia are of no concern to us. But it is a matter of most vital concern to us that European and Asiatic war-makers should not gain control of the oceans which lead to this hemisphere. . . .

Does anyone seriously believe that we need to fear attack while a free Britain remains our most powerful naval neighbor in the Atlantic? Does any one seriously believe, on the other hand, that we could rest easy if the Axis powers were our neighbor there?

If Great Britain goes down, the Axis powers will control the continents of Europe, Asia, Africa, Australia, and the high seas—and they will be in a position to bring enormous military and naval resources against this hemisphere. It is no exaggeration to say that all of us in the Americas would be living at the point of a gun—a gun loaded with explosive bullets, economic as well as military.

We should enter upon a new and terrible era in which the whole world, our hemisphere included, would be run by threats of brute force. To survive in such a world, we would have to convert ourselves permanently into a militaristic power on the basis of war economy.

Some of us like to believe that even if Great Britain falls, we are still safe, because of the broad expanse of the Atlantic and of the Pacific.

But the width of these oceans is not what it was in the days of clipper ships. At one point between Africa and Brazil the distance is less than from Washington to Denver—five hours for the latest type of bomber. And at the north of the Pacific Ocean, America and Asia almost touch each other.

Even today we have planes which could fly from the British Isles to New England and back without refueling. And the range of the modern bomber is ever being increased. . . .

There are those who say that the Axis powers would never have any desire to attack the Western Hemisphere. This is the same dangerous form of wishful thinking which has destroyed the powers of resistance of so many conquered peoples. The plain facts are that the Nazis have proclaimed, time and again, that all other races are their inferiors and therefore subject to their orders. And most important of all, the vast resources and wealth of this hemisphere constitute the most tempting loot in all the world. . . .

[Some] people not only believe that we can save our own skins by shutting our eyes to the fate of other nations. Some of them go much further than that. They say that we can and should become the friends and even the partners of the Axis powers. Some of them even suggest that we should imitate the methods of the dictatorships. Americans never can and never will do that.

The policy of the European leaders prior to World War II is referred to as appeasement. They gave in to the demands of Hitler and other dictators and allowed them to occupy certain countries in the hope that they would then be satisfied and war would be averted.

The experience of the past two years has proven beyond doubt that no nation can appease the Nazis. No man can tame a tiger into a kitten by stroking it. There can be no appeasement with ruthlessness. There can be no reasoning with an incendiary bomb. We know now that a nation can have peace with the Nazis only at the price of total surrender. . . .

Even the people of Italy have been forced to become accomplices of the Nazis; but at this moment they do not know how soon they will be embraced to death by their allies.

Thinking in terms of today and tomorrow, I make the direct statement to the American people that there is far less chance of the United States getting into war if we do all we can now to support the nations defending themselves against attack by the Axis than if we acquiesce in [agree to] their defeat, submit tamely to an Axis victory, and wait our turn to be the object of attack in another war later on.

If we are to be completely honest with ourselves, we must admit there is risk in *any* course we may take. But I deeply believe that the great majority of our people agree that the course that I advocate involves the least risk now and the greatest hope for world peace in the future.

The people of Europe who are defending themselves do not ask us to do their fighting. They ask us for the implements of war, the planes, the tanks, the guns, the freighters, which will enable them to fight for their liberty and our security. Emphatically we must get these weapons to them in sufficient volume and quickly enough, so that we and our children will be saved the agony and suffering of war which others have had to endure. . . .

On December 20, Roosevelt had created the Office of Production Management headed by William S. Knudsen to coordinate defense production and send necessary materials to the Allies.

Nine days ago I announced the setting up of a more effective organization to direct our gigantic efforts to increase the production of munitions. The appropriation of vast sums of money and a well-coordinated executive direction of our defense efforts are not in themselves enough. Guns, planes, and ships have to be built in the factories and arsenals of America. They have to be produced by workers and managers and engineers with the aid of machines, which in turn have to be built by hundreds of thousands of workers throughout the land. . . .

But all our present efforts are not enough. We must have more ships, more guns, more planes—more of everything. This can only be accomplished if we discard the notion of "business as usual." This job cannot be done merely by superimposing on the existing productive facilities the added requirements for defense. . . .

I want to make it clear that it is the purpose of the Nation to build now with all possible speed every machine and arsenal and factory that we need to manufacture our defense material. We have the men, the skill, the wealth, and above all, the will.

I am confident that if and when production of consumer or luxury goods in certain industries requires the use of machines and raw materials essential for defense purposes, then such production must yield to our primary and compelling purpose. . . .

We must be the great arsenal of democracy. For us this is an emergency as serious as war itself. We must apply ourselves to our task with the same resolution, the same sense of urgency, the same spirit of patriotism, and sacrifice, as we would show were we at war. . . .

As President of the United States I call for that national effort. I call for it in the name of this Nation which we love and honor and which we are privileged and proud to serve. I call upon our people with absolute confidence that our common cause will succeed.

Lindbergh: "A Policy not of Isolation, but of Independence"

The America First Committee was organized in 1940 to work toward keeping the United States out of the war. It drew support from businessmen who opposed Roosevelt, from reformers who wanted the government to concentrate on domestic problems, from pacifists and members of the disillusioned World War I generation, and from certain ethnic groups such as the German-Americans with pro-German feelings and Irish-Americans with traditional anti-British feelings. Lindbergh addressed a large America First rally in New York in early 1941.

Charles A. Lindbergh, **Address, New York, April 23, 1941.** Chicago: America First Committee, 1941, pp. 4–5, 6–7, 9–10, 12–13.

. . . I say we should not enter a war unless we have a reasonable chance of winning. . . . I do not believe that our American ideals, and our way of life, will gain through an unsuccessful war. And I know that the United States is not prepared to wage war in Europe successfully at this time. . . .

The American Expeditionary Force, commanded by General John J. Pershing, was sent to France in 1917. Pershing originally intended to have Americans fight as a separate army, but in 1918 the A.E.F. was fighting with the French and British under the unified command of Marshal Foch.

I have said before, and I will say again, that I believe it will be a tragedy to the entire world if the British Empire collapses. That is one of the main reasons why I opposed this war before it was declared, and why I have constantly advocated a negotiated peace. I did not feel that England and France had a reasonable chance of winning. France has now been defeated; and, . . . [the British] have one last desperate plan remaining. They hope that they may be able to persuade us to send another American Expeditionary Force to Europe, and to share with England militarily, as well as financially, the fiasco [complete failure] of this war. . . . I have been forced to the conclusion that we cannot win this war for England, regardless of how much assistance we extend. . . .

There is a policy open to this nation that *will* lead to success—a policy that leaves us free to follow our own way of life, and to develop our own civilization. It is not a new and untried idea. It was advocated by Washington. It was incorporated in the Monroe Doctrine. Under its guidance, the United States became the greatest nation in the world. It is based upon the belief that the security of a nation lies in the strength and character of its own people. It recommends the maintenance of armed forces sufficient to defend this hemisphere from attack by any combination of foreign powers. It demands faith in an independent American destiny. This is the policy of the America First Committee today. It is a policy not of isolation, but of independence; not of defeat, but of courage. It is a policy that led this nation to success during the most trying years of our history, and it is a policy that will lead us to success again. . . .

103 Congress Considers Lend-Lease

"The battle of France is over. I expect that the Battle of Britain is about to begin," Winston Churchill, Britain's great wartime leader, told his countrymen on July 1, 1940. While German submarines stepped up the Battle of the Atlantic, in an attempt to cut Britain's vital trade links with its Empire and with the United States, Hitler's famed *Luftwaffe* (as Germany's air force was called) rained tons of bombs upon English cities during the summer and fall of 1940. The war also spread to the east as Mussolini's forces hit Greece; the Nazis planned to attack the Balkans.

Isolationist sentiment weakened in America. Most Americans still wanted to stay out of the war, but they believed they could best do so through assisting Great Britain. Roosevelt's release of fifty destroyers to Britain stirred up considerable controversy, for his opponents thought this action drew America one step closer to war. Yet, in his successful campaign for re-election to an unprecedented third term, Roosevelt told the American people, "Your boys are not going to be sent into any foreign war."

Roosevelt added privately that an attack on the United States would not be considered a foreign war.

The Republicans rejected as their Presidential candidate two well-known isolationists, Senator Arthur Vandenberg of Michigan and Senator Robert A. Taft of Ohio. They turned instead to Wendell Wilkie who believed as strongly as Roosevelt that fascist aggression posed a genuine threat to America. The mood of the country had clearly changed by 1940.

Early in 1941, President Roosevelt proposed to implement his "arsenal of democracy" speech in order to help the British withstand massive German attacks. He asked Congress to pass a law authorizing him to sell, exchange, or lease arms and other equipment to any nation whose defense he considered vital to the security of the United States. When Roosevelt's proposal for a Lend-Lease Act became public, the diminishing, but still vocal, isolationists protested quickly. Before the full Congress debated the bill, the Senate Committee on Foreign Relations held public hearings on the proposal. Reading 103 comes from the testimony taken during those hearings. As you read, try to answer these questions:

1. What arguments did Dr. Niebuhr use in support of the bill? What arguments did Secretary Knox present? To what kinds of Americans might each man's testimony have been meaningful?
2. In what specific ways did Niebuhr and Knox reinforce arguments made by Roosevelt in his "arsenal of democracy" speech?
3. What point was Senator Clark trying to make with his question about Niebuhr's role in World War I? What point was Senator Nye trying to make with his newspaper quotation?
4. On the basis of the questioning, what other issues seem to have been involved in the debate over Lend-Lease?

"An Unofficial Declaration of War"

With the Lend-Lease Bill, Congress and the country considered a critical commitment. One historian has written, "It [Lend-Lease] was more than an abandonment of neutrality, for neutrality had already been abandoned; it was an unofficial declaration of war on the Axis—. . ." The following comes from the Lend-Lease debate before the Senate Foreign Relations Committee.

Senate Committee on Foreign Relations, **To Promote the Defense of the United States,** 77th Congress, 1st Session (January–February 1941). Washington, D.C.: Government Printing Office, 1941, pp. 169–75.

Statement of Dr. Reinhold Niebuhr

Reinhold Niebuhr (born 1892) is a clergyman and theologian. His prolific writings have aroused clerical interest in social reform.

DR. NIEBUHR: . . . If Nazi tyranny establishes its supremacy in Europe and makes all trade with the continent subject to its decrees, penetrates into South America through economic and political and cultural pressure, and challenges us in the Orient through its allies and satellites, we would be faced with the alternatives of either conniving [cooperating secretly] with this tyranny or spending more billions than have yet been envisaged to challenge it. Connivance would mean, among other things, participation in world trade on Nazi terms.

The Nazi unification of Europe would combine the conditions of slavery with the efficiency of a technical civilization for the first time in history. We have known slavery before and we know what the efficiency of modern industry is. But we have never had these two together. . . .

It is difficult to understand why those who are not willing that we spend a comparatively small sum in aid of the nations which are resisting totalitarianism are quite willing that we spend many more billions preparing for the eventuality of facing the totalitarian powers alone. . . .

Beyond the problem of our national interest is the larger problem of the very quality of our civilization, with its historic liberties and standards of justice, which the Nazis are sworn to destroy. No nation can be unmindful of its obligations to a civilization of which it is a part, even though no nation is able to think of these obligations in terms disassociated from its national interest. If we should define the present struggle in Europe as merely a clash between rival imperialisms, it would merely mean that a strange combination of cynicism and abstract idealism had so corrupted the commonsense moral insights of a people that we could no longer distinguish between right and wrong. History never presents us with choices of pure good against pure evil. But the Nazis have achieved something which is so close to the very negation of justice that if we cannot recognize it and react to it with a decent sense of moral indignation, we would prove ourselves incapable of preserving the heritage of our Western culture. Fortunately the various tests of public opinion prove that the common people have not lost this moral capacity, however much some intellectuals and religious idealists may be confused.

The Nazis have declared their intention of annihilating the Jewish race. This maniacal fury against a great race goes beyond anything previously known in the category of race prejudice. They have also declared their intention of subordinating the other nations of Europe to the dominion of a master race. In the case of Poland and Czechoslovakia their policy goes to the length of systematically destroying the whole fabric of the national life of these unhappy nations so that, were the Nazis to control Europe only for a decade, they would destroy some nations beyond hope of reconstruction. . . .

The term "Aryan" refers to people speaking an Indo-European dialect. In Nazi racist literature, German "racial" descent was traced back to a supposedly racial Aryan ancestry. Nazis classified Jews as non-Aryan, or Semitic, and considered them an inferior people.

Nor ought we forget that the Nazis are intent upon destroying the religious and cultural heritages of western Christendom, that they have debased all culture . . . and that violation of solemn undertakings, corruption of leaders in subordinate nations and every strategy in the arsenal of deception has been combined by them with a strategy of cruelty and terror in a new and terrible total policy of tyrannical imperialism. . . .

Democracies must be vigilant of their liberties. But if they do not also trust themselves by trusting their leaders, so that they can match the speed of tyrannies, they may awake to discover that they have, as some anxious mothers have done, smothered what they highly prized by guarding it too frantically. . . .

THE CHAIRMAN: Are there any questions? Senator Johnson.

Senator Walter F. George, Democrat from Georgia, was chairman.

SEN. JOHNSON OF CALIFORNIA: Is it your belief that the bill will keep us out of war?

Senator Hiram Johnson was an extreme isolationist. He had fought to keep the United States out of the League of Nations. Prior to World War II, he voted against all bills aimed to prepare the United States for war.

DR. NIEBUHR: I should hope so, Senator. I do not think that anybody could guarantee it. I should think the bill offers us a better opportunity to keep out of war than anything else I know.

SEN. JOHNSON OF CALIFORNIA: But, even if it did not have that effect, you would still be in favor of it, would you not?

DR. NIEBUHR: Yes, I would. As I said in my statement, I believe one has to take some risks or involve one's self in even greater risks.

SEN. JOHNSON OF CALIFORNIA: But it has no terrors for you at all?

DR. NIEBUHR: Yes; it has. War has terrors for me.

SEN. JOHNSON OF CALIFORNIA: Really? Really? I did not think so.

DR. NIEBUHR: Well, I do not see how any human being could be without a terror of war. I think we all have to face this proposition, whether a war is the worst terror we can conceive, and I am frank to say that I am not certain that it is, . . .

SEN. CLARK OF MISSOURI: Doctor, you are a man of the cloth [clergyman]—do you consider that your profession as a clergyman would prevent your entering into a war, about which you speak so complacently, if we were to have a war?

This was Senator Bennett Clark.

DR. NIEBUHR: No; it does not, Senator. I do not believe in clerical exemption.

SEN. CLARK OF MISSOURI: I am very glad to hear you say that, in view of the fact you were speaking so very complacently about the United States engaging in war.

You were 25 years old when the last war started, were you not?

DR. NIEBUHR: Yes.

SEN. CLARK OF MISSOURI: Where did you put in your time during the time that the United States was engaged in war?

DR. NIEBUHR: I put my time in as chairman of the Wartime Commission of my denomination, working with soldiers in the camps.

SEN. CLARK OF MISSOURI: You were a minister during that time?

DR. NIEBUHR: Yes, sir.

SEN. CLARK OF MISSOURI: You never wore the uniform of the United States during that period, did you?

DR. NIEBUHR: I did not; no, sir.

SEN. CLARK OF MISSOURI: That is all.

In 1940, Frank Knox, a Republican, was appointed Secretary of the Navy by President Roosevelt.

Statement of Hon. Frank Knox

SECRETARY KNOX: . . . I reiterate [repeat] here my belief that the chief question that confronts us is whether we shall now take steps to keep Europe's wars in Europe, or shall drift along and permit those wars to be transferred to the Americas. We need time to get ready to meet out at sea a strong, aggressive Germany, if we are to keep the fighting away from the lands of this hemisphere. . . .

In public speeches I have warned the American people that if Britain is defeated, we ought then to be fully prepared to repel attempts by Germany to seize bases on this side of the Atlantic. Germany would use these bases either to attack us directly, or else first to establish herself solidly in South America. Many of our people and many of the speakers who have opposed giving ample aid to Great Britain apparently believe it fantastic to think that there is any real danger of invasion. I disagree with such people, and believe that a victorious Germany would move over to this hemisphere just as soon as she could accumulate the strength to do so, and certainly very soon unless we now take the steps to check her career of reckless aggression.

SEN. NYE: How dangerous or how large is the chance of attack upon the United States in the event the worst should happen to Great Britain, Mr. Secretary?

SECRETARY KNOX: Well, that is all purely speculative. I do not know. I would hazard as my judgment that it would not come directly on us, anyway. It would come indirectly.

SEN. NYE: I did not catch that.

SECRETARY KNOX: I said I would just hazard a guess that it would come indirectly rather than directly.

SEN. NYE: In an economic way, perhaps?

The Secretary is referring to Latin America.

SECRETARY KNOX: Beginning that way, south of us.

SEN. NYE: You have felt, have you not, that it has often been true that emergencies have been created in the interest of accomplishing some purpose that was rather indirect?

SECRETARY KNOX: Yes; on both sides.

SEN. NYE: On both sides. You have known times when you felt very strongly that the so-called drums of emergency were being beaten to the end that there could be larger powers accomplished for an executive, have you not?

SECRETARY KNOX: Not in this emergency; no, sir.

SEN. NYE: Not in this emergency?

SECRETARY KNOX: I feel very deeply that this is a real one. It is impossible to exaggerate its gravity.

SEN. NYE: I am quoting now. "It is a disturbing quality, but Mr. Roosevelt seems to delight in catching people off guard."

The excerpt was from an editorial that appeared in the **Chicago Daily News.** Knox had been the publisher of the paper at that time.

SECRETARY KNOX: When was this written?

SEN. NYE: Just a moment [continuing reading]: "One technique is to beat the drums of emergency and try to force legislation "now"; the other technique is to slip something across quietly. The inevitable result is that he has engendered a feeling that he has to be watched—and watched continuously." Does that have a familiar ring to it, Mr. Secretary?

SEN. CONNALLY: Mr. Chairman, I want to intervene. The Secretary asked when this was written, and the Senator declined to give him that information. I think that is an unfair method of interrogation. I want to insist that he be advised of the information he asked for.

Senator Tom Connally of Texas later became a member of the delegation sent to San Francisco to draw up the charter for the United Nations.

SEN. NYE: Very well. The publication of this particular statement was in 1938.

SECRETARY KNOX: I thought so.

SEN. NYE: You do not feel that an emergency has been created and magnified to the end that there could be a hurrying and a speeding of this legislation that is pending at the present time?

SECRETARY KNOX: No, sir; and, on the contrary, I think we are awfully slow in meeting the crisis. Perfectly vital time right now is being lost. . . .

104 From Isolation to Total War

HISTORICAL ESSAY

America's refusal to join the League of Nations after World War I set the tone of American diplomacy in the 1920's. American hostility to the League declined somewhat as the decade passed, and United States representatives eventually cooperated with several international commissions set up by the League. American public opinion and Congress remained deeply suspicious of international organizations. Despite the urging of Presidents Coolidge and Hoover, for example, Congress refused to allow the United States to cooperate with the new World Court, set up to arbitrate international disputes.

As a dominant industrial power, however, the United States could not disengage itself from world affairs. As a result, American diplomacy during this period reflected a curious blend of moralism and self-interest. Woodrow Wilson had interpreted World War I in moral terms, that is, as a war to make the world safe for democracy. Although most of the American people eventually rejected this interpretation, the United States continued to take a moralistic approach to world affairs. In 1921, the United States sponsored the Washington Naval Conference, which resulted in agreements by the major powers to limit naval disarmament. In 1927, the United States played a leading role in drawing up the Kellogg-Briand Pact in which sixty-two nations agreed to outlaw war. But the participants in these agreements provided no way to enforce them.

During this same period, American businessmen helped support American policy with investments abroad. The success of the German Republic, a moderate regime in Japan, and friendly South American governments seemed to contribute to the self interest of the United States. Americans invested heavily in all three areas. The attitude toward the war debt piled up by the Allies during the war, also reflected a business approach to foreign policy. Resentment and misunderstanding developed on all sides, and Europe made only token payments on the debt. Although the Allies were certainly not blameless in this dispute, the tendency of American political leaders and the American people to interpret delicate matters of international politics and economics in business terms made a difficult situation even worse. In retrospect, this example seems almost symbolic. Americans in the 1920's wanted a world of peace and understanding—provided it cost them nothing.

From Isolation to Intervention, 1931–1941

Isolationism dominated America's foreign policy in 1931. Ten years later, the nation willingly provided assistance just short of war to support the defense of Great Britain. This reversal of attitudes represented a dramatic response to the rise of fascist governments in Germany, Italy, and Japan, whose aggressive conquests forced Americans to reconsider their foreign policy.

The Fascists were a political group that arose in Italy in 1919. The term fascist is also applied to other political groups that believe in strong central government, control of industry, and other totalitarian principles.

Fascist aggression began in 1931 when Japan attacked China without provocation and converted Manchuria into a Japanese satellite. Although this action violated both the American Open Door Policy in China and the Kellogg-Briand Pact, President Hoover refused to apply military or economic sanctions against Japan. But Secretary of State Henry Stimson did announce in the Stimson Doctrine, that the United States government would not recognize the validity of any Japanese actions taken in violation of existing treaty rights. The next year Japan attacked Shanghai, China. The

United States again protested Japan's action, and the League of Nations censured Japan. Japan withdrew from the League.

President Roosevelt was inaugurated in 1933, the same year that Japan left the League of Nations, and one year before Hitler assumed power in Germany. A former Assistant Secretary of the Navy under Wilson, Roosevelt had strong internationalist convictions. Problems of the Depression absorbed him during this first Administration. Except for a more constructive approach to Latin America, the United States played a minor role in world affairs.

The high point in American isolationism came in the mid-1930's. In 1935, Hitler imposed a military draft on Germany and began to raise an army and air force in clear violation of the Treaty of Versailles. During the same year, Italy attacked Ethiopia. As fascist aggression and the possibility of general war increased, so did Americans' insistence that their nation should not become involved. The Nye Committee suggested, by considerably distorting the facts, that America's entrance into World War I had really been plotted by greedy munitions manufacturers. This theme, taken up by successful novelists and playwrights, contributed to the tide of isolationist feeling. Congress passed neutrality legislation in 1935, 1936, and 1937 aimed at keeping the United States out of another war. When, in October 1937, President Roosevelt called for an international quarantine of aggressors, American isolationists protested vigorously. Most Americans favored a policy designed to keep America out of war rather than one to keep wars from breaking out.

Events in Europe from 1937 to 1939 played a vital role in changing American attitudes. The United States was not the only country that wanted peace. Great Britain and France had stood by passively while Hitler rebuilt his army and air force, reoccupied the Rhineland, and annexed Austria. In the Munich Conference, they practically handed Czechoslovakia to Hitler in the interests of peace. Meanwhile, Mussolini invaded Albania. Britain and France finally acted when Hitler attacked Poland in September 1939. True to their treaty promises, England and France declared war on Germany. In less than a year Poland, the Netherlands, Belgium, Norway, and France had all fallen to Germany, now allied with Italy. German air raids left British cities in flames. If Britain fell, no friendly power would stand between the United States and the fascist aggressors in Europe; no allies except a weak, divided, war-torn China would support America against Japan in the Pacific.

Between January and December 1941, the United States moved rapidly toward becoming a partner with England in the war against fascism. Congress passed the Lend-Lease Bill in March with an initial appropriation of a billion dollars. In May, President Roosevelt declared an unlimited national emergency and closed all German

The United States tried to improve relations with Latin America by replacing its imperialistic policy with a Good Neighbor policy. The Roosevelt Administration tried to improve trade, political, and cultural relations with the nations of the Western Hemisphere. It canceled the Platt Amendment which had proclaimed the right of the United States to intervene in the affairs of Cuba, and also removed troops from Haiti.

In a speech delivered on October 5, 1937, in the isolationist city of Chicago, Roosevelt moved away from his position of isolation and neutrality and came out against the aggressor nations, particularly Japan, which had just launched its attack against China. He urged an international quarantine of the aggressor nations, to be accomplished presumably by economic boycotts.

The Treaty of Versailles (1919) provided for the demilitarization and Allied occupation of the Rhineland, a region of West Germany located west of the Rhine River. Allied troops were withdrawn in 1930. In 1936, in violation of the Treaty, Germany began to remilitarize the Rhineland.

Hitler demanded that Czechoslovakia give him the Sudetan region which contained many German-speaking people. In order to prevent war, British Prime Minister Neville Chamberlain, French Premier Edouard Daladier, Hitler, and Mussolini met at Munich and signed a pact on September 30, 1938, giving Germany the Sudetan region and all important Czech fortresses.

On May 21, 1941, a German submarine sunk the **Robin Moor,** an unarmed American merchantman in the South Atlantic, outside a designated war zone. In retaliation, the United States ordered that all Italian and German consulates be closed, claiming that they were centers for subversive activities.

and Italian consulates in the United States. In June, when Germany violated the Non-Aggression Pact and invaded the Soviet Union, Roosevelt promised American aid to the Soviets. By autumn, the United States Navy convoyed supply ships as far as Iceland, and German submarines sank American destroyers and merchant ships.

As the United States became increasingly involved in the war in Europe, American-Japanese relations continued to deteriorate. Japan purchased oil from the United States to supply its military forces, but the United States government banned sales of scrap iron and machine tools. The United States, through Secretary of State Cordell Hull, sought to get Japan to withdraw from China and to promise not to attack unprotected French and Dutch colonies in Southeast Asia. When Japan moved into French Indo-China in July 1941, the United States froze Japanese assets in the United States and placed a total embargo on oil. Japan offered to limit further expansion if the United States would lift the embargo and allow "a just peace" in China. When the United States refused, the military party in power in Tokyo prepared a coordinated assault on the Dutch East Indies, British Malaya, and the Philippines. But they decided first to immobilize the American Pacific Fleet with a surprise air attack on the United States naval base at Pearl Harbor.

Bank balances in the United States were frozen, and the Japanese could neither withdraw the money nor spend it here. Trade relations between the two countries were completely terminated. In order to get oil, iron, steel, and other vital war materials, Japan would either have to attack Southeast Asia and risk war, or induce the United States to resume trade.

American intelligence experts knew that Japan planned an attack somewhere. The government sent general alerts to Pacific forces but the strike was expected somewhere in Southeast Asia. Consequently, the Hawaiian Islands lacked adequate protection. On December 7, 1941, Japanese planes reduced the American navy and air force at Pearl Harbor to flaming ruins. The next day the United States Congress declared war on Japan. On December 11, Germany and Italy declared war on the United States.

War on Two Fronts—The Strategy of Victory, 1941–1944

In January 1942, Manila surrendered. Douglas MacArthur, the American general who was recalled from the area in March 1942, remarked, "I shall return." He did three years later, and in February 1945, the Japanese were defeated.

The year 1942 was critical for the Allied cause. In the Pacific, Japan rapidly overran almost all of Southeast Asia, the Philippines, and most of China. In Europe, Germany controlled western Europe and penetrated deep into the Soviet Union. Italian and German forces held most of North Africa. At the same time, German submarines threatened to break the Atlantic supply line.

Before 1942 ended, however, the Allies launched a counteroffensive. British and American military leaders agreed that Germany was the most powerful enemy and should be dealt with first. In November 1942, a combined British and American force landed in North Africa and moved against German and Italian forces in the first phase of a campaign which, under General Dwight D. Eisenhower's leadership, eventually resulted in the first major allied

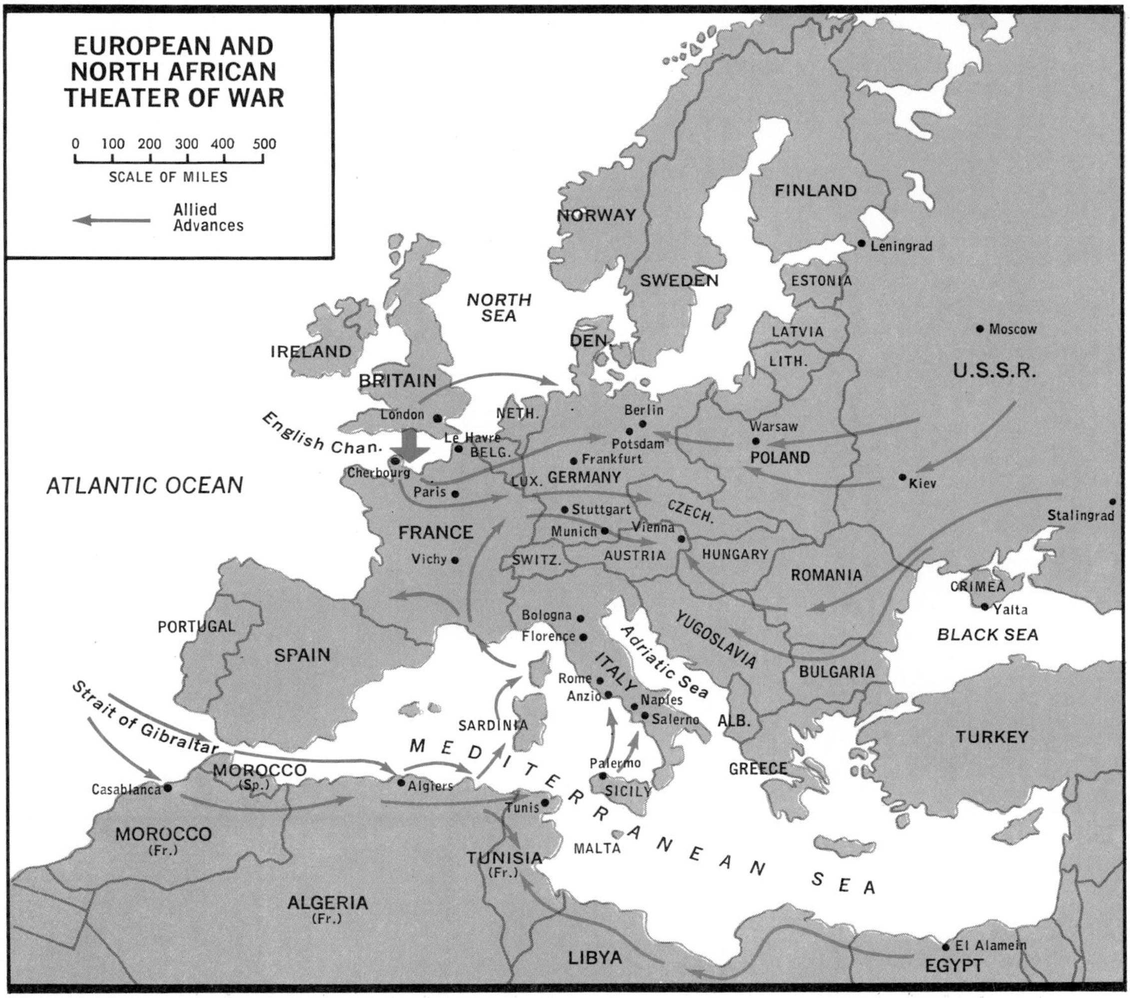

victory of the war. At the same time, the Soviet Union, after absorbing enormous losses, stalled the Nazi offensive on the northern front. In the Pacific, the American navy thwarted the Japanese threat against Australia in the Battle of the Coral Sea. The Japanese also lost a major naval engagement in their attempt to seize Midway Island. In August 1942, United States marines landed at Guadalcanal in the Solomon Islands. Under the leadership of General Douglas MacArthur and Admiral Chester Nimitz, American forces began the "island-hopping" strategy that would bring victory.

In the spring of 1943, the Allies crushed enemy resistance in North Africa, captured 250,000 troops and invaded Italy. At about the same time, Soviet forces began to push back the German front

The American strategy in the Pacific was to advance to Tokyo by "island-hopping," destroying Japanese strongholds in the Pacific. Led by General MacArthur, Allied troops won victories at Guadalcanal in the Solomon Islands, the Gilbert, Marshall, and Caroline Islands, Guam, and the Philippines. From these bases destructive raids were launched on the Japanese mainland.

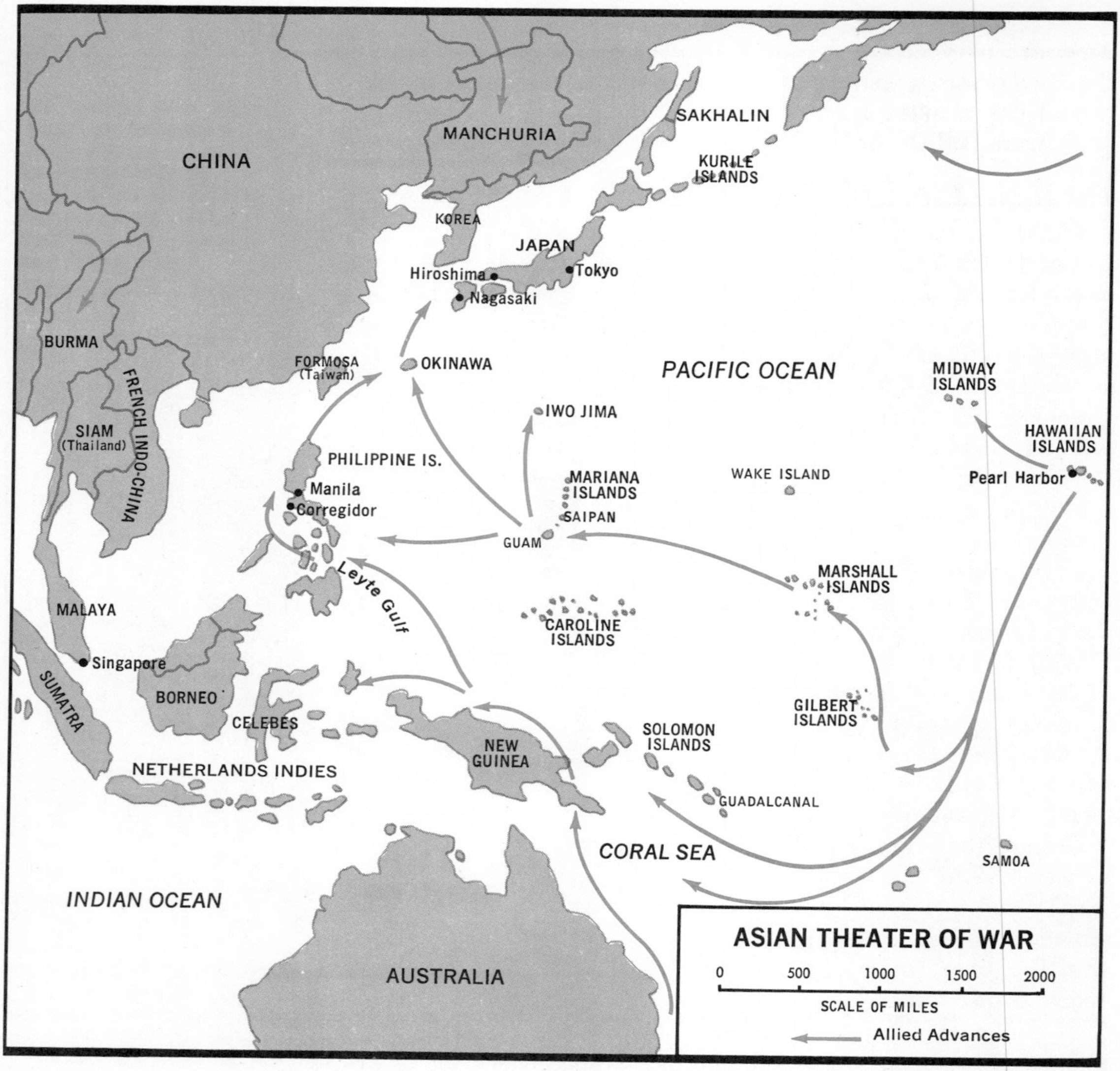

in Russia. A year later, on June 6, 1944, Great Britain and the United States launched the Normandy invasion successfully. Under General Eisenhower's command, 176,000 troops initially moved across the English Channel supported by 4600 ships and 11,000 planes. With British troops pushing the Germans from the south and west and the Soviets driving from the east, victory seemed assured.

In the Pacific, events moved somewhat more slowly. The Americans cut off the Japanese forces in the Solomons from their supply lines while landing in the Marshalls and the Marianas within effective bombing distance of Tokyo. In October 1944, MacArthur invaded the Philippines, and in the Battle of Leyte Gulf the

American navy decisively crushed Japanese sea power. Victory in the Pacific was within sight, but American military strategists expected that a massive and costly offensive on the Japanese mainland would still be required to attain it.

The Home Front

Victory in the war depended as much upon the ability of the United States to produce war materiel as upon the valor and skill of the fighting men. Between 1941 and 1945, the American government spent twice as much money as the total government expenditures since 1790! Annual production of such critical equipment as airplanes and ships increased at an incredible rate. In 1939, the United States produced 6000 airplanes and 237,000 tons of shipping; in 1944, the assembly lines yielded 96,000 airplanes and 10,000,000 tons of shipping.

Ship tonnage is the carrying capacity of freighters or tankers measured in long tons (1 ton equals 2240 pounds). It includes the cargo, crew, fuel, supplies, and spare parts. Ship tonnage also refers to the weight of a volume of water occupied by a naval ship, also measured in long tons.

Mobilizing gigantic resources and allocating scarce materials required a massive extension of the federal bureaucracy. Government organizations were established to oversee war production and scientific research, to regulate prices and wages, and to control the rationing of scarce materials, such as tires, gasoline, and meat.

With the expansion of the army from 334,000 in 1939 to 12,000,000 in 1945 and of the work force, unemployment practically disappeared. Wages went up, and almost everyone started paying taxes. Women joined the labor force in great numbers, and Negroes found better job opportunities, particularly in northern factories. Union membership increased, and there were few strikes.

After Pearl Harbor, many union leaders promised President Roosevelt that their workers would not strike during the wartime period. In return, the workers would be promised fair treatment. In January 1942, Roosevelt set up a National War Labor Board to act where a dispute had not been settled. As the cost of living increased in 1943, labor grew restless, but disputes were quickly settled.

Despite the enormous drain on the economy, the standard of living did not drop. Many items needed in the war—nylon, rubber, metals, and many foods—were rationed by the government. Government controls, although irritating, were not particularly oppressive. The American people as a whole showed restraint, good humor, and a strong sense of national purpose. Hysteria and intolerance were minimal—with one major exception. More than 100,000 loyal Japanese-Americans were removed to relocation centers. These American citizens had to sell their property (usually at a loss) or lose it entirely and move into camps until the end of the war.

The strength of the American economy, the stability of the people, and the flexibility of the American political system all showed to good advantage on the Home Front. In 1941, as in 1861, Americans were blessed with superior leadership at the time of grave crisis. Franklin Roosevelt's qualities of exuberance, optimism, and self-confidence that had captured the imagination of the American people in the 1930's, helped unite the country and reinforce the national purpose. Roosevelt was no administrative genius—his bureaucracy often seemed to work at cross purposes—but he had a keen sense of military strategy and knew what was required of the civilian population. Roosevelt knew what America was fighting for, and he communicated his convictions to the American people.

Political Strategy

American political strategy during the war was neither as clear-cut nor as successful as the military strategy. Most Americans believed they were fighting for survival. Beyond that, they pointed to a larger moral purpose in the Four Freedoms which Roosevelt had enunciated as world goals in 1941—freedom of speech, freedom of religion, freedom from want, and freedom from fear. Before the United States entered the war, Roosevelt had met on ship with Prime Minister Churchill to formulate the broad postwar principles of the United States and Great Britain. The Atlantic Charter, drawn up at this meeting, emphasized the principles of self-determination, respect for treaties, disarmament of aggressors, renunciation of territorial gain, freedom of the seas, and world economic and political cooperation.

Once the United States joined the war, Roosevelt and Churchill worked closely together as did the military chiefs of the two countries. The alliance was probably the most successful in history largely because of the respect and admiration the two men had for each other.

The alliance with the U.S.S.R., however, involved formidable political problems. The communist ideology of the U.S.S.R. rejected Western values and anticipated their eventual destruction. Moreover, the events just prior to the war had left a heritage of ill will and suspicion between the Soviet Union and the Western countries. Joseph Stalin, the Soviet dictator, believed that England and France had compromised with Germany in the 1930's because they opposed communism more strongly than they opposed fascism. On the other hand, the Allies had watched the Soviet Union suddenly reverse an anti-Nazi policy and sign a Non-Aggression Pact with Germany in 1939, invade Poland from the east after Germany's attack on September 1, and launch an attack on Finland, October 1940.

Once Germany attacked the Soviet Union, however, public opinion among the Allies changed remarkably, especially in the United States. The people of the Soviet Union had to bear the brunt of the war until the United States could mobilize men and materiel to help Britain mount an offensive against Germany. The toughness of the Soviet army and the tenacity and heroism of the Soviet people during the darkest days of the war, won the admiration of Americans. To help sustain their Soviet allies, the United States government supplied them with billions of dollars of lend-lease aid.

The Soviet Union professed a willingness to work with the Allies on military and postwar problems. In 1942, it signed the Declaration of the United Nations in which the Allies agreed to take no new territory after the war. In 1934, it dissolved the Comintern, the official agency for promoting world revolution. In November 1943, Roosevelt, Churchill, and Stalin met for the first time at Teheran, Iran, and agreed to coordinate the Normandy invasion with a Russian offensive against Germany. Stalin promised to enter the war against Japan after Germany's defeat, and the three heads of state formulated a general plan for a postwar international organization.

Roosevelt and Churchill had conferred at Washington, Casablanca, and Quebec to plan military strategy. Prior to the Teheran Conference, Churchill and Roosevelt met with Generalissimo Chiang Kai-shek, head of the Nationalist government of China, in Cairo to plan action against Japan.

The most important and controversial wartime conference was held in the Crimea, in the southern part of the Soviet Union, in 1945. At the Yalta Conference, the three major powers made important agreements for ending the war and organizing the postwar world. They agreed that Germany would pay heavy reparations and, pending a peace treaty, be divided into American, Soviet, British, and French military zones; that the Soviet Union would enter the war against Japan and in return would receive the Kurile Islands north of Japan, the southern part of the island of Sakhalin, and railroad and port concessions in Manchuria; that new Polish borders would be established giving Polish territory to the Soviet Union in the east and German territory to Poland in the west; and that the Polish government would be set up by the U.S.S.R. temporarily while preparations were made for democratic elections.

After the war, when the U.S.S.R. and the United States had become more enemies than allies, many Americans severely criticized the Yalta agreements. They accused Roosevelt of "selling out" to Stalin. The Soviet's most flagrant violation of the Yalta agreements came in Poland where democratic elections were never held. Poland became a Soviet satellite after the war, thus thrusting Soviet power to the heart of Europe. The criticisms of the commitments made at Yalta, however, came after the Cold War had already begun. In 1945, Allied victory was made possible because the three great powers had cooperated in war. Roosevelt, far more than Churchill, believed that they could cooperate in peace, as well. The Yalta agreements were based on the assumption that the U.S.S.R. would live up to her obligations. To Roosevelt and his advisors, and to most Americans, this seemed possible in 1945.

Victory and the Bomb

In April 1945, American and Soviet troops met each other at the Elbe River. By the end of the month, the Soviets reached Berlin. Italian partisans captured and killed Mussolini, and Hitler committed suicide in a Berlin bomb shelter. Germany surrendered unconditionally, as the Allies had demanded, May 8, 1945.

Partisans are resistance fighters working behind enemy lines, performing reconaissance and sabotage, and upsetting enemy movements as much as possible. They do not belong to the regular army but usually operate under orders from a professional military commander.

President Roosevelt did not live to see Germany's surrender. He died of a cerebral hemorrhage on April 12, after having led the nation through a longer and more perilous period than any other American President.

Roosevelt's successor, Harry S Truman, had to carry the war against Japan to a conclusion. To do this he had to make the most momentous decision of the war. In 1939, President Roosevelt, in response to information that Germany was working on a similar project, authorized the government to launch a program of atomic research. In July 1945, government scientists succeeded in exploding the first atomic bomb in the New Mexico desert. The United States now possessed the most terrible weapon in history. Should it be employed against the Japanese to end the war in the Pacific?

Truman based his decision to use the bomb on the assumption that Japan would fight to the end and that thousands of American lives would be lost in an invasion of the Japanese mainland. American military leaders predicted at least eighteen more months of fighting before final victory. On July 26, Truman and Churchill demanded that Japan surrender or face "utter destruction." Japan refused on July 29. One week later, on August 6, an American superfortress airplane dropped an atomic bomb on Hiroshima killing 75,000 people and injuring nearly 100,000 out of a total population of 344,000. The Soviet Union declared war on Japan two days later. On August 15, 1945, after a second atomic bomb had hit Nagasaki, Japan surrendered.

The United States emerged victorious from the most devastating war in history. Over twelve million Americans had served in the armed forces. More than 300,000 had given their lives. The totalitarian aggressors had been destroyed, but a large part of the world lay in ruins. The United States moved into the postwar world, searching for lasting peace, but armed with a weapon that could destroy mankind.

SUGGESTED READINGS

SEARS, STEPHEN W., *Carrier War in the Pacific* and *Desert War in North Africa.* These excellently illustrated volumes present dramatic accounts of the actual strategy and fighting of the war on land and sea.

SHERWOOD, ROBERT E., *Roosevelt and Hopkins.* Sherwood has written a somewhat longer but very vivid and personal account of the war years from the point of view of Roosevelt and a trusted advisor.

WILTZ, JOHN E., *From Isolation to War: 1931–1941.* This is a short narrative history of the period based on recent scholarly studies.

The Cold War, 1945–1969

CHAPTER 27

STATING THE ISSUE

Peace came to a troubled world in 1945. Millions of homeless men, women, and children faced starvation in Asia and Europe. Millions more who had been pressed into the service of the Axis powers were stranded far from home. Governments had collapsed in numerous European and Asian countries, and people in colonies all over the world demanded independence. The European economy was shattered and the countryside lay in ruins.

For a time, hope for a better world seemed well founded. The aggressor nations had been defeated thoroughly. The United Nations Organization, chartered by fifty nations in the spring of 1945, promised a new era of international order, cooperation, and peace.

The world soon recognized, however, that differences between the United States and the Soviet Union could not be reconciled at the conference table. Stalin turned eastern Europe into a Soviet sphere of influence and, after the Communists gained control of China in 1949, the threat of expanding communist empires grew.

Americans remembered that their isolationist policy as well as British and French acquiescence to the demands of the fascist dictators had enlarged those dictators' appetites for territory in the 1930's. In the late 1940's, only the United States remained strong enough to oppose communist expansion. American leaders, supported by the American people, formulated policies aimed at stopping communist encroachments on the noncommunist world without starting a third world war. Such policies required billions of dollars in military and economic assistance to friendly nations linked to the United States by treaties. Ultimately thousands of American servicemen died on distant battlefields in "limited" wars.

The Cold War showed little sign of slackening in the 1960's. The easing of the United States–Soviet relations was offset by heightened tensions between Communist China and the United States, by the Vietnamese War, and by a communist threat in South America.

Chapter 27 examines America's role in the Cold War. What were the major problems of the postwar world? How did the United States try to meet the challenges of the Cold War? How successful were American policies? These are the major issues raised in Chapter 27.

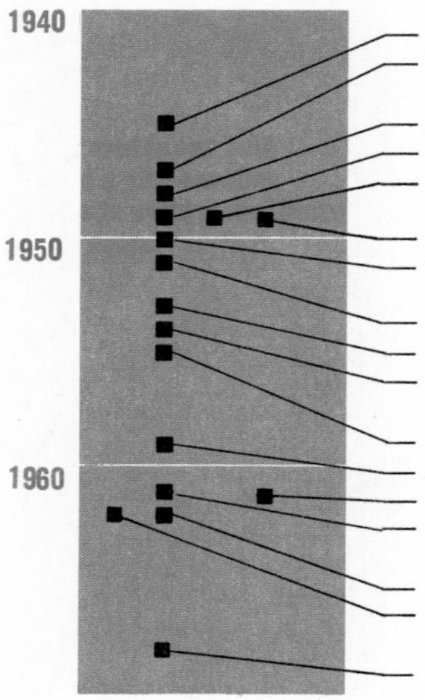

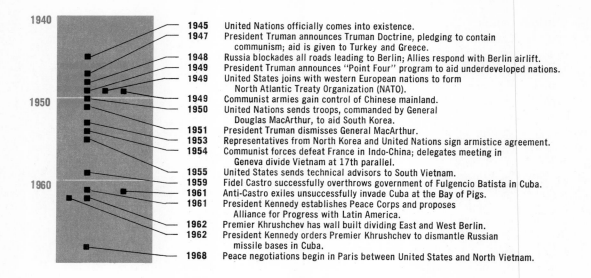

1945 United Nations officially comes into existence.
1947 President Truman announces Truman Doctrine, pledging to contain communism; aid is given to Turkey and Greece.
1948 Russia blockades all roads leading to Berlin; Allies respond with Berlin airlift.
1949 President Truman announces "Point Four" program to aid underdeveloped nations.
1949 United States joins with western European nations to form North Atlantic Treaty Organization (NATO).
1949 Communist armies gain control of Chinese mainland.
1950 United Nations sends troops, commanded by General Douglas MacArthur, to aid South Korea.
1951 President Truman dismisses General MacArthur.
1953 Representatives from North Korea and United Nations sign armistice agreement.
1954 Communist forces defeat France in Indo-China; delegates meeting in Geneva divide Vietnam at 17th parallel.
1955 United States sends technical advisors to South Vietnam.
1959 Fidel Castro successfully overthrows government of Fulgencio Batista in Cuba.
1961 Anti-Castro exiles unsuccessfully invade Cuba at the Bay of Pigs.
1961 President Kennedy establishes Peace Corps and proposes Alliance for Progress with Latin America.
1962 Premier Khrushchev has wall built dividing East and West Berlin.
1962 President Kennedy orders Premier Khrushchev to dismantle Russian missile bases in Cuba.
1968 Peace negotiations begin in Paris between United States and North Vietnam.

105 Foreign Aid and the Containment of Communism

The word **containment** first appeared in an article published anonymously in **Foreign Affairs** magazine. The author, later identified as George Kennan, a foreign service officer, recommended stopping the further spread of communism by stifling minor incidents before they broke into full-scale war.

In June 1946, United States Representative Bernard Baruch, proposed at the first meeting of the United Nations Atomic Energy Commission, that an international agency be set up to control the use of atomic energy. The United States insisted that the Big Five on the Security Council give up their veto power on atomic matters. Andrei Gromyko, the Soviet representative, rejected broad international control and substituted counterproposals unacceptable to the United States.

President Roosevelt had based his hope for world peace after the war on the continued cooperation of the United States and the Soviet Union. His optimism suited the mood of the American people, who were weary of the sacrifices and regimentation of war. During 1945 and 1946, Congress severely cut back the strength of the armed forces and refused to back universal military training.

Truman and his Secretary of State, James Byrnes, recognized that a cleavage was already developing between the Soviet Union and Western countries. The Soviets seemed intent upon consolidating political power over every inch of territory in eastern Europe through which their armies had marched while pursuing the Germans. While they denounced the people of the West as "warmongers," the Soviets refused to cooperate in attempts to work out peace treaties for Germany and Austria or to consider an American proposal for atomic controls. In March 1946, Stalin announced that war was "inevitable" between the capitalist and communist nations. Then in 1949, the Communists gained control of China. How would the United States act against the threat of communist power?

The answer came in Greece, where since the end of the war the royalist government had been harassed by rebel forces supported by the neighboring communist states of Albania, Bulgaria, and Yugoslavia. Since 1946, Great Britain had provided military aid to the Greek government, but when the fighting developed into civil war, Britain notified the United States of its inability to continue assistance. President Truman outlined the United States policy in Greece.

On March 12, 1947, President Truman asked Congress to appropriate $400 million for economic and military aid to both Greece and Turkey in order to check the spread of communism in northeastern Mediterranean.

Meanwhile, western European countries were in almost as critical a situation as Greece. Most of the great European manufacturing centers had been destroyed; agricultural fields had been devastated; and the entire financial structure of most Allied nations had been wrecked. Moreover, Communist parties in western European countries, particularly in France and Italy, gained supporters rapidly. How would the United States respond to these difficulties? George C. Marshall, Truman's new Secretary of State, announced the government's policy in a speech given on June 5, 1947.

The Truman Doctrine and the Marshall Plan, as the policy for Greece and for western Europe were known, became the cornerstones of American foreign policy in the immediate postwar period. As you read these policy statements, keep these questions in mind:

The Marshall Plan offered aid to any European nation, including the Soviet Union and its satellite countries in eastern Europe. The Soviet government denounced the plan as "Yankee imperialism" and refused to cooperate.

1. Why did Truman think the communists had been able to threaten the Greek government?
2. What was Truman's basic policy?
3. What did Secretary Marshall want the United States to do with respect to the devastation in western Europe?
4. Why did Truman and Marshall think that their plans were in the self-interest of the United States? Do you agree? Should a nation base its foreign policy on its own self-interest or should it try unselfishly to help others?

The Truman Doctrine

Portions of President Truman's address to Congress in which he outlined the Truman Doctrine follow.

Congressional Record, 80th Congress, 1st Session (March 12, 1947), pp. 1980 ff.

I am fully aware of the broad implications involved if the United States extends assistance to Greece and Turkey, and I shall discuss these implications with you at this time.

One of the primary objectives of the foreign policy of the United States is the creation of conditions in which we and other nations will be able to work out a way of life free from coercion [force or the threat of force]. This was a fundamental issue in the war with Germany and Japan. Our victory was won over countries which sought to impose their will, and way of life, on other nations.

To insure the peaceful development of nations, free from coercion, the United States has taken a leading part in establishing the United Nations. The United Nations is designed to make possible lasting freedom and independence for all its members. We shall not realize our objectives, however, unless we are willing to help free people to maintain their free institutions and their national integrity against aggressive movements that seek to impose upon them totalitarian regimes. This is no more than a frank recognition that totalitarian regimes imposed on free peoples, by direct or indirect aggression, undermine the foundations of international peace and hence the security of the United States.

The peoples of a number of countries of the world have recently had totalitarian regimes forced upon them against their will. The government of the United States has made frequent protests against coercion and intimidation, in violation of the Yalta agreement, in Poland, Romania and Bulgaria. I must also state that in a number of other countries there have been similar developments.

By the spring of 1947, Russia controlled Finland, Poland, Hungary, Czechoslovakia, Yugoslavia, Romania, Bulgaria, and parts of Germany and Austria. At Yalta, Stalin had agreed to allow elections in those countries and to support democratically elected governments there.

At the present moment in world history nearly every nation must choose between alternative ways of life. The choice is too often not a free one.

One way of life is based upon the will of the majority, and is distinguished by free institutions, representative government, free elections, guarantees of individual liberty, freedom of speech and religion, and freedom from political oppression.

The second way of life is based upon the will of a minority forcibly imposed upon the majority. It relies upon terror and oppression, a controlled press and radio, fixed elections and the suppression of personal freedoms.

I believe that it must be the policy of the United States to support peoples who are resisting attempted subjugation by armed minorities or by outside pressures. . . . I believe that our help should be primarily through economic and financial aid, which is essential to economic stability and orderly political processes.

The world is not static [motionless] and the status quo [present situation] is not sacred. But we cannot allow changes in the status quo in violation of the charter of the United Nations by such methods as coercion, or by such subterfuges [deceptions] as political infiltration. In helping free and independent nations to maintain their freedom, the United States will be giving effect to the principles of the charter of the United Nations.

It is necessary only to glance at a map to realize that the survival and integrity of the Greek nation are of grave importance in a much wider situation. If Greece should fall under the control of an armed minority, the effect upon its neighbor, Turkey, would be immediate and serious. Confusion and disorder might well spread throughout the entire Middle East. . . .

It would be an unspeakable tragedy if these countries, which have struggled so long against overwhelming odds, should lose that victory for which they sacrificed so much. Collapse of free institutions and loss of independence would be disastrous not only for them but for the world. Discouragement and possibly failure would quickly be the lot of neighboring peoples striving to maintain their freedom and independence. . . .

The seeds of totalitarian regimes are nurtured by misery and want. They spread and grow in the evil soil of poverty and strife. They reach their full growth when the hope of a people for a better life has died. We must keep that hope alive.

The free peoples of the world look to us for support in maintaining their freedoms. If we falter in our leadership, we may endanger the peace of the world—and we shall surely endanger the welfare of our own nation. Great responsibilities have been placed upon us by the swift movement of events. I am confident that the Congress will face these responsibilities squarely.

The Marshall Plan

Secretary of State George C. Marshall gave a speech at Harvard in which he outlined a plan for European recovery.

Congressional Record, 80th Congress, 1st Session (June 5, 1947), Appendix, pp. 3248 ff.

. . . [I]t has become obvious during recent months that this visible destruction [of Europe] was probably less serious than the dislocation of the entire fabric of [the] European economy. For the past 10 years conditions have been highly abnormal. The feverish preparation for war and the more feverish maintenance of the war effort engulfed all aspects of national economies. Machinery has fallen into disrepair or is entirely obsolete [outdated]. Under the arbitrary and destructive Nazi rule, virtually every possible enterprise was geared into the German war machine. . . .

At the present time the town and city industries are not producing adequate goods to exchange with the food-producing farmer. Raw materials and fuel are in short supply. Machinery is lacking or worn out. The farmer or the peasant cannot find the goods for sale which he desires to purchase. So the sale of his farm produce for money which he cannot use seems to him an unprofitable transaction. He, therefore, has withdrawn many fields from crop cultivation and is using them for grazing. He feeds more grain to stock and finds for himself and his family an ample supply of food, however short he may be on clothing and the other ordinary gadgets of civilization. Meanwhile people in the cities are short of food and fuel. So the governments are forced to use their foreign money and credits to procure these necessities abroad. This process exhausts funds which are urgently needed for reconstruction. . . .

The truth of the matter is that Europe's requirements for the next 3 or 4 years of foreign food and other essential products—principally from America—are so much greater than her present ability to pay that she must have substantial additional help, or face economic, social, and political deterioration of a very grave character.

The remedy lies in breaking the vicious circle and restoring the confidence of the European people in the economic future of their own countries and of Europe as a whole. The manufacturer and the farmer throughout wide areas must be able and willing to exchange their products for currencies the continuing value of which is not open to question.

Aside from the demoralizing effect on the world at large and the possibilities of disturbances arising as a result of the desperation of the people concerned, the consequences to the economy of the United States should be apparent to all. It is logical that the United States should do whatever it is able to do to assist in the return of normal economic health in the world, without which there can be no political stability and no assured peace. Our policy is directed not against any country or doctrine but against hunger, poverty, desperation and chaos. Its purpose should be the revival of a working economy in the world so as to permit the emergence of political and social conditions in which free institutions can exist. Such assistance, I am convinced, must not be on a piecemeal basis as various crises develop. Any assistance that this Government may render in the future should provide a cure rather than a mere palliative [something to cover up the symptoms]. Any government that is willing to assist in the task of recovery will find full cooperation, I am sure, on the part of the United States Government. Any government which maneuvers to block the recovery of other countries cannot expect help from us. Furthermore, governments, political parties, or groups which seek to perpetuate human misery in order to profit therefrom politically or otherwise will encounter the opposition of the United States.

. . . It would be neither fitting nor efficacious [effective] for this Government to undertake to draw up unilaterally a program designed to place Europe on its feet economically. This is the business of the Europeans. The initiative, I think, must come from Europe. The role of this country should consist of friendly aid in the drafting of a European program and of later support of such a program so far as it may be practical for us to do so. The program should be a joint one, agreed to by a number, if not all European nations.

An essential part of any successful action on the part of the United States is an understanding on the part of the people of America of the character of the problem and the remedies to be applied. Political passion and prejudice should have no part. With foresight, and a willingness on the part of our people to face up to the vast responsibility which history has clearly placed upon our country, the difficulties I have outlined can and will be overcome.

106 The United States and the Emerging Nations of the World

In 1945, there were seventy-three independent nations in the world; by 1968, the number of independent nations had grown to one hundred thirty-six. The introduction of sixty-three new nations into the world community within a single generation bears evidence of the revolutionary character of the postwar world.

These emerging nations posed new challenges for American foreign policy. Most of the new nations were located in Asia or Africa, parts of the world generally unfamiliar to most Americans. Almost all the new nations gained independence after a long period of colonial rule by western European nations. Naturally they guarded their independence jealously and looked suspiciously upon their former masters in the West with whom the United States had close cultural, economic, and diplomatic ties. The citizens of the emerging nations often associated democracy and capitalism with imperialism.

The new nations were "underdeveloped" in terms of Western science and technology. Their farmers and artisans followed agricultural and manufacturing practices that their ancestors had used hundreds of years ago. Facilities for public health and public education hardly existed, and the degree of poverty and social and economic inequality was greater than in Europe and North America.

Since World War II, the United States, the Soviet Union, and Communist China have competed with each other to gain the friendship and support of the new, underdeveloped nations, many of which prefer to remain uncommitted, or neutral, in the Cold War. Each of the major world powers promised that its political, economic, and social system held the key to rapid development. They have waged their competition with economic, military, and diplomatic support for the emerging nations, and have turned two newly independent nations, Korea and Vietnam, into battlefields.

Since the end of the war, Americans have confronted no problem more difficult than determining the policy their nation should follow in its relations with the new nations. Reading 106 contains the suggestions of one foreign policy expert and the policy President Truman developed in 1949. As you read, consider these questions:

1. What did Miss Dean believe was the basic difference between the West and the non-West? Why did she caution Americans about preaching the advantages of political democracy and private enterprise to non-Western peoples?
2. According to her, what advantages did the Soviet Union and China have in competing for the friendship of the new nations?

3. How did President Truman want the United States to deal with underdeveloped nations? What practical steps could be taken to put his policy into effect?
4. What similarities and differences do you find between the Marshall Plan and the Point Four Policy?

The West and the Non-West

Vera Micheles Dean is an authority on Russian affairs who has had extensive experience as editor of the Foreign Policy Bulletin *and as research director of the Foreign Policy Association. In 1957, she published* The Nature of the Non-Western World.

Vera Micheles Dean, **The Nature of the Non-Western World.** New York: The New American Library, Inc., 1957, pp. 17, 18, 20, 21, 22, 23, 24, 25 **passim.**

Feudal society means the political, social, and economic relationships of the Middle Ages based on a personal loyalty of men to other men either below or above them in the political system. Manorialism refers to the medieval economic system in which lords owned manors which were worked by serfs.

Rapid industrialization began in Great Britain during the late eighteenth century.

Anyone who has even glanced at elementary histories of western Europe and the United States must realize it was not magic, but centuries of travail [toil] and sacrifice, marked by a series of bloody wars and revolutions, that saw the peoples of the Atlantic community gradually move from the feudal society and manorial economy of the Middle Ages to industrialization, universal suffrage, separation of church and state (in the United States and France), scientific invention, enlightened social legislation, and the continuing expansion of intellectual inquiry.

But because by the clock and the calendar we are all living approximately at the same time around the globe, it is easy to assume that we are also all living in the same century. . . . The harsh truth is that today—and this has been true since the beginning of industrialization—the inhabitants of the globe live in widely differing stages of development. . . . It is only in recent years that towns have begun to grow on a considerable scale in non-Western areas. . . .

[I]n the West, the growth of towns brought with it the rise of the middle class of merchants, the bankers, and professional people. . . . As the middle class acquired position and influence, it encouraged creative ideas. From its ranks sprang men who were determined to destroy the restrictions of feudalism, and to take authority out of the hands of kings, aristocrats, and ecclesiastics [clergymen]. This they accomplished through revolutions in England and France, which cleared the way for the rise of modern democracy.

So far the middle class is still weak in most of the non-Western areas. It has not yet acquired the influence which would enable it to destroy the remnants of old regimes. The result is that when revolutions occur, they are often led either by military men or by those who come from the ranks of the workers or make their fortunes by appealing to the workers over the heads of the aristocrats and the middle class. Because of the lack or meagerness of the middle class, which in the Western world served to cushion political and social shocks, changes in non-Western areas are more fierce, and involve prolonged struggles for power, often marked by great cruelty and efforts to stamp out opposing ideas.

It is not an accident that Russia has been more closely associated in this century with the peoples east of the Oder than with those of the West. Russia, too, for the most part, belongs historically to that sector of the world which has had only indirect, and often unhappy, contacts with the "advanced" nations. . . .

The Oder River flows through central Europe and forms the boundary between Germany and Poland.

For it is not communism as an ideology, or the Russian system established by Stalin and his associates, that impressed people in Asia, Africa, Latin America, and the Middle East. It was, instead, the fact, made manifest [evident] every day, that a nation which had lagged a hundred or more years behind the West has succeeded, haltingly and at great sacrifice of men and materials, in fulfilling Stalin's injunction that the U.S.S.R. must "catch up with" and, he added, overtake the "capitalist" world. . . .

In short, peoples who are still living all the way along the arduous [difficult] route from the age of bronze weapons to the nineteenth century wonder whether Russia's experience, so close in time to their own, may not offer them a short cut for the jump they feel they must make from their own age into the nuclear age. And if Communist China should succeed in effecting this historic transition within a relatively short period of time, its experience will have an even greater impact on the non-Western world.

Unlike Russia, which at least has geographic links with Europe and a white population that has been exposed over the centuries, however remotely, to Western ideas, China is non-Western. Other peoples outside the Atlantic orbit will say to themselves, "What the Chinese can do, we can do," and some may even say, as India does, "We can do it better, with no resort to force and violence."

Given the far-reaching impression created by Russia and, more recently, China, we should carefully weigh the value of preaching today to non-Western peoples the advantages of political democracy and private enterprise. Desirable as these assets may seem to them, and particularly to their small elites who have studied and lived in the West, our concepts and practices simply do not yet correspond to their actual experience and therefore must remain alien to them, at least until such time as they, in turn, achieve the conditions which produced Western democratic institutions and a competitive economy.

Universal suffrage would have sounded ludicrous to the feudal barons and, later, the absolute monarchs of western Europe. Louis XIV, "L'état, c'est moi," [I am the state] is much closer to the current

Louis XIV was the divine-right monarch who ruled France from 1643 to 1715. All the powers of the state were consolidated in him, and he alone made the decisions that determined the destiny of France. He believed himself to be God's agent on earth, and to challenge him was to challenge God.

experience of Russia and China, of Egypt and Japan, than he is to Churchill or Eisenhower. . . .

If the barrier between Western and non-Western peoples is to be broken down, both sides must perform an act of imagination. Instead of urging the neolithic [new stone age] man of Central Africa, or the fanatically religious nomad of Arab lands, or the pre-industrial Chinese or Latin-American to become like ourselves, Westerners must strive to see the contemporary world through his eyes.

Instead of pressing on him a tractor which may erode his soil already impoverished by centuries of hard use and which cannot be serviced for lack of parts and skilled mechanics, let us look at his plow, no matter how ancient, and discover whether it can be improved by slight alterations.

Instead of expecting him to be thoroughly versed in the ideas of Thomas Jefferson or Abraham Lincoln—a happy state not yet achieved by every literate American—let us inquire who among his people has uttered thoughts which he has found a source of inspiration over the ages.

We shall thereby strengthen the roots of his past, instead of tearing them out. What is more, we shall also enrich our own, hitherto parochial [narrow, limited], outlook, which until recently tended to assume that all wisdom flowed from the West. . . .

For Westerners this should be reassuring. For we need not spend astronomical sums of dollars over incalculable eons [ages] of time to remake every people in our own image. What we need to do is to share our technical knowledge, our skills, and our managerial capacity in such a way as to ease the transition of widely diverse peoples who have their own ideas of how they want to live, from whatever century they may find themselves in today into our own. . . .

Truman's "Point Four Program"

In his inaugural address delivered on January 20, 1949, President Truman proposed a Four Point Foreign Policy. He pledged continued support for the United Nations and the European Recovery Program, and announced common defense arrangements planned for the nations of the North Atlantic and the Western Hemisphere. His fourth point, which follows, provided America's answer to the challenges of the underdeveloped areas of the world.

The Marshall Plan was officially known as the European Recovery Program.

We must embark on a bold new program for making the benefits of our scientific advances and industrial progress available for the improvement and growth of underdeveloped areas.

Congressional Record, 81st Congress, 1st Session,

More than half the people of the world are living in conditions approaching misery. Their food is inadequate. They are victims of disease. Their economic life is primitive and stagnant. Their poverty is a handicap and a threat both to them and prosperous areas.

For the first time in history, humanity possesses the knowledge and the skill to relieve the suffering of these people.

The United States is pre-eminent among nations in the development of industrial and scientific techniques. The material resources which we can afford to use for the assistance of other peoples are limited. But our imponderable resources in technical knowledge are constantly growing and are inexhaustible.

I believe that we should make available to peace-loving peoples the benefits of our store of technical knowledge in order to help them realize their aspirations for a better life. And, in cooperation with other nations, we should foster capital investment in areas needing development.

Our aim should be to help the free peoples of the world, through their own efforts, to produce more food, more clothing, more materials for housing, and more mechanical power to lighten their burdens.

We invite other countries to pool their technological resources in this undertaking. Their contributions will be warmly welcomed. This should be a cooperative enterprise in which all nations work together through the United Nations and its specialized agencies wherever practicable. It must be a worldwide effort for the achievement of peace, plenty, and freedom.

With the cooperation of business, private capital, agriculture, and labor in this country, this program can greatly increase the industrial activity in other nations and can raise substantially their standards of living.

Such new economic developments must be devised and controlled to benefit the peoples of the areas in which they are established. Guarantees to the investor must be balanced by guarantees in the interest of the people whose resources and whose labor go into these developments.

The old imperialism—exploitation for foreign profit—has no place in our plans. What we envisage is a program of development based on the concepts of democratic fair-dealing.

All countries, including our own, will greatly benefit from a constructive program for the better use of the world's human and natural resources. Experience shows that our commerce with other countries expands as they progress industrially and economically.

Greater production is the key to prosperity and peace. And the key to greater production is a wider and more vigorous application of modern scientific and technical knowledge.

Only by helping the least fortunate of its members to help themselves can the human family achieve the decent, satisfying life that is the right of all people.

Democracy alone can supply the vitalizing force to stir the peoples of the world into triumphant action, not only against their human oppressors, but also against their ancient enemies—hunger, misery, and despair. . . .

107 The Crisis in Vietnam

America's attempt to contain communism involved the United States in two costly wars in emerging nations—the Korean War in the early 1950's and the Vietnamese War in the 1960's.

After Japan's defeat, France reorganized the colony of Indo-China, setting up three governments, Laos, Cambodia, and Vietnam, each headed by pro-French leaders. Ho Chi Minh, a communist leader in Vietnam, who wanted complete independence for the Vietnamese people, challenged French authority immediately. Guerrilla warfare broke out in which Communist China and the U.S.S.R. supported Ho Chi Minh, while America supported France.

In 1954, the French faced military defeat in Vietnam and called upon the United States government for military assistance. The United States took no action because President Eisenhower, the Congress, and most of the American people did not want to participate in another Asian war. Consequently, France, Great Britain, China, and the Soviet Union met at Geneva, Switzerland, and signed a peace agreement which divided North and South Vietnam at the 17th parallel. Ho Chi Minh controlled the North and a pro-Western government under Ngo Dinh Diem was set up in the South. France then withdrew from Vietnam. The United States did not participate in the Geneva Agreement but agreed to its terms.

The Geneva Agreement divided Vietnam until free elections scheduled for two years later determined its political future. These elections never took place.

The American government attempted to strengthen South Vietnam with military and economic aid. In 1955, the United States sent technical specialists, including United States Army officers and enlisted men, to South Vietnam. In 1962, the United States increased its aid as Viet-Cong guerrillas, apparently supported by the North Vietnamese, took over large sections of the South Vietnamese countryside. In February 1965, President Johnson ordered American air strikes against North Vietnamese military targets, and by spring of that year, American ground troops were fighting communist guerrillas. By 1968, over a half million American servicemen were in Vietnam and over 17,000 had died there. Preliminary peace negotiations between North Vietnam and the United States began in the spring of 1968, but the savage war continued.

The Vietminh was a coalition group composed of Communists and nationalists, who fought against the French and were led by Ho Chi Minh. The Communist faction later became the Viet-Cong.

The Vietnamese War deeply divided the American public as debate raged in and out of Congress and as pro- and anti-war demonstrations spread across the United States. Central to the arguments was the question of precisely what was the central issue at stake in the war. Reading 107, taken from the speeches of two American Senators and from the captured diary of a Viet-Cong soldier, investigates that question. As you read, try to answer these questions:

1. How did Senator Dodd and Senator Fulbright differ on America's goals in Vietnam?
2. What different assumptions did the senators make about the nature of the war?
3. Did Do Luc's testimony support the views of Dodd? of Fulbright? of both men?
4. Do you think that the United States should have fought in Vietnam? Why or why not?

Senator Dodd on the Vietnamese War

The debate on America's role in the Vietnamese War has continued unabated since American troops were first committed to the fighting in 1965. Senator Thomas J. Dodd, Democrat from Connecticut, presented one side of the argument in a Senate speech given February 23, 1965.

Speech in U.S. Senate, February 23, 1965.

I disagree strongly with my colleagues who have spoken up to urge negotiations.

But if there is any way in which my voice could reach to Peiping [capital of Communist China] and to Moscow, I would warn the Communist leaders that they should not construe the debate that is now taking place in this Chamber as a sign of weakness; it is, on the contrary, a testimony to our strength.

Nor should they believe that those who speak up in favor of negotiations are the forerunners of a larger host of Americans who are prepared to accept surrender. Because there is no one here who believes in surrender or believes in capitulation [giving in]. . . .

I have been amazed by a number of letters I have received asking the question, "Why are we in Viet-Nam?" or "What is our policy in Viet-Nam?" I have been even more amazed to have the same questions put to me by sophisticated members of the press.

To me the reasons for our presence in Viet-Nam are so crystal clear that I find it difficult to comprehend the confusion which now appears to exist on this subject.

We are in Viet-Nam because our own security and the security of the entire free world demands that a firm line be drawn against the further advance of Communist imperialism—in Asia, in Africa, in Latin America, and in Europe.

We are in Viet-Nam because it is our national interest to assist every nation, large and small, which is seeking to defend itself against Communist subversion, infiltration, and aggression. There is nothing new about this policy; it is a policy, in fact, to which every administration has adhered since the proclamation of the Truman Doctrine.

Ngo Dinh Diem, the first president of the republic of Vietnam, requested American assistance. In response, the United States sent advisors to Vietnam in 1955 to help to train the army.

We are in Viet-Nam because our assistance was invited by the legitimate government of that country.

We are in Viet-Nam because, as the distinguished majority leader, the Senator from Montana [Mike Mansfield], pointed out in his 1963 report, Chinese Communist hostility to the United States threatens "the whole structure of our own security in the Pacific."

We are in Viet-Nam not merely to help the 14 million South Vietnamese defend themselves against communism, but because what is at stake is the independence and freedom of 240 million people in Southeast Asia and the future of freedom throughout the western Pacific.

These are the reasons why we are in Viet-Nam. There is nothing new about them and nothing very complex. They have never been obscure. They have never been concealed. I cannot, for the life of me, see why people fail to understand them.

Senator Fulbright on the Vietnamese War

Senator William Fulbright, Democrat from Arkansas and Chairman of the Senate Foreign Relations Committee since 1959 has frequently urged changes in American foreign policy. He was an outspoken critic of the Vietnamese War. Portions of one of his Senate speeches follows.

Speech in U.S. Senate, June 15, 1965.

I wish to say a few words about Viet-Nam.

It is clear to all reasonable Americans that a complete military victory in Viet-Nam, though theoretically attainable, can in fact be attained only at a cost far exceeding the requirements of our interest and our honor. It is equally clear that the unconditional withdrawal of American support from South Viet-Nam would have disastrous consequences, including but by no means confined to the victory of the Viet-Cong in South Viet-Nam. Our policy therefore has been—and should remain—one of determination to end the war at the earliest possible time by a negotiated settlement involving major concessions by both sides.

I am opposed to an unconditional American withdrawal from South Viet-Nam because such action would betray our obligation to people we have promised to defend, because it would weaken or destroy the credibility [belief in the truth] of American guarantees to other countries, and because such a withdrawal would encourage the view in Peiping and elsewhere that guerrilla wars supported from outside are a relatively safe and inexpensive way of expanding Communist power.

I am no less opposed to further escalation [stepping up] of the war, because the bombing thus far of North Viet-Nam has failed to weaken the military capacity of the Viet-Cong in any visible way; because escalation would invite the intervention—or infiltration—on a large scale of great numbers of North Vietnamese troops; because this in turn would probably draw the United States into a bloody and protracted [lengthy] jungle war in which the strategic advantages would be with the other side; and, finally, because the only available alternative to such a land war would then be the further expansion of the air war to such an extent as to invite either massive Chinese military intervention in many vulnerable areas in Southeast Asia or general nuclear war. . . .

Looking beyond a possible settlement of the Vietnamese war, it may be that the major lesson of this tragic conflict will be a new appreciation of the power of nationalism in Southeast Asia and, indeed, in all of the world's emerging nations. Generally, American foreign policy in Asia, in Africa, and in Latin America has been successful and constructive insofar as American aims have coincided with the national aims of the peoples concerned. The tragedy of Viet-Nam is that for many reasons, including the intransigence [refusal to compromise] of a colonial power [France] and the initial failure of the United States to appreciate the consequences of that intransigence, the nationalist movement became associated with and largely subordinate to the Communist movement.

In the postwar era it has been demonstrated repeatedly that nationalism is a stronger force than communism and that the association of the two, which has created so many difficulties for the United States, is neither inevitable nor natural. In the past it has come about when, for one reason or another, the West has set itself in opposition to the national aspirations of the emerging peoples. It is to be hoped that we will not do so again; it is to be hoped that in the future the United States will leave no country in doubt as to its friendship and support for legitimate national aspirations. If we do this, I do not think that we will soon find ourselves in another conflict like the one in Viet-Nam.

A Viet-Cong Soldier's Reasons for Fighting

Beginning with the entry in his diary for August 14, 1960, Do Luc, a Viet-Cong soldier reviews his life and explains his reasons for fighting.

Department of State Publication 7308

I answered the call of the Party when I was very young, and what did I do for the people of my village? I devoted myself to the people. I took part in propaganda and aroused the people to carry out the policy of the Party and the Government and helped organize village defense and fighting forces. On March 25, 1954, I began my fighting career and I contributed my part in fighting the French Expeditionary Force. With the army of Interzone 5, I saw the end of the war on July 20, 1954, and then on April 26, 1955, I left my native place and all the ties with my family and friends to go north as a victorious fighter. Since that day, my spirit has matured together with that of the regular army. We have built up a beautiful and prosperous and strong North; the construction sites and factories spring up quickly everywhere under a bright sky and under the superior socialist regime. Close to me there was a unique source of consolation in my life. My life was beautiful, my happiness immeasureable. Enough to eat; warm clothing in my daily life; earning a living was fairly easy; often I enjoyed songs and dances which deal with the healthy life of all the people in the North and with the maturity of the Army.

Then, one morning, while my life was touched with a fresh, joyous and peaceful atmosphere, in harmony with the reconstruction program in the North, while my life was a normal one and I was happy with my only love . . .

Suddenly, on December 15, 1960, . . .

I answered the needs of the international solidarity of the Vietnamese-Laotian proletariat. I had to leave my beloved Fatherland and my sweet life and go to help our friends with a spirit of unselfishness, of class solidarity, of love for my Fatherland, and the spirit of the international proletarian revolution, in order to annihilate the reactionary clique of Pumi Buon Um [Phoumi-Buon Oum] so that mankind and the two countries, Viet-Nam and Laos, could achieve prosperity and happiness.

In 1962, a fourteen-nation conference divided Laos into three political factions—Communist, pro-Western, and neutral. Prince Phoumi-Buon Oum became head of the right-wing pro-Western faction of the government.

Thus, I succeeded in meeting the needs of a friendly country.

Our friends' war has stopped and the guns are silent. On the call of the Party, I returned to my beloved Fatherland. My life returned to normal. I enjoyed again the peaceful atmosphere and my happiness. I continued training daily for the defense of the territory of the North and for the continuation of the liberation of the South. But

I was back with my only love. Hurrah! How happy and how sweet. But my life could not continue that way!

For the third time my life turned to war again. For the liberation of our compatriots in the South, a situation of boiling oil and burning fire is necessary! A situation in which husband is separated from wife, father from son, brother from brother is necessary. I joined the ranks of the liberation army in answer to the call of the front for liberation of the South.

Now my life is full of hardship—not enough rice to eat nor enough salt to give a taste to my tongue, not enough clothing to keep myself warm! But in my heart I keep loyal to the Party and to the people. I am proud and happy.

I am writing down this story for my sons and my grandsons of the future to know of my life and activities during the revolution when the best medicine available was the root of the wild banana tree and the best bandage was the leaf of rau lui, when there was no salt to give a taste to our meals, when there was no such food as meat or fish like we enjoy in a time of peace and happiness such as I have known and left behind. But that day will not take long to return to my life.

Rau lui is a plant growing in Southeast Asia.

108 American Involvement in a Divided World

HISTORICAL ESSAY

Since 1945, the government of the United States has become increasingly involved politically, economically, and militarily with other nations throughout the world. Some nations, such as Great Britain and France, are old friends; others, such as Pakistan and South Vietnam, are new nations which did not exist before World War II. In Europe, American foreign policy has been relatively successful; in non-Western countries and in Latin America, it has been less successful. Despite an enormous expenditure of money, lives, and natural resources, Americans continue to live in an unstable world that is neither at war nor at peace.

A high point in Soviet-American cooperation came on June 26, 1945, when Vyacheslav Molotov, the Russian Foreign Minister, signed the charter for the United Nations in San Francisco. Agreement had been reached on an international organization divided into two major parts: a General Assembly and a Security Council.

In 1944, delegates from the United States, Britain, China, and the Soviet Union met at Dumbarton Oaks in Washington, D.C., to prepare a plan for a postwar peace organization. At Yalta, the Big Three settled certain differences concerning the United Nations and agreed to call a conference in San Francisco to draw up a charter for the new organization.

The U.S.S.R. has three votes in the General Assembly. Two of the Soviet Union's sixteen republics, the Ukrainian and Byelorussian, were admitted to the United Nations as independent nations. Originally, the Soviets had demanded admission and a vote for each of the sixteen republics.

Nationalist China has a permanent seat in the Security Council because it was the legitimate government of China in 1945. Attempts have been made each year to admit Communist China to the United Nations.

Although Yugoslavia had a Communist government after the war, Marshal Tito, the country's leader, maintained its independence from the U.S.S.R. The American government gave assistance to Yugoslavia through trade agreements and financial aid. Many Americans criticized this aid program.

All member nations had one vote in the Assembly, which discussed issues and recommended action to settle disputes to the Security Council. The Security Council consisted of five permanent members, the United States, the Soviet Union, Great Britain, France, and China and six other nations elected for two-year terms. The United Nations Charter authorized the Council to apply diplomatic, economic, or military sanctions against nations that threatened world peace. The charter stipulated, however, that the Council could not take any action without the approval of all five permanent members. Therefore, any of the five could veto a proposed United Nations action.

Divisions and Alliances in Europe

The years immediately following World War II showed clearly that the nations of the world were united in name only. The main obstacle to peace was Stalin's apparent determination to turn all his wartime territorial gains into permanent political gains. The Soviet Union emerged from the war in military possession of Poland, the eastern half of Germany, all the Balkan states (Hungary, Romania, Bulgaria, Yugoslavia, Albania), and the Baltic states (Latvia, Lithuania, Estonia). By 1948, the Soviet Union had incorporated the Baltic states into its own government and had installed Moscow-dominated communist governments in East Germany, Poland, Czechoslovakia, and the Balkan countries.

In March 1946, Winston Churchill, the British prime minister, visited the United States. In a famous speech at Clayton, Missouri, he told his listeners that Stalin had lowered an "Iron Curtain" over Europe and had split the continent in half. Churchill did not believe that Stalin wanted war, but he warned the American people that Stalin respected only force and urged them to be strong.

Churchill's speech met a mixed reception. Many Americans still hoped that the Soviet Union would cooperate in peace as it had in war. The United States government, however, took Churchill's warning seriously. In March 1947, President Truman announced that the United States would provide economic and military aid to the legitimate government of Greece which was threatened by communist guerrillas. The United States later expanded this so-called Truman Doctrine by committing itself to support any nation threatened by outside military pressure or armed aggression. Later in 1947, Secretary of State Marshall announced the Marshall Plan designed to buttress the free nations of Europe through economic aid. The United States government made these commitments, which became known collectively as the "containment policy," in order to prevent the Soviet Union and later Communist China from extending their power over weaker neighbors.

The Soviet Union denounced the Marshall Plan as a capitalist plot, but the noncommunist countries in Europe subscribed to it eagerly. Congress appropriated $13 billion for the program, which brought nations such as Britain, France, Belgium, and the Netherlands closer together politically. These nations also realized that their economic recovery depended to a considerable extent upon a free and economically stable Germany.

Germany was still split between the Allied zones in the west and the Soviet zone in the east. All Allied attempts to get Soviet agreement on a peace treaty to unify Germany failed, so in 1948 the Western nations announced plans for creating the Republic of West Germany. The Soviets reacted to the success of the Marshall Plan and the proposed autonomy of West Germany by blockading the roads to Berlin in June 1948. When the Soviets refused to let Allied convoys into Berlin, the citizens of West Berlin faced starvation. Any Allied attempt to break through the blockade might mean war with the Soviet Union. The Allies solved the crisis by dropping supplies from the air. May 1949, the U.S.S.R. lifted the blockade but Berlin continued to play a potentially explosive role in the Cold War, partly because thousands of refugees from the Soviet zone of the city fled to the Allied zone. In order to halt the flow of refugees, Soviet Premier Nikita Khrushchev had a wall built in 1961 along the line dividing the city.

Berlin is located within the Soviet sector of Germany. All communication and transportation lines from West Germany must go through one hundred miles of Soviet-occupied territory before reaching the city. Before 1949, when East Germany proclaimed itself the German Democratic Republic, the city of Berlin had been jointly occupied by France, Britain, the U.S.S.R., and the United States.

The United States depended upon military power to support its containment policy. In April 1949, it signed—with eleven other nations—a mutual defense pact that set up the North Atlantic Treaty Organization (NATO). The twelve nations agreed to consider an attack on any treaty member "an attack against them all," and they pledged themselves to support treaty members with whatever action might be necessary "including the use of armed force." The United States Senate ratified the North Atlantic Treaty, and Congress passed the Mutual Defense Assistance Act to provide military aid largely to other NATO members. By the late 1940's, the United States had come full circle from isolationism.

Involvement in Asia

The policy of containment based on economic aid and a military alliance succeeded in Europe, for no European nation came under communist control after 1948. In the non-Western world, however, the United States confronted two formidable problems, making peace with Japan and gaining the friendship of the "new" underdeveloped non-Western nations, and ending communist expansion.

President Truman successfully kept the Soviet Union from playing an important role in the occupation of Japan. Under the able command of General MacArthur, American troops ran the country, introduced a series of political and economic reforms which included the break-up of industrial trusts, the organization of parliamentary government, the encouragement of labor unions, and de-emphasis of emperor worship. The old Japanese empire was dissolved, including Japan's claims in China and Korea. Meanwhile, stimulated by American aid, the Japanese economy recovered remarkably. In 1951, the Japanese Peace Treaty was signed, which formally ended American occupation, even though the United States continued to maintain troops in Japan. The United States achieved its goal of building a new democratic Japan, friendly to the United States and free of communist control.

Although American policies succeeded in Japan, they failed hopelessly in China. At the end of the war, China was a divided nation. The nominal head of the government was Chiang Kai-shek, who with the Nationalist party, founded by Sun Yat-sen, had begun to bring political unity to modern China. Mao Tse-tung, leader of the Chinese Communist party, opposed Chiang after the Communists and the Nationalists had split in 1927. In 1945, the Communists controlled most of the northern provinces of China and about one fourth of the total population. The Soviet Union formally recognized the Communists as the real rulers in China and gave them some aid. The United States supported Chiang Kai-shek, but took the position that no Chinese government could succeed unless the Nationalists and the Communists cooperated. In 1946, President Truman sent General Marshall to China to try to bring Chiang and Mao together. Marshall's attempt at mediation failed, and in 1947, a full-scale civil war broke out in China. By 1949, the Communists defeated the Nationalists, and Chiang and his army took refuge on Formosa.

Sun Yat-sen (1866–1925) was a revolutionary leader who founded the Kuomintang or Nationalist party, which overthrew the Manchu Dynasty and established the republic of China in 1912. Thereafter, Sun Yat-sen and his party fought against the local warlords to unify China and establish a stable government based on the economic and political philosophy he described in **Three People's Principles** (democracy, nationalism, and socialism). In 1921, he was elected president of a national government proclaimed at Canton.

The loss of China to the Communists provoked an intense political debate in the United States. President Truman's opponents accused him of betraying Chiang Kai-shek and the free world. Truman and his advisors probably underestimated the strength of the Chinese Communists; their swift success surprised even Stalin who had given them only a modest amount of aid. Moreover, Truman felt that Chiang lacked strong support among the Chinese people and that only massive American military assistance, which the American people would have been unlikely to give, could have sustained him. The unhappy truth seems to be that the Communists identified themselves with a revolutionary movement in China which had widespread popular support and carried them to power.

On August 5, 1949, the State Department issued a White Paper, a collection of documents blaming the Nationalist regime of China and not American foreign policy for the collapse of the Chiang government. This White Paper which depicted the Nationalist government as inept, selfish, and short-sighted, was favorably received by the American public, and denounced by many Republicans.

With a new communist power dominating the Asian continent, how would the United States apply its containment policy in the Far East? The answer came in Korea. Located on a narrow peninsula, close to Japan and bordering on both China and the Soviet Union, Korea had become a Japanese colony early in the twentieth century. After World War II, it was divided into two zones, with Soviet troops occupying the north and American troops occupying the south. The United States tried to refer the question of Korean unity and independence to the United Nations, but the U.S.S.R. refused to allow such action. Finally, North and South Korea set up separate governments, each claiming authority over the whole country. The Soviet Union and China backed North Korea; the United States supported South Korea.

On June 25, 1950, North Korean troops invaded South Korea. The United States immediately took the issue to the U.N. Security Council which the Soviets were boycotting at the time. Without the threat of a Soviet veto, Council members demanded that North Korea withdraw and urged the United Nations to aid the South.

The U.S.S.R. was boycotting the U.N. in protest against the decision not to admit Communist China.

Responding to the United Nations request, President Truman ordered American forces into the conflict under General MacArthur. Fifteen other nations sent troops to Korea, but Americans and South Koreans always made up at least ninety percent of MacArthur's United Nations army. During the first few months of fighting, the North Korean armies almost drove the U.N. forces off the peninsula and into the sea. Then MacArthur executed a brilliant amphibious landing behind the enemy lines at Inchon which turned the tide. The North Korean armies lost their momentum as they retreated.

The original objective of the U.N. military force had been to restore the South Korean border along the 38th parallel. President Truman then consented to MacArthur's request that he be permitted to pursue the North Koreans toward the China border. As the U.N. troops approached China along the Yalu River, President Truman and General MacArthur considered the possibility of direct Chinese intervention in the war. MacArthur assured Truman that Chinese intervention was most unlikely, even though China was threatening to join the war. Then in November 1950, Chinese troops crossed the Yalu River in force and sent MacArthur's troops reeling to the South. MacArthur demanded permission from President Truman to bomb Chinese bases, and suggested that a naval blockade be mounted on the China coast. President Truman rejected MacArthur's proposals fearing that the Soviet Union might join the Chinese and thus create a third World War. When MacArthur objected to this decision publicly, Truman removed him from command. MacArthur returned to a hero's welcome in the United States, and debate over the controversy raged throughout the country. During the Congressional investigation that followed, the Joint Chiefs of Staff supported Truman's decision not to extend the war.

Within the Department of Defense, Congress set up an agency called the Joint Chiefs of Staff in 1949. It consists of the military advisors to the President, the National Security Council, and the Secretary of Defense. The four permanent members are the chairman appointed by the President, and the chiefs of staff for the army, navy, and air force.

United Nations troops finally stabilized the Korean front close to the old North-South Korea border. In June 1951, agreement was reached to negotiate an armistice. The crisis subsided, but sporadic

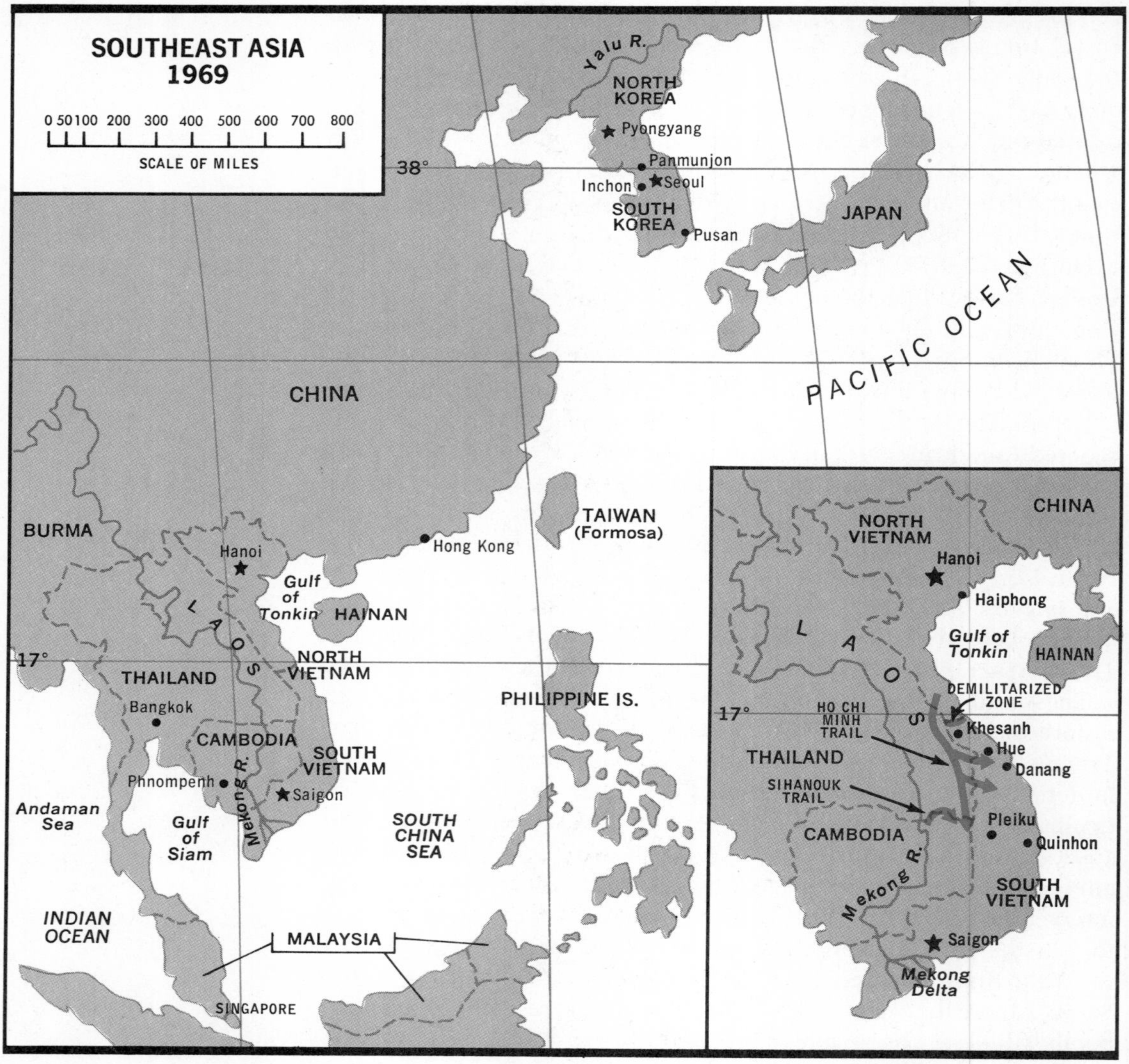

Fighting was fierce during negotiations, particularly the air war between Russian-built MIGS and American Sabre Jets.

fighting continued for two years before the armistice was finally signed in July 1953.

The Korean War was highly unpopular in the United States. Americans were frustrated at having to fight a war they could not "win" in any conventional sense. Yet for the first time in history, an international army had acted to preserve peace. The United States had shown that it would fight to prevent overt aggression in Asia, and an American President had refused to surrender his constitutional powers as Commander-in-Chief of the armed forces to a military officer.

The Korean crisis had no sooner eased before Americans found themselves involved in a similar crisis in Vietnam. Like the Korean War, the Vietnamese War was not popular. The government was criticized by those who complained that the United States was following the same kind of "no-win" policy that it had followed in Korea. These critics argued that instead of limiting itself to the bombing of strategic military targets in North Vietnam, the United States should destroy major cities such as Hanoi. Another group argued that any attempt to escalate the conflict could result in a war with China. These critics also believed that the war was not so much one of aggression from the North as it was a civil war for national independence. They cautioned that the United States should beware of insisting on its own kind of government.

In the late 1960's, Americans continued to fight in Vietnam. Preliminary peace talks began in the spring of 1968, but genuine peace seemed far away. Nobody knew whether "containment" would work.

Relations with Latin America

America's failure to find any final solution for the expansion of communist power in Asia has been matched by its inability to prevent the rise of hostile governments in Latin America. Although the Latin American countries had existed as independent states for long periods of time, they had more in common socially and economically with the "new nations" than with the United States.

In the twentieth century, relationships between the United States and Latin American nations have been both good and bad. The "gunboat diplomacy" of the early part of the century, when the United States interpreted the Monroe Doctrine as giving it the right to interfere in the internal affairs of Latin American nations, damaged American prestige throughout the area. President Franklin Roosevelt's more constructive Good Neighbor policy repaired some of this damage. Immediately after World War II, the United States concentrated on European and Asian problems to the neglect of Latin America. Many South American countries, beset with serious social and economic problems, often blamed the United States for their troubles. Conservatives berated America for not giving more aid to relieve the plight of their people. Radicals accused the United States of supporting corrupt and undemocratic political leaders. Resentment against the United States reached a high point in 1958 when Vice-President Nixon received such a hostile reception on his "good-will" tour of South America that he was forced to cancel his trip and return to the United States.

In 1969, Governor Rockefeller of New York met a similar reception on a "good-will" tour of Latin America for President Nixon.

Recognizing that poverty, inequality, and political disorder are breeding grounds for communism, American leaders sought a Latin American policy that would promote reforms in these countries, gain the friendship of the Latin American people, and at the same time, inhibit the growth of communism. With painful clarity, Cuba illustrated the difficulties of making such a policy work.

In 1959, Fidel Castro led a successful revolution to overthrow the government of Fulgencio Batista, one of the most corrupt and dictatorial regimes in the Western Hemisphere. President Eisenhower quickly granted diplomatic recognition to the Castro government. Castro, however, was violently anti-American. He harangued the United States in long speeches, seized American-owned property without adequate compensation, and openly courted the support of the Soviet Union as he set up a communist state in Cuba.

The Central Intelligence Agency (CIA) was established in 1947 under the National Security Act. Its main functions are to advise on security and to coordinate the many aspects of intelligence gathering, reporting, and evaluation. The CIA has been criticized at times for secretly influencing the affairs of other nations.

The prospect of an unfriendly communist power so close to the United States bewildered and infuriated the American people. Their government tried to meet the threat Castro posed to the hemisphere. On April 17, 1961, a band of anti-Castro exiles trained by the Central Intelligence Agency of the United States invaded Cuba at the Bay of Pigs in an unsuccessful attempt to dislodge Castro. Castro, in turn, established even closer relationships with the Soviet Union. In 1962, American aerial reconnaissance photographs taken over Cuba showed that Soviet technicians were installing intermediate range missile sites. A dangerous encounter between the United States and the Soviet Union followed as President Kennedy demanded that Premier Khrushchev dismantle the bases, and ordered the United States Navy to turn back any Russian ships en route to Cuba with "offensive" weapons. At the same time, he warned that any nuclear attack on the United States from Cuba would result in "a full retaliatory response upon the Soviet Union."

The sites were for ballistic missiles, self-propelled rockets that are aimed before firing and not directed during flight.

The world trembled, apparently at the brink of war, until Khrushchev withdrew his missiles. Communist influence—Chinese as well as Soviet—remained strong in Cuba. To help counteract the spread of "Castroism" to other South American countries, the United States, offered billions of dollars of aid to Latin America in an "Alliance for Progress."

American foreign policy in the postwar period did not always achieve its goals, but it remained reasonably consistent. During President Eisenhower's Administration, when John Foster Dulles was Secretary of State, the United States attempted to extend the containment policy in order to "liberate" the "captive" peoples in Soviet satellites and to counteract Soviet aggression with the threat of massive nuclear retaliation. The modification, however, proved to be without much substance. After the Soviet Union developed the hydrogen bomb in 1953, any massive nuclear attack by either the United States or the Soviet Union would invite retaliation by the other and result only in mutual annihilation. When the United States failed to help the Hungarians during their rebellion against Russia

On October 23, 1956, students and workers in Budapest, Hungary, rioted in the streets against the Soviets. Soviet tanks and jet planes moved in to crush the revolt which was spreading as the Hungarian army joined the rebels. The premier of Hungary asked the United Nations for aid. It passed a resolution condemning the Soviet action and demanded the withdrawal of Soviet troops.

in 1956, "liberation" proved to be no more feasible than massive retaliation. Meanwhile, Eisenhower supported NATO strongly, and he negotiated similar treaty organizations for the Middle East and Southeast Asia, thus following the pattern set by Truman.

Presidents Kennedy and Johnson tried to contain communism and continued to apply the principle of the Marshall Plan through ambitious economic aid programs to nations in Africa, Asia, and South America. One of the most imaginative developments in American policy came in 1961 when President Kennedy established the Peace Corps, an agency through which Americans volunteered to work on community action, education, and health projects in underdeveloped countries. The enthusiastic response of thousands of young Americans to this program testified eloquently to their idealism.

Stalin's death in 1953 shifted the alignment among the communist nations themselves. Although the Cold War continued, Stalin's successors indicated that the Soviet Union might be able to live in "peaceful coexistence" with the West. China refused to accept this change in communist ideology, and a serious rift developed between the two powers with most of the smaller communist nations supporting the Soviet Union. Some American observers believed that the prospect of several varieties of communism vying with each other might lessen the threat of aggression against other nations. Others feared the belligerent recklessness of the Chinese, made more dangerous after the Chinese exploded their first nuclear device in 1964.

In the late 1960's, the American people still tried to puzzle out the road to peace in a world of turmoil, conflict, and revolutionary change—a world in which their nation was fully involved but which it could not control.

The ANZUS pact signed in 1951 is a mutual defense treaty between the United States, Australia, and New Zealand. The Southeast Asia Collective Defense and Economic Treaty (SEATO) was signed in 1954 by the United States, Great Britain, France, Australia, New Zealand, Pakistan, Thailand, and the Philippines. The members pledged themselves to protect Laos, Cambodia, and South Vietnam against attacks. The Central Treaty Organization (CENTO) was formed in 1955 for the military defense of the Middle East. The United States is pledged to cooperate with its members although it did not join.

SUGGESTED READINGS

GATZKE, HANS W., *The Present in Perspective: A Look at the World Since 1945.* This is a short readable history which places the American experience in world perspective.

KENNEDY, ROBERT, *Thirteen Days.* The late Senator Kennedy has written a tense, first-hand account of the Cuban missile crisis from the point of view of a man intimately involved in formulating American policy.

WARD, BARBARA, *The Rich Nations and the Poor Nations.* Here is a readable discussion of the differences and tensions between the old and "developing" nations which have presented so many problems for American policy makers since World War II.

CHAPTER 28

America at Home, 1945–1968

STATING THE ISSUE

The American people had had their fill of crises by 1945. They had survived a dreary decade of depression and four fierce years of war. Americans yearned to have national peace and security and fresh opportunities to lead the good life. These dreams were soon shattered. A round of bitter disputes marked the transition from war to peace at home. Abroad, the outbreak of the Cold War forced the United States to support vast expenditures for economic and military assistance to its allies. Meanwhile, the grim threat of atomic annihilation hung over the world's people.

Four Presidents—Truman, Eisenhower, Kennedy, and Johnson—occupied the White House between 1945 and 1968. One—Eisenhower—was a Republican, and the remaining three were Democrats. All four men faced similar problems, although the intensity of each problem varied from one administration to another. Each one had to cope with war and the threat of even larger wars. Each faced charges that various subversives or agitators—Communists, students, blacks, racists—threatened the welfare of the country. And each recognized that the nation faced a host of serious problems in housing, education, civil rights, and other areas.

In some ways, these four Presidents had excellent resources with which to solve the nation's problems. The United States had become far more prosperous during these twenty-five years than any nation before in history. Although the economies of a few other countries, such as Japan, Sweden, and—in some years—the Soviet Union, grew at a faster rate than that of the United States, the huge lead that America had built up in the past provided a higher starting point for growth and enabled total output to climb rapidly. Technical competence and an early lead in the production of atomic bombs also provided a potent lever in dealings with foreign nations. Despite these advantages, the nation seemed to be torn asunder.

Chapter 28 analyzes and describes the United States during these two-and-a-half decades since the end of World War II. What accounted for American prosperity? How did Americans use their new wealth? What issues divided the nation? What were its greatest achievements and most conspicuous failures? These are the major issues of Chapter 28.

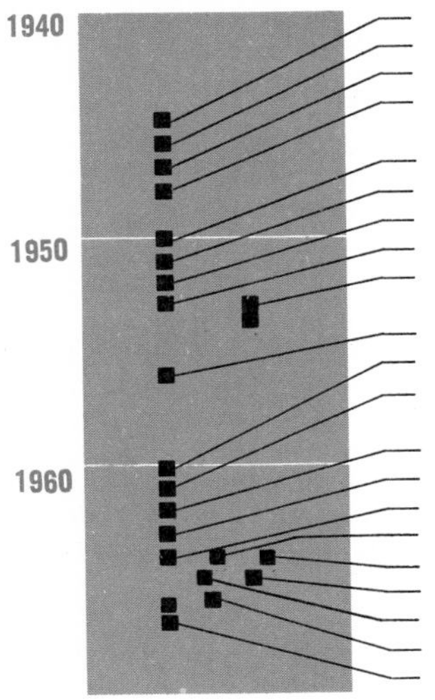

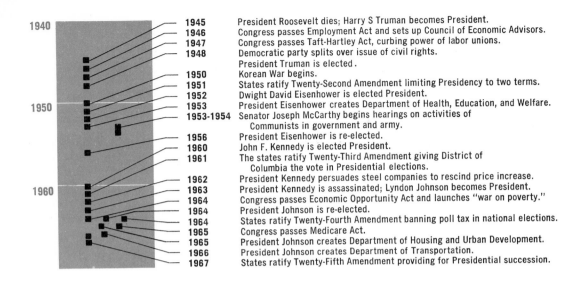

1945	President Roosevelt dies; Harry S Truman becomes President.
1946	Congress passes Employment Act and sets up Council of Economic Advisors.
1947	Congress passes Taft-Hartley Act, curbing power of labor unions.
1948	Democratic party splits over issue of civil rights. President Truman is elected.
1950	Korean War begins.
1951	States ratify Twenty-Second Amendment limiting Presidency to two terms.
1952	Dwight David Eisenhower is elected President.
1953	President Eisenhower creates Department of Health, Education, and Welfare.
1953-1954	Senator Joseph McCarthy begins hearings on activities of Communists in government and army.
1956	President Eisenhower is re-elected.
1960	John F. Kennedy is elected President.
1961	The states ratify Twenty-Third Amendment giving District of Columbia the vote in Presidential elections.
1962	President Kennedy persuades steel companies to rescind price increase.
1963	President Kennedy is assassinated; Lyndon Johnson becomes President.
1964	Congress passes Economic Opportunity Act and launches "war on poverty."
1964	President Johnson is re-elected.
1964	States ratify Twenty-Fourth Amendment banning poll tax in national elections.
1965	Congress passes Medicare Act.
1965	President Johnson creates Department of Housing and Urban Development.
1966	President Johnson creates Department of Transportation.
1967	States ratify Twenty-Fifth Amendment providing for Presidential succession.

109 The Economy, 1945–1968

Signs of prosperity abound in modern America. They can be seen in American clothing, housing, automobiles, television sets, and the thousands of luxury items which crowd the shelves of stores in glittering new shopping plazas. Amidst this plenty, the barren years of the depression decade seem part of another world. The United States seems to have entered a new age.

No one factor can account for all the changes in American society during the twenty-five years between the end of World War II and 1970. Underlying many of these changes, however, was the amazing growth of the American economy. This growth sustained a rapidly rising standard of living at the same time that the nation spent billions of dollars for national defense, gave its allies more billions to stabilize their economies and defend their borders, and made additional huge expenditures to explore space.

What accounts for this remarkable growth in the economy? The tables and graphs that follow present data which will enable you to answer this question. Study questions accompany each table or graph.

1: Gross National Product

1. By how much (in both dollars and in percentage) did the GNP increase over this period?

2. Does this increase necessarily mean that the standard of living for all Americans improved during this period?

Economic Report of the President (Transmitted to the Congress January 1969). Washington, D.C.: Government Printing Office, Appendix, p. 228.

(in billions of dollars adjusted to 1958 prices)			
Year	GNP	Year	GNP
1945	355.2	1957	452.5
1946	312.6	1958	447.3
1947	309.9	1959	475.9
1948	323.7	1960	487.7
1949	324.1	1961	497.2
1950	355.3	1962	529.8
1951	383.4	1963	551.0
1952	395.1	1964	581.1
1953	412.8	1965	616.7
1954	407.0	1966	652.6
1955	438.0	1967	673.1
1956	446.1	1968	706.9

The civilian labor force includes employed and unemployed.

2: *Total Population and Civilian Labor Force*

Economic Report of the President, pp. 251–52.

Figures for 1945–1947 are for workers 14 years and over; figures for 1948 and after are for workers 16 years and over.

1. By how much (in both numbers and percentage) did total population and the civilian labor force increase?
2. Compare the percentage increase in GNP with that of total population and of the percentage increase in civilian labor force. What happened to GNP per capita? What happened to GNP per worker?

Year	Estimated Total Population (rounded to nearest million)	Civilian Labor Force (rounded to nearest million)	Year	Estimated Total Population (rounded to nearest million)	Civilian Labor Force (rounded to nearest million)
1945	140	54	1957	172	67
1946	141	58	1958	175	68
1947	144	60	1959	178	68
1948	147	61	1960	181	70
1949	149	61	1961	184	70
1950	152	62	1962	187	71
1951	155	62	1963	189	72
1952	158	62	1964	192	73
1953	160	63	1965	195	74
1954	163	64	1966	197	76
1955	166	65	1967	199	77
1956	169	67	1968	201	79

3: Index of Output Per Man-Hour in the Private Economy

A man-hour is the amount of work one man can do in one hour. It is used in cost accounting and in determining wages.

1. By what percentage did output per man-hour increase during this time period?
2. Did output per man-hour increase more in the agricultural or the non-agricultural sectors of the economy?

Economic Report of the President, p. 266.

Year	Total Output	Agricultural Output	NonAgricultural Output	Year	Total Output	Agricultural Output	NonAgricultural Output
	(1957–1959 = 100)				(1957–1959 = 100)		
1945	72	50	79	1957	97	93	97
1946	70	52	76	1958	100	103	100
1947	69	50	74	1959	103	105	103
1948	72	58	77	1960	105	111	104
1949	74	57	80	1961	109	119	107
1950	81	64	85	1962	114	122	112
1951	83	65	86	1963	118	133	116
1952	84	70	87	1964	122	136	120
1953	88	80	90	1965	126	148	127
1954	90	84	92	1966	131	153	128
1955	94	84	96	1967	134	172	129
1956	94	88	95	1968	138	172	133

4: Business Expenditures on New Plants and Equipment

1. By what percentage did private investment on plants and equipment increase between 1947 (after the effects of the war had been reduced) and 1968?
2. How may this figure be related to GNP, the growth of the labor force, and output per man?

Economic Report of the President, p. 271.

Year	Total (in billions of dollars)	Year	Total (in billions of dollars)
1945	8.69	1957	36.96
1946	14.85	1958	30.53
1947	20.61	1959	32.54
1948	22.06	1960	35.68
1949	19.28	1961	34.37
1950	20.60	1962	37.31
1951	25.64	1963	39.22
1952	26.49	1964	44.90
1953	28.32	1965	51.96
1954	26.83	1966	60.63
1955	28.70	1967	61.66
1956	35.08	1968	64.53

Agricultural expenditures are not included.

5: *Spending on Education and Research and Development*

U.S. Office of Education, **Digest of Educational Statistics 1968.** Washington, D.C.: Government Printing Office, 1968, pp. 28–29, 59, 127.

1. How rapidly have expenditures increased for education? for research and development?
2. What effect may spending on each have had on output per man-hour?

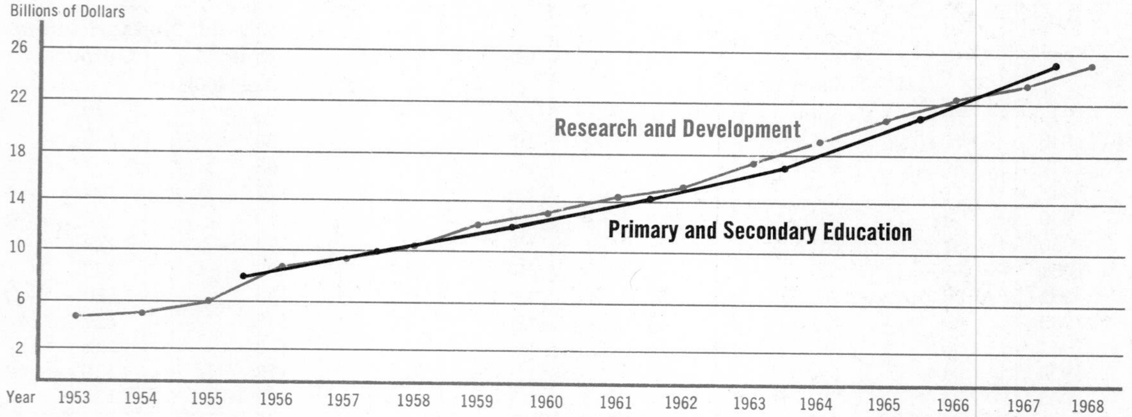

6: *Spending by Major Components*

Economic Report of the President, pp. 228–29.

1. Which has risen more rapidly, government or personal spending?
2. To what degree do war expenditures account for the increase in government expenditures?

Year	Personal Consumption Expenditures	Gross Private Investment	Government Purchases of Goods and Services		
			Federal		State and Local
			Defense	Other	
1946	$143.4 billion	$ 30.6 billion	$14.7 billion	$ 2.5 billion	$ 9.8 billion
1948	173.6	46.0	10.7	5.8	15.0
1950	191.0	54.1	14.1	4.3	19.5
1952	216.7	51.9	45.9	5.9	22.9
1954	236.5	51.7	41.2	6.2	27.4
1956	266.7	70.0	40.3	5.3	33.0
1958	290.1	60.9	45.9	7.7	40.6
1960	325.2	74.8	44.9	8.6	46.1
1962	355.1	83.0	51.6	11.8	53.7
1964	401.2	94.0	50.0	15.2	63.5
1966	465.5	120.8	60.6	16.8	78.8
1968	533.7	127.5	78.9	21.1	97.1

110 The Affluent Society

Dwight D. Eisenhower was unquestionably one of America's most popular Presidents. His election in 1952 and his re-election in 1956 by a margin of more than nine and a half million votes over his Democratic opponent, Adlai E. Stevenson, indicated the satisfaction of the American people with him and with the state of the nation in the mid-1950's.

During Eisenhower's Administration, the standard of living in America reached unprecedented heights. A television set, refrigerator, and at least one car had become standard equipment in most households. The majority of American families owned their own homes, and such luxuries as air conditioners and swimming pools became more and more common. On the average, American men and women earned more money, spent more, and lived more comfortably than ever before.

Many Americans attributed this unprecedented prosperity to the effectiveness of democracy and free enterprise in a country rich with natural resources. Such Americans tended to be confident and optimistic about the future. Critics of American society, however, believed that the outward signs of American prosperity concealed serious flaws in a society unwilling to put traditional American values into practice. They argued that in their concern for private goods, Americans ignored the need for public goods and services, such as schools, hospitals, parks, highways, and low-income housing.

These critics pointed out that even in the affluent 1950's, the poorest classes remained in poverty or became even poorer. In 1956, one out of every ten families had an annual income of less than $1000. Some of these families lived in rural areas and worked unprofitable farms; many lived in city slums where housing conditions were abominable. Critics argued that the deterioration of public services and the persistence of a substantial class of underprivileged Americans posed a grave threat to the nation's future.

Affluent is a term commonly used to describe the economic state of the United States during the 1950's and 1960's. It means wealthy, or having an abundance of goods.

Reading 110 examines optimistic and critical views of America that characterized the thought of the 1950's. As you read, try to answer these questions:

1. Upon what values did the author of the article from *U.S. News and World Report* place emphasis in his discussion of the American "accomplishment"?
2. What did Galbraith mean by "social imbalance"? How did he account for "social imbalance" in America? What solutions to this problem can you suggest?
3. Which author best expresses your own feelings about American society today? Why?

An Optimistic View of America in the 1950's

In its issue for December 27, 1957, the influential American magazine U.S. News and World Report *summarized American progress at home between 1947 and 1957.*

"10 Amazing Years, 1947–1957; A Decade of Miracles," **U.S. News & World Report,** XLIII (December 27, 1957), pp. 42 ff. Copyright © 1957 by **U.S. News & World Report.**

The last year of an amazing decade is about to end. These 10 years have been a time of change and accomplishment unmatched in the history of America, or of any other nation.

In one brief, 10-year period, America's face was remade. Vast suburban areas sprang up to receive millions of Americans pressing out from cities. Ribbons of superhighways were laid across the country. A huge expansion of air facilities helped tie the nation into a compact unity.

Whole regions changed their complexion. Deserts were turned into boom areas. Power was harnessed on a stupendous scale to ease the burden of work.

Nearly 30 million added people were provided for, and on a steadily rising standard of living. A car was put in every garage, two in many. TV sets came into almost every home. There was a chicken, packaged and frozen, for every pot, with more to spare. Never had so many people, anywhere, been so well off. . . .

Republican campaigners in the election of 1928 claimed that a victory for Herbert Hoover would bring "a chicken in every pot, a car in every garage."

Ten Years Ago. Look back 10 years, and you see how far America has come, how fast changes can occur at this period in history.

As 1947 was ending, the nation contained 144 million people, not the 172 million of today. Television was in its infancy. The four-engine plane was only beginning to appear on civilian airlines. Toll highways were a rarity. The superhighway was little more than a gleam in planners' eyes. Supermarkets had just begun to dot the landscape. The ranch-type house had hardly made a dent in the building market, and split-levels were all but unknown. The "modern kitchen" lacked many of the appliances that are standard today.

A ranch house is a one-story house with a wide, overhanging roof, usually very spacious. A split-level has rooms on several different levels, each level being one half story above or below the adjoining one. Both styles are modern.

Food packaging was primitive by modern standards. Nobody had heard of the heat-and-serve dinner. Passenger cars, with few exceptions, lacked automatic transmissions, power steering, power brakes and tubeless tires. Most had only six-cylinder engines. Air conditioning was the exception in average stores and homes. Polio had not been licked. Today's wide ranges of antibiotics and hormones were not available. The company pension was more the exception than the rule. So was hospital insurance. So was the long vacation.

In the 10 years that followed, amazing changes came over America. . . . The things that people enjoy increased immensely in number and volume. . . .

Home ownership spread until, today, every other family owns its own home. Families themselves have increased 10 million in number, and the average married couple has more children. Physical comforts of family homes were increased to a level not even approached in past decades. Millions of homes acquired their own air conditioning for summer and winter. Automatic dishwashers became standard equipment for millions. Freezers were acquired for even more homes. All kinds of electric gadgets were developed and bought in vast numbers—for disposing of garbage down the drain, for quick preparation of meals, for performing household chores with speed and ease.

People quickly accepted new products and new inventions. TV sets, only a curiosity 10 years ago, were acquired by most American families during the decade. High-fidelity phonographs were developed and sold in huge numbers. So were filtered cigarettes of many kinds. Housewives took to detergents. FM radios caught on. Lawn work was made easier with a wide variety of power mowers. People began to buy tape recorders, boats of glass fiber, instant foods, long-playing records. . . .

People, more prosperous than ever before, spent record amounts on travel and recreation. More than 8 million civilians traveled abroad. In addition, Americans flocked in record numbers to resorts in the U.S., bought boats, built summer cottages, went to dude ranches, built their own swimming pools, took up fishing and other forms of recreation—spending about 113 billion dollars on these activities in the process.

Recreation became big business. People bought 4 million power boats, 500,000 sailboats. More than 15 million hunters bought guns and licenses, while 4 million took to golf and 18 million bought tackle and went fishing.

Most of the 11 million new homes built during the decade were of the new rambler or split-level designs. More and more had two-car garages. Nearly all had picture windows of some kind. For the first time, the majority were heated by gas or oil rather than coal, had "revolutionized" kitchens. Many had new wall refrigerators, built-in vacuum-cleaning systems, even built-in "intercom" arrangements.

A rambler is a type of ranch house. Ranch houses are more common in the West.

An "intercom" or intercommunication system allows people to talk to one another in different rooms. It has a radio system placed in the wall, with a microphone and loudspeaker in each room.

With the growth of suburban developments, many families found they needed two cars to transport all members of the family to schools, shopping centers and jobs. Traffic increased enormously, with a net increase of 25 million new cars on the road. Huge traffic arteries were built. So were thousands of parking garages, to help ease the ensuing parking jams.

At the same time, the big cities began gigantic rebuilding plans during the decade. Billions were poured into these projects. They involved expressways to clear new routes for commuters, shoppers and freight. They have included huge new civic centers, modern office buildings, new apartment developments, parks and public auditoriums. Belt roads also were begun by many cities to speed service, help heavy industries escape from downtown. . . .

A belt road is one built around a city, enabling drivers to avoid going through urban areas.

Jobs became more technical, less routine. Demand increased rapidly for engineers, technicians, skilled workers in many fields. The number of jobs created by the technological revolution rose, with 8.3 million more Americans working at paid jobs at the decade's end than at its beginning.

Education took on more importance, as a result. Never had such a high percentage of U.S. youths gone on to higher schooling. In this 10-year period, 12.3 million youths acquired high-school diplomas, while 3.2 million went on to get college degrees. . . .

More to Eat. Food production reached a record high, even with a cut in the number of farms and farmers. . . . In the single decade, the figures now show, U.S. farms produced more than 230 billion pounds of meat, 11 billion bushels of wheat, 31 billion bushels of corn—far more than in any other 10-year period in history. . . .

All told, the decade just ending has been a real age of miracles, an unprecedented era of change and expansion, of jet planes and color TV, of great alterations in the face of America, coupled with a technological revolution that promises even greater miracles in the decade that now lies ahead.

A Critical View of America in the 1950's

John Kenneth Galbraith is a Harvard economist who has served as an ambassador to India. His book The Affluent Society, *published in 1958, was one of the most influential critiques of American society to appear since World War II.*

John Kenneth Galbraith, **The Affluent Society.** Boston: Houghton Mifflin Company, 1958, pp. 251–53, 266–67. Reprinted by permission.

A feature of the years immediately following World War II was a remarkable attack on the notion of expanding and improving public services. During the depression years such services had been elaborated and improved partly in order to fill some small part of the vacuum left by the shrinkage of private production. During the war years the role of government was vastly expanded. After that came the reaction. Much of it, unquestionably, was motivated by a desire to rehabilitate the prestige of private production and therewith of producers. . . .

In this discussion a certain mystique [awe] was attributed to the satisfaction of privately supplied wants. A community decision to have a new school means that the individual surrenders the necessary amount, willy-nilly, in his taxes. But if he is left with that income, he is a free man. He can decide between a better car or a television set. This was advanced with some solemnity as an argument for the TV set. The difficulty is that this argument leaves the community with no way of preferring the school. All private wants, where the individual can choose, are inherently superior to all public desires which must be paid for by taxation and with an inevitable component of compulsion. . . .

The final problem of the productive society is what it produces. This manifests itself in an implacable [inflexible] tendency to provide an opulent [abundant] supply of some things and a niggardly [scanty] yield of others. This disparity carries to the point where it is a cause of social discomfort and social unhealth. The line which divides our area of wealth from our area of poverty is roughly that which divides privately produced and marketed goods and services from publicly rendered services. Our wealth in the first is not only in startling contrast with the meagerness of the latter, but our wealth in privately produced goods is, to a marked degree, the cause of crisis in the supply of public services. For we have failed to see the importance, indeed the urgent need, of maintaining a balance . . .

This disparity between our flow of private and public goods and services is no matter of subjective judgment. On the contrary, it is the source of the most extensive comment which only stops short of the direct contrast being made here. In the years following World War II, the papers of any major city—those of New York were an excellent example—told daily of the shortages and shortcomings in the elementary municipal and metropolitan services. The schools were old and overcrowded. The police force was under strength and underpaid. The parks and playgrounds were insufficient. Streets and empty lots were filthy, and the sanitation staff was underequipped and in need of men. Access to the city by those who work there was uncertain and painful and becoming more so. Internal transportation was overcrowded, unhealthful, and dirty. So was the air. Parking on the streets had to be prohibited, and there was no space elsewhere. These deficiencies were not in new and novel services but in old and established ones. . . .

The discussion of this public poverty competed, on the whole successfully, with the stories of ever-increasing opulence in privately produced goods. The Gross National Product was rising. So were retail sales. So was personal income. Labor productivity had also advanced. The automobiles that could not be parked were being produced at an expanded rate. The children, though without schools, subject in the playgrounds to the affectionate interest of adults with odd tastes, and disposed to increasingly imaginative forms of delinquency, were admirably equipped with television sets. We had difficulty finding storage space for the great surpluses of food despite a national disposition to obesity [overweight]. Food was grown and packaged under private auspices. The care and refreshment of the mind, in contrast with the stomach, was principally in the public domain. Our colleges and universities were severely overcrowded and underprovided, and the same was true of the mental hospitals.

Mauve is a pale purple; cerise is a bright cherry pink. Cars in such exotic colors had been rare in the 1930's and 1940's.

The contrast was and remains evident not alone to those who read. The family which takes its mauve and cerise, airconditioned, power-steered, and power-braked automobile out for a tour passes through cities that are badly paved, made hideous by litter, blighted buildings, billboards, and posts for wires that should long since have been put underground. They pass on into a countryside that has been rendered largely invisible by commercial art. (The goods which the latter advertise have an absolute priority in our value system. Such aesthetic [concerned with beauty] considerations as a view of the countryside accordingly come second. On such matters we are consistent.) They picnic on exquisitely packaged food from a portable icebox by a polluted stream and go on to spend the night at a park which is a menace to public health and morals. Just before dozing off on an air mattress, beneath a nylon tent, amid the stench of decaying refuse, they may reflect vaguely on the curious unevenness of their blessings. Is this, indeed, the American genius?

111 From the New Frontier to the Great Society

In 1960, John F. Kennedy regained the Presidency for the Democrats. He was the first Roman Catholic and the youngest man ever to be elected to that high office. During his campaign, Kennedy had called the American people to advance on a "New Frontier," but his slender margin of victory over the Republican candidate, Richard M. Nixon, suggested that Americans were not ready for a radical transformation of their society. Nevertheless, President Kennedy proposed new legislation in the fields of medical care, urban redevelopment, civil rights, and federal aid to education, most of which failed to pass Congress.

John F. Kennedy received 303 electoral votes to Richard Nixon's 219. Kennedy won 34,227,000 popular votes while Nixon won 34,109,000.

Meanwhile, Kennedy's personal popularity grew enormously. His youth, eloquence, and energy, and his success in making Premier Khrushchev back down in the Cuban missile crisis won him the support of millions of Americans who had voted for Nixon in 1960. His re-election in 1964 seemed assured, and many observers believed that the important legislation of the New Frontier would be passed early in Kennedy's second term.

Then came one of the darkest days in American history. On November 22, 1963, John F. Kennedy was killed in Dallas, Texas, by bullets from a sniper's rifle. That same day Vice-President Lyndon B. Johnson took the Presidential oath of office.

President Kennedy's alleged assassin, Lee Harvey Oswald, was shot fatally while in the custody of the Dallas, Texas, police. His killer, Jack Ruby, was found guilty and died in prison.

During the remaining year of the term, President Johnson devoted himself, with remarkable success, to getting Congress to pass Kennedy's domestic program. In February 1964, Congress passed the $11.5 billion tax that Kennedy had proposed to stimulate economic growth. The passage of the Economic Opportunity Act, which established an Office of Economic Opportunity (OEO), launched a "war on poverty." With an initial authorization of $1 billion the OEO directed programs aimed at providing job training for unemployed workers, especially unemployed young people. Congress also passed the historic Civil Rights Act of 1964 which opened privately owned public facilities—such as restaurants and motels—and public facilities—such as parks and swimming pools—to all Americans regardless of race. The act also guaranteed every citizen's right to register and vote and banned discrimination in employment on the basis of either race or sex.

With the approach of the 1964 election, President Johnson outlined his own version of the New Frontier. He called upon Americans to create a Great Society. As you read Johnson's vision of the Great Society, try to answer these questions.

1. How did President Johnson compare the challenges America faces in the future with those it has faced in the past?
2. What particular domestic problems did Johnson single out for future action? To what extent have these problems been solved?
3. What relationship do you find between Johnson's speech and Galbraith's ideas about "social balance"?

The Great Society

The Great Society became the theme of President Johnson's successful Presidential campaign in 1964. He defined the Great Society in a speech given at the University of Michigan on May 22, 1964.

White House Press Release.

I have come today from the turmoil of your Capitol to the tranquility of your campus to speak about the future of our country. The purpose of protecting the life of our Nation and preserving the liberty of our citizens is to pursue the happiness of our people. Our success in that pursuit is the test of our success as a nation. For a century we labored to settle and to subdue a continent. For half a century, we called upon unbounded invention and untiring industry to create an order of plenty for all of our people. The challenge of the next half century is whether we have the wisdom to use that wealth to enrich and elevate our national life, and to advance the quality of our American civilization.

Your imagination, your initiative and your indignation will determine whether we build a society where progress is the servant of our needs, or a society where old values and new visions are buried under unbridled growth. For in your time we have the opportunity to move not only toward the rich society and the powerful society, but upward to the Great Society.The Great Society rests on abundance and liberty for all. It demands an end to poverty and racial injustice, to which we are totally committed in our time. But that is just the beginning. The Great Society is a place where every child can find knowledge to enrich his mind and to enlarge his talents. It is a place where leisure is a welcome chance to build and reflect, not a feared cause of boredom and restlessness. It is a place where the city of man serves not only the needs of the body and the demands of commerce, but the desire for beauty and the hunger for community.

It is a place where man can renew contact with nature. It is a place which honors creation for its own sake and for what it adds to the understanding of the race. It is a place where men are more concerned with the quality of their goals than the quantity of their goods. But most of all, the great society is not a safe harbor, a resting place, a final objective, a finished work. It is a challenge constantly renewed, beckoning us toward a destiny where the meaning of our lives matches the marvelous products of our labor.

So I want to talk to you today about three places where we begin to build the Great Society—in our cities, in our countryside, and in our classrooms. Many of you will live to see the day, perhaps 50 years from now, when there will be 400 million Americans; four-fifths of them in urban areas. In the remainder of this century urban population will double, city land will double, and we will have to build homes, highways and facilities equal to all those built since this country was first settled. So in the next 40 years we must rebuild the entire urban United States.

Aristotle was a Greek philosopher who lived in the fourth century B.C.

Aristotle said, "Men come together in cities in order to live, but they remain together in order to live the good life."

It is harder and harder to live the good life in American cities today. The catalogue of ills is long: There is the decay of the centers and the despoiling of the suburbs. There is not enough housing for our people or transportation for our traffic. Open land is vanishing and old landmarks are violated. Worst of all, expansion is eroding the precious and time honored values of community with neighbors and communion with nature. The loss of these values breeds loneliness and boredom and indifference. Our society will never be great until our cities are great. Today the frontier of imagination and innovation is inside those cities, and not beyond their borders. New experiments are already going on. It will be the task of your generation to make the American city a place where future generations will come, not only to live but to live the good life. . . .

A second place where we begin to build the Great Society is in our countryside. We have always prided ourselves on being not only America the strong and America the free, but America the beautiful. Today that beauty is in danger. The water we drink, the food we eat, the very air that we breathe, are threatened with pollution. Our parks are overcrowded. Our seashores overburdened. Green fields and dense forests are disappearing.

A few years ago we were greatly concerned about the Ugly American. Today we must act to prevent an Ugly America.

The Ugly American is the title of a book that criticized Americans who went to other countries and made no attempt to respect or understand the customs and cultures of those countries. Although in the book, the "Ugly American" is sympathetic to the countries he visits, the term was used popularly to mean a person who was unsympathetic.

For once the battle is lost, once our natural splendor is destroyed, it can never be recaptured. And once man can no longer walk with beauty or wonder at nature, his spirit will wither and his sustenance be wasted.

A third place to build the Great Society is in the classrooms of America. There your children's lives will be shaped. Our society will not be great until every young mind is set free to scan the farthest reaches of thought and imagination. We are still far from that goal. Today, eight million adult Americans, more than the entire population of Michigan, have not finished five years of school. Nearly 20 million have not finished eight years of school. Nearly 54 million, more than one-quarter of all America, have not even finished high school.

Each year more than 100,000 high school graduates, with proved ability, do not enter college because they cannot afford it. And if we cannot educate today's youth, what will we do in 1970 when elementary school enrollment will be 5 million greater than 1960? And high school enrollment will rise by five million. College enrollment will increase by more than three million. In many places, classrooms are overcrowded and curricula are outdated. Most of our qualified teachers are underpaid, and many of our paid teachers are unqualified. So we must give every child a place to sit and a teacher to learn from. Poverty must not be a bar to learning, and learning must offer an escape from poverty.

But more classrooms and more teachers are not enough. We must seek an educational system which grows in excellence as it grows in size. This means better training for our teachers. It means preparing youth to enjoy their hours of leisure as well as their hours of labor. It means exploring new techniques of teaching, to find new ways to stimulate the love of learning and the capacity for creation.

These are three of the central issues of the Great Society. While our government has many programs directed at those issues, I do not pretend that we have the full answer to those problems. But I do promise this: We are going to assemble the best thought and the broadest knowledge from all over the world to find those answers for America. I intend to establish working groups to prepare a series of White House conferences and meetings on the cities, on natural beauty, on the quality of education, and on other emerging challenges. And from these meetings and from this inspiration and from these studies we will begin to set our course toward the Great Society.

The solution to these problems does not rest on a massive program in Washington, nor can it rely solely on the strained resources of local authority. They require us to create new concepts of cooperation, a creative federalism, between the national capital and the leaders of local communities.

Woodrow Wilson once wrote: "Every man sent out from his university should be a man of his Nation as well as a man of his time."

Within your lifetime powerful forces, already loosed, will take us toward a way of life beyond the realm of our experience, almost beyond the bounds of our imagination. For better or for worse, your generation has been appointed by history to deal with those problems and to lead America toward a new age. You have the chance never before afforded to any people in any age. You can help build a society where the demands of morality, and the needs of the spirit, can be realized in the life of the nation. So will you join in the battle to give every citizen the full equality which God enjoins and the law requires, whatever his belief, or race, or the color of his skin? Will you join in the battle to give every citizen an escape from the crushing weight of poverty? Will you join in the battle to make it possible for all nations to live in enduring peace as neighbors and not as mortal enemies? Will you join in the battle to build the Great Society, to prove that our material progress is only the foundation on which we will build a richer life of mind and spirit?

There are those timid souls who say this battle cannot be won, that we are condemned to a soulless wealth. I do not agree. We have the power to shape the civilization that we want. But we need your will, your labor, your hearts, if we are to build that kind of society.

Those who came to this land sought to build more than just a new country. They sought a free world.

So I have come here today to your campus to say that you can make their vision our reality. Let us from this moment begin our work so that in the future men will look back and say: It was then, after a long and weary way, that man turned the exploits of his genius to the full enrichment of his life.

112 Domestic Politics 1945–1964

HISTORICAL ESSAY

When Truman became President after Roosevelt's death in 1945, the American people did not know him well. A former officer in World War I and a small businessman in Independence, Missouri, he had risen in politics largely through his loyalty to the Democratic party organization. In 1934, he had been elected to the Senate, where he supported New Deal legislation consistently. During the war, he had headed an important Senate committee investigating the defense program, thus gaining national recognition for the first time. After the dynamic personality of Franklin Roosevelt, Truman seemed unimpressive and singularly colorless. Despite these apparent limitations, he proved to be one of the nation's most vigorous Presidents, and made some of the most far-reaching decisions of any American chief executive.

Demobilization of the armed forces posed an immediate challenge to Truman when he became President. The American people expected that with the return of peace the men who had gone off to war would return home as soon as possible. They also expected to be relieved of the troublesome wage, price, and rent controls that had been imposed during the war. With the cancellation of vast defense contracts, defense plants had to be revamped for the production of consumer goods, such as automobiles and home appliances, which had not been manufactured during the war. Americans wanted all these things to be done quickly, but in a way that would avoid a depression.

In order to get rid of price controls without causing inflationary price increases, Truman wanted to reduce controls gradually. Republicans, supported by the business community, wanted them abolished immediately. Congress passed a law limiting the control program, which Truman vetoed. Consequently all controls ended. Prices immediately rose twenty-five percent, and when Congress reinstated controls cattlemen withheld their beef from the market. At the same time, a series of strikes crippled the economy. American

To prevent wartime inflation, Congress had authorized the Office of Price Administration to establish rent controls and set ceilings on prices. The War Labor Board had been authorized to "freeze" wages at a level that had been adjusted to cost-of-living increases.

voters blamed Truman for the inflation, the shortages, and the strikes, and in the Congressional elections of 1948, the Republicans gained majorities in both houses of Congress.

Each Congress of the United States has a lifetime of two years, beginning in January of an odd-numbered year. There are two regular sessions of each Congress, each beginning on January 3rd, although special sessions may be called by the President.

The struggle that followed between the Democratic President and the Republican-controlled 80th Congress centered on the issue of whether or not to extend New Deal welfare legislation. In a series of messages to Congress in 1945 and 1946, Truman called for laws to provide public housing, price supports for farmers, health insurance, and the improvement of existing laws regulating conservation, social security, and minimum wages. Except for the Employment Act of 1946, which established a Council of Economic Advisors to assist the President and directed the government to pursue policies aimed at promoting full employment and maximum purchasing power, Congress refused to enact his program. The Congress, strongly influenced by Republican Senator Robert A. Taft of Ohio, who believed that the American people wanted "a definite end to overgrown bureaucracy, overgrown taxing, and overgrown regulation of everybody—all abuses of the New Deal," tried to limit the further extension of government services. Congress, however, took vigorous action of its own when it passed the Taft-Hartley Bill over Truman's veto in June 1947. The Taft-Hartley Act, which curbed the power of unions, expressed the fear which had developed among many Americans that organized labor had grown too powerful and irresponsible. The new law banned the closed shop, allowed employers to sue unions for breach of contract, and required a sixty-day "cooling off" period before a union was allowed to strike. The Republicans had long complained that "labor bosses" had too much power in the Democratic party. Their passage of the Taft-Hartley Bill as well as their support for the Twenty-Second Amendment forbidding Presidential third terms (a belated slap at Franklin Roosevelt) seemed sure signs that the conservatism of the Republican party had been revitalized.

A bureaucracy is an administrative system characterized by a hierarchy of authority, fixed rules, and red tape.

The closed shop was replaced by the union shop. In a closed shop, an employer may hire only those workers who are members of a certain union. In a union shop, the employer may hire whom he prefers, but the men he hires must join the union in a specified time or lose their jobs.

As the election of 1948 approached, Truman's prestige sank perilously low. He had lost most of his legislative battles to the Republicans in the Congress and faced dissension within his own party. His recommendation for a federal Fair Employment Practices Commission and for anti-lynching and anti-poll tax legislation alienated southern Democrats. His strong resistance to communist aggression offended some northern liberals, such as former Vice-President Henry Wallace, who believed that friendly relations could be maintained with the Soviet Union. Truman's renomination resulted more from his party's inability to agree on another candidate than from a positive endorsement for his candidacy.

The 24th Amendment (1964) banned the collection of a poll tax in a national election.

The Republicans nominated Governor Thomas E. Dewey of New York for President and Governor Earl Warren of California for

Vice-President. Political observers thought Dewey would surely win after southern Democrats, headed by Strom Thurmond of South Carolina, formed their own Dixiecrat party, and Henry Wallace headed the communist-influenced Progressive party. Truman appeared doomed.

At the Democratic convention of 1948, liberals pushed through a strong civil-rights platform calling for federal legislation to end lynching, the poll tax, and employment discrimination. The southern delegates protested and formed the Dixiecrat party.

The President disagreed, however, and he decided to campaign not against Dewey, but against the "do-nothing, good-for-nothing" 80th Congress which had refused to enact his program. As his campaign train carried him over 30,000 miles, he gave more than 300 speeches in which he outlined his Fair Deal. On election night the pollsters predicted a sure Republican victory; before all returns had been counted, some newspapers and magazines actually appeared on the newsstands announcing Dewey's election. When the final results were tabulated, however, the American voters had given Truman twenty-four million votes to Dewey's twenty-two million and an electoral edge of 303 to 189. Thurmond and Wallace each polled 1.2 million votes, and Thurmond carried four southern states.

The first public-opinion poll was used in the election of 1824. Until the 1900's, newspapers and magazines conducted most of the polls. In 1935, George Gallup established the American Institute of Public Opinion or the Gallup poll. It had been relatively accurate until 1948, when it and all the other polls predicted the defeat of President Truman.

What accounted for this amazing upset? The Dixiecrats had turned northern Negroes to the Democrats in a bloc. At the same time, Wallace's defection from the Democratic party reassured conservatives who worried about possible communist penetration into the Democratic party. Both the farmers in the midwestern corn belt, who feared the Republican's agricultural policy, and organized labor, who were angered by the Taft-Hartley Act, gave Truman their votes. Finally, Truman's gallant fight against long odds proved more attractive to the independent voter than the lackluster campaign of Governor Dewey.

The election of 1948 demonstrated again that the Democrats in the country outnumbered the Republicans. Truman's success in attacking the 80th Congress suggested that a majority of the American people still identified the Republican party with the Depression and that they wanted to hold on to the kinds of government programs the Democrats had developed during the New Deal. On the other hand, Truman's victory did not give a mandate to extend New Deal legislation. Although Congress passed his public housing law, improved the social security system, and raised the minimum wage, his bolder Fair Deal program involving federal health insurance and direct income support to farmers received little support. During most of Truman's second term, the crises abroad occupied the nation's energy and attention.

During the early years of the Cold War many Americans believed that the communist threat at home was just as real as the threat of communist expansion abroad. The existence of a Communist party in the United States helped to sustain this fear, and the disclosure in 1946 of a Communist spy ring in Canada which had operated across the United States boundary gave it new impetus. President Truman directed the federal government to establish loyalty boards and to check the loyalty of all federal employees. In 1948 and 1949, public concern about the possibility of Communist infiltration mounted when Alger Hiss, a former State Department official, was convicted of perjury when he denied having committed espionage ten years earlier.

The conviction of Hiss and the subsequent revelation that a high-ranking English physicist had delivered atomic secrets to the Soviet Union with the help of American collaborators intensified Americans' concern about the Communist threat at home and helped prepare the way for the spectacular career of Senator Joseph R. McCarthy of Wisconsin. On February 9, 1950, McCarthy gave a speech in Wheeling, West Virginia, in which he claimed that he had a list of Communists "known to the Secretary of State" and "still working and making policy" for the United States government. McCarthy's charge transformed him suddenly from an obscure senator into a national celebrity. A Senate subcommittee, appointed to investigate his charges, reported that they were false, but McCarthy continued to claim that the government was infested with Communists. The outbreak of the Korean War helped create a public atmosphere that tolerated McCarthy's reckless attacks on institutions and individuals. He frequently identified Communism and treason with the Democratic party, and thereby contributed heavily to the mounting political problems which the Democrats faced as the 1952 elections approached.

The Republicans Take Control

In 1952, the Democratic party, which had held the Presidency for twenty years, faced serious trouble with the American voters. The most imaginative features of President Truman's program had been stalled in the Congress. Corruption had been uncovered in the Department of Revenue. Meanwhile, the indecisive course of the Korean War and the fear of Communist subversion at home disturbed Americans deeply.

The Democrats nominated Adlai Stevenson as their Presidential candidate. Stevenson had worked for the Roosevelt Administration during the Depression, with the State Department during the war, and as a delegate to the United Nations General Assembly in the postwar period. He had also made a progressive record as Governor of Illinois. As a Presidential candidate, he promised to continue the kinds of domestic programs and international commitments that had characterized the Roosevelt and Truman Administrations.

General Eisenhower, the Republican candidate, suited the mood of Americans ideally and promised to unify a divided nation. He was an authentic war hero without previous political connections, who had also served with distinction as Commander-in-Chief of the NATO forces. To the American people, Eisenhower represented such basic values as patriotism, individualism, and fair play. He based his campaign on a pledge to end the war in Korea and on a "middle-of-the-road" political philosophy which opposed "big government" but supported responsible public programs. He so appealed to Americans that he defeated Stevenson overwhelmingly in 1952 and again in 1956.

The twenty years of domestic legislation passed under the previous Democratic administrations had increased government involvement with business, agriculture, and organized labor. Federal expenditures for public welfare had increased as had the size of the federal bureaucracy. Republicans, as the opposition party, had charged repeatedly that Democratic programs required excessively high taxes and put too much power in the hands of government agencies, particularly those headed by the President. They claimed the Democrats had undermined the traditional American values of individualism and free enterprise.

Entering office in 1952 with the support of Republican control of both Houses of Congress, President Eisenhower presided over the most conservative period in the administration of national affairs since 1932. To some extent an analogy can be made between the return to "normalcy" in the 1920's and the Eisenhower Administration. Like Harding and Coolidge, Eisenhower sympathized with business leaders and he appointed several successful businessmen to his cabinet.

Unlike Roosevelt and Truman, Eisenhower preferred not to use the full powers of the executive office. He believed that his predecessors had assumed too much power, and he worked to restore what he called a "proper" balance between the executive and legislative branches of the government. He opposed the deficit financing which had characterized the New Deal and he resisted the extension of such New Deal innovations as TVA. Eisenhower's Secretary of the Treasury, George M. Humphrey, believed that economic prosperity depended upon lower taxes and government expenditures—a retreat from New Deal policies.

Although Eisenhower approached domestic affairs more conservatively than the Democratic Presidents immediately preceding and following him, the similarity with the 1920's should not be carried too far. In foreign affairs, Eisenhower was a convinced internationalist, committed to the United Nations and the principle of collective security. In domestic affairs, he recognized that ever since the

Depression the Democrats had effectively attacked the Republicans for caring more about "special interests than for the welfare of the whole people. The "Modern Republicanism" which Eisenhower believed in "yielded to no one in its concern for the human needs of human beings." He worked to extend social security benefits to an additional ten million people, to establish the new Cabinet-level Department of Health, Education and Welfare, and to support federal aid for schools and for highway construction. Even though he relied heavily on the advice of economic conservatives, Eisenhower believed that in times of severe economic difficulties the government should be prepared to use "any and all weapons in the federal arsenal," including public spending, if necessary, to prevent depression.

The "subversive" issue, which had contributed to the defeat of the Democrats in 1952, continued to plague President Eisenhower during his first term. Senator McCarthy continued to dominate the news media with attacks against an alleged communist conspiracy in the State Department and in the United States Army. Finally, in December 1954, McCarthy's colleagues in the Senate decided that his undocumented accusations had gone too far. In an action rarely taken in American history the Senate censured McCarthy by a vote of 67 to 22. By the middle of the decade, Senator McCarthy and the issue of loyalty had largely dropped from view.

To censure a senator or congressman means simply to reprimand him and curb his statements and actions.

Although the issue was dropped, many people lost their jobs or were denied new ones because they had been labeled subversive by McCarthy.

Despite its conservative emphasis the Eisenhower Administration was more a continuation than a repudiation of previous national policy. The censuring of Senator McCarthy, the support of the principle of collective security abroad, and the willingness to rely on public spending to promote the public welfare at home were all consistent with the Democratic administrations of the 1930's and 1940's. The fact that the Democrats controlled Congress through most of Eisenhower's two terms suggests that American voters supported him more because of strong personal attachment than because they wanted to reverse the government policies and programs since the New Deal.

The Democrats Return

Although he was one of the nation's most popular Presidents, Eisenhower did not rebuild the Republican party or pass on his popularity to a successor. In 1960, Senator John F. Kennedy of Massachusetts defeated Eisenhower's Vice-President, Richard M. Nixon, in one of the closest Presidential elections in American history.

Although only forty-three years old, the new President was rich in political experience. Kennedy had served six years in the House of Representatives and eight years in the Senate. The most intellectual

President since Wilson, he had written two books, one of which had won a Pulitzer prize. His conception of the Presidency had more in common with Roosevelt and Truman than with Eisenhower.

The "New Frontier" which Kennedy called upon his countrymen to conquer had two dimensions. Internationally, it meant the challenge of securing freedom without a nuclear holocaust. Domestically, it meant employing modern technology in such a way as to eliminate poverty and provide abundance and social justice for all.

A coalition of Republicans and southern Democrats stalled most of Kennedy's proposed legislation, and Kennedy, conscious of the slender margin of his victory in 1960, did not push it aggressively through Congress. Kennedy's tentative approach to the Congress contrasted strikingly with his full use of executive powers in the Cuba missile crisis. The President, however, moved just as forcefully in a domestic crisis created in 1962, when the steel companies attempted to raise prices after the government had persuaded the steel workers to cooperate with its anti-inflation program by not demanding a major wage increase. Kennedy immediately marshalled the weight of public opinion against the steel industry, threatened an antitrust suit, and forced the industry to rescind the price increase.

At the time of his assassination in November 1963, Kennedy had been able to get little of his program enacted. But he had dramatized important issues to the public and had captured the American imagination. Kennedy had said the President "must serve as a catalyst, an energizer." He did just that. The enduring impact of his brief tenure in the White House may well have been his ability to reawaken a sense of national purpose and, especially for members of the younger generation who so much admired him, to enhance the value of public service. Then an assassin's bullet struck him down.

A catalyst is something that causes changes without changing itself.

Lyndon B. Johnson, who succeeded Kennedy as President, had served in Congress since 1937. He had grown up politically with the New Deal, and in his years on Capitol Hill had earned a reputation as one of the most knowledgeable and skillful legislators in Washington. As Senate majority leader under Eisenhower, Johnson had refused to let party differences prevent him from cooperating with the President in directing important legislation through Congress. Johnson's success with Congress in enacting Kennedy's proposals was due partly to the fact that after Kennedy's death the nation united in common shame and mourning, and thus reached agreement on common goals and values more easily. Also Johnson demonstrated that his political experience and skill would assist him in using the executive power to speed legislative processes.

In 1964, Johnson sought re-election, urging the voters to follow him in creating the Great Society. Johnson's Republican opponent

Consensus refers to the beliefs and ideology agreed upon by most Americans.

In 1935, President Roosevelt appointed the 26-year old Lyndon Johnson director of the National Youth Administration (NYA) in Texas. In 1937, Johnson resigned to run for Congress. While in Congress, he consistently supported all New Deal measures.

was Senator Barry S. Goldwater of Arizona. The contrast between Johnson and Goldwater was as sharp as it has ever been between Presidential candidates representing the two major parties. Johnson assumed that the social welfare legislation of the New Deal had become a part of the national consensus and should be extended. Goldwater, on the other hand, gave the impression that he and his party opposed everything the government had done since 1933. He spoke of the government stagnating "in a swampland of collectivism." His attacks on big government aroused fear in the minds of many voters that if elected he would work to have Congress repeal most of the legislation which had originated with the New Deal, including social security and the Tennessee Valley Authority. At the same time that he talked of cutting taxes drastically, he insisted that the United States take a more forceful position against "the bully of Communism."

In November 1964, Johnson defeated Goldwater by a huge margin, winning over 61 percent of the popular vote. Even though his outspoken stand on civil rights lost him five states in the traditionally Democratic South, Johnson drew massive support from Republicans as well as Democrats. Most political analysts believed Americans repudiated Goldwater because they feared he would conduct foreign policy too recklessly and pursue domestic policy too conservatively. The mass of American voters still seemed interested in domestic legislation that would maintain political continuity with the pre-war period. The New Deal, the Fair Deal, Modern Republicanism, the New Frontier, and the Great Society all pointed in the same direction. Barry Goldwater, who promised he would provide the voters with "a choice not an echo," pointed in another direction. The voters repudiated him overwhelmingly.

SUGGESTED READINGS

GOLDMAN, ERIC, *The Crucial Decade & After: America 1945–1960.* Goldman has written a lively narrative which concentrates heavily on the leading public personalities of the time.

WHITE, THEODORE H., *The Making of the President, 1964.* This is an exciting account of American politics at work during the presidential campaign of 1964.

WHYTE, WILLIAM H., *The Organization Man.* Here is an interesting study of American middle-class values in the post-war years.

Equal Opportunity in a Democratic Society

STATING THE ISSUE

CHAPTER 29

As Americans entered the last decades of the twentieth century they were acutely aware that the relationships of blacks and whites in the United States had recently changed dramatically. The changes grew largely out of a rising concern for equality of opportunity for black Americans. The campaign for equality produced new educational and job opportunities but its by-products included riots and assassinations. The fate of the campaign appeared uncertain. What did seem certain was that the success or failure of the quest for equal opportunity would help to determine the meaning and future of American democracy.

The black Americans' search for equality in civil rights and equal access to jobs, education, and housing stretched back to the Revolutionary War. Their battle overlapped the struggles, past and present, of other minority groups for equality in American society; it resembled them in some ways but differed significantly in others.

Immigrant groups arriving in the nineteenth century often met the same sorts of prejudice and discrimination faced by Negroes. They often worked as laborers or at menial jobs, clustered in slums under dismal conditions, and struggled to deal with unfamiliar customs and language. Women, who constituted half of Americans, also suffered legal and political discrimination. The Indians who survived the loss of their land to the dominant whites were treated as separate and inferior dependents by an indifferent American society. Even recent arrivals like the Mexican-Americans in the Southwest and the Puerto Ricans of the cities on the east coast encountered discrimination of many kinds.

Each of these groups can tell a story that reveals much about the history of American democracy. Yet only among the ten percent of Americans who are identified as Negroes has the problem of achieving equality proved so serious as to constitute a crisis. To examine the reasons this is so, this chapter turns first to the American descendants of African immigrants, through readings that reveal their protests in the twentieth century. The historical essay, the last reading in the chapter, will relate the experience of blacks to those of other minority groups in recent American history.

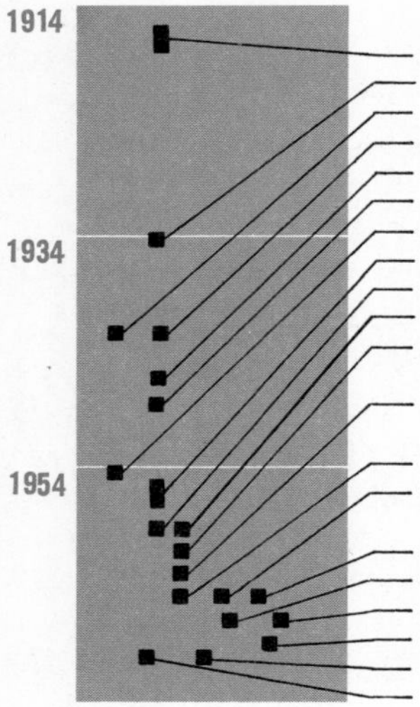

1917-1918	Marcus Garvey organizes "return to Africa" movement.
1934	Elijah Muhammad assumes leadership of Black Muslim movement.
1942	James Farmer organizes Congress of Racial Equality (CORE).
1942	President Roosevelt ends discrimination in hiring in defense plants.
1946	President Truman creates President's Committee on Civil Rights.
1948	President Truman orders armed forces desegregated.
1954	Supreme Court orders desegregation of public schools.
1955-1956	Martin Luther King leads boycott in Montgomery, Alabama, against bus system.
1957	Church-oriented groups form Southern Christian Leadership Conference (SCLC).
1957	President Eisenhower sends national guard to Little Rock, Arkansas.
1960	Students organize Student Non-Violent Coordinating Committee (SNCC) and begin program of "sit-ins" and "freedom-rides."
1963	Negroes and whites conduct peaceful "March on Washington" to demand civil-rights legislation.
1964	States ratify Twenty-Fourth Amendment, outlawing poll tax in federal elections.
1964	Congress passes Civil Rights Act outlawing discrimination in voting and in public accommodations.
1964	Martin Luther King wins Nobel Peace Prize.
1965	Malcolm X is assassinated.
1965	Congress passes Voting Rights Act.
1966	Riots break out in New York, Los Angeles, Newark, and Detroit.
1968	Congress passes Civil Rights Act ending discrimination in rental and sale of houses.
1968	Martin Luther King is assassinated; riots break out in major cities.

113 Protests and Programs after World War I

In 1900, the ten million black heirs of the slave system occupied the bottom of the ladder of achievement in American life. As a group they were poorer by far than whites; their children died younger, as did their adults; they were more often hungry and ill.

Yet there was hope. Literacy was increasing rapidly among blacks. Despite some coercion by whites who depended on their labor in the South, blacks moved fairly freely and sought economic opportunity where they could find it. Their educational leader, Booker T. Washington, urged them to work hard in order to take advantage of American life and pledged his faith in American democracy.

As Washington was speaking in the early 1900's, however, racial segregation was increasing rapidly in the South and border states. In public facilities such as railroads and streetcars, restaurants and theaters, and in private businesses and organizations, Negroes were rigidly segregated or excluded. It reached the point, as one historian has remarked, where whites and Negroes took oaths on separate Bibles in some southern courtrooms. In the North and West, informal segregation of neighborhoods was common. The process resulted in virtually segregated schools. But laws enforcing segregation were rapidly being eliminated in the North and West at the same time that they were spreading in the South.

Other Negro leaders argued vehemently that Washington's protests against segregation were too weak, amounting to passive acceptance, and that his emphasis on vocational education was shortsighted. W. E. B. Du Bois declared that Washington's program betrayed the "talented tenth"—those Negroes who should be admitted to higher education for training as leaders.

Two related events of great significance helped change the basis of this controversy and give the eventual victory to Du Bois's more militant point of view. In 1909, a group of whites and Negroes formed the National Association for the Advancement of Colored People to fight segregation and illegal violence against Negroes; the organization quickly became the most effective agency working for equal rights for Negroes. And between 1910 and 1920, southern Negroes by the hundreds of thousands poured northward to seek employment. They found jobs in industries and in service occupations during a labor shortage created by the reduction in immigration and the booming of production during World War I. The shape of the future became visible: American Negroes, traditionally southern and rural, were on the way to becoming a predominantly northern and urban people.

Immediately after the war a new militancy and a new consciousness of racial identity became apparent among American blacks. The two excerpts in Reading 113, written by W.E.B. Du Bois and Marcus Garvey, illustrate these trends. As you read them, think about the following questions:

1. What is the major point of Du Bois's argument? of Garvey's?
2. Do you think the demands which Du Bois made were justified? Why?
3. How practical was Garvey's plan? Why would it attract a large following?
4. In what ways did Du Bois and Garvey want the same things? In what ways did they want something different?

A Call for Justice and for Negro Militancy

As they had in every previous war, Negroes served valiantly in segregated troops in World War I. Nearly 400,000 Negroes answered the call to the colors in 1917 and 1918. The return of Negro troops from France in 1919 prompted W.E.B. Du Bois, the editor of the NAACP organ The Crisis, *to ask some searching questions about the future of the Negro in America.*

W.E.B. Du Bois, "A Call for Democracy After the War," **The Crisis,** XVIII (May 1919), pp. 13–14. Reprinted by permission of The Crisis Publishing Company, Inc.

We are returning from war! *The Crisis* and tens of thousands of black men were drafted into a great struggle. For bleeding France

An oligarchy is a select, elite, governing group. Du Bois was probably referring to the control of key Congressional committees by white, southern congressmen.

and what she means and has meant and will mean to us and humanity and against the threat of German race arrogance, we fought gladly and to the last drop of blood; for America and her highest ideals, we fought in far-off hope; for the dominant southern oligarchy entrenched in Washington, we fought in bitter resignation. For the America that represents and gloats in lynching, disfranchisement, caste, brutality and devilish insult—for this, in the hateful upturning and mixing of things, we were forced by vindictive fate to fight also.

But today we return! We return from the slavery of uniform which the world's madness demanded us to don, to the freedom of civil garb. We stand again to look America squarely in the face and call a spade a spade. We sing: This country of ours, despite all its better souls have done and dreamed, is yet a shameful land.

It *lynches.*

And lynching is barbarism of a degree of contemptible nastiness unparalleled in human history. Yet for fifty years we have lynched two Negroes a week, and we have kept this up right through the war.

It *disfranchises* its own citizens.

See page 434.

Disfranchisement is the deliberate theft and robbery of the only protection of poor against rich and black against white. The land that disfranchises its citizens and calls itself a democracy lies and knows it lies.

It encourages *ignorance.*

It has never really tried to educate the Negro. A dominant minority does not want Negroes educated. It wants servants, dogs, whores, and monkeys. And when this land allows a reactionary group by its stolen political power to force as many black folk into these categories as it possibly can, it cries in contemptible hypocrisy: "They threaten us with degeneracy; they cannot be educated."

It *steals* from us.

It organizes industry to cheat us. It cheats us out of our land; it cheats us out of our labor. It confiscates our savings. It reduces our wages. It raises our rent. It steals our profit. It taxes us without representation. It keeps us consistently and universally poor, and then feeds us on charity and derides our poverty.

It *insults* us.

It has organized a nation-wide and latterly a world-wide propaganda of deliberate and continuous insult and defamation of black blood wherever found. It decrees that it shall not be possible in travel nor residence, work nor play, education nor instruction for a black man to exist without tacit [silent] or open acknowledgment of his inferiority to the dirtiest white dog. And it looks upon any attempt to question or even discuss this dogma as arrogance, unwarranted assumption and treason.

This is the country to which we Soldiers of Democracy return. This the fatherland for which we fought! But it is *our* fatherland. It was right for us to fight. The faults of *our* country are *our* faults. Under similar circumstances, we would fight again. But by the God of Heaven, we are cowards and jackasses if now that that war is over, we do not marshal every ounce of our brain and brawn to fight a sterner, longer, more unbending battle against the forces of hell in our own land.

We return. We return from fighting. We return fighting.

Make way for Democracy! We saved it in France, and by the Great Jehovah, we will save it in the United States of America, or know the reason why.

Marcus Garvey Proposes an African Homeland

Marcus Garvey, a Negro leader born in the West Indies, organized a mass movement in the United States in the 1920's to procure an African homeland to which American Negroes might emigrate.

Marcus Garvey, **Philosophy and Opinions of Marcus Garvey,** compiled by Amy Jacques-Garvey. New York: Universal Publishing House, 1926, vol. II, pp. 34–36.

On every side we hear the cry of white supremacy—in America, Canada, Australia, Europe, and even South America. There is no white supremacy beyond the power and strength of the white man to hold himself against the others. The supremacy of any race is not permanent; it is a thing only of the time in which the race finds itself powerful. The whole world of white men is becoming nervous as touching its own future and that of other races. With the desire of self-preservation, which naturally is the first law of nature, they raise the hue and cry that the white race must be first in government and in control. What must the Negro do in the face of such a universal attitude but to align all his forces in the direction of protecting himself from the threatened disaster of race domination and ultimate extermination?

During the war, Marcus Garvey organized the Universal Negro Improvement Association, which offered a nationalistic solution for the plight of American Negroes.

Without a desire to harm anyone, the Universal Negro Improvement Association feels that the Negro should without compromise or any apology appeal to the same spirit of racial pride and love as the great white race is doing for its own preservation, so that while others are raising the cry of a white America, a white Canada, a white Australia, we also without reservation raise the cry of a "Black Africa." The critic asks, "Is this possible?" and the four hundred million courageous Negroes of the world answer, "Yes."

Out of this very reconstruction of world affairs will come the glorious opportunity for Africa's freedom. Out of the present chaos and European confusion will come an opportunity for the Negro never enjoyed in any other age, for the expansion of himself and the consolidation of his manhood in the direction of building himself a national power in Africa.

Garvey is referring to the provisions of the Versailles Treaty which ended World War I and disabled Germany.

No one believes in the permanent disablement of Germany, but all thoughtful minds realize that France is but laying the foundation through revenge for a greater conflict than has as yet been seen. With such another upheaval, there is absolutely no reason why organized Negro opinion could not be felt and directed in the channel of their own independence in Africa.

To fight for African redemption does not mean that we must give up our domestic fights for political justice and industrial rights. It does not mean that we must become disloyal to any government or to any country wherein we were born. Each and every race outside of its domestic national loyalty has a loyalty to itself; therefore, it is foolish for the Negro to talk about not being interested in his own racial, political, social and industrial destiny. We can be as loyal American citizens or British subjects as the Irishman or the Jew, and yet fight for the redemption of Africa, a complete emancipation of the race.

Many American Jews had supported the creation of a new state in Palestine as a Jewish homeland, and Irish-Americans had supported Ireland's independence from Britain. When the state of Israel was eventually carved out of Palestine, and when part of Ireland was established as the independent state of Eire, American Jews and Irish-Americans continued to consider themselves Americans.

Fighting for the establishment of Palestine does not make the American Jew disloyal; fighting for the independence of Ireland does not make the Irish-American a bad citizen. Why should fighting for the freedom of Africa make the Afro-American disloyal or a bad citizen?

The Universal Negro Improvement Association teaches loyalty to all governments outside of Africa; but when it comes to Africa, we feel that the Negro has absolutely no obligation to any one but himself.

114 Breakthrough in Civil Rights: Laws and Reactions

The slow and painstaking efforts of civil-rights groups, led by the NAACP, to strike down laws requiring or permitting segregation in public facilities and discrimination in other civil rights, achieved full success in the years after World War II. Both the United States Supreme Court and lower courts declared all segregation laws illegal, and governmental agencies began enforcing desegregation in public facilities. By the 1960's, also, an increasing number of Negroes had won election to public offices. They included, for example, the first Negroes to sit in the Georgia legislature since Reconstruction, the first southern Negro sheriffs since that era, the first Negro United States Senator ever elected from a northern state, and the first Negro mayors of large northern cities.

As far back as 1915, the Supreme Court had begun striking down segregation laws. Among the first of these laws were Maryland and Oklahoma constitutional provisions that discriminated against Negro voting and a Louisville, Kentucky, city law that tried to enforce racial segregation by neighborhoods. In the years between the two World Wars, the Supreme Court cut down little by little the areas in which segregation could legally operate. For example, it prohibited political parties from holding primary elections restricted to white voters and ordered states to admit Negroes to university graduate schools where no separate and equal facilities were available for them. The resulting changes were significant, but they came slowly and affected only a few people.

World War II, in which about a million American Negroes served in the armed forces, marked a dividing line. In the years immediately after the war many states, led by New York, adopted Fair Employment Practice Acts designed to prohibit discrimination in employment. The federal government moved to integrate the armed forces. And the Supreme Court struck down a variety of segregation laws in the vast area of the use of public facilities. The most crucial and controversial of the Court's decisions came on May 17, 1954, when, in *Brown* vs. *The Board of Education,* the Court declared that segregation in the public schools was illegal. In a subsequent ruling, the Court added that segregated schools had to desegregate "with all deliberate speed." Although many whites, especially from the South, protested this decision strongly, there was relatively little open conflict over it. Most school districts in border states moved gradually to comply with the law, while most of those in the deep South maintained segregation.

The 1954 decision reversed the **Plessy** vs. **Ferguson** decision of 1896, in which the Court said that "separate but equal" facilities were acceptable.

Reading 114 contains two excerpts related to subsequent events. The first describes the reaction of the federal government to opposition by the local and state governments to the desegregation in 1957 of Central High School in Little Rock, Arkansas. The second presents some results of a nationwide survey of white attitudes toward Negroes and their efforts to obtain equal opportunities. As you read, think about the following questions:

1. What did President Eisenhower do in the Little Rock crisis? Why was this action significant?
2. Do you think that the federal government ought to support the courts with force, if necessary? Why, or why not?

3. How can many American whites hold deep prejudices against Negroes but at the same time agree to their having equal rights?
4. What is the meaning of the surveys that show overwhelming white approval of equality of opportunity but also strong opposition to law enforcement designed to achieve equality?

President Eisenhower Intervenes at Little Rock

In the fall of 1957, trouble erupted in Little Rock, Arkansas, where the Supreme Court had ordered the city to admit a few Negro children to Central High School. Governor Orval Faubus of Arkansas intervened by calling out National Guardsmen who prevented blacks from entering the school. When he later withdrew the Guard, mobs of whites blocked the school entrance without interference by police and threatened the children. At this point, President Dwight Eisenhower, acting to uphold the authority of the federal courts, ordered army troops to Little Rock to guarantee the black children safe access to Central High. Excerpts from Eisenhower's radio message to the nation explaining his action appears as the first part of Reading 114.

Vital Speeches of the Day, vol. XXIV, no. 1 (October 15, 1957), pp. 11–12.

For a few minutes this evening I want to talk to you about the serious situation that has arisen in Little Rock. To make this talk I have come to the President's office in the White House. I could have spoken from Rhode Island, where I have been staying recently, but I felt that, in speaking from the house of Lincoln, of Jackson and of Wilson, my words would better convey both the sadness I feel in the action I was compelled today to take and the firmness with which I intend to pursue this course until the orders of the Federal Court at Little Rock can be executed without unlawful interference.

In that city, under the leadership of demagogic extremists, disorderly mobs have deliberately prevented the carrying out of proper orders from a Federal Court. Local authorities have not eliminated that violent opposition and, under the law, I yesterday issued a Proclamation calling upon the mob to disperse.

This morning the mob again gathered in front of the Central High School of Little Rock, obviously for the purpose of again preventing the carrying out of the Court's order relating to the admission of Negro children to that school.

Whenever normal agencies prove inadequate to the task and it becomes necessary for the Executive Branch of the Federal Government to use its powers and authority to uphold Federal Courts, the President's responsibility is inescapable.

In accordance with that responsibility, I have today issued an Executive Order directing the use of troops under Federal authority to aid in the execution of Federal law at Little Rock, Arkansas. This became necessary when my Proclamation of yesterday was not observed, and the obstruction of justice still continues.

It is important that the reasons for my action be understood by all our citizens.

As you know, the Supreme Court of the United States has decided that separate public educational facilities for the races are inherently unequal and therefore compulsory school segregation laws are unconstitutional.

Our personal opinions about the decision have no bearing on the matter of enforcement; the responsibility and authority of the Supreme Court to interpret the Constitution are very clear. Local Federal Courts were instructed by the Supreme Court to issue such orders and decrees as might be necessary to achieve admission to public schools without regard to race—and with all deliberate speed. . . .

The very basis of our individual rights and freedoms rests upon the certainty that the President and the Executive Branch of Government will support and insure the carrying out of the decisions of the Federal Courts, even, when necessary, with all the means at the President's command.

Unless the President did so, anarchy would result.

There would be no security for any except that which each one of us could provide for himself.

The interest of the nation in the proper fulfillment of the law's requirements cannot yield to opposition and demonstrations by some few persons. Mob rule cannot be allowed to override the decisions of our courts. . . .

Nationwide Survey Reveals White Attitudes Toward Negroes

In 1963, Newsweek *magazine conducted a nationwide survey of both white and black attitudes. The survey was made at a time when blacks and sympathetic whites were conducting protest marches, sit-in demonstrations, boycotts, and voter-registration drives, while antagonistic whites condemned their actions. The following selection, based on that survey, appeared after a section that described white prejudices against Negroes as people.*

William Brink and Louis Harris, **The Negro Revolution in America.** New York: Simon and Schuster, Inc., 1964, pp. 141–48.

If views such as these comprised the total white attitude toward Negroes, then the only logical conclusion to draw would be that

America is on the threshold of a bloody race war. But whites hold a whole roster [list] of other beliefs that are in direct conflict with their emotions about Negroes as people. One is that Negroes have rights as citizens which must be guaranteed under the laws of the United States. Whites were asked about some of the Negro's demands:

The White View of Negro Rights

Approve:	Nationwide %	South %
Voting in elections	93	88
Unrestricted use of buses and trains	88	75
Job opportunities	88	80
Decent housing	82	76

The most startling figures in this table are those that reflect Southern attitudes. Even in the South, a large majority of whites feel Negroes should be guaranteed these rights. What is more, sizable majorities of whites feel that further legislation is needed from Congress to strengthen Negro rights. On this question, however, Southern whites disagree sharply with white people elsewhere:

White Support for Civil-Rights Legislation

Approve:	Nationwide %	South %
Federal vote-enforcement law	57	31
Federal Fair Employment Practices law	62	40
Kennedy civil-rights bill	63	31
Public-accommodations bill	66	29

In June 1963, President Kennedy proposed a civil-rights bill prohibiting discrimination in public accommodations and giving the Attorney-General power to speed up school desegregation. Provisions of this bill became law in 1964.

Comparison of these two tables reveals an interesting anomaly [contradiction]: 88 percent of the white Southerners believe that Negroes have the right to vote, but only 31 percent favor legislation backing up that right. There is a similar though less striking contrast on the subject of jobs. Legislation seems to be the sticking point; all whites are more ready to approve other forms of Federal intervention for equal rights. . . .

How do whites rationalize this acceptance of equality under the law with the personal aversions to Negroes so many of them apparently feel? Timing plays a part. By better than a 2 to 1 margin, whites feel that Negroes are moving too fast in their revolution. . . .

When asked in detail about the methods of the Negro revolution, whites went on record as 2 to 1 in opposition to the lunch-counter sit-ins, 4 to 3 against Negro willingness to go to jail voluntarily for their cause, 5 to 3 against picketing of stores and over 10 to 1 against the "lie-downs" in front of trucks and construction sites. However, by slim margins, whites do accept the general idea of demonstrating and think that the Negroes are justified in having conducted the March on Washington. . . .

These very demonstrations appear to have driven home the whole point of the Negro protest. But the majority view of whites was clearly that the Negroes were pressing too hard, asking for too much. Whites have remarkably clear understanding of Negro demands. The following table drawn from volunteered comments, shows what whites think Negroes want:

What Whites Think Negroes Want

	Whites Nationwide %
Equal treatment	41
Better jobs	14
Better education	11
Make America aware of their problem	8
Better housing	7
Dignity, respect, status	6
Publicity for the problem	6
Representation in government	5
Be able to go anywhere, do anything	2

There is a remarkable parallel between what whites think Negroes want and what Negroes themselves said they want.

Furthermore, there is widespread recognition among whites that Negroes are discriminated against. Fully 71 percent of all whites in the country and even a majority of 56 percent in the South acknowledged this fact. By better than 3 to 2, white people feel Negroes do not have job opportunities equal to whites. By a somewhat closer margin whites also believe Negro children receive an inferior education. And by almost 3 to 1, whites believe Negro housing is not nearly so good as that for whites. . . .

If whites are thus able to understand in human terms just what it means to be a Negro in America, how far are they willing to go toward integration? This is obviously a key question, and in large part American history of the next ten years will be written by the answer. The survey investigated the limits of white viability [capacity to accept], from willingness to work side by side with a Negro to allowing a teen-age daughter to date a Negro boy:

The "previous social contact group" was composed of people who had had social contact with Negroes.

White Feelings about Contact with Negroes

	Nationwide %	South %	Previous Social Contact %
Would object to:			
Working next to a Negro on the job	17	31	8
Sitting next to a Negro at a lunch counter	20	50	4
Sitting next to a Negro on a bus	20	47	5
Sitting next to a Negro in a movie theater	23	54	6
Own children going to school with Negroes	23	55	9
Using same restroom as Negroes	24	56	9
Trying on same suit or dress that Negro had tried on in store	32	57	16
Having own child bring Negro friend home to supper	41	76	16
Having Negro family as next-door neighbors	51	74	26
Close friend or relative marrying a Negro	84	91	70
Own teen-age daughter dating a Negro	90	97	80

It is immediately apparent from these results that the vast majority of white America is prepared to accept a great deal more contact with Negroes than has taken place up to now. The degree of Southern viability may come as a surprise. Nationwide, in view of the revulsion [strong dislike] expressed by many earlier in this chapter, the over-all results testify to white willingness—grudging though it may be—to accommodate. But white America is not at all ready for social integration to the extent of dating and intermarriage. Even among those who have had social contact with Negroes, 70 percent would object to a close friend or relative marrying a Negro and 80 percent would be worried if their teen-age daughter dated a Negro.

115 The New Black Militancy

To most Negro leaders, as to most Americans, the ideal of black separatism embraced by Marcus Garvey in the 1920's seemed for many years an undesirable or impossible solution. Their hope of gaining the equal opportunity that was promised by the American democratic political system still seemed a brighter and more genuine possibility. But in the years after 1950 new developments threw fresh doubt into the minds of many persons that integration into a color-blind American society was possible.

The achievement of the principle of desegregation in public schools, however much it might mean to the ideal of equal opportunity, meant little in practice for most Negroes. Ten years after the Supreme Court's famous decision in 1954, fewer than 11 percent of the Negro pupils in southern and border states were enrolled in desegregated school districts; in the Deep South, the figure was lower than 1 percent. In the North, most Negro pupils attended schools that were nearly all black because they lived in segregated areas because of poverty, prejudice, and sometimes preference.

As the big cities of the North took in more and more black migrants from the South, more and more whites left for the suburbs. The most extreme case of such transfer of populations was Washington, D.C., whose population rose from 35.4 percent Negro in 1950 to 54.8 percent Negro in 1960, and whose public school enrollment rose from 45.2 percent Negro in 1960 to 88 percent Negro in 1965. Despite a disproportionately large expenditure of funds for ghetto schools in such cities as New York, heavy turnovers of both teacher and student populations in such schools contributed to educational difficulties there.

A far more potent source of Negro dissatisfaction was inequality of opportunity in employment and in housing. Despite progress made in overcoming discrimination in hiring practices and in admission to unions, unemployment among Negroes remained far higher than among whites. Housing conditions in the black ghettoes of American cities were often miserable, and discrimination in housing—which by 1969 was usually illegal—prevented many Negroes from obtaining living quarters elsewhere.

The continuing vast difference between the living and working conditions of whites and blacks prompted a new sense of militancy among Negroes. This spirit affected the older protest and welfare groups, such as the NAACP and the Urban League, to some extent, but was most evident in newer organizations. Reading 115 offers the voices of two Negro leaders—Rev. Martin Luther King and Stokely Carmichael—who described themselves as militants. As you read, consider these questions:

The Civil Rights Act of 1968 prohibits discrimination in the sale and rental of houses. It also provides stiff penalties for those guilty of injuring civil-rights workers, traveling from one state to another to incite a riot, or providing firearms for a riot.

The National Urban League, founded in 1911, is directed more toward offering services to Negroes than toward organizing protest movements. Its membership is primarily middle class.

1. What did King want? What did Carmichael want? How did they propose to reach these goals?
2. Why did King and Carmichael argue that blacks had to win their rights through their own efforts and their own organizations? Were the views of the two identical?

3. Do you agree with King's position? with Carmichael's?
4. Do you think that the use of violence is justified to obtain civil rights if non-violent techniques have failed in the past?

Martin Luther King Explains His Philosophy

The Rev. Dr. Martin Luther King, Jr., acted as spokesman for the Montgomery, Alabama, Negroes who in 1955 carried on a year-long successful boycott against the city transit system because it insisted on segregated seating in buses. King later led his Southern Christian Leadership Conference (SCLC) into protest marches, boycotts, and other kinds of direct action for equal opportunity. He won the Nobel Peace Prize in 1964 for his support of the principle and practice of nonviolence. He was assassinated in 1968 while preparing to assist in demonstrations for higher wages by sanitation workers in Memphis, Tennessee. The excerpts below are from a letter he wrote from jail where he was being held after a demonstration. It was addressed to a group of southern white clergymen.

The Southern Christian Leadership Conference is an agency with headquarters in Atlanta. It was founded in 1957 as an extension of the Montgomery Improvement Association, headed by Martin Luther King, and advocates nonviolent demonstrations.

Excerpts from "Letter from Birmingham Jail" (April 16, 1963), in Martin Luther King, Jr., **Why We Can't Wait.** New York: Harper & Row, Publishers, 1963, pp. 87, 90. Copyright © 1963 by Martin Luther King, Jr. Reprinted by permission of Joan Daves.

I must make two honest confessions to you, my Christian and Jewish brothers. First, I must confess that over the past few years I have been gravely disappointed with the white moderate. I have almost reached the regrettable conclusion that the Negro's great stumbling block in his stride toward freedom is not the White Citizens' Counciler or the Ku Klux Klanner, but the white moderate, who is more devoted to "order" than to justice; who prefers a negative peace which is the absence of tension to a positive peace which is the presence of justice; who constantly says: "I agree with you in the goal you seek, but I cannot agree with your methods of direct action"; who paternalistically believes he can set the timetable for another man's freedom; who lives by a mythical concept of time and who constantly advises the Negro to wait for a "more convenient season." Shallow understanding from people of good will is more frustrating than absolute misunderstanding from people of ill will. Lukewarm acceptance is much more bewildering than outright rejection.

White Citizens' Councils began to appear in the South after the **Brown** vs. **Board of Education** decision. Their aim was to maintain segregation through threats, economic pressure, and occasional violence.

You speak of our activity in Birmingham as extreme. At first I was rather disappointed that fellow clergymen would see my nonviolent efforts as those of an extremist. I began thinking about the fact that I stand in the middle of two opposing forces in the Negro community. One is a force of complacency, made up in part of Negroes who, as a result of long years of oppression, are so drained of self-respect and a sense of "somebodiness" that they have adjusted to segregation; and in part of a few middle-class Negroes who, because of a degree of academic and economic security and because in some ways they profit by segregation, have become insensitive to the problems of the masses. The other force is one of bitterness and hatred, and it comes perilously close to advocating violence. It is expressed in the various black nationalist groups that are springing up across the nation, the largest and best-known being Elijah Muhammad's Muslim movement. Nourished by the Negro's frustration over the continued existence of racial discrimination, this movement is made up of people who have lost faith in America, who have absolutely repudiated Christianity, and who have concluded that the white man is an incorrigible "devil."

The Nation of Islam, usually known as the "Black Muslim" movement, was organized in 1930 by Wali Farad, whom his followers believed to be an incarnation of Allah who came to America to rescue all black men from white bondage. In 1934, he was succeeded by Elijah Muhammad. The group is opposed to integration, has renounced Christianity, and seldom cooperates with other black groups.

I have tried to stand between these two forces, saying that we need emulate neither the "do-nothingism" of the complacent nor the hatred and despair of the black nationalist. For there is the more excellent way of love and nonviolent protest. I am grateful to God that, through the influence of the Negro church, the way of nonviolence became an integral part of our struggle.

Stokely Carmichael Explains "Black Power"

Like Marcus Garvey, Stokely Carmichael was born in the West Indies, but received his school and college education in the United States. He first won national prominence as chairman of the Student Nonviolent Coordinating Committee (SNCC), a group which engaged in many direct action projects, notably in voter registration drives among Negroes in the Deep South. He wrote the following explanation of the term "black power" in 1966.

Stokely Carmichael, "What We Want," **The New York Review of Books,** vol. VII, no. 4 (September 22, 1966), pp. 5, 6, 7 **passim.** Reprinted by permission of International Affairs Commission of SNCC.

One of the tragedies of the struggle against racism is that up to now there has been no national organization which could speak to the growing militancy of young black people in the urban ghetto. There has been only a civil rights movement, whose tone of voice was adapted to an audience of liberal whites. It served as a sort of buffer zone between them and angry young blacks. None of its so-called leaders could go into a rioting community and be listened to. In a sense, I blame ourselves—together with the mass media—for what has happened in Watts, Harlem, Chicago, Cleveland, Omaha. Each time the people in those cities saw Martin Luther King get slapped, they became angry; when they saw four little black girls bombed to death, they were angrier; and when nothing happened, they were steaming. We had nothing to offer that they could see,

Watts is a section of Los Angeles; Harlem is a section of Manhattan. The five places mentioned were scenes of Negro riots during the 1960's.

In 1963, a church bombing in Birmingham, Alabama, killed four Negro girls attending Sunday school.

except to go out and be beaten again. We helped to build their frustration.

For too many years, black Americans marched and had their heads broken and got shot. They were saying to the country, "Look, you guys are supposed to be nice guys and we are only going to do what we are supposed to do—why do you beat us up, why don't you give us what we ask, why don't you straighten yourselves out?" After years of this, we are at almost the same point—because we demonstrated from a position of weakness. We cannot be expected any longer to march and have our heads broken in order to say to whites: come on, you're nice guys. For you are not nice guys.

An organization which claims to speak for the needs of a community—as does the Student Nonviolent Coordinating Committee—must speak in the tone of that community, not as somebody else's buffer zone. This is the significance of black power as a slogan. For once, black people are going to use the words they want to use—not just the words whites want to hear. And they will do this no matter how often the press tries to stop the use of the slogan by equating it with racism or separatism.

. . . The concept of "black power" is not a recent or isolated phenomenon: It has grown out of the ferment of agitation and activity by different people and organizations in many black communities over the years. Our last year of work in Alabama added a new concrete possibility. In Lowndes county, for example, black power will mean that if a Negro is elected sheriff, he can end police brutality. If a black man is elected tax assessor, he can collect and channel funds for the building of better roads and schools serving black people—thus advancing the move from political power into the economic arena. In such areas as Lowndes, where black men have a majority, they will attempt to use it to exercise control. This is what they seek: control. Where Negroes lack a majority, black power means proper representation and sharing of control. It means the creation of power bases from which black people can work to change statewide or nationwide patterns of oppression through pressure from strength—instead of weakness. . . .

. . . Integration speaks not at all to the problem of poverty, only to the problem of blackness. Integration today means the man who "makes it," leaving his black brothers behind in the ghetto as fast as his new sports car will take him. It has no relevance to the Harlem wino or the cottonpicker making three dollars a day. . . . As a goal, it has been based on complete acceptance of the fact that *in order to have* a decent house or education, blacks must move into a white neighborhood or send their children to a white school. This reinforces, among both black and white, the idea that "white" is automatically better and "black" is by definition inferior.

This is why integration is a subterfuge for the maintenance of white supremacy. It allows the nation to focus on a handful of Southern children who get into white schools, at great price, and to ignore the 94 percent who are left behind in unimproved all-black schools. Such situations will not change until black people have power—to control their own school boards, in this case. Then Negroes become equal in a way that means something, and integration ceases to be a one-way street. . . .

See margin note, page 538.

The need for psychological equality is the reason why SNCC today believes that blacks must organize in the black community. Only black people can convey the revolutionary idea that black people are able to do things themselves; they must get poverty money they will control and spend themselves, they must conduct tutorial programs themselves so that black children can identify with black people. This is one reason Africa has such importance: The reality of black men ruling their own natives gives blacks elsewhere a sense of possibility, of power, which they do not now have.

This does not mean we don't welcome help, or friends. But we want the right to decide whether anyone is, in fact, our friend. In the past, black Americans have been almost the only people whom everybody and his momma could jump up and call their friends. We have been tokens, symbols, objects—as I was in high school to many young whites, who liked having "a Negro friend." We want to decide who is our friend, and we will not accept someone who comes to us and says: "If you do X, Y, and Z, then I'll help you." We will not be told whom we should choose as allies. We will not be isolated from any group or nation except by our own choice. We cannot have the oppressors telling the oppressed how to rid themselves of the oppressor. . . .

But our vision is not merely of a society in which all black men have enough to buy the good things of life. When we urge that black money go into black pockets, we mean the communal pocket. We want to see the cooperative concept applied in business and banking. We want to see black ghetto residents demand that an exploiting landlord or storekeeper sell them, at minimal cost, a building or a shop that they will own and improve cooperatively; they can back their demand with a rent strike, or a boycott, and a community so unified behind them that no one else will move into the building or buy at the store. The society we seek to build among black people, then, is not a capitalist one. It is a society in which the spirit of community and humanistic love prevail. . . . The love we seek to encourage is within the black community, the only American community where men call each other "brother" when they meet. We can build a community of love only where we have the ability and power to do so: among blacks.

A rent strike occurs when ghetto residents hold back their rent until the landlord makes substantial improvements.

116 The Uncertain Quest for Equality

HISTORICAL ESSAY

In 1944 a distinguished Swedish economist, Gunnar Myrdal, wrote a book about Negroes and whites in the United States called *An American Dilemma.* Whites had created a deep dilemma, Myrdal thought, by denying equality to Negroes while they themselves preached equality as a central part of the American democratic system. As a result, eighty years after the end of slavery, Negroes remained victims of prejudice, limited opportunity, poverty, and segregation in the midst of the world's greatest democracy, while whites were troubled by the contradiction between their principles and their practices.

Even in 1944, however, the groundwork for change had been established. Industrialization and urbanization had shifted Negroes out of the rural South. Political action by both whites and Negroes had begun to make an impact on discrimination. Since World War II, the contest between those who have sought to end the dilemma and those who have tried to preserve it has created a dramatic story. Why were Negroes, of all American minority groups, the chief victims of the dilemma described by Myrdal?

Minorities and Their Strengths

Many immigrant groups have suffered prejudice and discrimination in American society. Those who arrived in the late nineteenth and twentieth centuries—the years when most Negroes were living for the first time as free men—were not exceptions. Newcomers from Europe, Asia, Canada, and Latin America found many doors closed to them. Catholics had long experienced hardships in a largely Protestant society. Jews, both the newly arrived and the long established, felt a new wave of animosity, part of a tide of racism which rose in the early twentieth century throughout the Western world. Later arrivals, especially those from Puerto Rico, Mexico, and Cuba, repeated the experiences of earlier immigrants.

Yet the newcomers often possessed important resources that helped them come to terms with American society. They identified themselves with the cultures of their homelands and took pride in their religions. Their sense of being Germans, or Poles, or Chinese, or Catholics, or Jews served as a basis for group solidarity. Out of this solidarity emerged organizations designed to promote their economic interests, to use their political power effectively, to sustain their religious faith, and to encourage pride in their identities.

Most of the immigrants adopted American ways and came to think of themselves as Americans. But they did so gradually, maintaining their "old world" identities as long as they wished. They were Americans, but they were also Irishmen, Hungarians, or Japanese. Above all, both the immigrants and their organizations gained power from the strength of family groups which gave individual immigrants security in a strange new land.

Black freedmen, on the other hand, lacked many of these sources of strength. Although their African ancestors, like other immigrants, came from complex societies with rich cultures, American Negroes had been cut off from their heritage by slavery. They quickly lost specific knowledge of the customs, traditions, and languages of their African homelands. Under the conditions of slavery they adopted the language and ways of the whites. But the slave system blocked their access to American education, literature, and politics. They also lacked the support of strong families to help them make use of American ways. Their family ties, as well as their broader social ties, were undermined by the operations of the slave system.

Although the term "Negro" refers to a member of one of the three major races, in the United States it is often applied to people of mixed racial background who have any African ancestry.

Thus the freedman emerging from slavery was not really an Afro-American, a man who could find part of his identity in a knowledge of another country and culture. He was simply a black American, who drew his sense of who he was from the ways his former masters treated him. As bad as this treatment often was, few freedmen emigrated to Africa or elsewhere from the only homes they had ever known. Most blacks continued to live in the rural South, in a well-defined place in society. Migration to the city, which gave them a new kind of life, did not change their standing in society. One fact illustrates the distinctive position of Negroes in American society. Although blacks and whites had intermixed from the earliest times until millions of Americans had some white and some black ancestors, most whites classified all these people as "Negroes." To most whites, any sign of African ancestry was a sign of inferiority.

A comparison of the experience of Negroes with those of Indians and Spanish-speaking Americans during the last century gives perspective to the history of all three groups. Whites herded most Indians who survived the white occupation of the country into reservations, where they lived almost entirely separate from the rest of American society. Even though their lands were often cramped and infertile, they continued to remain apart in order to preserve tribal life. But despite tribalism, Indians suffered a sharp cultural shock. Their cultures had usually given glory to the achievements of hunters, fishermen, and warriors. Now the restrictions of reservation life made it virtually impossible to live by hunting and fishing, and the army stopped warfare. Many Indians on reservations came to depend increasingly on government rations of food and clothing to keep alive. Both tribal and individual morale declined sharply. Dominant American values, as taught in the white-run schools on the reservations did little to foster a favorable self-concept among Indian youth; children learned, in effect, that whites regarded them and their traditional cultures as inferior. American society has still not solved the problem of the separateness of Indian life.

Americans from Spanish-speaking countries constitute a loosely related set of minority groups whose experiences have been influenced both by length of residence in the United States and by ethnic identity. The original Indian population of Mexico and the West Indies became intermixed with both Spanish and African peoples. The earliest Spanish-speaking peoples in the American Southwest came from this mixed group. They increased in number gradually, then rapidly. Since 1924, when large-scale European immigration to the United States was cut off, Mexico has been the chief source of immigrants to this country. More than three million Mexican-Americans now live in the Southwest and West.

One Mexican-American laborer, Cesar Chavez, organized the grape-pickers of California into a union, the United Farm Workers Organizing Committee, which is affiliated with the AFL-CIO. He launched a campaign and boycott against those vineyards that did not recognize his union. His boycott won support in the East.

Most Mexican immigrants have been agricultural workers who encountered widespread prejudice and discrimination from native Americans. They also suffered from educational handicaps and lacked political power. Yet they have begun to achieve a higher economic, social, and political place fairly rapidly in recent years. About 250,000 Mexican-Americans served in the armed forces during World War II, thus taking a step towards merging with American society. The election to Congress after World War II of its first Mexican-Americans, Edward Roybal of California and Henry Gonzalez of Texas, suggests growing political participation and strength. School segregation of Mexican-Americans has begun to weaken recently. The conditions of agricultural labor in the Southwest, especially those of the "braceros" who migrated to the United States each year to work at harvesting crops, have been improved, partly through government action but also through the efforts of such organizations as the Alianza Hispana-Americana.

In 1960, more than 900,000 Puerto Ricans lived in the continental United States. Most of them came to the mainland after World War II. While all Puerto Ricans are American citizens, the Spanish-speaking arrivals, many of whom have dark skins, constituted a clearly defined minority, set off from both white and black native Americans by their language and customs. They concentrated in eastern cities, especially in New York City, where they reached a strength of nearly 700,000 in 1960.

Puerto Ricans, too, encountered discrimination and segregation. Typically they were poor, lacked skills needed for urban industrial or commercial jobs, and often had little education. Yet in the relatively few years after they became a sizeable minority, Puerto

Ricans adapted rapidly to their new circumstances. Like Mexican-Americans, they began to make their political weight felt, and benefited from activities of their social and religious organizations.

Both Puerto Ricans and Mexican-Americans came from westernized cultures which gave them a base from which to adapt to American society. American Indians did not; in order to adjust, they had to abandon tribal culture completely. American blacks occupied a still different position. They had neither cultural ties to a homeland, such as those of Spanish-speaking Americans, nor a traditional tribal culture with few points of contact with an urban, industrial society. But if they were neither an immigrant group, nor a traditional tribe, nor full members of American society, who were they?

The Problem of Assimilation

When different social groups come in contact, one or more of four processes takes place. One group may exterminate the other, as whites did to some Indian tribes. At the other extreme, the groups may amalgamate through intermarriage until they lose separate identities, as many English, Dutch, Swedish, German, and Scotch-Irish immigrants did in the eighteenth and nineteenth centuries. Between these two extremes lie accommodation, in which conflicting groups learn to live with each other while retaining their separate identities, and assimilation, a process through which cultural differences between groups are gradually reduced until their members accept each other fully.

Until recent years, most Negroes have probably wanted to assimilate with the white community. The barriers to assimilation did not at first seem to be of major importance. In the late nineteenth and early twentieth centuries, Negroes were far more interested in getting equal treatment before the law and winning a chance at jobs and education than in gaining full acceptance by whites. Since the issue of assimilation was not then important, and since Negroes started from a position of severe disadvantage, Negro leaders sought white aid and accepted it gladly in organizing protest and welfare movements. But they maintained the ideal of integration as a goal.

The industrial training programs of such institutions as Booker T. Washington's Tuskegee Institute depended heavily on the gifts of such white philanthropists as Andrew Carnegie. Both the NAACP and the National Urban League were joint Negro-white organizations. Most of the direct-action organizations that grew up after World War II, such as the Congress of Racial Equality (CORE) and the Student Non-Violent Coordinating Committee (SNCC) were also interracial in membership and control when founded.

Racism prevailed in the early years of the twentieth century. More than 100 Negroes suffered death by lynching in some years.

CORE, originally a local group set up to fight discrimination in Chicago, was organized by James Farmer on a national level in 1942. SNCC, organized in 1960, draws its support primarily from college students. Like CORE, it engages in such direct action protests as "freedom-rides" and "sit-ins." After 1966, CORE and SNCC became more militant, favoring the "black power" philosophy of Stokely Carmichael. By 1967, SNCC numbered only a few hundred members.

Between 1900 and World War II, riots aimed at Negroes broke out periodically in cities in both South and North. Considering that these developments were only the most extreme signs of a prejudice that could be found in almost every aspect of life, remarkable gains took place toward equality of treatment and opportunity for Negroes in America. Whites and Negroes worked together to spark reform movements. They called on American society to live up to its own professed ideals, as stated in the Declaration of Independence, the Constitution, and the Judeo-Christian religious tradition.

Between the two World Wars a small minority of Negroes emerged as a middle class. They were still largely separate from white society. Their higher education was obtained mainly in predominantly Negro colleges; their businesses, usually small, often provided services mainly for Negroes. But they acquired the economic power and position which made them leaders of their communities. Although Negro workingmen were still denied entry by most unions, they made significant gains during the 1930's when newly organized industrial unions like the United Automobile Workers and the United Steel Workers admitted them as members. State and national politics provided openings for a few Negro leaders, but in the 1930's civil-service jobs provided many more.

Perhaps the greatest opportunities for Negroes to establish equality of economic opportunity came in two widely separated areas. The massive public works and welfare programs of the New Deal served in many places to set a minimum to the income of both Negro and white unemployed, which meant that private employers of labor were obliged to offer them at least a subsistence wage. The greatest rewards for a few, in combined money and prestige, came in the fields of sports and entertainment, where such figures as the heavyweight boxer Joe Louis, the actor-dancer Bill Robinson, and singers Paul Robeson and Marian Anderson gained international fame. American Negro artists and writers, too, began to attract international attention.

Much more substantial gains, however, have come in the years since 1945. Most of the million black Americans serving in World War II were placed in segregated units. They were usually kept in the rear echelons, although some combat units, such as the Ninety-Second Infantry Division in Italy, were made up primarily of Negroes. Then after the war, by order of President Harry S Truman, all branches of the armed services eliminated segregation. In both the Korean War and the Vietnamese War black servicemen fought beside whites and established excellent combat records. The success of integration in the services can be judged by both the achievements of the fighting men and the decline in the number of objections to integration.

On the home front, A. Philip Randolph, a union leader, threatened to march on Washington in 1942 to protest job discrimination. President Franklin D. Roosevelt then issued an executive order prohibiting discrimination in industries with government war contracts. After the war, other executive orders and Congressional legislation broadened the guarantees of equal opportunities in employment and in business dealings with the federal government.

Congress took even more significant actions in 1964 and 1965. It adopted laws which guaranteed equal access to public facilities and provided for ways to register citizens who were being kept from voting on account of race. The latter law led to the registration of numbers of black voters in some parts of the Deep South for the first time in more than half a century. Negroes had been playing an increasingly important part in politics, both local and national, for a long time before then, however. Heavy Negro support had helped to reelect President Truman in a close election in 1948, and to elect President John F. Kennedy in a closer election in 1960.

Perhaps the most crucial role in the movement to guarantee equal opportunity fell to the Supreme Court. The Court, led by Chief Justice Earl Warren, rendered literally dozens of decisions striking down segregation laws and upholding legal guarantees of equal rights in the years after 1952. Critics of the Court argued that the judges were making political decisions that properly belonged to legislators. Defenders of the Court argued in return that it was responsible for interpreting the Constitution when constitutional questions were raised. Moreover, they said, the critics were usually defenders of a racial status quo which the Court was not obligated to maintain. The Supreme Court's decision of 1954 invalidating racial segregation in the public schools illustrates the way in which the judicial arm of government became caught in public controversy over racial relations.

By no means all action taken to secure equality of opportunity came through the federal government. State and local legislatures and agencies throughout the North and West, and including some states bordering the South, also took a variety of actions to suppress open segregation or discrimination in the years after World War II. Among the most important laws they passed were ones that forbade discrimination in employment and housing.

Partly as a result of legislation and of increasing acceptance of Negroes by whites, but also because of threats of boycotts and other economic and political pressures, Negroes made substantial gains in employment after World War II. The number of Negro union members rose steadily. Although they were concentrated in big industrial unions, they also entered some craft unions that had traditionally barred Negroes. For the first time, large businesses

A Philip Randolph, born 1889, organized the Brotherhood of Sleeping Car Porters, a union he still heads. In 1957, he became a vice-president of the AFL-CIO. He was one of the organizers and principal speakers at the "March on Washington" on August 28, 1963.

The Civil Rights Act of 1964 declared a sixth-grade education as proof of literacy for voting; forbade discrimination in public accommodations and government-owned facilities; authorized the withholding of federal funds from programs engaged in discrimination; and created an Equal Opportunity Commission and a Community Relations Service. The Voting Rights Act of 1965 authorized the Attorney-General to send federal examiners to any county accused of voter discrimination and register all qualified voters.

In 1947, Jackie Robinson was signed by the Brooklyn Dodgers and became the first Negro to play in the major leagues.

and industries, especially those operating on a national scale, began seeking Negro employees actively, and began recruiting them to serve in lower management positions. The upper levels were still reserved for whites.

Negroes cracked the wall of segregation in professional baseball, football, basketball, and other sports, and began to appear in movie, television, and stage roles in parts different from the stereotyped character parts to which they had been restricted. In the field of law and government, Negroes made distinguished contributions. The most notable were those of Thurgood Marshall, an NAACP attorney who organized the successful legal fight against school segregation and who, in 1968, became the first Negro Justice of the Supreme Court, and Ralph Bunche who served as Undersecretary of State and then as Undersecretary of the United Nations. The man who won the greatest international recognition, however, was Martin Luther King, Jr., who was awarded the Nobel Prize for Peace for his efforts to maintain non-violent processes in seeking equality.

But while these notable gains were being made, the question of ultimate assimilation occasionally emerged. The attitudes of many whites made it increasingly clear to Negroes that assimilation was an unrealistic goal in the near future. Hence, some Negroes turned to the development of all-black organizations whose goals often emphasized separatism, and to the development of an identity with African traditions and modern Africans. In the 1920's, Marcus Garvey's Universal Negro Improvement Association drew members by the hundreds of thousands from the black masses, rather than from the well educated Negro minority who supported and staffed the NAACP and Urban League. The UNIA gave its members a sense of belonging to something much larger than themselves which was really theirs. In addition, Garvey's ideal of an African homeland drew effectively on one of the most potent ideological forces of modern times: nationalism. The educated and sophisticated W. E. B. Du Bois, who opposed Garvey's movement, was himself active in a Pan-African movement designed to unite those of African descent everywhere in opposition to European colonialism in Africa; Du Bois ended his life as a citizen of the newly independent nation of Ghana in Africa.

In the years after World War II, black nationalism, spurred by the achievement of independence of dozens of former European colonies in Africa, and separatism both grew rapidly. The successes of the Southern Christian Leadership Conference, led by Dr. King until his death, of sit-in demonstrations by black groups to obtain the use of public facilities, and of boycotts to persuade businesses to hire more Negroes, helped stimulate the growth of all-black movements. Of these one of the most striking all-black groups was the Muslim religious organization, whose size was undetermined but which possessed societies, buildings, and other property in dozens of cities, mostly in the North. The Muslims preached a doctrine of black racism which portrayed whites as creatures of the devil. The assassination of Negro leaders like King and Medgar Evers, an NAACP leader in Mississippi, strengthened the militancy of blacks engaged in civil rights movements. Such tragic resorts to violence probably weakened the spirit of non-violence so successfully fostered by King and others, and encouraged blacks in urban ghettos toward violence and destruction of property (usually white-owned) when riots broke out.

In 1963, one of Elijah Muhammad's followers, Malcolm X, broke from the group and formed the Organization of Afro-American Unity. After his assassination in 1965, he became a folk hero for many black militants.

The emergence of black nationalism and separatism puzzled many Americans, including some Negroes. This trend seemed to reject the ideal of integration in American life at the very time when Negroes were making significant gains toward equality of opportunity. Many persons were also puzzled by the rise of black militancy, which seemed to suggest hatred of whites, at the very time when white cooperation in interracial ventures reached its height. Perhaps one answer to these ironies lies in the depth and extent of black resentment and suspicion which always were there but seldom were revealed because of the danger of violent repression. And perhaps another answer lies in the deeply felt need of many blacks for a group identity which does not depend in any way on the favor or support of white society. Perhaps black power will become a permanent ideology. On the other hand, strong feelings of racial pride may eventually make genuine assimilation possible among white and black citizens, each proud of his heritage and insistent upon his full rights in a democratic society. No more vital issue faces modern Americans.

SUGGESTED READINGS

ISAACS, HAROLD R., *The New World of Negro Americans.* Isaacs' volume emphasizes the impact of world events, especially African nationalism, on black Americans.

LANDES, RUTH, *Latin Americans of the Southwest.* This brief and simply written volume analyzes the history and culture of Americans of Mexican ancestry.

MALCOLM X and A. HALEY, *Autobiography of Malcolm X.* This powerful story of the progress of a Negro through crime and imprisonment to leadership in the Black Muslim organization and then his death by assassination has quickly become a minor classic.

WRIGHT, RICHARD, *Black Boy.* This is a gripping account of boyhood in the South a generation ago, written by a distinguished black writer.

The Present and the Future

CHAPTER 30

117 A SUMMARY ESSAY

The agriculture revolution marked mankind's first dramatic turning point. The ability to grow food freed man from ceaseless wandering over the face of the earth in pursuit of game or wild plants and made civilization possible. Scientific knowledge and industrialization began to mark a second great turning point about two or three hundred years ago. In the twentieth century the long-run effects unleashed by these two developments is becoming clear. Our era may well be a watershed as significant to mankind as the domestication of plants and animals.

The Twentieth Century as a Turning Point

Twenty-five percent of all people who have ever lived are now alive; in the near future, the percentage may reach fifty. World population now increases at a rate of 2.2 per second, 132 per minute, 190,000 per day, more than 1.3 million per week, about 72 million a year, or about one billion in fifteen years. World population reached one billion about 1800 and two billion about 1930; in 1975, it will probably pass the four billion mark. This fantastic explosion of people may well be the most significant development of the late twentieth century.

Knowledge grows at a similar rate. About every ten years, the total amount of mankind's knowledge doubles. About a million significant articles now appear each year, in more than 15,000 learned journals printed in hundreds of languages. Like population growth, the increase in knowledge will transform the modern world.

During this century, the world's population has shifted from rural to urban areas. Experts predict that by the year 2000, one quarter of the world's population will live in cities whose population exceeds 100,000. By 2050, half the world's people will live in such cities. The 1960 United States census indicated that 70 percent of Americans already lived in urban areas. This great transition has become possible because scientific knowledge and mechanization have made farmers so productive. About five percent of the population of the United States can now feed the entire nation.

Two sets of figures may help to indicate the growth of technology in the twentieth century. About half of all the energy used by mankind throughout history has been consumed within the last hundred years. And about half of the metals mined from the earth have been removed since about 1910, a period within the lifetime of most grandparents of today's high school students. No wonder that change tumbles upon change with bewildering rapidity.

The twentieth century has seen a host of new developments. Movies, radio, and television have revolutionized communications. Airplanes have linked every corner of the world. The new 490-passenger jets will fly from New York to London in five hours. Rockets now link man to the moon and to planets far in space. Scientists use nuclear energy to power ships and manufacture electricity. The computer is working an electronic revolution in industry. With the discovery of DNA, scientists may be able to control evolution. They have already transplanted hearts and fitted plastic organs into human bodies. The list is endless. In 1967, the United States government issued almost 70,000 patents to inventors.

DNA is a complex compound, a nucleic acid, which is the chief material found in chromosomes, the cell bodies that determine the heredity of plants and animals. In 1957, Dr. Arthur Kornberg, an American biochemist, demonstrated that DNA could reproduce outside a cell.

The Next Thirty Years

Prediction is risky, particularly in a world where one scientific advance can change a whole era. Still some trends seem certain. Take the nature of the American people, for example. By the year 2000, the present 200,000,000 population will have grown to 360,000,000. Many Americans will live well beyond retirement age as medical advances permit more and more people to reach their eighties. A greater proportion of all these people will live in the western states. They will have moved increasingly to metropolitan areas. They will be incredibly wealthy by the standards of any past society, although pockets of poverty may still exist, particularly among the aged and among minority groups. Wealth and mass communications will probably turn most Americans more and more toward middle-class standards which may alienate a future younger generation, just as present American society has driven hippies, campus protesters, and black militants to revolt. Whether or not the society moves in the direction of a melting pot or continues to marry primarily within religious and racial groups remains to be seen.

There is no question, however, about the progress of industrialization. The computer is changing mass-production industries into vast, automated complexes of machinery where a few men control entire manufacturing processes. This process will continue. New energy sources and machines will enable a far smaller percentage of the labor force to produce an enormously increased output of goods.

Here the GNP is quoted in 1969 prices.

GNP will continue to rise. In 1968, it was $860 billion. By the year 2000, it will be $2 trillion if it rises at a three percent rate, $2.8 trillion if at four percent, and $3.9 trillion at five percent. What will the nation do with all those goods and services?

Some resources must be allocated to combat pollution, the by-product of industrialization. Billions of dollars must be spent to clean Lake Erie which has become one vast cesspool. Thousands of other lakes and rivers are now polluted. The air over our major cities poisons man's lungs. Tin cans and bottles threaten to overwhelm our dumps. During the next three decades, we will probably junk 400 million cars. Millions more will blight roadways unless we learn to handle such waste products more efficiently.

Nor will the problems of the rest of the world go away. The population explosion threatens life itself in much of the non-Western world. Outside the United States, the world spends about $80 million each year for population control; the world's military budget totals $154 billion, of which the United States and the Soviet Union spend two thirds. Money taken from guns and given to population control might possibly stem the tide of people which seems inevitably destined to overwhelm man's food resources.

In January 1968, the North Koreans seized the U.S. Navy ship **Pueblo.** In April 1969, they shot down a Navy reconnaissance plane. Both times the United States protested, but did not retaliate. "The weak can be rash. The powerful must be restrained." said Secretary of State William Rogers.

People in developing lands, recently freed from colonial rule, demand a better life. They will not sit quiet and hungry as they watch American families buy their second home, their third automobile, and their fourth television set. They need capital goods and skilled people to help them start the difficult process of economic growth. In the near future, many of them will control hydrogen bombs; more can raise enormous armed forces. As the world's richest nation, the United States will face the responsibilities of power in a world where other nations, disturbed by our dominance, will grasp every opportunity to force us to face our human responsibilities, to provoke us, and to make us share our wealth. If we become impatient, we can set off an atomic war. A few strategically placed cobalt bombs can kill everyone on earth.

A cobalt bomb is an atomic bomb to which cobalt, a silver-white metallic element is added. Scientists have not yet produced a cobalt bomb, because it would produce large quantities of radiation fallout.

In the near future, living and working patterns of Americans will change drastically. Although the exodus from American farms to cities is almost at an end, metropolitan areas will continue to grow, and people will become even more crowded. More of them will live in apartments rather than houses. Suburbs will sprawl over what is now open countryside. Traffic congestion, already of frightening proportions, will become infinitely worse. People will have more leisure—the twenty-hour work week seems quite possible three decades hence. Moreover, with the society in such rapid transition, a man may hold several quite different jobs in a lifetime as new machines or new techniques eliminate the job he originally trained for. Unless he has learned how to learn, and unless education becomes a continuous process extending throughout a lifetime, a man in his early thirties may well find himself unemployable.

Sooner or later, governments must deal with problems like these. Governments can reallocate resources among the great variety of needs in a modern society. Governments can raise enough money for significant economic aid to foreign nations. Governments can use taxes to purify air and water. Governments can make urban life attractive. Governments can develop an educational system which can help a man keep pace with a society in rapid flux. And if government assumes these tasks, the taxpayer must foot the bill, although a rapid rise in GNP may make paying the bill relatively painless.

Citizens may be caught in competition between private and public wants. Americans demand steadily increasing real wages. But if private incomes rise too rapidly, there may not be enough public money to end poverty, clean up pollution, make the cities livable, revolutionize education, expand foreign aid enormously, and perform all the other tasks which government must do in an international, urbanized, industrialized society. The cost of providing vital public services may well be reducing private expenditures, or seeing them rise slowly. The battle over which sector of the economy gets what will take place in the political arena. Its outcome may well determine the quality of life for the entire world.

Johnson's Second Term

Many of the trends which seem likely to dominate the next three decades became noticeable during Lyndon B. Johnson's two terms. Chapters 27, 28, and 29 touched upon various events during the Johnson administration. The following analysis traces these events and explains others which have not been mentioned.

President Kennedy had worked hard to combat poverty and to bring justice to America's minorities, but Congress had balked. His death, Johnson's ability to work with Congress, and a sweeping electoral victory in 1964 produced new legislation. Johnson sponsored a series of measures in the tradition of Roosevelt's Second New Deal. The Eighty-Ninth Congress passed more reform and welfare legislation than any Congress in the previous thirty years.

During Johnson's first term, a tax cut helped to maintain spending and hence to reduce unemployment and increase GNP, which grew from $681 billion in 1965 to $857 billion in 1968. Through the 1960's, this growth rate averaged more than five percent a year, one of the highest in American history and in the contemporary world. This growth widened the gap between the wealth of a typical American and of the poverty-stricken citizens of developing nations.

Head Start, composed of professional teachers and volunteer aids, seeks to broaden the experiences of preschool children from low-income families and prepare them for formal schooling. Volunteers in Service to America (VISTA) is often referred to as the Domestic Peace Corps. Men and women over 18 live and work in poor communities throughout the country. The Neighborhood Youth Corps is sponsored by local Sanitation Departments. Young residents are employed to clean up their neighborhoods.

Soon after assuming office, Johnson launched a War on Poverty. The Economic Opportunity Bill set up the Office of Economic Opportunity to sponsor activities to benefit America's poor. The OEO developed the Job Corps, which set up training programs for young men who had been unable to find jobs in modern industry, and organized programs such as Head Start, Upward Bound, VISTA, and the Neighborhood Youth Corps. Bills to assist the poor in the Appalachian region, to set up health insurance for the aged, and to increase social security benefits, however, failed to pass Congress.

The Urban Mass Transportation Act (1964) appropriated $375 million to study ways to improve mass transportation. Urban areas had been increasingly choked with traffic as workers and shoppers drove automobiles into central cities rather than rely upon inadequate public transportation. With cities increasing both in number and size, this legislation clearly looked to the future.

Finally, Congress passed a Civil Rights Act in June 1964. The Act required identical voting requirements for whites and blacks, prohibited discrimination in most public accommodations, gave the Attorney General powers to speed school desegregation, assisted school districts that were desegregating, and prohibited discrimination in employment in firms whose products entered interstate commerce. Although some states and some private citizens continued to drag their feet, the new law steadily added to the rights enjoyed by black citizens.

In 1964, Johnson soundly defeated Senator Barry Goldwater, the Republican nominee for President. The election swept Democratic senators and representatives into office with Johnson. He faced fewer conservative opponents in Congress than any President since the mid 1930's.

The Eighty-Ninth Congress passed a number of measures to aid the aged and the poor. Medicare, a health plan for people over sixty-five, finally got through Congress (1965), where it had been rejected frequently since World War II. Amendments to the Social Security Act provided larger pensions and extended coverage to millions of additional workers. Amendments to the Fair Labor Standards Act raised the minimum wage to $1.40 in 1967 and to $1.60 a year later and extended coverage to eight million additional persons. In 1965, the War on Poverty received an appropriation of $1.5 billion, twice as much as the year before. Congress also passed a bill appropriating $1.1 billion to improve economic conditions in Appalachia, one of the nation's most depressed areas.

President Johnson appointed Robert C. Weaver Secretary of the Department of Housing and Urban Development. He became the first black to hold a Cabinet position.

To make the cities more livable, Johnson created the Department of Housing and Urban Development. In 1966, he created another Cabinet position, the Department of Transportation, to begin a concerted attack on that vital urban problem. The Demonstration Cities and the Metropolitan Development Acts of 1966 provided federal funds to plan and develop model neighborhoods in some eighty cities across the entire nation. But despite these attempts at reform, urban housing continued to deteriorate faster than society could clear slums and erect modern apartments.

Several measures helped to reform American education. The Elementary and Secondary Education Act appropriated $1.3 billion for a wide variety of programs in education leading to improved teacher training, funds for books and equipment, and similar goals. The Higher Education Act provided scholarships for college students and money for books and laboratories, and established the National Teacher Corps to prepare teachers for substandard schools. The Cold War GI Bill offered financial support to veterans who had served for more than six months in the armed services since when the original GI Bill, passed during World War II, had expired. Finally, Congress established the National Foundation of Arts and Humanities.

Veterans serving after January 31, 1955, became eligible for benefits under the 1966 act. All who have served at least 180 days and received an honorable discharge are eligible for such benefits as education loans up to $17,500 and $100 a month grants for veterans without dependents.

The Foundation assists individuals, states, and non-profit organizations engaged in artistic endeavors. It also encourages training and research in the humanities by a program of fellowships and grants.

Two measures affected civil rights. The Voting Rights Act of 1965 removed barriers to Negro voting, particularly literacy tests. In addition, the Immigration Act of 1965 abolished both the national origins and the quota systems which had been in force since the 1920's. A new annual ceiling on immigration, 120,000 from the Western hemisphere, and 170,000 from elsewhere, went into effect.

Finally, Congress passed a number of minor measures which had to do with safety or with the pollution of the environment. A Truth-in-Packaging Act required manufacturers to state what their products contained. The Motor Safety Vehicle Act established safety standards for new cars. Highway beautification projects, supported strongly by Mrs. Johnson, and increased programs to prevent air and water pollution, made a start in these directions.

This significant legislative spurt ended in 1966. The Republicans made a comeback in Congress in the off-year elections, gaining 47 seats in the House and 3 in the Senate. Perhaps more important, however, were the influence of the Vietnamese War, the racial troubles which haunted American cities, and revolts by young people, particularly on college campuses. These issues divided American society more deeply than anything else since the 1930's.

Vietnam; The Black Revolt; The Student Protests

In 1964, about 25,000 American soldiers served in Vietnam. By 1968, this number had increased to more than a half million. American battle deaths rose steadily—1728 in 1965; 6053 in 1966; 11,048 in 1967; 14,592 in 1968. During 1967, the government spent about $67.5 billion on defense, largely on Vietnam; during 1968, it spent $80.5 billion. Little could be done about domestic issues so long as the war drained the attention, the energy, and the money of the American people. Towards the end of the Johnson period, federal spending diminished in most non-military areas.

The Kennedy administration had escalated the war slightly. Early in 1965 after the election was over, Johnson sent American bombers over North Vietnam in response to North Vietnamese ground raids. Although no one knew it at the time, the war was on—and it was very hot. During the next few months, the U.S. government mounted increasing air attacks, sent more troops to Vietnam, and began to take over more and more of the fighting.

The conflict between Doves and Hawks escalated in turn. At first a minority, the Doves steadily increased in number and influence. By late 1967, polls revealed that the majority of Americans considered the Vietnamese war a mistake. The Hawks lost ground when predictions of success from military leaders consistently proved false. The so-called Tet Offensive, which began on January 31, 1968, proved that the Viet-Cong and their allies could launch attacks under the noses of American troops. This offensive brought the Vietnamese issue to a head.

The Communist offensive was launched during the cease-fire called during the lunar New Year (Tet). During the offensive, an estimated 14,000 South Vietnamese soldiers and 13,000 civilians were killed or wounded; 2000 Americans were killed; and an estimated 50,000 Communist troops were killed.

As Chapter 29 has indicated, the momentum of the movement for Negro rights picked up steadily after World War II. Congress passed five Civil Rights Acts between 1957 and 1968. Blacks and whites worked closely together to obtain most of this legislation and to organize the sit-ins and protest marches which dramatized the cause of black citizens. But in the 1960's, the black movement changed steadily toward a new emphasis on black power and black separatism. Black leaders more than forty years old had grown up in integrated organizations such as the NAACP and the Urban League. The younger generation, impatient of gradualism, began to found militant all-black organizations and led the civil disturbances which swept the nation, beginning with the Watts riot in Los Angeles in 1965. During the next three years, riots broke out in dozens of cities, particularly after the murder of the Rev. Martin Luther King, Jr. in April 1968. The change in the black revolution, like the war in Vietnam, deeply divided the American people.

After the riots of 1965, President Johnson appointed an Advisory Commission on Civil Disorders headed by Governor Otto Kerner of Illinois and Mayor John Lindsay of New York. The two Negro members of the group were Roy Wilkins, head of the NAACP, and Senator Edward Brooke of Massachusetts. The Commission or Kerner Report issued in March 1968 stated that the riots were not the result of a conspiracy but resulted from urban conditions caused by "white racism." The overall conclusion was that "our nation is moving toward two societies, one black, one white —separate and unequal."

So did campus revolts. Throughout the 1950's, critics complained that college students wanted only a steady job, a suburban home, and future security. The few "beatniks" who opposed this complacent attitude were vastly outnumbered. But the 1960's saw a sharp generational conflict spring up. "You can't trust anyone over thirty," one student protester proclaimed. The alienation represented by this slogan took both passive and active forms.

The passive resisters often became hippies, dropped out of "straight" society, and made their way to hippy colonies such as those in the Haight-Ashbury district of San Francisco or New York City's East Village. But the activists were determined to destroy the society. Led by militants organized in the Students for a Democratic Society (SDS), they began to occupy college buildings and make strident demands of college presidents and deans. Turned off by the Vietnam War and by the conflicts over civil rights, they were convinced that American society was not worth saving. By 1967, some SDS leaders counseled violence. Their activities at Berkeley, Columbia, Harvard, and many other universities alarmed many Americans. Thousands of other students joined campus revolts, partly in opposition to tactics by police against students and partly because America's universities had long been rife with abuses ignored by trustees, administrators, and faculty members alike.

Hippies are young people, predominately white, who have rejected the values and rewards of affluent middle-class society. Hippy philosophy is committed to living for the "now," a belief in love, and abhorence of violence. Although alienated by the work ethic which demands a 9-5 routine, many hippies will work on projects that do not violate their philosophy. Several groups are known for their community activities—organizing schools, communes, camps, and neighborhood work details.

These developments—the war, the black revolt, and the campus uprisings—disturbed the body politic. In November 1967, Senator Eugene McCarthy of Minnesota announced that he would seek the Democratic nomination for President, concentrating on opposition to the war as a campaign issue. Although most voters refused to take his candidacy seriously, he won the Democratic primary in New Hampshire in March, about five weeks after the Tet Offensive had begun. Soon afterward, Senator Robert F. Kennedy of New York, brother of the late President, declared himself a candidate.

Two weeks later, Lyndon Johnson announced that he would halt bombing in North Vietnam and start movements for peace talks. In order to separate these peace moves from partisan politics, Johnson announced that he would not be a candidate for another term. Four days later, an assassin killed Martin Luther King, Jr. in Memphis, Tennessee. Riots swept through Negro ghettos all over the country. Shortly afterward, Vice-President Hubert H. Humphrey announced his candidacy. Then on June 4, after winning the California primary, Robert Kennedy was assassinated in Los Angeles. During this period, riots prompted by a student revolt broke out at Columbia University. The national consensus of 1966 had burst.

Martin Luther King's assassin, James Earl Ray, was tried, found guilty, and sentenced to life imprisonment.

Robert Kennedy's murderer, Sirhan Sirhan, an Arab immigrant, was found guilty and received the death sentence.

Richard M. Nixon moved steadily toward nomination by the Republicans despite the opposition of such liberals as Governors George Romney of Michigan and Nelson Rockefeller of New York, and of conservatives such as California's Governor Ronald Reagen. Nixon won the Republican nomination easily and chose Maryland's little-known governor, Spiro T. Agnew, as his running mate. In the South, ex-Governor George Wallace of Alabama started a third party movement. An avowed conservative, he promised to shoot looters and to suppress student rebels with clubs. He chose retired Air Force

Anti-war demonstrators, chiefly students, professors, and hippies, came from all over the country to Chicago to protest the Vietnam policy of the Democratic administration. Fighting broke out in downtown Chicago and at the Hilton Hotel between demonstrators, police, and some delegates. In retaliation for obscene comments and other harassing tactics, the Chicago police, unrestrained by Mayor Daley, began assaulting innocent and guilty alike. Many viewed Daley as the villain of the Chicago convention; others lauded him for siding with law and order.

General Curtis LeMay as his vice-presidential candidate. In the meantime, the Democrats had nominated Humphrey with Maine's able senator, Edmund S. Muskie, filling out the ticket. But bitter debate at the Democratic Convention and the activities of Chicago police, supported by Democratic Mayor Daley of Chicago against student protesters near the Convention Hall, provoked a cry of dissatisfaction.

Although polls indicated that Nixon began the campaign with a generous lead, he lost ground steadily. The vote was unusually close. Nixon polled only about a third of a million plurality in a total vote of about 71 million, and the Democrats retained control of both the House and the Senate. With no clear mandate from the voters and with an opposing party in control of Congress, Nixon entered office with severe handicaps.

Toward the 1970's

President Nixon must cope with all the problems which haunted his predecessor: war, the cities, population growth, automation, pollution, the problems of the aged, student unrest, education, the war against poverty, civil rights, and foreign relations. Each of these problems may worsen in the immediate future. On the other hand, the remarkable health of the economy, faint signs of peace in Vietnam, and most of all, the proven ability of the American people to solve their problems all bring hope.

Whether or not our country becomes a great society depends primarily upon its citizens. They must make the hard choices between war and peace, between consumer goods and a healthy environment, between racial hatred and freedom for all men to pursue the American dream, that each individual shall receive the opportunity to develop to the limits of his ability in a free society. The study of history can give us perspective on choices like these. Intelligence, determination, and high courage can help us choose wisely while there is still time.

SUGGESTED READINGS

CONANT, JAMES B., *Slums and Suburbs.* This slim volume analyzes the differences between schools in white suburbs and in non-white urban areas and makes suggestions for change.

GATZKE, HANS W., *The Present in Perspective.* Gatzke's book describes major developments in the world since 1945 and places the history of the United States in its global setting.

HARRINGTON, MICHAEL, *The Other America: Poverty in the United States.* Harrington's influential volume describes both the society of affluence and the society of poverty. The original edition of this book helped to spark the war on poverty.

Appendix

The Declaration of Independence

WHEN in the course of human events, it becomes necessary for one people to dissolve the political bands which have connected them with another, and to assume among the powers of the earth, the separate and equal station to which the laws of Nature and of Nature's God entitle them, a decent respect to the opinions of mankind requires that they should declare the causes which impel them to the separation.

We hold these truths to be self-evident, that all men are created equal, that they are endowed by their Creator with certain unalienable rights, that among these are life, liberty and the pursuit of happiness. That to secure these rights, governments are instituted among men, deriving their just powers from the consent of the governed, That whenever any form of government becomes destructive of these ends, it is the right of the people to alter or to abolish it, and to institute new government laying its foundation on such principles and organizing its powers in such form, as to them shall seem most likely to effect their safety and happiness. Prudence, indeed, will dictate that governments long established should not be changed for light and transient causes; and accordingly all experience hath shown, that mankind are more disposed to suffer, while evils are sufferable, than to right themselves by abolishing the forms to which they are accustomed. But when a long train of abuses and usurpations, pursuing invariably the same object evinces a design to reduce them under absolute despotism, it is their right, it is their duty, to throw off such government, and to provide new guards for their future security. — Such has been the patient sufferance of these colonies; and such is now the necessity which constrains them to alter their former systems of government. The history of the present King of Great Britain is a history of repeated injuries and usurpations, all having in direct object the establishment of an absolute tyranny over these states. To prove this, let facts be submitted to a candid world.

He has refused his assent to laws, the most wholesome and necessary for the public good.

He has forbidden his governors to pass laws of immediate and pressing importance, unless suspended in their operation till his assent should be obtained; and when so suspended, he has utterly neglected to attend them.

He has refused to pass other laws for the accommodation of large districts of people, unless those people would relinquish the right of representation in the legislature, a right inestimable to them and formidable to tyrants only.

He has called together legislative bodies at places unusual, uncomfortable, and distant from the depository of their public records, for the sole purpose of fatiguing them into compliance with his measures.

He has dissolved representative houses repeatedly, for opposing with manly firmness his invasions on the rights of the people.

He has refused for a long time, after such dissolutions, to cause others to be elected; whereby the legislative powers, incapable of annihilation, have returned to the people at large for their exercise; the state remaining in the meantime exposed to all the dangers of invasion from without, and convulsions within.

He has endeavored to prevent the population of these states; for that purpose obstructing the laws for naturalization of foreigners; refusing to pass others to encourage their migration hither, and raising the conditions of new appropriations of lands.

He has obstructed the administration of justice, by refusing his assent to laws for establishing judiciary powers.

He has made judges dependent on his will alone, for the tenure of their offices, and the amount and payment of their salaries.

He has erected a multitude of new offices, and sent hither swarms of officers to harass our people, and eat out their substance.

He has kept among us, in times of peace, standing armies without the consent of our legislature.

He has affected to render the military independent of and superior to the civil power.

He has combined with others to subject us to a jurisdiction foreign to our constitution, and unacknowledged by our laws; giving his assent to their acts of pretended legislation:

For quartering large bodies of armed troops among us:

For protecting them, by a mock trial, from punishment for any murders which they should commit on the inhabitants of these states:

For cutting off our trade with all parts of the world:

For imposing taxes on us without our consent:

For depriving us in many cases, of the benefits of trial by jury:

For transporting us beyond seas to be tried for pretended offenses:

For abolishing the free system of English laws in a neighboring province, establishing therein an arbitrary government, and enlarging its boundaries so as to render it at once an example and fit instrument for introducing the same absolute rule into these colonies:

For taking away our charters, abolishing our most valuable laws; and altering fundamentally the forms of our governments:

For suspending our own legislatures, and declaring themselves invested with power to legislate for us in all cases whatsoever.

He has abdicated government here, by declaring us out of his protection and waging war against us.

He has plundered our seas, ravaged our coasts, burnt our towns, and destroyed the lives of our people.

He is at this time transporting large armies of foreign mercenaries to complete the works of death, desolation and tyranny, already begun with circumstances of cruelty and perfidy scarcely paralleled in the most barbarous ages, and totally unworthy the head of a civilized nation.

He has constrained our fellow citizens taken captive on the high seas to bear arms against their country, to become the executioners of their friends and brethren, or to fall themselves by their hands.

He has excited domestic insurrections amongst us, and has endeavored to bring on the inhabitants of our frontiers, the merciless Indian savages, whose known rule of warfare, is an undistinguished destruction of all ages, sexes and conditions.

In every stage of these oppressions we have petitioned for redress in the most humble terms. Our repeated petitions have been answered only by repeated injury. A prince, whose character is thus marked by every act which may define a tyrant, is unfit to be the ruler of a free people.

Nor have we been wanting in attention to our British brethren. We have warned them from time to time of attempts by their legislature to extend an unwarrantable jurisdiction over us. We have reminded them of the circumstances of our emigration and settlement here. We have appealed to their native justice and magnanimity, and we have conjured them by the ties of our common kindred to disavow these usurpations, which would inevitably interrupt our connections and correspondence. They too have been deaf to the voice of justice and of consanguinity. We must, therefore, acquiesce in the necessity, which denounces our separation, and hold them, as we hold the rest of mankind, enemies in war, in peace friends.

We, therefore, the representatives of the united states of America, in General Congress, assembled, appealing to the Supreme Judge of the world for the rectitude of our intentions, do, in the name, and by authority of the good people of these colonies, solemnly publish and declare, that these united colonies are, and of right ought to be free and independent states; that they are absolved from all allegiance to the British Crown, and that all political connection between them and the state of Great Britain, is and ought to be totally dissolved; and that as free and independent states, they have full power to levy war, conclude peace, contract alliances, establish commerce, and to do all other acts and things which independent states may of right do. And for the support of this Declaration, with a firm reliance on the protection of Divine Providence, we mutually pledge to each other our lives, our fortunes and our sacred honor.

The Constitution of the United States of America

(The portions of the Constitution printed in brackets are either out of date or changed by amendment. The descriptive headings have been added for your convenience.)

Preamble

We the people of the United States, in order to form a more perfect Union, establish justice, insure domestic tranquility, provide for the common defense, promote the general welfare, and secure the blessings of liberty to ourselves and our posterity, do ordain and establish this CONSTITUTION for the United States of America.

Article 1. Legislative Department

SECTION 1. CONGRESS

All legislative powers herein granted shall be vested in a Congress of the United States, which shall consist of a Senate and House of Representatives.

SECTION 2. HOUSE OF REPRESENTATIVES

1. *Election and term of office.* The House of Representatives shall be composed of members chosen every second year by the people of the several states, and the electors in each state shall have the qualifications requisite for electors of the most numerous branch of the state legislature.

2. *Qualifications for representatives.* No person shall be a representative who shall not have attained to the age of twenty-five years, and been seven years a citizen of the United States, and who shall not, when elected, be an inhabitant of that state in which he shall be chosen.

3. *Apportionment of representatives and direct taxes.* Representatives [and direct taxes] shall be apportioned among the several states which may be included within this Union, according to their respective numbers, [which shall be determined by adding to the whole number of free persons, including those bound to service for a term of years, and excluding Indians not taxed, three-fifths of all other persons.] The actual enumeration shall be made within three years after the first meeting of the Congress of the United States, and within every subsequent term of ten years, in such manner as they shall by law direct. The number of representatives shall not exceed 1 for every 30,000, but each state shall have at least 1 representative; [and until such enumeration shall be made, the state of New Hampshire shall be entitled to choose 3; Massachusetts, 8; Rhode Island and Providence Plantations, 1; Connecticut, 5; New

York, 6; New Jersey, 4; Pennsylvania, 8; Delaware, 1; Maryland, 6; Virginia, 10; North Carolina, 5; South Carolina 5; and Georgia 3.]

4. *Filling vacancies.* When vacancies happen in the representation from any state, the executive authority thereof shall issue writs of election to fill such vacancies.

5. *Election of officers; impeachment.* The House of Representatives shall choose their Speaker and other officers; and shall have the sole power of impeachment.

SECTION 3. SENATE

1. *Number of senators and term of office.* The Senate of the United States shall be composed of two senators from each state, [chosen by the legislature thereof,] for six years, and each senator shall have one vote.

2. *Classification; filling vacancies.* [Immediately after they shall be assembled in consequence of the first election, they shall be divided as equally as may be into three classes. The seats of the senators of the first class shall be vacated at the expiration of the second year, of the second class at the expiration of the fourth year, and of the third class at the expiration of the sixth year, so that one-third may be chosen every second year; and if vacancies happen by resignation, or otherwise, during the recess of the legislature of any state, the executive thereof may make temporary appointments until the next meeting of the legislature, which shall then fill such vacancies.]

3. *Qualifications for senators.* No person shall be a senator who shall not have attained to the age of thirty years, and been nine years a citizen of the United States, and who shall not, when elected, be an inhabitant of that state for which he shall be chosen.

4. *President of the Senate.* The Vice-President of the United States shall be president of the Senate, but shall have no vote, unless they be equally divided.

5. *Other officers.* The Senate shall choose their other officers, and also a President *pro tempore*, in the absence of the Vice-President, or when he shall exercise the office of President of the United States.

6. *Trials of impeachment.* The Senate shall have the sole power to try all impeachments. When sitting for that purpose, they shall be on oath or affirmation. When the President of the United States is tried, the Chief Justice shall preside; and no person shall be convicted without the concurrence of two thirds of the members present.

7. *Punishment for conviction.* Judgment in cases of impeachment shall not extend further than to removal from office, and disqualification to hold and enjoy any office of honor, trust, or profit under the United States; but the party convicted shall nevertheless be liable and subject to indictment, trial, judgment, and punishment, according to law.

SECTION 4. ELECTIONS AND MEETINGS OF CONGRESS

1. *Regulation of elections.* The times, places, and manner of holding elections for senators and representatives shall be prescribed in each state by the legislature thereof; but the Congress may at any time by law make or alter such regulations, except as to the places of choosing senators.

2. *Meetings.* The Congress shall assemble at least once in every year, [and such meeting shall be on the first Monday in December,] unless they shall by law appoint a different day.

SECTION 5. RULES OF PROCEDURE

1. *Membership and sittings.* Each house shall be the judge of the elections, returns, and qualifications of its own members, and a majority of each shall constitute a quorum to do business; but a smaller number may adjourn from day to day, and may be authorized to compel the attendance of absent members, in such manner, and under such penalties, as each house may provide.

2. *Proceedings.* Each house may determine the rules of its proceedings, punish its members for disorderly behavior, and with the concurrence of two thirds, expel a member.

3. *Journal.* Each house shall keep a journal of its proceedings, and from time to time publish the same, excepting such parts as may in their judgment require secrecy; and the yeas and nays of the members of either house on any question shall, at the desire of one fifth of those present, be entered on the journal.

4. *Adjournment.* Neither house, during the session of Congress, shall, without the consent of the other, adjourn for more than three days, nor to any other place than that in which the two houses shall be sitting.

SECTION 6. PRIVILEGES AND RESTRICTIONS

1. *Salary and privileges.* The senators and representatives shall receive a compensation for their services, to be ascertained by law and

paid out of the Treasury of the United States. They shall in all cases, except treason, felony, and breach of the peace, be privileged from arrest during their attendance at the session of their respective houses, and in going to and returning from the same; and for any speech or debate in either house, they shall not be questioned in any other place.

2. *Restrictions.* No senator or representative shall, during the time for which he was elected, be appointed to any civil office under the authority of the United States, which shall have been created, or the emoluments whereof shall have been increased, during such time; and no person holding any office under the United States shall be a member of either house during his continuance in office.

SECTION 7. METHOD OF PASSING LAWS

1. *Revenue bills.* All bills for raising revenue shall originate in the House of Representatives; but the Senate may propose or concur with amendments as on other bills.

2. *How a bill becomes a law.* Every bill which shall have passed the House of Representatives and the Senate shall, before it becomes a law, be presented to the President of the United States; if he approve, he shall sign it, but if not, he shall return it, with his objections, to that house in which it shall have originated, who shall enter the objections at large on their journal, and proceed to reconsider it. If after such reconsideration two thirds of that house shall agree to pass the bill, it shall be sent, together with the objections, to the other house, by which it shall likewise be reconsidered, and, if approved by two thirds of that house, it shall become a law. But in all such cases the votes of both houses shall be determined by yeas and nays, and the names of the persons voting for and against the bill shall be entered on the journal of each house respectively. If any bill shall not be returned by the President within ten days (Sundays excepted) after it shall have been presented to him, the same shall be a law, in like manner as if he had signed it, unless the Congress by their adjournment prevent its return, in which case it shall not be a law.

3. *Presidential approval or veto.* Every order, resolution, or vote to which the concurrence of the Senate and House of Representatives may be necessary (except on a question of adjournment) shall be presented to the President of the United States; and before the same shall take effect, shall be approved by him, or being disapproved by him shall be repassed by two thirds of the Senate and House of Representatives, according to the rules and limitations prescribed in the case of a bill.

SECTION 8. POWERS DELEGATED TO CONGRESS

The Congress shall have power

1. To lay and collect taxes, duties, imposts, and excises, to pay the debts and provide for the common defense and general welfare of the United States; but all duties, imposts, and excises shall be uniform throughout the United States;

2. To borrow money on the credit of the United States;

3. To regulate commerce with foreign nations, and among the several states, and with the Indian tribes;

4. To establish a uniform rule of naturalization, and uniform laws on the subject of bankruptcies throughout the United States;

5. To coin money, regulate the value thereof, and of foreign coin, and fix the standard of weights and measures;

6. To provide for the punishment of counterfeiting the securities and current coin of the United States;

7. To establish post offices and post roads;

8. To promote the progress of science and useful arts by securing for limited times to authors and inventors the exclusive right to their respective writings and discoveries;

9. To constitute tribunals inferior to the Supreme Court;

10. To define and punish piracies and felonies committed on the high seas and offenses against the law of nations;

11. To declare war, [grant letters of marque and reprisal,] and make rules concerning captures on land and water;

12. To raise and support armies, but no appropriation of money to that use shall be for a longer term than two years;

13. To provide and maintain a navy;

14. To make rules for the government and regulation of the land and naval forces;

15. To provide for calling forth the militia to execute the laws of the Union, suppress insurrections, and repel invasions;

16. To provide for organizing, arming, and disciplining the militia, and for governing such part of them as may be employed in the service of the United States, reserving to the states,

respectively, the appointment of the officers, and the authority of training the militia according to the discipline prescribed by Congress;

17. To exercise exclusive legislation in all cases whatsoever, over such district (not exceeding ten miles square) as may, by cession of particular states, and the acceptance of Congress, become the seat of government of the United States, and to exercise like authority over all places purchased by the consent of the legislature of the state in which the same shall be, for the erection of forts, magazines, arsenals, dockyards, and other needful buildings;—and

18. To make all laws which shall be necessary and proper for carrying into execution the foregoing powers, and all other powers vested by this Constitution in the government of the United States, or in any department or officer thereof.

SECTION 9. POWERS DENIED TO THE FEDERAL GOVERNMENT

1. [The migration or importation of such persons as any of the states now existing shall think proper to admit shall not be prohibited by the Congress prior to the year 1808; but a tax or duty may be imposed on such importation, not exceeding $10 for each person.]

2. The privilege of the writ of *habeas corpus* shall not be suspended, unless when in cases of rebellion or invasion the public safety may require it.

3. No bill of attainder or *ex post facto* law shall be passed.

4. No capitation or other direct tax shall be laid, unless in proportion to the census or enumeration herein before directed to be taken.

5. No tax or duty shall be laid on articles exported from any state.

6. No preference shall be given by any regulation of commerce or revenue to the ports of one state over those of another; nor shall vessels bound to, or from, one state, be obliged to enter, clear, or pay duties in another.

7. No money shall be drawn from the Treasury, but in consequence of appropriations made by law; and a regular statement and account of the receipts and expenditures of all public money shall be published from time to time.

8. No title of nobility shall be granted by the United States; and no person holding any office of profit or trust under them, shall, without the consent of the Congress, accept of any present, emolument, office, or title, of any kind whatever, from any king, prince, or foreign state.

SECTION 10. POWERS DENIED TO THE STATES

1. No state shall enter into any treaty, alliance, or confederation; grant letters of marque and reprisal; coin money; emit bills of credit; make anything but gold and silver coin a tender in payment of debts; pass any bill of attainder, *ex post facto* law, or law impairing the obligation of contracts, or grant any title of nobility.

2. No state shall, without the consent of the Congress, lay any imposts or duties on imports or exports, except what may be absolutely necessary for executing its inspection laws; and the net produce of all duties and imposts, laid by any state on imports or exports, shall be for the use of the Treasury of the United States; and all such laws shall be subject to the revision and control of the Congress.

3. No state shall, without the consent of Congress, lay any duty of tonnage, keep troops, or ships of war in time of peace, enter into any agreement or compact with another state, or with a foreign power, or engage in war, unless actually invaded, or in such imminent danger as will not admit of delay.

Article 2. Executive Department

SECTION 1. PRESIDENT AND VICE-PRESIDENT

1. *Term of office.* The executive power shall be vested in a President of the United States of America. He shall hold his office during the term of four years, and together with the Vice-President, chosen for the same term, be elected as follows:

2. *Electoral system.* Each state shall appoint, in such manner as the legislature thereof may direct, a number of electors, equal to the whole number of senators and representatives to which the state may be entitled in the Congress; but no senator or representative, or person holding an office of trust or profit under the United States, shall be appointed an elector.

3. *Election of President and Vice-President.* [The electors shall meet in their respective states, and vote by ballot for two persons, of whom one at least shall not be an inhabitant of the same state with themselves. And they shall make a list of all the persons voted for, and of

the number of votes for each; which list they shall sign and certify, and transmit sealed to the seat of the government of the United States, directed to the president of the Senate. The president of the Senate shall, in the presence of the Senate and House of Representatives, open all the certificates, and the votes shall then be counted. The person having the greatest number of votes shall be the President; if such number be a majority of the whole number of electors appointed; and if there be more than one who have such majority, and have an equal number of votes, then the House of Representatives shall immediately choose by ballot one of them for President; and if no person have a majority, then from the five highest on the list the said House shall in like manner choose the President. But in choosing the President the votes shall be taken by states, the representation from each state having one vote. A quorum for this purpose shall consist of a member or members from two-thirds of the states, and a majority of all the states shall be necessary to a choice. In every case, after the choice of the President, the person having the greatest number of votes of the electors shall be the Vice-President. But if there should remain two or more who have equal votes, the Senate shall choose from them by ballot the Vice-President.]

4. *Time of elections.* The Congress may determine the time of choosing the electors, and the day on which they shall give their votes; which day shall be the same throughout the United States.

5. *Qualifications for President.* No person except a natural-born citizen, [or a citizen of the United States, at the time of the adoption of this Constitution,] shall be eligible to the office of President; neither shall any person be eligible to that office who shall not have attained to the age of thirty-five years, and been fourteen years a resident within the United States.

6. *Filling vacancies.* [In case of the removal of the President from office, or of his death, resignation, or inability to discharge the powers and duties of the said office, the same shall devolve on the Vice-President, and the Congress may by law provide for the case of removal, death, resignation, or inability, both of the President and Vice-President, declaring what officer shall then act as President, and such officer shall act accordingly, until the disability be removed, or a President shall be elected.]

7. *Salary.* The President shall, at stated times, receive for his services, a compensation, which shall neither be increased nor diminished during the period for which he shall have been elected, and he shall not receive within that period any other emolument from the United States, or any of them.

8. *Oath of office.* Before he enter on the execution of his office, he shall take the following oath or affirmation:—"I do solemnly swear (or affirm) that I will faithfully execute the office of President of the United States, and will to the best of my ability, preserve, protect, and defend the Constitution of the United States."

SECTION 2. POWERS OF THE PRESIDENT

1. *Powers over the military and executive departments; reprieves and pardons.* The President shall be Commander in Chief of the Army and Navy of the United States, and of the militia of the several states, when called into the actual service of the United States; he may require the opinion, in writing, of the principal officer in each of the executive departments, upon any subject relating to the duties of their respective offices, and he shall have power to grant reprieves and pardons for offenses against the United States, except in cases of impeachment.

2. *Treaties and appointments.* He shall have power, by and with the advice and consent of the Senate, to make treaties, provided two thirds of the senators present concur; and he shall nominate, and by and with the advice and consent of the Senate, shall appoint ambassadors, other public ministers and consuls, judges of the Supreme Court, and all other officers of the United States, whose appointments are not herein otherwise provided for, and which shall be established by law; but the Congress may by law vest the appointment of such inferior officers, as they think proper, in the President alone, in the courts of law, or in the heads of departments.

3. *Filling vacancies.* The President shall have power to fill up all vacancies that may happen during the recess of the Senate, by granting commissions which shall expire at the end of their next session.

SECTION 3. DUTIES OF THE PRESIDENT

He shall from time to time give to the Congress information of the state of the Union, and recommend to their consideration such measures as he shall judge necessary and expedient; he may, on extraordinary occasions, convene both houses, or either of them, and in case of disagreement between them, with respect to the time of adjournment, he may adjourn them to such time as he shall think proper; he shall receive ambassadors and other public ministers; he shall take care that the laws be faithfully executed, and shall commission all the officers of the United States.

SECTION 4. IMPEACHMENT

The President, Vice-President, and all civil officers of the United States, shall be removed from office on impeachment for, and conviction of, treason, bribery, or other high crimes and misdemeanors.

Article 3. Judicial Department

SECTION 1. FEDERAL COURTS

The judicial power of the United States shall be vested in one Supreme Court, and in such inferior courts as the Congress may from time to time ordain and establish. The judges, both of the Supreme and inferior courts, shall hold their offices during good behavior, and shall, at stated times, receive for their services a compensation, which shall not be diminished during their continuance in office.

SECTION 2. JURISDICTION OF FEDERAL COURTS

1. *General jurisdiction.* The judicial power shall extend to all cases, in law and equity, arising under this Constitution, the laws of the United States, and treaties made or which shall be made, under their authority; to all cases affecting ambassadors, other public ministers and consuls; to all cases of admiralty and maritime jurisdiction; to controversies to which the United States shall be a party; to controversies between two or more states; between a state and citizens of another state; between citizens of different states; between citizens of the same state claiming lands under grants of different states, and between a state, or the citizens thereof, and foreign states, citizens, or subjects.

2. *Supreme Court.* In all cases affecting ambassadors, other public ministers and consuls, and those in which a state shall be a party, the Supreme Court shall have original jurisdiction. In all the other cases before mentioned, the Supreme Court shall have appellate jurisdiction, both as to law and fact, with such exceptions, and under such regulations as the Congress shall make.

3. *Conduct of trials.* The trial of all crimes, except in cases of impeachment, shall be by jury; and such trial shall be held in the state where the said crimes shall have been committed; but when not committed within any state, the trial shall be at such place or places as the Congress may by law have directed.

SECTION 3. TREASON

1. *Definition.* Treason against the United States shall consist only in levying war against them, or in adhering to their enemies, giving them aid and comfort. No person shall be convicted of treason unless on the testimony of two witnesses to the same overt act, or on confession in open court.

2. *Punishment.* The Congress shall have power to declare the punishment of treason, but no attainder of treason shall work corruption of blood or forfeiture except during the life of the person attainted.

Article 4. Relations Among the States

SECTION 1. OFFICIAL ACTS

Full faith and credit shall be given in each state to the public acts, records, and judicial proceedings of every other state. And the Congress may by general laws prescribe the manner in which such acts, records, and proceedings shall be proved, and the effect thereof.

SECTION 2. PRIVILEGES OF CITIZENS

1. *Privileges.* The citizens of each state shall be entitled to all privileges and immunities of citizens in the several states.

2. *Extradition.* A person charged in any state with treason, felony, or other crime, who shall flee from justice, and be found in another state, shall on demand of the executive authority of the state from which he fled, be delivered up, to be removed to the state having jurisdiction of the crime.

3. *Fugitive slaves.* [No person held in service or labor in one state, under the laws thereof, escaping into another, shall in consequence of any law or regulation therein, be discharged from such service or labor, but shall be delivered

up on claim of the party to whom such service or labor may be due.]

SECTION 3. NEW STATES AND TERRITORIES

1. *Admission of new states.* New states may be admitted by the Congress into this Union; but no new state shall be formed or erected within the jurisdiction of any other state; nor any state be formed by the junction of two or more states, or parts of states, without the consent of the legislatures of the states concerned as well as of the Congress.

2. *Power of Congress over territories and other property.* The Congress shall have power to dispose of and make all needful rules and regulations respecting the territory or other property belonging to the United States; and nothing in this Constitution shall be so construed as to prejudice any claims of the United States, or of any particular state.

SECTION 4. GUARANTEES TO THE STATES

The United States shall guarantee to every state in this Union a republican form of government, and shall protect each of them against invasion; and on application of the legislature, or of the executive (when the legislature cannot be convened) against domestic violence.

Article 5. Methods of Amendment

The Congress, whenever two thirds of both houses shall deem it necessary, shall propose amendments to this Constitution, or, on the application of the legislatures of two thirds of the several states, shall call a convention for proposing amendments, which, in either case, shall be valid to all intents and purposes, as part of this Constitution, when ratified by the legislatures of three fourths of the several states, or by conventions in three fourths thereof, as the one or the other mode of ratification may be proposed by the Congress; provided that [no amendments which may be made prior to the year 1808 shall in any manner affect the first and fourth clauses in the Ninth Section of the First Article; and that] no state, without its consent, shall be deprived of its equal suffrage in the Senate.

Article 6. General Provisions

1. *Public debts.* All debts contracted and engagements entered into, before the adoption of this Constitution, shall be as valid against the United States under this Constitution, as under the Confederation.

2. *The supreme law of the land.* This Constitution, and the laws of the United States which shall be made in pursuance thereof, and all treaties made, or which shall be made, under the authority of the United States, shall be the supreme law of the land; and the judges in every state shall be bound thereby, anything in the constitution or laws of any state to the contrary notwithstanding.

3. *Oaths of office; no religious test.* The senators and representatives before mentioned, and the members of the several state legislatures, and all executive and judicial officers, both of the United States and of the several states, shall be bound by oath or affirmation, to support this Constitution; but no religious test shall ever be required as a qualification to any office or public trust under the United States.

Article 7. Ratification

The ratification of the conventions of nine states shall be sufficient for the establishment of this Constitution between the states so ratifying the same.

Done in Convention by the unanimous consent of the States present the seventeenth day of September in the year of our Lord one thousand seven hundred and eighty-seven and of the independence of the United States of America the twelfth. In witness whereof we have hereunto subscribed our names.

Amendment 1. Freedom of Religion, Speech, Press, Assembly, and Petition (1791)

Congress shall make no law respecting an establishment of religion, or prohibiting the free exercise thereof; or abridging the freedom of speech, or of the press; or the right of the people peaceably to assemble, and to petition the government for a redress of grievances.

Amendment 2. Right to Keep Arms (1791)

A well-regulated militia, being necessary to the security of a free state, the right of the people to keep and bear arms shall not be infringed.

Amendment 3. Quartering of Troops (1791)

No soldier shall, in time of peace, be quartered in any house, without the consent of the owner; nor in time of war, but in a manner to be prescribed by law.

Amendment 4. Searches and Seizures; Warrants (1791)

The right of the people to be secure in their persons, houses, papers, and effects, against unreasonable searches and seizures, shall not be violated; and no warrants shall issue but upon probable cause, supported by oath or affirmation, and particularly describing the place to be searched, and the person or things to be seized.

Amendment 5. Rights of Accused Persons (1791)

No person shall be held to answer for a capital, or otherwise infamous, crime, unless on a presentment or indictment of a grand jury, except in cases arising in the land or naval forces, or in the militia, when in actual service in time of war or public danger; nor shall any person be subject for the same offense to be twice put in jeopardy of life or limb; nor shall be compelled, in any criminal case, to be a witness against himself; nor be deprived of life, liberty, or property, without due process of law; nor shall private property be taken for public use, without just compensation.

Amendment 6. Right to Speedy and Public Trial (1791)

In all criminal prosecutions, the accused shall enjoy the right to a speedy and public trial, by an impartial jury of the state and district wherein the crime shall have been committed, which district shall have been previously ascertained by law, and to be informed of the nature and cause of the accusation; to be confronted with the witnesses against him; to have compulsory process for obtaining witnesses in his favor, and to have the assistance of counsel for his defense.

Amendment 7. Jury Trial in Civil Cases (1791)

In suits at common law, where the value in controversy shall exceed twenty dollars, the right of trial by jury shall be preserved, and no fact tried by a jury shall be otherwise reexamined in any court of the United States than according to the rules of the common law.

Amendment 8. Bail, Fines, Punishments (1791)

Excessive bail shall not be required, nor excessive fines imposed, nor cruel and unusual punishments inflicted.

Amendment 9. Powers Reserved to the People (1791)

The enumeration in the Constitution, of certain rights, shall not be construed to deny or disparage others retained by the people.

Amendment 10. Powers Reserved to the States (1791)

The powers not delegated to the United States by the Constitution, nor prohibited by it to the states, are reserved to the states respectively, or to the people.

Amendment 11. Suits Against States (1798)

The judicial power of the United States shall not be construed to extend to any suit in law or equity, commenced or prosecuted against one of the United States, by citizens of another state, or by citizens or subjects of any foreign state.

Amendment 12. Election of President and Vice-President (1804)

The electors shall meet in their respective states, and vote by ballot for President and Vice-President, one of whom, at least, shall not be an inhabitant of the same state with themselves; they shall name in their ballots the person voted for as President, and in distinct ballots the person voted for as Vice-President, and they shall make distinct lists of all persons voted for as President, and of all persons voted for as Vice-President, and of the number of votes for each, which lists they shall sign and certify, and transmit, sealed, to the seat of government of the United States, directed to the President of the Senate; the President of the Senate shall, in the presence of the Senate and House of Representatives, open all the certificates and the votes shall then be counted; the person having the greatest number of votes for President shall be the President, if such number be a majority of the whole number of electors appointed; and if no person have such majority, then from the persons having the highest numbers not exceeding three on the list of those voted for as President, the House of Representatives shall choose immediately, by ballot, the President. But in choosing the President, the votes shall be taken by states, the representation from each state having one vote; a quorum for this purpose shall consist of a member or members from two thirds of the states, and a majority of all the states shall be necessary to a choice. [And if the House of Representatives shall not choose a President whenever the right of choice shall devolve upon them, before the fourth day of March next following, then the Vice-President shall act as President, as in the case of the death or other constitutional disability of the President.] The person having the greatest number of votes as Vice-President, shall be the Vice-President, if such number be a majority of the whole number of electors appointed, and if no person have a majority, then, from the two highest numbers on the list, the Senate shall choose the Vice-President; a quorum for the purpose shall consist of two thirds of the whole number of senators, and a majority of the whole number shall be necessary to a choice. But no person constitutionally ineligible to the office of President shall be eligible to that of Vice-President of the United States.

Amendment 13. Slavery Abolished (1865)

SECTION 1. Neither slavery nor involuntary servitude, except as a punishment for crime whereof the party shall have been duly convicted, shall exist within the United States, or any place subject to their jurisdiction.

SECTION 2. Congress shall have power to enforce this article by appropriate legislation.

Amendment 14. Rights of Citizens (1868)

SECTION 1. *Citizenship defined.* All persons born or naturalized in the United States and subject to the jurisdiction thereof, are citizens of the United States and of the state wherein they reside. No state shall make or enforce any law which shall abridge the privileges or immunities of citizens of the United States; nor shall any state deprive any person of life, liberty, or property, without due process of law; nor deny to any person within its jurisdiction the equal protection of the laws.

SECTION 2. *Apportionment of representatives.* Representatives shall be apportioned among the several states according to their respective numbers, counting the whole number of persons in each state, excluding Indians not taxed. But when the right to vote at any election for the choice of electors for President and Vice-President of the United States, representatives in Congress, the executive and judicial officers of a state, or the members of the legislature thereof, is denied to any of the male inhabitants of such state, being twenty-one years of age and citizens of the United States, or in any way abridged, except for participation in rebellion, or other crime, the basis of representation therein shall be reduced in the proportion which the number of such male citizens shall bear to the whole number of male citizens twenty-one years of age in such state.

SECTION 3. *Disability for engaging in insurrection.* No person shall be a senator or representative in Congress, or elector of President and Vice-President, or hold any office, civil or military, under the United States, or under any state, who, having previously taken an oath, as a member of Congress, or as an officer of the United States, or as a member of any state legislature, or as an executive or judicial officer of any state, to support the Constitution of the United States, shall have engaged in insurrection or rebellion against the same, or given aid or comfort to the enemies thereof. But Congress may, by a vote of two thirds of each house, remove such disability.

SECTION 4. *Public debt.* The validity of the public debt of the United States, authorized by law, including debts incurred for payment of pensions and bounties for services in suppressing insurrection or rebellion, shall not be questioned. But neither the United States nor any state shall assume or pay any debt or obligation incurred in aid of insurrection or rebellion against the United States, [or any claim for the loss or emancipation of any slave;] but all such debts, obligations, and claims shall be held illegal and void.

SECTION 5. *Enforcement.* The Congress shall have power to enforce, by appropriate legislation, the provisions of this article.

Amendment 15. Rights of Suffrage (1870)

SECTION 1. The right of citizens of the United States to vote shall not be denied or abridged by the United States or any state on account of race, color, or previous condition of servitude.

SECTION 2. The Congress shall have power to enforce this article by appropriate legislation.

Amendment 16. Income Tax (1913)

The Congress shall have power to lay and collect taxes on incomes, from whatever source derived, without apportionment among the several states, and without regard to any census or enumeration.

Amendment 17. Election of Senators (1913)

SECTION 1. *Method of election.* The Senate of the United States shall be composed of two senators from each state, elected by the people thereof, for six years; and each senator shall have one vote. The electors in each state shall have the qualifications requisite for electors of the most numerous branch of the state legislatures.

SECTION 2. *Filling vacancies.* When vacancies happen in the representation of any state in the Senate, the executive authority of such state shall issue writs of election to fill such vacancies: *Provided* that the legislature of any state may empower the executive thereof to make temporary appointments until the people fill the vacancies by election as the legislature may direct.

[SECTION 3. *Not retroactive.* This amendment shall not be so construed as to affect the election or term of any senator chosen before it becomes valid as part of the Constitution.]

Amendment 18. National Prohibition (1919)

[SECTION 1. After one year from the ratification of this article the manufacture, sale, or transportation of intoxicating liquors within, the importation thereof into, or the exportation thereof from, the United States and all territory subject to the jurisdiction thereof for beverage purposes is hereby prohibited.

SECTION 2. The Congress and the several states shall have concurrent power to enforce this article by appropriate legislation.

SECTION 3. This article shall be inoperative unless it shall have been ratified as an amendment to the Constitution by the legislatures of the several states, as provided in the Constitution, within seven years from the date of the submission hereof to the states by the Congress.]

Amendment 19. Woman Suffrage (1920)

SECTION 1. The right of citizens of the United States to vote shall not be denied or abridged by the United States or by any state on account of sex.

SECTION 2. Congress shall have power to enforce this article by appropriate legislation.

Amendment 20. "Lame Duck" Amendment (1933)

SECTION 1. *Beginning of terms.* The terms of the President and Vice-President shall end at noon on the 20th day of January, and the terms of senators and representatives at noon on the 3d day of January, of the years in which such terms would have ended if this article had not been ratified; and the terms of their successors shall then begin.

SECTION 2. *Beginning of congressional sessions.* The Congress shall assemble at least once in every year, and such meeting shall begin at noon on the 3d day of January, unless they shall by law appoint a different day.

SECTION 3. *Presidential succession.* If at the time fixed for the beginning of the term of the President, the President-elect shall have died, the Vice-President-elect shall become President. If a President shall not have been chosen before the time fixed for the beginning of his term, or if the President-elect shall have failed to qualify, then the Vice-President-elect shall act as President until a President shall have qualified; and the Congress may by law provide for the case wherein neither a President-elect nor a Vice-President-elect shall have qualified, declaring who shall then act as President, or the manner in which one who is to act shall be selected, and such person shall act accordingly until a President or Vice-President shall have qualified.

SECTION 4. *Filling Presidential vacancy.* The Congress may by law provide for the case of the death of any of the persons from whom the House of Representatives may choose a President whenever the right of choice shall have devolved upon them, and for the case of the death of any of the persons from whom the Senate may choose a Vice-President whenever the right of choice shall have devolved upon them.

[SECTION 5. *Effective date.* Sections 1 and 2 shall take effect on the 15th day of October following the ratification of this article.

SECTION 6. *Time limit for ratification.* This article shall be inoperative unless it shall have been ratified as an amendment to the Constitution by the legislatures of three fourths of the several states within seven years from the date of its submission.]

Amendment 21. Repeal of Prohibition (1933)

SECTION 1. The eighteenth article of amendment to the Constitution of the United States is hereby repealed.

SECTION 2. The transportation or importation into any state, territory, or possession of the United States for delivery or use therein of intoxicating liquors, in violation of the laws thereof, is hereby prohibited.

[SECTION 3. This article shall be inoperative unless it shall have been ratified as an amendment to the Constitution by conventions in the several states, as provided in the Constitution, within seven years from the date of the submission hereof to the states by the Congress.]

Amendment 22. Two-Term Limit for Presidents (1951)

SECTION 1. No person shall be elected to the office of the President more than twice, and no person who has held the office of President, or acted as President, for more than two years of a term to which some other person was elected President shall be elected to the office of the President more than once. [But this Article shall not apply to any person holding the office of President when this Article was proposed by the Congress, and shall not prevent any person who may be holding the office of President, or acting as President, during the term within which this Article becomes operative from holding the office of President or acting as President during the remainder of such term.]

[SECTION 2. This article shall be inoperative unless it shall have been ratified as an amendment to the Constitution by the legislatures of three fourths of the several states within seven years from the date of its submission to the states by the Congress.]

Amendment 23. Presidential Electors for District of Columbia (1961)

SECTION 1. The District constituting the seat of Government of the United States shall appoint in such manner as the Congress may direct:

A number of electors of President and Vice-President equal to the whole number of senators and representatives in Congress to which the District would be entitled if it were a State, but in no event more than the least populous State; they shall be in addition to those appointed by the States, but they shall be considered, for the purposes of the election of President and Vice-President, to be electors appointed by a State; and they shall meet in the District and perform such duties as provided by the twelfth article of amendment.

SECTION 2. The Congress shall have power to enforce this article by appropriate legislation.

Amendment 24. Poll Tax Banned in National Elections (1964)

SECTION 1. The right of citizens of the United States to vote in any primary or other election for President or Vice-President, for electors for President or Vice-President, or for senator or representative in Congress, shall not be denied or abridged by the United States or any state by reason of failure to pay any poll tax or other tax.

SECTION 2. The Congress shall have the power to enforce this article by appropriate legislation.

Amendment 25. Presidential Disability and Succession (1967)

1. In case of the removal of the President from office or his death or resignation, the Vice-President shall become President.

2. Whenever there is a vacancy in the office of the Vice-President, the President shall nominate a Vice-President who shall take the office upon confirmation of a majority vote of both houses of Congress.

3. Whenever the President transmits to the President *pro tempore* of the Senate and the Speaker of the House of Representatives his written declaration that he is unable to discharge the powers and duties of his office and until he transmits to them a written declaration to the contrary, such powers and duties shall be discharged by the Vice-President as Acting President.

4. Whenever the Vice-President and a majority of either the principal officers of the executive departments or of such other body as Congress may by law provide, transmit to the President *pro tempore* of the Senate and the Speaker of the House of Representatives their written declaration that the President is unable to discharge the powers and duties of his office, the Vice-President shall immediately assume the powers and duties of the office as Acting President.

Thereafter, when the President transmits to the President *pro tempore* of the Senate and the Speaker of the House of Representatives his written declaration that no inability exists, he shall resume the powers and duties of his office unless the Vice-President and a majority of either the principal officers of the executive department or of such other body as Congress may by law provide, transmit within four days to the President *pro tempore* of the Senate and the Speaker of the House of Representatives their written declaration that the President is unable to discharge the powers and duties of his office. Thereupon Congress shall decide the issue, assembling within forty-eight hours for that purpose if not in session. If the Congress, within twenty-one days after receipt of the latter written declaration, or, if Congress is not in session, within twenty-one days after Congress is required to assemble, determines by two thirds vote of both houses that the President is unable to discharge the powers and duties of his office, the Vice-President shall continue to discharge the same as Acting President; otherwise, the President shall resume the powers and duties of his office.

Index